MW01228126

West's Federal/National Criminal Law Library

Check on an evidence question...
research a procedural issue...
study the sentencing guidelines...
all without leaving your office!

Choose from these invaluable titles:

- ☐ *Criminal Law Defenses*, by Robinson
- ☐ *Criminal Procedure*, by LaFave and Israel
- ☐ *Federal Sentencing Law and Practice, 2d*, by Hutchison and Yellen
- ☐ *Search and Seizure, 2d*, by LaFave
- ☐ *Substantive Criminal Law*, by LaFave and Scott
- ☐ *Uniform Rules of Criminal Procedure*
- ☐ *Handbook of Federal Evidence, 3rd*
- ☐ *West's® Federal Forms, District Courts—Criminal*
- ☐ *Criminal Law News®*
- ☐ *Photographic Evidence, 2d*, by Scott
- ☐ *Federal Jury Practice and Instructions*, by Devitt, Blackmar and O'Malley
- ☐ *Federal Jury Instructions–Document Assembly* (disk product)
- ☐ *Federal Court of Appeals Manual, 2d*, by Knibb
- ☐ *Federal Practice and Procedure—Criminal, 2nd*
- ☐ *Federal Criminal Code and Rules*
- ☐ *Federal Criminal Code and Rules\FAST* (disk product)
- ☐ *Federal Sentencing Guidelines Manual*
- ☐ *Mandatory Minimum Penalties in the Federal Criminal Justice System*
- ☐ *Federal Criminal Practice: Prosecution and Defense*, by Subin, Mirsky and Weinstein

CALL
1-800-328-9352
TO REQUEST YOUR FREE TRIAL COPY!

West Publishing
More ways to win

4-9766-8/10-94 452166

COORDINATED RESEARCH IN CRIMINAL LAW AND PRACTICE FROM WEST

WEST'S CRIMINAL PRACTICE SERIES

Search and Seizure
Wayne R. LaFave

Substantive Criminal Law
Wayne R. LaFave and Austin W. Scott, Jr.

Criminal Law Defenses
Paul H. Robinson

Criminal Procedure
Wayne R. LaFave and Jerold H. Israel

Federal Sentencing Law and Practice
Thomas W. Hutchison and David Yellen

Federal Criminal Practice: Prosecution and Defense
Harry I. Subin, Chester L. Mirsky and Ian S. Weinstein

Federal Practice and Procedure
Vols. 1, 2, 3 and 3A – Criminal
Charles Alan Wright

Federal Jury Practice and Instructions
Volumes 1 and 2 – Civil and Criminal
Hon. Edward J. Devitt, Hon. Charles B. Blackmar,
Michael A. Wolff and Kevin F. O'Malley

Federal Criminal Code and Rules Pamphlet

Federal Sentencing Guidelines Manual
United States Sentencing Commission

WEST'S STATE PRACTICE SERIES

West has the following specialized criminal practice and procedure volumes in the state practice series:

Arizona Criminal Procedure Forms

California Criminal Trialbook

California Jury Instructions – Criminal

Colorado Jury Instructions – Criminal

Connecticut Criminal Jury Instructions

Illinois Criminal Practice and Procedure

Illinois Pattern Jury Instructions – Criminal

Indiana Criminal Procedure

Iowa Criminal Law and Procedure

Kansas Criminal Code and Code of Criminal Procedure

Kentucky Criminal Practice and Procedure

Kentucky Substantive Criminal Law

Massachusetts Criminal Practice and Procedure

Massachusetts Criminal Law

Michigan Criminal Law

Minnesota Criminal Law and Procedure

Mississippi Model Jury Instructions – Civil and Criminal

Missouri Criminal Practice and Procedure

New Jersey Criminal Practice and Procedure

New Jersey Criminal Law

McKinney's Forms for NY Laws – Criminal Procedure

Pennsylvania Criminal Procedure Forms and Commentary

Tennessee Criminal Practice and Procedure

Texas Criminal Forms

Washington Criminal Practice and Procedure

Washington Criminal Law

WESTLAW CRIMINAL JUSTICE DATABASES

FCJ–FSG Federal Sentencing Guidelines

FSLP Federal Sentencing Law and Practice

CJ–SCJ ABA Standards for Criminal Justice

CJ–CJA Criminal Justice Abstracts

WTH–CJ WESTLAW Highlights – Criminal Justice

CJ–TP Law Reviews, Texts and Journals

FEDERAL SENTENCING GUIDELINES MANUAL

1994–95 EDITION

UNITED STATES SENTENCING COMMISSION

Effective November 1, 1987

Including

November 1, 1994 Amendments
to
Guidelines, Policy Statements, and Commentary
—Also—
Highlights of the 1994 Amendments
Supreme Court Consideration of the Guidelines
Highlights of the 1994 Crime Legislation
Selected Provisions of 1994 Crime Act Relating to the Guidelines
Questions Most Frequently Asked About The Guidelines
Sentencing Worksheets
Model Sentencing Forms
Related Criminal Statutes and Rules
Table of Cases Applying Guidelines
History of 1988–1994 Amendments

ST. PAUL, MINN.
WEST PUBLISHING CO.
1994

ISBN 0-314-05374-3

PUBLISHER'S PREFACE

This 1994–95 Edition contains the current text of the Sentencing Guidelines, Commentary, and Policy Statements of the United States Sentencing Commission as most recently amended effective November 1, 1994. The most significant changes are summarized in the "Highlights of 1994 Amendments" feature that follows. See also Appendix C for descriptions of specific amendments.

Provisions of the Violent Crime Control and Law Enforcement Act of 1994 relating to the Sentencing Guidelines and the United States Sentencing Commission are included in Appendix G, as well as expert commentary on some of these provisions in a separate Highlights section.

Also included are revised Appendices A and C as issued by the Sentencing Commission. Appendix "A" provides a "Statutory Index" of the particular guideline section or sections ordinarily applicable to the specific offense statute. Appendix "C" chronicles the 1988–1994 amendments to the guidelines.

Other features in this 1994–95 Edition include:

- Highlights of 1994 Amendments to Guidelines, Policy Statements, and Commentary.
- Relevant Supreme Court Decisions.
- Selected federal statutes relating to sentencing. See App. B.
- Revised Organizational Worksheets of U.S. Sentencing Commission. See App. D.
- Revised Questions Most Frequently Asked About the Sentencing Guidelines. See App. E.
- Federal Rules of Criminal Procedure Relating to Sentencing. See App. F.
- Model Sentencing Forms as issued by Federal Judicial Center. See App. H.
- Table of Cases that have applied specific sentencing guidelines. See App. I.
- WESTLAW Electronic Research Guide for access to the very latest cases construing or applying specific guidelines.
- Quick-reference "Sentencing Table" on inside back cover.

For further coverage of the federal sentencing guidelines and related sentencing issues, reference should be made to Hutchison & Yellen, *Federal Sentencing Law and Practice, Second Edition*. This comprehensive publication fully explains and annotates each Guideline and Policy Statement, and provides many related reference materials not readily available elsewhere.

Retention of Prior Editions

The 1994 Edition of this *Federal Sentencing Guidelines Manual* should be retained —along with prior editions—in the event there is a need to refer to the text of a specific Guideline, Commentary, or Policy Statement at a particular point in time. See also

Appendix C of this 1994–95 Edition for reference to specific amendments as made in 1988, 1989, 1990, 1991, 1992, 1993 and 1994.

THE PUBLISHER

October, 1994

HIGHLIGHTS OF THE 1994 AMENDMENTS

by

David Yellen

The Sentencing Commission, on April 28, 1994, promulgated and sent to Congress six amendments to the *Sentencing Guidelines Manual*.[1] Those amendments, which have been designated amendments 503 through 508, took effect on November 1, 1994. The Commission also promulgated two other amendment.[2] Exercising authority given it by the Violent Crime Control And Law Enforcement Act of 1994, the Commission promulgated a new guideline dealing with the mandatory minimum safety valve provision of that Act.[3] The new guideline took effect on September 24, 1994. The Commission also promulgated an amendment making two amendments retroactive.[4] That amendment took effect November 1, 1994.[5] An outline of the changes made by all of these amendments follows.

The Commission revised commentary pertaining to the definition of (1) "jointly undertaken criminal activity" and (2) "same course of conduct". With regard to the former, amendment 503 adds language to application note 2 stating that "a defendant's relevant conduct does not include the conduct of members of a conspiracy prior to the defendant's joining the conspiracy, even if the defendant knew of that conduct . . . ." This change overturns two cases holding that a defendant could be held accountable under § 1B1.3 for conduct occurring before a defendant entered a conspiracy on the ground that such conduct was reasonably foreseeable.[6] Amendment 503, however, also revises the commentary to state that an upward departure may be warranted in "some unusual set of circumstances in which the exclusion of such conduct may not adequately reflect the defendant's culpability . . . ."

Application note 9 to § 1B1.3 explains what factors should be considered in determining whether multiple offenses constitute the "same course of conduct" for purposes of the relevant conduct rule. Amendment 503 adds language to application note 9 stating that "the regularity (repetitions) of the offense" is a factor appropriate to such a determination.[7] Amendment 503 also adds language stating that "when one of the above factors is absent, a stronger presence of a least one of the other factors is required."

---

[1]59 Fed. Register 23608-23610 (1994).

[2]*Id.* at __ (1994).

[3]Violent Crime Control and Law Enforcement Act of 1994, Pub. L. No. 103–322, § 80001(b), 108 Stat. 1796, __. *See* Highlights of the 1994 Crime Legislation, *infra*.

[4]59 Fed. Register __ (1994).

[5]*Id.*

[6]United States v. Miranda-Ortiz, 926 F.2d 172, 178 (2d Cir. 1991); United States v. Collado, 975 F.2d 985, 997 (3d Cir. 1992) (defendant can be held accountable for such conduct in "unusual circumstances"); United States v. Edwards, 945 F.2d 1387, 1393 (7th Cir. 1991), *cert. denied*, 112 S.Ct. 1590 (1992). *Contra.* United States v. O'Campo, 973 F.2d 1015, 1026 (1st Cir. 1992); United States v. Carreon, 11 F.3d 1225 (5th Cir. 1994); United States v. Petty, 982 F.2d 1374, 1377 (9th Cir. 1991).

[7]This language is derived from United States v. Hahn, 960 F.2d 903 (9th Cir. 1992).

§ 1B1.10. Retroactivity of Amended Guideline Range (Policy Statement).

The Commission made several changes to this policy statement.[8] Amendment 504 deletes the subsection prohibiting a reduction in sentence that is greater than the number of months by which the maximum of the applicable guideline range has been reduced.

Amendment 504 also revises subsection (b) to state that when a court is determining whether and to what extent to reduce a sentence under 18 U.S.C. § 3582(c)(2), "the court should consider the sentence that is would have imposed had the amendment(s) to the guidelines listed in subsection (c) been in effect at the time the defendant was sentenced." Consequently, a defendant will not benefit from any favorable amendment that takes effect after initial sentencing, unless that amendment is made retroactive. For example, D is sentenced in 1991 for trafficking in LSD. D moves for resentencing under 18 U.S.C. § 3682(c)(2) because amendment 484 changed the method of determining the quantity of LSD for guideline purposes, and § 1B1.10, p.s. makes amendment 484 retroactive. D would not benefit from the 1992 amendment that provides an additional one-level reduction for timely acceptance of responsibility (amendment 459) because that amendment has not been made retroactive.

The Commission also added two amendments to the list of amendments that are retroactive.[9] The two are amendment 371, which took effect November 1, 1991, and amendment 506, which took effect November 1, 1994. Amendment 371 adds several drug guidelines dealing with listed chemicals, drug paraphernalia, and evading reporting and recordkeeping requirements. Amendment 506 amends commentary to the career offender guideline, § 4B1.1, to revise the definition of "offense statutory maximum."

§ 2D1.1. Unlawful Manufacturing, Importing, Exporting, or Trafficking (Including Possession with Intent to Commit These Offenses); Attempt or Conspiracy.

Amendment 505 revises the drug table to make the highest base offense level 38 instead of 42. Quantities that produced a level 40 or 42 will now produce level 38. The Commission also has added language to the commentary stating that an upward departure may be warranted if the quantity of drugs attributable to the defendant is at least ten times the quantity required for level 38.[10]

§ 4B1.1. Career Offender.

Amendment 506 revises the definition of "offense statutory maximum" as that term is used in the career offender guideline. As revised, the term "offense statutory maximum" does not include any statutory

[8]This policy statement has a unique status. 18 U.S.C. § 3582(c)(2), which authorizes the sentencing court to modify a sentence under certain circumstances, requires that any reduction in sentence made in response to a motion filed under that section be "consistent with applicable policy statements issued by the Commission." The Commission issued § 1B1.10 to implement 18 U.S.C. § 3582(c)(2). *See* U.S.S.G. § 1B1.10, p.s., comment. (backg'd). *See also* Thomas W. Hutchison & David Yellen, Federal Sentencing Law and Practice § 1B1.10 Authors' Comment 2 (2d ed. 1994).

[9]U.S.S.G. App. C (amend. 510). *See* 59 Fed. Register __ (1994). Because the Commission was amending a policy statement, its action does not violate 28 U.S.C. § 994(p), which requires that the Sentencing Commission transmit to Congress by May 1 "amendments to *guidelines*" (emphasis added).

[10]59 Fed. Register __ (1994). This change was not a part of the amendment submitted to Congress. Because the change is to commentary, the Commission's action does not violate 28 U.S.C. § 994(p), which requires that the Sentencing Commission transmit to Congress by May 1 "amendments to *guidelines*" (emphasis added).

enhancements that would apply based on a defendant's prior convictions. For instance, when the statute provides for a higher maximum sentence because the defendant was previously convicted under the same statute, that higher maximum would not be used to determine the offense level under § 4B1.1.

§ 5C1.2. Limitation on Applicability of Statutory Minimums in Certain Cases.

Exercising authority given it by section 80001(b) of the Violent Crime Control and Law Enforcement Act of 1994, the Commission promulgated this guideline to implement the "safety valve" provision of that legislation.[11] The guideline took effect September 24, 1994.[12]

The new guideline provides that when a defendant is subject to a mandatory minimum sentence under specified provisions of title 21, United States Code, "the court shall impose a sentence in accordance with the applicable guidelines without regard to any statutory minimum sentence, if the court finds that the defendant meets the criteria in 18 U.S.C. § 3553(f)(1)–(5) set forth verbatim below . . . ." The use of the phrase "set forth verbatim below" means that the Commission is not seeking to modify any of the conditions set by Congress.

The Congressional intention in enacting the safety valve provision of the Violent Crime Control and Law Enforcement Act of 1994 appears to be that the most deserving defendant subject to a five-year mandatory minimum who qualifies for the safety valve—a defendant who receives a four-level downward adjustment for minimal participation and a three-level downward adjustment for acceptance of responsibility—should have a guideline range the bottom of which can be as low as 24 months.[13] Under the guidelines as presently drafted, such a defendant will in most instances have an offense level of 26. Deducting four levels for minimal participation and three levels for acceptance of responsibility results in an adjusted offense level of 19. For a defendant with no more than one criminal history point (a requirement to be eligible for the safety valve), that offense level results in a guideline range of 30–37 months.

It is possible for some defendants who qualify for the safety valve to have an adjusted offense level of less than 19. For example, a defendant convicted of trafficking in 1,000 doses of LSD will have a guideline quantity of 400 milligrams. If the jurisdiction uses the actual weight of the carrier when determining if a mandatory minimum applies and if the carrier is heavy, a five-year mandatory minimum will apply. A quantity of 400 milligrams yields an offense level of 20 under § 2D1.1. Assuming that the only adjustments to that offense level are for minimal participation (four levels) and acceptance of responsibility (three levels), the resulting offense level of 13 yields a guideline range of 12-18 months. A sentence within that range is required by 18 U.S.C. § 3553(b), unless the court has a basis for departing.

---

[11]*See* Highlights of the 1994 Crime Legislation, *infra*.

[12]59 Fed. Register __ (1994).

[13]Violent Crime Control and Law Enforcement Act of 1994, Pub. L. No. 103–322, § 80001(b)(1)(B), 108 Stat. 1796, __. *See* H.R. Rep. No. 460, 103d Cong. 2d Sess. 4–5 (1994) (the legislation "permits greater integration between sentencing guideline mitigating factors and mandatory minimum for the least culpable offenders").

§ 5G1.2. Sentencing on Multiple Counts of Conviction.

The Commission revised the commentary to this guideline to overturn two decisions holding that under certain circumstances a sentencing court can order that terms of supervised release run consecutively.[14] Amendment 507 adds language to the commentary stating "any term of supervised release imposed is to run concurrently with any other term of supervised release imposed."

§ 5K2.0. Grounds for Departure (Policy Statement).

The Commission, probably in response to a Seventh Circuit case,[15] has revised this policy statement and its commentary, and the introductory commentary to Chapter 5, part H, to indicate that the term "ordinarily" is to be given its plain meaning. Amendment 508 adds language to the policy statement providing that a factor that is not ordinarily relevant to a determination of whether to depart can be relevant to such a determination if the factor "is present to an unusual degree and distinguishes the case from the 'heartland' cases covered by the guidelines in a way that is important to the statutory purposes of sentencing." Commentary to the policy statement that amendment 508 adds states that "the Commission believes that such cases will be extremely rare."

---

[14]United States v. Shorthouse, 7 F.3d 149 (9th Cir. 1993); United States v. Maxwell, 966 F.2d 545, 551 (10th Cir. 1992). *Contra*, United States v. Gullickson, 982 F.2d 1231, 1236 (8th Cir. 1993).

[15]United States v. Thomas, 930 F.2d 526, 529–30 (7th Cir.), *cert. denied*, 112 S.Ct. 171 (1991).

SUPREME COURT CONSIDERATION OF THE GUIDELINES

by

David Yellen

The Supreme Court did not decide any cases directly involving the sentencing guidelines during the October 1993 term. The Court did decide three cases that are relevant to the guidelines—United States v. Granderson, 114 S.Ct. 1259 (1994), Custis v. United States, 114 S.Ct. 1732 (1994), and Nichols v. United States, 114 S.Ct. 1921 (1994).

United States v. Granderson, 114 S.Ct. 1259 (1994).

This case affects chapter seven of the guidelines, Violations of Probation and Supervised Release. In this case, the Court attempted to interpret the phrase "original sentence" in a statutory provision, 18 U.S.C. § 3565(a), that member of the Court called "wretchedly drafted"[1] and "far from transparent".[2]

Granderson was sentenced to five years' probation and a $2,000 fine after pleading guilty to one count of destruction of mail. This sentence was within the applicable guideline range of 0–6 months. After Granderson tested positive for cocaine, the District Court revoked Granderson's sentence of probation for violating a condition of probation. Under 18 U.S.C. § 3565(a), if a probationer possesses a controlled substance, "the court shall revoke the sentence of probation and sentence the defendant to not less than one-third of the original sentence." The District Court concluded that under this provision, the sentence upon revocation must be a term of imprisonment at least equal to one third of the term of probation actually imposed (60 months). The District Court therefore sentenced Granderson to 20 months' imprisonment. Ironically, and according to the Supreme Court startlingly, this sentence was harsher than the top of the guideline range applicable to the original offense (6 months), plus the one-year statutory maximum Granderson would have faced had the Government prosecuted him for cocaine possession.[3]

The Court of Appeals for the Eleventh Circuit vacated the sentence, and invoking the rule of lenity in interpreting an unclear provision, concluded that "original sentence" refers to "the [0–6 month] sentence of incarceration faced by Granderson under the Guidelines."[4] The Court of Appeals ordered Granderson released from custody because he had already served 11 months of his revocation sentence.

The Supreme Court affirmed the Eleventh Circuit's decision. While noting that § 3565(a) is far from clear, because of the "unexacting process" by which Congress enacted the provision,[5] the Court reached several conclusions. First, as urged by the Government, the Court determined that a sentence upon revocation under § 3565(a) must be a term of imprisonment. Otherwise, the Court noted, "the proviso at issue would

---

[1]S.Ct. at 1270 (Scalia, J., concurring in the judgment).

[2]*Id.* at 1270 (Kennedy, J., concurring in the judgment).

[3]*Id.* at 1264. However, as the dissent points out, this sentence is within the statutory maximum for destruction of mail. *Id.* at 1279 n.8.

[4]*Id.* at 1263.

[5]According to the Court, although § 3565(a) was enacted in 1988, the provision may have been drafted with the pre–1984 sentencing system, in which a sentence of imprisonment could be suspended and the defendant placed on probation, in mind. *Id.* at 1267.

make little sense", because the sentence after revocation could be a term of probation shorter than the original sentence of probation.

The Court rejected the Government's second argument, though, that the term "original" sentence refers to the duration of the original term of probation. Instead, the Court concluded that the "original sentence refers to the top of the applicable range of the sentencing guidelines. Thus, under the Court's reading, the minimum revocation sentence under § 3565(a) is a term of imprisonment equal to one third of the maximum of the guideline range applicable to the defendant's original conviction, and the maximum revocation sentence is the maximum of that guideline range.

Subsequent to this decision, Congress amended § 3565.[6] Under the amended statute, if the court applies the mandatory revocation provision (which would be the case with an offender such as Granderson, who possessed a controlled substance), the court must resentence the offender under the sentencing guidelines, and the resulting sentence must include a term of imprisonment. The amended statute does not specify the length of such a term of imprisonment.

Custis v. United States, 114 S.Ct. 1732 (1994).

The Armed Career Criminal Act of 1984, 18 U.S.C. § 924(e) (ACCA), enhances the penalty for the crime of possession of a firearm by a felon[7] to a mandatory minimum sentence of 15 years in prison and a maximum of life if a defendant "has three previous convictions . . . for a violent felony or a serious drug offense."[8] This case addresses whether a defendant facing an enhanced sentence under the ACCA may challenge the constitutional validity of the predicate convictions. The Supreme Court's answer is that a defendant in an ACCA proceeding may only challenge a previous conviction where there was a denial of the right to counsel.

Custis was convicted under 18 U.S.C. § 922(g)(1) of possession of a firearm by a felon. At sentencing, the Government sought to enhance Custis' sentence under the ACCA based on three prior felony convictions: (1) a 1985 Pennsylvania conviction for robbery; (2) a 1985 Maryland conviction for burglary; and (3) a 1989 Maryland conviction for attempted burglary. Custis objected to consideration of the two Maryland convictions on the ground, among others, that in those proceedings he had received ineffective assistance of counsel. The District Court concluded that the only basis for challenging a prior conviction is if there was a complete denial of counsel in that proceeding. The District Court then sentenced Custis under the ACCA. The Fourth Circuit affirmed.

The Supreme Court affirmed the Fourth Circuit's decision. The Court first concluded that the language of the ACCA did not expressly or impliedly support Custis' position that prior final convictions could be attacked for constitutional errors. The Court further held that the Sixth and Fourteenth Amendments to the Constitution do not require that defendants such as Custis be allowed to challenge previous convictions. Distinguishing cases such as Burgett v. Texas, 389 U.S. 109, 88 S.Ct. 258, 19 L.Ed.2d 319 (1967), and United States v. Tucker, 404 U.S. 443, 92 S.Ct. 589, 30 L.Ed.2d 592 (1972), the Court held that the right to collaterally attack convictions for violations of the right to appointed counsel is unique and should not be extended to claims such as Custis' allegations of ineffective assistance of counsel.

---

[6]Violent Crime Control and Law Enforcement Act of 1994, Pub. L. No. 103–322, § 110506(b), 108 Stat. 1796, ___.

[7]18 U.S.C. § 922(g)(1).

[8]For a defendant convicted of being a felon in possession of a firearm who is not covered by the ACCA, the maximum term of imprisonment is 10 years, and there is no mandatory minimum. 18 U.S.C. § 924(a)(2).

The Court thus rejected Custis' argument that he should be entitled to challenge his previous convictions in the ACCA proceeding. Finally, the Court did note that Custis may attack his Maryland convictions in state court or through federal habeas review, and if successful, he may then apply for resentencing on the federal sentence enhanced by the state conviction. The Court expressly noted, however, that is was expressing no opinion as to the appropriate disposition of such an application.

Justice Souter, writing for three dissenting members of the Court, disagreed with the majority's interpretation of the ACCA. In his view, "conviction" in the ACCA only refers to a "lawful conviction", a position he supports with reference to the text of the ACCA, the legal framework within which Congress drafted the ACCA, and Congress' failure to amend the statute in light of "the consistent interpretation of the ACCA as permitting attacks on prior convictions during sentencing". Further, according to Justice Souter, even if the language of the ACCA is ambiguous, the Court should construe the statute to avoid the serious constitutional issues raised by Custis.[9]

Nichols v. United States, 114 S.Ct. 1921 (1994).

In this case the Supreme Court overruled Baldasar v. Illinois, 446 U.S. 222, 100 S.Ct. 1585, 64 L.Ed.2d 169 (1980), and ruled that neither the Sixth nor Fourteenth Amendments prohibit a sentencing court from considering a defendant's previous uncounseled misdemeanor conviction that did not result in a sentence of imprisonment.

In Scott v. Illinois, 440 U.S. 367, 99 S.Ct. 1158, 59 L.Ed.2d 383 (1979), the Court held that a defendant charged with a misdemeanor has no constitutional right to the appointment of counsel, as long as no sentence of imprisonment is imposed. One year later, in *Baldasar*, the Court held, *per curiam*, that a prior uncounseled misdemeanor conviction, valid under *Scott*, could not be used to elevate a second misdemeanor conviction to a felony, as required by the applicable state sentencing enhancement statute.

In *Nichols*, the defendant pleaded guilty to conspiracy to possess cocaine with the intent to distribute. In determining the defendant's criminal history score under the sentencing guidelines, the District Court added one point for the defendant's 1983 state misdemeanor conviction for driving under the influence. In the DUI case, which resulted in a fine but no incarceration, Nichols was not represented by counsel. Distinguishing *Baldasar*, the District Court ruled that this previous uncounseled misdemeanor could be considered at sentencing because it was not being used to convert a misdemeanor to a felony (as was the case in *Scott*), even though including the DUI conviction did result in a sentence 25 months longer than would otherwise have been applicable. The Sixth Circuit affirmed.

The Supreme Court also affirmed, but the Court overruled, rather than distinguished, *Baldasar*. The Court agreed with the *Baldasar* dissent that a conviction, valid under *Scott*, should not be excluded in a sentencing for a subsequent offense. According to the Court, a recidivist statute, as in *Baldasar*, or the criminal history component of the sentencing guidelines, does not impose punishment for the previous offense; rather only the last offense committed by the defendant is penalized.

Justice Souter, concurring in the judgment, emphasized that because the applicable guideline range is a *presumptive*, not a mandatory, sentence, a defendant may still argue for a departure under § 4A1.3 if

[9] *Id.* at 1743 (citing Ashwander v. TVA, 297 U.S. 288, 348, 56 S.Ct. 466, 80 L.Ed. 688 (1936) (Brandeis, J., concurring)).

inclusion of the uncounseled misdemeanor "significantly over-represents the seriousness of [the] defendant's criminal history or the likelihood that the defendant will commit further crimes."[10]

The dissent would have clarified *Baldasar* and announced a rule that "an uncounseled misdemeanor conviction never can form the basis for a term of imprisonment" or for an increase in a prison term.

[10]For example, Justice Souter contends, a defendant might show "that his prior conviction resulted from railroading an unsophisticated indigent, from a frugal preference for a low fine with no counsel fee, or from a desire to put the matter behind him instead of investing time to fight the charges." 114. S.Ct. at 1930.

HIGHLIGHTS OF THE 1994 CRIME LEGISLATION[1]

by

David Yellen

The Violent Crime Control and Law Enforcement Act of 1994, which the President signed into law on September 13, 1994, is lengthy and affects a wide range of matters, from establishment of a National Commission on Crime Control and Prevention to the death penalty.[2] An outline of the provisions relating to sentencing follows:

I. Mandatory Minimum Sentences.

The legislation enacted one new mandatory minimum provision (the "three strikes" provision) and one provision enabling certain defendants to be sentenced under the guidelines, without regard to an otherwise applicable mandatory minimum (the "safety valve" provision).

A. Three Strikes. Title VII of the legislation amends 18 U.S.C. § 3559 to require life imprisonment for a person convicted of a serious violent felony, if that person has two or more prior final convictions for a serious violent felony or one prior conviction for a serious drug offense and one or more convictions for a serious violent felony. 18 U.S.C. § 3559(c)(1). Each predicate offense (other than the first) and the offense subject to the enhancement must have occurred on separate occasions and be separated by a conviction. 18 U.S.C. § 3559(c)(1)(B).

The term "serious violent felony" is defined to mean (1) any of certain specified offenses (such as murder, aggravated sexual abuse, robbery, and arson) and (2) a federal or state offense that is "punishable by a maximum term of imprisonment of 10 years or more that has as an element the use, attempted use, or threatened use of physical force against the person of another or that, by its nature involves a substantial risk that physical force against the person of another may be used in the course of committing the offense. 18 U.S.C. § 3559(c)(2)(F).[3] The term "serious drug offense" is defined to mean (1) a federal drug trafficking offense punishable by imprisonment for at least ten years and (2) a state offense that, had it been prosecuted in federal court, would have been a drug trafficking offense punishable by imprisonment for at least ten years. 18 U.S.C. § 3559(c)(2)(H).

For the three strikes enhancement to apply, the government must comply with the notice procedures in 21 U.S.C. § 851. 18 U.S.C. § 3559(c)(4). Failure to comply means that the defendant will not be subject to the enhancement. *See* 21 U.S.C. § 851(a)(1).

---

[1]Excerpts from the Violent Crime Control and Law Enforcement Act of 1994 may be found in Appendix G, below.

[2]Pub. L. No. 103–460, 108 Stat. 1796. The National Commission is authorized in title XXVII of the legislation, and the death penalty is addressed title VI of the legislation.

[3]An arson or robbery conviction will not qualify as a serious violent felony under certain conditions. 18 U.S.C. § 3559(c)(3). A robbery does not qualify as a serious violent felony if the defendant establishes by clear and convincing evidence that the offense did not involve the use or threatened use of a firearm or other dangerous weapon and that the offense did not result in death or serious bodily injury to any person. 18 U.S.C. § 3559(c)(3)(A). An arson does not qualify if the defendant establishes by clear and convincing evidence that the offense posed no threat to human life and the defendant reasonably believed that the offense posed no threat to human life. 18 U.S.C. § 3559(c)(3)(B).

There are two mitigating provisions. First, if a conviction used as a basis for applying the three strikes enhancement is subsequently determined to be unconstitutional or is "vitiated on the explicit basis of innocence or if the convicted person is pardoned on the explicit basis of innocence," the defendant must be resentenced to any sentence available at the time of the original sentencing. 18 U.S.C. § 3559(c)(7). Second, § 70002 of the legislation amends 18 U.S.C. § 3582(c)(1)(A) to authorized a sentencing court, upon motion of the Director of the Bureau of Prisons, to reduce the sentence of a prisoner who is 70 years of age or older and who has served at least 30 years of the life term imposed under the three strikes provision. The Director of the Bureau of Prisons, however, must determine that the prisoner "is not a danger to the safety of any other person or the community."

B. Safety Valve. Section 80001 of the legislation—the safety valve provision—contains two directives. One directive, in section 80001(a), is addressed to the sentencing court, and the other, in section 80001(b), is addressed to the Sentencing Commission.

Section 80001(a) requires the sentencing court to "impose a sentence pursuant to guidelines promulgated by the United States Sentencing Commission under section 994 of title 28 without regard to any statutory minimum sentence" if the defendant is convicted of certain drug trafficking offenses and meets five conditions. Because the court can sentence "without regard to any statutory minimum sentence," the court retains the authority under 18 U.S.C. § 3553(b) to impose a sentence below the guideline range if there is a mitigating circumstance for which the guidelines do not adequately account.[4]

The five conditions are—

> (1) the defendant does not have more than 1 criminal history point under the sentencing guidelines;
>
> (2) the defendant did not use violence or credible threats of violence or possess a firearm or other dangerous weapon in connection with the offense (or induce another participant to do so);
>
> (3) the offense did not result in death or serious bodily injury to any person;
>
> (4) the defendant was not an organizer, leader, manager, or supervisor and was not engaged in a continuing criminal enterprise; and
>
> (5) not later than the sentencing hearing, the defendant has truthfully provided to the government "all information and evidence the defendant has concerning the offense or offenses that were part of the same course of conduct or of a common scheme or plan . . . ." That the defendant has no relevant or useful other information to provide, or that the government is already aware of the information, does not preclude the court from finding that the defendant has complied with the requirement.

Section 80001(b)(1)(A) of the legislation directs the Commission to amend guidelines, and authorizes the Commission to amend policy statements, to carry out the purposes of the safety valve

[4]*See* 59 Fed. Register ___ (1994).

provision.[5] Section 8001(b)(1)(B) provides that, for a defendant subject to a mandatory minimum prison term of five years, the minimum of the guideline range must be not less than 24 months.[6]

Section 80001 did not take effect on September 13, 1994, when the President signed the legislation into law. Section 80001(c) provides that the safety valve provision applies to sentences imposed on and after the tenth day after the date of enactment—on September 23, 1994.

II. Probation.

A. Imposition of Probation. Under 18 U.S.C. § 3561(a), a defendant can be sentenced to probation unless (1) the offense of conviction is a class A or B felony and the defendant is an individual; (2) probation has been expressly precluded for the offense of conviction; and (3) "the defendant is sentenced at the same time to a term of imprisonment for the same or different offense." Section 280004 of the legislation narrows the last provision. As amended, 18 U.S.C. § 3651(a)(3) permits imposition of probation if the term of imprisonment imposed at the same time is for a petty offense.

B. Mandatory Conditions of Probation. Section 20414(b) of the legislation amends 18 U.S.C. § 3563(a) to add drug testing to the mandatory conditions of probation.[7] The court can suspend or ameliorate this condition if the court finds that there is a low risk of future substance abuse by the defendant.

C. Revocation of Probation. Section 280001 of the legislation amends 18 U.S.C. § 3553(a)(4) to require the court to consider applicable guidelines and policy statements when imposing punishment for violation of probation. Two other changes made by the legislation give the court greater power after revoking probation.

First, if the revocation is for other than drug possession, 18 U.S.C. § 3565 now requires the court to impose a sentence available "at the time of the initial sentencing." Section 110506 amends 18 U.S.C. § 3565 to direct the court to "resentence the defendant." Thus, the court will no longer be bound by the guideline range determined when the defendant was sentenced to probation. If the revocation is based upon a defendant's conviction of a state crime, for example the defendant's criminal history score will be increased based on the state conviction.

Second, if the revocation is for drug possession, 18 U.S.C. § 3565(a) mandates that the court "sentence the defendant to not less than one–third of the original sentence," a phrase that the Supreme Court has interpreted to mean one–third of the top of the applicable guideline range.[8] Section 110506 of the legislation amends 18 U.S.C. § 3565 to delete the one–third requirement and to require instead "a sentence that includes a term of imprisonment." In addition, section 110506 of the legislation amends 18 U.S.C. §

---

[5]Section 8001(b)(2) of the legislation provides that the Commission can promulgate such amendments "in accordance with the procedures set forth in section 21(a) of the Sentencing Act of 1987, as though the [Commission's] authority under that section had not expired." Section 21(a) of the Sentencing Act of 1987, Pub. L. No. 100–182, 101 Stat. 1266, 1271, authorizes the Commission to promulgate amendments without submitting them to Congress. Such amendments are in effect until November 1 of the year following the year of promulgation.

[6]The 24 month provision limits only the Sentencing Commission's discretion, and does not limit the sentencing court's discretion.

[7]18 U.S.C. § 3563(a) currently mandates a condition that the defendant "not possess illegal controlled substances." Section 280002 of the legislation changes this phrase to "not unlawfully possess a controlled substances."

[8]United States v. Granderson, 114 S.Ct. 1259 (1994).

3565 to mandate a sentence that includes a term of imprisonment if the revocation is for failing to submit to a drug test or for possessing a firearm.

III. Supervised Release.

A. Mandatory Conditions of Supervised Release. Section 20414(c) of the legislation makes drug testing a mandatory condition of supervised release. The court can suspend or ameliorate this condition if the court finds that there is a low risk of future substance abuse by the defendant.

B. Revocation of Supervised Release. Section 11505 of the legislation revises 18 U.S.C. § 3583(e)(3), which deals with revocation of supervised release. Revised 18 U.S.C. § 3583(e)(3) authorizes the court to revoke a term of supervised release and require the defendant to serve in prison "all or part of the term of supervised release authorized by statute for the offense" for which supervised release was imposed.

Section 110505 also revises 18 U.S.C. § 3583(g). Revised 19 U.S.C. § 3583(g) mandates revocation for possession of a firearm and for failing to submit to drug testing, as well as for unlawful possession of a controlled substance.

Finally, section 110505 adds new subsections to 18 U.S.C. § 3583. New 18 U.S.C. § 3583(h) authorize imposition of a term of supervised release to follow imprisonment for revocation of supervised release. The new term of supervised release plus the period of imprisonment, however, cannot exceed the statutorily–authorized maximum period of supervised release (5 years for a class A or B felony, 3 years for class C or D felony, and one year for a class E felony or a misdemeanor other than a petty offense). New 18 U.S.C. § 3583(i) authorizes revocation after the term of supervised release has expired if, before expiration, a warrant or summons was issued alleging a violation of supervised release.

IV. Fines and Restitution.

A. Fines. Section 20403 of the legislation amends 18 U.S.C. § 3572 to require the court, when deciding whether to impose a fine or the amount of a fine, to consider the cost to the government of any imprisonment, supervised release, or probation that is imposed.

B. Restitution. Section 40113(a) of the legislation adds a section to 18 U.S.C. ch. 109A that requires the court to order restitution as part of a sentence for a sex offense set forth in that chapter. Section 40113(b) of the legislation adds a new section to 18 U.S.C. ch. 110 that requires the court to order restitution as a part of a sentence for a child abuse offense set forth in that chapter.

Two provisions of the legislation amend 18 U.S.C. § 3663, which sets forth the sentencing court's authority to order restitution. Section 40504 amends 18 U.S.C. § 3663(b) to permit the court to require the defendant to reimburse the victim for costs related to the investigation or prosecution or to attendance at proceedings related to the offense. Section 40505 adds a new subsection to 18 U.S.C. § 3663 that requires federal agencies to suspend federal benefits to a defendant who the court finds to be delinquent in making restitution.

V. Victim Allocution.

Section 230101 of the legislation amends Rule 32 of the Federal Rules of Criminal Procedure to require the court, when imposing sentence for a crime of violence or sexual abuse, to allow the victim "to make a statement or present any information in relation to the sentence."

VI. Good Time.

Before enactment of the Violent Crime Control and Law Enforcement Act of 1994, 18 U.S.C. § 3624(b) provided that a prisoner earned 54 days of good time credit per year unless the Bureau of Prisons determined that the prisoner had not satisfactorily complied with institutional disciplinary regulations. Good time credit vested when received, and once vested, good time credit could not be taken away. Id. Section 20405 of the legislation amends 18 U.S.C. § 3624(b) to revise the awarding of good time credit. The former rule applies to prisoners who are not imprisoned for a "crime of violence." A prisoner imprisoned for a crime of violence may receive up to 54 days credit per year if the Bureau of Prisons determines that the prisoner "has displayed exemplary compliance" with institutional disciplinary regulations.

Section 20412 of the legislation amends 18 U.S.C. § 3624(b) by revising the vesting rule. Revised 18 U.S.C. § 3624(b) provides that good time credit does not vest "unless the prisoner has earned or is making satisfactory progress toward a high school diploma or an equivalent degree." Revised 18 U.S.C. § 3624(b) authorizes the Bureau of Prisons to make exemptions to this requirement.

VII. Directives to the Sentencing Commission.

The legislation contains some 16 provisions directing the Sentencing Commission to take specified action or expanding the Sentencing Commission's authority regarding the guidelines.

- Section 20403(a) amends 28 U.S.C. § 994 to authorize the Commission to include, as a component of a fine, the expected cost to the government of imprisonment, supervised release, and probation.

- Section 40111(b) directs the Commission to promulgate amendments to guidelines applicable to sexual abuse offenses to implement the provisions of a new section of title 18, United States Code, which doubles the maximum prison term authorized for a sexual abuse offense if the defendant committed the offense after a conviction for a prior sexual abuse offense had become final.

- Section 40112(a) directs the Commission to review and, if necessary, amend the guidelines applicable to offenses under 18 U.S.C. §§ 2241 (aggravated sexual abuse) and 2242 (sexual abuse) with regard to four factors.

- Section 90102 requires the Commission to amend the guidelines "to provide an appropriate enhancement for a defendant convicted of violating" 21 U.S.C. § 860 (drug distribution in a school zone).

- Section 90103(b) requires the Commission to amend the guidelines "to appropriately enhance the penalty for a person convicted" of simple possession of a controlled substance in a federal prison and of smuggling a controlled substance into, or distributing a controlled substance within, a federal prison.

- Section 110501(a) directs the Commission to amend the guidelines "to provide an appropriate enhancement" for a crime of violence (as defined in 18 U.S.C. § 924(c)(3)) and for a drug trafficking crime (as defined in 18 U.S.C. § 924(c)(2)) if a semiautomatic firearm is used.

- Section 110502 directs the Commission to amend the guidelines "to appropriately enhance penalties" for a conviction under 18 U.S.C. § 844(h) (carrying or using an explosive to commit a felony) if the defendant has a prior conviction under that provision.

- Section 110512 directs the Commission to amend the guidelines "to provide an appropriate enhancement" for a defendant convicted of a counterfeiting or forgery offense if the defendant used or carried a firearm during and in relation to the offense.

- Section 110513 requires the Commission to amend the guidelines to enhance the penalty for a defendant convicted of a firearm possession offense if the defendant has a prior conviction for a violent felony (as defined in 18 U.S.C. § 924(e)(2)(B)) or a serious drug offense (as defined in 18 U.S.C. § 924(e)(2)(A)).

- Section 120004 requires the Commission to amend the guidelines to provide an "appropriate enhancement" if a felony "involves or is intended to promote international terrorism."

- Section 14008 requires the Commission to amend the guidelines to provide "an appropriate sentence enhancement" if the defendant is 21 years of age or older and the defendant involved a minor in the commission of the offense.

- Section 180201(c) requires the Commission to amend the guidelines "to provide an appropriate enhancement" for a defendant convicted of trafficking in drugs at a truck stop or highway safety rest area.

- Section 240002 directs the Commission to "ensure that the applicable guideline range for a defendant convicted of a crime of violence against an elderly victim is sufficiently stringent to deter such a crime, to protect the public from additional crimes of such a defendant, and to adequately reflect the heinous nature of such an offense.

- Section 250003 requires the Commission to review and, if necessary, amend the guidelines "to ensure that victim related adjustments for fraud offenses against older victims over the age of 55 are adequate." Section 250003 also requires the Commission to report the results of the review to Congress within 180 days.

- Section 280003 directs the Commission to amend the guidelines to provide an enhancement of a least three levels "for offenses that the finder of fact at trial determines beyond a reasonable doubt are hate crimes."

- Section 280006 directs the Commission to submit to Congress by December 31, 1994, a report "on issues relating to sentences applicable to offenses involving the possessio or distribution of all forms of cocaine."

UNITED STATES SENTENCING COMMISSION
ONE COLUMBUS CIRCLE, NE
SUITE 2-500, SOUTH LOBBY
WASHINGTON, DC 20002-8002
(202) 273-4500
FAX (202) 273-4529

October 15, 1994

To all recipients of the *Guidelines Manual*:

The Sentencing Commission is pleased to transmit this edition of the *Guidelines Manual* which incorporates an "emergency" amendment effective September 23, 1994 (directed by the recently enacted Crime Bill), and six amendments effective November 1, 1994 (a result of the normal amendment cycle).

The emergency amendment implements Section 80001 of the Violent Crime Control and Law Enforcement Act of 1994. Under this section of the Act, defendants sentenced for certain drug offenses who meet the criteria in 18 U.S.C. § 3553(f), as incorporated into the *Manual* through §5C1.2, will qualify for a sentence under the guidelines without regard to an otherwise applicable statutory minimum sentence.

The *Manual* also includes the six amendments to the guidelines issued by the Commission pursuant to its authority under 28 U.S.C. § 994(p) and sent to Congress on April 28, 1994. These amendments take effect following 180 days of Congressional review on the date specified by the Commission unless Congress takes action to the contrary. It appears that these amendments are acceptable to the Congress; consequently, the revised *Manual* is mailed to you at this time so that you will have it in advance of the November 1 effective date.

As always, the Commission encourages judges, probation officers, prosecuting and defense attorneys, and other interested individuals to submit suggestions for improving the guidelines. Please send comments to: United States Sentencing Commission, Federal Judiciary Building, One Columbus Circle, N.E., Suite 2-500, South Lobby, Washington, D.C. 20002-8002, Attention: Public Information Office.

Thank you.

WILLIAM W. WILKINS, JR.
Chairman

UNITED STATES SENTENCING COMMISSION GUIDELINES MANUAL

William W. Wilkins, Jr.
Chairman

Julie E. Carnes
Commissioner

Michael S. Gelacak
Commissioner

A. David Mazzone
Commissioner

Ilene H. Nagel
Commissioner

Jo Ann Harris
Commissioner, Ex-officio

Edward F. Reilly, Jr.
Commissioner, Ex-officio

This document contains the text of the Guidelines Manual incorporating amendments effective January 15, 1988; June 15, 1988; October 15, 1988; November 1, 1989; November 1, 1990; November 1, 1991; November 27, 1991; November 1, 1992; November 1, 1993; September 23, 1994; and November 1, 1994.

*

RECOMMENDED CITATION FORM

United States Sentencing Commission Guidelines, Policy Statements, and Commentary may be cited as follows:

I. Full citation form

United States Sentencing Commission, *Guidelines Manual*, § 3E1.1 (Nov. 1994)

II. Abbreviated citation form

[using U.S.S.G. as the designated short form for United States Sentencing Guidelines]

- a guideline —

  U.S.S.G. § 2D1.1

- a policy statement —

  U.S.S.G. § 6A1.1, p.s.

- commentary designated as an application note —

  U.S.S.G. § 2F1.1, comment. (n.1)

- commentary designated as background —

  U.S.S.G. § 2F1.1, comment. (backg'd.)

- commentary designated as an introduction —

  U.S.S.G. Ch.3, Pt.D, intro. comment.

- an appendix to the Guidelines Manual —

  U.S.S.G. App. C

*

November 1, 1994

WESTLAW® ELECTRONIC RESEARCH GUIDE

Coordinating Legal Research With WESTLAW

The *Federal Sentencing Guidelines Manual* is an essential aid to legal research. WESTLAW provides additional resources. This guide will assist your use of WESTLAW to supplement research begun in this publication.

Databases

A database is a collection of documents with some features in common. It may contain statutes, court decisions, administrative materials, commentaries, news or other information. Each database has a unique identifier, used in many WESTLAW commands to select a database of interest. For example, the database containing cases decided by the United States Courts of Appeal has the identifier CTA; the cases of a specific state are contained in a database having identifier XX-CS, where XX is the state's postal code.

The WESTLAW Directory is a comprehensive list of databases with information about each database, including the types of documents each contains. The first page of a standard or customized WESTLAW Directory is displayed upon signing on to WESTLAW, except when prior, saved research is resumed. To access the WESTLAW Directory at any time, enter DB.

A special subdirectory, accessible from the main WESTLAW Directory, lists databases applicable to Criminal Justice research.

Databases of potential interest in connection with your research include:

FCJ-FSG	Federal Sentencing Guidelines
FCJ-CS	Federal Cases - Criminal Justice
MCJ-CS	Multistate Cases - Criminal Justice
XXCJ-CS	State Cases - Criminal Justice
XXETH-CS	State Cases - Legal Ethics & Professional Responsibility
XX-JLR	State Journals and Law Reviews
WLD-CJ	West Legal Directory - Criminal
LAFAVE1	Search and Seizure
CJ-CJAREP	Criminal Justice Act Reports
CJ-SCJ	ABA Standards for Criminal Justice

For information as to currentness and search tips regarding any WESTLAW database, enter the SCOPE command SC followed by the database identifier (e.g., SC CTA). It is not necessary to include the identifier to obtain scope information about the currently selected database.

WESTLAW Highlights

Use of this publication may be supplemented through the WESTLAW Bulletins (WLB and WSB-XX) and various Topical Highlights, including Criminal Justice Highlights (WTH-CJ). Highlights databases contain summaries of significant judicial, legislative and administrative developments and are updated daily; they are searchable both from an automatic list of recent documents and using general WESTLAW search methods for documents accumulated over time. The full text of any judicial decision may be retrieved by entering FIND.

Consult the WESTLAW Directory (enter DB) for a complete, current listing of other highlights databases.

Retrieving a Specific Case

The FIND command can be used to quickly retrieve a case whose citation is known. For example:

FI 830 S.W.2d 79

Updating Caselaw Research

There are a variety of citator services on WESTLAW for use in updating research.

Insta-Cite® may be used to verify citations, find parallel citations, ascertain the history of a case, and see whether it remains valid law. References are also provided to secondary sources, such as Corpus Juris Secundum®, that cite the case. To view the Insta-Cite history of a displayed case, simply enter the command IC. To view the Insta-Cite history of a selected case, enter a command in this form:

IC 982 F.2d 199

Shepard's® Citations provides a comprehensive list of cases and publications that have cited a particular case, with explanatory analysis to indicate how the citing cases have treated the case, e.g., "followed," "explained." To view the Shepard's Citations about a displayed case, enter the command SH. Add a case citation, if necessary, as in the prior Insta-Cite example.

For the latest citing references, not yet incorporated in Shepard's Citations, use Shepard's PreView® (SP command) and QuickCite™ (QC command), in the same way.

To see a complete list of publications covered by any of the citator services, enter its service abbreviation (IC, SH, SP or QC) followed by PUBS. To ascertain the scope of coverage for any of the services, enter the SCOPE command (SC) followed by the appropriate service abbreviation. For the complete list of commands available in a citator service, enter its service abbreviation (IC, SH, SP or QC) followed by CMDS.

Retrieving Statutes, Regulations, Court Rules and Guidelines

The United States Code and United States Code - Annotated are searchable databases on WESTLAW (identifiers USC and USCA, respectively), as are federal court rules (US-RULES) and regulations (CFR).

Annotated and/or unannotated versions of state statutes (XX-ST and XX-ST-ANN, respectively) and state court rules (XX-RULES) are also searchable on WESTLAW, as are the administrative codes of many states (XX-ADC).

In addition, the FIND command may be used to retrieve specific provisions by citation, obviating the need for database selection or search. To FIND a desired document, enter FI, followed by the citation of the desired document, using the full name of the publication, or one of the abbreviated styles recognized by WESTLAW.

For example, entering either FI FSG 5K1.1, FI Fed. Sent. Guideline, FI USSG 5K1.1, or FI Federal Sentencing Guidelines 5K1.1 displays the requested guideline.

If the forms attempted are not recognized, you may enter one of the following, using US or a state code in place of XX:

FI XX-ST	Displays templates for compiled statutes
FI XX-LEGIS	Displays templates for legislation
FI XX-RULES	Displays templates for rules
FI XX-ORDERS	Displays templates for court orders

Alternatively, entering FI followed by the publication's full name or an accepted abbreviation will normally display templates, useful jump possibilities, or helpful information necessary to complete the FIND process. For example:

FI USCA	Displays templates for United States Code - Annotated
FI FRAP	Displays templates for Federal Rules of Appellate Procedure
FI FRCP	Displays templates for Federal Rules of Civil Procedure
FI FRCRP	Displays templates for Federal Rules of Criminal Procedure
FI FRE	Displays templates for Federal Rules of Evidence
FI CFR	Displays templates for Code of Federal Regulations
FI FR	Displays templates for Federal Register

To view the complete list of FINDable documents and associated prescribed forms, enter FI PUBS.

Updating Research in re Statutes, Rules and Regulations

When viewing a statute, rule or regulation on WESTLAW after a search or FIND command, it is easy to update your research. A message will appear if relevant amendments, repeals or other new material are available through the UPDATE feature. Entering the UPDATE command will display such material.

Documents used to update federal statutes, rules, and regulations are searchable in the United States Public Laws (US-PL), Federal Orders (US-ORDERS) and Federal Register (FR) databases, respectively. For many states, similar material is contained in Legislative Service (XX-LEGIS), Court Orders (XX-ORDERS) and Administrative Register (XX-ADR) databases. Consult the WESTLAW Directory for availability in a specific state.

When documents citing a statute, rule or regulation are of interest, Shepard's Citations on WESTLAW may be of assistance. That service covers federal constitutional provisions, statutes and administrative provisions, and corresponding materials from many states. The command SH PUBS displays a directory of publications which may be Shepardized on WESTLAW. Consult the WESTLAW manual for more information about citator services.

Using WESTLAW as a Citator

For research beyond the coverage of any citator service, go directly to the databases (cases, for example) containing citing documents and use standard WESTLAW search techniques to retrieve documents citing specific constitutional provisions, statutes, standard jury instructions or other authorities.

Fortunately, the specific portion of a citation is often reasonably distinctive, such as 1B1.3, 22:636.1, 301.65, 401(k), 12-21-5, 12052. When it is, a search on that specific portion alone may retrieve applicable documents without any substantial number of inapplicable ones (unless the number happens to be coincidentally popular in another context).

Similarly, if the citation involves more than one number, such as 42 U.S.C.A. 1201, a search containing both numbers (e.g., 42 +5 1201) is likely to produce mostly desired information, even though the component numbers are common.

If necessary, the search may be limited in several ways:

A. Switch from a general database to one containing mostly cases within the subject area of the cite being researched;

B. Use a connector (&, /S, /P, etc.) to narrow the search to documents including terms which are highly likely to accompany the correct citation in the context of the issue being researched;

C. Include other citation information in the query. Because of the variety of citation formats used in documents, this option should be used primarily where other options prove insufficient. Illustrative queries for any database containing Federal cases:

amend! const.amend! /7 8 VIII Eighth

will retrieve cases citing the Eighth Amendment to the U.S. Constitution;

Fed.R.Civ! F.R.Civ! F.R.C.P! R.Civ! Civil Civ.! /7 16

will retrieve cases citing Federal Civil Rule 16; and

Bankruptcy Bankr.! /7 Rule (Procedure Proc. Proc.Rule) /7 1007

will retrieve cases citing Bankruptcy Procedure Rule 1007.

Alternative Retrieval Methods

WIN® (WESTLAW Is Natural™) allows you to frame your issue in plain English to retrieve documents:

Is larceny (theft stealing) a crime of violence under the career offender (4B1.1) provisions of the Sentencing Guidelines?

Alternatively, retrieval may be focused by use of the Terms and Connectors method:

DI(LARCENY THEFT STEAL! VIOLEN** /P 4B1.1 "CAREER OFFENDER")

In databases with Key Numbers, either of the above examples will identify Criminal Law ⚷1202.3(1), 1202.5(3), and 1202.5(4) as Key Numbers collecting headnotes relevant to this issue if there are pertinent cases.

Since the Key Numbers are affixed to points of law by trained specialists based on conceptual understanding of the case, relevant cases that were not retrieved by either of the language-dependent methods will often be found at a Key Number.

Similarly, citations in retrieved documents (to cases, statutes, rules, etc.) may suggest additional, fruitful research using other WESTLAW databases (e.g., annotated statutes, rules) or services (e.g., citator services).

Key Number Search

Frequently, caselaw research rapidly converges on a few topics, headings and Key Numbers within West's Key Number System that are likely to contain relevant cases. These may be discovered from known, relevant reported cases from any jurisdiction; Library References in West publications; browsing in a digest; or browsing the Key Number System on WESTLAW using the JUMP feature or the KEY command.

Once discovered, topics, subheadings or Key Numbers are useful as search terms (in databases containing reported cases) alone or with other search terms, to focus the search within a narrow range of potentially relevant material.

For example, to retrieve cases with at least one headnote classified to Criminal Law 🔑1202.5(3), sign on to a caselaw database and enter

110k1202.5(3) [use with other search terms, if desired]

The topic name (Criminal Law) is replaced by its numerical equivalent (110) and the 🔑 by the letter k. A list of topics and their numerical equivalents is in the WESTLAW Reference Manual and is displayed in WESTLAW when the KEY command is entered.

Other topics of special interest are listed below.

Adulteration (18)
Adultery (19)
Arrest (35)
Arson (36)
Assault and Battery (37)
Bigamy (55)
Breach of the Peace (62)
Bribery (63)
Burglary (67)
Compounding Offenses (88)
Conspiracy (91)
Convicts (98)
Counterfeiting (103)
Disorderly Conduct (129)
Disorderly House (130)
Disturbance of Public Assemblage (133)
Double Jeopardy (135H)
Drugs and Narcotics (138)
Embezzlement (146)
Escape (151)
Extortion and Threats (165)
Extradition and Detainers (166)
False Personation (169)
False Pretenses (170)
Fines (174)
Fires (175)
Forfeitures (180)
Forgery (181)
Fraud (184)
Grand Jury (193)
Habeas Corpus (197)
Homicide (203)
Incest (207)
Indictment and Information (210)
Insurrection and Sedition (218)
Kidnapping (232)
Larceny (234)
Lewdness (236)
Malicious Mischief (248)
Mayhem (256)
Neutrality Laws (273)
Obscenity (281)
Obstructing Justice (282)
Pardon and Parole (284)
Perjury (297)
Prisons (310)
Prostitution (316)
Racketeer Influenced and Corrupt Organizations (319H)
Rape (321)
Receiving Stolen Goods (324)
Rescue (337)
Riot (341)
Robbery (342)
Searches and Seizures (349)
Sodomy (357)
Suicide (368)
Treason (384)
Unlawful Assembly (396)
Vagrancy (399)
Weapons (406)
Witnesses (410)

Using JUMP

WESTLAW's JUMP feature allows you to move from one document to another or from one part of a document to another, then easily return to your original place, without losing your original result. Opportunities to move in this manner are marked in the text with a JUMP symbol (►). Whenever you see the JUMP symbol, you may move to the place designated by the adjacent reference by using the Tab, arrow keys or mouse click to position the cursor on the JUMP symbol, then pressing Enter or clicking again with the mouse.

Within the text of a court opinion, JUMP arrows are adjacent to case cites and federal statute cites, and adjacent to parenthesized numbers marking discussions corresponding to headnotes.

On a screen containing the text of a headnote, the JUMP arrows allow movement to the corresponding discussion in the text of the opinion,

► (3)

and allow browsing West's Key Number System beginning at various heading levels:

► 110 CRIMINAL LAW
► 110XXV Habitual and Second Offenders
► 110XXV(A) In General
► 110k1202.3 Offenses useable for Enhancement
► 110k1202.3(1) k. In general.

To return from a JUMP, enter GB (except for JUMPs between a headnote and the corresponding discussion in opinion, for which there is a matching number in parenthesis in both headnote and opinion). Returns from successive JUMPs (e.g., from case to cited case to case cited by cited case) without intervening returns may be accomplished by repeated entry of GB or by using the MAP command.

General Information

The information provided above illustrates some of the ways WESTLAW can complement research using this publication. However, this brief overview illustrates only some of the power of WESTLAW. The full range of WESTLAW search techniques is available to support your research.

Please consult the WESTLAW Reference Manual for additional information or assistance or call West's Reference Attorneys at 1–800–REF–ATTY (1–800–733–2889).

For information about subscribing to WESTLAW, please call 1–800–328–0109.

TABLE OF CONTENTS

CHAPTER ONE - INTRODUCTION AND GENERAL APPLICATION PRINCIPLES

PART A - INTRODUCTION

1. Authority

The United States Sentencing Commission ("Commission") is an independent agency in the judicial branch composed of seven voting and two non-voting, ex officio members. Its principal purpose is to establish sentencing policies and practices for the federal criminal justice system that will assure the ends of justice by promulgating detailed guidelines prescribing the appropriate sentences for offenders convicted of federal crimes.

The guidelines and policy statements promulgated by the Commission are issued pursuant to Section 994(a) of Title 28, United States Code.

2. The Statutory Mission

The Sentencing Reform Act of 1984 (Title II of the Comprehensive Crime Control Act of 1984) provides for the development of guidelines that will further the basic purposes of criminal punishment: deterrence, incapacitation, just punishment, and rehabilitation. The Act delegates broad authority to the Commission to review and rationalize the federal sentencing process.

The Act contains detailed instructions as to how this determination should be made, the most important of which directs the Commission to create categories of offense behavior and offender characteristics. An offense behavior category might consist, for example, of "bank robbery/committed with a gun/$2500 taken." An offender characteristic category might be "offender with one prior conviction not resulting in imprisonment." The Commission is required to prescribe guideline ranges that specify an appropriate sentence for each class of convicted persons determined by coordinating the offense behavior categories with the offender characteristic categories. Where the guidelines call for imprisonment, the range must be narrow: the maximum of the range cannot exceed the minimum by more than the greater of 25 percent or six months. 28 U.S.C. § 994(b)(2).

Pursuant to the Act, the sentencing court must select a sentence from within the guideline range. If, however, a particular case presents atypical features, the Act allows the court to depart from the guidelines and sentence outside the prescribed range. In that case, the court must specify reasons for departure. 18 U.S.C. § 3553(b). If the court sentences within the guideline range, an appellate court may review the sentence to determine whether the guidelines were correctly applied. If the court departs from the guideline range, an appellate court may review the reasonableness of the departure. 18 U.S.C. § 3742. The Act also abolishes parole, and substantially reduces and restructures good behavior adjustments.

The Commission's initial guidelines were submitted to Congress on April 13, 1987. After the prescribed period of Congressional review, the guidelines took effect on November 1, 1987, and apply to all offenses committed on or after that date. The Commission has the authority to submit guideline amendments each year to Congress between the beginning of a regular Congressional session and May 1. Such amendments automatically take effect 180 days after submission unless a law is enacted to the contrary. 28 U.S.C. § 994(p).

The initial sentencing guidelines and policy statements were developed after extensive hearings, deliberation, and consideration of substantial public comment. The Commission emphasizes, however, that it views the guideline-writing process as evolutionary. It expects, and the governing statute anticipates, that continuing research, experience, and analysis will result in modifications and revisions to the guidelines through submission of amendments to Congress. To this end, the Commission is established as a permanent agency to monitor sentencing practices in the federal courts.

3. The Basic Approach (Policy Statement)

To understand the guidelines and their underlying rationale, it is important to focus on the three objectives that Congress sought to achieve in enacting the Sentencing Reform Act of 1984. The Act's basic objective was to enhance the ability of the criminal justice system to combat crime through an effective, fair sentencing system. To achieve this end, Congress first sought honesty in sentencing. It sought to avoid the confusion and implicit deception that arose out of the pre-guidelines sentencing system which required the court to impose an indeterminate sentence of imprisonment and empowered the parole commission to determine how much of the sentence an offender actually would serve in prison. This practice usually resulted in a substantial reduction in the effective length of the sentence imposed, with defendants often serving only about one-third of the sentence imposed by the court.

Second, Congress sought reasonable uniformity in sentencing by narrowing the wide disparity in sentences imposed for similar criminal offenses committed by similar offenders. Third, Congress sought proportionality in sentencing through a system that imposes appropriately different sentences for criminal conduct of differing severity.

Honesty is easy to achieve: the abolition of parole makes the sentence imposed by the court the sentence the offender will serve, less approximately fifteen percent for good behavior. There is a tension, however, between the mandate of uniformity and the mandate of proportionality. Simple uniformity -- sentencing every offender to five years -- destroys proportionality. Having only a few simple categories of crimes would make the guidelines uniform and easy to administer, but might lump together offenses that are different in important respects. For example, a single category for robbery that included armed and unarmed robberies, robberies with and without injuries, robberies of a few dollars and robberies of millions, would be far too broad.

A sentencing system tailored to fit every conceivable wrinkle of each case would quickly become unworkable and seriously compromise the certainty of punishment and its deterrent effect. For example: a bank robber with (or without) a gun, which the robber kept hidden (or brandished), might have frightened (or merely warned), injured seriously (or less seriously), tied up (or simply pushed) a guard, teller, or customer, at night (or at noon), in an effort to obtain money for other crimes (or for other purposes), in the company of a few (or many) other robbers, for the first (or fourth) time.

The list of potentially relevant features of criminal behavior is long; the fact that they can occur in multiple combinations means that the list of possible permutations of factors is virtually endless. The appropriate relationships among these different factors are exceedingly difficult to establish, for they are often context specific. Sentencing courts do not treat the occurrence of a simple bruise identically in all cases, irrespective of whether that bruise occurred in the context of a bank robbery or in the context of a breach of peace. This is so, in part, because the risk that such a harm will occur differs depending on the underlying offense with which it is connected; and also because, in part, the relationship between punishment and multiple harms is not simply additive. The relation varies depending on how much other harm has occurred. Thus, it would not be proper to assign points for each kind of harm and simply add them up, irrespective of context and total amounts.

The larger the number of subcategories of offense and offender characteristics included in the guidelines, the greater the complexity and the less workable the system. Moreover, complex combinations of offense and offender characteristics would apply and interact in unforeseen ways to unforeseen situations, thus failing to cure the unfairness of a simple, broad category system. Finally, and perhaps most importantly, probation officers and courts, in applying a complex system having numerous subcategories, would be required to make a host of decisions regarding whether the underlying facts were sufficient to bring the case within a particular subcategory. The greater the number of decisions required and the greater their complexity, the greater the risk that different courts would apply the guidelines differently to situations that, in fact, are similar, thereby reintroducing the very disparity that the guidelines were designed to reduce.

In view of the arguments, it would have been tempting to retreat to the simple, broad category approach and to grant courts the discretion to select the proper point along a broad sentencing range. Granting such broad discretion, however, would have risked correspondingly broad disparity in sentencing, for different courts may exercise their discretionary powers in different ways. Such an approach would have risked a return to the wide disparity that Congress established the Commission to reduce and would have been contrary to the Commission's mandate set forth in the Sentencing Reform Act of 1984.

In the end, there was no completely satisfying solution to this problem. The Commission had to balance the comparative virtues and vices of broad, simple categorization and detailed, complex subcategorization, and within the constraints established by that balance, minimize the discretionary powers of the sentencing court. Any system will, to a degree, enjoy the benefits and suffer from the drawbacks of each approach.

A philosophical problem arose when the Commission attempted to reconcile the differing perceptions of the purposes of criminal punishment. Most observers of the criminal law agree that the ultimate aim of the law itself, and of punishment in particular, is the control of crime. Beyond this point, however, the consensus seems to break down. Some argue that appropriate punishment should be defined primarily on the basis of the principle of "just deserts." Under this principle, punishment should be scaled to the offender's culpability and the resulting harms. Others argue that punishment should be imposed primarily on the basis of practical "crime control" considerations. This theory calls for sentences that most effectively lessen the likelihood of future crime, either by deterring others or incapacitating the defendant.

Adherents of each of these points of view urged the Commission to choose between them and accord one primacy over the other. As a practical matter, however, this choice was unnecessary because in most sentencing decisions the application of either philosophy will produce the same or similar results.

In its initial set of guidelines, the Commission sought to solve both the practical and philosophical problems of developing a coherent sentencing system by taking an empirical approach that used as a starting point data estimating pre-guidelines sentencing practice. It analyzed data drawn from 10,000 presentence investigations, the differing elements of various crimes as distinguished in substantive criminal statutes, the United States Parole Commission's guidelines and statistics, and data from other relevant sources in order to determine which distinctions were important in pre-guidelines practice. After consideration, the Commission accepted, modified, or rationalized these distinctions.

This empirical approach helped the Commission resolve its practical problem by defining a list of relevant distinctions that, although of considerable length, was short enough to create a manageable set of guidelines. Existing categories are relatively broad and omit distinctions that some may believe important, yet they include most of the major distinctions that statutes and data suggest made a significant difference in sentencing decisions. Relevant distinctions not reflected in the guidelines probably will occur rarely and sentencing courts may take such unusual cases into account by departing from the guidelines.

The Commission's empirical approach also helped resolve its philosophical dilemma. Those who adhere to a just deserts philosophy may concede that the lack of consensus might make it difficult to say exactly what punishment is deserved for a particular crime. Likewise, those who subscribe to a philosophy of crime control may acknowledge that the lack of sufficient data might make it difficult to determine exactly the punishment that will best prevent that crime. Both groups might therefore recognize the wisdom of looking to those distinctions that judges and legislators have, in fact, made over the course of time. These established distinctions are ones that the community believes, or has found over time, to be important from either a just deserts or crime control perspective.

The Commission did not simply copy estimates of pre-guidelines practice as revealed by the data, even though establishing offense values on this basis would help eliminate disparity because the data represent averages. Rather, it departed from the data at different points for various important reasons. Congressional statutes, for example, suggested or required departure, as in the case of the Anti-Drug Abuse Act of 1986 that imposed increased and mandatory minimum sentences. In addition, the data revealed inconsistencies in treatment, such as punishing economic crime less severely than other apparently equivalent behavior.

Despite these policy-oriented departures from pre-guidelines practice, the guidelines represent an approach that begins with, and builds upon, empirical data. The guidelines will not please those who wish the Commission to adopt a single philosophical theory and then work deductively to establish a simple and perfect set of categorizations and distinctions. The guidelines may prove acceptable, however, to those who seek more modest, incremental improvements in the status quo, who believe the best is often the enemy of the good, and who recognize that these guidelines are, as the Act contemplates, but the first step in an evolutionary process. After spending considerable time and resources exploring alternative approaches, the Commission developed these guidelines as a practical effort toward the achievement of a more honest, uniform, equitable, proportional, and therefore effective sentencing system.

4. <u>The Guidelines' Resolution of Major Issues</u> (Policy Statement)

The guideline-drafting process required the Commission to resolve a host of important policy questions typically involving rather evenly balanced sets of competing considerations. As an aid to understanding the guidelines, this introduction briefly discusses several of those issues; commentary in the guidelines explains others.

(a) <u>Real Offense vs. Charge Offense Sentencing.</u>

One of the most important questions for the Commission to decide was whether to base sentences upon the actual conduct in which the defendant engaged regardless of the charges for which he was indicted or convicted ("real offense" sentencing), or upon the conduct that constitutes the elements of the offense for which the defendant was charged and of which he was convicted ("charge offense" sentencing). A bank robber, for example, might have used a gun, frightened bystanders, taken $50,000, injured a teller, refused to stop when ordered, and raced away damaging property during his escape. A pure real offense system would sentence on the basis of all identifiable conduct. A pure charge offense system would overlook some of the harms that did not constitute statutory elements of the offenses of which the defendant was convicted.

The Commission initially sought to develop a pure real offense system. After all, the pre-guidelines sentencing system was, in a sense, this type of system. The sentencing court and the parole commission took account of the conduct in which the defendant actually engaged, as determined in a presentence report, at the sentencing hearing, or before a parole commission hearing officer. The Commission's initial efforts in this direction, carried out in the spring and early summer of 1986, proved unproductive, mostly for practical reasons. To make such a system work, even to formalize and rationalize the status quo, would have required the Commission to decide precisely which harms to take into account, how to add them up, and what kinds of procedures the courts should use to determine the presence or absence of disputed factual elements. The Commission found no practical way to combine and account for the large number of diverse harms arising in different circumstances; nor did it find a practical way to reconcile the need for a fair adjudicatory procedure with the need for a speedy sentencing process given the potential existence of hosts of adjudicated "real harm" facts in many typical cases. The effort proposed as a solution to these problems required the use of, for example, quadratic roots and other mathematical operations that the Commission considered too complex to be workable. In the Commission's view, such a system risked return to wide disparity in sentencing practice.

In its initial set of guidelines submitted to Congress in April 1987, the Commission moved closer to a charge offense system. This system, however, does contain a significant number of real offense elements. For one thing, the hundreds of overlapping and duplicative statutory provisions that make up the federal criminal law forced the Commission to write guidelines that are descriptive of generic conduct rather than guidelines that track purely statutory language. For another, the guidelines take account of a number of important, commonly occurring real offense elements such as role in the offense, the presence of a gun, or the amount of money actually taken, through alternative base offense levels, specific offense characteristics, cross references, and adjustments.

The Commission recognized that a charge offense system has drawbacks of its own. One of the most important is the potential it affords prosecutors to influence sentences by increasing or decreasing the number of counts in an indictment. Of course, the defendant's actual conduct (that which the prosecutor can prove in court) imposes a natural limit upon the prosecutor's ability to increase a defendant's sentence. Moreover, the Commission has written its rules for the treatment of multicount convictions with an eye toward eliminating unfair treatment that might flow from count manipulation. For example, the guidelines treat a three-count indictment, each count of which charges sale of 100 grams of heroin or theft of $10,000, the same as a single-count indictment charging sale of 300 grams of heroin or theft of $30,000. Furthermore, a sentencing court may control any inappropriate manipulation of the indictment through use of its departure power. Finally, the Commission will closely monitor charging and plea agreement practices and will make appropriate adjustments should they become necessary.

(b) <u>Departures</u>.

The sentencing statute permits a court to depart from a guideline-specified sentence only when it finds "an aggravating or mitigating circumstance of a kind, or to a degree, not adequately taken into consideration by the Sentencing Commission in formulating the guidelines that should result in a sentence different from that described." 18 U.S.C. § 3553(b). The Commission intends the sentencing courts to treat each guideline as carving out a "heartland," a set of typical cases embodying the conduct that each guideline describes. When a court finds an atypical case, one to which a particular guideline linguistically applies but where conduct significantly differs from the norm, the court may consider whether a departure is warranted. Section 5H1.10 (Race, Sex, National Origin, Creed, Religion, and Socio-Economic Status), §5H1.12 (Lack of Guidance as a Youth and Similar Circumstances), the third sentence of §5H1.4 (Physical Condition, Including Drug Dependence and Alcohol Abuse), and the last sentence of §5K2.12 (Coercion and Duress) list several factors that the court cannot take into account as grounds for departure. With those specific exceptions, however, the Commission does not intend to limit the kinds of factors, whether or not mentioned anywhere else in the guidelines, that could constitute grounds for departure in an unusual case.

The Commission has adopted this departure policy for two reasons. First, it is difficult to prescribe a single set of guidelines that encompasses the vast range of human conduct potentially relevant to a sentencing decision. The Commission also recognizes that the initial set of guidelines need not do so. The Commission is a permanent body, empowered by law to write and rewrite guidelines, with progressive changes, over many years. By monitoring when courts depart from the guidelines and by analyzing their stated reasons for doing so and court decisions with references thereto, the Commission, over time, will be able to refine the guidelines to specify more precisely when departures should and should not be permitted.

Second, the Commission believes that despite the courts' legal freedom to depart from the guidelines, they will not do so very often. This is because the guidelines, offense by offense, seek to take account of those factors that the Commission's data indicate made a significant difference in pre-guidelines sentencing practice. Thus, for example, where the presence of physical injury made an important difference in pre-guidelines sentencing practice (as in the case of robbery or assault), the guidelines specifically include this factor to enhance the sentence. Where the guidelines do not specify an augmentation or diminution, this is generally because the sentencing data did not permit the Commission to conclude that the factor was empirically important in relation to the particular offense. Of course, an important factor (e.g., physical injury) may infrequently occur in connection with a particular crime (e.g., fraud). Such rare occurrences are precisely the type of events that the courts' departure powers were designed to cover -- unusual cases outside the range of the more typical offenses for which the guidelines were designed.

It is important to note that the guidelines refer to two different kinds of departure. The first involves instances in which the guidelines provide specific guidance for departure by analogy or by other numerical or non-numerical suggestions. For example, the Commentary to §2G1.1 (Transportation for the Purpose of Prostitution or Prohibited Sexual Conduct) recommends a downward departure of eight levels where a commercial purpose was not involved. The Commission intends such suggestions as policy guidance for the courts. The Commission expects that most departures will reflect the suggestions and that the courts of appeals may prove more likely to find departures "unreasonable" where they fall outside suggested levels.

A second type of departure will remain unguided. It may rest upon grounds referred to in Chapter Five, Part K (Departures) or on grounds not mentioned in the guidelines. While Chapter Five, Part K lists factors that the Commission believes may constitute grounds for departure, the list is not exhaustive. The Commission recognizes that there may be other grounds for departure that are not mentioned; it also believes there may be cases in which a departure outside suggested levels is warranted. In its view, however, such cases will be highly infrequent.

(c) Plea Agreements.

Nearly ninety percent of all federal criminal cases involve guilty pleas and many of these cases involve some form of plea agreement. Some commentators on early Commission guideline drafts urged the Commission not to attempt any major reforms of the plea agreement process on the grounds that any set of guidelines that threatened to change pre-guidelines practice radically also threatened to make the federal system unmanageable. Others argued that guidelines that failed to control and limit plea agreements would leave untouched a "loophole" large enough to undo the good that sentencing guidelines would bring.

The Commission decided not to make major changes in plea agreement practices in the initial guidelines, but rather to provide guidance by issuing general policy statements concerning the acceptance of plea agreements in Chapter Six, Part B (Plea Agreements). The rules set forth in Fed. R. Crim. P. 11(e) govern the acceptance or rejection of such agreements. The Commission will collect data on the courts' plea practices and will analyze this information to determine when and why the courts accept or reject plea agreements and whether plea agreement practices are undermining the intent of the Sentencing Reform Act. In light of this information and analysis, the Commission will seek to further regulate the plea agreement process as appropriate. Importantly, if the policy statements relating to plea agreements are followed, circumvention of the Sentencing Reform Act and the guidelines should not occur.

The Commission expects the guidelines to have a positive, rationalizing impact upon plea agreements for two reasons. First, the guidelines create a clear, definite expectation in respect to the sentence that a court will impose if a trial takes place. In the event a prosecutor and defense attorney explore the possibility of a negotiated plea, they will no longer work in the dark. This fact alone should help to reduce irrationality in respect to actual sentencing outcomes. Second, the guidelines create a norm to which courts will likely refer when they decide whether, under Rule 11(e), to accept or to reject a plea agreement or recommendation.

(d) <u>Probation and Split Sentences</u>.

The statute provides that the guidelines are to "reflect the general appropriateness of imposing a sentence other than imprisonment in cases in which the defendant is a first offender who has not been convicted of a crime of violence or an otherwise serious offense . . . ." 28 U.S.C. § 994(j). Under pre-guidelines sentencing practice, courts sentenced to probation an inappropriately high percentage of offenders guilty of certain economic crimes, such as theft, tax evasion, antitrust offenses, insider trading, fraud, and embezzlement, that in the Commission's view are "serious."

The Commission's solution to this problem has been to write guidelines that classify as serious many offenses for which probation previously was frequently given and provide for at least a short period of imprisonment in such cases. The Commission concluded that the definite prospect of prison, even though the term may be short, will serve as a significant deterrent, particularly when compared with pre-guidelines practice where probation, not prison, was the norm.

More specifically, the guidelines work as follows in respect to a first offender. For offense levels one through six, the sentencing court may elect to sentence the offender to probation (with or without confinement conditions) or to a prison term. For offense levels seven through ten, the court may substitute probation for a prison term, but the probation must include confinement conditions (community confinement, intermittent confinement, or home detention). For offense levels eleven and twelve, the court must impose at least one-half the minimum confinement sentence in the form of prison confinement, the remainder to be served on supervised release with a condition of community confinement or home detention. The Commission, of course, has not dealt with the single acts of aberrant behavior that still may justify probation at higher offense levels through departures.

(e) Multi-Count Convictions.

The Commission, like several state sentencing commissions, has found it particularly difficult to develop guidelines for sentencing defendants convicted of multiple violations of law, each of which makes up a separate count in an indictment. The difficulty is that when a defendant engages in conduct that causes several harms, each additional harm, even if it increases the extent to which punishment is warranted, does not necessarily warrant a proportionate increase in punishment. A defendant who assaults others during a fight, for example, may warrant more punishment if he injures ten people than if he injures one, but his conduct does not necessarily warrant ten times the punishment. If it did, many of the simplest offenses, for reasons that are often fortuitous, would lead to sentences of life imprisonment -- sentences that neither just deserts nor crime control theories of punishment would justify.

Several individual guidelines provide special instructions for increasing punishment when the conduct that is the subject of that count involves multiple occurrences or has caused several harms. The guidelines also provide general rules for aggravating punishment in light of multiple harms charged separately in separate counts. These rules may produce occasional anomalies, but normally they will permit an appropriate degree of aggravation of punishment for multiple offenses that are the subjects of separate counts.

These rules are set out in Chapter Three, Part D (Multiple Counts). They essentially provide: (1) when the conduct involves fungible items (e.g., separate drug transactions or thefts of money), the amounts are added and the guidelines apply to the total amount; (2) when nonfungible harms are involved, the offense level for the most serious count is increased (according to a diminishing scale) to reflect the existence of other counts of conviction. The guidelines have been written in order to minimize the possibility that an arbitrary casting of a single transaction into several counts will produce a longer sentence. In addition, the sentencing court will have adequate power to prevent such a result through departures.

(f) Regulatory Offenses.

Regulatory statutes, though primarily civil in nature, sometimes contain criminal provisions in respect to particularly harmful activity. Such criminal provisions often describe not only substantive offenses, but also more technical, administratively-related offenses such as failure to keep accurate records or to provide requested information. These statutes pose two problems: first, which criminal regulatory provisions should the Commission initially consider, and second, how should it treat technical or administratively-related criminal violations?

In respect to the first problem, the Commission found that it could not comprehensively treat all regulatory violations in the initial set of guidelines. There are hundreds of such provisions scattered throughout the United States Code. To find all potential violations would involve examination of each individual federal regulation. Because of this practical difficulty, the Commission sought to determine, with the assistance of the Department of Justice and several regulatory agencies, which criminal regulatory offenses were particularly important in light of the need for enforcement of the general regulatory scheme. The Commission addressed these offenses in the initial guidelines.

In respect to the second problem, the Commission has developed a system for treating technical recordkeeping and reporting offenses that divides them into four categories. First, in the simplest of cases, the offender may have failed to fill out a form intentionally, but without knowledge or intent that substantive harm would likely follow. He might fail, for example, to keep an accurate record of toxic substance transport, but that failure may not lead, nor be likely to lead, to the release or improper handling of any toxic substance. Second, the same failure may be accompanied by a significant likelihood that substantive harm will occur; it may make a release of a toxic substance more likely. Third, the same failure may have led to substantive harm. Fourth, the failure may represent an effort to conceal a substantive harm that has occurred.

The structure of a typical guideline for a regulatory offense provides a low base offense level (e.g., 6) aimed at the first type of recordkeeping or reporting offense. Specific offense characteristics designed to reflect substantive harms that do occur in respect to some regulatory offenses, or that are likely to occur, increase the offense level. A specific offense characteristic also provides that a recordkeeping or reporting offense that conceals a substantive offense will have the same offense level as the substantive offense.

(g) Sentencing Ranges.

In determining the appropriate sentencing ranges for each offense, the Commission estimated the average sentences served within each category under the pre-guidelines sentencing system. It also examined the sentences specified in federal statutes, in the parole guidelines, and in other relevant, analogous sources. The Commission's Supplementary Report on the Initial Sentencing Guidelines (1987) contains a comparison between estimates of pre-guidelines sentencing practice and sentences under the guidelines.

While the Commission has not considered itself bound by pre-guidelines sentencing practice, it has not attempted to develop an entirely new system of sentencing on the basis of theory alone. Guideline sentences, in many instances, will approximate average pre-guidelines practice and adherence to the guidelines will help to eliminate wide disparity. For example, where a high percentage of persons received probation under pre-guidelines practice, a guideline may include one or more specific offense characteristics in an effort to distinguish those types of defendants who received probation from those who received more severe sentences. In some instances, short sentences of incarceration for all offenders in a category have been substituted for a pre-guidelines sentencing practice of very wide variability in which some defendants received probation while others received several years in prison for the same offense. Moreover, inasmuch as those who pleaded guilty under pre-guidelines practice often received lesser sentences, the guidelines permit the court to impose lesser sentences on those defendants who accept responsibility for their misconduct. For defendants who provide substantial assistance to the government in the investigation or prosecution of others, a downward departure may be warranted.

The Commission has also examined its sentencing ranges in light of their likely impact upon prison population. Specific legislation, such as the Anti-Drug Abuse Act of 1986 and the career offender provisions of the Sentencing Reform Act of 1984 (28 U.S.C. § 994(h)), required the Commission to promulgate guidelines that will lead to substantial prison population increases. These increases will occur irrespective of the guidelines. The guidelines themselves, insofar as they reflect policy decisions made by the Commission (rather than legislated mandatory minimum or career offender sentences), are projected to lead to an increase in prison population that computer models, produced by the Commission and the Bureau of Prisons in 1987, estimated at approximately 10 percent over a period of ten years.

(h) The Sentencing Table.

The Commission has established a sentencing table that for technical and practical reasons contains 43 levels. Each level in the table prescribes ranges that overlap with the ranges in the preceding and succeeding levels. By overlapping the ranges, the table should discourage unnecessary litigation. Both prosecution and defense will realize that the difference between one level and another will not necessarily make a difference in the sentence that the court imposes. Thus, little purpose will be served in protracted litigation trying to determine, for example, whether $10,000 or $11,000 was obtained as a result of a fraud. At the same time, the levels work to increase a sentence proportionately. A change of six levels roughly doubles the sentence irrespective of the level at which one starts. The guidelines, in keeping with the statutory requirement that the maximum of any range cannot exceed the minimum by more than the greater of 25 percent or six months (28 U.S.C. § 994(b)(2)), permit courts to exercise the greatest permissible range of sentencing discretion. The table overlaps offense levels meaningfully, works proportionately, and at the same time preserves the maximum degree of allowable discretion for the court within each level.

Similarly, many of the individual guidelines refer to tables that correlate amounts of money with offense levels. These tables often have many rather than a few levels. Again, the reason is to minimize the likelihood of unnecessary litigation. If a money table were to make only a few distinctions, each distinction would become more important and litigation over which category an offender fell within would become more likely. Where a table has many small monetary distinctions, it minimizes the likelihood of litigation because the precise amount of money involved is of considerably less importance.

5. <u>A Concluding Note</u>

The Commission emphasizes that it drafted the initial guidelines with considerable caution. It examined the many hundreds of criminal statutes in the United States Code. It began with those that were the basis for a significant number of prosecutions and sought to place them in a rational order. It developed additional distinctions relevant to the application of these provisions and it applied sentencing ranges to each resulting category. In doing so, it relied upon pre-guidelines sentencing practice as revealed by its own statistical analyses based on summary reports of some 40,000 convictions, a sample of 10,000 augmented presentence reports, the parole guidelines, and policy judgments.

The Commission recognizes that some will criticize this approach as overly cautious, as representing too little a departure from pre-guidelines sentencing practice. Yet, it will cure wide disparity. The Commission is a permanent body that can amend the guidelines each year. Although the data available to it, like all data, are imperfect, experience with the guidelines will lead to additional information and provide a firm empirical basis for consideration of revisions.

Finally, the guidelines will apply to more than 90 percent of all felony and Class A misdemeanor cases in the federal courts. Because of time constraints and the nonexistence of statistical information, some offenses that occur infrequently are not considered in the guidelines. Their exclusion does not reflect any judgment regarding their seriousness and they will be addressed as the Commission refines the guidelines over time.

<u>Historical Note</u>: Effective November 1, 1987. Amended effective November 1, 1989 (<u>see</u> Appendix C, amendments 67 and 68); November 1, 1990 (<u>see</u> Appendix C, amendment 307); November 1, 1992 (<u>see</u> Appendix C, amendment 466).

PART B - GENERAL APPLICATION PRINCIPLES

§1B1.1. Application Instructions

(a) Determine the applicable offense guideline section from Chapter Two. See §1B1.2 (Applicable Guidelines). The Statutory Index (Appendix A) provides a listing to assist in this determination.

(b) Determine the base offense level and apply any appropriate specific offense characteristics contained in the particular guideline in Chapter Two in the order listed.

(c) Apply the adjustments as appropriate related to victim, role, and obstruction of justice from Parts A, B, and C of Chapter Three.

(d) If there are multiple counts of conviction, repeat steps (a) through (c) for each count. Apply Part D of Chapter Three to group the various counts and adjust the offense level accordingly.

(e) Apply the adjustment as appropriate for the defendant's acceptance of responsibility from Part E of Chapter Three.

(f) Determine the defendant's criminal history category as specified in Part A of Chapter Four. Determine from Part B of Chapter Four any other applicable adjustments.

(g) Determine the guideline range in Part A of Chapter Five that corresponds to the offense level and criminal history category determined above.

(h) For the particular guideline range, determine from Parts B through G of Chapter Five the sentencing requirements and options related to probation, imprisonment, supervision conditions, fines, and restitution.

(i) Refer to Parts H and K of Chapter Five, Specific Offender Characteristics and Departures, and to any other policy statements or commentary in the guidelines that might warrant consideration in imposing sentence.

Commentary

Application Notes:

1. *The following are definitions of terms that are used frequently in the guidelines and are of general applicability (except to the extent expressly modified in respect to a particular guideline or policy statement):*

   (a) "Abducted" means that a victim was forced to accompany an offender to a different location. For example, a bank robber's forcing a bank teller from the bank into a getaway car would constitute an abduction.

   (b) "Bodily injury" means any significant injury; e.g., an injury that is painful and obvious, or is of a type for which medical attention ordinarily would be sought. As used in the

guidelines, the definition of this term is somewhat different than that used in various statutes.

(c) *"Brandished" with reference to a dangerous weapon (including a firearm) means that the weapon was pointed or waved about, or displayed in a threatening manner.*

(d) *"Dangerous weapon" means an instrument capable of inflicting death or serious bodily injury. Where an object that appeared to be a dangerous weapon was brandished, displayed, or possessed, treat the object as a dangerous weapon.*

(e) *"Firearm" means (i) any weapon (including a starter gun) which will or is designed to or may readily be converted to expel a projectile by the action of an explosive; (ii) the frame or receiver of any such weapon; (iii) any firearm muffler or silencer; or (iv) any destructive device. A weapon, commonly known as a "BB" or pellet gun, that uses air or carbon dioxide pressure to expel a projectile is a dangerous weapon but not a firearm.*

(f) *"More than minimal planning" means more planning than is typical for commission of the offense in a simple form. "More than minimal planning" also exists if significant affirmative steps were taken to conceal the offense, other than conduct to which §3C1.1 (Obstructing or Impeding the Administration of Justice) applies.*

"More than minimal planning" is deemed present in any case involving repeated acts over a period of time, unless it is clear that each instance was purely opportune. Consequently, this adjustment will apply especially frequently in property offenses.

In an assault, for example, waiting to commit the offense when no witnesses were present would not alone constitute more than minimal planning. By contrast, luring the victim to a specific location, or wearing a ski mask to prevent identification, would constitute more than minimal planning.

In a commercial burglary, for example, checking the area to make sure no witnesses were present would not alone constitute more than minimal planning. By contrast, obtaining building plans to plot a particular course of entry, or disabling an alarm system, would constitute more than minimal planning.

In a theft, going to a secluded area of a store to conceal the stolen item in one's pocket would not alone constitute more than minimal planning. However, repeated instances of such thefts on several occasions would constitute more than minimal planning. Similarly, fashioning a special device to conceal the property, or obtaining information on delivery dates so that an especially valuable item could be obtained, would constitute more than minimal planning.

In an embezzlement, a single taking accomplished by a false book entry would constitute only minimal planning. On the other hand, creating purchase orders to, and invoices from, a dummy corporation for merchandise that was never delivered would constitute more than minimal planning, as would several instances of taking money, each accompanied by false entries.

(g) *"Otherwise used" with reference to a dangerous weapon (including a firearm) means that the conduct did not amount to the discharge of a firearm but was more than brandishing, displaying, or possessing a firearm or other dangerous weapon.*

(h) "Permanent or life-threatening bodily injury" means injury involving a substantial risk of death; loss or substantial impairment of the function of a bodily member, organ, or mental faculty that is likely to be permanent; or an obvious disfigurement that is likely to be permanent. In the case of a kidnapping, for example, maltreatment to a life-threatening degree (e.g., by denial of food or medical care) would constitute life-threatening bodily injury.

(i) "Physically restrained" means the forcible restraint of the victim such as by being tied, bound, or locked up.

(j) "Serious bodily injury" means injury involving extreme physical pain or the impairment of a function of a bodily member, organ, or mental faculty; or requiring medical intervention such as surgery, hospitalization, or physical rehabilitation. As used in the guidelines, the definition of this term is somewhat different than that used in various statutes.

(k) "Destructive device" means any article described in 26 U.S.C. § 5845(f) (including an explosive, incendiary, or poison gas - (i) bomb, (ii) grenade, (iii) rocket having a propellant charge of more than four ounces, (iv) missile having an explosive or incendiary charge of more than one-quarter ounce, (v) mine, or (vi) device similar to any of the devices described in the preceding clauses).

(l) "Offense" means the offense of conviction and all relevant conduct under §1B1.3 (Relevant Conduct) unless a different meaning is specified or is otherwise clear from the context.

2. *Definitions of terms also may appear in other sections. Such definitions are not designed for general applicability; therefore, their applicability to sections other than those expressly referenced must be determined on a case by case basis.*

   The term "includes" is not exhaustive; the term "e.g." is merely illustrative.

3. *The list of "Statutory Provisions" in the Commentary to each offense guideline does not necessarily include every statute covered by that guideline. In addition, some statutes may be covered by more than one guideline.*

4. *The offense level adjustments from more than one specific offense characteristic within an offense guideline are cumulative (added together) unless the guideline specifies that only the greater (or greatest) is to be used. Within each specific offense characteristic subsection, however, the offense level adjustments are alternative; only the one that best describes the conduct is to be used. E.g., in §2A2.2(b)(3), pertaining to degree of bodily injury, the subdivision that best describes the level of bodily injury is used; the adjustments for different degrees of bodily injury (subdivisions (A)-(E)) are not added together.*

   Absent an instruction to the contrary, the adjustments from different guideline sections are applied cumulatively (added together). For example, the adjustments from §2F1.1(b)(2) (more than minimal planning) and §3B1.1 (aggravating role) are applied cumulatively.

5. *Where two or more guideline provisions appear equally applicable, but the guidelines authorize the application of only one such provision, use the provision that results in the greater offense level. E.g., in §2A2.2(b)(2), if a firearm is both discharged and brandished, the provision applicable to the discharge of the firearm would be used.*

6. *In the case of a defendant subject to a sentence enhancement under 18 U.S.C. § 3147 (Penalty for an Offense Committed While on Release), see §2J1.7 (Commission of Offense While on Release).*

Historical Note: Effective November 1, 1987. Amended effective January 15, 1988 (see Appendix C, amendment 1); November 1, 1989 (see Appendix C, amendments 69-72 and 303); November 1, 1990 (see Appendix C, amendment 361); November 1, 1991 (see Appendix C, amendment 388); November 1, 1993 (see Appendix C, amendment 497).

§1B1.2. Applicable Guidelines

(a) Determine the offense guideline section in Chapter Two (Offense Conduct) most applicable to the offense of conviction (i.e., the offense conduct charged in the count of the indictment or information of which the defendant was convicted). *Provided*, however, in the case of a plea agreement (written or made orally on the record) containing a stipulation that specifically establishes a more serious offense than the offense of conviction, determine the offense guideline section in Chapter Two most applicable to the stipulated offense.

(b) After determining the appropriate offense guideline section pursuant to subsection (a) of this section, determine the applicable guideline range in accordance with §1B1.3 (Relevant Conduct).

(c) A plea agreement (written or made orally on the record) containing a stipulation that specifically establishes the commission of additional offense(s) shall be treated as if the defendant had been convicted of additional count(s) charging those offense(s).

(d) A conviction on a count charging a conspiracy to commit more than one offense shall be treated as if the defendant had been convicted on a separate count of conspiracy for each offense that the defendant conspired to commit.

Commentary

Application Notes:

1. *This section provides the basic rules for determining the guidelines applicable to the offense conduct under Chapter Two (Offense Conduct). As a general rule, the court is to use the guideline section from Chapter Two most applicable to the offense of conviction. The Statutory Index (Appendix A) provides a listing to assist in this determination. When a particular statute proscribes only a single type of criminal conduct, the offense of conviction and the conduct proscribed by the statute will coincide, and there will be only one offense guideline referenced. When a particular statute proscribes a variety of conduct that might constitute the subject of different offense guidelines, the court will determine which guideline section applies based upon the nature of the offense conduct charged in the count of which the defendant was convicted.*

However, there is a limited exception to this general rule. Where a stipulation that is set forth in a written plea agreement or made between the parties on the record during a plea proceeding specifically establishes facts that prove a more serious offense or offenses than the offense or offenses of conviction, the court is to apply the guideline most applicable to the more serious offense or offenses established. The sentence that may be imposed is limited, however, to the maximum authorized by the statute under which the defendant is convicted. See Chapter Five,

Part G (Implementing the Total Sentence of Imprisonment). For example, if the defendant pleads guilty to theft, but admits the elements of robbery as part of the plea agreement, the robbery guideline is to be applied. The sentence, however, may not exceed the maximum sentence for theft. See H. Rep. 98-1017, 98th Cong., 2d Sess. 99 (1984).

The exception to the general rule has a practical basis. In cases where the elements of an offense more serious than the offense of conviction are established by a plea agreement, it may unduly complicate the sentencing process if the applicable guideline does not reflect the seriousness of the defendant's actual conduct. Without this exception, the court would be forced to use an artificial guideline and then depart from it to the degree the court found necessary based upon the more serious conduct established by the plea agreement. The probation officer would first be required to calculate the guideline for the offense of conviction. However, this guideline might even contain characteristics that are difficult to establish or not very important in the context of the actual offense conduct. As a simple example, §2B1.1 (Larceny, Embezzlement, and Other Forms of Theft) contains monetary distinctions which are more significant and more detailed than the monetary distinctions in §2B3.1 (Robbery). Then, the probation officer might need to calculate the robbery guideline to assist the court in determining the appropriate degree of departure in a case in which the defendant pled guilty to theft but admitted committing robbery. This cumbersome, artificial procedure is avoided by using the exception rule in guilty or nolo contendere plea cases where it is applicable.

As with any plea agreement, the court must first determine that the agreement is acceptable, in accordance with the policies stated in Chapter Six, Part B (Plea Agreements). The limited exception provided here applies only after the court has determined that a plea, otherwise fitting the exception, is acceptable.

2. *Section 1B1.2(b) directs the court, once it has determined the applicable guideline (i.e., the applicable guideline section from Chapter Two) under §1B1.2(a) to determine any applicable specific offense characteristics (under that guideline), and any other applicable sentencing factors pursuant to the relevant conduct definition in §1B1.3. Where there is more than one base offense level within a particular guideline, the determination of the applicable base offense level is treated in the same manner as a determination of a specific offense characteristic. Accordingly, the "relevant conduct" criteria of §1B1.3 are to be used, unless conviction under a specific statute is expressly required.*

3. *In many instances, it will be appropriate that the court consider the actual conduct of the offender, even when such conduct does not constitute an element of the offense. As described above, this may occur when an offender stipulates certain facts in a plea agreement. It is more typically so when the court considers the applicability of specific offense characteristics within individual guidelines, when it considers various adjustments, and when it considers whether or not to depart from the guidelines for reasons relating to offense conduct. See §§1B1.3 (Relevant Conduct) and 1B1.4 (Information to be Used in Imposing Sentence).*

4. *Subsections (c) and (d) address circumstances in which the provisions of Chapter Three, Part D (Multiple Counts) are to be applied although there may be only one count of conviction. Subsection (c) provides that in the case of a stipulation to the commission of additional offense(s), the guidelines are to be applied as if the defendant had been convicted of an additional count for each of the offenses stipulated. For example, if the defendant is convicted of one count of robbery but, as part of a plea agreement, admits to having committed two additional robberies, the guidelines are to be applied as if the defendant had been convicted of three counts of robbery. Subsection (d) provides that a conviction on a conspiracy count charging conspiracy to commit more than one offense is treated as if the defendant had been convicted of a separate conspiracy count for each offense that he conspired to commit. For*

example, where a conviction on a single count of conspiracy establishes that the defendant conspired to commit three robberies, the guidelines are to be applied as if the defendant had been convicted on one count of conspiracy to commit the first robbery, one count of conspiracy to commit the second robbery, and one count of conspiracy to commit the third robbery.

5. *Particular care must be taken in applying subsection (d) because there are cases in which the verdict or plea does not establish which offense(s) was the object of the conspiracy. In such cases, subsection (d) should only be applied with respect to an object offense alleged in the conspiracy count if the court, were it sitting as a trier of fact, would convict the defendant of conspiring to commit that object offense. Note, however, if the object offenses specified in the conspiracy count would be grouped together under §3D1.2(d) (e.g., a conspiracy to steal three government checks) it is not necessary to engage in the foregoing analysis, because §1B1.3(a)(2) governs consideration of the defendant's conduct.*

Historical Note: Effective November 1, 1987. Amended effective January 15, 1988 (see Appendix C, amendment 2); November 1, 1989 (see Appendix C, amendments 73-75 and 303); November 1, 1991 (see Appendix C, amendment 434); November 1, 1992 (see Appendix C, amendment 438).

§1B1.3. Relevant Conduct (Factors that Determine the Guideline Range)

(a) Chapters Two (Offense Conduct) and Three (Adjustments). Unless otherwise specified, (i) the base offense level where the guideline specifies more than one base offense level, (ii) specific offense characteristics and (iii) cross references in Chapter Two, and (iv) adjustments in Chapter Three, shall be determined on the basis of the following:

(1) (A) all acts and omissions committed, aided, abetted, counseled, commanded, induced, procured, or willfully caused by the defendant; and

(B) in the case of a jointly undertaken criminal activity (a criminal plan, scheme, endeavor, or enterprise undertaken by the defendant in concert with others, whether or not charged as a conspiracy), all reasonably foreseeable acts and omissions of others in furtherance of the jointly undertaken criminal activity,

that occurred during the commission of the offense of conviction, in preparation for that offense, or in the course of attempting to avoid detection or responsibility for that offense;

(2) solely with respect to offenses of a character for which §3D1.2(d) would require grouping of multiple counts, all acts and omissions described in subdivisions (1)(A) and (1)(B) above that were part of the same course of conduct or common scheme or plan as the offense of conviction;

(3) all harm that resulted from the acts and omissions specified in subsections (a)(1) and (a)(2) above, and all harm that was the object of such acts and omissions; and

(4) any other information specified in the applicable guideline.

(b) Chapters Four (Criminal History and Criminal Livelihood) and Five (Determining the Sentence). Factors in Chapters Four and Five that establish the guideline range shall be determined on the basis of the conduct and information specified in the respective guidelines.

Commentary

Application Notes:

1. *The principles and limits of sentencing accountability under this guideline are not always the same as the principles and limits of criminal liability. Under subsections (a)(1) and (a)(2), the focus is on the specific acts and omissions for which the defendant is to be held accountable in determining the applicable guideline range, rather than on whether the defendant is criminally liable for an offense as a principal, accomplice, or conspirator.*

2. *A "jointly undertaken criminal activity" is a criminal plan, scheme, endeavor, or enterprise undertaken by the defendant in concert with others, whether or not charged as a conspiracy.*

In the case of a jointly undertaken criminal activity, subsection (a)(1)(B) provides that a defendant is accountable for the conduct (acts and omissions) of others that was both:

(i) *in furtherance of the jointly undertaken criminal activity; and*

(ii) *reasonably foreseeable in connection with that criminal activity.*

Because a count may be worded broadly and include the conduct of many participants over a period of time, the scope of the criminal activity jointly undertaken by the defendant (the "jointly undertaken criminal activity") is not necessarily the same as the scope of the entire conspiracy, and hence relevant conduct is not necessarily the same for every participant. In order to determine the defendant's accountability for the conduct of others under subsection (a)(1)(B), the court must first determine the scope of the criminal activity the particular defendant agreed to jointly undertake (i.e., the scope of the specific conduct and objectives embraced by the defendant's agreement). The conduct of others that was both in furtherance of, and reasonably foreseeable in connection with, the criminal activity jointly undertaken by the defendant is relevant conduct under this provision. The conduct of others that was not in furtherance of the criminal activity jointly undertaken by the defendant, or was not reasonably foreseeable in connection with that criminal activity, is not relevant conduct under this provision.

In determining the scope of the criminal activity that the particular defendant agreed to jointly undertake (i.e., the scope of the specific conduct and objectives embraced by the defendant's agreement), the court may consider any explicit agreement or implicit agreement fairly inferred from the conduct of the defendant and others.

Note that the criminal activity that the defendant agreed to jointly undertake, and the reasonably foreseeable conduct of others in furtherance of that criminal activity, are not necessarily identical. For example, two defendants agree to commit a robbery and, during the course of that robbery, the first defendant assaults and injures a victim. The second defendant is accountable for the assault and injury to the victim (even if the second defendant had not agreed to the assault and had cautioned the first defendant to be careful not to hurt anyone) because the assaultive conduct was in furtherance of the jointly undertaken criminal activity (the robbery) and was reasonably foreseeable in connection with that criminal activity (given the nature of the offense).

With respect to offenses involving contraband (including controlled substances), the defendant is accountable for all quantities of contraband with which he was directly involved and, in the case of a jointly undertaken criminal activity, all reasonably foreseeable quantities of contraband that were within the scope of the criminal activity that he jointly undertook.

The requirement of reasonable foreseeability applies only in respect to the conduct (i.e., acts and omissions) of others under subsection (a)(1)(B). It does not apply to conduct that the defendant personally undertakes, aids, abets, counsels, commands, induces, procures, or willfully causes; such conduct is addressed under subsection (a)(1)(A).

A defendant's relevant conduct does not include the conduct of members of a conspiracy prior to the defendant joining the conspiracy, even if the defendant knows of that conduct (e.g., in the case of a defendant who joins an ongoing drug distribution conspiracy knowing that it had been selling two kilograms of cocaine per week, the cocaine sold prior to the defendant joining the conspiracy is not included as relevant conduct in determining the defendant's offense level). The Commission does not foreclose the possibility that there may be some unusual set of circumstances in which the exclusion of such conduct may not adequately reflect the defendant's culpability; in such a case, an upward departure may be warranted.

Illustrations of Conduct for Which the Defendant is Accountable

(a) Acts and omissions aided or abetted by the defendant

(1) Defendant A is one of ten persons hired by Defendant B to off-load a ship containing marihuana. The off-loading of the ship is interrupted by law enforcement officers and one ton of marihuana is seized (the amount on the ship as well as the amount off-loaded). Defendant A and the other off-loaders are arrested and convicted of importation of marihuana. Regardless of the number of bales he personally unloaded, Defendant A is accountable for the entire one-ton quantity of marihuana. Defendant A aided and abetted the off-loading of the entire shipment of marihuana by directly participating in the off-loading of that shipment (i.e., the specific objective of the criminal activity he joined was the off-loading of the entire shipment). Therefore, he is accountable for the entire shipment under subsection (a)(1)(A) without regard to the issue of reasonable foreseeability. This is conceptually similar to the case of a defendant who transports a suitcase knowing that it contains a controlled substance and, therefore, is accountable for the controlled substance in the suitcase regardless of his knowledge or lack of knowledge of the actual type or amount of that controlled substance.

In certain cases, a defendant may be accountable for particular conduct under more than one subsection of this guideline. As noted in the preceding paragraph, Defendant A is accountable for the entire one-ton shipment of marihuana under subsection (a)(1)(A). Defendant A also is accountable for the entire one-ton shipment of marihuana on the basis of subsection (a)(1)(B)(applying to a jointly undertaken criminal activity). Defendant A engaged in a jointly undertaken criminal activity (the scope of which was the importation of the shipment of marihuana). A finding that the one-ton quantity of marihuana was reasonably foreseeable is warranted from the nature of the undertaking itself (the importation of marihuana by ship typically involves very large quantities of marihuana). The specific circumstances of the case (the defendant was one of ten persons off-loading the marihuana in bales) also support this finding. In an actual case, of course, if a defendant's accountability for particular conduct is established under one provision of this guideline, it is not necessary to review alternative provisions under which such accountability might be established.

(b) Acts and omissions aided or abetted by the defendant; requirement that the conduct of others be in furtherance of the jointly undertaken criminal activity and reasonably foreseeable

(1) *Defendant C is the getaway driver in an armed bank robbery in which $15,000 is taken and a teller is assaulted and injured. Defendant C is accountable for the money taken under subsection (a)(1)(A) because he aided and abetted the act of taking the money (the taking of money was the specific objective of the offense he joined). Defendant C is accountable for the injury to the teller under subsection (a)(1)(B) because the assault on the teller was in furtherance of the jointly undertaken criminal activity (the robbery) and was reasonably foreseeable in connection with that criminal activity (given the nature of the offense).*

As noted earlier, a defendant may be accountable for particular conduct under more than one subsection. In this example, Defendant C also is accountable for the money taken on the basis of subsection (a)(1)(B) because the taking of money was in furtherance of the jointly undertaken criminal activity (the robbery) and was reasonably foreseeable (as noted, the taking of money was the specific objective of the jointly undertaken criminal activity).

(c) Requirement that the conduct of others be in furtherance of the jointly undertaken criminal activity and reasonably foreseeable; scope of the criminal activity

(1) *Defendant D pays Defendant E a small amount to forge an endorsement on an $800 stolen government check. Unknown to Defendant E, Defendant D then uses that check as a down payment in a scheme to fraudulently obtain $15,000 worth of merchandise. Defendant E is convicted of forging the $800 check and is accountable for the forgery of this check under subsection (a)(1)(A). Defendant E is not accountable for the $15,000 because the fraudulent scheme to obtain $15,000 was not in furtherance of the criminal activity he jointly undertook with Defendant D (i.e., the forgery of the $800 check).*

(2) *Defendants F and G, working together, design and execute a scheme to sell fraudulent stocks by telephone. Defendant F fraudulently obtains $20,000. Defendant G fraudulently obtains $35,000. Each is convicted of mail fraud. Defendants F and G each are accountable for the entire amount ($55,000). Each defendant is accountable for the amount he personally obtained under subsection (a)(1)(A). Each defendant is accountable for the amount obtained by his accomplice under subsection (a)(1)(B) because the conduct of each was in furtherance of the jointly undertaken criminal activity and was reasonably foreseeable in connection with that criminal activity.*

(3) *Defendants H and I engaged in an ongoing marihuana importation conspiracy in which Defendant J was hired only to help off-load a single shipment. Defendants H, I, and J are included in a single count charging conspiracy to import marihuana. Defendant J is accountable for the entire single shipment of*

marihuana he helped import under subsection (a)(1)(A) and any acts and omissions in furtherance of the importation of that shipment that were reasonably foreseeable (<u>see</u> the discussion in example (a)(1) above). He is not accountable for prior or subsequent shipments of marihuana imported by Defendants H or I because those acts were not in furtherance of his jointly undertaken criminal activity (the importation of the single shipment of marihuana).

(4) *Defendant K is a wholesale distributor of child pornography. Defendant L is a retail-level dealer who purchases child pornography from Defendant K and resells it, but otherwise operates independently of Defendant K. Similarly, Defendant M is a retail-level dealer who purchases child pornography from Defendant K and resells it, but otherwise operates independently of Defendant K. Defendants L and M are aware of each other's criminal activity but operate independently. Defendant N is Defendant K's assistant who recruits customers for Defendant K and frequently supervises the deliveries to Defendant K's customers. Each defendant is convicted of a count charging conspiracy to distribute child pornography. Defendant K is accountable under subsection (a)(1)(A) for the entire quantity of child pornography sold to Defendants L and M. Defendant N also is accountable for the entire quantity sold to those defendants under subsection (a)(1)(B) because the entire quantity was within the scope of his jointly undertaken criminal activity and reasonably foreseeable. Defendant L is accountable under subsection (a)(1)(A) only for the quantity of child pornography that he purchased from Defendant K because the scope of his jointly undertaken criminal activity is limited to that amount. For the same reason, Defendant M is accountable under subsection (a)(1)(A) only for the quantity of child pornography that he purchased from Defendant K.*

(5) *Defendant O knows about her boyfriend's ongoing drug-trafficking activity, but agrees to participate on only one occasion by making a delivery for him at his request when he was ill. Defendant O is accountable under subsection (a)(1)(A) for the drug quantity involved on that one occasion. Defendant O is not accountable for the other drug sales made by her boyfriend because those sales were not in furtherance of her jointly undertaken criminal activity (<u>i.e.,</u> the one delivery).*

(6) *Defendant P is a street-level drug dealer who knows of other street-level drug dealers in the same geographic area who sell the same type of drug as he sells. Defendant P and the other dealers share a common source of supply, but otherwise operate independently. Defendant P is not accountable for the quantities of drugs sold by the other street-level drug dealers because he is not engaged in a jointly undertaken criminal activity with them. In contrast, Defendant Q, another street-level drug dealer, pools his resources and profits with four other street-level drug dealers. Defendant Q is engaged in a jointly undertaken criminal activity and, therefore, he is accountable under subsection (a)(1)(B) for the quantities of drugs sold by the four other dealers during the course of his joint undertaking with them because those sales were in furtherance of the jointly undertaken criminal activity and reasonably foreseeable in connection with that criminal activity.*

(7) *Defendant R recruits Defendant S to distribute 500 grams of cocaine. Defendant S knows that Defendant R is the prime figure in a conspiracy involved in importing much larger quantities of cocaine. As long as Defendant S's agreement and conduct is limited to the distribution of the 500 grams, Defendant S is*

accountable only for that 500 gram amount (under subsection (a)(1)(A)), rather than the much larger quantity imported by Defendant R.

(8) Defendants T, U, V, and W are hired by a supplier to backpack a quantity of marihuana across the border from Mexico into the United States. Defendants T, U, V, and W receive their individual shipments from the supplier at the same time and coordinate their importation efforts by walking across the border together for mutual assistance and protection. Each defendant is accountable for the aggregate quantity of marihuana transported by the four defendants. The four defendants engaged in a jointly undertaken criminal activity, the object of which was the importation of the four backpacks containing marihuana (subsection (a)(1)(B)), and aided and abetted each other's actions (subsection (a)(1)(A)) in carrying out the jointly undertaken criminal activity. In contrast, if Defendants T, U, V, and W were hired individually, transported their individual shipments at different times, and otherwise operated independently, each defendant would be accountable only for the quantity of marihuana he personally transported (subsection (a)(1)(A)). As this example illustrates, in cases involving contraband (including controlled substances), the scope of the jointly undertaken criminal activity (and thus the accountability of the defendant for the contraband that was the object of that jointly undertaken activity) may depend upon whether, in the particular circumstances, the nature of the offense is more appropriately viewed as one jointly undertaken criminal activity or as a number of separate criminal activities.

3. "Offenses of a character for which §3D1.2(d) would require grouping of multiple counts," as used in subsection (a)(2), applies to offenses for which grouping of counts would be required under §3D1.2(d) had the defendant been convicted of multiple counts. Application of this provision does not require the defendant, in fact, to have been convicted of multiple counts. For example, where the defendant engaged in three drug sales of 10, 15, and 20 grams of cocaine, as part of the same course of conduct or common scheme or plan, subsection (a)(2) provides that the total quantity of cocaine involved (45 grams) is to be used to determine the offense level even if the defendant is convicted of a single count charging only one of the sales. If the defendant is convicted of multiple counts for the above noted sales, the grouping rules of Chapter Three, Part D (Multiple Counts) provide that the counts are grouped together. Although Chapter Three, Part D (Multiple Counts) applies to multiple counts of conviction, it does not limit the scope of subsection (a)(2). Subsection (a)(2) merely incorporates by reference the types of offenses set forth in §3D1.2(d); thus, as discussed above, multiple counts of conviction are not required for subsection (a)(2) to apply.

As noted above, subsection (a)(2) applies to offenses of a character for which §3D1.2(d) would require grouping of multiple counts, had the defendant been convicted of multiple counts. For example, the defendant sells 30 grams of cocaine (a violation of 21 U.S.C. § 841) on one occasion and, as part of the same course of conduct or common scheme or plan, attempts to sell an additional 15 grams of cocaine (a violation of 21 U.S.C. 846) on another occasion. The defendant is convicted of one count charging the completed sale of 30 grams of cocaine. The two offenses (sale of cocaine and attempted sale of cocaine), although covered by different statutory provisions, are of a character for which §3D1.2(d) would require the grouping of counts, had the defendant been convicted of both counts. Therefore, subsection (a)(2) applies and the total amount of cocaine (45 grams) involved is used to determine the offense level.

4. "Harm" includes bodily injury, monetary loss, property damage and any resulting harm.

5. *If the offense guideline includes creating a risk or danger of harm as a specific offense characteristic, whether that risk or danger was created is to be considered in determining the offense level. See, e.g., §2K1.4 (Arson; Property Damage by Use of Explosives); §2Q1.2 (Mishandling of Hazardous or Toxic Substances or Pesticides). If, however, the guideline refers only to harm sustained (e.g., §2A2.2 (Aggravated Assault); §2B3.1 (Robbery)) or to actual, attempted or intended harm (e.g., §2F1.1 (Fraud and Deceit); §2X1.1 (Attempt, Solicitation, or Conspiracy)), the risk created enters into the determination of the offense level only insofar as it is incorporated into the base offense level. Unless clearly indicated by the guidelines, harm that is merely risked is not to be treated as the equivalent of harm that occurred. When not adequately taken into account by the applicable offense guideline, creation of a risk may provide a ground for imposing a sentence above the applicable guideline range. See generally §1B1.4 (Information to be Used in Imposing Sentence); §5K2.0 (Grounds for Departure). The extent to which harm that was attempted or intended enters into the determination of the offense level should be determined in accordance with §2X1.1 (Attempt, Solicitation, or Conspiracy) and the applicable offense guideline.*

6. *A particular guideline (in the base offense level or in a specific offense characteristic) may expressly direct that a particular factor be applied only if the defendant was convicted of a particular statute. For example, in §2S1.1, subsection (a)(1) applies if the defendant "is convicted under 18 U.S.C. § 1956(a)(1)(A), (a)(2)(A), or (a)(3)(A)." Unless such an express direction is included, conviction under the statute is not required. Thus, use of a statutory reference to describe a particular set of circumstances does not require a conviction under the referenced statute. An example of this usage is found in §2A3.4(a)(2) ("if the offense was committed by the means set forth in 18 U.S.C. § 2242").*

An express direction to apply a particular factor only if the defendant was convicted of a particular statute includes the determination of the offense level where the defendant was convicted of conspiracy, attempt, solicitation, aiding or abetting, accessory after the fact, or misprision of felony in respect to that particular statute. For example, §2S1.1(a)(1) (which is applicable only if the defendant is convicted under 18 U.S.C. § 1956(a)(1)(A), (a)(2)(A), or (a)(3)(A)) would be applied in determining the offense level under §2X3.1 (Accessory After the Fact) where the defendant was convicted of accessory after the fact to a violation of 18 U.S.C. § 1956(a)(1)(A), (a)(2)(A), or (a)(3)(A).

7. *In the case of a partially completed offense (e.g., an offense involving an attempted theft of $800,000 and a completed theft of $30,000), the offense level is to be determined in accordance with §2X1.1 (Attempt, Solicitation, or Conspiracy) whether the conviction is for the substantive offense, the inchoate offense (attempt, solicitation, or conspiracy), or both. See Application Note 4 in the Commentary to §2X1.1. Note, however, that Application Note 4 is not applicable where the offense level is determined under §2X1.1(c)(1).*

8. *For the purposes of subsection (a)(2), offense conduct associated with a sentence that was imposed prior to the acts or omissions constituting the instant federal offense (the offense of conviction) is not considered as part of the same course of conduct or common scheme or plan as the offense of conviction.*

Examples: (1) The defendant was convicted for the sale of cocaine and sentenced to state prison. Immediately upon release from prison, he again sold cocaine to the same person, using the same accomplices and modus operandi. The instant federal offense (the offense of conviction) charges this latter sale. In this example, the offense conduct relevant to the state prison sentence is considered as prior criminal history, not as part of the same course of conduct or common scheme or plan as the offense of conviction. The prior state prison sentence is counted under Chapter Four (Criminal History and Criminal Livelihood). (2) The defendant engaged in two cocaine sales constituting part of the same course of conduct or common scheme or plan. Subsequently, he is arrested by state authorities for the first sale and by federal authorities for the second sale. He is convicted in state court for the first sale and sentenced to imprisonment; he is then convicted in federal court for the second sale. In this case, the cocaine sales are not separated by an intervening sentence. Therefore, under subsection (a)(2), the cocaine sale associated with the state conviction is considered as relevant conduct to the instant federal offense. The state prison sentence for that sale is not counted as a prior sentence; see §4A1.2(a)(1).

Note, however, in certain cases, offense conduct associated with a previously imposed sentence may be expressly charged in the offense of conviction. Unless otherwise provided, such conduct will be considered relevant conduct under subsection (a)(1), not (a)(2).

9. *"Common scheme or plan" and "same course of conduct" are two closely related concepts.*

(A) Common scheme or plan. For two or more offenses to constitute part of a common scheme or plan, they must be substantially connected to each other by at least one common factor, such as common victims, common accomplices, common purpose, or similar modus operandi. For example, the conduct of five defendants who together defrauded a group of investors by computer manipulations that unlawfully transferred funds over an eighteen-month period would qualify as a common scheme or plan on the basis of any of the above listed factors; i.e., the commonality of victims (the same investors were defrauded on an ongoing basis), commonality of offenders (the conduct constituted an ongoing conspiracy), commonality of purpose (to defraud the group of investors), or similarity of modus operandi (the same or similar computer manipulations were used to execute the scheme).

(B) Same course of conduct. Offenses that do not qualify as part of a common scheme or plan may nonetheless qualify as part of the same course of conduct if they are sufficiently connected or related to each other as to warrant the conclusion that they are part of a single episode, spree, or ongoing series of offenses. Factors that are appropriate to the determination of whether offenses are sufficiently connected or related to each other to be considered as part of the same course of conduct include the degree of similarity of the offenses, the regularity (repetitions) of the offenses, and the time interval between the offenses. When one of the above factors is absent, a stronger presence of at least one of the other factors is required. For example, where the conduct alleged to be relevant is relatively remote to the offense of conviction, a stronger showing of similarity or regularity is necessary to compensate for the absence of temporal proximity. The nature of the offenses may also be a relevant consideration (e.g., a defendant's failure to file tax returns in three consecutive years appropriately would be considered as part of the same course of conduct because such returns are only required at yearly intervals).

10. *In the case of solicitation, misprision, or accessory after the fact, the conduct for which the defendant is accountable includes all conduct relevant to determining the offense level for the underlying offense that was known, or reasonably should have been known, by the defendant.*

Background: This section prescribes rules for determining the applicable guideline sentencing range, whereas §1B1.4 (Information to be Used in Imposing Sentence) governs the range of information that the court may consider in adjudging sentence once the guideline sentencing range has been determined. Conduct that is not formally charged or is not an element of the offense of conviction may enter into the determination of the applicable guideline sentencing range. The range of information that may be considered at sentencing is broader than the range of information upon which the applicable sentencing range is determined.

Subsection (a) establishes a rule of construction by specifying, in the absence of more explicit instructions in the context of a specific guideline, the range of conduct that is relevant to determining the applicable offense level (except for the determination of the applicable offense guideline, which is governed by §1B1.2(a)). No such rule of construction is necessary with respect to Chapters Four and Five because the guidelines in those Chapters are explicit as to the specific factors to be considered.

Subsection (a)(2) provides for consideration of a broader range of conduct with respect to one class of offenses, primarily certain property, tax, fraud and drug offenses for which the guidelines depend substantially on quantity, than with respect to other offenses such as assault, robbery and burglary. The distinction is made on the basis of §3D1.2(d), which provides for grouping together (i.e., treating as a single count) all counts charging offenses of a type covered by this subsection. However, the applicability of subsection (a)(2) does not depend upon whether multiple counts are alleged. Thus, in an embezzlement case, for example, embezzled funds that may not be specified in any count of conviction are nonetheless included in determining the offense level if they were part of the same course of conduct or part of the same scheme or plan as the count of conviction. Similarly, in a drug distribution case, quantities and types of drugs not specified in the count of conviction are to be included in determining the offense level if they were part of the same course of conduct or part of a common scheme or plan as the count of conviction. On the other hand, in a robbery case in which the defendant robbed two banks, the amount of money taken in one robbery would not be taken into account in determining the guideline range for the other robbery, even if both robberies were part of a single course of conduct or the same scheme or plan. (This is true whether the defendant is convicted of one or both robberies.)

Subsections (a)(1) and (a)(2) adopt different rules because offenses of the character dealt with in subsection (a)(2) (i.e., to which §3D1.2(d) applies) often involve a pattern of misconduct that cannot readily be broken into discrete, identifiable units that are meaningful for purposes of sentencing. For example, a pattern of embezzlement may consist of several acts of taking that cannot separately be identified, even though the overall conduct is clear. In addition, the distinctions that the law makes as to what constitutes separate counts or offenses often turn on technical elements that are not especially meaningful for purposes of sentencing. Thus, in a mail fraud case, the scheme is an element of the offense and each mailing may be the basis for a separate count; in an embezzlement case, each taking may provide a basis for a separate count. Another consideration is that in a pattern of small thefts, for example, it is important to take into account the full range of related conduct. Relying on the entire range of conduct, regardless of the number of counts that are alleged or on which a conviction is obtained, appears to be the most reasonable approach to writing workable guidelines for these offenses. Conversely, when §3D1.2(d) does not apply, so that convictions on multiple counts are considered separately in determining the guideline sentencing range, the guidelines prohibit aggregation of quantities from other counts in order to prevent "double counting" of the conduct and harm from each count of conviction. Continuing offenses present similar practical problems. The reference to §3D1.2(d), which provides for grouping of multiple counts arising out of a continuing offense when the offense guideline takes the continuing nature into account, also prevents double counting.

Subsection (a)(4) requires consideration of any other information specified in the applicable guideline. For example, §2A1.4 (Involuntary Manslaughter) specifies consideration of the defendant's state of mind; §2K1.4 (Arson; Property Damage By Use of Explosives) specifies consideration of the risk of harm created.

Historical Note: Effective November 1, 1987. Amended effective January 15, 1988 (see Appendix C, amendment 3); November 1, 1989 (see Appendix C, amendments 76-78 and 303); November 1, 1990 (see Appendix C, amendment 309); November 1, 1991 (see Appendix C, amendment 389); November 1, 1992 (see Appendix C, amendment 439); November 1, 1994 (see Appendix C, amendment 503).

§1B1.4. Information to be Used in Imposing Sentence (Selecting a Point Within the Guideline Range or Departing from the Guidelines)

In determining the sentence to impose within the guideline range, or whether a departure from the guidelines is warranted, the court may consider, without limitation, any information concerning the background, character and conduct of the defendant, unless otherwise prohibited by law. See 18 U.S.C. § 3661.

Commentary

Background: This section distinguishes between factors that determine the applicable guideline sentencing range (§1B1.3) and information that a court may consider in imposing sentence within that range. The section is based on 18 U.S.C. § 3661, which recodifies 18 U.S.C. § 3577. The recodification of this 1970 statute in 1984 with an effective date of 1987 (99 Stat. 1728), makes it clear that Congress intended that no limitation would be placed on the information that a court may consider in imposing an appropriate sentence under the future guideline sentencing system. A court is not precluded from considering information that the guidelines do not take into account. For example, if the defendant committed two robberies, but as part of a plea negotiation entered a guilty plea to only one, the robbery that was not taken into account by the guidelines would provide a reason for sentencing at the top of the guideline range. In addition, information that does not enter into the determination of the applicable guideline sentencing range may be considered in determining whether and to what extent to depart from the guidelines. Some policy statements do, however, express a Commission policy that certain factors should not be considered for any purpose, or should be considered only for limited purposes. See, e.g., Chapter Five, Part H (Specific Offender Characteristics).

Historical Note: Effective November 1, 1987. Amended effective January 15, 1988 (see Appendix C, amendment 4); November 1, 1989 (see Appendix C, amendment 303).

§1B1.5. Interpretation of References to Other Offense Guidelines

(a) A cross reference (an instruction to apply another offense guideline) refers to the entire offense guideline (i.e., the base offense level, specific offense characteristics, cross references, and special instructions).

(b) (1) An instruction to use the offense level from another offense guideline refers to the offense level from the entire offense guideline (i.e., the base offense level, specific offense characteristics, cross references, and special instructions), except as provided in subdivision (2) below.

(2) An instruction to use a particular subsection or table from another offense guideline refers only to the particular subsection or table referenced, and not to the entire offense guideline.

(c) If the offense level is determined by a reference to another guideline under subsection (a) or (b)(1) above, the adjustments in Chapter Three (Adjustments) also are determined in respect to the referenced offense guideline, except as otherwise expressly provided.

(d) A reference to another guideline under subsection (a) or (b)(1) above may direct that it be applied only if it results in the greater offense level. In such case, the greater offense level means the greater final offense level (i.e., the greater offense level taking into account both the Chapter Two offense level and any applicable Chapter Three adjustments).

Commentary

Application Notes:

1. *References to other offense guidelines are most frequently designated "Cross References," but may also appear in the portion of the guideline entitled "Base Offense Level" (e.g., §§2D1.2(a)(1), (2), and 2H1.1(a)(2), or "Specific Offense Characteristics" (e.g., §2A4.1(b)(7)). These references may be to a specific guideline, or may be more general (e.g., to the guideline for the "underlying offense"). Such references incorporate the specific offense characteristics, cross references, and special instructions as well as the base offense level. For example, if the guideline reads "2 plus the offense level from §2A2.2 (Aggravated Assault)," the user would determine the offense level from §2A2.2, including any applicable adjustments for planning, weapon use, degree of injury and motive, and then increase by 2 levels.*

   A reference may also be to a specific subsection of another guideline; e.g., the reference in §2D1.10(a)(1) to "3 plus the offense level from the Drug Quantity Table in §2D1.1". In such case, only the specific subsection of that other guideline is used.

2. *A reference to another guideline may direct that such reference is to be used only if it results in a greater offense level. In such cases, the greater offense level means the greater final offense level (i.e., the greater offense level taking into account both the Chapter Two offense level and any applicable Chapter Three adjustments). Although the offense guideline that results in the greater offense level under Chapter Two will most frequently result in the greater final offense level, this will not always be the case. If, for example, a role or abuse of trust adjustment applies to the cross-referenced offense guideline, but not to the guideline initially applied, the greater Chapter Two offense level may not necessarily result in a greater final offense level.*

3. *A reference may direct that, if the conduct involved another offense, the offense guideline for such other offense is to be applied. Where there is more than one such other offense, the most serious such offense (or group of closely related offenses in the case of offenses that would be grouped together under §3D1.2(d)) is to be used. For example, if a defendant convicted of possession of a firearm by a felon, to which §2K2.1 (Unlawful Receipt, Possession, or Transportation of Firearms or Ammunition; Prohibited Transactions Involving Firearms or Ammunition) applies, is found to have possessed that firearm during commission of a series of offenses, the cross reference at §2K2.1(c) is applied to the offense resulting in the greatest offense level.*

Historical Note: Effective November 1, 1987. Amended effective November 1, 1989 (see Appendix C, amendments 79, 80, and 302); November 1, 1991 (see Appendix C, amendment 429); November 1, 1992 (see Appendix C, amendment 440).

§1B1.6. Structure of the Guidelines

The guidelines are presented in numbered chapters divided into alphabetical parts. The parts are divided into subparts and individual guidelines. Each guideline is identified by three numbers and a letter corresponding to the chapter, part, subpart and individual guideline.

The first number is the chapter, the letter represents the part of the chapter, the second number is the subpart, and the final number is the guideline. Section 2B1.1, for example, is the first guideline in the first subpart in Part B of Chapter Two. Or, §3A1.2 is the second guideline in the first subpart in Part A of Chapter Three. Policy statements are similarly identified.

To illustrate:

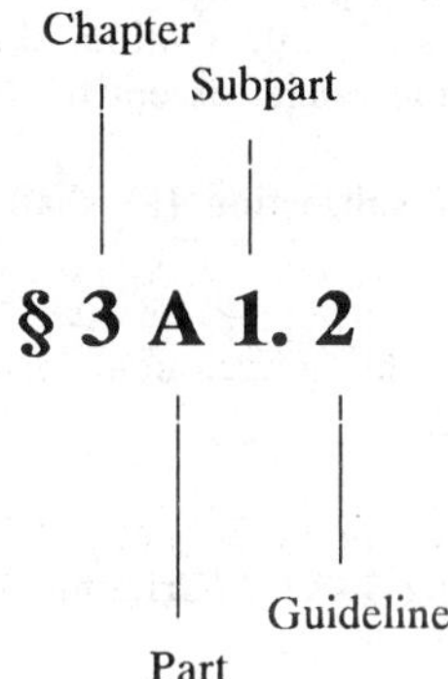

Historical Note: Effective November 1, 1987.

§1B1.7. **Significance of Commentary**

The Commentary that accompanies the guideline sections may serve a number of purposes. First, it may interpret the guideline or explain how it is to be applied. Failure to follow such commentary could constitute an incorrect application of the guidelines, subjecting the sentence to possible reversal on appeal. See 18 U.S.C. § 3742. Second, the commentary may suggest circumstances which, in the view of the Commission, may warrant departure from the guidelines. Such commentary is to be treated as the legal equivalent of a policy statement. Finally, the commentary may provide background information, including factors considered in promulgating the guideline or reasons underlying promulgation of the guideline. As with a policy statement, such commentary may provide guidance in assessing the reasonableness of any departure from the guidelines.

Commentary

Portions of this document not labeled as guidelines or commentary also express the policy of the Commission or provide guidance as to the interpretation and application of the guidelines. These are to be construed as commentary and thus have the force of policy statements.

"[C]ommentary in the Guidelines Manual that interprets or explains a guideline is authoritative unless it violates the Constitution or a federal statute, or is inconsistent with, or a plainly erroneous reading of, that guideline." Stinson v. United States, *113 S. Ct. 1913, 1915 (1993).*

Historical Note: Effective November 1, 1987. Amended effective November 1, 1993 (see Appendix C, amendment 498).

§1B1.8. Use of Certain Information

(a) Where a defendant agrees to cooperate with the government by providing information concerning unlawful activities of others, and as part of that cooperation agreement the government agrees that self-incriminating information provided pursuant to the agreement will not be used against the defendant, then such information shall not be used in determining the applicable guideline range, except to the extent provided in the agreement.

(b) The provisions of subsection (a) shall not be applied to restrict the use of information:

(1) known to the government prior to entering into the cooperation agreement;

(2) concerning the existence of prior convictions and sentences in determining §4A1.1 (Criminal History Category) and §4B1.1 (Career Offender);

(3) in a prosecution for perjury or giving a false statement;

(4) in the event there is a breach of the cooperation agreement by the defendant; or

(5) in determining whether, or to what extent, a downward departure from the guidelines is warranted pursuant to a government motion under §5K1.1 (Substantial Assistance to Authorities).

Commentary

Application Notes:

1. *This provision does not authorize the government to withhold information from the court but provides that self-incriminating information obtained under a cooperation agreement is not to be used to determine the defendant's guideline range. Under this provision, for example, if a defendant is arrested in possession of a kilogram of cocaine and, pursuant to an agreement to provide information concerning the unlawful activities of co-conspirators, admits that he assisted in the importation of an additional three kilograms of cocaine, a fact not previously known to the government, this admission would not be used to increase his applicable guideline range, except to the extent provided in the agreement. Although the guideline itself affects only the determination of the guideline range, the policy of the Commission, as a corollary, is that information prohibited from being used to determine the applicable guideline range shall not be used to increase the defendant's sentence above the applicable guideline range by upward departure. In contrast, subsection (b)(5) provides that consideration of such information is appropriate in determining whether, and to what extent, a downward departure is warranted*

pursuant to a government motion under §5K1.1 (Substantial Assistance to Authorities); e.g., a court may refuse to depart below the applicable guideline range on the basis of such information.

2. *Subsection (b)(2) prohibits any cooperation agreement from restricting the use of information as to the existence of prior convictions and sentences in determining adjustments under §4A1.1 (Criminal History Category) and §4B1.1 (Career Offender). The Probation Service generally will secure information relevant to the defendant's criminal history independent of information the defendant provides as part of his cooperation agreement.*

3. *On occasion the defendant will provide incriminating information to the government during plea negotiation sessions before a cooperation agreement has been reached. In the event no agreement is reached, use of such information in a sentencing proceeding is restricted by Rule 11(e)(6) (Inadmissibility of Pleas, Plea Discussions, and Related Statements) of the Federal Rules of Criminal Procedure and Rule 410 (Inadmissibility of Pleas, Plea Discussions, and Related Statements) of the Rules of Evidence.*

4. *As with the statutory provisions governing use immunity, 18 U.S.C. § 6002, this guideline does not apply to information used against the defendant in a prosecution for perjury, giving a false statement, or in the event the defendant otherwise fails to comply with the cooperation agreement.*

5. *This guideline limits the use of certain incriminating information furnished by a defendant in the context of a defendant-government agreement for the defendant to provide information concerning the unlawful activities of other persons. The guideline operates as a limitation on the use of such incriminating information in determining the applicable guideline range, and not merely as a restriction of the government's presentation of such information (e.g., where the defendant, subsequent to having entered into a cooperation agreement, provides such information to the probation officer preparing the presentence report, the use of such information remains protected by this section).*

6. *Unless the cooperation agreement relates to the provision of information concerning the unlawful activities of others, this guideline does not apply (i.e., an agreement by the defendant simply to detail the extent of his own unlawful activities, not involving an agreement to provide information concerning the unlawful activity of another person, is not covered by this guideline).*

Historical Note: Effective June 15, 1988 (see Appendix C, amendment 5). Amended effective November 1, 1990 (see Appendix C, amendment 308); November 1, 1991 (see Appendix C, amendment 390); November 1, 1992 (see Appendix C, amendment 441).

§1B1.9. Class B or C Misdemeanors and Infractions

The sentencing guidelines do not apply to any count of conviction that is a Class B or C misdemeanor or an infraction.

Commentary

Application Notes:

1. *Notwithstanding any other provision of the guidelines, the court may impose any sentence authorized by statute for each count that is a Class B or C misdemeanor or an infraction. A*

Class B misdemeanor is any offense for which the maximum authorized term of imprisonment is more than thirty days but not more than six months; a Class C misdemeanor is any offense for which the maximum authorized term of imprisonment is more than five days but not more than thirty days; an infraction is any offense for which the maximum authorized term of imprisonment is not more than five days.

2. *The guidelines for sentencing on multiple counts do not apply to counts that are Class B or C misdemeanors or infractions. Sentences for such offenses may be consecutive to or concurrent with sentences imposed on other counts. In imposing sentence, the court should, however, consider the relationship between the Class B or C misdemeanor or infraction and any other offenses of which the defendant is convicted.*

Background: *For the sake of judicial economy, the Commission has exempted all Class B and C misdemeanors and infractions from the coverage of the guidelines.*

Historical Note: Effective June 15, 1988 (see Appendix C, amendment 6). Amended effective November 1, 1989 (see Appendix C, amendment 81).

§1B1.10. Retroactivity of Amended Guideline Range (Policy Statement)

(a) Where a defendant is serving a term of imprisonment, and the guideline range applicable to that defendant has subsequently been lowered as a result of an amendment to the Guidelines Manual listed in subsection (c) below, a reduction in the defendant's term of imprisonment is authorized under 18 U.S.C. § 3582(c)(2). If none of the amendments listed in subsection (c) is applicable, a reduction in the defendant's term of imprisonment under 18 U.S.C. § 3582(c)(2) is not consistent with this policy statement and thus is not authorized.

(b) In determining whether, and to what extent, a reduction in sentence is warranted for a defendant eligible for consideration under 18 U.S.C. § 3582(c)(2), the court should consider the sentence that it would have imposed had the amendment(s) to the guidelines listed in subsection (c) been in effect at the time the defendant was sentenced.

(c) Amendments covered by this policy statement are listed in Appendix C as follows: 126, 130, 156, 176, 269, 329, 341, 371, 379, 380, 433, 454, 461, 484, 488, 490, 499, and 506.

Commentary

Application Notes:

1. *Eligibility for consideration under 18 U.S.C. § 3582(c)(2) is triggered only by an amendment listed in subsection (c) that lowers the applicable guideline range.*

2. *In determining the amended guideline range under subsection (b), the court shall substitute only the amendments listed in subsection (c) for the corresponding guideline provisions that were applied when the defendant was sentenced. All other guideline application decisions remain unaffected.*

Background: *Section 3582 (c)(2) of Title 18, United States Code, provides: "[I]n the case of a defendant who has been sentenced to a term of imprisonment based on a sentencing range that has subsequently been lowered by the Sentencing Commission pursuant to 28 U.S.C. § 994(o), upon motion of the defendant or the Director of the Bureau of Prisons, or on its own motion, the court may reduce the term of imprisonment, after considering the factors set forth in section 3553(a) to the extent that they are applicable, if such a reduction is consistent with applicable policy statements issued by the Sentencing Commission."*

This policy statement provides guidance for a court when considering a motion under 18 U.S.C. § 3582(c)(2) and implements 28 U.S.C. § 994(u), which provides: "If the Commission reduces the term of imprisonment recommended in the guidelines applicable to a particular offense or category of offenses, it shall specify in what circumstances and by what amount the sentences of prisoners serving terms of imprisonment for the offense may be reduced."

Among the factors considered by the Commission in selecting the amendments included in subsection (c) were the purpose of the amendment, the magnitude of the change in the guideline range made by the amendment, and the difficulty of applying the amendment retroactively.

The Commission has not included in this policy statement amendments that generally reduce the maximum of the guideline range by less than six months. This criterion is in accord with the legislative history of 28 U.S.C. § 994(u) (formerly § 994(t)), which states: "It should be noted that the Committee does not expect that the Commission will recommend adjusting existing sentences under the provision when guidelines are simply refined in a way that might cause isolated instances of existing sentences falling above the old guidelines or when there is only a minor downward adjustment in the guidelines. The Committee does not believe the courts should be burdened with adjustments in these cases." S. Rep. 98-225, 98th Cong., 1st Sess. 180 (1983).

Historical Note: Effective November 1, 1989 (see Appendix C, amendment 306). Amended effective November 1, 1990 (see Appendix C, amendment 360); November 1, 1991 (see Appendix C, amendment 423); November 1, 1992 (see Appendix C, amendment 469); November 1, 1993 (see Appendix C, amendment 502); November 1, 1994 (see Appendix C, amendment 504).

§1B1.11. Use of Guidelines Manual in Effect on Date of Sentencing (Policy Statement)

(a) The court shall use the Guidelines Manual in effect on the date that the defendant is sentenced.

(b) (1) If the court determines that use of the Guidelines Manual in effect on the date that the defendant is sentenced would violate the ex post facto clause of the United States Constitution, the court shall use the Guidelines Manual in effect on the date that the offense of conviction was committed.

(2) The Guidelines Manual in effect on a particular date shall be applied in its entirety. The court shall not apply, for example, one guideline section from one edition of the Guidelines Manual and another guideline section from a different edition of the Guidelines Manual. However, if a court applies an earlier edition of the Guidelines Manual, the court shall consider subsequent amendments, to the extent that such amendments are clarifying rather than substantive changes.

(3) If the defendant is convicted of two offenses, the first committed before, and the second after, a revised edition of the Guidelines Manual became effective, the revised edition of the Guidelines Manual is to be applied to both offenses.

Commentary

Application Notes:

1. *Subsection (b)(2) provides that if an earlier edition of the Guidelines Manual is used, it is to be used in its entirety, except that subsequent clarifying amendments are to be considered.*

   Example: A defendant is convicted of an antitrust offense committed in November 1989. He is to be sentenced in December 1992. Effective November 1, 1991, the Commission raised the base offense level for antitrust offenses. Effective November 1, 1992, the Commission lowered the guideline range in the Sentencing Table for cases with an offense level of 8 and criminal history category of I from 2-8 months to 0-6 months. Under the 1992 edition of the Guidelines Manual (effective November 1, 1992), the defendant has a guideline range of 4-10 months (final offense level of 9, criminal history category of I). Under the 1989 edition of the Guidelines Manual (effective November 1, 1989), the defendant has a guideline range of 2-8 months (final offense level of 8, criminal history category of I). If the court determines that application of the 1992 edition of the Guidelines Manual would violate the ex post facto clause of the United States Constitution, it shall apply the 1989 edition of the Guidelines Manual in its entirety. It shall not apply, for example, the offense level of 8 and criminal history category of I from the 1989 edition of the Guidelines Manual in conjunction with the amended guideline range of 0-6 months for this offense level and criminal history category from the 1992 edition of the Guidelines Manual.

2. *Under subsection (b)(1), the last date of the offense of conviction is the controlling date for ex post facto purposes. For example, if the offense of conviction (i.e., the conduct charged in the count of the indictment or information of which the defendant was convicted) was determined by the court to have been committed between October 15, 1991 and October 28, 1991, the date of October 28, 1991 is the controlling date for ex post facto purposes. This is true even if the defendant's conduct relevant to the determination of the guideline range under §1B1.3 (Relevant Conduct) included an act that occurred on November 2, 1991 (after a revised Guideline Manual took effect).*

Background: Subsections (a) and (b)(1) provide that the court should apply the Guidelines Manual in effect on the date the defendant is sentenced unless the court determines that doing so would violate the ex post facto clause in Article I, § 9 of the United States Constitution. Under 18 U.S.C. § 3553, the court is to apply the guidelines and policy statements in effect at the time of sentencing. Although aware of possible ex post facto clause challenges to application of the guidelines in effect at the time of sentencing, Congress did not believe that the ex post facto clause would apply to amended sentencing guidelines. S. Rep. No. 225, 98th Cong., 1st Sess. 77-78 (1983). While the Commission concurs in the policy expressed by Congress, courts to date generally have held that the ex post facto clause does apply to sentencing guideline amendments that subject the defendant to increased punishment.

Subsection (b)(2) provides that the Guidelines Manual in effect on a particular date shall be applied in its entirety.

Subsection (b)(3) provides that where the defendant is convicted of two offenses, the first committed before, and the second after, a revised edition of the Guidelines Manual became effective, the revised edition of the Guidelines Manual is to be applied to both offenses, even if the revised edition results in an increased penalty for the first offense. Because the defendant completed the second offense after the amendment to the guidelines took effect, the ex post facto clause does not prevent determining the sentence for that count based on the amended guidelines. For example, if a defendant pleads guilty to a single count of embezzlement that occurred after the most recent edition of the Guidelines Manual became effective, the guideline range applicable in sentencing will encompass any relevant conduct (e.g., related embezzlement offenses that may have occurred prior to the effective date of the guideline amendments) for the offense of conviction. The same would be true for a defendant convicted of two counts of embezzlement, one committed before the amendments were enacted, and the second after. In this example, the ex post facto clause would not bar application of the amended guideline to the first conviction; a contrary conclusion would mean that such defendant was subject to a lower guideline range than if convicted only of the second offense. Decisions from several appellate courts addressing the analogous situation of the constitutionality of counting pre-guidelines criminal activity as relevant conduct for a guidelines sentence support this approach. See United States v. Ykema, 887 F.2d 697 (6th Cir. 1989) (upholding inclusion of pre-November 1, 1987, drug quantities as relevant conduct for the count of conviction, noting that habitual offender statutes routinely augment punishment for an offense of conviction based on acts committed before a law is passed), cert. denied, 493 U.S. 1062 (1990); United States v. Allen, 886 F.2d 143 (8th Cir. 1989) (similar); see also United States v. Cusack, 901 F.2d 29 (4th Cir. 1990) (similar).

Moreover, the approach set forth in subsection (b)(3) should be followed regardless of whether the offenses of conviction are the type in which the conduct is grouped under §3D1.2(d). The ex post facto clause does not distinguish between groupable and nongroupable offenses, and unless that clause would be violated, Congress' directive to apply the sentencing guidelines in effect at the time of sentencing must be followed. Under the guideline sentencing system, a single sentencing range is determined based on the defendant's overall conduct, even if there are multiple counts of conviction (see §§3D1.1-3D1.5, 5G1.2). Thus, if a defendant is sentenced in January 1992 for a bank robbery committed in October 1988 and one committed in November 1991, the November 1991 Guidelines Manual should be used to determine a combined guideline range for both counts. See generally United States v. Stephenson, 921 F.2d 438 (2d Cir. 1990) (holding that the Sentencing Commission and Congress intended that the applicable version of the guidelines be applied as a "cohesive and integrated whole" rather than in a piecemeal fashion).

Consequently, even in a complex case involving multiple counts that occurred under several different versions of the Guidelines Manual, it will not be necessary to compare more than two manuals to determine the applicable guideline range -- the manual in effect at the time the last offense of conviction was completed and the manual in effect at the time of sentencing.

Historical Note: Effective November 1, 1992 (see Appendix C, amendment 442). Amended effective November 1, 1993 (see Appendix C, amendment 474).

§1B1.12. Persons Sentenced Under the Federal Juvenile Delinquency Act (Policy Statement)

The sentencing guidelines do not apply to a defendant sentenced under the Federal Juvenile Delinquency Act (18 U.S.C. §§ 5031-5042). However, the sentence imposed upon a juvenile delinquent may not exceed the maximum of the guideline range applicable to an otherwise similarly situated adult defendant unless the court finds an aggravating factor sufficient to warrant an upward departure from that guideline range. United States v. R.L.C., 112 S. Ct. 1329 (1992). Therefore, a necessary step in

ascertaining the maximum sentence that may be imposed upon a juvenile delinquent is the determination of the guideline range that would be applicable to a similarly situated adult defendant.

Historical Note: Effective November 1, 1993 (see Appendix C, amendment 475).

CHAPTER TWO - OFFENSE CONDUCT

Introductory Commentary

Chapter Two pertains to offense conduct. The chapter is organized by offenses and divided into parts and related sections that may cover one statute or many. Each offense has a corresponding base offense level and may have one or more specific offense characteristics that adjust the offense level upward or downward. Certain factors relevant to the offense that are not covered in specific guidelines in Chapter Two are set forth in Chapter Three, Parts A (Victim-Related Adjustments), B (Role in the Offense), and C (Obstruction); Chapter Four, Part B (Career Offenders and Criminal Livelihood); and Chapter Five, Part K (Departures).

Historical Note: Effective November 1, 1987.

PART A - OFFENSES AGAINST THE PERSON

1. HOMICIDE

§2A1.1. <u>**First Degree Murder**</u>

(a) Base Offense Level: **43**

<u>*Commentary*</u>

<u>Statutory Provisions</u>: 18 U.S.C. §§ 1111, 2113(e), 2118(c)(2); 21 U.S.C. § 848(e). For additional statutory provision(s), <u>see</u> Appendix A (Statutory Index).

<u>Application Notes:</u>

1. *The Commission has concluded that in the absence of capital punishment life imprisonment is the appropriate punishment for premeditated killing. However, this guideline also applies when death results from the commission of certain felonies. Life imprisonment is not necessarily appropriate in all such situations. For example, if in robbing a bank, the defendant merely passed a note to the teller, as a result of which she had a heart attack and died, a sentence of life imprisonment clearly would not be appropriate.*

   If the defendant did not cause the death intentionally or knowingly, a downward departure may be warranted. The extent of the departure should be based upon the defendant's state of mind (<u>e.g.</u>, recklessness or negligence), the degree of risk inherent in the conduct, and the nature of the underlying offense conduct. However, the Commission does not envision that departure below that specified in §2A1.2 (Second Degree Murder) is likely to be appropriate. Also, because death obviously is an aggravating factor, it necessarily would be inappropriate to impose a sentence at a level below that which the guideline for the underlying offense requires in the absence of death.

2. *If the defendant is convicted under 21 U.S.C. § 848(e), a sentence of death may be imposed under the specific provisions contained in that statute. This guideline applies when a sentence of death is not imposed.*

<u>Historical Note</u>: Effective November 1, 1987. Amended effective November 1, 1989 (<u>see</u> Appendix C, amendment 82); November 1, 1990 (<u>see</u> Appendix C, amendment 310); November 1, 1993 (<u>see</u> Appendix C, amendment 476).

§2A1.2. <u>**Second Degree Murder**</u>

(a) Base Offense Level: **33**

<u>*Commentary*</u>

<u>Statutory Provision:</u> 18 U.S.C. § 1111. For additional statutory provision(s), <u>see</u> Appendix A (Statutory Index).

Background: *The maximum term of imprisonment authorized by statute for second degree murder is life.*

Historical Note: Effective November 1, 1987.

§2A1.3. Voluntary Manslaughter

(a) Base Offense Level: **25**

Commentary

Statutory Provision: 18 U.S.C. § 1112. For additional statutory provision(s), see Appendix A (Statutory Index).

Background: The maximum term of imprisonment authorized by statute for voluntary manslaughter is ten years.

Historical Note: Effective November 1, 1987.

§2A1.4. Involuntary Manslaughter

(a) Base Offense Level:

(1) **10**, if the conduct was criminally negligent; or

(2) **14**, if the conduct was reckless.

Commentary

Statutory Provision: 18 U.S.C. § 1112. For additional statutory provision(s), see Appendix A (Statutory Index).

Application Notes:

1. *"Reckless" refers to a situation in which the defendant was aware of the risk created by his conduct and the risk was of such a nature and degree that to disregard that risk constituted a gross deviation from the standard of care that a reasonable person would exercise in such a situation. The term thus includes all, or nearly all, convictions for involuntary manslaughter under 18 U.S.C. § 1112. A homicide resulting from driving, or similarly dangerous actions, while under the influence of alcohol or drugs ordinarily should be treated as reckless.*

2. *"Criminally negligent" refers to conduct that involves a gross deviation from the standard of care that a reasonable person would exercise under the circumstances, but which is not reckless. Offenses with this characteristic usually will be encountered as assimilative crimes.*

Historical Note: Effective November 1, 1987.

§2A1.5. Conspiracy or Solicitation to Commit Murder

(a) Base Offense Level: **28**

(b) Specific Offense Characteristic

(1) If the offense involved the offer or the receipt of anything of pecuniary value for undertaking the murder, increase by **4** levels.

(c) Cross References

(1) If the offense resulted in the death of a victim, apply §2A1.1 (First Degree Murder).

(2) If the offense resulted in an attempted murder or assault with intent to commit murder, apply §2A2.1 (Assault With Intent to Commit Murder; Attempted Murder).

Commentary

Statutory Provisions: 18 U.S.C. §§ 351(d), 371, 373, 1117, 1751(d).

Historical Note: Effective November 1, 1990 (see Appendix C, amendment 311).

* * * * *

2. ASSAULT

§2A2.1. Assault With Intent to Commit Murder; Attempted Murder

(a) Base Offense Level:

(1) **28**, if the object of the offense would have constituted first degree murder; or

(2) **22**, otherwise.

(b) Specific Offense Characteristics

(1) (A) If the victim sustained permanent or life-threatening bodily injury, increase by **4** levels; (B) if the victim sustained serious bodily injury, increase by **2** levels; or (C) if the degree of injury is between that specified in subdivisions (A) and (B), increase by **3** levels.

(2) If the offense involved the offer or the receipt of anything of pecuniary value for undertaking the murder, increase by **4** levels.

Commentary

Statutory Provisions: 18 U.S.C. §§ 113(a), 351(c), 1113, 1116(a), 1751(c). For additional statutory provision(s), see Appendix A (Statutory Index).

Application Notes:

1. *Definitions of "serious bodily injury" and "permanent or life-threatening bodily injury" are found in the Commentary to §1B1.1 (Application Instructions).*

2. *"First degree murder," as used in subsection (a)(1), means conduct that, if committed within the special maritime and territorial jurisdiction of the United States, would constitute first degree murder under 18 U.S.C. § 1111.*

3. *If the offense created a substantial risk of death or serious bodily injury to more than one person, an upward departure may be warranted.*

Background: This section applies to the offenses of assault with intent to commit murder and attempted murder. An attempted manslaughter, or assault with intent to commit manslaughter, is covered under §2A2.2 (Aggravated Assault).

Historical Note: Effective November 1, 1987. Amended effective November 1, 1989 (see Appendix C, amendments 83 and 84); November 1, 1990 (see Appendix C, amendment 311); November 1, 1991 (see Appendix C, amendment 391).

§2A2.2. Aggravated Assault

(a) Base Offense Level: **15**

(b) Specific Offense Characteristics

(1) If the assault involved more than minimal planning, increase by **2** levels.

(2) (A) If a firearm was discharged, increase by **5** levels; (B) if a dangerous weapon (including a firearm) was otherwise used, increase by **4** levels; (C) if a dangerous weapon (including a firearm) was brandished or its use was threatened, increase by **3** levels.

(3) If the victim sustained bodily injury, increase the offense level according to the seriousness of the injury:

	Degree of Bodily Injury	Increase in Level
(A)	Bodily Injury	add **2**
(B)	Serious Bodily Injury	add **4**
(C)	Permanent or Life-Threatening Bodily Injury	add **6**

(D) If the degree of injury is between that specified in subdivisions (A) and (B), add **3** levels; or

(E) If the degree of injury is between that specified in subdivisions (B) and (C), add **5** levels.

Provided, however, that the cumulative adjustments from (2) and (3) shall not exceed **9** levels.

(4) If the assault was motivated by a payment or offer of money or other thing of value, increase by **2** levels.

Commentary

Statutory Provisions: 18 U.S.C. §§ 111, 112, 113(b),(c),(f), 114, 115(a), (b)(1), 351(e), 1751(e). For additional statutory provision(s), see Appendix A (Statutory Index).

Application Notes:

1. *"Aggravated assault" means a felonious assault that involved (a) a dangerous weapon with intent to do bodily harm (i.e., not merely to frighten), or (b) serious bodily injury, or (c) an intent to commit another felony.*

2. *Definitions of "more than minimal planning," "firearm," "dangerous weapon," "brandished," "otherwise used," "bodily injury," "serious bodily injury," and "permanent or life-threatening bodily injury," are found in the Commentary to §1B1.1 (Application Instructions).*

3. *This guideline also covers attempted manslaughter and assault with intent to commit manslaughter. Assault with intent to commit murder is covered by §2A2.1. Assault with intent to commit rape is covered by §2A3.1.*

Background: This section applies to serious (aggravated) assaults. Such offenses occasionally may involve planning or be committed for hire. Consequently, the structure follows §2A2.1.

There are a number of federal provisions that address varying degrees of assault and battery. The punishments under these statutes differ considerably, even among provisions directed to substantially similar conduct. For example, if the assault is upon certain federal officers "while engaged in or on account of . . . official duties," the maximum term of imprisonment under 18 U.S.C. § 111 is three years. If a dangerous weapon is used in the assault on a federal officer, the maximum term of imprisonment is ten years. However, if the same weapon is used to assault a person not otherwise specifically protected, the maximum term of imprisonment under 18 U.S.C. § 113(c) is five years. If the assault results in serious bodily injury, the maximum term of imprisonment under 18 U.S.C. § 113(f) is ten years, unless the injury constitutes maiming by scalding, corrosive, or caustic substances under 18 U.S.C. § 114, in which case the maximum term of imprisonment is twenty years.

Historical Note: Effective November 1, 1987. Amended effective November 1, 1989 (see Appendix C, amendments 85 and 86); November 1, 1990 (see Appendix C, amendment 311).

§2A2.3. Minor Assault

(a) Base Offense Level:

(1) **6**, if the conduct involved physical contact, or if a dangerous weapon (including a firearm) was possessed and its use was threatened; or

(2) **3**, otherwise.

Commentary

Statutory Provisions: 18 U.S.C. §§ 112, 115(a), 115(b)(1), 351(e), 1751(e). For additional statutory provision(s), see Appendix A (Statutory Index).

Application Notes:

1. *"Minor assault" means a misdemeanor assault, or a felonious assault not covered by §2A2.2.*

2. *Definitions of "firearm" and "dangerous weapon" are found in the Commentary to §1B1.1 (Application Instructions).*

Background: Minor assault and battery are covered in this section.

Historical Note: Effective November 1, 1987. Amended effective October 15, 1988 (see Appendix C, amendment 64); November 1, 1989 (see Appendix C, amendments 87 and 88).

§2A2.4. Obstructing or Impeding Officers

(a) Base Offense Level: **6**

(b) Specific Offense Characteristic

(1) If the conduct involved physical contact, or if a dangerous weapon (including a firearm) was possessed and its use was threatened, increase by **3** levels.

(c) Cross Reference

(1) If the conduct constituted aggravated assault, apply §2A2.2 (Aggravated Assault).

Commentary

Statutory Provisions: 18 U.S.C. §§ 111, 1501, 1502, 3056(d).

Application Notes:

1. *The base offense level reflects the fact that the victim was a governmental officer performing official duties. Therefore, do not apply §3A1.2 (Official Victim) unless subsection (c) requires the offense level to be determined under §2A2.2 (Aggravated Assault).*

2. *Definitions of "firearm" and "dangerous weapon" are found in the Commentary to §1B1.1 (Application Instructions).*

3. *The base offense level does not assume any significant disruption of governmental functions. In situations involving such disruption, an upward departure may be warranted. See §5K2.7 (Disruption of Governmental Function).*

Background: *Violations of 18 U.S.C. §§ 1501, 1502, and 3056(d) are misdemeanors; violation of 18 U.S.C. § 111 is a felony. The guideline has been drafted to provide offense levels that are identical to those otherwise provided for assaults involving an official victim; when no assault is involved, the offense level is 6.*

Historical Note: Effective October 15, 1988 (see Appendix C, amendment 64). Amended effective November 1, 1989 (see Appendix C, amendments 89 and 90); November 1, 1992 (see Appendix C, amendment 443).

* * * * *

3. CRIMINAL SEXUAL ABUSE

§2A3.1. Criminal Sexual Abuse; Attempt to Commit Criminal Sexual Abuse

(a) Base Offense Level: **27**

(b) Specific Offense Characteristics

(1) If the offense was committed by the means set forth in 18 U.S.C. § 2241(a) or (b) (including, but not limited to, the use or display of any dangerous weapon), increase by **4** levels.

(2) (A) If the victim had not attained the age of twelve years, increase by **4** levels; or (B) if the victim had attained the age of twelve years but had not attained the age of sixteen years, increase by **2** levels.

(3) If the victim was (A) in the custody, care, or supervisory control of the defendant; or (B) a person held in the custody of a correctional facility, increase by **2** levels.

(4) (A) If the victim sustained permanent or life-threatening bodily injury, increase by **4** levels; (B) if the victim sustained serious bodily injury, increase by **2** levels; or (C) if the degree of injury is between that specified in subdivisions (A) and (B), increase by **3** levels.

(5) If the victim was abducted, increase by **4** levels.

(c) Cross Reference

(1) If a victim was killed under circumstances that would constitute murder under 18 U.S.C. § 1111 had such killing taken place within the territorial or maritime jurisdiction of the United States, apply §2A1.1 (First Degree Murder).

(d) Special Instruction

(1) If the offense occurred in a correctional facility and the victim was a corrections employee, the offense shall be deemed to have an official victim for purposes of subsection (a) of §3A1.2 (Official Victim).

Commentary

Statutory Provisions: 18 U.S.C. §§ 2241, 2242. For additional statutory provision(s), see Appendix A (Statutory Index).

Application Notes:

1. *"Permanent or life-threatening bodily injury," "serious bodily injury," and "abducted" are defined in the Commentary to §1B1.1 (Application Instructions).*

2. *"The means set forth in 18 U.S.C. § 2241(a) or (b)" are: by using force against the victim; by threatening or placing the victim in fear that any person will be subject to death, serious bodily injury, or kidnapping; by rendering the victim unconscious; or by administering by force or threat of force, or without the knowledge or permission of the victim, a drug, intoxicant, or other similar substance and thereby substantially impairing the ability of the victim to appraise or control conduct. This provision would apply, for example, where any dangerous weapon was used, brandished, or displayed to intimidate the victim.*

3. *Subsection (b)(3), as it pertains to a victim in the custody, care, or supervisory control of the defendant, is intended to have broad application and is to be applied whenever the victim is entrusted to the defendant, whether temporarily or permanently. For example, teachers, day care providers, baby-sitters, or other temporary caretakers are among those who would be subject to this enhancement. In determining whether to apply this enhancement, the court should look to the actual relationship that existed between the defendant and the victim and not simply to the legal status of the defendant-victim relationship.*

4. *If the adjustment in subsection (b)(3) applies, do not apply §3B1.3 (Abuse of Position of Trust or Use of Special Skill).*

5. *If the defendant was convicted (A) of more than one act of criminal sexual abuse and the counts are grouped under §3D1.2 (Groups of Closely Related Counts), or (B) of only one such act but the court determines that the offense involved multiple acts of criminal sexual abuse of the same victim or different victims, an upward departure would be warranted.*

Background: Sexual offenses addressed in this section are crimes of violence. Because of their dangerousness, attempts are treated the same as completed acts of criminal sexual abuse. The maximum term of imprisonment authorized by statute is life imprisonment. The base offense level represents sexual abuse as set forth in 18 U.S.C. § 2242. An enhancement is provided for use of force; threat of death, serious bodily injury, or kidnapping; or certain other means as defined in 18 U.S.C. § 2241. This includes any use or threatened use of a dangerous weapon.

An enhancement is provided when the victim is less than sixteen years of age. An additional enhancement is provided where the victim is less than twelve years of age. Any criminal sexual abuse with a child less than twelve years of age, regardless of "consent," is governed by §2A3.1.

An enhancement for a custodial relationship between defendant and victim is also provided. Whether the custodial relationship is temporary or permanent, the defendant in such a case is a person the victim trusts or to whom the victim is entrusted. This represents the potential for greater and prolonged psychological damage. Also, an enhancement is provided where the victim was an inmate of, or a person employed in, a correctional facility. Finally, enhancements are provided for permanent, life-threatening, or serious bodily injury and abduction.

Historical Note: Effective November 1, 1987. Amended effective November 1, 1989 (see Appendix C, amendments 91 and 92); November 1, 1991 (see Appendix C, amendment 392); November 1, 1992 (see Appendix C, amendment 444); November 1, 1993 (see Appendix C, amendment 477).

§2A3.2. Criminal Sexual Abuse of a Minor (Statutory Rape) or Attempt to Commit Such Acts

(a) Base Offense Level: **15**

(b) Specific Offense Characteristic

(1) If the victim was in the custody, care, or supervisory control of the defendant, increase by **2** levels.

(c) Cross Reference

(1) If the offense involved criminal sexual abuse or attempt to commit criminal sexual abuse (as defined in 18 U.S.C. § 2241 or § 2242), apply §2A3.1 (Criminal Sexual Abuse; Attempt to Commit Criminal Sexual Abuse).

Commentary

Statutory Provision: 18 U.S.C. § 2243(a). For additional statutory provision(s), see Appendix A (Statutory Index).

Application Notes:

1. *If the defendant committed the criminal sexual act in furtherance of a commercial scheme such as pandering, transporting persons for the purpose of prostitution, or the production of pornography, an upward departure may be warranted. See Chapter Five, Part K (Departures).*

2. *Subsection (b)(1) is intended to have broad application and is to be applied whenever the victim is entrusted to the defendant, whether temporarily or permanently. For example, teachers, day care providers, baby-sitters, or other temporary caretakers are among those who would be subject to this enhancement. In determining whether to apply this enhancement, the court should look to the actual relationship that existed between the defendant and the victim and not simply to the legal status of the defendant-victim relationship.*

3. *If the adjustment in subsection (b)(1) applies, do not apply §3B1.3 (Abuse of Position of Trust or Use of Special Skill).*

Background: This section applies to sexual acts that would be lawful but for the age of the victim. It is assumed that at least a four-year age difference exists between the victim and the defendant, as specified in 18 U.S.C. § 2243(a). An enhancement is provided for a defendant who victimizes a minor under his supervision or care.

Historical Note: Effective November 1, 1987. Amended effective November 1, 1989 (see Appendix C, amendment 93); November 1, 1991 (see Appendix C, amendment 392); November 1, 1992 (see Appendix C, amendment 444).

§2A3.3. Criminal Sexual Abuse of a Ward or Attempt to Commit Such Acts

(a) Base Offense Level: **9**

Commentary

Statutory Provision: 18 U.S.C. § 2243(b). For additional statutory provision(s), see Appendix A (Statutory Index).

Application Note:

1. *A ward is a person in official detention under the custodial, supervisory, or disciplinary authority of the defendant.*

Background: The offense covered by this section is a misdemeanor. The maximum term of imprisonment authorized by statute is one year.

Historical Note: Effective November 1, 1987. Amended effective November 1, 1989 (see Appendix C, amendment 94).

§2A3.4. Abusive Sexual Contact or Attempt to Commit Abusive Sexual Contact

(a) Base Offense Level:

(1) **16**, if the offense was committed by the means set forth in 18 U.S.C. § 2241(a) or (b);

(2) **12**, if the offense was committed by the means set forth in 18 U.S.C. § 2242;

(3) **10**, otherwise.

(b) Specific Offense Characteristics

(1) If the victim had not attained the age of twelve years, increase by **4** levels; but if the resulting offense level is less than **16**, increase to level **16**.

(2) If the base offense level is determined under subsection (a)(1) or (2), and the victim had attained the age of twelve years but had not attained the age of sixteen years, increase by **2** levels.

(3) If the victim was in the custody, care, or supervisory control of the defendant, increase by **2** levels.

(c) Cross References

(1) If the offense involved criminal sexual abuse or attempt to commit criminal sexual abuse (as defined in 18 U.S.C. § 2241 or § 2242), apply §2A3.1 (Criminal Sexual Abuse; Attempt to Commit Criminal Sexual Abuse).

(2) If the offense involved criminal sexual abuse of a minor or attempt to commit criminal sexual abuse of a minor (as defined in 18 U.S.C. § 2243(a)), apply §2A3.2 (Criminal Sexual Abuse of a Minor or Attempt to Commit Such Acts), if the resulting offense level is greater than that determined above.

Commentary

Statutory Provisions: 18 U.S.C. § 2244(a)(1),(2),(3). For additional statutory provision(s), see Appendix A (Statutory Index).

Application Notes:

1. *"The means set forth in 18 U.S.C. § 2241(a) or (b)" are by using force against the victim; by threatening or placing the victim in fear that any person will be subjected to death, serious bodily injury, or kidnapping; by rendering the victim unconscious; or by administering by force or threat of force, or without the knowledge or permission of the victim, a drug, intoxicant, or other similar substance and thereby substantially impairing the ability of the victim to appraise or control conduct.*

2. *"The means set forth in 18 U.S.C. § 2242" are by threatening or placing the victim in fear (other than by threatening or placing the victim in fear that any person will be subjected to death, serious bodily injury, or kidnapping); or by victimizing an individual who is incapable of appraising the nature of the conduct or physically incapable of declining participation in, or communicating unwillingness to engage in, that sexual act.*

3. *Subsection (b)(3) is intended to have broad application and is to be applied whenever the victim is entrusted to the defendant, whether temporarily or permanently. For example, teachers, day care providers, baby-sitters, or other temporary caretakers are among those who would be subject to this enhancement. In determining whether to apply this enhancement, the court should look to the actual relationship that existed between the defendant and the victim and not simply to the legal status of the defendant-victim relationship.*

4. *If the adjustment in subsection (b)(3) applies, do not apply §3B1.3 (Abuse of Position of Trust or Use of Special Skill).*

Background: This section covers abusive sexual contact not amounting to criminal sexual abuse (criminal sexual abuse is covered under §§2A3.1-3.3). Alternative base offense levels are provided to take account of the different means used to commit the offense. Enhancements are provided for victimizing children or minors. The enhancement under subsection (b)(2) does not apply, however, where the base offense level is determined under subsection (a)(3) because an element of the offense to which that offense level applies is that the victim had attained the age of twelve years but had not attained the age of sixteen years. For cases involving consensual sexual contact involving victims that have achieved the age of 12 but are under age 16, the offense level assumes a substantial difference in sexual experience between the defendant and the victim. If the defendant and the victim are similar in sexual experience, a downward departure may be warranted. For such cases, the Commission recommends a downward departure to the equivalent of an offense level of 6.

Historical Note: Effective November 1, 1987. Amended effective November 1, 1989 (see Appendix C, amendment 95); November 1, 1991 (see Appendix C, amendment 392); November 1, 1992 (see Appendix C, amendment 444).

* * * * *

4. KIDNAPPING, ABDUCTION, OR UNLAWFUL RESTRAINT

§2A4.1. Kidnapping, Abduction, Unlawful Restraint

(a) Base Offense Level: **24**

(b) Specific Offense Characteristics

(1) If a ransom demand or a demand upon government was made, increase by **6** levels.

(2) (A) If the victim sustained permanent or life-threatening bodily injury, increase by **4** levels; (B) if the victim sustained serious bodily injury, increase by **2** levels; or (C) if the degree of injury is between that specified in subdivisions (A) and (B), increase by **3** levels.

(3) If a dangerous weapon was used, increase by **2** levels.

(4) (A) If the victim was not released before thirty days had elapsed, increase by **2** levels.

(B) If the victim was not released before seven days had elapsed, increase by **1** level.

(C) If the victim was released before twenty-four hours had elapsed, decrease by **1** level.

(5) If the victim was sexually exploited, increase by **3** levels.

(6) If the victim is a minor and, in exchange for money or other consideration, was placed in the care or custody of another person who had no legal right to such care or custody of the victim, increase by **3** levels.

(7) If the victim was kidnapped, abducted, or unlawfully restrained during the commission of, or in connection with, another offense or escape therefrom; or if another offense was committed during the kidnapping, abduction, or unlawful restraint, increase to --

(A) the offense level from the Chapter Two offense guideline applicable to that other offense if such offense guideline includes an adjustment for kidnapping, abduction, or unlawful restraint, or otherwise takes such conduct into account; or

(B) 4 plus the offense level from the offense guideline applicable to that other offense, but in no event greater than level **43**, in any other case,

if the resulting offense level is greater than that determined above.

(c) Cross Reference

(1) If the victim was killed under circumstances that would constitute murder under 18 U.S.C. § 1111 had such killing taken place within the territorial or maritime jurisdiction of the United States, apply §2A1.1 (First Degree Murder).

Commentary

Statutory Provisions: 18 U.S.C. §§ 115(b)(2), 351(b), (d), 1201, 1203, 1751(b). For additional statutory provision(s), see Appendix A (Statutory Index).

Application Notes:

1. *Definitions of "serious bodily injury" and "permanent or life-threatening bodily injury" are found in the Commentary to §1B1.1 (Application Instructions).*

2. *"A dangerous weapon was used" means that a firearm was discharged, or a "firearm" or "dangerous weapon" was "otherwise used" (as defined in the Commentary to §1B1.1 (Application Instructions)).*

3. *For the purpose of subsection (b)(4)(C), "released" includes allowing the victim to escape or turning him over to law enforcement authorities without resistance.*

4. *"Sexually exploited" includes offenses set forth in 18 U.S.C. §§ 2241-2244, 2251, and 2421-2423.*

5. *In the case of a conspiracy, attempt, or solicitation to kidnap, §2X1.1 (Attempt, Solicitation, or Conspiracy) requires that the court apply any adjustment that can be determined with reasonable certainty. Therefore, for example, if an offense involved conspiracy to kidnap for the purpose of committing murder, subsection (b)(7) would reference first degree murder (resulting in an offense level of 43, subject to a possible 3-level reduction under §2X1.1(b)). Similarly, for example, if an offense involved a kidnapping during which a participant attempted to murder the victim under circumstances that would have constituted first degree murder had death occurred, the offense referenced under subsection (b)(7) would be the offense of first degree murder.*

Background: Federal kidnapping cases generally encompass three categories of conduct: limited duration kidnapping where the victim is released unharmed; kidnapping that occurs as part of or to facilitate the commission of another offense (often, sexual assault); and kidnapping for ransom or political demand.

The guideline contains an adjustment for the length of time that the victim was detained. The adjustment recognizes the increased suffering involved in lengthy kidnappings and provides an incentive to release the victim.

An enhancement is provided when the offense is committed for ransom (subsection (b)(1)) or involves another federal, state, or local offense that results in a greater offense level (subsections (b)(7) and (c)(1)).

Section 401 of Public Law 101-647 amended 18 U.S.C. § 1201 to require that courts take into account certain specific offense characteristics in cases involving a victim under eighteen years of age and directed the Commission to include those specific offense characteristics within the guidelines.

Where the guidelines did not already take into account the conduct identified by the Act, additional specific offense characteristics have been provided.

Historical Note: Effective November 1, 1987. Amended effective November 1, 1989 (see Appendix C, amendment 96); November 1, 1991 (see Appendix C, amendment 363); November 1, 1992 (see Appendix C, amendment 445); November 1, 1993 (see Appendix C, amendment 478).

§2A4.2. Demanding or Receiving Ransom Money

(a) Base Offense Level: **23**

(b) Cross Reference

(1) If the defendant was a participant in the kidnapping offense, apply §2A4.1 (Kidnapping; Abduction; Unlawful Restraint).

Commentary

Statutory Provisions: 18 U.S.C. §§ 876, 877, 1202. For additional statutory provision(s), see Appendix A (Statutory Index).

Application Note:

1. *A "participant" is a person who is criminally responsible for the commission of the offense, but need not have been convicted.*

Background: This section specifically includes conduct prohibited by 18 U.S.C. § 1202, requiring that ransom money be received, possessed, or disposed of with knowledge of its criminal origins. The actual demand for ransom under these circumstances is reflected in §2A4.1. This section additionally includes extortionate demands through the use of the United States Postal Service, behavior proscribed by 18 U.S.C. §§ 876-877.

Historical Note: Effective November 1, 1987. Amended effective November 1, 1993 (see Appendix C, amendment 479).

* * * * *

5. AIR PIRACY

§2A5.1. Aircraft Piracy or Attempted Aircraft Piracy

(a) Base Offense Level: **38**

(b) Specific Offense Characteristic

(1) If death resulted, increase by **5** levels.

Commentary

Statutory Provisions: 49 U.S.C. § 1472(i), (n). For additional statutory provision(s), see Appendix A (Statutory Index).

Background: This section covers aircraft piracy both within the special aircraft jurisdiction of the United States, 49 U.S.C. § 1472(i), and aircraft piracy outside that jurisdiction when the defendant is later found in the United States, 49 U.S.C. § 1472(n). Seizure of control of an aircraft may be by force or violence, or threat of force or violence, or by any other form of intimidation. The presence of a weapon is assumed in the base offense level.

Historical Note: Effective November 1, 1987.

§2A5.2. Interference with Flight Crew Member or Flight Attendant

(a) Base Offense Level (Apply the greatest):

(1) **30**, if the offense involved intentionally endangering the safety of the aircraft and passengers; or

(2) **18**, if the offense involved recklessly endangering the safety of the aircraft and passengers; or

(3) if an assault occurred, the offense level from the most analogous assault guideline, §§2A2.1-2A2.4; or

(4) **9**.

Commentary

Statutory Provisions: 49 U.S.C. § 1472(c), (j). For additional statutory provision(s), see Appendix A (Statutory Index).

Background: An adjustment is provided where the defendant intentionally or recklessly endangered the safety of the aircraft and passengers. The offense of carrying a weapon aboard an aircraft, which is proscribed by 49 U.S.C. § 1472(l), is covered in §2K1.5 (Possessing Dangerous Weapons or Materials While Boarding or Aboard an Aircraft).

Historical Note: Effective November 1, 1987. Amended effective November 1, 1989 (see Appendix C, amendments 97 and 303); November 1, 1993 (see Appendix C, amendment 480).

§2A5.3. Committing Certain Crimes Aboard Aircraft

(a) Base Offense Level: The offense level applicable to the underlying offense.

Commentary

Statutory Provision: 49 U.S.C. § 1472(k)(1).

Application Notes:

1. *"Underlying offense" refers to the offense listed in 49 U.S.C. § 1472(k)(1) of which the defendant is convicted.*

2. *If the conduct intentionally or recklessly endangered the safety of the aircraft or passengers, an upward departure may be warranted.*

Historical Note: Effective October 15, 1988 (see Appendix C, amendment 65). Amended effective November 1, 1989 (see Appendix C, amendment 98).

* * * * *

6. THREATENING COMMUNICATIONS

§2A6.1. Threatening Communications

(a) Base Offense Level: **12**

(b) Specific Offense Characteristics

(1) If the offense involved any conduct evidencing an intent to carry out such threat, increase by **6** levels.

(2) If specific offense characteristic §2A6.1(b)(1) does not apply, and the offense involved a single instance evidencing little or no deliberation, decrease by **4** levels.

Commentary

Statutory Provisions: 18 U.S.C. §§ 871, 876, 877, 878(a), 879. For additional statutory provision(s), see Appendix A (Statutory Index).

Application Note:

1. *The Commission recognizes that this offense includes a particularly wide range of conduct and that it is not possible to include all of the potentially relevant circumstances in the offense level. Factors not incorporated in the guideline may be considered by the court in determining whether a departure from the guidelines is warranted. See Chapter Five, Part K (Departures).*

Background: These statutes cover a wide range of conduct, the seriousness of which depends upon the defendant's intent and the likelihood that the defendant would carry out the threat. The specific offense characteristics are intended to distinguish such cases.

Historical Note: Effective November 1, 1987. Amended effective November 1, 1993 (see Appendix C, amendment 480).

PART B - OFFENSES INVOLVING PROPERTY

1. THEFT, EMBEZZLEMENT, RECEIPT OF STOLEN PROPERTY, AND PROPERTY DESTRUCTION

<u>Introductory Commentary</u>

These sections address the most basic forms of property offenses: theft, embezzlement, transactions in stolen goods, and simple property damage or destruction. (Arson is dealt with separately in Part K, Offenses Involving Public Safety.) These guidelines apply to offenses prosecuted under a wide variety of federal statutes, as well as offenses that arise under the Assimilative Crimes Act.

<u>Historical Note</u>: Effective November 1, 1987. Amended effective November 1, 1989 (<u>see</u> Appendix C, amendment 303).

§2B1.1. <u>Larceny, Embezzlement, and Other Forms of Theft; Receiving, Transporting, Transferring, Transmitting, or Possessing Stolen Property</u>

(a) Base Offense Level: **4**

(b) Specific Offense Characteristics

(1) If the loss exceeded $100, increase the offense level as follows:

	<u>Loss</u> (Apply the Greatest)	<u>Increase in Level</u>
(A)	$100 or less	no increase
(B)	More than $100	add **1**
(C)	More than $1,000	add **2**
(D)	More than $2,000	add **3**
(E)	More than $5,000	add **4**
(F)	More than $10,000	add **5**
(G)	More than $20,000	add **6**
(H)	More than $40,000	add **7**
(I)	More than $70,000	add **8**
(J)	More than $120,000	add **9**
(K)	More than $200,000	add **10**
(L)	More than $350,000	add **11**
(M)	More than $500,000	add **12**
(N)	More than $800,000	add **13**
(O)	More than $1,500,000	add **14**
(P)	More than $2,500,000	add **15**
(Q)	More than $5,000,000	add **16**
(R)	More than $10,000,000	add **17**
(S)	More than $20,000,000	add **18**
(T)	More than $40,000,000	add **19**
(U)	More than $80,000,000	add **20**.

(2) If (A) a firearm, destructive device, or controlled substance was taken, or the taking of such item was an object of the offense; or (B) the

stolen property received, transported, transferred, transmitted, or possessed was a firearm, destructive device, or controlled substance, increase by **1** level; but if the resulting offense level is less than **7**, increase to level **7**.

(3) If the theft was from the person of another, increase by **2** levels.

(4) If (A) undelivered United States mail was taken, or the taking of such item was an object of the offense; or (B) the stolen property received, transported, transferred, transmitted, or possessed was undelivered United States mail, and the offense level as determined above is less than level **6**, increase to level **6**.

(5) (A) If the offense involved more than minimal planning, increase by **2** levels; or

(B) If the offense involved receiving stolen property, and the defendant was a person in the business of receiving and selling stolen property, increase by **4** levels.

(6) If the offense involved an organized scheme to steal vehicles or vehicle parts, and the offense level as determined above is less than level **14**, increase to level **14**.

(7) If the offense --

(A) substantially jeopardized the safety and soundness of a financial institution; or

(B) affected a financial institution and the defendant derived more than $1,000,000 in gross receipts from the offense,

increase by **4** levels. If the resulting offense level is less than level **24**, increase to level **24**.

<u>Commentary</u>

<u>Statutory Provisions</u>: 18 U.S.C. §§ 225, 553(a)(1), 641, 656, 657, 659, 662, 664, 1702, 1708, 2113(b), 2312-2317; 29 U.S.C. § 501(c). For additional statutory provision(s), <u>see</u> Appendix A (Statutory Index).

<u>Application Notes</u>:

1. *"More than minimal planning," "firearm," and "destructive device" are defined in the Commentary to §1B1.1 (Application Instructions).*

2. *"Loss" means the value of the property taken, damaged, or destroyed. Ordinarily, when property is taken or destroyed the loss is the fair market value of the particular property at issue. Where the market value is difficult to ascertain or inadequate to measure harm to the victim, the court may measure loss in some other way, such as reasonable replacement cost to the victim. Loss does not include the interest that could have been earned had the funds not been stolen. When property is damaged, the loss is the cost of repairs, not to exceed the loss had the property been*

destroyed. Examples: *(1) In the case of a theft of a check or money order, the loss is the loss that would have occurred if the check or money order had been cashed. (2) In the case of a defendant apprehended taking a vehicle, the loss is the value of the vehicle even if the vehicle is recovered immediately.*

Where the offense involved making a fraudulent loan or credit card application, or other unlawful conduct involving a loan or credit card, the loss is to be determined under the principles set forth in the Commentary to §2F1.1 (Fraud and Deceit).

In certain cases, an offense may involve a series of transactions without a corresponding increase in loss. For example, a defendant may embezzle $5,000 from a bank and conceal this embezzlement by shifting this amount from one account to another in a series of nine transactions over a six-month period. In this example, the loss is $5,000 (the amount taken), not $45,000 (the sum of the nine transactions), because the additional transactions did not increase the actual or potential loss.

In stolen property offenses (receiving, transporting, transferring, transmitting, or possessing stolen property), the loss is the value of the stolen property determined as in a theft offense.

*In the case of a partially completed offense (*e.g.*, an offense involving a completed theft that is part of a larger, attempted theft), the offense level is to be determined in accordance with the provisions of §2X1.1 (Attempt, Solicitation, or Conspiracy) whether the conviction is for the substantive offense, the inchoate offense (attempt, solicitation, or conspiracy), or both;* see *Application Note 4 in the Commentary to §2X1.1.*

3. *For the purposes of subsection (b)(1), the loss need not be determined with precision. The court need only make a reasonable estimate of the loss, given the available information. This estimate, for example, may be based upon the approximate number of victims and the average loss to each victim, or on more general factors such as the scope and duration of the offense.*

4. *The loss includes any unauthorized charges made with stolen credit cards, but in no event less than $100 per card.* See *Commentary to §§2X1.1 (Attempt, Solicitation, or Conspiracy) and 2F1.1 (Fraud and Deceit).*

5. *Controlled substances should be valued at their estimated street value.*

6. *"Undelivered United States mail" means mail that has not actually been received by the addressee or his agent (*e.g.*, it includes mail that is in the addressee's mail box).*

7. *"From the person of another" refers to property, taken without the use of force, that was being held by another person or was within arms' reach. Examples include pick-pocketing or non-forcible purse-snatching, such as the theft of a purse from a shopping cart.*

8. *Subsection (b)(6), referring to an "organized scheme to steal vehicles or vehicle parts," provides an alternative minimum measure of loss in the case of an ongoing, sophisticated operation such as an auto theft ring or "chop shop." "Vehicles" refers to all forms of vehicles, including aircraft and watercraft.*

9. *"Financial institution," as used in this guideline, is defined to include any institution described in 18 U.S.C. §§ 20, 656, 657, 1005-1007, and 1014; any state or foreign bank, trust company, credit union, insurance company, investment company, mutual fund, savings (building and loan) association, union or employee pension fund; any health, medical or hospital insurance association; brokers and dealers registered, or required to be registered, with the Securities and*

Exchange Commission; futures commodity merchants and commodity pool operators registered, or required to be registered, with the Commodity Futures Trading Commission; and any similar entity, whether or not insured by the federal government. "Union or employee pension fund" and "any health, medical, or hospital insurance association," as used above, primarily include large pension funds that serve many individuals (e.g., pension funds of large national and international organizations, unions, and corporations doing substantial interstate business), and associations that undertake to provide pension, disability, or other benefits (e.g., medical or hospitalization insurance) to large numbers of persons.

10. *An offense shall be deemed to have "substantially jeopardized the safety and soundness of a financial institution" if, as a consequence of the offense, the institution became insolvent; substantially reduced benefits to pensioners or insureds; was unable on demand to refund fully any deposit, payment, or investment; was so depleted of its assets as to be forced to merge with another institution in order to continue active operations; or was placed in substantial jeopardy of any of the above.*

11. *"The defendant derived more than $1,000,000 in gross receipts from the offense," as used in subsection (b)(7)(B), generally means that the gross receipts to the defendant individually, rather than to all participants, exceeded $1,000,000. "Gross receipts from the offense" includes all property, real or personal, tangible or intangible, which is obtained directly or indirectly as a result of such offense. See 18 U.S.C. § 982(a)(4).*

12. *If the defendant is convicted under 18 U.S.C. § 225 (relating to a continuing financial crimes enterprise), the offense level is that applicable to the underlying series of offenses comprising the "continuing financial crimes enterprise."*

13. *If subsection (b)(7)(A) or (B) applies, there shall be a rebuttable presumption that the offense involved "more than minimal planning."*

14. *If the offense involved theft or embezzlement from an employee pension or welfare benefit plan (a violation of 18 U.S.C. § 664) and the defendant was a fiduciary of the benefit plan, an adjustment under §3B1.3 (Abuse of Position of Trust or Use of Special Skill) will apply. "Fiduciary of the benefit plan" is defined in 29 U.S.C. § 1002(21)(A) to mean a person who exercises any discretionary authority or control in respect to the management of such plan or exercises authority or control in respect to management or disposition of its assets, or who renders investment advice for a fee or other direct or indirect compensation with respect to any moneys or other property of such plan, or has any authority or responsibility to do so, or who has any discretionary authority or responsibility in the administration of such plan.*

    If the offense involved theft or embezzlement from a labor union (a violation of 29 U.S.C. § 501(c)) and the defendant was a union officer or occupied a position of trust in the union as set forth in 29 U.S.C. § 501(a), an adjustment under §3B1.3 (Abuse of Position of Trust or Use of Special Skill) will apply.

Background: *The value of the property stolen plays an important role in determining sentences for theft and other offenses involving stolen property because it is an indicator of both the harm to the victim and the gain to the defendant. Because of the structure of the Sentencing Table (Chapter 5, Part A), subsection (b)(1) results in an overlapping range of enhancements based on the loss.*

The guidelines provide an enhancement for more than minimal planning, which includes most offense behavior involving affirmative acts on multiple occasions. Planning and repeated acts are indicative of an intention and potential to do considerable harm. Also, planning is often related to increased difficulties of detection and proof.

Consistent with statutory distinctions, an increased minimum offense level is provided for the theft of undelivered mail. Theft of undelivered mail interferes with a governmental function, and the scope of the theft may be difficult to ascertain.

Studies show that stolen firearms are used disproportionately in the commission of crimes. The guidelines provide an enhancement for theft of a firearm to ensure that some amount of imprisonment is required. An enhancement is also provided when controlled substances are taken. Such thefts may involve a greater risk of violence, as well as a likelihood that the substance will be abused.

Theft from the person of another, such as pickpocketing or non-forcible purse-snatching, receives an enhanced sentence because of the increased risk of physical injury. This guideline does not include an enhancement for thefts from the person by means of force or fear; such crimes are robberies.

A minimum offense level of 14 is provided for offenses involving an organized scheme to steal vehicles or vehicle parts. Typically, the scope of such activity is substantial (i.e., the value of the stolen property, combined with an enhancement for "more than minimal planning" would itself result in an offense level of at least 14), but the value of the property is particularly difficult to ascertain in individual cases because the stolen property is rapidly resold or otherwise disposed of in the course of the offense. Therefore, the specific offense characteristic of "organized scheme" is used as an alternative to "loss" in setting the offense level.

Subsection (b)(7)(A) implements, in a broader form, the instruction to the Commission in Section 961(m) of Public Law 101-73.

Subsection (b)(7)(B) implements the instruction to the Commission in Section 2507 of Public Law 101-647.

Historical Note: Effective November 1, 1987. Amended effective June 15, 1988 (see Appendix C, amendment 7); November 1, 1989 (see Appendix C, amendments 99-101 and 303); November 1, 1990 (see Appendix C, amendments 312, 317, and 361); November 1, 1991 (see Appendix C, amendments 364 and 393); November 1, 1993 (see Appendix C, amendments 481 and 482).

§2B1.2. [Deleted]

Historical Note: Section 2B1.2 (Receiving, Transporting, Transferring, Transmitting, or Possessing Stolen Property), effective November 1, 1987, amended effective January 15, 1988 (see Appendix C, amendment 8), June 15, 1988 (see Appendix C, amendment 9), November 1, 1989 (see Appendix C, amendments 102-104), and November 1, 1990 (see Appendix C, amendments 312 and 361), was deleted by consolidation with §2B1.1 effective November 1, 1993 (see Appendix C, amendment 481).

§2B1.3. Property Damage or Destruction

(a) Base Offense Level: 4

(b) Specific Offense Characteristics

(1) If the loss exceeded $100, increase by the corresponding number of levels from the table in §2B1.1.

(2) **If undelivered United States mail was destroyed, and the offense level as determined above is less than level 6, increase to level 6.**

(3) **If the offense involved more than minimal planning, increase by 2 levels.**

(c) Cross Reference

(1) **If the offense involved arson, or property damage by use of explosives, apply §2K1.4 (Arson; Property Damage by Use of Explosives).**

<u>Commentary</u>

<u>Statutory Provisions</u>: 18 U.S.C. §§ 1361, 1363, 1702, 1703 (if vandalism or malicious mischief, including destruction of mail is involved). For additional statutory provision(s), <u>see</u> Appendix A (Statutory Index).

<u>Application Notes</u>:

1. *"More than minimal planning" is defined in the Commentary to §1B1.1 (Application Instructions).*

2. *Valuation of loss is discussed in the Commentary to §2B1.1 (Larceny, Embezzlement, and Other Forms of Theft).*

3. *"Undelivered United States mail" means mail that has not been received by the addressee or his agent (<u>e.g.</u>, it includes mail that is in the addressee's mailbox).*

4. *In some cases, the monetary value of the property damaged or destroyed may not adequately reflect the extent of the harm caused. For example, the destruction of a $500 telephone line may cause an interruption in service to thousands of people for several hours. In such instances, an upward departure would be warranted.*

<u>Historical Note</u>: Effective November 1, 1987. Amended effective June 15, 1988 (<u>see</u> Appendix C, amendment 10); November 1, 1990 (<u>see</u> Appendix C, amendments 312 and 313).

* * * * *

2. BURGLARY AND TRESPASS

§2B2.1. <u>Burglary of a Residence or a Structure Other than a Residence</u>

(a) Base Offense Level:

(1) **17, if a residence; or**

(2) **12, if a structure other than a residence.**

(b) Specific Offense Characteristics

(1) If the offense involved more than minimal planning, increase by 2 levels.

(2) If the loss exceeded $2,500, increase the offense level as follows:

	Loss (Apply the Greatest)	Increase in Level
(A)	$2,500 or less	no increase
(B)	More than $2,500	add **1**
(C)	More than $10,000	add **2**
(D)	More than $50,000	add **3**
(E)	More than $250,000	add **4**
(F)	More than $800,000	add **5**
(G)	More than $1,500,000	add **6**
(H)	More than $2,500,000	add **7**
(I)	More than $5,000,000	add **8**.

(3) If a firearm, destructive device, or controlled substance was taken, or if the taking of such item was an object of the offense, increase by **1** level.

(4) If a dangerous weapon (including a firearm) was possessed, increase by **2** levels.

Commentary

Statutory Provisions: 18 U.S.C. §§ 1153, 2113(a), 2115, 2117, 2118(b). For additional statutory provision(s), see Appendix A (Statutory Index).

Application Notes:

1. *"More than minimal planning," "firearm," "destructive device," and "dangerous weapon" are defined in the Commentary to §1B1.1 (Application Instructions).*

2. *Valuation of loss is discussed in the Commentary to §2B1.1 (Larceny, Embezzlement, and Other Forms of Theft).*

3. *Subsection (b)(4) does not apply to possession of a dangerous weapon (including a firearm) that was stolen during the course of the offense.*

Background: The base offense level for residential burglary is higher than for other forms of burglary because of the increased risk of physical and psychological injury. Weapon possession, but not use, is a specific offense characteristic because use of a weapon (including to threaten) ordinarily would make the offense robbery. Weapon use would be a ground for upward departure.

Historical Note: Effective November 1, 1987. Amended effective January 15, 1988 (see Appendix C, amendment 11); June 15, 1988 (see Appendix C, amendment 12); November 1, 1989 (see Appendix C, amendments 105 and 106); November 1, 1990 (see Appendix C, amendments 315 and 361); November 1, 1993 (see Appendix C, amendment 481).

§2B2.2. [Deleted]

Historical Note: Section 2B2.2 (Burglary of Other Structures), effective November 1, 1987, amended effective June 15, 1988 (see Appendix C, amendment 13), November 1, 1989 (see Appendix C, amendment 107), and November 1, 1990 (see Appendix C, amendments 315 and 361), was deleted by consolidation with §2B2.1 effective November 1, 1993 (see Appendix C, amendment 481).

§2B2.3. Trespass

(a) Base Offense Level: **4**

(b) Specific Offense Characteristics

(1) If the trespass occurred at a secured government facility, a nuclear energy facility, or a residence, increase by **2** levels.

(2) If a dangerous weapon (including a firearm) was possessed, increase by **2** levels.

Commentary

Statutory Provision: 42 U.S.C. § 7270b. For additional statutory provision(s), see Appendix A (Statutory Index).

Application Note:

1. "Firearm" and "dangerous weapon" are defined in the Commentary to §1B1.1 (Application Instructions).

Background: Most trespasses punishable under federal law involve federal lands or property. The trespass section provides an enhancement for offenses involving trespass on secured government installations, such as nuclear facilities, to protect a significant federal interest. Additionally, an enhancement is provided for trespass at a residence.

Historical Note: Effective November 1, 1987. Amended effective November 1, 1989 (see Appendix C, amendments 108 and 109).

* * * * *

3. ROBBERY, EXTORTION, AND BLACKMAIL

§2B3.1. Robbery

(a) Base Offense Level: **20**

(b) Specific Offense Characteristics

(1) If (A) the property of a financial institution or post office was taken, or if the taking of such property was an object of the offense, or (B) the offense involved carjacking, increase by **2** levels.

(2) (A) If a firearm was discharged, increase by **7** levels; (B) if a firearm was otherwise used, increase by **6** levels; (C) if a firearm was brandished, displayed, or possessed, increase by **5** levels; (D) if a dangerous weapon was otherwise used, increase by **4** levels; (E) if a dangerous weapon was brandished, displayed, or possessed, increase by **3** levels; or (F) if an express threat of death was made, increase by **2** levels.

(3) If any victim sustained bodily injury, increase the offense level according to the seriousness of the injury:

	Degree of Bodily Injury	Increase in Level
(A)	Bodily Injury	add **2**
(B)	Serious Bodily Injury	add **4**
(C)	Permanent or Life-Threatening Bodily Injury	add **6**

(D) If the degree of injury is between that specified in subdivisions (A) and (B), add **3** levels; or

(E) If the degree of injury is between that specified in subdivisions (B) and (C), add **5** levels.

Provided, however, that the cumulative adjustments from (2) and (3) shall not exceed **11** levels.

(4) (A) If any person was abducted to facilitate commission of the offense or to facilitate escape, increase by **4** levels; or (B) if any person was physically restrained to facilitate commission of the offense or to facilitate escape, increase by **2** levels.

(5) If a firearm, destructive device, or controlled substance was taken, or if the taking of such item was an object of the offense, increase by **1** level.

(6) If the loss exceeded $10,000, increase the offense level as follows:

	Loss (Apply the Greatest)	Increase in Level
(A)	$10,000 or less	no increase
(B)	More than $10,000	add **1**
(C)	More than $50,000	add **2**
(D)	More than $250,000	add **3**
(E)	More than $800,000	add **4**
(F)	More than $1,500,000	add **5**
(G)	More than $2,500,000	add **6**
(H)	More than $5,000,000	add **7**.

(c) Cross Reference

(1) If a victim was killed under circumstances that would constitute murder under 18 U.S.C. § 1111 had such killing taken place within the territorial or maritime jurisdiction of the United States, apply §2A1.1 (First Degree Murder).

Commentary

Statutory Provisions: 18 U.S.C. §§ 1951, 2113, 2114, 2118(a), 2119. For additional statutory provision(s), see Appendix A (Statutory Index).

Application Notes:

1. *"Firearm," "destructive device," "dangerous weapon," "otherwise used," "brandished," "bodily injury," "serious bodily injury," "permanent or life-threatening bodily injury," "abducted," and "physically restrained" are defined in the Commentary to §1B1.1 (Application Instructions).*

   "Carjacking" means the taking or attempted taking of a motor vehicle from the person or presence of another by force and violence or by intimidation.

2. *When an object that appeared to be a dangerous weapon was brandished, displayed, or possessed, treat the object as a dangerous weapon for the purposes of subsection (b)(2)(E).*

3. *Valuation of loss is discussed in the Commentary to §2B1.1 (Larceny, Embezzlement, and Other Forms of Theft).*

4. *The combined adjustments for weapon involvement and injury are limited to a maximum enhancement of 11 levels.*

5. *If the defendant intended to murder the victim, an upward departure may be warranted; see §2A2.1 (Assault With Intent to Commit Murder; Attempted Murder).*

6. *An "express threat of death," as used in subsection (b)(2)(F), may be in the form of an oral or written statement, act, gesture, or combination thereof. For example, an oral or written demand using words such as "Give me the money or I will kill you", "Give me the money or I will pull the pin on the grenade I have in my pocket", "Give me the money or I will shoot you", "Give me your money or else (where the defendant draws his hand across his throat in a slashing motion)", or "Give me the money or you are dead" would constitute an express threat of death. The court should consider that the intent of the underlying provision is to provide an increased offense level for cases in which the offender(s) engaged in conduct that would instill in a reasonable person, who is a victim of the offense, significantly greater fear than that necessary to constitute an element of the offense of robbery.*

Background: Possession or use of a weapon, physical injury, and unlawful restraint sometimes occur during a robbery. The guideline provides for a range of enhancements where these factors are present.

Although in pre-guidelines practice the amount of money taken in robbery cases affected sentence length, its importance was small compared to that of the other harm involved. Moreover, because of the relatively high base offense level for robbery, an increase of 1 or 2 levels brings about a considerable increase in sentence length in absolute terms. Accordingly, the gradations for property loss increase more slowly than for simple property offenses.

The guideline provides an enhancement for robberies where a victim was forced to accompany the defendant to another location, or was physically restrained by being tied, bound, or locked up.

Historical Note: Effective November 1, 1987. Amended effective June 15, 1988 (see Appendix C, amendments 14 and 15); November 1, 1989 (see Appendix C, amendments 110 and 111); November 1, 1990 (see Appendix C, amendments 314, 315, and 361); November 1, 1991 (see Appendix C, amendment 365); November 1, 1993 (see Appendix C, amendment 483).

§2B3.2. Extortion by Force or Threat of Injury or Serious Damage

(a) Base Offense Level: **18**

(b) Specific Offense Characteristics

(1) If the offense involved an express or implied threat of death, bodily injury, or kidnapping, increase by **2** levels.

(2) If the greater of the amount demanded or the loss to the victim exceeded $10,000, increase by the corresponding number of levels from the table in §2B3.1(b)(6).

(3) (A)(i) If a firearm was discharged, increase by **7** levels; (ii) if a firearm was otherwise used, increase by **6** levels; (iii) if a firearm was brandished, displayed, or possessed, increase by **5** levels; (iv) if a dangerous weapon was otherwise used, increase by **4** levels; or (v) if a dangerous weapon was brandished, displayed, or possessed, increase by **3** levels; or

(B) If the offense involved preparation to carry out a threat of (i) death, (ii) serious bodily injury, (iii) kidnapping, or (iv) product tampering; or if the participant(s) otherwise demonstrated the ability to carry out such threat, increase by **3** levels.

(4) If any victim sustained bodily injury, increase the offense level according to the seriousness of the injury:

	Degree of Bodily Injury	Increase in Level
(A)	Bodily Injury	add **2**
(B)	Serious Bodily Injury	add **4**
(C)	Permanent or Life-Threatening Bodily Injury	add **6**

(D) If the degree of injury is between that specified in subdivisions (A) and (B), add **3** levels; or

(E) If the degree of injury is between that specified in subdivisions (B) and (C), add **5** levels.

Provided, however, that the cumulative adjustments from (3) and (4) shall not exceed **11** levels.

(5) (A) If any person was abducted to facilitate commission of the offense or to facilitate escape, increase by 4 levels; or (B) if any person was physically restrained to facilitate commission of the offense or to facilitate escape, increase by 2 levels.

(c) Cross References

(1) If a victim was killed under circumstances that would constitute murder under 18 U.S.C. § 1111 had such killing taken place within the territorial or maritime jurisdiction of the United States, apply §2A1.1 (First Degree Murder).

(2) If the offense was tantamount to attempted murder, apply §2A2.1 (Assault With Intent to Commit Murder; Attempted Murder) if the resulting offense level is greater than that determined above.

<u>Commentary</u>

<u>Statutory Provisions:</u> 18 U.S.C. §§ 875(b), 876, 877, 1951. For additional statutory provision(s), <u>see</u> Appendix A (Statutory Index).

<u>Application Notes:</u>

1. *"Firearm," "dangerous weapon," "otherwise used," "brandished," "bodily injury," "serious bodily injury," "permanent or life-threatening bodily injury," "abducted," and "physically restrained" are defined in the Commentary to §1B1.1 (Application Instructions).*

2. *This guideline applies if there was any threat, express or implied, that reasonably could be interpreted as one to injure a person or physically damage property, or any comparably serious threat, such as to drive an enterprise out of business. Even if the threat does not in itself imply violence, the possibility of violence or serious adverse consequences may be inferred from the circumstances of the threat or the reputation of the person making it. An ambiguous threat, such as "pay up or else," or a threat to cause labor problems, ordinarily should be treated under this section.*

3. *Guidelines for bribery involving public officials are found in Part C, Offenses Involving Public Officials. "Extortion under color of official right," which usually is solicitation of a bribe by a public official, is covered under §2C1.1 unless there is use of force or a threat that qualifies for treatment under this section. Certain other extortion offenses are covered under the provisions of Part E, Offenses Involving Criminal Enterprises and Racketeering.*

4. *The combined adjustments for weapon involvement and injury are limited to a maximum enhancement of 11 levels.*

5. *"Loss to the victim," as used in subsection (b)(2), means any demand paid plus any additional consequential loss from the offense (<u>e.g.,</u> the cost of defensive measures taken in direct response to the offense).*

6. *In certain cases, an extortionate demand may be accompanied by conduct that does not qualify as a display of a dangerous weapon under subsection (b)(3)(A)(v) but is nonetheless similar in seriousness, demonstrating the defendant's preparation or ability to carry out the threatened harm (<u>e.g.,</u> an extortionate demand containing a threat to tamper with a consumer product*

accompanied by a workable plan showing how the product's tamper-resistant seals could be defeated, or a threat to kidnap a person accompanied by information showing study of that person's daily routine). Subsection (b)(3)(B) addresses such cases.

7. *If the offense involved the threat of death or serious bodily injury to numerous victims (e.g., in the case of a plan to derail a passenger train or poison consumer products), an upward departure may be warranted.*

8. *If the offense involved organized criminal activity, or a threat to a family member of the victim, an upward departure may be warranted.*

Background: The Hobbs Act, 18 U.S.C. § 1951, prohibits extortion, attempted extortion, and conspiracy to extort. It provides for a maximum term of imprisonment of twenty years. 18 U.S.C. §§ 875-877 prohibits communication of extortionate demands through various means. The maximum penalty under these statutes varies from two to twenty years. Violations of 18 U.S.C. § 875 involve threats or demands transmitted by interstate commerce. Violations of 18 U.S.C. § 876 involve the use of the United States mails to communicate threats, while violations of 18 U.S.C. § 877 involve mailing threatening communications from foreign countries.

Historical Note: Effective November 1, 1987. Amended effective November 1, 1989 (see Appendix C, amendments 112, 113, and 303); November 1, 1990 (see Appendix C, amendment 316); November 1, 1991 (see Appendix C, amendment 366); November 1, 1993 (see Appendix C, amendment 479).

§2B3.3. Blackmail and Similar Forms of Extortion

(a) Base Offense Level: **9**

(b) Specific Offense Characteristic

(1) If the greater of the amount obtained or demanded exceeded $2,000, increase by the corresponding number of levels from the table in §2F1.1.

(c) Cross References

(1) If the offense involved extortion under color of official right, apply §2C1.1 (Offering, Giving, Soliciting, or Receiving a Bribe; Extortion Under Color of Official Right).

(2) If the offense involved extortion by force or threat of injury or serious damage, apply §2B3.2 (Extortion by Force or Threat of Injury or Serious Damage).

Commentary

Statutory Provisions: 18 U.S.C. §§ 873, 875-877, 1951. For additional statutory provision(s), see Appendix A (Statutory Index).

Application Note:

1. *This section applies only to blackmail and similar forms of extortion where there clearly is no threat of violence to person or property. "Blackmail" (18 U.S.C. § 873) is defined as a threat to disclose a violation of United States law unless money or some other item of value is given.*

Background: Under 18 U.S.C. § 873, the maximum term of imprisonment authorized for blackmail is one year. Extortionate threats to injure a reputation, or other threats that are less serious than those covered by §2B3.2, may also be prosecuted under 18 U.S.C. §§ 875-877, which carry higher maximum sentences.

Historical Note: Effective November 1, 1987. Amended effective November 1, 1989 (see Appendix C, amendment 114); November 1, 1993 (see Appendix C, amendment 479).

* * * * *

4. COMMERCIAL BRIBERY AND KICKBACKS

§2B4.1. Bribery in Procurement of Bank Loan and Other Commercial Bribery

(a) Base Offense Level: **8**

(b) Specific Offense Characteristics

(1) If the greater of the value of the bribe or the improper benefit to be conferred exceeded $2,000, increase the offense level by the corresponding number of levels from the table in §2F1.1.

(2) If the offense --

(A) substantially jeopardized the safety and soundness of a financial institution; or

(B) affected a financial institution and the defendant derived more than $1,000,000 in gross receipts from the offense,

increase by **4** levels. If the resulting offense level is less than level **24**, increase to level **24**.

(c) Special Instruction for Fines - Organizations

(1) In lieu of the pecuniary loss under subsection (a)(3) of §8C2.4 (Base Fine), use the greatest of: (A) the value of the unlawful payment; (B) the value of the benefit received or to be received in return for the unlawful payment; or (C) the consequential damages resulting from the unlawful payment.

Commentary

Statutory Provisions: 15 U.S.C. §§ 78dd-1, 78dd-2; 18 U.S.C. §§ 215, 224, 225; 26 U.S.C. §§ 9012(e), 9042(d); 41 U.S.C. §§ 53, 54; 42 U.S.C. §§ 1395nn(b)(1), (2), 1396h(b)(1),(2); 49 U.S.C. §§ 11907(a), (b). For additional statutory provision(s), see Appendix A (Statutory Index).

Application Notes:

1. *This guideline covers commercial bribery offenses and kickbacks that do not involve officials of federal, state, or local government. See Part C, Offenses Involving Public Officials, if governmental officials are involved.*

2. *The "value of the improper benefit to be conferred" refers to the value of the action to be taken or effected in return for the bribe. See Commentary to §2C1.1 (Offering, Giving, Soliciting, or Receiving a Bribe; Extortion Under Color of Official Right).*

3. *"Financial institution," as used in this guideline, is defined to include any institution described in 18 U.S.C. §§ 20, 656, 657, 1005-1007, and 1014; any state or foreign bank, trust company, credit union, insurance company, investment company, mutual fund, savings (building and loan) association, union or employee pension fund; any health, medical or hospital insurance association; brokers and dealers registered, or required to be registered, with the Securities and Exchange Commission; futures commodity merchants and commodity pool operators registered, or required to be registered, with the Commodity Futures Trading Commission; and any similar entity, whether or not insured by the federal government. "Union or employee pension fund" and "any health, medical, or hospital insurance association," as used above, primarily include large pension funds that serve many individuals (e.g., pension funds of large national and international organizations, unions, and corporations doing substantial interstate business), and associations that undertake to provide pension, disability, or other benefits (e.g., medical or hospitalization insurance) to large numbers of persons.*

4. *An offense shall be deemed to have "substantially jeopardized the safety and soundness of a financial institution" if, as a consequence of the offense, the institution became insolvent; substantially reduced benefits to pensioners or insureds; was unable on demand to refund fully any deposit, payment, or investment; was so depleted of its assets as to be forced to merge with another institution in order to continue active operations; or was placed in substantial jeopardy of any of the above.*

5. *"The defendant derived more than $1,000,000 in gross receipts from the offense," as used in subsection (b)(2)(B), generally means that the gross receipts to the defendant individually, rather than to all participants, exceeded $1,000,000. "Gross receipts from the offense" includes all property, real or personal, tangible or intangible, which is obtained directly or indirectly as a result of such offense. See 18 U.S.C. § 982(a)(4).*

6. *If the defendant is convicted under 18 U.S.C. § 225 (relating to a continuing financial crimes enterprise), the offense level is that applicable to the underlying series of offenses comprising the "continuing financial crimes enterprise."*

Background: This guideline applies to violations of various federal bribery statutes that do not involve governmental officials. The base offense level is to be enhanced based upon the value of the unlawful payment or the value of the action to be taken or effected in return for the unlawful payment, whichever is greater.

One of the more commonly prosecuted offenses to which this guideline applies is offering or accepting a fee in connection with procurement of a loan from a financial institution in violation of 18 U.S.C. § 215.

As with non-commercial bribery, this guideline considers not only the amount of the bribe but also the value of the action received in return. Thus, for example, if a bank officer agreed to the offer of a $25,000 bribe to approve a $250,000 loan under terms for which the applicant would not otherwise qualify, the court, in increasing the offense level, would use the greater of the $25,000 bribe, and the savings in interest over the life of the loan compared with alternative loan terms. If a gambler paid a player $5,000 to shave points in a nationally televised basketball game, the value of the action to the gambler would be the amount that he and his confederates won or stood to gain. If that amount could not be estimated, the amount of the bribe would be used to determine the appropriate increase in offense level.

This guideline also applies to making prohibited payments to induce the award of subcontracts on federal projects for which the maximum term of imprisonment authorized was recently increased from two to ten years. 41 U.S.C. §§ 51, 53-54. Violations of 42 U.S.C. §§ 1395nn(b)(1) and (b)(2), involve the offer or acceptance of a payment to refer an individual for services or items paid for under the Medicare program. Similar provisions in 42 U.S.C. §§ 1396h(b)(1) and (b)(2) cover the offer or acceptance of a payment for referral to the Medicaid program.

This guideline also applies to violations of law involving bribes and kickbacks in expenses incurred for a presidential nominating convention or presidential election campaign. These offenses are prohibited under 26 U.S.C. §§ 9012(e) and 9042(d), which apply to candidates for President and Vice President whose campaigns are eligible for federal matching funds.

This guideline also applies to violations of the Foreign Corrupt Practices Act, 15 U.S.C. §§ 78dd-1 and 78dd-2, and to violations of 18 U.S.C. § 224, sports bribery, as well as certain violations of the Interstate Commerce Act.

Subsection (b)(2)(A) implements, in a broader form, the instruction to the Commission in Section 961(m) of Public Law 101-73.

Subsection (b)(2)(B) implements the instruction to the Commission in Section 2507 of Public Law 101-647.

Historical Note: Effective November 1, 1987. Amended effective November 1, 1990 (see Appendix C, amendment 317); November 1, 1991 (see Appendix C, amendments 364 and 422); November 1, 1992 (see Appendix C, amendment 468).

* * * * *

5. COUNTERFEITING AND INFRINGEMENT OF COPYRIGHT OR TRADEMARK

Historical Note: Effective November 1, 1987. Amended effective November 1, 1993 (see Appendix C, amendment 481).

§2B5.1. Offenses Involving Counterfeit Bearer Obligations of the United States

(a) Base Offense Level: **9**

(b) Specific Offense Characteristics

(1) If the face value of the counterfeit items exceeded $2,000, increase by the corresponding number of levels from the table at §2F1.1 (Fraud and Deceit).

(2) If the defendant manufactured or produced any counterfeit obligation or security of the United States, or possessed or had custody of or control over a counterfeiting device or materials used for counterfeiting, and the offense level as determined above is less than **15**, increase to **15**.

Commentary

Statutory Provisions: 18 U.S.C. §§ 471-474, 476, 477, 500, 501, 1003. For additional statutory provision(s), see Appendix A (Statutory Index).

Application Notes:

1. *This guideline applies to counterfeiting of United States currency and coins, food stamps, postage stamps, treasury bills, bearer bonds and other items that generally could be described as bearer obligations of the United States, i.e., that are not made out to a specific payee.*

2. *"Counterfeit," as used in this section, means an instrument that purports to be genuine but is not, because it has been falsely made or manufactured in its entirety. Offenses involving genuine instruments that have been altered are covered under §2B5.2.*

3. *Subsection (b)(2) does not apply to persons who merely photocopy notes or otherwise produce items that are so obviously counterfeit that they are unlikely to be accepted even if subjected to only minimal scrutiny.*

Background: Possession of counterfeiting devices to copy obligations (including securities) of the United States is treated as an aggravated form of counterfeiting because of the sophistication and planning involved in manufacturing counterfeit obligations and the public policy interest in protecting the integrity of government obligations. Similarly, an enhancement is provided for a defendant who produces, rather than merely passes, the counterfeit items.

Historical Note: Effective November 1, 1987. Amended effective January 15, 1988 (see Appendix C, amendment 16); November 1, 1989 (see Appendix C, amendment 115).

§2B5.2. [Deleted]

Historical Note: Section 2B5.2 (Forgery; Offenses Involving Altered or Counterfeit Instruments Other than Counterfeit Bearer Obligations of the United States), effective November 1, 1987, amended effective January 15, 1988 (see Appendix C, amendment 17) and November 1, 1989 (see Appendix C, amendment 116), was deleted by consolidation with §2F1.1 effective November 1, 1993 (see Appendix C, amendment 481).

§2B5.3. Criminal Infringement of Copyright or Trademark

(a) Base Offense Level: **6**

(b) Specific Offense Characteristic

(1) If the retail value of the infringing items exceeded $2,000, increase by the corresponding number of levels from the table in §2F1.1 (Fraud and Deceit).

Commentary

Statutory Provisions: 17 U.S.C. § 506(a); 18 U.S.C. §§ 2318-2320, 2511. For additional statutory provision(s), see Appendix A (Statutory Index).

Application Note:

1. "Infringing items" means the items that violate the copyright or trademark laws (not the legitimate items that are infringed upon).

Background: This guideline treats copyright and trademark violations much like fraud. Note that the enhancement is based on the value of the infringing items, which will generally exceed the loss or gain due to the offense.

The Electronic Communications Act of 1986 prohibits the interception of satellite transmission for purposes of direct or indirect commercial advantage or private financial gain. Such violations are similar to copyright offenses and are therefore covered by this guideline.

Historical Note: Effective November 1, 1987. Amended effective November 1, 1993 (see Appendix C, amendments 481 and 482).

§2B5.4. [Deleted]

Historical Note: Section 2B5.4 (Criminal Infringement of Trademark), effective November 1, 1987, was deleted by consolidation with §2B5.3 effective November 1, 1993 (see Appendix C, amendment 481).

* * * * *

6. MOTOR VEHICLE IDENTIFICATION NUMBERS

§2B6.1. Altering or Removing Motor Vehicle Identification Numbers, or Trafficking in Motor Vehicles or Parts with Altered or Obliterated Identification Numbers

(a) Base Offense Level: **8**

(b) Specific Offense Characteristics

(1) If the retail value of the motor vehicles or parts involved exceeded $2,000, increase the offense level by the corresponding number of levels from the table in §2F1.1 (Fraud and Deceit).

(2) If the defendant was in the business of receiving and selling stolen property, increase by **2** levels.

(3) If the offense involved an organized scheme to steal vehicles or vehicle parts, or to receive stolen vehicles or vehicle parts, and the offense level as determined above is less than level **14**, increase to level **14**.

Commentary

Statutory Provisions: 18 U.S.C. §§ 511, 553(a)(2), 2321.

Application Notes:

1. *Subsection (b)(3), referring to an "organized scheme to steal vehicles or vehicle parts, or to receive stolen vehicles or vehicle parts," provides an alternative minimum measure of loss in the case of an ongoing, sophisticated operation such as an auto theft ring or "chop shop." "Vehicles" refers to all forms of vehicles, including aircraft and watercraft. See Commentary to §2B1.1 (Larceny, Embezzlement, and Other Forms of Theft).*

2. *The "corresponding number of levels from the table in §2F1.1 (Fraud and Deceit)," as used in subsection (b)(1), refers to the number of levels corresponding to the retail value of the motor vehicles or parts involved.*

Background: The statutes covered in this guideline prohibit altering or removing motor vehicle identification numbers, importing or exporting, or trafficking in motor vehicles or parts knowing that the identification numbers have been removed, altered, tampered with, or obliterated. Violations of 18 U.S.C. §§ 511 and 553(a)(2) carry a maximum of five years imprisonment. Violations of 18 U.S.C. § 2321 carry a maximum of ten years imprisonment.

Historical Note: Effective November 1, 1987. Amended effective November 1, 1989 (see Appendix C, amendments 117-119); November 1, 1993 (see Appendix C, amendment 482).

PART C - OFFENSES INVOLVING PUBLIC OFFICIALS

Introductory Commentary

The Commission believes that pre-guidelines sentencing practice did not adequately reflect the seriousness of public corruption offenses. Therefore, these guidelines provide for sentences that are considerably higher than average pre-guidelines practice.

Historical Note: Effective November 1, 1987.

§2C1.1. Offering, Giving, Soliciting, or Receiving a Bribe; Extortion Under Color of Official Right

(a) Base Offense Level: **10**

(b) Specific Offense Characteristics

(1) If the offense involved more than one bribe or extortion, increase by **2** levels.

(2) (If more than one applies, use the greater):

(A) If the value of the payment, the benefit received or to be received in return for the payment, or the loss to the government from the offense, whichever is greatest, exceeded $2,000, increase by the corresponding number of levels from the table in §2F1.1 (Fraud and Deceit).

(B) If the offense involved a payment for the purpose of influencing an elected official or any official holding a high-level decision-making or sensitive position, increase by **8** levels.

(c) Cross References

(1) If the offense was committed for the purpose of facilitating the commission of another criminal offense, apply the offense guideline applicable to a conspiracy to commit that other offense if the resulting offense level is greater than that determined above.

(2) If the offense was committed for the purpose of concealing, or obstructing justice in respect to, another criminal offense, apply §2X3.1 (Accessory After the Fact) or §2J1.2 (Obstruction of Justice), as appropriate, in respect to that other offense if the resulting offense level is greater than that determined above.

(3) If the offense involved a threat of physical injury or property destruction, apply §2B3.2 (Extortion by Force or Threat of Injury or Serious Damage) if the resulting offense level is greater than that determined above.

(d) Special Instruction for Fines - Organizations

(1) In lieu of the pecuniary loss under subsection (a)(3) of §8C2.4 (Base Fine), use the greatest of: (A) the value of the unlawful payment; (B) the value of the benefit received or to be received in return for the unlawful payment; or (C) the consequential damages resulting from the unlawful payment.

Commentary

Statutory Provisions: 18 U.S.C. §§ 201(b)(1), (2), 872, 1951. For additional statutory provision(s), see Appendix A (Statutory Index).

Application Notes:

1. *"Official holding a high-level decision-making or sensitive position" includes, for example, prosecuting attorneys, judges, agency administrators, supervisory law enforcement officers, and other governmental officials with similar levels of responsibility.*

2. *"Loss" is discussed in the Commentary to §2B1.1 (Larceny, Embezzlement, and Other Forms of Theft) and includes both actual and intended loss. The value of "the benefit received or to be received" means the net value of such benefit. Examples: (1) A government employee, in return for a $500 bribe, reduces the price of a piece of surplus property offered for sale by the government from $10,000 to $2,000; the value of the benefit received is $8,000. (2) A $150,000 contract on which $20,000 profit was made was awarded in return for a bribe; the value of the benefit received is $20,000. Do not deduct the value of the bribe itself in computing the value of the benefit received or to be received. In the above examples, therefore, the value of the benefit received would be the same regardless of the value of the bribe.*

3. *Do not apply §3B1.3 (Abuse of Position of Trust or Use of Special Skill) except where the offense level is determined under §2C1.1(c)(1), (2), or (3). In such cases, an adjustment from §3B1.3 (Abuse of Position of Trust or Use of Special Skill) may apply.*

4. *In some cases the monetary value of the unlawful payment may not be known or may not adequately reflect the seriousness of the offense. For example, a small payment may be made in exchange for the falsification of inspection records for a shipment of defective parachutes or the destruction of evidence in a major narcotics case. In part, this issue is addressed by the adjustments in §2C1.1(b)(2), and §2C1.1(c)(1), (2), and (3). However, in cases in which the seriousness of the offense is still not adequately reflected, an upward departure is warranted. See Chapter Five, Part K (Departures).*

5. *Where the court finds that the defendant's conduct was part of a systematic or pervasive corruption of a governmental function, process, or office that may cause loss of public confidence in government, an upward departure may be warranted. See Chapter Five, Part K (Departures).*

6. *Subsection (b)(1) provides an adjustment for offenses involving more than one incident of either bribery or extortion. Related payments that, in essence, constitute a single incident of bribery or extortion (e.g., a number of installment payments for a single action) are to be treated as a single bribe or extortion, even if charged in separate counts.*

Background: *This section applies to a person who offers or gives a bribe for a corrupt purpose, such as inducing a public official to participate in a fraud or to influence his official actions, or to a public official who solicits or accepts such a bribe. The maximum term of imprisonment authorized by statute for these offenses is fifteen years under 18 U.S.C. § 201(b) and (c), twenty years under 18 U.S.C. § 1951, and three years under 18 U.S.C. § 872.*

The object and nature of a bribe may vary widely from case to case. In some cases, the object may be commercial advantage (e.g., preferential treatment in the award of a government contract). In others, the object may be issuance of a license to which the recipient is not entitled. In still others, the object may be the obstruction of justice. Consequently, a guideline for the offense must be designed to cover diverse situations.

In determining the net value of the benefit received or to be received, the value of the bribe is not deducted from the gross value of such benefit; the harm is the same regardless of value of the bribe paid to receive the benefit. Where the value of the bribe exceeds the value of the benefit or the value of the benefit cannot be determined, the value of the bribe is used because it is likely that the payer of such a bribe expected something in return that would be worth more than the value of the bribe. Moreover, for deterrence purposes, the punishment should be commensurate with the gain to the payer or the recipient of the bribe, whichever is higher.

Under §2C1.1(b)(2)(B), if the payment was for the purpose of influencing an official act by certain officials, the offense level is increased by 8 levels if this increase is greater than that provided under §2C1.1(b)(2)(A).

Under §2C1.1(c)(1), if the payment was to facilitate the commission of another criminal offense, the guideline applicable to a conspiracy to commit that other offense will apply if the result is greater than that determined above. For example, if a bribe was given to a law enforcement officer to allow the smuggling of a quantity of cocaine, the guideline for conspiracy to import cocaine would be applied if it resulted in a greater offense level.

Under §2C1.1(c)(2), if the payment was to conceal another criminal offense or obstruct justice in respect to another criminal offense, the guideline from §2X3.1 (Accessory After the Fact) or §2J1.2 (Obstruction of Justice), as appropriate, will apply if the result is greater than that determined above. For example, if a bribe was given for the purpose of concealing the offense of espionage, the guideline for accessory after the fact to espionage would be applied.

Under §2C1.1(c)(3), if the offense involved forcible extortion, the guideline from §2B3.2 (Extortion by Force or Threat of Injury or Serious Damage) will apply if the result is greater than that determined above.

When the offense level is determined under §2C1.1(c)(1), (2), or (3), an adjustment from §3B1.3 (Abuse of Position of Trust or Use of Special Skill) may apply.

Section 2C1.1 also applies to extortion by officers or employees of the United States in violation of 18 U.S.C. § 872, and Hobbs Act extortion, or attempted extortion, under color of official right, in violation of 18 U.S.C. § 1951. The Hobbs Act, 18 U.S.C. § 1951(b)(2), applies in part to any person who acts "under color of official right." This statute applies to extortionate conduct by, among others, officials and employees of state and local governments. The panoply of conduct that may be prosecuted under the Hobbs Act varies from a city building inspector who demands a small amount of money from the owner of an apartment building to ignore code violations to a state court judge who extracts substantial interest-free loans from attorneys who have cases pending in his court.

Offenses involving attempted bribery are frequently not completed because the victim reports the offense to authorities or is acting in an undercover capacity. Failure to complete the offense does not lessen the defendant's culpability in attempting to use public position for personal gain. Therefore, solicitations and attempts are treated as equivalent to the underlying offense.

Historical Note: Effective November 1, 1987. Amended effective January 15, 1988 (see Appendix C, amendment 18); November 1, 1989 (see Appendix C, amendments 120-122); November 1, 1991 (see Appendix C, amendments 367 and 422).

§2C1.2. Offering, Giving, Soliciting, or Receiving a Gratuity

(a) Base Offense Level: **7**

(b) Specific Offense Characteristics

(1) If the offense involved more than one gratuity, increase by **2** levels.

(2) (If more than one applies, use the greater):

(A) If the value of the gratuity exceeded $2,000, increase by the corresponding number of levels from the table in §2F1.1 (Fraud and Deceit).

(B) If the gratuity was given, or to be given, to an elected official or any official holding a high-level decision-making or sensitive position, increase by **8** levels.

(c) Special Instruction for Fines - Organizations

(1) In lieu of the pecuniary loss under subsection (a)(3) of §8C2.4 (Base Fine), use the value of the unlawful payment.

Commentary

Statutory Provision: 18 U.S.C. § 201(c)(1). For additional statutory provision(s), see Appendix A (Statutory Index).

Application Notes:

1. *"Official holding a high-level decision-making or sensitive position" includes, for example, prosecuting attorneys, judges, agency administrators, supervisory law enforcement officers, and other governmental officials with similar levels of responsibility.*

2. *Do not apply the adjustment in §3B1.3 (Abuse of Position or Trust or Use of Special Skill).*

3. *In some cases, the public official is the instigator of the offense. In others, a private citizen who is attempting to ingratiate himself or his business with the public official may be the initiator. This factor may appropriately be considered in determining the placement of the sentence within the applicable guideline range.*

4. *Related payments that, in essence, constitute a single gratuity (e.g., separate payments for airfare and hotel for a single vacation trip) are to be treated as a single gratuity, even if charged in separate counts.*

Background: This section applies to the offering, giving, soliciting, or receiving of a gratuity to a public official in respect to an official act. A corrupt purpose is not an element of this offense. The maximum term of imprisonment authorized by statute for these offenses is two years. An adjustment is provided where the value of the gratuity exceeded $2,000, or where the public official was an elected official or held a high-level decision-making or sensitive position.

Historical Note: Effective November 1, 1987. Amended effective November 1, 1989 (see Appendix C, amendment 121); November 1, 1991 (see Appendix C, amendment 422).

§2C1.3. Conflict of Interest

(a) Base Offense Level: **6**

(b) Specific Offense Characteristic

(1) If the offense involved actual or planned harm to the government, increase by **4** levels.

Commentary

Statutory Provisions: 18 U.S.C. §§ 203, 205, 207, 208. For additional statutory provision(s), see Appendix A (Statutory Index).

Application Note:

1. *Do not apply the adjustment in §3B1.3 (Abuse of Position of Trust or Use of Special Skill).*

Background: This section applies to financial and non-financial conflicts of interest by present and former federal officers and employees. The maximum term of imprisonment authorized by statute is two years.

Historical Note: Effective November 1, 1987.

§2C1.4. Payment or Receipt of Unauthorized Compensation

(a) Base Offense Level: **6**

Commentary

Statutory Provisions: 18 U.S.C. §§ 209, 1909.

Application Note:

1. *Do not apply the adjustment in §3B1.3 (Abuse of Position of Trust or Use of Special Skill).*

Background: Violations of 18 U.S.C. § 209 involve the unlawful supplementation of salary of various federal employees. 18 U.S.C. § 1909 prohibits bank examiners from performing any service for compensation for banks or bank officials. Both offenses are misdemeanors for which the maximum term of imprisonment authorized by statute is one year.

Historical Note: Effective November 1, 1987.

§2C1.5. Payments to Obtain Public Office

(a) Base Offense Level: **8**

Commentary

Statutory Provisions: 18 U.S.C. §§ 210, 211.

Application Note:

1. *Do not apply the adjustment in §3B1.3 (Abuse of Position of Trust or Use of Special Skill).*

Background: Under 18 U.S.C. § 210, it is unlawful to pay, offer, or promise anything of value to a person, firm, or corporation in consideration of procuring appointive office. Under 18 U.S.C. § 211, it is unlawful to solicit or accept anything of value in consideration of a promise of the use of influence in obtaining appointive federal office. Both offenses are misdemeanors for which the maximum term of imprisonment authorized by statute is one year.

Historical Note: Effective November 1, 1987.

§2C1.6. Loan or Gratuity to Bank Examiner, or Gratuity for Adjustment of Farm Indebtedness, or Procuring Bank Loan, or Discount of Commercial Paper

(a) Base Offense Level: 7

(b) Specific Offense Characteristic

(1) If the value of the gratuity exceeded $2,000, increase by the corresponding number of levels from the table in §2F1.1 (Fraud and Deceit).

Commentary

Statutory Provisions: 18 U.S.C. §§ 212-214, 217.

Application Note:

1. *Do not apply the adjustment in §3B1.3 (Abuse of Position of Trust or Use of Special Skill).*

Background: Violations of 18 U.S.C. §§ 212 and 213 involve the offer to, or acceptance by, a bank examiner of a loan or gratuity. Violations of 18 U.S.C. § 214 involve the offer or receipt of anything of value for procuring a loan or discount of commercial paper from a Federal Reserve bank.

Violations of 18 U.S.C. § 217 involve the acceptance of a fee or other consideration by a federal employee for adjusting or cancelling a farm debt. These offenses are misdemeanors for which the maximum term of imprisonment authorized by statute is one year.

Historical Note: Effective November 1, 1987.

§2C1.7. Fraud Involving Deprivation of the Intangible Right to the Honest Services of Public Officials; Conspiracy to Defraud by Interference with Governmental Functions

(a) Base Offense Level: **10**

(b) Specific Offense Characteristic

(1) (If more than one applies, use the greater):

(A) If the loss to the government, or the value of anything obtained or to be obtained by a public official or others acting with a public official, whichever is greater, exceeded $2,000, increase by the corresponding number of levels from the table in §2F1.1 (Fraud and Deceit); or

(B) If the offense involved an elected official or any official holding a high-level decision-making or sensitive position, increase by **8** levels.

(c) Cross References

(1) If the offense was committed for the purpose of facilitating the commission of another criminal offense, apply the offense guideline applicable to a conspiracy to commit that other offense if the resulting offense level is greater than that determined above.

(2) If the offense was committed for the purpose of concealing, or obstructing justice in respect to, another criminal offense, apply §2X3.1 (Accessory After the Fact) or §2J1.2 (Obstruction of Justice), as appropriate, in respect to that other offense if the resulting offense level is greater than that determined above.

(3) If the offense involved a threat of physical injury or property destruction, apply §2B3.2 (Extortion by Force or Threat of Injury or Serious Damage) if the resulting offense level is greater than that determined above.

(4) If the offense is covered more specifically under §2C1.1 (Offering, Giving, Soliciting, or Receiving a Bribe; Extortion Under Color of Official Right), §2C1.2 (Offering, Giving, Soliciting, or Receiving a Gratuity), or §2C1.3 (Conflict of Interest), apply the offense guideline that most specifically covers the offense.

Commentary

Statutory Provisions: *18 U.S.C. §§ 371, 1341-1343.*

Application Notes:

1. *This guideline applies only to offenses committed by public officials or others acting with them that involve (A) depriving others of the intangible right to honest services (such offenses may be prosecuted under 18 U.S.C. §§ 1341-1343), or (B) conspiracy to defraud the United States by interfering with governmental functions (such offenses may be prosecuted under 18 U.S.C. § 371). "Public official," as used in this guideline, includes officers and employees of federal, state, or local government.*

2. *"Official holding a high-level decision-making or sensitive position" includes, for example, prosecuting attorneys, judges, agency administrators, supervisory law enforcement officers, and other governmental officials with similar levels of responsibility.*

3. *"Loss" is discussed in the Commentary to §2B1.1 (Larceny, Embezzlement, and Other Forms of Theft) and includes both actual and intended loss.*

4. *Do not apply §3B1.3 (Abuse of Position of Trust or Use of Special Skill) except where the offense level is determined under §2C1.7(c)(1), (2), or (3). In such cases, an adjustment from §3B1.3 (Abuse of Position of Trust or Use of Special Skill) may apply.*

5. *Where the court finds that the defendant's conduct was part of a systematic or pervasive corruption of a governmental function, process, or office that may cause loss of public confidence in government, an upward departure may be warranted.* See *Chapter Five, Part K (Departures).*

Background: *The maximum term of imprisonment authorized by statute under 18 U.S.C. §§ 371 and 1341-1343 is five years.*

Historical Note: Effective November 1, 1991 (see Appendix C, amendment 368). Amended effective November 1, 1992 (see Appendix C, amendment 468).

PART D - OFFENSES INVOLVING DRUGS

1. UNLAWFUL MANUFACTURING, IMPORTING, EXPORTING, TRAFFICKING, OR POSSESSION; CONTINUING CRIMINAL ENTERPRISE

§2D1.1. **Unlawful Manufacturing, Importing, Exporting, or Trafficking (Including Possession with Intent to Commit These Offenses); Attempt or Conspiracy**

(a) Base Offense Level (Apply the greatest):

(1) **43**, if the defendant is convicted under 21 U.S.C. § 841(b)(1)(A), (b)(1)(B), or (b)(1)(C), or 21 U.S.C. § 960(b)(1), (b)(2), or (b)(3), and the offense of conviction establishes that death or serious bodily injury resulted from the use of the substance and that the defendant committed the offense after one or more prior convictions for a similar offense; or

(2) **38**, if the defendant is convicted under 21 U.S.C. § 841(b)(1)(A), (b)(1)(B), or (b)(1)(C), or 21 U.S.C. § 960(b)(1), (b)(2), or (b)(3), and the offense of conviction establishes that death or serious bodily injury resulted from the use of the substance; or

(3) the offense level specified in the Drug Quantity Table set forth in subsection (c) below.

(b) Specific Offense Characteristics

(1) If a dangerous weapon (including a firearm) was possessed, increase by **2** levels.

(2) If the defendant unlawfully imported or exported a controlled substance under circumstances in which (A) an aircraft other than a regularly scheduled commercial air carrier was used to import or export the controlled substance, or (B) the defendant acted as a pilot, copilot, captain, navigator, flight officer, or any other operation officer aboard any craft or vessel carrying a controlled substance, increase by **2** levels. If the resulting offense level is less than level **26**, increase to level **26**.

[Subsection (c) (Drug Quantity Table) is set forth on the following pages.]

(d) Cross Reference

(1) If a victim was killed under circumstances that would constitute murder under 18 U.S.C. § 1111 had such killing taken place within the territorial or maritime jurisdiction of the United States, apply §2A1.1 (First Degree Murder).

(c) DRUG QUANTITY TABLE

Controlled Substances and Quantity*	Base Offense Level
(1) • 30 KG or more of Heroin (or the equivalent amount of other Schedule I or II Opiates); • 150 KG or more of Cocaine (or the equivalent amount of other Schedule I or II Stimulants); • 1.5 KG or more of Cocaine Base; • 30 KG or more of PCP, or 3 KG or more of PCP (actual); • 30 KG or more of Methamphetamine, or 3 KG or more of Methamphetamine (actual), or 3 KG or more of "Ice"; • 300 G or more of LSD (or the equivalent amount of other Schedule I or II Hallucinogens); • 12 KG or more of Fentanyl; • 3 KG or more of a Fentanyl Analogue; • 30,000 KG or more of Marihuana; • 6,000 KG or more of Hashish; • 600 KG or more of Hashish Oil.	Level 38
(2) • At least 10 KG but less than 30 KG of Heroin (or the equivalent amount of other Schedule I or II Opiates); • At least 50 KG but less than 150 KG of Cocaine (or the equivalent amount of other Schedule I or II Stimulants); • At least 500 G but less than 1.5 KG of Cocaine Base; • At least 10 KG but less than 30 KG of PCP, or at least 1 KG but less than 3 KG of PCP (actual); • At least 10 KG but less than 30 KG of Methamphetamine, or at least 1 KG but less than 3 KG of Methamphetamine (actual), or at least 1 KG but less than 3 KG of "Ice"; • At least 100 G but less than 300 G of LSD (or the equivalent amount of other Schedule I or II Hallucinogens); • At least 4 KG but less than 12 KG of Fentanyl; • At least 1 KG but less than 3 KG of a Fentanyl Analogue; • At least 10,000 KG but less than 30,000 KG of Marihuana; • At least 2,000 KG but less than 6,000 KG of Hashish; • At least 200 KG but less than 600 KG of Hashish Oil.	Level 36
(3) • At least 3 KG but less than 10 KG of Heroin (or the equivalent amount of other Schedule I or II Opiates); • At least 15 KG but less than 50 KG of Cocaine (or the equivalent amount of other Schedule I or II Stimulants); • At least 150 G but less than 500 G of Cocaine Base; • At least 3 KG but less than 10 KG of PCP, or at least 300 G but less than 1 KG of PCP (actual); • At least 3 KG but less than 10 KG of Methamphetamine, or at least 300 G but less than 1 KG of Methamphetamine (actual), or at least 300 G but less than 1 KG of "Ice"; • At least 30 G but less than 100 G of LSD (or the equivalent amount of other Schedule I or II Hallucinogens); • At least 1.2 KG but less than 4 KG of Fentanyl; • At least 300 G but less than 1 KG of a Fentanyl Analogue; • At least 3,000 KG but less than 10,000 KG of Marihuana; • At least 600 KG but less than 2,000 KG of Hashish; • At least 60 KG but less than 200 KG of Hashish Oil.	Level 34

Controlled Substances and Quantity* **Base Offense Level**

(4) • At least 1 KG but less than 3 KG of Heroin (or the equivalent amount of other Schedule I or II Opiates); **Level 32**
• At least 5 KG but less than 15 KG of Cocaine (or the equivalent amount of other Schedule I or II Stimulants);
• At least 50 G but less than 150 G of Cocaine Base;
• At least 1 KG but less than 3 KG of PCP, or at least 100 G but less than 300 G of PCP (actual);
• At least 1 KG but less than 3 KG of Methamphetamine, or at least 100 G but less than 300 G of Methamphetamine (actual), or at least 100 G but less than 300 G of "Ice";
• At least 10 G but less than 30 G of LSD (or the equivalent amount of other Schedule I or II Hallucinogens);
• At least 400 G but less than 1.2 KG of Fentanyl;
• At least 100 G but less than 300 G of a Fentanyl Analogue;
• At least 1,000 KG but less than 3,000 KG of Marihuana;
• At least 200 KG but less than 600 KG of Hashish;
• At least 20 KG but less than 60 KG of Hashish Oil.

(5) • At least 700 G but less than 1 KG of Heroin (or the equivalent amount of other Schedule I or II Opiates); **Level 30**
• At least 3.5 KG but less than 5 KG of Cocaine (or the equivalent amount of other Schedule I or II Stimulants);
• At least 35 G but less than 50 G of Cocaine Base;
• At least 700 G but less than 1 KG of PCP, or at least 70 G but less than 100 G of PCP (actual);
• At least 700 G but less than 1 KG of Methamphetamine, or at least 70 G but less than 100 G of Methamphetamine (actual), or at least 70 G but less than 100 G of "Ice";
• At least 7 G but less than 10 G of LSD (or the equivalent amount of other Schedule I or II Hallucinogens);
• At least 280 G but less than 400 G of Fentanyl;
• At least 70 G but less than 100 G of a Fentanyl Analogue;
• At least 700 KG but less than 1,000 KG of Marihuana;
• At least 140 KG but less than 200 KG of Hashish;
• At least 14 KG but less than 20 KG of Hashish Oil.

(6) • At least 400 G but less than 700 G of Heroin (or the equivalent amount of other Schedule I or II Opiates); **Level 28**
• At least 2 KG but less than 3.5 KG of Cocaine (or the equivalent amount of other Schedule I or II Stimulants);
• At least 20 G but less than 35 G of Cocaine Base;
• At least 400 G but less than 700 G of PCP, or at least 40 G but less than 70 G of PCP (actual);
• At least 400 G but less than 700 G of Methamphetamine, or at least 40 G but less than 70 G of Methamphetamine (actual), or at least 40 G but less than 70 G of "Ice";
• At least 4 G but less than 7 G of LSD (or the equivalent amount of other Schedule I or II Hallucinogens);
• At least 160 G but less than 280 G of Fentanyl;
• At least 40 G but less than 70 G of a Fentanyl Analogue;
• At least 400 KG but less than 700 KG of Marihuana;
• At least 80 KG but less than 140 KG of Hashish;
• At least 8 KG but less than 14 KG of Hashish Oil.

Controlled Substances and Quantity*	Base Offense Level
(7) • At least 100 G but less than 400 G of Heroin (or the equivalent amount of other Schedule I or II Opiates); • At least 500 G but less than 2 KG of Cocaine (or the equivalent amount of other Schedule I or II Stimulants); • At least 5 G but less than 20 G of Cocaine Base; • At least 100 G but less than 400 G of PCP, or at least 10 G but less than 40 G of PCP (actual); • At least 100 G but less than 400 G of Methamphetamine, or at least 10 G but less than 40 G of Methamphetamine (actual), or at least 10 G but less than 40 G of "Ice"; • At least 1 G but less than 4 G of LSD (or the equivalent amount of other Schedule I or II Hallucinogens); • At least 40 G but less than 160 G of Fentanyl; • At least 10 G but less than 40 G of a Fentanyl Analogue; • At least 100 KG but less than 400 KG of Marihuana; • At least 20 KG but less than 80 KG of Hashish; • At least 2 KG but less than 8 KG of Hashish Oil.	**Level 26**
(8) • At least 80 G but less than 100 G of Heroin (or the equivalent amount of other Schedule I or II Opiates); • At least 400 G but less than 500 G of Cocaine (or the equivalent amount of other Schedule I or II Stimulants); • At least 4 G but less than 5 G of Cocaine Base; • At least 80 G but less than 100 G of PCP, or at least 8 G but less than 10 G of PCP (actual); • At least 80 G but less than 100 G of Methamphetamine, or at least 8 G but less than 10 G of Methamphetamine (actual), or at least 8 G but less than 10 G of "Ice"; • At least 800 MG but less than 1 G of LSD (or the equivalent amount of other Schedule I or II Hallucinogens); • At least 32 G but less than 40 G of Fentanyl; • At least 8 G but less than 10 G of a Fentanyl Analogue; • At least 80 KG but less than 100 KG of Marihuana; • At least 16 KG but less than 20 KG of Hashish; • At least 1.6 KG but less than 2 KG of Hashish Oil.	**Level 24**
(9) • At least 60 G but less than 80 G of Heroin (or the equivalent amount of other Schedule I or II Opiates); • At least 300 G but less than 400 G of Cocaine (or the equivalent amount of other Schedule I or II Stimulants); • At least 3 G but less than 4 G of Cocaine Base; • At least 60 G but less than 80 G of PCP, or at least 6 G but less than 8 G of PCP (actual); • At least 60 G but less than 80 G of Methamphetamine, or at least 6 G but less than 8 G of Methamphetamine (actual), or at least 6 G but less than 8 G of "Ice"; • At least 600 MG but less than 800 MG of LSD (or the equivalent amount of other Schedule I or II Hallucinogens); • At least 24 G but less than 32 G of Fentanyl; • At least 6 G but less than 8 G of a Fentanyl Analogue; • At least 60 KG but less than 80 KG of Marihuana; • At least 12 KG but less than 16 KG of Hashish; • At least 1.2 KG but less than 1.6 KG of Hashish Oil.	**Level 22**

Controlled Substances and Quantity*	**Base Offense Level**
(10) • At least 40 G but less than 60 G of Heroin (or the equivalent amount of other Schedule I or II Opiates); • At least 200 G but less than 300 G of Cocaine (or the equivalent amount of other Schedule I or II Stimulants); • At least 2 G but less than 3 G of Cocaine Base; • At least 40 G but less than 60 G of PCP, or at least 4 G but less than 6 G of PCP (actual); • At least 40 G but less than 60 G of Methamphetamine, or at least 4 G but less than 6 G of Methamphetamine (actual), or at least 4 G but less than 6 G of "Ice"; • At least 400 MG but less than 600 MG of LSD (or the equivalent amount of other Schedule I or II Hallucinogens); • At least 16 G but less than 24 G of Fentanyl; • At least 4 G but less than 6 G of a Fentanyl Analogue; • At least 40 KG but less than 60 KG of Marihuana; • At least 8 KG but less than 12 KG of Hashish; • At least 800 G but less than 1.2 KG of Hashish Oil; • 20 KG or more of Secobarbital (or the equivalent amount of other Schedule I or II Depressants) or Schedule III substances (except Anabolic Steroids); • 40,000 or more units of Anabolic Steroids.	**Level 20**
(11) • At least 20 G but less than 40 G of Heroin (or the equivalent amount of other Schedule I or II Opiates); • At least 100 G but less than 200 G of Cocaine (or the equivalent amount of other Schedule I or II Stimulants); • At least 1 G but less than 2 G of Cocaine Base; • At least 20 G but less than 40 G of PCP, or at least 2 G but less than 4 G of PCP (actual); • At least 20 G but less than 40 G of Methamphetamine, or at least 2 G but less than 4 G of Methamphetamine (actual), or at least 2 G but less than 4 G of "Ice"; • At least 200 MG but less than 400 MG of LSD (or the equivalent amount of other Schedule I or II Hallucinogens); • At least 8 G but less than 16 G of Fentanyl; • At least 2 G but less than 4 G of a Fentanyl Analogue; • At least 20 KG but less than 40 KG of Marihuana; • At least 5 KG but less than 8 KG of Hashish; • At least 500 G but less than 800 G of Hashish Oil; • At least 10 KG but less than 20 KG of Secobarbital (or the equivalent amount of other Schedule I or II Depressants) or Schedule III substances (except Anabolic Steroids); • At least 20,000 but less than 40,000 units of Anabolic Steroids.	**Level 18**

Controlled Substances and Quantity* **Base Offense Level**

(12) • At least 10 G but less than 20 G of Heroin (or the equivalent amount of other Schedule I or II Opiates); **Level 16**
- At least 50 G but less than 100 G of Cocaine (or the equivalent amount of other Schedule I or II Stimulants);
- At least 500 MG but less than 1 G of Cocaine Base;
- At least 10 G but less than 20 G of PCP, or at least 1 G but less than 2 G of PCP (actual);
- At least 10 G but less than 20 G of Methamphetamine, or at least 1 G but less than 2 G of Methamphetamine (actual), or at least 1 G but less than 2 G of "Ice";
- At least 100 MG but less than 200 MG of LSD (or the equivalent amount of other Schedule I or II Hallucinogens);
- At least 4 G but less than 8 G of Fentanyl;
- At least 1 G but less than 2 G of a Fentanyl Analogue;
- At least 10 KG but less than 20 KG of Marihuana;
- At least 2 KG but less than 5 KG of Hashish;
- At least 200 G but less than 500 G of Hashish Oil;
- At least 5 KG but less than 10 KG of Secobarbital (or the equivalent amount of other Schedule I or II Depressants) or Schedule III substances (except Anabolic Steroids);
- At least 10,000 but less than 20,000 units of Anabolic Steroids.

(13) • At least 5 G but less than 10 G of Heroin (or the equivalent amount of other Schedule I or II Opiates); **Level 14**
- At least 25 G but less than 50 G of Cocaine (or the equivalent amount of other Schedule I or II Stimulants);
- At least 250 MG but less than 500 MG of Cocaine Base;
- At least 5 G but less than 10 G of PCP, or at least 500 MG but less than 1 G of PCP (actual);
- At least 5 G but less than 10 G of Methamphetamine, or at least 500 MG but less than 1 G of Methamphetamine (actual), or at least 500 MG but less than 1 G of "Ice";
- At least 50 MG but less than 100 MG of LSD (or the equivalent amount of other Schedule I or II Hallucinogens);
- At least 2 G but less than 4 G of Fentanyl;
- At least 500 MG but less than 1 G of a Fentanyl Analogue;
- At least 5 KG but less than 10 KG of Marihuana;
- At least 1 KG but less than 2 KG of Hashish;
- At least 100 G but less than 200 G of Hashish Oil;
- At least 2.5 KG but less than 5 KG of Secobarbital (or the equivalent amount of other Schedule I or II Depressants) or Schedule III substances (except Anabolic Steroids);
- At least 5,000 but less than 10,000 units of Anabolic Steroids.

Controlled Substances and Quantity*	**Base Offense Level**
(14) • Less than 5 G of Heroin (or the equivalent amount of other Schedule I or II Opiates); • Less than 25 G of Cocaine (or the equivalent amount of other Schedule I or II Stimulants); • Less than 250 MG of Cocaine Base; • Less than 5 G of PCP, or less than 500 MG of PCP (actual); • Less than 5 G of Methamphetamine, or less than 500 MG of Methamphetamine (actual), or less than 500 MG of "Ice"; • Less than 50 MG of LSD (or the equivalent amount of other Schedule I or II Hallucinogens); • Less than 2 G of Fentanyl; • Less than 500 MG of a Fentanyl Analogue; • At least 2.5 KG but less than 5 KG of Marihuana; • At least 500 G but less than 1 KG of Hashish; • At least 50 G but less than 100 G of Hashish Oil; • At least 1.25 KG but less than 2.5 KG of Secobarbital (or the equivalent amount of other Schedule I or II Depressants) or Schedule III substances (except Anabolic Steroids); • At least 2,500 but less than 5,000 units of Anabolic Steroids; • 20 KG or more of Schedule IV substances.	**Level 12**
(15) • At least 1 KG but less than 2.5 KG of Marihuana; • At least 200 G but less than 500 G of Hashish; • At least 20 G but less than 50 G of Hashish Oil; • At least 500 G but less than 1.25 KG of Secobarbital (or the equivalent amount of other Schedule I or II Depressants) or Schedule III substances (except Anabolic Steroids); • At least 1,000 but less than 2,500 units of Anabolic Steroids; • At least 8 KG but less than 20 KG of Schedule IV substances.	**Level 10**
(16) • At least 250 G but less than 1 KG of Marihuana; • At least 50 G but less than 200 G of Hashish; • At least 5 G but less than 20 G of Hashish Oil; • At least 125 G but less than 500 G of Secobarbital (or the equivalent amount of other Schedule I or II Depressants) or Schedule III substances (except Anabolic Steroids); • At least 250 but less than 1,000 units of Anabolic Steroids; • At least 2 KG but less than 8 KG of Schedule IV substances; • 20 KG or more of Schedule V substances.	**Level 8**
(17) • Less than 250 G of Marihuana; • Less than 50 G of Hashish; • Less than 5 G of Hashish Oil; • Less than 125 G of Secobarbital (or the equivalent amount of other Schedule I or II Depressants) or Schedule III substances (except Anabolic Steroids); • Less than 250 units of Anabolic Steroids; • Less than 2 KG of Schedule IV substances; • Less than 20 KG of Schedule V substances.	**Level 6**

---

* Unless otherwise specified, the weight of a controlled substance set forth in the table refers to the entire weight of any mixture or substance containing a detectable amount of the controlled substance. If a mixture or

substance contains more than one controlled substance, the weight of the entire mixture or substance is assigned to the controlled substance that results in the greater offense level.

The terms "PCP (actual)" and "Methamphetamine (actual)" refer to the weight of the controlled substance, itself, contained in the mixture or substance. For example, a mixture weighing 10 grams containing PCP at 50% purity contains 5 grams of PCP (actual). In the case of a mixture or substance containing PCP or methamphetamine, use the offense level determined by the entire weight of the mixture or substance, or the offense level determined by the weight of the PCP (actual) or methamphetamine (actual), whichever is greater.

"Ice," for the purposes of this guideline, means a mixture or substance containing d-methamphetamine hydrochloride of at least 80% purity.

"Cocaine base," for the purposes of this guideline, means "crack." "Crack" is the street name for a form of cocaine base, usually prepared by processing cocaine hydrochloride and sodium bicarbonate, and usually appearing in a lumpy, rocklike form.

In the case of an offense involving marihuana plants, if the offense involved (A) 50 or more marihuana plants, treat each plant as equivalent to 1 KG of marihuana; (B) fewer than 50 marihuana plants, treat each plant as equivalent to 100 G of marihuana. *Provided*, however, that if the actual weight of the marihuana is greater, use the actual weight of the marihuana.

In the case of anabolic steroids, one "unit" means a 10 cc vial of an injectable steroid or fifty tablets. All vials of injectable steroids are to be converted on the basis of their volume to the equivalent number of 10 cc vials (e.g., one 50 cc vial is to be counted as five 10 cc vials).

In the case of LSD on a carrier medium (e.g., a sheet of blotter paper), do not use the weight of the LSD/carrier medium. Instead, treat each dose of LSD on the carrier medium as equal to 0.4 mg of LSD for the purposes of the Drug Quantity Table.

Commentary

Statutory Provisions: 21 U.S.C. §§ 841(a), (b)(1)-(3), 960(a), (b). For additional statutory provision(s), see Appendix A (Statutory Index).

Application Notes:

1. *"Mixture or substance" as used in this guideline has the same meaning as in 21 U.S.C. § 841, except as expressly provided. Mixture or substance does not include materials that must be separated from the controlled substance before the controlled substance can be used. Examples of such materials include the fiberglass in a cocaine/fiberglass bonded suitcase, beeswax in a cocaine/beeswax statue, and waste water from an illicit laboratory used to manufacture a controlled substance. If such material cannot readily be separated from the mixture or substance that appropriately is counted in the Drug Quantity Table, the court may use any reasonable method to approximate the weight of the mixture or substance to be counted.*

   An upward departure nonetheless may be warranted when the mixture or substance counted in the Drug Quantity Table is combined with other, non-countable material in an unusually sophisticated manner in order to avoid detection.

2. *The statute and guideline also apply to "counterfeit" substances, which are defined in 21 U.S.C. § 802 to mean controlled substances that are falsely labeled so as to appear to have been legitimately manufactured or distributed.*

3. *Definitions of "firearm" and "dangerous weapon" are found in the Commentary to §1B1.1 (Application Instructions). The enhancement for weapon possession reflects the increased danger of violence when drug traffickers possess weapons. The adjustment should be applied if the weapon was present, unless it is clearly improbable that the weapon was connected with the offense. For example, the enhancement would not be applied if the defendant, arrested at his residence, had an unloaded hunting rifle in the closet. The enhancement also applies to offenses that are referenced to §2D1.1; see §§2D1.2(a)(1) and (2), 2D1.5(a)(1), 2D1.6, 2D1.7(b)(1), 2D1.8, 2D1.11(c)(1), 2D1.12(b)(1), and 2D2.1(b)(1).*

4. *Distribution of "a small amount of marihuana for no remuneration", 21 U.S.C. § 841(b)(4), is treated as simple possession, to which §2D2.1 applies.*

5. *Any reference to a particular controlled substance in these guidelines includes all salts, isomers, and all salts of isomers. Any reference to cocaine includes ecgonine and coca leaves, except extracts of coca leaves from which cocaine and ecgonine have been removed.*

6. *Where there are multiple transactions or multiple drug types, the quantities of drugs are to be added. Tables for making the necessary conversions are provided below.*

7. *Where a mandatory (statutory) minimum sentence applies, this mandatory minimum sentence may be "waived" and a lower sentence imposed (including a sentence below the applicable guideline range), as provided in 28 U.S.C. § 994(n), by reason of a defendant's "substantial assistance in the investigation or prosecution of another person who has committed an offense." See §5K1.1 (Substantial Assistance to Authorities). In addition, 18 U.S.C. § 3553(f) provides an exception to the applicability of mandatory minimum sentences in certain cases. See §5C1.2 (Limitation on Applicability of Statutory Minimum Sentences in Certain Cases).*

8. *A defendant who used special skills in the commission of the offense may be subject to an enhancement under §3B1.3 (Abuse of Position of Trust or Use of Special Skill). Certain*

professionals often occupy essential positions in drug trafficking schemes. These professionals include doctors, pilots, boat captains, financiers, bankers, attorneys, chemists, accountants, and others whose special skill, trade, profession, or position may be used to significantly facilitate the commission of a drug offense.

9. *Trafficking in controlled substances, compounds, or mixtures of unusually high purity may warrant an upward departure, except in the case of PCP or methamphetamine for which the guideline itself provides for the consideration of purity (see the footnote to the Drug Quantity Table). The purity of the controlled substance, particularly in the case of heroin, may be relevant in the sentencing process because it is probative of the defendant's role or position in the chain of distribution. Since controlled substances are often diluted and combined with other substances as they pass down the chain of distribution, the fact that a defendant is in possession of unusually pure narcotics may indicate a prominent role in the criminal enterprise and proximity to the source of the drugs. As large quantities are normally associated with high purities, this factor is particularly relevant where smaller quantities are involved.*

10. *The Commission has used the sentences provided in, and equivalences derived from, the statute (21 U.S.C. § 841(b)(1)), as the primary basis for the guideline sentences. The statute, however, provides direction only for the more common controlled substances, i.e., heroin, cocaine, PCP, methamphetamine, fentanyl, LSD and marihuana. The Drug Equivalency Tables set forth below provide conversion factors for other substances, which the Drug Quantity Table refers to as "equivalents" of these drugs. For example, one gram of a substance containing oxymorphone, a Schedule I opiate, is to be treated as the equivalent of five kilograms of marihuana in applying the Drug Quantity Table.*

The Drug Equivalency Tables also provide a means for combining differing controlled substances to obtain a single offense level. In each case, convert each of the drugs to its marihuana equivalent, add the quantities, and look up the total in the Drug Quantity Table to obtain the combined offense level.

For certain types of controlled substances, the marihuana equivalencies in the Drug Equivalency Tables are "capped" at specified amounts (e.g., the combined equivalent weight of all Schedule V controlled substances shall not exceed 999 grams of marihuana). Where there are controlled substances from more than one schedule (e.g., a quantity of a Schedule IV substance and a quantity of a Schedule V substance), determine the marihuana equivalency for each schedule separately (subject to the cap, if any, applicable to that schedule). Then add the marihuana equivalencies to determine the combined marihuana equivalency (subject to the cap, if any, applicable to the combined amounts).

Note: Because of the statutory equivalences, the ratios in the Drug Equivalency Tables do not necessarily reflect dosages based on pharmacological equivalents.

Examples:

a. *The defendant is convicted of selling 70 grams of a substance containing PCP (Level 22) and 250 milligrams of a substance containing LSD (Level 18). The PCP converts to 70 kilograms of marihuana; the LSD converts to 25 kilograms of marihuana. The total is therefore equivalent to 95 kilograms of marihuana, for which the Drug Quantity Table provides an offense level of 24.*

b. *The defendant is convicted of selling 500 grams of marihuana (Level 8) and five kilograms of diazepam (Level 8). The diazepam, a Schedule IV drug, is equivalent to 625 grams of marihuana. The total, 1.125 kilograms of marihuana, has an offense level of 10 in the Drug Quantity Table.*

c. *The defendant is convicted of selling 80 grams of cocaine (Level 16) and five kilograms of marihuana (Level 14). The cocaine is equivalent to 16 kilograms of marihuana. The total is therefore equivalent to 21 kilograms of marihuana, which has an offense level of 18 in the Drug Quantity Table.*

d. *The defendant is convicted of selling 28 kilograms of a Schedule III substance, 50 kilograms of a Schedule IV substance, and 100 kilograms of a Schedule V substance. The marihuana equivalency for the Schedule III substance is 56 kilograms of marihuana (below the cap of 59.99 kilograms of marihuana set forth as the maximum equivalent weight for Schedule III substances). The marihuana equivalency for the Schedule IV substance is subject to a cap of 4.99 kilograms of marihuana set forth as the maximum equivalent weight for Schedule IV substances (without the cap it would have been 6.25 kilograms). The marihuana equivalency for the Schedule V substance is subject to the cap of 999 grams of marihuana set forth as the maximum equivalent weight for Schedule V substances (without the cap it would have been 1.25 kilograms). The combined equivalent weight, determined by adding together the above amounts, is subject to the cap of 59.99 kilograms of marihuana set forth as the maximum combined equivalent weight for Schedule III, IV, and V substances. Without the cap, the combined equivalent weight would have been 61.99 (56 + 4.99 + .999) kilograms.*

DRUG EQUIVALENCY TABLES

Schedule I or II Opiates*

1 gm of Heroin =	1 kg of marihuana
1 gm of Alpha-Methylfentanyl =	10 kg of marihuana
1 gm of Dextromoramide =	670 gm of marihuana
1 gm of Dipipanone =	250 gm of marihuana
1 gm of 3-Methylfentanyl =	10 kg of marihuana
1 gm of 1-Methyl-4-phenyl-4-propionoxypiperidine/MPPP =	700 gm of marihuana
1 gm of 1-(2-Phenylethyl)-4-phenyl-4-acetyloxypiperidine/ PEPAP =	700 gm of marihuana
1 gm of Alphaprodine =	100 gm of marihuana
1 gm of Fentanyl (N-phenyl-N-[1-(2-phenylethyl)-4-piperidinyl] Propanamide) =	2.5 kg of marihuana
1 gm of Hydromorphone/Dihydromorphinone =	2.5 kg of marihuana
1 gm of Levorphanol =	2.5 kg of marihuana
1 gm of Meperidine/Pethidine =	50 gm of marihuana
1 gm of Methadone =	500 gm of marihuana
1 gm of 6-Monoacetylmorphine =	1 kg of marihuana
1 gm of Morphine =	500 gm of marihuana
1 gm of Oxycodone =	500 gm of marihuana
1 gm of Oxymorphone =	5 kg of marihuana

1 gm of Racemorphan =	800 gm of marihuana
1 gm of Codeine =	80 gm of marihuana
1 gm of Dextropropoxyphene/Propoxyphene-Bulk =	50 gm of marihuana
1 gm of Ethylmorphine =	165 gm of marihuana
1 gm of Hydrocodone/Dihydrocodeinone =	500 gm of marihuana
1 gm of Mixed Alkaloids of Opium/Papaveretum =	250 gm of marihuana
1 gm of Opium =	50 gm of marihuana

**Provided*, that the minimum offense level from the Drug Quantity Table for any of these controlled substances individually, or in combination with another controlled substance, is level 12.

<u>Cocaine and Other Schedule I and II Stimulants (and their immediate precursors)</u>*

1 gm of Cocaine =	200 gm of marihuana
1 gm of N-Ethylamphetamine =	80 gm of marihuana
1 gm of Fenethylline =	40 gm of marihuana
1 gm of Amphetamine =	200 gm of marihuana
1 gm of Dextroamphetamine =	200 gm of marihuana
1 gm of Methamphetamine =	1 kg of marihuana
1 gm of Methamphetamine (Actual) =	10 kg of marihuana
1 gm of "Ice" =	10 kg of marihuana
1 gm of L-Methamphetamine/Levo-methamphetamine/ L-Desoxyephedrine =	40 gm of marihuana
1 gm of 4-Methylaminorex ("Euphoria") =	100 gm of marihuana
1 gm of Methylphenidate (Ritalin) =	100 gm of marihuana
1 gm of Phenmetrazine =	80 gm of marihuana
1 gm Phenylacetone/P_2P (when possessed for the purpose of manufacturing methamphetamine) =	416 gm of marihuana
1 gm Phenylacetone/P_2P (in any other case) =	75 gm of marihuana
1 gm of Cocaine Base ("Crack") =	20 kg of marihuana
1 gm of Aminorex =	100 gm of marihuana
1 gm of Methcathinone =	380 gm of marihuana
1 gm of N-N-Dimethylamphetamine =	40 gm of marihuana

**Provided*, that the minimum offense level from the Drug Quantity Table for any of these controlled substances individually, or in combination with another controlled substance, is level 12.

<u>LSD, PCP, and Other Schedule I and II Hallucinogens (and their immediate precursors)</u>*

1 gm of Bufotenine =	70 gm of marihuana
1 gm of D-Lysergic Acid Diethylamide/Lysergide/LSD =	100 kg of marihuana
1 gm of Diethyltryptamine/DET =	80 gm of marihuana
1 gm of Dimethyltryptamine/DMT =	100 gm of marihuana
1 gm of Mescaline =	10 gm of marihuana

1 gm of Mushrooms containing Psilocin and/or Psilocybin (Dry) =	1 gm of marihuana
1 gm of Mushrooms containing Psilocin and/or Psilocybin (Wet) =	0.1 gm of marihuana
1 gm of Peyote (Dry) =	0.5 gm of marihuana
1 gm of Peyote (Wet) =	0.05 gm of marihuana
1 gm of Phencyclidine/PCP =	1 kg of marihuana
1 gm of Phencyclidine (actual) /PCP (actual) =	10 kg of marihuana
1 gm of Psilocin =	500 gm of marihuana
1 gm of Psilocybin =	500 gm of marihuana
1 gm of Pyrrolidine Analog of Phencyclidine/PHP =	1 kg of marihuana
1 gm of Thiophene Analog of Phencyclidine/TCP =	1 kg of marihuana
1 gm of 4-Bromo-2,5-Dimethoxyamphetamine/DOB =	2.5 kg of marihuana
1 gm of 2,5-Dimethoxy-4-methylamphetamine/DOM =	1.67 kg of marihuana
1 gm of 3,4-Methylenedioxyamphetamine/MDA =	50 gm of marihuana
1 gm of 3,4-Methylenedioxymethamphetamine/MDMA =	35 gm of marihuana
1 gm of 3,4-Methylenedioxy-N-ethylamphetamine/MDEA =	30 gm of marihuana
1 gm of 1-Piperidinocyclohexanecarbonitrile/PCC =	680 gm of marihuana
1 gm of N-ethyl-1-phenylcyclohexylamine (PCE) =	1 kg of marihuana

**Provided*, that the minimum offense level from the Drug Quantity Table for any of these controlled substances individually, or in combination with another controlled substance, is level 12.

Schedule I Marihuana

1 gm of Marihuana/Cannabis, granulated, powdered, etc. =	1 gm of marihuana
1 gm of Hashish Oil =	50 gm of marihuana
1 gm of Cannabis Resin or Hashish =	5 gm of marihuana
1 gm of Tetrahydrocannabinol, Organic =	167 gm of marihuana
1 gm of Tetrahydrocannabinol, Synthetic =	167 gm of marihuana

Secobarbital and Other Schedule I or II Depressants**

1 gm of Amobarbital =	2 gm of marihuana
1 gm of Glutethimide =	0.4 gm of marihuana
1 gm of Methaqualone =	0.7 gm of marihuana
1 gm of Pentobarbital =	2 gm of marihuana
1 gm of Secobarbital =	2 gm of marihuana

***Provided*, that the combined equivalent weight of all Schedule I or II depressants, Schedule III substances, Schedule IV substances, and Schedule V substances shall not exceed 59.99 kilograms of marihuana.

Schedule III Substances***

1 gm of a Schedule III Substance (except anabolic steroids) =	2 gm of marihuana
1 unit of anabolic steroids =	1 gm of marihuana

****Provided*, that the combined equivalent weight of all Schedule III substances, Schedule I or II depressants, Schedule IV substances, and Schedule V substances shall not exceed 59.99 kilograms of marihuana.

Schedule IV Substances****

1 gm of a Schedule IV Substance =	0.125 gm of marihuana

*****Provided*, that the combined equivalent weight of all Schedule IV and V substances shall not exceed 4.99 kilograms of marihuana.

Schedule V Substances*****

1 gm of a Schedule V Substance =	0.0125 gm of marihuana

******Provided*, that the combined equivalent weight of Schedule V substances shall not exceed 999 grams of marihuana.

To facilitate conversions to drug equivalencies, the following table is provided:

MEASUREMENT CONVERSION TABLE

1 oz = 28.35 gm
1 lb = 453.6 gm
1 lb = 0.4536 kg
1 gal = 3.785 liters
1 qt = 0.946 liters
1 gm = 1 ml (liquid)
1 liter = 1,000 ml
1 kg = 1,000 gm
1 gm = 1,000 mg
1 grain = 64.8 mg.

11. *If the number of doses, pills, or capsules but not the weight of the controlled substance is known, multiply the number of doses, pills, or capsules by the typical weight per dose in the table below to estimate the total weight of the controlled substance (e.g., 100 doses of Mescaline at 500 mg per dose = 50 gms of mescaline). The Typical Weight Per Unit Table, prepared from information provided by the Drug Enforcement Administration, displays the typical weight per dose, pill, or capsule for certain controlled substances. Do not use this table if any more reliable estimate of the total weight is available from case-specific information.*

TYPICAL WEIGHT PER UNIT (DOSE, PILL, OR CAPSULE) TABLE

Hallucinogens

*MDA**	*100 mg*
Mescaline	*500 mg*
*PCP**	*5 mg*
Peyote (dry)	*12 gm*
Peyote (wet)	*120 gm*
*Psilocin**	*10 mg*
Psilocybe mushrooms (dry)	*5 gm*
Psilocybe mushrooms (wet)	*50 gm*
*Psilocybin**	*10 mg*
*2,5-Dimethoxy-4-methylamphetamine (STP, DOM)**	*3 mg*

Depressants

*Methaqualone**	*300 mg*

Marihuana

1 marihuana cigarette	*0.5 gm*

Stimulants

*Amphetamine**	*10 mg*
*Methamphetamine**	*5 mg*
*Phenmetrazine (Preludin)**	*75 mg*

**For controlled substances marked with an asterisk, the weight per unit shown is the weight of the actual controlled substance, and not generally the weight of the mixture or substance containing the controlled substance. Therefore, use of this table provides a very conservative estimate of the total weight.*

12. *Types and quantities of drugs not specified in the count of conviction may be considered in determining the offense level. See §1B1.3(a)(2) (Relevant Conduct). Where there is no drug seizure or the amount seized does not reflect the scale of the offense, the court shall approximate the quantity of the controlled substance. In making this determination, the court may consider, for example, the price generally obtained for the controlled substance, financial or other records, similar transactions in controlled substances by the defendant, and the size or capability of any laboratory involved.*

If the offense involved both a substantive drug offense and an attempt or conspiracy (e.g., sale of five grams of heroin and an attempt to sell an additional ten grams of heroin), the total quantity involved shall be aggregated to determine the scale of the offense.

In an offense involving negotiation to traffic in a controlled substance, the weight under negotiation in an uncompleted distribution shall be used to calculate the applicable amount. However, where the court finds that the defendant did not intend to produce and was not reasonably capable of producing the negotiated amount, the court shall exclude from the guideline calculation the amount that it finds the defendant did not intend to produce and was not reasonably capable of producing.

13. *If subsection (b)(2)(B) applies, do not apply §3B1.3 (Abuse of Position of Trust or Use of Special Skill).*

14. *D-lysergic acid, which is generally used to make LSD, is classified as a Schedule III controlled substance (to which §2D1.1 applies) and as a listed precursor (to which §2D1.11 applies). Where the defendant is convicted under 21 U.S.C. §§ 841(b)(1)(D) or 960(b)(4) of an offense involving d-lysergic acid, apply §2D1.1 or §2D1.11, whichever results in the greater offense level. See Application Note 5 in the Commentary to §1B1.1 (Application Instructions). Where the defendant is accountable for an offense involving the manufacture of LSD, see Application Note 12 above pertaining to the determination of the scale of the offense.*

15. *Certain pharmaceutical preparations are classified as Schedule III, IV, or V controlled substances by the Drug Enforcement Administration under 21 C.F.R. § 1308.13-15 even though they contain a small amount of a Schedule I or II controlled substance. For example, Tylenol 3 is classified as a Schedule III controlled substance even though it contains a small amount of codeine, a Schedule II opiate. For the purposes of the guidelines, the classification of the controlled substance under 21 C.F.R. § 1308.13-15 is the appropriate classification.*

16. *Where (A) the amount of the controlled substance for which the defendant is accountable under §1B1.3 (Relevant Conduct) results in a base offense level greater than 36, (B) the court finds that this offense level overrepresents the defendant's culpability in the criminal activity, and (C) the defendant qualifies for a mitigating role adjustment under §3B1.2 (Mitigating Role), a downward departure may be warranted. The court may depart to a sentence no lower than the guideline range that would have resulted if the defendant's Chapter Two offense level had been offense level 36. Provided, that a defendant is not eligible for a downward departure under this provision if the defendant:*

    (a) *has one or more prior felony convictions for a crime of violence or a controlled substance offense as defined in §4B1.2 (Definitions of Terms Used in Section 4B1.1);*

    (b) *qualifies for an adjustment under §3B1.3 (Abuse of Position of Trust or Use of Special Skill);*

    (c) *possessed or induced another participant to use or possess a firearm in the offense;*

    (d) *had decision-making authority;*

    (e) *owned the controlled substance or financed any part of the offense; or*

    (f) *sold the controlled substance or played a substantial part in negotiating the terms of the sale.*

    Example: A defendant, who the court finds meets the criteria for a downward departure under this provision, has a Chapter Two offense level of 38, a 2-level reduction for a minor role from §3B1.2, and a 3-level reduction for acceptance of responsibility from §3E1.1. His final offense level is 33. If the defendant's Chapter Two offense level had been 36, the 2-level reduction for a minor role and 3-level reduction for acceptance of responsibility would have resulted in a final offense level of 31. Therefore, under this provision, a downward departure not to exceed 2 levels (from level 33 to level 31) would be authorized.

17. *If, in a reverse sting (an operation in which a government agent sells or negotiates to sell a controlled substance to a defendant), the court finds that the government agent set a price for the controlled substance that was substantially below the market value of the controlled substance, thereby leading to the defendant's purchase of a significantly greater quantity of the controlled substance than his available resources would have allowed him to purchase except for the artificially low price set by the government agent, a downward departure may be warranted.*

18. *LSD on a blotter paper carrier medium typically is marked so that the number of doses ("hits") per sheet readily can be determined. When this is not the case, it is to be presumed that each 1/4 inch by 1/4 inch section of the blotter paper is equal to one dose.*

In the case of liquid LSD (LSD that has not been placed onto a carrier medium), using the weight of the LSD alone to calculate the offense level may not adequately reflect the seriousness of the offense. In such a case, an upward departure may be warranted.

19. *In an extraordinary case, an upward departure above offense level 38 on the basis of drug quantity may be warranted. For example, an upward departure may be warranted where the quantity is at least ten times the minimum quantity required for level 38.*

Background: *Offenses under 21 U.S.C. §§ 841 and 960 receive identical punishment based upon the quantity of the controlled substance involved, the defendant's criminal history, and whether death or serious bodily injury resulted from the offense.*

The base offense levels in §2D1.1 are either provided directly by the Anti-Drug Abuse Act of 1986 or are proportional to the levels established by statute, and apply to all unlawful trafficking. Levels 32 and 26 in the Drug Quantity Table are the distinctions provided by the Anti-Drug Abuse Act; however, further refinement of drug amounts is essential to provide a logical sentencing structure for drug offenses. To determine these finer distinctions, the Commission consulted numerous experts and practitioners, including authorities at the Drug Enforcement Administration, chemists, attorneys, probation officers, and members of the Organized Crime Drug Enforcement Task Forces, who also advocate the necessity of these distinctions.

The base offense levels at levels 26 and 32 establish guideline ranges with a lower limit as close to the statutory minimum as possible; e.g., level 32 ranges from 121 to 151 months, where the statutory minimum is ten years or 120 months.

In cases involving fifty or more marihuana plants, an equivalency of one plant to one kilogram of marihuana is derived from the statutory penalty provisions of 21 U.S.C. § 841(b)(1)(A), (B), and (D). In cases involving fewer than fifty plants, the statute is silent as to the equivalency. For cases involving fewer than fifty plants, the Commission has adopted an equivalency of 100 grams per plant, or the actual weight of the usable marihuana, whichever is greater. The decision to treat each plant as equal to 100 grams is premised on the fact that the average yield from a mature marihuana plant equals 100 grams of marihuana. In controlled substance offenses, an attempt is assigned the same offense level as the object of the attempt. Consequently, the Commission adopted the policy that, in the case of fewer than fifty marihuana plants, each plant is to be treated as the equivalent of an attempt to produce 100 grams of marihuana, except where the actual weight of the usable marihuana is greater.

Specific Offense Characteristic (b)(2) is derived from Section 6453 of the Anti-Drug Abuse Act of 1988.

Frequently, a term of supervised release to follow imprisonment is required by statute for offenses covered by this guideline. Guidelines for the imposition, duration, and conditions of supervised release are set forth in Chapter Five, Part D (Supervised Release).

Because the weights of LSD carrier media vary widely and typically far exceed the weight of the controlled substance itself, the Commission has determined that basing offense levels on the entire weight of the LSD and carrier medium would produce unwarranted disparity among offenses involving the same quantity of actual LSD (but different carrier weights), as well as sentences disproportionate to those for other, more dangerous controlled substances, such as PCP. Consequently, in cases involving LSD contained in a carrier medium, the Commission has established a weight per dose of 0.4 milligram for purposes of determining the base offense level.

The dosage weight of LSD selected exceeds the Drug Enforcement Administration's standard dosage unit for LSD of 0.05 milligram (i.e., the quantity of actual LSD per dose) in order to assign some weight to the carrier medium. Because LSD typically is marketed and consumed orally on a carrier medium, the inclusion of some weight attributable to the carrier medium recognizes (A) that offense levels for most other controlled substances are based upon the weight of the mixture containing the controlled substance without regard to purity, and (B) the decision in Chapman v. United States, 111 S. Ct. 1919 (1991) (holding that the term "mixture or substance" in 21 U.S.C. § 841(b)(1) includes the carrier medium in which LSD is absorbed). At the same time, the weight per dose selected is less than the weight per dose that would equate the offense level for LSD on a carrier medium with that for the same number of doses of PCP, a controlled substance that comparative assessments indicate is more likely to induce violent acts and ancillary crime than is LSD. (Treating LSD on a carrier medium as weighing 0.5 milligram per dose would produce offense levels equivalent to those for PCP.) Thus, the approach decided upon by the Commission will harmonize offense levels for LSD offenses with those for other controlled substances and avoid an undue influence of varied carrier weight on the applicable offense level. Nonetheless, this approach does not override the applicability of "mixture or substance" for the purpose of applying any mandatory minimum sentence (see Chapman; §5G1.1(b)).

Historical Note: Effective November 1, 1987. Amended effective January 15, 1988 (see Appendix C, amendments 19, 20, and 21); November 1, 1989 (see Appendix C, amendments 123-134, 302, and 303); November 1, 1990 (see Appendix C, amendment 318); November 1, 1991 (see Appendix C, amendments 369-371 and 394-396); November 1, 1992 (see Appendix C, amendments 446 and 447); November 1, 1993 (see Appendix C, amendments 479, 484-488, and 499); September 23, 1994 (see Appendix C, amendment 509); November 1, 1994 (see Appendix C, amendment 505).

§2D1.2. Drug Offenses Occurring Near Protected Locations or Involving Underage or Pregnant Individuals; Attempt or Conspiracy

(a) Base Offense Level (Apply the greatest):

(1) **2** plus the offense level from §2D1.1 applicable to the quantity of controlled substances directly involving a protected location or an underage or pregnant individual; or

(2) **1** plus the offense level from §2D1.1 applicable to the total quantity of controlled substances involved in the offense; or

(3) **26**, if the offense involved a person less than eighteen years of age; or

(4) **13**, otherwise.

Commentary

Statutory Provisions: 21 U.S.C. §§ 859 (formerly 21 U.S.C. § 845), 860 (formerly 21 U.S.C. § 845a), 861 (formerly 21 U.S.C. § 845b).

Application Note:

1. *Where only part of the relevant offense conduct directly involved a protected location or an underage or pregnant individual, subsections (a)(1) and (a)(2) may result in different offense levels. For example, if the defendant, as part of the same course of conduct or common scheme or plan, sold 5 grams of heroin near a protected location and 10 grams of heroin elsewhere, the offense level from subsection (a)(1) would be level 16 (2 plus the offense level for the sale of 5 grams of heroin, the amount sold near the protected location); the offense level from subsection (a)(2) would be level 17 (1 plus the offense level for the sale of 15 grams of heroin, the total amount of heroin involved in the offense).*

Background: This section implements the direction to the Commission in Section 6454 of the Anti-Drug Abuse Act of 1988.

Historical Note: Effective November 1, 1987. Amended effective January 15, 1988 (see Appendix C, amendment 22); November 1, 1989 (see Appendix C, amendment 135); November 1, 1990 (see Appendix C, amendment 319); November 1, 1991 (see Appendix C, amendment 421); November 1, 1992 (see Appendix C, amendment 447).

§2D1.3. [Deleted]

Historical Note: Section 2D1.3 (Distributing Controlled Substances to Individuals Younger than Twenty-One Years, to Pregnant Women, or Within 1000 Feet of a School or College), effective November 1, 1987, amended effective January 15, 1988 (see Appendix C, amendment 23), was deleted by consolidation with §2D1.2 effective November 1, 1989 (see Appendix C, amendment 135).

§2D1.4. [Deleted]

Historical Note: Section 2D1.4 (Attempts and Conspiracies), effective November 1, 1987, amended effective November 1, 1989 (see Appendix C, amendments 136-138), was deleted by consolidation with the guidelines applicable to the underlying substantive offenses effective November 1, 1992 (see Appendix C, amendment 447).

§2D1.5. Continuing Criminal Enterprise; Attempt or Conspiracy

(a) Base Offense Level (Apply the greater):

(1) **4** plus the offense level from §2D1.1 applicable to the underlying offense; or

(2) **38.**

Commentary

Statutory Provision: 21 U.S.C. § 848.

Application Notes:

1. *Do not apply any adjustment from Chapter Three, Part B (Role in the Offense).*

2. *If as part of the enterprise the defendant sanctioned the use of violence, or if the number of persons managed by the defendant was extremely large, an upward departure may be warranted.*

3. *Under 21 U.S.C. § 848, certain conduct for which the defendant has previously been sentenced may be charged as part of the instant offense to establish a "continuing series of violations." A sentence resulting from a conviction sustained prior to the last overt act of the instant offense is to be considered a prior sentence under §4A1.2(a)(1) and not part of the instant offense.*

4. *Violations of 21 U.S.C. § 848 will be grouped with other drug offenses for the purpose of applying Chapter Three, Part D (Multiple Counts).*

Background: *Because a conviction under 21 U.S.C. § 848 establishes that a defendant controlled and exercised authority over one of the most serious types of ongoing criminal activity, this guideline provides a minimum base offense level of 38. An adjustment from Chapter Three, Part B is not authorized because the offense level of this guideline already reflects an adjustment for role in the offense.*

Title 21 U.S.C. § 848 provides a 20-year minimum mandatory penalty for the first conviction, a 30-year minimum mandatory penalty for a second conviction, and a mandatory life sentence for principal administrators of extremely large enterprises. If the application of the guidelines results in a sentence below the minimum sentence required by statute, the statutory minimum shall be the guideline sentence. See *§5G1.1(b).*

Historical Note: Effective November 1, 1987. Amended effective October 15, 1988 (see Appendix C, amendment 66); November 1, 1989 (see Appendix C, amendment 139); November 1, 1992 (see Appendix C, amendment 447).

§2D1.6. Use of Communication Facility in Committing Drug Offense; Attempt or Conspiracy

(a) Base Offense Level: the offense level applicable to the underlying offense.

Commentary

Statutory Provision: *21 U.S.C. § 843(b).*

Application Note:

1. *Where the offense level for the underlying offense is to be determined by reference to §2D1.1,* see *Application Note 12 of the Commentary to §2D1.1 for guidance in determining the scale of the offense. Note that the Drug Quantity Table in §2D1.1 provides a minimum offense level of 12 where the offense involves heroin (or other Schedule I or II opiates), cocaine (or other Schedule I or II stimulants), cocaine base, PCP, methamphetamine, LSD (or other Schedule I or II hallucinogens), fentanyl, or fentanyl analogue (§2D1.1(c)(14)); and a minimum offense level of 6 otherwise (§2D1.1(c)(17)).*

Background: This section covers the use of a communication facility in committing a drug offense. A communication facility includes any public or private instrument used in the transmission of writing, signs, signals, pictures, and sound; e.g., telephone, wire, radio.

Historical Note: Effective November 1, 1987. Amended effective November 1, 1990 (see Appendix C, amendment 320); November 1, 1992 (see Appendix C, amendment 447); November 1, 1994 (see Appendix C, amendment 505).

§2D1.7. Unlawful Sale or Transportation of Drug Paraphernalia; Attempt or Conspiracy

(a) Base Offense Level: **12**

(b) Cross Reference

(1) If the offense involved a controlled substance, apply §2D1.1 (Unlawful Manufacturing, Importing, Exporting, or Trafficking) or §2D2.1 (Unlawful Possession), as appropriate, if the resulting offense level is greater than that determined above.

Commentary

Statutory Provision: 21 U.S.C. § 863 (formerly 21 U.S.C. § 857).

Application Note:

1. The typical case addressed by this guideline involves small-scale trafficking in drug paraphernalia (generally from a retail establishment that also sells items that are not unlawful). In a case involving a large-scale dealer, distributor, or manufacturer, an upward departure may be warranted. Conversely, where the offense was not committed for pecuniary gain (e.g., transportation for the defendant's personal use), a downward departure may be warranted.

Historical Note: Effective November 1, 1987. Amended effective November 1, 1991 (see Appendix C, amendment 397); November 1, 1992 (see Appendix C, amendment 447).

§2D1.8. Renting or Managing a Drug Establishment; Attempt or Conspiracy

(a) Base Offense Level:

(1) The offense level from §2D1.1 applicable to the underlying controlled substance offense, except as provided below.

(2) If the defendant had no participation in the underlying controlled substance offense other than allowing use of the premises, the offense level shall be **4** levels less than the offense level from §2D1.1 applicable to the underlying controlled substance offense, but not greater than level **16**.

(b) Special Instruction

(1) If the offense level is determined under subsection (a)(2), do not apply an adjustment under §3B1.2 (Mitigating Role).

Commentary

Statutory Provision: 21 U.S.C. § 856.

Application Note:

1. *Subsection (a)(2) does not apply unless the defendant had no participation in the underlying controlled substance offense other than allowing use of the premises. For example, subsection (a)(2) would not apply to a defendant who possessed a dangerous weapon in connection with the offense, a defendant who guarded the cache of controlled substances, a defendant who arranged for the use of the premises for the purpose of facilitating a drug transaction, a defendant who allowed the use of more than one premises, a defendant who made telephone calls to facilitate the underlying controlled substance offense, or a defendant who otherwise assisted in the commission of the underlying controlled substance offense. Furthermore, subsection (a)(2) does not apply unless the defendant initially leased, rented, purchased, or otherwise acquired a possessory interest in the premises for a legitimate purpose. Finally, subsection (a)(2) does not apply if the defendant had previously allowed any premises to be used as a drug establishment without regard to whether such prior misconduct resulted in a conviction.*

Background: This section covers the offense of knowingly opening, maintaining, managing, or controlling any building, room, or enclosure for the purpose of manufacturing, distributing, storing, or using a controlled substance contrary to law (e.g., a "crack house").

Historical Note: Effective November 1, 1987. Amended effective November 1, 1991 (see Appendix C, amendment 394); November 1, 1992 (see Appendix C, amendments 447 and 448).

§2D1.9. Placing or Maintaining Dangerous Devices on Federal Property to Protect the Unlawful Production of Controlled Substances; Attempt or Conspiracy

(a) Base Offense Level: **23**

Commentary

Statutory Provision: 21 U.S.C. § 841(e)(1).

Background: This section covers the offense of assembling, placing, or causing to be placed, or maintaining a "booby-trap" on federal property where a controlled substance is being manufactured or distributed.

Historical Note: Effective November 1, 1987. Amended effective November 1, 1992 (see Appendix C, amendment 447).

§2D1.10. Endangering Human Life While Illegally Manufacturing a Controlled Substance; Attempt or Conspiracy

(a) Base Offense Level (Apply the greater):

(1) **3** plus the offense level from the Drug Quantity Table in §2D1.1; or

(2) **20**.

Commentary

Statutory Provision: 21 U.S.C. § 858.

Historical Note: Effective November 1, 1989 (see Appendix C, amendment 140). Amended effective November 1, 1992 (see Appendix C, amendment 447).

§2D1.11. Unlawfully Distributing, Importing, Exporting or Possessing a Listed Chemical; Attempt or Conspiracy

(a) Base Offense Level: The offense level from the Chemical Quantity Table set forth in subsection (d) below.

(b) Specific Offense Characteristics

(1) If a dangerous weapon (including a firearm) was possessed, increase by **2** levels.

(2) If the defendant is convicted of violating 21 U.S.C. §§ 841(d)(2), (g)(1), or 960(d)(2), decrease by **3** levels, unless the defendant knew or believed that the listed chemical was to be used to manufacture a controlled substance unlawfully.

(c) Cross Reference

(1) If the offense involved unlawfully manufacturing a controlled substance, or attempting to manufacture a controlled substance unlawfully, apply §2D1.1 (Unlawful Manufacturing, Importing, Exporting, Trafficking) if the resulting offense level is greater than that determined above.

(d) CHEMICAL QUANTITY TABLE*

Listed Chemicals and Quantity **Base Offense Level**

(1) Listed Precursor Chemicals **Level 28**
20 KG or more of Benzyl Cyanide;
200 G or more of D-Lysergic Acid;
20 KG or more of Ephedrine;
200 G or more of Ergonovine;
400 G or more of Ergotamine;
20 KG or more of Ethylamine;
44 KG or more of Hydriodic Acid;
320 KG or more of Isoafrole;
4 KG or more of Methylamine;
500 KG or more of N-Methylephedrine;
500 KG or more of N-Methylpseudoephedrine;
200 KG or more of Norpseudoephedrine;
20 KG or more of Phenylacetic Acid;
200 KG or more of Phenylpropanolamine;
10 KG or more of Piperidine;
320 KG or more of Piperonal;
1.6 KG or more of Propionic Anhydride;
20 KG or more of Pseudoephedrine;
320 KG or more of Safrole;
400 KG or more of 3, 4-Methylenedioxyphenyl-2-propanone;

Listed Essential Chemicals
11 KG or more of Acetic Anhydride;
1175 KG or more of Acetone;
20 KG or more of Benzyl Chloride;
1075 KG or more of Ethyl Ether;
1200 KG or more of Methyl Ethyl Ketone;
10 KG or more of Potassium Permanganate;
1300 KG or more of Toluene.

(2) Listed Precursor Chemicals **Level 26**
At least 6 KG but less than 20 KG of Benzyl Cyanide;
At least 60 G but less than 200 G of D-Lysergic Acid;
At least 6 KG but less than 20 KG of Ephedrine;
At least 60 G but less than 200 G of Ergonovine;
At least 120 G but less than 400 G of Ergotamine;
At least 6 KG but less than 20 KG of Ethylamine;
At least 13.2 KG but less than 44 KG of Hydriodic Acid;
At least 96 KG but less than 320 KG of Isoafrole;
At least 1.2 KG but less than 4 KG of Methylamine;
At least 150 KG but less than 500 KG of N-Methylephedrine;
At least 150 KG but less than 500 KG of N-Methylpseudoephedrine;
At least 60 KG but less than 200 KG of Norpseudoephedrine;
At least 6 KG but less than 20 KG of Phenylacetic Acid;
At least 60 KG but less than 200 KG of Phenylpropanolamine;
At least 3 KG but less than 10 KG of Piperidine;
At least 96 KG but less than 320 KG of Piperonal;

At least 480 G but less than 1.6 KG of Propionic Anhydride;
At least 6 KG but less than 20 KG of Pseudoephedrine;
At least 96 KG but less than 320 KG of Safrole;
At least 120 KG but less than 400 KG of 3, 4-Methylenedioxyphenyl-2-propanone;

Listed Essential Chemicals
At least 3.3 KG but less than 11 KG of Acetic Anhydride;
At least 352.5 KG but less than 1175 KG of Acetone;
At least 6 KG but less than 20 KG of Benzyl Chloride;
At least 322.5 KG but less than 1075 KG of Ethyl Ether;
At least 360 KG but less than 1200 KG of Methyl Ethyl Ketone;
At least 3 KG but less than 10 KG of Potassium Permanganate;
At least 390 KG but less than 1300 KG of Toluene.

(3) Listed Precursor Chemicals **Level 24**
At least 2 KG but less than 6 KG of Benzyl Cyanide;
At least 20 G but less than 60 G of D-Lysergic Acid;
At least 2 KG but less than 6 KG of Ephedrine;
At least 20 G but less than 60 G of Ergonovine;
At least 40 G but less than 120 G of Ergotamine;
At least 2 KG but less than 6 KG of Ethylamine;
At least 4.4 KG but less than 13.2 KG of Hydriodic Acid;
At least 32 KG but less than 96 KG of Isoafrole;
At least 400 G but less than 1.2 KG of Methylamine;
At least 50 KG but less than 150 KG of N-Methylephedrine;
At least 50 KG but less than 150 KG of N-Methylpseudoephedrine;
At least 20 KG but less than 60 KG of Norpseudoephedrine;
At least 2 KG but less than 6 KG of Phenylacetic Acid;
At least 20 KG but less than 60 KG of Phenylpropanolamine;
At least 1 KG but less than 3 KG of Piperidine;
At least 32 KG but less than 96 KG of Piperonal;
At least 160 G but less than 480 G of Propionic Anhydride;
At least 2 KG but less than 6 KG of Pseudoephedrine;
At least 32 KG but less than 96 KG of Safrole;
At least 40 KG but less than 120 KG of 3, 4-Methylenedioxyphenyl-2-propanone;

Listed Essential Chemicals
At least 1.1 KG but less than 3.3 KG of Acetic Anhydride;
At least 117.5 KG but less than 352.5 KG of Acetone;
At least 2 KG but less than 6 KG of Benzyl Chloride;
At least 107.5 KG but less than 322.5 KG of Ethyl Ether;
At least 120 KG but less than 360 KG of Methyl Ethyl Ketone;
At least 1 KG but less than 3 KG of Potassium Permanganate;
At least 130 KG but less than 390 KG of Toluene.

(4) Listed Precursor Chemicals **Level 22**
At least 1.4 KG but less than 2 KG of Benzyl Cyanide;
At least 14 G but less than 20 G of D-Lysergic Acid;
At least 1.4 KG but less than 2 KG of Ephedrine;
At least 14 G but less than 20 G of Ergonovine;
At least 28 G but less than 40 G of Ergotamine;

At least 1.4 KG but less than 2 KG of Ethylamine;
At least 3.08 KG but less than 4.4 KG of Hydriodic Acid;
At least 22.4 KG but less than 32 KG of Isoafrole;
At least 280 G but less than 400 G of Methylamine;
At least 35 KG but less than 50 KG of N-Methylephedrine;
At least 35 KG but less than 50 KG of N-Methylpseudoephedrine;
At least 14 KG but less than 20 KG of Norpseudoephedrine;
At least 1.4 KG but less than 2 KG of Phenylacetic Acid;
At least 14 KG but less than 20 KG of Phenylpropanolamine;
At least 700 G but less than 1 KG of Piperidine;
At least 22.4 KG but less than 32 KG of Piperonal;
At least 112 G but less than 160 G of Propionic Anhydride;
At least 1.4 KG but less than 2 KG of Pseudoephedrine;
At least 22.4 KG but less than 32 KG of Safrole;
At least 28 KG but less than 40 KG of 3, 4-Methylenedioxyphenyl-2-propanone;

Listed Essential Chemicals
At least 726 G but less than 1.1 KG of Acetic Anhydride;
At least 82.25 KG but less than 117.5 KG of Acetone;
At least 1.4 KG but less than 2 KG of Benzyl Chloride;
At least 75.25 KG but less than 107.5 KG of Ethyl Ether;
At least 84 KG but less than 120 KG of Methyl Ethyl Ketone;
At least 700 G but less than 1 KG of Potassium Permanganate;
At least 91 KG but less than 130 KG of Toluene.

(5) Listed Precursor Chemicals **Level 20**
At least 800 G but less than 1.4 KG of Benzyl Cyanide;
At least 8 G but less than 14 G of D-Lysergic Acid;
At least 800 G but less than 1.4 KG of Ephedrine;
At least 8 G but less than 14 G of Ergonovine;
At least 16 G but less than 28 G of Ergotamine;
At least 800 G but less than 1.4 KG of Ethylamine;
At least 1.76 KG but less than 3.08 KG of Hydriodic Acid;
At least 12.8 KG but less than 22.4 KG of Isoafrole;
At least 160 G but less than 280 G of Methylamine;
At least 20 KG but less than 35 KG of N-Methylephedrine;
At least 20 KG but less than 35 KG of N-Methylpseudoephedrine;
At least 8 KG but less than 14 KG of Norpseudoephedrine;
At least 800 G but less than 1.4 KG of Phenylacetic Acid;
At least 8 KG but less than 14 KG of Phenylpropanolamine;
At least 400 G but less than 700 G of Piperidine;
At least 12.8 KG but less than 22.4 KG of Piperonal;
At least 64 G but less than 112 G of Propionic Anhydride;
At least 800 G but less than 1.4 KG of Pseudoephedrine;
At least 12.8 KG but less than 22.4 KG of Safrole;
At least 16 KG but less than 28 KG of 3, 4-Methylenedioxyphenyl-2-propanone;

Listed Essential Chemicals
At least 440 G but less than 726 G of Acetic Anhydride;
At least 47 KG but less than 82.25 KG of Acetone;
At least 800 G but less than 1.4 KG of Benzyl Chloride;
At least 43 KG but less than 75.25 KG of Ethyl Ether;

At least 48 KG but less than 84 KG of Methyl Ethyl Ketone;
At least 400 G but less than 700 G of Potassium Permanganate;
At least 52 KG but less than 91 KG of Toluene.

(6) Listed Precursor Chemicals **Level 18**

At least 200 G but less than 800 G of Benzyl Cyanide;
At least 2 G but less than 8 G of D-Lysergic Acid;
At least 200 G but less than 800 G of Ephedrine;
At least 2 G but less than 8 G of Ergonovine;
At least 4 G but less than 16 G of Ergotamine;
At least 200 G but less than 800 G of Ethylamine;
At least 440 G but less than 1.76 KG of Hydriodic Acid;
At least 3.2 KG but less than 12.8 KG of Isoafrole;
At least 40 G but less than 160 G of Methylamine;
At least 5 KG but less than 20 KG of N-Methylephedrine;
At least 5 KG but less than 20 KG of N-Methylpseudoephedrine;
At least 2 KG but less than 8 KG of Norpseudoephedrine;
At least 200 G but less than 800 G of Phenylacetic Acid;
At least 2 KG but less than 8 KG of Phenylpropanolamine;
At least 100 G but less than 400 G of Piperidine;
At least 3.2 KG but less than 12.8 KG of Piperonal;
At least 16 G but less than 64 G of Propionic Anhydride;
At least 200 G but less than 800 G of Pseudoephedrine;
At least 3.2 KG but less than 12.8 KG of Safrole;
At least 4 KG but less than 16 KG of 3, 4-Methylenedioxyphenyl-2-propanone;

Listed Essential Chemicals

At least 110 G but less than 440 G of Acetic Anhydride;
At least 11.75 KG but less than 47 KG of Acetone;
At least 200 G but less than 800 G of Benzyl Chloride;
At least 10.75 KG but less than 43 KG of Ethyl Ether;
At least 12 KG but less than 48 KG of Methyl Ethyl Ketone;
At least 100 G but less than 400 G of Potassium Permanganate;
At least 13 KG but less than 52 KG of Toluene.

(7) Listed Precursor Chemicals **Level 16**

At least 160 G but less than 200 G of Benzyl Cyanide;
At least 1.6 G but less than 2 G of D-Lysergic Acid;
At least 160 G but less than 200 G of Ephedrine;
At least 1.6 G but less than 2 G of Ergonovine;
At least 3.2 G but less than 4 G of Ergotamine;
At least 160 G but less than 200 G of Ethylamine;
At least 352 G but less than 440 G of Hydriodic Acid;
At least 2.56 KG but less than 3.2 KG of Isoafrole;
At least 32 G but less than 40 G of Methylamine;
At least 4 KG but less than 5 KG of N-Methylephedrine;
At least 4 KG but less than 5 KG of N-Methylpseudoephedrine;
At least 1.6 KG but less than 2 KG of Norpseudoephedrine;
At least 160 G but less than 200 G of Phenylacetic Acid;
At least 1.6 KG but less than 2 KG of Phenylpropanolamine;
At least 80 G but less than 100 G of Piperidine;

At least 2.56 KG but less than 3.2 KG of Piperonal;
At least 12.8 G but less than 16 G of Propionic Anhydride;
At least 160 G but less than 200 G of Pseudoephedrine;
At least 2.56 KG but less than 3.2 KG of Safrole;
At least 3.2 KG but less than 4 KG of 3, 4-Methylenedioxyphenyl-2-propanone;

Listed Essential Chemicals
At least 88 G but less than 110 G of Acetic Anhydride;
At least 9.4 KG but less than 11.75 KG of Acetone;
At least 160 G but less than 200 G of Benzyl Chloride;
At least 8.6 KG but less than 10.75 KG of Ethyl Ether;
At least 9.6 KG but less than 12 KG of Methyl Ethyl Ketone;
At least 80 G but less than 100 G of Potassium Permanganate;
At least 10.4 KG but less than 13 KG of Toluene.

(8) Listed Precursor Chemicals **Level 14**
3.6 KG or more of Anthranilic Acid;
At least 120 G but less than 160 G of Benzyl Cyanide;
At least 1.2 G but less than 1.6 G of D-Lysergic Acid;
At least 120 G but less than 160 G of Ephedrine;
At least 1.2 G but less than 1.6 G of Ergonovine;
At least 2.4 G but less than 3.2 G of Ergotamine;
At least 120 G but less than 160 G of Ethylamine;
At least 264 G but less than 352 G of Hydriodic Acid;
At least 1.92 KG but less than 2.56 KG of Isoafrole;
At least 24 G but less than 32 G of Methylamine;
4.8 KG or more of N-Acetylanthranilic Acid;
At least 3 KG but less than 4 KG of N-Methylephedrine;
At least 3 KG but less than 4 KG of N-Methylpseudoephedrine;
At least 1.2 KG but less than 1.6 KG of Norpseudoephedrine;
At least 120 G but less than 160 G of Phenylacetic Acid;
At least 1.2 KG but less than 1.6 KG of Phenylpropanolamine;
At least 60 G but less than 80 G of Piperidine;
At least 1.92 KG but less than 2.56 KG of Piperonal;
At least 9.6 G but less than 12.8 G of Propionic Anhydride;
At least 120 G but less than 160 G of Pseudoephedrine;
At least 1.92 KG but less than 2.56 KG of Safrole;
At least 2.4 KG but less than 3.2 KG of 3, 4-Methylenedioxyphenyl-2-propanone;

Listed Essential Chemicals
At least 66 G but less than 88 G of Acetic Anhydride;
At least 7.05 KG but less than 9.4 KG of Acetone;
At least 120 G but less than 160 G of Benzyl Chloride;
At least 6.45 KG but less than 8.6 KG of Ethyl Ether;
At least 7.2 KG but less than 9.6 KG of Methyl Ethyl Ketone;
At least 60 G but less than 80 G of Potassium Permanganate;
At least 7.8 KG but less than 10.4 KG of Toluene.

(9) Listed Precursor Chemicals **Level 12**
Less than 3.6 KG of Anthranilic Acid;
Less than 120 G of Benzyl Cyanide;
Less than 1.2 G of D-Lysergic Acid;
Less than 120 G of Ephedrine;
Less than 1.2 G of Ergonovine;
Less than 2.4 G of Ergotamine;
Less than 120 G of Ethylamine;
Less than 264 G of Hydriodic Acid;
Less than 1.92 KG of Isoafrole;
Less than 24 G of Methylamine;
Less than 4.8 KG of N-Acetylanthranilic Acid;
Less than 3 KG of N-Methylephedrine;
Less than 3 KG of N-Methylpseudoephedrine;
Less than 1.2 KG of Norpseudoephedrine;
Less than 120 G of Phenylacetic Acid;
Less than 1.2 KG of Phenylpropanolamine;
Less than 60 G of Piperidine;
Less than 1.92 KG of Piperonal;
Less than 9.6 G of Propionic Anhydride;
Less than 120 G of Pseudoephedrine;
Less than 1.92 KG of Safrole;
Less than 2.4 KG of 3, 4-Methylenedioxyphenyl-2-propanone;

Listed Essential Chemicals
Less than 66 G of Acetic Anhydride;
Less than 7.05 KG of Acetone;
Less than 120 G of Benzyl Chloride;
Less than 6.45 KG of Ethyl Ether;
Less than 7.2 KG of Methyl Ethyl Ketone;
Less than 60 G of Potassium Permanganate;
Less than 7.8 KG of Toluene.

---

*Notes:

(A) If more than one listed precursor chemical is involved, use the Precursor Chemical Equivalency Table to determine the offense level.

(B) If more than one listed essential chemical is involved, use the single listed essential chemical resulting in the greatest offense level.

(C) If both listed precursor and listed essential chemicals are involved, use the offense level determined under (A) or (B) above, whichever is greater.

(D) The Precursor Chemical Equivalency Table provides a means for combining different listed precursor chemicals to obtain a single offense level. In cases involving multiple precursor chemicals, convert each to its ephedrine equivalency from the table below, add the quantities, and apply the Chemical Quantity Table to obtain the applicable offense level.

PRECURSOR CHEMICAL EQUIVALENCY TABLE

1 gm of Anthranilic Acid* =	0.033 gm of Ephedrine
1 gm of Benzyl Cyanide =	1 gm of Ephedrine
1 gm of D-Lysergic Acid =	100 gm of Ephedrine
1 gm of Ergonovine =	100 gm of Ephedrine
1 gm of Ergotamine =	50 gm of Ephedrine
1 gm of Ethylamine =	1 gm of Ephedrine
1 gm of Hydriodic Acid** =	0.4545 gm of Ephedrine
1 gm of Isoafrole =	0.0625 gm of Ephedrine
1 gm of Methylamine =	5 gm of Ephedrine
1 gm of N-Acetylanthranilic Acid* =	0.025 gm of Ephedrine
1 gm of N-Methylephedrine =	0.04 gm of Ephedrine
1 gm of N-Methylpseudoephedrine =	0.04 gm of Ephedrine
1 gm of Norpseudoephedrine =	0.1 gm of Ephedrine
1 gm of Phenylacetic Acid =	1 gm of Ephedrine
1 gm of Phenylpropanolamine =	0.1 gm of Ephedrine
1 gm of Piperidine =	2 gm of Ephedrine
1 gm of Piperonal =	0.0625 gm of Ephedrine
1 gm of Propionic Anhydride =	12.5 gm of Ephedrine
1 gm of Pseudoephedrine =	1 gm of Ephedrine
1 gm of Safrole =	0.0625 gm of Ephedrine
1 gm of 3,4-Methylenedioxyphenyl-2-propanone =	0.05 gm of Ephedrine

* The ephedrine equivalency for anthranilic acid or N-acetylanthranilic acid, or both, shall not exceed 159.99 grams of ephedrine.

**In cases involving both hydriodic acid and ephedrine, calculate the offense level for each separately and use the quantity that results in the greater offense level.

Commentary

Statutory Provisions: *21 U.S.C. §§ 841(d)(1), (2), (g)(1), 960(d)(1), (2).*

Application Notes:

1. *"Firearm" and "dangerous weapon" are defined in the Commentary to §1B1.1 (Application Instructions). The adjustment in subsection (b)(1) should be applied if the weapon was present, unless it is improbable that the weapon was connected with the offense.*

2. *"Offense involved unlawfully manufacturing a controlled substance or attempting to manufacture a controlled substance unlawfully," as used in subsection (c)(1), means that the defendant, or a person for whose conduct the defendant is accountable under §1B1.3 (Relevant Conduct), completed the actions sufficient to constitute the offense of unlawfully manufacturing a controlled substance or attempting to manufacture a controlled substance unlawfully.*

3. *In certain cases, the defendant will be convicted of an offense involving a listed chemical covered under this guideline, and a related offense involving an immediate precursor or other controlled substance covered under §2D1.1 (Unlawfully Manufacturing, Importing, Exporting, or Trafficking). For example, P2P (an immediate precursor) and 3,4-methylenedioxyphenyl-2-propanone (a listed chemical) are used together to produce methamphetamine. Determine the*

offense level under each guideline separately. The offense level for 3,4-methylenedioxyphenyl-2-propanone is determined by using §2D1.11. The offense level for P2P is determined by using §2D1.1 (P2P is listed in the Drug Equivalency Table under LSD, PCP, and Other Schedule I and II Hallucinogens (and their immediate precursors)). Under the grouping rules of §3D1.2(b), the counts will be grouped together. Note that in determining the scale of the offense under §2D1.1, the quantity of both the controlled substance and listed chemical should be considered (see Application Note 12 in the Commentary to §2D1.1).

4. *Where there are multiple listed precursor chemicals, the quantities of all listed precursors are added together for purposes of determining the base offense level, except as expressly noted (see Note A to the Chemical Quantity Table). This reflects that only one listed precursor typically is used in a given manufacturing process. For example, in the case of an offense involving 300 grams of piperidine and 800 grams of benzyl cyanide, the piperidine is converted to 600 grams of ephedrine and the benzyl cyanide is converted to 800 grams of ephedrine, using the Precursor Chemical Equivalency Table, for a total of 1400 grams of ephedrine. Applying the Chemical Quantity Table to 1400 grams (1.4 kilograms) of ephedrine results in a base offense level of 22.*

5. *Where there are multiple listed essential chemicals, all quantities of the same listed essential chemical are added together for purposes of determining the base offense level. However, quantities of different listed essential chemicals are not aggregated (see Note B to the Chemical Quantity Table). Thus, where multiple listed essential chemicals are involved in the offense, the base offense level is determined by using the base offense level for the single listed essential chemical resulting in the greatest base offense level. For example, in the case of an offense involving seven kilograms of methyl ethyl ketone and eight kilograms of acetone, the base offense level for the methyl ethyl ketone is 12 and the base offense level for the acetone is 14; therefore, the base offense level is 14.*

6. *Where both listed precursor chemicals and listed essential chemicals are involved, use the greater of the base offense level for the listed precursor chemicals or the listed essential chemicals (see Note C to the Chemical Quantity Table).*

7. *Convictions under 21 U.S.C. §§ 841(d)(2), (g)(1), and 960(d)(2) do not require that the defendant have knowledge or an actual belief that the listed chemical was to be used to manufacture a controlled substance unlawfully. Where the defendant possessed or distributed the listed chemical without such knowledge or belief, a 3-level reduction is provided to reflect that the defendant is less culpable than one who possessed or distributed listed chemicals knowing or believing that they would be used to manufacture a controlled substance unlawfully.*

Background: *Offenses covered by this guideline involve listed precursor chemicals and listed essential chemicals. Listed precursor chemicals are critical to the formation of a controlled substance and become part of the final product. For example, ephedrine reacts with other chemicals to form methamphetamine. The amount of ephedrine directly affects the amount of methamphetamine produced. Listed essential chemicals are generally solvents, catalysts, and reagents, and do not become part of the finished product.*

Historical Note: Effective November 1, 1991 (see Appendix C, amendment 371). Amended effective November 1, 1992 (see Appendix C, amendment 447).

§2D1.12. Unlawful Possession, Manufacture, Distribution, or Importation of Prohibited Flask or Equipment; Attempt or Conspiracy

(a) Base Offense Level: **12**

(b) Cross Reference

(1) If the offense involved unlawfully manufacturing a controlled substance, or attempting to manufacture a controlled substance unlawfully, apply §2D1.1 (Unlawful Manufacturing, Importing, Exporting, Trafficking) if the resulting offense level is greater than that determined above.

Commentary

Statutory Provisions: *21 U.S.C. § 843(a)(6), (7).*

Application Notes:

1. *If the offense involved the large-scale manufacture, distribution, or importation of prohibited flasks or equipment, an upward departure may be warranted.*

2. *"Offense involved unlawfully manufacturing a controlled substance or attempting to manufacture a controlled substance unlawfully," as used in subsection (b)(1), means that the defendant, or a person for whose conduct the defendant is accountable under §1B1.3 (Relevant Conduct), completed the actions sufficient to constitute the offense of unlawfully manufacturing a controlled substance or attempting to manufacture a controlled substance unlawfully.*

Historical Note: Effective November 1, 1991 (see Appendix C, amendment 371). Amended effective November 1, 1992 (see Appendix C, amendment 447).

§2D1.13. Structuring Chemical Transactions or Creating a Chemical Mixture to Evade Reporting or Recordkeeping Requirements; Presenting False or Fraudulent Identification to Obtain a Listed Chemical; Attempt or Conspiracy

(a) Base Offense Level (Apply the greatest):

(1) The offense level from §2D1.11 (Unlawfully Distributing, Importing, Exporting, or Possessing a Listed Chemical) if the defendant knew or believed that the chemical was to be used to manufacture a controlled substance unlawfully; or

(2) The offense level from §2D1.11 (Unlawfully Distributing, Importing, Exporting or Possessing a Listed Chemical) reduced by **3** levels if the defendant had reason to believe that the chemical was to be used to manufacture a controlled substance unlawfully; or

(3) **6**, otherwise.

Commentary

Statutory Provisions: 21 U.S.C. §§ 841(d)(3), (g)(1), 843(a)(4)(B), (a)(8).

Application Note:

1. *"The offense level from §2D1.11" includes the base offense level and any applicable specific offense characteristic or cross reference; see §1B1.5 (Interpretation of References to Other Offense Guidelines).*

Historical Note: Effective November 1, 1991 (see Appendix C, amendment 371). Amended effective November 1, 1992 (see Appendix C, amendment 447).

* * * * *

2. UNLAWFUL POSSESSION

§2D2.1. Unlawful Possession; Attempt or Conspiracy

(a) Base Offense Level:

(1) **8**, if the substance is heroin or any Schedule I or II opiate, an analogue of these, or cocaine base; or

(2) **6**, if the substance is cocaine, LSD, or PCP; or

(3) **4**, if the substance is any other controlled substance.

(b) Cross Reference

(1) If the defendant is convicted of possession of more than 5 grams of a mixture or substance containing cocaine base, apply §2D1.1 (Unlawful Manufacturing, Importing, Exporting, or Trafficking) as if the defendant had been convicted of possession of that mixture or substance with intent to distribute.

Commentary

Statutory Provision: 21 U.S.C. § 844(a). For additional statutory provision(s), see Appendix A (Statutory Index).

Background: Mandatory (statutory) minimum penalties for several categories of cases, ranging from fifteen days' to five years' imprisonment, are set forth in 21 U.S.C. § 844(a). When a mandatory minimum penalty exceeds the guideline range, the mandatory minimum becomes the guideline sentence. See §5G1.1(b). Note, however, that 18 U.S.C. § 3553(f) provides an exception to the applicability of mandatory minimum sentences in certain cases. See §5C1.2 (Limitation on Applicability of Statutory Minimum Sentences in Certain Cases).

Section 2D2.1(b)(1) provides a cross reference to §2D1.1 for possession of more than five grams of a mixture or substance containing cocaine base, an offense subject to an enhanced penalty under Section 6371 of the Anti-Drug Abuse Act of 1988. Other cases for which enhanced penalties are provided under Section 6371 of the Anti-Drug Abuse Act of 1988 (e.g., for a person with one prior conviction, possession of more than three grams of a mixture or substance containing cocaine base; for a person with two or more prior convictions, possession of more than one gram of a mixture or substance containing cocaine base) are to be sentenced in accordance with §5G1.1(b).

Historical Note: Effective November 1, 1987. Amended effective January 15, 1988 (see Appendix C, amendment 24); November 1, 1989 (see Appendix C, amendment 304); November 1, 1990 (see Appendix C, amendment 321); November 1, 1992 (see Appendix C, amendment 447); September 23, 1994 (see Appendix C, amendment 509).

§2D2.2. Acquiring a Controlled Substance by Forgery, Fraud, Deception, or Subterfuge; Attempt or Conspiracy

(a) Base Offense Level: **8**

Commentary

Statutory Provision: 21 U.S.C. § 843(a)(3).

Historical Note: Effective November 1, 1987. Amended effective November 1, 1992 (see Appendix C, amendment 447).

§2D2.3. Operating or Directing the Operation of a Common Carrier Under the Influence of Alcohol or Drugs

(a) Base Offense Level (Apply the greatest):

(1) **26**, if death resulted; or

(2) **21**, if serious bodily injury resulted; or

(3) **13**, otherwise.

(b) Special Instruction:

(1) If the defendant is convicted of a single count involving the death or serious bodily injury of more than one person, apply Chapter Three, Part D (Multiple Counts) as if the defendant had been convicted of a separate count for each such victim.

Commentary

Statutory Provision: 18 U.S.C. § 342.

Background: This section implements the direction to the Commission in Section 6482 of the Anti-Drug Abuse Act of 1988. Offenses covered by this guideline may vary widely with regard to harm and risk of harm. The offense levels assume that the offense involved the operation of a common carrier carrying a number of passengers, e.g., a bus. If no or only a few passengers were placed at risk, a downward departure may be warranted. If the offense resulted in the death or serious bodily injury of a large number of persons, such that the resulting offense level under subsection (b) would not adequately reflect the seriousness of the offense, an upward departure may be warranted.

Historical Note: Effective November 1, 1987. Amended effective January 15, 1988 (see Appendix C, amendment 25); November 1, 1989 (see Appendix C, amendment 141).

* * * * *

3. REGULATORY VIOLATIONS

§2D3.1. Illegal Use of Registration Number to Manufacture, Distribute, Acquire, or Dispense a Controlled Substance; Attempt or Conspiracy

(a) Base Offense Level: **6**

Commentary

Statutory Provisions: 21 U.S.C. §§ 842(a)(1), 843(a)(1), (2).

Background: The maximum term of imprisonment authorized by statute is four years, except in a case with a prior drug-related felony where the maximum term of imprisonment authorized by statute is eight years.

Historical Note: Effective November 1, 1987. Amended effective November 1, 1991 (see Appendix C, amendment 421); November 1, 1992 (see Appendix C, amendment 447).

§2D3.2. Regulatory Offenses Involving Controlled Substances; Attempt or Conspiracy

(a) Base Offense Level: **4**

Commentary

Statutory Provisions: 21 U.S.C. §§ 842(a)(2), (9), (10), (b), 954, 961.

Background: These offenses are misdemeanors. The maximum term of imprisonment authorized by statute is one year.

Historical Note: Effective November 1, 1987. Amended effective November 1, 1991 (see Appendix C, amendment 421); November 1, 1992 (see Appendix C, amendment 447); November 1, 1993 (see Appendix C, amendment 481).

§2D3.3. [Deleted]

Historical Note: Section 2D3.3 (Illegal Use of Registration Number to Distribute or Dispense a Controlled Substance to Another Registrant or Authorized Person; Attempt or Conspiracy), effective November 1, 1987, amended effective November 1, 1991 (see Appendix C, amendment 421) and November 1, 1992 (see Appendix C, amendment 447), was deleted by consolidation with §2D3.2 effective November 1, 1993 (see Appendix C, amendment 481).

§2D3.4. [Deleted]

Historical Note: Section 2D3.4 (Illegal Transfer or Transshipment of a Controlled Substance; Attempt or Conspiracy), effective November 1, 1987, amended effective November 1, 1990 (see Appendix C, amendment 359) and November 1, 1992 (see Appendix C, amendment 447), was deleted by consolidation with §2D3.2 effective November 1, 1993 (see Appendix C, amendment 481).

§2D3.5. [Deleted]

Historical Note: Section 2D3.5 (Violation of Recordkeeping or Reporting Requirements for Listed Chemicals and Certain Machines; Attempt or Conspiracy), effective November 1, 1991 (see Appendix C, amendment 371), amended effective November 1, 1992 (see Appendix C, amendment 447), was deleted by consolidation with §2D3.2 effective November 1, 1993 (see Appendix C, amendment 481).

PART E - OFFENSES INVOLVING CRIMINAL ENTERPRISES AND RACKETEERING

1. RACKETEERING

<u>*Introductory Commentary*</u>

Because of the jurisdictional nature of the offenses included, this subpart covers a wide variety of criminal conduct. The offense level usually will be determined by the offense level of the underlying conduct.

<u>Historical Note</u>: Effective November 1, 1987.

§2E1.1. <u>Unlawful Conduct Relating to Racketeer Influenced and Corrupt Organizations</u>

(a) Base Offense Level (Apply the greater):

(1) **19**; or

(2) the offense level applicable to the underlying racketeering activity.

<u>*Commentary*</u>

<u>*Statutory Provisions:*</u> *18 U.S.C. §§ 1962, 1963.*

<u>*Application Notes:*</u>

1. *Where there is more than one underlying offense, treat each underlying offense as if contained in a separate count of conviction for the purposes of subsection (a)(2). To determine whether subsection (a)(1) or (a)(2) results in the greater offense level, apply Chapter Three, Parts A, B, C, and D to both (a)(1) and (a)(2). Use whichever subsection results in the greater offense level.*

2. *If the underlying conduct violates state law, the offense level corresponding to the most analogous federal offense is to be used.*

3. *If the offense level for the underlying racketeering activity is less than the alternative minimum level specified (<u>i.e.</u>, 19), the alternative minimum base offense level is to be used.*

4. *Certain conduct may be charged in the count of conviction as part of a "pattern of racketeering activity" even though the defendant has previously been sentenced for that conduct. Where such previously imposed sentence resulted from a conviction prior to the last overt act of the instant offense, treat as a prior sentence under §4A1.2(a)(1) and not as part of the instant offense. This treatment is designed to produce a result consistent with the distinction between the instant offense and criminal history found throughout the guidelines. If this treatment produces an anomalous result in a particular case, a guideline departure may be warranted.*

<u>Historical Note</u>: Effective November 1, 1987. Amended effective June 15, 1988 (<u>see</u> Appendix C, amendment 26); November 1, 1989 (<u>see</u> Appendix C, amendment 142).

§2E1.2. Interstate or Foreign Travel or Transportation in Aid of a Racketeering Enterprise

(a) Base Offense Level (Apply the greater):

(1) **6**; or

(2) the offense level applicable to the underlying crime of violence or other unlawful activity in respect to which the travel or transportation was undertaken.

Commentary

Statutory Provision: 18 U.S.C. § 1952.

Application Notes:

1. *Where there is more than one underlying offense, treat each underlying offense as if contained in a separate count of conviction for the purposes of subsection (a)(2). To determine whether subsection (a)(1) or (a)(2) results in the greater offense level, apply Chapter Three, Parts A, B, C, and D to both (a)(1) and (a)(2). Use whichever subsection results in the greater offense level.*

2. *If the underlying conduct violates state law, the offense level corresponding to the most analogous federal offense is to be used.*

3. *If the offense level for the underlying conduct is less than the alternative minimum base offense level specified (i.e., 6), the alternative minimum base offense level is to be used.*

Historical Note: Effective November 1, 1987. Amended effective June 15, 1988 (see Appendix C, amendment 27).

§2E1.3. Violent Crimes in Aid of Racketeering Activity

(a) Base Offense Level (Apply the greater):

(1) **12**; or

(2) the offense level applicable to the underlying crime or racketeering activity.

Commentary

Statutory Provision: 18 U.S.C. § 1959 (formerly 18 U.S.C. § 1952B).

Application Notes:

1. *If the underlying conduct violates state law, the offense level corresponding to the most analogous federal offense is to be used.*

2. *If the offense level for the underlying conduct is less than the alternative minimum base offense level specified (i.e., 12), the alternative minimum base offense level is to be used.*

Background: The conduct covered under this section ranges from threats to murder. The maximum term of imprisonment authorized by statute ranges from three years to life imprisonment.

Historical Note: Effective November 1, 1987. Amended effective November 1, 1989 (see Appendix C, amendment 143).

§2E1.4. Use of Interstate Commerce Facilities in the Commission of Murder-For-Hire

(a) Base Offense Level (Apply the greater):

(1) **32**; or

(2) the offense level applicable to the underlying unlawful conduct.

Commentary

Statutory Provision: 18 U.S.C. § 1958 (formerly 18 U.S.C. § 1952A).

Application Note:

1. *If the underlying conduct violates state law, the offense level corresponding to the most analogous federal offense is to be used.*

Background: This guideline and the statute to which it applies do not require that a murder actually have been committed.

Historical Note: Effective November 1, 1987. Amended effective November 1, 1989 (see Appendix C, amendment 144); November 1, 1990 (see Appendix C, amendment 311); November 1, 1992 (see Appendix C, amendment 449).

§2E1.5. [Deleted]

Historical Note: Section 2E1.5 (Hobbs Act Extortion or Robbery), effective November 1, 1987, amended effective November 1, 1989 (see Appendix C, amendment 145), was deleted by consolidation with §§2B3.1, 2B3.2, 2B3.3, and 2C1.1 effective November 1, 1993 (see Appendix C, amendment 481).

* * * * *

2. EXTORTIONATE EXTENSION OF CREDIT

§2E2.1. Making or Financing an Extortionate Extension of Credit; Collecting an Extension of Credit by Extortionate Means

(a) Base Offense Level: **20**

(b) Specific Offense Characteristics

(1) (A) If a firearm was discharged increase by **5** levels; or

(B) if a dangerous weapon (including a firearm) was otherwise used, increase by **4** levels; or

(C) if a dangerous weapon (including a firearm) was brandished, displayed or possessed, increase by **3** levels.

(2) If any victim sustained bodily injury, increase the offense level according to the seriousness of the injury:

	Degree of Bodily Injury	Increase in Level
(A)	Bodily Injury	add **2**
(B)	Serious Bodily Injury	add **4**
(C)	Permanent or Life-Threatening Bodily Injury	add **6**

(D) If the degree of injury is between that specified in subdivisions (A) and (B), add **3** levels; or

(E) If the degree of injury is between that specified in subdivisions (B) and (C), add **5** levels.

Provided, however, that the combined increase from (1) and (2) shall not exceed **9** levels.

(3) (A) If any person was abducted to facilitate commission of the offense or to facilitate escape, increase by **4** levels; or

(B) if any person was physically restrained to facilitate commission of the offense or to facilitate escape, increase by **2** levels.

(c) Cross Reference

(1) If a victim was killed under circumstances that would constitute murder under 18 U.S.C. § 1111 had such killing taken place within the territorial or maritime jurisdiction of the United States, apply §2A1.1 (First Degree Murder).

Commentary

Statutory Provisions: 18 U.S.C. §§ 892-894.

Application Notes:

1. Definitions of "firearm," "dangerous weapon," "otherwise used," "brandished," "bodily injury," "serious bodily injury," "permanent or life-threatening bodily injury," "abducted," and "physically restrained" are found in the Commentary to §1B1.1 (Application Instructions).

2. *See also Commentary to §2B3.2 (Extortion by Force or Threat of Injury or Serious Damage) regarding the interpretation of the specific offense characteristics.*

Background: This section refers to offenses involving the making or financing of extortionate extensions of credit, or the collection of loans by extortionate means. These "loan-sharking" offenses typically involve threats of violence and provide economic support for organized crime. The base offense level for these offenses is higher than the offense level for extortion because loan sharking is in most cases a continuing activity. In addition, the guideline does not include the amount of money involved because the amount of money in such cases is often difficult to determine. Other enhancements parallel those in §2B3.2 (Extortion by Force or Threat of Injury or Serious Damage).

Historical Note: Effective November 1, 1987. Amended effective November 1, 1989 (see Appendix C, amendments 146-148); November 1, 1991 (see Appendix C, amendment 398); November 1, 1993 (see Appendix C, amendment 479).

* * * * *

3. GAMBLING

Introductory Commentary

This subpart covers a variety of proscribed conduct. The adjustments in Chapter Three, Part B (Role in the Offense) are particularly relevant in providing a measure of the scope of the offense and the defendant's participation.

Historical Note: Effective November 1, 1987.

§2E3.1. Gambling Offenses

(a) Base Offense Level:

(1) **12**, if the offense was (A) engaging in a gambling business; (B) transmission of wagering information; or (C) committed as part of, or to facilitate, a commercial gambling operation; or

(2) **6**, otherwise.

Commentary

Statutory Provisions: 15 U.S.C. §§ 1172-1175; 18 U.S.C. §§ 1082, 1301-1304, 1306, 1511, 1953, 1955. For additional statutory provision(s), see Appendix A (Statutory Index).

Historical Note: Effective November 1, 1987. Amended effective November 1, 1993 (see Appendix C, amendment 481).

§2E3.2. [Deleted]

Historical Note: Section 2E3.2 (Transmission of Wagering Information), effective November 1, 1987, was deleted by consolidation with §2E3.1 effective November 1, 1993 (see Appendix C, amendment 481).

§2E3.3. [Deleted]

Historical Note: Section 2E3.3 (Other Gambling Offenses), effective November 1, 1987, was deleted by consolidation with §2E3.1 effective November 1, 1993 (see Appendix C, amendment 481).

* * * * *

4. TRAFFICKING IN CONTRABAND CIGARETTES

§2E4.1. Unlawful Conduct Relating to Contraband Cigarettes

(a) Base Offense Level (Apply the greater):

(1) 9; or

(2) the offense level from the table in §2T4.1 (Tax Table) corresponding to the amount of the tax evaded.

Commentary

Statutory Provisions: 18 U.S.C. §§ 2342(a), 2344(a).

Application Note:

1. "Tax evaded" refers to state excise tax.

Background: The conduct covered by this section generally involves evasion of state excise taxes. At least 60,000 cigarettes must be involved. Because this offense is basically a tax matter, it is graded by use of the tax table in §2T4.1.

Historical Note: Effective November 1, 1987.

* * * * *

5. LABOR RACKETEERING

Introductory Commentary

The statutes included in this subpart protect the rights of employees under the Taft-Hartley Act, members of labor organizations under the Labor-Management Reporting and Disclosure Act of 1959, and participants of employee pension and welfare benefit plans covered under the Employee Retirement Income Security Act.

The base offense levels for many of the offenses in this subpart have been determined by reference to analogous sections of the guidelines. Thus, the base offense levels for bribery, theft, and fraud in this subpart generally correspond to similar conduct under other parts of the guidelines. The base offense levels for bribery and graft have been set higher than the level for commercial bribery due to the particular vulnerability to exploitation of the organizations covered by this subpart.

Historical Note: Effective November 1, 1987.

§2E5.1. Offering, Accepting, or Soliciting a Bribe or Gratuity Affecting the Operation of an Employee Welfare or Pension Benefit Plan; Prohibited Payments or Lending of Money by Employer or Agent to Employees, Representatives, or Labor Organizations

(a) Base Offense Level:

(1) **10**, if a bribe; or

(2) **6**, if a gratuity.

(b) Specific Offense Characteristics

(1) If the defendant was a fiduciary of the benefit plan or labor organization, increase by **2** levels.

(2) Increase by the number of levels from the table in §2F1.1 (Fraud and Deceit) corresponding to the value of the prohibited payment or the value of the improper benefit to the payer, whichever is greater.

(c) Special Instruction for Fines - Organizations

(1) In lieu of the pecuniary loss under subsection (a)(3) of §8C2.4 (Base Fine), use the greatest of: (A) the value of the unlawful payment; (B) if a bribe, the value of the benefit received or to be received in return for the unlawful payment; or (C) if a bribe, the consequential damages resulting from the unlawful payment.

Commentary

Statutory Provisions: 18 U.S.C. § 1954; 29 U.S.C. § 186.

Application Notes:

1. *"Bribe" refers to the offer or acceptance of an unlawful payment with the specific understanding that it will corruptly affect an official action of the recipient.*

2. *"Gratuity" refers to the offer or acceptance of an unlawful payment other than a bribe.*

3. *"Fiduciary of the benefit plan" is defined in 29 U.S.C. § 1002(21)(A) to mean a person who exercises any discretionary authority or control in respect to the management of such plan or exercises authority or control in respect to management or disposition of its assets, or who renders investment advice for a fee or other direct or indirect compensation with respect to any moneys or other property of such plan, or has any authority or responsibility to do so, or who has any discretionary authority or responsibility in the administration of such plan.*

4. *"Value of the improper benefit to the payer" is explained in the Commentary to §2C1.1 (Offering, Giving, Soliciting, or Receiving a Bribe; Extortion Under Color of Official Right).*

5. *If the adjustment for a fiduciary at §2E5.1(b)(1) applies, do not apply the adjustment at §3B1.3 (Abuse of Position of Trust or Use of Special Skill).*

Background: This section covers the giving or receipt of bribes and other unlawful gratuities involving employee welfare or pension benefit plans, or labor organizations. The seriousness of the offense is determined by several factors, including the value of the bribe or gratuity and the magnitude of the loss resulting from the transaction.

Historical Note: Effective November 1, 1987. Amended effective November 1, 1989 (see Appendix C, amendment 149); November 1, 1991 (see Appendix C, amendment 422); November 1, 1993 (see Appendix C, amendment 481).

§2E5.2. [Deleted]

Historical Note: Section 2E5.2 (Theft or Embezzlement from Employee Pension and Welfare Benefit Plans), effective November 1, 1987, amended effective June 15, 1988 (see Appendix C, amendment 28), November 1, 1989 (see Appendix C, amendment 150), and November 1, 1991 (see Appendix C, amendment 399), was deleted by consolidation with §2B1.1 effective November 1, 1993 (see Appendix C, amendment 481).

§2E5.3. False Statements and Concealment of Facts in Relation to Documents Required by the Employee Retirement Income Security Act; Failure to Maintain and Falsification of Records Required by the Labor Management Reporting and Disclosure Act

(a) Base Offense Level (Apply the greater):

(1) **6**; or

(2) If the offense was committed to facilitate or conceal a theft or embezzlement, or an offense involving a bribe or a gratuity, apply §2B1.1 or §2E5.1, as applicable.

Commentary

Statutory Provisions: 18 U.S.C. § 1027; 29 U.S.C. §§ 439, 461, 1131. For additional statutory provision(s), see Appendix A (Statutory Index).

Background: This section covers the falsification of documents or records relating to a benefit plan covered by ERISA. It also covers failure to maintain proper documents required by the LMRDA or falsification of such documents. Such violations sometimes occur in connection with the criminal conversion of plan funds or schemes involving bribery or graft. Where a violation under this section occurs in connection with another offense, the offense level is determined by reference to the offense facilitated by the false statements or documents.

Historical Note: Effective November 1, 1987. Amended effective November 1, 1989 (see Appendix C, amendment 151); November 1, 1993 (see Appendix C, amendment 481).

§2E5.4. [Deleted]

Historical Note: Section 2E5.4 (Embezzlement or Theft from Labor Unions in the Private Sector), effective November 1, 1987, amended effective June 15, 1988 (see Appendix C, amendment 29) and November 1, 1989 (see Appendix C, amendment 152), was deleted by consolidation with §2B1.1 effective November 1, 1993 (see Appendix C, amendment 481).

§2E5.5. [Deleted]

Historical Note: Section 2E5.5 (Failure to Maintain and Falsification of Records Required by the Labor Management Reporting and Disclosure Act), effective November 1, 1987, amended effective November 1, 1989 (see Appendix C, amendment 153), was deleted by consolidation with §2E5.3 effective November 1, 1993 (see Appendix C, amendment 481).

§2E5.6. [Deleted]

Historical Note: Section 2E5.6 (Prohibited Payments or Lending of Money by Employer or Agent to Employees, Representatives, or Labor Organizations), effective November 1, 1987, amended effective November 1, 1991 (see Appendix C, amendment 422), was deleted by consolidation with §2E5.1 effective November 1, 1993 (see Appendix C, amendment 481).

PART F - OFFENSES INVOLVING FRAUD OR DECEIT

§2F1.1. Fraud and Deceit; Forgery; Offenses Involving Altered or Counterfeit Instruments Other than Counterfeit Bearer Obligations of the United States

(a) Base Offense Level: **6**

(b) Specific Offense Characteristics

(1) If the loss exceeded $2,000, increase the offense level as follows:

	Loss (Apply the Greatest)	Increase in Level
(A)	$2,000 or less	no increase
(B)	More than $2,000	add **1**
(C)	More than $5,000	add **2**
(D)	More than $10,000	add **3**
(E)	More than $20,000	add **4**
(F)	More than $40,000	add **5**
(G)	More than $70,000	add **6**
(H)	More than $120,000	add **7**
(I)	More than $200,000	add **8**
(J)	More than $350,000	add **9**
(K)	More than $500,000	add **10**
(L)	More than $800,000	add **11**
(M)	More than $1,500,000	add **12**
(N)	More than $2,500,000	add **13**
(O)	More than $5,000,000	add **14**
(P)	More than $10,000,000	add **15**
(Q)	More than $20,000,000	add **16**
(R)	More than $40,000,000	add **17**
(S)	More than $80,000,000	add **18**.

(2) If the offense involved (A) more than minimal planning, or (B) a scheme to defraud more than one victim, increase by **2** levels.

(3) If the offense involved (A) a misrepresentation that the defendant was acting on behalf of a charitable, educational, religious or political organization, or a government agency, or (B) violation of any judicial or administrative order, injunction, decree, or process not addressed elsewhere in the guidelines, increase by **2** levels. If the resulting offense level is less than level **10**, increase to level **10**.

(4) If the offense involved the conscious or reckless risk of serious bodily injury, increase by **2** levels. If the resulting offense level is less than level **13**, increase to level **13**.

(5) If the offense involved the use of foreign bank accounts or transactions to conceal the true nature or extent of the fraudulent conduct, and the offense level as determined above is less than level **12**, increase to level **12**.

(6) If the offense --

(A) substantially jeopardized the safety and soundness of a financial institution; or

(B) affected a financial institution and the defendant derived more than $1,000,000 in gross receipts from the offense,

increase by **4** levels. If the resulting offense level is less than level **24**, increase to level **24**.

<u>Commentary</u>

<u>Statutory Provisions</u>: 7 U.S.C. §§ 6, 6b, 6c, 6h, 6o, 13, 23; 15 U.S.C. §§ 50, 77e, 77q, 77x, 78d, 78j, 78ff, 80b-6, 1644; 18 U.S.C. §§ 225, 285-289, 471-473, 500, 510, 659, 1001-1008, 1010-1014, 1016-1022, 1025, 1026, 1028, 1029, 1031, 1341-1344, 2314, 2315. For additional statutory provision(s), <u>see</u> Appendix A (Statutory Index).

<u>Application Notes</u>:

1. *The adjustments in §2F1.1(b)(3) are alternative rather than cumulative. If in a particular case, however, both of the enumerated factors applied, an upward departure might be warranted.*

2. *"More than minimal planning" (subsection (b)(2)(A)) is defined in the Commentary to §1B1.1 (Application Instructions).*

3. *"Scheme to defraud more than one victim," as used in subsection (b)(2)(B), refers to a design or plan to obtain something of value from more than one person. In this context, "victim" refers to the person or entity from which the funds are to come directly. Thus, a wire fraud in which a single telephone call was made to three distinct individuals to get each of them to invest in a pyramid scheme would involve a scheme to defraud more than one victim, but passing a fraudulently endorsed check would not, even though the maker, payee and/or payor all might be considered victims for other purposes, such as restitution.*

4. *Subsection (b)(3)(A) provides an adjustment for a misrepresentation that the defendant was acting on behalf of a charitable, educational, religious or political organization, or a government agency. Examples of conduct to which this factor applies would include a group of defendants who solicit contributions to a non-existent famine relief organization by mail, a defendant who diverts donations for a religiously affiliated school by telephone solicitations to church members in which the defendant falsely claims to be a fund-raiser for the school, or a defendant who poses as a federal collection agent in order to collect a delinquent student loan.*

5. *Subsection (b)(3)(B) provides an adjustment for violation of any judicial or administrative order, injunction, decree, or process. If it is established that an entity the defendant controlled was a party to the prior proceeding, and the defendant had knowledge of the prior decree or order, this provision applies even if the defendant was not a specifically named party in that prior case. For example, a defendant whose business was previously enjoined from selling a dangerous product, but who nonetheless engaged in fraudulent conduct to sell the product, would be subject to this provision. This subsection does not apply to conduct addressed elsewhere in the guidelines; <u>e.g.</u>, a violation of a condition of release (addressed in §2J1.7 (Offense Committed While on Release)) or a violation of probation (addressed in §4A1.1 (Criminal History Category)).*

6. *Some fraudulent schemes may result in multiple-count indictments, depending on the technical elements of the offense. The cumulative loss produced by a common scheme or course of conduct should be used in determining the offense level, regardless of the number of counts of conviction. See Chapter Three, Part D (Multiple Counts).*

7. *Valuation of loss is discussed in the Commentary to §2B1.1 (Larceny, Embezzlement, and Other Forms of Theft). As in theft cases, loss is the value of the money, property, or services unlawfully taken; it does not, for example, include interest the victim could have earned on such funds had the offense not occurred. Consistent with the provisions of §2X1.1 (Attempt, Solicitation or Conspiracy), if an intended loss that the defendant was attempting to inflict can be determined, this figure will be used if it is greater than the actual loss. Frequently, loss in a fraud case will be the same as in a theft case. For example, if the fraud consisted of selling or attempting to sell $40,000 in worthless securities, or representing that a forged check for $40,000 was genuine, the loss would be $40,000.*

   There are, however, instances where additional factors are to be considered in determining the loss or intended loss:

   (a) Fraud Involving Misrepresentation of the Value of an Item or Product Substitution

   A fraud may involve the misrepresentation of the value of an item that does have some value (in contrast to an item that is worthless). Where, for example, a defendant fraudulently represents that stock is worth $40,000 and the stock is worth only $10,000, the loss is the amount by which the stock was overvalued (i.e., $30,000). In a case involving a misrepresentation concerning the quality of a consumer product, the loss is the difference between the amount paid by the victim for the product and the amount for which the victim could resell the product received.

   (b) Fraudulent Loan Application and Contract Procurement Cases

   In fraudulent loan application cases and contract procurement cases, the loss is the actual loss to the victim (or if the loss has not yet come about, the expected loss). For example, if a defendant fraudulently obtains a loan by misrepresenting the value of his assets, the loss is the amount of the loan not repaid at the time the offense is discovered, reduced by the amount the lending institution has recovered (or can expect to recover) from any assets pledged to secure the loan. However, where the intended loss is greater than the actual loss, the intended loss is to be used.

   In some cases, the loss determined above may significantly understate or overstate the seriousness of the defendant's conduct. For example, where the defendant substantially understated his debts to obtain a loan, which he nevertheless repaid, the loss determined above (zero loss) will tend not to reflect adequately the risk of loss created by the defendant's conduct. Conversely, a defendant may understate his debts to a limited degree to obtain a loan (e.g., to expand a grain export business), which he genuinely expected to repay and for which he would have qualified at a higher interest rate had he made truthful disclosure, but he is unable to repay the loan because of some unforeseen event (e.g., an embargo imposed on grain exports) which would have caused a default in any event. In such a case, the loss determined above may overstate the seriousness of the defendant's conduct. Where the loss determined above significantly understates or overstates the seriousness of the defendant's conduct, an upward or downward departure may be warranted.

(c) Consequential Damages in Procurement Fraud and Product Substitution Cases

In contrast to other types of cases, loss in a procurement fraud or product substitution case includes not only direct damages, but also consequential damages that were reasonably foreseeable. For example, in a case involving a defense product substitution offense, the loss includes the government's reasonably foreseeable costs of making substitute transactions and handling or disposing of the product delivered or retrofitting the product so that it can be used for its intended purpose, plus the government's reasonably foreseeable cost of rectifying the actual or potential disruption to government operations caused by the product substitution. Similarly, in the case of fraud affecting a defense contract award, loss includes the reasonably foreseeable administrative cost to the government and other participants of repeating or correcting the procurement action affected, plus any increased cost to procure the product or service involved that was reasonably foreseeable. Inclusion of reasonably foreseeable consequential damages directly in the calculation of loss in procurement fraud and product substitution cases reflects that such damages frequently are substantial in such cases.

(d) Diversion of Government Program Benefits

In a case involving diversion of government program benefits, loss is the value of the benefits diverted from intended recipients or uses.

(e) Davis-Bacon Act Cases

In a case involving a Davis-Bacon Act violation (a violation of 40 U.S.C. § 276a, criminally prosecuted under 18 U.S.C. § 1001), the loss is the difference between the legally required and actual wages paid.

8. *For the purposes of subsection (b)(1), the loss need not be determined with precision. The court need only make a reasonable estimate of the loss, given the available information. This estimate, for example, may be based on the approximate number of victims and an estimate of the average loss to each victim, or on more general factors, such as the nature and duration of the fraud and the revenues generated by similar operations. The offender's gain from committing the fraud is an alternative estimate that ordinarily will underestimate the loss.*

9. *In the case of a partially completed offense (e.g., an offense involving a completed fraud that is part of a larger, attempted fraud), the offense level is to be determined in accordance with the provisions of §2X1.1 (Attempt, Solicitation, or Conspiracy) whether the conviction is for the substantive offense, the inchoate offense (attempt, solicitation, or conspiracy), or both; see Application Note 4 in the Commentary to §2X1.1.*

10. *In cases in which the loss determined under subsection (b)(1) does not fully capture the harmfulness and seriousness of the conduct, an upward departure may be warranted. Examples may include the following:*

    (a) *a primary objective of the fraud was non-monetary; or the fraud caused or risked reasonably foreseeable, substantial non-monetary harm;*

    (b) *false statements were made for the purpose of facilitating some other crime;*

    (c) *the offense caused reasonably foreseeable, physical or psychological harm or severe emotional trauma;*

(d) the offense endangered national security or military readiness;

(e) the offense caused a loss of confidence in an important institution;

(f) the offense involved the knowing endangerment of the solvency of one or more victims.

In a few instances, the loss determined under subsection (b)(1) may overstate the seriousness of the offense. This may occur, for example, where a defendant attempted to negotiate an instrument that was so obviously fraudulent that no one would seriously consider honoring it. In such cases, a downward departure may be warranted.

11. *Offenses involving fraudulent identification documents and access devices, in violation of 18 U.S.C. §§ 1028 and 1029, are also covered by this guideline. Where the primary purpose of the offense involved the unlawful production, transfer, possession, or use of identification documents for the purpose of violating, or assisting another to violate, the laws relating to naturalization, citizenship, or legal resident status, apply §2L2.1 or §2L2.2, as appropriate, rather than §2F1.1. In the case of an offense involving false identification documents or access devices, an upward departure may be warranted where the actual loss does not adequately reflect the seriousness of the conduct.*

12. *If the fraud exploited vulnerable victims, an enhancement will apply. See §3A1.1 (Vulnerable Victim).*

13. *Sometimes, offenses involving fraudulent statements are prosecuted under 18 U.S.C. § 1001, or a similarly general statute, although the offense is also covered by a more specific statute. Examples include false entries regarding currency transactions, for which §2S1.3 would be more apt, and false statements to a customs officer, for which §2T3.1 likely would be more apt. In certain other cases, the mail or wire fraud statutes, or other relatively broad statutes, are used primarily as jurisdictional bases for the prosecution of other offenses. For example, a state arson offense where a fraudulent insurance claim was mailed might be prosecuted as mail fraud. Where the indictment or information setting forth the count of conviction (or a stipulation as described in §1B1.2(a)) establishes an offense more aptly covered by another guideline, apply that guideline rather than §2F1.1. Otherwise, in such cases, §2F1.1 is to be applied, but a departure from the guidelines may be considered.*

14. *"Financial institution," as used in this guideline, is defined to include any institution described in 18 U.S.C. §§ 20, 656, 657, 1005-1007, and 1014; any state or foreign bank, trust company, credit union, insurance company, investment company, mutual fund, savings (building and loan) association, union or employee pension fund; any health, medical or hospital insurance association; brokers and dealers registered, or required to be registered, with the Securities and Exchange Commission; futures commodity merchants and commodity pool operators registered, or required to be registered, with the Commodity Futures Trading Commission; and any similar entity, whether or not insured by the federal government. "Union or employee pension fund" and "any health, medical, or hospital insurance association," as used above, primarily include large pension funds that serve many individuals (e.g., pension funds of large national and international organizations, unions, and corporations doing substantial interstate business), and associations that undertake to provide pension, disability, or other benefits (e.g., medical or hospitalization insurance) to large numbers of persons.*

15. *An offense shall be deemed to have "substantially jeopardized the safety and soundness of a financial institution" if, as a consequence of the offense, the institution became insolvent; substantially reduced benefits to pensioners or insureds; was unable on demand to refund fully any deposit, payment, or investment; was so depleted of its assets as to be forced to merge with*

another institution in order to continue active operations; or was placed in substantial jeopardy of any of the above.

16. *"The defendant derived more than $1,000,000 in gross receipts from the offense," as used in subsection (b)(6)(B), generally means that the gross receipts to the defendant individually, rather than to all participants, exceeded $1,000,000. "Gross receipts from the offense" includes all property, real or personal, tangible or intangible, which is obtained directly or indirectly as a result of such offense. See 18 U.S.C. § 982(a)(4).*

17. *If the defendant is convicted under 18 U.S.C. § 225 (relating to a continuing financial crimes enterprise), the offense level is that applicable to the underlying series of offenses comprising the "continuing financial crimes enterprise."*

18. *If subsection (b)(6)(A) or (B) applies, there shall be a rebuttable presumption that the offense involved "more than minimal planning."*

Background: *This guideline is designed to apply to a wide variety of fraud cases. The statutory maximum term of imprisonment for most such offenses is five years. The guideline does not link offense characteristics to specific code sections. Because federal fraud statutes are so broadly written, a single pattern of offense conduct usually can be prosecuted under several code sections, as a result of which the offense of conviction may be somewhat arbitrary. Furthermore, most fraud statutes cover a broad range of conduct with extreme variation in severity.*

Empirical analyses of pre-guidelines practice showed that the most important factors that determined sentence length were the amount of loss and whether the offense was an isolated crime of opportunity or was sophisticated or repeated. Accordingly, although they are imperfect, these are the primary factors upon which the guideline has been based.

The extent to which an offense is planned or sophisticated is important in assessing its potential harmfulness and the dangerousness of the offender, independent of the actual harm. A complex scheme or repeated incidents of fraud are indicative of an intention and potential to do considerable harm. In pre-guidelines practice, this factor had a significant impact, especially in frauds involving small losses. Accordingly, the guideline specifies a 2-level enhancement when this factor is present.

Use of false pretenses involving charitable causes and government agencies enhances the sentences of defendants who take advantage of victims' trust in government or law enforcement agencies or their generosity and charitable motives. Taking advantage of a victim's self-interest does not mitigate the seriousness of fraudulent conduct. However, defendants who exploit victims' charitable impulses or trust in government create particular social harm. A defendant who has been subject to civil or administrative proceedings for the same or similar fraudulent conduct demonstrates aggravated criminal intent and is deserving of additional punishment for not conforming with the requirements of judicial process or orders issued by federal, state, or local administrative agencies.

Offenses that involve the use of transactions or accounts outside the United States in an effort to conceal illicit profits and criminal conduct involve a particularly high level of sophistication and complexity. These offenses are difficult to detect and require costly investigations and prosecutions. Diplomatic processes often must be used to secure testimony and evidence beyond the jurisdiction of United States courts. Consequently, a minimum level of 12 is provided for these offenses.

Subsection (b)(6)(A) implements, in a broader form, the instruction to the Commission in Section 961(m) of Public Law 101-73.

Subsection (b)(6)(B) implements the instruction to the Commission in Section 2507 of Public Law 101-647.

Historical Note: Effective November 1, 1987. Amended effective June 15, 1988 (see Appendix C, amendment 30); November 1, 1989 (see Appendix C, amendments 154-156 and 303); November 1, 1990 (see Appendix C, amendment 317); November 1, 1991 (see Appendix C, amendments 364 and 393); November 1, 1992 (see Appendix C, amendment 470); November 1, 1993 (see Appendix C, amendments 481 and 482).

§2F1.2. Insider Trading

(a) Base Offense Level: **8**

(b) Specific Offense Characteristic

(1) Increase by the number of levels from the table in §2F1.1 corresponding to the gain resulting from the offense.

Commentary

Statutory Provisions: 15 U.S.C. § 78j and 17 C.F.R. § 240.10b-5. For additional statutory provision(s), see Appendix A (Statutory Index).

Application Note:

1. *Section 3B1.3 (Abuse of Position of Trust or Use of Special Skill) should be applied only if the defendant occupied and abused a position of special trust. Examples might include a corporate president or an attorney who misused information regarding a planned but unannounced takeover attempt. It typically would not apply to an ordinary "tippee."*

Background: This guideline applies to certain violations of Rule 10b-5 that are commonly referred to as "insider trading." Insider trading is treated essentially as a sophisticated fraud. Because the victims and their losses are difficult if not impossible to identify, the gain, i.e., the total increase in value realized through trading in securities by the defendant and persons acting in concert with him or to whom he provided inside information, is employed instead of the victims' losses.

Certain other offenses, e.g., 7 U.S.C. § 13(e), that involve misuse of inside information for personal gain also may appropriately be covered by this guideline.

Historical Note: Effective November 1, 1987.

PART G - OFFENSES INVOLVING PROSTITUTION, SEXUAL EXPLOITATION OF MINORS, AND OBSCENITY

1. PROSTITUTION

§2G1.1. Transportation for the Purpose of Prostitution or Prohibited Sexual Conduct

(a) Base Offense Level: **14**

(b) Specific Offense Characteristic

(1) If the offense involved the use of physical force, or coercion by threats or drugs or in any manner, increase by **4** levels.

(c) Special Instruction

(1) If the offense involved the transportation of more than one person, Chapter Three, Part D (Multiple Counts) shall be applied as if the transportation of each person had been contained in a separate count of conviction.

Commentary

Statutory Provisions: 8 U.S.C. § 1328; 18 U.S.C. §§ 2421, 2422.

Application Notes:

1. *The base offense level assumes that the offense was committed for profit. In the infrequent case where the defendant did not commit the offense for profit and the offense did not involve physical force or coercion, the Commission recommends a downward departure of 8 levels.*

2. *The enhancement for physical force, or coercion, anticipates no bodily injury. If bodily injury results, an upward departure may be warranted. See Chapter Five, Part K (Departures).*

3. *"Coercion," as used in this guideline, includes any form of conduct that negates the voluntariness of the behavior of the person transported. This factor would apply, for example, where the ability of the person being transported to appraise or control conduct was substantially impaired by drugs or alcohol. In the case of transportation involving an adult, rather than a minor, this characteristic generally will not apply where the alcohol or drug was voluntarily taken.*

4. *For the purposes of §3B1.1 (Aggravating Role), the persons transported are considered participants only if they assisted in the unlawful transportation of others.*

5. *For the purposes of Chapter Three, Part D (Multiple Counts), each person transported is to be treated as a separate victim. Consequently, multiple counts involving the transportation of different persons are not to be grouped together under §3D1.2 (Groups of Closely Related Counts). Special instruction (c)(1) directs that if the relevant conduct of an offense of conviction includes more than one person being transported, whether specifically cited in the*

count of conviction or not, each such person shall be treated as if contained in a separate count of conviction.

Historical Note: Effective November 1, 1987. Amended effective November 1, 1989 (see Appendix C, amendments 157 and 158); November 1, 1990 (see Appendix C, amendment 322).

§2G1.2. Transportation of a Minor for the Purpose of Prostitution or Prohibited Sexual Conduct

(a) Base Offense Level: **16**

(b) Specific Offense Characteristics

(1) If the offense involved the use of physical force, or coercion by threats or drugs or in any manner, increase by **4** levels.

(2) If the offense involved the transportation of a minor under the age of twelve years, increase by **4** levels.

(3) If the offense involved the transportation of a minor at least twelve years of age but under the age of sixteen years, increase by **2** levels.

(4) If the defendant was a parent, relative, or legal guardian of the minor involved in the offense, or if the minor was otherwise in the custody, care, or supervisory control of the defendant, increase by **2** levels.

(c) Cross References

(1) If the offense involved causing, transporting, permitting, or offering or seeking by notice or advertisement, a minor to engage in sexually explicit conduct for the purpose of producing a visual depiction of such conduct, apply §2G2.1 (Sexually Exploiting a Minor by Production of Sexually Explicit Visual or Printed Material; Custodian Permitting Minor to Engage in Sexually Explicit Conduct; Advertisement for Minors to Engage in Production).

(2) If the offense involved criminal sexual abuse, attempted criminal sexual abuse, or assault with intent to commit criminal sexual abuse, apply §2A3.1 (Criminal Sexual Abuse; Attempt to Commit Criminal Sexual Abuse).

(3) If neither subsection (c)(1) nor (c)(2) is applicable, and the offense did not involve transportation for the purpose of prostitution, apply §2A3.2 (Criminal Sexual Abuse of a Minor or Attempt to Commit Such Acts) or §2A3.4 (Abusive Sexual Contact or Attempt to Commit Abusive Sexual Contact), as appropriate.

(d) Special Instruction

(1) If the offense involved the transportation of more than one person, Chapter Three, Part D (Multiple Counts) shall be applied as if the

transportation of each person had been contained in a separate count of conviction.

Commentary

Statutory Provisions: *8 U.S.C. § 1328; 18 U.S.C. §§ 2421, 2422, 2423.*

Application Notes:

1. *For the purposes of Chapter Three, Part D (Multiple Counts), each person transported is to be treated as a separate victim. Consequently, multiple counts involving the transportation of different persons are not to be grouped together under §3D1.2 (Groups of Closely Related Counts). Special instruction (d)(1) directs that if the relevant conduct of an offense of conviction includes more than one person being transported, whether specifically cited in the count of conviction or not, each such person shall be treated as if contained in a separate count of conviction.*

2. *The enhancement for physical force, or coercion, anticipates no bodily injury. If bodily injury results, an upward departure may be warranted.* See *Chapter Five, Part K (Departures).*

3. *"Coercion," as used in this guideline, includes any form of conduct that negates the voluntariness of the behavior of the person transported. This factor would apply, for example, where the ability of the person being transported to appraise or control conduct was substantially impaired by drugs or alcohol.*

4. *"Sexually explicit conduct," as used in this guideline, has the meaning set forth in 18 U.S.C. § 2256.*

5. *Subsection (b)(4) is intended to have broad application and includes offenses involving a minor entrusted to the defendant, whether temporarily or permanently. For example, teachers, day care providers, baby-sitters, or other temporary caretakers are among those who would be subject to this enhancement. In determining whether to apply this adjustment, the court should look to the actual relationship that existed between the defendant and the child and not simply to the legal status of the defendant-child relationship.*

6. *If the adjustment in subsection (b)(4) applies, do not apply §3B1.3 (Abuse of Position of Trust or Use of Special Skill).*

7. *The cross reference in subsection (c)(1) is to be construed broadly to include all instances where the offense involved employing, using, persuading, inducing, enticing, coercing, transporting, permitting, or offering or seeking by notice or advertisement, a minor to engage in sexually explicit conduct for the purpose of producing any visual depiction of such conduct.*

Historical Note: Effective November 1, 1987. Amended effective November 1, 1989 (see Appendix C, amendments 159 and 160); November 1, 1990 (see Appendix C, amendment 323); November 1, 1991 (see Appendix C, amendment 400); November 1, 1992 (see Appendix C, amendment 444).

* * * * *

2. SEXUAL EXPLOITATION OF A MINOR

§2G2.1. Sexually Exploiting a Minor by Production of Sexually Explicit Visual or Printed Material; Custodian Permitting Minor to Engage in Sexually Explicit Conduct; Advertisement for Minors to Engage in Production

(a) Base Offense Level: **25**

(b) Specific Offense Characteristics

(1) If the offense involved a minor under the age of twelve years, increase by **4** levels; otherwise, if the offense involved a minor under the age of sixteen years, increase by **2** levels.

(2) If the defendant was a parent, relative, or legal guardian of the minor involved in the offense, or if the minor was otherwise in the custody, care, or supervisory control of the defendant, increase by **2** levels.

(c) Special Instruction

(1) If the offense involved the exploitation of more than one minor, Chapter Three, Part D (Multiple Counts) shall be applied as if the exploitation of each minor had been contained in a separate count of conviction.

Commentary

Statutory Provisions: *18 U.S.C. § 2251(a), (b), (c)(1)(B).*

Application Notes:

1. *For the purposes of Chapter Three, Part D (Multiple Counts), each minor exploited is to be treated as a separate victim. Consequently, multiple counts involving the exploitation of different minors are not to be grouped together under §3D1.2 (Groups of Closely Related Counts). Special instruction (c)(1) directs that if the relevant conduct of an offense of conviction includes more than one minor being exploited, whether specifically cited in the count of conviction or not, each such minor shall be treated as if contained in a separate count of conviction.*

2. *Subsection (b)(2) is intended to have broad application and includes offenses involving a minor entrusted to the defendant, whether temporarily or permanently. For example, teachers, day care providers, baby-sitters, or other temporary caretakers are among those who would be subject to this enhancement. In determining whether to apply this adjustment, the court should look to the actual relationship that existed between the defendant and the child and not simply to the legal status of the defendant-child relationship.*

3. *If the adjustment in subsection (b)(2) applies, do not apply §3B1.3 (Abuse of Position of Trust or Use of Special Skill).*

Historical Note: Effective November 1, 1987. Amended effective November 1, 1989 (see Appendix C, amendment 161); November 1, 1990 (see Appendix C, amendment 324); November 1, 1991 (see Appendix C, amendment 400).

§2G2.2. Trafficking in Material Involving the Sexual Exploitation of a Minor; Receiving, Transporting, Shipping, or Advertising Material Involving the Sexual Exploitation of a Minor; Possessing Material Involving the Sexual Exploitation of a Minor with Intent to Traffic

(a) Base Offense Level: **15**

(b) Specific Offense Characteristics

(1) If the material involved a prepubescent minor or a minor under the age of twelve years, increase by **2** levels.

(2) If the offense involved distribution, increase by the number of levels from the table in §2F1.1 corresponding to the retail value of the material, but in no event by less than **5** levels.

(3) If the offense involved material that portrays sadistic or masochistic conduct or other depictions of violence, increase by **4** levels.

(4) If the defendant engaged in a pattern of activity involving the sexual abuse or exploitation of a minor, increase by **5** levels.

(c) Cross Reference

(1) If the offense involved causing, transporting, permitting, or offering or seeking by notice or advertisement, a minor to engage in sexually explicit conduct for the purpose of producing a visual depiction of such conduct, apply §2G2.1 (Sexually Exploiting a Minor by Production of Sexually Explicit Visual or Printed Material; Custodian Permitting Minor to Engage in Sexually Explicit Conduct; Advertisement for Minors to Engage in Production) if the resulting offense level is greater than that determined above.

Commentary

Statutory Provisions: *18 U.S.C. §§ 2251(c)(1)(A), 2252(a)(1)-(3).*

Application Notes:

1. *"Distribution," as used in this guideline, includes any act related to distribution for pecuniary gain, including production, transportation, and possession with intent to distribute.*

2. *"Sexually explicit conduct," as used in this guideline, has the meaning set forth in 18 U.S.C. § 2256.*

3. *The cross reference in (c)(1) is to be construed broadly to include all instances where the offense involved employing, using, persuading, inducing, enticing, coercing, transporting, permitting, or offering or seeking by notice or advertisement, a minor to engage in sexually explicit conduct for the purpose of producing any visual depiction of such conduct.*

4. *"Pattern of activity involving the sexual abuse or exploitation of a minor," for the purposes of subsection (b)(4), means any combination of two or more separate instances of the sexual abuse or the sexual exploitation of a minor, whether involving the same or different victims.*

5. *If the defendant sexually exploited or abused a minor at any time, whether or not such sexual abuse occurred during the course of the offense, an upward departure may be warranted. In determining the extent of such a departure, the court should take into consideration the offense levels provided in §§2A3.1, 2A3.2, and 2A3.4 most commensurate with the defendant's conduct, as well as whether the defendant has received an enhancement under subsection (b)(4) on account of such conduct.*

Historical Note: Effective November 1, 1987. Amended effective June 15, 1988 (see Appendix C, amendment 31); November 1, 1990 (see Appendix C, amendment 325); November 1, 1991 (see Appendix C, amendment 372); November 27, 1991 (see Appendix C, amendment 435).

§2G2.3. Selling or Buying of Children for Use in the Production of Pornography

(a) Base Offense Level: **38**

Commentary

Statutory Provision: 18 U.S.C. § 2251A.

Background: The statutory minimum sentence for a defendant convicted under 18 U.S.C. § 2251A is twenty years imprisonment.

Historical Note: Effective November 1, 1989 (see Appendix C, amendment 162).

§2G2.4. Possession of Materials Depicting a Minor Engaged in Sexually Explicit Conduct

(a) Base Offense Level: **13**

(b) Specific Offense Characteristics

(1) If the material involved a prepubescent minor or a minor under the age of twelve years, increase by **2** levels.

(2) If the offense involved possessing ten or more books, magazines, periodicals, films, video tapes, or other items, containing a visual depiction involving the sexual exploitation of a minor, increase by **2** levels.

(c) Cross References

(1) If the offense involved causing, transporting, permitting, or offering or seeking by notice or advertisement, a minor to engage in sexually explicit conduct for the purpose of producing a visual depiction of such conduct, apply §2G2.1 (Sexually Exploiting a Minor by Production of Sexually Explicit Visual or Printed Material; Custodian Permitting

Minor to Engage in Sexually Explicit Conduct; Advertisement for Minors to Engage in Production).

(2) If the offense involved trafficking in material involving the sexual exploitation of a minor (including receiving, transporting, shipping, advertising, or possessing material involving the sexual exploitation of a minor with intent to traffic), apply §2G2.2 (Trafficking in Material Involving the Sexual Exploitation of a Minor; Receiving, Transporting, Shipping, or Advertising Material Involving the Sexual Exploitation of a Minor; Possessing Material Involving the Sexual Exploitation of a Minor with Intent to Traffic).

Commentary

Statutory Provision: 18 U.S.C. § 2252(a)(4).

Historical Note: Effective November 1, 1991 (see Appendix C, amendment 372). Amended effective November 27, 1991 (see Appendix C, amendment 436).

§2G2.5. Recordkeeping Offenses Involving the Production of Sexually Explicit Materials

(a) Base Offense Level: **6**

(b) Cross References

(1) If the offense reflected an effort to conceal a substantive offense that involved causing, transporting, permitting, or offering or seeking by notice or advertisement, a minor to engage in sexually explicit conduct for the purpose of producing a visual depiction of such conduct, apply §2G2.1 (Sexually Exploiting a Minor by Production of Sexually Explicit Visual or Printed Material; Custodian Permitting Minor to Engage in Sexually Explicit Conduct; Advertisement for Minors to Engage in Production).

(2) If the offense reflected an effort to conceal a substantive offense that involved trafficking in material involving the sexual exploitation of a minor (including receiving, transporting, advertising, or possessing material involving the sexual exploitation of a minor with intent to traffic), apply §2G2.2 (Trafficking in Material Involving the Sexual Exploitation of a Minor; Receiving, Transporting, Advertising, or Possessing Material Involving the Sexual Exploitation of a Minor with Intent to Traffic).

Commentary

Statutory Provision: 18 U.S.C. § 2257.

Historical Note: Effective November 1, 1991 (see Appendix C, amendment 372).

* * * * *

3. OBSCENITY

§2G3.1. Importing, Mailing, or Transporting Obscene Matter

(a) Base Offense Level: **10**

(b) Specific Offense Characteristics

(1) If the offense involved an act related to distribution for pecuniary gain, increase by the number of levels from the table in §2F1.1 corresponding to the retail value of the material, but in no event by less than **5** levels.

(2) If the offense involved material that portrays sadistic or masochistic conduct or other depictions of violence, increase by **4** levels.

(c) Cross Reference

(1) If the offense involved transporting, distributing, receiving, possessing, or advertising to receive material involving the sexual exploitation of a minor, apply §2G2.2 (Trafficking in Material Involving the Sexual Exploitation of a Minor; Receiving, Transporting, Shipping, or Advertising Material Involving the Sexual Exploitation of a Minor; Possessing Material Involving the Sexual Exploitation of a Minor with Intent to Traffic) or §2G2.4 (Possession of Materials Depicting a Minor Engaged in Sexually Explicit Conduct), as appropriate.

Commentary

Statutory Provisions: 18 U.S.C. §§ 1460-1463, 1465, 1466. For additional statutory provision(s), see Appendix A (Statutory Index).

Application Note:

1. *"Act related to distribution," as used in this guideline, is to be construed broadly and includes production, transportation, and possession with intent to distribute.*

Background: Most federal prosecutions for offenses covered in this guideline are directed to offenses involving distribution for pecuniary gain. Consequently, the offense level under this section generally will be at least 15.

Historical Note: Effective November 1, 1987. Amended effective November 1, 1989 (see Appendix C, amendment 163); November 1, 1990 (see Appendix C, amendment 326); November 1, 1991 (see Appendix C, amendment 372); November 27, 1991 (see Appendix C, amendment 437).

§2G3.2. **Obscene Telephone Communications for a Commercial Purpose; Broadcasting Obscene Material**

(a) Base Offense Level: **12**

(b) Specific Offense Characteristics

(1) If a person who received the telephonic communication was less than eighteen years of age, or if a broadcast was made between six o'clock in the morning and eleven o'clock at night, increase by **4** levels.

(2) If **6** plus the offense level from the table at 2F1.1(b)(1) corresponding to the volume of commerce attributable to the defendant is greater than the offense level determined above, increase to that offense level.

Commentary

Statutory Provisions: 18 U.S.C. §§ 1464, 1468; 47 U.S.C. § 223(b)(1)(A).

Background: Subsection (b)(1) provides an enhancement where an obscene telephonic communication was received by a minor less than 18 years of age or where a broadcast was made during a time when such minors were likely to receive it. Subsection (b)(2) provides an enhancement for large-scale "dial-a-porn" or obscene broadcasting operations that results in an offense level comparable to the offense level for such operations under §2G3.1 (Importing, Mailing, or Transporting Obscene Matter). The extent to which the obscene material was distributed is approximated by the volume of commerce attributable to the defendant.

Historical Note: Effective November 1, 1989 (see Appendix C, amendment 164). A former §2G3.2 (Obscene or Indecent Telephone Communications), effective November 1, 1987, was deleted effective November 1, 1989 (see Appendix C, amendment 164).

PART H - OFFENSES INVOLVING INDIVIDUAL RIGHTS

1. CIVIL RIGHTS

<u>Introductory Commentary</u>

This subpart covers violations of civil rights statutes that typically penalize conduct involving death or bodily injury more severely than discriminatory or intimidating conduct not involving such injury.

The addition of two levels to the offense level applicable to the underlying offense in this subpart reflects the fact that the harm involved both the underlying conduct and activity intended to deprive a person of his civil rights. An added penalty is imposed on an offender who was a public official at the time of the offense to reflect the likely damage to public confidence in the integrity and fairness of government, and the added likely force of the threat because of the official's involvement.

<u>Historical Note</u>: Effective November 1, 1987.

§2H1.1. <u>Conspiracy to Interfere with Civil Rights; Going in Disguise to Deprive of Rights</u>

(a) Base Offense Level (Apply the greater):

(1) **15**; or

(2) **2** plus the offense level applicable to any underlying offense.

(b) Specific Offense Characteristic

(1) If the defendant was a public official at the time of the offense, increase by **4** levels.

<u>Commentary</u>

<u>Statutory Provision</u>: 18 U.S.C. § 241.

<u>Application Notes</u>:

1. *"Underlying offense," as used in this guideline, includes any offense under federal, state, or local law other than an offense that is itself covered under Chapter Two, Part H, Subpart 1, 2, or 4. For example, in the case of a conspiracy to interfere with a person's civil rights (a violation of 18 U.S.C. § 241) that involved an aggravated assault (the use of force) to deny certain rights or benefits in furtherance of discrimination (a violation of 18 U.S.C. § 245), the underlying offense in respect to both the violation of 18 U.S.C. § 241 (to which §2H1.1 applies) and the violation of 18 U.S.C. § 245 (to which §2H1.3 applies) would be the aggravated assault.*

   "2 plus the offense level applicable to any underlying offense" means 2 levels above the offense level (base offense level plus any applicable specific offense characteristics and cross references) from the offense guideline in Chapter Two that most closely corresponds to the underlying

offense. For example, if the underlying offense was second degree murder, which under §2A1.2 has an offense level of 33, "2 plus the offense level applicable to any underlying offense" would be 33 + 2 = 35. If the underlying offense was assault, criminal sexual conduct, kidnapping, abduction or unlawful restraint, the offense level from the guideline for the most comparable offense in §§2A2.1-2A4.2 (Assault, Criminal Sexual Abuse, and Kidnapping, Abduction, or Unlawful Restraint) would first be determined, and 2 levels then would be added. If the underlying offense was damage to property by means of arson or an explosive device, the offense level from §2K1.4 (Arson; Property Damage By Use of Explosives) would first be determined and 2 levels would be added. If the offense was property damage by other means, the offense level from §2B1.3 (Property Damage or Destruction) would first be determined and 2 levels would be added. If the offense was a conspiracy or attempt to commit arson, "2 plus the offense level applicable to any underlying offense" would be the offense level from the guideline applicable to a conspiracy or attempt to commit arson plus 2 levels.

In certain cases, the count of which the defendant is convicted may set forth conduct that constitutes more than one underlying offense (e.g., two instances of assault, or one instance of assault and one instance of arson). In such cases, determine the offense level for the underlying offense by treating each underlying offense as if contained in a separate count of conviction. To determine which of the alternative base offense levels (e.g., §2H1.1(a)(1) or (a)(2)) results in the greater offense level, apply Chapter Three, Parts A, B, C, and D to each alternative base offense level. Use whichever results in the greater offense level. Example: The defendant is convicted of one count of conspiracy to violate civil rights that included two level 12 underlying offenses (of a type not grouped together under Chapter Three, Part D). No adjustment from Chapter Three, Parts A, B, or C applies. The base offense level from §2H1.1(a)(1) is 15. The offense level for each underlying offense from §2H1.1(a)(2) is 14 (2 + 12). Under Chapter Three, Part D (Multiple Counts), the two level 14 underlying offenses result in a combined offense level of 16. This offense level is greater than the alternative base offense level of 15 under §2H1.1(a)(1). Therefore, the case is treated as if there were two counts, one for each underlying offense, with a base offense level under §2H1.1(a)(2) of 14 for each underlying offense.

2. *Where the adjustment in §2H1.1(b)(1) is applied, do not apply §3B1.3 (Abuse of Position of Trust or Use of Special Skill).*

Background: *This section applies to intimidating activity by various groups, including formally and informally organized groups as well as hate groups. The maximum term of imprisonment authorized by statute is ten years; except where death results, the maximum term of imprisonment authorized by statute is life imprisonment. The base offense level for this guideline assumes threatening or otherwise serious conduct.*

Historical Note: Effective November 1, 1987. Amended effective November 1, 1989 (see Appendix C, amendment 303); November 1, 1990 (see Appendix C, amendments 313 and 327); November 1, 1991 (see Appendix C, amendment 430).

§2H1.2. [Deleted]

Historical Note: Section 2H1.2 (Conspiracy to Interfere with Civil Rights), effective November 1, 1987, amended effective November 1, 1989 (see Appendix C, amendment 303), was deleted by consolidation with §2H1.1 effective November 1, 1990 (see Appendix C, amendment 327).

§2H1.3. Use of Force or Threat of Force to Deny Benefits or Rights in Furtherance of Discrimination; Damage to Religious Real Property

(a) Base Offense Level (Apply the greatest):

(1) **10**, if no injury occurred; or

(2) **15**, if injury occurred; or

(3) **2** plus the offense level applicable to any underlying offense.

(b) Specific Offense Characteristic

(1) If the defendant was a public official at the time of the offense, increase by **4** levels.

Commentary

Statutory Provisions: 18 U.S.C. §§ 245, 247; 42 U.S.C. § 3631. For additional statutory provision(s), see Appendix A (Statutory Index).

Application Notes:

1. *"2 plus the offense level applicable to any underlying offense" is defined in the Commentary to §2H1.1.*

2. *"Injury" means "bodily injury," "serious bodily injury," or "permanent or life-threatening bodily injury" as defined in the Commentary to §1B1.1 (Application Instructions).*

3. *Where the adjustment in §2H1.3(b)(1) is applied, do not apply §3B1.3 (Abuse of Position of Trust or Use of Special Skill).*

4. *In the case of a violation of 42 U.S.C. § 3631, apply this guideline where the offense involved the threat or use of force. Otherwise, apply §2H1.5.*

Background: The statutes covered by this guideline provide federal protection for the exercise of civil rights in a variety of contexts (e.g., voting, employment, public accommodations, etc.). The base offense level in §2H1.3(a) reflects that the threat or use of force is inherent in the offense. The maximum term of imprisonment authorized by statute is one year if no bodily injury results, ten years if bodily injury results, and life imprisonment if death results.

Historical Note: Effective November 1, 1987. Amended effective November 1, 1989 (see Appendix C, amendment 165).

§2H1.4. Interference with Civil Rights Under Color of Law

(a) Base Offense Level (Apply the greater):

(1) **10**; or

(2) **6** plus the offense level applicable to any underlying offense.

Commentary

Statutory Provision: 18 U.S.C. § 242.

Application Notes:

1. *"6 plus the offense level applicable to any underlying offense" means 6 levels above the offense level for any underlying criminal conduct. See the discussion in the Commentary to §2H1.1.*

2. *Do not apply the adjustment from §3B1.3 (Abuse of Position of Trust or Use of Special Skill).*

Background: This maximum term of imprisonment authorized by 18 U.S.C. § 242 is one year if no bodily injury results, ten years if bodily injury results, and life imprisonment if death results. A base offense level of 10 is prescribed at §2H1.4(a)(1) providing a guideline sentence near the one-year statutory maximum for cases not resulting in death or bodily injury because of the compelling public interest in deterring and adequately punishing those who violate civil rights under color of law. The Commission intends to recommend that this one-year statutory maximum penalty be increased. An alternative base offense level is provided at §2H1.4(a)(2). The 6-level increase under subsection (a)(2) reflects the 2-level increase that is applied to other offenses covered in this Part plus a 4-level increase for the commission of the offense under actual or purported legal authority. This 4-level increase is inherent in the base offense level of 10 under subsection (a)(1).

Enhancement under §3B1.3 (Abuse of Position of Trust or Use of Special Skill) is inappropriate because the base offense level in §2H1.4(a) reflects that the abuse of actual or purported legal authority is inherent in the offense.

Historical Note: Effective November 1, 1987. Amended effective November 1, 1989 (see Appendix C, amendment 166).

§2H1.5. Other Deprivations of Rights or Benefits in Furtherance of Discrimination

(a) Base Offense Level (Apply the greater):

(1) **6**; or

(2) **2** plus the offense level applicable to any underlying offense.

(b) Specific Offense Characteristic

(1) If the defendant was a public official at the time of the offense, increase by **4** levels.

Commentary

Statutory Provision: 18 U.S.C. § 246.

Application Notes:

1. *"2 plus the offense level applicable to any underlying offense" is defined in the Commentary to §2H1.1.*

2. *Where the adjustment in §2H1.5(b)(1) is applied, do not apply §3B1.3 (Abuse of Position of Trust or Use of Special Skill).*

Background: Violations of the statutes covered by this provision do not necessarily involve the use of force or threatening conduct or violations by public officials. Accordingly, the minimum base offense level (level 6) provided is lower than that of the other guidelines in this subpart.

Historical Note: Effective November 1, 1987. Amended effective November 1, 1989 (see Appendix C, amendment 167); November 1, 1990 (see Appendix C, amendment 328).

* * * * *

2. POLITICAL RIGHTS

§2H2.1. Obstructing an Election or Registration

(a) Base Offense Level (Apply the greatest):

(1) **18**, if the obstruction occurred by use of force or threat of force against person(s) or property; or

(2) **12**, if the obstruction occurred by forgery, fraud, theft, bribery, deceit, or other means, except as provided in (3) below; or

(3) **6**, if the defendant (A) solicited, demanded, accepted, or agreed to accept anything of value to vote, refrain from voting, vote for or against a particular candidate, or register to vote, (B) gave false information to establish eligibility to vote, or (C) voted more than once in a federal election.

Commentary

Statutory Provisions: 18 U.S.C. §§ 241, 242, 245(b)(1)(A), 592, 593, 594, 597; 42 U.S.C. §§ 1973i, 1973j. For additional statutory provision(s), see Appendix A (Statutory Index).

Application Note:

1. *If the offense resulted in bodily injury or significant property damage, or involved corrupting a public official, an upward departure may be warranted. See Chapter Five, Part K (Departures).*

Background: Alternative base offense levels cover three major ways of obstructing an election: by force, by deceptive or dishonest conduct, or by bribery. A defendant who is a public official or who directs others to engage in criminal conduct is subject to an enhancement from Chapter Three, Part B (Role in the Offense).

Historical Note: Effective November 1, 1987. Amended effective November 1, 1989 (see Appendix C, amendment 168).

* * * * *

3. PRIVACY AND EAVESDROPPING

§2H3.1. Interception of Communications or Eavesdropping

(a) Base Offense Level: **9**

(b) Specific Offense Characteristic

(1) If the purpose of the conduct was to obtain direct or indirect commercial advantage or economic gain, increase by **3** levels.

(c) Cross Reference

(1) If the purpose of the conduct was to facilitate another offense, apply the guideline applicable to an attempt to commit that offense, if the resulting offense level is greater than that determined above.

Commentary

Statutory Provisions: 18 U.S.C. § 2511; 47 U.S.C. § 605. For additional statutory provision(s), see Appendix A (Statutory Index).

Application Note:

1. *If the offense involved interception of satellite cable transmissions for purposes of commercial advantage or private financial gain (including avoiding payment of fees), apply §2B5.3 (Criminal Infringement of Copyright) rather than this guideline.*

Background: This section refers to conduct proscribed by 47 U.S.C. § 605 and the Electronic Communications Privacy Act of 1986, which amends 18 U.S.C. § 2511 and other sections of Title 18 dealing with unlawful interception and disclosure of communications. These statutes proscribe the interception and divulging of wire, oral, radio, and electronic communications. The Electronic Communications Privacy Act of 1986 provides for a maximum term of imprisonment of five years for violations involving most types of communication.

Historical Note: Effective November 1, 1987. Amended effective November 1, 1989 (see Appendix C, amendment 169).

§2H3.2. Manufacturing, Distributing, Advertising, or Possessing an Eavesdropping Device

(a) Base Offense Level: **6**

(b) Specific Offense Characteristic

(1) If the offense was committed for pecuniary gain, increase by **3** levels.

Commentary

Statutory Provision: 18 U.S.C. § 2512.

Historical Note: Effective November 1, 1987.

§2H3.3. Obstructing Correspondence

(a) Base Offense Level:

(1) **6**; or

(2) if the conduct was theft of mail, apply §2B1.1 (Larceny, Embezzlement, and Other Forms of Theft);

(3) if the conduct was destruction of mail, apply §2B1.3 (Property Damage or Destruction).

Commentary

Statutory Provision: 18 U.S.C. § 1702. For additional statutory provision(s), see Appendix A (Statutory Index).

Background: The statutory provision covered by this guideline is sometimes used to prosecute offenses more accurately described as theft or destruction of mail. In such cases, §2B1.1 (Larceny, Embezzlement, and Other Forms of Theft) or §2B1.3 (Property Damage or Destruction) is to be applied.

Historical Note: Effective November 1, 1987. Amended effective November 1, 1990 (see Appendix C, amendment 313).

* * * * *

4. PEONAGE, INVOLUNTARY SERVITUDE, AND SLAVE TRADE

§2H4.1. Peonage, Involuntary Servitude, and Slave Trade

(a) Base Offense Level (Apply the greater):

(1) **15**; or

(2) **2** plus the offense level applicable to any underlying offense.

Commentary

Statutory Provisions: 18 U.S.C. §§ 1581-1588.

Application Note:

1. *"2 plus the offense level applicable to the underlying offense" is explained in the Commentary to §2H1.1.*

Background: This section covers statutes that prohibit peonage, involuntary servitude, and slave trade. For purposes of deterrence and just punishment, the minimum base offense level is 15. However, these offenses frequently involve other serious offenses. In such cases, the offense level will be increased under §2H4.1(a)(2).

Historical Note: Effective November 1, 1987.

PART J - OFFENSES INVOLVING THE ADMINISTRATION OF JUSTICE

§2J1.1. Contempt

Apply §2X5.1 (Other Offenses).

Commentary

Statutory Provisions: 18 U.S.C. §§ 401, 228. For additional statutory provision(s), see Appendix A (Statutory Index).

Application Notes:

1. *Because misconduct constituting contempt varies significantly and the nature of the contemptuous conduct, the circumstances under which the contempt was committed, the effect the misconduct had on the administration of justice, and the need to vindicate the authority of the court are highly context-dependent, the Commission has not provided a specific guideline for this offense. In certain cases, the offense conduct will be sufficiently analogous to §2J1.2 (Obstruction of Justice) for that guideline to apply.*

2. *For offenses involving the willful failure to pay court-ordered child support (violations of 18 U.S.C. § 228), the most analogous guideline is §2B1.1 (Larceny, Embezzlement, and Other Forms of Theft). The amount of the loss is the amount of child support that the defendant willfully failed to pay. Note: This guideline applies to second and subsequent offenses under 18 U.S.C. § 228. A first offense under 18 U.S.C. § 228 is not covered by this guideline because it is a Class B misdemeanor.*

Historical Note: Effective November 1, 1987. Amended effective November 1, 1989 (see Appendix C, amendments 170 and 171); November 1, 1993 (see Appendix C, amendment 496).

§2J1.2. Obstruction of Justice

(a) Base Offense Level: **12**

(b) Specific Offense Characteristics

(1) If the offense involved causing or threatening to cause physical injury to a person, or property damage, in order to obstruct the administration of justice, increase by **8** levels.

(2) If the offense resulted in substantial interference with the administration of justice, increase by **3** levels.

(c) Cross Reference

(1) If the offense involved obstructing the investigation or prosecution of a criminal offense, apply §2X3.1 (Accessory After the Fact) in respect to that criminal offense, if the resulting offense level is greater than that determined above.

Commentary

Statutory Provisions: 18 U.S.C. §§ 1503, 1505-1513, 1516. For additional statutory provision(s), see Appendix A (Statutory Index).

Application Notes:

1. *"Substantial interference with the administration of justice" includes a premature or improper termination of a felony investigation; an indictment, verdict, or any judicial determination based upon perjury, false testimony, or other false evidence; or the unnecessary expenditure of substantial governmental or court resources.*

2. *For offenses covered under this section, Chapter Three, Part C (Obstruction) does not apply, unless the defendant obstructed the investigation or trial of the obstruction of justice count.*

3. *In the event that the defendant is convicted under this section as well as for the underlying offense (i.e., the offense that is the object of the obstruction), see the Commentary to Chapter Three, Part C (Obstruction), and to §3D1.2(c) (Groups of Closely Related Counts).*

4. *If a weapon was used, or bodily injury or significant property damage resulted, a departure may be warranted. See Chapter Five, Part K (Departures).*

5. *The inclusion of "property damage" under subsection (b)(1) is designed to address cases in which property damage is caused or threatened as a means of intimidation or retaliation (e.g., to intimidate a witness from, or retaliate against a witness for, testifying). Subsection (b)(1) is not intended to apply, for example, where the offense consisted of destroying a ledger containing an incriminating entry.*

Background: This section addresses offenses involving the obstruction of justice generally prosecuted under the above-referenced statutory provisions. Numerous offenses of varying seriousness may constitute obstruction of justice: using threats or force to intimidate or influence a juror or federal officer; obstructing a civil or administrative proceeding; stealing or altering court records; unlawfully intercepting grand jury deliberations; obstructing a criminal investigation; obstructing a state or local investigation of illegal gambling; using intimidation or force to influence testimony, alter evidence, evade legal process, or obstruct the communication of a judge or law enforcement officer; or causing a witness bodily injury or property damage in retaliation for providing testimony, information or evidence in a federal proceeding. The conduct that gives rise to the violation may, therefore, range from a mere threat to an act of extreme violence.

The specific offense characteristics reflect the more serious forms of obstruction. Because the conduct covered by this guideline is frequently part of an effort to avoid punishment for an offense that the defendant has committed or to assist another person to escape punishment for an offense, a cross reference to §2X3.1 (Accessory After the Fact) is provided. Use of this cross reference will provide an enhanced offense level when the obstruction is in respect to a particularly serious offense, whether such offense was committed by the defendant or another person.

Historical Note: Effective November 1, 1987. Amended effective November 1, 1989 (see Appendix C, amendments 172-174); November 1, 1991 (see Appendix C, amendment 401).

§2J1.3. Perjury or Subornation of Perjury; Bribery of Witness

(a) Base Offense Level: **12**

(b) Specific Offense Characteristics

(1) If the offense involved causing or threatening to cause physical injury to a person, or property damage, in order to suborn perjury, increase by **8** levels.

(2) If the perjury, subornation of perjury, or witness bribery resulted in substantial interference with the administration of justice, increase by **3** levels.

(c) Cross Reference

(1) If the offense involved perjury, subornation of perjury, or witness bribery in respect to a criminal offense, apply §2X3.1 (Accessory After the Fact) in respect to that criminal offense, if the resulting offense level is greater than that determined above.

(d) Special Instruction

(1) In the case of counts of perjury or subornation of perjury arising from testimony given, or to be given, in separate proceedings, do not group the counts together under §3D1.2 (Groups of Closely Related Counts).

Commentary

Statutory Provisions: 18 U.S.C. §§ 201 (b)(3), (4), 1621-1623. For additional statutory provision(s), see Appendix A (Statutory Index).

Application Notes:

1. *"Substantial interference with the administration of justice" includes a premature or improper termination of a felony investigation; an indictment, verdict, or any judicial determination based upon perjury, false testimony, or other false evidence; or the unnecessary expenditure of substantial governmental or court resources.*

2. *For offenses covered under this section, Chapter Three, Part C (Obstruction) does not apply, unless the defendant obstructed the investigation or trial of the perjury count.*

3. *In the event that the defendant is convicted under this section as well as for the underlying offense (i.e., the offense with respect to which he committed perjury, subornation of perjury, or witness bribery), see the Commentary to Chapter Three, Part C (Obstruction), and to §3D1.2(c) (Groups of Closely Related Counts).*

4. *If a weapon was used, or bodily injury or significant property damage resulted, an upward departure may be warranted. See Chapter Five, Part K (Departures).*

5. *"Separate proceedings," as used in subsection (d)(1), includes different proceedings in the same case or matter (e.g., a grand jury proceeding and a trial, or a trial and retrial), and proceedings*

in separate cases or matters (e.g., separate trials of codefendants), but does not include multiple grand jury proceedings in the same case.

Background: This section applies to perjury, subornation of perjury, and witness bribery, generally prosecuted under the referenced statutes. The guidelines provide a higher penalty for perjury than the pre-guidelines practice estimate of ten months imprisonment. The Commission believes that perjury should be treated similarly to obstruction of justice. Therefore, the same considerations for enhancing a sentence are applied in the specific offense characteristics, and an alternative reference to the guideline for accessory after the fact is made.

Historical Note: Effective November 1, 1987. Amended effective November 1, 1989 (see Appendix C, amendment 175); November 1, 1991 (see Appendix C, amendments 401 and 402); November 1, 1993 (see Appendix C, amendment 481).

§2J1.4. Impersonation

(a) Base Offense Level: **6**

(b) Specific Offense Characteristic

(1) If the impersonation was committed for the purpose of conducting an unlawful arrest, detention, or search, increase by **6** levels.

(c) Cross Reference

(1) If the impersonation was to facilitate another offense, apply the guideline for an attempt to commit that offense, if the resulting offense level is greater than the offense level determined above.

Commentary

Statutory Provisions: 18 U.S.C. §§ 912, 913.

Background: This section applies to impersonation of a federal officer, agent, or employee; and impersonation to conduct an unlawful search or arrest.

Historical Note: Effective November 1, 1987. Amended effective November 1, 1989 (see Appendix C, amendment 176).

§2J1.5. Failure to Appear by Material Witness

(a) Base Offense Level:

(1) **6**, if in respect to a felony; or

(2) **4**, if in respect to a misdemeanor.

(b) Specific Offense Characteristic

(1) If the offense resulted in substantial interference with the administration of justice, increase by **3** levels.

Commentary

Statutory Provision: 18 U.S.C. § 3146(b)(2). For additional statutory provision(s), see Appendix A (Statutory Index).

Application Notes:

1. *"Substantial interference with the administration of justice" includes a premature or improper termination of a felony investigation; an indictment, verdict, or any judicial determination based upon perjury, false testimony, or other false evidence; or the unnecessary expenditure of substantial governmental or court resources.*

2. *By statute, a term of imprisonment imposed for this offense runs consecutively to any other term of imprisonment imposed. 18 U.S.C. § 3146(b)(2).*

Background: This section applies to a failure to appear by a material witness. The base offense level incorporates a distinction as to whether the failure to appear was in respect to a felony or misdemeanor prosecution. This offense covered by this section is a misdemeanor for which the maximum period of imprisonment authorized by statute is one year.

Historical Note: Effective November 1, 1987. Amended effective November 1, 1989 (see Appendix C, amendment 177); November 1, 1991 (see Appendix C, amendment 401).

§2J1.6. Failure to Appear by Defendant

(a) Base Offense Level:

(1) **11**, if the offense constituted a failure to report for service of sentence; or

(2) **6**, otherwise.

(b) Specific Offense Characteristics

(1) If the base offense level is determined under subsection (a)(1), and the defendant --

(A) voluntarily surrendered within 96 hours of the time he was originally scheduled to report, decrease by **5** levels; or

(B) was ordered to report to a community corrections center, community treatment center, "halfway house," or similar facility, and subdivision (A) above does not apply, decrease by **2** levels.

Provided, however, that this reduction shall not apply if the defendant, while away from the facility, committed any federal, state, or local offense punishable by a term of imprisonment of one year or more.

(2) If the base offense level is determined under subsection (a)(2), and the underlying offense is --

(A) punishable by death or imprisonment for a term of fifteen years or more, increase by **9** levels; or

(B) punishable by a term of imprisonment of five years or more, but less than fifteen years, increase by **6** levels; or

(C) a felony punishable by a term of imprisonment of less than five years, increase by **3** levels.

Commentary

Statutory Provision: 18 U.S.C. § 3146(b)(1).

Application Notes:

1. *"Underlying offense" means the offense in respect to which the defendant failed to appear.*

2. *For offenses covered under this section, Chapter Three, Part C (Obstruction) does not apply, unless the defendant obstructed the investigation or trial of the failure to appear count.*

3. *In the case of a failure to appear for service of sentence, any term of imprisonment imposed on the failure to appear count is to be imposed consecutively to any term of imprisonment imposed for the underlying offense. See §5G1.3(a). The guideline range for the failure to appear count is to be determined independently and the grouping rules of §§3D1.2-3D1.5 do not apply.*

   Otherwise, in the case of a conviction on both the underlying offense and the failure to appear, the failure to appear is treated under §3C1.1 (Obstructing or Impeding the Administration of Justice) as an obstruction of the underlying offense; and the failure to appear count and the count(s) for the underlying offense are grouped together under §3D1.2(c). Note that although 18 U.S.C. § 3146(b)(2) does not require a sentence of imprisonment on a failure to appear count, it does require that any sentence of imprisonment on a failure to appear count be imposed consecutively to any other sentence of imprisonment. Therefore, in such cases, the combined sentence must be constructed to provide a "total punishment" that satisfies the requirements both of §5G1.2 (Sentencing on Multiple Counts of Conviction) and 18 U.S.C. § 3146(b)(2). For example, where the combined applicable guideline range for both counts is 30-37 months and the court determines a "total punishment" of 36 months is appropriate, a sentence of thirty months for the underlying offense plus a consecutive six months sentence for the failure to appear count would satisfy these requirements.

4. *In some cases, the defendant may be sentenced on the underlying offense (the offense in respect to which the defendant failed to appear) before being sentenced on the failure to appear offense. In such cases, criminal history points for the sentence imposed on the underlying offense are to be counted in determining the guideline range on the failure to appear offense only where the offense level is determined under subsection (a)(1) (i.e., where the offense constituted a failure to report for service of sentence).*

Background: This section applies to a failure to appear by a defendant who was released pending trial, sentencing, appeal, or surrender for service of sentence. Where the base offense level is determined under subsection (a)(2), the offense level increases in relation to the statutory maximum of the underlying offense.

Historical Note: Effective November 1, 1987. Amended effective November 1, 1990 (see Appendix C, amendment 329); November 1, 1991 (see Appendix C, amendment 403).

§2J1.7. Commission of Offense While on Release

If an enhancement under 18 U.S.C. § 3147 applies, add **3** levels to the offense level for the offense committed while on release as if this section were a specific offense characteristic contained in the offense guideline for the offense committed while on release.

Commentary

Statutory Provision: 18 U.S.C. § 3147.

Application Notes:

1. *Because 18 U.S.C. § 3147 is an enhancement provision, rather than an offense, this section provides a specific offense characteristic to increase the offense level for the offense committed while on release.*

2. *Under 18 U.S.C. § 3147, a sentence of imprisonment must be imposed in addition to the sentence for the underlying offense, and the sentence of imprisonment imposed under 18 U.S.C. § 3147 must run consecutively to any other sentence of imprisonment. Therefore, the court, in order to comply with the statute, should divide the sentence on the judgment form between the sentence attributable to the underlying offense and the sentence attributable to the enhancement. The court will have to ensure that the "total punishment" (i.e., the sentence for the offense committed while on release plus the sentence enhancement under 18 U.S.C. § 3147) is in accord with the guideline range for the offense committed while on release, as adjusted by the enhancement in this section. For example, if the applicable adjusted guideline range is 30-37 months and the court determines "total punishment" of 36 months is appropriate, a sentence of 30 months for the underlying offense plus 6 months under 18 U.S.C. § 3147 would satisfy this requirement.*

Background: An enhancement under 18 U.S.C. § 3147 may be imposed only after sufficient notice to the defendant by the government or the court, and applies only in the case of a conviction for a federal offense that is committed while on release on another federal charge.

Legislative history indicates that the mandatory nature of the penalties required by 18 U.S.C. § 3147 was to be eliminated upon the implementation of the sentencing guidelines. "Section 213(h) [renumbered as §200(g) in the Crime Control Act of 1984] amends the new provision in title I of this Act relating to consecutive enhanced penalties for committing an offense on release (new 18 U.S.C. § 3147) by eliminating the mandatory nature of the penalties in favor of utilizing sentencing guidelines." (Senate Report 98-225 at 186). Not all of the phraseology relating to the requirement of a mandatory sentence, however, was actually deleted from the statute. Consequently, it appears that the court is required to impose a consecutive sentence of imprisonment under this provision, but there is no requirement as to any minimum term. This guideline is drafted to enable the court to determine and implement a combined "total punishment" consistent with the overall structure of the guidelines, while at the same time complying with the statutory requirement. Guideline provisions that prohibit the grouping of counts of conviction requiring consecutive sentences (e.g., the introductory paragraph of §3D1.2; §5G1.2(a)) do not apply to this section because 18 U.S.C. § 3147 is an enhancement, not a count of conviction.

Historical Note: Effective November 1, 1987. Amended effective January 15, 1988 (see Appendix C, amendment 32); November 1, 1989 (see Appendix C, amendment 178); November 1, 1991 (see Appendix C, amendment 431).

§2J1.8. [Deleted]

Historical Note: Section 2J1.8 (Bribery of Witness), effective November 1, 1987, amended effective January 15, 1988 (see Appendix C, amendment 33), November 1, 1989 (see Appendix C, amendment 179), and November 1, 1991 (see Appendix C, amendment 401), was deleted by consolidation with §2J1.3 effective November 1, 1993 (see Appendix C, amendment 481).

§2J1.9. Payment to Witness

(a) Base Offense Level: **6**

(b) Specific Offense Characteristic

(1) If the payment was made or offered for refusing to testify or for the witness absenting himself to avoid testifying, increase by **4** levels.

Commentary

Statutory Provisions: 18 U.S.C. § 201(c)(2), (3).

Application Notes:

1. *For offenses covered under this section, Chapter Three, Part C (Obstruction) does not apply unless the defendant obstructed the investigation or trial of the payment to witness count.*

2. *In the event that the defendant is convicted under this section as well as for the underlying offense (i.e., the offense with respect to which the payment was made), see the Commentary to Chapter Three, Part C (Obstruction), and to §3D1.2(c) (Groups of Closely Related Counts).*

Background: This section applies to witness gratuities in federal proceedings.

Historical Note: Effective November 1, 1987. Amended effective November 1, 1989 (see Appendix C, amendments 180 and 181).

PART K - OFFENSES INVOLVING PUBLIC SAFETY

1. EXPLOSIVES AND ARSON

§2K1.1. Failure to Report Theft of Explosive Materials; Improper Storage of Explosive Materials

(a) Base Offense Level: **6**

Commentary

Statutory Provisions: 18 U.S.C. §§ 842(j), (k), 844(b). For additional statutory provision(s), see Appendix A (Statutory Index).

Background: The above-referenced provisions are misdemeanors. The maximum term of imprisonment authorized by statute is one year.

Historical Note: Effective November 1, 1987. Amended effective November 1, 1991 (see Appendix C, amendment 404); November 1, 1993 (see Appendix C, amendment 481).

§2K1.2. [Deleted]

Historical Note: Section 2K1.2 (Improper Storage of Explosive Materials), effective November 1, 1987, amended effective November 1, 1991 (see Appendix C, amendment 404), was deleted by consolidation with §2K1.1 effective November 1, 1993 (see Appendix C, amendment 481).

§2K1.3. Unlawful Receipt, Possession, or Transportation of Explosive Materials; Prohibited Transactions Involving Explosive Materials

(a) Base Offense Level (Apply the Greatest):

(1) **24**, if the defendant had at least two prior felony convictions of either a crime of violence or a controlled substance offense; or

(2) **20**, if the defendant had one prior felony conviction of either a crime of violence or a controlled substance offense; or

(3) **16**, if the defendant is a prohibited person; or knowingly distributed explosive materials to a prohibited person; or

(4) **12**, otherwise.

(b) Specific Offense Characteristics

(1) If the offense involved twenty-five pounds or more of explosive materials, increase as follows:

	Weight of Explosive Material	Increase in Level
(A)	At least 25 but less than 100 lbs.	add **1**
(B)	At least 100 but less than 250 lbs.	add **2**
(C)	At least 250 but less than 500 lbs.	add **3**
(D)	At least 500 but less than 1000 lbs.	add **4**
(E)	1000 lbs. or more	add **5**.

(2) If the offense involved any explosive material that the defendant knew or had reason to believe was stolen, increase by **2** levels.

Provided, that the cumulative offense level determined above shall not exceed level **29**.

(3) If the defendant used or possessed any explosive material in connection with another felony offense; or possessed or transferred any explosive material with knowledge, intent, or reason to believe that it would be used or possessed in connection with another felony offense, increase by **4** levels. If the resulting offense level is less than level **18**, increase to level **18**.

(c) Cross Reference

(1) If the defendant used or possessed any explosive material in connection with the commission or attempted commission of another offense, or possessed or transferred any explosive material with knowledge or intent that it would be used or possessed in connection with another offense, apply --

(A) §2X1.1 (Attempt, Solicitation, or Conspiracy) in respect to that other offense if the resulting offense level is greater than that determined above; or

(B) if death resulted, the most analogous offense guideline from Chapter Two, Part A, Subpart 1 (Homicide), if the resulting offense level is greater than that determined above.

<u>Commentary</u>

<u>Statutory Provisions:</u> *18 U.S.C. §§ 842(a)-(e), (h), (i), 844(d), (g), 1716; 26 U.S.C. § 5865.*

<u>Application Notes:</u>

1. "Explosive material(s)" include explosives, blasting agents, and detonators. <u>See</u> 18 U.S.C. § 841(c). "Explosives" is defined at 18 U.S.C. § 844(j). A destructive device, defined in the Commentary to §1B1.1 (Application Instructions), may contain explosive materials. Where the conduct charged in the count of which the defendant was convicted establishes that the offense involved a destructive device, apply §2K2.1 (Unlawful Receipt, Possession, or Transportation of Firearms or Ammunition; Prohibited Transactions Involving Firearms or Ammunition) if the resulting offense level is greater.

2. *"Crime of violence," "controlled substance offense," and "prior felony conviction(s)," as used in subsections (a)(1) and (a)(2), are defined at §4B1.2 (Definitions of Terms Used in Section 4B1.1), subsections (1) and (2), and Application Note 3 of the Commentary, respectively. For purposes of determining the number of such convictions under subsections (a)(1) and (a)(2), count any such prior conviction that receives any points under §4A1.1 (Criminal History Category).*

3. *"Prohibited person," as used in subsection (a)(3), means anyone who: (i) is under indictment for, or has been convicted of, a "crime punishable by imprisonment for a term exceeding one year," as defined at 18 U.S.C. § 841(l); (ii) is a fugitive from justice; (iii) is an unlawful user of, or is addicted to, any controlled substance; or (iv) has been adjudicated as a mental defective or involuntarily committed to a mental institution.*

4. *"Felony offense," as used in subsection (b)(3), means any offense (federal, state, or local) punishable by imprisonment for a term exceeding one year, whether or not a criminal charge was brought, or conviction obtained.*

5. *For purposes of calculating the weight of explosive materials under subsection (b)(1), include only the weight of the actual explosive material and the weight of packaging material that is necessary for the use or detonation of the explosives. Exclude the weight of any other shipping or packaging materials. For example, the paper and fuse on a stick of dynamite would be included; the box that the dynamite was shipped in would not be included.*

6. *For purposes of calculating the weight of explosive materials under subsection (b)(1), count only those explosive materials that were unlawfully sought to be obtained, unlawfully possessed, or unlawfully distributed, including any explosive material that a defendant attempted to obtain by making a false statement.*

7. *If the defendant is convicted under 18 U.S.C. § 842(h) (offense involving stolen explosive materials), and is convicted of no other offenses subject to this guideline, do not apply the adjustment in subsection (b)(2) because the base offense level itself takes such conduct into account.*

8. *Under subsection (c)(1), the offense level for the underlying offense (which may be a federal, state, or local offense) is to be determined under §2X1.1 (Attempt, Solicitation, or Conspiracy) or, if death results, under the most analogous guideline from Chapter Two, Part A, Subpart 1 (Homicide).*

9. *Prior felony conviction(s) resulting in an increased base offense level under subsection (a)(1), (a)(2), or (a)(3) are also counted for purposes of determining criminal history points pursuant to Chapter Four, Part A (Criminal History).*

10. *An upward departure may be warranted in any of the following circumstances: (1) the quantity of explosive materials significantly exceeded 1000 pounds; (2) the explosive materials were of a nature more volatile or dangerous than dynamite or conventional powder explosives (e.g., plastic explosives); (3) the defendant knowingly distributed explosive materials to a person under twenty-one years of age; or (4) the offense posed a substantial risk of death or bodily injury to multiple individuals.*

11. *As used in subsections (b)(3) and (c)(1), "another felony offense" and "another offense" refer to offenses other than explosives or firearms possession or trafficking offenses. However, where the defendant used or possessed a firearm or explosive to facilitate another firearms or explosives offense (e.g., the defendant used or possessed a firearm to protect the delivery of an*

unlawful shipment of explosives), an upward departure under §5K2.6 (Weapons and Dangerous Instrumentalities) may be warranted.

Historical Note: Effective November 1, 1987. Amended effective November 1, 1989 (see Appendix C, amendment 183); November 1, 1991 (see Appendix C, amendment 373); November 1, 1992 (see, Appendix C, amendment 471); November 1, 1993 (see, Appendix C, amendment 478).

§2K1.4. Arson; Property Damage by Use of Explosives

(a) Base Offense Level (Apply the Greatest):

(1) **24**, if the offense (A) created a substantial risk of death or serious bodily injury to any person other than a participant in the offense, and that risk was created knowingly; or (B) involved the destruction or attempted destruction of a dwelling;

(2) **20**, if the offense (A) created a substantial risk of death or serious bodily injury to any person other than a participant in the offense; (B) involved the destruction or attempted destruction of a structure other than a dwelling; or (C) endangered a dwelling, or a structure other than a dwelling;

(3) **2** plus the offense level from §2F1.1 (Fraud and Deceit) if the offense was committed in connection with a scheme to defraud; or

(4) **2** plus the offense level from §2B1.3 (Property Damage or Destruction).

(b) Specific Offense Characteristic

(1) If the offense was committed to conceal another offense, increase by **2** levels.

(c) Cross Reference

(1) If death resulted, or the offense was intended to cause death or serious bodily injury, apply the most analogous guideline from Chapter Two, Part A (Offenses Against the Person) if the resulting offense level is greater than that determined above.

Commentary

Statutory Provisions: 18 U.S.C. §§ 32(a), (b), 33, 81, 844(f), (h) (only in the case of an offense committed prior to November 18, 1988), (i), 1153, 1855, 2275. For additional statutory provision(s), see Appendix A (Statutory Index).

Application Notes:

1. *If bodily injury resulted, an upward departure may be warranted. See Chapter Five, Part K (Departures).*

2. *Creating a substantial risk of death or serious bodily injury includes creating that risk to fire fighters and other emergency and law enforcement personnel who respond to or investigate an offense.*

3. *"Explosives," as used in the title of this guideline, includes any explosive, explosive material, or destructive device.*

Historical Note: Effective November 1, 1987. Amended effective November 1, 1989 (see Appendix C, amendments 182, 184, and 185); November 1, 1990 (see Appendix C, amendment 330); November 1, 1991 (see Appendix C, amendment 404).

§2K1.5. Possessing Dangerous Weapons or Materials While Boarding or Aboard an Aircraft

(a) Base Offense Level: **9**

(b) Specific Offense Characteristics

If more than one applies, use the greatest:

(1) If the offense was committed willfully and without regard for the safety of human life, or with reckless disregard for the safety of human life, increase by **15** levels.

(2) If the defendant was prohibited by another federal law from possessing the weapon or material, increase by **2** levels.

(3) If the defendant's possession of the weapon or material would have been lawful but for 49 U.S.C. § 1472(l) and he acted with mere negligence, decrease by **3** levels.

(c) Cross Reference

(1) If the defendant used or possessed the weapon or material in committing or attempting another offense, apply the guideline for such other offense, or §2X1.1 (Attempt, Solicitation, or Conspiracy), as appropriate, if the resulting offense level is greater than that determined above.

Commentary

Statutory Provision: *49 U.S.C. § 1472(l).*

Background: *Except under the circumstances specified in 49 U.S.C. § 1472(l)(2), the offense covered by this section is a misdemeanor for which the maximum term of imprisonment authorized by statute is one year. An enhancement is provided where the defendant was a person prohibited by federal law from possession of the weapon or material. A decrease is provided in a case of mere negligence where the defendant was otherwise authorized to possess the weapon or material.*

Historical Note: Effective November 1, 1987. Amended effective November 1, 1989 (see Appendix C, amendments 182, 186, 187, and 303); November 1, 1991 (see Appendix C, amendment 404); November 1, 1992 (see Appendix C, amendment 443).

§2K1.6. Licensee Recordkeeping Violations Involving Explosive Materials

(a) Base Offense Level: **6**

(b) Cross Reference

(1) If a recordkeeping offense reflected an effort to conceal a substantive explosive materials offense, apply §2K1.3 (Unlawful Receipt, Possession, or Transportation of Explosives Materials; Prohibited Transactions Involving Explosive Materials).

Commentary

Statutory Provisions: 18 U.S.C. § 842(f), (g).

Background: The above-referenced provisions are recordkeeping offenses applicable only to "licensees," who are defined at 18 U.S.C. § 841(m).

Historical Note: Effective November 1, 1991 (see Appendix C, amendment 373). A former §2K1.6 (Shipping, Transporting, or Receiving Explosives with Felonious Intent or Knowledge; Using or Carrying Explosives in Certain Crimes), effective November 1, 1987, amended effective November 1, 1989 (see Appendix C, amendment 303) and November 1, 1990 (see Appendix C, amendment 331), was deleted by consolidation with §2K1.3 effective November 1, 1991 (see Appendix C, amendment 373).

§2K1.7. [Deleted]

Historical Note: Section 2K1.7 (Use of Fire or Explosives to Commit a Federal Felony), effective November 1, 1989 (see Appendix C, amendment 188), amended effective November 1, 1990 (see Appendix C, amendment 332), was deleted by consolidation with §2K2.4 effective November 1, 1993 (see Appendix C, amendment 481).

* * * * *

2. FIREARMS

§2K2.1. Unlawful Receipt, Possession, or Transportation of Firearms or Ammunition; Prohibited Transactions Involving Firearms or Ammunition

(a) Base Offense Level (Apply the Greatest):

(1) **26**, if the defendant had at least two prior felony convictions of either a crime of violence or a controlled substance offense, and the instant offense involved a firearm listed in 26 U.S.C. § 5845(a); or

(2) **24**, if the defendant had at least two prior felony convictions of either a crime of violence or a controlled substance offense; or

(3) **22**, if the defendant had one prior felony conviction of either a crime of violence or a controlled substance offense, and the instant offense involved a firearm listed in 26 U.S.C. § 5845(a); or

(4) **20**, if the defendant --

(A) had one prior felony conviction of either a crime of violence or a controlled substance offense; or

(B) is a prohibited person, and the offense involved a firearm listed in 26 U.S.C. § 5845(a); or

(5) **18**, if the offense involved a firearm listed in 26 U.S.C. § 5845(a); or

(6) **14**, if the defendant is a prohibited person; or

(7) **12**, except as provided below; or

(8) **6**, if the defendant is convicted under 18 U.S.C. § 922(c), (e), (f), or (m).

(b) Specific Offense Characteristics

(1) If the offense involved three or more firearms, increase as follows:

	Number of Firearms	Increase in Level
(A)	3-4	add **1**
(B)	5-7	add **2**
(C)	8-12	add **3**
(D)	13-24	add **4**
(E)	25-49	add **5**
(F)	50 or more	add **6**.

(2) If the defendant, other than a defendant subject to subsection (a)(1), (a)(2), (a)(3), (a)(4), or (a)(5), possessed all ammunition and firearms solely for lawful sporting purposes or collection, and did not unlawfully discharge or otherwise unlawfully use such firearms or ammunition, decrease the offense level determined above to level **6**.

(3) If the offense involved a destructive device, increase by **2** levels.

(4) If any firearm was stolen, or had an altered or obliterated serial number, increase by **2** levels.

Provided, that the cumulative offense level determined above shall not exceed level **29**.

(5) If the defendant used or possessed any firearm or ammunition in connection with another felony offense; or possessed or transferred any firearm or ammunition with knowledge, intent, or reason to believe that it would be used or possessed in connection with another felony offense, increase by **4** levels. If the resulting offense level is less than level **18**, increase to level **18**.

(6) If a recordkeeping offense reflected an effort to conceal a substantive offense involving firearms or ammunition, increase to the offense level for the substantive offense.

(c) Cross Reference

(1) If the defendant used or possessed any firearm or ammunition in connection with the commission or attempted commission of another offense, or possessed or transferred a firearm or ammunition with knowledge or intent that it would be used or possessed in connection with another offense, apply --

(A) §2X1.1 (Attempt, Solicitation, or Conspiracy) in respect to that other offense, if the resulting offense level is greater than that determined above; or

(B) if death resulted, the most analogous offense guideline from Chapter Two, Part A, Subpart 1 (Homicide), if the resulting offense level is greater than that determined above.

Commentary

Statutory Provisions: 18 U.S.C. §§ 922(a)-(p), (r), 924(a), (b), (e), (f), (g); 26 U.S.C. § 5861(a)-(l). For additional statutory provisions, see Appendix A (Statutory Index).

Application Notes:

1. *"Firearm" includes (i) any weapon (including a starter gun) which will or is designed to or may readily be converted to expel a projectile by the action of an explosive; (ii) the frame or receiver of any such weapon; (iii) any firearm muffler or silencer; or (iv) any destructive device. See 18 U.S.C. § 921(a)(3).*

2. *"Ammunition" includes ammunition or cartridge cases, primer, bullets, or propellent powder designed for use in any firearm. See 18 U.S.C. § 921(a)(17)(A).*

3. *"Firearm listed in 26 U.S.C. § 5845(a)" includes: (i) any short-barreled rifle or shotgun or any weapon made therefrom; (ii) a machinegun; (iii) a silencer; (iv) a destructive device; or (v) any "other weapon," as that term is defined by 26 U.S.C. § 5845(e). A firearm listed in 26 U.S.C. § 5845(a) does not include unaltered handguns or regulation-length rifles or shotguns. For a more detailed definition, refer to 26 U.S.C. § 5845.*

4. *"Destructive device" is a type of firearm listed in 26 U.S.C. § 5845(a), and includes any explosive, incendiary, or poison gas -- (i) bomb, (ii) grenade, (iii) rocket having a propellant charge of more than four ounces, (iv) missile having an explosive or incendiary charge of more than one-quarter ounce, (v) mine, or (vi) device similar to any of the devices described in the preceding clauses; any type of weapon which will, or which may be readily converted to, expel a projectile by the action of an explosive or other propellant, and which has any barrel with a bore of more than one-half inch in diameter; or any combination of parts either designed or intended for use in converting any device into any destructive device listed above. For a more detailed definition, refer to 26 U.S.C. § 5845(f).*

5. *"Crime of violence," "controlled substance offense," and "prior felony conviction(s)," are defined in §4B1.2 (Definitions of Terms Used in Section 4B1.1), subsections (1) and (2), and Application Note 3 of the Commentary, respectively. For purposes of determining the number of such convictions under subsections (a)(1), (a)(2), (a)(3), and (a)(4)(A), count any such prior conviction that receives any points under §4A1.1 (Criminal History Category).*

6. *"Prohibited person," as used in subsections (a)(4)(B) and (a)(6), means anyone who: (i) is under indictment for, or has been convicted of, a "crime punishable by imprisonment for more than one year," as defined by 18 U.S.C. § 921(a)(20); (ii) is a fugitive from justice; (iii) is an unlawful user of, or is addicted to, any controlled substance; (iv) has been adjudicated as a mental defective or involuntarily committed to a mental institution; or (v) being an alien, is illegally or unlawfully in the United States.*

7. *"Felony offense," as used in subsection (b)(5), means any offense (federal, state, or local) punishable by imprisonment for a term exceeding one year, whether or not a criminal charge was brought, or conviction obtained.*

8. *Subsection (a)(7) includes the interstate transportation or interstate distribution of firearms, which is frequently committed in violation of state, local, or other federal law restricting the possession of firearms, or for some other underlying unlawful purpose. In the unusual case in which it is established that neither avoidance of state, local, or other federal firearms law, nor any other underlying unlawful purpose was involved, a reduction in the base offense level to no lower than level 6 may be warranted to reflect the less serious nature of the violation.*

9. *For purposes of calculating the number of firearms under subsection (b)(1), count only those firearms that were unlawfully sought to be obtained, unlawfully possessed, or unlawfully distributed, including any firearm that a defendant obtained or attempted to obtain by making a false statement to a licensed dealer.*

10. *Under subsection (b)(2), "lawful sporting purposes or collection" as determined by the surrounding circumstances, provides for a reduction to an offense level of 6. Relevant surrounding circumstances include the number and type of firearms, the amount and type of ammunition, the location and circumstances of possession and actual use, the nature of the defendant's criminal history (e.g., prior convictions for offenses involving firearms), and the extent to which possession was restricted by local law. Note that where the base offense level is determined under subsections (a)(1) - (a)(5), subsection (b)(2) is not applicable.*

11. *A defendant whose offense involves a destructive device receives both the base offense level from the subsection applicable to a firearm listed in 26 U.S.C. § 5845(a) (e.g., subsection (a)(1), (a)(3), (a)(4)(B), or (a)(5)), and a two-level enhancement under subsection (b)(3). Such devices pose a considerably greater risk to the public welfare than other National Firearms Act weapons.*

12. *If the defendant is convicted under 18 U.S.C. § 922(i), (j), or (k), or 26 U.S.C. § 5861(g) or (h) (offenses involving stolen firearms or ammunition), and is convicted of no other offense subject to this guideline, do not apply the adjustment in subsection (b)(4) because the base offense level itself takes such conduct into account.*

13. *Under subsection (b)(6), if a record-keeping offense was committed to conceal a substantive firearms or ammunition offense, the offense level is increased to the offense level for the substantive firearms or ammunition offense (e.g., if the defendant falsifies a record to conceal the sale of a firearm to a prohibited person, the offense level is increased to the offense level applicable to the sale of a firearm to a prohibited person).*

14. *Under subsection (c)(1), the offense level for the underlying offense (which may be a federal, state, or local offense) is to be determined under §2X1.1 (Attempt, Solicitation, or Conspiracy) or, if death results, under the most analogous guideline from Chapter Two, Part A, Subpart 1 (Homicide).*

15. *Prior felony conviction(s) resulting in an increased base offense level under subsection (a)(1), (a)(2), (a)(3), (a)(4)(A), (a)(4)(B), or (a)(6) are also counted for purposes of determining criminal history points pursuant to Chapter Four, Part A (Criminal History).*

16. *An upward departure may be warranted in any of the following circumstances: (1) the number of firearms significantly exceeded fifty; (2) the offense involved multiple National Firearms Act weapons (e.g., machineguns, destructive devices), military type assault rifles, non-detectable ("plastic") firearms (defined at 18 U.S.C. § 922(p)); (3) the offense involved large quantities of armor-piercing ammunition (defined at 18 U.S.C. § 921(a)(17)(B)); or (4) the offense posed a substantial risk of death or bodily injury to multiple individuals.*

17. *A defendant who is subject to an enhanced sentence under the provisions of 18 U.S.C. § 924(e) is an Armed Career Criminal. See §4B1.4.*

18. *As used in subsections (b)(5) and (c)(1), "another felony offense" and "another offense" refer to offenses other than explosives or firearms possession or trafficking offenses. However, where the defendant used or possessed a firearm or explosive to facilitate another firearms or explosives offense (e.g., the defendant used or possessed a firearm to protect the delivery of an unlawful shipment of explosives), an upward departure under §5K2.6 (Weapons and Dangerous Instrumentalities) may be warranted.*

19. *The enhancement under subsection (b)(4) for a stolen firearm or a firearm with an altered or obliterated serial number applies whether or not the defendant knew or had reason to believe that the firearm was stolen or had an altered or obliterated serial number.*

Historical Note: Effective November 1, 1987. Amended effective November 1, 1989 (see Appendix C, amendment 189); November 1, 1990 (see Appendix C, amendment 333); November 1, 1991 (see Appendix C, amendment 374); November 1, 1992 (see Appendix C, amendment 471); November 1, 1993 (see Appendix C, amendment 478).

§2K2.2. [Deleted]

Historical Note: Section 2K2.2 (Unlawful Trafficking and Other Prohibited Transactions Involving Firearms), effective November 1, 1987, amended effective January 15, 1988 (see Appendix C, amendment 34), November 1, 1989 (see Appendix C, amendment 189), and November 1, 1990 (see Appendix C, amendment 333), was deleted by consolidation with §2K2.1 effective November 1, 1991 (see Appendix C, amendment 374).

§2K2.3. [Deleted]

Historical Note: Section 2K2.3 (Receiving, Transporting, Shipping or Transferring a Firearm or Ammunition With Intent to Commit Another Offense, or With Knowledge that It Will Be Used in Committing Another Offense), effective November 1, 1989 (see Appendix C, amendment 189), was deleted by consolidation with §2K2.1 effective November 1, 1991 (see Appendix C, amendment 374). A former §2K2.3 (Prohibited Transactions in or Shipment of Firearms and Other Weapons), effective November 1, 1987, was deleted by consolidation with §2K2.2 effective November 1, 1989 (see Appendix C, amendment 189).

§2K2.4. Use of Firearm, Armor-Piercing Ammunition, or Explosive During or in Relation to Certain Crimes

(a) If the defendant, whether or not convicted of another crime, was convicted under 18 U.S.C. § 844(h), § 924(c), or § 929(a), the term of imprisonment is that required by statute.

(b) Special Instructions for Fines

(1) Where there is a federal conviction for the underlying offense, the fine guideline shall be the fine guideline that would have been applicable had there only been a conviction for the underlying offense. This guideline shall be used as a consolidated fine guideline for both the underlying offense and the conviction underlying this section.

Commentary

Statutory Provisions: 18 U.S.C. §§ 844(h), 924(c), 929(a).

Application Notes:

1. *In each case, the statute requires a term of imprisonment imposed under this section to run consecutively to any other term of imprisonment.*

2. *Where a sentence under this section is imposed in conjunction with a sentence for an underlying offense, any specific offense characteristic for the possession, use, or discharge of an explosive or firearm (e.g., §2B3.1(b)(2)(A)-(F) (Robbery)) is not to be applied in respect to the guideline for the underlying offense.*

In a few cases, the offense level for the underlying offense determined under the preceding paragraph may result in a guideline range that, when combined with the mandatory consecutive sentence under 18 U.S.C. § 844(h), § 924(c), or § 929(a), produces a total maximum penalty that is less than the maximum of the guideline range that would have resulted had there not been a count of conviction under 18 U.S.C. § 844(h), § 924(c), or § 929(a) (i.e., the guideline range that would have resulted if the enhancements for possession, use, or discharge of a firearm had been applied). In such a case, an upward departure may be warranted so that the conviction under 18 U.S.C. § 844(h), § 924(c), or § 929(a) does not result in a decrease in the total punishment. An upward departure under this paragraph shall not exceed the maximum of the guideline range that would have resulted had there not been a count of conviction under 18 U.S.C. § 844(h), § 924(c), or § 929(a).

3. *Imposition of a term of supervised release is governed by the provisions of §5D1.1 (Imposition of a Term of Supervised Release).*

4. *Subsection (b) sets forth special provisions concerning the imposition of fines. Where there is also a conviction for the underlying offense, a consolidated fine guideline is determined by the offense level that would have applied to the underlying offense absent a conviction under 18 U.S.C. § 844(h), § 924(c), or § 929(a). This is required because the offense level for the underlying offense may be reduced when there is also a conviction under 18 U.S.C. § 844(h), § 924(c), or § 929(a) in that any specific offense characteristic for possession, use, or discharge of a firearm is not applied (see Application Note 2). The Commission has not established a*

fine guideline range for the unusual case in which there is no conviction for the underlying offense, although a fine is authorized under 18 U.S.C. § 3571.

Background: 18 U.S.C. §§ 844(h), 924(c), and 929(a) provide mandatory minimum penalties for the conduct proscribed. To avoid double counting, when a sentence under this section is imposed in conjunction with a sentence for an underlying offense, any specific offense characteristic for explosive or firearm discharge, use, or possession is not applied in respect to such underlying offense.

Historical Note: Effective November 1, 1987. Amended effective November 1, 1989 (see Appendix C, amendment 190); November 1, 1990 (see Appendix C, amendment 332); November 1, 1991 (see Appendix C, amendment 405); November 1, 1993 (see Appendix C, amendments 481 and 489).

§2K2.5. Possession of Firearm or Dangerous Weapon in Federal Facility; Possession or Discharge of Firearm in School Zone

(a) Base Offense Level: **6**

(b) Specific Offense Characteristic

(1) If --

(A) the defendant unlawfully possessed or caused any firearm or dangerous weapon to be present in a federal court facility; or

(B) the defendant unlawfully possessed or caused any firearm to be present in a school zone,

increase by **2** levels.

(c) Cross Reference

(1) If the defendant used or possessed any firearm or dangerous weapon in connection with the commission or attempted commission of another offense, or possessed or transferred a firearm or dangerous weapon with knowledge or intent that it would be used or possessed in connection with another offense, apply --

(A) §2X1.1 (Attempt, Solicitation, or Conspiracy) in respect to that other offense if the resulting offense level is greater than that determined above; or

(B) if death resulted, the most analogous offense guideline from Chapter Two, Part A, Subpart 1 (Homicide), if the resulting offense level is greater than that determined above.

Commentary

Statutory Provisions: 18 U.S.C. §§ 922(q), 930.

Application Notes:

1. *"Dangerous weapon" and "firearm" are defined in the Commentary to §1B1.1 (Application Instructions).*

2. *"Federal court facility" includes the courtroom; judges' chambers; witness rooms; jury deliberation rooms; attorney conference rooms; prisoner holding cells; offices and parking facilities of the court clerks, the United States attorney, and the United States marshal; probation and parole offices; and adjoining corridors and parking facilities of any court of the United States. See 18 U.S.C. § 930(f)(3).*

3. *"School zone" is defined at 18 U.S.C. § 922(q). A sentence of imprisonment under 18 U.S.C. § 922(q) must run consecutively to any sentence of imprisonment imposed for any other offense. In order to comply with the statute, when the guideline range is based on the underlying offense, and the defendant is convicted both of the underlying offense and 18 U.S.C. § 922(q), the court should apportion the sentence between the count for the underlying offense and the count under 18 U.S.C. § 922(q). For example, if the guideline range is 30-37 months and the court determines "total punishment" of 36 months is appropriate, a sentence of 30 months for the underlying offense, plus 6 months under 18 U.S.C. § 922(q) would satisfy this requirement.*

4. *Where the firearm was brandished, discharged, or otherwise used, in a federal facility, federal court facility, or school zone, and the cross reference from subsection (c)(1) does not apply, an upward departure may be warranted.*

Historical Note: Effective November 1, 1989 (see Appendix C, amendment 191). Amended effective November 1, 1991 (see Appendix C, amendment 374).

* * * * *

3. MAILING INJURIOUS ARTICLES

Historical Note: Effective November 1, 1987. Amended effective November 1, 1993 (see Appendix C, amendment 481).

§2K3.1. [Deleted]

Historical Note: Section 2K3.1 (Unlawfully Transporting Hazardous Materials in Commerce), effective November 1, 1987, was deleted by consolidation with §2Q1.2 effective November 1, 1993 (see Appendix C, amendment 481).

§2K3.2. Feloniously Mailing Injurious Articles

(a) Base Offense Level (Apply the greater):

(1) If the offense was committed with intent (A) to kill or injure any person, or (B) to injure the mails or other property, apply §2X1.1 (Attempt, Solicitation, or Conspiracy) in respect to the intended offense; or

(2) If death resulted, apply the most analogous offense guideline from Chapter Two, Part A, Subpart 1 (Homicide).

Commentary

Statutory Provision: *18 U.S.C. § 1716 (felony provisions only).*

Background: *This guideline applies only to the felony provisions of 18 U.S.C. § 1716. The Commission has not promulgated a guideline for the misdemeanor provisions of this statute.*

Historical Note: Effective November 1, 1990 (see Appendix C, amendment 334).

PART L - OFFENSES INVOLVING IMMIGRATION, NATURALIZATION, AND PASSPORTS

1. IMMIGRATION

§2L1.1. Smuggling, Transporting, or Harboring an Unlawful Alien

(a) Base Offense Level:

(1) **20**, if the defendant was convicted under 8 U.S.C. § 1327 of a violation involving an alien who previously was deported after a conviction for an aggravated felony; or

(2) **9**, otherwise.

(b) Specific Offense Characteristics

(1) If the defendant committed the offense other than for profit, and the base offense level is determined under subsection (a)(2), decrease by **3** levels.

(2) If the offense involved the smuggling, transporting, or harboring of six or more unlawful aliens, increase as follows:

	Number of Unlawful Aliens Smuggled, Transported, or Harbored	Increase in Level
(A)	6-24	add **2**
(B)	25-99	add **4**
(C)	100 or more	add **6**.

(3) If the defendant is an unlawful alien who has been deported (voluntarily or involuntarily) on one or more occasions prior to the instant offense, and the offense level determined above is less than level **8**, increase to level **8**.

Commentary

Statutory Provisions: 8 U.S.C. §§ 1324(a), 1327. For additional statutory provision(s), see Appendix A (Statutory Index).

Application Notes:

1. *"For profit" means for financial gain or commercial advantage, but this definition does not include a defendant who commits the offense solely in return for his own entry or transportation. The "number of unlawful aliens smuggled, transported, or harbored" does not include the defendant.*

2. *For the purposes of §3B1.1 (Aggravating Role), the aliens smuggled, transported, or harbored are not considered participants unless they actively assisted in the smuggling, transporting, or harboring of others.*

3. *For the purposes of §3B1.2 (Mitigating Role), a defendant who commits the offense solely in return for his own entry or transportation is not entitled to a reduction for a minor or minimal role. This is because the reduction at §2L1.1(b)(1) applies to such a defendant.*

4. *Where the defendant smuggled, transported, or harbored an alien knowing that the alien intended to enter the United States to engage in subversive activity, drug trafficking, or other serious criminal behavior, an upward departure may be warranted.*

5. *If the offense involved dangerous or inhumane treatment, death or bodily injury, possession of a dangerous weapon, or substantially more than 100 aliens, an upward departure may be warranted.*

6. *"Aggravated felony" is defined in the Commentary to §2L1.2 (Unlawfully Entering or Remaining in the United States).*

Background: *This section includes the most serious immigration offenses covered under the Immigration Reform and Control Act of 1986. A specific offense characteristic provides a reduction if the defendant did not commit the offense for profit. The offense level increases with the number of unlawful aliens smuggled, transported, or harbored. In large scale cases, an additional adjustment from §3B1.1 (Aggravating Role) typically will apply to the most culpable defendants.*

Historical Note: Effective November 1, 1987. Amended effective January 15, 1988 (see Appendix C, amendments 35, 36, and 37); November 1, 1989 (see Appendix C, amendment 192); November 1, 1990 (see Appendix C, amendment 335); November 1, 1991 (see Appendix C, amendment 375); November 1, 1992 (see Appendix C, amendment 450).

§2L1.2. Unlawfully Entering or Remaining in the United States

(a) Base Offense Level: **8**

(b) Specific Offense Characteristics

If more than one applies, use the greater:

(1) If the defendant previously was deported after a conviction for a felony, other than a felony involving violation of the immigration laws, increase by **4** levels.

(2) If the defendant previously was deported after a conviction for an aggravated felony, increase by **16** levels.

Commentary

Statutory Provisions: 8 U.S.C. § 1325(a) (second or subsequent offense only), 8 U.S.C. § 1326. For additional statutory provision(s), see Appendix A (Statutory Index).

Application Notes:

1. *This guideline applies only to felonies. A first offense under 8 U.S.C. § 1325(a) is a Class B misdemeanor for which no guideline has been promulgated. A prior sentence for such offense, however, is to be considered under the provisions of Chapter Four, Part A (Criminal History).*

2. *In the case of a defendant with repeated prior instances of deportation without criminal conviction, a sentence at or near the maximum of the applicable guideline range may be warranted.*

3. *A 4-level increase is provided under subsection (b)(1) in the case of a defendant who was previously deported after a conviction for a felony, other than a felony involving a violation of the immigration laws.*

4. *A 16-level increase is provided under subsection (b)(2) in the case of a defendant who was previously deported after a conviction for an aggravated felony.*

5. *An adjustment under subsection (b)(1) or (b)(2) for a prior felony conviction applies in addition to any criminal history points added for such conviction in Chapter Four, Part A (Criminal History).*

6. *"Deported after a conviction," as used in subsections (b)(1) and (b)(2), means that the deportation was subsequent to the conviction, whether or not the deportation was in response to such conviction.*

7. *"Aggravated felony," as used in subsection (b)(2), means murder; any illicit trafficking in any controlled substance (as defined in 21 U.S.C. § 802), including any drug trafficking crime as defined in 18 U.S.C. § 924(c)(2); any illicit trafficking in any firearms or destructive devices as defined in 18 U.S.C. § 921; any offense described in 18 U.S.C. § 1956 (relating to laundering of monetary instruments); any crime of violence (as defined in 18 U.S.C. § 16, not including a purely political offense) for which the term of imprisonment imposed (regardless of any suspension of such imprisonment) is at least five years; or any attempt or conspiracy to commit any such act. The term "aggravated felony" applies to offenses described in the previous sentence whether in violation of federal or state law and also applies to offenses described in the previous sentence in violation of foreign law for which the term of imprisonment was completed within the previous 15 years. See 8 U.S.C. § 1101(a)(43).*

Historical Note: Effective November 1, 1987. Amended effective January 15, 1988 (see Appendix C, amendment 38); November 1, 1989 (see Appendix C, amendment 193); November 1, 1991 (see Appendix C, amendment 375).

§2L1.3. [Deleted]

Historical Note: Section 2L1.3 (Engaging in a Pattern of Unlawful Employment of Aliens), effective November 1, 1987, was deleted effective November 1, 1989 (see Appendix C, amendment 194).

* * * * *

2. NATURALIZATION AND PASSPORTS

§2L2.1. Trafficking in a Document Relating to Naturalization, Citizenship, or Legal Resident Status, or a United States Passport; False Statement in Respect to the Citizenship or Immigration Status of Another; Fraudulent Marriage to Assist Alien to Evade Immigration Law

(a) Base Offense Level: **9**

(b) Specific Offense Characteristics

(1) If the defendant committed the offense other than for profit, decrease by **3** levels.

(2) If the offense involved six or more sets of documents or passports, increase as follows:

	Number of Sets of Documents/Passports	Increase in Level
(A)	6-24	add **2**
(B)	25-99	add **4**
(C)	100 or more	add **6**.

Commentary

Statutory Provisions: 8 U.S.C. §§ 1160(b)(7)(A), 1185(a)(3), (4), 1325(b), (c); 18 U.S.C. §§ 1015, 1028, 1425-1427, 1542, 1544, 1546.

Application Notes:

1. *"For profit" means for financial gain or commercial advantage.*

2. *Where it is established that multiple documents are part of a set intended for use by a single person, treat the documents as one set.*

Historical Note: Effective November 1, 1987. Amended effective November 1, 1989 (see Appendix C, amendment 195); November 1, 1992 (see Appendix C, amendment 450); November 1, 1993 (see Appendix C, amendment 481).

§2L2.2. Fraudulently Acquiring Documents Relating to Naturalization, Citizenship, or Legal Resident Status for Own Use; False Personation or Fraudulent Marriage by Alien to Evade Immigration Law; Fraudulently Acquiring or Improperly Using a United States Passport

(a) Base Offense Level: **6**

(b) Specific Offense Characteristic

(1) If the defendant is an unlawful alien who has been deported (voluntarily or involuntarily) on one or more occasions prior to the instant offense, increase by **2** levels.

Commentary

Statutory Provisions: 8 U.S.C. §§ 1160(b)(7)(A), 1185(a)(3), (5), 1325(b), (c); 18 U.S.C. §§ 911, 1015, 1028, 1423-1426, 1542-1544, 1546.

Application Note:

1. *For the purposes of Chapter Three, Part D (Multiple Counts), a conviction for unlawfully entering or remaining in the United States (§2L1.2) arising from the same course of conduct is treated as a closely related count, and is therefore grouped with an offense covered by this guideline.*

Historical Note: Effective November 1, 1987. Amended effective January 15, 1988 (see Appendix C, amendment 39); November 1, 1989 (see Appendix C, amendment 196); November 1, 1992 (see Appendix C, amendment 450); November 1, 1993 (see Appendix C, amendment 481).

§2L2.3. [Deleted]

Historical Note: Section 2L2.3 (Trafficking in a United States Passport), effective November 1, 1987, amended effective November 1, 1989 (see Appendix C, amendment 197) and November 1, 1992 (see Appendix C, amendment 450), was deleted by consolidation with §2L2.1 effective November 1, 1993 (see Appendix C, amendment 481).

§2L2.4. [Deleted]

Historical Note: Section 2L2.4 (Fraudulently Acquiring or Improperly Using a United States Passport), effective November 1, 1987, amended effective January 15, 1988 (see Appendix C, amendment 40) and November 1, 1989 (see Appendix C, amendment 198), was deleted by consolidation with §2L2.2 effective November 1, 1993 (see Appendix C, amendment 481).

§2L2.5. Failure to Surrender Canceled Naturalization Certificate

(a) Base Offense Level: **6**

Commentary

Statutory Provision: 18 U.S.C. § 1428.

Historical Note: Effective November 1, 1987.

PART M - OFFENSES INVOLVING NATIONAL DEFENSE

1. TREASON

§2M1.1. Treason

(a) Base Offense Level:

(1) **43**, if the conduct is tantamount to waging war against the United States;

(2) the offense level applicable to the most analogous offense, otherwise.

Commentary

Statutory Provision: 18 U.S.C. § 2381.

Background: Treason is a rarely prosecuted offense that could encompass a relatively broad range of conduct, including many of the more specific offenses in this Part. The guideline contemplates imposition of the maximum penalty in the most serious cases, with reference made to the most analogous offense guideline in lesser cases.

Historical Note: Effective November 1, 1987.

* * * * *

2. SABOTAGE

§2M2.1. Destruction of, or Production of Defective, War Material, Premises, or Utilities

(a) Base Offense Level: **32**

Commentary

Statutory Provisions: 18 U.S.C. § 2153, 2154; 42 U.S.C. § 2284.

Application Note:

1. *Violations of 42 U.S.C. § 2284 are included in this section where the defendant was convicted of acting with intent to injure the United States or aid a foreign nation.*

Historical Note: Effective November 1, 1987. Amended effective November 1, 1993 (see Appendix C, amendment 481).

§2M2.2. [Deleted]

Historical Note: Section 2M2.2 (Production of Defective War Material, Premises, or Utilities), effective November 1, 1987, was deleted by consolidation with §2M2.1 effective November 1, 1993 (see Appendix C, amendment 481).

§2M2.3. Destruction of, or Production of Defective, National Defense Material, Premises, or Utilities

(a) Base Offense Level: **26**

Commentary

Statutory Provisions: 18 U.S.C. § 2155, 2156; 42 U.S.C. § 2284.

Application Note:

1. *Violations of 42 U.S.C. § 2284 not included in §2M2.1 are included in this section.*

Historical Note: Effective November 1, 1987. Amended effective November 1, 1993 (see Appendix C, amendment 481).

§2M2.4. [Deleted]

Historical Note: Section 2M2.4 (Production of Defective National Defense Material, Premises, or Utilities), effective November 1, 1987, was deleted by consolidation with §2M2.3 effective November 1, 1993 (see Appendix C, amendment 481).

* * * * *

3. ESPIONAGE AND RELATED OFFENSES

§2M3.1. Gathering or Transmitting National Defense Information to Aid a Foreign Government

(a) Base Offense Level:

(1) **42**, if top secret information was gathered or transmitted; or

(2) **37**, otherwise.

Commentary

Statutory Provisions: 18 U.S.C. § 794; 42 U.S.C. §§ 2274(a), (b), 2275.

Application Notes:

1. *"Top secret information" is information that, if disclosed, "reasonably could be expected to cause exceptionally grave damage to the national security." Executive Order 12356.*

2. *The Commission has set the base offense level in this subpart on the assumption that the information at issue bears a significant relation to the nation's security, and that the revelation will significantly and adversely affect security interests. When revelation is likely to cause little or no harm, a downward departure may be warranted. See Chapter Five, Part K (Departures).*

3. *The court may depart from the guidelines upon representation by the President or his duly authorized designee that the imposition of a sanction other than authorized by the guideline is necessary to protect national security or further the objectives of the nation's foreign policy.*

Background: Offense level distinctions in this subpart are generally based on the classification of the information gathered or transmitted. This classification, in turn, reflects the importance of the information to the national security.

Historical Note: Effective November 1, 1987.

§2M3.2. Gathering National Defense Information

(a) Base Offense Level:

(1) **35**, if top secret information was gathered; or

(2) **30**, otherwise.

Commentary

Statutory Provisions: 18 U.S.C. § 793(a), (b), (c), (d), (e), (g). For additional statutory provision(s), see Appendix A (Statutory Index).

Application Notes:

1. *See Commentary to §2M3.1.*

2. *If the defendant is convicted under 18 U.S.C. § 793(d) or (e), §2M3.3 may apply. See Commentary to §2M3.3.*

Background: The statutes covered in this section proscribe diverse forms of obtaining and transmitting national defense information with intent or reason to believe the information would injure the United States or be used to the advantage of a foreign government.

Historical Note: Effective November 1, 1987.

§2M3.3. Transmitting National Defense Information; Disclosure of Classified Cryptographic Information; Unauthorized Disclosure to a Foreign Government or a Communist Organization of Classified Information by Government Employee; Unauthorized Receipt of Classified Information

(a) Base Offense Level:

(1) **29**, if top secret information; or

(2) **24**, otherwise.

Commentary

Statutory Provisions: 18 U.S.C. §§ 793(d), (e), (g), 798; 50 U.S.C. § 783(b), (c).

Application Notes:

1. *See Commentary to §2M3.1.*

2. *If the defendant was convicted of 18 U.S.C. § 793(d) or (e) for the willful transmission or communication of intangible information with reason to believe that it could be used to the injury of the United States or the advantage of a foreign nation, apply §2M3.2.*

Background: The statutes covered in this section proscribe willfully transmitting or communicating to a person not entitled to receive it a document, writing, code book, signal book, sketch, photograph, photographic negative, blueprint, plan, map, model, instrument, appliance, or note relating to the national defense. Proof that the item was communicated with reason to believe that it could be used to the injury of the United States or the advantage of a foreign nation is required only where intangible information is communicated under 18 U.S.C. § 793(d) or (e).

This section also covers statutes that proscribe the disclosure of classified information concerning cryptographic or communication intelligence to the detriment of the United States or for the benefit of a foreign government, the unauthorized disclosure to a foreign government or a communist organization of classified information by a government employee, and the unauthorized receipt of classified information.

Historical Note: Effective November 1, 1987. Amended effective November 1, 1993 (see Appendix C, amendment 481).

§2M3.4. Losing National Defense Information

(a) Base Offense Level:

(1) **18**, if top secret information was lost; or

(2) **13**, otherwise.

Commentary

Statutory Provision: 18 U.S.C. § 793(f).

Application Note:

1. See Commentary to §2M3.1.

Background: Offenses prosecuted under this statute generally do not involve subversive conduct on behalf of a foreign power, but rather the loss of classified information by the gross negligence of an employee of the federal government or a federal contractor.

Historical Note: Effective November 1, 1987.

§2M3.5. Tampering with Restricted Data Concerning Atomic Energy

(a) Base Offense Level: **24**

Commentary

Statutory Provision: 42 U.S.C. § 2276.

Application Note:

1. See Commentary to §2M3.1.

Historical Note: Effective November 1, 1987.

§2M3.6. [Deleted]

Historical Note: Section 2M3.6 (Disclosure of Classified Cryptographic Information), effective November 1, 1987, was deleted by consolidation with §2M3.3 effective November 1, 1993 (see Appendix C, amendment 481).

§2M3.7. [Deleted]

Historical Note: Section 2M3.7 (Unauthorized Disclosure to Foreign Government or a Communist Organization of Classified Information by Government Employee), effective November 1, 1987, was deleted by consolidation with §2M3.3 effective November 1, 1993 (see Appendix C, amendment 481).

§2M3.8. [Deleted]

Historical Note: Section 2M3.8 (Receipt of Classified Information), effective November 1, 1987, was deleted by consolidation with §2M3.3 effective November 1, 1993 (see Appendix C, amendment 481).

§2M3.9. <u>Disclosure of Information Identifying a Covert Agent</u>

(a) Base Offense Level:

(1) **30**, if the information was disclosed by a person with, or who had authorized access to classified information identifying a covert agent; or

(2) **25**, if the information was disclosed by a person with authorized access only to other classified information.

<u>*Commentary*</u>

<u>Statutory Provision</u>: 50 U.S.C. § 421.

<u>Application Notes</u>:

1. *<u>See</u> Commentary to §2M3.1.*

2. *This guideline applies only to violations of 50 U.S.C. § 421 by persons who have or previously had authorized access to classified information. This guideline does not apply to violations of 50 U.S.C. § 421 by defendants, including journalists, who disclosed such information without having or having had authorized access to classified information. Violations of 50 U.S.C. § 421 not covered by this guideline may vary in the degree of harm they inflict, and the court should impose a sentence that reflects such harm. <u>See</u> §2X5.1 (Other Offenses).*

<u>Background</u>: The alternative base offense levels reflect a statutory distinction by providing a greater base offense level for a violation of 50 U.S.C. § 421 by an official who has or had authorized access to classified information identifying a covert agent than for a violation by an official with authorized access only to other classified information. This guideline does not apply to violations of 50 U.S.C. § 421 by defendants who disclosed such information without having, or having had, authorized access to classified information.

<u>Historical Note</u>: Effective November 1, 1987.

* * * * *

4. EVASION OF MILITARY SERVICE

§2M4.1. <u>Failure to Register and Evasion of Military Service</u>

(a) Base Offense Level: **6**

(b) Specific Offense Characteristic

(1) If the offense occurred at a time when persons were being inducted for compulsory military service, increase by **6** levels.

Commentary

Statutory Provision: 50 U.S.C. App. § 462.

Application Note:

1. *Subsection (b)(1) does not distinguish between whether the offense was committed in peacetime or during time of war or armed conflict. If the offense was committed when persons were being inducted for compulsory military service during time of war or armed conflict, an upward departure may be warranted.*

Historical Note: Effective November 1, 1987. Amended effective November 1, 1990 (see Appendix C, amendment 336).

* * * * *

5. PROHIBITED FINANCIAL TRANSACTIONS AND EXPORTS

§2M5.1. Evasion of Export Controls

(a) Base Offense Level (Apply the greater):

(1) **22**, if national security or nuclear proliferation controls were evaded; or

(2) **14.**

Commentary

Statutory Provisions: 50 U.S.C. App. §§ 2401-2420.

Application Notes:

1. *In the case of a violation during time of war or armed conflict, an upward departure may be warranted.*

2. *In determining the sentence within the applicable guideline range, the court may consider the degree to which the violation threatened a security interest of the United States, the volume of commerce involved, the extent of planning or sophistication, and whether there were multiple occurrences. Where such factors are present in an extreme form, a departure from the guidelines may be warranted. See Chapter Five, Part K (Departures).*

3. *In addition to the provisions for imprisonment, 50 U.S.C. App. § 2410 contains provisions for criminal fines and forfeiture as well as civil penalties. The maximum fine for individual defendants is $250,000. In the case of corporations, the maximum fine is five times the value of the exports involved or $1 million, whichever is greater. When national security controls are violated, in addition to any other sanction, the defendant is subject to forfeiture of any interest in, security of, or claim against: any goods or tangible items that were the subject of the*

violation; property used to export or attempt to export that was the subject of the violation; and any proceeds obtained directly or indirectly as a result of the violation.

Historical Note: Effective November 1, 1987.

§2M5.2. Exportation of Arms, Munitions, or Military Equipment or Services Without Required Validated Export License

(a) Base Offense Level:

(1) **22**, except as provided in subdivision (2) below;

(2) **14**, if the offense involved only non-fully automatic small arms (rifles, handguns, or shotguns), and the number of weapons did not exceed ten.

Commentary

Statutory Provisions: 22 U.S.C. §§ 2778, 2780.

Application Notes:

1. *Under 22 U.S.C. § 2778, the President is authorized, through a licensing system administered by the Department of State, to control exports of defense articles and defense services that he deems critical to a security or foreign policy interest of the United States. The items subject to control constitute the United States Munitions List, which is set out in 22 C.F.R. Part 121.1. Included in this list are such things as military aircraft, helicopters, artillery, shells, missiles, rockets, bombs, vessels of war, explosives, military and space electronics, and certain firearms.*

   The base offense level assumes that the offense conduct was harmful or had the potential to be harmful to a security or foreign policy interest of the United States. In the unusual case where the offense conduct posed no such risk, a downward departure may be warranted. In the case of a violation during time of war or armed conflict, an upward departure may be warranted. See Chapter Five, Part K (Departures).

2. *In determining the sentence within the applicable guideline range, the court may consider the degree to which the violation threatened a security or foreign policy interest of the United States, the volume of commerce involved, the extent of planning or sophistication, and whether there were multiple occurrences. Where such factors are present in an extreme form, a departure from the guidelines may be warranted.*

Historical Note: Effective November 1, 1987. Amended effective November 1, 1990 (see Appendix C, amendment 337).

* * * * *

6. ATOMIC ENERGY

§2M6.1. Unlawful Acquisition, Alteration, Use, Transfer, or Possession of Nuclear Material, Weapons, or Facilities

(a) Base Offense Level: **30**

(b) Specific Offense Characteristic

(1) If the offense was committed with intent to injure the United States or to aid a foreign nation, increase by **12** levels.

Commentary

Statutory Provisions: 42 U.S.C. §§ 2077(b), 2122, 2131. Also, 18 U.S.C. § 831 (only where the conduct is similar to that proscribed by the aforementioned statutory provisions). For additional statutory provision(s), see Appendix A (Statutory Index).

Historical Note: Effective November 1, 1987.

§2M6.2. Violation of Other Federal Atomic Energy Agency Statutes, Rules, and Regulations

(a) Base Offense Level (Apply the greater):

(1) **30**, if the offense was committed with intent to injure the United States or to aid a foreign nation; or

(2) **6**.

Commentary

Statutory Provision: 42 U.S.C. § 2273.

Background: This section applies to offenses related to nuclear energy not specifically addressed elsewhere. This provision covers, for example, violations of statutes dealing with rules and regulations, license conditions, and orders of the Nuclear Regulatory Commission and the Department of Energy.

Historical Note: Effective November 1, 1987. Amended effective November 1, 1990 (see Appendix C, amendment 359).

PART N - OFFENSES INVOLVING FOOD, DRUGS, AGRICULTURAL PRODUCTS, AND ODOMETER LAWS

1. TAMPERING WITH CONSUMER PRODUCTS

§2N1.1. Tampering or Attempting to Tamper Involving Risk of Death or Bodily Injury

(a) Base Offense Level: **25**

(b) Specific Offense Characteristic

(1) (A) If any victim sustained permanent or life-threatening bodily injury, increase by **4** levels; (B) if any victim sustained serious bodily injury, increase by **2** levels; or (C) if the degree of injury is between that specified in subdivisions (A) and (B), increase by **3** levels.

(c) Cross References

(1) If the offense resulted in death, apply §2A1.1 (First Degree Murder) if the death was caused intentionally or knowingly, or §2A1.2 (Second Degree Murder) in any other case.

(2) If the offense was tantamount to attempted murder, apply §2A2.1 (Assault With Intent to Commit Murder; Attempted Murder) if the resulting offense level is greater than that determined above.

(3) If the offense involved extortion, apply §2B3.2 (Extortion by Force or Threat of Injury or Serious Damage) if the resulting offense level is greater than that determined above.

(d) Special Instruction

(1) If the defendant is convicted of a single count involving (A) the death or permanent, life-threatening, or serious bodily injury of more than one victim, or (B) conduct tantamount to the attempted murder of more than one victim, Chapter Three, Part D (Multiple Counts) shall be applied as if the defendant had been convicted of a separate count for each such victim.

<u>Commentary</u>

<u>Statutory Provisions:</u> *18 U.S.C. § 1365(a), (e).*

<u>Application Notes:</u>

1. *The base offense level reflects that this offense typically poses a risk of death or serious bodily injury to one or more victims; or causes, or is intended to cause, bodily injury. Where the offense posed a substantial risk of death or serious bodily injury to numerous victims, or caused extreme psychological injury or substantial property damage or monetary loss, an upward departure may be warranted. In the unusual case in which the offense did not cause a risk of*

death or serious bodily injury, and neither caused nor was intended to cause bodily injury, a downward departure may be warranted.

2. *The special instruction in subsection (d)(1) applies whether the offense level is determined under subsection (b)(1) or by use of a cross reference in subsection (c).*

Historical Note: Effective November 1, 1987. Amended effective November 1, 1990 (see Appendix C, amendment 338); November 1, 1991 (see Appendix C, amendment 376).

§2N1.2. Providing False Information or Threatening to Tamper with Consumer Products

(a) Base Offense Level: **16**

(b) Cross Reference

(1) If the offense involved extortion, apply §2B3.2 (Extortion by Force or Threat of Injury or Serious Damage).

Commentary

Statutory Provisions: 18 U.S.C. § 1365(c), (d).

Application Note:

1. *If death or bodily injury, extreme psychological injury, or substantial property damage or monetary loss resulted, an upward departure may be warranted. See Chapter Five, Part K (Departures).*

Historical Note: Effective November 1, 1987. Amended effective November 1, 1990 (see Appendix C, amendment 339).

§2N1.3. Tampering With Intent to Injure Business

(a) Base Offense Level: **12**

Commentary

Statutory Provision: 18 U.S.C. § 1365(b).

Application Note:

1. *If death or bodily injury, extreme psychological injury, or substantial property damage or monetary loss resulted, an upward departure may be warranted. See Chapter Five, Part K (Departures).*

Historical Note: Effective November 1, 1987.

* * * * *

2. FOOD, DRUGS, AND AGRICULTURAL PRODUCTS

§2N2.1. Violations of Statutes and Regulations Dealing With Any Food, Drug, Biological Product, Device, Cosmetic, or Agricultural Product

(a) Base Offense Level: **6**

(b) Cross References

(1) If the offense involved fraud, apply §2F1.1 (Fraud and Deceit).

(2) If the offense was committed in furtherance of, or to conceal, an offense covered by another offense guideline, apply that other offense guideline if the resulting offense level is greater than that determined above.

Commentary

Statutory Provisions: 7 U.S.C. §§ 150bb, 150gg; 21 U.S.C. §§ 115, 117, 122, 134-134e, 151-158, 331, 333(a)(1), (a)(2), (b), 458-461, 463, 466, 610, 611, 614, 617, 619, 620, 642-644, 676; 42 U.S.C. § 262. For additional statutory provision(s), see Appendix A (Statutory Index).

Application Notes:

1. *This guideline assumes a regulatory offense that involved knowing or reckless conduct. Where only negligence was involved, a downward departure may be warranted. See Chapter Five, Part K (Departures).*

2. *The cross reference at subsection (b)(1) addresses cases in which the offense involved fraud. The cross reference at subsection (b)(2) addresses cases in which the offense was committed in furtherance of, or to conceal, an offense covered by another offense guideline (e.g., theft, bribery, revealing trade secrets, or destruction of property).*

3. *If death or bodily injury, extreme psychological injury, property damage or monetary loss resulted, an upward departure may be warranted. See Chapter Five, Part K (Departures).*

4. *The Commission has not promulgated a guideline for violations of 21 U.S.C. § 333(e) (offenses involving human growth hormones). Offenses involving anabolic steroids are covered by Chapter Two, Part D (Offenses Involving Drugs). In the case of an offense involving a substance purported to be an anabolic steroid, but not containing any active ingredient, apply §2F1.1 (Fraud and Deceit) with "loss" measured by the amount paid, or to be paid, by the victim for such substance.*

Historical Note: Effective November 1, 1987. Amended effective November 1, 1990 (see Appendix C, amendment 340); November 1, 1991 (see Appendix C, amendment 432); November 1, 1992 (see Appendix C, amendment 451).

* * * * *

3. ODOMETER LAWS AND REGULATIONS

§2N3.1. Odometer Laws and Regulations

(a) Base Offense Level: **6**

(b) Cross Reference

(1) If the offense involved more than one vehicle, apply §2F1.1 (Fraud and Deceit).

Commentary

Statutory Provisions: 15 U.S.C. §§ 1983-1988, 1990c.

Background: The base offense level takes into account the deceptive aspect of the offense assuming a single vehicle was involved. If more than one vehicle was involved, the guideline for fraud and deception, §2F1.1, is to be applied because it is designed to deal with a pattern or scheme.

Historical Note: Effective November 1, 1987. Amended effective November 1, 1989 (see Appendix C, amendment 199).

PART P - OFFENSES INVOLVING PRISONS AND CORRECTIONAL FACILITIES

§2P1.1. Escape, Instigating or Assisting Escape

(a) Base Offense Level:

(1) **13**, if the custody or confinement is by virtue of an arrest on a charge of felony, or conviction of any offense;

(2) **8**, otherwise.

(b) Specific Offense Characteristics

(1) If the use or the threat of force against any person was involved, increase by **5** levels.

(2) If the defendant escaped from non-secure custody and returned voluntarily within ninety-six hours, decrease the offense level under §2P1.1(a)(1) by **7** levels or the offense level under §2P1.1(a)(2) by **4** levels. *Provided*, however, that this reduction shall not apply if the defendant, while away from the facility, committed any federal, state, or local offense punishable by a term of imprisonment of one year or more.

(3) If the defendant escaped from the non-secure custody of a community corrections center, community treatment center, "halfway house," or similar facility, and subsection (b)(2) is not applicable, decrease the offense level under subsection (a)(1) by **4** levels or the offense level under subsection (a)(2) by **2** levels. *Provided*, however, that this reduction shall not apply if the defendant, while away from the facility, committed any federal, state, or local offense punishable by a term of imprisonment of one year or more.

(4) If the defendant was a law enforcement or correctional officer or employee, or an employee of the Department of Justice, at the time of the offense, increase by **2** levels.

Commentary

Statutory Provisions: 18 U.S.C. §§ 751, 752, 755; 28 U.S.C. § 1826. For additional statutory provision(s), see Appendix A (Statutory Index).

Application Notes:

1. "Non-secure custody" means custody with no significant physical restraint (e.g., where a defendant walked away from a work detail outside the security perimeter of an institution; where a defendant failed to return to any institution from a pass or unescorted furlough; or where a defendant escaped from an institution with no physical perimeter barrier).

2. *"Returned voluntarily" includes voluntarily returning to the institution or turning one's self in to a law enforcement authority as an escapee (not in connection with an arrest or other charges).*

3. *If the adjustment in subsection (b)(4) applies, no adjustment is to be made under §3B1.3 (Abuse of Position of Trust or Use of Special Skill).*

4. *If death or bodily injury resulted, an upward departure may be warranted. See Chapter Five, Part K (Departures).*

5. *Criminal history points under Chapter Four, Part A (Criminal History) are to be determined independently of the application of this guideline. For example, in the case of a defendant serving a one-year sentence of imprisonment at the time of the escape, criminal history points from §4A1.1(b) (for the sentence being served at the time of the escape), §4A1.1(d) (custody status), and §4A1.1(e) (recency) would be applicable.*

6. *If the adjustment in subsection (b)(1) applies as a result of conduct that involves an official victim, do not apply §3A1.2 (Official Victim).*

Historical Note: Effective November 1, 1987. Amended effective November 1, 1989 (see Appendix C, amendments 200 and 201); November 1, 1990 (see Appendix C, amendment 341); November 1, 1991 (see Appendix C, amendment 406).

§2P1.2. Providing or Possessing Contraband in Prison

(a) Base Offense Level:

(1) **23**, if the object was a firearm or destructive device.

(2) **13**, if the object was a weapon (other than a firearm or a destructive device), any object that might be used as a weapon or as a means of facilitating escape, ammunition, LSD, PCP, or a narcotic drug.

(3) **6**, if the object was an alcoholic beverage, United States or foreign currency, or a controlled substance (other than LSD, PCP, or a narcotic drug).

(4) **4**, if the object was any other object that threatened the order, discipline, or security of the institution or the life, health, or safety of an individual.

(b) Specific Offense Characteristic

(1) If the defendant was a law enforcement or correctional officer or employee, or an employee of the Department of Justice, at the time of the offense, increase by **2** levels.

(c) Cross Reference

(1) If the defendant is convicted under 18 U.S.C. § 1791(a)(1) and is punishable under 18 U.S.C. § 1791(b)(1), the offense level is **2** plus the offense level from §2D1.1, but in no event less than level **26**.

Commentary

Statutory Provision: 18 U.S.C. § 1791.

Application Notes:

1. *If the adjustment in §2P1.2(b)(1) applies, no adjustment is to be made under §3B1.3 (Abuse of Position of Trust or Use of Special Skill).*

2. *Pursuant to 18 U.S.C. § 1791(c), as amended, a sentence imposed upon an inmate for a violation of 18 U.S.C. § 1791 shall be consecutive to the sentence being served at the time of the violation.*

Historical Note: Effective November 1, 1987. Amended effective November 1, 1989 (see Appendix C, amendments 202 and 203).

§2P1.3. Engaging In, Inciting or Attempting to Incite a Riot Involving Persons in a Facility for Official Detention

(a) Base Offense Level:

(1) **22**, if the offense was committed under circumstances creating a substantial risk of death or serious bodily injury to any person.

(2) **16**, if the offense involved a major disruption to the operation of an institution.

(3) **10**, otherwise.

Commentary

Statutory Provision: 18 U.S.C. § 1792.

Application Note:

1. *If death or bodily injury resulted, an upward departure may be warranted. See Chapter Five, Part K (Departures).*

Historical Note: Effective November 1, 1987.

§2P1.4. [Deleted]

Historical Note: Section 2P1.4 (Trespass on Bureau of Prisons Facilities), effective November 1, 1987, was deleted effective November 1, 1989 (see Appendix C, amendment 204).

PART Q - OFFENSES INVOLVING THE ENVIRONMENT

1. ENVIRONMENT

§2Q1.1. Knowing Endangerment Resulting From Mishandling Hazardous or Toxic Substances, Pesticides or Other Pollutants

(a) Base Offense Level: **24**

Commentary

Statutory Provisions: 33 U.S.C. § 1319(c)(3); 42 U.S.C. § 6928(e).

Application Note:

1. *If death or serious bodily injury resulted, an upward departure may be warranted. See Chapter Five, Part K (Departures).*

Background: This section applies to offenses committed with knowledge that the violation placed another person in imminent danger of death or serious bodily injury.

Historical Note: Effective November 1, 1987.

§2Q1.2. Mishandling of Hazardous or Toxic Substances or Pesticides; Recordkeeping, Tampering, and Falsification; Unlawfully Transporting Hazardous Materials in Commerce

(a) Base Offense Level: **8**

(b) Specific Offense Characteristics

(1) (A) If the offense resulted in an ongoing, continuous, or repetitive discharge, release, or emission of a hazardous or toxic substance or pesticide into the environment, increase by **6** levels; or

(B) if the offense otherwise involved a discharge, release, or emission of a hazardous or toxic substance or pesticide, increase by **4** levels.

(2) If the offense resulted in a substantial likelihood of death or serious bodily injury, increase by **9** levels.

(3) If the offense resulted in disruption of public utilities or evacuation of a community, or if cleanup required a substantial expenditure, increase by **4** levels.

(4) If the offense involved transportation, treatment, storage, or disposal without a permit or in violation of a permit, increase by **4** levels.

(5) If a recordkeeping offense reflected an effort to conceal a substantive environmental offense, use the offense level for the substantive offense.

(6) If the offense involved a simple recordkeeping or reporting violation only, decrease by **2** levels.

Commentary

Statutory Provisions: 7 U.S.C. §§ 136j-136l; 15 U.S.C. §§ 2614 and 2615; 33 U.S.C. §§ 1319(c)(1), (2), 1321(b)(5), 1517(b); 42 U.S.C. §§ 300h-2, 6928(d), 7413, 9603(b), (c), (d); 43 U.S.C. §§ 1350, 1816(a), 1822(b); 49 U.S.C. § 1809(b). For additional statutory provision(s), see Appendix A (Statutory Index).

Application Notes:

1. *"Recordkeeping offense" includes both recordkeeping and reporting offenses. The term is to be broadly construed as including failure to report discharges, releases, or emissions where required; the giving of false information; failure to file other required reports or provide necessary information; and failure to prepare, maintain, or provide records as prescribed.*

2. *"Simple recordkeeping or reporting violation" means a recordkeeping or reporting offense in a situation where the defendant neither knew nor had reason to believe that the recordkeeping offense would significantly increase the likelihood of any substantive environmental harm.*

3. *This section applies to offenses involving pesticides or substances designated toxic or hazardous at the time of the offense by statute or regulation. A listing of hazardous and toxic substances in the guidelines would be impractical. Several federal statutes (or regulations promulgated thereunder) list toxics, hazardous wastes and substances, and pesticides. These lists, such as those of toxic pollutants for which effluent standards are published under the Federal Water Pollution Control Act (e.g., 33 U.S.C. § 1317) as well as the designation of hazardous substances under the Comprehensive Environmental Response, Compensation and Liability Act (e.g., 42 U.S.C. § 9601(14)), are revised from time to time. "Toxic" and "hazardous" are defined differently in various statutes, but the common dictionary meanings of the words are not significantly different.*

4. *Except when the adjustment in subsection (b)(6) for simple recordkeeping offenses applies, this section assumes knowing conduct. In cases involving negligent conduct, a downward departure may be warranted.*

5. *Subsection (b)(1) assumes a discharge or emission into the environment resulting in actual environmental contamination. A wide range of conduct, involving the handling of different quantities of materials with widely differing propensities, potentially is covered. Depending upon the harm resulting from the emission, release or discharge, the quantity and nature of the substance or pollutant, the duration of the offense and the risk associated with the violation, a departure of up to two levels in either direction from the offense levels prescribed in these specific offense characteristics may be appropriate.*

6. *Subsection (b)(2) applies to offenses where the public health is seriously endangered. Depending upon the nature of the risk created and the number of people placed at risk, a departure of up to three levels upward or downward may be warranted. If death or serious bodily injury results, a departure would be called for. See Chapter Five, Part K (Departures).*

7. *Subsection (b)(3) provides an enhancement where a public disruption, evacuation or cleanup at substantial expense has been required. Depending upon the nature of the contamination involved, a departure of up to two levels either upward or downward could be warranted.*

8. *Subsection (b)(4) applies where the offense involved violation of a permit, or where there was a failure to obtain a permit when one was required. Depending upon the nature and quantity of the substance involved and the risk associated with the offense, a departure of up to two levels either upward or downward may be warranted.*

9. *Where a defendant has previously engaged in similar misconduct established by a civil adjudication or has failed to comply with an administrative order, an upward departure may be warranted. See §4A1.3 (Adequacy of Criminal History Category).*

Background: This section applies both to substantive violations of the statute governing the handling of pesticides and toxic and hazardous substances and to recordkeeping offenses. The first four specific offense characteristics provide enhancements when the offense involved a substantive violation. The last two specific offense characteristics apply to recordkeeping offenses. Although other sections of the guidelines generally prescribe a base offense level of 6 for regulatory violations, §2Q1.2 prescribes a base offense level of 8 because of the inherently dangerous nature of hazardous and toxic substances and pesticides. A decrease of 2 levels is provided, however, for "simple recordkeeping or reporting violations" under §2Q1.2(b)(6).

Historical Note: Effective November 1, 1987. Amended effective November 1, 1993 (see Appendix C, amendment 481).

§2Q1.3. Mishandling of Other Environmental Pollutants; Recordkeeping, Tampering, and Falsification

(a) Base Offense Level: **6**

(b) Specific Offense Characteristics

(1) (A) If the offense resulted in an ongoing, continuous, or repetitive discharge, release, or emission of a pollutant into the environment, increase by **6** levels; or

(B) if the offense otherwise involved a discharge, release, or emission of a pollutant, increase by **4** levels.

(2) If the offense resulted in a substantial likelihood of death or serious bodily injury, increase by **11** levels.

(3) If the offense resulted in disruption of public utilities or evacuation of a community, or if cleanup required a substantial expenditure, increase by **4** levels.

(4) If the offense involved a discharge without a permit or in violation of a permit, increase by **4** levels.

(5) If a recordkeeping offense reflected an effort to conceal a substantive environmental offense, use the offense level for the substantive offense.

Commentary

Statutory Provisions: *33 U.S.C. §§ 403, 406, 407, 411, 1319(c)(1), (c)(2), 1415(b), 1907, 1908; 42 U.S.C. § 7413. For additional statutory provision(s), see Appendix A (Statutory Index).*

Application Notes:

1. *"Recordkeeping offense" includes both recordkeeping and reporting offenses. The term is to be broadly construed as including failure to report discharges, releases, or emissions where required; the giving of false information; failure to file other required reports or provide necessary information; and failure to prepare, maintain, or provide records as prescribed.*

2. *If the offense involved mishandling of nuclear material, apply §2M6.2 (Violation of Other Federal Atomic Energy Statutes, Rules, and Regulations) rather than this guideline.*

3. *The specific offense characteristics in this section assume knowing conduct. In cases involving negligent conduct, a downward departure may be warranted.*

4. *Subsection (b)(1) assumes a discharge or emission into the environment resulting in actual environmental contamination. A wide range of conduct, involving the handling of different quantities of materials with widely differing propensities, potentially is covered. Depending upon the harm resulting from the emission, release or discharge, the quantity and nature of the substance or pollutant, the duration of the offense and the risk associated with the violation a departure of up to two levels in either direction from that prescribed in these specific offense characteristics may be appropriate.*

5. *Subsection (b)(2) applies to offenses where the public health is seriously endangered. Depending upon the nature of the risk created and the number of people placed at risk, a departure of up to three levels upward or downward may be warranted. If death or serious bodily injury results, a departure would be called for. See Chapter Five, Part K (Departures).*

6. *Subsection (b)(3) provides an enhancement where a public disruption, evacuation or cleanup at substantial expense has been required. Depending upon the nature of the contamination involved, a departure of up to two levels in either direction could be warranted.*

7. *Subsection (b)(4) applies where the offense involved violation of a permit, or where there was a failure to obtain a permit when one was required. Depending upon the nature and quantity of the substance involved and the risk associated with the offense, a departure of up to two levels in either direction may be warranted.*

8. *Where a defendant has previously engaged in similar misconduct established by a civil adjudication or has failed to comply with an administrative order, an upward departure may be warranted. See §4A1.3 (Adequacy of Criminal History Category).*

Background: *This section parallels §2Q1.2 but applies to offenses involving substances which are not pesticides and are not designated as hazardous or toxic.*

Historical Note: Effective November 1, 1987. Amended effective November 1, 1989 (see Appendix C, amendment 205).

§2Q1.4. Tampering or Attempted Tampering with Public Water System

(a) Base Offense Level: **18**

(b) Specific Offense Characteristics

(1) If a risk of death or serious bodily injury was created, increase by **6** levels.

(2) If the offense resulted in disruption of a public water system or evacuation of a community, or if cleanup required a substantial expenditure, increase by **4** levels.

(3) If the offense resulted in an ongoing, continuous, or repetitive release of a contaminant into a public water system or lasted for a substantial period of time, increase by **2** levels.

(4) If the purpose of the offense was to influence government action or to extort money, increase by **6** levels.

Commentary

Statutory Provision: 42 U.S.C. § 300i-1.

Application Note:

1. *"Serious bodily injury" is defined in the Commentary to §1B1.1 (Application Instructions).*

Historical Note: Effective November 1, 1987. Amended effective November 1, 1989 (see Appendix C, amendment 206).

§2Q1.5. Threatened Tampering with Public Water System

(a) Base Offense Level: **10**

(b) Specific Offense Characteristic

(1) If the threat or attempt resulted in disruption of a public water system or evacuation of a community or a substantial public expenditure, increase by **4** levels.

(c) Cross Reference

(1) If the purpose of the offense was to influence government action or to extort money, apply §2B3.2 (Extortion by Force or Threat of Injury or Serious Damage).

Commentary

Statutory Provision: 42 U.S.C. § 300i-1.

Historical Note: Effective November 1, 1987. Amended effective November 1, 1989 (see Appendix C, amendment 207).

§2Q1.6. Hazardous or Injurious Devices on Federal Lands

(a) Base Offense Level (Apply the greatest):

(1) If the intent was to violate the Controlled Substance Act, apply §2D1.9 (Placing or Maintaining Dangerous Devices on Federal Property to Protect the Unlawful Production of Controlled Substances);

(2) If the intent was to obstruct the harvesting of timber, and property destruction resulted, apply §2B1.3 (Property Damage or Destruction);

(3) If the offense involved reckless disregard to the risk that another person would be placed in danger of death or serious bodily injury under circumstances manifesting extreme indifference to such risk, the offense level from §2A2.2 (Aggravated Assault);

(4) **6**, otherwise.

Commentary

Statutory Provision: 18 U.S.C. § 1864.

Background: The statute covered by this guideline proscribes a wide variety of conduct, ranging from placing nails in trees to interfere with harvesting equipment to placing anti-personnel devices capable of causing death or serious bodily injury to protect the unlawful production of a controlled substance. Subsections (a)(1)-(a)(3) cover the more serious forms of this offense. Subsection (a)(4) provides a minimum offense level of 6 where the intent was to obstruct the harvesting of timber and little or no property damage resulted.

Historical Note: Effective November 1, 1989 (see Appendix C, amendment 208). Amended effective November 1, 1990 (see Appendix C, amendment 313).

* * * * *

2. CONSERVATION AND WILDLIFE

§2Q2.1. Specially Protected Fish, Wildlife, and Plants; Smuggling and Otherwise Unlawfully Dealing in Fish, Wildlife, and Plants

(a) Base Offense Level: **6**

(b) Specific Offense Characteristics

(1) If the offense (A) was committed for pecuniary gain or otherwise involved a commercial purpose; or (B) involved a pattern of similar violations, increase by **2** levels.

(2) If the offense (A) involved fish, wildlife, or plants that were not quarantined as required by law; or (B) otherwise created a significant risk of infestation or disease transmission potentially harmful to humans, fish, wildlife, or plants, increase by **2** levels.

(3) (If more than one applies, use the greater):

(A) If the market value of the fish, wildlife, or plants exceeded $2,000, increase the offense level by the corresponding number of levels from the table in §2F1.1 (Fraud and Deceit); or

(B) If the offense involved (i) marine mammals that are listed as depleted under the Marine Mammal Protection Act (as set forth in 50 C.F.R. § 216.15); (ii) fish, wildlife, or plants that are listed as endangered or threatened by the Endangered Species Act (as set forth in 50 C.F.R. Part 17); or (iii) fish, wildlife, or plants that are listed in Appendix I to the Convention on International Trade in Endangered Species of Wild Fauna or Flora (as set forth in 50 C.F.R. Part 23), increase by **4** levels.

Commentary

Statutory Provisions: 16 U.S.C. §§ 668(a), 707(b), 1174(a), 1338(a), 1375(b), 1540(b), 3373(d); 18 U.S.C. § 545. For additional statutory provision(s), see Appendix A (Statutory Index).

Application Notes:

1. *"For pecuniary gain" means for receipt of, or in anticipation of receipt of, anything of value, whether monetary or in goods or services. Thus, offenses committed for pecuniary gain include both monetary and barter transactions. Similarly, activities designed to increase gross revenue are considered to be committed for pecuniary gain.*

2. *The acquisition of fish, wildlife, or plants for display to the public, whether for a fee or donation and whether by an individual or an organization, including a governmental entity, a private non-profit organization, or a private for-profit organization, shall be considered to involve a "commercial purpose."*

3. *For purposes of subsection (b)(2), the quarantine requirements include those set forth in 9 C.F.R. Part 92, and 7 C.F.R. Chapter III. State quarantine laws are included as well.*

4. *When information is reasonably available, "market value" under subsection (b)(3)(A) shall be based on the fair-market retail price. Where the fair-market retail price is difficult to ascertain, the court may make a reasonable estimate using any reliable information, such as the reasonable replacement or restitution cost or the acquisition and preservation (e.g., taxidermy)*

cost. Market value, however, shall not be based on measurement of aesthetic loss (so called "contingent valuation" methods).

5. *If the offense involved the destruction of a substantial quantity of fish, wildlife, or plants, and the seriousness of the offense is not adequately measured by the market value, an upward departure may be warranted.*

Background: This section applies to violations of the Endangered Species Act, the Bald Eagle Protection Act, the Migratory Bird Treaty, the Marine Mammal Protection Act, the Wild Free-Roaming Horses and Burros Act, the Fur Seal Act, the Lacey Act, and to violations of 18 U.S.C. § 545 where the smuggling activity involved fish, wildlife, or plants.

Historical Note: Effective November 1, 1987. Amended effective January 15, 1988 (see Appendix C, amendment 41); November 1, 1989 (see Appendix C, amendments 209 and 210); November 1, 1991 (see Appendix C, amendment 407); November 1, 1992 (see Appendix C, amendment 452).

§2Q2.2. [Deleted]

Historical Note: Section 2Q2.2 (Lacey Act; Smuggling and Otherwise Unlawfully Dealing in Fish, Wildlife, and Plants), effective November 1, 1987, was deleted by consolidation with §2Q2.1 effective November 1, 1989 (see Appendix C, amendment 209).

PART R - ANTITRUST OFFENSES

§2R1.1. Bid-Rigging, Price-Fixing or Market-Allocation Agreements Among Competitors

(a) Base Offense Level: **10**

(b) Specific Offense Characteristics

(1) If the conduct involved participation in an agreement to submit non-competitive bids, increase by **1** level.

(2) If the volume of commerce attributable to the defendant was more than $400,000, adjust the offense level as follows:

	Volume of Commerce(Apply the Greatest)	Adjustment to Offense Level
(A)	More than $400,000	add **1**
(B)	More than $1,000,000	add **2**
(C)	More than $2,500,000	add **3**
(D)	More than $6,250,000	add **4**
(E)	More than $15,000,000	add **5**
(F)	More than $37,500,000	add **6**
(G)	More than $100,000,000	add **7**.

For purposes of this guideline, the volume of commerce attributable to an individual participant in a conspiracy is the volume of commerce done by him or his principal in goods or services that were affected by the violation. When multiple counts or conspiracies are involved, the volume of commerce should be treated cumulatively to determine a single, combined offense level.

(c) Special Instruction for Fines

(1) For an individual, the guideline fine range shall be from one to five percent of the volume of commerce, but not less than $20,000.

(d) Special Instructions for Fines - Organizations

(1) In lieu of the pecuniary loss under subsection (a)(3) of §8C2.4 (Base Fine), use 20 percent of the volume of affected commerce.

(2) When applying §8C2.6 (Minimum and Maximum Multipliers), neither the minimum nor maximum multiplier shall be less than 0.75.

(3) In a bid-rigging case in which the organization submitted one or more complementary bids, use as the organization's volume of commerce the greater of (A) the volume of commerce done by the organization in the goods or services that were affected by the violation, or (B) the largest contract on which the organization submitted a complementary bid in connection with the bid-rigging conspiracy.

<u>Commentary</u>

<u>Statutory Provision</u>: 15 U.S.C. § 1. For additional statutory provision(s), <u>see</u> Appendix A (Statutory Index).

<u>Application Notes</u>:

1. *The provisions of §3B1.1 (Aggravating Role) and §3B1.2 (Mitigating Role) should be applied to an individual defendant as appropriate to reflect the individual's role in committing the offense. For example, if a sales manager organizes or leads the price-fixing activity of five or more participants, a 4-level increase is called for under §3B1.1. An individual defendant should be considered for a downward adjustment under §3B1.2 for a mitigating role in the offense only if he was responsible in some minor way for his firm's participation in the conspiracy.*

2. *In setting the fine for individuals, the court should consider the extent of the defendant's participation in the offense, his role, and the degree to which he personally profited from the offense (including salary, bonuses, and career enhancement). If the court concludes that the defendant lacks the ability to pay the guideline fine, it should impose community service in lieu of a portion of the fine. The community service should be equally as burdensome as a fine.*

3. *The fine for an organization is determined by applying Chapter Eight (Sentencing of Organizations). In selecting a fine for an organization within the guideline fine range, the court should consider both the gain to the organization from the offense and the loss caused by the organization. It is estimated that the average gain from price-fixing is 10 percent of the selling price. The loss from price-fixing exceeds the gain because, among other things, injury is inflicted upon consumers who are unable or for other reasons do not buy the product at the higher prices. Because the loss from price-fixing exceeds the gain, subsection (d)(1) provides that 20 percent of the volume of affected commerce is to be used in lieu of the pecuniary loss under §8C2.4(a)(3). The purpose for specifying a percent of the volume of commerce is to avoid the time and expense that would be required for the court to determine the actual gain or loss. In cases in which the actual monopoly overcharge appears to be either substantially more or substantially less than 10 percent, this factor should be considered in setting the fine within the guideline fine range.*

4. *Another consideration in setting the fine is that the average level of mark-up due to price-fixing may tend to decline with the volume of commerce involved.*

5. *It is the intent of the Commission that alternatives such as community confinement not be used to avoid imprisonment of antitrust offenders.*

6. *Understatement of seriousness is especially likely in cases involving complementary bids. If, for example, the defendant participated in an agreement not to submit a bid, or to submit an unreasonably high bid, on one occasion, in exchange for his being allowed to win a subsequent bid that he did not in fact win, his volume of commerce would be zero, although he would have contributed to harm that possibly was quite substantial. The court should consider sentences near the top of the guideline range in such cases.*

7. *In the case of a defendant with previous antitrust convictions, a sentence at or even above the maximum of the applicable guideline range may be warranted. <u>See</u> §4A1.3 (Adequacy of Criminal History Category).*

Background: *These guidelines apply to violations of the antitrust laws. Although they are not unlawful in all countries, there is near universal agreement that restrictive agreements among competitors, such as horizontal price-fixing (including bid rigging) and horizontal market-allocation, can cause serious economic harm. There is no consensus, however, about the harmfulness of other types of antitrust offenses, which furthermore are rarely prosecuted and may involve unsettled issues of law. Consequently, only one guideline, which deals with horizontal agreements in restraint of trade, has been promulgated.*

The agreements among competitors covered by this section are almost invariably covert conspiracies that are intended to and serve no purpose other than to restrict output and raise prices, and that are so plainly anticompetitive that they have been recognized as illegal per se, i.e., without any inquiry in individual cases as to their actual competitive effect. The Commission believes that the most effective method to deter individuals from committing this crime is through imposing short prison sentences coupled with large fines. The controlling consideration underlying this guideline is general deterrence.

Under the guidelines, prison terms for these offenders should be much more common, and usually somewhat longer, than typical under pre-guidelines practice. Absent adjustments, the guidelines require confinement of six months or longer in the great majority of cases that are prosecuted, including all bid-rigging cases. The court will have the discretion to impose considerably longer sentences within the guideline ranges. Adjustments from Chapter Three, Part E (Acceptance of Responsibility) and, in rare instances, Chapter Three, Part B (Role in the Offense), may decrease these minimum sentences; nonetheless, in very few cases will the guidelines not require that some confinement be imposed. Adjustments will not affect the level of fines.

Tying the offense level to the scale or scope of the offense is important in order to ensure that the sanction is in fact punitive and that there is an incentive to desist from a violation once it has begun. The offense levels are not based directly on the damage caused or profit made by the defendant because damages are difficult and time consuming to establish. The volume of commerce is an acceptable and more readily measurable substitute. The limited empirical data available as to pre-guidelines practice showed that fines increased with the volume of commerce and the term of imprisonment probably did as well.

The Commission believes that the volume of commerce is liable to be an understated measure of seriousness in some bid-rigging cases. For this reason, and consistent with pre-guidelines practice, the Commission has specified a 1-level increase for bid-rigging.

Substantial fines are an essential part of the sentence. For an individual, the guideline fine range is from one to five percent of the volume of commerce, but not less than $20,000. For an organization, the guideline fine range is determined under Chapter Eight (Sentencing of Organizations), but pursuant to subsection (d)(2), the minimum multiplier is at least 0.75. This multiplier, which requires a minimum fine of 15 percent of the volume of commerce for the least serious case, was selected to provide an effective deterrent to antitrust offenses. At the same time, this minimum multiplier maintains incentives for desired organizational behavior. Because the Department of Justice has a well-established amnesty program for organizations that self-report antitrust offenses, no lower minimum multiplier is needed as an incentive for self-reporting. A minimum multiplier of at least 0.75 ensures that fines imposed in antitrust cases will exceed the average monopoly overcharge.

The Commission believes that most antitrust defendants have the resources and earning capacity to pay the fines called for by this guideline, at least over time on an installment basis. The statutory *maximum fine is $350,000 for individuals and $10,000,000 for organizations, but is increased when there are convictions on multiple counts.*

Historical Note: Effective November 1, 1987. Amended effective November 1, 1989 (see Appendix C, amendments 211 and 303); November 1, 1991 (see Appendix C, amendments 377 and 422).

PART S - MONEY LAUNDERING AND MONETARY TRANSACTION REPORTING

Historical Note: Introductory Commentary to this Part, effective November 1, 1987, was deleted effective November 1, 1990 (see Appendix C, amendment 342).

§2S1.1. Laundering of Monetary Instruments

(a) Base Offense Level:

(1) **23**, if convicted under 18 U.S.C. § 1956(a)(1)(A), (a)(2)(A), or (a)(3)(A);

(2) **20**, otherwise.

(b) Specific Offense Characteristics

(1) If the defendant knew or believed that the funds were the proceeds of an unlawful activity involving the manufacture, importation, or distribution of narcotics or other controlled substances, increase by **3** levels.

(2) If the value of the funds exceeded $100,000, increase the offense level as follows:

	Value (Apply the Greatest)	Increase in Level
(A)	$100,000 or less	no increase
(B)	More than $100,000	add **1**
(C)	More than $200,000	add **2**
(D)	More than $350,000	add **3**
(E)	More than $600,000	add **4**
(F)	More than $1,000,000	add **5**
(G)	More than $2,000,000	add **6**
(H)	More than $3,500,000	add **7**
(I)	More than $6,000,000	add **8**
(J)	More than $10,000,000	add **9**
(K)	More than $20,000,000	add **10**
(L)	More than $35,000,000	add **11**
(M)	More than $60,000,000	add **12**
(N)	More than $100,000,000	add **13**.

(c) Special Instruction for Fines - Organizations

(1) In lieu of the applicable amount from the table in subsection (d) of §8C2.4 (Base Fine), use:

(A) the greater of $250,000 or 100 percent of the value of the funds if subsections (a)(1) and (b)(1) are used to determine the offense level; or

(B) the greater of $200,000 or 70 percent of the value of the funds if subsections (a)(2) and (b)(1) are used to determine the offense level; or

(C) the greater of $200,000 or 70 percent of the value of the funds if subsection (a)(1) but not (b)(1) is used to determine the offense level; or

(D) the greater of $150,000 or 50 percent of the value of the funds if subsection (a)(2) but not (b)(1) is used to determine the offense level.

Commentary

Statutory Provision: 18 U.S.C. § 1956.

Background: The statute covered by this guideline is a part of the Anti-Drug Abuse Act of 1986, and prohibits financial transactions involving funds that are the proceeds of "specified unlawful activity," if such transactions are intended to facilitate that activity, or conceal the nature of the proceeds or avoid a transaction reporting requirement. The maximum term of imprisonment authorized is twenty years.

In keeping with the clear intent of the legislation, this guideline provides for substantial punishment. The punishment is higher than that specified in §2S1.2 and §2S1.3 because of the higher statutory maximum, and the added elements as to source of funds, knowledge, and intent.

A higher base offense level is specified if the defendant is convicted under 18 U.S.C. § 1956(a)(1)(A), (a)(2)(A), or (a)(3)(A) because those subsections apply to defendants who encouraged or facilitated the commission of further crimes. Effective November 18, 1988, 18 U.S.C. § 1956(a)(1)(A) contains two subdivisions. The base offense level of 23 applies to § 1956(a)(1)(A)(i) and (ii).

The amount of money involved is included as a factor because it is an indicator of the magnitude of the criminal enterprise, and the extent to which the defendant aided the enterprise. Narcotics trafficking is included as a factor because of the clearly expressed Congressional intent to adequately punish persons involved in that activity.

Historical Note: Effective November 1, 1987. Amended effective November 1, 1989 (see Appendix C, amendments 212-214); November 1, 1991 (see Appendix C, amendments 378 and 422).

§2S1.2. Engaging in Monetary Transactions in Property Derived from Specified Unlawful Activity

(a) Base Offense Level: **17**

(b) Specific Offense Characteristics

(1) If the defendant knew that the funds were the proceeds of:

(A) an unlawful activity involving the manufacture, importation, or distribution of narcotics or other controlled substances, increase by **5** levels; or

(B) any other specified unlawful activity (see 18 U.S.C. § 1956(c)(7)), increase by **2** levels.

(2) If the value of the funds exceeded $100,000, increase the offense level as specified in §2S1.1(b)(2).

(c) Special Instruction for Fines - Organizations

(1) In lieu of the applicable amount from the table in subsection (d) of §8C2.4 (Base Fine), use:

(A) the greater of $175,000 or 60 percent of the value of the funds if subsection (b)(1)(A) is used to determine the offense level; or

(B) the greater of $150,000 or 50 percent of the value of the funds if subsection (b)(1)(B) is used to determine the offense level.

Commentary

Statutory Provision: 18 U.S.C. § 1957.

Application Note:

1. *"Specified unlawful activity" is defined in 18 U.S.C. § 1956(c)(7) to include racketeering offenses (18 U.S.C. § 1961(1)), drug offenses, and most other serious federal crimes but does not include other money-laundering offenses.*

Background: The statute covered by this guideline is a part of the Anti-Drug Abuse Act of 1986, and prohibits monetary transactions that exceed $10,000 and involve the proceeds of "specified unlawful activity" (as defined in 18 U.S.C. § 1956), if the defendant knows that the funds are "criminally derived property." (Knowledge that the property is from a specified unlawful activity is not an element of the offense.) The maximum term of imprisonment specified is ten years.

The statute is similar to 18 U.S.C. § 1956, but does not require that the recipient exchange or "launder" the funds, that he have knowledge that the funds were proceeds of a specified unlawful activity, nor that he have any intent to further or conceal such an activity. In keeping with the intent of the legislation, this guideline provides for substantial punishment. The offense levels are higher than in §2S1.3 because of the higher statutory maximum and the added element of knowing that the funds were criminally derived property.

The 2-level increase in subsection (b)(1)(B) applies if the defendant knew that the funds were not merely criminally derived, but were in fact the proceeds of a specified unlawful activity. Such a distinction is not made in §2S1.1, because the level of intent required in that section effectively precludes an inference that the defendant was unaware of the nature of the activity.

Historical Note: Effective November 1, 1987. Amended effective November 1, 1989 (see Appendix C, amendment 215); November 1, 1991 (see Appendix C, amendment 422).

§2S1.3. Structuring Transactions to Evade Reporting Requirements; Failure to Report Cash or Monetary Transactions; Failure to File Currency and Monetary Instrument Report; Knowingly Filing False Reports

(a) Base Offense Level: **6** plus the number of offense levels from the table in §2F1.1 (Fraud and Deceit) corresponding to the value of the funds.

(b) Specific Offense Characteristics:

(1) If the defendant knew or believed that the funds were proceeds of unlawful activity, or were intended to promote unlawful activity, increase by **2** levels.

(2) If (A) subsection (b)(1) does not apply; (B) the defendant did not act with reckless disregard of the source of the funds; (C) the funds were the proceeds of lawful activity; and (D) the funds were to be used for a lawful purpose, decrease the offense level to level **6**.

(c) Cross Reference

(1) If the offense was committed for the purposes of violating the Internal Revenue laws, apply the most appropriate guideline from Chapter Two, Part T (Offenses Involving Taxation) if the resulting offense level is greater than that determined above.

Commentary

Statutory Provisions: 26 U.S.C. § 7203 (if a violation based upon 26 U.S.C. § 6050I), § 7206 (if a violation based upon 26 U.S.C. § 6050I); 31 U.S.C. §§ 5313, 5314, 5316, 5324. For additional statutory provision(s), see Appendix A (Statutory Index).

Application Note:

1. *For purposes of this guideline, "value of the funds" means the amount of the funds involved in the structuring or reporting conduct. The relevant statutes require monetary reporting without regard to whether the funds were lawfully or unlawfully obtained.*

Background: The offenses covered by this guideline relate to records and reports of certain transactions involving currency and monetary instruments. These reports include Currency Transaction Reports, Currency and Monetary Instrument Reports, Reports of Foreign Bank and Financial Accounts, and Reports of Cash Payments Over $10,000 Received in a Trade or Business.

Historical Note: Effective November 1, 1987. Amended effective November 1, 1989 (see Appendix C, amendments 216-218); November 1, 1991 (see Appendix C, amendments 379 and 422); November 1, 1993 (see Appendix C, amendment 490).

§2S1.4. [Deleted]

<u>Historical Note</u>: Section 2S1.4 (Failure to File Currency and Monetary Instrument Report), effective November 1, 1991 (<u>see</u> Appendix C, amendments 379 and 422), was deleted by consolidation with §2S1.3 effective November 1, 1993 (<u>see</u> Appendix C, amendment 490).

PART T - OFFENSES INVOLVING TAXATION

1. INCOME TAXES, EMPLOYMENT TAXES, ESTATE TAXES, GIFT TAXES, AND EXCISE TAXES (OTHER THAN ALCOHOL, TOBACCO, AND CUSTOMS TAXES)

Historical Note: Effective November 1, 1987. Amended effective November 1, 1993 (see Appendix C, amendment 491).

Introductory Commentary

The criminal tax laws are designed to protect the public interest in preserving the integrity of the nation's tax system. Criminal tax prosecutions serve to punish the violator and promote respect for the tax laws. Because of the limited number of criminal tax prosecutions relative to the estimated incidence of such violations, deterring others from violating the tax laws is a primary consideration underlying these guidelines. Recognition that the sentence for a criminal tax case will be commensurate with the gravity of the offense should act as a deterrent to would-be violators.

Historical Note: Effective November 1, 1987.

§2T1.1. Tax Evasion; Willful Failure to File Return, Supply Information, or Pay Tax; Fraudulent or False Returns, Statements, or Other Documents

(a) Base Offense Level:

(1) Level from §2T4.1 (Tax Table) corresponding to the tax loss; or

(2) **6**, if there is no tax loss.

(b) Specific Offense Characteristics

(1) If the defendant failed to report or to correctly identify the source of income exceeding $10,000 in any year from criminal activity, increase by **2** levels. If the resulting offense level is less than level **12**, increase to level **12**.

(2) If sophisticated means were used to impede discovery of the existence or extent of the offense, increase by **2** levels.

(c) Special Instructions

For the purposes of this guideline --

(1) If the offense involved tax evasion or a fraudulent or false return, statement, or other document, the tax loss is the total amount of loss that was the object of the offense (i.e., the loss that would have resulted had the offense been successfully completed).

Notes:

(A) If the offense involved filing a tax return in which gross income was underreported, the tax loss shall be treated as equal to 28% of the unreported gross income (34% if the taxpayer is a corporation) plus 100% of any false credits claimed against tax, unless a more accurate determination of the tax loss can be made.

(B) If the offense involved improperly claiming a deduction or an exemption, the tax loss shall be treated as equal to 28% of the amount of the improperly claimed deduction or exemption (34% if the taxpayer is a corporation) plus 100% of any false credits claimed against tax, unless a more accurate determination of the tax loss can be made.

(C) If the offense involved improperly claiming a deduction to provide a basis for tax evasion in the future, the tax loss shall be treated as equal to 28% of the amount of the improperly claimed deduction (34% if the taxpayer is a corporation) plus 100% of any false credits claimed against tax, unless a more accurate determination of the tax loss can be made.

(2) If the offense involved failure to file a tax return, the tax loss is the amount of tax that the taxpayer owed and did not pay.

Note: If the offense involved failure to file a tax return, the tax loss shall be treated as equal to 20% of the gross income (25% if the taxpayer is a corporation) less any tax withheld or otherwise paid, unless a more accurate determination of the tax loss can be made.

(3) If the offense involved willful failure to pay tax, the tax loss is the amount of tax that the taxpayer owed and did not pay.

(4) If the offense involved improperly claiming a refund to which the claimant was not entitled, the tax loss is the amount of the claimed refund to which the claimant was not entitled.

(5) The tax loss is not reduced by any payment of the tax subsequent to the commission of the offense.

Commentary

Statutory Provisions: *26 U.S.C. §§ 7201, 7203 (other than a violation based upon 26 U.S.C. § 6050I), 7206 (other than a violation based upon 26 U.S.C. § 6050I or § 7206(2)), and 7207.*

Application Notes:

1. *"Tax loss" is defined in subsection (c). The tax loss does not include interest or penalties. Although the definition of tax loss corresponds to what is commonly called the "criminal figures," its amount is to be determined by the same rules applicable in determining any other sentencing factor. In some instances, such as when indirect methods of proof are used, the amount of the tax loss may be uncertain; the guidelines contemplate that the court will simply make a reasonable estimate based on the available facts.*

Notes under subsections (c)(1) and (c)(2) address certain situations in income tax cases in which the tax loss may not be reasonably ascertainable. In these situations, the "presumptions" set forth are to be used unless the government or defense provides sufficient information for a more accurate assessment of the tax loss. In cases involving other types of taxes, the presumptions in the notes under subsections (c)(1) and (c)(2) do not apply.

Example 1: A defendant files a tax return reporting income of $40,000 when his income was actually $90,000. Under Note (A) to subsection (c)(1), the tax loss is treated as $14,000 ($90,000 of actual gross income minus $40,000 of reported gross income = $50,000 x 28%) unless sufficient information is available to make a more accurate assessment of the tax loss.

Example 2: A defendant files a tax return reporting income of $60,000 when his income was actually $130,000. In addition, the defendant claims $10,000 in false tax credits. Under Note (A) to subsection (c)(1), the tax loss is treated as $29,600 ($130,000 of actual gross income minus $60,000 of reported gross income = $70,000 x 28% = $19,600, plus $10,000 of false tax credits) unless sufficient information is available to make a more accurate assessment of the tax loss.

Example 3: A defendant fails to file a tax return for a year in which his salary was $24,000, and $2,600 in income tax was withheld by his employer. Under the note to subsection (c)(2), the tax loss is treated as $2,200 ($24,000 of gross income x 20% = $4,800, minus $2,600 of tax withheld) unless sufficient information is available to make a more accurate assessment of the tax loss.

In determining the tax loss attributable to the offense, the court should use as many methods set forth in subsection (c) and this commentary as are necessary given the circumstances of the particular case. If none of the methods of determining the tax loss set forth fit the circumstances of the particular case, the court should use any method of determining the tax loss that appears appropriate to reasonably calculate the loss that would have resulted had the offense been successfully completed.

2. *In determining the total tax loss attributable to the offense (see §1B1.3(a)(2)), all conduct violating the tax laws should be considered as part of the same course of conduct or common scheme or plan unless the evidence demonstrates that the conduct is clearly unrelated. The following examples are illustrative of conduct that is part of the same course of conduct or common scheme or plan: (a) there is a continuing pattern of violations of the tax laws by the defendant; (b) the defendant uses a consistent method to evade or camouflage income, e.g., backdating documents or using off-shore accounts; (c) the violations involve the same or a related series of transactions; (d) the violation in each instance involves a false or inflated claim of a similar deduction or credit; and (e) the violation in each instance involves a failure to report or an understatement of a specific source of income, e.g., interest from savings accounts or income from a particular business activity. These examples are not intended to be exhaustive.*

3. *"Criminal activity" means any conduct constituting a criminal offense under federal, state, local, or foreign law.*

4. *"Sophisticated means," as used in subsection (b)(2), includes conduct that is more complex or demonstrates greater intricacy or planning than a routine tax-evasion case. An enhancement would be applied, for example, where the defendant used offshore bank accounts, or transactions through corporate shells or fictitious entities.*

5. *A "credit claimed against tax" is an item that reduces the amount of tax directly. In contrast, a "deduction" is an item that reduces the amount of taxable income.*

6. *"Gross income," for the purposes of this section, has the same meaning as it has in 26 U.S.C. § 61 and 26 C.F.R. § 1.61.*

7. *If the offense involves both individual and corporate tax returns, the tax loss is the aggregate tax loss from the offenses taken together.*

Background: *This guideline relies most heavily on the amount of loss that was the object of the offense. Tax offenses, in and of themselves, are serious offenses; however, a greater tax loss is obviously more harmful to the treasury and more serious than a smaller one with otherwise similar characteristics. Furthermore, as the potential benefit from the offense increases, the sanction necessary to deter also increases.*

Under pre-guidelines practice, roughly half of all tax evaders were sentenced to probation without imprisonment, while the other half received sentences that required them to serve an average prison term of twelve months. This guideline is intended to reduce disparity in sentencing for tax offenses and to somewhat increase average sentence length. As a result, the number of purely probationary sentences will be reduced. The Commission believes that any additional costs of imprisonment that may be incurred as a result of the increase in the average term of imprisonment for tax offenses are inconsequential in relation to the potential increase in revenue. According to estimates current at the time this guideline was originally developed (1987), income taxes are underpaid by approximately $90 billion annually. Guideline sentences should result in small increases in the average length of imprisonment for most tax cases that involve less than $100,000 in tax loss. The increase is expected to be somewhat larger for cases involving more taxes.

Failure to report criminally derived income is included as a factor for deterrence purposes. Criminally derived income is generally difficult to establish, so that the tax loss in such cases will tend to be substantially understated. An enhancement for offenders who violate the tax laws as part of a pattern of criminal activity from which they derive a substantial portion of their income also serves to implement the mandate of 28 U.S.C. § 994(i)(2).

Although tax offenses always involve some planning, unusually sophisticated efforts to conceal the offense decrease the likelihood of detection and therefore warrant an additional sanction for deterrence purposes.

The guideline does not make a distinction for an employee who prepares fraudulent returns on behalf of his employer. The adjustments in Chapter Three, Part B (Role in the Offense) should be used to make appropriate distinctions.

Historical Note: Effective November 1, 1987. Amended effective November 1, 1989 (see Appendix C, amendments 219-223); November 1, 1990 (see Appendix C, amendment 343); November 1, 1992 (see Appendix C, amendment 468); November 1, 1993 (see Appendix C, amendment 491).

§2T1.2. [Deleted]

Historical Note: Section 2T1.2 (Willful Failure To File Return, Supply Information, or Pay Tax), effective November 1, 1987, amended effective November 1, 1989 (see Appendix C, amendments 224-227), November 1, 1990 (see Appendix C, amendment 343), and November 1, 1991 (see Appendix C, amendment 408), was deleted by consolidation with §2T1.1 effective November 1, 1993 (see Appendix C, amendment 491).

§2T1.3. [Deleted]

Historical Note: Section 2T1.3 (Fraud and False Statements Under Penalty of Perjury), effective November 1, 1987, amended effective November 1, 1989 (see Appendix C, amendments 228-230), November 1, 1990 (see Appendix C, amendment 343), and November 1, 1991 (see Appendix C, amendment 426), was deleted by consolidation with §2T1.1 effective November 1, 1993 (see Appendix C, amendment 491).

§2T1.4. Aiding, Assisting, Procuring, Counseling, or Advising Tax Fraud

(a) Base Offense Level:

(1) Level from §2T4.1 (Tax Table) corresponding to the tax loss; or

(2) **6**, if there is no tax loss.

For purposes of this guideline, the "tax loss" is the tax loss, as defined in §2T1.1, resulting from the defendant's aid, assistance, procurance or advice.

(b) Specific Offense Characteristics

(1) If (A) the defendant committed the offense as part of a pattern or scheme from which he derived a substantial portion of his income; or (B) the defendant was in the business of preparing or assisting in the preparation of tax returns, increase by **2** levels.

(2) If sophisticated means were used to impede discovery of the existence or extent of the offense, increase by **2** levels.

Commentary

Statutory Provision: 26 U.S.C. § 7206(2) (other than a violation based upon 26 U.S.C. § 6050I).

Application Notes:

1. *For the general principles underlying the determination of tax loss, see §2T1.1(c) and Application Note 1 of the Commentary to §2T1.1 (Tax Evasion; Willful Failure to File Return, Supply Information, or Pay Tax; Fraudulent or False Returns, Statements, or Other Documents). In certain instances, such as promotion of a tax shelter scheme, the defendant may advise other persons to violate their tax obligations through filing returns that find no support in the tax laws. If this type of conduct can be shown to have resulted in the filing of false returns (regardless of whether the principals were aware of their falsity), the misstatements in all such returns will contribute to one aggregate "tax loss."*

2. *Subsection (b)(1) has two prongs. The first prong applies to persons who derive a substantial portion of their income through the promotion of tax schemes, e.g., through promoting fraudulent tax shelters. The second prong applies to persons who regularly prepare or assist in the preparation of tax returns for profit. If an enhancement from this subsection applies, do not apply §3B1.3 (Abuse of Position of Trust or Use of Special Skill).*

3. *"Sophisticated means," as used in §2T1.4(b)(2), includes conduct that is more complex or demonstrates greater intricacy or planning than a routine tax-evasion case. An enhancement*

would be applied, for example, where the defendant used offshore bank accounts or transactions through corporate shells or fictitious entities.

Background: An increased offense level is specified for those in the business of preparing or assisting in the preparation of tax returns and those who make a business of promoting tax fraud because their misconduct poses a greater risk of revenue loss and is more clearly willful. Other considerations are similar to those in §2T1.1.

Historical Note: Effective November 1, 1987. Amended effective November 1, 1989 (see Appendix C, amendments 231 and 303); November 1, 1990 (see Appendix C, amendment 343); November 1, 1993 (see Appendix C, amendment 491).

§2T1.5. [Deleted]

Historical Note: Section 2T1.5 (Fraudulent Returns, Statements, or Other Documents), effective November 1, 1987, was deleted by consolidation with §2T1.1 effective November 1, 1993 (see Appendix C, amendment 491).

§2T1.6. Failing to Collect or Truthfully Account for and Pay Over Tax

(a) Base Offense Level: Level from §2T4.1 (Tax Table) corresponding to the tax not collected or accounted for and paid over.

(b) Cross Reference

(1) Where the offense involved embezzlement by withholding tax from an employee's earnings and willfully failing to account to the employee for it, apply §2B1.1 (Larceny, Embezzlement, and Other Forms of Theft) if the resulting offense level is greater than that determined above.

Commentary

Statutory Provision: 26 U.S.C. § 7202.

Application Note:

1. *In the event that the employer not only failed to account to the Internal Revenue Service and pay over the tax, but also collected the tax from employees and did not account to them for it, it is both tax evasion and a form of embezzlement. Subsection (b)(1) addresses such cases.*

Background: The offense is a felony that is infrequently prosecuted. The failure to collect or truthfully account for the tax must be willful, as must the failure to pay. Where no effort is made to defraud the employee, the offense is a form of tax evasion, and is treated as such in the guidelines.

Historical Note: Effective November 1, 1987. Amended effective November 1, 1989 (see Appendix C, amendment 232); November 1, 1991 (see Appendix C, amendment 409).

§2T1.7. Failing to Deposit Collected Taxes in Trust Account as Required After Notice

(a) Base Offense Level (Apply the greater):

(1) **4**; or

(2) **5** less than the level from §2T4.1 (Tax Table) corresponding to the amount not deposited.

Commentary

Statutory Provisions: 26 U.S.C. §§ 7215, 7512(b).

Application Notes:

1. *If funds are deposited and withdrawn without being paid to the Internal Revenue Service, they should be treated as never having been deposited.*

2. *It is recommended that the fine be based on the total amount of funds not deposited.*

Background: This offense is a misdemeanor that does not require any intent to evade taxes, nor even that taxes have not been paid. The more serious offense is 26 U.S.C. § 7202 (see §2T1.6).

This offense should be relatively easy to detect and fines may be feasible. Accordingly, the offense level has been set considerably lower than for tax evasion, although some effort has been made to tie the offense level to the level of taxes that were not deposited.

Historical Note: Effective November 1, 1987.

§2T1.8. Offenses Relating to Withholding Statements

(a) Base Offense Level: **4**

Commentary

Statutory Provisions: 26 U.S.C. §§ 7204, 7205.

Application Note:

1. *If the defendant was attempting to evade, rather than merely delay, payment of taxes, a sentence above the guidelines may be warranted.*

Background: The offenses are misdemeanors. Under pre-guidelines practice, imprisonment was unusual.

Historical Note: Effective November 1, 1987.

§2T1.9. Conspiracy to Impede, Impair, Obstruct, or Defeat Tax

(a) Base Offense Level (Apply the greater):

(1) Offense level determined from §2T1.1 or §2T1.4, as appropriate; or

(2) **10**.

(b) Specific Offense Characteristics

If more than one applies, use the greater:

(1) If the offense involved the planned or threatened use of violence to impede, impair, obstruct, or defeat the ascertainment, computation, assessment, or collection of revenue, increase by **4** levels.

(2) If the conduct was intended to encourage persons other than or in addition to co-conspirators to violate the internal revenue laws or impede, impair, obstruct, or defeat the ascertainment, computation, assessment, or collection of revenue, increase by **2** levels. Do not, however, apply this adjustment if an adjustment from §2T1.4(b)(1) is applied.

Commentary

Statutory Provision: 18 U.S.C. § 371.

Application Notes:

1. *This section applies to conspiracies to "defraud the United States by impeding, impairing, obstructing and defeating . . . the collection of revenue." United States v. Carruth, 699 F.2d 1017, 1021 (9th Cir. 1983), cert. denied, 464 U.S. 1038 (1984). See also United States v. Browning, 723 F.2d 1544 (11th Cir. 1984); United States v. Klein, 247 F.2d 908, 915 (2d Cir. 1957), cert. denied, 355 U.S. 924 (1958). It does not apply to taxpayers, such as a husband and wife, who merely evade taxes jointly or file a fraudulent return.*

2. *The base offense level is the offense level (base offense level plus any applicable specific offense characteristics) from §2T1.1 or §2T1.4 (whichever guideline most closely addresses the harm that would have resulted had the conspirators succeeded in impeding, impairing, obstructing, or defeating the Internal Revenue Service) if that offense level is greater than 10. Otherwise, the base offense level is 10.*

3. *Specific offense characteristics from §2T1.9(b) are to be applied to the base offense level determined under §2T1.9(a)(1) or (2).*

4. *Subsection (b)(2) provides an enhancement where the conduct was intended to encourage persons, other than the participants directly involved in the offense, to violate the tax laws (e.g., an offense involving a "tax protest" group that encourages persons to violate the tax laws, or an offense involving the marketing of fraudulent tax shelters or schemes).*

Background: This type of conspiracy generally involves substantial sums of money. It also typically is complex and may be far-reaching, making it quite difficult to evaluate the extent of the revenue loss caused. Additional specific offense characteristics are included because of the potential for these tax conspiracies to subvert the revenue system and the danger to law enforcement agents and the public.

Historical Note: Effective November 1, 1987. Amended effective November 1, 1989 (see Appendix C, amendments 233 and 234); November 1, 1993 (see Appendix C, amendment 491).

* * * * *

2. ALCOHOL AND TOBACCO TAXES

Introductory Commentary

This section deals with offenses contained in Parts I-IV of Subchapter J of Title 26, chiefly 26 U.S.C. §§ 5601-5605, 5607, 5608, 5661, 5671, 5691, and 5762, where the essence of the conduct is tax evasion or a regulatory violation. Because these offenses are no longer a major enforcement priority, no effort has been made to provide a section-by-section set of guidelines. Rather, the conduct is dealt with by dividing offenses into two broad categories: tax evasion offenses and regulatory offenses.

Historical Note: Effective November 1, 1987.

§2T2.1. Non-Payment of Taxes

(a) Base Offense Level: Level from §2T4.1 (Tax Table) corresponding to the tax loss.

For purposes of this guideline, the "tax loss" is the amount of taxes that the taxpayer failed to pay or attempted not to pay.

Commentary

Statutory Provisions: 26 U.S.C. §§ 5601-5605, 5607, 5608, 5661, 5671, 5691, 5762, provided the conduct constitutes non-payment, evasion or attempted evasion of taxes. For additional statutory provision(s), see Appendix A (Statutory Index).

Application Notes:

1. *The tax loss is the total amount of unpaid taxes that were due on the alcohol and/or tobacco, or that the defendant was attempting to evade.*

2. *Offense conduct directed at more than tax evasion (e.g., theft or fraud) may warrant an upward departure.*

Background: The most frequently prosecuted conduct violating this section is operating an illegal still. 26 U.S.C. § 5601(a)(1).

Historical Note: Effective November 1, 1987.

§2T2.2. <u>Regulatory Offenses</u>

(a) Base Offense Level: **4**

<u>Commentary</u>

<u>Statutory Provisions:</u> 26 U.S.C. §§ 5601, 5603-5605, 5661, 5671, 5762, provided the conduct is tantamount to a record-keeping violation rather than an effort to evade payment of taxes. For additional statutory provision(s), <u>see</u> Appendix A (Statutory Index).

<u>Background:</u> Prosecutions of this type are infrequent.

<u>Historical Note</u>: Effective November 1, 1987. Amended effective November 1, 1990 (<u>see</u> Appendix C, amendment 359).

* * * * *

3. CUSTOMS TAXES

<u>Introductory Commentary</u>

This Subpart deals with violations of 18 U.S.C. §§ 496, 541-545, 547, 548, 550, 551, 1915 and 19 U.S.C. §§ 283, 1436, 1464, 1465, 1586(e), 1708(b), and is designed to address violations involving revenue collection or trade regulation. It is not intended to deal with the importation of contraband, such as drugs, or other items such as obscene material, firearms or pelts of endangered species, the importation of which is prohibited or restricted for non-economic reasons. Other, more specific criminal statutes apply to most of these offenses. Importation of contraband or stolen goods would be a reason for referring to another, more specific guideline, if applicable, or for imposing a sentence above that specified in the guideline in this Subpart.

<u>Historical Note</u>: Effective November 1, 1987. Amended effective November 1, 1992 (<u>see</u> Appendix C, amendment 453).

§2T3.1. <u>Evading Import Duties or Restrictions (Smuggling); Receiving or Trafficking in Smuggled Property</u>

(a) Base Offense Level:

(1) The level from §2T4.1 (Tax Table) corresponding to the tax loss, if the tax loss exceeded $1,000; or

(2) **5**, if the tax loss exceeded $100 but did not exceed $1,000; or

(3) **4**, if the tax loss did not exceed $100.

For purposes of this guideline, the "tax loss" is the amount of the duty.

(b) Specific Offense Characteristic

(1) If sophisticated means were used to impede discovery of the nature or existence of the offense, increase by **2** levels.

(c) Cross Reference

(1) If the offense involves a contraband item covered by another offense guideline, apply that offense guideline if the resulting offense level is greater than that determined above.

Commentary

Statutory Provisions: 18 U.S.C. §§ 496, 541-545, 547, 548, 550, 551, 1915; 19 U.S.C. §§ 283, 1436, 1464, 1465, 1586(e), 1708(b). For additional statutory provision(s), see Appendix A (Statutory Index).

Application Notes:

1. *A sentence at or near the minimum of the guideline range typically would be appropriate for cases involving tourists who bring in items for their own use. Such conduct generally poses a lesser threat to revenue collection.*

2. *Particular attention should be given to those items for which entry is prohibited, limited, or restricted. Especially when such items are harmful or protective quotas are in effect, the duties evaded on such items may not adequately reflect the harm to society or protected industries resulting from their importation. In such instances, an upward departure may be warranted. A sentence based upon an alternative measure of the "duty" evaded, such as the increase in market value due to importation, or 25 percent of the items' fair market value in the United States if the increase in market value due to importation is not readily ascertainable, might be considered.*

Historical Note: Effective November 1, 1987. Amended effective November 1, 1989 (see Appendix C, amendment 235); November 1, 1991 (see Appendix C, amendment 410); November 1, 1992 (see Appendix C, amendment 453).

§2T3.2. [Deleted]

Historical Note: Section 2T3.2 (Receiving or Trafficking in Smuggled Property), effective November 1, 1987, amended effective November 1, 1989 (see Appendix C, amendment 236) and November 1, 1991 (see Appendix C, amendment 410), was deleted by consolidation with §2T3.1 effective November 1, 1992 (see Appendix C, amendment 453).

* * * * *

4. TAX TABLE

§2T4.1. Tax Table

	Tax Loss (Apply the Greatest)	Offense Level
(A)	$1,700 or less	6
(B)	More than $1,700	7
(C)	More than $3,000	8
(D)	More than $5,000	9
(E)	More than $8,000	10
(F)	More than $13,500	11
(G)	More than $23,500	12
(H)	More than $40,000	13
(I)	More than $70,000	14
(J)	More than $120,000	15
(K)	More than $200,000	16
(L)	More than $325,000	17
(M)	More than $550,000	18
(N)	More than $950,000	19
(O)	More than $1,500,000	20
(P)	More than $2,500,000	21
(Q)	More than $5,000,000	22
(R)	More than $10,000,000	23
(S)	More than $20,000,000	24
(T)	More than $40,000,000	25
(U)	More than $80,000,000	26.

Historical Note: Effective November 1, 1987. Amended effective November 1, 1989 (see Appendix C, amendment 237); November 1, 1993 (see Appendix C, amendment 491).

PART X - OTHER OFFENSES

1. CONSPIRACIES, ATTEMPTS, SOLICITATIONS

§2X1.1. Attempt, Solicitation, or Conspiracy (Not Covered by a Specific Offense Guideline)

(a) Base Offense Level: The base offense level from the guideline for the substantive offense, plus any adjustments from such guideline for any intended offense conduct that can be established with reasonable certainty.

(b) Specific Offense Characteristics

(1) If an attempt, decrease by **3** levels, unless the defendant completed all the acts the defendant believed necessary for successful completion of the substantive offense or the circumstances demonstrate that the defendant was about to complete all such acts but for apprehension or interruption by some similar event beyond the defendant's control.

(2) If a conspiracy, decrease by **3** levels, unless the defendant or a co-conspirator completed all the acts the conspirators believed necessary on their part for the successful completion of the substantive offense or the circumstances demonstrate that the conspirators were about to complete all such acts but for apprehension or interruption by some similar event beyond their control.

(3) (A) If a solicitation, decrease by **3** levels unless the person solicited to commit or aid the substantive offense completed all the acts he believed necessary for successful completion of the substantive offense or the circumstances demonstrate that the person was about to complete all such acts but for apprehension or interruption by some similar event beyond such person's control.

(B) If the statute treats solicitation of the substantive offense identically with the substantive offense, do not apply subdivision (A) above; i.e., the offense level for solicitation is the same as that for the substantive offense.

(c) Cross Reference

(1) When an attempt, solicitation, or conspiracy is expressly covered by another offense guideline section, apply that guideline section.

Commentary

Statutory Provisions: 18 U.S.C. §§ 371, 372, 2271. For additional statutory provision(s), see Appendix A (Statutory Index).

Application Notes:

1. *Certain attempts, conspiracies, and solicitations are expressly covered by other offense guidelines.*

   Offense guidelines that expressly cover attempts include:

   §§2A2.1, 2A3.1, 2A3.2, 2A3.3, 2A3.4, 2A4.2, 2A5.1;
   §§2C1.1, 2C1.2;
   §§2D1.1, 2D1.2, 2D1.5, 2D1.6, 2D1.7, 2D1.8, 2D1.9, 2D1.10, 2D1.11, 2D1.12, 2D1.13, 2D2.1, 2D2.2, 2D3.1, 2D3.2;
   §2E5.1;
   §2N1.1;
   §2Q1.4.

   Offense guidelines that expressly cover conspiracies include:

   §2A1.5;
   §§2D1.1, 2D1.2, 2D1.5, 2D1.6, 2D1.7, 2D1.8, 2D1.9, 2D1.10, 2D1.11, 2D1.12, 2D1.13, 2D2.1, 2D2.2, 2D3.1, 2D3.2;
   §2H1.1;
   §2T1.9.

   Offense guidelines that expressly cover solicitations include:

   §2A1.5;
   §§2C1.1, 2C1.2;
   §2E5.1.

2. *"Substantive offense," as used in this guideline, means the offense that the defendant was convicted of soliciting, attempting, or conspiring to commit. Under §2X1.1(a), the base offense level will be the same as that for the substantive offense. But the only specific offense characteristics from the guideline for the substantive offense that apply are those that are determined to have been specifically intended or actually occurred. Speculative specific offense characteristics will not be applied. For example, if two defendants are arrested during the conspiratorial stage of planning an armed bank robbery, the offense level ordinarily would not include aggravating factors regarding possible injury to others, hostage taking, discharge of a weapon, or obtaining a large sum of money, because such factors would be speculative. The offense level would simply reflect the level applicable to robbery of a financial institution, with the enhancement for possession of a weapon. If it was established that the defendants actually intended to physically restrain the teller, the specific offense characteristic for physical restraint would be added. In an attempted theft, the value of the items that the defendant attempted to steal would be considered.*

3. *If the substantive offense is not covered by a specific guideline, see §2X5.1 (Other Offenses).*

4. *In certain cases, the participants may have completed (or have been about to complete but for apprehension or interruption) all of the acts necessary for the successful completion of part, but not all, of the intended offense. In such cases, the offense level for the count (or group of closely related multiple counts) is whichever of the following is greater: the offense level for the intended offense minus 3 levels (under §2X1.1(b)(1), (b)(2), or (b)(3)(A)), or the offense level for the part of the offense for which the necessary acts were completed (or about to be completed but for apprehension or interruption). For example, where the intended offense was*

the theft of $800,000 but the participants completed (or were about to complete) only the acts necessary to steal $30,000, the offense level is the offense level for the theft of $800,000 minus 3 levels, or the offense level for the theft of $30,000, whichever is greater.

In the case of multiple counts that are not closely related counts, whether the 3-level reduction under §2X1.1(b)(1), (b)(2), or (b)(3)(A) applies is determined separately for each count.

Background: In most prosecutions for conspiracies or attempts, the substantive offense was substantially completed or was interrupted or prevented on the verge of completion by the intercession of law enforcement authorities or the victim. In such cases, no reduction of the offense level is warranted. Sometimes, however, the arrest occurs well before the defendant or any co-conspirator has completed the acts necessary for the substantive offense. Under such circumstances, a reduction of 3 levels is provided under §2X1.1(b)(1) or (2).

Historical Note: Effective November 1, 1987. Amended effective January 15, 1988 (see Appendix C, amendment 42); November 1, 1989 (see Appendix C, amendments 238-242); November 1, 1990 (see Appendix C, amendments 311 and 327); November 1, 1991 (see Appendix C, amendment 411); November 1, 1992 (see Appendix C, amendments 444 and 447); November 1, 1993 (see Appendix C, amendment 496).

* * * * *

2. AIDING AND ABETTING

§2X2.1. Aiding and Abetting

The offense level is the same level as that for the underlying offense.

Commentary

Statutory Provision: 18 U.S.C. § 2.

Application Note:

1. *"Underlying offense" means the offense the defendant is convicted of aiding or abetting.*

Background: A defendant convicted of aiding and abetting is punishable as a principal. 18 U.S.C. § 2. This section provides that aiding and abetting the commission of an offense has the same offense level as the underlying offense. An adjustment for a mitigating role (§3B1.2) may be applicable.

Historical Note: Effective November 1, 1987. Amended effective November 1, 1990 (see Appendix C, amendment 359).

* * * * *

3. ACCESSORY AFTER THE FACT

§2X3.1. Accessory After the Fact

(a) Base Offense Level: **6** levels lower than the offense level for the underlying offense, but in no event less than **4**, or more than **30**. *Provided*, that where the conduct is limited to harboring a fugitive, the offense level shall not be more than level **20**.

Commentary

Statutory Provisions: 18 U.S.C. §§ 3, 757, 1071, 1072.

Application Notes:

1. *"Underlying offense" means the offense as to which the defendant is convicted of being an accessory. Apply the base offense level plus any applicable specific offense characteristics that were known, or reasonably should have been known, by the defendant; see Application Note 10 of the Commentary to §1B1.3 (Relevant Conduct).*

2. *The adjustment from §3B1.2 (Mitigating Role) normally would not apply because an adjustment for reduced culpability is incorporated in the base offense level.*

Historical Note: Effective November 1, 1987. Amended effective November 1, 1989 (see Appendix C, amendment 243); November 1, 1991 (see Appendix C, amendment 380); November 1, 1993 (see Appendix C, amendment 496).

* * * * *

4. MISPRISION OF FELONY

§2X4.1. Misprision of Felony

(a) Base Offense Level: **9** levels lower than the offense level for the underlying offense, but in no event less than **4**, or more than **19**.

Commentary

Statutory Provision: 18 U.S.C. § 4.

Application Notes:

1. *"Underlying offense" means the offense as to which the defendant is convicted of committing the misprision. Apply the base offense level plus any applicable specific offense characteristics that were known, or reasonably should have been known, by the defendant; see Application Note 10 of the Commentary to §1B1.3 (Relevant Conduct).*

2. *The adjustment from §3B1.2 (Mitigating Role) normally would not apply because an adjustment for reduced culpability is incorporated in the base offense level.*

Historical Note: Effective November 1, 1987. Amended effective November 1, 1989 (see Appendix C, amendment 244); November 1, 1993 (see Appendix C, amendment 496).

* * * * *

5. ALL OTHER OFFENSES

§2X5.1. Other Offenses

If the offense is a felony or Class A misdemeanor for which no guideline expressly has been promulgated, apply the most analogous offense guideline. If there is not a sufficiently analogous guideline, the provisions of 18 U.S.C. § 3553(b) shall control, except that any guidelines and policy statements that can be applied meaningfully in the absence of a Chapter Two offense guideline shall remain applicable.

Commentary

Application Note:

1. *Guidelines and policy statements that can be applied meaningfully in the absence of a Chapter Two offense guideline include: §5B1.3 (Conditions of Probation); §5B1.4 (Recommended Conditions of Probation and Supervised Release); §5D1.1 (Imposition of a Term of Supervised Release); §5D1.2 (Term of Supervised Release); §5D1.3 (Conditions of Supervised Release); §5E1.1 (Restitution); §5E1.3 (Special Assessments); §5E1.4 (Forfeiture); Chapter Five, Part F (Sentencing Options); §5G1.3 (Imposition of a Sentence on a Defendant Subject to an Undischarged Term of Imprisonment); Chapter Five, Part H (Specific Offender Characteristics); Chapter Five, Part J (Relief from Disability); Chapter Five, Part K (Departures); Chapter Six, Part A (Sentencing Procedures); Chapter Six, Part B (Plea Agreements).*

Background: Many offenses, especially assimilative crimes, are not listed in the Statutory Index or in any of the lists of Statutory Provisions that follow each offense guideline. Nonetheless, the specific guidelines that have been promulgated cover the type of criminal behavior that most such offenses proscribe. The court is required to determine if there is a sufficiently analogous offense guideline, and, if so, to apply the guideline that is most analogous. Where there is no sufficiently analogous guideline, the provisions of 18 U.S.C. § 3553(b) control. That statute provides in relevant part as follows: "In the absence of an applicable sentencing guideline, the court shall impose an appropriate sentence, having due regard for the purposes set forth in [18 U.S.C. § 3553] subsection (a)(2). In the absence of an applicable sentencing guideline in the case of an offense other than a petty offense, the court shall also have due regard for the relationship of the sentence imposed to sentences prescribed by guidelines applicable to similar offenses and offenders, and to the applicable policy statements of the Sentencing Commission."

The sentencing guidelines apply to convictions under 18 U.S.C. § 13 (Assimilative Crimes Act) and 18 U.S.C. § 1153 (Indian Major Crimes Act); see 18 U.S.C. § 3551(a), as amended by section 1602 of Public Law 101-647.

Historical Note: Effective November 1, 1987. Amended effective June 15, 1988 (see Appendix C, amendment 43); November 1, 1991 (see Appendix C, amendment 412).

[Page intentionally blank]

CHAPTER THREE - ADJUSTMENTS

PART A - VICTIM-RELATED ADJUSTMENTS

Introductory Commentary

The following adjustments are included in this Part because they may apply to a wide variety of offenses.

Historical Note: Effective November 1, 1987. Amended effective November 1, 1990 (see Appendix C, amendment 344).

§3A1.1. Vulnerable Victim

If the defendant knew or should have known that a victim of the offense was unusually vulnerable due to age, physical or mental condition, or that a victim was otherwise particularly susceptible to the criminal conduct, increase by 2 levels.

Commentary

Application Notes:

1. *This adjustment applies to offenses where an unusually vulnerable victim is made a target of criminal activity by the defendant. The adjustment would apply, for example, in a fraud case where the defendant marketed an ineffective cancer cure or in a robbery where the defendant selected a handicapped victim. But it would not apply in a case where the defendant sold fraudulent securities by mail to the general public and one of the victims happened to be senile. Similarly, for example, a bank teller is not an unusually vulnerable victim solely by virtue of the teller's position in a bank.*

2. *Do not apply this adjustment if the offense guideline specifically incorporates this factor. For example, where the offense guideline provides an enhancement for the age of the victim, this guideline should not be applied unless the victim was unusually vulnerable for reasons unrelated to age.*

Historical Note: Effective November 1, 1987. Amended effective November 1, 1989 (see Appendix C, amendment 245); November 1, 1990 (see Appendix C, amendment 344); November 1, 1992 (see Appendix C, amendment 454).

§3A1.2. Official Victim

If --

(a) the victim was a government officer or employee; a former government officer or employee; or a member of the immediate family of any of the above, and the offense of conviction was motivated by such status; or

(b) during the course of the offense or immediate flight therefrom, the defendant or a person for whose conduct the defendant is otherwise accountable, knowing or having reasonable cause to believe that a person was a law enforcement or corrections officer, assaulted such officer in a manner creating a substantial risk of serious bodily injury,

increase by **3** levels.

Commentary

Application Notes:

1. *This guideline applies when specified individuals are victims of the offense. This guideline does not apply when the only victim is an organization, agency, or the government.*

2. *Certain high-level officials, e.g., the President and Vice President, although covered by this section, do not represent the heartland of the conduct covered. An upward departure to reflect the potential disruption of the governmental function in such cases typically would be warranted.*

3. *Do not apply this adjustment if the offense guideline specifically incorporates this factor. In most cases, the offenses to which subdivision (a) will apply will be from Chapter Two, Part A (Offenses Against the Person). The only offense guideline in Chapter Two, Part A, that specifically incorporates this factor is §2A2.4 (Obstructing or Impeding Officers).*

4. *"Motivated by such status" in subdivision (a) means that the offense of conviction was motivated by the fact that the victim was a government officer or employee, or a member of the immediate family thereof. This adjustment would not apply, for example, where both the defendant and victim were employed by the same government agency and the offense was motivated by a personal dispute. This adjustment also would not apply in the case of a robbery of a postal employee because the offense guideline for robbery contains an enhancement (§2B3.1(a)) that takes such conduct into account.*

5. *Subdivision (b) applies in circumstances tantamount to aggravated assault against a law enforcement or corrections officer, committed in the course of, or in immediate flight following, another offense, such as bank robbery. While this subdivision may apply in connection with a variety of offenses that are not by nature targeted against official victims, its applicability is limited to assaultive conduct against law enforcement or corrections officers that is sufficiently serious to create at least a "substantial risk of serious bodily injury" and that is proximate in time to the commission of the offense.*

6. *The phrase "substantial risk of serious bodily injury" in subdivision (b) is a threshold level of harm that includes any more serious injury that was risked, as well as actual serious bodily injury (or more serious harm) if it occurs.*

Historical Note: Effective November 1, 1987. Amended effective January 15, 1988 (see Appendix C, amendment 44); November 1, 1989 (see Appendix C, amendments 246-248); November 1, 1992 (see Appendix C, amendment 455).

§3A1.3. <u>Restraint of Victim</u>

If a victim was physically restrained in the course of the offense, increase by **2** levels.

<u>*Commentary*</u>

<u>*Application Notes:*</u>

1. *"Physically restrained" is defined in the Commentary to §1B1.1 (Application Instructions).*

2. *Do not apply this adjustment where the offense guideline specifically incorporates this factor, or where the unlawful restraint of a victim is an element of the offense itself (<u>e.g.</u>, this adjustment does not apply to offenses covered by §2A4.1 (Kidnapping, Abduction, Unlawful Restraint)).*

3. *If the restraint was sufficiently egregious, an upward departure may be warranted. <u>See</u> §5K2.4 (Abduction or Unlawful Restraint).*

<u>Historical Note</u>: Effective November 1, 1987. Amended effective November 1, 1989 (<u>see</u> Appendix C, amendments 249 and 250); November 1, 1991 (<u>see</u> Appendix C, amendment 413).

PART B - ROLE IN THE OFFENSE

Introductory Commentary

This Part provides adjustments to the offense level based upon the role the defendant played in committing the offense. The determination of a defendant's role in the offense is to be made on the basis of all conduct within the scope of §1B1.3 (Relevant Conduct), i.e., all conduct included under §1B1.3(a)(1)-(4), and not solely on the basis of elements and acts cited in the count of conviction.

When an offense is committed by more than one participant, §3B1.1 or §3B1.2 (or neither) may apply. Section 3B1.3 may apply to offenses committed by any number of participants.

Historical Note: Effective November 1, 1987. Amended effective November 1, 1990 (see Appendix C, amendment 345); November 1, 1992 (see Appendix C, amendment 456).

§3B1.1. Aggravating Role

Based on the defendant's role in the offense, increase the offense level as follows:

(a) If the defendant was an organizer or leader of a criminal activity that involved five or more participants or was otherwise extensive, increase by **4** levels.

(b) If the defendant was a manager or supervisor (but not an organizer or leader) and the criminal activity involved five or more participants or was otherwise extensive, increase by **3** levels.

(c) If the defendant was an organizer, leader, manager, or supervisor in any criminal activity other than described in (a) or (b), increase by **2** levels.

Commentary

Application Notes:

1. *A "participant" is a person who is criminally responsible for the commission of the offense, but need not have been convicted. A person who is not criminally responsible for the commission of the offense (e.g., an undercover law enforcement officer) is not a participant.*

2. *To qualify for an adjustment under this section, the defendant must have been the organizer, leader, manager, or supervisor of one or more other participants. An upward departure may be warranted, however, in the case of a defendant who did not organize, lead, manage, or supervise another participant, but who nevertheless exercised management responsibility over the property, assets, or activities of a criminal organization.*

3. *In assessing whether an organization is "otherwise extensive," all persons involved during the course of the entire offense are to be considered. Thus, a fraud that involved only three participants but used the unknowing services of many outsiders could be considered extensive.*

4. *In distinguishing a leadership and organizational role from one of mere management or supervision, titles such as "kingpin" or "boss" are not controlling. Factors the court should*

consider include the exercise of decision making authority, the nature of participation in the commission of the offense, the recruitment of accomplices, the claimed right to a larger share of the fruits of the crime, the degree of participation in planning or organizing the offense, the nature and scope of the illegal activity, and the degree of control and authority exercised over others. There can, of course, be more than one person who qualifies as a leader or organizer of a criminal association or conspiracy. This adjustment does not apply to a defendant who merely suggests committing the offense.

Background: This section provides a range of adjustments to increase the offense level based upon the size of a criminal organization (i.e., the number of participants in the offense) and the degree to which the defendant was responsible for committing the offense. This adjustment is included primarily because of concerns about relative responsibility. However, it is also likely that persons who exercise a supervisory or managerial role in the commission of an offense tend to profit more from it and present a greater danger to the public and/or are more likely to recidivate. The Commission's intent is that this adjustment should increase with both the size of the organization and the degree of the defendant's responsibility.

In relatively small criminal enterprises that are not otherwise to be considered as extensive in scope or in planning or preparation, the distinction between organization and leadership, and that of management or supervision, is of less significance than in larger enterprises that tend to have clearly delineated divisions of responsibility. This is reflected in the inclusiveness of §3B1.1(c).

Historical Note: Effective November 1, 1987. Amended effective November 1, 1991 (see Appendix C, amendment 414); November 1, 1993 (see Appendix C, amendment 500).

§3B1.2. Mitigating Role

Based on the defendant's role in the offense, decrease the offense level as follows:

(a) If the defendant was a minimal participant in any criminal activity, decrease by **4** levels.

(b) If the defendant was a minor participant in any criminal activity, decrease by **2** levels.

In cases falling between (a) and (b), decrease by **3** levels.

Commentary

Application Notes:

1. *Subsection (a) applies to a defendant who plays a minimal role in concerted activity. It is intended to cover defendants who are plainly among the least culpable of those involved in the conduct of a group. Under this provision, the defendant's lack of knowledge or understanding of the scope and structure of the enterprise and of the activities of others is indicative of a role as minimal participant.*

2. *It is intended that the downward adjustment for a minimal participant will be used infrequently. It would be appropriate, for example, for someone who played no other role in a very large drug smuggling operation than to offload part of a single marihuana shipment, or in a case where*

an individual was recruited as a courier for a single smuggling transaction involving a small amount of drugs.

3. *For purposes of §3B1.2(b), a minor participant means any participant who is less culpable than most other participants, but whose role could not be described as minimal.*

4. *If a defendant has received a lower offense level by virtue of being convicted of an offense significantly less serious than warranted by his actual criminal conduct, a reduction for a mitigating role under this section ordinarily is not warranted because such defendant is not substantially less culpable than a defendant whose only conduct involved the less serious offense. For example, if a defendant whose actual conduct involved a minimal role in the distribution of 25 grams of cocaine (an offense having a Chapter Two offense level of 14 under §2D1.1) is convicted of simple possession of cocaine (an offense having a Chapter Two offense level of 6 under §2D2.1), no reduction for a mitigating role is warranted because the defendant is not substantially less culpable than a defendant whose only conduct involved the simple possession of cocaine.*

Background: This section provides a range of adjustments for a defendant who plays a part in committing the offense that makes him substantially less culpable than the average participant. The determination whether to apply subsection (a) or subsection (b), or an intermediate adjustment, involves a determination that is heavily dependent upon the facts of the particular case.

Historical Note: Effective November 1, 1987. Amended effective November 1, 1992 (see Appendix C, amendment 456).

§3B1.3. Abuse of Position of Trust or Use of Special Skill

If the defendant abused a position of public or private trust, or used a special skill, in a manner that significantly facilitated the commission or concealment of the offense, increase by **2** levels. This adjustment may not be employed if an abuse of trust or skill is included in the base offense level or specific offense characteristic. If this adjustment is based upon an abuse of a position of trust, it may be employed in addition to an adjustment under §3B1.1 (Aggravating Role); if this adjustment is based solely on the use of a special skill, it may not be employed in addition to an adjustment under §3B1.1 (Aggravating Role).

Commentary

Application Notes:

1. *"Public or private trust" refers to a position of public or private trust characterized by professional or managerial discretion (i.e., substantial discretionary judgment that is ordinarily given considerable deference). Persons holding such positions ordinarily are subject to significantly less supervision than employees whose responsibilities are primarily non-discretionary in nature. For this enhancement to apply, the position of trust must have contributed in some significant way to facilitating the commission or concealment of the offense (e.g., by making the detection of the offense or the defendant's responsibility for the offense more difficult). This adjustment, for example, would apply in the case of an embezzlement of a client's funds by an attorney serving as a guardian, a bank executive's fraudulent loan scheme, or the criminal sexual abuse of a patient by a physician under the guise of an examination. This adjustment would not apply in the case of an embezzlement or theft by an*

ordinary bank teller or hotel clerk because such positions are not characterized by the above-described factors.

Notwithstanding the preceding paragraph, because of the special nature of the United States mail an adjustment for an abuse of a position of trust will apply to any employee of the U.S. Postal Service who engages in the theft or destruction of undelivered United States mail.

2. *"Special skill" refers to a skill not possessed by members of the general public and usually requiring substantial education, training or licensing. Examples would include pilots, lawyers, doctors, accountants, chemists, and demolition experts.*

Background: *This adjustment applies to persons who abuse their positions of trust or their special skills to facilitate significantly the commission or concealment of a crime. Such persons generally are viewed as more culpable.*

Historical Note: Effective November 1, 1987. Amended effective November 1, 1990 (see Appendix C, amendment 346); November 1, 1993 (see Appendix C, amendment 492).

§3B1.4. In any other case, no adjustment is made for role in the offense.

Commentary

Many offenses are committed by a single individual or by individuals of roughly equal culpability so that none of them will receive an adjustment under this Part. In addition, some participants in a criminal organization may receive increases under §3B1.1 (Aggravating Role) while others receive decreases under §3B1.2 (Mitigating Role) and still other participants receive no adjustment.

Historical Note: Effective November 1, 1987. Amended effective November 1, 1989 (see Appendix C, amendment 303).

PART C - OBSTRUCTION

§3C1.1. <u>Obstructing or Impeding the Administration of Justice</u>

If the defendant willfully obstructed or impeded, or attempted to obstruct or impede, the administration of justice during the investigation, prosecution, or sentencing of the instant offense, increase the offense level by **2** levels.

<u>*Commentary*</u>

<u>*Application Notes:*</u>

1. *This provision is not intended to punish a defendant for the exercise of a constitutional right. A defendant's denial of guilt (other than a denial of guilt under oath that constitutes perjury), refusal to admit guilt or provide information to a probation officer, or refusal to enter a plea of guilty is not a basis for application of this provision. In applying this provision in respect to alleged false testimony or statements by the defendant, such testimony or statements should be evaluated in a light most favorable to the defendant.*

2. *Obstructive conduct can vary widely in nature, degree of planning, and seriousness. Application Note 3 sets forth examples of the types of conduct to which this enhancement is intended to apply. Application Note 4 sets forth examples of less serious forms of conduct to which this enhancement is not intended to apply, but that ordinarily can appropriately be sanctioned by the determination of the particular sentence within the otherwise applicable guideline range. Although the conduct to which this enhancement applies is not subject to precise definition, comparison of the examples set forth in Application Notes 3 and 4 should assist the court in determining whether application of this enhancement is warranted in a particular case.*

3. *The following is a non-exhaustive list of examples of the types of conduct to which this enhancement applies:*

   (a) threatening, intimidating, or otherwise unlawfully influencing a co-defendant, witness, or juror, directly or indirectly, or attempting to do so;

   (b) committing, suborning, or attempting to suborn perjury;

   (c) producing or attempting to produce a false, altered, or counterfeit document or record during an official investigation or judicial proceeding;

   (d) destroying or concealing or directing or procuring another person to destroy or conceal evidence that is material to an official investigation or judicial proceeding (<u>e.g.</u>, shredding a document or destroying ledgers upon learning that an official investigation has commenced or is about to commence), or attempting to do so; however, if such conduct occurred contemporaneously with arrest (<u>e.g.</u>, attempting to swallow or throw away a controlled substance), it shall not, standing alone, be sufficient to warrant an adjustment for obstruction unless it resulted in a material hindrance to the official investigation or prosecution of the instant offense or the sentencing of the offender;

(e) *escaping or attempting to escape from custody before trial or sentencing; or willfully failing to appear, as ordered, for a judicial proceeding;*

(f) *providing materially false information to a judge or magistrate;*

(g) *providing a materially false statement to a law enforcement officer that significantly obstructed or impeded the official investigation or prosecution of the instant offense;*

(h) *providing materially false information to a probation officer in respect to a presentence or other investigation for the court;*

(i) *conduct prohibited by 18 U.S.C. §§ 1501-1516.*

This adjustment also applies to any other obstructive conduct in respect to the official investigation, prosecution, or sentencing of the instant offense where there is a separate count of conviction for such conduct.

4. *The following is a non-exhaustive list of examples of the types of conduct that, absent a separate count of conviction for such conduct, do not warrant application of this enhancement, but ordinarily can appropriately be sanctioned by the determination of the particular sentence within the otherwise applicable guideline range:*

   (a) *providing a false name or identification document at arrest, except where such conduct actually resulted in a significant hindrance to the investigation or prosecution of the instant offense;*

   (b) *making false statements, not under oath, to law enforcement officers, unless Application Note 3(g) above applies;*

   (c) *providing incomplete or misleading information, not amounting to a material falsehood, in respect to a presentence investigation;*

   (d) *avoiding or fleeing from arrest (see, however, §3C1.2 (Reckless Endangerment During Flight)).*

5. *"Material" evidence, fact, statement, or information, as used in this section, means evidence, fact, statement, or information that, if believed, would tend to influence or affect the issue under determination.*

6. *Where the defendant is convicted for an offense covered by §2J1.1 (Contempt), §2J1.2 (Obstruction of Justice), §2J1.3 (Perjury or Subornation of Perjury; Bribery of Witness), §2J1.5 (Failure to Appear by Material Witness), §2J1.6 (Failure to Appear by Defendant), §2J1.9 (Payment to Witness), §2X3.1 (Accessory After the Fact), or §2X4.1 (Misprision of Felony), this adjustment is not to be applied to the offense level for that offense except where a significant further obstruction occurred during the investigation, prosecution, or sentencing of the obstruction offense itself (e.g., where the defendant threatened a witness during the course of the prosecution for the obstruction offense). Where the defendant is convicted both of the obstruction offense and the underlying offense, the count for the obstruction offense will be grouped with the count for the underlying offense under subsection (c) of §3D1.2 (Groups of Closely Related Counts). The offense level for that group of closely related counts will be the offense level for the underlying offense increased by the 2-level adjustment specified by this section, or the offense level for the obstruction offense, whichever is greater.*

7. *Under this section, the defendant is accountable for his own conduct and for conduct that he aided or abetted, counseled, commanded, induced, procured, or willfully caused.*

Historical Note: Effective November 1, 1987. Amended effective November 1, 1989 (see Appendix C, amendments 251 and 252); November 1, 1990 (see Appendix C, amendment 347); November 1, 1991 (see Appendix C, amendment 415); November 1, 1992 (see Appendix C, amendment 457); November 1, 1993 (see Appendix C, amendment 496).

§3C1.2. Reckless Endangerment During Flight

If the defendant recklessly created a substantial risk of death or serious bodily injury to another person in the course of fleeing from a law enforcement officer, increase by **2** levels.

Commentary

Application Notes:

1. *Do not apply this enhancement where the offense guideline in Chapter Two, or another adjustment in Chapter Three, results in an equivalent or greater increase in offense level solely on the basis of the same conduct.*

2. *"Reckless" is defined in the Commentary to §2A1.4 (Involuntary Manslaughter). For the purposes of this guideline, "reckless" means that the conduct was at least reckless and includes any higher level of culpability. However, where a higher degree of culpability was involved, an upward departure above the 2-level increase provided in this section may be warranted.*

3. *"During flight" is to be construed broadly and includes preparation for flight. Therefore, this adjustment also is applicable where the conduct occurs in the course of resisting arrest.*

4. *"Another person" includes any person, except a participant in the offense who willingly participated in the flight.*

5. *Under this section, the defendant is accountable for his own conduct and for conduct that he aided or abetted, counseled, commanded, induced, procured, or willfully caused.*

6. *If death or bodily injury results or the conduct posed a substantial risk of death or bodily injury to more than one person, an upward departure may be warranted. See Chapter Five, Part K (Departures).*

Historical Note: Effective November 1, 1990 (see Appendix C, amendment 347). Amended effective November 1, 1991 (see Appendix C, amendment 416); November 1, 1992 (see Appendix C, amendment 457).

PART D - MULTIPLE COUNTS

Introductory Commentary

This Part provides rules for determining a single offense level that encompasses all the counts of which the defendant is convicted. The single, "combined" offense level that results from applying these rules is used, after adjustment pursuant to the guidelines in subsequent parts, to determine the sentence. These rules have been designed primarily with the more commonly prosecuted federal offenses in mind.

The rules in this Part seek to provide incremental punishment for significant additional criminal conduct. The most serious offense is used as a starting point. The other counts determine how much to increase the offense level. The amount of the additional punishment declines as the number of additional offenses increases.

Some offenses that may be charged in multiple-count indictments are so closely intertwined with other offenses that conviction for them ordinarily would not warrant increasing the guideline range. For example, embezzling money from a bank and falsifying the related records, although legally distinct offenses, represent essentially the same type of wrongful conduct with the same ultimate harm, so that it would be more appropriate to treat them as a single offense for purposes of sentencing. Other offenses, such as an assault causing bodily injury to a teller during a bank robbery, are so closely related to the more serious offense that it would be appropriate to treat them as part of the more serious offense, leaving the sentence enhancement to result from application of a specific offense characteristic.

In order to limit the significance of the formal charging decision and to prevent multiple punishment for substantially identical offense conduct, this Part provides rules for grouping offenses together. Convictions on multiple counts do not result in a sentence enhancement unless they represent additional conduct that is not otherwise accounted for by the guidelines. In essence, counts that are grouped together are treated as constituting a single offense for purposes of the guidelines.

Some offense guidelines, such as those for theft, fraud and drug offenses, contain provisions that deal with repetitive or ongoing behavior. Other guidelines, such as those for assault and robbery, are oriented more toward single episodes of criminal behavior. Accordingly, different rules are required for dealing with multiple-count convictions involving these two different general classes of offenses. More complex cases involving different types of offenses may require application of one rule to some of the counts and another rule to other counts.

Some offenses, e.g., racketeering and conspiracy, may be "composite" in that they involve a pattern of conduct or scheme involving multiple underlying offenses. The rules in this Part are to be used to determine the offense level for such composite offenses from the offense level for the underlying offenses.

Essentially, the rules in this Part can be summarized as follows: (1) If the offense guidelines in Chapter Two base the offense level primarily on the amount of money or quantity of substance involved (e.g., theft, fraud, drug trafficking, firearms dealing), or otherwise contain provisions dealing with repetitive or ongoing misconduct (e.g., many environmental offenses), add the numerical quantities and apply the pertinent offense guideline, including any specific offense characteristics for the conduct taken as a whole. (2) When offenses are closely interrelated, group them together for purposes of the multiple-count rules, and use only the offense level for the most serious offense in that group. (3) As to other offenses (e.g., independent instances of assault or robbery), start with the offense level for the most serious count and use the number and severity of additional counts to determine the amount by which to increase that offense level.

Historical Note: Effective November 1, 1987. Amended effective November 1, 1989 (see Appendix C, amendment 121).

§3D1.1. Procedure for Determining Offense Level on Multiple Counts

(a) When a defendant has been convicted of more than one count, the court shall:

(1) Group the counts resulting in conviction into distinct Groups of Closely Related Counts ("Groups") by applying the rules specified in §3D1.2.

(2) Determine the offense level applicable to each Group by applying the rules specified in §3D1.3.

(3) Determine the combined offense level applicable to all Groups taken together by applying the rules specified in §3D1.4.

(b) Any count for which the statute mandates imposition of a consecutive sentence is excluded from the operation of §§3D1.2-3D1.5. Sentences for such counts are governed by the provisions of §5G1.2(a).

Commentary

Application Note:

1. *Counts for which a statute mandates imposition of a consecutive sentence are excepted from application of the multiple count rules. Convictions on such counts are not used in the determination of a combined offense level under this Part, but may affect the offense level for other counts. A conviction for 18 U.S.C. § 924(c) (use of firearm in commission of a crime of violence) provides a common example. In the case of a conviction under 18 U.S.C. § 924(c), the specific offense characteristic for weapon use in the primary offense is to be disregarded to avoid double counting. See Commentary to §2K2.4. Example: The defendant is convicted of one count of bank robbery (18 U.S.C. § 2113), and one count of use of a firearm in the commission of a crime of violence (18 U.S.C. § 924(c)). The two counts are not grouped together, and the offense level for the bank robbery count is computed without application of an enhancement for weapon possession or use. The mandatory five-year sentence on the weapon-use count runs consecutively, as required by law. See §5G1.2(a).*

Background: This section outlines the procedure to be used for determining the combined offense level. After any adjustments from Chapter 3, Part E (Acceptance of Responsibility) and Chapter 4, Part B (Career Offenders and Criminal Livelihood) are made, this combined offense level is used to determine the guideline sentence range. Chapter Five (Determining the Sentence) discusses how to determine the sentence from the (combined) offense level; §5G1.2 deals specifically with determining the sentence of imprisonment when convictions on multiple counts are involved. References in Chapter Five (Determining the Sentence) to the "offense level" should be treated as referring to the combined offense level after all subsequent adjustments have been made.

Historical Note: Effective November 1, 1987. Amended effective November 1, 1990 (see Appendix C, amendment 348).

§3D1.2. Groups of Closely Related Counts

All counts involving substantially the same harm shall be grouped together into a single Group. Counts involve substantially the same harm within the meaning of this rule:

(a) When counts involve the same victim and the same act or transaction.

(b) When counts involve the same victim and two or more acts or transactions connected by a common criminal objective or constituting part of a common scheme or plan.

(c) When one of the counts embodies conduct that is treated as a specific offense characteristic in, or other adjustment to, the guideline applicable to another of the counts.

(d) When the offense level is determined largely on the basis of the total amount of harm or loss, the quantity of a substance involved, or some other measure of aggregate harm, or if the offense behavior is ongoing or continuous in nature and the offense guideline is written to cover such behavior.

Offenses covered by the following guidelines are to be grouped under this subsection:

§§2B1.1, 2B1.3, 2B4.1, 2B5.1, 2B5.3, 2B6.1;
§§2C1.1, 2C1.2, 2C1.7;
§§2D1.1, 2D1.2, 2D1.5, 2D1.11, 2D1.13;
§§2E4.1, 2E5.1;
§§2F1.1, 2F1.2;
§2K2.1;
§§2L1.1, 2L2.1;
§2N3.1;
§2Q2.1;
§2R1.1;
§§2S1.1, 2S1.2, 2S1.3;
§§2T1.1, 2T1.4, 2T1.6, 2T1.7, 2T1.9, 2T2.1, 2T3.1.

Specifically excluded from the operation of this subsection are:

all offenses in Chapter Two, Part A;
§§2B2.1, 2B2.3; 2B3.1, 2B3.2, 2B3.3;
§2C1.5;
§§2D2.1, 2D2.2, 2D2.3;
§§2E1.3, 2E1.4, 2E2.1;
§§2G1.1, 2G1.2, 2G2.1;
§§2H1.1, 2H1.2, 2H1.3, 2H1.4, 2H2.1, 2H4.1;
§§2L2.2, 2L2.5;
§§2M2.1, 2M2.3, 2M3.1, 2M3.2, 2M3.3, 2M3.4, 2M3.5, 2M3.9;
§§2P1.1, 2P1.2, 2P1.3.

For multiple counts of offenses that are not listed, grouping under this subsection may or may not be appropriate; a case-by-case determination must be made based upon the facts of the case and the applicable guidelines (including specific offense characteristics and other adjustments) used to determine the offense level.

Exclusion of an offense from grouping under this subsection does not necessarily preclude grouping under another subsection.

Commentary

Application Notes:

1. *Subsections (a)-(d) set forth circumstances in which counts are to be grouped together into a single Group. Counts are to be grouped together into a single Group if any one or more of the subsections provide for such grouping. Counts for which the statute mandates imposition of a consecutive sentence are excepted from application of the multiple count rules.* See *§3D1.1(b).*

2. *The term "victim" is not intended to include indirect or secondary victims. Generally, there will be one person who is directly and most seriously affected by the offense and is therefore identifiable as the victim. For offenses in which there are no identifiable victims (*e.g.*, drug or immigration offenses, where society at large is the victim), the "victim" for purposes of subsections (a) and (b) is the societal interest that is harmed. In such cases, the counts are grouped together when the societal interests that are harmed are closely related. Where one count, for example, involves unlawfully entering the United States and the other involves possession of fraudulent evidence of citizenship, the counts are grouped together because the societal interests harmed (the interests protected by laws governing immigration) are closely related. In contrast, where one count involves the sale of controlled substances and the other involves an immigration law violation, the counts are not grouped together because different societal interests are harmed. Ambiguities should be resolved in accordance with the purpose of this section as stated in the lead paragraph,* i.e., *to identify and group "counts involving substantially the same harm."*

3. *Under subsection (a), counts are to be grouped together when they represent essentially a single injury or are part of a single criminal episode or transaction involving the same victim.*

   When one count charges an attempt to commit an offense and the other charges the commission of that offense, or when one count charges an offense based on a general prohibition and the other charges violation of a specific prohibition encompassed in the general prohibition, the counts will be grouped together under subsection (a).

   Examples: *(1) The defendant is convicted of forging and uttering the same check. The counts are to be grouped together. (2) The defendant is convicted of kidnapping and assaulting the victim during the course of the kidnapping. The counts are to be grouped together. (3) The defendant is convicted of bid rigging (an antitrust offense) and of mail fraud for signing and mailing a false statement that the bid was competitive. The counts are to be grouped together. (4) The defendant is convicted of two counts of assault on a federal officer for shooting at the same officer twice while attempting to prevent apprehension as part of a single criminal episode. The counts are to be grouped together. (5) The defendant is convicted of three counts of unlawfully bringing aliens into the United States, all counts arising out of a single incident. The three counts are to be grouped together.* But: *(6) The defendant is convicted of two counts of assault on a federal officer for shooting at the officer on two separate days. The counts* are not *to be grouped together.*

4. *Subsection (b) provides that counts that are part of a single course of conduct with a single criminal objective and represent essentially one composite harm to the same victim are to be grouped together, even if they constitute legally distinct offenses occurring at different times. This provision does not authorize the grouping of offenses that cannot be considered to represent essentially one composite harm (e.g., robbery of the same victim on different occasions involves multiple, separate instances of fear and risk of harm, not one composite harm).*

   When one count charges a conspiracy or solicitation and the other charges a substantive offense that was the sole object of the conspiracy or solicitation, the counts will be grouped together under subsection (b).

   Examples: (1) The defendant is convicted of one count of conspiracy to commit extortion and one count of extortion for the offense he conspired to commit. The counts are to be grouped together. (2) The defendant is convicted of two counts of mail fraud and one count of wire fraud, each in furtherance of a single fraudulent scheme. The counts are to be grouped together, even if the mailings and telephone call occurred on different days. (3) The defendant is convicted of one count of auto theft and one count of altering the vehicle identification number of the car he stole. The counts are to be grouped together. (4) The defendant is convicted of two counts of distributing a controlled substance, each count involving a separate sale of 10 grams of cocaine that is part of a common scheme or plan. In addition, a finding is made that there are two other sales, also part of the common scheme or plan, each involving 10 grams of cocaine. The total amount of all four sales (40 grams of cocaine) will be used to determine the offense level for each count under §1B1.3(a)(2). The two counts will then be grouped together under either this subsection or subsection (d) to avoid double counting. But: (5) The defendant is convicted of two counts of rape for raping the same person on different days. The counts are not to be grouped together.

5. *Subsection (c) provides that when conduct that represents a separate count, e.g., bodily injury or obstruction of justice, is also a specific offense characteristic in or other adjustment to another count, the count represented by that conduct is to be grouped with the count to which it constitutes an aggravating factor. This provision prevents "double counting" of offense behavior. Of course, this rule applies only if the offenses are closely related. It is not, for example, the intent of this rule that (assuming they could be joined together) a bank robbery on one occasion and an assault resulting in bodily injury on another occasion be grouped together. The bodily injury (the harm from the assault) would not be a specific offense characteristic to the robbery and would represent a different harm. On the other hand, use of a firearm in a bank robbery and unlawful possession of that firearm are sufficiently related to warrant grouping of counts under this subsection. Frequently, this provision will overlap subsection (a), at least with respect to specific offense characteristics. However, a count such as obstruction of justice, which represents a Chapter Three adjustment and involves a different harm or societal interest than the underlying offense, is covered by subsection (c) even though it is not covered by subsection (a).*

   Sometimes there may be several counts, each of which could be treated as an aggravating factor to another more serious count, but the guideline for the more serious count provides an adjustment for only one occurrence of that factor. In such cases, only the count representing the most serious of those factors is to be grouped with the other count. For example, if in a robbery of a credit union on a military base the defendant is also convicted of assaulting two employees, one of whom is injured seriously, the assault with serious bodily injury would be grouped with the robbery count, while the remaining assault conviction would be treated separately.

A cross reference to another offense guideline does not constitute "a specific offense characteristic . . . or other adjustment" within the meaning of subsection (c). For example, the guideline for bribery of a public official contains a cross reference to the guideline for a conspiracy to commit the offense that the bribe was to facilitate. Nonetheless, if the defendant were convicted of one count of securities fraud and one count of bribing a public official to facilitate the fraud, the two counts would not be grouped together by virtue of the cross reference. If, however, the bribe was given for the purpose of hampering a criminal investigation into the offense, it would constitute obstruction and under §3C1.1 would result in a 2-level enhancement to the offense level for the fraud. Under the latter circumstances, the counts would be grouped together.

6. *Subsection (d) likely will be used with the greatest frequency. It provides that most property crimes (except robbery, burglary, extortion and the like), drug offenses, firearms offenses, and other crimes where the guidelines are based primarily on quantity or contemplate continuing behavior are to be grouped together. The list of instances in which this subsection should be applied is not exhaustive. Note, however, that certain guidelines are specifically excluded from the operation of subsection (d).*

   A conspiracy, attempt, or solicitation to commit an offense is covered under subsection (d) if the offense that is the object of the conspiracy, attempt, or solicitation is covered under subsection (d).

   Counts involving offenses to which different offense guidelines apply are grouped together under subsection (d) if the offenses are of the same general type and otherwise meet the criteria for grouping under this subsection. In such cases, the offense guideline that results in the highest offense level is used; <u>see</u> §3D1.3(b). The "same general type" of offense is to be construed broadly, and would include, for example, larceny, embezzlement, forgery, and fraud.

   <u>Examples</u>: (1) The defendant is convicted of five counts of embezzling money from a bank. The five counts are to be grouped together. (2) The defendant is convicted of two counts of theft of social security checks and three counts of theft from the mail, each from a different victim. All five counts are to be grouped together. (3) The defendant is convicted of five counts of mail fraud and ten counts of wire fraud. Although the counts arise from various schemes, each involves a monetary objective. All fifteen counts are to be grouped together. (4) The defendant is convicted of three counts of unlicensed dealing in firearms. All three counts are to be grouped together. (5) The defendant is convicted of one count of selling heroin, one count of selling PCP, and one count of selling cocaine. The counts are to be grouped together. The Commentary to §2D1.1 provides rules for combining (adding) quantities of different drugs to determine a single combined offense level. (6) The defendant is convicted of three counts of tax evasion. The counts are to be grouped together. (7) The defendant is convicted of three counts of discharging toxic substances from a single facility. The counts are to be grouped together. (8) The defendant is convicted on two counts of check forgery and one count of uttering the first of the forged checks. All three counts are to be grouped together. Note, however, that the uttering count is first grouped with the first forgery count under subsection (a) of this guideline, so that the monetary amount of that check counts only once when the rule in §3D1.3(b) is applied. <u>But</u>: (9) The defendant is convicted of three counts of bank robbery. The counts <u>are</u> <u>not</u> to be grouped together, nor are the amounts of money involved to be added.

7. *A single case may result in application of several of the rules in this section. Thus, for example, example (8) in the discussion of subsection (d) involves an application of §3D1.2(a) followed by an application of §3D1.2(d). Note also that a Group may consist of a single count; conversely, all counts may form a single Group.*

8. *A defendant may be convicted of conspiring to commit several substantive offenses and also of committing one or more of the substantive offenses. In such cases, treat the conspiracy count as if it were several counts, each charging conspiracy to commit one of the substantive offenses. See §1B1.2(d) and accompanying commentary. Then apply the ordinary grouping rules to determine the combined offense level based upon the substantive counts of which the defendant is convicted and the various acts cited by the conspiracy count that would constitute behavior of a substantive nature. Example: The defendant is convicted of two counts: conspiring to commit offenses A, B, and C, and committing offense A. Treat this as if the defendant was convicted of (1) committing offense A; (2) conspiracy to commit offense A; (3) conspiracy to commit offense B; and (4) conspiracy to commit offense C. Count (1) and count (2) are grouped together under §3D1.2(b). Group the remaining counts, including the various acts cited by the conspiracy count that would constitute behavior of a substantive nature, according to the rules in this section.*

Background: Ordinarily, the first step in determining the combined offense level in a case involving multiple counts is to identify those counts that are sufficiently related to be placed in the same Group of Closely Related Counts ("Group"). This section specifies four situations in which counts are to be grouped together. Although it appears last for conceptual reasons, subsection (d) probably will be used most frequently.

A primary consideration in this section is whether the offenses involve different victims. For example, a defendant may stab three prison guards in a single escape attempt. Some would argue that all counts arising out of a single transaction or occurrence should be grouped together even when there are distinct victims. Although such a proposal was considered, it was rejected because it probably would require departure in many cases in order to capture adequately the criminal behavior. Cases involving injury to distinct victims are sufficiently comparable, whether or not the injuries are inflicted in distinct transactions, so that each such count should be treated separately rather than grouped together. Counts involving different victims (or societal harms in the case of "victimless" crimes) are grouped together only as provided in subsection (c) or (d).

Even if counts involve a single victim, the decision as to whether to group them together may not always be clear cut. For example, how contemporaneous must two assaults on the same victim be in order to warrant grouping together as constituting a single transaction or occurrence? Existing case law may provide some guidance as to what constitutes distinct offenses, but such decisions often turn on the technical language of the statute and cannot be controlling. In interpreting this Part and resolving ambiguities, the court should look to the underlying policy of this Part as stated in the Introductory Commentary.

Historical Note: Effective November 1, 1987. Amended effective June 15, 1988 (see Appendix C, amendment 45); November 1, 1989 (see Appendix C, amendments 121, 253-256, and 303); November 1, 1990 (see Appendix C, amendments 309, 348, and 349); November 1, 1991 (see Appendix C, amendment 417); November 1, 1992 (see Appendix C, amendment 458); November 1, 1993 (see Appendix C, amendment 496).

§3D1.3. Offense Level Applicable to Each Group of Closely Related Counts

Determine the offense level applicable to each of the Groups as follows:

(a) In the case of counts grouped together pursuant to §3D1.2(a)-(c), the offense level applicable to a Group is the offense level, determined in accordance with Chapter Two and Parts A, B, and C of Chapter Three, for the most serious of the counts comprising the Group, i.e., the highest offense level of the counts in the Group.

(b) In the case of counts grouped together pursuant to §3D1.2(d), the offense level applicable to a Group is the offense level corresponding to the aggregated quantity, determined in accordance with Chapter Two and Parts A, B and C of Chapter Three. When the counts involve offenses of the same general type to which different guidelines apply (e.g., theft and fraud), apply the offense guideline that produces the highest offense level.

Commentary

Application Notes:

1. *The "offense level" for a count refers to the offense level from Chapter Two after all adjustments from Parts A, B, and C of Chapter Three.*

2. *When counts are grouped pursuant to §3D1.2(a)-(c), the highest offense level of the counts in the group is used. Ordinarily, it is necessary to determine the offense level for each of the counts in a Group in order to ensure that the highest is correctly identified. Sometimes, it will be clear that one count in the Group cannot have a higher offense level than another, as with a count for an attempt or conspiracy to commit the completed offense. The formal determination of the offense level for such a count may be unnecessary.*

3. *When counts are grouped pursuant to §3D1.2(d), the offense guideline applicable to the aggregate behavior is used. If the counts in the Group are covered by different guidelines (e.g., theft and fraud), use the guideline that produces the highest offense level. Determine whether the specific offense characteristics or adjustments from Chapter Three, Parts A, B, and C apply based upon the combined offense behavior taken as a whole. Note that guidelines for similar property offenses have been coordinated to produce identical offense levels, at least when substantial property losses are involved. However, when small sums are involved the differing specific offense characteristics that require increasing the offense level to a certain minimum may affect the outcome. In addition, the adjustment for "more than minimal planning" frequently will apply to multiple count convictions for property offenses.*

4. *Sometimes the rule specified in this section may not result in incremental punishment for additional criminal acts because of the grouping rules. For example, if the defendant commits forcible criminal sexual abuse (rape), aggravated assault, and robbery, all against the same victim on a single occasion, all of the counts are grouped together under §3D1.2. The aggravated assault will increase the guideline range for the rape. The robbery, however, will not. This is because the offense guideline for rape (§2A3.1) includes the most common aggravating factors, including injury, that data showed to be significant in actual practice. The additional factor of property loss ordinarily can be taken into account adequately within the guideline range for rape, which is fairly wide. However, an exceptionally large property loss in the course of the rape would provide grounds for a sentence above the guideline range. See §5K2.5 (Property Damage or Loss).*

Background: This section provides rules for determining the offense level associated with each Group of Closely Related Counts. Summary examples of the application of these rules are provided at the end of the Commentary to this Part.

Historical Note: Effective November 1, 1987. Amended effective November 1, 1989 (see Appendix C, amendments 257 and 303).

§3D1.4. Determining the Combined Offense Level

The combined offense level is determined by taking the offense level applicable to the Group with the highest offense level and increasing that offense level by the amount indicated in the following table:

Number of Units	Increase in Offense Level
1	none
1 1/2	add 1 level
2	add 2 levels
2 1/2 - 3	add 3 levels
3 1/2 - 5	add 4 levels
More than 5	add 5 levels.

In determining the number of Units for purposes of this section:

(a) Count as one Unit the Group with the highest offense level. Count one additional Unit for each Group that is equally serious or from 1 to 4 levels less serious.

(b) Count as one-half Unit any Group that is 5 to 8 levels less serious than the Group with the highest offense level.

(c) Disregard any Group that is 9 or more levels less serious than the Group with the highest offense level. Such Groups will not increase the applicable offense level but may provide a reason for sentencing at the higher end of the sentencing range for the applicable offense level.

Commentary

Application Notes:

1. *Application of the rules in §§3D1.2 and 3D1.3 may produce a single Group of Closely Related Counts. In such cases, the combined offense level is the level corresponding to the Group determined in accordance with §3D1.3.*

2. *The procedure for calculating the combined offense level when there is more than one Group of Closely Related Counts is as follows: First, identify the offense level applicable to the most serious Group; assign it one Unit. Next, determine the number of Units that the remaining Groups represent. Finally, increase the offense level for the most serious Group by the number of levels indicated in the table corresponding to the total number of Units.*

Background: When Groups are of roughly comparable seriousness, each Group will represent one Unit. When the most serious Group carries an offense level substantially higher than that applicable to the other Groups, however, counting the lesser Groups fully for purposes of the table could add excessive punishment, possibly even more than those offenses would carry if prosecuted separately. To avoid this anomalous result and produce declining marginal punishment, Groups 9 or more levels less serious than the most serious Group should not be counted for purposes of the table, and that Groups 5 to 8 levels less serious should be treated as equal to one-half of a Group. Thus, if the most serious Group is at offense level 15 and if two other Groups are at level 10, there would be a total of two Units for purposes of the table (one plus one-half plus one-half) and the combined offense level would be 17. Inasmuch as the maximum increase provided in the guideline is 5 levels, departure would be warranted in the unusual case where the additional offenses resulted in a total of significantly more than 5 Units.

In unusual circumstances, the approach adopted in this section could produce adjustments for the additional counts that are inadequate or excessive. If there are several groups and the most serious offense is considerably more serious than all of the others, there will be no increase in the offense level resulting from the additional counts. Ordinarily, the court will have latitude to impose added punishment by sentencing toward the upper end of the range authorized for the most serious offense. Situations in which there will be inadequate scope for ensuring appropriate additional punishment for the additional crimes are likely to be unusual and can be handled by departure from the guidelines. Conversely, it is possible that if there are several minor offenses that are not grouped together, application of the rules in this Part could result in an excessive increase in the sentence range. Again, such situations should be infrequent and can be handled through departure. An alternative method for ensuring more precise adjustments would have been to determine the appropriate offense level adjustment through a more complicated mathematical formula; that approach was not adopted because of its complexity.

Historical Note: Effective November 1, 1987. Amended effective November 1, 1990 (see Appendix C, amendment 350).

§3D1.5. Determining the Total Punishment

Use the combined offense level to determine the appropriate sentence in accordance with the provisions of Chapter Five.

Commentary

This section refers the court to Chapter Five (Determining the Sentence) in order to determine the total punishment to be imposed based upon the combined offense level. The combined offense level is subject to adjustments from Chapter Three, Part E (Acceptance of Responsibility) and Chapter Four, Part B (Career Offenders and Criminal Livelihood).

Historical Note: Effective November 1, 1987.

* * * * *

Illustrations of the Operation of the Multiple-Count Rules

The following examples, drawn from presentence reports in the Commission's files, illustrate the operation of the guidelines for multiple counts. The examples are discussed summarily; a more thorough, step-by-step approach is recommended until the user is thoroughly familiar with the guidelines.

1. *Defendant A was convicted on four counts, each charging robbery of a different bank. Each would represent a distinct Group. §3D1.2. In each of the first three robberies, the offense level was 22 (20 plus a 2-level increase because a financial institution was robbed) (§2B3.1(b)). In the fourth robbery $12,000 was taken and a firearm was displayed; the offense level was therefore 28. As the first three counts are 6 levels lower than the fourth, each of the first three represents one-half unit for purposes of §3D1.4. Altogether there are 2 1/2 Units, and the*

offense level for the most serious (28) is therefore increased by 3 levels under the table. The combined offense level is 31.

2. *Defendant B was convicted on the following seven counts: (1) theft of a $2,000 check; (2) uttering the same $2,000 check; (3) possession of a stolen $1,200 check; (4) forgery of a $600 check; (5) possession of a stolen $1,000 check; (6) forgery of the same $1,000 check; (7) uttering the same $1,000 check. Counts 1, 3 and 5 involve offenses under Part B (Theft), while Counts 2, 4, 6 and 7 involve offenses under Part F (Fraud and Deceit). For purposes of §3D1.2(d), fraud and theft are treated as offenses of the same kind, and therefore all counts are grouped into a single Group, for which the offense level depends on the aggregate harm. The total value of the checks is $4,800. The fraud guideline is applied, because it produces an offense level that is as high as or higher than the theft guideline. The base offense level is 6; 1 level is added because of the value of the property (§2F1.1(b)(1)); and 2 levels are added because the conduct involved repeated acts with some planning (§2F1.1(b)(2)(A)). The resulting offense level is 9.*

3. *Defendant C was convicted on four counts: (1) distribution of 230 grams of cocaine; (2) distribution of 150 grams of cocaine; (3) distribution of seventy-five grams of heroin; (4) offering a DEA agent $20,000 to avoid prosecution. The combined offense level for drug offenses is determined by the total quantity of drugs, converted to heroin equivalents. The first count translates into forty-six grams of heroin; the second count translates into thirty grams of heroin. The total is 151 grams of heroin. Under §2D1.1, the combined offense level for the drug offenses is 26. In addition, because of the attempted bribe of the DEA agent, this offense level is increased by 2 levels to 28 under §3C1.1 (Obstructing or Impeding the Administration of Justice). Because the conduct constituting the bribery offense is accounted for by §3C1.1, it becomes part of the same Group as the drug offenses pursuant to §3D1.2(c). The combined offense level is 28 pursuant to §3D1.3(a), because the offense level for bribery (22) is less than the offense level for the drug offenses (28).*

4. *Defendant D was convicted of four counts arising out of a scheme pursuant to which he received kickbacks from subcontractors. The counts were as follows: (1) The defendant received $27,000 from subcontractor A relating to contract X (Mail Fraud). (2) The defendant received $12,000 from subcontractor A relating to contract X (Commercial Bribery). (3) The defendant received $15,000 from subcontractor A relating to contract Y (Mail Fraud). (4) The defendant received $20,000 from subcontractor B relating to contract Z (Commercial Bribery). The mail fraud counts are covered by §2F1.1 (Fraud and Deceit). The bribery counts are covered by §2B4.1 (Bribery in Procurement of Bank Loan and Other Commercial Bribery), which treats the offense as a sophisticated fraud. The total money involved is $74,000, which results in an offense level of 14 under either §2B4.1 or §2F1.1. Since these two guidelines produce identical offense levels, the combined offense level is 14.*

Historical Note: Effective November 1, 1987. Amended effective November 1, 1989 (see Appendix C, amendment 303); November 1, 1990 (see Appendix C, amendment 350); November 1, 1991 (see Appendix C, amendment 417).

PART E - ACCEPTANCE OF RESPONSIBILITY

§3E1.1. Acceptance of Responsibility

(a) If the defendant clearly demonstrates acceptance of responsibility for his offense, decrease the offense level by **2** levels.

(b) If the defendant qualifies for a decrease under subsection (a), the offense level determined prior to the operation of subsection (a) is level **16** or greater, and the defendant has assisted authorities in the investigation or prosecution of his own misconduct by taking one or more of the following steps:

(1) timely providing complete information to the government concerning his own involvement in the offense; or

(2) timely notifying authorities of his intention to enter a plea of guilty, thereby permitting the government to avoid preparing for trial and permitting the court to allocate its resources efficiently,

decrease the offense level by **1** additional level.

Commentary

Application Notes:

1. *In determining whether a defendant qualifies under subsection (a), appropriate considerations include, but are not limited to, the following:*

   (a) *truthfully admitting the conduct comprising the offense(s) of conviction, and truthfully admitting or not falsely denying any additional relevant conduct for which the defendant is accountable under §1B1.3 (Relevant Conduct). Note that a defendant is not required to volunteer, or affirmatively admit, relevant conduct beyond the offense of conviction in order to obtain a reduction under subsection (a). A defendant may remain silent in respect to relevant conduct beyond the offense of conviction without affecting his ability to obtain a reduction under this subsection. However, a defendant who falsely denies, or frivolously contests, relevant conduct that the court determines to be true has acted in a manner inconsistent with acceptance of responsibility;*

   (b) *voluntary termination or withdrawal from criminal conduct or associations;*

   (c) *voluntary payment of restitution prior to adjudication of guilt;*

   (d) *voluntary surrender to authorities promptly after commission of the offense;*

   (e) *voluntary assistance to authorities in the recovery of the fruits and instrumentalities of the offense;*

   (f) *voluntary resignation from the office or position held during the commission of the offense;*

   (g) *post-offense rehabilitative efforts (e.g., counseling or drug treatment); and*

(h) the timeliness of the defendant's conduct in manifesting the acceptance of responsibility.

2. *This adjustment is not intended to apply to a defendant who puts the government to its burden of proof at trial by denying the essential factual elements of guilt, is convicted, and only then admits guilt and expresses remorse. Conviction by trial, however, does not automatically preclude a defendant from consideration for such a reduction. In rare situations a defendant may clearly demonstrate an acceptance of responsibility for his criminal conduct even though he exercises his constitutional right to a trial. This may occur, for example, where a defendant goes to trial to assert and preserve issues that do not relate to factual guilt (e.g., to make a constitutional challenge to a statute or a challenge to the applicability of a statute to his conduct). In each such instance, however, a determination that a defendant has accepted responsibility will be based primarily upon pre-trial statements and conduct.*

3. *Entry of a plea of guilty prior to the commencement of trial combined with truthfully admitting the conduct comprising the offense of conviction, and truthfully admitting or not falsely denying any additional relevant conduct for which he is accountable under §1B1.3 (Relevant Conduct) (see Application Note 1(a)), will constitute significant evidence of acceptance of responsibility for the purposes of subsection (a). However, this evidence may be outweighed by conduct of the defendant that is inconsistent with such acceptance of responsibility. A defendant who enters a guilty plea is not entitled to an adjustment under this section as a matter of right.*

4. *Conduct resulting in an enhancement under §3C1.1 (Obstructing or Impeding the Administration of Justice) ordinarily indicates that the defendant has not accepted responsibility for his criminal conduct. There may, however, be extraordinary cases in which adjustments under both §§3C1.1 and 3E1.1 may apply.*

5. *The sentencing judge is in a unique position to evaluate a defendant's acceptance of responsibility. For this reason, the determination of the sentencing judge is entitled to great deference on review.*

6. *Subsection (a) provides a 2-level decrease in offense level. Subsection (b) provides an additional 1-level decrease in offense level for a defendant at offense level 16 or greater prior to the operation of subsection (a) who both qualifies for a decrease under subsection (a) and who has assisted authorities in the investigation or prosecution of his own misconduct by taking one or both of the steps set forth in subsection (b). The timeliness of the defendant's acceptance of responsibility is a consideration under both subsections, and is context specific. In general, the conduct qualifying for a decrease in offense level under subsection (b)(1) or (2) will occur particularly early in the case. For example, to qualify under subsection (b)(2), the defendant must have notified authorities of his intention to enter a plea of guilty at a sufficiently early point in the process so that the government may avoid preparing for trial and the court may schedule its calendar efficiently.*

Background: The reduction of offense level provided by this section recognizes legitimate societal interests. For several reasons, a defendant who clearly demonstrates acceptance of responsibility for his offense by taking, in a timely fashion, one or more of the actions listed above (or some equivalent action) is appropriately given a lower offense level than a defendant who has not demonstrated acceptance of responsibility.

Subsection (a) provides a 2-level decrease in offense level. Subsection (b) provides an additional 1-level decrease for a defendant at offense level 16 or greater prior to operation of subsection (a) who both qualifies for a decrease under subsection (a) and has assisted authorities in the investigation or prosecution of his own misconduct by taking one or more of the steps specified in subsection (b). Such a defendant has accepted responsibility in a way that ensures the certainty of his just punishment in a timely manner, thereby appropriately meriting an addition Subsection (b) does not apply, however, to a defendant whose offense level is level 15 c to application of subsection (a). At offense level 15 or lower, the reduction in the gu. provided by a 2-level decrease in offense level under subsection (a) (which is a greater reduction in the guideline range than at higher offense levels due to the structure of th. Table) is adequate for the court to take into account the factors set forth in subsectio the applicable guideline range.

Historical Note: Effective November 1, 1987. Amended effective January 15, 1988 (see Appendix C, ar November 1, 1989 (see Appendix C, amendment 258); November 1, 1990 (see Appendix C, amendment 351] 1992 (see Appendix C, amendment 459).

CHAPTER FOUR - CRIMINAL HISTORY AND CRIMINAL LIVELIHOOD

PART A - CRIMINAL HISTORY

Introductory Commentary

The Comprehensive Crime Control Act sets forth four purposes of sentencing. (See 18 U.S.C. § 3553(a)(2).) A defendant's record of past criminal conduct is directly relevant to those purposes. A defendant with a record of prior criminal behavior is more culpable than a first offender and thus deserving of greater punishment. General deterrence of criminal conduct dictates that a clear message be sent to society that repeated criminal behavior will aggravate the need for punishment with each recurrence. To protect the public from further crimes of the particular defendant, the likelihood of recidivism and future criminal behavior must be considered. Repeated criminal behavior is an indicator of a limited likelihood of successful rehabilitation.

The specific factors included in §4A1.1 and §4A1.3 are consistent with the extant empirical research assessing correlates of recidivism and patterns of career criminal behavior. While empirical research has shown that other factors are correlated highly with the likelihood of recidivism, e.g., age and drug abuse, for policy reasons they were not included here at this time. The Commission has made no definitive judgment as to the reliability of the existing data. However, the Commission will review additional data insofar as they become available in the future.

Historical Note: Effective November 1, 1987.

§4A1.1. Criminal History Category

The total points from items (a) through (f) determine the criminal history category in the Sentencing Table in Chapter Five, Part A.

(a) Add **3** points for each prior sentence of imprisonment exceeding one year and one month.

(b) Add **2** points for each prior sentence of imprisonment of at least sixty days not counted in (a).

(c) Add **1** point for each prior sentence not counted in (a) or (b), up to a total of **4** points for this item.

(d) Add **2** points if the defendant committed the instant offense while under any criminal justice sentence, including probation, parole, supervised release, imprisonment, work release, or escape status.

(e) Add **2** points if the defendant committed the instant offense less than two years after release from imprisonment on a sentence counted under (a) or (b) or while in imprisonment or escape status on such a sentence. If **2** points are added for item (d), add only **1** point for this item.

(f) Add **1** point for each prior sentence resulting from a conviction of a crime of violence that did not receive any points under (a), (b), or (c) above because such sentence was considered related to another sentence resulting from a conviction of a crime of violence, up to a total of 3 points for this item. *Provided*, that this item does not apply where the sentences are considered related because the offenses occurred on the same occasion.

Commentary

The total criminal history points from §4A1.1 determine the criminal history category (I-VI) in the Sentencing Table in Chapter Five, Part A. The definitions and instructions in §4A1.2 govern the computation of the criminal history points. Therefore, §§4A1.1 and 4A1.2 must be read together. The following notes highlight the interaction of §§4A1.1 and 4A1.2.

Application Notes:

1. *§4A1.1(a). Three points are added for each prior sentence of imprisonment exceeding one year and one month. There is no limit to the number of points that may be counted under this item. The term "prior sentence" is defined at §4A1.2(a). The term "sentence of imprisonment" is defined at §4A1.2(b). Where a prior sentence of imprisonment resulted from a revocation of probation, parole, or a similar form of release, see §4A1.2(k).*

   Certain prior sentences are not counted or are counted only under certain conditions:

   A sentence imposed more than fifteen years prior to the defendant's commencement of the instant offense is not counted unless the defendant's incarceration extended into this fifteen-year period. See §4A1.2(e).

   A sentence imposed for an offense committed prior to the defendant's eighteenth birthday is counted under this item only if it resulted from an adult conviction. See §4A1.2(d).

   A sentence for a foreign conviction, a conviction that has been expunged, or an invalid conviction is not counted. See §4A1.2(h) and (j) and the Commentary to §4A1.2.

2. *§4A1.1(b). Two points are added for each prior sentence of imprisonment of at least sixty days not counted in §4A1.1(a). There is no limit to the number of points that may be counted under this item. The term "prior sentence" is defined at §4A1.2(a). The term "sentence of imprisonment" is defined at §4A1.2(b). Where a prior sentence of imprisonment resulted from a revocation of probation, parole, or a similar form of release, see §4A1.2(k).*

   Certain prior sentences are not counted or are counted only under certain conditions:

   A sentence imposed more than ten years prior to the defendant's commencement of the instant offense is not counted. See §4A1.2(e).

   An adult or juvenile sentence imposed for an offense committed prior to the defendant's eighteenth birthday is counted only if confinement resulting from such sentence extended into the five-year period preceding the defendant's commencement of the instant offense. See §4A1.2(d).

   Sentences for certain specified non-felony offenses are never counted. See §4A1.2(c)(2).

   A sentence for a foreign conviction or a tribal court conviction, an expunged conviction, or an invalid conviction is not counted. See §4A1.2(h), (i), (j), and the Commentary to §4A1.2.

A military sentence is counted only if imposed by a general or special court martial. See §4A1.2(g).

3. *§4A1.1(c). One point is added for each prior sentence not counted under §4A1.1(a) or (b). A maximum of four points may be counted under this item. The term "prior sentence" is defined at §4A1.2(a).*

Certain prior sentences are not counted or are counted only under certain conditions:

A sentence imposed more than ten years prior to the defendant's commencement of the instant offense is not counted. See §4A1.2(e).

An adult or juvenile sentence imposed for an offense committed prior to the defendant's eighteenth birthday is counted only if imposed within five years of the defendant's commencement of the current offense. See §4A1.2(d).

Sentences for certain specified non-felony offenses are counted only if they meet certain requirements. See §4A1.2(c)(1).

Sentences for certain specified non-felony offenses are never counted. See §4A1.2(c)(2).

A diversionary disposition is counted only where there is a finding or admission of guilt in a judicial proceeding. See §4A1.2(f).

A sentence for a foreign conviction, a tribal court conviction, an expunged conviction, or an invalid conviction, is not counted. See §4A1.2(h), (i), (j), and the Commentary to §4A1.2.

A military sentence is counted only if imposed by a general or special court martial. See §4A1.2(g).

4. *§4A1.1(d). Two points are added if the defendant committed any part of the instant offense (i.e., any relevant conduct) while under any criminal justice sentence, including probation, parole, supervised release, imprisonment, work release, or escape status. Failure to report for service of a sentence of imprisonment is to be treated as an escape from such sentence. See §4A1.2(n). For the purposes of this item, a "criminal justice sentence" means a sentence countable under §4A1.2 (Definitions and Instructions for Computing Criminal History) having a custodial or supervisory component, although active supervision is not required for this item to apply. For example, a term of unsupervised probation would be included; but a sentence to pay a fine, by itself, would not be included. A defendant who commits the instant offense while a violation warrant from a prior sentence is outstanding (e.g., a probation, parole, or supervised release violation warrant) shall be deemed to be under a criminal justice sentence for the purposes of this provision if that sentence is otherwise countable, even if that sentence would have expired absent such warrant. See §4A1.2(m).*

5. *§4A1.1(e). Two points are added if the defendant committed any part of the instant offense (i.e., any relevant conduct) less than two years following release from confinement on a sentence counted under §4A1.1(a) or (b). This also applies if the defendant committed the instant offense while in imprisonment or escape status on such a sentence. Failure to report for service of a sentence of imprisonment is to be treated as an escape from such sentence. See §4A1.2(n). However, if two points are added under §4A1.1(d), only one point is added under §4A1.1(e).*

6. §4A1.1(f). *Where the defendant received two or more prior sentences as a result of convictions for crimes of violence that are treated as related cases but did not arise from the same occasion (i.e., offenses committed on different occasions that were part of a single common scheme or plan or were consolidated for trial or sentencing; see Application Note 3 of the Commentary to §4A1.2), one point is added under §4A1.1(f) for each such sentence that did not result in any additional points under §4A1.1(a), (b), or (c). A total of up to 3 points may be added under §4A1.1(f). 'Crime of violence' is defined in §4B1.2(1); see §4A1.2(p).*

   For example, a defendant's criminal history includes two robbery convictions for offenses committed on different occasions that were consolidated for sentencing and therefore are treated as related. If the defendant received a five-year sentence of imprisonment for one robbery and a four-year sentence of imprisonment for the other robbery (consecutively or concurrently), a total of 3 points is added under §4A1.1(a). An additional point is added under §4A1.1(f) because the second sentence did not result in any additional point(s) (under §4A1.1(a), (b), or (c)). In contrast, if the defendant received a one-year sentence of imprisonment for one robbery and a nine-month consecutive sentence of imprisonment for the other robbery, a total of 3 points also is added under §4A1.1(a) (a one-year sentence of imprisonment and a consecutive nine-month sentence of imprisonment are treated as a combined one-year-nine-month sentence of imprisonment). But no additional point is added under §4A1.1(f) because the sentence for the second robbery already resulted in an additional point under §4A1.1(a). Without the second sentence, the defendant would only have received two points under §4A1.1(b) for the one-year sentence of imprisonment).

Background: *Prior convictions may represent convictions in the federal system, fifty state systems, the District of Columbia, territories, and foreign, tribal, and military courts. There are jurisdictional variations in offense definitions, sentencing structures, and manner of sentence pronouncement. To minimize problems with imperfect measures of past crime seriousness, criminal history categories are based on the maximum term imposed in previous sentences rather than on other measures, such as whether the conviction was designated a felony or misdemeanor. In recognition of the imperfection of this measure however, §4A1.3 permits information about the significance or similarity of past conduct underlying prior convictions to be used as a basis for imposing a sentence outside the applicable guideline range.*

Subdivisions (a), (b), and (c) of §4A1.1 distinguish confinement sentences longer than one year and one month, shorter confinement sentences of at least sixty days, and all other sentences, such as confinement sentences of less than sixty days, probation, fines, and residency in a halfway house.

Section 4A1.1(d) implements one measure of recency by adding two points if the defendant was under a criminal justice sentence during any part of the instant offense.

Section 4A1.1(e) implements another measure of recency by adding two points if the defendant committed any part of the instant offense less than two years immediately following his release from confinement on a sentence counted under §4A1.1(a) or (b). Because of the potential overlap of (d) and (e), their combined impact is limited to three points. However, a defendant who falls within both (d) and (e) is more likely to commit additional crimes; thus, (d) and (e) are not completely combined.

Historical Note: Effective November 1, 1987. Amended effective November 1, 1989 (see Appendix C, amendments 259-261); November 1, 1991 (see Appendix C, amendments 381 and 382).

§4A1.2. Definitions and Instructions for Computing Criminal History

(a) Prior Sentence Defined

(1) The term "prior sentence" means any sentence previously imposed upon adjudication of guilt, whether by guilty plea, trial, or plea of nolo contendere, for conduct not part of the instant offense.

(2) Prior sentences imposed in unrelated cases are to be counted separately. Prior sentences imposed in related cases are to be treated as one sentence for purposes of §4A1.1(a), (b), and (c). Use the longest sentence of imprisonment if concurrent sentences were imposed and the aggregate sentence of imprisonment imposed in the case of consecutive sentences.

(3) A conviction for which the imposition or execution of sentence was totally suspended or stayed shall be counted as a prior sentence under §4A1.1(c).

(4) Where a defendant has been convicted of an offense, but not yet sentenced, such conviction shall be counted as if it constituted a prior sentence under §4A1.1(c) if a sentence resulting from that conviction otherwise would be countable. In the case of a conviction for an offense set forth in §4A1.2(c)(1), apply this provision only where the sentence for such offense would be countable regardless of type or length.

"Convicted of an offense," for the purposes of this provision, means that the guilt of the defendant has been established, whether by guilty plea, trial, or plea of nolo contendere.

(b) Sentence of Imprisonment Defined

(1) The term "sentence of imprisonment" means a sentence of incarceration and refers to the maximum sentence imposed.

(2) If part of a sentence of imprisonment was suspended, "sentence of imprisonment" refers only to the portion that was not suspended.

(c) Sentences Counted and Excluded

Sentences for all felony offenses are counted. Sentences for misdemeanor and petty offenses are counted, except as follows:

(1) Sentences for the following prior offenses and offenses similar to them, by whatever name they are known, are counted only if (A) the sentence was a term of probation of at least one year or a term of imprisonment of at least thirty days, or (B) the prior offense was similar to an instant offense:

Careless or reckless driving
Contempt of court
Disorderly conduct or disturbing the peace

Driving without a license or with a revoked or suspended license
False information to a police officer
Fish and game violations
Gambling
Hindering or failure to obey a police officer
Insufficient funds check
Leaving the scene of an accident
Local ordinance violations (excluding local ordinance violations that are also criminal offenses under state law)
Non-support
Prostitution
Resisting arrest
Trespassing.

(2) Sentences for the following prior offenses and offenses similar to them, by whatever name they are known, are never counted:

Hitchhiking
Juvenile status offenses and truancy
Loitering
Minor traffic infractions (e.g., speeding)
Public intoxication
Vagrancy.

(d) **Offenses Committed Prior to Age Eighteen**

(1) If the defendant was convicted as an adult and received a sentence of imprisonment exceeding one year and one month, add **3** points under §4A1.1(a) for each such sentence.

(2) In any other case,

(A) add **2** points under §4A1.1(b) for each adult or juvenile sentence to confinement of at least sixty days if the defendant was released from such confinement within five years of his commencement of the instant offense;

(B) add **1** point under §4A1.1(c) for each adult or juvenile sentence imposed within five years of the defendant's commencement of the instant offense not covered in (A).

(e) **Applicable Time Period**

(1) Any prior sentence of imprisonment exceeding one year and one month that was imposed within fifteen years of the defendant's commencement of the instant offense is counted. Also count any prior sentence of imprisonment exceeding one year and one month, whenever imposed, that resulted in the defendant being incarcerated during any part of such fifteen-year period.

(2) Any other prior sentence that was imposed within ten years of the defendant's commencement of the instant offense is counted.

(3) Any prior sentence not within the time periods specified above is not counted.

(4) The applicable time period for certain sentences resulting from offenses committed prior to age eighteen is governed by §4A1.2(d)(2).

(f) **Diversionary Dispositions**

Diversion from the judicial process without a finding of guilt (e.g., deferred prosecution) is not counted. A diversionary disposition resulting from a finding or admission of guilt, or a plea of nolo contendere, in a judicial proceeding is counted as a sentence under §4A1.1(c) even if a conviction is not formally entered, except that diversion from juvenile court is not counted.

(g) **Military Sentences**

Sentences resulting from military offenses are counted if imposed by a general or special court martial. Sentences imposed by a summary court martial or Article 15 proceeding are not counted.

(h) **Foreign Sentences**

Sentences resulting from foreign convictions are not counted, but may be considered under §4A1.3 (Adequacy of Criminal History Category).

(i) **Tribal Court Sentences**

Sentences resulting from tribal court convictions are not counted, but may be considered under §4A1.3 (Adequacy of Criminal History Category).

(j) **Expunged Convictions**

Sentences for expunged convictions are not counted, but may be considered under §4A1.3 (Adequacy of Criminal History Category).

(k) **Revocations of Probation, Parole, Mandatory Release, or Supervised Release**

(1) In the case of a prior revocation of probation, parole, supervised release, special parole, or mandatory release, add the original term of imprisonment to any term of imprisonment imposed upon revocation. The resulting total is used to compute the criminal history points for §4A1.1(a), (b), or (c), as applicable.

(2) (A) Revocation of probation, parole, supervised release, special parole, or mandatory release may affect the points for §4A1.1(e) in respect to the recency of last release from confinement.

(B) Revocation of probation, parole, supervised release, special parole, or mandatory release may affect the time period under which certain sentences are counted as provided in §4A1.2(d)(2) and (e). For the purposes of determining the applicable time period, use the following: (i) in the case of an adult term of imprisonment totaling more than one year and one month, the date of last release from incarceration on such sentence (see §4A1.2(e)(1)); (ii) in the case of any other confinement sentence for an offense committed prior to the defendant's eighteenth birthday, the date of the defendant's last release from confinement on such sentence (see §4A1.2(d)(2)(A)); and (iii) in any other case, the date of the original sentence (see §4A1.2(d)(2)(B) and (e)(2)).

(l) **Sentences on Appeal**

Prior sentences under appeal are counted except as expressly provided below. In the case of a prior sentence, the execution of which has been stayed pending appeal, §4A1.1(a), (b), (c), (d), and (f) shall apply as if the execution of such sentence had not been stayed; §4A1.1(e) shall not apply.

(m) **Effect of a Violation Warrant**

For the purposes of §4A1.1(d), a defendant who commits the instant offense while a violation warrant from a prior sentence is outstanding (e.g., a probation, parole, or supervised release violation warrant) shall be deemed to be under a criminal justice sentence if that sentence is otherwise countable, even if that sentence would have expired absent such warrant.

(n) **Failure to Report for Service of Sentence of Imprisonment**

For the purposes of §4A1.1(d) and (e), failure to report for service of a sentence of imprisonment shall be treated as an escape from such sentence.

(o) **Felony Offense**

For the purposes of §4A1.2(c), a "felony offense" means any federal, state, or local offense punishable by death or a term of imprisonment exceeding one year, regardless of the actual sentence imposed.

(p) **Crime of Violence Defined**

For the purposes of §4A1.1(f), the definition of "crime of violence" is that set forth in §4B1.2(1).

Commentary

Application Notes:

1. *Prior Sentence. "Prior sentence" means a sentence imposed prior to sentencing on the instant offense, other than a sentence for conduct that is part of the instant offense. See §4A1.2(a). A sentence imposed after the defendant's commencement of the instant offense, but prior to sentencing on the instant offense, is a prior sentence if it was for conduct other than conduct that was part of the instant offense. Conduct that is part of the instant offense means conduct that is relevant conduct to the instant offense under the provisions of §1B1.3 (Relevant Conduct).*

Under §4A1.2(a)(4), a conviction for which the defendant has not yet been sentenced is treated as if it were a prior sentence under §4A1.1(c) if a sentence resulting from such conviction otherwise would have been counted. In the case of an offense set forth in §4A1.2(c)(1) (which lists certain misdemeanor and petty offenses), a conviction for which the defendant has not yet been sentenced is treated as if it were a prior sentence under §4A1.2(a)(4) only where the offense is similar to the instant offense (because sentences for other offenses set forth in §4A1.2(c)(1) are counted only if they are of a specified type and length).

2. *Sentence of Imprisonment. To qualify as a sentence of imprisonment, the defendant must have actually served a period of imprisonment on such sentence (or, if the defendant escaped, would have served time). See §4A1.2(a)(3) and (b)(2). For the purposes of applying §4A1.1(a), (b), or (c), the length of a sentence of imprisonment is the stated maximum (e.g., in the case of a determinate sentence of five years, the stated maximum is five years; in the case of an indeterminate sentence of one to five years, the stated maximum is five years; in the case of an indeterminate sentence for a term not to exceed five years, the stated maximum is five years; in the case of an indeterminate sentence for a term not to exceed the defendant's twenty-first birthday, the stated maximum is the amount of time in pre-trial detention plus the amount of time between the date of sentence and the defendant's twenty-first birthday). That is, criminal history points are based on the sentence pronounced, not the length of time actually served. See §4A1.2(b)(1) and (2). A sentence of probation is to be treated as a sentence under §4A1.1(c) unless a condition of probation requiring imprisonment of at least sixty days was imposed.*

3. *Related Cases. Prior sentences are not considered related if they were for offenses that were separated by an intervening arrest (i.e., the defendant is arrested for the first offense prior to committing the second offense). Otherwise, prior sentences are considered related if they resulted from offenses that (1) occurred on the same occasion, (2) were part of a single common scheme or plan, or (3) were consolidated for trial or sentencing. The court should be aware that there may be instances in which this definition is overly broad and will result in a criminal history score that underrepresents the seriousness of the defendant's criminal history and the danger that he presents to the public. For example, if a defendant was convicted of a number of serious non-violent offenses committed on different occasions, and the resulting sentences were treated as related because the cases were consolidated for sentencing, the assignment of a single set of points may not adequately reflect the seriousness of the defendant's criminal history or the frequency with which he has committed crimes. In such circumstances, an upward departure may be warranted. Note that the above example refers to serious non-violent offenses. Where prior related sentences result from convictions of crimes of violence, §4A1.1(f) will apply.*

4. *Sentences Imposed in the Alternative. A sentence which specifies a fine or other non-incarcerative disposition as an alternative to a term of imprisonment (e.g., $1,000 fine or ninety days' imprisonment) is treated as a non-imprisonment sentence.*

5. *Sentences for Driving While Intoxicated or Under the Influence. Convictions for driving while intoxicated or under the influence (and similar offenses by whatever name they are known) are counted. Such offenses are not minor traffic infractions within the meaning of §4A1.2(c).*

6. *Reversed, Vacated, or Invalidated Convictions. Sentences resulting from convictions that (A) have been reversed or vacated because of errors of law or because of subsequently discovered evidence exonerating the defendant, or (B) have been ruled constitutionally invalid in a prior case are not to be counted. With respect to the current sentencing proceeding, this guideline and commentary do not confer upon the defendant any right to attack collaterally a prior*

conviction or sentence beyond any such rights otherwise recognized in law (e.g., 21 U.S.C. § 851 expressly provides that a defendant may collaterally attack certain prior convictions).

Nonetheless, the criminal conduct underlying any conviction that is not counted in the criminal history score may be considered pursuant to §4A1.3 (Adequacy of Criminal History Category).

7. *Offenses Committed Prior to Age Eighteen. Section 4A1.2(d) covers offenses committed prior to age eighteen. Attempting to count every juvenile adjudication would have the potential for creating large disparities due to the differential availability of records. Therefore, for offenses committed prior to age eighteen, only those that resulted in adult sentences of imprisonment exceeding one year and one month, or resulted in imposition of an adult or juvenile sentence or release from confinement on that sentence within five years of the defendant's commencement of the instant offense are counted. To avoid disparities from jurisdiction to jurisdiction in the age at which a defendant is considered a "juvenile," this provision applies to all offenses committed prior to age eighteen.*

8. *Applicable Time Period. Section 4A1.2(d)(2) and (e) establishes the time period within which prior sentences are counted. As used in §4A1.2(d)(2) and (e), the term "commencement of the instant offense" includes any relevant conduct. See §1B1.3 (Relevant Conduct). If the court finds that a sentence imposed outside this time period is evidence of similar, or serious dissimilar, criminal conduct, the court may consider this information in determining whether an upward departure is warranted under §4A1.3 (Adequacy of Criminal History Category).*

9. *Diversionary Dispositions. Section 4A1.2(f) requires counting prior adult diversionary dispositions if they involved a judicial determination of guilt or an admission of guilt in open court. This reflects a policy that defendants who receive the benefit of a rehabilitative sentence and continue to commit crimes should not be treated with further leniency.*

10. *Convictions Set Aside or Defendant Pardoned. A number of jurisdictions have various procedures pursuant to which previous convictions may be set aside or the defendant may be pardoned for reasons unrelated to innocence or errors of law, e.g., in order to restore civil rights or to remove the stigma associated with a criminal conviction. Sentences resulting from such convictions are to be counted. However, expunged convictions are not counted. §4A1.2(j).*

11. *Revocations to be Considered. Section 4A1.2(k) covers revocations of probation and other conditional sentences where the original term of imprisonment imposed, if any, did not exceed one year and one month. Rather than count the original sentence and the resentence after revocation as separate sentences, the sentence given upon revocation should be added to the original sentence of imprisonment, if any, and the total should be counted as if it were one sentence. By this approach, no more than three points will be assessed for a single conviction, even if probation or conditional release was subsequently revoked. If the sentence originally imposed, the sentence imposed upon revocation, or the total of both sentences exceeded one year and one month, the maximum three points would be assigned. If, however, at the time of revocation another sentence was imposed for a new criminal conviction, that conviction would be computed separately from the sentence imposed for the revocation.*

Where a revocation applies to multiple sentences, and such sentences are counted separately under §4A1.2(a)(2), add the term of imprisonment imposed upon revocation to the sentence that will result in the greatest increase in criminal history points. Example: A defendant was serving two probationary sentences, each counted separately under §4A1.2(a)(2); probation was revoked on both sentences as a result of the same violation conduct; and the defendant was sentenced to a total of 45 days of imprisonment. If one sentence had been a "straight" probationary sentence and the other had been a probationary sentence that had required service of 15 days of imprisonment, the revocation term of imprisonment (45 days) would be added to the probationary sentence that had the 15-day term of imprisonment. This would result in a total of 2 criminal history points under §4A1.1(b) (for the combined 60-day term of imprisonment) and 1 criminal history point under §4A1.1(c) (for the other probationary sentence).

12. *Local Ordinance Violations. A number of local jurisdictions have enacted ordinances covering certain offenses (e.g., larceny and assault misdemeanors) that are also violations of state criminal law. This enables a local court (e.g., a municipal court) to exercise jurisdiction over such offenses. Such offenses are excluded from the definition of local ordinance violations in §4A1.2(c)(1) and, therefore, sentences for such offenses are to be treated as if the defendant had been convicted under state law.*

13. *Insufficient Funds Check. "Insufficient funds check," as used in §4A1.2(c)(1), does not include any conviction establishing that the defendant used a false name or non-existent account.*

Background: Prior sentences, not otherwise excluded, are to be counted in the criminal history score, including uncounseled misdemeanor sentences where imprisonment was not imposed.

Historical Note: Effective November 1, 1987. Amended effective November 1, 1989 (see Appendix C, amendments 262-265); November 1, 1990 (see Appendix C, amendments 352 and 353); November 1, 1991 (see Appendix C, amendments 381 and 382); November 1, 1992 (see Appendix C, amendment 472); November 1, 1993 (see Appendix C, amendment 493).

§4A1.3. Adequacy of Criminal History Category (Policy Statement)

If reliable information indicates that the criminal history category does not adequately reflect the seriousness of the defendant's past criminal conduct or the likelihood that the defendant will commit other crimes, the court may consider imposing a sentence departing from the otherwise applicable guideline range. Such information may include, but is not limited to, information concerning:

(a) prior sentence(s) not used in computing the criminal history category (e.g., sentences for foreign and tribal offenses);

(b) prior sentence(s) of substantially more than one year imposed as a result of independent crimes committed on different occasions;

(c) prior similar misconduct established by a civil adjudication or by a failure to comply with an administrative order;

(d) whether the defendant was pending trial or sentencing on another charge at the time of the instant offense;

(e) prior similar adult criminal conduct not resulting in a criminal conviction.

A departure under this provision is warranted when the criminal history category significantly under-represents the seriousness of the defendant's criminal history or the likelihood that the defendant will commit further crimes. Examples might include the case of a defendant who (1) had several previous foreign sentences for serious offenses, (2) had received a prior consolidated sentence of ten years for a series of serious assaults, (3) had a similar instance of large scale fraudulent misconduct established by an adjudication in a Securities and Exchange Commission enforcement proceeding, (4) committed the instant offense while on bail or pretrial release for another serious offense or (5) for appropriate reasons, such as cooperation in the prosecution of other defendants, had previously received an extremely lenient sentence for a serious offense. The court may, after a review of all the relevant information, conclude that the defendant's criminal history was significantly more serious than that of most defendants in the same criminal history category, and therefore consider an upward departure from the guidelines. However, a prior arrest record itself shall not be considered under §4A1.3.

There may be cases where the court concludes that a defendant's criminal history category significantly over-represents the seriousness of a defendant's criminal history or the likelihood that the defendant will commit further crimes. An example might include the case of a defendant with two minor misdemeanor convictions close to ten years prior to the instant offense and no other evidence of prior criminal behavior in the intervening period. The court may conclude that the defendant's criminal history was significantly less serious than that of most defendants in the same criminal history category (Category II), and therefore consider a downward departure from the guidelines.

In considering a departure under this provision, the Commission intends that the court use, as a reference, the guideline range for a defendant with a higher or lower criminal history category, as applicable. For example, if the court concludes that the defendant's criminal history category of III significantly under-represents the seriousness of the defendant's criminal history, and that the seriousness of the defendant's criminal history most closely resembles that of most defendants with Criminal History Category IV , the court should look to the guideline range specified for a defendant with Criminal History Category IV to guide its departure. The Commission contemplates that there may, on occasion, be a case of an egregious, serious criminal record in which even the guideline range for Criminal History Category VI is not adequate to reflect the seriousness of the defendant's criminal history. In such a case, a departure above the guideline range for a defendant with Criminal History Category VI may be warranted. In determining whether an upward departure from Criminal History Category VI is warranted, the court should consider that the nature of the prior offenses rather than simply their number is often more indicative of the seriousness of the defendant's criminal record. For example, a defendant with five prior sentences for very large-scale fraud offenses may have 15 criminal history points, within the range of points typical for Criminal History Category VI, yet have a substantially more serious criminal history overall because of the nature of the prior offenses. On the other hand, a defendant with nine prior 60-day jail sentences for offenses such as petty larceny, prostitution, or possession of gambling slips has a higher number of criminal history points (18 points) than the typical Criminal History Category VI defendant, but not necessarily a more serious criminal history overall. Where the court determines that the extent and nature of the defendant's criminal history, taken together, are sufficient to warrant an upward departure from Criminal History Category VI, the court should structure the departure by moving incrementally down the sentencing table to the next higher offense level in Criminal History Category VI until it finds a guideline range appropriate to the case.

However, this provision is not symmetrical. The lower limit of the range for Criminal History Category I is set for a first offender with the lowest risk of recidivism. Therefore, a departure below the lower limit of the guideline range for Criminal

History Category I on the basis of the adequacy of criminal history cannot be appropriate.

Commentary

Background: *This policy statement recognizes that the criminal history score is unlikely to take into account all the variations in the seriousness of criminal history that may occur. For example, a defendant with an extensive record of serious, assaultive conduct who had received what might now be considered extremely lenient treatment in the past might have the same criminal history category as a defendant who had a record of less serious conduct. Yet, the first defendant's criminal history clearly may be more serious. This may be particularly true in the case of younger defendants (e.g., defendants in their early twenties or younger) who are more likely to have received repeated lenient treatment, yet who may actually pose a greater risk of serious recidivism than older defendants. This policy statement authorizes the consideration of a departure from the guidelines in the limited circumstances where reliable information indicates that the criminal history category does not adequately reflect the seriousness of the defendant's criminal history or likelihood of recidivism, and provides guidance for the consideration of such departures.*

Historical Note: Effective November 1, 1987. Amended effective November 1, 1991 (see Appendix C, amendment 381); November 1, 1992 (see Appendix C, amendment 460).

PART B - CAREER OFFENDERS AND CRIMINAL LIVELIHOOD

§4B1.1. <u>Career Offender</u>

A defendant is a career offender if (1) the defendant was at least eighteen years old at the time of the instant offense, (2) the instant offense of conviction is a felony that is either a crime of violence or a controlled substance offense, and (3) the defendant has at least two prior felony convictions of either a crime of violence or a controlled substance offense. If the offense level for a career criminal from the table below is greater than the offense level otherwise applicable, the offense level from the table below shall apply. A career offender's criminal history category in every case shall be Category VI.

	Offense Statutory Maximum	Offense Level*
(A)	Life	**37**
(B)	25 years or more	**34**
(C)	20 years or more, but less than 25 years	**32**
(D)	15 years or more, but less than 20 years	**29**
(E)	10 years or more, but less than 15 years	**24**
(F)	5 years or more, but less than 10 years	**17**
(G)	More than 1 year, but less than 5 years	**12.**

*If an adjustment from §3E1.1 (Acceptance of Responsibility) applies, decrease the offense level by the number of levels corresponding to that adjustment.

<u>*Commentary*</u>

<u>*Application Notes:*</u>

1. *"Crime of violence," "controlled substance offense," and "two prior felony convictions" are defined in §4B1.2.*

2. *"Offense Statutory Maximum," for the purposes of this guideline, refers to the maximum term of imprisonment authorized for the offense of conviction that is a crime of violence or controlled substance offense, not including any increase in that maximum term under a sentencing enhancement provision that applies because of the defendant's prior criminal record (such sentencing enhancement provisions are contained, for example, in 21 U.S.C. § 841(b)(1)(A), (b)(1)(B), (b)(1)(C), and (b)(1)(D)). For example, where the statutory maximum term of imprisonment under 21 U.S.C. § 841(b)(1)(C) is increased from twenty years to thirty years because the defendant has one or more qualifying prior drug convictions, the "Offense Statutory Maximum" for the purposes of this guideline is twenty years and not thirty years. If more than one count of conviction is of a crime of violence or controlled substance offense, use the maximum authorized term of imprisonment for the count that authorizes the greatest maximum term of imprisonment.*

<u>*Background*</u>*: 28 U.S.C. § 994(h) mandates that the Commission assure that certain "career" offenders, as defined in the statute, receive a sentence of imprisonment "at or near the maximum term authorized." Section 4B1.1 implements this mandate. The legislative history of this provision suggests that the phrase "maximum term authorized" should be construed as the maximum term authorized by statute. <u>See</u> S. Rep. 98-225, 98th Cong., 1st Sess. 175 (1983), 128 Cong. Rec. 26, 511-*

12 (1982) (text of "Career Criminals" amendment by Senator Kennedy), 26, 515 (brief summary of amendment), 26, 517-18 (statement of Senator Kennedy).

Historical Note: Effective November 1, 1987. Amended effective January 15, 1988 (see Appendix C, amendments 47 and 48); November 1, 1989 (see Appendix C, amendments 266 and 267); November 1, 1992 (see Appendix C, amendment 459); November 1, 1994 (see Appendix C, amendment 506).

§4B1.2. Definitions of Terms Used in Section 4B1.1

(1) The term "crime of violence" means any offense under federal or state law punishable by imprisonment for a term exceeding one year that --

(i) has as an element the use, attempted use, or threatened use of physical force against the person of another, or

(ii) is burglary of a dwelling, arson, or extortion, involves use of explosives, or otherwise involves conduct that presents a serious potential risk of physical injury to another.

(2) The term "controlled substance offense" means an offense under a federal or state law prohibiting the manufacture, import, export, distribution, or dispensing of a controlled substance (or a counterfeit substance) or the possession of a controlled substance (or a counterfeit substance) with intent to manufacture, import, export, distribute, or dispense.

(3) The term "two prior felony convictions" means (A) the defendant committed the instant offense subsequent to sustaining at least two felony convictions of either a crime of violence or a controlled substance offense (i.e., two felony convictions of a crime of violence, two felony convictions of a controlled substance offense, or one felony conviction of a crime of violence and one felony conviction of a controlled substance offense), and (B) the sentences for at least two of the aforementioned felony convictions are counted separately under the provisions of §4A1.1(a), (b), or (c). The date that a defendant sustained a conviction shall be the date that the guilt of the defendant has been established, whether by guilty plea, trial, or plea of nolo contendere.

Commentary

Application Notes:

1. *The terms "crime of violence" and "controlled substance offense" include the offenses of aiding and abetting, conspiring, and attempting to commit such offenses.*

2. *"Crime of violence" includes murder, manslaughter, kidnapping, aggravated assault, forcible sex offenses, robbery, arson, extortion, extortionate extension of credit, and burglary of a dwelling. Other offenses are included where (A) that offense has as an element the use, attempted use, or threatened use of physical force against the person of another, or (B) the conduct set forth (i.e., expressly charged) in the count of which the defendant was convicted involved use of explosives (including any explosive material or destructive device) or, by its nature, presented a serious potential risk of physical injury to another. Under this section, the conduct of which the defendant was convicted is the focus of inquiry.*

The term "crime of violence" does not include the offense of unlawful possession of a firearm by a felon. Where the instant offense is the unlawful possession of a firearm by a felon, §2K2.1 (Unlawful Receipt, Possession, or Transportation of Firearms or Ammunition; Prohibited Transactions Involving Firearms or Ammunition) provides an increase in offense level if the defendant has one or more prior felony convictions for a crime of violence or controlled substance offense; and, if the defendant is sentenced under the provisions of 18 U.S.C. § 924(e), §4B1.4 (Armed Career Criminal) will apply.

3. *"Prior felony conviction" means a prior adult federal or state conviction for an offense punishable by death or imprisonment for a term exceeding one year, regardless of whether such offense is specifically designated as a felony and regardless of the actual sentence imposed. A conviction for an offense committed at age eighteen or older is an adult conviction. A conviction for an offense committed prior to age eighteen is an adult conviction if it is classified as an adult conviction under the laws of the jurisdiction in which the defendant was convicted (e.g., a federal conviction for an offense committed prior to the defendant's eighteenth birthday is an adult conviction if the defendant was expressly proceeded against as an adult).*

4. *The provisions of §4A1.2 (Definitions and Instructions for Computing Criminal History) are applicable to the counting of convictions under §4B1.1.*

Historical Note: Effective November 1, 1987. Amended effective January 15, 1988 (see Appendix C, amendment 49); November 1, 1989 (see Appendix C, amendment 268); November 1, 1991 (see Appendix C, amendment 433); November 1, 1992 (see Appendix C, amendment 461).

§4B1.3. Criminal Livelihood

If the defendant committed an offense as part of a pattern of criminal conduct engaged in as a livelihood, his offense level shall be not less than **13**, unless §3E1.1 (Acceptance of Responsibility) applies, in which event his offense level shall be not less than **11**.

Commentary

Application Notes:

1. *"Pattern of criminal conduct" means planned criminal acts occurring over a substantial period of time. Such acts may involve a single course of conduct or independent offenses.*

2. *"Engaged in as a livelihood" means that (1) the defendant derived income from the pattern of criminal conduct that in any twelve-month period exceeded 2,000 times the then existing hourly minimum wage under federal law; and (2) the totality of circumstances shows that such criminal conduct was the defendant's primary occupation in that twelve-month period (e.g., the defendant engaged in criminal conduct rather than regular, legitimate employment; or the defendant's legitimate employment was merely a front for his criminal conduct).*

Background: Section 4B1.3 implements 28 U.S.C. § 994(i)(2), which directs the Commission to ensure that the guidelines specify a "substantial term of imprisonment" for a defendant who committed an offense as part of a pattern of criminal conduct from which he derived a substantial portion of his income.

Historical Note: Effective November 1, 1987. Amended effective June 15, 1988 (see Appendix C, amendment 50); November 1, 1989 (see Appendix C, amendment 269); November 1, 1990 (see Appendix C, amendment 354).

§4B1.4. <u>Armed Career Criminal</u>

(a) A defendant who is subject to an enhanced sentence under the provisions of 18 U.S.C. § 924(e) is an armed career criminal.

(b) The offense level for an armed career criminal is the greatest of:

(1) the offense level applicable from Chapters Two and Three; or

(2) the offense level from §4B1.1 (Career Offender) if applicable; or

(3) (A) 34, if the defendant used or possessed the firearm or ammunition in connection with a crime of violence or controlled substance offense, as defined in §4B1.2(1), or if the firearm possessed by the defendant was of a type described in 26 U.S.C. § 5845(a)*; or

(B) 33, otherwise.*

*If an adjustment from §3E1.1 (Acceptance of Responsibility) applies, decrease the offense level by the number of levels corresponding to that adjustment.

(c) The criminal history category for an armed career criminal is the greatest of:

(1) the criminal history category from Chapter Four, Part A (Criminal History), or §4B1.1 (Career Offender) if applicable; or

(2) Category VI, if the defendant used or possessed the firearm or ammunition in connection with a crime of violence or controlled substance offense, as defined in §4B1.2(1), or if the firearm possessed by the defendant was of a type described in 26 U.S.C. § 5845(a); or

(3) Category IV.

<u>*Commentary*</u>

<u>*Application Note:*</u>

1. *This guideline applies in the case of a defendant subject to an enhanced sentence under 18 U.S.C. § 924(e). Under 18 U.S.C. § 924(e)(1), a defendant is subject to an enhanced sentence if the instant offense of conviction is a violation of 18 U.S.C. § 922(g) and the defendant has at least three prior convictions for a "violent felony" or "serious drug offense," or both, committed on occasions different from one another. The terms "violent felony" and "serious drug offense" are defined in 18 U.S.C. § 924(e)(2). It is to be noted that the definitions of "violent felony" and "serious drug offense" in 18 U.S.C. § 924(e)(2) are not identical to the definitions of "crime of violence" and "controlled substance offense" used in §4B1.1 (Career Offender), nor are the time periods for the counting of prior sentences under §4A1.2 (Definitions and Instructions for Computing Criminal History) applicable to the determination of whether a defendant is subject to an enhanced sentence under 18 U.S.C. § 924(e).*

It is also to be noted that the procedural steps relative to the imposition of an enhanced sentence under 18 U.S.C. § 924(e) are not set forth by statute and may vary to some extent from jurisdiction to jurisdiction.

Background: This section implements 18 U.S.C. § 924(e), which requires a minimum sentence of imprisonment of fifteen years for a defendant who violates 18 U.S.C. § 922(g) and has three previous convictions for a violent felony or a serious drug offense. If the offense level determined under this section is greater than the offense level otherwise applicable, the offense level determined under this section shall be applied. A minimum criminal history category (Category IV) is provided, reflecting that each defendant to whom this section applies will have at least three prior convictions for serious offenses. In some cases, the criminal history category may not adequately reflect the defendant's criminal history; see §4A1.3 (Adequacy of Criminal History Category).

Historical Note: Effective November 1, 1990 (see Appendix C, amendment 355). Amended effective November 1, 1992 (see Appendix C, amendment 459).

CHAPTER FIVE - DETERMINING THE SENTENCE

Introductory Commentary

For certain categories of offenses and offenders, the guidelines permit the court to impose either imprisonment or some other sanction or combination of sanctions. In determining the type of sentence to impose, the sentencing judge should consider the nature and seriousness of the conduct, the statutory purposes of sentencing, and the pertinent offender characteristics. A sentence is within the guidelines if it complies with each applicable section of this chapter. The court should impose a sentence sufficient, but not greater than necessary, to comply with the statutory purposes of sentencing. 18 U.S.C. § 3553(a).

Historical Note: Effective November 1, 1987.

PART A - SENTENCING TABLE

The Sentencing Table used to determine the guideline range follows:

SENTENCING TABLE
(in months of imprisonment)

	Offense Level	Criminal History Category (Criminal History Points)					
		I (0 or 1)	II (2 or 3)	III (4, 5, 6)	IV (7, 8, 9)	V (10, 11, 12)	VI (13 or more)
	1	0 - 6	0 - 6	0 - 6	0 - 6	0 - 6	0 - 6
	2	0 - 6	0 - 6	0 - 6	0 - 6	0 - 6	1 - 7
	3	0 - 6	0 - 6	0 - 6	0 - 6	2 - 8	3 - 9
Zone A	4	0 - 6	0 - 6	0 - 6	2 - 8	4 - 10	6 - 12
	5	0 - 6	0 - 6	1 - 7	4 - 10	6 - 12	9 - 15
	6	0 - 6	1 - 7	2 - 8	6 - 12	9 - 15	12 - 18
	7	0 - 6	2 - 8	4 - 10	8 - 14	12 - 18	15 - 21
	8	0 - 6	4 - 10	6 - 12	10 - 16	15 - 21	18 - 24
	9	4 - 10	6 - 12	8 - 14	12 - 18	18 - 24	21 - 27
Zone B							
	10	6 - 12	8 - 14	10 - 16	15 - 21	21 - 27	24 - 30
	11	8 - 14	10 - 16	12 - 18	18 - 24	24 - 30	27 - 33
Zone C	12	10 - 16	12 - 18	15 - 21	21 - 27	27 - 33	30 - 37
	13	12 - 18	15 - 21	18 - 24	24 - 30	30 - 37	33 - 41
	14	15 - 21	18 - 24	21 - 27	27 - 33	33 - 41	37 - 46
	15	18 - 24	21 - 27	24 - 30	30 - 37	37 - 46	41 - 51
	16	21 - 27	24 - 30	27 - 33	33 - 41	41 - 51	46 - 57
	17	24 - 30	27 - 33	30 - 37	37 - 46	46 - 57	51 - 63
	18	27 - 33	30 - 37	33 - 41	41 - 51	51 - 63	57 - 71
	19	30 - 37	33 - 41	37 - 46	46 - 57	57 - 71	63 - 78
	20	33 - 41	37 - 46	41 - 51	51 - 63	63 - 78	70 - 87
	21	37 - 46	41 - 51	46 - 57	57 - 71	70 - 87	77 - 96
	22	41 - 51	46 - 57	51 - 63	63 - 78	77 - 96	84 - 105
	23	46 - 57	51 - 63	57 - 71	70 - 87	84 - 105	92 - 115
	24	51 - 63	57 - 71	63 - 78	77 - 96	92 - 115	100 - 125
Zone D	25	57 - 71	63 - 78	70 - 87	84 - 105	100 - 125	110 - 137
	26	63 - 78	70 - 87	78 - 97	92 - 115	110 - 137	120 - 150
	27	70 - 87	78 - 97	87 - 108	100 - 125	120 - 150	130 - 162
	28	78 - 97	87 - 108	97 - 121	110 - 137	130 - 162	140 - 175
	29	87 - 108	97 - 121	108 - 135	121 - 151	140 - 175	151 - 188
	30	97 - 121	108 - 135	121 - 151	135 - 168	151 - 188	168 - 210
	31	108 - 135	121 - 151	135 - 168	151 - 188	168 - 210	188 - 235
	32	121 - 151	135 - 168	151 - 188	168 - 210	188 - 235	210 - 262
	33	135 - 168	151 - 188	168 - 210	188 - 235	210 - 262	235 - 293
	34	151 - 188	168 - 210	188 - 235	210 - 262	235 - 293	262 - 327
	35	168 - 210	188 - 235	210 - 262	235 - 293	262 - 327	292 - 365
	36	188 - 235	210 - 262	235 - 293	262 - 327	292 - 365	324 - 405
	37	210 - 262	235 - 293	262 - 327	292 - 365	324 - 405	360 - life
	38	235 - 293	262 - 327	292 - 365	324 - 405	360 - life	360 - life
	39	262 - 327	292 - 365	324 - 405	360 - life	360 - life	360 - life
	40	292 - 365	324 - 405	360 - life	360 - life	360 - life	360 - life
	41	324 - 405	360 - life	360 - life	360 - life	360 - life	360 - life
	42	360 - life	360 - life	360 - life	360 - life	360 - life	360 - life
	43	life	life	life	life	life	life

Commentary to Sentencing Table

Application Notes:

1. *The Offense Level (1-43) forms the vertical axis of the Sentencing Table. The Criminal History Category (I-VI) forms the horizontal axis of the Table. The intersection of the Offense Level and Criminal History Category displays the Guideline Range in months of imprisonment. "Life" means life imprisonment. For example, the guideline range applicable to a defendant with an Offense Level of 15 and a Criminal History Category of III is 24-30 months of imprisonment.*

2. *In rare cases, a total offense level of less than 1 or more than 43 may result from application of the guidelines. A total offense level of less than 1 is to be treated as an offense level of 1. An offense level of more than 43 is to be treated as an offense level of 43.*

3. *The Criminal History Category is determined by the total criminal history points from Chapter Four, Part A, except as provided in §§4B1.1 (Career Offender) and 4B1.4 (Armed Career Criminal). The total criminal history points associated with each Criminal History Category are shown under each Criminal History Category in the Sentencing Table.*

Historical Note: Effective November 1, 1987. Amended effective November 1, 1989 (see Appendix C, amendment 270); November 1, 1991 (see Appendix C, amendment 418); November 1, 1992 (see Appendix C, amendment 462).

PART B - PROBATION

Introductory Commentary

The Comprehensive Crime Control Act of 1984 makes probation a sentence in and of itself. 18 U.S.C. § 3561. Probation may be used as an alternative to incarceration, provided that the terms and conditions of probation can be fashioned so as to meet fully the statutory purposes of sentencing, including promoting respect for law, providing just punishment for the offense, achieving general deterrence, and protecting the public from further crimes by the defendant.

Historical Note: Effective November 1, 1987.

§5B1.1. Imposition of a Term of Probation

(a) Subject to the statutory restrictions in subsection (b) below, a sentence of probation is authorized if:

(1) the applicable guideline range is in Zone A of the Sentencing Table; or

(2) the applicable guideline range is in Zone B of the Sentencing Table and the court imposes a condition or combination of conditions requiring intermittent confinement, community confinement, or home detention as provided in subsection (c)(3) of §5C1.1 (Imposition of a Term of Imprisonment).

(b) A sentence of probation may not be imposed in the event:

(1) the offense of conviction is a Class A or B felony, 18 U.S.C. § 3561(a)(1);

(2) the offense of conviction expressly precludes probation as a sentence, 18 U.S.C. § 3561(a)(2);

(3) the defendant is sentenced at the same time to a sentence of imprisonment for the same or a different offense, 18 U.S.C. § 3561(a)(3).

Commentary

Application Notes:

1. *Except where prohibited by statute or by the guideline applicable to the offense in Chapter Two, the guidelines authorize, but do not require, a sentence of probation in the following circumstances:*

   (a) *Where the applicable guideline range is in Zone A of the Sentencing Table (i.e., the minimum term of imprisonment specified in the applicable guideline range is zero months). In such cases, a condition requiring a period of community confinement, home detention, or intermittent confinement may be imposed but is not required.*

(b) *__Where the applicable guideline range is in Zone B of the Sentencing Table (i.e., the minimum term of imprisonment specified in the applicable guideline range is at least one but not more than six months)__. In such cases, the court may impose probation only if it imposes a condition or combination of conditions requiring a period of community confinement, home detention, or intermittent confinement sufficient to satisfy the minimum term of imprisonment specified in the guideline range. For example, where the offense level is 7 and the criminal history category is II, the guideline range from the Sentencing Table is 2-8 months. In such case, the court may impose a sentence of probation only if it imposes a condition or conditions requiring at least two months of community confinement, home detention, or intermittent confinement, or a combination of community confinement, home detention, and intermittent confinement totalling at least two months.*

2. *Where the applicable guideline range is in Zone C or D of the Sentencing Table (__i.e.__, the minimum term of imprisonment specified in the applicable guideline range is eight months or more), the guidelines do not authorize a sentence of probation. __See__ §5C1.1 (Imposition of a Term of Imprisonment).*

__Background__: This section provides for the imposition of a sentence of probation. The court may sentence a defendant to a term of probation in any case unless (1) prohibited by statute, or (2) where a term of imprisonment is required under §5C1.1 (Imposition of a Term of Imprisonment). Under 18 U.S.C. § 3561(a)(3), the imposition of a sentence of probation is prohibited where the defendant is sentenced at the same time to a sentence of imprisonment for the same or a different offense. Although this provision has effectively abolished the use of "split sentences" imposable pursuant to the former 18 U.S.C. § 3651, the drafters of the Sentencing Reform Act noted that the functional equivalent of the split sentence could be "achieved by a more direct and logically consistent route" by providing that a defendant serve a term of imprisonment followed by a period of supervised release. (S. Rep. No. 225, 98th Cong., 1st Sess. 89 (1983)). Section 5B1.1(a)(2) provides a transition between the circumstances under which a "straight" probationary term is authorized and those where probation is prohibited.

__Historical Note__: Effective November 1, 1987. Amended effective November 1, 1989 (__see__ Appendix C, amendment 302); November 1, 1992 (__see__ Appendix C, amendment 462).

§5B1.2. __Term of Probation__

(a) When probation is imposed, the term shall be:

(1) at least one year but not more than five years if the offense level is 6 or greater;

(2) no more than three years in any other case.

__*Commentary*__

__Background__: This section governs the length of a term of probation. Subject to statutory restrictions, the guidelines provide that a term of probation may not exceed three years if the offense level is less than 6. If a defendant has an offense level of 6 or greater, the guidelines provide that a term of probation be at least one year but not more than five years. Although some distinction in the length of a term of probation is warranted based on the circumstances of the case, a term of probation may also be used to enforce conditions such as fine or restitution payments, or attendance in a program *of treatment such as drug rehabilitation. Often, it may not be possible to determine the amount of time required for the satisfaction of such payments or programs in advance. This issue has been resolved by setting forth two broad ranges for the duration of a term of probation depending upon the offense level. Within the guidelines set forth in this section, the determination of the length of a term of probation is within the discretion of the sentencing judge.*

Historical Note: Effective November 1, 1987.

§5B1.3. Conditions of Probation

(a) If a term of probation is imposed, the court shall impose a condition that the defendant shall not commit another federal, state, or local crime during the term of probation. 18 U.S.C. § 3563(a)(1). The court shall also impose a condition that the defendant not possess illegal controlled substances. 18 U.S.C. § 3563(a)(3).

(b) The court may impose other conditions that (1) are reasonably related to the nature and circumstances of the offense, the history and characteristics of the defendant, and the purposes of sentencing and (2) involve only such deprivations of liberty or property as are reasonably necessary to effect the purposes of sentencing. 18 U.S.C. § 3563(b). Recommended conditions are set forth in §5B1.4.

(c) If a term of probation is imposed for a felony, the court shall impose at least one of the following as a condition of probation: a fine, an order of restitution, or community service, unless the court finds on the record that extraordinary circumstances exist that would make such a condition plainly unreasonable, in which event the court shall impose one or more of the other conditions set forth under 18 U.S.C. § 3563(b). 18 U.S.C. § 3563(a)(2).

(d) Intermittent confinement (custody for intervals of time) may be ordered as a condition of probation during the first year of probation. 18 U.S.C. § 3563(b)(11). Intermittent confinement shall be credited toward the guideline term of imprisonment at §5C1.1 as provided in the schedule at §5C1.1(e).

Commentary

A broader form of the condition required under 18 U.S.C. § 3563(a)(3) (pertaining to possession of controlled substances) is set forth as recommended condition (7) at §5B1.4 (Recommended Conditions of Probation and Supervised Release).

Historical Note: Effective November 1, 1987. Amended effective November 1, 1989 (see Appendix C, amendments 273, 274, and 302).

§5B1.4. Recommended Conditions of Probation and Supervised Release (Policy Statement)

(a) The following "standard" conditions (1-13) are generally recommended for both probation and supervised release:

(1) the defendant shall not leave the judicial district or other specified geographic area without the permission of the court or probation officer;

(2) the defendant shall report to the probation officer as directed by the court or probation officer and shall submit a truthful and complete written report within the first five days of each month;

(3) the defendant shall answer truthfully all inquiries by the probation officer and follow the instructions of the probation officer;

(4) the defendant shall support his dependents and meet other family responsibilities;

(5) the defendant shall work regularly at a lawful occupation unless excused by the probation officer for schooling, training, or other acceptable reasons;

(6) the defendant shall notify the probation officer within seventy-two hours of any change in residence or employment;

(7) the defendant shall refrain from excessive use of alcohol and shall not purchase, possess, use, distribute, or administer any narcotic or other controlled substance, or any paraphernalia related to such substances, except as prescribed by a physician;

(8) the defendant shall not frequent places where controlled substances are illegally sold, used, distributed, or administered, or other places specified by the court;

(9) the defendant shall not associate with any persons engaged in criminal activity, and shall not associate with any person convicted of a felony unless granted permission to do so by the probation officer;

(10) the defendant shall permit a probation officer to visit him at any time at home or elsewhere and shall permit confiscation of any contraband observed in plain view by the probation officer;

(11) the defendant shall notify the probation officer within seventy-two hours of being arrested or questioned by a law enforcement officer;

(12) the defendant shall not enter into any agreement to act as an informer or a special agent of a law enforcement agency without the permission of the court;

(13) as directed by the probation officer, the defendant shall notify third parties of risks that may be occasioned by the defendant's criminal record or personal history or characteristics, and shall permit the probation officer to make such notifications and to confirm the defendant's compliance with such notification requirement.

(b) The following "special" conditions of probation and supervised release (14-24) are either recommended or required by law under the circumstances described, or may be appropriate in a particular case:

(14) Possession of Weapons

If the instant conviction is for a felony, or if the defendant was previously convicted of a felony or used a firearm or other dangerous weapon in the course of the instant offense, it is recommended that the court impose a condition prohibiting the defendant from possessing a firearm or other dangerous weapon.

(15) Restitution

If the court imposes an order of restitution, it is recommended that the court impose a condition requiring the defendant to make payment of restitution or adhere to a court ordered installment schedule for payment of restitution. See §5E1.1 (Restitution).

(16) Fines

If the court imposes a fine, it is recommended that the court impose a condition requiring the defendant to pay the fine or adhere to a court ordered installment schedule for payment of the fine.

(17) Debt Obligations

If an installment schedule of payment of restitution or fines is imposed, it is recommended that the court impose a condition prohibiting the defendant from incurring new credit charges or opening additional lines of credit without approval of the probation officer unless the defendant is in compliance with the payment schedule.

(18) Access to Financial Information

If the court imposes an order of restitution, forfeiture, or notice to victims, or orders the defendant to pay a fine, it is recommended that the court impose a condition requiring the defendant to provide the probation officer access to any requested financial information.

(19) Community Confinement

Residence in a community treatment center, halfway house or similar facility may be imposed as a condition of probation or supervised release. See §5F1.1 (Community Confinement).

(20) Home Detention

Home detention may be imposed as a condition of probation or supervised release, but only as a substitute for imprisonment. See §5F1.2 (Home Detention).

(21) Community Service

Community service may be imposed as a condition of probation or supervised release. See §5F1.3 (Community Service).

(22) Occupational Restrictions

Occupational restrictions may be imposed as a condition of probation or supervised release. See §5F1.5 (Occupational Restrictions).

(23) Substance Abuse Program Participation

If the court has reason to believe that the defendant is an abuser of narcotics, other controlled substances or alcohol, it is recommended that the court impose a condition requiring the defendant to participate in a program approved by the United States Probation Office for substance abuse, which program may include testing to determine whether the defendant has reverted to the use of drugs or alcohol.

(24) Mental Health Program Participation

If the court has reason to believe that the defendant is in need of psychological or psychiatric treatment, it is recommended that the court impose a condition requiring that the defendant participate in a mental health program approved by the United States Probation Office.

(25) Curfew

If the court concludes that restricting the defendant to his place of residence during evening and nighttime hours is necessary to provide just punishment for the offense, to protect the public from crimes that the defendant might commit during those hours, or to assist in the rehabilitation of the defendant, a condition of curfew is recommended. Electronic monitoring may be used as a means of surveillance to ensure compliance with a curfew order.

Commentary

Application Note:

1. *Home detention, as defined by §5F1.2, may only be used as a substitute for imprisonment.* See *§5C1.1 (Imposition of a Term of Imprisonment). Under home detention, the defendant, with specified exceptions, is restricted to his place of residence during all non-working hours. Curfew, which limits the defendant to his place of residence during evening and nighttime hours, is less restrictive than home detention and may be imposed as a condition of probation whether or not imprisonment could have been ordered.*

Historical Note: Effective November 1, 1987. Amended effective November 1, 1989 (see Appendix C, amendments 271, 272, and 302).

PART C - IMPRISONMENT

§5C1.1. Imposition of a Term of Imprisonment

(a) A sentence conforms with the guidelines for imprisonment if it is within the minimum and maximum terms of the applicable guideline range.

(b) If the applicable guideline range is in Zone A of the Sentencing Table, a sentence of imprisonment is not required, unless the applicable guideline in Chapter Two expressly requires such a term.

(c) If the applicable guideline range is in Zone B of the Sentencing Table, the minimum term may be satisfied by --

(1) a sentence of imprisonment; or

(2) a sentence of imprisonment that includes a term of supervised release with a condition that substitutes community confinement or home detention according to the schedule in subsection (e), provided that at least one month is satisfied by imprisonment; or

(3) a sentence of probation that includes a condition or combination of conditions that substitute intermittent confinement, community confinement, or home detention for imprisonment according to the schedule in subsection (e).

(d) If the applicable guideline range is in Zone C of the Sentencing Table, the minimum term may be satisfied by --

(1) a sentence of imprisonment; or

(2) a sentence of imprisonment that includes a term of supervised release with a condition that substitutes community confinement or home detention according to the schedule in subsection (e), provided that at least one-half of the minimum term is satisfied by imprisonment.

(e) Schedule of Substitute Punishments:

(1) One day of intermittent confinement in prison or jail for one day of imprisonment (each 24 hours of confinement is credited as one day of intermittent confinement, provided, however, that one day shall be credited for any calendar day during which the defendant is employed in the community and confined during all remaining hours);

(2) One day of community confinement (residence in a community treatment center, halfway house, or similar residential facility) for one day of imprisonment;

(3) One day of home detention for one day of imprisonment.

(f) If the applicable guideline range is in Zone D of the Sentencing Table, the minimum term shall be satisfied by a sentence of imprisonment.

<u>Commentary</u>

<u>*Application Notes:*</u>

1. *Subsection (a) provides that a sentence conforms with the guidelines for imprisonment if it is within the minimum and maximum terms of the applicable guideline range specified in the Sentencing Table in Part A of this Chapter. For example, if the defendant has an Offense Level of 20 and a Criminal History Category of I, the applicable guideline range is 33-41 months of imprisonment. Therefore, a sentence of imprisonment of at least thirty-three months, but not more than forty-one months, is within the applicable guideline range.*

2. *Subsection (b) provides that where the applicable guideline range is in Zone A of the Sentencing Table (<u>i.e.,</u> the minimum term of imprisonment specified in the applicable guideline range is zero months), the court is not required to impose a sentence of imprisonment unless a sentence of imprisonment or its equivalent is specifically required by the guideline applicable to the offense. Where imprisonment is not required, the court, for example, may impose a sentence of probation. In some cases, a fine appropriately may be imposed as the sole sanction.*

3. *Subsection (c) provides that where the applicable guideline range is in Zone B of the Sentencing Table (<u>i.e.,</u> the minimum term of imprisonment specified in the applicable guideline range is at least one but not more than six months), the court has three options:*

   It may impose a sentence of imprisonment.

   It may impose a sentence of probation provided that it includes a condition of probation requiring a period of intermittent confinement, community confinement, or home detention, or combination of intermittent confinement, community confinement, and home detention, sufficient to satisfy the minimum period of imprisonment specified in the guideline range. For example, where the guideline range is 4-10 months, a sentence of probation with a condition requiring at least four months of intermittent confinement, community confinement, or home detention would satisfy the minimum term of imprisonment specified in the guideline range.

   Or, it may impose a sentence of imprisonment that includes a term of supervised release with a condition that requires community confinement or home detention. In such case, at least one month must be satisfied by actual imprisonment and the remainder of the minimum term specified in the guideline range must be satisfied by community confinement or home detention. For example, where the guideline range is 4-10 months, a sentence of imprisonment of one month followed by a term of supervised release with a condition requiring three months of community confinement or home detention would satisfy the minimum term of imprisonment specified in the guideline range.

   The preceding examples illustrate sentences that satisfy the minimum term of imprisonment required by the guideline range. The court, of course, may impose a sentence at a higher point within the applicable guideline range. For example, where the guideline range is 4-10 months, both a sentence of probation with a condition requiring six months of community confinement or home detention (under subsection (c)(3)) and a sentence of two months imprisonment followed by a term of supervised release with a condition requiring four months of community confinement or home detention (under subsection (c)(2)) would be within the guideline range.

4. *Subsection (d) provides that where the applicable guideline range is in Zone C of the Sentencing Table (i.e., the minimum term specified in the applicable guideline range is eight, nine, or ten months), the court has two options:*

   It may impose a sentence of imprisonment.

   Or, it may impose a sentence of imprisonment that includes a term of supervised release with a condition requiring community confinement or home detention. In such case, at least one-half of the minimum term specified in the guideline range must be satisfied by imprisonment, and the remainder of the minimum term specified in the guideline range must be satisfied by community confinement or home detention. For example, where the guideline range is 8-14 months, a sentence of four months imprisonment followed by a term of supervised release with a condition requiring four months community confinement or home detention would satisfy the minimum term of imprisonment required by the guideline range.

   The preceding example illustrates a sentence that satisfies the minimum term of imprisonment required by the guideline range. The court, of course, may impose a sentence at a higher point within the guideline range. For example, where the guideline range is 8-14 months, both a sentence of four months imprisonment followed by a term of supervised release with a condition requiring six months of community confinement or home detention (under subsection (d)), and a sentence of five months imprisonment followed by a term of supervised release with a condition requiring four months of community confinement or home detention (also under subsection (d)) would be within the guideline range.

5. *Subsection (e) sets forth a schedule of imprisonment substitutes.*

6. *There may be cases in which a departure from the guidelines by substitution of a longer period of community confinement than otherwise authorized for an equivalent number of months of imprisonment is warranted to accomplish a specific treatment purpose (e.g., substitution of twelve months in an approved residential drug treatment program for twelve months of imprisonment). Such a substitution should be considered only in cases where the defendant's criminality is related to the treatment problem to be addressed and there is a reasonable likelihood that successful completion of the treatment program will eliminate that problem.*

7. *The use of substitutes for imprisonment as provided in subsections (c) and (d) is not recommended for most defendants with a criminal history category of III or above. Generally, such defendants have failed to reform despite the use of such alternatives.*

8. *Subsection (f) provides that, where the applicable guideline range is in Zone D of the Sentencing Table (i.e., the minimum term specified in the applicable guideline range is twelve months or more), the minimum term must be satisfied by a sentence of imprisonment without the use of any of the imprisonment substitutes in subsection(e).*

Historical Note: Effective November 1, 1987. Amended effective January 15, 1988 (see Appendix C, amendment 51); November 1, 1989 (see Appendix C, amendments 271, 275, and 302); November 1, 1992 (see Appendix C, amendment 462).

§5C1.2. Limitation on Applicability of Statutory Minimum Sentences in Certain Cases

In the case of an offense under 21 U.S.C. § 841, 844, 846, 960, or 963, the court shall impose a sentence in accordance with the applicable guidelines without regard to any statutory minimum sentence, if the court finds that the defendant meets the criteria in 18 U.S.C. § 3553(f)(1)-(5) set forth verbatim below:

(1) the defendant does not have more than 1 criminal history point, as determined under the sentencing guidelines;

(2) the defendant did not use violence or credible threats of violence or possess a firearm or other dangerous weapon (or induce another participant to do so) in connection with the offense;

(3) the offense did not result in death or serious bodily injury to any person;

(4) the defendant was not an organizer, leader, manager, or supervisor of others in the offense, as determined under the sentencing guidelines and was not engaged in a continuing criminal enterprise, as defined in 21 U.S.C. § 848; and

(5) not later than the time of the sentencing hearing, the defendant has truthfully provided to the Government all information and evidence the defendant has concerning the offense or offenses that were part of the same course of conduct or of a common scheme or plan, but the fact that the defendant has no relevant or useful other information to provide or that the Government is already aware of the information shall not preclude a determination by the court that the defendant has complied with this requirement.

Commentary

Application Notes:

1. *"More than 1 criminal history point, as determined under the sentencing guidelines," as used in subdivision (1), means more than one criminal history point as determined under §4A1.1 (Criminal History Category).*

2. *"Dangerous weapon" and "firearm," as used in subdivision (2), and "serious bodily injury," as used in subdivision (3), are defined in the Commentary to §1B1.1 (Application Instructions).*

3. *"Offense," as used in subdivisions (2)-(4), and "offense or offenses that were part of the same course of conduct or of a common scheme or plan," as used in subdivision (5), mean the offense of conviction and all relevant conduct.*

4. *Consistent with §1B1.3 (Relevant Conduct), the term "defendant," as used in subdivision (2), limits the accountability of the defendant to his own conduct and conduct that he aided or abetted, counseled, commanded, induced, procured, or willfully caused.*

5. *"Organizer, leader, manager, or supervisor of others in the offense, as determined under the sentencing guidelines," as used in subdivision (4), means a defendant who receives an adjustment for an aggravating role under §3B1.1 (Aggravating Role).*

6. *"Engaged in a continuing criminal enterprise," as used in subdivision (4), is defined in 21 U.S.C. § 848(c). As a practical matter, it should not be necessary to apply this prong of subdivision (4) because (i) this section does not apply to a conviction under 21 U.S.C. § 848, and (ii) any defendant who "engaged in a continuing criminal enterprise" but is convicted of an offense to which this section applies will be a "leader, organizer, manager, or supervisor of others in the offense."*

7. *Information disclosed by the defendant with respect to subdivision (5) may be considered in determining the applicable guideline range, except where the use of such information is restricted under the provisions of §1B1.8 (Use of Certain Information). That is, subdivision (5) does not provide an independent basis for restricting the use of information disclosed by the defendant.*

8. *Under 18 U.S.C. § 3553(f), prior to its determination, the court shall afford the government an opportunity to make a recommendation. See also Rule 32(a)(1), Fed. R. Crim. P.*

Background: This section sets forth the relevant provisions of 18 U.S.C. § 3553(f), as added by section 80001(a) of the Violent Crime Control and Law Enforcement Act of 1994, which limit the applicability of statutory minimum sentences in certain cases. Under the authority of section 80001(b) of that Act, the Commission has promulgated application notes to provide guidance in the application of 18 U.S.C. § 3553(f). See also H. Rep. No. 103-460, 103d Cong., 2d Sess. 3 (1994) (expressing intent to foster greater coordination between mandatory minimum sentencing and the sentencing guideline system).

Historical Note: Effective September 23, 1994 (see Appendix C, amendment 509).

PART D - SUPERVISED RELEASE

§5D1.1. Imposition of a Term of Supervised Release

(a) The court shall order a term of supervised release to follow imprisonment when a sentence of imprisonment of more than one year is imposed, or when required by statute.

(b) The court may order a term of supervised release to follow imprisonment in any other case.

Commentary

Application Notes:

1. *Subsection 5D1.1(a) requires imposition of supervised release following any sentence of imprisonment for a term of more than one year or if required by a specific statute. While there may be cases within this category that do not require post release supervision, these cases are the exception and may be handled by a departure from this guideline.*

2. *Under §5D1.1(b), the court may impose a term of supervised release in cases involving imprisonment for a term of one year or less. The court may consider the need for a term of supervised release to facilitate the reintegration of the defendant into the community; to enforce a fine, restitution order, or other condition; or to fulfill any other purpose authorized by statute.*

Historical Note: Effective November 1, 1987. Amended effective November 1, 1989 (see Appendix C, amendment 302).

§5D1.2. Term of Supervised Release

(a) If a defendant is convicted under a statute that requires a term of supervised release, the term shall be at least three years but not more than five years, or the minimum period required by statute, whichever is greater.

(b) Otherwise, when a term of supervised release is ordered, the length of the term shall be:

(1) at least three years but not more than five years for a defendant convicted of a Class A or B felony;

(2) at least two years but not more than three years for a defendant convicted of a Class C or D felony;

(3) one year for a defendant convicted of a Class E felony or a Class A misdemeanor.

Commentary

Background: This section specifies the length of a term of supervised release that is to be imposed. Subsection (a) applies to statutes, such as the Anti-Drug Abuse Act of 1986, that require imposition of a specific minimum term of supervised release. Subsection (b) applies to all other statutes.

Historical Note: Effective November 1, 1987. Amended effective January 15, 1988 (see Appendix C, amendment 52); November 1, 1989 (see Appendix C, amendment 302).

§5D1.3. Conditions of Supervised Release

(a) If a term of supervised release is imposed, the court shall impose a condition that the defendant not commit another federal, state, or local crime. 18 U.S.C. § 3583(d). The court shall also impose a condition that the defendant not possess illegal controlled substances. 18 U.S.C. § 3563(a)(3).

(b) The court may impose other conditions of supervised release, to the extent that such conditions are reasonably related to (1) the nature and circumstances of the offense and the history and characteristics of the defendant, and (2) the need for the sentence imposed to afford adequate deterrence to criminal conduct, to protect the public from further crimes of the defendant, and to provide the defendant with needed educational or vocational training, medical care, or other correctional treatment in the most effective manner. 18 U.S.C. §§ 3553(a)(2) and 3583(d).

(c) Recommended conditions of supervised release are set forth in §5B1.4.

Commentary

Background: This section applies to conditions of supervised release. The conditions generally recommended for supervised release are those recommended for probation. See §5B1.4. A broader form of the condition required under 18 U.S.C. § 3563(a)(3) (pertaining to possession of controlled substances) is set forth as recommended condition (7) at §5B1.4 (Recommended Conditions of Probation and Supervised Release).

Historical Note: Effective November 1, 1987. Amended effective November 1, 1989 (see Appendix C, amendments 276, 277, and 302).

PART E - RESTITUTION, FINES, ASSESSMENTS, FORFEITURES

§5E1.1. Restitution

(a) The court shall --

(1) enter a restitution order if such order is authorized under 18 U.S.C. §§ 3663-3664; or

(2) if a restitution order would be authorized under 18 U.S.C. §§ 3663-3664, except for the fact that the offense of conviction is not an offense set forth in Title 18, United States Code, or 49 U.S.C. § 1472(h), (i), (j), or (n), impose a term of probation or supervised release with a condition requiring restitution.

(b) *Provided*, that the provisions of subsection (a) do not apply when full restitution has been made, or to the extent the court determines that the complication and prolongation of the sentencing process resulting from the fashioning of a restitution requirement outweighs the need to provide restitution to any victims through the criminal process.

(c) If a defendant is ordered to make restitution and to pay a fine, the court shall order that any money paid by the defendant shall first be applied to satisfy the order of restitution.

(d) With the consent of the victim of the offense, the court may order a defendant to perform services for the benefit of the victim in lieu of monetary restitution or in conjunction therewith. 18 U.S.C. § 3663(b)(4).

<u>*Commentary*</u>

<u>Background</u>: Section 3553(a)(7) of Title 18 requires the court, "in determining the particular sentence to be imposed," to consider "the need to provide restitution to any victims of the offense." Section 3556 of Title 18 authorizes the court to impose restitution in accordance with 18 U.S.C. §§ 3663 and 3664, which authorize restitution for violations of Title 18 and of designated subdivisions of 49 U.S.C. § 1472. For other offenses, restitution may be imposed as a condition of probation or supervised release. <u>See</u> 18 U.S.C. § 3563(b)(3) <u>as amended by</u> Section 7110 of Pub. L. No. 100-690 (1988).

A court's authority to decline to order restitution is limited. Subsection (a)(1) of this guideline requires the court to order restitution for offenses under Title 18, United States Code, or 49 U.S.C. § 1472(h), (i), (j), or (n), unless full restitution has already been made or "the court determines that the complication and prolongation of the sentencing process resulting from the fashioning of an order of restitution . . . outweighs the need to provide restitution to any victims." 18 U.S.C. § 3663(d). The legislative history of 18 U.S.C. § 3579, the precursor of 18 U.S.C. § 3663, states that even "[i]n those unusual cases where the precise amount owed is difficult to determine, the section authorizes the court to reach an expeditious, reasonable determination of appropriate restitution by resolving uncertainties with a view toward achieving fairness to the victim." S. Rep. No. 532, 97th Cong., 2d Sess. 31, reprinted in 1982 U.S. Code Cong. & Ad. News 2515, 2537. If the court does not order restitution, or orders only partial restitution, it must state its reasons for doing so. 18 U.S.C. § 3553(c). Subsection (a)(2) provides for restitution as a condition of probation or supervised release for offenses not set forth in Title 18, United States Code, or 49 U.S.C. § 1472(h), (i), (j), or (n).

In determining whether to impose an order of restitution, and the amount of restitution, the court shall consider the amount of loss the victim suffered as a result of the offense, the financial resources of the defendant, the financial needs of the defendant and his dependents, and other factors the court deems appropriate. 18 U.S.C. § 3664(a).

Pursuant to Rule 32(c)(2)(D), Federal Rules of Criminal Procedure, the probation officer's presentence investigation report must contain a victim impact statement. That report must contain information about the financial impact on the victim and the defendant's financial condition. The sentencing judge may base findings on the presentence report or other testimony or evidence supported by a preponderance of the evidence. 18 U.S.C. § 3664(d).

Unless the court orders otherwise, restitution must be made immediately. 18 U.S.C. § 3663(f)(3). The court may permit the defendant to make restitution within a specified period or in specified installments, provided that the last installment is paid not later than the expiration of probation, five years after the end of the defendant's term of imprisonment, or in any other case five years after the date of sentencing. 18 U.S.C. § 3663(f)(1) and (2). The restitution order should specify the manner in which, and the persons to whom, payment is to be made.

Historical Note: Effective November 1, 1987. Amended effective January 15, 1988 (see Appendix C, amendment 53); November 1, 1989 (see Appendix C, amendments 278, 279, and 302); November 1, 1991 (see Appendix C, amendment 383); November 1, 1993 (see Appendix C, amendment 501).

§5E1.2. Fines for Individual Defendants

(a) The court shall impose a fine in all cases, except where the defendant establishes that he is unable to pay and is not likely to become able to pay any fine.

(b) Except as provided in subsections (f) and (i) below, or otherwise required by statute, the fine imposed shall be within the range specified in subsection (c) below. If, however, the guideline for the offense in Chapter Two provides a specific rule for imposing a fine, that rule takes precedence over subsection (c) of this section.

(c) (1) The minimum of the fine range is the amount shown in column A of the table below.

(2) Except as specified in (4) below, the maximum of the fine range is the amount shown in column B of the table below.

(3) Fine Table

Offense Level	A Minimum	B Maximum
3 and below	$100	$5,000
4-5	$250	$5,000
6-7	$500	$5,000
8-9	$1,000	$10,000
10-11	$2,000	$20,000
12-13	$3,000	$30,000
14-15	$4,000	$40,000

16-17	$5,000	$50,000
18-19	$6,000	$60,000
20-22	$7,500	$75,000
23-25	$10,000	$100,000
26-28	$12,500	$125,000
29-31	$15,000	$150,000
32-34	$17,500	$175,000
35-37	$20,000	$200,000
38 and above	$25,000	$250,000.

(4) Subsection (c)(2), limiting the maximum fine, does not apply if the defendant is convicted under a statute authorizing (A) a maximum fine greater than $250,000, or (B) a fine for each day of violation. In such cases, the court may impose a fine up to the maximum authorized by the statute.

(d) In determining the amount of the fine, the court shall consider:

(1) the need for the combined sentence to reflect the seriousness of the offense (including the harm or loss to the victim and the gain to the defendant), to promote respect for the law, to provide just punishment and to afford adequate deterrence;

(2) any evidence presented as to the defendant's ability to pay the fine (including the ability to pay over a period of time) in light of his earning capacity and financial resources;

(3) the burden that the fine places on the defendant and his dependents relative to alternative punishments;

(4) any restitution or reparation that the defendant has made or is obligated to make;

(5) any collateral consequences of conviction, including civil obligations arising from the defendant's conduct;

(6) whether the defendant previously has been fined for a similar offense; and

(7) any other pertinent equitable considerations.

(e) The amount of the fine should always be sufficient to ensure that the fine, taken together with other sanctions imposed, is punitive.

(f) If the defendant establishes that (1) he is not able and, even with the use of a reasonable installment schedule, is not likely to become able to pay all or part of the fine required by the preceding provisions, or (2) imposition of a fine would unduly burden the defendant's dependents, the court may impose a lesser fine or waive the fine. In these circumstances, the court shall consider alternative sanctions in lieu of all or a portion of the fine, and must still impose a total combined sanction that is punitive. Although any additional sanction not proscribed by the guidelines is permissible, community service is the generally preferable alternative in such instances.

(g) If the defendant establishes that payment of the fine in a lump sum would have an unduly severe impact on him or his dependents, the court should establish an installment schedule for payment of the fine. The length of the installment schedule generally should not exceed twelve months, and shall not exceed the maximum term of probation authorized for the offense. The defendant should be required to pay a substantial installment at the time of sentencing. If the court authorizes a defendant sentenced to probation or supervised release to pay a fine on an installment schedule, the court shall require as a condition of probation or supervised release that the defendant pay the fine according to the schedule. The court also may impose a condition prohibiting the defendant from incurring new credit charges or opening additional lines of credit unless he is in compliance with the payment schedule.

(h) If the defendant knowingly fails to pay a delinquent fine, the court shall resentence him in accordance with 18 U.S.C. § 3614.

(i) Notwithstanding of the provisions of subsection (c) of this section, but subject to the provisions of subsection (f) herein, the court shall impose an additional fine amount that is at least sufficient to pay the costs to the government of any imprisonment, probation, or supervised release ordered.

<u>Commentary</u>

<u>Application Notes:</u>

1. *A fine may be the sole sanction if the guidelines do not require a term of imprisonment. If, however, the fine is not paid in full at the time of sentencing, it is recommended that the court sentence the defendant to a term of probation, with payment of the fine as a condition of probation. If a fine is imposed in addition to a term of imprisonment, it is recommended that the court impose a term of supervised release following imprisonment as a means of enforcing payment of the fine.*

2. *In general, the maximum fine permitted by law as to each count of conviction is $250,000 for a felony or for any misdemeanor resulting in death; $100,000 for a Class A misdemeanor; and $5,000 for any other offense. 18 U.S.C. § 3571(b)(3)-(7). However, higher or lower limits may apply when specified by statute. 18 U.S.C. § 3571(b)(1), (e). As an alternative maximum, the court may fine the defendant up to the greater of twice the gross gain or twice the gross loss. 18 U.S.C. § 3571(b)(2), (d).*

3. *The determination of the fine guideline range may be dispensed with entirely upon a court determination of present and future inability to pay any fine. The inability of a defendant to post bail bond (having otherwise been determined eligible for release) and the fact that a defendant is represented by (or was determined eligible for) assigned counsel are significant indicators of present inability to pay any fine. In conjunction with other factors, they may also indicate that the defendant is not likely to become able to pay any fine.*

4. *The Commission envisions that for most defendants, the maximum of the guideline fine range from subsection (c) will be at least twice the amount of gain or loss resulting from the offense. Where, however, two times either the amount of gain to the defendant or the amount of loss caused by the offense exceeds the maximum of the fine guideline, an upward departure from the fine guideline may be warranted.*

Moreover, where a sentence within the applicable fine guideline range would not be sufficient to ensure both the disgorgement of any gain from the offense that otherwise would not be disgorged (e.g., by restitution or forfeiture) and an adequate punitive fine, an upward departure from the fine guideline range may be warranted.

5. *Subsection (c)(4) applies to statutes that contain special provisions permitting larger fines; the guidelines do not limit maximum fines in such cases. These statutes include, among others: 21 U.S.C. §§ 841(b) and 960(b), which authorize fines up to $8 million in offenses involving the manufacture, distribution, or importation of certain controlled substances; 21 U.S.C. § 848(a), which authorizes fines up to $4 million in offenses involving the manufacture or distribution of controlled substances by a continuing criminal enterprise; 18 U.S.C. § 1956(a), which authorizes a fine equal to the greater of $500,000 or two times the value of the monetary instruments or funds involved in offenses involving money laundering of financial instruments; 18 U.S.C. § 1957(b)(2), which authorizes a fine equal to two times the amount of any criminally derived property involved in a money laundering transaction; 33 U.S.C. § 1319(c), which authorizes a fine of up to $50,000 per day for violations of the Water Pollution Control Act; 42 U.S.C. § 6928(d), which authorizes a fine of up to $50,000 per day for violations of the Resource Conservation Act; and 42 U.S.C. § 7413(c), which authorizes a fine of up to $25,000 per day for violations of the Clean Air Act.*

6. *The existence of income or assets that the defendant failed to disclose may justify a larger fine than that which otherwise would be warranted under §5E1.2. The court may base its conclusion as to this factor on information revealing significant unexplained expenditures by the defendant or unexplained possession of assets that do not comport with the defendant's reported income. If the court concludes that the defendant willfully misrepresented all or part of his income or assets, it may increase the offense level and resulting sentence in accordance with Chapter Three, Part C (Obstruction).*

7. *Subsection (i) provides for an additional fine sufficient to pay the costs of any imprisonment, probation, or supervised release ordered, subject to the defendant's ability to pay as prescribed in subsection (f). In making a determination as to the amount of any fine to be imposed under this provision, the court may be guided by reports published by the Bureau of Prisons and the Administrative Office of the United States Courts concerning average costs.*

Historical Note: Effective November 1, 1987. Amended effective January 15, 1988 (see Appendix C, amendment 54); November 1, 1989 (see Appendix C, amendments 280, 281, and 302); November 1, 1990 (see Appendix C, amendment 356); November 1, 1991 (see Appendix C, amendment 384).

§5E1.3. Special Assessments

A special assessment must be imposed on a convicted defendant in the amount prescribed by statute.

Commentary

Background: *The Victims of Crime Act of 1984, Pub. L. No. 98-473, Title II, Chap. XIV, requires the courts to impose special assessments on convicted defendants for the purpose of funding the Crime Victims Fund established by the same legislation. Monies deposited in the fund are awarded to the states by the Attorney General for victim assistance and compensation programs. Under the Victims of Crime Act, as amended by Section 7085 of the Anti-Drug Abuse Act of 1988, the court is required to impose assessments in the following amounts with respect to offenses committed on or after November 18, 1988:*

Individuals:

$5, if the defendant is an individual convicted of an infraction or a Class C misdemeanor;
$10, if the defendant is an individual convicted of a Class B misdemeanor;
$25, if the defendant is an individual convicted of a Class A misdemeanor; and
$50, if the defendant is an individual convicted of a felony.

Organizations:

$50, if the defendant is an organization convicted of a Class B misdemeanor;
$125, if the defendant is an organization convicted of a Class A misdemeanor; and
$200, if the defendant is an organization convicted of a felony. 18 U.S.C. § 3013.

With respect to offenses committed prior to November 18, 1988, the court is required to impose assessments in the following amounts:

$25, if the defendant is an individual convicted of a misdemeanor;
$50, if the defendant is an individual convicted of a felony;
$100, if the defendant is an organization convicted of a misdemeanor; and
$200, if the defendant is an organization convicted of a felony. 18 U.S.C. § 3013.

The Act does not authorize the court to waive imposition of the assessment.

Historical Note: Effective November 1, 1987. Amended effective November 1, 1989 (see Appendix C, amendments 282 and 302).

§5E1.4. Forfeiture

Forfeiture is to be imposed upon a convicted defendant as provided by statute.

Commentary

Background: Forfeiture provisions exist in various statutes. For example, 18 U.S.C. § 3554 requires the court imposing a sentence under 18 U.S.C. § 1962 (proscribing the use of the proceeds of racketeering activities in the operation of an enterprise engaged in interstate commerce) or Titles II and III of the Comprehensive Drug Abuse Prevention and Control Act of 1970 (proscribing the manufacture and distribution of controlled substances) to order the forfeiture of property in accordance with 18 U.S.C. § 1963 and 21 U.S.C. § 853, respectively. Those provisions require the automatic forfeiture of certain property upon conviction of their respective underlying offenses.

In addition, the provisions of 18 U.S.C. §§ 3681-3682 authorizes the court, in certain circumstances, to order the forfeiture of a violent criminal's proceeds from the depiction of his crime in a book, movie, or other medium. Those sections authorize the deposit of proceeds in an escrow account in the Crime Victims Fund of the United States Treasury. The money is to remain available in the account for five years to satisfy claims brought against the defendant by the victim(s) of his offenses. At the end of the five-year period, the court may require that any proceeds remaining in the account be released from escrow and paid into the Fund. 18 U.S.C. § 3681(c)(2).

Historical Note: Effective November 1, 1987. Amended effective November 1, 1989 (see Appendix C, amendment 302).

§5E1.5. Costs of Prosecution (Policy Statement)

Costs of prosecution shall be imposed on a defendant as required by statute.

Commentary

Background: *Various statutes require the court to impose the costs of prosecution: 7 U.S.C. § 13 (larceny or embezzlement in connection with commodity exchanges); 21 U.S.C. § 844 (simple possession of controlled substances) (unless the court finds that the defendant lacks the ability to pay); 26 U.S.C. § 7201 (attempt to defeat or evade income tax); 26 U.S.C. § 7202 (willful failure to collect or pay tax); 26 U.S.C. § 7203 (willful failure to file income tax return, supply information, or pay tax); 26 U.S.C. 7206 (fraud and false statements); 26 U.S.C. § 7210 (failure to obey summons); 26 U.S.C. § 7213 (unauthorized disclosure of information); 26 U.S.C. § 7215 (offenses with respect to collected taxes); 26 U.S.C. § 7216 (disclosure or use of information by preparers of returns); 26 U.S.C. § 7232 (failure to register or false statement by gasoline manufacturer or producer); 42 U.S.C. § 1302c-9 (improper FOIA disclosure); 43 U.S.C. § 942-6 (rights of way for Alaskan wagon roads).*

Historical Note: Effective November 1, 1992 (see Appendix C, amendment 463).

PART F - SENTENCING OPTIONS

§5F1.1. Community Confinement

Community confinement may be imposed as a condition of probation or supervised release.

Commentary

Application Notes:

1. *"Community confinement" means residence in a community treatment center, halfway house, restitution center, mental health facility, alcohol or drug rehabilitation center, or other community facility; and participation in gainful employment, employment search efforts, community service, vocational training, treatment, educational programs, or similar facility-approved programs during non-residential hours.*

2. *Community confinement generally should not be imposed for a period in excess of six months. A longer period may be imposed to accomplish the objectives of a specific rehabilitative program, such as drug rehabilitation. The sentencing judge may impose other discretionary conditions of probation or supervised release appropriate to effectuate community confinement.*

Historical Note: Effective November 1, 1987. Amended effective November 1, 1989 (see Appendix C, amendment 302).

§5F1.2. Home Detention

Home detention may be imposed as a condition of probation or supervised release, but only as a substitute for imprisonment.

Commentary

Application Notes:

1. *"Home detention" means a program of confinement and supervision that restricts the defendant to his place of residence continuously, except for authorized absences, enforced by appropriate means of surveillance by the probation office. When an order of home detention is imposed, the defendant is required to be in his place of residence at all times except for approved absences for gainful employment, community service, religious services, medical care, educational or training programs, and such other times as may be specifically authorized. Electronic monitoring is an appropriate means of surveillance and ordinarily should be used in connection with home detention. However, alternative means of surveillance may be used so long as they are as effective as electronic monitoring.*

2. *The court may impose other conditions of probation or supervised release appropriate to effectuate home detention. If the court concludes that the amenities available in the residence of a defendant would cause home detention not to be sufficiently punitive, the court may limit the amenities available.*

3. *The defendant's place of residence, for purposes of home detention, need not be the place where the defendant previously resided. It may be any place of residence, so long as the owner of the residence (and any other person(s) from whom consent is necessary) agrees to any conditions that may be imposed by the court, e.g., conditions that a monitoring system be installed, that there will be no "call forwarding" or "call waiting" services, or that there will be no cordless telephones or answering machines.*

Background: *The Commission has concluded that the surveillance necessary for effective use of home detention ordinarily requires electronic monitoring. However, in some cases home detention may effectively be enforced without electronic monitoring, e.g., when the defendant is physically incapacitated, or where some other effective means of surveillance is available. Accordingly, the Commission has not required that electronic monitoring be a necessary condition for home detention. Nevertheless, before ordering home detention without electronic monitoring, the court should be confident that an alternative form of surveillance will be equally effective.*

In the usual case, the Commission assumes that a condition requiring that the defendant seek and maintain gainful employment will be imposed when home detention is ordered.

Historical Note: Effective November 1, 1987. Amended effective November 1, 1989 (see Appendix C, amendments 271 and 302).

§5F1.3. Community Service

Community service may be ordered as a condition of probation or supervised release.

Commentary

Application Note:

1. *Community service generally should not be imposed in excess of 400 hours. Longer terms of community service impose heavy administrative burdens relating to the selection of suitable placements and the monitoring of attendance.*

Historical Note: Effective November 1, 1987. Amended effective November 1, 1989 (see Appendix C, amendments 283 and 302); November 1, 1991 (see Appendix C, amendment 419).

§5F1.4. Order of Notice to Victims

The court may order the defendant to pay the cost of giving notice to victims pursuant to 18 U.S.C. § 3555. This cost may be set off against any fine imposed if the court determines that the imposition of both sanctions would be excessive.

Commentary

Background: *In cases where a defendant has been convicted of an offense involving fraud or "other intentionally deceptive practices," the court may order the defendant to "give reasonable notice and explanation of the conviction, in such form as the court may approve" to the victims of the offense. 18 U.S.C. § 3555. The court may order the notice to be given by mail, by advertising in specific areas or through specific media, or by other appropriate means. In determining whether a notice is* *appropriate, the court must consider the generally applicable sentencing factors listed in 18 U.S.C. § 3553(a) and the cost involved in giving the notice as it relates to the loss caused by the crime. The court may not require the defendant to pay more than $20,000 to give notice.*

If an order of notice to victims is under consideration, the court must notify the government and the defendant. 18 U.S.C. § 3553(d). Upon motion of either party, or on its own motion, the court must: (1) permit the parties to submit affidavits and memoranda relevant to the imposition of such an order; (2) provide counsel for both parties the opportunity to address orally, in open court, the appropriateness of such an order; and (3) if it issues such an order, state its reasons for doing so. The court may also order any additional procedures that will not unduly complicate or prolong the sentencing process.

Historical Note: Effective November 1, 1987. Amended effective November 1, 1989 (see Appendix C, amendments 284 and 302).

§5F1.5. Occupational Restrictions

(a) The court may impose a condition of probation or supervised release prohibiting the defendant from engaging in a specified occupation, business, or profession, or limiting the terms on which the defendant may do so, only if it determines that:

(1) a reasonably direct relationship existed between the defendant's occupation, business, or profession and the conduct relevant to the offense of conviction; and

(2) imposition of such a restriction is reasonably necessary to protect the public because there is reason to believe that, absent such restriction, the defendant will continue to engage in unlawful conduct similar to that for which the defendant was convicted.

(b) If the court decides to impose a condition of probation or supervised release restricting a defendant's engagement in a specified occupation, business, or profession, the court shall impose the condition for the minimum time and to the minimum extent necessary to protect the public.

Commentary

Background: The Comprehensive Crime Control Act authorizes the imposition of occupational restrictions as a condition of probation, 18 U.S.C. § 3563(b)(6), or supervised release, 18 U.S.C. § 3583(d). Pursuant to section 3563(b)(6), a court may require a defendant to:

> *[R]efrain, in the case of an individual, from engaging in a specified occupation, business, or profession bearing a reasonably direct relationship to the conduct constituting the offense, or engage in such a specified occupation, business, or profession only to a stated degree or under stated circumstances.*

Section 3583(d) incorporates this section by reference. The Senate Judiciary Committee Report on the Comprehensive Crime Control Act explains that the provision was "intended to be used to preclude the continuation or repetition of illegal activities while avoiding a bar from employment that exceeds that needed to achieve that result." S. Rep. No. 225, 98th Cong., 1st Sess. 96-97. The condition "should only be used as reasonably necessary to protect the public. It should not be used as a means of punishing the convicted person." Id. at 96. Section 5F1.5 accordingly limits the use of the condition and, if imposed, limits its scope, to the minimum reasonably necessary to protect the public.

The appellate review provisions permit a defendant to challenge the imposition of a probation condition under 18 U.S.C. § 3563(b)(6) if "the sentence includes . . . a more limiting condition of probation or supervised release under section 3563(b)(6) . . . than the maximum established in the guideline." 18 U.S.C. § 3742(a)(3)(A). The government may appeal if the sentence includes a "less limiting" condition of probation than the minimum established in the guideline. 18 U.S.C. § 3742(b)(3)(A).

Historical Note: Effective November 1, 1987. Amended effective November 1, 1989 (see Appendix C, amendments 285 and 302); November 1, 1991 (see Appendix C, amendment 428).

§5F1.6. Denial of Federal Benefits to Drug Traffickers and Possessors

The court, pursuant to 21 U.S.C. § 862, may deny the eligibility for certain Federal benefits of any individual convicted of distribution or possession of a controlled substance.

Commentary

Application Note:

1. *"Federal benefit" is defined in 21 U.S.C. § 862(d) to mean "any grant, contract, loan, professional license, or commercial license provided by an agency of the United States or by appropriated funds of the United States" but "does not include any retirement, welfare, Social Security, health, disability, veterans benefit, public housing, or other similar benefit, or any other benefit for which payments or services are required for eligibility."*

Background: Subsections (a) and (b) of 21 U.S.C. § 862 provide that an individual convicted of a state or federal drug trafficking or possession offense may be denied certain federal benefits. Except for an individual convicted of a third or subsequent drug distribution offense, the period of benefit ineligibility, within the applicable maximum term set forth in 21 U.S.C. § 862(a)(1) (for distribution offenses) and (b)(1)(for possession offenses), is at the discretion of the court. In the case of an individual convicted of a third or subsequent drug distribution offense, denial of benefits is mandatory and permanent under 21 U.S.C. § 862(a)(1)(C)(unless suspended by the court under 21 U.S.C. § 862(c)).

Subsection (b)(2) of 21 U.S.C. § 862 provides that the period of benefit ineligibility that may be imposed in the case of a drug possession offense "shall be waived in the case of a person who, if there is a reasonable body of evidence to substantiate such declaration, declares himself to be an addict and submits himself to a long-term treatment program for addiction, or is deemed to be rehabilitated pursuant to rules established by the Secretary of Health and Human Services."

Subsection (c) of 21 U.S.C. § 862 provides that the period of benefit ineligibility shall be suspended "if the individual (A) completes a supervised drug rehabilitation program after becoming ineligible under this section; (B) has otherwise been rehabilitated; or (C) has made a good faith effort to gain admission to a supervised drug rehabilitation program, but is unable to do so because of inaccessibility or unavailability of such a program, or the inability of the individual to pay for such a program."

Subsection (e) of 21 U.S.C. § 862 provides that a period of benefit ineligibility "shall not apply to any individual who cooperates or testifies with the Government in the prosecution of a Federal or State offense or who is in a Government witness protection program."

Historical Note: Effective November 1, 1989 (see Appendix C, amendment 305); November 1, 1992 (see Appendix C, amendment 464).

§5F1.7. Shock Incarceration Program (Policy Statement)

The court, pursuant to 18 U.S.C. §§ 3582(a) and 3621(b)(4), may recommend that a defendant who meets the criteria set forth in 18 U.S.C. § 4046 participate in a shock incarceration program.

Commentary

Section 4046 of Title 18, United States Code, provides --

"(a) the Bureau of Prisons may place in a shock incarceration program any person who is sentenced to a term of more than 12, but not more than 30 months, if such person consents to that placement.

(b) For such initial portion of the term of imprisonment as the Bureau of Prisons may determine, not to exceed six months, an inmate in the shock incarceration program shall be required to -

(1) adhere to a highly regimented schedule that provides the strict discipline, physical training, hard labor, drill, and ceremony characteristic of military basic training; and

(2) participate in appropriate job training and educational programs (including literacy programs) and drug, alcohol, and other counseling programs.

(c) An inmate who in the judgment of the Director of the Bureau of Prisons has successfully completed the required period of shock incarceration shall remain in the custody of the Bureau for such period (not to exceed the remainder of the prison term otherwise required by law to be served by that inmate), and under such conditions, as the Bureau deems appropriate. 18 U.S.C. § 4046."

The Bureau of Prisons has issued an operations memorandum (174-90 (5390), November 20, 1990) that outlines eligibility criteria and procedures for the implementation of this program (which the Bureau of Prisons has titled "intensive confinement program"). Under these procedures, the Bureau will not place a defendant in an intensive confinement program unless the sentencing court has approved, either at the time of sentencing or upon consultation after the Bureau has determined that the defendant is otherwise eligible. In return for the successful completion of the "intensive confinement" portion of the program, the defendant is eligible to serve the remainder of his term of

imprisonment in a graduated release program comprised of community corrections center and home confinement phases.

Historical Note: Effective November 1, 1991 (see Appendix C, amendment 424).

PART G - IMPLEMENTING THE TOTAL SENTENCE OF IMPRISONMENT

§5G1.1. Sentencing on a Single Count of Conviction

(a) Where the statutorily authorized maximum sentence is less than the minimum of the applicable guideline range, the statutorily authorized maximum sentence shall be the guideline sentence.

(b) Where a statutorily required minimum sentence is greater than the maximum of the applicable guideline range, the statutorily required minimum sentence shall be the guideline sentence.

(c) In any other case, the sentence may be imposed at any point within the applicable guideline range, provided that the sentence --

(1) is not greater than the statutorily authorized maximum sentence, and

(2) is not less than any statutorily required minimum sentence.

Commentary

This section describes how the statutorily authorized maximum sentence, or a statutorily required minimum sentence, may affect the determination of a sentence under the guidelines. For example, if the applicable guideline range is 51-63 months and the maximum sentence authorized by statute for the offense of conviction is 48 months, the sentence required by the guidelines under subsection (a) is 48 months; a sentence of less than 48 months would be a guideline departure. If the applicable guideline range is 41-51 months and there is a statutorily required minimum sentence of 60 months, the sentence required by the guidelines under subsection (b) is 60 months; a sentence of more than 60 months would be a guideline departure. If the applicable guideline range is 51-63 months and the maximum sentence authorized by statute for the offense of conviction is 60 months, the guideline range is restricted to 51-60 months under subsection (c).

Historical Note: Effective November 1, 1987. Amended effective November 1, 1989 (see Appendix C, amendment 286).

§5G1.2. Sentencing on Multiple Counts of Conviction

(a) The sentence to be imposed on a count for which the statute mandates a consecutive sentence shall be determined and imposed independently.

(b) Except as otherwise required by law (see §5G1.1(a), (b)), the sentence imposed on each other count shall be the total punishment as determined in accordance with Part D of Chapter Three, and Part C of this Chapter.

(c) If the sentence imposed on the count carrying the highest statutory maximum is adequate to achieve the total punishment, then the sentences on all counts shall run concurrently, except to the extent otherwise required by law.

(d) If the sentence imposed on the count carrying the highest statutory maximum is less than the total punishment, then the sentence imposed on one or more of the other counts shall run consecutively, but only to the extent necessary to produce a combined sentence equal to the total punishment. In all other respects sentences on all counts shall run concurrently, except to the extent otherwise required by law.

Commentary

This section specifies the procedure for determining the specific sentence to be formally imposed on each count in a multiple-count case. The combined length of the sentences ("total punishment") is determined by the adjusted combined offense level. To the extent possible, the total punishment is to be imposed on each count. Sentences on all counts run concurrently, except as required to achieve the total sentence, or as required by law.

This section applies to multiple counts of conviction (1) contained in the same indictment or information, or (2) contained in different indictments or informations for which sentences are to be imposed at the same time or in a consolidated proceeding.

Usually, at least one of the counts will have a statutory maximum adequate to permit imposition of the total punishment as the sentence on that count. The sentence on each of the other counts will then be set at the lesser of the total punishment and the applicable statutory maximum, and be made to run concurrently with all or part of the longest sentence. If no count carries an adequate statutory maximum, consecutive sentences are to be imposed to the extent necessary to achieve the total punishment.

Counts for which a statute mandates a consecutive sentence, such as counts charging the use of a firearm in a violent crime (18 U.S.C. § 924(c)) are treated separately. The sentence imposed on such a count is the sentence indicated for the particular offense of conviction. That sentence then runs consecutively to the sentences imposed on the other counts. See Commentary to §§2K2.4 and 3D1.1 regarding determination of the offense levels for related counts when a conviction under 18 U.S.C. § 924(c) is involved. Note, however, that even in the case of a consecutive term of imprisonment imposed under subsection (a), any term of supervised release imposed is to run concurrently with any other term of supervised release imposed. See 18 U.S.C. § 3624(e).

Historical Note: Effective November 1, 1987. Amended effective November 1, 1989 (see Appendix C, amendments 287 and 288); November 1, 1994 (see Appendix C, amendment 507).

§5G1.3. Imposition of a Sentence on a Defendant Subject to an Undischarged Term of Imprisonment

(a) If the instant offense was committed while the defendant was serving a term of imprisonment (including work release, furlough, or escape status) or after sentencing for, but before commencing service of, such term of imprisonment, the sentence for the instant offense shall be imposed to run consecutively to the undischarged term of imprisonment.

(b) If subsection (a) does not apply, and the undischarged term of imprisonment resulted from offense(s) that have been fully taken into account in the determination of the offense level for the instant offense, the sentence for the instant offense shall be imposed to run concurrently to the undischarged term of imprisonment.

(c) (Policy Statement) In any other case, the sentence for the instant offense shall be imposed to run consecutively to the prior undischarged term of imprisonment to the extent necessary to achieve a reasonable incremental punishment for the instant offense.

<u>Commentary</u>

<u>Application Notes:</u>

1. Under subsection (a), the court shall impose a consecutive sentence where the instant offense (or any part thereof) was committed while the defendant was serving an undischarged term of imprisonment or after sentencing for, but before commencing service of, such term of imprisonment.

2. Subsection (b) (which may apply only if subsection (a) does not apply), addresses cases in which the conduct resulting in the undischarged term of imprisonment has been fully taken into account under §1B1.3 (Relevant Conduct) in determining the offense level for the instant offense. This can occur, for example, where a defendant is prosecuted in both federal and state court, or in two or more federal jurisdictions, for the same criminal conduct or for different criminal transactions that were part of the same course of conduct.

When a sentence is imposed pursuant to subsection (b), the court should adjust for any term of imprisonment already served as a result of the conduct taken into account in determining the sentence for the instant offense. <u>Example:</u> The defendant has been convicted of a federal offense charging the sale of 30 grams of cocaine. Under §1B1.3 (Relevant Conduct), the defendant is held accountable for the sale of an additional 15 grams of cocaine that is part of the same course of conduct for which the defendant has been convicted and sentenced in state court (the defendant received a nine-month sentence of imprisonment, of which he has served six months at the time of sentencing on the instant federal offense). The guideline range applicable to the defendant is 10-16 months (Chapter Two offense level of 14 for sale of 45 grams of cocaine; 2-level reduction for acceptance of responsibility; final offense level of 12; Criminal History Category I). The court determines that a sentence of 13 months provides the appropriate total punishment. Because the defendant has already served six months on the related state charge, a sentence of seven months, imposed to run concurrently with the remainder of the defendant's state sentence, achieves this result. For clarity, the court should note on the Judgment in a Criminal Case Order that the sentence imposed is not a departure from the guidelines because the defendant has been credited for guideline purposes under §5G1.3(b) with six months served in state custody.

3. Where the defendant is subject to an undischarged term of imprisonment in circumstances other than those set forth in subsections (a) or (b), subsection (c) applies and the court shall impose a consecutive sentence to the extent necessary to fashion a sentence resulting in a reasonable incremental punishment for the multiple offenses. In some circumstances, such incremental punishment can be achieved by the imposition of a sentence that is concurrent with the remainder of the unexpired term of imprisonment. In such cases, a consecutive sentence is not required. To the extent practicable, the court should consider a reasonable incremental penalty to be a sentence for the instant offense that results in a combined sentence of imprisonment that approximates the total punishment that would have been imposed under §5G1.2 (Sentencing on Multiple Counts of Conviction) had all of the offenses been federal offenses for which sentences were being imposed at the same time. It is recognized that this determination frequently will require an approximation. Where the defendant is serving a term of imprisonment for a state offense, the information available may permit only a rough estimate of the total punishment that would have been imposed under the guidelines. Where the offense resulting in the undischarged term of imprisonment is a federal offense for which a guideline determination has previously been made, the task will be somewhat more straightforward, although even in such cases a precise determination may not be possible.

It is not intended that the above methodology be applied in a manner that unduly complicates or prolongs the sentencing process. Additionally, this methodology does not, itself, require the court to depart from the guideline range established for the instant federal offense. Rather, this methodology is meant to assist the court in determining the appropriate sentence (e.g., the appropriate point within the applicable guideline range, whether to order the sentence to run concurrently or consecutively to the undischarged term of imprisonment, or whether a departure is warranted). Generally, the court may achieve an appropriate sentence through its determination of an appropriate point within the applicable guideline range for the instant federal offense, combined with its determination of whether that sentence will run concurrently or consecutively to the undischarged term of imprisonment.

Illustrations of the Application of Subsection (c):

(A) The guideline range applicable to the instant federal offense is 24-30 months. The court determines that a total punishment of 36 months' imprisonment would appropriately reflect the instant federal offense and the offense resulting in the undischarged term of imprisonment. The undischarged term of imprisonment is an indeterminate sentence of imprisonment with a 60-month maximum. At the time of sentencing on the instant federal offense, the defendant has served ten months on the undischarged term of imprisonment. In this case, a sentence of 26 months' imprisonment to be served concurrently with the remainder of the undischarged term of imprisonment would (1) be within the guideline range for the instant federal offense, and (2) achieve an appropriate total punishment (36 months).

(B) The applicable guideline range for the instant federal offense is 24-30 months. The court determines that a total punishment of 36 months' imprisonment would appropriately reflect the instant federal offense and the offense resulting in the undischarged term of imprisonment. The undischarged term of imprisonment is a six-month determinate sentence. At the time of sentencing on the instant federal offense, the defendant has served three months on the undischarged term of imprisonment. In this case, a sentence of 30 months' imprisonment to be served consecutively to the undischarged term of imprisonment would (1) be within the guideline range for the instant federal offense, and (2) achieve an appropriate total punishment (36 months).

(C) The applicable guideline range for the instant federal offense is 24-30 months. The court determines that a total punishment of 60 months' imprisonment would appropriately reflect the instant federal offense and the offense resulting in the undischarged term of imprisonment. The undischarged term of imprisonment is a 12-month determinate sentence. In this case, a sentence of 30 months' imprisonment to be served consecutively to the undischarged term of imprisonment would be the greatest sentence imposable without departure for the instant federal offense.

(D) The applicable guideline range for the instant federal offense is 24-30 months. The court determines that a total punishment of 36 months' imprisonment would appropriately reflect the instant federal offense and the offense resulting in the undischarged term of imprisonment. The undischarged term of imprisonment is an indeterminate sentence with a 60-month maximum. At the time of sentencing on the instant federal offense, the

defendant has served 22 months on the undischarged term of imprisonment. In this case, a sentence of 24 months to be served concurrently with the remainder of the undischarged term of imprisonment would be the lowest sentence imposable without departure for the instant federal offense.

4. *If the defendant was on federal or state probation, parole, or supervised release at the time of the instant offense, and has had such probation, parole, or supervised release revoked, the sentence for the instant offense should be imposed to be served consecutively to the term imposed for the violation of probation, parole, or supervised release in order to provide an incremental penalty for the violation of probation, parole, or supervised release (in accord with the policy expressed in §§7B1.3 and 7B1.4).*

Background: This guideline provides direction to the court when a term of imprisonment is imposed on a defendant who is already subject to an undischarged term of imprisonment. See 18 U.S.C. § 3584. Except in the cases in which subsection (a) applies, this guideline is intended to result in an appropriate incremental punishment for the instant offense that most nearly approximates the sentence that would have been imposed had all the sentences been imposed at the same time.

Historical Note: Effective November 1, 1987. Amended effective November 1, 1989 (see Appendix C, amendment 289); November 1, 1991 (see Appendix C, amendment 385); November 1, 1992 (see Appendix C, amendment 465); November 1, 1993 (see Appendix C, amendment 494).

PART H - SPECIFIC OFFENDER CHARACTERISTICS

Introductory Commentary

The following policy statements address the relevance of certain offender characteristics to the determination of whether a sentence should be outside the applicable guideline range and, in certain cases, to the determination of a sentence within the applicable guideline range. Under 28 U.S.C. § 994(d), the Commission is directed to consider whether certain specific offender characteristics "have any relevance to the nature, extent, place of service, or other incidents of an appropriate sentence" and to take them into account only to the extent they are determined to be relevant by the Commission.

The Commission has determined that certain factors are not ordinarily relevant to the determination of whether a sentence should be outside the applicable guideline range. Unless expressly stated, this does not mean that the Commission views such factors as necessarily inappropriate to the determination of the sentence within the applicable guideline range or to the determination of various other incidents of an appropriate sentence (e.g., the appropriate conditions of probation or supervised release). Furthermore, although these factors are not ordinarily relevant to the determination of whether a sentence should be outside the applicable guideline range, they may be relevant to this determination in exceptional cases. See §5K2.0 (Grounds for Departure).

In addition, 28 U.S.C. § 994(e) requires the Commission to assure that its guidelines and policy statements reflect the general inappropriateness of considering the defendant's education, vocational skills, employment record, family ties and responsibilities, and community ties in determining whether a term of imprisonment should be imposed or the length of a term of imprisonment.

Historical Note: Effective November 1, 1987. Amended effective November 1, 1990 (see Appendix C, amendment 357); November 1, 1991 (see Appendix C, amendment 386); November 1, 1994 (see Appendix C, amendment 508).

§5H1.1. Age (Policy Statement)

Age (including youth) is not ordinarily relevant in determining whether a sentence should be outside the applicable guideline range. Age may be a reason to impose a sentence below the applicable guideline range when the defendant is elderly and infirm and where a form of punishment such as home confinement might be equally efficient as and less costly than incarceration. Physical condition, which may be related to age, is addressed at §5H1.4 (Physical Condition, Including Drug or Alcohol Dependence or Abuse).

Historical Note: Effective November 1, 1987. Amended effective November 1, 1991 (see Appendix C, amendment 386); November 1, 1993 (see Appendix C, amendment 475).

§5H1.2. Education and Vocational Skills (Policy Statement)

Education and vocational skills are not ordinarily relevant in determining whether a sentence should be outside the applicable guideline range, but the extent to which a defendant may have misused special training or education to facilitate criminal activity is an express guideline factor. See §3B1.3 (Abuse of Position of Trust or Use of Special Skill).

Education and vocational skills may be relevant in determining the conditions of probation or supervised release for rehabilitative purposes, for public protection by restricting activities that allow for the utilization of a certain skill, or in determining the appropriate type of community service.

Historical Note: Effective November 1, 1987. Amended effective November 1, 1991 (see Appendix C, amendment 386).

§5H1.3. Mental and Emotional Conditions (Policy Statement)

Mental and emotional conditions are not ordinarily relevant in determining whether a sentence should be outside the applicable guideline range, except as provided in Chapter Five, Part K, Subpart 2 (Other Grounds for Departure).

Mental and emotional conditions may be relevant in determining the conditions of probation or supervised release; e.g., participation in a mental health program (see recommended condition (24) at §5B1.4 (Recommended Conditions of Probation and Supervised Release)).

Historical Note: Effective November 1, 1987. Amended effective November 1, 1991 (see Appendix C, amendment 386).

§5H1.4. Physical Condition, Including Drug or Alcohol Dependence or Abuse (Policy Statement)

Physical condition or appearance, including physique, is not ordinarily relevant in determining whether a sentence should be outside the applicable guideline range. However, an extraordinary physical impairment may be a reason to impose a sentence below the applicable guideline range; e.g., in the case of a seriously infirm defendant, home detention may be as efficient as, and less costly than, imprisonment.

Drug or alcohol dependence or abuse is not a reason for imposing a sentence below the guidelines. Substance abuse is highly correlated to an increased propensity to commit crime. Due to this increased risk, it is highly recommended that a defendant who is incarcerated also be sentenced to supervised release with a requirement that the defendant participate in an appropriate substance abuse program (see recommended condition (23) at §5B1.4 (Recommended Conditions of Probation and Supervised Release)). If participation in a substance abuse program is required, the length of supervised release should take into account the length of time necessary for the supervisory body to judge the success of the program.

Similarly, where a defendant who is a substance abuser is sentenced to probation, it is strongly recommended that the conditions of probation contain a requirement that the defendant participate in an appropriate substance abuse program (see recommended condition (23) at §5B1.4 (Recommended Conditions of Probation and Supervised Release)).

Historical Note: Effective November 1, 1987. Amended effective November 1, 1991 (see Appendix C, amendment 386).

§5H1.5. Employment Record (Policy Statement)

Employment record is not ordinarily relevant in determining whether a sentence should be outside the applicable guideline range.

Employment record may be relevant in determining the conditions of probation or supervised release (e.g., the appropriate hours of home detention).

Historical Note: Effective November 1, 1987. Amended effective November 1, 1991 (see Appendix C, amendment 386).

§5H1.6. Family Ties and Responsibilities, and Community Ties (Policy Statement)

Family ties and responsibilities and community ties are not ordinarily relevant in determining whether a sentence should be outside the applicable guideline range.

Family responsibilities that are complied with may be relevant to the determination of the amount of restitution or fine.

Historical Note: Effective November 1, 1987. Amended effective November 1, 1991 (see Appendix C, amendment 386).

§5H1.7. Role in the Offense (Policy Statement)

A defendant's role in the offense is relevant in determining the appropriate sentence. See Chapter Three, Part B (Role in the Offense).

Historical Note: Effective November 1, 1987.

§5H1.8. Criminal History (Policy Statement)

A defendant's criminal history is relevant in determining the appropriate sentence. See Chapter Four (Criminal History and Criminal Livelihood).

Historical Note: Effective November 1, 1987.

§5H1.9. Dependence upon Criminal Activity for a Livelihood (Policy Statement)

The degree to which a defendant depends upon criminal activity for a livelihood is relevant in determining the appropriate sentence. See Chapter Four, Part B (Career Offenders and Criminal Livelihood).

Historical Note: Effective November 1, 1987.

§5H1.10. Race, Sex, National Origin, Creed, Religion, and Socio-Economic Status (Policy Statement)

These factors are not relevant in the determination of a sentence.

Historical Note: Effective November 1, 1987.

§5H1.11. Military, Civic, Charitable, or Public Service; Employment-Related Contributions; Record of Prior Good Works (Policy Statement)

Military, civic, charitable, or public service; employment-related contributions; and similar prior good works are not ordinarily relevant in determining whether a sentence should be outside the applicable guideline range.

Historical Note: Effective November 1, 1991 (see Appendix C, amendment 386).

§5H1.12. Lack of Guidance as a Youth and Similar Circumstances (Policy Statement)

Lack of guidance as a youth and similar circumstances indicating a disadvantaged upbringing are not relevant grounds for imposing a sentence outside the applicable guideline range.

Historical Note: Effective November 1, 1992 (see Appendix C, amendment 466).

PART J - RELIEF FROM DISABILITY

Historical Note: Effective November 1, 1987. Amended effective June 15, 1988 (see Appendix C, amendment 55).

§5J1.1. Relief from Disability Pertaining to Convicted Persons Prohibited from Holding Certain Positions (Policy Statement)

A collateral consequence of conviction of certain crimes described in 29 U.S.C. §§ 504 and 1111 is the prohibition of convicted persons from service and employment with labor unions, employer associations, employee pension and welfare benefit plans, and as labor relations consultants in the private sector. A convicted person's prohibited service or employment in such capacities without having been granted one of the following three statutory procedures of administrative or judicial relief is subject to criminal prosecution. First, a disqualified person whose citizenship rights have been fully restored to him or her in the jurisdiction of conviction, following the revocation of such rights as a result of the disqualifying conviction, is relieved of the disability. Second, a disqualified person convicted after October 12, 1984, may petition the sentencing court to reduce the statutory length of disability (thirteen years after date of sentencing or release from imprisonment, whichever is later) to a lesser period (not less than three years after date of conviction or release from imprisonment, whichever is later). Third, a disqualified person may petition either the United States Parole Commission or a United States District Court judge to exempt his or her service or employment in a particular prohibited capacity pursuant to the procedures set forth in 29 U.S.C. §§ 504(a)(B) and 1111(a)(B). In the case of a person convicted of a disqualifying crime committed before November 1, 1987, the United States Parole Commission will continue to process such exemption applications.

In the case of a person convicted of a disqualifying crime committed on or after November 1, 1987, however, a petition for exemption from disability must be directed to a United States District Court. If the petitioner was convicted of a disqualifying federal offense, the petition is directed to the sentencing judge. If the petitioner was convicted of a disqualifying state or local offense, the petition is directed to the United States District Court for the district in which the offense was committed. In such cases, relief shall not be given to aid rehabilitation, but may be granted only following a clear demonstration by the convicted person that he or she has been rehabilitated since commission of the disqualifying crime and can therefore be trusted not to endanger the organization in the position for which he or she seeks relief from disability.

Historical Note: Effective November 1, 1987. Amended effective June 15, 1988 (see Appendix C, amendment 56).

PART K - DEPARTURES

1. SUBSTANTIAL ASSISTANCE TO AUTHORITIES

§5K1.1. Substantial Assistance to Authorities (Policy Statement)

Upon motion of the government stating that the defendant has provided substantial assistance in the investigation or prosecution of another person who has committed an offense, the court may depart from the guidelines.

(a) The appropriate reduction shall be determined by the court for reasons stated that may include, but are not limited to, consideration of the following:

(1) the court's evaluation of the significance and usefulness of the defendant's assistance, taking into consideration the government's evaluation of the assistance rendered;

(2) the truthfulness, completeness, and reliability of any information or testimony provided by the defendant;

(3) the nature and extent of the defendant's assistance;

(4) any injury suffered, or any danger or risk of injury to the defendant or his family resulting from his assistance;

(5) the timeliness of the defendant's assistance.

<u>Commentary</u>

<u>Application Notes:</u>

1. *Under circumstances set forth in 18 U.S.C. § 3553(e) and 28 U.S.C. § 994(n), as amended, substantial assistance in the investigation or prosecution of another person who has committed an offense may justify a sentence below a statutorily required minimum sentence.*

2. *The sentencing reduction for assistance to authorities shall be considered independently of any reduction for acceptance of responsibility. Substantial assistance is directed to the investigation and prosecution of criminal activities by persons other than the defendant, while acceptance of responsibility is directed to the defendant's affirmative recognition of responsibility for his own conduct.*

3. *Substantial weight should be given to the government's evaluation of the extent of the defendant's assistance, particularly where the extent and value of the assistance are difficult to ascertain.*

<u>Background:</u> *A defendant's assistance to authorities in the investigation of criminal activities has been recognized in practice and by statute as a mitigating sentencing factor. The nature, extent, and significance of assistance can involve a broad spectrum of conduct that must be evaluated by the court on an individual basis. Latitude is, therefore, afforded the sentencing judge to reduce a sentence based upon variable relevant factors, including those listed above. The sentencing judge*

must, however, state the reasons for reducing a sentence under this section. 18 U.S.C. § 3553(c). The court may elect to provide its reasons to the defendant in camera and in writing under seal for the safety of the defendant or to avoid disclosure of an ongoing investigation.

Historical Note: Effective November 1, 1987. Amended effective November 1, 1989 (see Appendix C, amendment 290).

§5K1.2. Refusal to Assist (Policy Statement)

A defendant's refusal to assist authorities in the investigation of other persons may not be considered as an aggravating sentencing factor.

Historical Note: Effective November 1, 1987. Amended effective November 1, 1989 (see Appendix C, amendment 291).

* * * * *

2. OTHER GROUNDS FOR DEPARTURE

Historical Note: Effective November 1, 1987. Amended effective November 1, 1990 (see Appendix C, amendment 358).

§5K2.0. Grounds for Departure (Policy Statement)

Under 18 U.S.C. § 3553(b) the sentencing court may impose a sentence outside the range established by the applicable guideline, if the court finds "that there exists an aggravating or mitigating circumstance of a kind, or to a degree, not adequately taken into consideration by the Sentencing Commission in formulating the guidelines that should result in a sentence different from that described." Circumstances that may warrant departure from the guidelines pursuant to this provision cannot, by their very nature, be comprehensively listed and analyzed in advance. The controlling decision as to whether and to what extent departure is warranted can only be made by the courts. Nonetheless, this subpart seeks to aid the court by identifying some of the factors that the Commission has not been able to take into account fully in formulating the guidelines. Any case may involve factors in addition to those identified that have not been given adequate consideration by the Commission. Presence of any such factor may warrant departure from the guidelines, under some circumstances, in the discretion of the sentencing court. Similarly, the court may depart from the guidelines, even though the reason for departure is taken into consideration in the guidelines (e.g., as a specific offense characteristic or other adjustment), if the court determines that, in light of unusual circumstances, the guideline level attached to that factor is inadequate.

Where, for example, the applicable offense guideline and adjustments do take into consideration a factor listed in this subpart, departure from the applicable guideline range is warranted only if the factor is present to a degree substantially in excess of that which ordinarily is involved in the offense. Thus, disruption of a governmental function, §5K2.7, would have to be quite serious to warrant departure from the guidelines when the applicable offense guideline is bribery or obstruction of justice. When the theft offense guideline is applicable, however, and the theft caused disruption of a governmental function, departure from the applicable guideline range more readily would be appropriate. Similarly, physical injury would not warrant departure from the guidelines when the robbery offense guideline is applicable because the robbery guideline includes a specific adjustment based on the extent of any injury. However, because the robbery guideline does not deal with injury to more than one victim, departure would be warranted if several persons were injured.

Also, a factor may be listed as a specific offense characteristic under one guideline but not under all guidelines. Simply because it was not listed does not mean that there may not be circumstances when that factor would be relevant to sentencing. For example, the use of a weapon has been listed as a specific offense characteristic under many guidelines, but not under immigration violations. Therefore, if a weapon is a relevant factor to sentencing for an immigration violation, the court may depart for this reason.

An offender characteristic or other circumstance that is not ordinarily relevant in determining whether a sentence should be outside the applicable guideline range may be relevant to this determination if such characteristic or circumstance is present to an unusual degree and distinguishes the case from the "heartland" cases covered by the guidelines in a way that is important to the statutory purposes of sentencing.

<u>Commentary</u>

The last paragraph of this policy statement sets forth the conditions under which an offender characteristic or other circumstance that is not ordinarily relevant to a departure from the applicable guideline range may be relevant to this determination. The Commission does not foreclose the possibility of an extraordinary case that, because of a combination of such characteristics or circumstances, differs significantly from the "heartland" cases covered by the guidelines in a way that is important to the statutory purposes of sentencing, even though none of the characteristics or circumstances individually distinguishes the case. However, the Commission believes that such cases will be extremely rare.

In the absence of a characteristic or circumstance that distinguishes a case as sufficiently atypical to warrant a sentence different from that called for under the guidelines, a sentence outside the guideline range is not authorized. <u>See</u> 18 U.S.C. § 3553(b). For example, dissatisfaction with the available sentencing range or a preference for a different sentence than that authorized by the guidelines is not an appropriate basis for a sentence outside the applicable guideline range.

<u>Historical Note</u>: Effective November 1, 1987. Amended effective June 15, 1988 (<u>see</u> Appendix C, amendment 57); November 1, 1990 (<u>see</u> Appendix C, amendment 358); November 1, 1994 (<u>see</u> Appendix C, amendment 508).

§5K2.1. <u>Death</u> (Policy Statement)

If death resulted, the court may increase the sentence above the authorized guideline range.

Loss of life does not automatically suggest a sentence at or near the statutory maximum. The sentencing judge must give consideration to matters that would normally distinguish among levels of homicide, such as the defendant's state of mind and the degree of planning or preparation. Other appropriate factors are whether multiple deaths resulted, and the means by which life was taken. The extent of the increase should depend on the dangerousness of the defendant's conduct, the extent to which death or serious injury was intended or knowingly risked, and the extent to which the offense level for the offense of conviction, as determined by the other Chapter Two guidelines, already reflects the risk of personal injury. For example, a substantial increase may be appropriate if the death was intended or knowingly risked or if the underlying offense was one for which base offense levels do not reflect an allowance for the risk of personal injury, such as fraud.

Historical Note: Effective November 1, 1987.

§5K2.2. Physical Injury (Policy Statement)

If significant physical injury resulted, the court may increase the sentence above the authorized guideline range. The extent of the increase ordinarily should depend on the extent of the injury, the degree to which it may prove permanent, and the extent to which the injury was intended or knowingly risked. When the victim suffers a major, permanent disability and when such injury was intentionally inflicted, a substantial departure may be appropriate. If the injury is less serious or if the defendant (though criminally negligent) did not knowingly create the risk of harm, a less substantial departure would be indicated. In general, the same considerations apply as in §5K2.1.

Historical Note: Effective November 1, 1987.

§5K2.3. Extreme Psychological Injury (Policy Statement)

If a victim or victims suffered psychological injury much more serious than that normally resulting from commission of the offense, the court may increase the sentence above the authorized guideline range. The extent of the increase ordinarily should depend on the severity of the psychological injury and the extent to which the injury was intended or knowingly risked.

Normally, psychological injury would be sufficiently severe to warrant application of this adjustment only when there is a substantial impairment of the intellectual, psychological, emotional, or behavioral functioning of a victim, when the impairment is likely to be of an extended or continuous duration, and when the impairment manifests itself by physical or psychological symptoms or by changes in behavior patterns. The court should consider the extent to which such harm was likely, given the nature of the defendant's conduct.

Historical Note: Effective November 1, 1987.

§5K2.4. Abduction or Unlawful Restraint (Policy Statement)

If a person was abducted, taken hostage, or unlawfully restrained to facilitate commission of the offense or to facilitate the escape from the scene of the crime, the court may increase the sentence above the authorized guideline range.

Historical Note: Effective November 1, 1987.

§5K2.5. Property Damage or Loss (Policy Statement)

If the offense caused property damage or loss not taken into account within the guidelines, the court may increase the sentence above the authorized guideline range. The extent of the increase ordinarily should depend on the extent to which the harm was intended or knowingly risked and on the extent to which the harm to property is more serious than other harm caused or risked by the conduct relevant to the offense of conviction.

Historical Note: Effective November 1, 1987.

§5K2.6. Weapons and Dangerous Instrumentalities (Policy Statement)

If a weapon or dangerous instrumentality was used or possessed in the commission of the offense the court may increase the sentence above the authorized guideline range. The extent of the increase ordinarily should depend on the dangerousness of the weapon, the manner in which it was used, and the extent to which its use endangered others. The discharge of a firearm might warrant a substantial sentence increase.

Historical Note: Effective November 1, 1987.

§5K2.7. Disruption of Governmental Function (Policy Statement)

If the defendant's conduct resulted in a significant disruption of a governmental function, the court may increase the sentence above the authorized guideline range to reflect the nature and extent of the disruption and the importance of the governmental function affected. Departure from the guidelines ordinarily would not be justified when the offense of conviction is an offense such as bribery or obstruction of justice; in such cases interference with a governmental function is inherent in the offense, and unless the circumstances are unusual the guidelines will reflect the appropriate punishment for such interference.

Historical Note: Effective November 1, 1987.

§5K2.8. Extreme Conduct (Policy Statement)

If the defendant's conduct was unusually heinous, cruel, brutal, or degrading to the victim, the court may increase the sentence above the guideline range to reflect the nature of the conduct. Examples of extreme conduct include torture of a victim, gratuitous infliction of injury, or prolonging of pain or humiliation.

Historical Note: Effective November 1, 1987.

§5K2.9. Criminal Purpose (Policy Statement)

If the defendant committed the offense in order to facilitate or conceal the commission of another offense, the court may increase the sentence above the guideline range to reflect the actual seriousness of the defendant's conduct.

Historical Note: Effective November 1, 1987.

§5K2.10. Victim's Conduct (Policy Statement)

If the victim's wrongful conduct contributed significantly to provoking the offense behavior, the court may reduce the sentence below the guideline range to reflect the nature and circumstances of the offense. In deciding the extent of a sentence reduction, the court should consider:

(a) the size and strength of the victim, or other relevant physical characteristics, in comparison with those of the defendant;

(b) the persistence of the victim's conduct and any efforts by the defendant to prevent confrontation;

(c) the danger reasonably perceived by the defendant, including the victim's reputation for violence;

(d) the danger actually presented to the defendant by the victim; and

(e) any other relevant conduct by the victim that substantially contributed to the danger presented.

Victim misconduct ordinarily would not be sufficient to warrant application of this provision in the context of offenses under Chapter Two, Part A.3 (Criminal Sexual Abuse). In addition, this provision usually would not be relevant in the context of non-violent offenses. There may, however, be unusual circumstances in which substantial victim misconduct would warrant a reduced penalty in the case of a non-violent offense. For example, an extended course of provocation and harassment might lead a defendant to steal or destroy property in retaliation.

Historical Note: Effective November 1, 1987.

§5K2.11. Lesser Harms (Policy Statement)

Sometimes, a defendant may commit a crime in order to avoid a perceived greater harm. In such instances, a reduced sentence may be appropriate, provided that the circumstances significantly diminish society's interest in punishing the conduct, for example, in the case of a mercy killing. Where the interest in punishment or deterrence is not reduced, a reduction in sentence is not warranted. For example, providing defense secrets to a hostile power should receive no lesser punishment simply because the defendant believed that the government's policies were misdirected.

In other instances, conduct may not cause or threaten the harm or evil sought to be prevented by the law proscribing the offense at issue. For example, where a war

veteran possessed a machine gun or grenade as a trophy, or a school teacher possessed controlled substances for display in a drug education program, a reduced sentence might be warranted.

Historical Note: Effective November 1, 1987.

§5K2.12. Coercion and Duress (Policy Statement)

If the defendant committed the offense because of serious coercion, blackmail or duress, under circumstances not amounting to a complete defense, the court may decrease the sentence below the applicable guideline range. The extent of the decrease ordinarily should depend on the reasonableness of the defendant's actions and on the extent to which the conduct would have been less harmful under the circumstances as the defendant believed them to be. Ordinarily coercion will be sufficiently serious to warrant departure only when it involves a threat of physical injury, substantial damage to property or similar injury resulting from the unlawful action of a third party or from a natural emergency. The Commission considered the relevance of economic hardship and determined that personal financial difficulties and economic pressures upon a trade or business do not warrant a decrease in sentence.

Historical Note: Effective November 1, 1987.

§5K2.13. Diminished Capacity (Policy Statement)

If the defendant committed a non-violent offense while suffering from significantly reduced mental capacity not resulting from voluntary use of drugs or other intoxicants, a lower sentence may be warranted to reflect the extent to which reduced mental capacity contributed to the commission of the offense, provided that the defendant's criminal history does not indicate a need for incarceration to protect the public.

Historical Note: Effective November 1, 1987.

§5K2.14. Public Welfare (Policy Statement)

If national security, public health, or safety was significantly endangered, the court may increase the sentence above the guideline range to reflect the nature and circumstances of the offense.

Historical Note: Effective November 1, 1987.

§5K2.15. Terrorism (Policy Statement)

If the defendant committed the offense in furtherance of a terroristic action, the court may increase the sentence above the authorized guideline range.

Historical Note: Effective November 1, 1989 (see Appendix C, amendment 292).

§5K2.16. <u>Voluntary Disclosure of Offense</u> (Policy Statement)

If the defendant voluntarily discloses to authorities the existence of, and accepts responsibility for, the offense prior to the discovery of such offense, and if such offense was unlikely to have been discovered otherwise, a departure below the applicable guideline range for that offense may be warranted. For example, a downward departure under this section might be considered where a defendant, motivated by remorse, discloses an offense that otherwise would have remained undiscovered. This provision does not apply where the motivating factor is the defendant's knowledge that discovery of the offense is likely or imminent, or where the defendant's disclosure occurs in connection with the investigation or prosecution of the defendant for related conduct.

<u>Historical Note</u>: Effective November 1, 1991 (<u>see</u> Appendix C, amendment 420).

[Page intentionally blank]

CHAPTER SIX - SENTENCING PROCEDURES AND PLEA AGREEMENTS

PART A - SENTENCING PROCEDURES

Introductory Commentary

This Part addresses sentencing procedures that are applicable in all cases, including those in which guilty or nolo contendere pleas are entered with or without a plea agreement between the parties, and convictions based upon judicial findings or verdicts. It sets forth the procedures for establishing the facts upon which the sentence will be based. Reliable fact-finding is essential to procedural due process and to the accuracy and uniformity of sentencing.

Historical Note: Effective November 1, 1987.

§6A1.1. Presentence Report (Policy Statement)

A probation officer shall conduct a presentence investigation and report to the court before the imposition of sentence unless the court finds that there is information in the record sufficient to enable the meaningful exercise of sentencing authority pursuant to 18 U.S.C. § 3553, and the court explains this finding on the record. Rule 32(c)(1), Fed. R. Crim. P. The defendant may not waive preparation of the presentence report.

Commentary

A thorough presentence investigation is essential in determining the facts relevant to sentencing. In order to ensure that the sentencing judge will have information sufficient to determine the appropriate sentence, Congress deleted provisions of Rule 32(c), Fed. R. Crim. P., which previously permitted the defendant to waive the presentence report. Rule 32(c)(1) permits the judge to dispense with a presentence report, but only after explaining, on the record, why sufficient information is already available.

Historical Note: Effective November 1, 1987. Amended effective June 15, 1988 (see Appendix C, amendment 58); November 1, 1989 (see Appendix C, amendment 293).

§6A1.2. Disclosure of Presentence Report; Issues in Dispute (Policy Statement)

Courts should adopt procedures to provide for the timely disclosure of the presentence report; the narrowing and resolution, where feasible, of issues in dispute in advance of the sentencing hearing; and the identification for the court of issues remaining in dispute. See Model Local Rule for Guideline Sentencing prepared by the Probation Committee of the Judicial Conference (August 1987).

Commentary

Application Note:

1. *Under Rule 32, Fed.R.Crim. P., if the court intends to consider a sentence outside the applicable guideline range on a ground not identified as a ground for departure either in the presentence report or a pre-hearing submission, it shall provide reasonable notice that it is contemplating such ruling, specifically identifying the ground for the departure. Burns v. United States, 111 S.Ct. 2182 (1991).*

Background: In order to focus the issues prior to sentencing, the parties are required to respond to the presentence report and to identify any issues in dispute. The potential complexity of factors important to the sentencing determination normally requires that the position of the parties be presented in writing. However, because courts differ greatly with respect to their reliance on written plea agreements and with respect to the feasibility of written statements under guidelines, district courts are encouraged to consider the approach that is most appropriate under local conditions. The Commission intends to reexamine this issue in light of experience under the guidelines.

Historical Note: Effective November 1, 1987. Amended effective June 15, 1988 (see Appendix C, amendment 59); November 1, 1991 (see Appendix C, amendment 425).

§6A1.3. Resolution of Disputed Factors (Policy Statement)

(a) When any factor important to the sentencing determination is reasonably in dispute, the parties shall be given an adequate opportunity to present information to the court regarding that factor. In resolving any reasonable dispute concerning a factor important to the sentencing determination, the court may consider relevant information without regard to its admissibility under the rules of evidence applicable at trial, provided that the information has sufficient indicia of reliability to support its probable accuracy.

(b) The court shall resolve disputed sentencing factors in accordance with Rule 32(a)(1), Fed. R. Crim. P. (effective Nov. 1, 1987), notify the parties of its tentative findings and provide a reasonable opportunity for the submission of oral or written objections before imposition of sentence.

Commentary

In pre-guidelines practice, factors relevant to sentencing were often determined in an informal fashion. The informality was to some extent explained by the fact that particular offense and offender characteristics rarely had a highly specific or required sentencing consequence. This situation will no longer exist under sentencing guidelines. The court's resolution of disputed sentencing factors will usually have a measurable effect on the applicable punishment. More formality is therefore unavoidable if the sentencing process is to be accurate and fair. Although lengthy sentencing hearings should seldom be necessary, disputes about sentencing factors must be resolved with care. When a reasonable dispute exists about any factor important to the sentencing determination, the court must ensure that the parties have an adequate opportunity to present relevant information. Written statements of counsel or affidavits of witnesses may be adequate under many circumstances. An evidentiary hearing may sometimes be the only reliable way to resolve disputed issues. See United States v. Fatico, 603 F.2d 1053, 1057 n.9 (2d Cir. 1979) cert. denied, 444 U.S. 1073 (1980). The sentencing court must determine the appropriate procedure in light of the nature of the dispute, its relevance to the sentencing determination, and applicable case law.

In determining the relevant facts, sentencing judges are not restricted to information that would be admissible at trial. 18 U.S.C. § 3661. Any information may be considered, so long as it has "sufficient indicia of reliability to support its probable accuracy." United States v. Marshall, 519 F. Supp. 751 (E.D. Wis. 1981), aff'd, 719 F.2d 887 (7th Cir. 1983); United States v. Fatico, 579 F.2d 707 (2d Cir. 1978) cert. denied, 444 U.S. 1073 (1980). Reliable hearsay evidence may be considered. Out-of-court declarations by an unidentified informant may be considered "where there is good cause for the nondisclosure of his identity and there is sufficient corroboration by other means." United States v. Fatico, 579 F.2d at 713. Unreliable allegations shall not be considered. United States v. Weston, 448 F.2d 626 (9th Cir. 1971) cert. denied, 404 U.S. 1061 (1972).

The Commission believes that use of a preponderance of the evidence standard is appropriate to meet due process requirements and policy concerns in resolving disputes regarding application of the guidelines to the facts of a case.

If sentencing factors are the subject of reasonable dispute, the court should, where appropriate, notify the parties of its tentative findings and afford an opportunity for correction of oversight or error before sentence is imposed.

Historical Note: Effective November 1, 1987. Amended effective November 1, 1989 (see Appendix C, amendment 294); November 1, 1991 (see Appendix C, amendment 387).

PART B - PLEA AGREEMENTS

Introductory Commentary

Policy statements governing the acceptance of plea agreements under Rule 11(e)(1), Fed. R. Crim. P., are intended to ensure that plea negotiation practices:

(1) promote the statutory purposes of sentencing prescribed in 18 U.S.C. § 3553(a); and

(2) do not perpetuate unwarranted sentencing disparity.

These policy statements are a first step toward implementing 28 U.S.C. § 994(a)(2)(E). Congress indicated that it expects judges "to examine plea agreements to make certain that prosecutors have not used plea bargaining to undermine the sentencing guidelines." S. Rep. 98-225, 98th Cong., 1st Sess. 63, 167 (1983). In pursuit of this goal, the Commission shall study plea agreement practice under the guidelines and ultimately develop standards for judges to use in determining whether to accept plea agreements. Because of the difficulty in anticipating problems in this area, and because the sentencing guidelines are themselves to some degree experimental, substantive restrictions on judicial discretion would be premature at this stage of the Commission's work.

The present policy statements move in the desired direction in two ways. First, the policy statements make clear that sentencing is a judicial function and that the appropriate sentence in a guilty plea case is to be determined by the judge. This is a reaffirmation of pre-guidelines practice. Second, the policy statements ensure that the basis for any judicial decision to depart from the guidelines will be explained on the record. Explanations will be carefully analyzed by the Commission and will pave the way for more detailed policy statements presenting substantive criteria to achieve consistency in this aspect of the sentencing process.

Historical Note: Effective November 1, 1987.

§6B1.1. Plea Agreement Procedure (Policy Statement)

(a) If the parties have reached a plea agreement, the court shall, on the record, require disclosure of the agreement in open court or, on a showing of good cause, in camera. Rule 11(e)(2), Fed. R. Crim. P.

(b) If the plea agreement includes a nonbinding recommendation pursuant to Rule 11(e)(1)(B), the court shall advise the defendant that the court is not bound by the sentencing recommendation, and that the defendant has no right to withdraw the defendant's guilty plea if the court decides not to accept the sentencing recommendation set forth in the plea agreement.

(c) The court shall defer its decision to accept or reject any nonbinding recommendation pursuant to Rule 11(e)(1)(B), and the court's decision to accept or reject any plea agreement pursuant to Rules 11(e)(1)(A) and 11(e)(1)(C) until there has been an opportunity to consider the presentence report, unless a report is not required under §6A1.1.

<u>Commentary</u>

This provision parallels the procedural requirements of Rule 11(e), Fed. R. Crim. P. Plea agreements must be fully disclosed and a defendant whose plea agreement includes a nonbinding recommendation must be advised that the court's refusal to accept the sentencing recommendation will not entitle the defendant to withdraw the plea.

Section 6B1.1(c) deals with the timing of the court's decision whether to accept the plea agreement. Rule 11(e)(2) gives the court discretion to accept the plea agreement immediately or defer acceptance pending consideration of the presentence report. Prior to the guidelines, an immediate decision was permissible because, under Rule 32(c), Fed. R. Crim. P., the defendant could waive preparation of the presentence report. Section 6B1.1(c) reflects the changes in practice required by §6A1.1 and amended Rule 32(c)(1). Since a presentence report normally will be prepared, the court must defer acceptance of the plea agreement until the court has had an opportunity to consider the presentence report.

<u>Historical Note</u>: Effective November 1, 1987.

§6B1.2. <u>Standards for Acceptance of Plea Agreements</u> (Policy Statement)

(a) In the case of a plea agreement that includes the dismissal of any charges or an agreement not to pursue potential charges [Rule 11(e)(1)(A)], the court may accept the agreement if the court determines, for reasons stated on the record, that the remaining charges adequately reflect the seriousness of the actual offense behavior and that accepting the agreement will not undermine the statutory purposes of sentencing or the sentencing guidelines.

Provided, that a plea agreement that includes the dismissal of a charge or a plea agreement not to pursue a potential charge shall not preclude the conduct underlying such charge from being considered under the provisions of §1B1.3 (Relevant Conduct) in connection with the count(s) of which the defendant is convicted.

(b) In the case of a plea agreement that includes a nonbinding recommendation [Rule 11(e)(1)(B)], the court may accept the recommendation if the court is satisfied either that:

(1) the recommended sentence is within the applicable guideline range; or

(2) the recommended sentence departs from the applicable guideline range for justifiable reasons.

(c) In the case of a plea agreement that includes a specific sentence [Rule 11(e)(1)(C)], the court may accept the agreement if the court is satisfied either that:

(1) the agreed sentence is within the applicable guideline range; or

(2) the agreed sentence departs from the applicable guideline range for justifiable reasons.

Commentary

The court may accept an agreement calling for dismissal of charges or an agreement not to pursue potential charges if the remaining charges reflect the seriousness of the actual offense behavior. This requirement does not authorize judges to intrude upon the charging discretion of the prosecutor. If the government's motion to dismiss charges or statement that potential charges will not be pursued is not contingent on the disposition of the remaining charges, the judge should defer to the government's position except under extraordinary circumstances. Rule 48(a), Fed. R. Crim. P. However, when the dismissal of charges or agreement not to pursue potential charges is contingent on acceptance of a plea agreement, the court's authority to adjudicate guilt and impose sentence is implicated, and the court is to determine whether or not dismissal of charges will undermine the sentencing guidelines.

Similarly, the court should accept a recommended sentence or a plea agreement requiring imposition of a specific sentence only if the court is satisfied either that such sentence is an appropriate sentence within the applicable guideline range or, if not, that the sentence departs from the applicable guideline range for justifiable reasons (i.e., that such departure is authorized by 18 U.S.C. § 3553(b)). See generally Chapter 1, Part A (4)(b)(Departures).

A defendant who enters a plea of guilty in a timely manner will enhance the likelihood of his receiving a reduction in offense level under §3E1.1 (Acceptance of Responsibility). Further reduction in offense level (or sentence) due to a plea agreement will tend to undermine the sentencing guidelines.

The second paragraph of subsection (a) provides that a plea agreement that includes the dismissal of a charge, or a plea agreement not to pursue a potential charge, shall not prevent the conduct underlying that charge from being considered under the provisions of §1B1.3 (Relevant Conduct) in connection with the count(s) of which the defendant is convicted. This paragraph prevents a plea agreement from restricting consideration of conduct that is within the scope of §1B1.3 (Relevant Conduct) in respect to the count(s) of which the defendant is convicted; it does not in any way expand or modify the scope of §1B1.3 (Relevant Conduct).

The Commission encourages the prosecuting attorney prior to the entry of a plea of guilty or nolo contendere under Rule 11 of the Federal Rules of Criminal Procedure to disclose to the defendant the facts and circumstances of the offense and offender characteristics, then known to the prosecuting attorney, that are relevant to the application of the sentencing guidelines. This recommendation, however, shall not be construed to confer upon the defendant any right not otherwise recognized in law.

Historical Note: Effective November 1, 1987. Amended effective November 1, 1989 (see Appendix C, amendment 295); November 1, 1992 (see Appendix C, amendment 467); November 1, 1993 (see Appendix C, amendment 495).

§6B1.3. Procedure Upon Rejection of a Plea Agreement (Policy Statement)

If a plea agreement pursuant to Rule 11(e)(1)(A) or Rule 11(e)(1)(C) is rejected, the court shall afford the defendant an opportunity to withdraw the defendant's guilty plea. Rule 11(e)(4), Fed. R. Crim. P.

Commentary

This provision implements the requirements of Rule 11(e)(4). It assures the defendant an opportunity to withdraw his plea when the court has rejected a plea agreement that would require dismissal of charges or imposition of a specific sentence.

Historical Note: Effective November 1, 1987.

§6B1.4. Stipulations (Policy Statement)

(a) A plea agreement may be accompanied by a written stipulation of facts relevant to sentencing. Except to the extent that a party may be privileged not to disclose certain information, stipulations shall:

(1) set forth the relevant facts and circumstances of the actual offense conduct and offender characteristics;

(2) not contain misleading facts; and

(3) set forth with meaningful specificity the reasons why the sentencing range resulting from the proposed agreement is appropriate.

(b) To the extent that the parties disagree about any facts relevant to sentencing, the stipulation shall identify the facts that are in dispute.

(c) A district court may, by local rule, identify categories of cases for which the parties are authorized to make the required stipulation orally, on the record, at the time the plea agreement is offered.

(d) The court is not bound by the stipulation, but may with the aid of the presentence report, determine the facts relevant to sentencing.

Commentary

This provision requires that when a plea agreement includes a stipulation of fact, the stipulation must fully and accurately disclose all factors relevant to the determination of sentence. This provision does not obligate the parties to reach agreement on issues that remain in dispute or to present the court with an appearance of agreement in areas where agreement does not exist. Rather, the overriding principle is full disclosure of the circumstances of the actual offense and the agreement of the parties. The stipulation should identify all areas of agreement, disagreement and uncertainty that may be relevant to the determination of sentence. Similarly, it is not appropriate for the parties to stipulate to misleading or non-existent facts, even when both parties are willing to assume the existence of such "facts" for purposes of the litigation. Rather, the parties should fully disclose the actual facts and then explain to the court the reasons why the disposition of the case should differ from that which such facts ordinarily would require under the guidelines.

Because of the importance of the stipulations and the potential complexity of the factors that can affect the determination of sentences, stipulations ordinarily should be in writing. However, exceptions to this practice may be allowed by local rule. The Commission intends to pay particular attention to this aspect of the plea agreement procedure as experience under the guidelines develops. See Commentary to §6A1.2.

Section 6B1.4(d) makes clear that the court is not obliged to accept the stipulation of the parties. Even though stipulations are expected to be accurate and complete, the court cannot rely exclusively upon stipulations in ascertaining the factors relevant to the determination of sentence. Rather, in determining the factual basis for the sentence, the court will consider the stipulation, together with the results of the presentence investigation, and any other relevant information.

Historical Note: Effective November 1, 1987.

CHAPTER SEVEN - VIOLATIONS OF PROBATION AND SUPERVISED RELEASE

PART A - INTRODUCTION TO CHAPTER SEVEN

1. Authority

Under 28 U.S.C. § 994(a)(3), the Sentencing Commission is required to issue guidelines or policy statements applicable to the revocation of probation and supervised release. At this time, the Commission has chosen to promulgate policy statements only. These policy statements will provide guidance while allowing for the identification of any substantive or procedural issues that require further review. The Commission views these policy statements as evolutionary and will review relevant data and materials concerning revocation determinations under these policy statements. Revocation guidelines will be issued after federal judges, probation officers, practitioners, and others have the opportunity to evaluate and comment on these policy statements.

2. Background

(a) Probation.

Prior to the implementation of the federal sentencing guidelines, a court could stay the imposition or execution of sentence and place a defendant on probation. When a court found that a defendant violated a condition of probation, the court could continue probation, with or without extending the term or modifying the conditions, or revoke probation and either impose the term of imprisonment previously stayed, or, where no term of imprisonment had originally been imposed, impose any term of imprisonment that was available at the initial sentencing.

The statutory authority to "suspend" the imposition or execution of sentence in order to impose a term of probation was abolished upon implementation of the sentencing guidelines. Instead, the Sentencing Reform Act recognized probation as a sentence in itself. 18 U.S.C. § 3561. Under current law, if the court finds that a defendant violated a condition of probation, the court may continue probation, with or without extending the term or modifying the conditions, or revoke probation and impose any other sentence that initially could have been imposed. 18 U.S.C. § 3565. For certain violations, revocation is required by statute.

(b) Supervised Release.

Supervised release, a new form of post-imprisonment supervision created by the Sentencing Reform Act, accompanied implementation of the guidelines. A term of supervised release may be imposed by the court as a part of the sentence of imprisonment at the time of initial sentencing. 18 U.S.C. § 3583(a). Unlike parole, a term of supervised release does not replace a portion of the sentence of imprisonment, but rather is an order of supervision in addition to any term of imprisonment imposed by the court. Accordingly, supervised release is more analogous to the additional "special parole term" previously authorized for certain drug offenses.

With the exception of intermittent confinement, which is available only for a sentence of probation, the conditions of supervised release authorized by statute are the same as those for a sentence of probation. When the court finds that the defendant violated a condition of supervised release, it may continue the defendant on supervised release, with or without extending the term or modifying the conditions, or revoke supervised release and impose a term of imprisonment. The periods of imprisonment authorized by statute for a violation of the conditions of supervised release generally are more limited, however, than those available for a violation of the conditions of probation. 18 U.S.C. § 3583(e)(3).

3. **Resolution of Major Issues**

(a) Guidelines versus Policy Statements.

At the outset, the Commission faced a choice between promulgating guidelines or issuing advisory policy statements for the revocation of probation and supervised release. After considered debate and input from judges, probation officers, and prosecuting and defense attorneys, the Commission decided, for a variety of reasons, initially to issue policy statements. Not only was the policy statement option expressly authorized by statute, but this approach provided greater flexibility to both the Commission and the courts. Unlike guidelines, policy statements are not subject to the May 1 statutory deadline for submission to Congress, and the Commission believed that it would benefit from the additional time to consider complex issues relating to revocation guidelines provided by the policy statement option.

Moreover, the Commission anticipates that, because of its greater flexibility, the policy statement option will provide better opportunities for evaluation by the courts and the Commission. This flexibility is important, given that supervised release as a method of post-incarceration supervision and transformation of probation from a suspension of sentence to a sentence in itself represent recent changes in federal sentencing practices. After an adequate period of evaluation, the Commission intends to promulgate revocation guidelines.

(b) Choice Between Theories.

The Commission debated two different approaches to sanctioning violations of probation and supervised release.

The first option considered a violation resulting from a defendant's failure to follow the court-imposed conditions of probation or supervised release as a "breach of trust." While the nature of the conduct leading to the revocation would be considered in measuring the extent of the breach of trust, imposition of an appropriate punishment for any new criminal conduct would not be the primary goal of a revocation sentence. Instead, the sentence imposed upon revocation would be intended to sanction the violator for failing to abide by the conditions of the court-ordered supervision, leaving the punishment for any new criminal conduct to the court responsible for imposing the sentence for that offense.

The second option considered by the Commission sought to sanction violators for the particular conduct triggering the revocation as if that conduct were being sentenced as new federal criminal conduct. Under this approach, offense guidelines in Chapters Two and Three of the Guidelines Manual would be applied to any criminal conduct that formed the basis of the violation, after which the criminal history in Chapter Four of the Guidelines Manual would be recalculated to determine the appropriate revocation sentence. This option would also address a violation not constituting a criminal offense.

After lengthy consideration, the Commission adopted an approach that is consistent with the theory of the first option; i.e., at revocation the court should sanction primarily the defendant's breach of trust, while taking into account, to a limited degree, the seriousness of the underlying violation and the criminal history of the violator.

The Commission adopted this approach for a variety of reasons. First, although the Commission found desirable several aspects of the second option that provided for a detailed revocation guideline system similar to that applied at the initial sentencing, extensive testing proved it to be impractical. In particular, with regard to new criminal conduct that constituted a violation of state or local law, working groups expert in the functioning of federal criminal law noted that it would be difficult in many instances for the court or the parties to obtain the information necessary to apply properly the guidelines to this new conduct. The potential unavailability of information and witnesses necessary for a determination of specific offense characteristics or other guideline adjustments could create questions about the accuracy of factual findings concerning the existence of those factors.

In addition, the Commission rejected the second option because that option was inconsistent with its views that the court with jurisdiction over the criminal conduct leading to revocation is the more appropriate body to impose punishment for that new criminal conduct, and that, as a breach of trust inherent in the conditions of supervision, the sanction for the violation of trust should be in addition, or consecutive, to any sentence imposed for the new conduct. In contrast, the second option would have the revocation court substantially duplicate the sanctioning role of the court with jurisdiction over a defendant's new criminal conduct and would provide for the punishment imposed upon revocation to run concurrently with, and thus generally be subsumed in, any sentence imposed for that new criminal conduct.

Further, the sanctions available to the courts upon revocation are, in many cases, more significantly restrained by statute. Specifically, the term of imprisonment that may be imposed upon revocation of supervised release is limited by statute to not more than five years for persons convicted of Class A felonies, except for certain Title 21 drug offenses; not more than three years for Class B felonies; not more than two years for Class C or D felonies; and not more than one year for Class E felonies. 18 U.S.C. § 3583(e)(3).

Given the relatively narrow ranges of incarceration available in many cases, combined with the potential difficulty in obtaining information necessary to determine specific offense characteristics, the Commission felt that it was undesirable at this time to develop guidelines that attempt to distinguish, in detail, the wide variety of behavior that can lead to revocation. Indeed, with the relatively low ceilings set by statute, revocation policy statements that attempted to delineate with great particularity the gradations of conduct leading to revocation would frequently result in a sentence at the statutory maximum penalty.

Accordingly, the Commission determined that revocation policy statements that provided for three broad grades of violations would permit proportionally longer terms for more serious violations and thereby would address adequately concerns about proportionality, without creating the problems inherent in the second option.

4. **The Basic Approach**

The revocation policy statements categorize violations of probation and supervised release in three broad classifications ranging from serious new felonious criminal conduct to less serious criminal conduct and technical violations. The grade of the violation, together with the violator's criminal history category calculated at the time of the initial sentencing, fix the applicable sentencing range.

The Commission has elected to develop a single set of policy statements for revocation of both probation and supervised release. In reviewing the relevant literature, the Commission determined that the purpose of supervision for probation and supervised release should focus on the integration of the violator into the community, while providing the supervision designed to limit further criminal conduct. Although there was considerable debate as to whether the sanction imposed upon revocation of probation should be different from that imposed upon revocation of supervised release, the Commission has initially concluded that a single set of policy statements is appropriate.

5. A Concluding Note

The Commission views these policy statements for revocation of probation and supervised release as the first step in an evolutionary process. The Commission expects to issue revocation guidelines after judges, probation officers, and practitioners have had an opportunity to apply and comment on the policy statements.

In developing these policy statements, the Commission assembled two outside working groups of experienced probation officers representing every circuit in the nation, officials from the Probation Division of the Administrative Office of the U.S. Courts, the General Counsel's office at the Administrative Office of the U.S. Courts, and the U.S. Parole Commission. In addition, a number of federal judges, members of the Criminal Law and Probation Administration Committee of the Judicial Conference, and representatives from the Department of Justice and federal and community defenders provided considerable input into this effort.

Historical Note: Effective November 1, 1990 (see Appendix C, amendment 362).

§§7A1.1 - 7A1.4 [Deleted]

Historical Note: Sections 7A1.1 (Reporting of Violations of Probation and Supervised Release), 7A1.2 (Revocation of Probation), 7A1.3 (Revocation of Supervised Release), and 7A1.4 (No Credit for Time Under Supervision), effective November 1, 1987, were deleted as part of an overall revision of this chapter effective November 1, 1990 (see Appendix C, amendment 362).

PART B - PROBATION AND SUPERVISED RELEASE VIOLATIONS

<u>*Introductory Commentary*</u>

The policy statements in this chapter seek to prescribe penalties only for the violation of the judicial order imposing supervision. Where a defendant is convicted of a criminal charge that also is a basis of the violation, these policy statements do not purport to provide the appropriate sanction for the criminal charge itself. The Commission has concluded that the determination of the appropriate sentence on any new criminal conviction should be a separate determination for the court having jurisdiction over such conviction.

Because these policy statements focus on the violation of the court-ordered supervision, this chapter, to the extent permitted by law, treats violations of the conditions of probation and supervised release as functionally equivalent.

Under 18 U.S.C. § 3584, the court, upon consideration of the factors set forth in 18 U.S.C. § 3553(a), including applicable guidelines and policy statements issued by the Sentencing Commission, may order a term of imprisonment to be served consecutively or concurrently to an undischarged term of imprisonment. It is the policy of the Commission that the sanction imposed upon revocation is to be served consecutively to any other term of imprisonment imposed for any criminal conduct that is the basis of the revocation.

This chapter is applicable in the case of a defendant under supervision for a felony or Class A misdemeanor. Consistent with §1B1.9 (Class B or C Misdemeanors and Infractions), this chapter does not apply in the case of a defendant under supervision for a Class B or C misdemeanor or an infraction.

<u>Historical Note</u>: Effective November 1, 1990 (<u>see</u> Appendix C, amendment 362).

§7B1.1. <u>Classification of Violations</u> (Policy Statement)

(a) There are three grades of probation and supervised release violations:

(1) <u>Grade A Violations</u> -- conduct constituting (A) a federal, state, or local offense punishable by a term of imprisonment exceeding one year that (i) is a crime of violence, (ii) is a controlled substance offense, or (iii) involves possession of a firearm or destructive device of a type described in 26 U.S.C. § 5845(a); or (B) any other federal, state, or local offense punishable by a term of imprisonment exceeding twenty years;

(2) <u>Grade B Violations</u> -- conduct constituting any other federal, state, or local offense punishable by a term of imprisonment exceeding one year;

(3) <u>Grade C Violations</u> -- conduct constituting (A) a federal, state, or local offense punishable by a term of imprisonment of one year or less; or (B) a violation of any other condition of supervision.

(b) Where there is more than one violation of the conditions of supervision, or the violation includes conduct that constitutes more than one offense, the grade of the violation is determined by the violation having the most serious grade.

Commentary

Application Notes:

1. *Under 18 U.S.C. §§ 3563(a)(1) and 3583(d), a mandatory condition of probation and supervised release is that the defendant not commit another federal, state, or local crime. A violation of this condition may be charged whether or not the defendant has been the subject of a separate federal, state, or local prosecution for such conduct. The grade of violation does not depend upon the conduct that is the subject of criminal charges or of which the defendant is convicted in a criminal proceeding. Rather, the grade of the violation is to be based on the defendant's actual conduct.*

2. *"Crime of violence" is defined in §4B1.2 (Definitions of Terms Used in Section 4B1.1). See §4B1.2(1) and Application Notes 1 and 2 of the Commentary to §4B1.2.*

3. *"Controlled substance offense" is defined in §4B1.2 (Definitions of Terms Used in Section 4B1.1). See §4B1.2(2) and Application Note 1 of the Commentary to §4B1.2.*

4. *A "firearm or destructive device of a type described in 26 U.S.C. § 5845(a)" includes a shotgun, or a weapon made from a shotgun, with a barrel or barrels of less than 18 inches in length; a weapon made from a shotgun or rifle with an overall length of less than 26 inches; a rifle, or a weapon made from a rifle, with a barrel or barrels of less than 16 inches in length; a machine gun; a muffler or silencer for a firearm; a destructive device; and certain large bore weapons.*

5. *Where the defendant is under supervision in connection with a felony conviction, or has a prior felony conviction, possession of a firearm (other than a firearm of a type described in 26 U.S.C. § 5845(a)) will generally constitute a Grade B violation, because 18 U.S.C. § 922(g) prohibits a convicted felon from possessing a firearm. The term "generally" is used in the preceding sentence, however, because there are certain limited exceptions to the applicability of 18 U.S.C. § 922(g). See, e.g., 18 U.S.C. § 925(c).*

Historical Note: Effective November 1, 1990 (see Appendix C, amendment 362). Amended effective November 1, 1992 (see Appendix C, amendment 473).

§7B1.2. Reporting of Violations of Probation and Supervised Release (Policy Statement)

(a) The probation officer shall promptly report to the court any alleged Grade A or B violation.

(b) The probation officer shall promptly report to the court any alleged Grade C violation unless the officer determines: (1) that such violation is minor, and not part of a continuing pattern of violations; and (2) that non-reporting will not present an undue risk to an individual or the public or be inconsistent with any directive of the court relative to the reporting of violations.

Commentary

Application Note:

1. *Under subsection (b), a Grade C violation must be promptly reported to the court unless the probation officer makes an affirmative determination that the alleged violation meets the criteria for non-reporting. For example, an isolated failure to file a monthly report or a minor traffic infraction generally would not require reporting.*

Historical Note: Effective November 1, 1990 (see Appendix C, amendment 362).

§7B1.3. **Revocation of Probation or Supervised Release** (Policy Statement)

(a) (1) Upon a finding of a Grade A or B violation, the court shall revoke probation or supervised release.

(2) Upon a finding of a Grade C violation, the court may (A) revoke probation or supervised release; or (B) extend the term of probation or supervised release and/or modify the conditions of supervision.

(b) In the case of a revocation of probation or supervised release, the applicable range of imprisonment is that set forth in §7B1.4 (Term of Imprisonment).

(c) In the case of a Grade B or C violation --

(1) Where the minimum term of imprisonment determined under §7B1.4 (Term of Imprisonment) is at least one month but not more than six months, the minimum term may be satisfied by (A) a sentence of imprisonment; or (B) a sentence of imprisonment that includes a term of supervised release with a condition that substitutes community confinement or home detention according to the schedule in §5C1.1(e) for any portion of the minimum term; and

(2) Where the minimum term of imprisonment determined under §7B1.4 (Term of Imprisonment) is more than six months but not more than ten months, the minimum term may be satisfied by (A) a sentence of imprisonment; or (B) a sentence of imprisonment that includes a term of supervised release with a condition that substitutes community confinement or home detention according to the schedule in §5C1.1(e), provided that at least one-half of the minimum term is satisfied by imprisonment.

(3) In the case of a revocation based, at least in part, on a violation of a condition specifically pertaining to community confinement, intermittent confinement, or home detention, use of the same or a less restrictive sanction is not recommended.

(d) Any restitution, fine, community confinement, home detention, or intermittent confinement previously imposed in connection with the sentence for which revocation is ordered that remains unpaid or unserved at the time of revocation shall be ordered to be paid or served in addition to the sanction determined under §7B1.4 (Term of Imprisonment), and any such unserved period of community confinement, home detention, or intermittent confinement may be converted to an equivalent period of imprisonment.

(e) Where the court revokes probation or supervised release and imposes a term of imprisonment, it shall increase the term of imprisonment determined under subsections (b), (c), and (d) above by the amount of time in official detention that will be credited toward service of the term of imprisonment under 18 U.S.C. § 3585(b), other than time in official detention resulting from the federal probation or supervised release violation warrant or proceeding.

(f) Any term of imprisonment imposed upon the revocation of probation or supervised release shall be ordered to be served consecutively to any sentence of imprisonment that the defendant is serving, whether or not the sentence of imprisonment being served resulted from the conduct that is the basis of the revocation of probation or supervised release.

(g) (1) Where probation is revoked and a term of imprisonment is imposed, the provisions of §§5D1.1-1.3 shall apply to the imposition of a term of supervised release.

(2) Where supervised release is revoked and the term of imprisonment imposed is less than the maximum term of imprisonment imposable upon revocation, the defendant may, to the extent permitted by law, be ordered to recommence supervised release upon release from imprisonment.

<u>Commentary</u>

<u>Application Notes:</u>

1. *Revocation of probation or supervised release generally is the appropriate disposition in the case of a Grade C violation by a defendant who, having been continued on supervision after a finding of violation, again violates the conditions of his supervision.*

2. *The provisions for the revocation, as well as early termination and extension, of a term of supervised release are found in 18 U.S.C. § 3583(e). This statute, however, neither expressly authorizes nor precludes a court from ordering that a term of supervised release recommence after revocation. Under §7B1.3(g)(2), the court may order, to the extent permitted by law, the recommencement of a supervised release term following revocation.*

3. *Subsection (c) provides for the use of certain alternatives to imprisonment upon revocation. It is to be noted, however, that a court may decide that not every alternative is authorized by statute in every circumstance. For example, in <u>United States v. Behnezhad</u>, 907 F.2d 896 (9th Cir. 1990), the Ninth Circuit held that where a term of supervised release was revoked there was no statutory authority to impose a further term of supervised release. Under this decision, in the case of a revocation of a term of supervised release, an alternative that is contingent upon imposition of a further term of supervised release (<u>e.g.</u>, a period of imprisonment followed by a period of community confinement or detention as a condition of supervised release) cannot be implemented. The Commission has transmitted to the Congress a proposal for a statutory amendment to address this issue.*

4. *Subsection (e) is designed to ensure that the revocation penalty is not decreased by credit for time in official detention other than time in official detention resulting from the federal probation or supervised release violation warrant or proceeding. Example: A defendant, who was in pre-trial detention for three months, is placed on probation, and subsequently violates that probation. The court finds the violation to be a Grade C violation, determines that the applicable range of imprisonment is 4-10 months, and determines that revocation of probation and imposition of a term of imprisonment of four months is appropriate. Under subsection (e), a sentence of seven months imprisonment would be required because the Bureau of Prisons, under 18 U.S.C. § 3585(b), will allow the defendant three months' credit toward the term of imprisonment imposed upon revocation.*

5. *Subsection (f) provides that any term of imprisonment imposed upon the revocation of probation or supervised release shall run consecutively to any sentence of imprisonment being served by the defendant. Similarly, it is the Commission's recommendation that any sentence of imprisonment for a criminal offense that is imposed after revocation of probation or supervised release be run consecutively to any term of imprisonment imposed upon revocation.*

6. *Intermittent confinement is authorized only as a condition of probation during the first year of the term of probation. 18 U.S.C. § 3563(b)(11). Intermittent confinement is not authorized as a condition of supervised release. 18 U.S.C. § 3583(d).*

7. *"Maximum term of imprisonment imposable upon revocation," as used in subsection (g)(2), refers to the maximum term of imprisonment authorized by statute for the violation of supervised release, not to the maximum of the guideline range.*

Historical Note: Effective November 1, 1990 (see Appendix C, amendment 362). Amended effective November 1, 1991 (see Appendix C, amendment 427).

§7B1.4. Term of Imprisonment (Policy Statement)

(a) The range of imprisonment applicable upon revocation is set forth in the following table:

Revocation Table
(in months of imprisonment)

Grade of Violation		Criminal History Category*					
		I	II	III	IV	V	VI
Grade C		3-9	4-10	5-11	6-12	7-13	8-14
Grade B		4-10	6-12	8-14	12-18	18-24	21-27
Grade A	(1)	Except as provided in subdivision (2) below:					
		12-18	15-21	18-24	24-30	30-37	33-41
	(2)	Where the defendant was on probation or supervised release as a result of a sentence for a Class A felony:					
		24-30	27-33	30-37	37-46	46-57	51-63.

*The criminal history category is the category applicable at the time the defendant originally was sentenced to a term of supervision.

(b) *Provided*, that --

(1) Where the statutorily authorized maximum term of imprisonment that is imposable upon revocation is less than the minimum of the applicable range, the statutorily authorized maximum term shall be substituted for the applicable range; and

(2) Where the minimum term of imprisonment required by statute, if any, is greater than the maximum of the applicable range, the minimum term of imprisonment required by statute shall be substituted for the applicable range.

(3) In any other case, the sentence upon revocation may be imposed at any point within the applicable range, provided that the sentence --

(A) is not greater than the maximum term of imprisonment authorized by statute; and

(B) is not less than any minimum term of imprisonment required by statute.

Commentary

Application Notes:

1. *The criminal history category to be used in determining the applicable range of imprisonment in the Revocation Table is the category determined at the time the defendant originally was sentenced to the term of supervision. The criminal history category is not to be recalculated because the ranges set forth in the Revocation Table have been designed to take into account that the defendant violated supervision. In the rare case in which no criminal history category was determined when the defendant originally was sentenced to the term of supervision being revoked, the court shall determine the criminal history category that would have been applicable at the time the defendant originally was sentenced to the term of supervision. (See the criminal history provisions of §§4A1.1-4B1.4.)*

2. *Departure from the applicable range of imprisonment in the Revocation Table may be warranted when the court departed from the applicable range for reasons set forth in §4A1.3 (Adequacy of Criminal History Category) in originally imposing the sentence that resulted in supervision. Additionally, an upward departure may be warranted when a defendant, subsequent to the federal sentence resulting in supervision, has been sentenced for an offense that is not the basis of the violation proceeding.*

3. *In the case of a Grade C violation that is associated with a high risk of new felonious conduct (e.g., a defendant, under supervision for conviction of criminal sexual abuse, violates the condition that he not associate with children by loitering near a schoolyard), an upward departure may be warranted.*

4. *Where the original sentence was the result of a downward departure (e.g., as a reward for substantial assistance), or a charge reduction that resulted in a sentence below the guideline range applicable to the defendant's underlying conduct, an upward departure may be warranted.*

5. *Under 18 U.S.C. § 3565(a), upon a finding that a defendant violated a condition of probation by being in possession of a controlled substance, the court is required "to revoke the sentence of probation and sentence the defendant to not less than one-third of the original sentence." Under 18 U.S.C. § 3583(g), upon a finding that a defendant violated a condition of supervised release by being in possession of a controlled substance, the court is required "to terminate supervised release and sentence the defendant to serve in prison not less than one-third of the term of supervised release." The Commission leaves to the court the determination of whether evidence of drug usage established solely by laboratory analysis constitutes "possession of a controlled substance" as set forth in 18 U.S.C. §§ 3565(a) and 3583(g).*

6. *Under 18 U.S.C. § 3565(b), upon a finding that a defendant violated a condition of probation by the actual possession of a firearm, the court is required "to revoke the sentence of probation and impose any other sentence that was available ... at the time of initial sentencing."*

Historical Note: Effective November 1, 1990 (see Appendix C, amendment 362).

§7B1.5. No Credit for Time Under Supervision (Policy Statement)

(a) Upon revocation of probation, no credit shall be given (toward any sentence of imprisonment imposed) for any portion of the term of probation served prior to revocation.

(b) Upon revocation of supervised release, no credit shall be given (toward any term of imprisonment ordered) for time previously served on post-release supervision.

(c) *Provided,* that in the case of a person serving a period of supervised release on a foreign sentence under the provisions of 18 U.S.C. § 4106A, credit shall be given for time on supervision prior to revocation, except that no credit shall be given for any time in escape or absconder status.

Commentary

Application Note:

1. *Subsection (c) implements 18 U.S.C. § 4106A(b)(1)(C), which provides that the combined periods of imprisonment and supervised release in transfer treaty cases shall not exceed the term of imprisonment imposed by the foreign court.*

Background: This section provides that time served on probation or supervised release is not to be credited in the determination of any term of imprisonment imposed upon revocation. Other aspects of the defendant's conduct, such as compliance with supervision conditions and adjustment while under supervision, appropriately may be considered by the court in the determination of the sentence to be imposed within the applicable revocation range.

Historical Note: Effective November 1, 1990 (see Appendix C, amendment 362).

CHAPTER EIGHT - SENTENCING OF ORGANIZATIONS

Introductory Commentary

The guidelines and policy statements in this chapter apply when the convicted defendant is an organization. Organizations can act only through agents and, under federal criminal law, generally are vicariously liable for offenses committed by their agents. At the same time, individual agents are responsible for their own criminal conduct. Federal prosecutions of organizations therefore frequently involve individual and organizational co-defendants. Convicted individual agents of organizations are sentenced in accordance with the guidelines and policy statements in the preceding chapters. This chapter is designed so that the sanctions imposed upon organizations and their agents, taken together, will provide just punishment, adequate deterrence, and incentives for organizations to maintain internal mechanisms for preventing, detecting, and reporting criminal conduct.

This chapter reflects the following general principles: First, the court must, whenever practicable, order the organization to remedy any harm caused by the offense. The resources expended to remedy the harm should not be viewed as punishment, but rather as a means of making victims whole for the harm caused. Second, if the organization operated primarily for a criminal purpose or primarily by criminal means, the fine should be set sufficiently high to divest the organization of all its assets. Third, the fine range for any other organization should be based on the seriousness of the offense and the culpability of the organization. The seriousness of the offense generally will be reflected by the highest of the pecuniary gain, the pecuniary loss, or the amount in a guideline offense level fine table. Culpability generally will be determined by the steps taken by the organization prior to the offense to prevent and detect criminal conduct, the level and extent of involvement in or tolerance of the offense by certain personnel, and the organization's actions after an offense has been committed. Fourth, probation is an appropriate sentence for an organizational defendant when needed to ensure that another sanction will be fully implemented, or to ensure that steps will be taken within the organization to reduce the likelihood of future criminal conduct.

Historical Note: Effective November 1, 1991 (see Appendix C, amendment 422).

PART A - GENERAL APPLICATION PRINCIPLES

§8A1.1. Applicability of Chapter Eight

This chapter applies to the sentencing of all organizations for felony and Class A misdemeanor offenses.

Commentary

Application Notes:

1. *"Organization" means "a person other than an individual." 18 U.S.C. § 18. The term includes corporations, partnerships, associations, joint-stock companies, unions, trusts, pension funds, unincorporated organizations, governments and political subdivisions thereof, and non-profit organizations.*

2. *The fine guidelines in §§8C2.2 through 8C2.9 apply only to specified types of offenses. The other provisions of this chapter apply to the sentencing of all organizations for all felony and Class A misdemeanor offenses. For example, the restitution and probation provisions in Parts B and D of this chapter apply to the sentencing of an organization, even if the fine guidelines in §§8C2.2 through 8C2.9 do not apply.*

Historical Note: Effective November 1, 1991 (see Appendix C, amendment 422).

§8A1.2. Application Instructions - Organizations

(a) Determine from Part B (Remedying Harm from Criminal Conduct) the sentencing requirements and options relating to restitution, remedial orders, community service, and notice to victims.

(b) Determine from Part C (Fines) the sentencing requirements and options relating to fines:

(1) If the organization operated primarily for a criminal purpose or primarily by criminal means, apply §8C1.1 (Determining the Fine - Criminal Purpose Organizations).

(2) Otherwise, apply §8C2.1 (Applicability of Fine Guidelines) to identify the counts for which the provisions of §§8C2.2 through 8C2.9 apply. For such counts:

(A) Refer to §8C2.2 (Preliminary Determination of Inability to Pay Fine) to determine whether an abbreviated determination of the guideline fine range may be warranted.

(B) Apply §8C2.3 (Offense Level) to determine the offense level from Chapter Two (Offense Conduct) and Chapter Three, Part D (Multiple Counts).

(C) Apply §8C2.4 (Base Fine) to determine the base fine.

(D) Apply §8C2.5 (Culpability Score) to determine the culpability score.

(E) Apply §8C2.6 (Minimum and Maximum Multipliers) to determine the minimum and maximum multipliers corresponding to the culpability score.

(F) Apply §8C2.7 (Guideline Fine Range - Organizations) to determine the minimum and maximum of the guideline fine range.

(G) Refer to §8C2.8 (Determining the Fine Within the Range) to determine the amount of the fine within the applicable guideline range.

(H) Apply §8C2.9 (Disgorgement) to determine whether an increase to the fine is required.

For any count or counts not covered under §8C2.1 (Applicability of Fine Guidelines), apply §8C2.10 (Determining the Fine for Other Counts).

(3) Apply the provisions relating to the implementation of the sentence of a fine in Part C, Subpart 3 (Implementing the Sentence of a Fine).

(4) For grounds for departure from the applicable guideline fine range, refer to Part C, Subpart 4 (Departures from the Guideline Fine Range).

(c) Determine from Part D (Organizational Probation) the sentencing requirements and options relating to probation.

(d) Determine from Part E (Special Assessments, Forfeitures, and Costs) the sentencing requirements relating to special assessments, forfeitures, and costs.

<u>Commentary</u>

<u>Application Notes:</u>

1. *Determinations under this chapter are to be based upon the facts and information specified in the applicable guideline. Determinations that reference other chapters are to be made under the standards applicable to determinations under those chapters.*

2. *The definitions in the Commentary to §1B1.1 (Application Instructions) and the guidelines and commentary in §§1B1.2 through 1B1.8 apply to determinations under this chapter unless otherwise specified. The adjustments in Chapter Three, Parts A (Victim-Related Adjustments), B (Role in the Offense), C (Obstruction), and E (Acceptance of Responsibility) do not apply. The provisions of Chapter Six (Sentencing Procedures and Plea Agreements) apply to proceedings in which the defendant is an organization. Guidelines and policy statements not referenced in this chapter, directly or indirectly, do not apply when the defendant is an organization; <u>e.g.</u>, the policy statements in Chapter Seven (Violations of Probation and Supervised Release) do not apply to organizations.*

3. *The following are definitions of terms used frequently in this chapter:*

(a) *"Offense" means the offense of conviction and all relevant conduct under §1B1.3 (Relevant Conduct) unless a different meaning is specified or is otherwise clear from the context.*

(b) *"High-level personnel of the organization" means individuals who have substantial control over the organization or who have a substantial role in the making of policy within the organization. The term includes: a director; an executive officer; an individual in charge of a major business or functional unit of the organization, such as sales, administration, or finance; and an individual with a substantial ownership interest. "High-level personnel of a unit of the organization" is defined in the Commentary to §8C2.5 (Culpability Score).*

(c) *"Substantial authority personnel" means individuals who within the scope of their authority exercise a substantial measure of discretion in acting on behalf of an organization. The term includes high-level personnel, individuals who exercise substantial supervisory authority (e.g., a plant manager, a sales manager), and any other individuals who, although not a part of an organization's management, nevertheless exercise substantial discretion when acting within the scope of their authority (e.g., an individual with authority in an organization to negotiate or set price levels or an individual authorized to negotiate or approve significant contracts). Whether an individual falls within this category must be determined on a case-by-case basis.*

(d) *"Agent" means any individual, including a director, an officer, an employee, or an independent contractor, authorized to act on behalf of the organization.*

(e) *An individual "condoned" an offense if the individual knew of the offense and did not take reasonable steps to prevent or terminate the offense.*

(f) *"Similar misconduct" means prior conduct that is similar in nature to the conduct underlying the instant offense, without regard to whether or not such conduct violated the same statutory provision. For example, prior Medicare fraud would be misconduct similar to an instant offense involving another type of fraud.*

(g) *"Prior criminal adjudication" means conviction by trial, plea of guilty (including an Alford plea), or plea of nolo contendere.*

(h) *"Pecuniary gain" is derived from 18 U.S.C. § 3571(d) and means the additional before-tax profit to the defendant resulting from the relevant conduct of the offense. Gain can result from either additional revenue or cost savings. For example, an offense involving odometer tampering can produce additional revenue. In such a case, the pecuniary gain is the additional revenue received because the automobiles appeared to have less mileage, i.e., the difference between the price received or expected for the automobiles with the apparent mileage and the fair market value of the automobiles with the actual mileage. An offense involving defense procurement fraud related to defective product testing can produce pecuniary gain resulting from cost savings. In such a case, the pecuniary gain is the amount saved because the product was not tested in the required manner.*

(i) *"Pecuniary loss" is derived from 18 U.S.C. § 3571(d) and is equivalent to the term "loss" as used in Chapter Two (Offense Conduct).* <u>See</u> *Commentary to §§2B1.1 (Larceny, Embezzlement, and Other Forms of Theft), 2F1.1 (Fraud and Deceit), and definitions of "tax loss" in Chapter Two, Part T (Offenses Involving Taxation).*

(j) *An individual was "willfully ignorant of the offense" if the individual did not investigate the possible occurrence of unlawful conduct despite knowledge of circumstances that would lead a reasonable person to investigate whether unlawful conduct had occurred.*

(k) *An "effective program to prevent and detect violations of law" means a program that has been reasonably designed, implemented, and enforced so that it generally will be effective in preventing and detecting criminal conduct. Failure to prevent or detect the instant offense, by itself, does not mean that the program was not effective. The hallmark of an effective program to prevent and detect violations of law is that the organization exercised due diligence in seeking to prevent and detect criminal conduct by its employees and other agents. Due diligence requires at a minimum that the organization must have taken the following types of steps:*

(1) *The organization must have established compliance standards and procedures to be followed by its employees and other agents that are reasonably capable of reducing the prospect of criminal conduct.*

(2) *Specific individual(s) within high-level personnel of the organization must have been assigned overall responsibility to oversee compliance with such standards and procedures.*

(3) *The organization must have used due care not to delegate substantial discretionary authority to individuals whom the organization knew, or should have known through the exercise of due diligence, had a propensity to engage in illegal activities.*

(4) *The organization must have taken steps to communicate effectively its standards and procedures to all employees and other agents,* <u>e.g.</u>, *by requiring participation in training programs or by disseminating publications that explain in a practical manner what is required.*

(5) *The organization must have taken reasonable steps to achieve compliance with its standards,* <u>e.g.</u>, *by utilizing monitoring and auditing systems reasonably designed to detect criminal conduct by its employees and other agents and by having in place and publicizing a reporting system whereby employees and other agents could report criminal conduct by others within the organization without fear of retribution.*

(6) *The standards must have been consistently enforced through appropriate disciplinary mechanisms, including, as appropriate, discipline of individuals responsible for the failure to detect an offense. Adequate discipline of individuals responsible for an offense is a necessary component of enforcement; however, the form of discipline that will be appropriate will be case specific.*

(7) *After an offense has been detected, the organization must have taken all reasonable steps to respond appropriately to the offense and to prevent further similar offenses -- including any necessary modifications to its program to prevent and detect violations of law.*

The precise actions necessary for an effective program to prevent and detect violations of law will depend upon a number of factors. Among the relevant factors are:

(i) Size of the organization -- The requisite degree of formality of a program to prevent and detect violations of law will vary with the size of the organization: the larger the organization, the more formal the program typically should be. A larger organization generally should have established written policies defining the standards and procedures to be followed by its employees and other agents.

(ii) Likelihood that certain offenses may occur because of the nature of its business -- If because of the nature of an organization's business there is a substantial risk that certain types of offenses may occur, management must have taken steps to prevent and detect those types of offenses. For example, if an organization handles toxic substances, it must have established standards and procedures designed to ensure that those substances are properly handled at all times. If an organization employs sales personnel who have flexibility in setting prices, it must have established standards and procedures designed to prevent and detect price-fixing. If an organization employs sales personnel who have flexibility to represent the material characteristics of a product, it must have established standards and procedures designed to prevent fraud.

(iii) Prior history of the organization -- An organization's prior history may indicate types of offenses that it should have taken actions to prevent. Recurrence of misconduct similar to that which an organization has previously committed casts doubt on whether it took all reasonable steps to prevent such misconduct.

An organization's failure to incorporate and follow applicable industry practice or the standards called for by any applicable governmental regulation weighs against a finding of an effective program to prevent and detect violations of law.

<u>Historical Note</u>: Effective November 1, 1991 (<u>see</u> Appendix C, amendment 422).

PART B - REMEDYING HARM FROM CRIMINAL CONDUCT

Introductory Commentary

As a general principle, the court should require that the organization take all appropriate steps to provide compensation to victims and otherwise remedy the harm caused or threatened by the offense. A restitution order or an order of probation requiring restitution can be used to compensate identifiable victims of the offense. A remedial order or an order of probation requiring community service can be used to reduce or eliminate the harm threatened, or to repair the harm caused by the offense, when that harm or threatened harm would otherwise not be remedied. An order of notice to victims can be used to notify unidentified victims of the offense.

Historical Note: Effective November 1, 1991 (see Appendix C, amendment 422).

§8B1.1. Restitution - Organizations

(a) The court shall --

(1) enter a restitution order if such order is authorized under 18 U.S.C. §§ 3663-3664; or

(2) if a restitution order would be authorized under 18 U.S.C. §§ 3663-3664, except for the fact that the offense of conviction is not an offense set forth in Title 18, United States Code, or 49 U.S.C. § 1472(h), (i), (j), or (n), sentence the organization to probation with a condition requiring restitution.

(b) *Provided*, that the provisions of subsection (a) do not apply when the organization has made full restitution, or to the extent the court determines that the complication and prolongation of the sentencing process resulting from the fashioning of a restitution requirement outweighs the need to provide restitution to any victims through the criminal process.

Commentary

Background: *This guideline provides for restitution either as a sentence under 18 U.S.C. §§ 3663-3664 or as a condition of probation.*

Historical Note: Effective November 1, 1991 (see Appendix C, amendment 422).

§8B1.2. Remedial Orders - Organizations (Policy Statement)

(a) To the extent not addressed under §8B1.1 (Restitution - Organizations), a remedial order imposed as a condition of probation may require the organization to remedy the harm caused by the offense and to eliminate or reduce the risk that the instant offense will cause future harm.

(b) If the magnitude of expected future harm can be reasonably estimated, the court may require the organization to create a trust fund sufficient to address that expected harm.

Commentary

Background: *The purposes of a remedial order are to remedy harm that has already occurred and to prevent future harm. A remedial order requiring corrective action by the organization may be necessary to prevent future injury from the instant offense,* e.g., *a product recall for a food and drug violation or a clean-up order for an environmental violation. In some cases in which a remedial order potentially may be appropriate, a governmental regulatory agency,* e.g., *the Environmental Protection Agency or the Food and Drug Administration, may have authority to order remedial measures. In such cases, a remedial order by the court may not be necessary. If a remedial order is entered, it should be coordinated with any administrative or civil actions taken by the appropriate governmental regulatory agency.*

Historical Note: Effective November 1, 1991 (see Appendix C, amendment 422).

§8B1.3. Community Service - Organizations (Policy Statement)

Community service may be ordered as a condition of probation where such community service is reasonably designed to repair the harm caused by the offense.

Commentary

Background: *An organization can perform community service only by employing its resources or paying its employees or others to do so. Consequently, an order that an organization perform community service is essentially an indirect monetary sanction, and therefore generally less desirable than a direct monetary sanction. However, where the convicted organization possesses knowledge, facilities, or skills that uniquely qualify it to repair damage caused by the offense, community service directed at repairing damage may provide an efficient means of remedying harm caused.*

In the past, some forms of community service imposed on organizations have not been related to the purposes of sentencing. Requiring a defendant to endow a chair at a university or to contribute to a local charity would not be consistent with this section unless such community service provided a means for preventive or corrective action directly related to the offense and therefore served one of the purposes of sentencing set forth in 18 U.S.C. § 3553(a).

Historical Note: Effective November 1, 1991 (see Appendix C, amendment 422).

§8B1.4. Order of Notice to Victims - Organizations

Apply §5F1.4 (Order of Notice to Victims).

Historical Note: Effective November 1, 1991 (see Appendix C, amendment 422).

PART C - FINES

1. DETERMINING THE FINE - CRIMINAL PURPOSE ORGANIZATIONS

§8C1.1. Determining the Fine - Criminal Purpose Organizations

If, upon consideration of the nature and circumstances of the offense and the history and characteristics of the organization, the court determines that the organization operated primarily for a criminal purpose or primarily by criminal means, the fine shall be set at an amount (subject to the statutory maximum) sufficient to divest the organization of all its net assets. When this section applies, Subpart 2 (Determining the Fine - Other Organizations) and §8C3.4 (Fines Paid by Owners of Closely Held Organizations) do not apply.

Commentary

Application Note:

1. *"Net assets," as used in this section, means the assets remaining after payment of all legitimate claims against assets by known innocent bona fide creditors.*

Background: *This guideline addresses the case in which the court, based upon an examination of the nature and circumstances of the offense and the history and characteristics of the organization, determines that the organization was operated primarily for a criminal purpose (e.g., a front for a scheme that was designed to commit fraud; an organization established to participate in the illegal manufacture, importation, or distribution of a controlled substance) or operated primarily by criminal means (e.g., a hazardous waste disposal business that had no legitimate means of disposing of hazardous waste). In such a case, the fine shall be set at an amount sufficient to remove all of the organization's net assets. If the extent of the assets of the organization is unknown, the maximum fine authorized by statute should be imposed, absent innocent bona fide creditors.*

Historical Note: Effective November 1, 1991 (see Appendix C, amendment 422).

* * * * *

2. DETERMINING THE FINE - OTHER ORGANIZATIONS

§8C2.1. Applicability of Fine Guidelines

The provisions of §§8C2.2 through 8C2.9 apply to each count for which the applicable guideline offense level is determined under:

(a) §§2B1.1, 2B1.3, 2B2.3, 2B4.1, 2B5.3, 2B6.1;
§§2C1.1, 2C1.2, 2C1.4, 2C1.6, 2C1.7;
§§2D1.7, 2D3.1, 2D3.2;
§§2E3.1, 2E4.1, 2E5.1, 2E5.3;
§§2F1.1, 2F1.2;

§2G3.1;
§§2K1.1, 2K2.1;
§2L1.1;
§2N3.1;
§2R1.1;
§§2S1.1, 2S1.2, 2S1.3;
§§2T1.1, 2T1.4, 2T1.6, 2T1.7, 2T1.8, 2T1.9, 2T2.1, 2T2.2, 2T3.1; or

(b) §§2E1.1, 2X1.1, 2X2.1, 2X3.1, 2X4.1, with respect to cases in which the offense level for the underlying offense is determined under one of the guideline sections listed in subsection (a) above.

<u>*Commentary*</u>

<u>*Application Notes:*</u>

1. If the Chapter Two offense guideline for a count is listed in subsection (a) or (b) above, and the applicable guideline results in the determination of the offense level by use of one of the listed guidelines, apply the provisions of §§8C2.2 through 8C2.9 to that count. For example, §§8C2.2 through 8C2.9 apply to an offense under §2K2.1 (an offense guideline listed in subsection (a)), unless the cross reference in that guideline requires the offense level to be determined under an offense guideline section not listed in subsection (a).

2. If the Chapter Two offense guideline for a count is not listed in subsection (a) or (b) above, but the applicable guideline results in the determination of the offense level by use of a listed guideline, apply the provisions of §§8C2.2 through 8C2.9 to that count. For example, where the conduct set forth in a count of conviction ordinarily referenced to §2N2.1 (an offense guideline not listed in subsection (a)) establishes §2F1.1 (Fraud and Deceit) as the applicable offense guideline (an offense guideline listed in subsection (a)), §§8C2.2 through 8C2.9 would apply because the actual offense level is determined under §2F1.1 (Fraud and Deceit).

<u>*Background:*</u> *The fine guidelines of this subpart apply only to offenses covered by the guideline sections set forth in subsection (a) above. For example, the provisions of §§8C2.2 through 8C2.9 do not apply to counts for which the applicable guideline offense level is determined under Chapter Two, Part Q (Offenses Involving the Environment). For such cases, §8C2.10 (Determining the Fine for Other Counts) is applicable.*

<u>Historical Note</u>: Effective November 1, 1991 (<u>see</u> Appendix C, amendment 422). Amended effective November 1, 1992 (<u>see</u> Appendix C, amendment 453); November 1, 1993 (<u>see</u> Appendix C, amendment 496).

§8C2.2. <u>Preliminary Determination of Inability to Pay Fine</u>

(a) Where it is readily ascertainable that the organization cannot and is not likely to become able (even on an installment schedule) to pay restitution required under §8B1.1 (Restitution - Organizations), a determination of the guideline fine range is unnecessary because, pursuant to §8C3.3(a), no fine would be imposed.

(b) Where it is readily ascertainable through a preliminary determination of the minimum of the guideline fine range (<u>see</u> §§8C2.3 through 8C2.7) that the organization cannot and is not likely to become able (even on an installment schedule) to pay such minimum guideline fine, a further determination of the guideline fine range is unnecessary. Instead, the court may use the preliminary determination and impose the fine that would result from the application of §8C3.3 (Reduction of Fine Based on Inability to Pay).

<u>Commentary</u>

<u>Application Notes:</u>

1. *In a case of a determination under subsection (a), a statement that "the guideline fine range was not determined because it is readily ascertainable that the defendant cannot and is not likely to become able to pay restitution" is recommended.*

2. *In a case of a determination under subsection (b), a statement that "no precise determination of the guideline fine range is required because it is readily ascertainable that the defendant cannot and is not likely to become able to pay the minimum of the guideline fine range" is recommended.*

<u>Background</u>: Many organizational defendants lack the ability to pay restitution. In addition, many organizational defendants who may be able to pay restitution lack the ability to pay the minimum fine called for by §8C2.7(a). In such cases, a complete determination of the guideline fine range may be a needless exercise. This section provides for an abbreviated determination of the guideline fine range that can be applied where it is readily ascertainable that the fine within the guideline fine range determined under §8C2.7 (Guideline Fine Range - Organizations) would be reduced under §8C3.3 (Reduction of Fine Based on Inability to Pay).

<u>Historical Note</u>: Effective November 1, 1991 (<u>see</u> Appendix C, amendment 422).

§8C2.3. <u>Offense Level</u>

(a) For each count covered by §8C2.1 (Applicability of Fine Guidelines), use the applicable Chapter Two guideline to determine the base offense level and apply, in the order listed, any appropriate adjustments contained in that guideline.

(b) Where there is more than one such count, apply Chapter Three, Part D (Multiple Counts) to determine the combined offense level.

<u>Commentary</u>

<u>Application Notes:</u>

1. *In determining the offense level under this section, "defendant," as used in Chapter Two, includes any agent of the organization for whose conduct the organization is criminally responsible.*

2. *In determining the offense level under this section, apply the provisions of §§1B1.2 through 1B1.8. Do not apply the adjustments in Chapter Three, Parts A (Victim-Related Adjustments), B (Role in the Offense), C (Obstruction), and E (Acceptance of Responsibility).*

Historical Note: Effective November 1, 1991 (see Appendix C, amendment 422).

§8C2.4. Base Fine

(a) The base fine is the greatest of:

(1) the amount from the table in subsection (d) below corresponding to the offense level determined under §8C2.3 (Offense Level); or

(2) the pecuniary gain to the organization from the offense; or

(3) the pecuniary loss from the offense caused by the organization, to the extent the loss was caused intentionally, knowingly, or recklessly.

(b) *Provided*, that if the applicable offense guideline in Chapter Two includes a special instruction for organizational fines, that special instruction shall be applied, as appropriate.

(c) *Provided, further*, that to the extent the calculation of either pecuniary gain or pecuniary loss would unduly complicate or prolong the sentencing process, that amount, i.e., gain or loss as appropriate, shall not be used for the determination of the base fine.

(d) Offense Level Fine Table

Offense Level	Amount
6 or less	$5,000
7	$7,500
8	$10,000
9	$15,000
10	$20,000
11	$30,000
12	$40,000
13	$60,000
14	$85,000
15	$125,000
16	$175,000
17	$250,000
18	$350,000
19	$500,000
20	$650,000
21	$910,000
22	$1,200,000
23	$1,600,000
24	$2,100,000
25	$2,800,000
26	$3,700,000

27	$4,800,000
28	$6,300,000
29	$8,100,000
30	$10,500,000
31	$13,500,000
32	$17,500,000
33	$22,000,000
34	$28,500,000
35	$36,000,000
36	$45,500,000
37	$57,500,000
38 or more	$72,500,000

<u>*Commentary*</u>

<u>*Application Notes:*</u>

1. *"Pecuniary gain," "pecuniary loss," and "offense" are defined in the Commentary to §8A1.2 (Application Instructions - Organizations). Note that subsections (a)(2) and (a)(3) contain certain limitations as to the use of pecuniary gain and pecuniary loss in determining the base fine. Under subsection (a)(2), the pecuniary gain used to determine the base fine is the pecuniary gain to the organization from the offense. Under subsection (a)(3), the pecuniary loss used to determine the base fine is the pecuniary loss from the offense caused by the organization, to the extent that such loss was caused intentionally, knowingly, or recklessly.*

2. *Under 18 U.S.C. § 3571(d), the court is not required to calculate pecuniary loss or pecuniary gain to the extent that determination of loss or gain would unduly complicate or prolong the sentencing process. Nevertheless, the court may need to approximate loss in order to calculate offense levels under Chapter Two. <u>See</u> Commentary to §2B1.1 (Larceny, Embezzlement, and Other Forms of Theft). If loss is approximated for purposes of determining the applicable offense level, the court should use that approximation as the starting point for calculating pecuniary loss under this section.*

3. *In a case of an attempted offense or a conspiracy to commit an offense, pecuniary loss and pecuniary gain are to be determined in accordance with the principles stated in §2X1.1 (Attempt, Solicitation, or Conspiracy).*

4. *In a case involving multiple participants (<u>i.e.</u>, multiple organizations, or the organization and individual(s) unassociated with the organization), the applicable offense level is to be determined without regard to apportionment of the gain from or loss caused by the offense. <u>See</u> §1B1.3 (Relevant Conduct). However, if the base fine is determined under subsections (a)(2) or (a)(3), the court may, as appropriate, apportion gain or loss considering the defendant's relative culpability and other pertinent factors. Note also that under §2R1.1(d)(1), the volume of commerce, which is used in determining a proxy for loss under §8C2.4(a)(3), is limited to the volume of commerce attributable to the defendant.*

5. *Special instructions regarding the determination of the base fine are contained in: §2B4.1 (Bribery in Procurement of Bank Loan and Other Commercial Bribery); §2C1.1 (Offering, Giving, Soliciting, or Receiving a Bribe; Extortion Under Color of Official Right); §2C1.2 (Offering, Giving, Soliciting, or Receiving a Gratuity); §2E5.1 (Offering, Accepting, or Soliciting a Bribe or Gratuity Affecting the Operation of an Employee Welfare or Pension Benefit Plan; Prohibited Payments or Lending of Money by Employer or Agent to Employees, Representatives,*

or Labor Organizations); §2R1.1 (Bid-Rigging, Price-Fixing or Market-Allocation Agreements Among Competitors); §2S1.1 (Laundering of Monetary Instruments); §2S1.2 (Engaging in Monetary Transactions in Property Derived from Specified Unlawful Activity); and §2S1.3 (Structuring Transactions to Evade Reporting Requirements; Failure to Report Cash or Monetary Transactions; Failure to File Currency and Monetary Instrument Report; Knowingly Filing False Reports).

Background: Under this section, the base fine is determined in one of three ways: (1) by the amount, based on the offense level, from the table in subsection (d); (2) by the pecuniary gain to the organization from the offense; and (3) by the pecuniary loss caused by the organization, to the extent that such loss was caused intentionally, knowingly, or recklessly. In certain cases, special instructions for determining the loss or offense level amount apply. As a general rule, the base fine measures the seriousness of the offense. The determinants of the base fine are selected so that, in conjunction with the multipliers derived from the culpability score in §8C2.5 (Culpability Score), they will result in guideline fine ranges appropriate to deter organizational criminal conduct and to provide incentives for organizations to maintain internal mechanisms for preventing, detecting, and reporting criminal conduct. In order to deter organizations from seeking to obtain financial reward through criminal conduct, this section provides that, when greatest, pecuniary gain to the organization is used to determine the base fine. In order to ensure that organizations will seek to prevent losses intentionally, knowingly, or recklessly caused by their agents, this section provides that, when greatest, pecuniary loss is used to determine the base fine in such circumstances. Chapter Two provides special instructions for fines that include specific rules for determining the base fine in connection with certain types of offenses in which the calculation of loss or gain is difficult, e.g., price-fixing and money laundering. For these offenses, the special instructions tailor the base fine to circumstances that occur in connection with such offenses and that generally relate to the magnitude of loss or gain resulting from such offenses.

Historical Note: Effective November 1, 1991 (see Appendix C, amendment 422). Amended effective November 1, 1993 (see Appendix C, amendment 496).

§8C2.5. Culpability Score

(a) Start with 5 points and apply subsections (b) through (g) below.

(b) Involvement in or Tolerance of Criminal Activity

If more than one applies, use the greatest:

(1) If --

(A) the organization had 5,000 or more employees and

(i) an individual within high-level personnel of the organization participated in, condoned, or was willfully ignorant of the offense; or

(ii) tolerance of the offense by substantial authority personnel was pervasive throughout the organization; or

(B) the unit of the organization within which the offense was committed had 5,000 or more employees and

(i) an individual within high-level personnel of the unit participated in, condoned, or was willfully ignorant of the offense; or

(ii) tolerance of the offense by substantial authority personnel was pervasive throughout such unit,

add 5 points; or

(2) If --

(A) the organization had 1,000 or more employees and

(i) an individual within high-level personnel of the organization participated in, condoned, or was willfully ignorant of the offense; or

(ii) tolerance of the offense by substantial authority personnel was pervasive throughout the organization; or

(B) the unit of the organization within which the offense was committed had 1,000 or more employees and

(i) an individual within high-level personnel of the unit participated in, condoned, or was willfully ignorant of the offense; or

(ii) tolerance of the offense by substantial authority personnel was pervasive throughout such unit,

add 4 points; or

(3) If --

(A) the organization had 200 or more employees and

(i) an individual within high-level personnel of the organization participated in, condoned, or was willfully ignorant of the offense; or

(ii) tolerance of the offense by substantial authority personnel was pervasive throughout the organization; or

(B) the unit of the organization within which the offense was committed had 200 or more employees and

(i) an individual within high-level personnel of the unit participated in, condoned, or was willfully ignorant of the offense; or

(ii) tolerance of the offense by substantial authority personnel was pervasive throughout such unit,

add **3** points; or

(4) If the organization had 50 or more employees and an individual within substantial authority personnel participated in, condoned, or was willfully ignorant of the offense, add **2** points; or

(5) If the organization had 10 or more employees and an individual within substantial authority personnel participated in, condoned, or was willfully ignorant of the offense, add **1** point.

(c) Prior History

If more than one applies, use the greater:

(1) If the organization (or separately managed line of business) committed any part of the instant offense less than 10 years after (A) a criminal adjudication based on similar misconduct; or (B) civil or administrative adjudication(s) based on two or more separate instances of similar misconduct, add **1** point; or

(2) If the organization (or separately managed line of business) committed any part of the instant offense less than 5 years after (A) a criminal adjudication based on similar misconduct; or (B) civil or administrative adjudication(s) based on two or more separate instances of similar misconduct, add **2** points.

(d) Violation of an Order

If more than one applies, use the greater:

(1) (A) If the commission of the instant offense violated a judicial order or injunction, other than a violation of a condition of probation; or (B) if the organization (or separately managed line of business) violated a condition of probation by engaging in similar misconduct, i.e., misconduct similar to that for which it was placed on probation, add **2** points; or

(2) If the commission of the instant offense violated a condition of probation, add **1** point.

(e) Obstruction of Justice

If the organization willfully obstructed or impeded, attempted to obstruct or impede, or aided, abetted, or encouraged obstruction of justice during the investigation, prosecution, or sentencing of the instant offense, or, with knowledge thereof, failed to take reasonable steps to prevent such obstruction or impedance or attempted obstruction or impedance, add **3** points.

(f) Effective Program to Prevent and Detect Violations of Law

If the offense occurred despite an effective program to prevent and detect violations of law, subtract 3 points.

Provided, that this subsection does not apply if an individual within high-level personnel of the organization, a person within high-level personnel of the unit of the organization within which the offense was committed where the unit had 200 or more employees, or an individual responsible for the administration or enforcement of a program to prevent and detect violations of law participated in, condoned, or was willfully ignorant of the offense. Participation of an individual within substantial authority personnel in an offense results in a rebuttable presumption that the organization did not have an effective program to prevent and detect violations of law.

Provided, further, that this subsection does not apply if, after becoming aware of an offense, the organization unreasonably delayed reporting the offense to appropriate governmental authorities.

(g) Self-Reporting, Cooperation, and Acceptance of Responsibility

If more than one applies, use the greatest:

(1) If the organization (A) prior to an imminent threat of disclosure or government investigation; and (B) within a reasonably prompt time after becoming aware of the offense, reported the offense to appropriate governmental authorities, fully cooperated in the investigation, and clearly demonstrated recognition and affirmative acceptance of responsibility for its criminal conduct, subtract **5** points; or

(2) If the organization fully cooperated in the investigation and clearly demonstrated recognition and affirmative acceptance of responsibility for its criminal conduct, subtract **2** points; or

(3) If the organization clearly demonstrated recognition and affirmative acceptance of responsibility for its criminal conduct, subtract **1** point.

Commentary

Application Notes:

1. *"Substantial authority personnel," "condoned," "willfully ignorant of the offense," "similar misconduct," "prior criminal adjudication," and "effective program to prevent and detect violations of law," are defined in the Commentary to §8A1.2 (Application Instructions - Organizations).*

2. *For purposes of subsection (b), "unit of the organization" means any reasonably distinct operational component of the organization. For example, a large organization may have several large units such as divisions or subsidiaries, as well as many smaller units such as specialized manufacturing, marketing, or accounting operations within these larger units. For purposes of*

this definition, all of these types of units are encompassed within the term "unit of the organization."

3. *"High-level personnel of the organization" is defined in the Commentary to §8A1.2 (Application Instructions - Organizations). With respect to a unit with 200 or more employees, "high-level personnel of a unit of the organization" means agents within the unit who set the policy for or control that unit. For example, if the managing agent of a unit with 200 employees participated in an offense, three points would be added under subsection (b)(3); if that organization had 1,000 employees and the managing agent of the unit with 200 employees were also within high-level personnel of the entire organization, four points (rather than three) would be added under subsection (b)(2).*

4. *Pervasiveness under subsection (b) will be case specific and depend on the number, and degree of responsibility, of individuals within substantial authority personnel who participated in, condoned, or were willfully ignorant of the offense. Fewer individuals need to be involved for a finding of pervasiveness if those individuals exercised a relatively high degree of authority. Pervasiveness can occur either within an organization as a whole or within a unit of an organization. For example, if an offense were committed in an organization with 1,000 employees but the tolerance of the offense was pervasive only within a unit of the organization with 200 employees (and no high-level personnel of the organization participated in, condoned, or was willfully ignorant of the offense), three points would be added under subsection (b)(3). If, in the same organization, tolerance of the offense was pervasive throughout the organization as a whole, or an individual within high-level personnel of the organization participated in the offense, four points (rather than three) would be added under subsection (b)(2).*

5. *A "separately managed line of business," as used in subsections (c) and (d), is a subpart of a for-profit organization that has its own management, has a high degree of autonomy from higher managerial authority, and maintains its own separate books of account. Corporate subsidiaries and divisions frequently are separately managed lines of business. Under subsection (c), in determining the prior history of an organization with separately managed lines of business, only the prior conduct or criminal record of the separately managed line of business involved in the instant offense is to be used. Under subsection (d), in the context of an organization with separately managed lines of business, in making the determination whether a violation of a condition of probation involved engaging in similar misconduct, only the prior misconduct of the separately managed line of business involved in the instant offense is to be considered.*

6. *Under subsection (c), in determining the prior history of an organization or separately managed line of business, the conduct of the underlying economic entity shall be considered without regard to its legal structure or ownership. For example, if two companies merged and became separate divisions and separately managed lines of business within the merged company, each division would retain the prior history of its predecessor company. If a company reorganized and became a new legal entity, the new company would retain the prior history of the predecessor company. In contrast, if one company purchased the physical assets but not the ongoing business of another company, the prior history of the company selling the physical assets would not be transferred to the company purchasing the assets. However, if an organization is acquired by another organization in response to solicitations by appropriate federal government officials, the prior history of the acquired organization shall not be attributed to the acquiring organization.*

7. *Under subsections (c)(1)(B) and (c)(2)(B), the civil or administrative adjudication(s) must have occurred within the specified period (ten or five years) of the instant offense.*

8. *Adjust the culpability score for the factors listed in subsection (e) whether or not the offense guideline incorporates that factor, or that factor is inherent in the offense.*

9. *Subsection (e) applies where the obstruction is committed on behalf of the organization; it does not apply where an individual or individuals have attempted to conceal their misconduct from the organization. The Commentary to §3C1.1 (Obstructing or Impeding the Administration of Justice) provides guidance regarding the types of conduct that constitute obstruction.*

10. *The second proviso in subsection (f) contemplates that the organization will be allowed a reasonable period of time to conduct an internal investigation. In addition, no reporting is required by this proviso if the organization reasonably concluded, based on the information then available, that no offense had been committed.*

11. *"Appropriate governmental authorities," as used in subsections (f) and (g)(1), means the federal or state law enforcement, regulatory, or program officials having jurisdiction over such matter. To qualify for a reduction under subsection (g)(1), the report to appropriate governmental authorities must be made under the direction of the organization.*

12. *To qualify for a reduction under subsection (g)(1) or (g)(2), cooperation must be both timely and thorough. To be timely, the cooperation must begin essentially at the same time as the organization is officially notified of a criminal investigation. To be thorough, the cooperation should include the disclosure of all pertinent information known by the organization. A prime test of whether the organization has disclosed all pertinent information is whether the information is sufficient for law enforcement personnel to identify the nature and extent of the offense and the individual(s) responsible for the criminal conduct. However, the cooperation to be measured is the cooperation of the organization itself, not the cooperation of individuals within the organization. If, because of the lack of cooperation of particular individual(s), neither the organization nor law enforcement personnel are able to identify the culpable individual(s) within the organization despite the organization's efforts to cooperate fully, the organization may still be given credit for full cooperation.*

13. *Entry of a plea of guilty prior to the commencement of trial combined with truthful admission of involvement in the offense and related conduct ordinarily will constitute significant evidence of affirmative acceptance of responsibility under subsection (g), unless outweighed by conduct of the organization that is inconsistent with such acceptance of responsibility. This adjustment is not intended to apply to an organization that puts the government to its burden of proof at trial by denying the essential factual elements of guilt, is convicted, and only then admits guilt and expresses remorse. Conviction by trial, however, does not automatically preclude an organization from consideration for such a reduction. In rare situations, an organization may clearly demonstrate an acceptance of responsibility for its criminal conduct even though it exercises its constitutional right to a trial. This may occur, for example, where an organization goes to trial to assert and preserve issues that do not relate to factual guilt (e.g., to make a constitutional challenge to a statute or a challenge to the applicability of a statute to its conduct). In each such instance, however, a determination that an organization has accepted responsibility will be based primarily upon pretrial statements and conduct.*

14. *In making a determination with respect to subsection (g), the court may determine that the chief executive officer or highest ranking employee of an organization should appear at sentencing in order to signify that the organization has clearly demonstrated recognition and affirmative acceptance of responsibility.*

Background: *The increased culpability scores under subsection (b) are based on three interrelated principles. First, an organization is more culpable when individuals who manage the organization or who have substantial discretion in acting for the organization participate in, condone, or are willfully ignorant of criminal conduct. Second, as organizations become larger and their managements become more professional, participation in, condonation of, or willful ignorance of criminal conduct by such management is increasingly a breach of trust or abuse of position. Third, as organizations increase in size, the risk of criminal conduct beyond that reflected in the instant offense also increases whenever management's tolerance of that offense is pervasive. Because of the continuum of sizes of organizations and professionalization of management, subsection (b) gradually increases the culpability score based upon the size of the organization and the level and extent of the substantial authority personnel involvement.*

Historical Note: Effective November 1, 1991 (see Appendix C, amendment 422).

§8C2.6. Minimum and Maximum Multipliers

Using the culpability score from §8C2.5 (Culpability Score) and applying any applicable special instruction for fines in Chapter Two, determine the applicable minimum and maximum fine multipliers from the table below.

Culpability Score	Minimum Multiplier	Maximum Multiplier
10 or more	2.00	4.00
9	1.80	3.60
8	1.60	3.20
7	1.40	2.80
6	1.20	2.40
5	1.00	2.00
4	0.80	1.60
3	0.60	1.20
2	0.40	0.80
1	0.20	0.40
0 or less	0.05	0.20.

Commentary

Application Note:

1. *A special instruction for fines in §2R1.1 (Bid-Rigging, Price-Fixing or Market-Allocation Agreements Among Competitors) sets a floor for minimum and maximum multipliers in cases covered by that guideline.*

Historical Note: Effective November 1, 1991 (see Appendix C, amendment 422).

§8C2.7. Guideline Fine Range - Organizations

(a) The minimum of the guideline fine range is determined by multiplying the base fine determined under §8C2.4 (Base Fine) by the applicable minimum multiplier determined under §8C2.6 (Minimum and Maximum Multipliers).

(b) The maximum of the guideline fine range is determined by multiplying the base fine determined under §8C2.4 (Base Fine) by the applicable maximum multiplier determined under §8C2.6 (Minimum and Maximum Multipliers).

Historical Note: Effective November 1, 1991 (see Appendix C, amendment 422).

§8C2.8. Determining the Fine Within the Range (Policy Statement)

(a) In determining the amount of the fine within the applicable guideline range, the court should consider:

(1) the need for the sentence to reflect the seriousness of the offense, promote respect for the law, provide just punishment, afford adequate deterrence, and protect the public from further crimes of the organization;

(2) the organization's role in the offense;

(3) any collateral consequences of conviction, including civil obligations arising from the organization's conduct;

(4) any nonpecuniary loss caused or threatened by the offense;

(5) whether the offense involved a vulnerable victim;

(6) any prior criminal record of an individual within high-level personnel of the organization or high-level personnel of a unit of the organization who participated in, condoned, or was willfully ignorant of the criminal conduct;

(7) any prior civil or criminal misconduct by the organization other than that counted under §8C2.5(c);

(8) any culpability score under §8C2.5 (Culpability Score) higher than 10 or lower than 0;

(9) partial but incomplete satisfaction of the conditions for one or more of the mitigating or aggravating factors set forth in §8C2.5 (Culpability Score); and

(10) any factor listed in 18 U.S.C. § 3572(a).

(b) In addition, the court may consider the relative importance of any factor used to determine the range, including the pecuniary loss caused by the offense, the pecuniary gain from the offense, any specific offense characteristic used to determine the offense level, and any aggravating or mitigating factor used to determine the culpability score.

Commentary

Application Notes:

1. *Subsection (a)(2) provides that the court, in setting the fine within the guideline fine range, should consider the organization's role in the offense. This consideration is particularly appropriate if the guideline fine range does not take the organization's role in the offense into account. For example, the guideline fine range in an antitrust case does not take into consideration whether the organization was an organizer or leader of the conspiracy. A higher fine within the guideline fine range ordinarily will be appropriate for an organization that takes a leading role in such an offense.*

2. *Subsection (a)(3) provides that the court, in setting the fine within the guideline fine range, should consider any collateral consequences of conviction, including civil obligations arising from the organization's conduct. As a general rule, collateral consequences that merely make victims whole provide no basis for reducing the fine within the guideline range. If criminal and civil sanctions are unlikely to make victims whole, this may provide a basis for a higher fine within the guideline fine range. If punitive collateral sanctions have been or will be imposed on the organization, this may provide a basis for a lower fine within the guideline fine range.*

3. *Subsection (a)(4) provides that the court, in setting the fine within the guideline fine range, should consider any nonpecuniary loss caused or threatened by the offense. To the extent that nonpecuniary loss caused or threatened (e.g., loss of or threat to human life; psychological injury; threat to national security) by the offense is not adequately considered in setting the guideline fine range, this factor provides a basis for a higher fine within the range. This factor is more likely to be applicable where the guideline fine range is determined by pecuniary loss or gain, rather than by offense level, because the Chapter Two offense levels frequently take actual or threatened nonpecuniary loss into account.*

4. *Subsection (a)(6) provides that the court, in setting the fine within the guideline fine range, should consider any prior criminal record of an individual within high-level personnel of the organization or a unit of the organization. Since an individual within high-level personnel either exercises substantial control over the organization or a unit of the organization or has a substantial role in the making of policy within the organization or a unit of the organization, any prior criminal misconduct of such an individual may be relevant to the determination of the appropriate fine for the organization.*

5. *Subsection (a)(7) provides that the court, in setting the fine within the guideline fine range, should consider any prior civil or criminal misconduct by the organization other than that counted under §8C2.5(c). The civil and criminal misconduct counted under §8C2.5(c) increases the guideline fine range. Civil or criminal misconduct other than that counted under §8C2.5(c) may provide a basis for a higher fine within the range. In a case involving a pattern of illegality, an upward departure may be warranted.*

6. *Subsection (a)(8) provides that the court, in setting the fine within the guideline fine range, should consider any culpability score higher than ten or lower than zero. As the culpability score increases above ten, this may provide a basis for a higher fine within the range. Similarly, as the culpability score decreases below zero, this may provide a basis for a lower fine within the range.*

7. *Under subsection (b), the court, in determining the fine within the range, may consider any factor that it considered in determining the range. This allows for courts to differentiate between cases that have the same offense level but differ in seriousness (e.g., two fraud cases*

at offense level 12, one resulting in a loss of $21,000, the other $40,000). Similarly, this allows for courts to differentiate between two cases that have the same aggravating factors, but in which those factors vary in their intensity (e.g., two cases with upward adjustments to the culpability score under §8C2.5(c)(2) (prior criminal adjudications within 5 years of the commencement of the instant offense, one involving a single conviction, the other involving two or more convictions).

Background: *Subsection (a) includes factors that the court is required to consider under 18 U.S.C. §§ 3553(a) and 3572(a) as well as additional factors that the Commission has determined may be relevant in a particular case. A number of factors required for consideration under 18 U.S.C. § 3572(a) (e.g., pecuniary loss, the size of the organization) are used under the fine guidelines in this subpart to determine the fine range, and therefore are not specifically set out again in subsection (a) of this guideline. In unusual cases, factors listed in this section may provide a basis for departure.*

Historical Note: Effective November 1, 1991 (see Appendix C, amendment 422).

§8C2.9. Disgorgement

The court shall add to the fine determined under §8C2.8 (Determining the Fine Within the Range) any gain to the organization from the offense that has not and will not be paid as restitution or by way of other remedial measures.

Commentary

Application Note:

1. *This section is designed to ensure that the amount of any gain that has not and will not be taken from the organization for remedial purposes will be added to the fine. This section typically will apply in cases in which the organization has received gain from an offense but restitution or remedial efforts will not be required because the offense did not result in harm to identifiable victims, e.g., money laundering, obscenity, and regulatory reporting offenses. Money spent or to be spent to remedy the adverse effects of the offense, e.g., the cost to retrofit defective products, should be considered as disgorged gain. If the cost of remedial efforts made or to be made by the organization equals or exceeds the gain from the offense, this section will not apply.*

Historical Note: Effective November 1, 1991 (see Appendix C, amendment 422).

§8C2.10. Determining the Fine for Other Counts

For any count or counts not covered under §8C2.1 (Applicability of Fine Guidelines), the court should determine an appropriate fine by applying the provisions of 18 U.S.C. §§ 3553 and 3572. The court should determine the appropriate fine amount, if any, to be imposed in addition to any fine determined under §8C2.8 (Determining the Fine Within the Range) and §8C2.9 (Disgorgement).

Commentary

Background: The Commission has not promulgated guidelines governing the setting of fines for counts not covered by §8C2.1 (Applicability of Fine Guidelines). For such counts, the court should determine the appropriate fine based on the general statutory provisions governing sentencing. In cases that have a count or counts not covered by the guidelines in addition to a count or counts covered by the guidelines, the court shall apply the fine guidelines for the count(s) covered by the guidelines, and add any additional amount to the fine, as appropriate, for the count(s) not covered by the guidelines.

Historical Note: Effective November 1, 1991 (see Appendix C, amendment 422).

* * * * *

3. IMPLEMENTING THE SENTENCE OF A FINE

§8C3.1. Imposing a Fine

(a) Except to the extent restricted by the maximum fine authorized by statute or any minimum fine required by statute, the fine or fine range shall be that determined under §8C1.1 (Determining the Fine - Criminal Purpose Organizations); §8C2.7 (Guideline Fine Range - Organizations) and §8C2.9 (Disgorgement); or §8C2.10 (Determining the Fine for Other Counts), as appropriate.

(b) Where the minimum guideline fine is greater than the maximum fine authorized by statute, the maximum fine authorized by statute shall be the guideline fine.

(c) Where the maximum guideline fine is less than a minimum fine required by statute, the minimum fine required by statute shall be the guideline fine.

Commentary

Background: This section sets forth the interaction of the fines or fine ranges determined under this chapter with the maximum fine authorized by statute and any minimum fine required by statute for the count or counts of conviction. The general statutory provisions governing a sentence of a fine are set forth in 18 U.S.C. § 3571.

When the organization is convicted of multiple counts, the maximum fine authorized by statute may increase. For example, in the case of an organization convicted of three felony counts related to a $200,000 fraud, the maximum fine authorized by statute will be $500,000 on each count, for an aggregate maximum authorized fine of $1,500,000.

Historical Note: Effective November 1, 1991 (see Appendix C, amendment 422).

§8C3.2. Payment of the Fine - Organizations

(a) If the defendant operated primarily for a criminal purpose or primarily by criminal means, immediate payment of the fine shall be required.

(b) In any other case, immediate payment of the fine shall be required unless the court finds that the organization is financially unable to make immediate payment or that such payment would pose an undue burden on the organization. If the court permits other than immediate payment, it shall require full payment at the earliest possible date, either by requiring payment on a date certain or by establishing an installment schedule.

Commentary

Application Note:

1. *When the court permits other than immediate payment, the period provided for payment shall in no event exceed five years. 18 U.S.C. § 3572(d).*

Historical Note: Effective November 1, 1991 (see Appendix C, amendment 422).

§8C3.3. Reduction of Fine Based on Inability to Pay

(a) The court shall reduce the fine below that otherwise required by §8C1.1 (Determining the Fine - Criminal Purpose Organizations), or §8C2.7 (Guideline Fine Range - Organizations) and §8C2.9 (Disgorgement), to the extent that imposition of such fine would impair its ability to make restitution to victims.

(b) The court may impose a fine below that otherwise required by §8C2.7 (Guideline Fine Range - Organizations) and §8C2.9 (Disgorgement) if the court finds that the organization is not able and, even with the use of a reasonable installment schedule, is not likely to become able to pay the minimum fine required by §8C2.7 (Guideline Fine Range - Organizations) and §8C2.9 (Disgorgement).

Provided, that the reduction under this subsection shall not be more than necessary to avoid substantially jeopardizing the continued viability of the organization.

Commentary

Application Note:

1. *For purposes of this section, an organization is not able to pay the minimum fine if, even with an installment schedule under §8C3.2 (Payment of the Fine - Organizations), the payment of that fine would substantially jeopardize the continued existence of the organization.*

Background: Subsection (a) carries out the requirement in 18 U.S.C. § 3572(b) that the court impose a fine or other monetary penalty only to the extent that such fine or penalty will not impair the ability of the organization to make restitution for the offense; however, this section does not authorize a criminal purpose organization to remain in business in order to pay restitution.

Historical Note: Effective November 1, 1991 (see Appendix C, amendment 422).

§8C3.4. Fines Paid by Owners of Closely Held Organizations

The court may offset the fine imposed upon a closely held organization when one or more individuals, each of whom owns at least a 5 percent interest in the organization, has been fined in a federal criminal proceeding for the same offense conduct for which the organization is being sentenced. The amount of such offset shall not exceed the amount resulting from multiplying the total fines imposed on those individuals by those individuals' total percentage interest in the organization.

Commentary

Application Notes:

1. *For purposes of this section, an organization is closely held, regardless of its size, when relatively few individuals own it. In order for an organization to be closely held, ownership and management need not completely overlap.*

2. *This section does not apply to a fine imposed upon an individual that arises out of offense conduct different from that for which the organization is being sentenced.*

Background: For practical purposes, most closely held organizations are the alter egos of their owner-managers. In the case of criminal conduct by a closely held corporation, the organization and the culpable individual(s) both may be convicted. As a general rule in such cases, appropriate punishment may be achieved by offsetting the fine imposed upon the organization by an amount that reflects the percentage ownership interest of the sentenced individuals and the magnitude of the fines imposed upon those individuals. For example, an organization is owned by five individuals, each of whom has a twenty percent interest; three of the individuals are convicted; and the combined fines imposed on those three equals $100,000. In this example, the fine imposed upon the organization may be offset by up to 60 percent of their combined fine amounts, i.e., by $60,000.

Historical Note: Effective November 1, 1991 (see Appendix C, amendment 422).

* * * * *

4. DEPARTURES FROM THE GUIDELINE FINE RANGE

Introductory Commentary

The statutory provisions governing departures are set forth in 18 U.S.C. § 3553(b). Departure may be warranted if the court finds "that there exists an aggravating or mitigating circumstance of a kind, or to a degree, not adequately taken into consideration by the Sentencing Commission in formulating the guidelines that should result in a sentence different from that described." This subpart sets forth certain factors that, in connection with certain offenses, may not have been adequately taken into consideration by the guidelines. In deciding whether departure is warranted, the court should consider the extent to which that factor is adequately taken into consideration by the guidelines and the relative importance or substantiality of that factor in the particular case.

To the extent that any policy statement from Chapter Five, Part K (Departures) is relevant to the organization, a departure from the applicable guideline fine range may be warranted. Some factors listed in Chapter Five, Part K that are particularly applicable to organizations are listed in this subpart. Other factors listed in Chapter Five, Part K may be applicable in particular cases. While this subpart lists factors that the Commission believes may constitute grounds for departure, the list is not exhaustive.

Historical Note: Effective November 1, 1991 (see Appendix C, amendment 422).

§8C4.1. Substantial Assistance to Authorities - Organizations (Policy Statement)

(a) Upon motion of the government stating that the defendant has provided substantial assistance in the investigation or prosecution of another organization that has committed an offense, or in the investigation or prosecution of an individual not directly affiliated with the defendant who has committed an offense, the court may depart from the guidelines.

(b) The appropriate reduction shall be determined by the court for reasons stated on the record that may include, but are not limited to, consideration of the following:

(1) the court's evaluation of the significance and usefulness of the organization's assistance, taking into consideration the government's evaluation of the assistance rendered;

(2) the nature and extent of the organization's assistance; and

(3) the timeliness of the organization's assistance.

Commentary

Application Note:

1. Departure under this section is intended for cases in which substantial assistance is provided in the investigation or prosecution of crimes committed by individuals not directly affiliated with the organization or by other organizations. It is not intended for assistance in the investigation or prosecution of the agents of the organization responsible for the offense for which the organization is being sentenced.

Historical Note: Effective November 1, 1991 (see Appendix C, amendment 422).

§8C4.2. Risk of Death or Bodily Injury (Policy Statement)

If the offense resulted in death or bodily injury, or involved a foreseeable risk of death or bodily injury, an upward departure may be warranted. The extent of any such departure should depend, among other factors, on the nature of the harm and the extent to which the harm was intended or knowingly risked, and the extent to which such harm or risk is taken into account within the applicable guideline fine range.

Historical Note: Effective November 1, 1991 (see Appendix C, amendment 422).

§8C4.3. Threat to National Security (Policy Statement)

If the offense constituted a threat to national security, an upward departure may be warranted.

Historical Note: Effective November 1, 1991 (see Appendix C, amendment 422).

§8C4.4. Threat to the Environment (Policy Statement)

If the offense presented a threat to the environment, an upward departure may be warranted.

Historical Note: Effective November 1, 1991 (see Appendix C, amendment 422).

§8C4.5. Threat to a Market (Policy Statement)

If the offense presented a risk to the integrity or continued existence of a market, an upward departure may be warranted. This section is applicable to both private markets (e.g., a financial market, a commodities market, or a market for consumer goods) and public markets (e.g., government contracting).

Historical Note: Effective November 1, 1991 (see Appendix C, amendment 422).

§8C4.6. Official Corruption (Policy Statement)

If the organization, in connection with the offense, bribed or unlawfully gave a gratuity to a public official, or attempted or conspired to bribe or unlawfully give a gratuity to a public official, an upward departure may be warranted.

Historical Note: Effective November 1, 1991 (see Appendix C, amendment 422).

§8C4.7. Public Entity (Policy Statement)

If the organization is a public entity, a downward departure may be warranted.

Historical Note: Effective November 1, 1991 (see Appendix C, amendment 422).

§8C4.8. **Members or Beneficiaries of the Organization as Victims (Policy Statement)**

If the members or beneficiaries, other than shareholders, of the organization are direct victims of the offense, a downward departure may be warranted. If the members or beneficiaries of an organization are direct victims of the offense, imposing a fine upon the organization may increase the burden upon the victims of the offense without achieving a deterrent effect. In such cases, a fine may not be appropriate. For example, departure may be appropriate if a labor union is convicted of embezzlement of pension funds.

Historical Note: Effective November 1, 1991 (see Appendix C, amendment 422).

§8C4.9. **Remedial Costs that Greatly Exceed Gain (Policy Statement)**

If the organization has paid or has agreed to pay remedial costs arising from the offense that greatly exceed the gain that the organization received from the offense, a downward departure may be warranted. In such a case, a substantial fine may not be necessary in order to achieve adequate punishment and deterrence. In deciding whether departure is appropriate, the court should consider the level and extent of substantial authority personnel involvement in the offense and the degree to which the loss exceeds the gain. If an individual within high-level personnel was involved in the offense, a departure would not be appropriate under this section. The lower the level and the more limited the extent of substantial authority personnel involvement in the offense, and the greater the degree to which remedial costs exceeded or will exceed gain, the less will be the need for a substantial fine to achieve adequate punishment and deterrence.

Historical Note: Effective November 1, 1991 (see Appendix C, amendment 422).

§8C4.10. **Mandatory Programs to Prevent and Detect Violations of Law (Policy Statement)**

If the organization's culpability score is reduced under §8C2.5(f) (Effective Program to Prevent and Detect Violations of Law) and the organization had implemented its program in response to a court order or administrative order specifically directed at the organization, an upward departure may be warranted to offset, in part or in whole, such reduction.

Historical Note: Effective November 1, 1991 (see Appendix C, amendment 422).

§8C4.11. **Exceptional Organizational Culpability (Policy Statement)**

If the organization's culpability score is greater than 10, an upward departure may be appropriate.

If no individual within substantial authority personnel participated in, condoned, or was willfully ignorant of the offense; the organization at the time of the offense had an effective program to prevent and detect violations of law; and the base fine is determined under §8C2.4(a)(1), §8C2.4(a)(3), or a special instruction for fines in Chapter Two (Offense Conduct), a downward departure may be warranted. In a case

meeting these criteria, the court may find that the organization had exceptionally low culpability and therefore a fine based on loss, offense level, or a special Chapter Two instruction results in a guideline fine range higher than necessary to achieve the purposes of sentencing. Nevertheless, such fine should not be lower than if determined under §8C2.4(a)(2).

Historical Note: Effective November 1, 1991 (see Appendix C, amendment 422).

PART D - ORGANIZATIONAL PROBATION

Introductory Commentary

Section 8D1.1 sets forth the circumstances under which a sentence to a term of probation is required. Sections 8D1.2 through 8D1.5 address the length of the probation term, conditions of probation, and violations of probation conditions.

Historical Note: Effective November 1, 1991 (see Appendix C, amendment 422).

§8D1.1. Imposition of Probation - Organizations

(a) The court shall order a term of probation:

(1) if such sentence is necessary to secure payment of restitution (§8B1.1), enforce a remedial order (§8B1.2), or ensure completion of community service (§8B1.3);

(2) if the organization is sentenced to pay a monetary penalty (e.g., restitution, fine, or special assessment), the penalty is not paid in full at the time of sentencing, and restrictions are necessary to safeguard the organization's ability to make payments;

(3) if, at the time of sentencing, an organization having 50 or more employees does not have an effective program to prevent and detect violations of law;

(4) if the organization within five years prior to sentencing engaged in similar misconduct, as determined by a prior criminal adjudication, and any part of the misconduct underlying the instant offense occurred after that adjudication;

(5) if an individual within high-level personnel of the organization or the unit of the organization within which the instant offense was committed participated in the misconduct underlying the instant offense and that individual within five years prior to sentencing engaged in similar misconduct, as determined by a prior criminal adjudication, and any part of the misconduct underlying the instant offense occurred after that adjudication;

(6) if such sentence is necessary to ensure that changes are made within the organization to reduce the likelihood of future criminal conduct;

(7) if the sentence imposed upon the organization does not include a fine; or

(8) if necessary to accomplish one or more of the purposes of sentencing set forth in 18 U.S.C. § 3553(a)(2).

Commentary

Background: Under 18 U.S.C. § 3561(a), an organization may be sentenced to a term of probation. Under 18 U.S.C. § 3551(c), imposition of a term of probation is required if the sentence imposed upon the organization does not include a fine.

Historical Note: Effective November 1, 1991 (see Appendix C, amendment 422).

§8D1.2. Term of Probation - Organizations

(a) When a sentence of probation is imposed --

(1) In the case of a felony, the term of probation shall be at least one year but not more than five years.

(2) In any other case, the term of probation shall be not more than five years.

Commentary

Application Note:

1. *Within the limits set by the guidelines, the term of probation should be sufficient, but not more than necessary, to accomplish the court's specific objectives in imposing the term of probation. The terms of probation set forth in this section are those provided in 18 U.S.C. § 3561(b).*

Historical Note: Effective November 1, 1991 (see Appendix C, amendment 422).

§8D1.3. Conditions of Probation - Organizations

(a) Pursuant to 18 U.S.C. § 3563(a)(1), any sentence of probation shall include the condition that the organization shall not commit another federal, state, or local crime during the term of probation.

(b) Pursuant to 18 U.S.C. § 3563(a)(2), if a sentence of probation is imposed for a felony, the court shall impose as a condition of probation at least one of the following: a fine, restitution, or community service, unless the court finds on the record that extraordinary circumstances exist that would make such condition plainly unreasonable, in which event the court shall impose one or more other conditions set forth in 18 U.S.C. § 3563(b).

(c) The court may impose other conditions that (1) are reasonably related to the nature and circumstances of the offense or the history and characteristics of the organization; and (2) involve only such deprivations of liberty or property as are necessary to effect the purposes of sentencing.

Historical Note: Effective November 1, 1991 (see Appendix C, amendment 422).

§8D1.4. <u>**Recommended Conditions of Probation - Organizations**</u> **(Policy Statement)**

(a) The court may order the organization, at its expense and in the format and media specified by the court, to publicize the nature of the offense committed, the fact of conviction, the nature of the punishment imposed, and the steps that will be taken to prevent the recurrence of similar offenses.

(b) If probation is imposed under §8D1.1(a)(2), the following conditions may be appropriate to the extent they appear necessary to safeguard the organization's ability to pay any deferred portion of an order of restitution, fine, or assessment:

(1) The organization shall make periodic submissions to the court or probation officer, at intervals specified by the court, reporting on the organization's financial condition and results of business operations, and accounting for the disposition of all funds received.

(2) The organization shall submit to: (A) a reasonable number of regular or unannounced examinations of its books and records at appropriate business premises by the probation officer or experts engaged by the court; and (B) interrogation of knowledgeable individuals within the organization. Compensation to and costs of any experts engaged by the court shall be paid by the organization.

(3) The organization shall be required to notify the court or probation officer immediately upon learning of (A) any material adverse change in its business or financial condition or prospects, or (B) the commencement of any bankruptcy proceeding, major civil litigation, criminal prosecution, or administrative proceeding against the organization, or any investigation or formal inquiry by governmental authorities regarding the organization.

(4) The organization shall be required to make periodic payments, as specified by the court, in the following priority: (1) restitution; (2) fine; and (3) any other monetary sanction.

(c) If probation is ordered under §8D1.1(a)(3), (4), (5), or (6), the following conditions may be appropriate:

(1) The organization shall develop and submit to the court a program to prevent and detect violations of law, including a schedule for implementation.

(2) Upon approval by the court of a program to prevent and detect violations of law, the organization shall notify its employees and shareholders of its criminal behavior and its program to prevent and detect violations of law. Such notice shall be in a form prescribed by the court.

(3) The organization shall make periodic reports to the court or probation officer, at intervals and in a form specified by the court, regarding the organization's progress in implementing the program to prevent and detect violations of law. Among other things, such reports shall disclose

any criminal prosecution, civil litigation, or administrative proceeding commenced against the organization, or any investigation or formal inquiry by governmental authorities of which the organization learned since its last report.

(4) In order to monitor whether the organization is following the program to prevent and detect violations of law, the organization shall submit to: (A) a reasonable number of regular or unannounced examinations of its books and records at appropriate business premises by the probation officer or experts engaged by the court; and (B) interrogation of knowledgeable individuals within the organization. Compensation to and costs of any experts engaged by the court shall be paid by the organization.

Commentary

Application Notes:

1. *In determining the conditions to be imposed when probation is ordered under §8D1.1(a)(3) through (6), the court should consider the views of any governmental regulatory body that oversees conduct of the organization relating to the instant offense. To assess the efficacy of a program to prevent and detect violations of law submitted by the organization, the court may employ appropriate experts who shall be afforded access to all material possessed by the organization that is necessary for a comprehensive assessment of the proposed program. The court should approve any program that appears reasonably calculated to prevent and detect violations of law, provided it is consistent with any applicable statutory or regulatory requirement.*

2. *Periodic reports submitted in accordance with subsection (c)(3) should be provided to any governmental regulatory body that oversees conduct of the organization relating to the instant offense.*

Historical Note: Effective November 1, 1991 (see Appendix C, amendment 422).

§8D1.5. Violations of Conditions of Probation - Organizations (Policy Statement)

Upon a finding of a violation of a condition of probation, the court may extend the term of probation, impose more restrictive conditions of probation, or revoke probation and resentence the organization.

Commentary

Application Note:

1. *In the event of repeated, serious violations of conditions of probation, the appointment of a master or trustee may be appropriate to ensure compliance with court orders.*

Historical Note: Effective November 1, 1991 (see Appendix C, amendment 422).

PART E - SPECIAL ASSESSMENTS, FORFEITURES, AND COSTS

§8E1.1. Special Assessments - Organizations

A special assessment must be imposed on an organization in the amount prescribed by statute.

Commentary

Background: Pursuant to 18 U.S.C. § 3013(a), the court is required to impose assessments in the following amounts:

$50, if the organization is convicted of a Class B misdemeanor;
$125, if the organization is convicted of a Class A misdemeanor; and
$200, if the organization is convicted of a felony. 18 U.S.C. § 3013.

The Act does not authorize the court to waive imposition of the assessment.

Historical Note: Effective November 1, 1991 (see Appendix C, amendment 422).

§8E1.2. Forfeiture - Organizations

Apply §5E1.4 (Forfeiture).

Historical Note: Effective November 1, 1991 (see Appendix C, amendment 422).

§8E1.3. Assessment of Costs - Organizations

As provided in 28 U.S.C. § 1918, the court may order the organization to pay the costs of prosecution. In addition, specific statutory provisions mandate assessment of costs.

Historical Note: Effective November 1, 1991 (see Appendix C, amendment 422).

[Page intentionally blank]

APPENDIX A - STATUTORY INDEX

INTRODUCTION

This index specifies the guideline section or sections ordinarily applicable to the statute of conviction. If more than one guideline section is referenced for the particular statute, use the guideline most appropriate for the nature of the offense conduct charged in the count of which the defendant was convicted. If, in an atypical case, the guideline section indicated for the statute of conviction is inappropriate because of the particular conduct involved, use the guideline section most applicable to the nature of the offense conduct charged in the count of which the defendant was convicted. (See §1B1.2.)

If the offense involved a conspiracy, attempt, or solicitation, refer to §2X1.1 as well as the guideline for the substantive offense.

For those offenses not listed in this index, the most analogous guideline is to be applied. (See §2X5.1.)

The guidelines do not apply to any count of conviction that is a Class B or C misdemeanor or an infraction. (See §1B1.9.)

Historical Note: Effective November 1, 1987. Amended effective November 1, 1989 (see Appendix C, amendments 296 and 297); November 1, 1993 (see Appendix C, amendment 496).

INDEX

Statute	Guideline
7 U.S.C. § 6	2F1.1
7 U.S.C. § 6b(A)	2F1.1
7 U.S.C. § 6b(B)	2F1.1
7 U.S.C. § 6b(C)	2F1.1
7 U.S.C. § 6c	2F1.1
7 U.S.C. § 6h	2F1.1
7 U.S.C. § 6o	2F1.1
7 U.S.C. § 13(a)(1)	2B1.1
7 U.S.C. § 13(a)(2)	2F1.1
7 U.S.C. § 13(a)(3)	2F1.1
7 U.S.C. § 13(a)(4)	2F1.1
7 U.S.C. § 13(c)	2C1.3
7 U.S.C. § 13(d)	2F1.2
7 U.S.C. § 13(f)	2F1.2
7 U.S.C. § 23	2F1.1
7 U.S.C. § 87b	2N2.1
7 U.S.C. § 136	2Q1.2
7 U.S.C. § 136j	2Q1.2
7 U.S.C. § 136k	2Q1.2
7 U.S.C. § 136l	2Q1.2
7 U.S.C. § 149	2N2.1
7 U.S.C. § 150bb	2N2.1
7 U.S.C. § 150gg	2N2.1
7 U.S.C. § 154	2N2.1
7 U.S.C. § 156	2N2.1
7 U.S.C. § 157	2N2.1
7 U.S.C. § 158	2N2.1
7 U.S.C. § 161	2N2.1
7 U.S.C. § 163	2N2.1
7 U.S.C. § 195	2N2.1
7 U.S.C. § 270	2F1.1
7 U.S.C. § 281	2N2.1
7 U.S.C. § 472	2N2.1
7 U.S.C. § 473c-1	2N2.1
7 U.S.C. § 491	2N2.1
7 U.S.C. § 499n	2N2.1
7 U.S.C. § 503	2N2.1
7 U.S.C. § 511d	2N2.1
7 U.S.C. § 511i	2N2.1
7 U.S.C. § 516	2N2.1
7 U.S.C. § 610(g)	2C1.3
7 U.S.C. § 2024(b)	2F1.1
7 U.S.C. § 2024(c)	2F1.1
8 U.S.C. § 1160(b)(7)(A)	2L2.1, 2L2.2

Statute	Guideline
8 U.S.C. § 1185(a)(1)	2L1.2
8 U.S.C. § 1185(a)(2)	2L1.1
8 U.S.C. § 1185(a)(3)	2L2.1, 2L2.2
8 U.S.C. § 1185(a)(4)	2L2.1
8 U.S.C. § 1185(a)(5)	2L2.2
8 U.S.C. § 1252(e)	2L1.2
8 U.S.C. § 1324(a)	2L1.1
8 U.S.C. § 1325(a)	2L1.2
8 U.S.C. § 1325(b)	2L2.1, 2L2.2
8 U.S.C. § 1325(c)	2L2.1, 2L2.2
8 U.S.C. § 1326	2L1.2
8 U.S.C. § 1327	2L1.1
8 U.S.C. § 1328	2G1.1, 2G1.2
12 U.S.C. § 631	2F1.1
15 U.S.C. § 1	2R1.1
15 U.S.C. § 50	2F1.1, 2J1.1, 2J1.5
15 U.S.C. § 77e	2F1.1
15 U.S.C. § 77q	2F1.1
15 U.S.C. § 77x	2F1.1
15 U.S.C. § 78j	2F1.1, 2F1.2
15 U.S.C. § 78dd-1	2B4.1
15 U.S.C. § 78dd-2	2B4.1
15 U.S.C. § 78ff	2B4.1, 2F1.1
15 U.S.C. § 80b-6	2F1.1
15 U.S.C. § 158	2F1.1
15 U.S.C. § 645(a)	2F1.1
15 U.S.C. § 645(b)	2B1.1, 2F1.1
15 U.S.C. § 645(c)	2B1.1, 2F1.1
15 U.S.C. § 714m(a)	2F1.1
15 U.S.C. § 714m(b)	2B1.1, 2F1.1
15 U.S.C. § 714m(c)	2B1.1
15 U.S.C. § 1172	2E3.1
15 U.S.C. § 1173	2E3.1
15 U.S.C. § 1174	2E3.1
15 U.S.C. § 1175	2E3.1
15 U.S.C. § 1176	2E3.1
15 U.S.C. § 1281	2B1.3
15 U.S.C. § 1644	2F1.1
15 U.S.C. § 1681q	2F1.1
15 U.S.C. § 1693n(a)	2F1.1
15 U.S.C. § 1983	2N3.1

Statute	Guideline
15 U.S.C. § 1984	2N3.1
15 U.S.C. § 1985	2N3.1
15 U.S.C. § 1986	2N3.1
15 U.S.C. § 1987	2N3.1
15 U.S.C. § 1988	2N3.1
15 U.S.C. § 1990c	2N3.1
15 U.S.C. § 2614	2Q1.2
15 U.S.C. § 2615	2Q1.2
16 U.S.C. § 114	2B1.1, 2B1.3
16 U.S.C. § 117c	2B1.1, 2B1.3
16 U.S.C. § 123	2B1.1, 2B1.3, 2B2.3
16 U.S.C. § 146	2B1.1, 2B1.3, 2B2.3
16 U.S.C. § 413	2B1.1, 2B1.3
16 U.S.C. § 433	2B1.1, 2B1.3
16 U.S.C. § 668(a)	2Q2.1
16 U.S.C. § 707(b)	2Q2.1
16 U.S.C. § 742j-1(a)	2Q2.1
16 U.S.C. § 773c(a)(2), (3),(4),(6)	2A2.4
16 U.S.C. § 773g	2A2.4
16 U.S.C. § 831t(a)	2B1.1
16 U.S.C. § 831t(b)	2F1.1
16 U.S.C. § 831t(c)	2F1.1, 2X1.1
16 U.S.C. § 916c	2Q2.1
16 U.S.C. § 916f	2Q2.1
16 U.S.C. § 973c(a)(8), (10),(11),(12)	2A2.4
16 U.S.C. § 973e	2A2.4
16 U.S.C. § 1029	2A2.4
16 U.S.C. § 1030	2A2.4
16 U.S.C. § 1174(a)	2Q2.1
16 U.S.C. § 1338(a)	2Q2.1
16 U.S.C. § 1375(b)	2Q2.1
16 U.S.C. § 1417(a)(5), (6),(b)(2)	2A2.4
16 U.S.C. § 1540(b)	2Q2.1
16 U.S.C. § 1857(1)(D)	2A2.4
16 U.S.C. § 1857(1)(E)	2A2.4
16 U.S.C. § 1857(1)(F)	2A2.4
16 U.S.C. § 1857(1)(H)	2A2.4
16 U.S.C. § 1859	2A2.4
16 U.S.C. § 2435(4)	2A2.4

Statute	Guideline
16 U.S.C. § 2435(5)	2A2.4
16 U.S.C. § 2435(6)	2A2.4
16 U.S.C. § 2435(7)	2A2.4
16 U.S.C. § 2438	2A2.4
16 U.S.C. § 3373(d)	2Q2.1
16 U.S.C. § 3606	2A2.4
16 U.S.C. § 3637(a)(2), (3),(4),(6),(c)	2A2.4
16 U.S.C. § 4223	2Q2.1
16 U.S.C. § 4224	2Q2.1
16 U.S.C. § 4910(a)	2Q2.1
16 U.S.C. § 4912(a)(2)(A)	2Q2.1
16 U.S.C. § 5009(5),(6), (7),(8)	2A2.4
16 U.S.C. § 5010(b)	2A2.4
17 U.S.C. § 506(a)	2B5.3
18 U.S.C. § 2	2X2.1
18 U.S.C. § 3	2X3.1
18 U.S.C. § 4	2X4.1
18 U.S.C. § 32(a),(b)	2A1.1, 2A1.2, 2A1.3, 2A1.4, 2A2.1, 2A2.2 2A2.3, 2A4.1, 2A5.1, 2A5.2, 2B1.3, 2K1.4
18 U.S.C. § 32(c)	2A6.1
18 U.S.C. § 33	2A2.1, 2A2.2, 2B1.3, 2K1.4
18 U.S.C. § 34	2A1.1, 2A1.2, 2A1.3, 2A1.4
18 U.S.C. § 35(b)	2A6.1
18 U.S.C. § 43	2B1.3
18 U.S.C. § 81	2K1.4
18 U.S.C. § 111	2A2.2, 2A2.4
18 U.S.C. § 112(a)	2A2.1, 2A2.2, 2A2.3, 2A4.1, 2B1.3, 2K1.4
18 U.S.C. § 113(a)	2A2.1
18 U.S.C. § 113(b)	2A2.2
18 U.S.C. § 113(c)	2A2.2
18 U.S.C. § 113(f)	2A2.2
18 U.S.C. § 114	2A2.2
18 U.S.C. § 115(a)	2A1.1, 2A1.2, 2A1.3, 2A2.1, 2A2.2, 2A2.3, 2A4.1, 2A6.1
18 U.S.C. § 115(b)(1)	2A2.1, 2A2.2, 2A2.3
18 U.S.C. § 115(b)(2)	2A4.1
18 U.S.C. § 115(b)(3)	2A1.1, 2A1.2, 2A2.1

Statute	Guideline
18 U.S.C. § 115(b)(4)	2A6.1
18 U.S.C. § 152	2B4.1, 2F1.1, 2J1.3
18 U.S.C. § 153	2B1.1, 2F1.1
18 U.S.C. § 155	2F1.1
18 U.S.C. § 201(b)(1)	2C1.1
18 U.S.C. § 201(b)(2)	2C1.1
18 U.S.C. § 201(b)(3)	2J1.3
18 U.S.C. § 201(b)(4)	2J1.3
18 U.S.C. § 201(c)(1)	2C1.2
18 U.S.C. § 201(c)(2)	2J1.9
18 U.S.C. § 201(c)(3)	2J1.9
18 U.S.C. § 203	2C1.3
18 U.S.C. § 204	2C1.3
18 U.S.C. § 205	2C1.3
18 U.S.C. § 207	2C1.3
18 U.S.C. § 208	2C1.3
18 U.S.C. § 209	2C1.4
18 U.S.C. § 210	2C1.5
18 U.S.C. § 211	2C1.5
18 U.S.C. § 212	2C1.6
18 U.S.C. § 213	2C1.6
18 U.S.C. § 214	2C1.6
18 U.S.C. § 215	2B4.1
18 U.S.C. § 217	2C1.6
18 U.S.C. § 219	2C1.3
18 U.S.C. § 224	2B4.1
18 U.S.C. § 225	2B1.1, 2B4.1, 2F1.1
18 U.S.C. § 228	2J1.1
18 U.S.C. § 241	2H1.1, 2H2.1
18 U.S.C. § 242	2H1.4, 2H2.1
18 U.S.C. § 245(b)	2H1.3, 2H2.1, 2J1.2
18 U.S.C. § 246	2H1.5
18 U.S.C. § 247	2H1.3
18 U.S.C. § 281	2C1.3
18 U.S.C. § 285	2B1.1, 2F1.1
18 U.S.C. § 286	2F1.1
18 U.S.C. § 287	2F1.1
18 U.S.C. § 288	2F1.1
18 U.S.C. § 289	2F1.1
18 U.S.C. § 332	2B1.1, 2F1.1
18 U.S.C. § 335	2F1.1

Statute	Guideline
18 U.S.C. § 342	2D2.3
18 U.S.C. § 351(a)	2A1.1, 2A1.2, 2A1.3, 2A1.4
18 U.S.C. § 351(b)	2A1.1, 2A4.1
18 U.S.C. § 351(c)	2A2.1, 2A4.1
18 U.S.C. § 351(d)	2A1.5, 2A4.1
18 U.S.C. § 351(e)	2A2.2, 2A2.3
18 U.S.C. § 371	2A1.5, 2C1.7, 2T1.9, 2X1.1
18 U.S.C. § 372	2X1.1
18 U.S.C. § 373	2A1.5, 2X1.1
18 U.S.C. § 401	2J1.1
18 U.S.C. § 403	2J1.1
18 U.S.C. § 440	2C1.3
18 U.S.C. § 442	2C1.3
18 U.S.C. § 471	2B5.1, 2F1.1
18 U.S.C. § 472	2B5.1, 2F1.1
18 U.S.C. § 473	2B5.1, 2F1.1
18 U.S.C. § 474	2B5.1, 2F1.1
18 U.S.C. § 476	2B5.1, 2F1.1
18 U.S.C. § 477	2B5.1, 2F1.1
18 U.S.C. § 478	2F1.1
18 U.S.C. § 479	2F1.1
18 U.S.C. § 480	2F1.1
18 U.S.C. § 481	2F1.1
18 U.S.C. § 482	2F1.1
18 U.S.C. § 483	2F1.1
18 U.S.C. § 484	2B5.1, 2F1.1
18 U.S.C. § 485	2B5.1, 2F1.1
18 U.S.C. § 486	2B5.1, 2F1.1
18 U.S.C. § 487	2B5.1
18 U.S.C. § 488	2F1.1
18 U.S.C. § 490	2B5.1
18 U.S.C. § 491	2F1.1
18 U.S.C. § 493	2B5.1, 2F1.1
18 U.S.C. § 494	2F1.1
18 U.S.C. § 495	2F1.1
18 U.S.C. § 496	2F1.1, 2T3.1
18 U.S.C. § 497	2F1.1
18 U.S.C. § 498	2F1.1
18 U.S.C. § 499	2F1.1
18 U.S.C. § 500	2B1.1, 2B5.1, 2F1.1
18 U.S.C. § 501	2B5.1, 2F1.1
18 U.S.C. § 502	2F1.1
18 U.S.C. § 503	2F1.1
18 U.S.C. § 505	2F1.1, 2J1.2
18 U.S.C. § 506	2F1.1
18 U.S.C. § 507	2F1.1
18 U.S.C. § 508	2F1.1
18 U.S.C. § 509	2F1.1
18 U.S.C. § 510	2F1.1
18 U.S.C. § 511	2B6.1
18 U.S.C. § 513	2F1.1
18 U.S.C. § 541	2T3.1
18 U.S.C. § 542	2T3.1
18 U.S.C. § 543	2T3.1
18 U.S.C. § 544	2T3.1
18 U.S.C. § 545	2Q2.1, 2T3.1
18 U.S.C. § 547	2T3.1
18 U.S.C. § 548	2T3.1
18 U.S.C. § 549	2B1.1, 2T3.1
18 U.S.C. § 550	2T3.1
18 U.S.C. § 551	2J1.2, 2T3.1
18 U.S.C. § 552	2G3.1
18 U.S.C. § 553(a)(1)	2B1.1
18 U.S.C. § 553(a)(2)	2B1.1, 2B6.1
18 U.S.C. § 592	2H2.1
18 U.S.C. § 593	2H2.1
18 U.S.C. § 594	2H2.1
18 U.S.C. § 597	2H2.1
18 U.S.C. § 608	2H2.1
18 U.S.C. § 641	2B1.1
18 U.S.C. § 642	2B5.1, 2F1.1
18 U.S.C. § 643	2B1.1
18 U.S.C. § 644	2B1.1
18 U.S.C. § 645	2B1.1
18 U.S.C. § 646	2B1.1
18 U.S.C. § 647	2B1.1
18 U.S.C. § 648	2B1.1
18 U.S.C. § 649	2B1.1
18 U.S.C. § 650	2B1.1
18 U.S.C. § 651	2B1.1

Statute	Guideline
18 U.S.C. § 652	2B1.1
18 U.S.C. § 653	2B1.1
18 U.S.C. § 654	2B1.1
18 U.S.C. § 655	2B1.1
18 U.S.C. § 656	2B1.1, 2F1.1
18 U.S.C. § 657	2B1.1, 2F1.1
18 U.S.C. § 658	2B1.1
18 U.S.C. § 659	2B1.1, 2F1.1
18 U.S.C. § 660	2B1.1
18 U.S.C. § 661	2B1.1
18 U.S.C. § 662	2B1.1
18 U.S.C. § 663	2B1.1, 2F1.1
18 U.S.C. § 664	2B1.1
18 U.S.C. § 665(a)	2B1.1, 2F1.1
18 U.S.C. § 665(b)	2B3.3, 2C1.1
18 U.S.C. § 665(c)	2J1.2
18 U.S.C. § 666(a)(1)(A)	2B1.1, 2F1.1
18 U.S.C. § 666(a)(1)(B)	2C1.1, 2C1.2
18 U.S.C. § 666(a)(2)	2C1.1, 2C1.2
18 U.S.C. § 667	2B1.1
18 U.S.C. § 709	2F1.1
18 U.S.C. § 712	2F1.1
18 U.S.C. § 751	2P1.1
18 U.S.C. § 752	2P1.1
18 U.S.C. § 753	2P1.1
18 U.S.C. § 755	2P1.1
18 U.S.C. § 756	2P1.1
18 U.S.C. § 757	2P1.1, 2X3.1
18 U.S.C. § 793(a)-(c)	2M3.2
18 U.S.C. § 793(d),(e)	2M3.2, 2M3.3
18 U.S.C. § 793(f)	2M3.4
18 U.S.C. § 793(g)	2M3.2, 2M3.3
18 U.S.C. § 794	2M3.1
18 U.S.C. § 798	2M3.3
18 U.S.C. § 831	2M6.1
18 U.S.C. § 842(a)-(e)	2K1.3
18 U.S.C. § 842(f)	2K1.6
18 U.S.C. § 842(g)	2K1.6
18 U.S.C. § 842(h),(i)	2K1.3
18 U.S.C. § 842(j)	2K1.1
18 U.S.C. § 842(k)	2K1.1
18 U.S.C. § 844(d)	2K1.3
18 U.S.C. § 844(e)	2A6.1
18 U.S.C. § 844(f)	2K1.4, 2X1.1
18 U.S.C. § 844(h)	2K2.4 (2K1.4 for offenses committed prior to November 18, 1988)
18 U.S.C. § 844(i)	2K1.4
18 U.S.C. § 871	2A6.1
18 U.S.C. § 872	2C1.1
18 U.S.C. § 873	2B3.3
18 U.S.C. § 874	2B3.2, 2B3.3
18 U.S.C. § 875(a)	2A4.2, 2B3.2
18 U.S.C. § 875(b)	2B3.2
18 U.S.C. § 875(c)	2A6.1
18 U.S.C. § 875(d)	2B3.2, 2B3.3
18 U.S.C. § 876	2A4.2, 2A6.1, 2B3.2, 2B3.3
18 U.S.C. § 877	2A4.2, 2A6.1, 2B3.2, 2B3.3
18 U.S.C. § 878(a)	2A6.1
18 U.S.C. § 878(b)	2B3.2
18 U.S.C. § 879	2A6.1
18 U.S.C. § 892	2E2.1
18 U.S.C. § 893	2E2.1
18 U.S.C. § 894	2E2.1
18 U.S.C. § 911	2F1.1, 2L2.2
18 U.S.C. § 912	2J1.4
18 U.S.C. § 913	2J1.4
18 U.S.C. § 914	2F1.1
18 U.S.C. § 915	2F1.1
18 U.S.C. § 917	2F1.1
18 U.S.C. § 922(a)-(p)	2K2.1
18 U.S.C. § 922(q)	2K2.5
18 U.S.C. § 922(r)	2K2.1
18 U.S.C. § 923	2K2.1
18 U.S.C. § 924(a)	2K2.1
18 U.S.C. § 924(b)	2K2.1
18 U.S.C. § 924(c)	2K2.4
18 U.S.C. § 924(e)	2K2.1 (see also 4B1.4)
18 U.S.C. § 924(f)	2K2.1
18 U.S.C. § 924(g)	2K2.1
18 U.S.C. § 924(h)	2K2.1

Statute	Guideline
18 U.S.C. § 929(a)	2K2.4
18 U.S.C. § 930	2K2.5
18 U.S.C. § 970(a)	2B1.3, 2K1.4
18 U.S.C. § 1001	2F1.1
18 U.S.C. § 1002	2F1.1
18 U.S.C. § 1003	2B5.1, 2F1.1
18 U.S.C. § 1004	2F1.1
18 U.S.C. § 1005	2F1.1
18 U.S.C. § 1006	2F1.1, 2S1.3
18 U.S.C. § 1007	2F1.1, 2S1.3
18 U.S.C. § 1008	2F1.1, 2S1.3
18 U.S.C. § 1010	2F1.1
18 U.S.C. § 1011	2F1.1
18 U.S.C. § 1012	2C1.3, 2F1.1
18 U.S.C. § 1013	2F1.1
18 U.S.C. § 1014	2F1.1
18 U.S.C. § 1015	2F1.1, 2J1.3, 2L2.1, 2L2.2
18 U.S.C. § 1016	2F1.1
18 U.S.C. § 1017	2F1.1
18 U.S.C. § 1018	2F1.1
18 U.S.C. § 1019	2F1.1
18 U.S.C. § 1020	2F1.1
18 U.S.C. § 1021	2F1.1
18 U.S.C. § 1022	2F1.1
18 U.S.C. § 1023	2B1.1, 2F1.1
18 U.S.C. § 1024	2B1.1
18 U.S.C. § 1025	2F1.1
18 U.S.C. § 1026	2F1.1
18 U.S.C. § 1027	2E5.3
18 U.S.C. § 1028	2F1.1, 2L2.1, 2L2.2
18 U.S.C. § 1029	2F1.1
18 U.S.C. § 1030(a)(1)	2M3.2
18 U.S.C. § 1030(a)(2)	2F1.1
18 U.S.C. § 1030(a)(3)	2F1.1
18 U.S.C. § 1030(a)(4)	2F1.1
18 U.S.C. § 1030(a)(5)	2F1.1
18 U.S.C. § 1030(a)(6)	2F1.1
18 U.S.C. § 1030(b)	2X1.1
18 U.S.C. § 1031	2F1.1
18 U.S.C. § 1032	2B4.1, 2F1.1

Statute	Guideline
18 U.S.C. § 1071	2X3.1
18 U.S.C. § 1072	2X3.1
18 U.S.C. § 1082	2E3.1
18 U.S.C. § 1084	2E3.1
18 U.S.C. § 1091	2H1.3
18 U.S.C. § 1111(a)	2A1.1, 2A1.2
18 U.S.C. § 1112	2A1.3, 2A1.4
18 U.S.C. § 1113	2A2.1, 2A2.2
18 U.S.C. § 1114	2A1.1, 2A1.2, 2A1.3, 2A1.4, 2A2.1
18 U.S.C. § 1115	2A1.4
18 U.S.C. § 1116	2A1.1, 2A1.2, 2A1.3, 2A1.4, 2A2.1
18 U.S.C. § 1117	2A1.5
18 U.S.C. § 1153	2A1.1, 2A1.2, 2A1.3, 2A1.4, 2A2.1, 2A2.2, 2A3.1, 2A3.2, 2A3.3, 2A3.4, 2A4.1, 2B1.1, 2B2.1, 2B3.1, 2K1.4
18 U.S.C. § 1163	2B1.1
18 U.S.C. § 1167	2B1.1
18 U.S.C. § 1168	2B1.1
18 U.S.C. § 1201(a)	2A4.1
18 U.S.C. § 1201(c),(d)	2X1.1
18 U.S.C. § 1202	2A4.2
18 U.S.C. § 1203	2A4.1
18 U.S.C. § 1301	2E3.1
18 U.S.C. § 1302	2E3.1
18 U.S.C. § 1303	2E3.1
18 U.S.C. § 1304	2E3.1
18 U.S.C. § 1306	2E3.1
18 U.S.C. § 1341	2C1.7, 2F1.1
18 U.S.C. § 1342	2C1.7, 2F1.1
18 U.S.C. § 1343	2C1.7, 2F1.1
18 U.S.C. § 1344	2F1.1
18 U.S.C. § 1361	2B1.3
18 U.S.C. § 1362	2B1.3, 2K1.4
18 U.S.C. § 1363	2B1.3, 2K1.4
18 U.S.C. § 1364	2K1.4
18 U.S.C. § 1365(a)	2N1.1
18 U.S.C. § 1365(b)	2N1.3
18 U.S.C. § 1365(c)	2N1.2
18 U.S.C. § 1365(d)	2N1.2

Statute	Guideline
18 U.S.C. § 1365(e)	2N1.1
18 U.S.C. § 1366	2B1.3
18 U.S.C. § 1422	2C1.2, 2F1.1
18 U.S.C. § 1423	2L2.2
18 U.S.C. § 1424	2L2.2
18 U.S.C. § 1425	2L2.1, 2L2.2
18 U.S.C. § 1426	2L2.1, 2L2.2
18 U.S.C. § 1427	2L2.1
18 U.S.C. § 1428	2L2.5
18 U.S.C. § 1429	2J1.1
18 U.S.C. § 1460	2G3.1
18 U.S.C. § 1461	2G3.1
18 U.S.C. § 1462	2G3.1
18 U.S.C. § 1463	2G3.1
18 U.S.C. § 1464	2G3.2
18 U.S.C. § 1465	2G3.1
18 U.S.C. § 1466	2G3.1
18 U.S.C. § 1468	2G3.2
18 U.S.C. § 1501	2A2.2, 2A2.4
18 U.S.C. § 1502	2A2.4
18 U.S.C. § 1503	2J1.2
18 U.S.C. § 1505	2J1.2
18 U.S.C. § 1506	2J1.2
18 U.S.C. § 1507	2J1.2
18 U.S.C. § 1508	2J1.2
18 U.S.C. § 1509	2J1.2
18 U.S.C. § 1510	2J1.2
18 U.S.C. § 1511	2E3.1, 2J1.2
18 U.S.C. § 1512(a)	2A1.1, 2A1.2, 2A1.3, 2A2.1
18 U.S.C. § 1512(b)	2A1.2, 2A2.2, 2J1.2
18 U.S.C. § 1512(c)	2J1.2
18 U.S.C. § 1513	2J1.2
18 U.S.C. § 1516	2J1.2
18 U.S.C. § 1517	2J1.2
18 U.S.C. § 1541	2L2.1
18 U.S.C. § 1542	2L2.1, 2L2.2
18 U.S.C. § 1543	2L2.1, 2L2.2
18 U.S.C. § 1544	2L2.1, 2L2.2
18 U.S.C. § 1546	2L2.1, 2L2.2
18 U.S.C. § 1581	2H4.1
18 U.S.C. § 1582	2H4.1
18 U.S.C. § 1583	2H4.1
18 U.S.C. § 1584	2H4.1
18 U.S.C. § 1585	2H4.1
18 U.S.C. § 1586	2H4.1
18 U.S.C. § 1587	2H4.1
18 U.S.C. § 1588	2H4.1
18 U.S.C. § 1621	2J1.3
18 U.S.C. § 1622	2J1.3
18 U.S.C. § 1623	2J1.3
18 U.S.C. § 1700	2H3.3
18 U.S.C. § 1702	2B1.1, 2B1.3, 2H3.3
18 U.S.C. § 1703	2B1.1, 2B1.3, 2H3.3
18 U.S.C. § 1704	2B1.1, 2F1.1
18 U.S.C. § 1705	2B1.3
18 U.S.C. § 1706	2B1.3
18 U.S.C. § 1707	2B1.1
18 U.S.C. § 1708	2B1.1, 2F1.1
18 U.S.C. § 1709	2B1.1
18 U.S.C. § 1710	2B1.1
18 U.S.C. § 1711	2B1.1
18 U.S.C. § 1712	2F1.1
18 U.S.C. § 1716 (felony provisions only)	2K1.3, 2K3.2
18 U.S.C. § 1716C	2F1.1
18 U.S.C. § 1720	2F1.1
18 U.S.C. § 1721	2B1.1
18 U.S.C. § 1728	2F1.1
18 U.S.C. § 1735	2G3.1
18 U.S.C. § 1737	2G3.1
18 U.S.C. § 1751(a)	2A1.1, 2A1.2, 2A1.3, 2A1.4
18 U.S.C. § 1751(b)	2A4.1
18 U.S.C. § 1751(c)	2A2.1, 2A4.1, 2X1.1
18 U.S.C. § 1751(d)	2A1.5, 2A4.1, 2X1.1
18 U.S.C. § 1751(e)	2A2.2, 2A2.3
18 U.S.C. § 1791	2P1.2
18 U.S.C. § 1792	2P1.3
18 U.S.C. § 1851	2B1.1
18 U.S.C. § 1852	2B1.1, 2B1.3
18 U.S.C. § 1853	2B1.1, 2B1.3

Statute	Guideline
18 U.S.C. § 1854	2B1.1, 2B1.3
18 U.S.C. § 1855	2K1.4
18 U.S.C. § 1857	2B1.3, 2B2.3
18 U.S.C. § 1860	2R1.1
18 U.S.C. § 1861	2F1.1
18 U.S.C. § 1864	2Q1.6
18 U.S.C. § 1901	2C1.3
18 U.S.C. § 1902	2F1.2
18 U.S.C. § 1903	2C1.3
18 U.S.C. § 1905	2H3.1
18 U.S.C. § 1909	2C1.3, 2C1.4
18 U.S.C. § 1915	2T3.1
18 U.S.C. § 1919	2F1.1
18 U.S.C. § 1920	2F1.1
18 U.S.C. § 1923	2F1.1
18 U.S.C. § 1951	2B3.1, 2B3.2, 2B3.3, 2C1.1
18 U.S.C. § 1952	2E1.2
18 U.S.C. § 1952A	2E1.4
18 U.S.C. § 1952B	2E1.3
18 U.S.C. § 1953	2E3.1
18 U.S.C. § 1954	2E5.1
18 U.S.C. § 1955	2E3.1
18 U.S.C. § 1956	2S1.1
18 U.S.C. § 1957	2S1.2
18 U.S.C. § 1958	2E1.4
18 U.S.C. § 1959	2E1.3
18 U.S.C. § 1962	2E1.1
18 U.S.C. § 1963	2E1.1
18 U.S.C. § 1991	2A2.1, 2X1.1
18 U.S.C. § 1992	2A1.1, 2B1.3, 2K1.4, 2X1.1
18 U.S.C. § 2071	2B1.1, 2B1.3
18 U.S.C. § 2072	2F1.1
18 U.S.C. § 2073	2F1.1
18 U.S.C. § 2111	2B3.1
18 U.S.C. § 2112	2B3.1
18 U.S.C. § 2113(a)	2B1.1, 2B2.1, 2B3.1, 2B3.2
18 U.S.C. § 2113(b)	2B1.1
18 U.S.C. § 2113(c)	2B1.1
18 U.S.C. § 2113(d)	2B3.1
18 U.S.C. § 2113(e)	2A1.1, 2B3.1
18 U.S.C. § 2114	2B3.1
18 U.S.C. § 2115	2B2.1
18 U.S.C. § 2116	2A2.2, 2A2.3, 2B2.1, 2B3.1
18 U.S.C. § 2117	2B2.1
18 U.S.C. § 2118(a)	2B3.1
18 U.S.C. § 2118(b)	2B2.1
18 U.S.C. § 2118(c)(1)	2A2.1, 2A2.2, 2B3.1
18 U.S.C. § 2118(c)(2)	2A1.1
18 U.S.C. § 2118(d)	2X1.1
18 U.S.C. § 2119	2B3.1
18 U.S.C. § 2153	2M2.1
18 U.S.C. § 2154	2M2.1
18 U.S.C. § 2155	2M2.3
18 U.S.C. § 2156	2M2.3
18 U.S.C. § 2197	2F1.1
18 U.S.C. § 2199	2B1.1, 2B2.3
18 U.S.C. § 2231	2A2.2, 2A2.3
18 U.S.C. § 2232	2J1.2
18 U.S.C. § 2233	2B1.1, 2B3.1
18 U.S.C. § 2241	2A3.1
18 U.S.C. § 2242	2A3.1
18 U.S.C. § 2243(a)	2A3.2
18 U.S.C. § 2243(b)	2A3.3
18 U.S.C. § 2244	2A3.4
18 U.S.C. § 2251(a),(b)	2G2.1
18 U.S.C. § 2251(c)(1)(A)	2G2.2
18 U.S.C. § 2251(c)(1)(B)	2G2.1
18 U.S.C. § 2251A	2G2.3
18 U.S.C. § 2252	2G2.2, 2G2.4
18 U.S.C. § 2257	2G2.5
18 U.S.C. § 2271	2X1.1
18 U.S.C. § 2272	2F1.1
18 U.S.C. § 2275	2B1.3, 2K1.4
18 U.S.C. § 2276	2B1.3, 2B2.1
18 U.S.C. § 2312	2B1.1
18 U.S.C. § 2313	2B1.1
18 U.S.C. § 2314	2B1.1, 2F1.1
18 U.S.C. § 2315	2B1.1, 2F1.1
18 U.S.C. § 2316	2B1.1

Statute	Guideline
18 U.S.C. § 2317	2B1.1
18 U.S.C. § 2318	2B5.3
18 U.S.C. § 2319	2B5.3
18 U.S.C. § 2320	2B5.3
18 U.S.C. § 2321	2B6.1
18 U.S.C. § 2322	2B6.1
18 U.S.C. § 2332(a)	2A1.1, 2A1.2, 2A1.3, 2A1.4
18 U.S.C. § 2332(b)(1)	2A2.1
18 U.S.C. § 2332(b)(2)	2A1.5
18 U.S.C. § 2332(c)	2A2.2
18 U.S.C. § 2342(a)	2E4.1
18 U.S.C. § 2344(a)	2E4.1
18 U.S.C. § 2381	2M1.1
18 U.S.C. § 2421	2G1.1, 2G1.2
18 U.S.C. § 2422	2G1.1, 2G1.2
18 U.S.C. § 2423	2G1.2
18 U.S.C. § 2511	2B5.3, 2H3.1
18 U.S.C. § 2512	2H3.2
18 U.S.C. § 3056(d)	2A2.4
18 U.S.C. § 3146(b)(1)(A)	2J1.6
18 U.S.C. § 3146(b)(1)(B)	2J1.5
18 U.S.C. § 3147	2J1.7
19 U.S.C. § 283	2T3.1
19 U.S.C. § 1304	2T3.1
19 U.S.C. § 1433	2T3.1
19 U.S.C. § 1434	2F1.1, 2T3.1
19 U.S.C. § 1435	2F1.1, 2T3.1
19 U.S.C. § 1436	2F1.1, 2T3.1
19 U.S.C. § 1464	2T3.1
19 U.S.C. § 1465	2T3.1
19 U.S.C. § 1586(e)	2T3.1
19 U.S.C. § 1707	2T3.1
19 U.S.C. § 1708(b)	2T3.1
19 U.S.C. § 1919	2F1.1
19 U.S.C. § 2316	2F1.1
20 U.S.C. § 1097(a)	2B1.1, 2F1.1
20 U.S.C. § 1097(b)	2F1.1
20 U.S.C. § 1097(c)	2B4.1
20 U.S.C. § 1097(d)	2F1.1
21 U.S.C. § 101	2N2.1

Statute	Guideline
21 U.S.C. § 102	2N2.1
21 U.S.C. § 103	2N2.1
21 U.S.C. § 104	2N2.1
21 U.S.C. § 105	2N2.1
21 U.S.C. § 111	2N2.1
21 U.S.C. § 115	2N2.1
21 U.S.C. § 117	2N2.1
21 U.S.C. § 120	2N2.1
21 U.S.C. § 121	2N2.1
21 U.S.C. § 122	2N2.1
21 U.S.C. § 124	2N2.1
21 U.S.C. § 126	2N2.1
21 U.S.C. § 134a-e	2N2.1
21 U.S.C. § 135a	2N2.1
21 U.S.C. § 141	2N2.1
21 U.S.C. § 143	2N2.1
21 U.S.C. § 144	2N2.1
21 U.S.C. § 145	2N2.1
21 U.S.C. § 151	2N2.1
21 U.S.C. § 152	2N2.1
21 U.S.C. § 153	2N2.1
21 U.S.C. § 154	2N2.1
21 U.S.C. § 155	2N2.1
21 U.S.C. § 156	2N2.1
21 U.S.C. § 157	2N2.1
21 U.S.C. § 158	2N2.1
21 U.S.C. § 331	2N2.1
21 U.S.C. § 333(a)(1)	2N2.1
21 U.S.C. § 333(a)(2)	2F1.1, 2N2.1
21 U.S.C. § 333(b)	2N2.1
21 U.S.C. § 458	2N2.1
21 U.S.C. § 459	2N2.1
21 U.S.C. § 460	2N2.1
21 U.S.C. § 461	2N2.1
21 U.S.C. § 463	2N2.1
21 U.S.C. § 466	2N2.1
21 U.S.C. § 610	2N2.1
21 U.S.C. § 611	2N2.1
21 U.S.C. § 614	2N2.1
21 U.S.C. § 617	2N2.1
21 U.S.C. § 619	2N2.1

Statute	Guideline
21 U.S.C. § 620	2N2.1
21 U.S.C. § 622	2C1.1
21 U.S.C. § 642	2N2.1
21 U.S.C. § 643	2N2.1
21 U.S.C. § 644	2N2.1
21 U.S.C. § 675	2A1.1, 2A1.2, 2A1.3, 2A1.4, 2A2.1, 2A2.2, 2A2.3
21 U.S.C. § 676	2N2.1
21 U.S.C. § 841(a)	2D1.1
21 U.S.C. § 841(b)(1)-(3)	2D1.1
21 U.S.C. § 841(b)(4)	2D2.1
21 U.S.C. § 841(d)(1),(2)	2D1.11
21 U.S.C. § 841(d)(3)	2D1.13
21 U.S.C. § 841(e)	2D1.9
21 U.S.C. § 841(g)(1)	2D1.11, 2D1.13
21 U.S.C. § 842(a)(1)	2D3.1
21 U.S.C. § 842(a)(2),(9), (10)	2D3.2
21 U.S.C. § 842(b)	2D3.2
21 U.S.C. § 843(a)(1),(2)	2D3.1
21 U.S.C. § 843(a)(3)	2D2.2
21 U.S.C. § 843(a)(4)(B)	2D1.13
21 U.S.C. § 843(a)(6),(7)	2D1.12
21 U.S.C. § 843(a)(8)	2D1.13
21 U.S.C. § 843(b)	2D1.6
21 U.S.C. § 844(a)	2D2.1
21 U.S.C. § 845	2D1.2
21 U.S.C. § 845a	2D1.2
21 U.S.C. § 845b	2D1.2
21 U.S.C. § 846	2D1.1, 2D1.2, 2D1.5, 2D1.6, 2D1.7, 2D1.8, 2D1.9, 2D1.10, 2D1.11, 2D1.12, 2D1.13, 2D2.1, 2D2.2, 2D3.1, 2D3.2
21 U.S.C. § 848(a)	2D1.5
21 U.S.C. § 848(b)	2D1.5
21 U.S.C. § 848(e)	2A1.1
21 U.S.C. § 856	2D1.8
21 U.S.C. § 857	2D1.7
21 U.S.C. § 858	2D1.10
21 U.S.C. § 859	2D1.2
21 U.S.C. § 860	2D1.2

Statute	Guideline
21 U.S.C. § 861	2D1.2
21 U.S.C. § 863	2D1.7
21 U.S.C. § 952	2D1.1
21 U.S.C. § 953	2D1.1
21 U.S.C. § 954	2D3.2
21 U.S.C. § 955	2D1.1
21 U.S.C. § 955a(a)-(d)	2D1.1
21 U.S.C. § 957	2D1.1
21 U.S.C. § 959	2D1.1
21 U.S.C. § 960(a),(b)	2D1.1
21 U.S.C. § 960(d)(1),(2)	2D1.11
21 U.S.C. § 961	2D3.2
21 U.S.C. § 963	2D1.1, 2D1.2, 2D1.5, 2D1.6, 2D1.7, 2D1.8, 2D1.9, 2D1.10, 2D1.11, 2D1.12, 2D1.13, 2D2.1, 2D2.2, 2D3.1, 2D3.2
22 U.S.C. § 1980(g)	2F1.1
22 U.S.C. § 2197(n)	2F1.1
22 U.S.C. § 2778	2M5.2
22 U.S.C. § 2780	2M5.2
22 U.S.C. § 4217	2B1.1
22 U.S.C. § 4221	2F1.1
25 U.S.C. § 450d	2B1.1, 2F1.1
26 U.S.C. § 5148(1)	2T2.1
26 U.S.C. § 5214(a)(1)	2T2.1
26 U.S.C. § 5273(b)(2)	2T2.1
26 U.S.C. § 5273(c)	2T2.1
26 U.S.C. § 5291(a)	2T2.1, 2T2.2
26 U.S.C. § 5601(a)	2T2.1, 2T2.2
26 U.S.C. § 5602	2T2.1
26 U.S.C. § 5603	2T2.1, 2T2.2
26 U.S.C. § 5604(a)	2T2.1, 2T2.2
26 U.S.C. § 5605	2T2.1, 2T2.2
26 U.S.C. § 5607	2T2.1
26 U.S.C. § 5608	2T2.1
26 U.S.C. § 5661	2T2.1, 2T2.2
26 U.S.C. § 5662	2T2.2
26 U.S.C. § 5671	2T2.1, 2T2.2
26 U.S.C. § 5684	2T2.1
26 U.S.C. § 5685	2K1.3, 2K2.1
26 U.S.C. § 5691(a)	2T2.1

Statute	Guideline
26 U.S.C. § 5751(a)(1),(2)	2T2.1
26 U.S.C. § 5752	2T2.2
26 U.S.C. § 5762(a)(1), (2),(4),(5),(6)	2T2.2
26 U.S.C. § 5762(a)(3)	2T2.1
26 U.S.C. § 5861(a)-(l)	2K2.1
26 U.S.C. § 5871	2K2.1
26 U.S.C. § 7201	2T1.1
26 U.S.C. § 7202	2T1.6
26 U.S.C. § 7203	2S1.3, 2T1.1
26 U.S.C. § 7204	2T1.8
26 U.S.C. § 7205	2T1.8
26 U.S.C. § 7206(1),(3), (4),(5)	2S1.3, 2T1.1
26 U.S.C. § 7206(2)	2S1.3, 2T1.4
26 U.S.C. § 7207	2T1.1
26 U.S.C. § 7208	2F1.1
26 U.S.C. § 7210	2J1.1
26 U.S.C. § 7211	2T1.1
26 U.S.C. § 7212(a)	2A2.4
26 U.S.C. § 7212(a) (omnibus clause)	2J1.2, 2T1.1
26 U.S.C. § 7214	2C1.1, 2C1.2, 2F1.1
26 U.S.C. § 7215	2T1.7
26 U.S.C. § 7232	2F1.1
26 U.S.C. § 7512(b)	2T1.7
26 U.S.C. § 9012(e)	2B4.1
26 U.S.C. § 9042(d)	2B4.1
28 U.S.C. § 1826(c)	2P1.1
28 U.S.C. § 2902(e)	2P1.1
29 U.S.C. § 186	2E5.1
29 U.S.C. § 431	2E5.3
29 U.S.C. § 432	2E5.3
29 U.S.C. § 433	2E5.3
29 U.S.C. § 439	2E5.3
29 U.S.C. § 461	2E5.3
29 U.S.C. § 501(c)	2B1.1
29 U.S.C. § 530	2B3.2
29 U.S.C. § 1131	2E5.3
29 U.S.C. § 1141	2B3.2, 2F1.1
30 U.S.C. § 1461(a)(3), (4),(5),(7)	2A2.4
30 U.S.C. § 1463	2A2.4
31 U.S.C. § 5313	2S1.3
31 U.S.C. § 5314	2S1.3
31 U.S.C. § 5316	2S1.3
31 U.S.C. § 5322	2S1.3
31 U.S.C. § 5324	2S1.3
33 U.S.C. § 403	2Q1.3
33 U.S.C. § 406	2Q1.3
33 U.S.C. § 407	2Q1.3
33 U.S.C. § 411	2Q1.3
33 U.S.C. § 506	2J1.1
33 U.S.C. § 1227(b)	2J1.1
33 U.S.C. § 1232(b)(2)	2A2.4
33 U.S.C. § 1319(c)(1), (2),(4)	2Q1.2, 2Q1.3
33 U.S.C. § 1319(c)(3)	2Q1.1
33 U.S.C. § 1321	2Q1.2, 2Q1.3
33 U.S.C. § 1342	2Q1.2, 2Q1.3
33 U.S.C. § 1415(b)	2Q1.2, 2Q1.3
33 U.S.C. § 1517	2Q1.2, 2Q1.3
33 U.S.C. § 1907	2Q1.3
33 U.S.C. § 1908	2Q1.3
38 U.S.C. § 787	2F1.1
38 U.S.C. § 3501(a)	2B1.1
38 U.S.C. § 3502	2F1.1
41 U.S.C. § 53	2B4.1
41 U.S.C. § 54	2B4.1
42 U.S.C. § 261(a)	2D1.1
42 U.S.C. § 262	2N2.1
42 U.S.C. § 300h-2	2Q1.2
42 U.S.C. § 300i-1	2Q1.4, 2Q1.5
42 U.S.C. § 408	2F1.1
42 U.S.C. § 1307(a)	2F1.1
42 U.S.C. § 1320a-7b	2B1.1, 2B4.1, 2F1.1
42 U.S.C. § 1383(d)(2)	2F1.1
42 U.S.C. § 1383a(a)	2F1.1
42 U.S.C. § 1383a(b)	2F1.1
42 U.S.C. § 1395nn(a)	2F1.1
42 U.S.C. § 1395nn(b)(1)	2B4.1
42 U.S.C. § 1395nn(b)(2)	2B4.1
42 U.S.C. § 1395nn(c)	2F1.1

Statute	Guideline
42 U.S.C. § 1396h(a)	2F1.1
42 U.S.C. § 1396h(b)(1)	2B4.1
42 U.S.C. § 1396h(b)(2)	2B4.1
42 U.S.C. § 1713	2F1.1
42 U.S.C. § 1760(g)	2B1.1, 2F1.1
42 U.S.C. § 1761(o)(1)	2F1.1
42 U.S.C. § 1761(o)(2)	2B1.1, 2F1.1
42 U.S.C. § 1973i(c)	2H2.1
42 U.S.C. § 1973i(d)	2H2.1
42 U.S.C. § 1973i(e)	2H2.1
42 U.S.C. § 1973j(a)	2H2.1
42 U.S.C. § 1973j(b)	2H2.1
42 U.S.C. § 1973j(c)	2X1.1
42 U.S.C. § 1973aa	2H2.1
42 U.S.C. § 1973aa-1	2H2.1
42 U.S.C. § 1973aa-1a	2H2.1
42 U.S.C. § 1973aa-3	2H2.1
42 U.S.C. § 1973bb	2H2.1
42 U.S.C. § 1973gg-10	2H2.1
42 U.S.C. § 2000e-13	2A1.1, 2A1.2, 2A1.3, 2A1.4, 2A2.1, 2A2.2, 2A2.3
42 U.S.C. § 2077	2M6.1
42 U.S.C. § 2122	2M6.1
42 U.S.C. § 2131	2M6.1
42 U.S.C. § 2272	2M6.1
42 U.S.C. § 2273	2M6.2
42 U.S.C. § 2274(a),(b)	2M3.1
42 U.S.C. § 2275	2M3.1
42 U.S.C. § 2276	2M3.5
42 U.S.C. § 2278a(c)	2B2.3
42 U.S.C. § 2283(a)	2A1.1, 2A1.2, 2A1.3, 2A1.4
42 U.S.C. § 2283(b)	2A2.2, 2A2.3
42 U.S.C. § 2284(a)	2M2.1, 2M2.3
42 U.S.C. § 3220(a)	2F1.1
42 U.S.C. § 3220(b)	2B1.1, 2F1.1
42 U.S.C. § 3426	2F1.1
42 U.S.C. § 3611(f)	2J1.1
42 U.S.C. § 3631	2H1.3
42 U.S.C. § 3791	2B1.1, 2F1.1
42 U.S.C. § 3792	2F1.1
42 U.S.C. § 3795	2B1.1, 2F1.1
42 U.S.C. § 5157(a)	2F1.1
42 U.S.C. § 6928(d)	2Q1.2
42 U.S.C. § 6928(e)	2Q1.1
42 U.S.C. § 7270b	2B2.3
42 U.S.C. § 7413	2Q1.2, 2Q1.3
42 U.S.C. § 9151(2),(3), (4),(5),	2A2.4
42 U.S.C. § 9152(d)	2A2.4
42 U.S.C. § 9603(b)	2Q1.2
42 U.S.C. § 9603(c)	2Q1.2
42 U.S.C. § 9603(d)	2Q1.2
43 U.S.C. § 1350	2Q1.2
43 U.S.C. § 1733(a) (43 C.F.R. 4140.1 (b)(1)(i))	2B2.3
43 U.S.C. § 1816(a)	2Q1.2
43 U.S.C. § 1822(b)	2Q1.2
45 U.S.C. § 359(a)	2F1.1
46 U.S.C. § 1276	2F1.1
46 U.S.C. § 3718(b)	2Q1.2
46 U.S.C. App. § 1707a (f)(2)	2B1.1
46 U.S.C. App. § 1903(a)	2D1.1
46 U.S.C. App. § 1903(g)	2D1.1
46 U.S.C. App. § 1903(j)	2D1.1
47 U.S.C. § 223(b)(1)(A)	2G3.2
47 U.S.C. § 553(b)(2)	2B5.3
47 U.S.C. § 605	2B5.3, 2H3.1
49 U.S.C. § 121	2F1.1
49 U.S.C. § 1472(c)	2A5.2
49 U.S.C. § 1472(h)(2)	2Q1.2
49 U.S.C. § 1472(i)(1)	2A5.1
49 U.S.C. § 1472(j)	2A5.2
49 U.S.C. § 1472(k)(1)	2A5.3
49 U.S.C. § 1472(l)	2K1.5
49 U.S.C. § 1472(n)(1)	2A5.1
49 U.S.C. § 1809(b)	2Q1.2
49 U.S.C. § 11904	2B4.1
49 U.S.C. § 11907(a)	2B4.1
49 U.S.C. § 11907(b)	2B4.1
49 U.S.C. App. § 1687(g)	2B1.3

Statute	Guideline	Statute	Guideline
50 U.S.C. § 421	2M3.9	50 U.S.C. App. § 462	2M4.1
50 U.S.C. § 783(b)	2M3.3	50 U.S.C. App. § 2410	2M5.1
50 U.S.C. § 783(c)	2M3.3		

Historical Note: Effective November 1, 1987. Amended effective January 15, 1988 (see Appendix C, amendments 60 and 61); June 15, 1988 (see Appendix C, amendments 62 and 63); October 15, 1988 (see Appendix C, amendments 64 and 65); November 1, 1989 (see Appendix C, amendments 297-301); November 1, 1990 (see Appendix C, amendment 359); November 1, 1991 (see Appendix C, amendment 421); November 1, 1992 (see Appendix C, amendment 468); November 1, 1993 (see Appendix C, amendment 496).

[Page intentionally blank]

INDEX TO GUIDELINES MANUAL

APPENDIX B - SELECTED SENTENCING STATUTES

This appendix sets forth the principal statutory provisions governing sentencing, the Sentencing Commission, and the drafting of sentencing guidelines as extracted from the following sources:

- 18 U.S.C. chapter 227 ("Sentences");
- 18 U.S.C. chapter 229 ("Postsentence Administration");
- 18 U.S.C. chapter 232 ("Miscellaneous Sentencing Provisions");
- 18 U.S.C. chapter 235 ("Appeal");
- 28 U.S.C. chapter 58 ("United States Sentencing Commission"); and
- The Anti-Drug Abuse Act of 1988 (Pub.L. 100-690), the Major Fraud Act of 1988 (Pub.L. 100-700), the Financial Institutions Reform, Recovery, and Enforcement Act of 1989 (Pub.L. 101-73), the Crime Control Act of 1990 (Pub.L. 101-647), the Treasury, Postal Service and General Government Appropriations Act, 1992 (Pub.L. 102-141), and the Violent Crime Control and Law Enforcement Act of 1994 (Pub.L. 103-322) (set out as notes under 28 U.S.C. § 994).

The legal authority for the United States Sentencing Commission ("Commission") and the related authority and procedures for sentencing in federal courts have their legislative foundation in the Sentencing Reform Act of 1984 (Chapter II of the Comprehensive Crime Control Act of 1984, Pub.L. 98-473, October 12, 1984).

These statutory provisions are presented in this appendix solely for the purpose of providing a reference to federal sentencing law as it currently stands. For the sake of brevity, certain miscellaneous provisions are omitted. The Commission makes no representations concerning the accuracy of these provisions and recommends that authoritative sources be consulted where legal reliance is necessary.

Title 18

CRIMES AND CRIMINAL PROCEDURE

—

CHAPTER 227[1]–SENTENCES

SUBCHAPTER A–GENERAL PROVISIONS

Section

§ 3551. Authorized sentences

(a) In general.–Except as otherwise specifically provided, a defendant who has been found guilty of an offense described in any Federal statute, including sections 13 and 1153 of this title, other than an Act of Congress applicable exclusively in the District of Columbia or the Uniform Code of Military Justice, shall be sentenced in accordance with the provisions of this chapter so as to achieve the purposes set forth in subparagraphs (A) through (D) of section 3553(a)(2) to the extent that they are applicable in light of all the circumstances of the case.

(b) Individuals.–An individual found guilty of an offense shall be sentenced, in accordance with the provisions of section 3553, to–

(1) a term of probation as authorized by subchapter B;
(2) a fine as authorized by subchapter C; or
(3) a term of imprisonment as authorized by subchapter D.

A sentence to pay a fine may be imposed in addition to any other sentence. A sanction authorized by section 3554, 3555, or 3556 may be imposed in addition to the sentence required by this subsection.

(c) Organizations.–An organization found guilty of an offense shall be sentenced, in accordance with the provisions of section 3553, to–

(1) a term of probation as authorized by subchapter B; or
(2) a fine as authorized by subchapter C.

A sentence to pay a fine may be imposed in addition to a sentence to probation. A sanction authorized by section 3554, 3555, or 3556 may be imposed in addition to the sentence required by this subsection.

(Added Pub.L. 98-473, Title II, § 212(a)(2), Oct. 12, 1984, 98 Stat. 1988, and amended Pub.L. 101-647, Title XVI, § 1602, Nov. 29, 1990, 104 Stat. 4843.)

---

[1]Another chapter 227 "SENTENCE, JUDGMENT, AND EXECUTION" (§§ 3561 to 3580) was repealed, effective Nov. 1, 1987.

EDITORIAL NOTES

Effective Date and Savings Provisions of Sentencing Reform Act of 1984 (Pub.L. 98-473, Title II, c. II, §§ 211 to 239); Terms of Members of U.S. Sentencing Commission and U.S. Parole Commission; Parole Release Dates; Membership of National Institute of Corrections, Advisory Corrections Council, and U.S. Sentencing Commission. Section 235 of Pub.L. 98-473, Title II, c. II, Oct. 12, 1984, 98 Stat. 2031, as amended by Pub.L. 99-217, §§ 2, 4, Dec. 26, 1985, 99 Stat. 1728; Pub.L. 99-646, § 35, Nov. 10, 1986, 100 Stat. 3599; Pub.L. 100-182, § 2, Dec. 7, 1987, 101 Stat. 1266, provided:

"(a)(1) This chapter [chapter II, §§ 211-239, of Title II of Pub.L. 98-473] shall take effect on the first day of the first calendar month beginning 36 months after the date of enactment [Oct. 12, 1984] and shall apply only to offenses committed after the taking effect of this chapter, except that–

"(A) the repeal of chapter 402 of title 18, United States Code, shall take effect on the date of enactment;

"(B)(i) chapter 58 of title 28, United States Code, shall take effect on the date of enactment of this Act or October 1, 1983, whichever occurs later, and the United States Sentencing Commission shall submit the initial sentencing guidelines promulgated under section 994(a)(1) of title 28 to the Congress within 30 months of the effective date of such chapter 58; and

"(ii) the sentencing guidelines promulgated pursuant to section 994(a)(1) shall not go into effect until–

"(I) the United States Sentencing Commission has submitted the initial set of sentencing guidelines to the Congress pursuant to subparagraph (B)(i), along with a report stating the reasons for the Commission's recommendations;

"(II) the General Accounting Office has undertaken a study of the guidelines, and their potential impact in comparison with the operation of the existing sentencing and parole release system, and has, within one hundred and fifty days of submission of the guidelines, reported to the Congress the results of its study; and

"(III) the day after the Congress has had six months after the date described in subclause (I) in which to examine the guidelines and consider the reports; and

"(IV) section 212(a)(2) [enacting chapter 227, 'Sentences', comprised of sections 3551 to 3559, 3561 to 3566, 3571 to 3574, and 3581 to 3586; and chapter 229, 'Postsentence administration', comprised of sections 3601 to 3607, 3611 to 3615, and 3621 to 3625 of this title; and repealing former chapter 227, 'Sentence, judgment, and execution', comprised of sections 3561 to 3580; former chapter 229, 'Fines, penalties, and forfeitures', comprised of sections 3611 to 3620; and former chapter 231, 'Probation', comprised of sections 3651 to 3656 of this title] takes effect, in the case of the initial sentencing guidelines so promulgated.

"(2) For the purposes of section 992(a) of title 28, the terms of the first members of the United States Sentencing Commission shall not begin to run until the sentencing guidelines go into effect pursuant to paragraph (1)(B)(ii).

"(b)(1) The following provisions of law in effect on the day before the effective date of this Act shall remain in effect for five years after the effective date as to an individual who committed an offense or an act of juvenile delinquency before the effective date and as to a term of imprisonment during the period described in subsection (a)(1)(B):

"(A) Chapter 311 of title 18, United States Code.

"(B) Chapter 309 of title 18, United States Code.

"(C) Sections 4251 through 4255 of title 18, United States Code.

"(D) Sections 5041 and 5042 of title 18, United States Code.

"(E) Sections 5017 through 5020 of title 18, United States Code, as to a sentence imposed before the date of enactment.

"(F) The maximum term of imprisonment in effect on the effective date for an offense committed before the effective date.

"(G) Any other law relating to a violation of a condition of release or to arrest authority with regard to a person who violates a condition of release.

"(2) Notwithstanding the provisions of section 4202 of title 18, United States Code, as in effect on the day before the effective date of this Act, the term of office of a Commissioner who is in office on the effective date is extended to the end of the five-year period after the effective date of this Act.

"(3) The United States Parole Commission shall set a release date, for an individual who will be in its jurisdiction the day before the expiration of five years after the effective date of this Act, pursuant to section 4206 of title 18, United States Code. A release date set pursuant to this paragraph shall be set early enough to permit consideration of an appeal of the release date, in accordance with Parole Commission procedures, before the expiration of five years following the effective date of this Act.

"(4) Notwithstanding the other provisions of this subsection, all laws in effect on the day before the effective date of this Act pertaining to an individual who is–

"(A) released pursuant to a provision listed in paragraph (1); and

"(B)(i) subject to supervision on the day before the expiration of the five-year period following the effective date of this Act; or

"(ii) released on a date set pursuant to paragraph (3); "including laws pertaining to terms and conditions of release, revocation of release, provision of counsel, and payment of transportation costs, shall remain in effect as to the individual until the expiration of his sentence, except that the district court shall determine, in accord with the Federal Rules of Criminal Procedure, whether release should be revoked or the conditions of release amended for violation of a condition of release.

"(5) Notwithstanding the provisions of section 991 of title 28, United States Code, and sections 4351 and 5002 of title 18, United States Code, the Chairman of the United States Parole Commission or his designee shall be a member of the National Institute of Corrections, and the Chairman of the United States Parole Commission shall be a member of the Advisory Corrections Council and a nonvoting member of the United States Sentencing Commission, ex officio, until the expiration of the five-year period following the effective date of this Act. Notwithstanding the provisions of section 4351 of title 18, during the five-year period the National Institute of Corrections shall have seventeen members, including seven ex officio members. Notwithstanding the provisions of section 991 of title 28, during the five-year period the United States Sentencing Commission shall consist of nine members, including two ex officio, nonvoting members."

[Pub.L. 101-650, Title III, § 316, Dec. 1, 1990, 104 Stat. 5115, provided that: "For the purposes of section 235(b) of Public Law 98-473 [set out as a note under this section] as it relates to chapter 311 of title 18, United States Code [section 4201 et seq. of this title], and the United States Parole Commission, each reference in such section to 'five years' or a 'five-year period' shall be deemed a reference to 'ten years' or a 'ten-year period', respectively."]

Sentencing Considerations Prior to Enactment of Guidelines. Section 239 of Pub.L. 98-473, Title II, c. II, Oct. 12, 1984, 98 Stat. 2039, provided:

"Since, due to an impending crisis in prison over-crowding, available Federal prison space must be treated as a scarce resource in the sentencing of criminal defendants;

"Since, sentencing decisions should be designed to ensure that prison resources are, first and foremost, reserved for those violent and serious criminal offenders who pose the most dangerous threat to society;

"Since, in cases of nonviolent and nonserious offenders, the interests of society as a whole as well as individual victims of crime can continue to be served through the imposition of alternative sentences, such as restitution and community service;

"Since, in the two years preceding the enactment of sentencing guidelines, Federal sentencing practice should ensure that scarce prison resources are available to house violent and serious criminal offenders by the increased use of restitution, community service, and other alternative sentences in cases of nonviolent and nonserious offenders: Now, therefore, be it

"Declared, That it is the sense of the Senate that in the two years preceding the enactment of the sentencing guidelines, Federal judges, in determining the particular sentence to be imposed, consider–

"(1) the nature and circumstances of the offense and the history and characteristics of the defendant;

"(2) the general appropriateness of imposing a sentence other than imprisonment in cases in which the defendant has not been convicted of a crime of violence or otherwise serious offense; and

"(3) the general appropriateness of imposing a sentence of imprisonment in cases in which the defendant has been convicted of a crime of violence or otherwise serious offense."

§ 3552. Presentence reports

(a) Presentence investigation and report by probation officer.–A United States probation officer shall make a presentence investigation of a defendant that is required pursuant to the provisions of Rule 32(c) of the Federal Rules of Criminal Procedure, and shall, before the imposition of sentence, report the results of the investigation to the court.

(b) Presentence study and report by bureau of prisons.–If the court, before or after its receipt of a report specified in subsection (a) or (c), desires more information than is otherwise available to it as a basis for determining the sentence to be imposed on a defendant found guilty of a misdemeanor or felony, it may order a study of the defendant. The study shall be conducted in the local community by qualified consultants unless the sentencing judge finds that there is a compelling reason for the study to be done by the Bureau of Prisons or there are no adequate professional resources available in the local community to perform the study. The period of the study shall be no more than sixty days. The order shall specify the additional information that the court needs before determining the sentence to be imposed. Such an order shall be treated for administrative purposes as a provisional sentence of imprisonment for the maximum term authorized by section 3581(b) for the offense committed. The study shall inquire into such matters as are specified by the court and any other matters that the Bureau of Prisons or the professional consultants believe are pertinent to the factors set forth in section 3553(a). The period of the study may, in the discretion of the court, be extended for an additional period of not more than sixty days. By the expiration of the period of the study, or by the expiration of any extension granted by the court, the United States marshal shall, if the defendant is in custody, return the defendant to the court for final sentencing. The Bureau of Prisons or the professional consultants shall provide the court with a written report of the pertinent results of the study and make to the court whatever recommendations the Bureau or the consultants believe will be helpful to a proper resolution of the case. The report shall include recommendations of the Bureau or the consultants concerning the guidelines and policy statements, promulgated by the Sentencing Commission pursuant to 28 U.S.C. 994(a), that they believe are applicable to the defendant's case. After receiving the report and the recommendations, the court shall proceed finally to sentence the defendant in accordance with the sentencing alternatives and procedures available under this chapter.

(c) Presentence examination and report by psychiatric or psychological examiners.–If the court, before or after its receipt of a report specified in subsection (a) or (b) desires more information than is otherwise available to it as a basis for determining the mental condition of the defendant, the court may order the same psychiatric or psychological examination and report thereon as may be ordered under section 4244(b) of this title.

(d) Disclosure of presentence reports.–The court shall assure that a report filed pursuant to this section is disclosed to the defendant, the counsel for the defendant, and the attorney for the Government at least ten days prior to the date set for sentencing, unless this minimum period is waived by the defendant. The court shall provide a copy of the presentence report to the attorney for the Government to use in collecting an assessment, criminal fine, forfeiture or restitution imposed.

(Added Pub.L. 98-473, Title II, § 212(a)(2), Oct. 12, 1984, 98 Stat. 1988, and amended Pub.L. 99-646, § 7(a), Nov. 10, 1986, 100 Stat. 3593; Pub.L. 101-647, Title XXXVI, § 3625, Nov. 29, 1990, 104 Stat. 4965).

EDITORIAL NOTES

Effective Date of 1990 Amendment. Amendment by section 3625 of Pub.L. 101-647 effective 180 days after Nov. 29, 1990, see section 3631 of Pub.L. 101-647.

Effective Date of 1986 Amendment. Section 7(b) of Pub.L. 99-646 provided that: "The amendments made by this section [amending this section] shall take effect on the date of the taking effect of section 3552 of title 18, United States Code [this section]."

Effective Date. Section effective on the first day of first calendar month beginning thirty six months after Oct. 12, 1984, applicable only to offenses committed after taking effect of sections 211 to 239 of Pub.L. 98-473, and except as otherwise provided for therein, see section 235 of Pub.L. 98-473, as amended, set out as a note under section 3551 of this title.

§ 3553. Imposition of a sentence

(a) Factors to be considered in imposing a sentence.–The court shall impose a sentence sufficient, but not greater than necessary, to comply with the purposes set forth in paragraph (2) of this subsection. The court, in determining the particular sentence to be imposed, shall consider–

(1) the nature and circumstances of the offense and the history and characteristics of the defendant;

(2) the need for the sentence imposed–

(A) to reflect the seriousness of the offense, to promote respect for the law, and to provide just punishment for the offense;

(B) to afford adequate deterrence to criminal conduct;

(C) to protect the public from further crimes of the defendant; and

(D) to provide the defendant with needed educational or vocational training, medical care, or other correctional treatment in the most effective manner;

(3) the kinds of sentences available;

(4) the kinds of sentence and the sentencing range established for–

(A) the applicable category of offense committed by the applicable category of defendant as set forth in the guidelines issued by the Sentencing Commission pursuant to section 994(a)(1) of title 28, United States Code, and that are in effect on the date the defendant is sentenced; or

(B) in the case of a violation of probation or supervised release, the applicable guidelines or policy statements issued by the Sentencing Commission pursuant to section 994(a)(3) of title 28, United States Code;

(5) any pertinent policy statement issued by the Sentencing Commission pursuant to 28 U.S.C. 994(a)(2) that is in effect on the date the defendant is sentenced;

(6) the need to avoid unwarranted sentence disparities among defendants with similar records who have been found guilty of similar conduct; and

(7) the need to provide restitution to any victims of the offense.

(b) Application of guidelines in imposing a sentence.–The court shall impose a sentence of the kind, and within the range, referred to in subsection (a)(4) unless the court finds that there exists an aggravating or mitigating circumstance of a kind, or to a degree, not adequately taken into consideration by the Sentencing Commission in formulating the guidelines that should result in a sentence different from that described. In determining whether a circumstance was adequately taken into consideration, the court shall consider only the sentencing guidelines, policy statements, and official commentary of the Sentencing Commission. In the absence of an applicable sentencing guideline, the court shall impose an appropriate sentence, having due regard for the purposes set forth in subsection (a)(2). In the absence of an applicable sentencing guideline in the case of an offense other than a petty offense, the court shall also have due regard for the relationship of the sentence imposed to sentences prescribed by guidelines applicable to similar offenses and offenders, and to the applicable policy statements of the Sentencing Commission.

(c) Statement of reasons for imposing a sentence.–The court, at the time of sentencing, shall state in open court the reasons for its imposition of the particular sentence, and, if the sentence–

(1) is of the kind, and within the range, described in subsection (a)(4), and that range exceeds 24 months, the reason for imposing a sentence at a particular point within the range; or

(2) is not of the kind, or is outside the range, described in subsection (a)(4), the specific reason for the imposition of a sentence different from that described.

If the court does not order restitution, or orders only partial restitution, the court shall include in the statement the reason therefor. The court shall provide a transcription or other appropriate public record of the court's statement of reasons to the Probation System, and, if the sentence includes a term of imprisonment, to the Bureau of Prisons.

(d) Presentence procedure for an order of notice.–Prior to imposing an order of notice pursuant to section 3555, the court shall give notice to the defendant and the Government that it is considering imposing such an order. Upon motion of the defendant or the Government, or on its own motion, the court shall–

(1) permit the defendant and the Government to submit affidavits and written memoranda addressing matters relevant to the imposition of such an order;

(2) afford counsel an opportunity in open court to address orally the appropriateness of the imposition of such an order; and

(3) include in its statement of reasons pursuant to subsection (c) specific reasons underlying its determinations regarding the nature of such an order.

Upon motion of the defendant or the Government, or on its own motion, the court may in its discretion employ any additional procedures that it concludes will not unduly complicate or prolong the sentencing process.

(e) Limited authority to impose a sentence below a statutory minimum.–Upon motion of the Government, the court shall have the authority to impose a sentence below a level established by statute as minimum sentence so as to reflect a defendant's substantial assistance in the investigation or prosecution of another person who has committed an offense. Such sentence shall be imposed in accordance with the guidelines and policy statements issued by the Sentencing Commission pursuant to section 994 of title 28, United States Code.

(f) Limitation on Applicability of Statutory Minimums in Certain Cases.–Notwithstanding any other provision of law, in the case of an offense under section 401, 404, or 406 of the Controlled Substances Act (21 U.S.C. 841, 844, 846) or section 1010 or 1013 of the Controlled Substances Import and Export Act (21 U.S.C. 961,[1] 963), the court shall impose a sentence pursuant to guidelines promulgated by the United States Sentencing Commission under section 994 of title 28 without regard to any statutory minimum sentence, if the court finds at sentencing, after the Government has been afforded the opportunity to make a recommendation, that–

(1) the defendant does not have more than 1 criminal history point, as determined under the sentencing guidelines;

(2) the defendant did not use violence or credible threats of violence or possess a firearm or other dangerous weapon (or induce another participant to do so) in connection with the offense;

(3) the offense did not result in death or serious bodily injury to any person;

(4) the defendant was not an organizer, leader, manager, or supervisor of others in the offense, as determined under the sentencing guidelines and was not engaged in a continuing criminal enterprise, as defined in 21 U.S.C. 848; and

(5) not later than the time of the sentencing hearing, the defendant has truthfully provided to the Government all information and evidence the defendant has concerning the offense or offenses that were part of the same course of conduct or of a common scheme or plan, but the fact that the defendant has no relevant or useful other information to provide or that the Government is already aware of the information shall not preclude a determination by the court that the defendant has complied with this requirement.

(Added Pub.L. 98-473, Title II, § 212(a)(2), Oct. 12, 1984, 98 Stat. 1989, and amended Pub.L. 99-570, Title I, § 1007(b), Oct. 27, 1986, 100 Stat. 3707-7; Pub.L. 99-646, §§ 8(a), 9(a), 80(a), 81(a), Nov. 10, 1986, 100 Stat. 3593, 3619; Pub.L. 100-182, §§ 3, 16(a), (17), Dec. 7, 1987, 101 Stat. 1266, 1269, 1270; Pub.L. 100-690, Title VII, § 7102, Nov. 18, 1988, 102 Stat. 4416; Pub.L. 103-322, Title VIII, § 80001(a), Title XXVIII, § 280001, Sept. 13, 1994, 108 Stat. ___, __.)

[1]So in original. Probably should be "960" (section 1010 of the Controlled Substances Import and Export Act is 21 U.S.C. § 960).

EDITORIAL NOTES

Effective Date of 1994 Amendment. Section 80001(c) of Pub.L. 103-322 provided that: "The amendment made by subsection (a) [adding 18 U.S.C. § 3553(f)] shall apply to all sentences imposed on or after [Sept. 23, 1994] the 10th day beginning after the date of enactment of this Act [Sept. 13, 1994]."

Effective Date of 1987 Amendment. Amendment by Pub.L. 100-182 applicable with respect to offenses committed after enactment of Pub.L. 100-182, which was approved Dec. 7, 1987, see section 26 of Pub.L. 100-182.

Effective Date of 1986 Amendment. Section 8(c) of Pub.L. 99-646 provided that: "The amendments made by this section [amending subsec. (a) of this section and section 3663 of this title] shall take effect on the date of the taking effect of section 3553 of title 18, United States Code [this section]."

Section 9(b) of Pub.L. 99-646 provided that: "The amendments made by this section [subsec. (b) of this section] shall take effect on the date of the taking effect of section 3553 of title 18, United States Code [this section]."

Section 80(b) of Pub.L. 99-646 provided that: "The amendments made by this section [amending subsec. (d) of this section] shall take effect on the date of the taking effect of section 212(a)(2) of the Sentencing Reform Act of 1984 [see Effective Date note below]."

Section 81(b) of Pub.L. 99-646 provided that: "–The amendments made by this section [amending subsec. (a) of this section] shall take effect on the date of the taking effect of section 212(a)(2) of the Sentencing Reform Act of 1984 [see Effective Date note below]."

Section 1007(b) of Pub.L. 99-570 provided that: "(b) The amendment made by this section [enacting subsec. (d) of this section] shall take effect on the date of the taking effect of section 3553 of title 18, United States Code [this section]."

Effective Date. Section effective on the first day of first calendar month beginning thirty six months after Oct. 12, 1984, applicable only to offenses committed after taking effect of sections 211 to 239 of Pub.L. 98-473, and except as otherwise provided for therein, see section 235 of Pub.L. 98-473, as amended, set out as a note under section 3551 of this title.

Authority to Lower Sentences Below Statutory Minimum for Old Offenses. Section 24 of Pub.L. 100-182 provided that: "Notwithstanding section 235 of the Comprehensive Crime Control Act of 1984 [section 235 of Pub.L. 98-473, set out as a note under section 3551 of this title]–

"(1) section 3553(e) of title 18, United States Code [subsec. (e) of this section];

"(2) rule 35(b) of the Federal Rules of Criminal Procedure as amended by section 215(b) of such Act; and

"(3) rule 35(b) as in effect before the taking effect of the initial set of guidelines promulgated by the United States Sentencing Commission pursuant to chapter 58 of title 28, United States Code [sections 991 et seq. of Title 28, Judiciary and Judicial Procedure],

shall apply in the case of an offense committed before the taking effect of such guidelines."

§ 3554. Order of criminal forfeiture

The court, in imposing a sentence on a defendant who has been found guilty of an offense described in section 1962 of this title or in title II or III of the Comprehensive Drug Abuse Prevention and Control Act of 1970 shall order, in addition to the sentence that is imposed pursuant to the provisions of section 3551, that the defendant forfeit property to the United States in accordance with the provisions of section 1963 of this title or section 413 of the Comprehensive Drug Abuse and Control Act of 1970.

(Added Pub.L. 98-473, Title II, § 212(a)(2), Oct. 12, 1984, 98 Stat. 1990.)

EDITORIAL NOTES

References in Text. Title II or III of the Comprehensive Drug Abuse Prevention and Control Act of 1970, referred to in text, are Titles II and III of Pub.L. 91-513, Oct. 27, 1970, 84 Stat. 1242, which are principally classified to subchapters I and II of chapter 13 of Title 21, Food and Drugs.

Section 413 of such Act, referred to in text, is section 413 of Pub.L. 91-513, added Pub.L. 98-473, Title II, c. III, part B, § 303, Oct. 12, 1984, 98 Stat. 2044, which is classified to section 853 of Title 21.

Effective Date. Section effective on the first day of first calendar month beginning thirty six months after Oct. 12, 1984, applicable only to offenses committed after taking effect of sections 211 to 239 of Pub.L. 98-473, and except as otherwise provided for therein, see section 235 of Pub.L. 98-473, as amended, set out as a note under section 3551 of this title.

§ 3555. Order of notice to victims

The court, in imposing a sentence on a defendant who has been found guilty of an offense involving fraud or other intentionally deceptive practices, may order, in addition to the sentence that is imposed pursuant to the provisions of section 3551, that the defendant give reasonable notice and explanation of the conviction, in such form as the court may approve, to the victims of the offense. The notice may be ordered to be given by mail, by advertising in designated areas or through designated media, or by other appropriate means. In determining whether to require the defendant to give such notice, the court shall consider the factors set forth in section 3553(a) to the extent that they are applicable and shall consider the cost involved in giving the notice as it relates to the loss caused by the offense, and shall not require the defendant to bear the costs of notice in excess of $20,000.

(Added Pub.L. 98-473, Title II, § 212(a)(2), Oct. 12, 1984, 98 Stat. 1991.)

EDITORIAL NOTES

Effective Date. Section effective on the first day of first calendar month beginning thirty six months after Oct. 12, 1984, applicable only to offenses committed after taking effect of sections 211 to 239 of Pub.L. 98-473, and except as otherwise provided for therein, see section 235 of Pub.L. 98-473, as amended, set out as a note under section 3551 of this title.

§ 3556. Order of restitution

The court, in imposing a sentence on a defendant who has been found guilty of an offense may order restitution in accordance with sections 3663 and 3664.

(Added Pub.L. 98-473, Title II, § 212(a)(2), Oct. 12, 1984, 98 Stat. 1991, and amended Pub.L. 99-646, § 20(b), Nov. 10, 1986, 100 Stat. 3596.)

EDITORIAL NOTES

Effective Date of 1986 Amendment. Section 20(c) of Pub.L. 99-646 provided that: "The amendments made by this section [amending this section and section 3663 of this title] shall take effect on the date of the taking effect of section 212(a)(2) of the Sentencing Reform Act of 1984 [see Effective Date note below]."

Effective Date. Section effective on the first day of first calendar month beginning thirty six months after Oct. 12, 1984, applicable only to offenses committed after taking effect of sections 211 to 239 of Pub.L. 98-473, and except as otherwise provided for therein, see section 235 of Pub.L. 98-473, as amended, set out as a note under section 3551 of this title.

§ 3557. Review of a sentence

The review of a sentence imposed pursuant to section 3551 is governed by the provisions of section 3742.

(Added Pub.L. 98-473, Title II, § 212(a)(2), Oct. 12, 1984, 98 Stat. 1991.)

EDITORIAL NOTES

Effective Date. Section effective on the first day of first calendar month beginning thirty six months after Oct. 12, 1984, applicable only to offenses committed after taking effect of sections 211 to 239 of Pub.L. 98-473, and except as otherwise provided for therein, see section 235 of Pub.L. 98-473, as amended, set out as a note under section 3551 of this title.

§ 3558. Implementation of a sentence

The implementation of a sentence imposed pursuant to section 3551 is governed by the provisions of chapter 229.

(Added Pub.L. 98-473, Title II, § 212(a)(2), Oct. 12, 1984, 98 Stat. 1991.)

EDITORIAL NOTES

Effective Date. Section effective on the first day of first calendar month beginning thirty six months after Oct. 12, 1984, applicable only to offenses committed after taking effect of sections 211 to 239 of Pub.L. 98-473, and except as otherwise provided for therein, see section 235 of Pub.L. 98-473, as amended, set out as a note under section 3551 of this title.

§ 3559. Sentencing classification of offenses

(a) Classification.–An offense that is not specifically classified by a letter grade in the section defining it, is classified if the maximum term of imprisonment authorized is–

(1) life imprisonment, or if the maximum penalty is death, as a Class A felony;
(2) twenty-five years or more, as a Class B felony;
(3) less than twenty-five years but ten or more years, as a Class C felony;
(4) less than ten years but five or more years, as a Class D felony;
(5) less than five years but more than one year, as a Class E felony;
(6) one year or less but more than six months, as a Class A misdemeanor;
(7) six months or less but more than thirty days, as a Class B misdemeanor;
(8) thirty days or less but more than five days, as a Class C misdemeanor; or
(9) five days or less, or if no imprisonment is authorized, as an infraction.

(b) Effect of classification.–Except as provided in subsection (c), an offense classified under subsection (a) carries all the incidents assigned to the applicable letter designation, except that the maximum term of imprisonment is the term authorized by the law describing the offense.

(c) Imprisonment of Certain Violent Felons.–

(1) Mandatory life imprisonment.–Notwithstanding any other provision of law, a person who is convicted in a court of the United States of a serious violent felony shall be sentenced to life imprisonment if–

(A) the person has been convicted (and those convictions have become final) on separate prior occasions in a court of the United States or of a State of–

(i) 2 or more serious violent felonies; or

(ii) one or more serious violent felonies and one or more serious drug offenses; and

(B) each serious violent felony or serious drug offense used as a basis for sentencing under this subsection, other than the first, was committed after the defendant's conviction of the preceding serious violent felony or serious drug offense.

(2) Definitions.–For purposes of this subsection–

(A) the term "assault with the intent to commit rape" means an offense that has as its elements engaging in physical contact with another person or using or brandishing a weapon against another person with intent to commit aggravated sexual abuse or sexual abuse (as described in sections 2241 and 2242);

(B) the term "arson" means an offense that has as its elements maliciously damaging or destroying any building, inhabited structure, vehicle, vessel, or real property by means of fire or an explosive;

(C) the term "extortion" means an offense that has as its elements the extraction of anything of value from another person by threatening or placing that person in fear of injury to any person or kidnapping of any person;

(D) the term "firearms use" means an offense that has as its elements those described in section 924(c) or 929(a), if the firearm was brandished, discharged, or otherwise used as a weapon and the crime of violence or drug trafficking crime during and relation[1] to which the firearm was used was subject to prosecution in a court of the United States or a court of a State, or both;

(E) the term "kidnapping" means an offense that has as its elements the abduction, restraining, confining, or carrying away of another person by force or threat of force;

(F) the term "serious violent felony" means–

(i) a Federal or State offense, by whatever designation and wherever committed, consisting of murder (as described in section 1111); manslaughter other than involuntary manslaughter (as described in section 1112); assault with intent to commit murder (as described in section 113(a)); assault with intent to commit rape; aggravated sexual abuse and sexual abuse (as described in sections 2241 and 2242); abusive sexual contact (as described in sections 2244 (a)(1) and (a)(2)); kidnapping; aircraft piracy (as described in section 46502 of Title 49); robbery (as described in section 2111, 2113, or 2118); carjacking (as described in section 2119); extortion; arson; firearms use; or attempt, conspiracy, or solicitation to commit any of the above offenses; and

(ii) any other offense punishable by a maximum term of imprisonment of 10 years or more that has as an element the use, attempted use, or threatened use of physical force against the person of another or that, by its nature, involves a substantial risk that physical force against the person of another may be used in the course of committing the offense;

(G) the term "State" means a State of the United States, the District of Columbia, and a commonwealth, territory, or possession of the United States; and

(H) the term "serious drug offense" means–

(i) an offense that is punishable under section 401(b)(1)(A) or 408 of the Controlled Substances Act (21 U.S.C. 841(b)(1)(A), 848) or section 1010(b)(1)(A) of the Controlled Substances Import and Export Act (21 U.S.C. § 960(b)(1)(A); or

(ii) an offense under State law that, had the offense been prosecuted in a court of the United States, would have been punishable under section 401(b)(1)(A) or 408 of the Controlled Substances Act (21 U.S.C. 841(b)(1)(A), 848) or section 1010(b)(1)(A) of the Controlled Substances Import and Export Act (21 U.S.C. 960(b)(1)(A)).

---

[1] So in original. Probably should be "in relation".

(3) Nonqualifying felonies–

(A) Robbery in certain cases.–Robbery, an attempt, conspiracy, or solicitation to commit robbery; or an offense described in paragraph (2)(F)(ii) shall not serve as a basis for sentencing under this subsection if the defendant establishes by clear and convincing evidence that–

(i) no firearm or other dangerous weapon was used in the offense and no threat of use of a firearm or other dangerous weapon was involved in the offense; and

(ii) the offense did not result in death or serious bodily injury (as defined in section 1365) to any person.–

(B) Arson in certain cases.–Arson shall not serve as a basis for sentencing under this subsection if the defendant establishes by clear and convincing evidence that–

(i) the offense posed no threat to human life; and

(ii) the defendant reasonably believed the offense posed no threat to human life.

(4) Information filed by united states attorney.–The provisions of section 411(a) of the Controlled Substances Act (21 U.S.C. § 851(a)) shall apply to the imposition of sentence under this subsection.

(5) Rule of construction.–This subsection shall not be construed to preclude imposition of the death penalty.

(6) Special provision for indian country.–No person subject to the criminal jurisdiction of an Indian tribal government shall be subject to this subsection for any offense for which Federal jurisdiction is solely predicated on Indian country (as defined in section 1151) and which occurs within the boundaries of such Indian country unless the governing body of the tribe has elected that this subsection have effect over land and persons subject to the criminal jurisdiction of the tribe.

(7) Resentencing upon overturning of prior conviction.–If the conviction for a serous violent felony or serious drug offense that was a basis for sentencing under this subsection is found, pursuant to any appropriate State or Federal procedure, to be unconstitutional or is vitiated on the explicit basis of innocence, or if the convicted person is pardoned on the explicit basis of innocence, the person serving a sentence imposed under this subsection shall be resentenced to any sentence that was available at the time of the original sentencing.

(Added Pub.L. 98-473, Title II, § 212(a)(2), Oct. 12, 1984, 98 Stat. 1991, and amended Pub.L. 100-185, § 5, Dec. 11, 1987, 101 Stat. 1279; Pub.L. 100-690, Title VII, § 7041, Nov. 18, 1988, 102 Stat. 4399); Pub.L. 103-322, Title VII § 70001, Sept. 13, 1994, 108 Stat.__.)

EDITORIAL NOTES

Effective Date. Section effective on the first day of first calendar month beginning thirty six months after Oct. 12, 1984, applicable only to offenses committed after taking effect of sections 211 to 239 of Pub.L. 98-473, and except as otherwise provided for therein, see section 235 of Pub.L. 98-473, as amended, set out as a note under section 3551 of this title.

SUBCHAPTER B–PROBATION

Section

3561. Sentence of probation.
3562. Imposition of a sentence of probation.
3563. Conditions of probation.
3564. Running of a term of probation.
3565. Revocation of probation.
3566. Implementation of a sentence of probation.

§ 3561. Sentence of probation

(a) In general.–A defendant who has been found guilty of an offense may be sentenced to a term of probation unless–

(1) the offense is a Class A or Class B felony and the defendant is an individual;

(2) the offense is an offense for which probation has been expressly precluded; or

(3) the defendant is sentenced at the same time to a term of imprisonment for the same or a different offense that is not a petty offense.

(b) Domestic Violence Offenders.–A defendant who has been convicted for the first time of a domestic violence crime shall be sentenced to a term of probation if not sentenced to a term of imprisonment. The term "domestic violence crime" means a crime of violence for which the defendant may be prosecuted in a court of the United States in which the victim or intended victim is the spouse, former spouse, intimate partner, former intimate partner, child, or former child of the defendant, or any relative defendant, child, or former child of the defendant,[1] or any other relative of the defendant.

(c) Authorized terms.–The authorized terms of probation are–

(1) for a felony, not less than one nor more than five years;

(2) for a misdemeanor, not more than five years; and

(3) for an infraction, not more than one year.

(Added Pub.L. 98-473, Title II, § 212(a)(2), Oct. 12, 1984, 98 Stat. 1992, and amended Pub.L. 99-646, § 10(a), Nov. 10, 1986, 100 Stat. 3593; Pub.L. 100-182, § 7, Dec. 7, 1987, 101 Stat. 1267; Pub.L. 103-322, Title XXVIII, § 280004, Title XXXII, § 320921(a), Sept. 13, 1994, 108 Stat. __, __.)

EDITORIAL NOTES

Effective Date of 1987 Amendment. Amendment by Pub.L. 100-182 applicable with respect to offenses committed after enactment of Pub.L. 100-182, which was approved Dec. 7, 1987, see section 26 of Pub.L. 100-182.

Effective Date of 1986 Amendment. Section 10(b) of Pub.L. 99-646 provided that: "The amendment made by this section [amending subsec. (a) of this section] shall take effect on the date of the taking effect of such section 3561(a) [subsec. (a) of this section]."

Effective Date. Section effective on the first day of first calendar month beginning thirty six months after Oct. 12, 1984, applicable only to offenses committed after taking effect of sections 211 to 239 of Pub.L. 98-473, and except as otherwise provided for therein, see section 235 of Pub.L. 98-473, as amended, set out as a note under section 3551 of this title.

§ 3562. Imposition of a sentence of probation

(a) Factors to be considered in imposing a term of probation.–The court, in determining whether to impose a term of probation, and, if a term of probation is to be imposed, in determining the length of the term and the conditions of probation, shall consider the factors set forth in section 3553(a) to the extent that they are applicable.

(b) Effect of finality of judgment.–Notwithstanding the fact that a sentence of probation can subsequently be–

(1) modified or revoked pursuant to the provisions of section 3564 or 3565;

[1]So in original.

(2) corrected pursuant to the provisions of rule 35 of the Federal Rules of Criminal Procedure and section 3742; or

(3) appealed and modified, if outside the guideline range, pursuant to the provisions of section 3742; a judgment of conviction that includes such a sentence constitutes a final judgment for all other purposes.

(Added Pub.L. 98-473, Title II, § 212(a)(2), Oct. 12, 1984, 98 Stat. 1992, and amended Pub.L. 101-647, Title XXXV, § 3583, Nov. 29, 1990, 104 Stat. 4930.)

EDITORIAL NOTES

Effective Date. Section effective on the first day of first calendar month beginning thirty six months after Oct. 12, 1984, applicable only to offenses committed after taking effect of sections 211 to 239 of Pub.L. 98-473, and except as otherwise provided for therein, see section 235 of Pub.L. 98-473, as amended, set out as a note under section 3551 of this title.

§ 3563. Conditions of probation

(a) Mandatory conditions.–The court shall provide, as an explicit condition of a sentence of probation–

(1) for a felony, a misdemeanor, or an infraction, that the defendant not commit another Federal, State, or local crime during the term of probation;

(2) for a felony, that the defendant also abide by at least one condition set forth in subsection (b)(2), (b)(3), or (b)(13), unless the court finds on the record that extraordinary circumstances exist that would make such a condition plainly unreasonable, in which event the court shall impose one or more of the other conditions set forth under subsection (b);

(3) for a felony, a misdemeanor, or an infraction, that the defendant not unlawfully possess a controlled substance; and

(4) for a felony, a misdemeanor, or an infraction, that the defendant refrain from any unlawful use of a controlled substance and submit to one drug test within 15 days of release on probation and at least 2 periodic drug tests thereafter (as determined by the court) for use of a controlled substance, but the condition stated in this paragraph may be ameliorated or suspended by the court for any individual defendant if the defendant's presentence report or other reliable sentencing information indicates a low risk of future substance abuse by the defendant.

(4)[1] for a domestic violence crime as defined in section 3561(b) by a defendant convicted of such an offense for the first time that the defendant attend a public, private, or private non-profit offender rehabilitation program that has been approved by the court, in consultation with a State Coalition Against Domestic Violence or other appropriate experts, if an approved program is readily available within a 50-mile radius of the legal residence of the defendant.

If the court has imposed and ordered execution of a fine and placed the defendant on probation, payment of the fine or adherence to the court-established installment schedule shall be a condition of the probation. The results of a drug test administered in accordance with paragraph (4) shall be subject to confirmation only if the results are positive, the defendant is subject to possible imprisonment for such failure, and either the defendant denies the accuracy of such test or there is some other reason to question the results of the test. A defendant who tests positive may be detained pending verification of a positive drug test result. A drug test confirmation shall be a urine drug test confirmed using gas chromatography/mass spectrometry techniques or such test as the Director of the Administrative Office of the United States Courts after consultation with the Secretary of Health and Human Services may determine to be of equivalent accuracy. The court shall consider whether the availability of appropriate substance abuse treatment programs, or an individual's current or past participation in such programs, warrants an exception in accordance with United States Sentencing Commission guidelines from the

[1]So in original.

rule of section 3565(b), when considering any action against a defendant who fails a drug test administered in accordance with paragraph (4).

(b) Discretionary conditions.–The court may provide, as further conditions of a sentence of probation, to the extent that such conditions are reasonably related to the factors set forth in section 3553(a)(1) and (a)(2) and to the extent that such conditions involve only such deprivations of liberty or property as are reasonably necessary for the purposes indicated in section 3553(a)(2), that the defendant–

(1) support his dependents and meet other family responsibilities;

(2) pay a fine imposed pursuant to the provisions of subchapter C;

(3) make restitution to a victim of the offense under sections 3663 and 3664 (but not subject to the limitations of section 3663(a));

(4) give to the victims of the offense the notice ordered pursuant to the provisions of section 3555;

(5) work conscientiously at suitable employment or pursue conscientiously a course of study or vocational training that will equip him for suitable employment;

(6) refrain, in the case of an individual, from engaging in a specified occupation, business, or profession bearing a reasonably direct relationship to the conduct constituting the offense, or engage in such a specified occupation, business, or profession only to a stated degree or under stated circumstances;

(7) refrain from frequenting specified kinds of places or from associating unnecessarily with specified persons;

(8) refrain from excessive use of alcohol, or any use of a narcotic drug or other controlled substance, as defined in section 102 of the Controlled Substances Act (21 U.S.C. 802), without a prescription by a licensed medical practitioner;

(9) refrain from possessing a firearm, destructive device, or other dangerous weapon;

(10) undergo available medical, psychiatric, or psychological treatment, including treatment for drug or alcohol dependency, as specified by the court, and remain in a specified institution if required for that purpose;

(11) remain in the custody of the Bureau of Prisons during nights, weekends, or other intervals of time, totaling no more than the lesser of one year or the term of imprisonment authorized for the offense, during the first year of the term of probation;

(12) reside at, or participate in the program of, a community corrections facility (including a facility maintained or under contract to the Bureau of Prisons) for all or part of the term of probation;

(13) work in community service as directed by the court;

(14) reside in a specified place or area, or refrain from residing in a specified place or area;

(15) remain within the jurisdiction of the court, unless granted permission to leave by the court or a probation officer;

(16) report to a probation officer as directed by the court or the probation officer;

(17) permit a probation officer to visit him at his home or elsewhere as specified by the court;

(18) answer inquiries by a probation officer and notify the probation officer promptly of any change in address or employment;

(19) notify the probation officer promptly if arrested or questioned by a law enforcement officer;

(20) remain at his place of residence during nonworking hours and, if the court finds it appropriate, that compliance with this condition be monitored by telephonic or electronic signaling devices, except that a condition under this paragraph may be imposed only as an alternative to incarceration;

(21) comply with the terms of any court order or order of an administrative process pursuant to the law of a State, the District of Columbia, or any other possession or territory of the United States, requiring payments by the defendant for the support and maintenance of a child or of a child and the parent with whom the child is living; or

(22) satisfy such other conditions as the court may impose.

(c) Modifications of conditions.–The court may modify, reduce, or enlarge the conditions of a sentence of probation at any time prior to the expiration or termination of the term of probation, pursuant to the provisions of the Federal Rules of Criminal Procedure relating to the modification of probation and the provisions applicable to the initial setting of the conditions of probation.

(d) Written statement of conditions.–The court shall direct that the probation officer provide the defendant with a written statement that sets forth all the conditions to which the sentence is subject, and that is sufficiently clear and specific to serve as a guide for the defendant's conduct and for such supervision as is required.

(Added Pub.L. 98-473, Title II, § 212(a)(2), Oct. 12, 1984, 98 Stat. 1993, and amended Pub.L. 99-646, §§ 11(a), 12(a), Nov. 10, 1986, 100 Stat. 3594; Pub.L. 100-182, §§ 10, 18, Dec. 7, 1987, 101 Stat. 1267, 1270; Pub.L. 100-690, Title VII, §§ 7086, 7110, 7303(a)(1), 7305(a), Nov. 18, 1988, 102 Stat. 4408, 4419, 4464, 4465; Pub.L. 101-647, Title XXXV, § 3584, Nov. 29, 1990, 104 Stat. 4430; Pub.L. 102-521, § 3, Oct. 25, 1992, 106 Stat. 3404; Pub.L. 103-322, Title II, § 20414(b), Title XXVIII, § 280002, Title XXXII, § 320921(b), Sept. 13, 1994, 108 Stat. __, __, __.)

EDITORIAL NOTES

Codification. Amendment by section 3584(1) of Pub.L. 101-647 directed the substitution of "defendant" for "defendent" in subsec. (a)(3). Such substitution had already been editorially executed, therefore, no further change was required.

Effective Date of 1988 Amendment. Section 7303(d) of Pub.L. 100-690 provided that: "The amendments made by this section [amending this section and sections 3565, 3583, 4209, and 4214 of this title] shall apply with respect to persons whose probation, supervised release, or parole begins after December 31, 1988."

Effective Date of 1987 Amendment. Amendment by Pub.L. 100-182 applicable with respect to offenses committed after enactment of Pub.L. 100-182, which was approved Dec. 7, 1987, see section 26 of Pub.L. 100-182.

Effective Date of 1986 Amendment. Section 11(b) of Pub.L. 99-646 provided that: "The amendment made by this section [amending subsec. (b)(11) of this section] shall take effect on the date of the taking effect of such section 3563(b)(11) [subsec. (b)(11) of this section]."

Section 12(c)(1) of Pub.L. 99-646 provided that: "The amendments made by subsection (a) [amending subsec. (c) of this section] shall take effect on the date of the taking effect of such section 3563(c) [subsec. (c) of this section]."

Effective Date. Section effective on the first day of first calendar month beginning thirty six months after Oct. 12, 1984, applicable only to offenses committed after taking effect of sections 211 to 239 of Pub.L. 98-473, and except as otherwise provided for therein, see section 235 of Pub.L. 98-473, as amended, set out as a note under section 3551 of this title.

§ 3564. Running of a term of probation

(a) Commencement.–A term of probation commences on the day that the sentence of probation is imposed, unless otherwise ordered by the court.

(b) Concurrence with other sentences.–Multiple terms of probation, whether imposed at the same time or at different times, run concurrently with each other. A term of probation runs concurrently with any Federal, State, or local term of probation, supervised release, or parole for another offense to which the defendant is subject or becomes subject during the term of probation. A term of probation does not run while the defendant is imprisoned in connection with a conviction for a Federal, State, or local crime unless the imprisonment is for a period of less than thirty consecutive days.

(c) Early termination.–The court, after considering the factors set forth in section 3553(a) to the extent that they are applicable, may, pursuant to the provisions of the Federal Rules of Criminal Procedure relating to the modification of probation, terminate a term of probation previously ordered and discharge the defendant at any time in the case of a misdemeanor or an infraction or at any time after the expiration of one year of probation in the case of a felony, if it is satisfied that such action is warranted by the conduct of the defendant and the interest of justice.

(d) Extension.–The court may, after a hearing, extend a term of probation, if less than the maximum authorized term was previously imposed, at any time prior to the expiration or termination of the term of probation, pursuant to the provisions applicable to the initial setting of the term of probation.

(e) Subject to revocation.–A sentence of probation remains conditional and subject to revocation until its expiration or termination.

(Added Pub.L. 98-473, Title II, § 212(a)(2), Oct. 12, 1984, 98 Stat. 1994, and amended Pub.L. 99-646, § 13(a), Nov. 10, 1986, 100 Stat. 3594; Pub.L. 100-182, § 11, Dec. 7, 1987, 101 Stat. 1268.)

EDITORIAL NOTES

Effective Date of 1987 Amendment. Amendment by Pub.L. 100-182 applicable with respect to offenses committed after enactment of Pub.L. 100-182, which was approved Dec. 7, 1987, see section 26 of Pub.L. 100-182.

Effective Date of 1986 Amendment. Section 13(b) of Pub.L. 99-646 provided that: "The amendments made by this section [amending subsec. (b) of this section] shall take effect on the date of the taking effect of such section 3564 [this section]."

Effective Date. Section effective on the first day of first calendar month beginning thirty six months after Oct. 12, 1984, applicable only to offenses committed after taking effect of sections 211 to 239 of Pub.L. 98-473, and except as otherwise provided for therein, see section 235 of Pub.L. 98-473, as amended, set out as a note under section 3551 of this title.

§ 3565. Revocation of probation

(a) Continuation or revocation.–If the defendant violates a condition of probation at any time prior to the expiration or termination of the term of probation, the court may, after a hearing pursuant to Rule 32.1 of the Federal Rules of Criminal Procedure, and after considering the factors set forth in section 3553(a) to the extent that they are applicable–

(1) continue him on probation, with or without extending the term or modifying or enlarging the conditions; or

(2) revoke the sentence of probation and resentence the defendant under subchapter A.

(b) Mandatory Revocation for Possession of Controlled Substance or Firearm or Refusal to Comply With Drug Testing.–If the defendant–

(1) possesses a controlled substance in violation of the condition set forth in section 3563(a)(3);

(2) possesses a firearm, as such term is defined in section 921 of this title, in violation of Federal law, or otherwise violates a condition of probation prohibiting the defendant from possessing a firearm; or

(3) refuses to comply with drug testing, thereby violating the condition imposed by section 3563(a)(4), the court shall revoke the sentence of probation and resentence the defendant under subchapter A to a sentence that includes a term of imprisonment.

(c) Delayed revocation.–The power of the court to revoke a sentence of probation for violation of a condition of probation, and to impose another sentence, extends beyond the expiration of the term of probation for any period reasonably necessary for the adjudication of matters arising before its expiration if, prior to its expiration, a warrant or summons has been issued on the basis of an allegation of such a violation.

(Added Pub.L. 98-473, Title II, § 212(a)(2), Oct. 12, 1984, 98 Stat. 1995, amended Pub.L. 100-690, Title VI, § 6214, Title VII, § 7303(a)(2), Nov. 18, 1988, 102 Stat. 4361, 4464; Pub.L. 101-647, Title XXXV, § 3585, Nov. 29, 1990, 104 Stat. 4930; Pub.L. 103-322, Title XI § 110506, Sept. 13, 1994, 108 Stat. __.)

EDITORIAL NOTES

Effective Date of 1988 Amendment. Amendment by section 7303(a)(2) of Pub.L. 100-690 applicable with respect to persons whose probation, supervised release, or parole begins after Dec. 31, 1988, see section 7303(d) of Pub.L. 100-690, set out as a note under section 3563 of this title.

Effective Date. Section effective on the first day of first calendar month beginning thirty six months after Oct. 12, 1984, applicable only to offenses committed after taking effect of sections 211 to 239 of Pub.L. 98-473, and except as otherwise provided for therein, see section 235 of Pub.L. 98-473, as amended, set out as a note under section 3551 of this title.

§ 3566. Implementation of a sentence of probation

The implementation of a sentence of probation is governed by the provisions of subchapter A of chapter 229.

(Added Pub.L. 98-473, Title II, § 212(a)(2), Oct. 12, 1984, 98 Stat. 1995.)

EDITORIAL NOTES

Effective Date. Section effective on the first day of first calendar month beginning thirty six months after Oct. 12, 1984, applicable only to offenses committed after taking effect of sections 211 to 239 of Pub.L. 98-473, and except as otherwise provided for therein, see section 235 of Pub.L. 98-473, as amended, set out as a note under section 3551 of this title.

SUBCHAPTER C–FINES

Section

§ 3571. Sentence of fine

(a) In general.–A defendant who has been found guilty of an offense may be sentenced to pay a fine.

(b) Fines for individuals.–Except as provided in subsection (e) of this section, an individual who has been found guilty of an offense may be fined not more than the greatest of–

(1) the amount specified in the law setting forth the offense;
(2) the applicable amount under subsection (d) of this section;
(3) for a felony, not more than $250,000;
(4) for a misdemeanor resulting in death, not more than $250,000;
(5) for a Class A misdemeanor that does not result in death, not more than $100,000;
(6) for a Class B or C misdemeanor that does not result in death, not more than $5,000; or
(7) for an infraction, not more than $5,000.

(c) Fines for organizations.–Except as provided in subsection (e) of this section, an organization that has been found guilty of an offense may be fined not more than the greatest of–

(1) the amount specified in the law setting forth the offense;
(2) the applicable amount under subsection (d) of this section;
(3) for a felony, not more than $500,000;
(4) for a misdemeanor resulting in death, not more than $500,000;
(5) for a Class A misdemeanor that does not result in death, not more than $200,000;
(6) for a Class B or C misdemeanor that does not result in death, not more than $10,000; and
(7) for an infraction, not more than $10,000.

(d) Alternative fine based on gain or loss.–If any person derives pecuniary gain from the offense, or if the offense results in pecuniary loss to a person other than the defendant, the defendant may be fined not more than the greater of twice the gross gain or twice the gross loss, unless imposition of a fine under this subsection would unduly complicate or prolong the sentencing process.

(e) Special rule for lower fine specified in substantive provision.–If a law setting forth an offense specifies no fine or a fine that is lower than the fine otherwise applicable under this section and such law, by specific reference, exempts the offense from the applicability of the fine otherwise applicable under this section, the defendant may not be fined more than the amount specified in the law setting forth the offense.

(Added Pub.L. 98-473, Title II, § 212(a)(2), Oct. 12, 1984, 98 Stat. 1995, and amended Pub.L. 100-185, § 6, Dec. 11, 1987, 101 Stat. 1280.)

EDITORIAL NOTES

Effective Date. Section effective on the first day of first calendar month beginning thirty six months after Oct. 12, 1984, applicable only to offenses committed after taking effect of sections 211 to 239 of Pub.L. 98-473, and except as otherwise provided for therein, see section 235 of Pub.L. 98-473, as amended, set out as a note under section 3551 of this title.

§ 3572. Imposition of a sentence of fine and related matters

(a) Factors to be considered.–In determining whether to impose a fine, and the amount, time for payment, and method of payment of a fine, the court shall consider, in addition to the factors set forth in section 3553(a)–

(1) the defendant's income, earning capacity, and financial resources;

(2) the burden that the fine will impose upon the defendant, any person who is financially dependent on the defendant, or any other person (including a government) that would be responsible for the welfare of any person financially dependent on the defendant, relative to the burden that alternative punishments would impose;

(3) any pecuniary loss inflicted upon others as a result of the offense;

(4) whether restitution is ordered or made and the amount of such restitution;

(5) the need to deprive the defendant of illegally obtained gains from the offense;

(6) the expected costs to the government of any imprisonment, supervised release, or probation component of the sentence;

(7) whether the defendant can pass on to consumers or other persons the expense of the fine; and

(8) if the defendant is an organization, the size of the organization and any measure taken by the organization to discipline any officer, director, employee, or agent of the organization responsible for the offense and to prevent a recurrence of such an offense.

(b) Fine not to impair ability to make restitution.–If, as a result of a conviction, the defendant has the obligation to make restitution to a victim of the offense, the court shall impose a fine or other monetary penalty only to the extent that such fine or penalty will not impair the ability of the defendant to make restitution.

(c) Effect of finality of judgment.–Notwithstanding the fact that a sentence to pay a fine can subsequently be–

(1) modified or remitted under section 3573;
(2) corrected under rule 35 of the Federal Rules of Criminal Procedure and section 3742; or
(3) appealed and modified under section 3742;

a judgment that includes such a sentence is a final judgment for all other purposes.

(d) Time, method of payment, and related items.–A person sentenced to pay a fine or other monetary penalty shall make such payment immediately, unless, in the interest of justice, the court provides for payment on a date certain or in installments. If the court provides for payment in installments, the installments shall be in equal monthly payments over the period provided by the court, unless the court establishes another schedule. If the judgment permits other than immediate payment, the period provided for shall not exceed five years, excluding any period served by the defendant as imprisonment for the offense.

(e) Alternative sentence precluded.–At the time a defendant is sentenced to pay a fine, the court may not impose an alternative sentence to be carried out if the fine is not paid.

(f) Responsibility for payment of monetary obligation relating to organization.–If a sentence includes a fine, special assessment, or other monetary obligation (including interest) with respect to an organization, each individual authorized to make disbursements for the organization has a duty to pay the obligation from assets of the organization. If such an obligation is imposed on a director, officer, shareholder, employee, or agent of an organization, payments may not be made, directly or indirectly, from assets of the organization, unless the court finds that such payment is expressly permissible under applicable State law.

(g) Security for stayed fine.–If a sentence imposing a fine is stayed, the court shall, absent exceptional circumstances (as determined by the court)–

(1) require the defendant to deposit, in the registry of the district court, any amount of the fine that is due;
(2) require the defendant to provide a bond or other security to ensure payment of the fine; or
(3) restrain the defendant from transferring or dissipating assets.

(h) Delinquency.–A fine is delinquent if a payment is more than 30 days late.

(i) Default.–A fine is in default if a payment is delinquent for more than 90 days. When a fine is in default, the entire amount of the fine is due within 30 days after notification of the default, notwithstanding any installment schedule.

[(j) Redesignated (i)]

(Added Pub.L. 98-473, Title II, § 212(a)(2), Oct. 12, 1984, 98 Stat. 1995, and amended Pub.L. 100-185, § 7, Dec. 11, 1987, 101 Stat. 1280; Pub.L. 101-647, Title XXXV, § 3587, Nov. 29, 1990, 104 Stat. 4930; Pub.L. 103-322, Title II, § 20403(a), Sept. 13, 1994, 108 Stat. __.)

EDITORIAL NOTES

Effective Date. Section effective on the first day of first calendar month beginning thirty six months after Oct. 12, 1984, applicable only to offenses committed after taking effect of sections 211 to 239 of Pub.L. 98-473, and except as otherwise provided for therein, see section 235 of Pub.L. 98-473, as amended, set out as a note under section 3551 of this title.

§ 3573. Petition of the Government for modification or remission

Upon petition of the Government showing that reasonable efforts to collect a fine or assessment are not likely to be effective, the court may, in the interest of justice–

(1) remit all or part of the unpaid portion of the fine or special assessment, including interest and penalties;

(2) defer payment of the fine or special assessment to a date certain or pursuant to an installment schedule; or

(3) extend a date certain or an installment schedule previously ordered.

A petition under this subsection shall be filed in the court in which sentence was originally imposed, unless the court transfers jurisdiction to another court. This section shall apply to all fines and assessments irrespective of the date of imposition.

(Added Pub.L. 98-473, Title II, § 212(a)(2), Oct. 12, 1984, 98 Stat. 1997, and amended Pub.L. 100-185, § 8(a), Dec. 11, 1987, 101 Stat. 1282; Pub.L. 100-690, Title VII, § 7082(a), Nov. 18, 1988, 102 Stat. 4407.)

EDITORIAL NOTES

Effective Date. Section effective on the first day of first calendar month beginning thirty six months after Oct. 12, 1984, applicable only to offenses committed after taking effect of sections 211 to 239 of Pub.L. 98-473, and except as otherwise provided for therein, see section 235 of Pub.L. 98-473, as amended, set out as a note under section 3551 of this title.

§ 3574. Implementation of a sentence of fine

The implementation of a sentence to pay a fine is governed by the provisions of subchapter B of chapter 229.

(Added Pub.L. 98-473, Title II, § 212(a)(2), Oct. 12, 1984, 98 Stat. 1997.)

EDITORIAL NOTES

Effective Date. Section effective on the first day of first calendar month beginning thirty six months after Oct. 12, 1984, applicable only to offenses committed after taking effect of sections 211 to 239 of Pub.L. 98-473, and except as otherwise provided for therein, see section 235 of Pub.L. 98-473, as amended, set out as a note under section 3551 of this title.

SUBCHAPTER D–IMPRISONMENT

Section

§ 3581. Sentence of imprisonment

(a) In general.–A defendant who has been found guilty of an offense may be sentenced to a term of imprisonment.

(b) Authorized terms.–The authorized terms of imprisonment are–

(1) for a Class A felony, the duration of the defendant's life or any period of time;
(2) for a Class B felony, not more than twenty-five years;
(3) for a Class C felony, not more than twelve years;
(4) for a Class D felony, not more than six years;
(5) for a Class E felony, not more than three years;
(6) for a Class A misdemeanor, not more than one year;
(7) for a Class B misdemeanor, not more than six months;
(8) for a Class C misdemeanor, not more than thirty days; and
(9) for an infraction, not more than five days.

(Added Pub.L. 98-473, Title II, § 212(a)(2), Oct. 12, 1984, 98 Stat. 1998.)

EDITORIAL NOTES

Effective Date. Section effective on the first day of first calendar month beginning thirty six months after Oct. 12, 1984, applicable only to offenses committed after taking effect of sections 211 to 239 of Pub.L. 98-473, and except as otherwise provided for therein, see section 235 of Pub.L. 98-473, as amended, set out as a note under section 3551 of this title.

§ 3582. Imposition of a sentence of imprisonment

(a) Factors to be considered in imposing a term of imprisonment.–The court, in determining whether to impose a term of imprisonment, and, if a term of imprisonment is to be imposed, in determining the length of the term, shall consider the factors set forth in section 3553(a) to the extent that they are applicable, recognizing that imprisonment is not an appropriate means of promoting correction and rehabilitation. In determining whether to make a recommendation concerning the type of prison facility appropriate for the defendant, the court shall consider any pertinent policy statements issued by the Sentencing Commission pursuant to 28 U.S.C. 994(a)(2).

(b) Effect of finality of judgment.–Notwithstanding the fact that a sentence to imprisonment can subsequently be–

(1) modified pursuant to the provisions of subsection (c);
(2) corrected pursuant to the provisions of rule 35 of the Federal Rules of Criminal Procedure and section 3742; or
(3) appealed and modified, if outside the guideline range, pursuant to the provisions of section 3742;

a judgment of conviction that includes such a sentence constitutes a final judgment for all other purposes.

(c) Modification of an imposed term of imprisonment.–The court may not modify a term of imprisonment once it has been imposed except that–

(1) in any case–

(A) the court, upon motion of the Director of the Bureau of Prisons, may reduce the term of imprisonment, after considering the factors set forth in section 3553(a) to the extent that they are applicable, if it finds that–

(i) extraordinary and compelling reasons warrant such a reduction;

(ii) the defendant is at least 70 years of age, has served at least 30 year in prison, pursuant to a sentence imposed under section 3559(c), for the offense or offenses for which the defendant is currently imprisoned, and a determination has been made by the Director of the Bureau of Prisons that the defendant is not a danger to the safety of any other person or the community, as provided under section 3142(g);

and that such a reduction is consistent with applicable policy statements issued by the Sentencing Commission; and

(B) the court may modify an imposed term of imprisonment to the extent otherwise expressly permitted by statute or by Rule 35 of the Federal Rules of Criminal Procedure; and

(2) in the case of a defendant who has been sentenced to a term of imprisonment based on a sentencing range that has subsequently been lowered by the Sentencing Commission pursuant to 28 U.S.C. 994(*o*), upon motion of the defendant or the Director of the Bureau of Prisons, or on its own motion, the court may reduce the term of imprisonment, after considering the factors set forth in section 3553(a) to the extent that they are applicable, if such a reduction is consistent with applicable policy statements issued by the Sentencing Commission.

(d) Inclusion of an order to limit criminal association of organized crime and drug offenders.–The court, in imposing a sentence to a term of imprisonment upon a defendant convicted of a felony set forth in chapter 95 (racketeering) or 96 (racketeer influenced and corrupt organizations) of this title or in the Comprehensive Drug Abuse Prevention and Control Act of 1970 (21 U.S.C. 801 et seq.), or at any time thereafter upon motion by the Director of the Bureau of Prisons or a United States attorney, may include as a part of the sentence an order that requires that the defendant not associate or communicate with a specified person, other than his attorney, upon a showing of probable cause to believe that association or communication with such person is for the purpose of enabling the defendant to control, manage, direct, finance, or otherwise participate in an illegal enterprise.

(Added Pub.L. 98-473, Title II, § 212(a)(2), Oct. 12, 1984, 98 Stat. 1998, amended Pub.L. 100-690, Title VII, § 7107, Nov. 18, 1988, 102 Stat. 4418; Pub.L. 101-647, Title XXXV, § 3588, Nov. 29, 1990, 104 Stat. 4930; Pub.L. 103-322, Title VII, § 70002, Sept. 13, 1994, 108 Stat. __.)

EDITORIAL NOTES

Effective Date. Section effective on the first day of first calendar month beginning thirty six months after Oct. 12, 1984, applicable only to offenses committed after taking effect of sections 211 to 239 of Pub.L. 98-473, and except as otherwise provided for therein, see section 235 of Pub.L. 98-473, as amended, set out as a note under section 3551 of this title.

§ 3583. Inclusion of a term of supervised release after imprisonment

(a) In general.–The court, in imposing a sentence to a term of imprisonment for a felony or a misdemeanor, may include as a part of the sentence a requirement that the defendant be placed on a term of supervised release after imprisonment, except that the court shall include as a part of the sentence a requirement that the defendant be placed on a term of supervised release if such a term is required by statute or if the defendant has been convicted for the first time of a domestic violence crime as defined in section 3561(b).

(b) Authorized terms of supervised release.–Except as otherwise provided, the authorized terms of supervised release are–

(1) for a Class A or Class B felony, not more than five years;

(2) for a Class C or Class D felony, not more than three years; and

(3) for a Class E felony, or for a misdemeanor (other than a petty offense), not more than one year.

(c) Factors to be considered in including a term of supervised release.–The court, in determining whether to include a term of supervised release, and, if a term of supervised release is to be included, in determining the length of the term and the conditions of supervised release, shall consider the factors set forth in section 3553(a)(1), (a)(2)(B), (a)(2)(C), (a)(2)(D), (a)(4), (a)(5), and (a)(6).

(d) Conditions of supervised release.–The court shall order, as an explicit condition of supervised release, that the defendant not commit another Federal, State, or local crime during the term of supervision and that the defendant not unlawfully possess a controlled substance. The court shall order as an explicit condition of supervised release for a defendant convicted for the first time of a domestic violence crime as defined in section 3561(b) that the defendant attend a public, private, or private nonprofit offender rehabilitation program that has been approved by the court, in consultation with a State Coalition Against Domestic Violence or other appropriate experts, if an approved program is readily available within a 50-mile radius of the legal residence of the defendant. The court shall also order, as an explicit condition of supervised release, that the defendant refrain from any unlawful use of a controlled substance and submit to a drug test within 15 days of release on supervised release and at least 2 periodic drug tests thereafter (as determined by the court) for use of a controlled substance. The condition stated in the preceding sentence may be ameliorated or suspended by the court as provided in section 3563(a)(4). The results of a drug test administered in accordance with the preceding subsection shall be subject to confirmation only if the results are positive, the defendant is subject to possible imprisonment for such failure, and either the defendant denies the accuracy of such test or there is some other reason to question the results of the test. A drug test confirmation shall be a urine drug test confirmed using gas chromatography/mass spectrometry techniques or such test as the Director of the Administrative Office of the United States Courts after consultation with the Secretary of Health and Human Services may determine to be of equivalent accuracy. The court shall consider whether the availability of appropriate substance abuse treatment programs, or an individual's current or past participation in such programs, warrants an exception in accordance with United States Sentencing Commission guidelines from the rule of section 3583(g) when considering any action against a defendant who fails a drug test. The court may order, as a further condition of supervised release, to the extent that such condition–

(1) is reasonably related to the factors set forth in section 3553(a)(1), (a)(2)(B), (a)(2)(C), and (a)(2)(D);

(2) involves no greater deprivation of liberty than is reasonably necessary for the purposes set forth in section 3553(a)(2)(B), (a)(2)(C), and (a)(2)(D); and

(3) is consistent with any pertinent policy statements issued by the Sentencing Commission pursuant to 28 U.S.C. 994(a);

any condition set forth as a discretionary condition of probation in section 3563(b)(1) through (b)(10) and (b)(12) through (b)(20), and any other condition it considers to be appropriate. If an alien defendant is subject to deportation, the court may provide, as a condition of supervised release, that he be deported and remain outside the United States, and may order that he be delivered to a duly authorized immigration official for such deportation.

(e) Modification of conditions or revocation.–The court may, after considering the factors set forth in section 3553(a)(1), (a)(2)(B), (a)(2)(C), (a)(2)(D), (a)(4), (a)(5), and (a)(6)–

(1) terminate a term of supervised release and discharge the defendant released[1] at any time after the expiration of one year of supervised release, pursuant to the provisions of the Federal Rules of Criminal Procedure relating to the modification of probation, if it is satisfied that such action is warranted by the conduct of the defendant released[1] and the interest of justice;

(2) extend a term of supervised release if less than the maximum authorized term was previously imposed, and may modify, reduce, or enlarge the conditions of supervised release, at any time prior to the expiration or termination of the term of supervised release, pursuant to the provisions of the Federal Rules of Criminal Procedure relating to the modification of probation and the provisions applicable to the initial setting of the terms and conditions of post-release supervision;

(3) revoke a term of supervised release, and require the defendant to serve in prison all or part of the term of supervised release authorized by statute for the offense that resulted in such term of supervised release without credit for time previously served on postrelease supervision, if the court, pursuant to the Federal Rules of Criminal Procedure applicable to revocation of probation or supervised release, finds by a preponderance of the evidence that the defendant violated a condition of supervised release, except that a defendant whose term is revoked under this paragraph may not be required to serve more than 5 years in prison if the offense that resulted in the term of supervised release is a class A felony, more than 3 years

---

[1]So in original. Probably "defendant released" should be "defendant".

in prison if such offense is a class B felony, more than 2 years in prison if such offense is a class C or D felony, or more than one year in any other case; or

(4) order the defendant to remain at his place of residence during nonworking hours and, if the court so directs, to have compliance monitored by telephone or electronic signaling devices, except that an order under this paragraph may be imposed only as an alternative to incarceration.

(f) Written statement of conditions.–The court shall direct that the probation officer provide the defendant with a written statement that sets forth all the conditions to which the term of supervised release is subject, and that is sufficiently clear and specific to serve as a guide for the defendant's conduct and for such supervision as is required.

(g) Mandatory Revocation for Possession of Controlled Substance or Firearm or for Refusal to Comply With Drug Testing.–If the defendant–

(1) possesses a controlled substance in violation of the condition set forth in subsection (d);

(2) possesses a firearm, as such term is defined in section 921 of this title, in violation of Federal law, or otherwise violates a condition of supervised release prohibiting the defendant from possessing a firearm; or

(3) refuses to comply with drug testing imposed as a condition of supervised release;

the court shall revoke the term of supervised release and require the defendant to serve a term of imprisonment not to exceed the maximum term of imprisonment authorized under subsection (e)(3).

(h) Supervised Release Following Revocation.–When a term of supervise release is revoked and the defendant is required to serve a term of imprisonment that is less than the maximum term of imprisonment authorized under subsection (e)(3), the court may include a requirement that the defendant be placed on a term of supervised release after imprisonment. The length of such a term of supervised release shall not exceed the term of supervised release authorized by statute for the offense that resulted in the original term of supervised release, less any term of imprisonment that was imposed upon revocation of supervised release.

(i) Delayed Revocation.–The power of the court to revoke a term of supervised release for violation for a condition of supervised release, and to order the defendant to serve a term of imprisonment and, subject to the limitations in subsection (h), a further term of supervised release, extends beyond the expiration of the term of supervised release for any period reasonably necessary for the adjudication of matters arising before its expiration if, before its expiration, a warrant or summons has been issued on the basis of an allegation of such a violation.

(Added Pub.L. 98-473, Title II, § 212(a)(2), Oct. 12, 1984, 98 Stat. 1999, and amended Pub.L. 99-570, Title I, § 1006(a), Oct. 27, 1986, 100 Stat. 3207-6, 3207-7; Pub.L. 99-646, § 14(a), Nov. 10, 1986, 100 Stat. 3594; Pub.L. 100-182, §§ 8, 9, 12, 25, Dec. 7, 1987, 101 Stat. 1267, 1268, 1272; Pub.L. 100-690, Title VII, §§ 7108, 7303(b), 7305(b), Nov. 18, 1988, 102 Stat. 4418, 4419, 4464-4466; Pub.L. 101-647, Title XXXV, § 3589, Nov. 29, 1990, 104 Stat. 4930; Pub.L. 103-322, Title II, § 20414(c), Title XI, § 110505, Title XXXII, § 320921(c), Sept. 13, 1994, 108 Stat.__, __, __.)

EDITORIAL NOTES

Codification. Amendment by section 7108(a)(2) of Pub.L. 100-690 to subsec. (d)(2), which directed that "(a)(2)(C)," be inserted after "(a)(2)(B),", was executed by inserting "(a)(2)(C)," after "(a)(2)(B)" since no comma appeared after "(a)(2)(B)".

Amendment by section 7305(b)(2) of Pub.L. 100-690 to subsec. (e) which struck out "or" at the end of par. (3), struck out the period at the end of par. (4) and inserted "; or", and added par. (5) could not be completely executed in view of prior amendment to such provision by section 7108(b) of Pub.L. 100-690 which redesignated former par. (4) as (3) thereby resulting in no par. (4) amended.

Amendment by section 14(a)(1) of Pub.L. 99-646 to subsec. (e) catchline duplicates amendment to such subsection catchline made by Pub.L. 99-570, § 1006(a)(3)(A).

Effective Date of 1988 Amendment. Amendment by section 7303(b) of Pub.L. 100-690 applicable with respect to persons whose probation, supervised release, or parole begins after Dec. 31, 1988, see section 7303(d) of Pub.L. 100-690, set out as a note under section 3563 of this title.

Effective Date of 1987 Amendment. Amendment by Pub.L. 100-182 applicable with respect to offenses committed after enactment of Pub.L. 100-182, which was approved Dec. 7, 1987, see section 26 of Pub.L. 100-182.

Effective Date of 1986 Amendment. Section 14(b) of Pub.L. 99-646 provided that: "The amendments made by this section [amending subsec. (e) of this section] shall take effect on the date of the taking effect of section 3583 of title 18, United States Code [this section]."

Section 1006(a)(4) of Pub.L. 99-570 provided that: "The amendments made by this subsection [amending this section] shall take effect on the date of the taking effect of section 3583 of title 18, United States Code [this section]."

Effective Date. Section effective on the first day of first calendar month beginning thirty six months after Oct. 12, 1984, applicable only to offenses committed after taking effect of sections 211 to 239 of Pub.L. 98-473, and except as otherwise provided for therein, see section 235 of Pub.L. 98-473, as amended, set out as a note under section 3551 of this title.

§ 3584. Multiple sentences of imprisonment

(a) Imposition of concurrent or consecutive terms.–If multiple terms of imprisonment are imposed on a defendant at the same time, or if a term of imprisonment is imposed on a defendant who is already subject to an undischarged term of imprisonment, the terms may run concurrently or consecutively, except that the terms may not run consecutively for an attempt and for another offense that was the sole objective of the attempt. Multiple terms of imprisonment imposed at the same time run concurrently unless the court orders or the statute mandates that the terms are to run consecutively. Multiple terms of imprisonment imposed at different times run consecutively unless the court orders that the terms are to run concurrently.

(b) Factors to be considered in imposing concurrent or consecutive terms.–The court, in determining whether the terms imposed are to be ordered to run concurrently or consecutively, shall consider, as to each offense for which a term of imprisonment is being imposed, the factors set forth in section 3553(a).

(c) Treatment of multiple sentence as an aggregate.–Multiple terms of imprisonment ordered to run consecutively or concurrently shall be treated for administrative purposes as a single, aggregate term of imprisonment.

(Added Pub.L. 98-473, Title II, § 212(a)(2), Oct. 12, 1984, 98 Stat. 2000.)

EDITORIAL NOTES

Effective Date. Section effective on the first day of first calendar month beginning thirty six months after Oct. 12, 1984, applicable only to offenses committed after taking effect of sections 211 to 239 of Pub.L. 98-473, and except as otherwise provided for therein, see section 235 of Pub.L. 98-473, as amended, set out as a note under section 3551 of this title.

§ 3585. Calculation of a term of imprisonment

(a) Commencement of sentence.–A sentence to a term of imprisonment commences on the date the defendant is received in custody awaiting transportation to, or arrives voluntarily to commence service of sentence at, the official detention facility at which the sentence is to be served.

(b) Credit for prior custody.–A defendant shall be given credit toward the service of a term of imprisonment for any time he has spent in official detention prior to the date the sentence commences–

(1) as a result of the offense for which the sentence was imposed; or

(2) as a result of any other charge for which the defendant was arrested after the commission of the offense for which the sentence was imposed;

that has not been credited against another sentence.

(Added Pub.L. 98-473, Title II, § 212(a)(2), Oct. 12, 1984, 98 Stat. 2001.)

EDITORIAL NOTES

Effective Date. Section effective on the first day of first calendar month beginning thirty six months after Oct. 12, 1984, applicable only to offenses committed after taking effect of sections 211 to 239 of Pub.L. 98-473, and except as otherwise provided for therein, see section 235 of Pub.L. 98-473, as amended, set out as a note under section 3551 of this title.

§ 3586. Implementation of a sentence of imprisonment

The implementation of a sentence of imprisonment is governed by the provisions of subchapter C of chapter 229 and, if the sentence includes a term of supervised release, by the provisions of subchapter A of chapter 229.

(Added Pub.L. 98-473, Title II, § 212(a)(2), Oct. 12, 1984, 98 Stat. 2001.)

EDITORIAL NOTES

Effective Date. Section effective on the first day of first calendar month beginning thirty six months after Oct. 12, 1984, applicable only to offenses committed after taking effect of sections 211 to 239 of Pub.L. 98-473, and except as otherwise provided for therein, see section 235 of Pub.L. 98-473, as amended, set out as a note under section 3551 of this title.

CHAPTER 229[1]–POSTSENTENCE ADMINISTRATION

SUBCHAPTER C–IMPRISONMENT

* * *

§ 3621. Imprisonment of a convicted person

(a) Commitment to custody of Bureau of Prisons.–A person who has been sentenced to a term of imprisonment pursuant to the provisions of subchapter D of chapter 227 shall be committed to the custody of the Bureau of Prisons until the expiration of the term imposed, or until earlier released for satisfactory behavior pursuant to the provisions of section 3624.

(b) Place of imprisonment.–The Bureau of Prisons shall designate the place of the prisoner's imprisonment. The Bureau may designate any available penal or correctional facility that meets minimum standards of health and habitability established by the Bureau, whether maintained by the Federal Government or otherwise and whether within or without the judicial district in which the person was convicted, that the Bureau determines to be appropriate and suitable, considering–

[1]Another chapter 229 "FINES, PENALTIES, AND FORFEITURES" (§§ 3611 to 3624) was repealed, effective Nov. 1, 1987.

(1) the resources of the facility contemplated;
(2) the nature and circumstances of the offense;
(3) the history and characteristics of the prisoner;
(4) any statement by the court that imposed the sentence–
(A) concerning the purposes for which the sentence to imprisonment was determined to be warranted; or
(B) recommending a type of penal or correctional facility as appropriate; and
(5) any pertinent policy statement issued by the Sentencing Commission pursuant to section 994(a)(2) of title 28.

In designating the place of imprisonment or making transfers under this subsection, there shall be no favoritism given to prisoners of high social or economic status. The Bureau may at any time, having regard for the same matters, direct the transfer of a prisoner from one penal or correctional facility to another. The Bureau shall make available appropriate substance abuse treatment for each prisoner the Bureau determines has a treatable condition of substance addiction or abuse.

(c) Delivery of order of commitment.–When a prisoner, pursuant to a court order, is placed in the custody of a person in charge of a penal or correctional facility, a copy of the order shall be delivered to such person as evidence of this authority to hold the prisoner, and the original order, with the return endorsed thereon, shall be returned to the court that issued it.

(d) Delivery of prisoner for court appearances.–The United States marshal shall, without charge, bring a prisoner into court or return him to a prison facility on order of a court of the United States or on written request of an attorney for the Government.

(e) Substance Abuse Treatment.–

(1) Phase-In.–In order to carry out the requirement of the last sentence of subsection (b) of this section, that every prisoner with a substance abuse problem have the opportunity to participate in appropriate substance abuse treatment, the Bureau of Prisons shall, subject to the availability of appropriations, provide residential substance abuse treatment (and make arrangements for appropriate aftercare)–

(A) for not less than 50 percent of eligible prisoners by the end of fiscal year 1995, with priority for such treatment accorded based on an eligible prisoner's proximity to release date;

(B) for not less than 75 percent of eligible prisoners by the end of fiscal year 1996, with priority for such treatment accorded based on an eligible prisoner's proximity to release date; and

(C) for all eligible prisoners by the end of fiscal year 1997 and thereafter, with priority for such treatment accorded based on an eligible prisoner's proximity to release date.

(2) Incentive for prisoners' successful completion of treatment program.–

(A) Generally.–Any prisoner who, in the judgment of the Director of the Bureau of Prisons, has successfully completed a program of residential substance abuse treatment provided under paragraph (1) of this subsection, shall remain in the custody of the Bureau under such conditions as the Bureau deems appropriate. If the conditions of confinement are different from those the prisoner would have experienced absent the successful completion of the treatment, the Bureau shall periodically test the prisoner for substance abuse and discontinue such conditions on determining that substance abuse has recurred.

(B) Period of custody.–The period a prisoner convicted of a nonviolent offense remains in custody after successfully completing a treatment program may be reduced by the Bureau of Prisons, but such reduction may not be more than one year from the term the prisoner must otherwise serve.

(3) Report.–The Bureau of Prisons shall transmit to the Committees on the Judiciary of the Senate and the House of Representatives on January 1, 1995, and on January 1 of each year thereafter, a report. Such report shall contain–

(A) a detailed quantitative and qualitative description of each substance abuse treatment program, residential or not, operated by the Bureau;

(B) a full explanation of how eligibility for such programs is determined, with complete information on what proportion of prisoners with substance abuse problems are eligible; and

(C) a complete statement of to what extent the Bureau has achieved compliance with the requirements of this title.

(4) Authorization of appropriations.–There are authorized to be appropriate to carry out this subsection–

(A) $13,500,000 for fiscal year 1996;

(B) $18,900,000 for fiscal year 1997;

(C) $25,200,000 for fiscal year 1998;

(D) $27,000,000 for fiscal year 1999; and

(E) $27,900,000 for fiscal year 2000.

(5) Definitions.–As used in this subsection–

(A) the term "residential substance abuse treatment" means a course of individual and group activities, lasting between 6 and 12 months, in residential treatment facilities set apart from the general prison population–

(i) directed at the substance abuse problems of the prisoner; and

(ii) intended to develop the prisoner's cognitive, behavioral, social, vocational, and other skills so as to solve the prisoner's substance abuse and related problems;

(B) the term "eligible prisoner" means a prisoner who is–

(i) determined by the Bureau of Prisons to have a substance abuse problem; and

(ii) willing to participate in a residential substance abuse treatment program; and

(C) the term "aftercare" means placement, case management and monitoring of the participants in a community-based substance abuse treatment program when the participant leaves the custody of the Bureau of Prisons.

(6) Coordination of federal assistance.–The Bureau of Prisons shall consult with the Department of Health and Human Services concerning substance abuse treatment and related services and the incorporation of applicable components existing comprehensive approaches including relapse prevention and aftercare services.

(Added Pub.L. 98-473, Title II, § 212(a)(2), Oct. 12, 1984, 98 Stat. 2007, and amended Pub.L. 101-647, Title XXIX, § 2903, Nov. 29, 1990, 104 Stat. 4913; Pub.L. 103-322, Title II, § 20401, Title III § 32001, Sept. 13, 1994, 108 Stat. __, __.)

EDITORIAL NOTES

Effective Date. Section effective on the first day of first calendar month beginning thirty six months after Oct. 12, 1984, applicable only to offenses committed after taking effect of sections 211 to 239 of Pub.L. 98-473, and except as otherwise provided for therein, see section 235 of Pub.L. 98-473, as amended, set out as a note under section 3551 of this title.

§ 3622. Temporary release of a prisoner

The Bureau of Prisons may release a prisoner from the place of his imprisonment for a limited period if such release appears to be consistent with the purpose for which the sentence was imposed and any pertinent policy statement issued by the Sentencing Commission pursuant to 28 U.S.C. 994(a)(2), if such release otherwise appears to be consistent with the public interest and if there is reasonable cause to believe that a prisoner will honor the trust to be imposed in him, by authorizing him, under prescribed conditions, to–

(a) visit a designated place for a period not to exceed thirty days, and

then return to the same or another facility, for the purpose of–

(1) visiting a relative who is dying;

(2) attending a funeral of a relative;

(3) obtaining medical treatment not otherwise available;

(4) contacting a prospective employer;

(5) establishing or reestablishing family or community ties; or

(6) engaging in any other significant activity consistent with the public interest;

(b) participate in a training or educational program in the community while continuing in official detention at the prison facility; or

(c) work at paid employment in the community while continuing in official detention at the penal or correctional facility if–

(1) the rates of pay and other conditions of employment will not be less than those paid or provided for work of a similar nature in the community; and

(2) the prisoner agrees to pay to the Bureau such costs incident to official detention as the Bureau finds appropriate and reasonable under all the circumstances, such costs to be collected by the Bureau and deposited in the Treasury to the credit of the appropriation available for such costs at the time such collections are made.

(Added Pub.L. 98-473, Title II, § 212(a)(2), Oct. 12, 1984, 98 Stat. 2007.)

EDITORIAL NOTES

Effective Date. Section effective on the first day of first calendar month beginning thirty six months after Oct. 12, 1984, applicable only to offenses committed after taking effect of sections 211 to 239 of Pub.L. 98-473, and except as otherwise provided for therein, see section 235 of Pub.L. 98-473, as amended, set out as a note under section 3551 of this title.

§ 3623. Transfer of a prisoner to State authority

The Director of the Bureau of Prisons shall order that a prisoner who has been charged in an indictment or information with, or convicted of, a State felony, be transferred to an official detention facility within such State prior to his release from a Federal prison facility if–

(1) the transfer has been requested by the Governor or other executive authority of the State;

(2) the State has presented to the Director a certified copy of the indictment, information, or judgment of conviction; and

(3) the Director finds that the transfer would be in the public interest.

If more than one request is presented with respect to a prisoner, the Director shall determine which request should receive preference. The expenses of such transfer shall be borne by the State requesting the transfer.

(Added Pub.L. 98-473, Title II, § 212(a)(2), Oct. 12, 1984, 98 Stat. 2008.)

EDITORIAL NOTES

Effective Date. Section effective on the first day of first calendar month beginning thirty six months after Oct. 12, 1984, applicable only to offenses committed after taking effect of sections 211 to 239 of Pub.L. 98-473, and except as otherwise provided for therein, see section 235 of Pub.L. 98-473, as amended, set out as a note under section 3551 of this title.

§ 3624. Release of a prisoner

(a) Date of release.–A prisoner shall be released by the Bureau of Prisons on the date of the expiration of the prisoner's term of imprisonment, less any time credited toward the service of the prisoner's sentence as provided in subsection (b). If the date for a prisoner's release falls on a Saturday, a Sunday, or a legal holiday at the place of confinement, the prisoner may be released by the Bureau on the last preceding weekday.

(b) Credit toward service of sentence for satisfactory behavior.–(1) A prisoner (other than a prisoner serving a sentence for a crime of violence) who is serving a term of imprisonment of more than one year, other than a term of imprisonment for the duration of the prisoner's life, shall receive credit toward the service of the prisoner's sentence, beyond the time served, of fifty-four days at the end of each year of the prisoner's term of imprisonment, beginning at the end of the first year of the term, unless the Bureau of Prisons determines that, during that year, the prisoner has not satisfactorily complied with such institutional disciplinary regulations as have been approved by the Attorney General and issued to the prisoner. A prisoner who is serving a term of imprisonment of more than 1 year for a crime of violence, other than a term of imprisonment for the duration of the prisoner's life, may receive credit toward the service of the prisoner's sentence, beyond the time served, of up to 54 days at the end of each year of the prisoner's term of imprisonment, beginning at the end of the first year of the term, subject to determination by the Bureau of Prisons that, during that year, the prisoner has displayed exemplary compliance with such institutional disciplinary regulations. If the Bureau determines that, during that year, the prisoner has not satisfactorily complied with such institutional regulations, the prisoner shall receive no such credit toward service of the prisoner's sentence or shall receive such lesser credit as the Bureau determines to be appropriate. The Bureau's determination shall be made within fifteen days after the end of each year of the sentence. Credit that has not been earned may not later be granted. Credit for the last year or portion of a year of the term of imprisonment shall be prorated and credited within the last six weeks of the sentence.

(2) Credit toward a prisoner's service of sentence shall not be vested unless the prisoner has earned or is making satisfactory progress toward a high school diploma or an equivalent degree.

(3) The Attorney General shall ensure that the Bureau of Prisons has in effect an optional General Educational Development program for inmates who have not earned a high school diploma or its equivalent.

(4) Exemptions to the General Educational Development requirement may be made as deemed appropriate by the Director of the Federal Bureau of Prisons.

(c) Pre-release custody.–The Bureau of Prisons shall, to the extent practicable, assure that a prisoner serving a term of imprisonment spends a reasonable part, not to exceed six months, of the last 10 per centum of the term to be served under conditions that will afford the prisoner a reasonable opportunity to adjust to and prepare for the prisoner's re-entry into the community. The authority provided by this subsection may be used to place a prisoner in home confinement. The United States Probation System shall, to the extent practicable, offer assistance to a prisoner during such pre-release custody.

(d) Allotment of clothing, funds, and transportation.–Upon the release of a prisoner on the expiration of the prisoner's term of imprisonment, the Bureau of Prisons shall furnish the prisoner with–

(1) suitable clothing;

(2) an amount of money, not more than $500, determined by the Director to be consistent with the needs of the offender and the public interest, unless the Director determines that the financial position of the offender is such that no sum should be furnished; and

(3) transportation to the place of the prisoner's conviction, to the prisoner's bona fide residence within the United States, or to such other place within the United States as may be authorized by the Director.

(e) Supervision after release.–A prisoner whose sentence includes a term of supervised release after imprisonment shall be released by the Bureau of Prisons to the supervision of a probation officer who shall, during the term imposed, supervise the person released to the degree warranted by the conditions specified by the sentencing court. The term of supervised release commences on the day the person is released from imprisonment and runs concurrently with any Federal, State, or local term of probation or supervised release or parole for another offense to which the person is subject or becomes subject during the term of supervised release. A term of supervised release does not run during any period in which the person is imprisoned in connection with a conviction for a Federal, State, or local crime unless the imprisonment is for a period of less than 30 consecutive days. No prisoner shall be released on supervision unless such prisoner agrees to adhere to an installment schedule, not to exceed two years except in special circumstances, to pay for any fine imposed for the offense committed by such prisoner.

(f) Mandatory functional literacy requirement.–

(1) The Attorney General shall direct the Bureau of Prisons to have in effect a mandatory functional literacy program for all mentally capable inmates who are not functionally literate in each Federal correctional institution within 6 months from the date of the enactment of this Act.

(2) Each mandatory functional literacy program shall include a requirement that each inmate participate in such program for a mandatory period sufficient to provide the inmate with an adequate opportunity to achieve functional literacy, and appropriate incentives which lead to successful completion of such programs shall be developed and implemented.

(3) As used in this section, the term "functional literacy" means-

(A) an eighth grade equivalence in reading and mathematics on a nationally recognized standardized test;

(B) functional competency or literacy on a nationally recognized criterion-referenced test; or

(C) a combination of subparagraphs (A) and (B).

(4) Non-English speaking inmates shall be required to participate in an English-As-A-Second-Language program until they function at the equivalence of the eighth grade on a nationally recognized educational achievement test.

(5) The Chief Executive Officer of each institution shall have authority to grant waivers for good cause as determined and documented on an individual basis.

(6) A report shall be provided to Congress on an annual basis summarizing the results of this program, including the number of inmate participants, the number successfully completing the program, the number who do not successfully complete the program, and the reasons for failure to successfully complete the program.

(Added Pub.L. 98-473, Title II, § 212(a)(2), Oct. 12, 1984, 98 Stat. 2008, and amended Pub.L. 99-646, §§ 16(a), 17(a), Nov. 10, 1986, 100 Stat. 3595; Pub.L. 101-647, Title XXIX, §§ 2902(a), 2904, Nov. 29, 1990, 104 Stat. 4913; Pub.L. 103-322, Title II, §§ 20405, 20412, Sept. 13, 1994, 108 Stat. __, __.)

EDITORIAL NOTES

References in Text. The date of enactment of this Act, referred to in subsec. (f)(1), probably means the date of enactment of Pub.L. 101-647, Nov. 29, 1990, 104 Stat. 4789, which was approved Nov. 29, 1990.

Effective Date of 1990 Amendment. Section 2902(b) of Pub.L. 101-647 provided that: "Section 3624(c) of title 18, United States Code, as amended by this section [subsec. (c) of this section] shall apply with respect to all inmates, regardless of the date of their offense."

Effective Date of 1986 Amendment. Section 16(b) of Pub.L. 99-646 provided that: "The amendment made by this section [amending subsec. (b) of this section] shall take effect on the date of the taking effect of such section 3624 [this section]."

Section 17(a) of Pub.L. 99-646 provided that: "The amendment made by this section [amending subsec. (e) of this section] shall take effect on the date of the taking effect of such section 3624 [this section]."

Effective Date. Section effective on the first day of first calendar month beginning thirty six months after Oct. 12, 1984, applicable only to offenses committed after taking effect of sections 211 to 239 of Pub.L. 98-473, and except as otherwise provided for therein, see section 235 of Pub.L. 98-473, as amended, set out as a note under section 3551 of this title.

* * *

CHAPTER 232 - MISCELLANEOUS SENTENCING PROVISIONS

* * *

§ 3661. Use of information for sentencing

No limitation shall be placed on the information concerning the background, character, and conduct of a person convicted of an offense which a court of the United States may receive and consider for the purpose of imposing an appropriate sentence.

(Added Pub.L. 91-452, Title X, § 1001(a), Oct. 15, 1970, 84 Stat. 951, § 3577, and renumbered Pub.L. 98-473, Title II, § 212(a)(1), Oct. 12, 1984, 98 Stat. 1987.)

EDITORIAL NOTES

Effective Date and Savings Provisions of 1984 Amendment. Amendment by Pub.L. 98-473 effective on the first day of first calendar month beginning thirty six months after Oct. 12, 1984, applicable only to offenses committed after taking effect of sections 211 to 239 of Pub.L. 98-473, and except as otherwise provided for therein, see section 225 of Pub.L. 98-473, as amended, set out as a note under section 3551 of this title.

* * *

§ 3663. Order of restitution

(a)(1) The court, when sentencing a defendant convicted of an offense under this title or under subsection (h), (i), (j), or (n) of section 902 of the Federal Aviation Act of 1958 (49 U.S.C. 1472), may order, in addition to or, in the case of a misdemeanor, in lieu of any other penalty authorized by law, that the defendant make restitution to any victim of such offense.

(2) For the purposes of restitution, a victim of an offense that involves as an element a scheme, a conspiracy, or a pattern of criminal activity means any person directly harmed by the defendant's criminal conduct in the course of the scheme, conspiracy, or pattern.

(3) The court may also order restitution in any criminal case to the extent agreed to by the parties in a plea agreement.

(b) The order may require that such defendant–

(1) in the case of an offense resulting in damage to or loss or destruction of property of a victim of the offense–

(A) return the property to the owner of the property or someone designated by the owner; or

(B) if return of the property under subparagraph (A) is impossible, impractical, or inadequate, pay an amount equal to the greater of–

(i) the value of the property on the date of the damage, loss, or destruction, or

(ii) the value of the property on the date of sentencing,

less the value (as of the date the property is returned) of any part of the property that is returned;

(2) in the case of an offense resulting in bodily injury to a victim including an offense under chapter 109A or chapter 110–

(A) pay an amount equal to the cost of necessary medical and related professional services and devices relating to physical, psychiatric, and psychological care, including nonmedical care and treatment rendered in accordance with a method of healing recognized by the law of the place of treatment;

(B) pay an amount equal to the cost of necessary physical and occupational therapy and rehabilitation; and

(C) reimburse the victim for income lost by such victim as a result of such offense;

(3) in the case of an offense resulting in bodily injury also results in the death of a victim, pay an amount equal to the cost of necessary funeral and related services;

(4) in any case, reimburse the victim for lost income and necessary child care, transportation, and other expenses related to participation in the investigation or prosecution of the offense or attendance at proceedings related to the offense; and

(5) in any case, if the victim (or if the victim is deceased, the victim's estate) consents, make restitution in services in lieu of money, or make restitution to a person or organization designated by the victim or the estate.

(c) If the court decides to order restitution under this section, the court shall, if the victim is deceased, order that the restitution be made to the victim's estate.

(d) To the extent that the court determines that the complication and prolongation of the sentencing process resulting from the fashioning of an order of restitution under this section outweighs the need to provide restitution to any victims, the court may decline to make such an order.

(e)(1) The court shall not impose restitution with respect to a loss for which the victim has received or is to receive compensation, except that the court may, in the interest of justice, order restitution to any person who has compensated the victim for such loss to the extent that such person paid the compensation. An order of restitution shall require that all restitution to victims under such order be made before any restitution to any other person under such order is made.

(2) Any amount paid to a victim under an order of restitution shall be set off against any amount later recovered as compensatory damages by such victim in–

(A) any Federal civil proceeding; and

(B) any State civil proceeding, to the extent provided by the law of that State.

(f)(1) The court may require that such defendant make restitution under this section within a specified period or in specified installments.

(2) The end of such period or the last such installment shall not be later than–

(A) the end of the period of probation, if probation is ordered;

(B) five years after the end of the term of imprisonment imposed, if the court does not order probation; and

(C) five years after the date of sentencing in any other case.

(3) If not otherwise provided by the court under this subsection, restitution shall be made immediately.

(4) The order of restitution shall require the defendant to make restitution directly to the victim or other person eligible under this section, or to deliver the amount or property due as restitution to the Attorney General or the person designated under section 604(a)(18) of title 28 for transfer to such victim or person.

(g) If such defendant is placed on probation or sentenced to a term of supervised release under this title, any restitution ordered under this section shall be a condition of such probation or supervised release. The court may revoke probation or a term of supervised release, or modify the term or conditions of probation or a term of supervised release, or hold a defendant in contempt pursuant to section 3583(e) if the defendant fails to comply with such order. In determining whether to revoke probation or a term of supervised release, or hold a defendant serving a term of supervised release in contempt, the court shall consider the defendant's employment status, earning ability, financial resources, the willfulness of the defendant's failure to pay, and any other special circumstances that may have a bearing on the defendant's ability to pay.

(h) An order of restitution may be enforced–

(1) by the United States–

(A) in the manner provided for the collection and payment of fines in subchapter B of chapter 229 of this title; or

(B) in the same manner as a judgment in a civil action; and

(2) by a victim named in the order to receive the restitution, in the same manner as a judgment in a civil action.

(i)(1) A Federal agency shall immediately suspend all Federal benefits provided by the agency to the defendant, and shall terminate the defendant's eligibility for Federal benefits administered by that agency, upon receipt of a certified copy of a written judicial finding that the defendant is delinquent in making restitution in accordance with any schedule of payments or any requirement of immediate payment imposed under this section.

(2) Any written finding of delinquency described in paragraph (1) shall be made by a court, after a hearing, upon motion of the victim named in the order to receive the restitution or upon motion of the United States.

(3) A defendant found to be delinquent may subsequently seek a written finding from the court that the defendant has rectified the delinquency or that the defendant has made and will make good faith efforts to rectify the delinquency. The defendant's eligibility for Federal benefits shall be reinstated upon receipt by the agency of a certified copy of such a finding.

(4) In this subsection, "Federal benefit" means a grant, contract, loan, professional license, or commercial license provided by an agency of the United States.

(Added Pub.L. 97-291, § 5(a), Oct. 12, 1982, 96 Stat. 1253, § 3579 renumbered and amended Pub.L. 98-473, Title II, § 212(a)(1), (3), Oct. 12, 1984, 98 Stat. 1987, 2010; Pub.L. 98-596, § 9, Oct. 30, 1984, 98 Stat. 3138; Nov. 10, 1986, Pub.L. 99-646, §§ 8(b), 20(a), 77(a), 78(a), 79(a), 100 Stat. 3593, 3596, 3618, 3619; Pub. L. 100-182, § 13, Dec. 7, 1987, 101 Stat. 1268; Pub.L. 100-185, § 12, Dec. 11, 1987, 101 Stat. 1285; Pub.L. 100-690, Title VII, § 7042, Nov. 18, 1988, 102 Stat. 4399; Pub.L. 101-647, Title XXV, § 2509, Title XXXV, § 3595, Nov. 29, 1990, 104 Stat. 4863, 4931; Pub.L. 103-322, Title IV, §§ 40504, 40505, Sept. 13, 1994, 108 Stat. __, __.)

EDITORIAL NOTES

Effective Date of 1987 Amendment. Amendment by Pub.L. 100-182 applicable with respect to offenses committed after enactment of Pub.L. 100-182, which was approved Dec. 7, 1987, see section 26 of Pub.L. 100-182.

Effective Date of 1986 Amendment. Amendment of subsec. (a) by section 8(b) of Pub.L. 99-646, effective on the day section 3553 takes effect, Nov. 1, 1987, see section 8(c) of Pub.L. 99-646, set out as a note under section 3553 of this title.

Amendment of subsec. (a)(1) by section 20(a) of Pub.L. 99-646, effective on the date of taking effect of section 212(a)(2) of Pub.L. 98-473, Nov. 1, 1987, see section 20(c) of Pub.L. 99-646, set out as a note under section 3556 of this title.

Section 77(b) of Pub.L. 99-646 provided that: "The amendment made by this section [amending this section] shall take effect on the 30th day after the date of the enactment of this Act [Nov. 10, 1986]."

Section 78(b) of Pub.L. 99-646 provided that: "The amendment made by this section [amending this section] shall take effect on the 30th day after the date of the enactment of this Act [Nov. 10, 1986]."

Section 79(b) of Pub.L. 99-646 provided that: "The amendment made by this section [amending this section] shall take effect on the date of the enactment of this Act [Nov. 10, 1986]."

Effective Date and Savings Provisions of 1984 Amendment. Amendment by Pub.L. 98-473 effective on the first day of first calendar month beginning thirty six months after Oct. 12, 1984, applicable only to offenses committed after taking effect of sections 211 to 239 of Pub.L. 98-473, and except as otherwise provided for therein, see section 235 of Pub.L. 98-473, as amended, set out as a note under section 3551 of this title.

Effective Date. Section effective with respect to offenses occurring after Jan. 1, 1983, pursuant to section 9(b)(2) of Pub.L. 97-291.

§ 3664. Procedure for issuing order of restitution

(a) The court, in determining whether to order restitution under section 3663 of this title and the amount of such restitution, shall consider the amount of the loss sustained by any victim as a result of the offense, the financial resources of the defendant, the financial needs and earning ability of the defendant and the defendant's dependents, and such other factors as the court deems appropriate.

(b) The court may order the probation service of the court to obtain information pertaining to the factors set forth in subsection (a) of this section. The probation service of the court shall include the information collected in the report of presentence investigation or in a separate report, as the court directs.

(c) The court shall disclose to both the defendant and the attorney for the Government all portions of the presentence or other report pertaining to the matters described in subsection (a) of this section.

(d) Any dispute as to the proper amount or type of restitution shall be resolved by the court by the preponderance of the evidence. The burden of demonstrating the amount of the loss sustained by a victim as a result of the offense shall be on the attorney for the Government. The burden of demonstrating the financial resources of the defendant and the financial needs of the defendant and such defendant's dependents shall be on the defendant. The burden of demonstrating such other matters as the court deems appropriate shall be upon the party designated by the court as justice requires.

(e) A conviction of a defendant for an offense involving the act giving rise to restitution under this section shall estop the defendant from denying the essential allegations of that offense in any subsequent Federal civil proceeding or State civil proceeding, to the extent consistent with State law, brought by the victim.

(Added Pub.L. 97-291, § 5(a), Oct. 12, 1982, 96 Stat. 1255, § 3580, renumbered Pub.L. 98-473, Title II, § 212(a)(1), Oct. 12, 1984; 98 Stat. 1987; Pub.L. 101-647, Title XXXV, § 3596, Nov. 29, 1990, 104 Stat. 4931.)

EDITORIAL NOTES

Effective Date and Savings Provisions of 1984 Amendment. Amendment by Pub.L. 98-473 effective on the first day of first calendar month beginning thirty six months after Oct. 12, 1984, applicable only to offenses committed after taking effect of sections 211 to 239 of Pub.L. 98-473, and except as otherwise provided for therein, see section 235 of Pub.L. 98-473, as amended, set out as a note under section 3551 of this title.

Effective Date. Section effective with respect to offenses occurring after Jan. 1, 1983, see section 9(b)(2) of Pub.L. 97-291.

* * *

CHAPTER 235–APPEAL

* * *

§ 3742. Review of a sentence

(a) Appeal by a defendant.–A defendant may file a notice of appeal in the district court for review of an otherwise final sentence if the sentence–

(1) was imposed in violation of law;

(2) was imposed as a result of an incorrect application of the sentencing guidelines; or

(3) is greater than the sentence specified in the applicable guideline range to the extent that the sentence includes a greater fine or term of imprisonment, probation, or supervised release than the maximum established in the guideline range, or includes a more limiting condition of probation or supervised release under section 3563(b)(6) or (b)(11) than the maximum established in the guideline range; or

(4) was imposed for an offense for which there is no sentencing guideline and is plainly unreasonable.

(b) Appeal by the Government.–The Government may file a notice of appeal in the district court for review of an otherwise final sentence if the sentence–

(1) was imposed in violation of law;

(2) was imposed as a result of an incorrect application of the sentencing guidelines;

(3) is less than the sentence specified in the applicable guideline range to the extent that the sentence includes a lesser fine or term of imprisonment, probation, or supervised release than the minimum established in the guideline range, or includes a less limiting condition of probation or supervised release under section 3563(b)(6) or (b)(11) than the minimum established in the guideline range; or

(4) was imposed for an offense for which there is no sentencing guideline and is plainly unreasonable.

The Government may not further prosecute such appeal without the personal approval of the Attorney General, the Solicitor General, or a deputy solicitor general designated by the Solicitor General.

(c) Plea agreements.–In the case of a plea agreement that includes a specific sentence under rule 11(e)(1)(C) of the Federal Rules of Criminal Procedure–

(1) a defendant may not file a notice of appeal under paragraph (3) or (4) of subsection (a) unless the sentence imposed is greater than the sentence set forth in such agreement; and

(2) the Government may not file a notice of appeal under paragraph (3) or (4) of subsection (b) unless the sentence imposed is less than the sentence set forth in such agreement.

(d) Record on review.–If a notice of appeal is filed in the district court pursuant to subsection (a) or (b), the clerk shall certify to the court of appeals–

(1) that portion of the record in the case that is designated as pertinent by either of the parties;

(2) the presentence report; and

(3) the information submitted during the sentencing proceeding.

(e) Consideration.–Upon review of the record, the court of appeals shall determine whether the sentence–

(1) was imposed in violation of law;

(2) was imposed as a result of an incorrect application of the sentencing guidelines;

(3) is outside of the applicable guideline range, and is unreasonable, having regard for–

(A) the factors to be considered in imposing a sentence, as set forth in chapter 227 of this title; and

(B) the reasons for the imposition of the particular sentence, as stated by the district court pursuant to the provisions of section 3553(c); or

(4) was imposed for an offense for which there is no applicable sentencing guideline and is plainly unreasonable.

The court of appeals shall give due regard to the opportunity of the district court to judge the credibility of the witnesses, and shall accept the findings of fact of the district court unless they are clearly erroneous and shall give due deference to the district court's application of the guidelines to the facts.

(f) Decision and disposition.–If the court of appeals determines that the sentence–

(1) was imposed in violation of law or imposed as a result of an incorrect application of the sentencing guidelines, the court shall remand the case for further sentencing proceedings with such instructions as the court considers appropriate;

(2) is outside the applicable guideline range and is unreasonable or was imposed for an offense for which there is no applicable sentencing guideline and is plainly unreasonable, it shall state specific reasons for its conclusions and–

(A) if it determines that the sentence is too high and the appeal has been filed under subsection (a), it shall set aside the sentence and remand the case for further sentencing proceedings with such instructions as the court considers appropriate;

(B) if it determines that the sentence is too low and the appeal has been filed under subsection (b), it shall set aside the sentence and remand the case for further sentencing proceedings with such instructions as the court considers appropriate;

(3) is not described in paragraph (1) or (2), it shall affirm the sentence.

(g) Application to a sentence by a magistrate.–An appeal of an otherwise final sentence imposed by a United States magistrate may be taken to a judge of the district court, and this section shall apply (except for the requirement of approval by the Attorney General or the Solicitor General in the case of a Government appeal) as though the appeal were to a court of appeals from a sentence imposed by a district court.

(h) Guideline not expressed as a range.–For the purpose of this section, the term "guideline range" includes a guideline range having the same upper and lower limits.

(Added Pub.L. 98-473, Title II, § 213(a), Oct. 12, 1984, 98 Stat. 2011, and amended Pub.L. 99-646, § 73(a), Nov. 10, 1986, 100 Stat. 3617; Pub.L. 100-182, §§ 4-6, Dec. 7, 1987, 101 Stat. 1266, 1267; Pub.L. 100-690, Title VII, § 7103(a), Nov. 18, 1988, 102 Stat. 4416, 4417; Pub.L. 101-647, Title XXXV, §§ 3501, 3503, Nov. 29, 1990, 104 Stat. 4921; Pub.L. 103-322, Title XXXIII, § 330002(k) Sept. 13, 1994, 108 Stat. __.)

EDITORIAL NOTES

Effective Date of 1987 Amendment. Amendment by Pub.L. 100-182 applicable with respect to offenses committed after enactment of Pub.L. 100-182, which was approved Dec. 7, 1987, see section 26 of Pub.L. 100-182.

Effective Date. Section effective on the first day of first calendar month beginning thirty six months after Oct. 12, 1984, applicable only to offenses committed after taking effect of sections 211 to 239 of Pub.L. 98-473, and except as otherwise provided for therein, see section 235 of Pub.L. 98-473, as amended, set out as a note under section 3551 of this title.

Change of Name of United States Magistrates. United States magistrates appointed under section 631 of the Title 28, Judiciary and Judicial Procedure, to be known as United States magistrate judge after Dec. 1, 1990, with any reference to any United States magistrate or magistrate contained in Title 28, in any other Federal statute, etc., deemed to refer to a United States magistrate judge appointed under section 631 of Title 28, see section 321 of Pub.L. 101-650.

* * *

Title 28

JUDICIARY AND JUDICIAL PROCEDURE

—

CHAPTER 58–UNITED STATES SENTENCING COMMISSION

Section

§ 991. United States Sentencing Commission; establishment and purposes

(a) There is established as an independent commission in the judicial branch of the United States a United States Sentencing Commission which shall consist of seven voting members and one nonvoting member. The President, after consultation with representatives of judges, prosecuting attorneys, defense attorneys, law enforcement officials, senior citizens, victims of crime, and others interested in the criminal justice process, shall appoint the voting members of the Commission, by and with the advice and consent of the Senate, one of whom shall be appointed, by and with the advice and consent of the Senate, as the Chair and three of whom shall be designated by the President as Vice Chairs. At least three of the members shall be Federal judges selected after considering a list of six judges recommended to the President by the Judicial Conference of the United States. Not more than four of the members of the Commission shall be members of the same political party, and of the three Vice Chairs, no more than two shall be members of the same political party. The Attorney General, or the Attorney General's designee, shall be an ex officio, nonvoting member of the Commission. The Chair, Vice Chairs, and members of the Commission shall be subject to removal from the Commission by the President only for neglect of duty or malfeasance in office or for other good cause shown.

(b) The purposes of the United States Sentencing Commission are to–

(1) establish sentencing policies and practices for the Federal criminal justice system that–

(A) assure the meeting of the purposes of sentencing as set forth in section 3553(a)(2) of title 18, United States Code;

(B) provide certainty and fairness in meeting the purposes of sentencing, avoiding unwarranted sentencing disparities among defendants with similar records who have been found guilty of similar criminal conduct while maintaining sufficient flexibility to permit individualized sentences when warranted by mitigating or aggravating factors not taken into account in the establishment of general sentencing practices; and

(C) reflect, to the extent practicable, advancement in knowledge of human behavior as it relates to the criminal justice process; and

(2) develop means of measuring the degree to which the sentencing, penal, and correctional practices are effective in meeting the purposes of sentencing as set forth in section 3553(a)(2) of title 18, United States Code.

(Added Pub.L. 98-473, Title II, § 217(a), Oct. 12, 1984, 98 Stat. 2017, and amended Pub.L. 99-22, § 1(1), Apr. 15, 1985, 99 Stat. 46; Pub.L. 103-322, Title XXVIII, § 280005, Sept. 13, 1994, 108 Stat. __.)

EDITORIAL NOTES

Effective Date. Section effective Oct. 12, 1984, see section 235(a)(1)(B)(i) of Pub.L. 98-473, set out as a note under section 3551 of Title 18, Crimes and Criminal Procedure.

§ 992. Terms of office; compensation

(a) The voting members of the United States Sentencing Commission shall be appointed for six-year terms, except that the initial terms of the first members of the Commission shall be staggered so that–

(1) two members, including the Chair, serve terms of six years;

(2) three members serve terms of four years; and

(3) two members serve terms of two years.

(b)(1) Subject to paragraph (2)–

(A) no voting member of the Commission may serve more than two full terms; and

(B) a voting member appointed to fill a vacancy that occurs before the expiration of the term for which a predecessor was appointed shall be appointed only for the remainder of such term.

(2) A voting member of the Commission whose term has expired may continue to serve until the earlier of–

(A) the date on which a successor has taken office; or

(B) the date on which the Congress adjourns sine die to end the session of Congress that commences after the date on which the member's term expired.

(c) The Chair and Vice Chairs of the Commission shall hold full-time positions and shall be compensated during their terms of office at the annual rate at which judges of the United States courts of appeals are compensated. The voting members of the Commission, other than the Chair and Vice Chair, shall hold full-time positions until the end of the first six years after the sentencing guidelines go into effect pursuant to section 235(a)(1)(B)(ii) of the Sentencing Reform Act of 1984, and shall be compensated at the annual rate at which judges of the United States courts of appeals are compensated. Thereafter, the voting members of the commission, other than the Chair and Vice Chairs, shall hold part-time positions and shall be paid at the daily rate at which judges of the United States courts of appeals are compensated. A Federal judge may serve as a member of the Commission without resigning the judge's appointment as a Federal judge.

(d) Sections 44(c) and 134(b) of this title (relating to the residence of judges) do not apply to any judge holding a full-time position on the Commission under subsection (c) of this section.

(Added Pub.L. 98-473, Title II, § 217(a), Oct. 12, 1984, 98 Stat. 2018, and amended Pub.L. 99-646, §§ 4, 6(a), Nov. 10, 1986; 100 Stat. 3592; Pub.L. 102-349, § 1, Aug. 26, 1992, 106 Stat. 933; Pub.L. 103-322, Tittle XXVIII, § 280005, Sept. 13, 1994, 108 Stat. __.)

EDITORIAL NOTES

References in Text. Section 235(a)(1)(B)(ii) of the Sentencing Reform Act of 1984, referred to in subsec. (c), is section 235(a)(1)(B)(ii) of Pub.L. 98-473, which is set out as a note under section 3551 of Title 18, Crimes and Criminal Procedure.

Effective Date. Section effective Oct. 12, 1984, see section 235(a)(1)(B)(i) of Pub.L. 98-473, set out as a note under section 3551 of Title 18, Crimes and Criminal Procedure.

Commencement of Terms of First Members of Commission. For provisions directing that, for purposes of subsec. (a) of this section, the terms of the first members of the United States Sentencing Commission shall not begin to run until the sentencing guidelines go into effect pursuant to section 235(a)(1)(B)(ii) of Pub.L. 98-473, set out as a note under section 994 of this title, see section 235(a)(2) of Pub.L. 98-473, set out as a note under section 3551 of Title 18, Crimes and Criminal Procedure.

§ 993. Powers and duties of Chair

The Chair shall–

(a) call and preside at meetings of the Commission, which shall be held for at least two weeks in each quarter after the members of the Commission hold part-time positions; and

(b) direct–
(1) the preparation of requests for appropriations for the Commission; and
(2) the use of funds made available to the Commission.

(Added Pub.L. 98-473, Title II, § 217(a), Oct. 12, 1984, 98 Stat. 2019, and amended Pub.L. 99-22, § 1(2), Apr. 15, 1985, 99 Stat. 46; Pub.L. 99-646, § 5, Nov. 10, 1986, 100 Stat. 3592; Pub.L. 103-322, Title XXVIII, § 280005(c)(1), Sept. 13, 1994, 108 Stat. __.)

EDITORIAL NOTES

Effective Date. Section effective Oct. 12, 1984, see section 235(a)(1)(B)(i) of Pub.L. 98-473, set out as a note under section 3551 of Title 18, Crimes and Criminal Procedure.

§ 994. Duties of the Commission

(a) The Commission, by affirmative vote of at least four members of the Commission, and pursuant to its rules and regulations and consistent with all pertinent provisions of this title and title 18, United States Code, shall promulgate and distribute to all courts of the United States and to the United States Probation System–
(1) guidelines, as described in this section, for use of a sentencing court in determining the sentence to be imposed in a criminal case, including–
(A) a determination whether to impose a sentence to probation, a fine, or a term of imprisonment;

(B) a determination as to the appropriate amount of a fine or the appropriate length of a term of probation or a term of imprisonment;

(C) a determination whether a sentence to a term of imprisonment should include a requirement that the defendant be placed on a term of supervised release after imprisonment, and, if so, the appropriate length of such a term;

(D) a determination whether multiple sentences to terms of imprisonment should be ordered to run concurrently or consecutively; and

(E) a determination under paragraphs (6) and (11) of section 3563(b) of title 18;

(2) general policy statements regarding application of the guidelines or any other aspect of sentencing or sentence implementation that in the view of the Commission would further the purposes set forth in section 3553(a)(2) of title 18, United States Code, including the appropriate use of–

(A) the sanctions set forth in sections 3554, 3555, and 3556 of title 18;

(B) the conditions of probation and supervised release set forth in sections 3563(b) and 3583(d) of title 18;

(C) the sentence modification provisions set forth in sections 3563(c), 3564, 3573, and 3582(c) of title 18;

(D) the fine imposition provisions set forth in section 3572 of title 18;

(E) the authority granted under rule 11(e)(2) of the Federal Rules of Criminal Procedure to accept or reject a plea agreement entered into pursuant to rule 11(e)(1); and

(F) the temporary release provisions set forth in section 3622 of title 18, and the prerelease custody provisions set forth in section 3624(c) of title 18; and

(3) guidelines or general policy statements regarding the appropriate use of the provisions for revocation of probation set forth in section 3565 of title 18, and the provisions for modification of the term or conditions of supervised release and revocation of supervised release set forth in section 3583(e) of title 18.

(b)(1) The Commission, in the guidelines promulgated pursuant to subsection (a)(1), shall, for each category of offense involving each category of defendant, establish a sentencing range that is consistent with all pertinent provisions of title 18, United States Code.

(2) If a sentence specified by the guidelines includes a term of imprisonment, the maximum of the range established for such a term shall not exceed the minimum of that range by more than the greater of 25 percent or 6 months, except that, if the minimum term of the range is 30 years or more, the maximum may be life imprisonment.

(c) The Commission, in establishing categories of offenses for use in the guidelines and policy statements governing the imposition of sentences of probation, a fine, or imprisonment, governing the imposition of other authorized sanctions, governing the size of a fine or the length of a term of probation, imprisonment, or supervised release, and governing the conditions of probation, supervised release, or imprisonment, shall consider whether the following matters, among others, have any relevance to the nature, extent, place of service, or other incidents[1] of an appropriate sentence, and shall take them into account only to the extent that they do have relevance–

(1) the grade of the offense;

(2) the circumstances under which the offense was committed which mitigate or aggravate the seriousness of the offense;

(3) the nature and degree of the harm caused by the offense, including whether it involved property, irreplaceable property, a person, a number of persons, or a breach of public trust;

(4) the community view of the gravity of the offense;

(5) the public concern generated by the offense;

(6) the deterrent effect a particular sentence may have on the commission of the offense by others; and

(7) the current incidence of the offense in the community and in the Nation as a whole.

[1]So in original. Probably should be "incidence".

(d) The Commission in establishing categories of defendants for use in the guidelines and policy statements governing the imposition of sentences of probation, a fine, or imprisonment, governing the imposition of other authorized sanctions, governing the size of a fine or the length of a term of probation, imprisonment, or supervised release, and governing the conditions of probation, supervised release, or imprisonment, shall consider whether the following matters, among others with respect to a defendant, have any relevance to the nature, extent, place of service, or other incidents[1] of an appropriate sentence, and shall take them into account only to the extent that they do have relevance–

(1) age;

(2) education;

(3) vocational skills;

(4) mental and emotional condition to the extent that such condition mitigates the defendant's culpability or to the extent that such condition is otherwise plainly relevant;

(5) physical condition, including drug dependence;

(6) previous employment record;

(7) family ties and responsibilities;

(8) community ties;

(9) role in the offense;

(10) criminal history; and

(11) degree of dependence upon criminal activity for a livelihood.

The Commission shall assure that the guidelines and policy statements are entirely neutral as to the race, sex, national origin, creed, and socioeconomic status of offenders.

(e) The Commission shall assure that the guidelines and policy statements, in recommending a term of imprisonment or length of a term of imprisonment, reflect the general inappropriateness of considering the education, vocational skills, employment record, family ties and responsibilities, and community ties of the defendant.

(f) The Commission, in promulgating guidelines pursuant to subsection (a)(1), shall promote the purposes set forth in section 991(b)(1), with particular attention to the requirements of subsection 991(b)(1)(B) for providing certainty and fairness in sentencing and reducing unwarranted sentence disparities.

(g) The Commission, in promulgating guidelines pursuant to subsection (a)(1) to meet the purposes of sentencing as set forth in section 3553(a)(2) of title 18, United States Code, shall take into account the nature and capacity of the penal, correctional, and other facilities and services available, and shall make recommendations concerning any change or expansion in the nature or capacity of such facilities and services that might become necessary as a result of the guidelines promulgated pursuant to the provisions of this chapter. The sentencing guidelines prescribed under this chapter shall be formulated to minimize the likelihood that the Federal prison population will exceed the capacity of the Federal prisons, as determined by the Commission.

(h) The Commission shall assure that the guidelines specify a sentence to a term of imprisonment at or near the maximum term authorized for categories of defendants in which the defendant is eighteen years old or older and–

(1) has been convicted of a felony that is–

(A) a crime of violence; or

(B) an offense described in section 401 of the Controlled Substances Act (21 U.S.C. 841), sections 1002(a), 1005, and 1009 of the Controlled Substances Import and Export Act (21 U.S.C. 952(a), 955, and 959), and the Maritime Drug Law Enforcement Act (46 U.S.C. App. 1901 et seq.) and

(2) has previously been convicted of two or more prior felonies, each of which is–

(A) a crime of violence; or

[1] So in original. Probably should be "incidence".

(B) an offense described in section 401 of the Controlled Substances Act (21 U.S.C. 841), sections 1002(a), 1005, and 1009 of the Controlled Substances Import and Export Act (21 U.S.C. 952(a), 955, and 959), and the Maritime Drug Law Enforcement Act (46 U.S.C. App. 1901 et seq.).

(i) The Commission shall assure that the guidelines specify a sentence to a substantial term of imprisonment for categories of defendants in which the defendant–

(1) has a history of two or more prior Federal, State, or local felony convictions for offenses committed on different occasions;

(2) committed the offense as part of a pattern of criminal conduct from which the defendant derived a substantial portion of the defendant's income;

(3) committed the offense in furtherance of a conspiracy with three or more persons engaging in a pattern of racketeering activity in which the defendant participated in a managerial or supervisory capacity;

(4) committed a crime of violence that constitutes a felony while on release pending trial, sentence, or appeal from a Federal, State, or local felony for which he was ultimately convicted; or

(5) committed a felony that is set forth in section 401 or 1010 of the Comprehensive Drug Abuse Prevention and Control Act of 1970 (21 U.S.C. 841 and 960), and that involved trafficking in a substantial quantity of a controlled substance.

(j) The Commission shall insure that the guidelines reflect the general appropriateness of imposing a sentence other than imprisonment in cases in which the defendant is a first offender who has not been convicted of a crime of violence or an otherwise serious offense, and the general appropriateness of imposing a term of imprisonment on a person convicted of a crime of violence that results in serious bodily injury.

(k) The Commission shall insure that the guidelines reflect the inappropriateness of imposing a sentence to a term of imprisonment for the purpose of rehabilitating the defendant or providing the defendant with needed educational or vocational training, medical care, or other correctional treatment.

(l) The Commission shall insure that the guidelines promulgated pursuant to subsection (a)(1) reflect–

(1) the appropriateness of imposing an incremental penalty for each offense in a case in which a defendant is convicted of–

(A) multiple offenses committed in the same course of conduct that result in the exercise of ancillary jurisdiction over one or more of the offenses; and

(B) multiple offenses committed at different times, including those cases in which the subsequent offense is a violation of section 3146 (penalty for failure to appear) or is committed while the person is released pursuant to the provisions of section 3147 (penalty for an offense committed while on release) of title 18; and

(2) the general inappropriateness of imposing consecutive terms of imprisonment for an offense of conspiring to commit an offense or soliciting commission of an offense and for an offense that was the sole object of the conspiracy or solicitation.

(m) The Commission shall insure that the guidelines reflect the fact that, in many cases, current sentences do not accurately reflect the seriousness of the offense. This will require that, as a starting point in its development of the initial sets of guidelines for particular categories of cases, the Commission ascertain the average sentences imposed in such categories of cases prior to the creation of the Commission, and in cases involving sentences to terms of imprisonment, the length of such terms actually served. The Commission shall not be bound by such average sentences, and shall independently develop a sentencing range that is consistent with the purposes of sentencing described in section 3553(a)(2) of Title 18, United States Code.

(n) The Commission shall assure that the guidelines reflect the general appropriateness of imposing a lower sentence than would otherwise be imposed, including a sentence that is lower than that established by statute as a minimum sentence, to take into account a defendant's substantial assistance in the investigation or prosecution of another person who has committed an offense.

(o) The Commission periodically shall review and revise, in consideration of comments and data coming to its attention, the guidelines promulgated pursuant to the provisions of this section. In fulfilling its duties and in exercising its powers, the Commission shall consult with authorities on, and individual and institutional representatives of, various aspects of the Federal criminal justice system. The United States Probation System, the Bureau of Prisons, the Judicial Conference of the United States, the Criminal Division of the United States Department of Justice, and a representative of the Federal Public Defenders shall submit to the Commission any observations, comments, or questions pertinent to the work of the Commission whenever they believe such communication would be useful, and shall, at least annually, submit to the Commission a written report commenting on the operation of the Commission's guidelines, suggesting changes in the guidelines that appear to be warranted, and otherwise assessing the Commission's work.

(p) The Commission, at or after the beginning of a regular session of Congress, but not later than the first day of May, may promulgate under subsection (a) of this section and submit to Congress amendments to the guidelines and modifications to previously submitted amendments that have not taken effect, including modifications to the effective dates of such amendments. Such an amendment or modification shall be accompanied by a statement of the reasons therefor and shall take effect on a date specified by the Commission, which shall be no earlier than 180 days after being so submitted and no later than the first day of November of the calendar year in which the amendment or modification is submitted, except to the extent that the effective date is revised or the amendment is otherwise modified or disapproved by Act of Congress.

(q) The Commission and the Bureau of Prisons shall submit to Congress an analysis and recommendations concerning maximum utilization of resources to deal effectively with the Federal prison population. Such report shall be based upon consideration of a variety of alternatives, including–

(1) modernization of existing facilities;

(2) inmate classification and periodic review of such classification for use in placing inmates in the least restrictive facility necessary to ensure adequate security; and

(3) use of existing Federal facilities, such as those currently within military jurisdiction.

(r) The Commission, not later than two years after the initial set of sentencing guidelines promulgated under subsection (a) goes into effect, and thereafter whenever it finds it advisable, shall recommend to the Congress that it raise or lower the grades, or otherwise modify the maximum penalties, of those offenses for which such an adjustment appears appropriate.

(s) The Commission shall give due consideration to any petition filed by a defendant requesting modification of the guidelines utilized in the sentencing of such defendant, on the basis of changed circumstances unrelated to the defendant, including changes in–

(1) the community view of the gravity of the offense;

(2) the public concern generated by the offense; and

(3) the deterrent effect particular sentences may have on the commission of the offense by others.

(t) The Commission, in promulgating general policy statements regarding the sentencing modification provisions in section 3582(c)(1)(A) of title 18, shall describe what should be considered extraordinary and compelling reasons for sentence reduction, including the criteria to be applied and a list of specific examples. Rehabilitation of the defendant alone shall not be considered an extraordinary and compelling reason.

(u) If the Commission reduces the term of imprisonment recommended in the guidelines applicable to a particular offense or category of offenses, it shall specify in what circumstances and by what amount the sentences of prisoners serving terms of imprisonment for the offense may be reduced.

(v) The Commission shall ensure that the general policy statements promulgated pursuant to subsection (a)(2) include a policy limiting consecutive terms of imprisonment for an offense involving a violation of a general prohibition and for an offense involving a violation of a specific prohibition encompassed within the general prohibition.

(w) The appropriate judge or officer shall submit to the Commission in connection with each sentence imposed (other than a sentence imposed for a petty offense, as defined in title 18, for which there is no applicable sentencing guideline) a written report of the sentence, the offense for which it is imposed, the age, race, and sex of the offender, information regarding factors made relevant by the guidelines, and such other information as the Commission finds appropriate. The Commission shall submit to Congress at least annually an analysis of these reports and any recommendations for legislation that the Commission concludes is warranted by that analysis.

(x) The provisions of section 553 of title 5, relating to publication in the Federal Register and public hearing procedure, shall apply to the promulgation of guidelines pursuant to this section.

(y) The Commission, in promulgating guidelines pursuant to subsection (a)(1), may include, as a component of a fine, the expected costs to the Government of any imprisonment, supervised release, or probation sentence that is ordered.

(Added Pub.L. 98-473, Title II, § 217(a), Oct. 12, 1984, 98 Stat. 2019, and amended Pub.L. 99-217, § 3, Dec. 26, 1985, 99 Stat. 1728; Pub.L. 99-363, § 2, July 11, 1986, 100 Stat. 770; Pub.L. 99-570, Title I, §§ 1006(b), 1008, Oct. 27, 1986, 100 Stat. 3214; Pub.L. 99-646, §§ 6(b), 56, Nov. 10, 1986, 100 Stat. 3592, 3611; Pub.L. 100-182, §§ 16(b), 23, Dec. 7, 1987, 101 Stat. 1269, 1271; Pub.L. 100-690, Title VII, §§ 7083, 7103(b), 7109, Nov. 18, 1988, 102 Stat. 4408, 4418, 4419; Pub.L. 103-322, Title II § 20403(b) Title XXVII, § 280005(c)(4), Title XXXIII, § 330003(f)(1), Sept. 13, 1994, 108 Stat. __, __, __.)

EDITORIAL NOTES

Codification. Amendment by Pub.L. 99-646 to subsec. (t) of this section has been executed to subsec. (u) as the probable intent of Congress in view of redesignation of subsec. (t) as (u) by Pub.L. 99-570.

Effective Date of 1987 Amendment. Amendment by Pub.L. 100-182 applicable with respect to offenses committed after Dec. 7, 1987, see section 26 of Pub.L. 100-182.

Effective Date. Section effective Oct. 12, 1984, see section 235(a)(1)(B)(i) of Pub.L. 98-473, set out as a note under section 3551 of Title 18, Crimes and Criminal Procedure.

Sexual Offenses by Repeat Offenders; Amendment of Sentencing Guidelines. Pub.L. 103-322, Title IV, § 40111(b), Sept. 13, 1994, 108 Stat. ___, provided that: "The Sentencing Commission shall implement the amendment made by subsection (a)[of this section (pertaining to repeat sexual offenders)] by promulgating amendments, if appropriate, in the sentencing guidelines applicable to chapter 109A [of title 18] offenses."

Sexual Offenses; Amendment of Sentencing Guidelines. Pub.L. 103-322, Title IV, § 40112, Sept. 13, 1994, 108 Stat. __, provided that:

"**(a) Amendment of Sentencing Guidelines.**–Pursuant to its authority under section 994(p) of title 28, United States Code, the United States Sentencing Commission shall review and amend, where necessary, its sentencing guidelines on aggravated sexual abuse under section 2241 of title 18, United States Code, or sexual abuse under section 2242 of title 18 United States Code, as follows:

"**(1)** The Commission shall review and promulgate amendments to the guidelines, if appropriate, to enhance penalties if more than 1 offender is involved in the offense.

"**(2)** The Commission shall review and promulgate amendments to the guidelines, if appropriate, to reduce unwarranted disparities between the sentences for sex offenders who are known to the victim and sentences for sex offenders who are not known to the victim.

"**(3)** The Commission shall review and promulgate amendments to the guidelines to enhance penalties, if appropriate, to render Federal penalties on Federal territory commensurate with penalties for similar offenses in the States.

"**(4)** The Commission shall review and promulgate amendments to the guidelines, if appropriate, to account for the general problem of recidivism in cases of sex offenses, the severity of the offense, and its devastating effects on survivors.

"**(b) Report.**–Not later than 180 days after the date of enactment of this Act, the United States Sentencing Commission shall review and submit to Congress a report containing an analysis of Federal rape sentencing, accompanied by comment from independent experts in the field, describing–

"**(1)** comparative Federal sentences for cases in which the rape victim is known to the defendant and cases in which the rape victim is not known to the defendant;

"**(2)** comparative Federal sentences for cases on Federal territory and sentences in surrounding States; and

"**(3)** an analysis of the effect of rape sentences on populations residing primarily on Federal territory relative to the impact of other Federal offenses in which the existence of Federal jurisdiction depends upon the offense's being committed on Federal territory."

Report on Penalties for Intentional Transmission of HIV. Pub.L. 103-322, Title IV, § 40503(c), Sept. 13, 1994, 108 Stat. __, provided that: "Not later than 6 months after the date of enactment of this Act, the United States Sentencing Commission shall conduct a study and prepare and submit to the committees on the Judiciary of the Senate and the House of Representatives a report concerning recommendations for the revision of sentencing guidelines that relate to offenses in which an HIV infected individual engages in sexual activity if the individual knows that he or she is infected with HIV and intends, through such sexual activity, to expose another to HIV."

Limitation on Applicability of Mandatory Minimum Penalties in Certain Cases; Sentencing Commission Authority. Pub.L. 103-322, Title VIII, § 80001(b), Sept. 13, 1994, 108 Stat. __, provided that:

"**(1) In General.**–(A) The United States Sentencing Commission (referred to in this subsection as the 'Commission'), under section 994(a)(1) and (p) of title 28–

"**(i)** shall promulgate guidelines, or amendments to guidelines, to carry out the purposes of this section and the amendment made by this section; and

"**(ii)** may promulgate policy statements, or amendments to policy statements, to assist in the application of this section and that amendment.

"**(B)** In the case of a defendant for whom the statutorily required minimum sentence of 5 years, such guidelines and amendments to guidelines issued under subparagraph (A) shall call for a guideline range in which the lowest term of imprisonment is at least 24 months.

"**(2) Procedures.**–If the Commission determines that it is necessary to do so in order that the amendments made under paragraph (1) may take effect on the effective date of the amendment made by subsection (a), the Commission may promulgate the amendments made under paragraph (1) in accordance with the procedures set forth in section 21(a) of the Sentencing Act of 1987, as though the authority under that section had not expired."

Increased Penalties for Drug-Dealing in "Drug-Free" Zones; Amendment of Sentencing Guidelines. Pub.L. 103-322, Title IX, § 90102, Sept. 13, 1994, 108 Stat. __, provided that: "Pursuant to its authority under section 994 of title 28, United States Code, the United States Sentencing Commission shall amend its sentencing guidelines to provide an appropriate enhancement for a defendant convicted of violating section 419 of the Controlled Substances Act (21 U.S.C. 860)."

Enhanced Penalties for Illegal Drug Use in Federal Prisons and for Smuggling Drugs into Federal Prisons; Amendment of Sentencing Guidelines. Pub.L. 103-322, Title IX, § 90103, Sept. 13, 1994, 108 Stat. __, provided that:

"(a) **Declaration of Policy.**–It is the policy of the Federal Government that the use or distribution of illegal drugs in the Nation's Federal prisons will not be tolerated and that such crimes shall be prosecuted to the fullest extent of the law.

"(b) **Sentencing Guidelines.**–Pursuant to its authority under section 994 of title 28, United States Code, the United States Sentencing Commission shall amend its sentencing guidelines to appropriately enhance the penalty for a person convicted of an offense–

"(1) under section 404 of the Controlled Substances Act involving simple possession of a controlled substance within a Federal prison or other Federal detention facility; or

"(2) under section 401(b) of the Controlled Substances Act involving the smuggling of a controlled substance into a Federal prison or other Federal detention facility or the distribution or intended distribution of a controlled substance within a Federal prison or other Federal detention facility.

"(c) **No Probation.**–Notwithstanding any other law, the court shall not sentence a person convicted of an offense described in subsection (b) to probation."

Enhanced Penalty for Use of a Semiautomatic Firearm During a Crime of Violence or a Drug Trafficking Crime; Amendment to Sentencing Guidelines. Pub.L. 103-322, Title XI, § 110501, Sept. 13, 1994, 108 Stat. __, provided that:

"(a) **Amendment to Sentencing Guidelines.**–Pursuant to its authority under section 994 of title 28, United States Code, the United States Sentencing Commission shall amend its sentencing guidelines to provide an appropriate enhancement of the punishment for a crime of violence (as defined in section 924(c)(3) of title 18, United States Code) or a drug trafficking crime (as defined in section 924(c)(2) of title 18, United States Code) if a semiautomatic firearm is involved.

"(b) **Semiautomatic Firearm.**–In subsection (a), 'semiautomatic firearm' means any repeating firearm that utilizes a portion of the energy of a firing cartridge to extract the fired cartridge case and chamber the next round and that requires a separate pull of the trigger to fire each cartridge."

Enhanced Penalty for Second Offense of Using an Explosive to Commit a Felony; Amendment of Sentencing Guidelines. Pub.L. 103-322, Title XI, § 110502, Sept. 13, 1994, 108 Stat. __, provided that: "Pursuant to its authority under section 994 of title 28, United States Code, the United States Sentencing Commission shall promulgate amendments to the sentencing guidelines to appropriately enhance penalties in a case in which a defendant convicted under section 844(h) of title 18, United States Code, has previously been convicted under that section."

Using a Firearm in the Commission of Counterfeiting or Forgery; Amendment of Sentencing Guidelines. Pub.L. 103-322, Title XI, § 110512, Sept. 13, 1994, 108 Stat. __, provided that: "Pursuant to its authority under section 994 of title 28, United States Code, the United States Sentencing Commission shall amend its sentencing guidelines to provide an appropriate enhancement of the punishment for a defendant convicted of a felony under chapter 25 of title 18, United States Code, if the defendant used or carried a firearm (as defined in section 921(a)(3) of title 18, United States Code) during and in relation to the felony."

Enhanced Penalties for Firearms Possession by Violent Felons and Serious Drug Offenders; Amendment of Sentencing Guidelines. Pub.L. 103-322, Title XI, § 110513, Sept. 13, 1994, 108 Stat. __, provided that: "Pursuant to its authority under section 994 of title 28, United States Code, the United States Sentencing Commission shall amend its sentencing guidelines to–

"(1) appropriately enhance penalties in cases in which a defendant convicted under section 922(g) of title 18, United States Code, has 1 prior conviction by any court referred to in section 922(g)(1) of title 18 for a violent felony (as defined in section 924(e)(2)(B) of that title) or a serious drug offense (as defined in section 924(e)(2)(A) of that title); and

"(2) appropriately enhance penalties in cases in which such a defendant has 2 prior convictions for a violent felony (as so defined) or a serious drug offense (as so defined)."

Sentencing Guidelines Increase for Terrorist Crimes. Pub.L. 103-322, Title XII, § 120004, Sept. 13, 1994, 108 Stat. __, provided that: "The United States Sentencing Commission is directed to amend its sentencing guidelines to provide an appropriate enhancement for any felony, whether committed within or outside the United States, that involves or is intended to promote international terrorism, unless such involvement or intent is itself an element of the crime."

Solicitation of Minor to Commit Crime; Amendment of Sentencing Guidelines. Pub.L. 103-322, Title XIV, § 140008, Sept. 13, 1994, 108 Stat. __, provided that:

"**(a) Directive to Sentencing Commission.**–(1) The United States Sentencing Commission shall promulgate guidelines or amend existing guidelines to provide that a defendant 21 years of age or older who has been convicted of an offense shall receive an appropriate sentence enhancement if the defendant involved a minor in the commission of the offense.

"(2) The Commission shall provide that the guidelines enhancement promulgated pursuant to paragraph (1) shall apply for any offense in relation to which the defendant has solicited, procured, recruited, counseled, encouraged, trained, directed, commanded, intimidated, or otherwise used or attempted to use any person less than 18 years of age with the intent that the minor would commit a Federal offense.

"**(b) Relevant Considerations.**–In implementing the directive in subsection (a), the Sentencing Commission shall consider–

"(1) the severity of the crime that the defendant intended the minor to commit;

"(2) the number of minors that the defendant used or attempted to use in relation to the offense;

"(3) the fact that involving a minor in a crime of violence is frequently of even greater seriousness than involving a minor in a drug trafficking offense, for which the guidelines already provide a two-level enhancement; and

"(4) the possible relevance of the proximity in age between the offender and the minor(s) involved in the offense."

Drug Free Truck Stops and Safety Rest Areas; Amendment of Sentencing Guidelines. Pub.L. 103-322, Title XVIII, § 180201(c), Sept. 13, 1994, 108 Stat. __, provided that: "Pursuant to its authority under section 994 of title 28, United States Code, and section 21 of the Sentencing Act of 1987 (28 U.S.C. 994 note), the United States Sentencing Commission shall promulgate guidelines, or shall amend existing guidelines, to provide an appropriate enhancement of punishment for a defendant convicted of violating section 409 of the Controlled Substances Act, as added by subsection (b) [of this section]."

Crimes Against the Elderly; Amendment of Sentencing Guidelines. Pub.L. 103-322, Title XXIV, § 240002, Sept. 13, 1994, 108 Stat. __, provided that:

"**(a) In General.**–Pursuant to its authority under the Sentencing Reform Act of 1984 and section 21 of the Sentencing Act of 1987 (including its authority to amend the sentencing guidelines and policy statements) and its authority to make such amendments on an emergency basis, the United States Sentencing Commission shall ensure that the applicable guideline range for a defendant convicted of a crime of violence against an elderly victim is sufficiently stringent to deter such a crime, to protect the public from additional crimes of such a defendant, and to adequately reflect the heinous nature of such an offense.

"**(b) Criteria.**–In carrying out subsection (a), the United States Sentencing Commission shall ensure that–

"(1) the guidelines provide for increasingly severe punishment for a defendant commensurate with the degree of physical harm caused to the elderly victim;

"(2) the guidelines take appropriate account of the vulnerability of the victim; and

"(3) the guidelines provide enhanced punishment for a defendant convicted of a crime of violence against an elderly victim who has previously been convicted of a crime of violence against an elderly victim, regardless of whether the conviction occurred in Federal or State court.

"**(c) Definitions.**–In this section–

"'crime of violence' means an offense under section 113, 114, 1111, 1112, 1113, 1117, 2241, 2242, or 2244 of title 18, United States Code.

"'elderly victim' means a victim who is 65 years of age or older at the time of an offense."

Increased Penalties for Fraud Against Older Victims; Amendment of Sentencing Guidelines. Pub.L. 103-322, Title XXV, § 250003, Sept. 13, 1994, 108 Stat. __, provided that:

"**(a) Review.**–The United States Sentencing Commission shall review and, if necessary, amend the sentencing guidelines to ensure that victim related adjustments for fraud offenses against older victims over the age of 55 are adequate.

"**(b) Report.**–Not later than 180 days after the date of enactment of this Act, the Sentencing Commission shall report to Congress the result of its review under subsection (a)."

Direction to United States Sentencing Commission regarding Sentencing Enhancements for Hate Crimes. Pub.L. 103-322, Title XXVIII, § 280003, Sept. 13, 1994, 108 Stat. __, provided that:

"**(a) Definition.**–In this section, 'hate crime' means a crime in which the defendant intentionally selects a victim, or in the case of a property crime, the property that is the object of the crime, because of the actual or perceived race, color, religion, national origin, ethnicity, gender, disability, or sexual orientation of any person.

"**(b) Sentencing Enhancement.**–Pursuant to section 994 of title 28, United States Code, the United States Sentencing Commission shall promulgate guidelines or amend existing guidelines to provide sentencing enhancements of not less than 3 offense levels for offenses that the finder of fact at trial determines beyond a reasonable doubt are hate crimes. In carrying out this section, the United States Sentencing Commission shall ensure that there is reasonable consistency with other guidelines, avoid duplicative punishments for substantially the same offense, and take into account any mitigating circumstances that might justify exceptions."

Cocaine Penalty Study. Pub.L. 103-322, Title XXVIII, § 280006, Sept. 13, 1994, 108 Stat. __, provided that: "Not later than December 31, 1994, the United States Sentencing Commission shall submit a report to Congress on issues relating to sentences applicable to offenses involving the possession or distribution of all forms of cocaine. The report shall address the differences in penalty levels that apply to different forms of cocaine and include any recommendations that the Commission may have for retention or modification of such differences in penalty levels."

Sexual Abuse and Exploitation of Minors; Amendment of Sentencing Guidelines. Pub.L. 102-141, Title VI, § 632, Oct. 28, 1991, 105 Stat. 876, provided that:

"(1) Pursuant to its authority under section 994 of title 28, United States Code [this section], the Sentencing Commission shall promulgate guidelines, or amend existing or proposed guidelines as follows:

"**(A)** Guideline 2G2.2 to provide a base offense level of not less than 15 and to provide at least a 5 level increase for offenders who have engaged in a pattern of activity involving the sexual abuse or exploitation of a minor.

"**(B)** Guideline 2G2.4 to provide that such guideline shall apply only to offense conduct that involves the simple possession of materials proscribed by chapter 110 of title 18, United States Code [section 2251 et seq. of Title 18, Crimes and Criminal Procedure] and guideline 2G2.2 to provide that such guideline shall apply to offense conduct that involves receipt or trafficking (including, but not limited to transportation, distribution, or shipping).

"**(C)** Guideline 2G2.4 to provide a base offense level of not less than 13, and to provide at least a 2 level increase for possessing 10 or more books, magazines, periodicals, films, video tapes or other items containing a visual depiction involving the sexual exploitation of a minor.

"**(D)** Section 2G3.1 to provide a base offense level of not less than 10.

"**(2)(A)** Notwithstanding any other provision of law, the Sentencing Commission shall promulgate the amendments mandated in subsection (1) by November 1, 1991, or within 30 days after enactment [probably means date of enactment of Pub.L. 102-141, which was approved Oct. 28, 1991], whichever is later. The amendments to the guidelines promulgated under subsection (1) shall take effect November 1, 1991, or 30 days after enactment, and shall supersede any amendment to the contrary contained in the amendments to the sentencing guidelines submitted to the Congress by the Sentencing Commission on or about May 1, 1991.

"**(B)** The provisions of section 944(x) of title 28, United States Code [subsec. (x) of this section], shall not apply to the promulgation or amendment of guidelines under this section."

Sexual Crimes Against Children; Amendment of Sentencing Guidelines. Pub.L. 101-647, Title III, § 321, Nov. 29, 1990, 104 Stat. 4817, provided that: "The United States Sentencing Commission shall amend existing guidelines for sentences involving sexual crimes against children, including offenses contained in chapter 109A of title 18 [chapter 109A of Title 18, Crimes and Criminal Procedure], so that more substantial penalties may be imposed if the Commission determines current penalties are inadequate."

Enhanced Penalties for Kidnapping Offenses Involving Children; Promulgation of Guidelines. Pub.L. 101-647, Title IV, § 401, Nov. 29, 1990, 104 Stat 4819, amended 18 U.S.C. § 1201 by adding the following new subsection:

"(g) Special Rule for Certain Offenses Involving Children.-

"**(1)** To Whom Applicable.-If-

"**(A)** the victim of an offense under this section has not attained the age of eighteen years; and

"**(B)** the offender-

"**(i)** has attained such age; and

"**(ii)** is not-

"**(I)** a parent;

"**(II)** a grandparent;

"**(III)** a brother;

"**(IV)** a sister;

"**(V)** an aunt;

"**(VI)** an uncle; or

"**(VII)** an individual having legal custody of the victim;

the sentence under this section for such offense shall be subject to paragraph (2) of this subsection.

"**(2)** Guidelines.-The United States Sentencing Commission is directed to amended the existing guidelines for the offense of 'kidnapping, abduction, or unlawful restraint,' by including the following additional specific offense characteristics: If the victim was intentionally maltreated (i.e., denied either food or medical care) to a life-threatening degree, increase by 4 levels; if the victim was sexually exploited (i.e., abused, used involuntarily for pornographic purposes) increase by 3 levels; if the victim was placed in the care or custody of another person who does not have a legal right to such care or custody of the child either in exchange for money or other consideration, increase by 3 levels; if the defendant allowed the child to be subjected to any of the conduct specified in this section by another person, then increase by 2 levels."

Sentencing Guidelines Increased Penalties in Major Bank Crimes Cases. Pub.L. 101-647, Title XXV, § 2507, Nov. 29, 1990, 104 Stat. 4862, provided that:

"**(a) Increased Penalties.**-Pursuant to section 994 of title 28, United States Code [this section], and section 21 of the Sentencing Act of 1987 [Pub.L. 100-182, § 21, set out as a note under this section] the United States Sentencing Commission shall promulgate guidelines, or amend existing guidelines, to provide that a defendant convicted of violating, or conspiring to violate, section 215, 656, 657, 1005, 1006, 1007, 1014, 1032, or 1344 of title 18, United States Code [sections 215, 656, 657, 1005, 1006, 1007, 1014, 1032, or 1344 of Title 18, Crimes and Criminal Procedure], or section 1341 or 1343 [section 1341 or 1343 of Title 18] affecting a financial institution (as defined in section 20 of title 18, United States Code) [section 20 of Title 18] shall be assigned not less than offense level 24 under chapter 2 of the sentencing guidelines if the defendant derives more than $1,000,000 in gross receipts from the offense.

"**(b) Amendments to Sentencing Guidelines.**-If the sentencing guidelines are amended after the effective date of this section, the Sentencing Commission shall implement the instruction set forth in subsection (a) so as to achieve a comparable result.

Sentencing Guidelines Relating to Methamphetamine Offenses. Pub.L. 101-647, Title XXVII, § 2701, Nov. 29, 1990, 104 Stat. 4912, provided that: "The United States Sentencing Commission is instructed to amend the existing guidelines for offenses involving smokable crystal methamphetamine under section 401(b) of the Controlled Substances Act (21 U.S.C. § 841(b)) [section 841(b) of Title 21, Food and Drugs] so that convictions for offenses involving smokable crystal methamphetamine will be assigned an offense level under the guidelines which is two levels above that which would have been assigned to the same offense involving other forms of methamphetamine."

Sentencing Guidelines for Crimes Involving Federally Insured Financial Institutions. Pub.L. 101-73, Title IX, § 961(m), Aug. 9, 1989, 103 Stat. 501, provided that:

"Pursuant to section 994 of title 28, United States Code [this section], and section 21 of the Sentencing Act of 1987 [Pub.L. 100-182, § 21, set out as a note under this section], the United States Sentencing Commission shall promulgate guidelines, or amend existing guidelines, to provide for a substantial period of incarceration for a violation of, or a conspiracy to violate, section 215, 656, 657, 1005, 1006, 1007, 1014, 1341, 1343, or 1344 of title 18, United States Code [sections 215, 656, 657, 1005, 1006, 1007, 1014, 1341, 1343, or 1344 of Title 18, Crimes and Criminal Procedure], that substantially jeopardizes the safety and soundness of a federally insured financial institution."

Sentencing Guidelines for Personal Injury From Fraud. Pub.L. 100-700, Chapter 47, § 2(b), Nov. 19, 1988, 102 Stat. 4632, provided that:

"Pursuant to its authority under section 994(p) of title 28, United States Code [section 994(p) of Title 28, Judiciary and Judicial Procedure] and section 21 of the Sentencing Act of 1987 [Pub.L. 100-182, § 21, set out as a note under this section], the United States Sentencing Commission shall promulgate guidelines, or shall amend existing guidelines, to provide for appropriate penalty enhancements, where conscious or reckless risk of serious personal injury resulting from the fraud has occurred. The Commission shall consider the appropriateness of assigning to such a defendant an offense level under Chapter Two of the sentencing guidelines that is at least two levels greater than the level that would have been assigned had conscious or reckless risk of serious personal injury not resulted from the fraud."

Penalties For Importation of Controlled Substances by Aircraft and Other Vessels; Promulgation of Sentencing Guidelines. Section 6453 of Pub.L. 100-690 provided that:

"**(a) In general.**–Pursuant to its authority under section 994(p) of title 28, United States Code [subsec. (p) of this section], and section 21 of the Sentencing Act of 1987 [section 21 of Pub.L. 100-182, set out as a note under this section], the United States Sentencing Commission shall promulgate guidelines, or shall amend existing guidelines, to provide that a defendant convicted of violating section 1010(a) of the Controlled Substances Import and Export Act (21 U.S.C. 960(a)) [section 960(a) of Title 21, Food and Drugs] under circumstances in which–

"**(1)** an aircraft other than a regularly scheduled commercial air carrier was used to import the controlled substance; or

"**(2)** the defendant acted as a pilot, copilot, captain, navigator, flight officer, or any other operation officer aboard any craft of vessel carrying a controlled substance.

shall be assigned an offense level under chapter 2 of the sentencing guidelines that is–

"**(A)** two levels greater than the level that would have been assigned had the offense not been committed under circumstances set forth in (A) or (B) above; and

"**(B)** in no event less than level 26.

"**(b) Effect of amendment.**–If the sentencing guidelines are amended after the effective date of this section [probably means date of enactment of this section, Nov. 18, 1988], the Sentencing Commission shall implement the instruction set forth in subsection (a) so as to achieve a comparable result."

Enhanced Penalties For Offenses Involving Children; Promulgation of Sentencing Guidelines. Section 6454 of Pub.L. 100-690 provided that:

"**(a) In general.**–Pursuant to its authority under section 994(p) of title 28, United States Code [subsec. (p) of this section], and section 21 of the Sentencing Act of 1987 [section 21 of Pub.L. 100-182, set out as a note under this section], the United States Sentencing Commission shall promulgate guidelines, or shall amend existing guidelines, to provide that a defendant convicted of violating sections 405, 405A, or 405B of the Controlled Substances Act (21 U.S.C. 845, 845a or 845b) [sections 845, 845a, and 845b of Title 21, Food and Drugs] involving a person under 18 years of age shall be assigned an offense level under chapter 2 of the sentencing guidelines that is–

"**(1)** two levels greater than the level that would have been assigned for the underlying controlled substance offense; and

"**(2)** in no event less than level 26.

"**(b) Effects of amendment.**–If the sentencing guidelines are amended after the effective date of this section [probably means date of enactment of this section, Nov. 18, 1988], the Sentencing Commission shall implement the instruction set forth in subsection (a) so as to achieve a comparable result.

"**(c) Multiple enhancements.**–The guidelines referred to in subsection (a), as promulgated or amended under such subsection, shall provide that an offense that could be subject to multiple enhancements pursuant to such subsection is subject to not more than one such enhancement."

Drug Offenses Within Federal Prisons; Promulgation of Sentencing Guidelines. Section 6468(c) and (d) of Pub.L. 100-690 provided that:

"**(c)** Pursuant to its authority under section 994(p) of title 28, United States Code [subsec. (p) of this section], and section 21 of the Sentencing Act of 1987 [section 21 of Pub.L. 100-182, set out as a note under this section], the United States Sentencing Commission shall promulgate guidelines, or shall amend existing guidelines, to provide that a defendant convicted of violating section 1791(a)(1) of title 18, United States Code [section 1791(a)(1) of Title 18, Crimes and Criminal Procedure], and punishable under section 1791(b)(1) of that title [section 1791(b)(1) of Title 18] as so redesignated, shall be assigned an offense level under chapter 2 of the sentencing guidelines that is–

"**(1)** two levels greater than the level that would have been assigned had the offense not been committed in prison; and

"**(2)** in no event less than level 26.

"**(d)** If the sentencing guidelines are amended after the effective date of this section [probably means the date of enactment of this section, Nov. 18, 1988], the Sentencing Commission shall implement the instruction set forth in subsection (c) so as to achieve a comparable result."

Common Carrier Operation Under Influence of Alcohol or Drugs; Promulgation of Sentencing Guidelines. Section 6482(c) of Pub.L. 100-690 provided that:

"**(1)** Pursuant to its authority under section 994(p) of title 28, United States Code [subsec. (p) of this section], and section 21 of the Sentencing Act of 1987 [section 21 of Pub.L. 100-182, set out as a note under this section], the United States Sentencing Commission shall promulgate guidelines, or shall amend existing guidelines, to provide that–

"**(A)** a defendant convicted of violating section 342 of title 18, United States Code [section 342 of Title 18, Crimes and Criminal Procedure], under circumstances in which death results, shall be assigned an offense level under chapter 2 of the sentencing guidelines that is not less than level 26; and

"**(B)** a defendant convicted of violating section 342 of title 18, United States Code [section 342 of Title 18, Crimes and Criminal Procedure], under circumstances in which serious bodily injury results, shall be assigned an offense level under chapter 2 of the sentencing guidelines that is not less than level 21.

"**(2)** If the sentencing guidelines are amended after the effective date of this section [probably means date of enactment of this section, Nov. 18, 1988], the Sentencing Commission shall implement the instruction set forth in paragraph (1) so as to achieve a comparable result."

Emergency Guidelines Promulgation Authority. Section 21 of Pub.L. 100-182 provided that:

"**(a) In general.**–In the case of–

"**(1)** an invalidated sentencing guideline;

"**(2)** the creation of a new offense or amendment of an existing offense; or

"**(3)** any other reason relating to the application of a previously established sentencing guideline, and determined by the United States Sentencing Commission to be urgent and compelling;

the Commission, by affirmative vote of at least four members of the Commission, and pursuant to its rules and regulations and consistent with all pertinent provisions of title 28 and title 18, United States Code, shall promulgate and distribute to all courts of the United States and to the United States Probation System a temporary guideline or amendment to an existing guideline, to remain in effect until and during the pendency of the next report to Congress under section 994(p) of title 28, United States Code [subsec. (p) of this section].

"**(b) Expiration of authority.**–The authority of the Commission under paragraphs (1) and (2) of subsection (a) shall expire on November 1, 1989. The authority of the Commission to promulgate and distribute guidelines under paragraph (3) of subsection (a) shall expire on May 1, 1988."

Initial Sentencing Guidelines. Provisions directing that the United States Sentencing Commission submit to Congress within 30 months of Oct. 12, 1984, the initial sentencing guidelines promulgated pursuant to subsec. (a)(1) of this section, see section 235(a)(1)(B)(i) of Pub.L. 98-473, as amended, set out as a note under section 3551 of Title 18, Crimes and Criminal Procedure.

Effective Date of Sentencing Guidelines. For provisions directing that the sentencing guidelines promulgated pursuant to subsec. (a)(1) of this section not go into effect until the day after–

(I) the United States Sentencing Commission has submitted the initial set of sentencing guidelines to the Congress, along with a report stating the reasons for the Commission's recommendations;

(II) the General Accounting Office has undertaken a study of the guidelines, and their potential impact in comparison with the operation of the existing sentencing and parole release system, and has, within one hundred and fifty days of submission of the guidelines, reported to the Congress the results of its study; and

(III) the Congress has had six months after the date described in subclause (I) in which to examine the guidelines and consider the reports, see section 235(a)(1)(B)(ii) of Pub.L. 98-473, set out as a note under section 3551 of Title 18, Crimes and Criminal Procedure.

General Accounting Office Study of Impact and Operation of Sentencing Guideline System. Section 236 of Pub.L. 98-473 provided that:

"**(a)(1)** Four years after the sentencing guidelines promulgated pursuant to section 994(a)(1) [subsec. (a)(1) of this section], and the provisions of section 3581, 3583, and 3624 of title 18, United States Code, go into effect, the General Accounting Office shall undertake a study of the guidelines in order to determine their impact and compare the guideline system with the operation of the previous sentencing and parole release system, and within six months of the undertaking of such study, report to the Congress the results of its study.

"**(2)** Within one month of the start of the study required under subsection (a), the United States Sentencing Commission shall submit a report to the General Accounting Office, all appropriate courts, the Department of Justice, and the Congress detailing the operation of the sentencing guideline system and discussing any problems with the system or reforms needed. The report shall include an evaluation of the impact of the sentencing guidelines on prosecutorial discretion, plea bargaining, disparities in sentencing, and the use of incarceration, and shall be issued by affirmative vote of a majority of the voting members of the Commission.

"**(b)** The Congress shall review the study submitted pursuant to subsection (a) in order to determine–

"**(1)** whether the sentencing guideline system has been effective;

"**(2)** whether any changes should be made in the sentencing guideline system; and

"**(3)** whether the parole system should be reinstated in some form and the life of the Parole Commission extended."

Study of Sentencing Guidelines. Section 236 of Pub.L. 98-473 provided that:

"**(a)(1)** Four years after the sentencing guidelines promulgated pursuant to section 994(a)(1) [subsec. (a)(1) of this section], and the provisions of sections 3581, 3583, and 3624 of title 18, United States Code, go into effect, the General Accounting Office shall undertake a study of the guidelines in order to determine their impact and compare the guidelines system with the operation of the previous sentencing and parole release system, and, within six months of the undertaking of such study, report to the Congress the results of its study.

"**(2)** Within one month of the start of the study required under subsection (a), the United States Sentencing Commission shall submit a report to the General Accounting Office, all appropriate courts, the Department of Justice, and the Congress detailing the operation of the sentencing guideline system and discussing any problems with the system or reforms needed. The report shall include an evaluation of the impact of the sentencing guidelines on prosecutorial discretion, plea bargaining, disparities in sentencing, and the use of incarceration, and shall be issued by affirmative vote of a majority of the voting members of the Commission.

"**(b)** The Congress shall review the study submitted pursuant to subsection (a) in order to determine–

"**(1)** whether the sentencing guideline system has been effective;

"**(2)** whether any changes should be made in the sentencing guideline system; and

"**(3)** whether the parole system should be reinstated in some form and the life of the Parole Commission extended."

§ 995. Powers of the Commission

(a) The Commission, by vote of a majority of the members present and voting, shall have the power to–

(1) establish general policies and promulgate such rules and regulations for the Commission as are necessary to carry out the purposes of this chapter;

(2) appoint and fix the salary and duties of the Staff Director of the Sentencing Commission, who shall serve at the discretion of the Commission and who shall be compensated at a rate not to exceed the highest rate now or hereafter prescribed for Level 6 of the Senior Executive Service Schedule (5 U.S.C. 5382);

(3) deny, revise, or ratify any request for regular, supplemental, or deficiency appropriations prior to any submission of such request to the Office of Management and Budget by the Chair;

(4) procure for the Commission temporary and intermittent services to the same extent as is authorized by section 3109(b) of title 5, United States Code;

(5) utilize, with their consent, the services, equipment, personnel, information, and facilities of other Federal, State, local, and private agencies and instrumentalities with or without reimbursement therefor;

(6) without regard to 31 U.S.C. 3324, enter into and perform such contracts, leases, cooperative agreements, and other transactions as may be necessary in the conduct of the functions of the Commission, with any public agency, or with any person, firm, association, corporation, educational institution, or nonprofit organization;

(7) accept and employ, in carrying out the provisions of this title, voluntary and uncompensated services, notwithstanding the provisions of 31 U.S.C. 1342, however, individuals providing such services shall not be considered Federal employees except for purposes of chapter 81 of title 5, United States Code, with respect to job-incurred disability and title 28, United States Code, with respect to tort claims;

(8) request such information, data, and reports from any Federal agency or judicial officer as the Commission may from time to time require and as may be produced consistent with other law;

(9) monitor the performance of probation officers with regard to sentencing recommendations, including application of the Sentencing Commission guidelines and policy statements;

(10) issue instructions to probation officers concerning the application of Commission guidelines and policy statements;

(11) arrange with the head of any other Federal agency for the performance by such agency of any function of the Commission, with or without reimbursement;

(12) establish a research and development program within the Commission for the purpose of–

(A) serving as a clearinghouse and information center for the collection, preparation, and dissemination of information on Federal sentencing practices; and

(B) assisting and serving in a consulting capacity to Federal courts, departments, and agencies in the development, maintenance, and coordination of sound sentencing practices;

(13) collect systematically the data obtained from studies, research, and the empirical experience of public and private agencies concerning the sentencing process;

(14) publish data concerning the sentencing process;

(15) collect systematically and disseminate information concerning sentences actually imposed, and the relationship of such sentences to the factors set forth in section 3553(a) of title 18, United States Code;

(16) collect systematically and disseminate information regarding effectiveness of sentences imposed;

(17) devise and conduct, in various geographical locations, seminars and workshops providing continuing studies for persons engaged in the sentencing field;

(18) devise and conduct periodic training programs of instruction in sentencing techniques for judicial and probation personnel and other persons connected with the sentencing process;

(19) study the feasibility of developing guidelines for the disposition of juvenile delinquents;

(20) make recommendations to Congress concerning modification or enactment of statutes relating to sentencing, penal, and correctional matters that the Commission finds to be necessary and advisable to carry out an effective, humane and rational sentencing policy;

(21) hold hearings and call witnesses that might assist the Commission in the exercise of its powers or duties;

(22) perform such other functions as are required to permit Federal courts to meet their responsibilities under section 3553(a) of title 18, United States Code, and to permit others involved in the Federal criminal justice system to meet their related responsibilities;

(23) retain private attorneys to provide legal advice to the Commission in the conduct of its work, or to appear for or represent the Commission in any case in which the Commission is authorized by law to

represent itself, or in which the Commission is representing itself with the consent of the Department of Justice; and the Commission may in its discretion pay reasonable attorney's fees to private attorneys employed by it out of its appropriated funds. When serving as officers or employees of the United States, such private attorneys shall be considered special government employees as defined in section 202(a) of title 18; and

(24) grant incentive awards to its employees pursuant to chapter 45 of title 5, United States Code.

(b) The Commission shall have such other powers and duties and shall perform such other functions as may be necessary to carry out the purposes of this chapter, and may delegate to any member or designated person such powers as may be appropriate other than the power to establish general policy statements and guidelines pursuant to section 994(a)(1) and (2), the issuance of general policies and promulgation of rules and regulations pursuant to subsection (a)(1) of this section, and the decisions as to the factors to be considered in establishment of categories of offenses and offenders pursuant to section 994(b). The Commission shall, with respect to its activities under subsections (a)(9), (a)(10), (a)(11), (a)(12), (a)(13), (a)(14), (a)(15), (a)(16), (a)(17), and (a)(18), to the extent practicable, utilize existing resources of the Administrative Office of the United States Courts and the Federal Judicial Center for the purpose of avoiding unnecessary duplication.

(c) Upon the request of the Commission, each Federal agency is authorized and directed to make its services, equipment, personnel, facilities, and information available to the greatest practicable extent to the Commission in the execution of its functions.

(d) A simple majority of the membership then serving shall constitute a quorum for the conduct of business. Other than for the promulgation of guidelines and policy statements pursuant to section 994, the Commission may exercise its powers and fulfill its duties by the vote of a simple majority of the members present.

(e) Except as otherwise provided by law, the Commission shall maintain and make available for public inspection a record of the final vote of each member on any action taken by it.

(Added Pub.L. 98-473, Title II, § 217(a), Oct. 12, 1984, 98 Stat. 2024; amended Pub.L. 100-690, Title VII, §§ 7104, 7105, 7106(b), Nov. 18, 1988, 102 Stat. 4418; Pub.L. 101-650, Title III, § 325(b)(5), Dec. 1, 1990, 104 Stat. 5121; Pub.L. 103-322, Title XXVIII, § 280005(c)(1), Sept. 13, 1994, 108 Stat. __.)

EDITORIAL NOTES

References in Text. The provisions of title 28, United States Code, with respect to tort claims, referred to in subsec. (a)(7), are classified generally to section 1346(b) and chapter 171 (section 2671 et seq.) of this title.

Effective Date. Section effective Oct. 12, 1984, see section 235(a)(1)(B)(i) of Pub.L. 98-473, set out as a note under section 3551 of Title 18, Crimes and Criminal Procedure.

§ 996. Director and staff

(a) The Staff Director shall supervise the activities of persons employed by the Commission and perform other duties assigned to the Staff Director by the Commission.

(b) The Staff Director shall, subject to the approval of the Commission, appoint such officers and employees as are necessary in the execution of the functions of the Commission. The officers and employees of the Commission shall be exempt from the provisions of part III of title 5, United States Code, except the following chapters: 45 (Incentive Awards), 81 (Compensation for Work Injuries), 83 (Retirement), 85 (Unemployment Compensation), 87 (Life Insurance), and 89 (Health Insurance).

(Added Pub.L. 98-473, Title II, § 217(a), Oct. 12, 1984, 98 Stat. 2026, and amended Pub.L. 100-690, Title VII, § 7106(c), Nov. 18, 1988, 102 Stat. 4418; Pub.L. 101-650, Title III, § 325(b)(6), Dec. 1, 1990, 104 Stat. 5121; Pub.L. 103-322, Title XXVIII, § 280005(c)(5), Sept. 13, 1994, 108 Stat. __.)

EDITORIAL NOTES

Effective Date. Section effective Oct. 12, 1984, see section 235(a)(1)(B)(i) of Pub.L. 98-473, set out as a note under section 3551 of Title 18, Crimes and Criminal Procedure.

§ 997. Annual report

The Commission shall report annually to the Judicial Conference of the United States, the Congress, and the President of the United States on the activities of the Commission.

(Added Pub.L. 98-473, Title II, § 217(a), Oct. 12, 1984, 98 Stat. 2026.)

EDITORIAL NOTES

Effective Date. Section effective Oct. 12, 1984, see section 235(a)(1)(B)(i) of Pub.L. 98-473, set out as a note under section 3551 of Title 18, Crimes and Criminal Procedure.

§ 998. Definitions

As used in this chapter–

(a) "Commission" means the United States Sentencing Commission;

(b) "Commissioner" means a member of the United States Sentencing Commission;

(c) "guidelines" means the guidelines promulgated by the Commission pursuant to section 994(a) of this title; and

(d) "rules and regulations" means rules and regulations promulgated by the Commission pursuant to section 995 of this title.

(Added Pub.L. 98-473, Title II, § 217(a), Oct. 12, 1984, 98 Stat. 2026.)

EDITORIAL NOTES

Effective Date. Section effective Oct. 12, 1984, see section 235(a)(1)(B)(i) of Pub.L. 98-473, set out as a note under section 3551 of Title 18, Crimes and Criminal Procedure.

———

APPENDIX C - AMENDMENTS TO THE GUIDELINES MANUAL

This Appendix presents the amendments to the guidelines, policy statements, and official commentary promulgated since issuance of the Guidelines Manual of October 1987.*

The format under which the amendments are presented in this Appendix is designed to facilitate a comparison between previously existing and amended provisions, in the event it becomes necessary to reference the former guideline, policy statement, or commentary language.

AMENDMENTS

1. Section 1B1.1(b) is amended by inserting "in the order listed" immediately following "Chapter Two".

   Section 1B1.1(d) is amended by deleting "one" and "three" and inserting in lieu thereof "(a)" and "(c)" respectively.

   The Commentary to §1B1.1 captioned "Application Notes" is amended by inserting the following additional note:

   > "4. The offense level adjustments from more than one specific offense characteristic within an offense guideline are cumulative (added together) unless the guideline specifies that only the greater (or greatest) is to be used. Within each specific offense characteristic subsection, however, the offense level adjustments are alternative; only the one that best describes the conduct is to be used. E.g., in §2A2.2(b)(3), pertaining to degree of bodily injury, the subsection that best describes the level of bodily injury is used; the adjustments for different degrees of bodily injury (subsections (A), (B), and (C)) are not added together.".

   The purposes of this amendment are to correct a clerical error and to clarify the operation of the guidelines by consolidating the former §1B1.4 (Determining the Offense Level) with this section. **The effective date of this amendment is January 15, 1988.**

2. Section 1B1.2(a) is amended by deleting "guideline" the first time it appears and inserting in lieu thereof "offense guideline section".

---

*In addition to the numbered amendments set forth in this Appendix, the following minor editorial revisions have been made to update the Manual to reflect that the guidelines system now constitutes current practice: the terms "current practice," "existing practice," and "present practice," where used to denote sentencing practice prior to guidelines, have been replaced by the term "pre-guidelines practice" and conforming tense changes have been made in §2B3.1, comment. (backg'd); Chapter Two, Part C, intro. comment., §2F1.1, comment. (backg'd); §2J1.3, comment. (backg'd); §2K2.1, comment. (backg'd); §2R1.1, comment. (backg'd); §2T1.1, comment. (backg'd); §2T1.2, comment. (backg'd); §2T1.8, comment. (backg'd); §6A1.3, comment.; and Chapter Six, Part B, intro. comment. Also, an additional sentence ("For additional statutory provision(s), see Appendix A (Statutory Index).") has been inserted for clarity in the Commentary captioned "Statutory Provision[s]" of each Chapter Two offense guideline that has additional statutory provision(s) listed in Appendix A (Statutory Index). **The effective date of this amendment is November 1, 1990.**

In addition, citations to court cases have been updated, as appropriate, in the Manual and this Appendix.

Section 1B1.2(a) is amended by inserting the following additional sentence at the end of the subsection: "Similarly, stipulations to additional offenses are treated as if the defendant had been convicted of separate counts charging those offenses.".

Section 1B1.2(b) is amended by deleting:

> "The court shall determine any applicable specific offense characteristic, victim- related adjustment, or departure from the guidelines attributable to offense conduct, according to the principles in §1B1.3 (Relevant Conduct).",

and inserting in lieu thereof:

> "After determining the appropriate offense guideline section pursuant to subsection (a) of this section, determine the applicable guideline range in accordance with §1B1.3 (Relevant Conduct).".

The Commentary to §1B1.2 captioned "Application Notes" is amended in Note 2 by deleting:

> "any applicable victim-related adjustment from Chapter Three, Part A, and any guideline departures attributable to the offense conduct from Chapter Five, Part K, using a 'relevant conduct' standard, as that standard is defined in §1B1.3.",

and inserting in lieu thereof:

> "and any other applicable sentencing factors pursuant to the relevant conduct definition in §1B1.3.".

The Commentary to §1B1.2 captioned "Application Notes" is amended in Note 3 by deleting:

> "In such instances, the court should consider all conduct, circumstances, and injury relevant to the offense (as well as all relevant offender characteristics). See §1B1.3 (Relevant Conduct).",

and inserting in lieu thereof:

> "See §§1B1.3 (Relevant Conduct) and 1B1.4 (Information to be Used in Imposing Sentence).".

The purposes of this amendment are to correct a clerical error and to clarify the operation of the guidelines. **The effective date of this amendment is January 15, 1988.**

3. Chapter One, Part B is amended by deleting §1B1.3 in its entirety as follows:

> "§1B1.3. Relevant Conduct
>
> To determine the seriousness of the offense conduct, all conduct, circumstances, and injuries relevant to the offense of conviction shall be taken into account.
>
> (a) Unless otherwise specified under the guidelines, conduct and circumstances relevant to the offense of conviction means:
>
> acts or omissions committed or aided and abetted by the defendant, or by a person for whose conduct the defendant is legally accountable, that (1) are part of the same course of conduct, or a common scheme or plan, as the offense of conviction, or (2) are relevant to the defendant's state of mind or motive in committing the offense of conviction, or (3)

indicate the defendant's degree of dependence upon criminal activity for a livelihood.

(b) Injury relevant to the offense of conviction means harm which is caused intentionally, recklessly or by criminal negligence in the course of conduct relevant to the offense of conviction.

Commentary

Application Note:

1. In sentencing, the court should consider all relevant offense and offender characteristics. For purposes of assessing offense conduct, the relevant conduct and circumstances of the offense of conviction are as follows:

   a. conduct directed toward preparation for or commission of the offense of conviction, and efforts to avoid detection and responsibility for the offense of conviction;

   b. conduct indicating that the offense of conviction was to some degree part of a broader purpose, scheme, or plan;

   c. conduct that is relevant to the state of mind or motive of the defendant in committing the crime;

   d. conduct that is relevant to the defendant's involvement in crime as a livelihood.

   The first three criteria are derived from two sources, Rule 8(a) of the Federal Rules of Criminal Procedure, governing joinder of similar or related offenses, and Rule 404(b) of the Federal Rules of Evidence, permitting admission of evidence of other crimes to establish motive, intent, plan, and common scheme. These rules provide standards that govern consideration at trial of crimes "of the same or similar character," and utilize concepts and terminology familiar to judges, prosecutors, and defenders. The governing standard should be liberally construed in favor of considering information generally appropriate to sentencing. When other crimes are inadmissible under the Rule 404(b) standard, such crimes may not be "relevant to the offense of conviction" under the criteria that determine this question for purposes of Chapter Two; such crimes would, however, be considered in determining the relevant offender characteristics to the extent authorized by Chapter Three (Adjustments), and Chapter Four (Criminal History and Criminal Livelihood) and Chapter Five, Part H (Specific Offender Characteristics). This construction is consistent with the existing rule that "[n]o limitation shall be placed on the information concerning the background, character, and conduct of a person convicted of an offense . . . for the purpose of imposing an appropriate sentence," 18 U.S.C. § 3577, so long as the information "has sufficient indicia of reliability to support its probable accuracy." United States v. Marshall, 519 F. Supp. 751 (D. Wis. 1981), aff'd, 719 F.2d 887 (7th Cir. 1983).

   The last of these criteria is intended to ensure that a judge may consider at sentencing, information that, although not specifically within other criteria of relevance, indicates that the defendant engages in crime for a living. Inclusion of this information in sentencing considerations is consistent with 28 U.S.C. § 994(d)(11).".

A replacement guideline with accompanying commentary is inserted as §1B1.3 (Relevant Conduct (Factors that Determine the Guideline Range)).

The purpose of this amendment is to clarify the guideline. The amended language restates the intent of §1B1.3 as originally promulgated. **The effective date of this amendment is January 15, 1988.**

4. Chapter One, Part B is amended by deleting §1B1.4 in its entirety as follows:

"§1B1.4. Determining the Offense Level

In determining the offense level:

(a) determine the base offense level from Chapter Two;

(b) make any applicable adjustments for specific offense characteristics from Chapter Two in the order listed;

(c) make any applicable adjustments from Chapter Three;

(d) make any applicable adjustments from Chapter Four, Part B (Career Offenders and Criminal Livelihood).

Commentary

Application Notes:

1. A particular guideline (in the base offense level or in a specific offense characteristic) may expressly direct that a particular factor be applied only if the defendant was convicted of a particular statute. E.g., in §2K2.3, a base offense level of 12 is used "if convicted under 26 U.S.C. § 5861." Unless such an express direction is included, conviction under the statute is not required. Thus, use of a statutory reference to describe a particular set of circumstances does not require a conviction under the referenced statute. Examples of this usage are found in §2K1.3(b)(4) ("if the defendant was a person prohibited from receiving explosives under 18 U.S.C. § 842(i), or if the defendant knowingly distributed explosives to a person prohibited from receiving explosives under 18 U.S.C. § 842(i), increase by 10 levels"); and §2A3.4(b)(2) ("if the abusive contact was accomplished as defined in 18 U.S.C. § 2242, increase by 4 levels"). In such cases, the particular circumstances described are to be evaluated under the "relevant conduct" standard of §1B1.3.

2. Once the appropriate base offense level is determined, all specific offense characteristics are to be applied in the order listed.

3. The offense level adjustments from more than one specific offense characteristic within an offense guideline are cumulative (added together) unless the guideline specifies that only the greater (or greatest) is to be used. Within each specific offense characteristic subsection, however, the offense level adjustments are alternative; only the one that best describes the conduct is to be used. E.g., in §2A2.2(b)(3), pertaining to degree of bodily injury, the subsection that best describes the level of bodily injury is used; the adjustments from different degrees of bodily injury (subsections (A), (B) and (C)) are not added together).

4. The adjustments in Chapter Three that may apply include Part A (Victim-Related Adjustments), Part B (Role in the Offense), Part C (Obstruction), Part D (Multiple Counts), and Part E (Acceptance of Responsibility).".

A replacement guideline with accompanying commentary is inserted as §1B1.4 (Information to be Used in Imposing Sentence (Selecting a Point Within the Guideline Range or Departing from the Guidelines)).

The purposes of this amendment are to remove material made redundant by the reorganization of this Part and to replace it with material that clarifies the operation of the guidelines. The material formerly in this section is now covered by §1B1.1. **The effective date of this amendment is January 15, 1988.**

5. Chapter One, Part B, is amended by inserting an additional guideline with accompanying commentary as §1B1.8 (Use of Certain Information).

The purpose of this amendment is to facilitate cooperation agreements by ensuring that certain information revealed by a defendant, as part of an agreement to cooperate with the government by providing information concerning unlawful activities of others, will not be used to increase the guideline sentence. **The effective date of this amendment is June 15, 1988.**

6. Chapter One, Part B, is amended by inserting an additional guideline with accompanying commentary as §1B1.9 (Petty Offenses).

The purpose of this guideline is to delete coverage of petty offenses. **The effective date of this amendment is June 15, 1988.**

7. Section 2B1.1(b)(1) is amended by deleting "value of the property taken" and inserting in lieu thereof "loss".

The Commentary to §2B1.1 captioned "Application Notes" is amended in Note 2 by deleting:

> "Loss is to be based upon replacement cost to the victim or market value of the property, whichever is greater.",

and inserting in lieu thereof:

> "'Loss' means the value of the property taken, damaged, or destroyed. Ordinarily, when property is taken or destroyed the loss is the fair market value of the particular property at issue. Where the market value is difficult to ascertain or inadequate to measure harm to the victim, the court may measure loss in some other way, such as reasonable replacement cost to the victim. When property is damaged the loss is the cost of repairs, not to exceed the loss had the property been destroyed. In cases of partially completed conduct, the loss is to be determined in accordance with the provisions of §2X1.1 (Attempt, Solicitation, or Conspiracy Not Covered by a Specific Guideline). E.g., in the case of the theft of a government check or money order, loss refers to the loss that would have occurred if the check or money order had been cashed. Similarly, if a defendant is apprehended in the process of taking a vehicle, the loss refers to the value of the vehicle even if the vehicle is recovered immediately.".

The purpose of this amendment is to clarify the guideline in respect to the determination of loss. **The effective date of this amendment is June 15, 1988.**

8. Section 2B1.2 is amended by transposing the texts of subsections (b)(2) and (3).

The Commentary to §2B1.2 captioned "Application Notes" is amended by deleting:

"3. For consistency with §2B1.1, it is the Commission's intent that specific offense characteristic (b)(3) be applied before (b)(2).",

and by renumbering Note 4 as Note 3.

The purpose of this amendment is to correct a clerical error in the guideline. Correction of the error makes the deleted commentary unnecessary. **The effective date of this amendment is January 15, 1988.**

9. Section 2B1.2(b)(1) is amended by deleting "taken", and inserting "stolen" immediately before "property".

The purpose of this amendment is to correct a clerical error. **The effective date of this amendment is June 15, 1988.**

10. Section 2B1.3(b)(1) is amended by deleting "amount of the property damage or destruction, or the cost of restoration," and inserting in lieu thereof "loss".

The Commentary to §2B1.3 captioned "Application Notes" is amended in Note 2 by deleting "property" and inserting in lieu thereof "loss".

The purpose of this amendment is to clarify the guideline in respect to the determination of loss. **The effective date of this amendment is June 15, 1988.**

11. The Commentary to §2B2.1 captioned "Application Notes" is amended in Note 4 by inserting "or other dangerous weapon" immediately following "firearm".

The purpose of the amendment is to correct a clerical error. **The effective date of this amendment is January 15, 1988.**

12. Section 2B2.1(b)(2) is amended by deleting "value of the property taken or destroyed" and inserting in lieu thereof "loss".

The Commentary to §2B2.1 captioned "Application Notes" is amended in Note 3 by deleting "property" and inserting in lieu thereof "loss".

The purpose of this amendment is to clarify the guideline in respect to the determination of loss. **The effective date of this amendment is June 15, 1988.**

13. Section 2B2.2(b)(2) is amended by deleting "value of the property taken or destroyed" and inserting in lieu thereof "loss".

The Commentary to §2B2.2 captioned "Application Notes" is amended in Note 3 by deleting "property" and inserting in lieu thereof "loss".

The purpose of this amendment is to clarify the guideline in respect to the determination of loss. **The effective date of this amendment is June 15, 1988.**

14. Section 2B3.1(b)(1) is amended by deleting "value of the property taken or destroyed" and inserting in lieu thereof "loss".

The Commentary to §2B3.1 captioned "Application Notes" is amended in Note 3 by deleting "property" and inserting in lieu thereof "loss".

The purpose of this amendment is to clarify the guideline in respect to the determination of loss. **The effective date of this amendment is June 15, 1988.**

15. The Commentary to §2B3.1 captioned "Application Notes" is amended in Note 2 by inserting "or attempted robbery" immediately following "robbery".

The purpose of this amendment is to clarify the guideline. **The effective date of this amendment is June 15, 1988.**

16. The Commentary to §2B5.1 captioned "Statutory Provisions" is amended by deleting "473" and inserting in lieu thereof "474", and by deleting "510," and ", 2314, 2315".

The purpose of this amendment is to correct a clerical error. **The effective date of this amendment is January 15, 1988.**

17. The Commentary to §2B5.2 is amended by deleting "Statutory Provision: 18 U.S.C. § 510" and inserting in lieu thereof "Statutory Provisions: 18 U.S.C. §§ 471-473, 500, 510, 1003, 2314, 2315".

The purpose of this amendment is to correct a clerical error. **The effective date of this amendment is January 15, 1988.**

18. The Commentary to §2C1.1 captioned "Application Notes" is amended in Note 3 by deleting "§3C1.1(c)(1)" and inserting in lieu thereof "§2C1.1(c)(1)".

The purpose of this amendment is to correct a typographical error. **The effective date of this amendment is January 15, 1988.**

19. The Commentary to §2D1.1 captioned "Application Notes" is amended in the Measurement Conversion Table in Note 10 by deleting "1 lb = .45 kg" and inserting in lieu thereof "1 lb = .4536 kg", by deleting "1 kg = 2.2 lbs", by deleting "1 gal = 3.8 liters" and inserting in lieu thereof "1 gal = 3.785 liters", and by deleting "1 qt = .95 liters" and inserting in lieu thereof "1 qt = .946 liters".

The purpose of this amendment is to correct a clerical error. **The effective date of this amendment is January 15, 1988.**

20. The Commentary to §2D1.1 captioned "Application Notes" is amended by deleting:

"11. If it is uncertain whether the quantity of drugs involved falls into one category in the table or an adjacent category, the court may use the intermediate level for sentencing purposes. For example, sale of 700-999 grams of heroin is at level 30, while sale of 400-699 grams is at level 28. If the exact quantity is uncertain, but near 700 grams, use of level 29 would be permissible.".

The purpose of this amendment is to delete an erroneous reference to interpolation, which cannot apply as the guideline is written. **The effective date of this amendment is January 15, 1988.**

21. The Commentary to §2D1.1 captioned "Application Notes" is amended by inserting the following additional note:

"11. Types and quantities of drugs not specified in the count of conviction may be considered in determining the offense level. See §1B1.3(a)(2) (Relevant Conduct). If the amount seized does not reflect the scale of the offense, see Application Note 2 of the Commentary to §2D1.4. If the offense involved negotiation to traffic in a controlled substance, see Application Note 1 of the Commentary to §2D1.4.".

The purpose of this amendment is to clarify the commentary. **The effective date of this amendment is January 15, 1988.**

22. Section 2D1.2(a)(1) is amended by deleting "less than fourteen years of age" and inserting in lieu thereof "fourteen years of age or less".

Section 2D1.2(a)(2) is amended by deleting "fourteen" and inserting in lieu thereof "fifteen".

The Commentary to §2D1.2 captioned "Statutory Provision" is amended by deleting "21 U.S.C. § 845(b)" and inserting in lieu thereof "21 U.S.C. § 845b".

The Commentary to §2D1.2 captioned "Background" is amended by deleting:

"(provided for by the minimum base offense level of 13) in addition to the punishment imposed for the applicable crime in which the defendant involved a juvenile. An increased penalty for the employment or use of persons under age fourteen is statutorily directed by 21 U.S.C. § 845b(d).",

and inserting in lieu thereof:

". An increased penalty for the employment or use of persons fourteen years of age or younger reflects the enhanced sentence authorized by 21 U.S.C. § 845b(d).".

The purpose of this amendment is to correct clerical errors in the guideline and commentary. **The effective date of this amendment is January 15, 1988.**

23. The Commentary to §2D1.3 captioned "Application Notes" is amended in Note 1 by deleting:

"If more than one enhancement provision is applicable in a particular case, the punishment imposed under the separate enhancement provisions should be added together in calculating the appropriate guideline sentence.",

and inserting in lieu thereof:

"If both subsections (a)(1) and (a)(2) apply to a single distribution (e.g., the distribution of 10 grams of a controlled substance to a pregnant woman under twenty-one years of age), the enhancements are applied cumulatively, i.e., by using four times rather than two times the amount distributed.".

The purpose of this amendment is to clarify the commentary. **The effective date of this amendment is January 15, 1988.**

24. Section 2D2.1(a)(1) is amended by deleting "or LSD," immediately following "opiate".

Section 2D2.1(a)(2) is amended by inserting ", LSD," immediately following "cocaine".

The purpose of this amendment is to correct a clerical error. **The effective date of this amendment is January 15, 1988.**

25. The Commentary to §2D2.3 captioned "Statutory Provision" is amended by deleting "21 U.S.C. § 342" and inserting in lieu thereof "18 U.S.C. § 342".

The purpose of this amendment is to correct a typographical error. **The effective date of this amendment is January 15, 1988.**

26. The Commentary to §2E1.1 captioned "Application Notes" is amended in Note 1 by deleting:

"For purposes of subsection (a)(2), determine the offense level for each underlying offense. Use the provisions of Chapter Three, Part D (Multiple Counts), to determine the offense level, treating each underlying offense as if contained in a separate count of conviction.",

and inserting in lieu thereof:

"Where there is more than one underlying offense, treat each underlying offense as if contained in a separate count of conviction for the purposes of subsection (a)(2). To determine whether subsection (a)(1) or (a)(2) results in the greater offense level, apply Chapter Three, Parts A, B, C, and D to both (a)(1) and (a)(2). Use whichever subsection results in the greater offense level.".

The purpose of this amendment is to clarify the guideline. **The effective date of this amendment is June 15, 1988.**

27. The Commentary to §2E1.2 captioned "Application Notes" is amended in Note 1 by deleting:

"For purposes of subsection (a)(2), determine the offense level for each underlying offense. Use the provisions of Chapter Three, Part D (Multiple Counts), to determine the offense level, treating each underlying offense as if contained in a separate count of conviction.",

and inserting in lieu thereof:

"Where there is more than one underlying offense, treat each underlying offense as if contained in a separate count of conviction for the purposes of subsection (a)(2). To determine whether subsection (a)(1) or (a)(2) results in the greater offense level, apply Chapter Three, Parts A, B, C, and D to both (a)(1) and (a)(2). Use whichever subsection results in the greater offense level.".

The purpose of this amendment is to clarify the guideline. **The effective date of this amendment is June 15, 1988.**

28. Section 2E5.2(b)(3) is amended by deleting "value of the property stolen" and inserting in lieu thereof "loss".

The Commentary to §2E5.2 captioned "Application Notes" is amended in Note 1 by inserting immediately following the first sentence: "Valuation of loss is discussed in the Commentary to §2B1.1 (Larceny, Embezzlement, and Other Forms of Theft).".

The purpose of this amendment is to clarify the guideline in respect to the determination of loss. **The effective date of this amendment is June 15, 1988.**

29. Section 2E5.4(b)(3) is amended by deleting "value of the property stolen" and inserting in lieu thereof "loss".

    The Commentary to §2E5.4 captioned "Application Notes" is amended in Note 1 by inserting immediately following the first sentence: "Valuation of loss is discussed in the Commentary to §2B1.1 (Larceny, Embezzlement, and Other Forms of Theft).".

    The purpose of this amendment is to clarify the guideline in respect to the determination of loss. **The effective date of this amendment is June 15, 1988.**

30. Section 2F1.1(b)(1) is amended by deleting "estimated, probable, or intended" immediately before "loss".

    The Commentary to §2F1.1 captioned "Statutory Provisions" is amended by deleting "291" and inserting in lieu thereof "290".

    The Commentary to §2F1.1 captioned "Application Notes" is amended in Note 7 by inserting as the first sentence: "Valuation of loss is discussed in the Commentary to §2B1.1 (Larceny, Embezzlement, and Other Forms of Theft).".

    The purposes of this amendment are to clarify the guideline in respect to the determination of loss and to delete an inadvertently included infraction. **The effective date of this amendment is June 15, 1988,**

31. Section 2G2.2(b)(1) is amended by inserting "a prepubescent minor or" immediately following "involved".

    The purpose of this amendment is to provide an alternative measure to be used in determining whether the material involved an extremely young minor for cases in which the actual age of the minor is unknown. **The effective date of this amendment is June 15, 1988.**

32. The Commentary to §2J1.7 captioned "Application Notes" is amended by deleting:

    "1. By statute, a term of imprisonment imposed for this offense runs consecutively to any other term of imprisonment. 18 U.S.C. § 3147.

    2. This guideline assumes that the sentence imposed for the offense committed while on release, which may have been imposed by a state court, is reasonably consistent with that which the guidelines would provide for a similar federal offense. If this is not the case, a departure may be warranted. <u>See</u> Chapter Five, Part K (Departures).

    3. If the defendant was convicted in state court for the offense committed while on release, the term of imprisonment referred to in subdivision (b) is the maximum term of imprisonment authorized under state law.",

    and inserting in lieu thereof:

    "1. This guideline applies whenever a sentence pursuant to 18 U.S.C. § 3147 is imposed.

    2. By statute, a term of imprisonment imposed for a violation of 18 U.S.C. § 3147 runs consecutively to any other term of imprisonment. Consequently, a sentence for such a violation is exempt from grouping under the multiple count rules. <u>See</u> §3D1.2.".

The Commentary to §2J1.7 captioned "Background" is amended by deleting "necessarily" and inserting in lieu thereof "generally".

The purposes of this amendment are to clarify the commentary and to delete erroneous references. **The effective date of this amendment is January 15, 1988.**

33. Section 2J1.8(c) is amended by deleting "perjury" and inserting in lieu thereof "bribery of a witness".

The Commentary to §2J1.8 captioned "Application Notes" is amended by deleting:

"4. Subsection (c) refers to bribing a witness regarding his testimony in respect to a criminal offense."

The purpose of this amendment is to correct a clerical error. Correction of this error makes the deleted commentary unnecessary. **The effective date of this amendment is January 15, 1988.**

34. The Commentary to §2K2.2 captioned "Application Note" is amended by deleting "Application Note" and inserting in lieu thereof "Application Notes", and by inserting the following additional note:

"2. Subsection (c)(1) refers to any situation in which the defendant possessed a firearm to facilitate another offense that he committed or attempted.".

The purpose of this amendment is to clarify the guideline. **The effective date of this amendment is January 15, 1988.**

35. Section 2L1.1(a) is amended by deleting "6" and inserting in lieu thereof "9".

Section 2L1.1(b)(1) is amended by deleting "for profit or with knowledge" and inserting in lieu thereof "other than for profit, and without knowledge", and by deleting "increase by 3 levels" and inserting in lieu thereof "decrease by 3 levels".

The Commentary to §2L1.1 captioned "Background" is amended by deleting:

"A specific offense characteristic provides an enhancement if the defendant committed the offense for profit or with knowledge that the alien was excludable as a subversive.",

and inserting in lieu thereof:

"A specific offense characteristic provides a reduction if the defendant did not commit the offense for profit and did not know that the alien was excludable as a subversive.".

The purpose of this amendment is to make the guideline conform to the typical case. **The effective date of this amendment is January 15, 1988.**

36. Section 2L1.1(b)(2) is amended by deleting "bringing illegal aliens into the United States" and inserting in lieu thereof "smuggling, transporting, or harboring an unlawful alien, or a related offense".

The Commentary to §2L1.1 captioned "Application Notes" is amended in Note 2 by deleting "bringing illegal aliens into the United States" and inserting in lieu thereof "smuggling, transporting, or harboring an unlawful alien, or a related offense".

The purpose of this amendment is to correct a clerical error in the guideline and conform the commentary to the corrected guideline. **The effective date of this amendment is January 15, 1988.**

37. The Commentary to §2L1.1 captioned "Application Notes" is amended by inserting the following additional note:

> "8. The Commission has not considered offenses involving large numbers of aliens or dangerous or inhumane treatment. An upward departure should be considered in those circumstances.".

The purpose of this amendment is to clarify the factors considered by the Commission in promulgating the guideline. **The effective date of this amendment is January 15, 1988.**

38. Section 2L1.2(a) is amended by deleting "6" and inserting in lieu thereof "8".

Section 2L1.2(b) is amended by deleting:

> "(b) Specific Offense Characteristic
>
> (1) If the defendant previously has unlawfully entered or remained in the United States, increase by 2 levels.".

The Commentary to §2L1.2 captioned "Statutory Provisions" is amended by deleting "§§ 1325, 1326" and inserting in lieu thereof "§ 1325 (second or subsequent offense only), 8 U.S.C. § 1326".

The Commentary to §2L1.2 captioned "Application Notes" is amended in Note 1 by deleting:

> "The adjustment at §2L1.2(b)(1) is to be applied where the previous entry resulted in deportation (voluntary or involuntary), with or without a criminal conviction. If the previous entry resulted in a conviction, this adjustment is to be applied in addition to any points added to the criminal history score for such conviction in Chapter Four, Part A (Criminal History).",

and inserting in lieu thereof:

> "This guideline applies only to felonies. First offenses under 8 U.S.C. § 1325 are petty offenses for which no guideline has been promulgated.".

The purpose of this amendment is to delete coverage of a petty offense. **The effective date of this amendment is January 15, 1988.**

39. The Commentary to §2L2.2 captioned "Application Notes" is amended in Note 1 by deleting "an enhancement equivalent to that at §2L1.2(b)(1)," and inserting in lieu thereof "a result equivalent to §2L1.2.".

The purpose of this amendment is to make the commentary consistent with §2L1.2, as amended. **The effective date of this amendment is January 15, 1988.**

40. **The Commentary to §2L2.4 captioned "Application Notes" is amended in Note 1 by deleting "an enhancement equivalent to that at §2L1.2(b)(1)," and inserting in lieu thereof "a result equivalent to §2L1.2.".**

The purpose of this amendment is to make the commentary consistent with §2L1.2, as amended. The effective date of this amendment is January 15, 1988.

41. **The Commentary to §2Q2.1 captioned "Statutory Provisions" is amended by deleting "707" and inserting in lieu thereof "707(b)".**

The purpose of this amendment is to correct a clerical error. The effective date of this amendment is January 15, 1988.

42. **The Commentary to §2X1.1 captioned "Application Notes" is amended in Note 1 by deleting "§2A4.1" and inserting in lieu thereof "§2D1.4".**

The purpose of this amendment is to correct a typographical error. The effective date of this amendment is January 15, 1988.

43. Chapter Two, Part X is amended by deleting §2X5.1 in its entirety as follows:

"§2X5.1. Other Offenses (Policy Statement)

For offenses for which no specific guideline has been promulgated:

(a) If the offense is a felony or class A misdemeanor, the most analogous guideline should be applied. If no sufficiently analogous guideline exists, any sentence that is reasonable and consistent with the purposes of sentencing should be imposed. See 18 U.S.C. § 3553(b).

(b) If the offense is a Class B or C misdemeanor or an infraction, any sentence that is reasonable and consistent with the purpose of sentencing should be imposed. See 18 U.S.C. § 3553(b).

Commentary

Background: This policy statement addresses cases in which a defendant has been convicted of an offense for which no specific guideline has been written. For a felony or a class A misdemeanor (see 18 U.S.C. §§ 3559(a) and 3581(b)), the court is directed to apply the most analogous guideline. If no sufficiently analogous guideline exists, the court is directed to sentence without reference to a specific guideline or guideline range, as provided in 18 U.S.C. § 3553(b).

For a class B or C misdemeanor or an infraction (see 18 U.S.C. §§ 3559(a) and 3581(b)) that is not covered by a specific guideline, the court is directed to sentence without reference to a specific guideline or guideline range, as provided in 18 U.S.C. § 3553(b). An inquiry as to whether there is a sufficiently analogous guideline that might be applied is not required. The Commission makes this distinction in treatment because for many lesser offenses (e.g., traffic infractions), generally handled under assimilative offense provisions by magistrates, there will be no sufficiently analogous guideline, and a case-by-case determination in respect to this issue for the high volume of cases processed each year would be unduly burdensome and would not significantly reduce disparity.".

A replacement guideline with accompanying commentary is inserted as §2X5.1 (Other Offenses).

The purposes of this amendment are to make the section a binding guideline (as the Commission originally intended with respect to felonies and Class A misdemeanors) rather than a policy statement, to delete language relating to petty offenses, and to conform and clarify the commentary. **The effective date of this amendment is June 15, 1988.**

44. The Commentary to §3A1.2 captioned "Application Notes" is amended in Note 1 by deleting:

" 'Victim' refers to an individual directly victimized by the offense. This term does not include an organization, agency, or the government itself.",

and inserting in lieu thereof:

"This guideline applies when specified individuals are victims of the offense. This guideline does not apply when the only victim is an organization, agency, or the government.".

The purpose of this amendment is to clarify the commentary. **The effective date of this amendment is January 15, 1988.**

45. Section 3D1.2(d) is amended by deleting:

"(d) When counts involve the same general type of offense and the guidelines for that type of offense determine the offense level primarily on the basis of the total amount of harm or loss, the quantity of a substance involved, or some other measure of aggregate harm. Offenses of this kind are found in Chapter Two, Part B (except §§2B2.1-2B3.3), Part D (except §§2D1.6-2D3.4), Part E (except §§2E1.1-2E2.1), Part F, Part G (§§2G2.2-2G3.1), Part K (§2K2.3), Part N (§§2N2.1, 2N3.1), Part Q (§§2Q2.1, 2Q2.2), Part R, Part S, and Part T. This rule also applies where the guidelines deal with offenses that are continuing, e.g.., §§2L1.3 and 2Q1.3(b)(1)(A).",

and inserting in lieu thereof:

"(d) Counts are grouped together if the offense level is determined largely on the basis of the total amount of harm or loss, the quantity of a substance involved, or some other measure of aggregate harm, or if the offense behavior is ongoing or continuous in nature and the offense guideline is written to cover such behavior.

Offenses covered by the following guidelines are specifically included under this subsection:

§§2B1.1, 2B1.2, 2B1.3, 2B4.1, 2B5.1, 2B5.2, 2B5.3, 2B5.4, 2B6.1;
§§2D1.1, 2D1.2, 2D1.3, 2D1.5;
§§2E4.1, 2E5.1, 2E5.2, 2E5.4, 2E5.6;
§§2F1.1, 2F1.2;
§2N3.1;
§2R1.1;
§§2S1.1, 2S1.2, 2S1.3;
§§2T1.1, 2T1.2, 2T1.3, 2T1.4, 2T1.6, 2T1.7, 2T1.9, 2T2.1, 2T3.1, 2T3.2.

Specifically excluded from the operation of this subsection are:

all offenses in Part A;
§§2B2.1, 2B2.2, 2B2.3, 2B3.1, 2B3.2, 2B3.3;
§§2C1.1, 2C1.5;
§§2D2.1, 2D2.2, 2D2.3;
§§2E1.3, 2E1.4, 2E1.5, 2E2.1;
§§2G1.1, 2G1.2, 2G2.1, 2G3.2;
§§2H1.1, 2H1.2, 2H1.3, 2H1.4, 2H2.1, 2H4.1;
§§2L1.1, 2L2.1, 2L2.2, 2L2.3, 2L2.4, 2L2.5;
§§2M2.1, 2M2.3, 2M3.1, 2M3.2, 2M3.3, 2M3.4, 2M3.5, 2M3.6, 2M3.7, 2M3.8, 2M3.9;
§§2P1.1, 2P1.2, 2P1.3, 2P1.4.

For multiple counts of offenses that are not listed, grouping under this subsection may or may not be appropriate; a case-by-case determination must be made based upon the facts of the case and the applicable guidelines (including specific offense characteristics and other adjustments) used to determine the offense level.

Exclusion of an offense from grouping under this subsection does not necessarily preclude grouping under another subsection.".

The purpose of this amendment is to clarify the guideline. **The effective date of this amendment is June 15, 1988.**

46. Section 3E1.1(a) is amended by deleting "the offense of conviction" and inserting in lieu thereof "his criminal conduct".

The purpose of this amendment is to clarify the guideline. **The effective date of this amendment is January 15, 1988.**

47. Section 4B1.1 is amended by deleting "(2) the instant offense is a crime of violence or trafficking in a controlled substance" and inserting in lieu thereof "(2) the instant offense of conviction is a felony that is either a crime of violence or a controlled substance offense".

The purposes of this amendment are to correct a clerical error and to clarify the guideline. **The effective date of this amendment is January 15, 1988.**

48. Section 4B1.1 is amended by deleting:

"<u>Offense Statutory Maximum</u>		<u>Offense Level</u>
(A)	Life	37
(B)	20 years or more	34
(C)	10 years or more, but less than 20 years	26
(D)	5 years or more, but less than 10 years	19
(E)	More than 1 year, but less than 5 years	12
(F)	1 year or less	4",

and inserting in lieu thereof:

"Offense Statutory Maximum		Offense Level
(A)	Life	37
(B)	25 years or more	34
(C)	20 years or more, but less than 25 years	32
(D)	15 years or more, but less than 20 years	29
(E)	10 years or more, but less than 15 years	24
(F)	5 years or more, but less than 10 years	17
(G)	More than 1 year, but less than 5 years	12".

The Commentary to §4B1.1 captioned "Background" is amended by deleting the last paragraph as follows:

"The guideline levels for career offenders were established by using the statutory maximum for the offense of conviction to determine the class of felony provided in 18 U.S.C. § 3559. Then the maximum authorized sentence of imprisonment for each class of felony was determined as provided by 18 U.S.C. § 3581. A guideline range for each class of felony was then chosen so that the maximum of the guideline range was at or near the maximum provided in 18 U.S.C. § 3581.".

The purpose of this amendment is to correct the guideline so that the table relating offense statutory maxima to offense levels is consistent with the current authorized statutory maximum terms. The effective date of this amendment is January 15, 1988.

49. **Section 4B1.2(2) is amended by inserting "845b, 856," immediately following "841," and by deleting "§§ 405B and 416 of the Controlled Substance Act as amended in 1986," immediately following "959;".**

Section 4B1.2(3) is amended by deleting:

"(1) the defendant committed the instant offense subsequent to sustaining at least two felony convictions for either a crime of violence or a controlled substance offense (i.e., two crimes of violence, two controlled substance offenses, or one crime of violence and one controlled substance offense), and (2)",

and inserting in lieu thereof:

"(A) the defendant committed the instant offense subsequent to sustaining at least two felony convictions of either a crime of violence or a controlled substance offense (i.e., two felony convictions of a crime of violence, two felony convictions of a controlled substance offense, or one felony conviction of a crime of violence and one felony conviction of a controlled substance offense), and (B)".

The Commentary to §4B1.2 captioned "Application Notes" is amended in Note 2 by deleting "means any of the federal offenses identified in the statutes referenced in §4B1.2, or substantially equivalent state offenses" and inserting in lieu thereof "includes any federal or state offense that is substantially similar to any of those listed in subsection (2) of the guideline", by inserting "importing," immediately following "manufacturing,", and by inserting "import," immediately following "manufacture,".

The Commentary to §4B1.2 captioned "Application Notes" is amended in Note 3 by deleting "Felony" and inserting in lieu thereof "Prior felony".

The purposes of this amendment are to correct a clerical error and to clarify the guideline. **The effective date of this amendment is January 15, 1988.**

50. Section 4B1.3 is amended by deleting:

". In no such case will the defendant be eligible for a sentence of probation."

and inserting in lieu thereof:

", unless §3E1.1 (Acceptance of Responsibility) applies, in which event his offense level shall be not less than 11.".

The Commentary to §4B1.3 captioned "Application Note" is amended by deleting "(e.g., an ongoing fraudulent scheme)" immediately following "course of conduct", "(e.g., a number of burglaries or robberies, or both)" immediately following "independent offenses", and "or petty" immediately following "to minor".

The Commentary to §4B1.3 captioned "Background" is amended by deleting "that offense" and inserting in lieu thereof "an offense", and by deleting the last sentence as follows: "Under this provision, the offense level is raised to 13, if it is not already 13 or greater".

The purpose of this amendment is to provide that the adjustment from §3E1.1 (Acceptance of Responsibility) applies to cases under §4B1.3 (Criminal Livelihood). **The effective date of this amendment is June 15, 1988.**

51. The Commentary to §5C2.1 captioned "Application Notes" is amended in Note 4 by deleting "at least six" and inserting in lieu thereof "more than six", by deleting "6-12" whenever it appears and inserting in lieu thereof in each instance "8-14", and by deleting "three" whenever it appears and inserting in lieu thereof in each instance "four".

The purpose of this amendment is to correct a clerical error. **The effective date of this amendment is January 15, 1988.**

52. Section 5D3.2(b) is amended by deleting:

"(1) three years for a defendant convicted of a Class A or B felony;

(2) two years for a defendant convicted of a Class C or D felony;

(3) one year for a defendant convicted of a Class E felony or a misdemeanor.",

and inserting in lieu thereof:

"(1) at least three years but not more than five years for a defendant convicted of a Class A or B felony;

(2) at least two years but not more than three years for a defendant convicted of a Class C or D felony;

(3) one year for a defendant convicted of a Class E felony or a Class A misdemeanor.".

The purpose of this amendment is to permit implementation of the longer terms of supervised release authorized by the Sentencing Act of 1987. **The effective date of this amendment is January 15, 1988.**

53. Section 5E4.1(a) is amended by inserting immediately before the period at the end of the subsection: ", and may be ordered as a condition of probation or supervised release in any other case".

The purpose of this amendment is to clarify the guideline. **The effective date of this amendment is January 15, 1988.**

54. Section 5E4.2 is amended by deleting:

"(b) The generally applicable minimum and maximum fine for each offense level is shown in the Fine Table in subsection (c) below. Unless a statute expressly authorizes a greater amount, no fine may exceed $250,000 for a felony or a misdemeanor resulting in the loss of human life; $25,000 for any other misdemeanor; or $1,000 for an infraction. 18 U.S.C. § 3571(b)(1).

(c) (1) The minimum fine range is the greater of:

(A) the amount shown in column A of the table below; or

(B) any monetary gain to the defendant, less any restitution made or ordered.

(2) Except as specified in (4) below, the maximum fine is the greater of:

(A) the amount shown in column B of the table below;

(B) twice the estimated loss caused by the offense; or

(C) three times the estimated gain to the defendant.",

and inserting in lieu thereof:

"(b) Except as provided in subsections (f) and (i) below, or otherwise required by statute, the fine imposed shall be within the range specified in subsection (c) below.

(c) (1) The minimum of the fine range is the greater of:

(A) the amount shown in column A of the table below; or

(B) the pecuniary gain to the defendant, less restitution made or ordered.

(2) Except as specified in (4) below, the maximum of the fine range is the greater of:

(A) the amount shown in column B of the table below;

(B) twice the gross pecuniary loss caused by the offense; or

(C) three times the gross pecuniary gain to all participants in the offense.".

The Commentary to §5E4.2 captioned "Application Notes" is amended by deleting:

"2. The maximum fines generally authorized by statute are restated in subsection (b). These apply to each count of conviction. Ordinarily, the maximum fines on each count are independent and cumulative. However, if the offenses 'arise from a common scheme or plan' and 'do not cause separable or distinguishable kinds of harm or damage,' the aggregate fine may not exceed 'twice the amount imposable for the most serious offense.' 18 U.S.C. § 3572(b) (former 18 U.S.C. § 3623(c)(2)).

3. Alternative fine limits are provided in subsection (c)(2). The term 'estimated gain' is used to emphasize that the Commission does not intend precise or detailed calculation of the monetary gain (nor of the loss) in using the alternative fine limits. In many cases, circumstances will make it unnecessary to consider these standards other than in the most general terms.",

and inserting in lieu thereof:

"2. In general, the maximum fine permitted by law as to each count of conviction is $250,000 for a felony or for any misdemeanor resulting in death; $100,000 for a Class A misdemeanor; and $5,000 for any other offense. 18 U.S.C. § 3571(b)(3)-(7). However, higher or lower limits may apply when specified by statute. 18 U.S.C. § 3571(b)(1), (e). As an alternative maximum, the court may fine the defendant up to the greater of twice the gross gain or twice the gross loss. 18 U.S.C. § 3571(b)(2), (d).

3. Alternative fine limits are provided in subsection (c). The terms 'pecuniary gain' and 'pecuniary loss' are taken from 18 U.S.C. § 3571(d). The Commission does not intend precise or detailed calculation of the gain or loss in using the alternative fine limits. In many cases, circumstances will make it unnecessary to consider these standards other than in the most general terms.".

The Commentary to §5E4.2 captioned "Application Notes" is amended in Note 4 by deleting "Any restitution" and inserting in lieu thereof "Restitution".

The Commentary to §5E4.2 captioned "Background" is amended by deleting:

"defendant. In addition, the Commission concluded that greater latitude with a gain-based fine was justified; when the court finds it necessary to rely on the gain, rather than the loss, to set the fine, ordering restitution usually will not be feasible because of the difficulty in computing the amount.",

and inserting in lieu thereof:

"participants. In addition, in many such cases restitution will not be feasible.".

The purposes of this amendment are to make the guideline consistent with 18 U.S.C. § 3571, as amended, to clarify the commentary, and to correct clerical errors in the guideline and commentary. **The effective date of this amendment is January 15, 1988.**

55. Chapter 5, Part J is amended in the title of the Part by deleting "PERTAINING TO CERTAIN EMPLOYMENT" immediately following "DISABILITY".

The purpose of this amendment is to eliminate the possible inference that this part covers only employment for compensation. **The effective date of this amendment is June 15, 1988.**

56. Chapter Five, Part J is amended by deleting §5J1.1 in its entirety as follows:

"§5J1.1. Relief From Disability Pertaining to Certain Employment (Policy Statement)

With regard to labor racketeering offenses, a part of the punishment imposed by 29 U.S.C. §§ 504 and 511 is the prohibition of convicted persons from service in labor unions, employer associations, employee benefit plans, and as labor relations consultants. Violations of these provisions are felony offenses. Persons convicted after October 12, 1984, may petition the sentencing court to reduce the statutory disability (thirteen years after sentence or imprisonment, whichever is later) to a lesser period (not less than three years after entry of judgment in the trial court). After November 1, 1987, petitions for exemption from the disability that were formerly administered by the United States Parole Commission will be transferred to the courts. Relief shall not be given in such cases to aid rehabilitation, but may be granted only following a clear demonstration by the convicted person that he has been rehabilitated since commission of the crime.".

A replacement policy statement is inserted as §5J1.1 (Relief from Disability Pertaining to Convicted Persons Prohibited from Holding Certain Positions (Policy Statement)).

The purpose of this amendment is to clarify the policy statement and conform it to the pertinent provisions of the Sentencing Act of 1987. **The effective date of this amendment is June 15, 1988.**

57. Section 5K2.0 is amended by deleting "an aggravating or mitigating circumstance exists that was" and inserting in lieu thereof "there exists an aggravating or mitigating circumstance of a kind, or to a degree".

The purpose of this amendment is to conform the quotation in this section to the wording in the Sentencing Act of 1987. **The effective date of this amendment is June 15, 1988.**

58. Section 6A1.1 is amended by deleting "(a)" immediately before "A probation officer", and by deleting:

"(b) The presentence report shall be disclosed to the defendant, counsel for the defendant and the attorney for the government, to the maximum extent permitted by Rule 32(c), Fed. R. Crim. P. Disclosure shall be made at least ten days prior to the date set for sentencing, unless this minimum period is waived by the defendant. 18 U.S.C. § 3552(d).".

The purpose of this amendment is to delete material more properly covered elsewhere. See §6A1.2 (Disclosure of Presentence Report; Issues in Dispute (Policy Statement)). **The effective date of this amendment is June 15, 1988.**

59. Section 6A1.2 is amended by deleting:

"Position of Parties with Respect to Sentencing Factors

(a) After receipt of the presentence report and within a reasonable time before sentencing, the attorney for the government and the attorney for the defendant, or the pro se defendant, shall each file with the court a written statement of the sentencing factors to be relied upon at sentencing. The parties are not precluded from asserting additional sentencing factors if notice of the intention to rely upon another factor is filed with the court within a reasonable time before sentencing.

(b) Copies of all sentencing statements filed with the court shall be contemporaneously served upon all other parties and submitted to the probation officer assigned to the case.

(c) In lieu of the written statement required by §6A1.2(a), any party may file:

(1) a written statement adopting the findings of the presentence report;

(2) a written statement adopting such findings subject to certain exceptions or additions; or

(3) a written stipulation in which the parties agree to adopt the findings of the presentence report or to adopt such findings subject to certain exceptions or additions.

(d) A district court may, by local rule, identify categories of cases for which the parties are authorized to make oral statements at or before sentencing, in lieu of the written statement required by this section.

(e) Except to the extent that a party may be privileged not to disclose certain information, all statements filed with the court or made orally to the court pursuant to this section shall:

(1) set forth, directly or by reference to the presentence report, the relevant facts and circumstances of the actual offense conduct and offender characteristics; and

(2) not contain misleading facts.",

and inserting in lieu thereof:

"Disclosure of Presentence Report; Issues in Dispute (Policy Statement)

Courts should adopt procedures to provide for the timely disclosure of the presentence report; the narrowing and resolution, where feasible, of issues in dispute in advance of the sentencing hearing; and the identification for the court of issues remaining in dispute. See Model Local Rule for Guideline Sentencing prepared by the Probation Committee of the Judicial Conference (August 1987).".

This amendment deletes this guideline and inserts in lieu thereof a general policy statement. The Commission has determined that this subject is more appropriately covered by the Model Local Rule for Guideline Sentencing prepared by the Probation Committee of the Judicial Conference. **The effective date of this amendment is June 15, 1988.**

60. Appendix A is amended by inserting the following statutes in the appropriate place according to statutory title and section number:

"7 U.S.C. § 2024(b) 2F1.1",
"7 U.S.C. § 2024(c) 2F1.1",
"18 U.S.C. § 874 2B3.2, 2B3.3",
"18 U.S.C. § 914 2F1.1",
"18 U.S.C. § 923 2K2.3",
"18 U.S.C. § 1030(a)(1) 2M3.2",
"18 U.S.C. § 1030(a)(2) 2F1.1",
"18 U.S.C. § 1030(a)(3) 2F1.1",
"18 U.S.C. § 1030(a)(4) 2F1.1",
"18 U.S.C. § 1030(a)(5) 2F1.1",
"18 U.S.C. § 1030(a)(6) 2F1.1",
"18 U.S.C. § 1030(b) 2X1.1",
"18 U.S.C. § 1501 2A2.2, 2A2.3",
"18 U.S.C. § 1720 2F1.1",
"18 U.S.C. § 4082(d) 2P1.1",

"19 U.S.C. § 1304	2T3.1",
"20 U.S.C. § 1097(c)	2B4.1",
"20 U.S.C. § 1097(d)	2F1.1",
"38 U.S.C. § 3502	2F1.1",
"42 U.S.C. § 1307(a)	2F1.1",
"42 U.S.C. § 1395nn(c)	2F1.1",
"45 U.S.C. § 359(a)	2F1.1".

The purpose of this amendment is to make the statutory index more comprehensive. The effective date of this amendment is January 15, 1988.

61. Appendix A is amended by deleting:

"16 U.S.C. § 703	2Q2.1",
"16 U.S.C. § 707	2Q2.1",

and inserting in lieu thereof:

"16 U.S.C. § 707(b)	2Q2.1";

by deleting:

"18 U.S.C. § 112(a)	2A2.1, 2A2.2, 2A2.3",

and inserting in lieu thereof:

"18 U.S.C. § 112(a)	2A2.2, 2A2.3";

by deleting:

"18 U.S.C. § 510(a)	2B5.1",

and inserting in lieu thereof:

"18 U.S.C. § 510	2B5.2";

by deleting:

"18 U.S.C. § 1005	2F1.1, 2S1.3",

and inserting in lieu thereof:

"18 U.S.C. § 1005	2F1.1";

by deleting:

"18 U.S.C. § 1701	2B1.1, 2H3.3",

and inserting in lieu thereof:

"18 U.S.C. § 1700	2H3.3";

by deleting:

"18 U.S.C. § 2113(a)	2B1.1, 2B3.1",

and inserting in lieu thereof:

"18 U.S.C. § 2113(a) 2B1.1, 2B2.2, 2B3.1, 2B3.2";

by deleting "2B5.1," from the line beginning with "18 U.S.C. § 2314"; and

by deleting "2B5.1," from the line beginning with "18 U.S.C. § 2315".

The purpose of this amendment is to correct clerical errors. **The effective date of this amendment is January 15, 1988.**

62. Appendix A is amended by inserting the following statutes in the appropriate place according to statutory title and section number:

"18 U.S.C. § 911	2F1.1, 2L2.2",
"18 U.S.C. § 922(n)	2K2.1",
"18 U.S.C. § 2071	2B1.1, 2B1.3",
"26 U.S.C. § 7212(a)	2A2.2, 2A2.3",
"42 U.S.C. § 2278(a)(c)	2B2.3",
"46 U.S.C. § 3718(b)	2K3.1",
"47 U.S.C. § 553(b)(2)	2B5.3",
"49 U.S.C. § 1472(h)(2)	2K3.1".

The purpose of this amendment is to make the statutory index more comprehensive. **The effective date of this amendment is June 15, 1988.**

63. Appendix A is amended by deleting:

"7 U.S.C. § 166	2N2.1",
"7 U.S.C. § 213	2F1.1",
"7 U.S.C. § 473	2N2.1";

by deleting:

"7 U.S.C. § 511e	2N2.1",
"7 U.S.C. § 511k	2N2.1",

and inserting in lieu thereof:

"7 U.S.C. § 511d	2N2.1",
"7 U.S.C. § 511i	2N2.1";

by deleting:

"7 U.S.C. § 586	2N2.1",
"7 U.S.C. § 596	2N2.1",
"7 U.S.C. § 608c-1	2N2.1";

by deleting:

"16 U.S.C. § 117(c) 2B1.1, 2B1.3",

and inserting in lieu thereof:

"16 U.S.C. § 117c 2B1.1, 2B1.3";

by deleting:

"16 U.S.C. § 414 2B2.3",

"16 U.S.C. § 426i	2B1.1, 2B1.3",
"16 U.S.C. § 428i	2B1.1, 2B1.3",
"18 U.S.C. § 291	2C1.3, 2F1.1",
"26 U.S.C. § 7269	2T1.2",
"41 U.S.C. § 51	2B4.1",
"42 U.S.C. § 4012	2Q1.3",
"50 U.S.C. § 2410	2M5.1";

and by deleting the first time it appears:

"50 U.S.C. App. § 462 2M4.1".

The purposes of this amendment are to correct clerical errors and delete inadvertently included statutes. **The effective date of this amendment is June 15, 1988.**

64. Chapter Two, Part A is amended by inserting an additional guideline with accompanying commentary as §2A2.4 (Obstructing or Impeding Officers).

The Commentary to §2A2.3 captioned "Statutory Provisions" is amended by deleting "111".

Appendix A is amended by deleting "2A2.3," from the line beginning with "18 U.S.C. § 111", and inserting in lieu thereof "2A2.4";

by deleting "2A2.3," from the line beginning with "18 U.S.C. § 1501", and inserting in lieu thereof "2A2.4";

by inserting the following statutes in the appropriate place according to statutory title and section number:

"18 U.S.C. § 1502	2A2.4",
"18 U.S.C. § 3056(d)	2A2.4".

The purpose of this amendment is to make the guidelines more comprehensive. **The effective date of this amendment is October 15, 1988.**

65. Chapter Two, Part A is amended by inserting an additional guideline with accompanying commentary as §2A5.3 (Committing Certain Crimes Aboard Aircraft).

Appendix A is amended by inserting the following statute in the appropriate place according to statutory title and section number:

"49 U.S.C. § 1472(k)(1) 2A5.3".

The purpose of this amendment is to make the guidelines more comprehensive. **The effective date of this amendment is October 15, 1988.**

66. Chapter Two, Part D is amended by deleting §2D1.5 in its entirety as follows:

"§2D1.5. Continuing Criminal Enterprise

(a) Base Offense Level:

(1) 32, for the first conviction of engaging in a continuing criminal enterprise; or

(2) 38, for the second or any subsequent conviction of engaging in a continuing criminal enterprise; or

(3) 43, for engaging in a continuing criminal enterprise as the principal administrator, leader, or organizer, if either the amount of drugs involved was 30 times the minimum in the first paragraph (i.e., the text corresponding to Level 36) of the Drug Quantity Table or 300 times the minimum in the third paragraph (i.e., the text corresponding to Level 32), or the principal received $10 million in gross receipts for any twelve-month period.

Commentary

Statutory Provision: 21 U.S.C. § 848.

Application Note:

1. Do not apply any adjustment from Chapter Three, Part B (Role in the Offense).

Background: The base offense levels for continuing criminal enterprises are mandatory minimum sentences provided by the statute that mandate imprisonment for leaders of large scale drug enterprises. A conviction establishes that the defendant controlled and exercised decision-making authority over one of the most serious forms of ongoing criminal activity. Therefore, an adjustment for role in the offense in Chapter Three, Part B, is not applicable.".

A replacement guideline with accompanying commentary is inserted as §2D1.5 (Continuing Criminal Enterprise).

The purpose of this amendment is to ensure that the guideline adequately reflects the seriousness of the criminal conduct. The previous guideline specified sentences that were lower than sentences typically imposed on defendants convicted of engaging in a continuing criminal enterprise, a result that the Commission did not intend. The guideline is also amended to delete, as unnecessary, provisions that referred to statutory minimum sentences. **The effective date of this amendment is October 15, 1988.**

67. Chapter One, Part A (4)(b) is amended in the first sentence by deleting "... that was" and inserting in lieu thereof "of a kind, or to a degree,".

Chapter One, Part A, section 4(b) is amended in the second sentence of the last paragraph by deleting "Part H" and inserting in lieu thereof "Part K (Departures)", and in the third sentence of the last paragraph by deleting "Part H" and inserting in lieu thereof "Part K".

The purposes of this amendment are to conform the quotation to the statute, as amended by Section 3 of the Sentencing Act of 1987, and to correct a clerical error. **The effective date of this amendment is November 1, 1989.**

68. Chapter One, Part A, section 4(b) is amended in the first sentence of the fourth paragraph by deleting "three" and inserting in lieu thereof "two"; in the fourth paragraph by deleting the second through eighth sentences as follows:

"The first kind, which will most frequently be used, is in effect an interpolation between two adjacent, numerically oriented guideline rules. A specific offense characteristic, for example, might require an increase of four levels for serious bodily injury but two levels for bodily injury. Rather than requiring a court to force middle instances into either the 'serious' or the 'simple' category, the guideline commentary suggests that the court may interpolate and select a midpoint increase of three levels. The Commission has decided to call such an interpolation a 'departure' in light of the legal views that a guideline providing for a range of increases in offense levels may violate the statute's 25 percent rule (though other have presented contrary legal arguments). Since interpolations are technically departures, the courts will have to provide reasons for their selection, and it will be subject to review for 'reasonableness' on appeal. The Commission believes, however, that a simple reference by the court to the 'mid-category' nature of the facts will typically provide sufficient reason. It does not foresee serious practical problems arising out of the application of the appeal provisions to this form of departure.";

in the first sentence of the fifth paragraph by deleting "second" and inserting in lieu thereof "first"; and, in the first sentence of the sixth paragraph by deleting "third" and inserting in lieu thereof "second".

The purpose of this amendment is to eliminate references to interpolation as a special type of departure. The Commission has reviewed the discussion of interpolation in Chapter One, which has been read as describing "interpolation" as a departure from an offense level rather than from the guideline range established after the determination of an offense level. The Commission concluded that it is simpler to add intermediate offense level adjustments to the guidelines in the cases where interpolation is most likely to be considered (i.e., degree of bodily injury). This amendment is not intended to preclude interpolation in other cases; where appropriate, the court will be able to achieve the same result by use of the regular departure provisions. **The effective date of this amendment is November 1, 1989.**

69. Section 1B1.1(a) is amended by deleting "guideline section in Chapter Two most applicable to the statute of conviction" and inserting in lieu thereof "applicable offense guideline section from Chapter Two", and by deleting the last sentence as follows: "If more than one guideline is referenced for the particular statute, select the guideline most appropriate for the conduct of which the defendant was convicted.".

The purposes of this amendment are to clarify the guideline and conform the language to §1B1.2. **The effective date of this amendment is November 1, 1989.**

70. Section 1B1.1(e) is amended by deleting the last sentence as follows: "The resulting offense level is the total offense level.".

Section 1B1.1(g) is amended by deleting "total", and by inserting "determined above" immediately following "category".

The purpose of this amendment is to clarify the guideline. **The effective date of this amendment is November 1, 1989.**

71. The Commentary to §1B1.1 captioned "Application Notes" is amended in Note 1(c) by deleting "firearm or other dangerous weapon" and inserting in lieu thereof "dangerous weapon (including a firearm)".

The Commentary to §1B1.1 captioned "Application Notes" is amended in Note 1(d) by inserting the following additional sentence at the end: "Where an object that appeared to be a dangerous weapon was brandished, displayed, or possessed, treat the object as a dangerous weapon.".

The Commentary to §1B1.1 captioned "Application Notes" is amended in Note 1(g) by deleting "firearm or other dangerous weapon" the first time it appears and inserting in lieu thereof "dangerous weapon (including a firearm)".

The Commentary to §1B1.1 captioned "Application Notes" is amended by inserting the following additional note:

"5. Where two or more guideline provisions appear equally applicable, but the guidelines authorize the application of only one such provision, use the provision that results in the greater offense level. E.g., in §2A2.2(b)(2), if a firearm is both discharged and brandished, the provision applicable to the discharge of the firearm would be used.".

The purposes of this amendment are to clarify the definition of a dangerous weapon; and to clarify that when two or more guideline provisions appear equally applicable, but the guidelines authorize the application of only one such provision, the provision that results in the greater offense level is to be used. **The effective date of this amendment is November 1, 1989.**

72. The Commentary to §1B1.1 captioned "Application Notes" is amended by inserting the following additional note:

"6. In the case of a defendant subject to a sentence enhancement under 18 U.S.C. § 3147 (Penalty for an Offense Committed While on Release), see §2J1.7 (Commission of Offense While on Release).".

The purpose of this amendment is to clarify the treatment of a specific enhancement provision. **The effective date of this amendment is November 1, 1989.**

73. Section 1B1.2(a) is amended in the first sentence by deleting "The court shall apply" and inserting in lieu thereof "Determine"; and in the second sentence by deleting "the court shall apply" and inserting in lieu thereof "determine", and by deleting "guideline in such chapter" and inserting in lieu thereof "offense guideline section in Chapter Two".

The purposes of this amendment are to clarify the guideline and to make the phraseology of this subsection more consistent with that of §§1B1.1 and 1B1.2(b). **The effective date of this amendment is November 1, 1989.**

74. Section 1B1.2(a) is amended in the first sentence by inserting immediately before the period: "(i.e., the offense conduct charged in the count of the indictment or information of which the defendant was convicted)".

The Commentary to §1B1.2 captioned "Application Notes" is amended in the first paragraph of Note 1 by deleting:

"As a general rule, the court is to apply the guideline covering the offense conduct most applicable to the offense of conviction. Where a particular statute proscribes a variety of conduct which might constitute the subject of different guidelines, the court will decide which guideline applies based upon the nature of the offense conduct charged.",

and inserting in lieu thereof:

"As a general rule, the court is to use the guideline section from Chapter Two most applicable to the offense of conviction. The Statutory Index (Appendix A) provides a listing to assist in this determination. When a particular statute proscribes only a single type of criminal conduct, the offense of conviction and the conduct proscribed by the statute will coincide, and there will be only one offense guideline referenced. When a particular statute proscribes a variety of conduct that might constitute the subject of different offense guidelines, the court will determine which guideline section applies based upon the nature of the offense conduct charged in the count of which the defendant was convicted.".

The purpose of this amendment is to clarify the guideline and commentary. **The effective date of this amendment is November 1, 1989.**

75. Section 1B1.2(a) is amended by deleting the last sentence as follows:

"Similarly, stipulations to additional offenses are treated as if the defendant had been convicted of separate counts charging those offenses.",

and by inserting the following additional subsections:

"(c) A conviction by a plea of guilty or nolo contendere containing a stipulation that specifically establishes the commission of additional offense(s) shall be treated as if the defendant had been convicted of additional count(s) charging those offense(s).

(d) A conviction on a count charging a conspiracy to commit more than one offense shall be treated as if the defendant had been convicted on a separate count of conspiracy for each offense that the defendant conspired to commit.".

The Commentary to §1B1.2 captioned "Application Notes" is amended in the second paragraph of Note 1 by deleting:

"Similarly, if the defendant pleads guilty to one robbery but admits the elements of two additional robberies as part of a plea agreement, the guideline applicable to three robberies is to be applied.",

and by inserting the following additional notes:

"4. Subsections (c) and (d) address circumstances in which the provisions of Chapter Three, Part D (Multiple Counts) are to be applied although there may be only one count of conviction. Subsection (c) provides that in the case of a stipulation to the commission of additional offense(s), the guidelines are to be applied as if the defendant had been convicted of an additional count for each of the offenses stipulated. For example, if the defendant is convicted of one count of robbery but, as part of a plea agreement, admits to having committed two additional robberies, the guidelines are to be applied as if the defendant had been convicted of three counts of robbery. Subsection (d) provides that a conviction on a conspiracy count charging conspiracy to commit more than one offense is treated as if the defendant had been convicted of a separate conspiracy count for each offense that he conspired to commit. For example, where a conviction on a single count of conspiracy establishes that the defendant conspired to commit three robberies, the guidelines are to be applied as if the defendant had been convicted on one count of conspiracy to commit the first robbery, one count of conspiracy to commit the second robbery, and one count of conspiracy to commit the third robbery.

5. Particular care must be taken in applying subsection (d) because there are cases in which the jury's verdict does not establish which offense(s) was the object of the conspiracy. In such cases, subsection (d) should only be applied with respect to an object offense alleged in the conspiracy count if the court, were it sitting as a trier of fact, would convict the defendant of conspiring to

commit that object offense. Note, however, if the object offenses specified in the conspiracy count would be grouped together under §3D1.2(d) (e.g., a conspiracy to steal three government checks) it is not necessary to engage in the foregoing analysis, because §1B1.3(a)(2) governs consideration of the defendant's conduct.".

The purpose of this amendment is to add a guideline subsection (subsection (d)) expressly providing that a conviction of conspiracy to commit more than one offense is treated for guideline purposes as if the defendant had been convicted of a separate conspiracy count for each offense that the defendant conspired to commit. The current instruction in Application Note 9 of §3D1.2 is inadequate. For consistency, material now contained at §1B1.2(a) concerning stipulations to having committed additional offenses is moved to a new subsection (subsection (c)).

Additional commentary (Application Note 5) is provided to address cases in which the jury's verdict does not specify how many or which offenses were the object of the conspiracy of which the defendant was convicted. Compare United States v. Johnson, 713 F.2d 633, 645-46 (11th Cir. 1983) (conviction stands if there is sufficient proof with respect to any one of the objectives) cert. denied sub nom. Wilkins v. United States, 465 U.S. 1081 (1984) with United States v. Tarnopol, 561 F.2d 466 (3d Cir. 1977) (failure of proof with respect to any one of the objectives renders the conspiracy conviction invalid). In order to maintain consistency with other §1B1.2(a) determinations, this decision should be governed by a reasonable doubt standard. A higher standard of proof should govern the creation of what is, in effect, a new count of conviction for the purposes of Chapter Three, Part D (Multiple Counts). Because the guidelines do not explicitly establish standards of proof, the proposed new application note calls upon the court to determine which offense(s) was the object of the conspiracy as if it were "sitting as a trier of fact." The foregoing determination is not required, however, in the case of offenses that are grouped together under §3D1.2(d) (e.g., fraud and theft) because §1B1.3(a)(2) governs consideration of the defendant's conduct. **The effective date of this amendment is November 1, 1989.**

76. Section 1B1.3 is amended in subsection (a)(3) by deleting "or risk of harm" immediately following "all harm", and by deleting "if the harm or risk was caused intentionally, recklessly or by criminal negligence, and all harm or risk" and inserting in lieu thereof "and all harm".

Section 1B1.3(a) is amended by deleting:

"(4) the defendant's state of mind, intent, motive and purpose in committing the offense; and",

by renumbering subsection (a)(5) as (a)(4), and by inserting "and" at the end of subsection (a)(3) immediately following the semicolon.

The Commentary to §1B1.3 captioned "Background" is amended by deleting:

" Subsection (a)(4) requires consideration of the defendant's 'state of mind, intent, motive or purpose in committing the offense.' The defendant's state of mind is an element of the offense that may constitute a specific offense characteristic. See, e.g., §2A1.4 (Involuntary Manslaughter) (distinction made between recklessness and criminal negligence). The guidelines also incorporate broader notions of intent or purpose that are not elements of the offense, e.g., whether the offense was committed for profit, or for the purpose of facilitating a more serious offense. Accordingly, such factors must be considered in determining the applicable guideline range.",

and inserting in lieu thereof:

" Subsection (a)(4) requires consideration of any other information specified in the applicable guideline. For example, §2A1.4 (Involuntary Manslaughter) specifies consideration of the defendant's state of mind; §2K1.4 (Arson; Property Damage By Use of Explosives) specifies consideration of the risk of harm created.".

The purpose of this amendment is to delete language pertaining to "risk of harm" and "state of mind" as unnecessary. Cases in which the guidelines specifically address risk of harm or state of mind are covered in the amended guideline under subsection (a)(4) [formerly subsection (a)(5)]. In addition, the amendment deletes reference to harm committed "intentionally, recklessly, or by criminal negligence" as unnecessary and potentially confusing. **The effective date of this amendment is November 1, 1989.**

77. Section 1B1.3 is amended by deleting the introductory sentence as follows: "The conduct that is relevant to determining the applicable guideline range includes that set forth below.".

Section 1B1.3(b) is amended by deleting:

"(b) Chapter Four (Criminal History and Criminal Livelihood). To determine the criminal history category and the applicability of the career offender and criminal livelihood guidelines, the court shall consider all conduct relevant to a determination of the factors enumerated in the respective guidelines in Chapter Four.",

and inserting in lieu thereof:

"(b) Chapters Four (Criminal History and Criminal Livelihood) and Five (Determining the Sentence). Factors in Chapters Four and Five that establish the guideline range shall be determined on the basis of the conduct and information specified in the respective guidelines.".

The Commentary to §1B1.3 captioned "Background" is amended in the second paragraph by deleting "Chapter Four" and inserting in lieu thereof "Chapters Four and Five", and by deleting "that Chapter" and inserting in lieu thereof "those Chapters".

The purpose of this amendment is to clarify the guideline. **The effective date of this amendment is November 1, 1989.**

78. The Commentary to §1B1.3 captioned "Application Notes" is amended in Note 1 by deleting:

"If the conviction is for conspiracy, it includes conduct in furtherance of the conspiracy that was known to or was reasonably foreseeable by the defendant. If the conviction is for solicitation, misprision or accessory after the fact, it includes all conduct relevant to determining the offense level for the underlying offense that was known to or reasonably should have been known by the defendant. See generally §§2X1.1-2X4.1.",

and inserting in lieu thereof:

"In the case of criminal activity undertaken in concert with others, whether or not charged as a conspiracy, the conduct for which the defendant 'would be otherwise accountable' also includes conduct of others in furtherance of the execution of the jointly-undertaken criminal activity that was reasonably foreseeable by the defendant. Because a count may be broadly worded and include the conduct of many participants over a substantial period of time, the scope of the jointly-undertaken criminal activity, and hence relevant conduct, is not necessarily the same for every participant. Where it is established that the conduct was neither within the scope of the defendant's agreement, nor was reasonably foreseeable in connection with the criminal activity the defendant agreed to jointly undertake, such conduct is not included in establishing the defendant's offense level under this guideline.

In the case of solicitation, misprision, or accessory after the fact, the conduct for which the defendant 'would be otherwise accountable' includes all conduct relevant to determining the offense level for the underlying offense that was known, or reasonably should have been known, by the defendant.

<u>Illustrations of Conduct for Which the Defendant is Accountable</u>

a. Defendant A, one of ten off-loaders hired by Defendant B, was convicted of importation of marihuana, as a result of his assistance in off-loading a boat containing a one-ton shipment of marihuana. Regardless of the number of bales of marihuana that he actually unloaded, and notwithstanding any claim on his part that he was neither aware of, nor could reasonably foresee, that the boat contained this quantity of marihuana, Defendant A is held accountable for the entire one-ton quantity of marihuana on the boat because he aided and abetted the unloading, and hence the importation, of the entire shipment.

b. Defendant C, the getaway driver in an armed bank robbery in which $15,000 is taken and a teller is injured, is convicted of the substantive count of bank robbery. Defendant C is accountable for the money taken because he aided and abetted the taking of the money. He is accountable for the injury inflicted because he participated in concerted criminal conduct that he could reasonably foresee might result in the infliction of injury.

c. Defendant D pays Defendant E a small amount to forge an endorsement on an $800 stolên government check. Unknown to Defendant E, Defendant D then uses that check as a down payment in a scheme to fraudulently obtain $15,000 worth of merchandise. Defendant E is convicted of forging the $800 check. Defendant E is not accountable for the $15,000 because the fraudulent scheme to obtain $15,000 was beyond the scope of, and not reasonably foreseeable in connection with, the criminal activity he jointly undertook with Defendant D.

d. Defendants F and G, working together, design and execute a scheme to sell fraudulent stocks by telephone. Defendant F fraudulently obtains $20,000. Defendant G fraudulently obtains $35,000. Each is convicted of mail fraud. Each defendant is accountable for the entire amount ($55,000) because each aided and abetted the other in the fraudulent conduct. Alternatively, because Defendants F and G engaged in concerted criminal activity, each is accountable for the entire $55,000 loss because the conduct of each was in furtherance of the jointly undertaken criminal activity and was reasonably foreseeable.

e. Defendants H and I engaged in an ongoing marihuana importation conspiracy in which Defendant J was hired only to help off-load a single shipment. Defendants H, I, and J are included in a single count charging conspiracy to import marihuana. For the purposes of determining the offense level under this guideline, Defendant J is accountable for the entire single shipment of marihuana he conspired to help import and any acts or omissions in furtherance of the importation that were reasonably foreseeable. He is not accountable for prior or subsequent shipments of marihuana imported by Defendants H or I if those acts were beyond the scope of, and not reasonably foreseeable in connection with, the criminal activity he agreed to jointly undertake with Defendants H and I (<u>i.e.</u>, the importation of the single shipment of marihuana).".

The purpose of this amendment is to clarify the definition of conduct for which the defendant is "otherwise accountable." **The effective date of this amendment is November 1, 1989.**

79. Section 1B1.5 is amended by deleting "adjustments for" immediately following "all applicable", and by inserting "and cross references" immediately before the period at the end of the sentence.

The Commentary to §1B1.5 captioned "Application Note" is amended in Note 1 by inserting "and cross references" immediately before "as well as the base offense level".

The purpose of this amendment is to clarify the guideline and commentary. **The effective date of this amendment is November 1, 1989.**

80. The Commentary to §1B1.5 captioned "Application Note" is amended in Note 1 by deleting the last sentence as follows: "If the victim was vulnerable, the adjustment from §3A1.1 (Vulnerable Victim) also would apply.".

The purpose of this amendment is to delete an unnecessary sentence. No substantive change is made. **The effective date of this amendment is November 1, 1989.**

81. Section 1B1.9 is amended in the title by deleting "Petty Offenses" and inserting in lieu thereof "Class B or C Misdemeanors and Infractions".

Section 1B1.9 is amended by deleting "(petty offense)" immediately following "infraction".

The Commentary to §1B1.9 captioned "Application Notes is amended in the first sentence of Note 1 by deleting "petty offense" and inserting in lieu thereof "Class B or C misdemeanor or an infraction", in the second sentence of Note 1 by deleting "A petty offense is any offense for which the maximum sentence that may be imposed does not exceed six months' imprisonment." and inserting in lieu thereof "A Class B misdemeanor is any offense for which the maximum authorized term of imprisonment is more than thirty days but not more than six months; a Class C misdemeanor is any offense for which the maximum authorized term of imprisonment is more than five days but not more than thirty days; an infraction is any offense for which the maximum authorized term of imprisonment is not more than five days.", in the first sentence of Note 2 by deleting "petty offenses" and inserting in lieu thereof "Class B or C misdemeanors or infractions", in the second sentence of Note 2 by deleting "petty" and inserting in lieu thereof "such", in the third sentence of Note 2 by deleting "petty offense" and inserting in lieu thereof "Class B or C misdemeanor or infraction" and, in Note 3 by deleting:

"3. All other provisions of the guidelines should be disregarded to the extent that they purport to cover petty offenses.".

The Commentary to §1B1.9 captioned "Background" is amended by deleting:

"voted to adopt a temporary amendment to exempt all petty offenses from the coverage of the guidelines. Consequently, to the extent that some published guidelines may appear to cover petty offenses, they should be disregarded even if they appear in the Statutory Index",

and inserting in lieu thereof:

"exempted all Class B and C misdemeanors and infractions from the coverage of the guidelines".

The purposes of this amendment are to conform the guideline to a revision in the statutory definition of a petty offense, and to convert the wording of the Commission's emergency amendment at §1B1.9 (effective June 15, 1988) to that appropriate for a permanent amendment. Section 7089 of the Anti-Drug Abuse Act of 1988 revises the definition of a petty offense so that it no longer exactly corresponds with a Class B or C misdemeanor or infraction. Under the revised definition, a Class B or C misdemeanor or infraction that has an authorized fine of more than $5,000 for an individual (or more than $10,000 for an organization) will not be a petty offense. This legislative revision does not affect the maximum terms of imprisonment authorized. The maximum authorized term of imprisonment remains controlled by the grade of the offense (i.e., the maximum term of imprisonment remains five days for an infraction, thirty days for a Class C misdemeanor, and six months for a Class B misdemeanor). Because the statutory grade of the offense (i.e., a Class B or C misdemeanor or an infraction) is the more relevant definition for guideline purposes, this amendment deletes the references in §1B1.9 to "petty offenses" and in lieu thereof inserts references to "Class B and C misdemeanors and infractions." **The effective date of this amendment is November 1, 1989.**

82. The Commentary to §2A1.1 captioned "Statutory Provision" is amended by deleting "Provision" and inserting in lieu thereof "Provisions", and by inserting "; 21 U.S.C. § 848(e)" at the end immediately before the period.

The Commentary to §2A1.1 captioned "Application Note" is amended in the caption by deleting "Note" and inserting in lieu thereof "Notes", and by inserting the following additional note:

"2. If the defendant is convicted under 21 U.S.C. § 848(e), a sentence of death may be imposed under the specific provisions contained in that statute. This guideline applies when a sentence of death is not imposed.".

The Commentary to §2A1.1 captioned "Background" is amended by deleting "statute" and inserting in lieu thereof "18 U.S.C. § 1111", and by inserting immediately after the first sentence:

"Prior to the applicability of the Sentencing Reform Act of 1984, a defendant convicted under this statute and sentenced to life imprisonment could be paroled (see 18 U.S.C. § 4205(a)). Because of the abolition of parole by that Act, the language of 18 U.S.C. § 1111(b) (which was not amended by the Act) appears on its face to provide a mandatory minimum sentence of life imprisonment for this offense. Other provisions of the Act, however, classify this offense as a Class A felony (see 18 U.S.C. § 3559(a)(1)), for which a term of imprisonment of any period of time is authorized as an alternative to imprisonment for the duration of the defendant's life (see 18 U.S.C. §§ 3559(b), 3581(b)(1), as amended); hence, the relevance of the discussion in Application Note 1, supra, regarding circumstances in which a sentence less than life may be appropriate for a conviction under this statute."

The Commentary to §2A1.1 captioned "Background" is amended by inserting the following additional paragraph at the end:

" The maximum penalty authorized under 21 U.S.C. § 848(e) is death or life imprisonment. If a term of imprisonment is imposed, the statutorily required minimum term is twenty years.".

The purpose of this amendment is to incorporate new first-degree murder offenses created by Section 7001 of the Anti-Drug Abuse Act of 1988 where the death penalty is not imposed. This amendment also clarifies the existing commentary to this guideline. **The effective date of this amendment is November 1, 1989.**

83. Section 2A2.1 is amended in subsection (b)(2)(B) by deleting "a firearm or a dangerous weapon" and inserting in lieu thereof "a dangerous weapon (including a firearm)", and in subsection (b)(2)(C) by deleting "a firearm or other dangerous weapon" and inserting in lieu thereof "a dangerous weapon (including a firearm)".

The purposes of this amendment are to clarify that a firearm is a type of dangerous weapon and to remove the inconsistency in the language between specific offense characteristic subdivisions (b)(2)(B) and (b)(2)(C). **The effective date of this amendment is November 1, 1989.**

84. Section 2A2.1(b)(3) is amended by inserting the following additional subdivisions:

"(D) If the degree of injury is between that specified in subdivisions (A) and (B), add 3 levels; or

(E) If the degree of injury is between that specified in subdivisions (B) and (C), add 5 levels.".

The Commentary to §2A2.1 captioned "Application Notes" is amended in the caption by deleting "Notes" and inserting in lieu thereof "Note", and by deleting:

"2. If the degree of bodily injury falls between two injury categories, use of the intervening level (i.e., interpolation) is appropriate."

The purpose of this amendment is to provide intermediate adjustment levels for the degree of bodily injury. **The effective date of this amendment is November 1, 1989.**

85. Section 2A2.2 is amended in subsection (b)(2)(B) by deleting "a firearm or a dangerous weapon" and inserting in lieu thereof "a dangerous weapon (including a firearm)", and in subsection (b)(2)(C) by deleting "a firearm or other dangerous weapon" and inserting in lieu thereof "a dangerous weapon (including a firearm)".

The purposes of this amendment are to clarify that a firearm is a type of dangerous weapon and to remove the inconsistency in language between specific offense characteristic subdivisions (b)(2)(B) and (b)(2)(C). **The effective date of this amendment is November 1, 1989.**

86. Section 2A2.2(b)(3) is amended by inserting the following additional subdivisions:

"(D) If the degree of injury is between that specified in subdivisions (A) and (B), add 3 levels; or

(E) If the degree of injury is between that specified in subdivisions (B) and (C), add 5 levels.".

The Commentary to §2A2.2 captioned "Application Notes" is amended by deleting:

"3. If the degree of bodily injury falls between two injury categories, use of the intervening level (i.e., interpolation) is appropriate.",

and by renumbering Note 4 as Note 3.

The purpose of this amendment is to provide intermediate adjustment levels for the degree of bodily injury. **The effective date of this amendment is November 1, 1989.**

87. Section 2A2.3(a)(1) is amended by deleting "striking, beating, or wounding" and inserting in lieu thereof "physical contact, or if a dangerous weapon (including a firearm) was possessed and its use was threatened".

The Commentary to §2A2.3 captioned "Application Notes" is amended by deleting:

"2. 'Striking, beating, or wounding' means conduct sufficient to violate 18 U.S.C. § 113(d).",

and inserting in lieu thereof:

"2. Definitions of 'firearm' and 'dangerous weapon' are found in the Commentary to §1B1.1 (Application Instructions).".

The Commentary to §2A2.3 captioned "Background" is amended by deleting the last sentence as follows: "The distinction for striking, beating, or wounding reflects the statutory distinction found in 18 U.S.C. § 113(d) and (e).".

The purpose of this amendment is to provide a clearer standard by replacing the phrase "striking, wounding, or beating" (a statutory phrase dealing with a petty offense) with "physical contact." The amendment also provides an enhanced offense level for the case in which a weapon is possessed and its use is threatened. **The effective date of this amendment is November 1, 1989.**

88. The Commentary to §2A2.3 captioned "Statutory Provisions" is amended by deleting "113(d), 113(e),".

The purpose of this amendment is to delete references to petty offenses. **The effective date of this amendment is November 1, 1989.**

89. The Commentary to §2A2.4 captioned "Application Notes" is amended in Note 1 by deleting the first sentence as follows:

"Do not apply §3A1.2 (Official Victim).",

and by inserting the following additional sentence at the end:

"Therefore, do not apply §3A1.2 (Official Victim) unless subsection (c) requires the offense level to be determined under §2A2.2 (Aggravated Assault).".

The purpose of this amendment is to clarify the commentary. **The effective date of this amendment is November 1, 1989.**

90. Section 2A2.4(b)(1) is amended by deleting "striking, beating, or wounding", and inserting in lieu thereof "physical contact, or if a dangerous weapon (including a firearm) was possessed and its use was threatened".

The Commentary to §2A2.4 captioned "Application Notes" is amended by deleting:

> "2. 'Striking, beating, or wounding' is discussed in the Commentary to §2A2.3 (Minor Assault).",

and inserting in lieu thereof:

> "2. Definitions of 'firearm' and 'dangerous weapon' are found in the Commentary to §1B1.1 (Application Instructions).".

The purpose of this amendment is to provide a clearer standard by replacing the phrase "striking, wounding, or beating" (a statutory phrase dealing with a petty offense) with "physical contact." The amendment also provides an enhanced offense level for the case in which a weapon is possessed and its use is threatened. **The effective date of this amendment is November 1, 1989.**

91. Section 2A3.1(b)(1) is amended by deleting:

> "criminal sexual abuse was accomplished as defined in 18 U.S.C. § 2241",

and inserting in lieu thereof:

> "offense was committed by the means set forth in 18 U.S.C. § 2241(a) or (b)".

The Commentary to §2A3.1 captioned "Application Notes" is amended in Note 2 by deleting:

> "'Accomplished as defined in 18 U.S.C. § 2241' means accomplished by force, threat, or other means as defined in 18 U.S.C. § 2241(a) or (b) (i.e., by using force against that person; by threatening or placing that other person",

and inserting in lieu thereof:

> "'The means set forth in 18 U.S.C. § 2241(a) or (b)' are: by using force against the victim; by threatening or placing the victim",

by deleting the parenthesis immediately before the period at the end of the Note, and by inserting the following additional sentence at the end of the Note:

> "This provision would apply, for example, where any dangerous weapon was used, brandished, or displayed to intimidate the victim.".

The Commentary to §2A3.1 captioned "Background" is amended in the fifth sentence of the first paragraph by deleting the comma immediately following "force" and inserting in lieu thereof a semicolon, and by deleting "kidnapping," and inserting in lieu thereof "or kidnapping;", and in the last sentence of the last paragraph by deleting "serious physical" and inserting in lieu thereof "permanent, life-threatening, or serious bodily".

The purpose of this amendment is to clarify the guideline and commentary. **The effective date of this amendment is November 1, 1989.**

92. Section 2A3.1(b)(4) is amended by inserting immediately before the period at the end of the sentence: "; or (C) if the degree of injury is between that specified in subdivisions (A) and (B), increase by 3 levels".

The purpose of this amendment is to provide an intermediate adjustment level for degree of bodily injury. **The effective date of this amendment is November 1, 1989.**

93. The Commentary to §2A3.2 captioned "Statutory Provision" and "Background" is amended by deleting "2243" wherever it appears and inserting in lieu thereof "2243(a)".

The Commentary to §2A3.2 captioned "Background" is amended by deleting "statutory rape, i.e.," immediately following "applies to", and by deleting "victim's incapacity to give lawful consent" and inserting in lieu thereof "age of the victim".

The purposes of this amendment are to clarify that the relevant factor is the age of the victim, and to provide a more specific reference to the underlying statute. **The effective date of this amendment is November 1, 1989.**

94. Section 2A3.3 is amended in the title by deleting "(Statutory Rape)" immediately following "a Ward".

The Commentary to §2A3.3 captioned "Statutory Provision" is amended by deleting "§2243" and inserting in lieu thereof "§2243(b)".

The purposes of this amendment are to delete inapt language from the title and to provide a more specific reference to the underlying statute. **The effective date of this amendment is November 1, 1989.**

95. Chapter Two, Part A is amended by deleting §2A3.4 in entirety as follows:

"§2A3.4. Abusive Sexual Contact or Attempt to Commit Abusive Sexual Contact

(a) Base Offense Level: 6

(b) Specific Offense Characteristics

(1) If the abusive sexual contact was accomplished as defined in 18 U.S.C. § 2241 (including, but not limited to, the use or display of any dangerous weapon), increase by 9 levels.

(2) If the abusive sexual contact was accomplished as defined in 18 U.S.C. § 2242, increase by 4 levels.

Commentary

Statutory Provisions: 18 U.S.C. §§ 2244, 2245.

Application Notes:

1. 'Accomplished as defined in 18 U.S.C. § 2241' means accomplished by force, threat, or other means as defined in 18 U.S.C. § 2241(a) or (b) (i.e., by using force against that person; by threatening or placing that other person in fear that any person will be subject to death, serious bodily injury, or kidnapping; by rendering the victim unconscious; or by administering by force or threat of force, or without the knowledge or permission of the victim, a drug, intoxicant, or other similar substance and thereby substantially impairing the ability of the victim to appraise or control conduct).

2. 'Accomplished as defined in 18 U.S.C. § 2242' means accomplished by threatening or placing the victim in fear (other than by threatening or placing the victim in fear that any person will be subjected to death, serious bodily injury, or kidnapping); or when the victim is incapable of appraising the nature of the conduct or physically incapable of declining participation in, or communicating unwillingness to engage in, that sexual act.

Background: This section covers abusive sexual contact not amounting to criminal sexual abuse (criminal sexual abuse is covered under §2A3.1-3.3). Enhancements are provided for the use of force or threats. The maximum term of imprisonment authorized by statute for offenses covered in this section is five years (if accomplished as defined in 18 U.S.C. § 2241), three years (if accomplished as defined in 18 U.S.C. § 2242), and six months otherwise. The base offense level applies to conduct that is consensual.".

A replacement guideline with accompanying commentary is inserted as §2A3.4 (Abusive Sexual Contact or Attempt to Commit Abusive Sexual Contact).

The purposes of the amendment are to make the offense levels under this guideline consistent with the structure of related guidelines (§§2A3.1, 2A3.2, 2G1.2, 2G2.1, and 2G2.2) and to reflect the increased maximum sentences for certain conduct covered by this guideline. The amendment increases all offense levels, but in particular provides enhanced punishment for victimization of minors and children. **The effective date of this amendment is November 1, 1989.**

96. Section 2A4.1(b)(2) is amended by inserting immediately before the period at the end of the sentence: "; or (C) if the degree of injury is between that specified in subdivisions (A) and (B), increase by 3 levels".

The purpose of this amendment is to provide an intermediate adjustment level for the degree of bodily injury. **The effective date of this amendment is November 1, 1989.**

97. The Commentary to §2A5.2 captioned "Application Note" is amended by deleting:

"Application Note:

1. If an assault occurred, apply the most analogous guideline from Part A, Subpart 2 (Assault) if the offense level under that guideline is greater.".

The purpose of this amendment is to simplify the guideline by deleting redundant material. **The effective date of this amendment is November 1, 1989.**

98. The Commentary to §2A5.3 captioned "Application Notes" is amended in Note 1 by deleting "that the defendant is convicted of violating" and inserting in lieu thereof "of which the defendant is convicted".

The purpose of this amendment is to clarify the commentary. **The effective date of this amendment is November 1, 1989.**

99. Section 2B1.1(b)(1) is amended by deleting:

	"Loss	Increase in Level
(A)	$100 or less	no increase
(B)	$101 - $1,000	add 1
(C)	$1,001 - $2,000	add 2
(D)	$2,001 - $5,000	add 3
(E)	$5,001 - $10,000	add 4
(F)	$10,001 - $20,000	add 5
(G)	$20,001 - $50,000	add 6
(H)	$50,001 - $100,000	add 7
(I)	$100,001 - $200,000	add 8
(J)	$200,001 - $500,000	add 9
(K)	$500,001 - $1,000,000	add 10
(L)	$1,000,001 - $2,000,000	add 11
(M)	$2,000,001 - $5,000,000	add 12
(N)	over $5,000,000	add 13",

and inserting in lieu thereof:

	"Loss (Apply the Greatest)	Increase in Level
(A)	$100 or less	no increase
(B)	More than $100	add 1
(C)	More than $1,000	add 2
(D)	More than $2,000	add 3
(E)	More than $5,000	add 4
(F)	More than $10,000	add 5
(G)	More than $20,000	add 6
(H)	More than $40,000	add 7
(I)	More than $70,000	add 8
(J)	More than $120,000	add 9
(K)	More than $200,000	add 10
(L)	More than $350,000	add 11
(M)	More than $500,000	add 12

(N)	More than $800,000	add 13
(O)	More than $1,500,000	add 14
(P)	More than $2,500,000	add 15
(Q)	More than $5,000,000	add 16
(R)	More than $10,000,000	add 17
(S)	More than $20,000,000	add 18
(T)	More than $40,000,000	add 19
(U)	More than $80,000,000	add 20.".

The purposes of this amendment are to conform the theft and fraud loss tables to the tax evasion table in order to remove an unintended inconsistency between these tables in cases where the amount is greater than $40,000, to increase the offense levels for larger losses to provide additional deterrence and better reflect the seriousness of the conduct, and to eliminate minor gaps in the loss table. **The effective date of this amendment is November 1, 1989.**

100. Section 2B1.1(b)(6) is amended by deleting "organized criminal activity" and inserting in lieu thereof "an organized scheme to steal vehicles or vehicle parts".

The Commentary to §2B1.1 captioned "Application Notes" is amended by deleting:

> "8. 'Organized criminal activity' refers to operations such as car theft rings or 'chop shops,' where the scope of the activity is clearly significant.",

and inserting in lieu thereof:

> "8. Subsection (b)(6), referring to an 'organized scheme to steal vehicles or vehicle parts,' provides an alternative minimum measure of loss in the case of an ongoing, sophisticated operation such as an auto theft ring or 'chop shop.' 'Vehicles' refers to all forms of vehicles, including aircraft and watercraft.".

The Commentary to §2B1.1 captioned "Background" is amended in the last paragraph by deleting:

> "A minimum offense level of 14 is provided for organized criminal activity, i.e., operations such as car theft rings or 'chop shops,' where the scope of the activity is clearly significant but difficult to estimate. The guideline is structured so that if reliable information enables the court to estimate a volume of property loss that would result in a higher offense level, the higher offense level would govern.",

and inserting in lieu thereof:

> "A minimum offense level of 14 is provided for offenses involving an organized scheme to steal vehicles or vehicle parts. Typically, the scope of such activity is substantial (i.e., the value of the stolen property, combined with an enhancement for 'more than minimal planning' would itself result in an offense level of at least 14), but the value of the property is particularly difficult to ascertain in individual cases because the stolen property is rapidly resold or otherwise disposed of in the course of the offense. Therefore, the specific offense characteristic of 'organized scheme' is used as an alternative to 'loss' in setting the offense level.".

The purpose of this amendment is to clarify the coverage of a specific offense characteristic. **The effective date of this amendment is November 1, 1989.**

101. The Commentary to §2B1.1 captioned "Background" is amended in the first paragraph by deleting "§5A1.1" and inserting in lieu thereof "Chapter Five, Part A".

The purpose of this amendment is to correct a clerical error. **The effective date of this amendment is November 1, 1989.**

102. Section 2B1.2 is amended in the title by inserting ", Transporting, Transferring, Transmitting, or Possessing" immediately after "Receiving".

Section 2B1.2(b)(3)(A) is amended by inserting "receiving and" immediately before "selling".

The Commentary to §2B1.2 captioned "Application Notes" is amended by deleting:

"1. If the defendant is convicted of transporting stolen property, either §2B1.1 or this guideline would apply, depending upon whether the defendant stole the property.",

and by renumbering Notes 2 and 3 as Notes 1 and 2 respectively.

The purpose of this amendment is to clarify the nature of the cases to which this guideline applies. **The effective date of this amendment is November 1, 1989.**

103. Section 2B1.2 is amended by renumbering subsection (b)(4) as (b)(5), and by inserting the following new subsection (b)(4):

"(4) If the property included undelivered United States mail and the offense level as determined above is less than level 6, increase to level 6.".

The Commentary to §2B1.2 captioned "Application Notes", as amended, is further amended by inserting the following additional note:

"3. 'Undelivered United States mail' means mail that has not actually been received by the addressee or his agent (<u>e.g.</u>, it includes mail that is in the addressee's mail box).".

The purpose of this amendment is to add a specific offense characteristic where stolen property involved "undelivered mail" to conform to §2B1.1. **The effective date of this amendment is November 1, 1989.**

104. Section 2B1.2(b)(5)[formerly (b)(4)] is amended by deleting "organized criminal activity" and inserting in lieu thereof "an organized scheme to receive stolen vehicles or vehicle parts".

The Commentary to §2B1.2 captioned "Application Notes" is amended by inserting the following additional note:

"4. Subsection (b)(5), referring to an 'organized scheme to receive stolen vehicles or vehicle parts,' provides an alternative minimum measure of loss in the case of an ongoing, sophisticated operation such as an auto theft ring or 'chop shop.' 'Vehicles' refers to all forms of vehicles, including aircraft and watercraft. See Commentary to §2B1.1 (Larceny, Embezzlement, and Other Forms of Theft).".

The purpose of this amendment is to clarify the coverage of a specific offense characteristic. **The effective date of this amendment is November 1, 1989.**

105. Section 2B2.1(b)(2) is amended by deleting:

	"Loss	Increase in Level
(A)	$2,500 or less	no increase
(B)	$2,501 - $10,000	add 1
(C)	$10,001 - $50,000	add 2
(D)	$50,001 - $250,000	add 3
(E)	$250,001 - $1,000,000	add 4
(F)	$1,000,001 - $5,000,000	add 5
(G)	more than $5,000,000	add 6",

and inserting in lieu thereof:

	"Loss (Apply the Greatest)	Increase in Level
(A)	$2,500 or less	no increase
(B)	More than $2,500	add 1
(C)	More than $10,000	add 2
(D)	More than $50,000	add 3
(E)	More than $250,000	add 4
(F)	More than $800,000	add 5
(G)	More than $1,500,000	add 6
(H)	More than $2,500,000	add 7
(I)	More than $5,000,000	add 8.".

The purposes of this amendment are to eliminate minor gaps in the loss table and to conform the offense levels for larger losses to the amended loss table at §2B1.1. **The effective date of this amendment is November 1, 1989.**

106. Section 2B2.1(b)(4) is amended by deleting "a firearm or other dangerous weapon" and inserting in lieu thereof "a dangerous weapon (including a firearm)".

The Commentary to §2B2.1 captioned "Application Notes" is amended in Note 4 by deleting "with respect to a firearm or other dangerous weapon" and inserting in lieu thereof "to possession of a dangerous weapon (including a firearm) that was".

The purpose of this amendment is to clarify the guideline and commentary. **The effective date of this amendment is November 1, 1989.**

107. Section 2B2.2(b)(4) is amended by deleting "a firearm or other dangerous weapon" and inserting in lieu thereof "a dangerous weapon (including a firearm)".

The Commentary to §2B2.2 captioned "Application Notes" is amended in Note 4 by deleting "with respect to a firearm", and inserting in lieu thereof "to possession of a dangerous weapon (including a firearm) that was".

The purpose of this amendment is to clarify the guideline and commentary. **The effective date of this amendment is November 1, 1989.**

108. Section 2B2.3(b)(2) is amended by deleting "a firearm or other dangerous weapon" and inserting in lieu thereof "a dangerous weapon (including a firearm)".

The purpose of this amendment is to clarify the guideline. **The effective date of this amendment is November 1, 1989.**

109. Section 2B2.3(b) is amended by deleting "Characteristic" and inserting in lieu thereof "Characteristics".

The Commentary to §2B2.3 captioned "Statutory Provisions" is amended by deleting "Provisions" and inserting in lieu thereof "Provision", and by deleting "18 U.S.C. §§ 1382, 1854" and inserting in lieu thereof "42 U.S.C. § 7270b".

The purposes of this amendment are to correct a clerical error, to delete a reference to a petty offense and an incorrect statutory reference, and to insert an additional statutory reference. **The effective date of this amendment is November 1, 1989.**

110. Section 2B3.1(a) is amended by deleting "18" and inserting in lieu thereof "20".

Section 2B3.1(b) is amended by deleting subdivisions (1) and (2) as follows:

"(1) If the loss exceeded $2,500, increase the offense level as follows:

	Loss	Increase in Level
(A)	$2,500 or less	no increase
(B)	$2,501 - $10,000	add 1
(C)	$10,001 - $50,000	add 2
(D)	$50,001 - $250,000	add 3
(E)	$250,001 - $1,000,000	add 4
(F)	$1,000,001 - $5,000,000	add 5
(G)	more than $5,000,000	add 6

Treat the loss for a financial institution or post office as at least $5,000.

(2) (A) If a firearm was discharged increase by 5 levels; (B) if a firearm or a dangerous weapon was otherwise used, increase by 4 levels; (C) if a firearm or other dangerous weapon was brandished, displayed or possessed, increase by 3 levels.",

and inserting in lieu thereof:

"(1) If the offense involved robbery or attempted robbery of the property of a financial institution or post office, increase by 2 levels.

(2) (A) If a firearm was discharged, increase by 5 levels; (B) if a dangerous weapon (including a firearm) was otherwise used, increase by 4 levels; (C) if a dangerous weapon (including a firearm) was brandished, displayed, or possessed, increase by 3 levels; or (D) if an express threat of death was made, increase by 2 levels.",

and by inserting the following additional subdivision:

"(6) If the loss exceeded $10,000, increase the offense level as follows:

	Loss (Apply the Greatest)	Increase in Level
(A)	$10,000 or less	no increase
(B)	More than $10,000	add 1
(C)	More than $50,000	add 2
(D)	More than $250,000	add 3
(E)	More than $800,000	add 4
(F)	More than $1,500,000	add 5
(G)	More than $2,500,000	add 6
(H)	More than $5,000,000	add 7.".

The Commentary to §2B3.1 captioned "Application Notes" is amended by deleting:

"2. Pursuant to the last sentence of §2B3.1(b)(1), robbery or attempted robbery of a bank or post office results in a minimum one-level enhancement. There is no special enhancement for banks and post offices if the loss exceeds $10,000, however.",

and inserting in lieu thereof:

"2. When an object that appeared to be a dangerous weapon was brandished, displayed, or possessed, treat the object as a dangerous weapon for the purposes of subsection (b)(2)(C).".

The Commentary to §2B3.1 captioned "Application Notes" is amended by inserting the following additional note:

"8. An 'express threat of death,' as used in subsection (b)(2)(D), may be in the form of an oral or written statement, act, gesture, or combination thereof. For example, an oral or written demand using words such as 'Give me the money or I will kill you', 'Give me the money or I will pull the pin on the grenade I have in my pocket', 'Give me the money or I will shoot you', 'Give me your money or else (where the defendant draws his hand across his throat in a slashing motion)', or 'Give me the money or you are dead' would constitute an express threat of death. The court should consider that the intent of the underlying provision is to provide an increased offense level for cases in which the offender(s) engaged in conduct that would instill in a reasonable person, who is a victim of the offense, significantly greater fear than that necessary to constitute an element of the offense of robbery.".

The Commentary to §2B3.1 captioned "Background" is amended in the first paragraph by deleting the third sentence as follows:

"Banks and post offices carry a minimum 1 level enhancement for property loss because such institutions generally have more cash readily available, and whether the defendant obtains more or less than $2,500 is largely fortuitous.".

The purposes of this amendment are to increase the offense level for robbery to better reflect the seriousness of the offense and past practice, to provide an increased enhancement for the robbery of the property of a financial institution or post office, to provide an enhancement for an express threat of death, and to provide that an object that appeared to be a dangerous weapon is to be treated as a dangerous weapon for the purposes of subsection (b)(2)(C). **The effective date of this amendment is November 1, 1989.**

111. Section 2B3.1(b)(3) is amended by inserting the following additional subdivisions:

"(D) If the degree of injury is between that specified in subdivisions (A) and (B), add 3 levels; or

(E) If the degree of injury is between that specified in subdivisions (B) and (C), add 5 levels.".

The Commentary to §2B3.1 captioned "Application Notes" is amended by deleting:

"4. If the degree of bodily injury falls between two injury categories, use of the intervening level (i.e., interpolation) is appropriate.",

and by renumbering Notes 5-8 as 4-7, respectively.

The purpose of this amendment is to provide intermediate adjustment levels for the degree of bodily injury. **The effective date of this amendment is November 1, 1989.**

112. Section 2B3.2 is amended in subsection (b)(2)(B) by deleting "a firearm or a dangerous weapon" and inserting in lieu thereof "a dangerous weapon (including a firearm)", and in subsection (b)(2)(C) by deleting "a firearm or other dangerous weapon" and inserting in lieu thereof "a dangerous weapon (including a firearm)".

The purposes of this amendment are to clarify that a firearm is a type of dangerous weapon and to remove the inconsistency in language between specific offense characteristic subdivisions (b)(2)(B) and (b)(2)(C). **The effective date of this amendment is November 1, 1989.**

113. Section 2B3.2(b)(3) is amended by inserting the following additional subdivisions:

"(D) If the degree of injury is between that specified in subdivisions (A) and (B), add 3 levels; or

(E) If the degree of injury is between that specified in subdivisions (B) and (C), add 5 levels.".

The Commentary to §2B3.2 captioned "Application Notes" is amended by deleting:

"4. If the degree of bodily injury falls between two injury categories, use of the intervening level (i.e., interpolation) is appropriate.",

and by renumbering Notes 5 and 6 as 4 and 5, respectively.

The purpose of this amendment is to provide intermediate adjustment levels for the degree of bodily injury. **The effective date of this amendment is November 1, 1989.**

114. Section 2B3.3(b) is amended by deleting "Characteristics" and inserting in lieu thereof "Characteristic".

The purpose of this amendment is to correct a clerical error. **The effective date of this amendment is November 1, 1989.**

115. Section 2B5.1 is amended in the title by inserting "Bearer" immediately before "Obligations".

The Commentary to §2B5.1 captioned "Application Notes" is amended by renumbering Note 2 as Note 3, and by inserting the following new note 2:

"2. 'Counterfeit,' as used in this section, means an instrument that purports to be genuine but is not, because it has been falsely made or manufactured in its entirety. Offenses involving genuine instruments that have been altered are covered under §2B5.2.".

The Commentary to §2B5.1 captioned "Application Notes" is amended in the renumbered Note 3 by deleting ", paste corners of notes on notes of a different denomination," immediately before "or otherwise produce".

The purpose of this amendment is to clarify the coverage and operation of this guideline. The amendment revises the title of §2B5.1 to make the coverage of the guideline clear from the title, and adopts the definition of "counterfeit" used in 18 U.S.C. § 513. "Altered" obligations (e.g., the corner of a note of one denomination pasted on a note of a different denomination) are covered under §2B5.2. **The effective date of this amendment is November 1, 1989.**

116. Section 2B5.2 is amended in the title by inserting "Altered or" immediately following "Involving" and by inserting "Counterfeit Bearer" immediately following "Other than".

The purpose of this amendment is to clarify the coverage of this guideline. **The effective date of this amendment is November 1, 1989.**

117. Section 2B6.1(b) is amended by renumbering subsection (b)(2) as (b)(3) and inserting the following new subsection (b)(2):

"(2) If the defendant was in the business of receiving and selling stolen property, increase by 2 levels.".

The purpose of this amendment is to resolve an inconsistency between this section and §2B1.2 created by the lack of an enhancement in this section for a person in the business of selling stolen property. This amendment eliminates this inconsistency by adding a 2-level increase if the defendant was in the business of selling stolen property. Two levels rather than four levels is the applicable increase to conform to §2B1.2 because the base offense level of §2B6.1 already incorporates the adjustment for more than minimal planning. **The effective date of this amendment is November 1, 1989.**

118. Section 2B6.1(b)(3)[formerly (b)(2)] is amended by deleting "organized criminal activity" and inserting in lieu thereof "an organized scheme to steal vehicles or vehicle parts, or to receive stolen vehicles or vehicle parts".

The Commentary to §2B6.1 captioned "Application Note" is amended by deleting:

"1. See Commentary to §2B1.1 (Larceny, Embezzlement, and other Forms of Theft) regarding the adjustment in subsection (b)(2) for organized criminal activity, such as car theft rings and 'chop shop' operations.",

and inserting in lieu thereof:

"1. Subsection (b)(3), referring to an 'organized scheme to steal vehicles or vehicle parts, or to receive stolen vehicles or vehicle parts,' provides an alternative minimum measure of loss in the case of an ongoing, sophisticated operation such as an auto theft ring or 'chop shop.' 'Vehicles' refers to all forms of vehicles, including aircraft and watercraft. See Commentary to §2B1.1 (Larceny, Embezzlement, and Other Forms of Theft).".

The purpose of this amendment is to clarify the coverage of a specific offense characteristic. **The effective date of this amendment is November 1, 1989.**

119. Section 2B6.1(b) is amended by deleting "Characteristic" and inserting in lieu thereof "Characteristics".

The Commentary to §2B6.1 captioned "Statutory Provisions" and "Background" is amended by deleting "2320" wherever it appears and inserting in lieu thereof in each instance "2321".

The purpose of this amendment is to correct clerical errors. **The effective date of this amendment is November 1, 1989.**

120. Section 2C1.1(b)(1) is amended by deleting "action received" and inserting in lieu thereof "benefit received, or to be received,".

The Commentary to §2C1.1 captioned "Application Notes" is amended in Note 2 in the first sentence by deleting "action received" and inserting in lieu thereof "benefit received, or to be received,", and by deleting "action (i.e., benefit or favor)" and inserting in lieu thereof "benefit"; in the second sentence by deleting "action received in return" and inserting in lieu thereof "benefit received or to be received", and by deleting "such action" and inserting in lieu thereof "such benefit"; and in the third sentence by deleting "action" and inserting in lieu thereof "benefit".

The purpose of this amendment is to clarify the guideline and commentary. **The effective date of this amendment is November 1, 1989.**

121. Section 2C1.1(b) is amended by deleting "(1)" and "(2)" and inserting in lieu thereof "(A)" and "(B)" respectively; and by deleting "Apply the greater" and inserting in lieu thereof:

"(1) If the offense involved more than one bribe, increase by 2 levels.

(2) (If more than one applies, use the greater):".

The Commentary to §2C1.1 captioned "Application Notes" is amended by deleting the text of Note 6 as follows:

"When multiple counts are involved, each bribe is to be treated as a separate, unrelated offense not subject to §3D1.2(d) or §3D1.3(b). Instead, apply §3D1.4. However, if a defendant makes several payments as part of a single bribe, that is to be treated as a single bribery offense involving the total amount of the bribe.",

and inserting in lieu thereof:

"Related payments that, in essence, constitute a single bribe (e.g., a number of installment payments for a single action) are to be treated as a single bribe, even if charged in separate counts.".

Section 2C1.2(b) is amended by deleting "(1)" and "(2)" and inserting in lieu thereof "(A)" and "(B)" respectively; and by deleting "Apply the greater" and inserting in lieu thereof:

"(1) If the offense involved more than one gratuity, increase by 2 levels.

(2) (If more than one applies, use the greater):".

The Commentary to §2C1.2 captioned "Application Notes" is amended by deleting the text of Note 4 as follows:

"When multiple counts of receiving a gratuity are involved, each count is to be treated as a separate, unrelated offense not subject to §3D1.2(d) or §3D1.3(b). Instead, apply §3D1.4.",

and inserting in lieu thereof:

"Related payments that, in essence, constitute a single gratuity (e.g., separate payments for airfare and hotel for a single vacation trip) are to be treated as a single gratuity, even if charged in separate counts.".

Section 3D1.2(d) is amended in the listing of offense sections in the third paragraph by deleting "§2C1.1,", and in the listing of offense sections in the second paragraph by inserting in order by section number "§§2C1.1, 2C1.2;".

The Introductory Commentary to Chapter Three, Part D, is amended in the fifth paragraph by deleting ", robbery, and bribery" and inserting in lieu thereof "and robbery", and in the seventh paragraph by deleting ", robbery, or bribery" and inserting in lieu thereof "or robbery".

Under the current bribery guideline, there is no enhancement for repeated instances of bribery if the conduct involves the same course of conduct or common scheme or plan and the same victim (as frequently is the case where the government is the victim) because such cases are grouped under §3D1.2(b). In contrast, the fraud and theft guidelines generally provide a 2-level increase in cases of repeated instances under the second prong of the "more than minimal planning" definition.

Unlike the theft and fraud guidelines, it is arguable that the value of any bribe that was part of the same course of conduct or a common scheme or plan as the offense of conviction, but not included in the count of conviction, is excluded from consideration. This is because §1B1.3(a)(2), which authorizes consideration of conduct not expressly included in the offense of conviction but part of the same course of conduct or common scheme or plan, applies only to offenses grouped under §3D1.2(d). Thus, if the defendant pleads to one count of a bribery offense involving one $10,000 bribe in satisfaction of a 15 count indictment involving an additional $80,000 in separate bribes that were part of the same course of conduct, the current bribery guideline, unlike the theft and fraud guidelines, would not take into account the additional $80,000, and there would be no increase for repeated instances.

The current guideline may also create various anomalies because the multiple count rule (which applies only where the offenses are not grouped under §3D1.2(b)) increases the offense level differently than the monetary table. For example, an elected public official who takes three unrelated $200 bribes has an offense level of 21; the same defendant who took two unrelated $500,000 bribes would have an offense level of 20.

The purpose of this amendment is to address the above noted issues. A specific offense characteristic is added to provide a 2-level increase where the offense involved more than one bribe or gratuity. In addition, such offenses will be grouped under §3D1.2(d) which allows for aggregation of the amount of the bribes from the same course of conduct or common scheme or plan under §1B1.3(a)(2) (as in theft and fraud offenses). **The effective date of this amendment is November 1, 1989.**

122. The Commentary to §2C1.1 captioned "Background" is amended in the eighth paragraph by deleting "extortions, conspiracies, and attempts" and inserting in lieu thereof "extortion, or attempted extortion,".

The purpose of this amendment is to correct a technical error. This section expressly covers extortion and attempted extortion; conspiracy is covered through the operation of §2X1.1. **The effective date of this amendment is November 1, 1989.**

123. Section 2D1.1(a) is amended by deleting:

"(a) Base Offense Level:

(1) 43, for an offense that results in death or serious bodily injury with a prior conviction for a similar drug offense; or

(2) 38, for an offense that results in death or serious bodily injury and involved controlled substances (except Schedule III, IV, and V controlled substances and less than: (A) fifty kilograms of marihuana, (B) ten kilograms of hashish, and (C) one kilogram of hashish oil); or

(3) For any other offense, the base offense level is the level specified in the Drug Quantity Table below.",

and inserting in lieu thereof:

"(a) Base Offense Level (Apply the greatest):

(1) 43, if the defendant is convicted under 21 U.S.C. § 841(b)(1)(A), (b)(1)(B), or (b)(1)(C), or 21 U.S.C. § 960(b)(1), (b)(2), or (b)(3), and the offense of conviction establishes that death or serious bodily injury resulted from the use of the substance and that the defendant committed the offense after one or more prior convictions for a similar offense; or

(2) 38, if the defendant is convicted under 21 U.S.C. § 841(b)(1)(A), (b)(1)(B), or (b)(1)(C), or 21 U.S.C. § 960(b)(1), (b)(2), or (b)(3), and the offense of conviction establishes that death or serious bodily injury resulted from the use of the substance; or

(3) the offense level specified in the Drug Quantity Table set forth in subsection (c) below.".

The Commentary to §2D1.1 captioned "Application Notes" is amended in Note 1 by deleting "'Similar drug offense' as used in §2D1.1(a)(1) means a prior conviction as described in 21 U.S.C. §§ 841(b) or 962(b).", and inserting in lieu thereof "'Mixture or substance' as used in this guideline has the same meaning as in 21 U.S.C. § 841.".

The purpose of this amendment is to provide that subsections (a)(1) and (a)(2) apply only in the case of a conviction under circumstances specified in the statutes cited. The amendment also clarifies that the term "mixture or substance" has the same meaning as it has in the statute. **The effective date of this amendment is November 1, 1989.**

124. Section 2D1.1(b) is amended by deleting "a firearm or other dangerous weapon" and inserting in lieu thereof "a dangerous weapon (including a firearm)".

The purpose of the amendment is to clarify the guideline. **The effective date of this amendment is November 1, 1989.**

125. Section 2D1.1 is amended by deleting the "Drug Quantity Table" in its entirety, including the title and footnotes, as follows:

"DRUG QUANTITY TABLE

Controlled Substances and Quantity*	Base Offense Level
10 KG Heroin or equivalent Schedule I or II Opiates, 50 KG Cocaine or equivalent Schedule I or II Stimulants, 500 G Cocaine Base, 10 KG PCP or 1 KG Pure PCP, 100 G LSD or equivalent Schedule I or II Hallucinogens, 4 KG Fentanyl or 1 KG Fentanyl Analogue, 10,000 KG Marihuana, 100,000 Marihuana Plants, 2000 KG Hashish, 200 KG Hashish Oil (or more of any of the above)	Level 36

3-9.9 KG Heroin or equivalent Schedule I or II Opiates, 15-49.9 KG Cocaine or equivalent Schedule I or II Stimulants, 150-499 G Cocaine Base, 3-9.9 KG PCP or 300-999 G Pure PCP, 30-99 G LSD or equivalent Schedule I or II Hallucinogens, 1.2-3.9 KG Fentanyl or 300-999 G Fentanyl Analogue, 3000-9999 KG Marihuana, 30,000-99,999 Marihuana Plants, 600-1999 KG Hashish, 60-199 KG Hashish Oil	Level 34
1-2.9 KG Heroin or equivalent Schedule I or II Opiates, 5-14.9 KG Cocaine or equivalent Schedule I or II Stimulants, 50-149 G Cocaine Base, 1-2.9 KG PCP or 100-299 G Pure PCP, 10-29 G LSD or equivalent Schedule I or II Hallucinogens, .4-1.1 KG Fentanyl or 100-299 G Fentanyl Analogue, 1000-2999 KG Marihuana, 10,000-29,999 Marihuana Plants, 200-599 KG Hashish, 20-59.9 KG Hashish Oil	Level 32**
700-999 G Heroin or equivalent Schedule I or II Opiates, 3.5-4.9 KG Cocaine or equivalent Schedule I or II Stimulants, 35-49 G Cocaine Base, 700-999 G PCP or 70-99 G Pure PCP, 7-9.9 G LSD or equivalent Schedule I or II Hallucinogens, 280-399 G Fentanyl or 70-99 G Fentanyl Analogue, 700-999 KG Marihuana, 7000-9999 Marihuana Plants, 140-199 KG Hashish, 14-19.9 KG Hashish Oil	Level 30
400-699 G Heroin or equivalent Schedule I or II Opiates, 2-3.4 KG Cocaine or equivalent Schedule I or II Stimulants, 20-34.9 G Cocaine Base, 400-699 G PCP or 40-69 G Pure PCP, 4-6.9 G LSD or equivalent Schedule I or II Hallucinogens, 160-279 G Fentanyl or 40-69 G Fentanyl Analogue, 400-699 KG Marihuana, 4000-6999 Marihuana Plants, 80-139 KG Hashish, 8.0-13.9 KG Hashish Oil	Level 28
100-399 G Heroin or equivalent Schedule I or II Opiates, .5-1.9 KG Cocaine or equivalent Schedule I or II Stimulants, 5-19 G Cocaine Base, 100-399 G PCP or 10-39 G Pure PCP, 1-3.9 G LSD or equivalent Schedule I or II Hallucinogens, 40-159 G Fentanyl or 10-39 G Fentanyl Analogue, 100-399 KG Marihuana, 1000-3999 Marihuana Plants, 20-79 KG Hashish, 2.0-7.9 KG Hashish Oil	Level 26**
80-99 G Heroin or equivalent Schedule I or II Opiates, 400-499 G Cocaine or equivalent Schedule I or II Stimulants, 4-4.9 G Cocaine Base, 80-99 G PCP or 8-9.9 G Pure PCP, 800-999 MG LSD or equivalent Schedule I or II Hallucinogens, 32-39 G Fentanyl or 8-9.9 G Fentanyl Analogue, 80-99 KG Marihuana, 800-999 Marihuana Plants, 16-19.9 KG Hashish, 1.6-1.9 KG Hashish Oil	Level 24
60-79 G Heroin or equivalent Schedule I or II Opiates, 300-399 G Cocaine or equivalent Schedule I or II Stimulants, 3-3.9 G Cocaine Base, 60-79 G PCP or 6-7.9 G Pure PCP, 600 -799 MG LSD or equivalent Schedule I or II Hallucinogens, 24-31.9 G Fentanyl or 6-7.9 G Fentanyl Analogue, 60-79 KG Marihuana, 600-799 Marihuana Plants, 12-15.9 KG Hashish, 1.2-1.5 KG Hashish Oil	Level 22
40-59 G Heroin or equivalent Schedule I or II Opiates, 200-299 G Cocaine or equivalent Schedule I or II Stimulants, 2-2.9 G Cocaine Base, 40-59 G PCP or 4-5.9 G Pure PCP, 400-599 MG LSD or equivalent Schedule I or II Hallucinogens, 16-23.9 G Fentanyl or 4-5.9 G Fentanyl Analogue, 40-59 KG Marihuana, 400-599 Marihuana Plants, 8-11.9 KG Hashish, .8-1.1 KG Hashish Oil, 20 KG+ Schedule III or other Schedule I or II controlled substances	Level 20
20-39 G Heroin or equivalent Schedule I or II Opiates, 100-199 G Cocaine or equivalent Schedule I or II Stimulants, 1-1.9 G Cocaine Base, 20-39 G PCP or 2-3.9 G Pure PCP, 200-399 MG LSD or equivalent Schedule I or II Hallucinogens, 8-15.9 G Fentanyl or 2-3.9 G Fentanyl Analogue, 20-39 KG Marihuana, 200-399 Marihuana Plants, 5-7.9 KG Hashish, 500-799 G Hashish Oil, 10-19 KG Schedule III or other Schedule I or II controlled substances	Level 18
10-19 G Heroin or equivalent Schedule I or II Opiates, 50-99 G Cocaine or equivalent Schedule I or II Stimulants, 500-999 MG Cocaine Base, 10-19.9 G PCP or 1-1.9 G Pure PCP, 100-199 MG LSD or equivalent Schedule I or II Hallucinogens, 4-7.9 G Fentanyl or 1-1.9 G Fentanyl Analogue, 10-19 KG Marihuana, 100-199 Marihuana Plants, 2-4.9 KG Hashish, 200-499 G Hashish Oil, 5-9.9 KG Schedule III or other Schedule I or II controlled substances	Level 16
5-9.9 G Heroin or equivalent Schedule I or II Opiates, 25-49 G Cocaine or equivalent Schedule I or II Stimulants, 250-499 MG Cocaine Base, 5-9.9 G PCP or 500-999 MG Pure PCP, 50-99 MG LSD or equivalent Schedule I or II Hallucinogens, 2-3.9 G Fentanyl or .5-.9 G Fentanyl Analogue, 5-9.9 KG Marihuana, 50-99 Marihuana Plants, 1-1.9 KG Hashish, 100-199 G Hashish Oil, 2.5-4.9 KG Schedule III or other Schedule I or II controlled substances	Level 14

Less than the following: 5 G Heroin or equivalent Schedule I or II Opiates, 25 G Cocaine or equivalent Schedule I or II Stimulants, 250 MG Cocaine Base, 5 G PCP or 500 MG Pure PCP, 50 MG LSD or equivalent Schedule I or II Hallucinogens, 2 G Fentanyl or 500 MG Fentanyl Analogue; 2.5-4.9 KG Marihuana, 25-49 Marihuana Plants, 500-999 G Hashish, 50-99 G Hashish Oil, 1.25-2.4 KG Schedule III or other Schedule I or II controlled substances, 20 KG+ Schedule IV	Level 12
1-2.4 KG Marihuana, 10-24 Marihuana Plants, 200-499 G Hashish, 20-49 G Hashish Oil, .50-1.24 KG Schedule III or other Schedule I or II controlled substances, 8-19 KG Schedule IV	Level 10
250-999 G Marihuana, 3-9 Marihuana Plants, 50-199 G Hashish, 10-19 G Hashish Oil, 125-449 G Schedule III or other Schedule I or II controlled substances, 2-7.9 KG Schedule IV, 20 KG+ Schedule V	Level 8
Less than the following: 250 G Marihuana, 3 Marihuana Plants, 50 G Hashish, 10 G Hashish Oil, 125 G Schedule III or other Schedule I or II controlled substances, 2 KG Schedule IV, 20 KG Schedule V	Level 6

---

* The scale amounts for all controlled substances refer to the total weight of the controlled substance. Consistent with the provisions of the Anti-Drug Abuse Act, if any mixture of a compound contains any detectable amount of a controlled substance, the entire amount of the mixture or compound shall be considered in measuring the quantity. If a mixture or compound contains a detectable amount of more than one controlled substance, the most serious controlled substance shall determine the categorization of the entire quantity.

** Statute specifies a mandatory minimum sentence.",

and inserting in lieu thereof:

"(c) DRUG QUANTITY TABLE

Controlled Substances and Quantity*		Base Offense Level
(1)	300 KG or more of Heroin (or the equivalent amount of other Schedule I or II Opiates); 1500 KG or more of Cocaine (or the equivalent amount of other Schedule I or II Stimulants); 15 KG or more of Cocaine Base; 300 KG or more of PCP, or 30 KG or more of Pure PCP; 300 KG or more of Methamphetamine, or 30 KG or more of Pure Methamphetamine; 3 KG or more of LSD (or the equivalent amount of other Schedule I or II Hallucinogens); 120 KG or more of Fentanyl; 30 KG or more of a Fentanyl Analogue; 300,000 KG or more of Marihuana; 60,000 KG or more of Hashish; 6,000 KG or more of Hashish Oil.	Level 42
(2)	At least 100 KG but less than 300 KG of Heroin (or the equivalent amount of other Schedule I or II Opiates); At least 500 KG but less than 1500 KG of Cocaine (or the equivalent amount of other Schedule I or II Stimulants); At least 5 KG but less than 15 KG of Cocaine Base; At least 100 KG but less than 300 KG of PCP, or at least 10 KG but less than 30 KG of Pure PCP; At least 100 KG but less than 300 KG of Methamphetamine, or at least 10 KG but less than 30 KG of Pure Methamphetamine; At least 1 KG but less than 3 KG of LSD (or the equivalent amount of other Schedule I or II Hallucinogens); At least 40 KG but less than 120 KG of Fentanyl; At least 10 KG but less than 30 KG of a Fentanyl Analogue; At least 100,000 KG but less than 300,000 KG of Marihuana; At least 20,000 KG but less than 60,000 KG of Hashish; At least 2,000 KG but less than 6,000 KG of Hashish Oil.	Level 40
(3)	At least 30 KG but less than 100 KG of Heroin (or the equivalent amount of other Schedule I or II Opiates); At least 150 KG but less than 500 KG of Cocaine (or the equivalent amount of other Schedule I or II Stimulants); At least 1.5 KG but less than 5 KG of Cocaine Base; At least 30 KG but less than 100 KG of PCP, or at least 3 KG but less than 10 KG of Pure PCP;	Level 38

At least 30 KG but less than 100 KG of Methamphetamine, or at least 3 KG but less than 10 KG of Pure Methamphetamine;
At least 300 G but less than 1 KG of LSD (or the equivalent amount of other Schedule I or II Hallucinogens);
At least 12 KG but less than 40 KG of Fentanyl;
At least 3 KG but less than 10 KG of a Fentanyl Analogue;
At least 30,000 KG but less than 100,000 KG of Marihuana;
At least 6,000 KG but less than 20,000 KG of Hashish;
At least 600 KG but less than 2,000 KG of Hashish Oil.

(4) At least 10 KG but less than 30 KG of Heroin (or the equivalent amount of other Schedule I or II Opiates); — Level 36
At least 50 KG but less than 150 KG of Cocaine (or the equivalent amount of other Schedule I or II Stimulants);
At least 500 G but less than 1.5 KG of Cocaine Base;
At least 10 KG but less than 30 KG of PCP, or at least 1 KG but less than 3 KG of Pure PCP;
At least 10 KG but less than 30 KG of Methamphetamine, or at least 1 KG but less than 3 KG of Pure Methamphetamine;
At least 100 G but less than 300 G of LSD (or the equivalent amount of other Schedule I or II Hallucinogens);
At least 4 KG but less than 12 KG of Fentanyl;
At least 1 KG but less than 3 KG of a Fentanyl Analogue;
At least 10,000 KG but less than 30,000 KG of Marihuana;
At least 2,000 KG but less than 6,000 KG of Hashish;
At least 200 KG but less than 600 KG of Hashish Oil.

(5) At least 3 KG but less than 10 KG of Heroin (or the equivalent amount of other Schedule I or II Opiates); — Level 34
At least 15 KG but less than 50 KG of Cocaine (or the equivalent amount of other Schedule I or II Stimulants);
At least 150 G but less than 500 G of Cocaine Base;
At least 3 KG but less than 10 KG of PCP, or at least 300 G but less than 1 KG of Pure PCP;
At least 3 KG but less than 10 KG of Methamphetamine, or at least 300 G but less than 1 KG of Pure Methamphetamine;
At least 30 G but less than 100 G of LSD (or the equivalent amount of other Schedule I or II Hallucinogens);
At least 1.2 KG but less than 4 KG of Fentanyl;
At least 300 G but less than 1 KG of a Fentanyl Analogue;
At least 3,000 KG but less than 10,000 KG of Marihuana;
At least 600 KG but less than 2,000 KG of Hashish;
At least 60 KG but less than 200 KG of Hashish Oil.

(6) At least 1 KG but less than 3 KG of Heroin (or the equivalent amount of other Schedule I or II Opiates); — Level 32
At least 5 KG but less than 15 KG of Cocaine (or the equivalent amount of other Schedule I or II Stimulants);
At least 50 G but less than 150 G of Cocaine Base;
At least 1 KG but less than 3 KG of PCP, or at least 100 G but less than 300 G of Pure PCP;
At least 1 KG but less than 3 KG of Methamphetamine, or at least 100 G but less than 300 G of Pure Methamphetamine;
At least 10 G but less than 30 G of LSD (or the equivalent amount of other Schedule I or II Hallucinogens);
At least 400 G but less than 1.2 KG of Fentanyl;
At least 100 G but less than 300 G of a Fentanyl Analogue;
At least 1,000 KG but less than 3,000 KG of Marihuana;
At least 200 KG but less than 600 KG of Hashish;
At least 20 KG but less than 60 KG of Hashish Oil.

(7) At least 700 G but less than 1 KG of Heroin (or the equivalent amount of other Schedule I or II Opiates); — Level 30
At least 3.5 KG but less than 5 KG of Cocaine (or the equivalent amount of other Schedule I or II Stimulants);
At least 35 G but less than 50 G of Cocaine Base;
At least 700 G but less than 1 KG of PCP, or at least 70 G but less than 100 G of Pure PCP;
At least 700 G but less than 1 KG of Methamphetamine, or at least 70 G but less than 100 G of Pure Methamphetamine;
At least 7 G but less than 10 G of LSD (or the equivalent amount of other Schedule I or II Hallucinogens);
At least 280 G but less than 400 G of Fentanyl;
At least 70 G but less than 100 G of a Fentanyl Analogue;
At least 700 KG but less than 1,000 KG of Marihuana;
At least 140 KG but less than 200 KG of Hashish;
At least 14 KG but less than 20 KG of Hashish Oil.

(8) At least 400 G but less than 700 G of Heroin (or the equivalent amount of other Schedule I or II Opiates);
At least 2 KG but less than 3.5 KG of Cocaine (or the equivalent amount of other Schedule I or II Stimulants);
At least 20 G but less than 35 G of Cocaine Base;
At least 400 G but less than 700 G of PCP, or at least 40 G but less than 70 G of Pure PCP;
At least 400 G but less than 700 G of Methamphetamine, or at least 40 G but less than 70 G of Pure Methamphetamine;
At least 4 G but less than 7 G of LSD (or the equivalent amount of other Schedule I or II Hallucinogens);
At least 160 G but less than 280 G of Fentanyl;
At least 40 G but less than 70 G of a Fentanyl Analogue;
At least 400 KG but less than 700 KG of Marihuana;
At least 80 KG but less than 140 KG of Hashish;
At least 8 KG but less than 14 KG of Hashish Oil. — Level 28

(9) At least 100 G but less than 400 G of Heroin (or the equivalent amount of other Schedule I or II Opiates);
At least 500 G but less than 2 KG of Cocaine (or the equivalent amount of other Schedule I or II Stimulants);
At least 5 G but less than 20 G of Cocaine Base;
At least 100 G but less than 400 G of PCP, or at least 10 G but less than 40 G of Pure PCP;
At least 100 G but less than 400 G of Methamphetamine, or at least 10 G but less than 40 G of Pure Methamphetamine;
At least 1 G but less than 4 G of LSD (or the equivalent amount of other Schedule I or II Hallucinogens);
At least 40 G but less than 160 G of Fentanyl;
At least 10 G but less than 40 G of a Fentanyl Analogue;
At least 100 KG but less than 400 KG of Marihuana;
At least 20 KG but less than 80 KG of Hashish;
At least 2 KG but less than 8 KG of Hashish Oil. — Level 26

(10) At least 80 G but less than 100 G of Heroin (or the equivalent amount of other Schedule I or II Opiates);
At least 400 G but less than 500 G of Cocaine (or the equivalent amount of other Schedule I or II Stimulants);
At least 4 G but less than 5 G of Cocaine Base;
At least 80 G but less than 100 G of PCP, or at least 8 G but less than 10 G of Pure PCP;
At least 80 G but less than 100 G of Methamphetamine, or at least 8 G but less than 10 G of Pure Methamphetamine;
At least 800 MG but less than 1 G of LSD (or the equivalent amount of other Schedule I or II Hallucinogens);
At least 32 G but less than 40 G of Fentanyl;
At least 8 G but less than 10 G of a Fentanyl Analogue;
At least 80 KG but less than 100 KG of Marihuana;
At least 16 KG but less than 20 KG of Hashish;
At least 1.6 KG but less than 2 KG of Hashish Oil. — Level 24

(11) At least 60 G but less than 80 G of Heroin (or the equivalent amount of other Schedule I or II Opiates);
At least 300 G but less than 400 G of Cocaine (or the equivalent amount of other Schedule I or II Stimulants);
At least 3 G but less than 4 G of Cocaine Base;
At least 60 G but less than 80 G of PCP, or at least 6 G but less than 8 G of Pure PCP;
At least 60 G but less than 80 G of Methamphetamine, or at least 6 G but less than 8 G of Pure Methamphetamine;
At least 600 MG but less than 800 MG of LSD (or the equivalent amount of other Schedule I or II Hallucinogens);
At least 24 G but less than 32 G of Fentanyl;
At least 6 G but less than 8 G of a Fentanyl Analogue;
At least 60 KG but less than 80 KG of Marihuana;
At least 12 KG but less than 16 KG of Hashish;
At least 1.2 KG but less than 1.6 KG of Hashish Oil. — Level 22

(12) At least 40 G but less than 60 G of Heroin (or the equivalent amount of other Schedule I or II Opiates);
At least 200 G but less than 300 G of Cocaine (or the equivalent amount of other Schedule I or II Stimulants);
At least 2 G but less than 3 G of Cocaine Base;
At least 40 G but less than 60 G of PCP, or at least 4 G but less than 6 G of Pure PCP;
At least 40 G but less than 60 G of Methamphetamine, or at least 4 G but less than 6 G of Pure Methamphetamine;
At least 400 MG but less than 600 MG of LSD (or the equivalent amount of other Schedule I or II Hallucinogens); — Level 20

At least 16 G but less than 24 G of Fentanyl;
At least 4 G but less than 6 G of a Fentanyl Analogue;
At least 40 KG but less than 60 KG of Marihuana;
At least 8 KG but less than 12 KG of Hashish;
At least 800 G but less than 1.2 KG of Hashish Oil;
20 KG or more of Schedule I or II Depressants or Schedule III substances.

(13) At least 20 G but less than 40 G of Heroin (or the equivalent amount of other Schedule I or II Opiates); Level 18
At least 100 G but less than 200 G of Cocaine (or the equivalent amount of other Schedule I or II Stimulants);
At least 1 G but less than 2 G of Cocaine Base;
At least 20 G but less than 40 G of PCP, or at least 2 G but less than 4 G of Pure PCP;
At least 20 G but less than 40 G of Methamphetamine, or at least 2 G but less than 4 G of Pure Methamphetamine;
At least 200 MG but less than 400 MG of LSD (or the equivalent amount of other Schedule I or II Hallucinogens);
At least 8 G but less than 16 G of Fentanyl;
At least 2 G but less than 4 G of a Fentanyl Analogue;
At least 20 KG but less than 40 KG of Marihuana;
At least 5 KG but less than 8 KG of Hashish;
At least 500 G but less than 800 G of Hashish Oil;
At least 10 KG but less than 20 KG of Schedule I or II Depressants or Schedule III substances.

(14) At least 10 G but less than 20 G of Heroin (or the equivalent amount of other Schedule I or II Opiates); Level 16
At least 50 G but less than 100 G of Cocaine (or the equivalent amount of other Schedule I or II Stimulants);
At least 500 MG but less than 1 G of Cocaine Base;
At least 10 G but less than 20 G of PCP, or at least 1 G but less than 2 G of Pure PCP;
At least 10 G but less than 20 G of Methamphetamine, or at least 1 G but less than 2 G of Pure Methamphetamine;
At least 100 MG but less than 200 MG of LSD (or the equivalent amount of other Schedule I or II Hallucinogens);
At least 4 G but less than 8 G of Fentanyl;
At least 1 G but less than 2 G of a Fentanyl Analogue;
At least 10 KG but less than 20 KG of Marihuana;
At least 2 KG but less than 5 KG of Hashish;
At least 200 G but less than 500 G of Hashish Oil;
At least 5 KG but less than 10 KG of Schedule I or II Depressants or Schedule III substances.

(15) At least 5 G but less than 10 G of Heroin (or the equivalent amount of other Schedule I or II Opiates); Level 14
At least 25 G but less than 50 G of Cocaine (or the equivalent amount of other Schedule I or II Stimulants);
At least 250 MG but less than 500 MG of Cocaine Base;
At least 5 G but less than 10 G of PCP, or at least 500 MG but less than 1 G of Pure PCP;
At least 5 G but less than 10 G of Methamphetamine, or at least 500 MG but less than 1 G of Pure Methamphetamine;
At least 50 MG but less than 100 MG of LSD (or the equivalent amount of other Schedule I or II Hallucinogens);
At least 2 G but less than 4 G of Fentanyl;
At least 500 MG but less than 1 G of a Fentanyl Analogue;
At least 5 KG but less than 10 KG of Marihuana;
At least 1 KG but less than 2 KG of Hashish;
At least 100 G but less than 200 G of Hashish Oil;
At least 2.5 KG but less than 5 KG of Schedule I or II Depressants or Schedule III substances.

(16) Less than 5 G Heroin (or the equivalent amount of other Schedule I or II Opiates); Level 12
Less than 25 G Cocaine (or the equivalent amount of other Schedule I or II Stimulants);
Less than 250 MG of Cocaine Base;
Less than 5 G of PCP, or less than 500 MG of Pure PCP;
Less than 5 G of Methamphetamine, or less than 500 MG of Pure Methamphetamine;
Less than 50 MG of LSD (or the equivalent amount of other Schedule I or II Hallucinogens);
Less than 2 G of Fentanyl;
Less than 500 MG of a Fentanyl Analogue;
At least 2.5 KG but less than 5 KG of Marihuana;
At least 500 G but less than 1 KG of Hashish;

	At least 50 G but less than 100 G of Hashish Oil; At least 1.25 KG but less than 2.5 KG of Schedule I or II Depressants or Schedule III substances; 20 KG or more of Schedule IV substances.	
(17)	At least 1 KG but less than 2.5 KG of Marihuana; At least 200 G but less than 500 G of Hashish; At least 20 G but less than 50 G of Hashish Oil; At least 500 G but less than 1.25 KG of Schedule I or II Depressants or Schedule III substances; At least 8 KG but less than 20 KG of Schedule IV substances.	Level 10
(18)	At least 250 G but less than 1 KG of Marihuana; At least 50 G but less than 200 G of Hashish; At least 5 G but less than 20 G of Hashish Oil; At least 125 G but less than 500 G of Schedule I or II Depressants or Schedule III substances; At least 2 KG but less than 8 KG of Schedule IV substances; 20 KG or more of Schedule V substances.	Level 8
(19)	Less than 250 G of Marihuana; Less than 50 G of Hashish; Less than 5 G of Hashish Oil; Less than 125 G of Schedule I or II Depressants or Schedule III substances; Less than 2 KG of Schedule IV substances; Less than 20 KG of Schedule V substances.	Level 6

---

*Unless otherwise specified, the weight of a controlled substance set forth in the table refers to the entire weight of any mixture or substance containing a detectable amount of the controlled substance. If a mixture or substance contains more than one controlled substance, the weight of the entire mixture or substance is assigned to the controlled substance that results in the greater offense level. In the case of a mixture or substance containing PCP or methamphetamine, use the offense level determined by the entire weight of the mixture or substance or the offense level determined by the weight of the pure PCP or methamphetamine, whichever is greater.

In the case of an offense involving marihuana plants, if the offense involved (A) 50 or more marihuana plants, treat each plant as equivalent to 1 KG of marihuana; (B) fewer than 50 marihuana plants, treat each plant as equivalent to 100 G of marihuana. Provided, however, that if the actual weight of the marihuana is greater, use the actual weight of the marihuana.".

The Commentary to §2D1.1 captioned "Application Notes" is amended in Note 9 by inserting immediately before the period at the end of the first sentence of the first paragraph:

> ", except in the case of PCP or methamphetamine for which the guideline itself provides for the consideration of purity (see the footnote to the Drug Quantity Table)",

and by deleting the second paragraph as follows:

> "Congress provided an exception to purity considerations in the case of phencyclidine (PCP). 21 U.S.C. § 841(b)(1)(A). The legislation designates amounts of pure PCP and mixtures in establishing mandatory sentences. The first row of the table illustrates this distinction as one kilogram of PCP or 100 grams of pure PCP. Allowance for higher sentences based on purity is not appropriate for PCP.".

The Commentary to §2D1.1 captioned "Application Notes" is amended in the first paragraph of Note 10 by inserting "methamphetamine, fentanyl," immediately following "i.e., heroin, cocaine, PCP," and by deleting:

"one gram of a substance containing methamphetamine, a Schedule I stimulant, is to be treated as the equivalent of two grams of a substance containing cocaine in applying the Drug Quantity Table.",

and inserting in lieu thereof:

"one gram of a substance containing oxymorphone, a Schedule I opiate, is to be treated as the equivalent of five grams of a substance containing heroin in applying the Drug Quantity Table.".

The Commentary to §2D1.1 captioned "Application Notes" is amended in Note 10, in the subdivision of the "Drug Equivalency Tables" captioned "Cocaine and Other Schedule I & II Stimulants" by deleting "2.0 gm. of cocaine/0.4 gm of heroin" immediately following "1 gm of Methamphetamine =" and inserting in lieu thereof "5.0 gm of cocaine/1.0 gm of heroin", and by deleting:

"1 gm of Phenylacetone/P_2P (amphetamine precursor) =	0.375 gm of cocaine/0.075 gm of heroin
1 gm of Phenylacebone/P_2P (methamphetamine precursor) =	0.833 gm of cocaine/0.167 gm of heroin",

and inserting in lieu thereof:

"1 gm Phenylacetone/P_2P (when possessed for the purpose of manufacturing methamphetamine) =	2.08 gm of cocaine/0.418 gm of heroin
1 gm Phenylacetone/P_2P (in any other case) =	0.375 gm of cocaine/0.075 gm of heroin".

The Commentary to §2D1.1 captioned "Application Notes" is amended in Note 10, in the subdivision of the "Drug Equivalency Tables" captioned "Schedule I Marihuana" by deleting:

"1 Marihuana/Cannabis Plant =	0.1 gm of heroin/100 gm of marihuana".

The Commentary to §2D1.1 captioned "Application Notes" is amended in Note 10 in the second paragraph by deleting "Other Schedule I or II Substances" and inserting in lieu thereof "Schedule I or II Depressants", and in the "Drug Equivalency Tables" by deleting "<u>Other Schedule I or II Substances</u>" and inserting in lieu thereof "<u>Schedule I or II Depressants</u>".

The Commentary to 2D1.1 captioned "Background" is amended in the third paragraph by deleting "with two asterisks represent mandatory minimum sentences established by the Anti-Drug Abuse Act of 1986. These levels reflect sentences" and inserting in lieu thereof "at levels 26 and 32 establish guideline ranges", and by deleting "requirement" and inserting in lieu thereof "minimum".

The purposes of this amendment are to expand the Drug Quantity Table to reflect offenses involving extremely large quantities of controlled substances, to eliminate minor gaps in the Drug Quantity Table, to reflect the statutory change with respect to methamphetamine (Section 6470 of the Anti-Drug Abuse Act of 1988) by inserting specific references to the quantity of this substance for each offense level set forth in the table, to reflect the statutory change with respect to fifty or more marihuana plants (Section 6479 of the Anti-Drug Abuse Act of 1988), to correct anomaly in the relationship of hashish oil to hashish in levels 6 and 8 of the Drug Quantity Table, to delete an unnecessary footnote, and to clarify the operation of the guideline. **The effective date of this amendment is November 1, 1989.**

126. The Commentary to §2D1.1 captioned "Application Notes" is amended in Note 10 in the subdivision of the "Drug Equivalency Tables" captioned "Schedule I or II Opiates" on the line beginning "piperidinyl] Propanamide) =" by deleting "31.25 gm" and inserting in lieu thereof "2.5 gm"; on the line beginning "1 gm of Alpha-Methylfentanyl" by deleting "100 gm" and inserting in lieu thereof "10 gm"; and on the line beginning "1 gm of 3-Methylfentanyl" by deleting "125 gm" and inserting in lieu thereof "10 gm".

The purpose of this amendment is to conform the equivalency for fentanyl and fentanyl analogues to that set forth in the Drug Quantity Table and statute. **The effective date of this amendment is November 1, 1989.**

127. The Commentary to §2D1.1 captioned "Application Notes" is amended in Note 10 in the subdivision of "Dosage Equivalency Table" captioned "Hallucinogens" by deleting "STP (DOM) Dimethoxyamphetamine" and inserting in lieu thereof "2, 5-Dimethoxy-4-methylamphetamine (STP, DOM)".

The Commentary to §2D1.1 captioned "Application Notes" is amended in Note 10 in the subdivision of the "Dosage Equivalency Table" captioned "Stimulants" by deleting "Preludin 25 mg" and inserting in lieu thereof "Phenmetrazine (Preludin) 75 mg".

The purposes of this amendment are to substitute generic names for two substances and to conform the dosage of Phenmetrazine to that currently being manufactured. **The effective date of this amendment is November 1, 1989.**

128. The Commentary to §2D1.1 captioned "Application Notes" is amended in Note 10 in the "Drug Equivalency Tables" in the subdivision captioned "Schedule III Substances" by deleting:

"1 gm of Thiohexethal = 2 mg of heroin/2 gm of marihuana",

in the "Dosage Equivalency Table" in the subdivision captioned "Hallucinogens" by deleting:

"Anhalamine	300 mg",
"Anhalonide	300 mg",
"Anhalonine	300 mg",
"Lophophorine	300 mg",
"Pellotine	300 mg",

and in the "Dosage Equivalency Table" in the subdivision captioned "Depressants" by deleting:

"Brallobarbital	30 mg",
"Eldoral	100 mg",
"Eunarcon	100 mg",
"Hexethel	100 mg",

"Thiohexethal 60 mg".

The purpose of this amendment is to delete substances that either are not controlled substances or are no longer manufactured. **The effective date of this amendment is November 1, 1989.**

129. The Commentary to §2D1.1 captioned "Application Notes" is amended in Note 10 in the "Drug Equivalency Tables" in the subdivision captioned "Cocaine and Other Schedule I and II Stimulants" by inserting the following as the eighth and ninth entries:

"1 gm of 4-Methylaminorex ('Euphoria') = 0.5 gm of cocaine/0.1 gm of heroin",
"1 gm of Methylphenidate (Ritalin) = 0.5gm of cocaine/0.1 gm of heroin",

in the subdivision captioned "LSD, PCP, and Other Schedule I and II Hallucinogens" by inserting the following as the twentieth entry:

"1 gm of 3, 4-Methylenedioxy
- N - ethylamphetamine/MDEA = 0.03 gm of heroin or PCP",

in the subdivision captioned "Schedule III Substances" by inserting the following as the fourth entry:

"1 gm of Benzphetamine = 4 mg of heroin/4 gm of marihuana",

and in the "Dosage Equivalency Table" in the subdivision captioned "Depressants" by inserting the following in the appropriate place in alphabetical order:

"Glutethimide (Doriden) 500 mg".

The Commentary to §2D1.1 captioned "Application Notes" is amended in Note 10 in the "Dosage Equivalency Table" by inserting the following immediately after the subdivision captioned "Depressants":

"Marihuana

1 marihuana cigarette 0.5 gm".

The purpose of this amendment is to make the Drug Equivalency Tables and Dosage Equivalency Table more comprehensive. **The effective date of this amendment is November 1, 1989.**

130. The Commentary to §2D1.1 captioned "Application Notes" is amended in Note 10 in the "Drug Equivalency Tables" in the subdivision captioned "Schedule III Substances" by deleting "2 mg of heroin/2 gm of marihuana" immediately following "1 gm of Glutethimide = " and inserting in lieu thereof "0.4 mg of heroin/0.4 gm of marihuana", and by deleting:

"1 gm of Paregoric = 2 mg of heroin/2 gm of marihuana
1 gm of Hydrocodone
Cough Syrups = 2 mg of heroin/2 gm of marihuana",

and inserting in lieu thereof:

"1 ml of Paregoric =	0.25 mg of heroin/0.25 gm of marihuana
1 ml of Hydrocodone Cough Syrup =	1 mg of heroin/1 gm of marihuana".

The Commentary to §2D1.1 captioned "Application Notes" is amended in Note 10 in the "Dosage Equivalency Table" in the subdivision captioned "Hallucinogens" by deleting ".1 mg" in the line beginning "LSD (Lysergic acid diethylamide)" and inserting in lieu thereof ".05 mg", by deleting "LSD tartrate .05 mg", by deleting "Peyote 12 mg", and by inserting the following in the appropriate place in alphabetical order:

"Peyote (dry)	12 gm",
"Peyote (wet)	120 gm",
"Psilocybe mushrooms (dry)	5 gm",
"Psilocybe mushrooms (wet)	50 gm".

The Commentary to §2D1.1 captioned "Application Notes" is amended in Note 10 in the "Dosage Equivalency Table" in the subdivision captioned "Stimulants" by deleting "Ethylamphetamine HCL 12 mg" and "Ethylamphetamine SO_4 12 mg", by deleting "Amphetamines" and inserting in lieu thereof "Amphetamine", by deleting "Methamphetamines" and inserting in lieu thereof "Methamphetamine", and by deleting "Methamphetamine combinations 5 mg".

The purposes of this amendment are to provide more accurate approximations of the equivalencies and dosages for certain controlled substances, and to eliminate unnecessary references. **The effective date of this amendment is November 1, 1989.**

131. The Commentary to §2D1.1 captioned "Application Notes" is amended in Note 10 in the subdivision of the "Drug Equivalency Tables" captioned "LSD, PCP, and Other Schedule I and II Hallucinogens" by deleting:

"1 gm of Liquid phencyclidine =	0.1 gm of heroin or PCP".

The purpose of this amendment is to delete an incorrect equivalency. **The effective date of this amendment is November 1, 1989.**

132. The Commentary to §2D1.1 captioned "Application Notes" is amended in Note 10 in the "Drug Equivalency Tables" by inserting immediately following the captions "Cocaine and Other Schedule I and II Stimulants" and "LSD, PCP, and Other Hallucinogens" in each instance "(<u>and their immediate precursors</u>)".

The purpose of this amendment is to clarify the commentary. **The effective date of this amendment is November 1, 1989.**

133. The Commentary to §2D1.1 captioned "Application Notes" is amended in Note 10 by deleting:

"The following dosage equivalents for certain common drugs are provided by the Drug Enforcement Administration to facilitate the application of §2D1.1 of the guidelines in cases where the number of doses, but not the weight of the controlled substances are known. The dosage equivalents provided in these tables reflect the amount of the pure drug contained in an average dose.

<u>DOSAGE EQUIVALENCY TABLE</u>",

and inserting in lieu thereof:

"11. If the number of doses, pills, or capsules but not the weight of the controlled substance is known, multiply the number of doses, pills, or capsules by the typical weight per dose to estimate the total weight of the controlled substance (<u>e.g.</u>, 100 doses of Bufotenine at 1 mg per dose = 100 mg of Bufotenine). The Typical Weight Per Unit Table, prepared from information provided by the Drug Enforcement Administration, displays the typical weight per dose, pill, or capsule for common controlled substances.

<u>TYPICAL WEIGHT PER UNIT (DOSE, PILL, OR CAPSULE) TABLE</u>".

The Commentary to §2D1.1 captioned "Application Notes" is amended by renumbering the current Note 11 as Note 12.

The purpose of this amendment is to clarify the commentary. **The effective date of this amendment is November 1, 1989.**

134. Section 2D1.1(b) is amended by deleting "Characteristic" and inserting in lieu thereof "Characteristics", and by inserting the following additional specific offense characteristic:

"(2) If the defendant is convicted of violating 21 U.S.C. § 960(a) under circumstances in which (A) an aircraft other than a regularly scheduled commercial air carrier was used to import the controlled substance, or (B) the defendant acted as a pilot, copilot, captain, navigator, flight officer, or any other operation officer aboard any craft or vessel carrying a controlled substance, increase by 2 levels. If the resulting offense level is less than level 26, increase to level 26.";

The Commentary to §2D1.1 captioned "Application Notes" is amended by inserting the following additional note:

"13. If subsection (b)(2)(B) applies, do not apply §3B1.3 (Abuse of Position of Trust or Use of Special Skill).";

The Commentary to §2D1.1 captioned "Background" is amended by inserting the following additional paragraph between the third and fourth paragraphs:

" Specific Offense Characteristic (b)(2) is mandated by Section 6453 of the Anti-Drug Abuse Act of 1988.".

The purpose of this amendment is to implement the directive to the Commission in Section 6453 of the Anti-Drug Abuse Act of 1988. **The effective date of this amendment is November 1, 1989.**

135. Chapter Two, Part D is amended by deleting §§2D1.2 and 2D1.3 in their entirety as follows:

"§2D1.2. Involving Juveniles in the Trafficking of Controlled Substances

(a) Base Offense Level:

(1) Level from §2D1.1, corresponding to triple the drug amount involved, but in no event less than level 13, for involving an individual fourteen years of age or less; or

(2) Level from §2D1.1, corresponding to double the drug amount involved, for involving an individual at least fifteen years of age and less than eighteen years of age.

Commentary

Statutory Provision: 21 U.S.C. § 845b.

Application Notes:

1. If multiple drugs or offenses occur and all or some of them involve juveniles, double or triple the drug amounts for those offenses involving juveniles before totalling the amounts. For example, if there are three drug offenses of conviction and only one involves juveniles in trafficking, add the amount from the first and second offense, double the amount for the offense involving juveniles, and total. Use that total to determine the base offense level.

2. The reference to the level from §2D1.1 includes the base offense level plus the specific offense characteristic dealing with a weapon. Under §2D1.1(b)(1) there is a 2-level increase for possession of a firearm or other dangerous weapon during commission of the offense.

Background: The statute addressed by this section punishes any person eighteen years of age or older who knowingly employs or uses any person younger than eighteen to violate or to conceal any violation of any provision of Title 21. Section 845b provides a minimum mandatory period of imprisonment of one year. An increased penalty for the employment or use of persons fourteen years of age or younger reflects the enhanced sentence authorized by 21 U.S.C. § 845b(d).

§2D1.3. Distributing Controlled Substances to Individuals Younger than Twenty-One Years, To Pregnant Women, or Within 1000 Feet of a School or College

(a) Base Offense Level:

(1) Level from §2D1.1, corresponding to double the drug amount involved, but in no event less than level 13, for distributing a controlled substance to a pregnant woman;

(2) (A) Level from §2D1.1, corresponding to double the drug amount involved, but in no event less than level 13, for distributing a controlled substance other than five grams or less of marihuana to an individual under the age of twenty-one years; or

(B) Level from §2D1.1, corresponding to double the drug amount involved, but in no event less than level 13, for distributing or manufacturing a controlled substance other than five grams or less of marihuana within 1000 feet of a schoolyard.

Commentary

Statutory Provisions: 21 U.S.C. §§ 845, 845a.

Application Notes:

1. The provisions addressed by this section contain a mandatory minimum period of imprisonment of one year. The base offense level is determined as in §2D1.2. If both subsections (a)(1) and (a)(2) apply to a single distribution (e.g., the distribution of 10 grams of a controlled substance to a pregnant woman under twenty-one years of age), the enhancements are applied cumulatively, i.e., by using four times rather than two times the amount distributed. However, only one of the enhancements in §2D1.3(a)(2) shall apply in a given case.

2. If multiple drugs or offenses occur, determine the offense level as described in the Commentary to §2D1.2.

3. The reference to the level from §2D1.1 includes the base offense level plus the specific offense characteristic dealing with a weapon. Under §2D1.1(b)(1) there is a 2-level increase for possession of a firearm, or other dangerous weapon during the commission of the offense.

Background: The guideline sentences for distribution of controlled substances to individuals under twenty-one years of age or within 1000 feet of a school or college treat the distribution of less than five grams of marihuana less harshly than other controlled substances. This distinction is based on the statutory provisions that specifically exempt convictions for the distribution of less than five grams of marihuana from the mandatory minimum one-year imprisonment requirement.".

A replacement guideline with accompanying commentary is inserted as §2D1.2 (Drug Offenses Occurring Near Protected Locations or Involving Underage or Pregnant Individuals).

The purposes of this amendment are to implement the directive in Section 6454 of the Anti-Drug Abuse Act of 1988, and to expand the coverage of the guideline to include the provision of Sections 6458 and 6459 of that Act. The amendment also covers the provisions of 21 U.S.C. § 845, 845a, and 845b not included in the statutory direction to the Commission. **The effective date of this amendment is November 1, 1989.**

136. The Commentary to §2D1.4 captioned "Application Notes" is amended in Note 1 by deleting:

> "Where the defendant was not reasonably capable of producing the negotiated amount, the court may depart and impose a sentence lower than the sentence that would otherwise result.",

and inserting in lieu thereof:

> "However, where the court finds that the defendant did not intend to produce and was not reasonably capable of producing the negotiated amount, the court shall exclude from the guideline calculation the amount that it finds the defendant did not intend to produce and was not reasonably capable of producing.".

Application Note 1 currently provides that the "weight under negotiation in an uncompleted distribution shall be used to calculate the applicable amount." The instruction then provides "Where the defendant was not reasonably capable of producing the negotiated amount the court may depart and impose a sentence lower than the sentence that would otherwise result." This provision may result in inflated offense levels in uncompleted offenses where a defendant is merely "puffing," even though the court is then authorized to address the situation by a downward departure. The purpose of this amendment is to provide a more direct procedure for calculating the offense level where the court finds that the defendant did not intend to produce and was not reasonably capable of producing the negotiated amount. **The effective date of this amendment is November 1, 1989.**

137. The Commentary to §2D1.4 captioned "Application Notes" is amended in Note 1 by deleting "the sentence should be imposed only on the basis of the defendant's conduct or the conduct of co-conspirators in furtherance of the conspiracy that was known to the defendant or was reasonably foreseeable" and inserting in lieu thereof "see Application Note 1 to §1B1.3 (Relevant Conduct)".

The purpose of this amendment is to conform this commentary to the revision of §1B1.3. **The effective date of this amendment is November 1, 1989.**

138. Section 2D1.4(a) is amended by deleting "participating in an incomplete" and inserting in lieu thereof "a".

The purpose of this amendment is to clarify the guideline. **The effective date of this amendment is November 1, 1989.**

139. Section 2D1.5 is amended by deleting: "(a) Base Offense Level: 36" and inserting in lieu thereof:

"(a) Base Offense Level (Apply the greater):

(1) 4 plus the offense level from §2D1.1 applicable to the underlying offense; or

(2) 38.".

The Commentary to §2D1.5 captioned "Application Notes" is amended in Note 2 by deleting "if the quantity of drugs substantially exceeds that required for level 36 in the drug quantity table," immediately before "or if", and by deleting "is extremely" and inserting in lieu thereof "was extremely".

The Commentary to §2D1.5 captioned "Background" is amended in the first paragraph by deleting "base offense level of 36" and inserting in lieu thereof "minimum base offense level of 38", and in the second paragraph by deleting "for second convictions" and inserting in lieu thereof "for the first conviction, a 30-year minimum mandatory penalty for a second conviction,".

The purpose of this amendment is to reflect the increased mandatory minimum penalty for this offense pursuant to Section 6481 of the Anti-Drug Abuse Act of 1988. **The effective date of this amendment is November 1, 1989.**

140. Chapter Two, Part D is amended by inserting an additional guideline with accompanying commentary as §2D1.10 (Endangering Human Life While Illegally Manufacturing a Controlled Substance).

The purpose of this amendment is to create a guideline covering the new offense in Section 6301 of the Anti-Drug Abuse Act of 1988. **The effective date of this amendment is November 1, 1989.**

141. Section 2D2.3 is amended by deleting : "(a) Base Offense Level: 8" and inserting in lieu thereof:

"(a) Base Offense Level (Apply the greatest):

(1) 26, if death resulted; or

(2) 21, if serious bodily injury resulted; or

(3) 13, otherwise.

(b) Special Instruction:

(1) If the defendant is convicted of a single count involving the death or serious bodily injury of more than one person, apply Chapter Three, Part D (Multiple Counts) as if the defendant had been convicted of a separate count for each such victim.".

The Commentary to §2D2.3 is amended by inserting at the end:

"Background: This section implements the direction to the Commission in Section 6482 of the Anti-Drug Abuse Act of 1988. Offenses covered by this guideline may vary widely with regard to harm and risk of harm. The offense levels assume that the offense involved the operation of a common carrier carrying a number of passengers, e.g., a bus. If no or only a few passengers were placed at risk, a downward departure may be warranted. If the offense resulted in the death or serious bodily injury of a large number of persons, such that the resulting offense level under subsection (b) would not adequately reflect the seriousness of the offense, an upward departure may be warranted.".

The purpose of this amendment is to implement the directive to the Commission in Section 6482 of the Anti-Drug Abuse Act of 1988. In addition, the base offense level under subsection (a)(3) is increased to reflect the seriousness of the offense. **The effective date of this amendment is November 1, 1989.**

142. The Commentary to §2E1.1 captioned "Application Notes" is amended by inserting the following additional note:

"4. Certain conduct may be charged in the count of conviction as part of a 'pattern of racketeering activity' even though the defendant has previously been sentenced for that conduct. Where such previously imposed sentence resulted from a conviction prior to the last overt act of the instant offense, treat as a prior sentence under §4A1.2(a)(1) and not as part of the instant offense. This treatment is designed to produce a result consistent with the distinction between the instant offense and criminal history found throughout the guidelines. If this treatment produces an anomalous result in a particular case, a guideline departure may be warranted.".

The purpose of this amendment is to clarify the treatment of certain conduct for which the defendant previously has been sentenced as either part of the instant offense or prior criminal record. **The effective date of this amendment is November 1, 1989.**

143. The Commentary to §2E1.3 captioned "Statutory Provision" is amended by deleting "1952B" and inserting in lieu thereof "1959 (formerly 18 U.S.C. § 1952B)".

The purpose of this amendment is to reflect the redesignation of this statute. **The effective date of this amendment is November 1, 1989.**

144. The Commentary to §2E1.4 captioned "Statutory Provision" is amended by deleting "1952A" and inserting in lieu thereof "1958 (formerly 18 U.S.C. § 1952A)".

The purpose of this amendment is to reflect the redesignation of this statute. **The effective date of this amendment is November 1, 1989.**

145. Section 2E1.5 is amended by deleting "the guideline provision for extortion or robbery" and inserting in lieu thereof "§2B3.1 (Robbery), §2B3.2 (Extortion by Force or Threat of Injury or Serious Damage), §2B3.3 (Blackmail and Similar Forms of Extortion), or §2C1.1 (Offering, Giving, Soliciting, or Receiving a Bribe; Extortion Under Color of Official Right)".

The Commentary to §2E1.5 captioned "Application Note" is amended by deleting:

"Application Note:

1. Apply the guideline most applicable to the underlying conduct, which may include §2B3.1(Robbery), §2B3.2 (Extortion by Force or Threat of Injury or Serious Damage), §2B3.3 (Blackmail and Similar Forms of Extortion), or §2C1.1 (Offering, Giving, Soliciting, or Receiving a Bribe).".

The purpose of this amendment is to move material from the commentary to the guideline where it more appropriately belongs. **The effective date of this amendment is November 1, 1989.**

146. Section 2E2.1 is amended in subsection (b)(1)(B) by deleting "a firearm or a dangerous weapon" and inserting in lieu thereof "a dangerous weapon (including a firearm)", and in subsection (b)(1)(C) by deleting "a firearm or other dangerous weapon" and inserting in lieu thereof "a dangerous weapon (including a firearm)".

The purposes of this amendment are to clarify that a firearm is a type of dangerous weapon and to remove the inconsistency in language between specific offense characteristic subdivisions (b)(1)(B) and (b)(1)(C). **The effective date of this amendment is November 1, 1989.**

147. Section 2E2.1(b)(2) is amended by inserting the following additional subdivisions:

"(D) If the degree of injury is between that specified in subdivisions (A) and (B), add 3 levels; or

(E) If the degree of injury is between that specified in subdivisions (B) and (C), add 5 levels.".

The purpose of this amendment is to provide intermediate adjustment levels for the degree of bodily injury. **The effective date of this amendment is November 1, 1989.**

148. Section 2E2.1(b)(3)(A) is amended by inserting "or" immediately following "4 levels;".

The purpose of this amendment is to correct a clerical error. **The effective date of this amendment is November 1, 1989.**

149. Section 2E5.1 is amended in the title by deleting "Bribery or Gratuity" and inserting in lieu thereof "Offering, Accepting, or Soliciting a Bribe or Gratuity".

The purpose of amending the title of this section is to ensure that attempts and solicitations are expressly covered by this guideline. **The effective date of this amendment is November 1, 1989.**

150. Section 2E5.2 is amended by deleting:

"(a) Base Offense Level: 4

(b) Specific Offense Characteristics

(1) If the offense involved more than minimal planning, increase by 2 levels.

(2) If the defendant had a fiduciary obligation under the Employee Retirement Income Security Act, increase by 2 levels.

(3) Increase by corresponding number of levels from the table in §2B1.1 (Larceny, Embezzlement, and Other Forms of Theft) according to the loss.",

and inserting in lieu thereof:

"Apply §2B1.1 (Larceny, Embezzlement, and Other Forms of Theft).".

The Commentary to §2E5.2 captioned "Application Notes" is amended by deleting:

"1. 'More than minimal planning' is defined in the Commentary to §1B1.1 (Application Instructions). Valuation of loss is discussed in the Commentary to §2B1.1 (Larceny, Embezzlement, and Other Forms of Theft)." and

"3. If the adjustment for a fiduciary obligation at §2E5.2(b)(2) is applied, do not apply the adjustment at §3B1.3 (Abuse of a Position of Trust or Use of a Special Skill).",

and by inserting in lieu of Note 1:

"1. In the case of a defendant who had a fiduciary obligation under the Employee Retirement Income Security Act, an adjustment under §3B1.3 (Abuse of Position of Trust or Use of Special Skill) would apply.".

The Commentary to §2E5.2 captioned "Background" is amended by deleting the second and third sentences as follows:

"The base offense level corresponds to the base offense level for other forms of theft. Specific offense characteristics address whether a defendant has a fiduciary relationship to the benefit plan, the sophistication of the offense, and the scale of the offense.".

The purpose of this amendment is to simplify application of the guidelines. **The effective date of this amendment is November 1, 1989.**

151. Section 2E5.3(a)(2) is amended by deleting "false records were used for criminal conversion of funds or a scheme" and inserting in lieu thereof "the offense was committed to facilitate or conceal a theft or embezzlement, or an offense".

The Commentary to §2E5.3 captioned "Application Note" is amended by deleting:

"<u>Application Note</u>:

1. 'Criminal conversion' means embezzlement.".

The purpose of this amendment is to ensure that subsection (a)(2) covers any conduct engaged in for the purpose of facilitating or concealing a theft or embezzlement, or an offense involving a bribe or gratuity. **The effective date of this amendment is November 1, 1989.**

152. Section 2E5.4 is amended by deleting:

"(a) Base Offense Level: 4

(b) Specific Offense Characteristics

(1) If the offense involved more than minimal planning, increase by 2 levels.

(2) If the defendant was a union officer or occupied a position of trust in the union, as set forth in 29 U.S.C. § 501(a), increase by 2 levels.

(3) Increase by the number of levels from the table in §2B1.1 (Larceny, Embezzlement, and Other Forms of Theft) corresponding to the loss.",

and inserting in lieu thereof:

"Apply §2B1.1 (Larceny, Embezzlement, and Other Forms of Theft).".

The Commentary to §2E5.4 captioned "Application Notes" is amended by deleting:

"1. 'More than minimal planning' is defined in the Commentary to §1B1.1 (Applicable Instructions). Valuation of loss is discussed in the Commentary to §2B1.1 (Larceny, Embezzlement, and Other Forms of Theft).

2. If the adjustment for being a union officer or occupying a position of trust in a union at §2E5.4(b)(2) is applied, do not apply the adjustment at §3B1.3 (Abuse of a Position of Trust or Use of a Special Skill).",

and inserting in lieu thereof:

"1. In the case of a defendant who was a union officer or occupied a position of trust in the union, as set forth in 29 U.S.C. § 501(a), an adjustment under §3B1.3 (Abuse of Position of Trust or Use of Special Skill) would apply.",

and by deleting in the caption "Notes" and inserting in lieu thereof "Note".

The Commentary to §2E5.4 captioned "Background" is amended by deleting the last sentence as follows:

"The seriousness of this offense is determined by the amount of money taken, the sophistication of the offense, and the nature of the defendant's position in the union.".

The purpose of this amendment is to simplify application of the guidelines. **The effective date of this amendment is November 1, 1989.**

153. Section 2E5.5(a)(2) is amended by deleting "false records were used for criminal conversion of funds or a scheme" and inserting in lieu thereof "the offense was committed to facilitate or conceal a theft or embezzlement, or an offense".

The purpose of this amendment is to ensure that subsection (a)(2) covers any conduct engaged in for the purpose of facilitating or concealing a theft or embezzlement, or an offense involving a bribe or gratuity. **The effective date of this amendment is November 1, 1989.**

154. Section 2F1.1(b)(1) is amended by deleting:

	"<u>Loss</u>	<u>Increase in Level</u>
(A)	$2,000 or less	no increase
(B)	$2,001 - $5,000	add 1
(C)	$5,001 - $10,000	add 2
(D)	$10,001 - $20,000	add 3
(E)	$20,001 - $50,000	add 4
(F)	$50,001 - $100,000	add 5
(G)	$100,001 - $200,000	add 6
(H)	$200,001 - $500,000	add 7
(I)	$500,001 - $1,000,000	add 8
(J)	$1,000,001 - $2,000,000	add 9
(K)	$2,000,001 - $5,000,000	add 10
(L)	over $5,000,000	add 11",

and inserting in lieu thereof:

	"<u>Loss</u> (Apply the Greatest)	<u>Increase in Level</u>
(A)	$2,000 or less	no increase
(B)	More than $2,000	add 1
(C)	More than $5,000	add 2
(D)	More than $10,000	add 3
(E)	More than $20,000	add 4
(F)	More than $40,000	add 5
(G)	More than $70,000	add 6
(H)	More than $120,000	add 7
(I)	More than $200,000	add 8
(J)	More than $350,000	add 9
(K)	More than $500,000	add 10
(L)	More than $800,000	add 11
(M)	More than $1,500,000	add 12
(N)	More than $2,500,000	add 13
(O)	More than $5,000,000	add 14
(P)	More than $10,000,000	add 15
(Q)	More than $20,000,000	add 16
(R)	More than $40,000,000	add 17
(S)	More than $80,000,000	add 18.".

The purposes of this amendment are to conform the theft and fraud loss tables to the tax evasion table in order to remove an unintended inconsistency between these tables in cases where the amount is greater than $40,000, to increase the offense levels for offenses with larger losses to provide additional deterrence and better reflect the seriousness of the conduct, and to eliminate minor gaps in the loss table. **The effective date of this amendment is November 1, 1989.**

155. The Commentary to §2F1.1 captioned "Application Notes" is amended beginning in Note 14 by deleting:

"In such instances, although §2F1.1 applies, a departure may be warranted.

15. In certain other cases, the mail or wire fraud statutes, or other relatively broad statutes, are used primarily as jurisdictional bases for the prosecution of other offenses. For example, a state law arson where a fraudulent insurance claim was mailed might be prosecuted as mail fraud. In such cases the most analogous guideline (in the above case, §2K1.4) is to be applied.",

and by inserting at the end of Note 14:

"In certain other cases, the mail or wire fraud statutes, or other relatively broad statutes, are used primarily as jurisdictional bases for the prosecution of other offenses. For example, a state arson offense where a fraudulent insurance claim was mailed might be prosecuted as mail fraud. Where the indictment or information setting forth the count of conviction (or a stipulation as described in §1B1.2(a)) establishes an offense more aptly covered by another guideline, apply that guideline rather than §2F1.1. Otherwise, in such cases, §2F1.1 is to be applied, but a departure from the guidelines may be considered.".

The Commentary to §2F1.1 captioned "Application Notes" is amended in the second sentence of Note 14 by deleting "in which" and inserting in lieu thereof "for which".

The purposes of this amendment are to ensure that this guideline is interpreted in a manner consistent with §1B1.2 and to correct a clerical error. **The effective date of this amendment is November 1, 1989.**

156. Section 2F1.1(b)(2) is amended by deleting "; (B)" and inserting in lieu thereof ", or (B)", and by deleting "; (C) a misrepresentation that the defendant was acting on behalf of a charitable, educational, religious or political organization, or a government agency; or (D) violation of any judicial or administrative order, injunction, decree or process; increase by 2 levels, but if the result is less than level 10, increase to level 10" and inserting in lieu thereof ", increase by 2 levels".

Section 2F1.1(b)(3) is renumbered as (b)(5), and the following are inserted as new subsections:

"(3) If the offense involved (A) a misrepresentation that the defendant was acting on behalf of a charitable, educational, religious or political organization, or a government agency, or (B) violation of any judicial or administrative order, injunction, decree or process, increase by 2 levels. If the resulting offense level is less than level 10, increase to level 10.

(4) If the offense involved the conscious or reckless risk of serious bodily injury, increase by 2 levels. If the resulting offense level is less than level 13, increase to level 13.".

The Commentary to §2F1.1 captioned "Statutory Provisions" is amended by inserting "1031," immediately following "1029,".

The Commentary to §2F1.1 captioned "Application Notes" is amended in Note 4 by deleting "(b)(2)(C)" and inserting in lieu thereof "(b)(3)(A)", in Note 5 by deleting "(b)(2)(D)" and inserting in lieu thereof "(b)(3)(B)", and in Note 9(c) by deleting "or risked" immediately following "caused".

The Commentary to §2F1.1 captioned "Background" is amended in the third paragraph by deleting "not only" immediately following "Accordingly, the guideline", by deleting ", but also specifies that the minimum offense level in such cases shall be 10" immediately following "is present", and by deleting the last sentence as follows:

"A number of special cases are specifically broken out under subdivision (b)(2) to ensure that defendants in such cases are adequately punished.".

The Commentary to §2F1.1 captioned "Application Notes" is amended by deleting:

"10. The adjustments for loss do not distinguish frauds involving losses greater than $5,000,000. Departure above the applicable guideline may be warranted if the loss substantially exceeds that amount.",

and by renumbering Notes 11-14 as 10-13 respectively.

The Commentary to §2F1.1 captioned "Application Notes" is amended in Note 1 by deleting "(b)(2)" and inserting in lieu thereof "(b)(3)", by deleting "several" and inserting in lieu thereof "both", and by deleting "upward" and inserting in lieu thereof "an upward".

The purpose of this amendment is to reflect the instruction to the Commission in Section 2(b) of the Major Fraud Act of 1988. The Commission has concluded that a 2-level enhancement with a minimum offense level of 13 should apply to all fraud cases involving a conscious or reckless risk of serious bodily injury. In addition, the amendment divides former subsection (b)(2) into two separate specific offenses characteristics to better reflect their separate nature. **The effective date of this amendment is November 1, 1989.**

157. Section 2G1.1(b)(1) is amended by deleting "defendant used" and inserting in lieu thereof "offense involved the use of", and by deleting "drugs or otherwise" and inserting in lieu thereof "threats or drugs or in any manner".

The Commentary to §2G1.1 captioned "Application Notes" is amended in Note 2 by deleting "by drugs or otherwise" immediately following "coercion".

The purpose of this amendment is to clarify the guideline and commentary. **The effective date of this amendment is November 1, 1989.**

158. Section 2G1.1 is amended by inserting the following additional subsection:

"(c) Special Instruction

(1) If the offense involves the transportation of more than one person, Chapter Three, Part D (Multiple Counts) shall be applied as if the transportation of each person had been contained in a separate count of conviction.".

The purpose of this amendment is to provide a special instruction for the application of the multiple count rule in cases involving the transportation of more than one person. **The effective date of this amendment is November 1, 1989.**

159. Section 2G1.2(b)(1) is amended by deleting "drugs or otherwise" and inserting in lieu thereof "threats or drugs or in any manner".

Section 2G1.2(b)(2) and (3) is amended by deleting "conduct" whenever it appears and inserting in lieu thereof in each instance "offense".

The Commentary to §2G1.2 captioned "Application Notes" is amended in Note 2 by deleting "by drugs or otherwise" immediately following "coercion", and in the caption by deleting "Note" and inserting in lieu thereof "Notes".

The purpose of this amendment is to clarify the guideline and commentary. **The effective date of this amendment is November 1, 1989.**

160. Section 2G1.2 is amended by inserting the following additional subsection:

"(c) Special Instruction

(1) If the offense involves the transportation of more than one person, Chapter Three, Part D (Multiple Counts) shall be applied as if the transportation of each person had been contained in a separate count of conviction.".

The purpose of this amendment is to provide a special instruction for the application of the multiple count rule in cases involving the transportation of more than one person. **The effective date of this amendment is November 1, 1989.**

161. The Commentary to §2G2.1 captioned "Application Note" is amended in Note 1 by deleting ", distinct offense, even if several are exploited simultaneously." and inserting in lieu thereof "victim. Consequently, multiple counts involving the exploitation of different minors are not to be grouped together under §3D1.2 (Groups of Closely-Related Counts).".

The purpose of this amendment is to clarify that multiple counts involving different minors are not grouped under §3D1.2. **The effective date of this amendment is November 1, 1989.**

162. Chapter Two, Part G, is amended by inserting an additional guideline with accompanying commentary as §2G2.3 (Selling or Buying of Children for Use in the Production of Pornography).

The purpose of this amendment is to create a guideline covering the new offense in Section 7512 of the Anti-Drug Abuse Act of 1988. **The effective date of this amendment is November 1, 1989.**

163. The Commentary to §2G3.1 captioned "Statutory Provisions" is amended by deleting "§§1461-1465" and inserting in lieu thereof "§§1460-1463, 1465-1466".

The purposes of this amendment are to conform the Statutory Provisions to the revision of §2G3.2 and to make them more comprehensive. **The effective date of this amendment is November 1, 1989.**

164. Chapter Two, Part G is amended by deleting §2G3.2 in its entirety as follows:

"§2G3.2. Obscene or Indecent Telephone Communications

(a) Base Offense Level: 6

Commentary

Statutory Provision: 47 U.S.C. § 223.

Background: This offense is a misdemeanor for which the maximum term of imprisonment authorized by statute is six months.".

A replacement guideline with accompanying commentary is inserted as §2G3.2 (Obscene Telephone Communications for a Commercial Purpose; Broadcasting Obscene Material).

The purposes of this amendment are to delete a guideline covering a petty offense; and to insert a guideline covering felony offenses, including two offenses created by Sections 7523 and 7524 of the Anti-Drug Abuse Act of 1988. **The effective date of this amendment is November 1, 1989.**

165. The title to §2H1.3 is amended by inserting at the end "; Damage to Religious Real Property".

The Commentary to §2H1.3 captioned "Application Notes" is amended in Note 3 by deleting "the adjustment at" immediately before "§3B1.3".

The Commentary to §2H1.3 captioned "Background" is amended in the third sentence by deleting "injury occurs, ten years if injury occurs," and inserting in lieu thereof "bodily injury results, ten years if bodily injury results".

The Commentary to §2H1.3 captioned "Statutory Provisions" is amended by deleting "18 U.S.C. § 245" and inserting in lieu thereof "18 U.S.C. §§ 245, 247".

The purposes of this amendment are to include a recently enacted offense (18 U.S.C. § 247) expressly in the title of this guideline and to make editorial improvements. **The effective date of this amendment is November 1, 1989.**

166. Section 2H1.4(a)(2) is amended by deleting "2 plus" and inserting in lieu thereof "6 plus".

The Commentary to §2H1.4 captioned "Application Notes" is amended in Note 1 by deleting "2 plus" and inserting in lieu thereof "6 plus", and by deleting "is defined" and inserting in lieu thereof "means 6 levels above the offense level for any underlying criminal conduct. See the discussion".

The Commentary to §2H1.4 captioned "Background" is amended in the first paragraph by deleting ", except where death results, in which case the maximum term of imprisonment authorized is life imprisonment" and inserting in lieu there of "if no bodily injury results, ten years if bodily injury results, and life imprisonment if death results", by deleting "Given this one-year statutory maximum, a" and inserting in lieu thereof "A", by inserting "one-year" immediately following "near the", and by inserting "or bodily injury" immediately following "resulting in death".

The Commentary to §2H1.4 captioned "Background" is amended by inserting the following sentences at the end of the first paragraph:

> "The 6-level increase under subsection (a)(2) reflects the 2-level increase that is applied to other offenses covered in this Part plus a 4-level increase for the commission of the offense under actual or purported legal authority. This 4-level increase is inherent in the base offense level of 10 under subsection (a)(1).".

The purpose of this amendment is to correct an anomaly between the offense level under this section and §2H1.5 when the offense level is determined under subsection (a)(2). Section 2H1.4 is similar to §2H1.5 in that it may or may not involve the use of force. Under §2H1.4, however, the offense must involve the abuse of actual or purported legal authority. The base offense level of 10 used in 2H1.4(a)(1) has a built-in 4-level enhancement (which corresponds to the base offense level of 6 under §2H1.5(a)(1) plus the 4-level increase for a public official). There is an anomaly, however, when the base offense level from (a)(2) is used. In such cases, §2H1.4 results in an offense level that is 4 levels less than §2H1.5 when the offense is committed by a public official. The Commentary to §2H1.4 is also amended to reflect the increase in the maximum authorized sentence from one to ten years in cases involving bodily injury. **The effective date of this amendment is November 1, 1989.**

167. The Commentary to §2H1.5 captioned "Application Notes" is amended in Note 1 by deleting "explained" and inserting in lieu thereof "defined".

The Commentary to §2H1.5 captioned "Application Notes" is amended in Note 2 by deleting "§2H1.4(b)(1)" and inserting in lieu thereof "§2H1.5(b)(1)", and by deleting "the adjustment at" immediately before "§3B1.3".

The purposes of this amendment are to correct a clerical error and to make editorial improvements. **The effective date of this amendment is November 1, 1989.**

168. Section 2H2.1(a)(1) is amended by deleting "persons" and inserting in lieu thereof "person(s)".

The Commentary to §2H2.1 captioned "Background" is amended by deleting "Specific offense characteristics" and inserting in lieu thereof "Alternative base offense levels".

The purpose of this amendment is to correct two clerical errors. **The effective date of this amendment is November 1, 1989.**

169. Section 2H3.1 is amended by deleting:

"(a) Base Offense Level (Apply the greater):

(1) 9; or

(2) If the purpose of the conduct was to facilitate another offense, apply the guideline applicable to an attempt to commit that offense.

(b) Specific Offense Characteristic

(1) If the purpose of the conduct was to obtain direct or indirect commercial advantage or economic gain not covered by §2H3.1(a)(2) above, increase by 3 levels.",

and inserting in lieu thereof:

"(a) Base Offense Level: 9

(b) Specific Offense Characteristic

(1) If the purpose of the conduct was to obtain direct or indirect commercial advantage or economic gain, increase by 3 levels.

(c) Cross Reference

(1) If the purpose of the conduct was to facilitate another offense, apply the guideline applicable to an attempt to commit that offense, if the resulting offense level is greater than that determined above.".

The purpose of this amendment is to correct an anomaly in §2H3.1. Currently, specific offense characteristic (b)(1) applies only to base offense level (a)(1). Consequently, conduct facilitating an offense for economic gain of level 8 or 9 would result in a greater offense level (11 or 12) than conduct facilitating a more serious (level 10 or 11) offense. **The effective date of this amendment is November 1, 1989.**

170. Section 2J1.1 is amended by deleting:

"If the defendant was adjudged guilty of contempt, the court shall impose a sentence based on stated reasons and the purposes of sentencing set forth in 18 U.S.C. § 3553(a)(2).",

and inserting in lieu thereof:

"Apply §2X5.1 (Other Offenses).".

The Commentary to §2J1.1 captioned "Application Note" is amended in Note 1 by deleting "See, however, §2X5.1 (Other Offenses)." and inserting in lieu thereof "In certain cases, the offense conduct will be sufficiently analogous to §2J1.2 (Obstruction of Justice) for that guideline to apply.".

This section is designated as a guideline, but it is not a guideline contemplated by the Sentencing Reform Act. The purpose of this amendment is to clarify the Commission's original intent by referencing this section to §2X5.1 (Other Offenses). **The effective date of this amendment is November 1, 1989.**

171. The Commentary to §2J1.1 captioned "Statutory Provisions" is amended by deleting "Provisions" and inserting in lieu thereof "Provision", and by deleting "§" and ", 402".

The purpose of this amendment is to delete a reference to a petty offense. **The effective date of this amendment is November 1, 1989.**

172. Section 2J1.2(b)(1) is amended by deleting "defendant obstructed or attempted to obstruct the administration of justice by" and inserting in lieu thereof "offense involved", and by deleting "or property," and inserting in lieu thereof ", or property damage, in order to obstruct the administration of justice".

Section 2J1.2(b)(2) is amended by deleting "defendant substantially interfered" and inserting in lieu thereof "offense resulted in substantial interference".

Section 2J1.2(c)(1) is amended by deleting "conduct was" and inserting in lieu thereof "offense involved", and by deleting "such" and inserting in lieu thereof "that".

The Commentary to §2J1.2 captioned "Application Notes" is amended in Note 1 by deleting "'Substantially interfered" and inserting in lieu thereof "'Substantial interference", and by deleting "offense conduct resulting in" immediately before "a premature".

The purposes of this amendment are to clarify the guideline and to ensure that an attempted obstruction is not excluded from subsection (c) because of the non-parallel language between (b)(1) and (c)(1). **The effective date of this amendment is November 1, 1989.**

173. The Commentary to §2J1.2 captioned "Statutory Provisions" is amended by deleting "1503-" and inserting in lieu thereof "1503, 1505-".

The purpose of this amendment is to delete a reference to a petty offense. **The effective date of this amendment is November 1, 1989.**

174. The Commentary to §2J1.2 captioned "Statutory Provisions" is amended by inserting ", 1516" immediately following "1513".

The purpose of this amendment is to expand the coverage of an existing guideline to include a new offense (Obstruction of a Federal Audit) created by Section 7078 of the Anti-Drug Abuse Act of 1988. **The effective date of this amendment is November 1, 1989.**

175. Section 2J1.3 is amended in the caption by inserting "or Subornation of Perjury" immediately following "Perjury".

Section 2J1.3(b)(1) is amended by deleting "defendant suborned perjury by" and inserting in lieu thereof "offense involved", and by deleting "or property" and inserting in lieu thereof ", or property damage, in order to suborn perjury".

Section 2J1.3(b)(2) is amended by deleting "defendant's" immediately following "If the", and by deleting "substantially interfered" and inserting in lieu thereof "resulted in substantial interference".

Section 2J1.3(c)(1) is amended by deleting "conduct was perjury" and inserting in lieu thereof "offense involved perjury or subornation of perjury", and by deleting "such" and inserting in lieu thereof "that".

The Commentary to §2J1.3 captioned "Application Notes" is amended in Note 1 by deleting "'Substantially interfered" and inserting in lieu thereof "'Substantial interference", and by deleting "offense conduct resulting in" immediately before "a premature".

The purposes of this amendment are to clarify the guideline and to ensure that subornation of perjury is not excluded from subsection (c) due to a lack of parallel wording in the subsections. **The effective date of this amendment is November 1, 1989.**

176. Section 2J1.4(b)(1) is amended by deleting:

"If the defendant falsely represented himself as a federal officer, agent or employee to demand or obtain any money, paper, document, or other thing of value or to conduct an unlawful arrest or search, increase by 6 levels.",

and inserting in lieu thereof:

"If the impersonation was committed for the purpose of conducting an unlawful arrest, detention, or search, increase by 6 levels.".

Section 2J1.4 is amended by inserting the following additional subsection:

"(c) Cross Reference

(1) If the impersonation was to facilitate another offense, apply the guideline for an attempt to commit that offense, if the resulting offense level is greater than the offense level determined above.".

The purpose of this amendment is to relate the offense levels more directly to the underlying offense where the impersonation is committed for the purpose of facilitating another offense. **The effective date of this amendment is November 1, 1989.**

177. Section 2J1.5(b)(1) is amended by deleting "substantially interfered" and inserting in lieu thereof "resulted in substantial interference".

The Commentary to §2J1.5 captioned "Application Notes" is amended in Note 1 by deleting "'Substantially interfered" and inserting in lieu thereof "'Substantial interference", and by deleting "offense conduct resulting in" immediately before "a premature".

The purpose of this amendment is to clarify the guideline. **The effective date of this amendment is November 1, 1989.**

178. Chapter Two, Part J is amended by deleting §2J1.7 in its entirety as follows:

"§2J1.7. Commission of Offense While on Release

(a) Base Offense Level: 6

(b) Specific Offense Characteristics

(1) If the offense committed while on release is punishable by death or imprisonment for a term of fifteen years or more, increase by 6 levels.

(2) If the offense committed while on release is punishable by a term of imprisonment of five or more years, but less than fifteen years, increase by 4 levels.

(3) If the offense committed while on release is a felony punishable by a maximum term of less than five years, increase by 2 levels.

Commentary

Statutory Provision: 18 U.S.C. § 3147.

Application Notes:

1. This guideline applies whenever a sentence pursuant to 18 U.S.C. § 3147 is imposed.

2. By statute, a term of imprisonment imposed for a violation of 18 U.S.C. § 3147 runs consecutively to any other term of imprisonment. Consequently, a sentence for such a violation is exempt from grouping under the multiple count rules. See §3D1.2.

Background: Because defendants convicted under this section will generally have a prior criminal history, the guideline sentences provided are greater than they otherwise might appear.".

A replacement guideline with accompanying commentary is inserted as §2J1.7 (Commission of Offense While on Release).

The purpose of this amendment is to reflect the fact that 18 U.S.C. § 3147 is an enhancement provision, not a distinct offense. Created in 1984 as part of the Comprehensive Crime Control Act, the statute contained interim provisions (mandatory consecutive sentences that were subject to the parole and good time provisions of prior law) that were to be in effect until the sentencing guidelines took effect. The Senate Report to S.1762 indicates that the mandatory nature of the interim provisions was to be eliminated when the sentencing guidelines took effect ("Section 213(h) [220(g) of the CCCA of 1984] amends the new provision in title I of this Act relating to consecutive enhanced penalties for committing an offense while on release (new 18 U.S.C. § 3147)) by eliminating the mandatory nature of the penalties in favor of utilizing sentencing guidelines" (Senate Report 98-225 at 186). The statute, as amended, however, did not actually eliminate all language referring to mandatory penalties. A mandatory consecutive term of imprisonment is required but, unlike other mandatory provisions, there is no minimum required.

The amendment converts this section into an offense level adjustment for the offense committed while on release, a treatment that is considerably more consistent with the treatment of other offense/offender characteristics. **The effective date of this amendment is November 1, 1989.**

179. Section 2J1.8(b)(1) is amended by deleting "substantially interfered" and inserting in lieu thereof "resulted in substantial interference".

Section 2J1.8(c)(1) is amended by deleting "conduct was" and inserting in lieu thereof "offense involved", and by deleting "such" and inserting in lieu thereof "that".

The Commentary to §2J1.8 captioned "Application Notes" is amended in Note 1 by deleting "Substantially interfered" and inserting in lieu thereof "Substantial interference", and by deleting "offense conduct resulting in" immediately before "a premature".

The Commentary to §2J1.8 captioned "Application Notes" is amended in Note 2 by deleting the first sentence as follows: "This section applies only in the case of a conviction under the above referenced (or equivalent) statute.".

The purpose of this amendment is to clarify the guideline. **The effective date of this amendment is November 1, 1989.**

180. The Commentary to §2J1.9 captioned "Application Notes" is amended in Note 2 by deleting the first sentence as follows: "This section applies only in the case of a conviction under the above referenced (or equivalent) statute.".

The purpose of this amendment is to clarify the commentary. **The effective date of this amendment is November 1, 1989.**

181. Section 2J1.9(b)(1) is amended by deleting "for refusing to testify" and inserting in lieu thereof "made or offered for refusing to testify or for the witness absenting himself to avoid testifying".

The Commentary to §2J1.9 captioned "Application Notes" is amended by deleting:

"1. 'Refusing to testify' includes absenting oneself for the purpose of avoiding testifying.",

and by renumbering Notes 2 and 3 as 1 and 2 respectively.

The purpose of this amendment is to move material from the commentary to the guideline itself where it more properly belongs. **The effective date of this amendment is November 1, 1989.**

182. Sections 2K1.4(c) and 2K1.5(c) are amended by deleting "higher" whenever it appears and inserting in lieu thereof "greater".

The purpose of this amendment is to correct a clerical error. **The effective date of this amendment is November 1, 1989.**

183. Section 2K1.3(b) is amended by deleting "any of the following" and inserting in lieu thereof "more than one".

Section 2K1.3(b)(5) is amended by deleting "firearm offense" and inserting in lieu thereof "offense involving explosives".

The purpose of this amendment is to clarify the guideline. **The effective date of this amendment is November 1, 1989.**

184. Section 2K1.4(b) is amended by deleting "any of the following" and inserting in lieu thereof "more than one".

The purpose of this amendment is to clarify the guideline. **The effective date of this amendment is November 1, 1989.**

185. Section 2K1.4 is amended by inserting the following additional subsection:

"(d) Note

(1) The specific offense characteristic in subsection (b)(4) applies only in the case of an offense committed prior to November 18, 1988.".

The Commentary to §2K1.4 captioned "Statutory Provisions" is amended by inserting "(only in the case of an offense committed prior to November 18, 1988)" immediately following "(h)".

The Commentary to §2K1.4 captioned "Background", is amended by deleting "used fire or an explosive in the commission of a felony," immediately before "used a destructive device", and by inserting the following additional sentences at the end of the paragraph:

"As amended by Section 6474(b) of the Anti-Drug Abuse Act of 1988 (effective November 18, 1988), 18 U.S.C. § 844(h) sets forth a mandatory sentencing enhancement of five years for the first offense and ten years for subsequent offenses if the defendant was convicted of using fire or an explosive to commit a felony or of carrying an explosive during the commission of a felony. See §2K1.7.".

The purpose of this amendment is to conform the guideline to a statutory revision to 18 U.S.C. § 844(h). **The effective date of this amendment is November 1, 1989.**

186. Section 2K1.5(b) is amended by deleting "any of the following" and inserting in lieu thereof "more than one".

The purpose of this amendment is to clarify the guideline. **The effective date of this amendment is November 1, 1989.**

187. Section 2K1.5(b)(1) is amended by deleting "(i.e., the defendant is convicted under 49 U.S.C. § 1472(l)(2)" immediately following "human life", and by inserting "is convicted under 49 U.S.C. § 1472(l)(2) (i.e., the defendant" immediately before "acted".

The purpose of this amendment is to clarify the guideline. **The effective date of this amendment is November 1, 1989.**

188. Chapter Two, Part K is amended by inserting an additional guideline with accompanying commentary as §2K1.7 (Use of Fire or Explosives to Commit a Federal Felony).

The purpose of this amendment is to conform the guideline to a statutory revision of 18 U.S.C. § 844(h). **The effective date of this amendment is November 1, 1989.**

189. Section 2K2.1 is amended by deleting the entire guideline and accompanying commentary, except for the commentary captioned "Background", as follows:

"§2K2.1. Receipt, Possession, or Transportation of Firearms and Other Weapons by Prohibited Persons

(a) Base Offense Level: 9

(b) Specific Offense Characteristics

(1) If the firearm was stolen or had an altered or obliterated serial number, increase by 1 level.

(2) If the defendant obtained or possessed the firearm solely for sport or recreation, decrease by 4 levels.

(c) Cross Reference

(1) If the defendant used the firearm in committing or attempting another offense, apply the guideline in respect to such other offense, or §2X1.1 (Attempt or Conspiracy) if the resulting offense level is higher than that determined above.

Commentary

Statutory Provisions: 18 U.S.C. §§ 922(a)(6), (g), (h).

Application Note:

1. Under §2K2.1(b)(2), intended lawful use, as determined by the surrounding circumstances, provides a decrease in offense level. Relevant circumstances include, among others, the number and type of firearms (sawed-off shotguns, for example, have few legitimate uses) and ammunition, the location and circumstances of possession, the nature of the defendant's criminal history (e.g., whether involving firearms), and the extent to which possession is restricted by local law.",

and inserting in lieu thereof:

"§2K2.1. Unlawful Receipt, Possession, or Transportation of Firearms or Ammunition

(a) Base Offense Level (Apply the greatest):

(1) 16, if the defendant is convicted under 18 U.S.C. § 922(o) or 26 U.S.C. § 5861; or

(2) 12, if the defendant is convicted under 18 U.S.C. § 922(g), (h), or (n); or if the defendant, at the time of the offense, had been convicted in any court of an offense punishable by imprisonment for a term exceeding one year; or

(3) 6, otherwise.

(b) Specific Offense Characteristics

(1) If the defendant obtained or possessed the firearm or ammunition solely for lawful sporting purposes or collection, decrease the offense level determined above to level 6.

(2) If the firearm was stolen or had an altered or obliterated serial number, increase by 2 levels.

(c) Cross References

(1) If the offense involved the distribution of a firearm or possession with intent to distribute, apply §2K2.2 (Unlawful Trafficking and Other Prohibited Transactions Involving Firearms) if the resulting offense level is greater than that determined above.

(2) If the defendant used or possessed the firearm in connection with commission or attempted commission of another offense, apply §2X1.1 (Attempt, Solicitation, or Conspiracy) in respect to that other offense, if the resulting offense level is greater than that determined above.

Commentary

Statutory Provisions: 18 U.S.C. § 922(a)(1), (a)(3), (a)(4), (a)(6), (e), (f), (g), (h), (i), (j),(k), (l), (n), and (o); 26 U.S.C. § 5861(b), (c), (d), (h), (i), (j), and (k).

Application Notes:

1. The definition of 'firearm' used in this section is that set forth in 18 U.S.C. § 921(a)(3) (if the defendant is convicted under 18 U.S.C. § 922) and 26 U.S.C. § 5845(a) (if the defendant is convicted under 26 U.S.C. § 5861). These definitions are somewhat broader than that used in Application Note 1(e) of the Commentary to §1B1.1 (Application Instructions). Under 18 U.S.C. § 921(a)(3), the term 'firearm' means (A) any weapon (including a starter gun) which will or is designed to or may readily be converted to expel a projectile by the action of an explosive; (B) the frame or receiver of any such weapon; (C) any firearm muffler or firearm silencer; or (D) any destructive device. Under 26 U.S.C. § 5845(a), the term 'firearm' includes a shotgun, or a weapon made from a shotgun, with a barrel or barrels of less than 18 inches in length; a weapon made from a shotgun or rifle with an overall length of less than 26 inches; a rifle, or weapon made from a rifle, with a barrel or barrels less than 16 inches in length; a machine gun; a muffler or silencer for a firearm; a destructive device; and certain other large bore weapons.

2. Under §2K2.1(b)(1), intended lawful use, as determined by the surrounding circumstances, provides a decrease in the offense level. Relevant circumstances include, among others, the number and type of firearms (sawed-

off shotguns, for example, have few legitimate uses) and ammunition, the location and circumstances of possession, the nature of the defendant's criminal history (e.g., whether involving firearms), and the extent to which possession was restricted by local law.".

The Commentary to §2K2.1 captioned "Background" is amended in the last paragraph by deleting "§2K2.1(c)" and inserting in lieu thereof "§2K2.1(c)(2)".

Chapter Two, Part K, Subpart 2 is amended by deleting §§2K2.2 and 2K2.3 in their entirety as follows:

"§2K2.2. Receipt, Possession, or Transportation of Firearms and Other Weapons in Violation of National Firearms Act

(a) Base Offense Level: 12

(b) Specific Offense Characteristics

(1) If the firearm was stolen or had an altered or obliterated serial number, increase by 1 level.

(2) If the firearm was a silencer, increase by 4 levels.

(3) If the defendant obtained or possessed the firearm solely for sport, recreation or collection, decrease by 6 levels.

(c) Cross Reference

(1) If the defendant used the firearm in committing or attempting another offense, apply the guideline for such other offense or §2X1.1 (Attempt or Conspiracy), if the resulting offense level is higher than that determined above.

Commentary

Statutory Provisions: 26 U.S.C. §§ 5861(b) through (l).

Application Notes:

1. Under §2K2.2(b)(3), intended lawful use, as determined by the surrounding circumstances, provides a decrease in offense level. Relevant circumstances include, among others, the number and type of firearms (sawed-off shotguns, for example, have few legitimate uses) and ammunition, the location and circumstances of possession, the nature of the defendant's criminal history (e.g., whether involving firearms), and the extent to which possession is restricted by local law.

2. Subsection (c)(1) refers to any situation in which the defendant possessed a firearm to facilitate another offense that he committed or attempted.

Background: 26 U.S.C. § 5861 prohibits the unlicensed receipt, possession, transportation, or manufacture of certain firearms, such as machine guns, silencers, rifles and shotguns with shortened barrels, and destructive devices. As with §2K2.1, there is considerable variation in the conduct included under this statutory provision and some violations may be relatively technical.

§2K2.3. Prohibited Transactions in or Shipment of Firearms and Other Weapons

(a) Base Offense Level:

(1) 12, if convicted under 26 U.S.C. § 5861; or

(2) 6, otherwise.

(b) Specific Offense Characteristics

(1) If the number of firearms unlawfully dealt in exceeded 5, increase as follows:

	Number of Firearms	Increase in Level
(A)	6 - 10	add 1
(B)	11 - 20	add 2
(C)	21 - 50	add 3
(D)	51 - 100	add 4
(E)	101 - 200	add 5
(F)	more than 200	add 6

(2) If any of the following applies, use the greatest:

(A) If the defendant knew or had reason to believe that a purchaser was a person prohibited by federal law from owning the firearm, increase by 2 levels.

(B) If the defendant knew or had reason to believe that a purchaser resided in another state in which he was prohibited from owning the firearm, increase by 1 level.

(C) If the defendant knew or had reason to believe that a firearm was stolen or had an altered or obliterated serial number, increase by 1 level.

(c) Cross Reference

(1) If the defendant provided the firearm to another for the purpose of committing another offense, or knowing that he planned to use it in committing another offense, apply §2X1.1 (Attempt or Conspiracy) in respect to such other offense, if the resulting offense level is higher.

Commentary

Statutory Provisions: 18 U.S.C. § 922 (a)(1), (a)(5), (b)(2), (b)(3), (d), (i), (j), (k), (l); 26 U.S.C. § 5861(a).

Background: This section applies to a variety of offenses involving prohibited transactions in or transportation of firearms and certain other weapons.".

A replacement guideline with accompanying commentary is inserted as §2K2.2 (Unlawful Trafficking and Other Prohibited Transactions Involving Firearms).

Chapter Two, Part K, Subpart 2 is amended by inserting an additional guideline with accompanying commentary as §2K2.3 (Receiving, Transporting, Shipping or Transferring a Firearm or Ammunition With Intent to Commit Another Offense, or With Knowledge that It Will Be Used in Committing Another Offense).

This amendment addresses a number of diverse substantive and technical issues, as well as the creation of several new offenses, and increased statutory maximum penalties for certain other offenses. Because there exist a large number of overlapping statutory provisions, the three basic guidelines, §2K2.1 (Possession by a prohibited person), §2K2.2 (Possession of certain types of weapons), and §2K2.3 (Unlawful trafficking) are not closely tied to the actual conduct. The amendment addresses this issue by consolidating the current three guidelines into two guidelines: (1) unlawful possession, receipt, or transportation, and (2) unlawful trafficking; and by more carefully drawing the distinctions between the base offense levels provided. The third guideline in this amendment is a new guideline to address transfer of a weapon with intent or knowledge that it will be used to commit another offense (formerly covered in a cross reference) and a new offense added by the Anti-Drug Abuse Act of 1988 (Section 6211)(Interstate travel to acquire a firearm for a criminal purpose).

The base offense level for conduct covered by the current §2K2.1 is increased in the amendment from 9 to 12. The statutorily authorized maximum sentence for the conduct covered under §2K2.1 was increased from five to ten years by the Anti-Drug Abuse Act of 1988 (Section 6462). Note, however, that the most aggravated conduct under §2K2.1 (possession of a weapon during commission of another offense) is handled by the cross-reference at subsection (c) and is based upon the offense level for an attempt to commit the underlying offense. See Background Commentary to current §2K2.1. The offense level for unlawful possession of a machine gun, sawed off shotgun, or destructive device is increased from 12 to 16. In addition, the amendment raises the enhancement for stolen weapons or obliterated serial numbers from 1 to 2 levels to better reflect the seriousness of this conduct. The numbers currently used in the table for the distribution of multiple weapons in §2K2.2 are amended to increase the offense level more rapidly for sale of multiple weapons. **The effective date of this amendment is November 1, 1989.**

190. Section 2K2.4 is amended by deleting "penalties are those" and inserting in lieu thereof "term of imprisonment is that".

The Commentary to §2K2.4 captioned "Application Notes" is amended by inserting the following additional note:

"3. Imposition of a term of supervised release is governed by the provisions of §5D1.1 (Imposition of a Term of Supervised Release).".

Section 2K2.4 is amended by inserting "(a)" immediately before "If", and by inserting the following additional subsection:

"(b) Special Instructions for Fines

(1) Where there is a federal conviction for the underlying offense, the fine guideline shall be the fine guideline that would have been applicable had there only been a conviction for the underlying offense. This guideline
shall be used as a consolidated fine guideline for both the underlying offense and the conviction underlying this section.".

The Commentary to §2K2.4 captioned "Application Notes" is amended by inserting the following additional note:

"4. Subsection (b) sets forth special provisions concerning the imposition of fines. Where there is also a conviction for the underlying offense, a consolidated fine guideline is determined by the offense level that would have applied to the underlying offense absent a conviction under 18 U.S.C. § 924(c) or 929(a). This is because the offense level for the underlying offense may be reduced when there is also a conviction under 18 U.S.C. § 924(c) or 929(a) in that any specific offense characteristic for possession, use, or discharge of a firearm is not applied (see Application Note 2). The Commission has not established a fine guideline range for the unusual case in which there is no conviction for the underlying offense.".

The purpose of this amendment is to address the imposition of a fine or term of supervised release when this guideline applies. **The effective date of this amendment is November 1, 1989.**

191. Chapter Two, Part K is amended by inserting an additional guideline with accompanying commentary as §2K2.5 (Possession of Firearms and Dangerous Weapons in Federal Facilities).

The purpose of this amendment is to reflect a new offense enacted by Section 6215 of the Anti-Drug Abuse Act of 1988. A base offense level of 6 is provided for the misdemeanor portion of this statute. The felony portion of this statute (possession with intent to commit another offense) is treated as if an attempt to commit that other offense. **The effective date of this amendment is November 1, 1989.**

192. Section 2L1.1(b) is amended by inserting the following additional subsection:

"(3) If the defendant is an unlawful alien who has been deported (voluntarily or involuntarily) on one or more occasions prior to the instant offense, and the offense level determined above is less than level 8, increase to level 8.".

The Commentary to §2L1.1 captioned "Application Notes" is amended in Note 6 by deleting "enhancement at §2L1.1(b)(1) does not apply" and inserting in lieu thereof "reduction at §2L1.1(b)(1) applies".

The purposes of this amendment are to provide an offense level that is no less than that provided under §2L1.2 in the case of a defendant who is a previously deported alien, and to conform Application Note 6 of the Commentary to §2L1.1 to the January 1988 revision of §2L1.1. **The effective date of this amendment is November 1, 1989.**

193. Section 2L1.2 is amended by inserting the following additional subsection:

"(b) Specific Offense Characteristic

(1) If the defendant previously was deported after sustaining a conviction for a felony, other than a felony involving violation of the immigration laws, increase by 4 levels.",

The Commentary to §2L1.2 captioned "Application Notes" is amended by inserting the following additional notes:

"3. A 4-level increase is provided under subsection (b)(1) in the case of a defendant who was previously deported after sustaining a conviction for a felony, other than a felony involving a violation of the immigration laws. In the case of a defendant previously deported after sustaining a conviction for an aggravated felony as defined in 8 U.S.C. § 1101(a), or for any other violent felony, an upward departure may be warranted.

4. The adjustment under §2L1.2(b)(1) is in addition to any criminal history points added for such conviction in Chapter 4, Part A (Criminal History).".

The purpose of this amendment is to add a specific offense characteristic to provide an increase in the case of an alien previously deported after conviction of a felony other than an immigration law violation. This specific offense characteristic is in addition to, and not in lieu of, criminal history points added for the prior sentence. The amendment provides for consideration of an upward departure where the previous deportation was for an "aggravated felony" or for any other violent felony. **The effective date of this amendment is November 1, 1989.**

194. Chapter Two, Part L, Subpart 1 is amended by deleting §2L1.3 in its entirety as follows:

"§2L1.3. Engaging in a Pattern of Unlawful Employment of Aliens

(a) Base Offense Level: 6

Commentary

Statutory Provision: 8 U.S.C. § 1324a(f)(1).

Background: The offense covered under this section is a misdemeanor for which the maximum term of imprisonment authorized by statute is six months.".

The purpose of this amendment is to delete a guideline applying only to a petty offense. Petty offenses were deleted from coverage of the guidelines by the adoption of §1B1.9 (effective June 15, 1988). **The effective date of this amendment is November 1, 1989.**

195. Section 2L2.1(a) is amended by deleting "6" and inserting in lieu thereof "9".

Section 2L2.1(b)(1) is amended by deleting "for profit, increase by 3 levels" and inserting in lieu thereof "other than for profit, decrease by 3 levels".

The purpose of this amendment is to conform the structure of this guideline to that of §2L1.1. **The effective date of this amendment is November 1, 1989.**

196. Section 2L2.2 is amended by inserting the following additional subsection:

"(b) Specific Offense Characteristic

(1) If the defendant is an unlawful alien who has been deported (voluntarily or involuntarily) on one or more occasions prior to the instant offense, increase by 2 levels.".

The Commentary to §2L2.2 captioned "Application Notes" is amended by deleting:

"1. In the case of a defendant who is an unlawful alien and has been deported (voluntarily or involuntarily) on one or more occasions prior to the instant offense, the Commission recommends an upward departure of 2 levels in order to provide a result equivalent to §2L1.2.",

by renumbering Note 2 as Note 1, and by deleting "Notes" and inserting in lieu thereof "Note".

The purpose of this amendment it to convert a departure recommendation into a specific offense characteristic. **The effective date of this amendment is November 1, 1989.**

197. Section 2L2.3(a) is amended by deleting "6" and inserting in lieu thereof "9".

Section 2L2.3(b)(1) is amended by deleting "for profit, increase by 3 levels" and inserting in lieu thereof "other than for profit, decrease by 3 levels".

The purpose of this amendment is to conform the structure of this guideline to that of §2L1.1. **The effective date of this amendment is November 1, 1989.**

198. Section 2L2.4 is amended by inserting the following additional subsection:

"(b) Specific Offense Characteristic

(1) If the defendant is an unlawful alien who has been deported (voluntarily or involuntarily) on one or more occasions prior to the instant offense, increase by 2 levels.".

The Commentary to §2L2.4 captioned "Application Notes" is amended by deleting:

"1. In the case of a defendant who is an unlawful alien and has been deported (voluntarily or involuntarily) on one or more occasions prior to the instant offense, the Commission recommends an upward departure of 2 levels in order to provide a result equivalent to §2L1.2.",

by renumbering Note 2 as Note 1, and by deleting "Notes" and inserting in lieu thereof "Note".

The purpose of this amendment is to convert a departure recommendation into a specific offense characteristic. **The effective date of this amendment is November 1, 1989.**

199. Section 2N3.1 is amended by deleting:

"(b) If more than one vehicle was involved, apply §2F1.1 (Offenses Involving Fraud or Deceit).",

and inserting in lieu thereof:

"(b) Cross Reference

(1) If the offense involved more than one vehicle, apply §2F1.1 (Fraud and Deceit).".

The purposes of this amendment are to correct a clerical error and to conform the phraseology of this subsection to that used elsewhere in the guidelines. **The effective date of this amendment is November 1, 1989.**

200. Section 2P1.1(a) is amended by deleting:

"(1) 13, if from lawful custody resulting from a conviction or as a result of a lawful arrest for a felony;

(2) 8, if from lawful custody awaiting extradition, pursuant to designation as a recalcitrant witness or as a result of a lawful arrest for a misdemeanor.",

and inserting in lieu thereof:

"(1) 13, if the custody or confinement is by virtue of an arrest on a charge of felony, or conviction of any offense;

(2) 8, otherwise.".

The purpose of this amendment is to clarify the language of the guideline by making it conform more closely to that used in 18 U.S.C. § 751, the statute from which it was derived. **The effective date of this amendment is November 1, 1989.**

201. Section 2P1.1(b)(3) is amended by deleting:

"If the defendant committed the offense while a correctional officer or other employee of the Department of Justice, increase by 2 levels.",

and inserting in lieu thereof:

"If the defendant was a law enforcement or correctional officer or employee, or an employee of the Department of Justice, at the time of the offense, increase by 2 levels.".

The current specific offense characteristic (b)(3) applies only to correctional officers or Justice Department employees, and not to local or state law enforcement officers who might have custody of a federal prisoner, or even to federal law enforcement officers who are not employed by the Department of Justice (e.g., Secret Service agents are employed by the Treasury Department). It also does not appear to apply to law enforcement or correctional employees who are not sworn officers unless they are Justice Department employees. The purpose of this amendment is to correct this anomaly. **The effective date of this amendment is November 1, 1989.**

202. Section 2P1.2(b)(1) is amended by deleting:

"If the defendant committed the offense while a correctional officer or other employee of the Department of Justice, increase by 2 levels.",

and inserting in lieu thereof:

"If the defendant was a law enforcement or correctional officer or employee, or an employee of the Department of Justice, at the time of the offense, increase by 2 levels.".

The current specific offense characteristic (b)(1) applies only to correctional officers or Justice Department employees, and not to local or state law enforcement officers who might have custody of a federal prisoner, or even to federal law enforcement officers who are not employed by the Department of Justice (e.g., Secret Service agents are employed by the Treasury Department). It also does not appear to apply to law enforcement or correctional employees who are not sworn officers unless they are Justice Department employees. The purpose of this amendment is to correct this anomaly. **The effective date of this amendment is November 1, 1989.**

203. Section 2P1.2 is amended by inserting the following additional subsection:

"(c) Cross Reference

(1) If the defendant is convicted under 18 U.S.C. § 1791(a)(1) and is punishable under 18 U.S.C. § 1791(b)(1), the offense level is 2 plus the offense level from §2D1.1, but in no event less than level 26.".

The Commentary to §2P1.2 captioned "Application Note" is amended by deleting "Note" and inserting in lieu thereof "Notes", and by inserting the following additional note:

"2. Pursuant to 18 U.S.C. § 1791(c), as amended, a sentence imposed upon an inmate for a violation of 18 U.S.C. § 1791 shall be consecutive to the sentence being served at the time of the violation.".

The purpose of this amendment is to implement the direction to the Commission in Section 6468 of the Anti-Drug Abuse Act of 1988. **The effective date of this amendment is November 1, 1989.**

204. Chapter Two, Part P is amended by deleting §2P1.4 in its entirety as follows:

"§2P1.4. Trespass on Bureau of Prisons Facilities

(a) Base Offense Level: 6

Commentary

Statutory Provision: 18 U.S.C. § 1793.".

The purpose of this amendment is to delete a guideline applying only to a petty offense. Petty offenses were deleted from coverage of the guidelines by the adoption of §1B1.9 (effective June 15, 1988). **The effective date of this amendment is November 1, 1989.**

205. The Commentary to §2Q1.3 captioned "Statutory Provisions" is amended by deleting "§ 4912,".

The purpose of this amendment is to delete a reference to a petty offense. **The effective date of this amendment is November 1, 1989.**

206. Section 2Q1.4(b)(1) is amended by inserting "bodily" immediately preceding "injury".

The Commentary to §2Q1.4 captioned "Application Note" is amended by deleting:

"1. 'Serious injury' means serious bodily injury as defined in the Commentary to §1B1.1 (Applicable Instructions).",

and inserting in lieu thereof:

"1. 'Serious bodily injury' is defined in the Commentary to §1B1.1 (Application Instructions).".

The purpose of this amendment is to correct a clerical error. **The effective date of this amendment is November 1, 1989.**

207. Section 2Q1.5(b) is amended by deleting:

"(2) If the purpose of the offense was to influence government action or to extort money, increase by 8 levels.",

and by inserting the following additional subsection:

"(c) Cross Reference

(1) If the purpose of the offense was to influence government action or to extort money, apply §2B3.2 (Extortion by Force or Threat of Injury or Serious Damage).".

Section 2Q1.5(b) is amended by deleting "Characteristics" and inserting in lieu thereof "Characteristic".

The purposes of this amendment are to convert a specific offense characteristic to a cross-reference and render the guidelines internally more consistent. **The effective date of this amendment is November 1, 1989.**

208. Chapter Two, Part Q, Subpart 1, is amended by inserting an additional guideline with accompanying commentary as §2Q1.6 (Hazardous or Injurious Devices on Federal Lands).

The purpose of this amendment is to reflect a new offense created by Section 6254(f) of the Anti-Drug Abuse Act of 1988. **The effective date of this amendment is November 1, 1989.**

209. Section 2Q2.1 is amended in the title by inserting at the end "; Smuggling and Otherwise Unlawfully Dealing in Fish, Wildlife, and Plants".

The Commentary to §2Q2.1 captioned "Statutory Provisions" is amended by inserting immediately before the period at the end ", 3373(d); 18 U.S.C. § 545".

The Commentary to §2Q2.1 captioned "Background" is amended by deleting "and the Fur Seal Act. These statutes provide special protection to particular species of fish, wildlife and plants." and inserting in lieu thereof "the Fur Seal Act, the Lacey Act, and to violations of 18 U.S.C. § 545 where the smuggling activity involved fish, wildlife, or plants.".

Chapter Two, Part Q, Subpart 2 is amended by deleting §2Q2.2 in its entirety as follows:

"§2Q2.2. <u>Lacey Act; Smuggling and Otherwise Unlawfully Dealing in Fish, Wildlife, and Plants</u>

(a) Base Offense Level:

(1) 6, if the defendant knowingly imported or exported fish, wildlife, or plants, or knowingly engaged in conduct involving the sale or purchase of fish, wildlife, or plants with a market value greater than $350; or

(2) 4.

(b) Specific Offense Characteristics

(1) If the offense involved a commercial purpose, increase by 2 levels.

(2) If the offense involved fish, wildlife, or plants that were not quarantined as required by law, increase by 2 levels.

(3) Apply the greater:

(A) If the market value of the fish, wildlife, or plants exceeded $2,000, increase the offense level by the corresponding number of levels from the table in §2F1.1 (Fraud and Deceit); or

(B) If the offense involved a quantity of fish, wildlife, or plants that was substantial in relation either to the overall population of the species or to a discrete subpopulation, increase by 4 levels.

Commentary

Statutory Provisions: 16 U.S.C. § 3773(d); 18 U.S.C. § 545.

Application Note:

1. This section applies to violations of 18 U.S.C. § 545 where the smuggling activity involved fish, wildlife, or plants. In other cases, see §§2T3.1 and 2T3.2.

Background: This section applies to violations of the Lacey Act Amendments of 1981, 16 U.S.C. § 3373(d), and to violations of 18 U.S.C. § 545 where the smuggling activity involved fish, wildlife, or plants. These are the principal enforcement statutes utilized to combat interstate and foreign commerce in unlawfully taken fish, wildlife, and plants. The adjustments for specific offense characteristics are identical to those in §2Q2.1.".

The purpose of this amendment is to consolidate two guidelines that cover very similar offenses. **The effective date of this amendment is November 1, 1989.**

210. Section 2Q2.1(b)(3) is amended by deleting "Apply the greater:" and inserting in lieu thereof "(If more than one applies, use the greater):".

The purpose of this amendment is to conform the guideline to the style of other guidelines. **The effective date of this amendment is November 1, 1989.**

211. Section 2R1.1(b)(2) is amended in the first column of the table by deleting:

"Volume of Commerce

(A) less than $1,000,000
(B) $1,000,000 - $4,000,000
(C) $4,000,001 - $15,000,000
(D) $15,000,001 - $50,000,000
(E) over $50,000,000",

and inserting in lieu thereof:

"Volume of Commerce (Apply the Greatest)

(A) Less than $1,000,000
(B) $1,000,000 - $4,000,000
(C) More than $4,000,000
(D) More than $15,000,000
(E) More than $50,000,000".

The purpose of this amendment is to eliminate minor gaps in the loss table. **The effective date of this amendment is November 1, 1989.**

212. Section 2S1.1(b)(2) is amended in the first column of the table by deleting:

	"Value
(A)	$100,000 or less
(B)	$100,001 - $200,000
(C)	$200,001 - $350,000
(D)	$350,001 - $600,000
(E)	$600,001 - $1,000,000
(F)	$1,000,001 - $2,000,000
(G)	$2,000,001 - $3,500,000
(H)	$3,500,001 - $6,000,000
(I)	$6,000,001 - $10,000,000
(J)	$10,000,001 - $20,000,000
(K)	$20,000,001 - $35,000,000
(L)	$35,000,001 - $60,000,000
(M)	$60,000,001 - $100,000,000
(N)	more than $100,000,000",

and inserting in lieu thereof:

	"Value (Apply the Greatest)
(A)	$100,000 or less
(B)	More than $100,000
(C)	More than $200,000
(D)	More than $350,000
(E)	More than $600,000
(F)	More than $1,000,000
(G)	More than $2,000,000
(H)	More than $3,500,000
(I)	More than $6,000,000
(J)	More than $10,000,000
(K)	More than $20,000,000
(L)	More than $35,000,000
(M)	More than $60,000,000
(N)	More than $100,000,000".

The purpose of this amendment is to eliminate minor gaps in the value table. **The effective date of this amendment is November 1, 1989.**

213. The Commentary to §2S1.1 captioned "Background" is amended in the third paragraph by inserting the following additional sentences at the end: "Effective November 18, 1988, 18 U.S.C. § 1956(a)(1)(A) contains two subdivisions. The base offense level of 23 applies to § 1956(a)(1)(A)(i) and (ii).".

The purpose of this amendment is to reflect a statutory revision made by Section 6471 of the Anti-Drug Abuse Act of 1988. **The effective date of this amendment is November 1, 1989.**

214. The Commentary to §2S1.1 captioned "Background" is amended in the fourth paragraph by deleting "scope of the criminal enterprise as well as the degree of the defendant's involvement" and inserting in lieu thereof "magnitude of the criminal enterprise, and the extent to which the defendant aided the enterprise".

The purpose of this amendment is to clarify the commentary. **The effective date of this amendment is November 1, 1989.**

215. Section 2S1.2(b)(1)(A) is amended by inserting at the end "or".

The Commentary to §2S1.2 captioned "Background" is amended in the third paragraph by deleting "(b)(1)" and inserting in lieu thereof "(b)(1)(B)".

The purpose of this amendment is to correct clerical errors. **The effective date of this amendment is November 1, 1989.**

216. Section 2S1.3(a)(1)(C) is amended by deleting "the proceeds of criminal activity" and inserting in lieu thereof "criminally derived property", and in subsection (b)(1) by inserting "property" immediately following "criminally derived".

The Commentary to §2S1.3 captioned "Application Note" is amended by deleting:

"1. As used in this guideline, funds or other property are the 'proceeds of criminal activity' or 'criminally derived' if they are 'criminally derived property,' within the meaning of 18 U.S.C. § 1957.",

and inserting in lieu thereof:

"1. 'Criminally derived property' means any property constituting, or derived from, proceeds obtained from a criminal offense. See 18 U.S.C. § 1957(f)(2).".

The purpose of this amendment is to clarify the guideline. **The effective date of this amendment is November 1, 1989.**

217. The Commentary to §2S1.3 captioned "Statutory Provisions" is amended by inserting "26 U.S.C. § 7203 (if a willful violation of 26 U.S.C. § 6050I);" immediately before "31 U.S.C.".

The purpose of this amendment is to conform the guideline to a revision of the relevant statute. **The effective date of this amendment is November 1, 1989.**

218. Section 2S1.3(a)(1)(A) is amended by inserting "or" immediately following "requirements;". Section 2S1.3(a)(1)(B) is amended by deleting "activity" and inserting in lieu thereof "evasion of reporting requirements".

The Commentary to §2S1.3 captioned "Application Note" is amended in the caption by deleting "Note" and inserting in lieu thereof "Notes", and by inserting the following additional note:

"2. Subsection (a)(1)(C) applies where a reasonable person would have believed from the circumstances that the funds were criminally derived property. Subsection (b)(1) applies if the defendant knew or believed the funds were criminally derived property. Subsection (b)(1) applies in addition to, and not in lieu of, subsection (a)(1)(C). Where subsection (b)(1) applies, subsection (a)(1)(C) also will apply. It is possible that a defendant 'believed' or 'reasonably should have believed' that the funds were criminally derived property even if, in fact, the funds were not so derived (e.g., in a 'sting' operation where the defendant is told the funds were derived from the unlawful sale of controlled substances).".

The Commentary to §2S1.3 captioned "Background" is amended in the second paragraph by deleting:

"The base offense level is set at 13 for the great majority of cases. However, the base offense level is set at 5 for those cases in which these offenses may be committed with innocent motives and the defendant reasonably believed that the funds were from legitimate sources. The higher base offense level applies in all other cases. The offense level is increased by 5 levels if the defendant knew that the funds were criminally derived.",

and inserting in lieu thereof:

"A base offense level of 13 is provided for those offenses where the defendant either structured the transaction to evade reporting requirements, made false statements to conceal or disguise the activity, or reasonably should have believed that the funds were criminally derived property. A lower alternative base offense level of 5 is provided in all other cases. The Commission anticipates that such cases will involve simple recordkeeping or other more minor technical violations of the regulatory scheme governing certain monetary transactions committed by defendants who reasonably believe that the funds at issue emanated from legitimate sources.

Where the defendant actually knew or believed that the funds were criminally derived property, subsection (b)(1) provides for a 5 level increase in the offense level.".

The Commentary to §2S1.3 captioned "Background" is amended in the last paragraph by deleting "The dollar value of the the transactions not reported is an important sentencing factor, except in rare cases. It is an" and inserting in lieu thereof "Except in rare cases, the dollar value of the transactions not reported is an important".

The Commentary to §2S1.3 captioned "Statutory Provisions" is amended by inserting "18 U.S.C. § 1005;" immediately following "Provisions".

The purposes of this amendment are to clarify the guideline and commentary, to provide more complete statutory references, and to conform the format of the guideline to that used in other guidelines. **The effective date of this amendment is November 1, 1989.**

219. Section 2T1.1(a) is amended by deleting the last sentence as follows: "When more than one year is involved, the tax losses are to be added.".

The Commentary to §2T1.1 captioned "Application Notes" is amended in Note 2 by deleting:

"The court is to determine this amount as it would any other guideline factor.",

and inserting in lieu thereof:

"Although the definition of tax loss corresponds to what is commonly called the 'criminal deficiency,' its amount is to be determined by the same rules applicable in determining any other sentencing factor.".

The Commentary to §2T1.1 captioned "Application Notes" is amended in Note 3 by deleting:

"Although the definition of tax loss corresponds to what is commonly called the 'criminal deficiency,' its amount is to be determined by the same rules applicable in determining any other sentencing factor. In accordance with the 'relevant conduct' approach adopted by the guidelines, tax losses resulting from more than one year are to be added whether or not the defendant is convicted of multiple counts.",

and inserting in lieu thereof:

> "In determining the total tax loss attributable to the offense (see §1B1.3(a)(2)), all conduct violating the tax laws should be considered as part of the same course of conduct or common scheme or plan unless the evidence demonstrates that the conduct is clearly unrelated. The following examples are illustrative of conduct that is part of the same course of conduct or common scheme or plan: (a) there is a continuing pattern of violations of the tax laws by the defendant; (b) the defendant uses a consistent method to evade or camouflage income, e.g., backdating documents or using off-shore accounts; (c) the violations involve the same or a related series of transactions; (d) the violation in each instance involves a false or inflated claim of a similar deduction or credit; and (e) the violation in each instance involves a failure to report or an understatement of a specific source of income, e.g., interest from savings accounts or income from a particular business activity. These examples are not intended to be exhaustive.".

The purposes of this amendment are to clarify the determination of tax loss and to make this instruction consistent among §§2T1.1-2T1.3. **The effective date of this amendment is November 1, 1989.**

220. Section 2T1.1(a) is amended by deleting ", including interest to the date of filing an indictment or information" immediately following "attempted to evade".

The Commentary to §2T1.1 captioned "Application Notes" is amended in Note 2 in the first sentence by deleting ", plus interest to the date of the filing of an indictment or information" immediately following "attempted to evade", and in the second sentence by inserting "interest or" immediately before "penalties.".

The purpose of this amendment is to simplify the application of the guideline by deleting interest from the calculation of tax loss. **The effective date of this amendment is November 1, 1989.**

221. Section 2T1.1(b)(1) is amended by deleting "(A)" immediately before "the defendant failed", by deleting ", or (B) the offense concealed or furthered criminal activity from which the defendant derived a substantial portion of his income" immediately following "criminal activity", by inserting "or to correctly identify the source of" immediately after "report", and by deleting "per" and inserting in lieu thereof "in any".

The purposes of this amendment are to provide a more objective test for application of this enhancement, and to make clear that this enhancement applies if the defendant fails to report or disguises income exceeding $10,000 from criminal activity in any year. **The effective date of this amendment is November 1, 1989.**

222. The Commentary to §2T1.1 captioned "Application Notes" is amended in Note 6 by deleting:

> "Whether 'sophisticated means' were employed (§2T1.1(b)(2)) requires a subjective determination similar to that in §2F1.1(b)(2).",

and inserting in lieu thereof:

> "'Sophisticated means,' as used in §2T1.1(b)(2), includes conduct that is more complex or demonstrates greater intricacy or planning than a routine tax-evasion case.".

The purpose of this amendment is to clarify the commentary. **The effective date of this amendment is November 1, 1989.**

223. The Commentary to §2T1.1 captioned "Background" is amended in the second paragraph by deleting "Tax Table" wherever it appears and inserting in lieu thereof in each instance "Sentencing Table".

The purpose of this amendment is to correct a clerical error. **The effective date of this amendment is November 1, 1989..**

224. Section 2T1.2(b)(1) is amended by deleting "(A)" immediately before "the defendant failed", by deleting ", or (B) the offense concealed or furthered criminal activity from which the defendant derived a substantial portion of his income" immediately following "criminal activity", by inserting "or to correctly identify the source of" immediately after "report", and by deleting "per" and inserting in lieu thereof "in any".

The purposes of this amendment are to provide a more objective test for application of this enhancement, and to make clear that this enhancement applies if the defendant fails to report or disguises income exceeding $10,000 from criminal activity in any year. **The effective date of this amendment is November 1, 1989.**

225. Section 2T1.2 is amended by inserting the following additional subsection:

"(c) Cross Reference

(1) If the defendant is convicted of a willful violation of 26 U.S.C. § 6050I, apply §2S1.3 (Failure to Report Monetary Transactions) in lieu of this guideline.".

The Commentary to §2T1.2 captioned "Statutory Provision" is amended by inserting immediately before the period at the end "(other than a willful violation of 26 U.S.C. § 6050I)".

The purpose of this amendment is to reflect a revision of 26 U.S.C. § 6050I made by Section 7601 of the Anti-Drug Abuse Act of 1988. **The effective date of this amendment is November 1, 1989.**

226. The Commentary to §2T1.2 captioned "Application Note" is amended in Note 2 by deleting:

"Whether 'sophisticated means' were employed (§2T1.2(b)(2)) requires a determination similar to that in §2F1.1(b)(2).",

and inserting in lieu thereof:

"'Sophisticated means,' as used in §2T1.2(b)(2), includes conduct that is more complex or demonstrates greater intricacy or planning than a routine tax-evasion case.".

The purpose of this amendment is to clarify the commentary. **The effective date of this amendment is November 1, 1989.**

227. The Commentary to §2T1.2 captioned "Application Note" is amended in the caption by deleting "Note" and inserting in lieu thereof "Notes", and by inserting the following additional note:

"3. In determining the total tax loss attributable to the offense (see §1B1.3(a)(2)), all conduct violating the tax laws should be considered as part of the same course of conduct or common scheme or plan unless the evidence demonstrates that the conduct is clearly unrelated. See Application Note 3 of the Commentary to §2T1.1.".

The purpose of this amendment is to clarify the determination of tax loss. **The effective date of this amendment is November 1, 1989.**

228. Section 2T1.3(b)(1) is amended by deleting "(A)" immediately before "the defendant failed", by deleting ", or (B) the offense concealed or furthered criminal activity from which the defendant derived a substantial portion of his income" immediately following "criminal activity", by inserting "or to correctly identify the source of" immediately after "report", and by deleting "per" and inserting in lieu thereof "in any".

The purposes of this amendment are to provide a more objective test for application of this enhancement, and to make clear that this enhancement applies if the defendant fails to report or disguises income exceeding $10,000 from criminal activity in any year. **The effective date of this amendment is November 1, 1989.**

229. The Commentary to §2T1.3 captioned "Application Notes" is amended in Note 2 by deleting:

"Whether 'sophisticated means' were employed (§2T1.3(b)(2)) requires a determination similar to that in §2F1.1(b)(2).",

and inserting in lieu thereof:

"'Sophisticated means,' as used in §2T1.3(b)(2), includes conduct that is more complex or demonstrates greater intricacy or planning than a routine tax-evasion case.".

The purpose of this amendment is to clarify the commentary. **The effective date of this amendment is November 1, 1989.**

230. The Commentary to §2T1.3 captioned "Application Notes" is amended by inserting the following additional note:

"3. In determining the total tax loss attributable to the offense (see §1B1.3(a)(2)), all conduct violating the tax laws should be considered as part of the same course of conduct or common scheme or plan unless the evidence demonstrates that the conduct is clearly unrelated. See Application Note 3 of the Commentary to §2T1.1.".

The purpose of this amendment is to clarify the determination of tax loss. **The effective date of this amendment is November 1, 1989.**

231. The Commentary to §2T1.4 captioned "Application Notes" is amended in Note 2 by deleting:

"Whether 'sophisticated means' were employed (§2T1.1(b)(2)) requires a determination similar to that in §2F1.1(b)(2).",

and inserting in lieu thereof:

"'Sophisticated means,' as used in §2T1.4(b)(2), includes conduct that is more complex or demonstrates greater intricacy or planning than a routine tax-evasion case.".

The purpose of this amendment is to clarify the commentary. **The effective date of this amendment is November 1, 1989.**

232. Section 2T1.6(a) is amended by deleting ", plus interest" immediately following "paid over".

The purpose of this amendment is to simplify the application of the guideline by deleting interest from the calculation of tax loss. **The effective date of this amendment is November 1, 1989.**

233. Section 2T1.9(b) is amended by deleting "either of the following adjustments" and inserting in lieu thereof "more than one".

The purpose of this amendment is to correct a clerical error. **The effective date of this amendment is November 1, 1989.**.

234. The Commentary to section 2T1.9 captioned "Application Notes" is amended by deleting:

"2. The minimum base offense level is 10. If a tax loss from the conspiracy can be established under either §2T1.1 or §2T1.3 (whichever applies to the underlying conduct), and that tax loss corresponds to a higher offense level in the Tax Table (§2T4.1), use that higher base offense level.

3. The specific offense characteristics are in addition to those specified in §2T1.1 and §2T1.3.

4. Because the offense is a conspiracy, adjustments from Chapter Three, Part B (Role in the Offense) usually will apply.",

and inserting in lieu thereof:

"2. The base offense level is the offense level (base offense level plus any applicable specific offense characteristics) from §2T1.1 or §2T1.3 (whichever is applicable to the underlying conduct), if that offense level is greater than 10. Otherwise, the base offense level is 10.

3. Specific offense characteristics from §2T1.9(b) are to be applied to the base offense level determined under §2T1.9(a)(1) or (2).".

The purpose of this amendment is to clarify Application Notes 2 and 3. Application Note 4 (the content of which does not appear in any of the other guidelines covering conspiracy) is deleted as unnecessary. **The effective date of this amendment is November 1, 1989.**

235. The Commentary to §2T3.1 captioned "Application Notes" is amended in Note 2 by inserting "if the increase in market value due to importation is not readily ascertainable" immediately following "United States".

The purpose of this amendment is to clarify the commentary. **The effective date of this amendment is November 1, 1989.**

236. The Commentary to §2T3.2 is amended by inserting at the end:

"Application Note:

1. Particular attention should be given to those items for which entry is prohibited, limited, or restricted. Especially when such items are harmful or protective quotas are in effect, the duties evaded on such items may not adequately reflect the harm to society or protected industries resulting from their importation. In such instances, the court should impose a sentence above

the guideline. A sentence based upon an alternative measure of the 'duty' evaded, such as the increase in market value due to importation, or 25 percent of the items' fair market value in the United States if the increase in market value due to importation is not readily ascertainable, might be considered.".

The purpose of this amendment is to clarify the application of the guideline by adding the text from Application Note 2 of the Commentary to §2T3.1, which applies equally to this guideline section. **The effective date of this amendment is November 1, 1989.**

237. Section 2T4.1 is amended by deleting:

	"Tax Loss	Offense Level
(A)	less than $2,000	6
(B)	$2,000 - $5,000	7
(C)	$5,001 - $10,000	8
(D)	$10,001 - $20,000	9
(E)	$20,001 - $40,000	10
(F)	$40,001 - $80,000	11
(G)	$80,001 - $150,000	12
(H)	$150,001 - $300,000	13
(I)	$300,001 - $500,000	14
(J)	$500,001 - $1,000,000	15
(K)	$1,000,001 - $2,000,000	16
(L)	$2,000,001 - $5,000,000	17
(M)	more than $5,000,000	18",

and inserting in lieu thereof:

	"Tax Loss (Apply the Greatest)	Offense Level
(A)	$2,000 or less	6
(B)	More than $2,000	7
(C)	More than $5,000	8
(D)	More than $10,000	9
(E)	More than $20,000	10
(F)	More than $40,000	11
(G)	More than $70,000	12
(H)	More than $120,000	13
(I)	More than $200,000	14
(J)	More than $350,000	15
(K)	More than $500,000	16
(L)	More than $800,000	17
(M)	More than $1,500,000	18
(N)	More than $2,500,000	19
(O)	More than $5,000,000	20
(P)	More than $10,000,000	21
(Q)	More than $20,000,000	22
(R)	More than $40,000,000	23
(S)	More than $80,000,000	24.".

The purposes of this amendment are to increase the offense levels for offenses with larger losses in order to provide additional deterrence and better reflect the seriousness of the conduct, and to eliminate minor gaps in the table. **The effective date of this amendment is November 1, 1989.**

238. Section 2X1.1(b)(1) is amended by deleting "or solicitation" immediately following "If an attempt".

Section 2X1.1(b) is amended by deleting:

"(3) If a solicitation, and the statute treats solicitation identically with the object of the offense, do not apply §2X1.1(b)(1); i.e., the offense level for solicitation is the same as that for the object offense.",

and inserting in lieu thereof:

"(3)(A) If a solicitation, decrease by 3 levels unless the person solicited to commit or aid the offense completed all the acts he believed necessary for successful completion of the object offense or the circumstances demonstrate that the person was about to complete all such acts but for apprehension or interruption by some similar event beyond such person's control.

(B) If the statute treats solicitation of the offense identically with the object offense, do not apply subdivision (A) above; i.e., the offense level for solicitation is the same as that for the object offense.".

The current subsection (b)(1) does not clearly address how a solicitation is to be treated where the person solicited to commit the offense completes all the acts necessary for the successful completion of the offense. The purpose of this amendment is to clarify the treatment of such cases in a manner consistent with the treatment of attempts and conspiracies. **The effective date of this amendment is November 1, 1989.**

239. Section 2X1.1 is amended in the title by deleting "Not Covered by a Specific Guideline" and inserting in lieu thereof "(Not Covered by a Specific Offense Guideline)".

Section 2X1.1 is amended by inserting the following additional subsection:

"(c) Cross Reference

(1) When an attempt, solicitation, or conspiracy is expressly covered by another offense guideline section, apply that guideline section.".

The Commentary to §2X1.1 captioned "Application Notes" is amended by deleting:

"1. Certain attempts, conspiracies, and solicitations are covered by specific guidelines (e.g., §2A2.1 includes attempt, conspiracy, or solicitation to commit murder; §2A3.1 includes attempted criminal sexual abuse; and §2D1.4 includes attempts and conspiracies to commit controlled substance offenses). Section 2X1.1 applies only in the absence of a more specific guideline.",

and inserting in lieu thereof:

"1. Certain attempts, conspiracies, and solicitations are expressly covered by other offense guidelines.

Offense guidelines that expressly cover attempts include: §2A2.1 (Assault With Intent to Commit Murder; Conspiracy or Solicitation to Commit Murder; Attempted Murder); §2A3.1 (Criminal Sexual Abuse; Attempt or Assault with the Intent to Commit Criminal Sexual Abuse); §2A3.2 (Criminal Sexual Abuse of a Minor (Statutory Rape) or Attempt to Commit Such Acts); §2A3.3 (Criminal Sexual Abuse of a Ward or Attempt to Commit Such Acts); §2A3.4 (Abusive Sexual Contact or Attempt to Commit Abusive Sexual Contact);

§2A4.2 (Demanding or Receiving Ransom Money); §2A5.1 (Aircraft Piracy or Attempted Aircraft Piracy); §2C1.1 (Offering, Giving, Soliciting, or Receiving a Bribe; Extortion Under Color of Official Right); §2C1.2 (Offering, Giving, Soliciting, or Receiving a Gratuity); §2D1.4 (Attempts and Conspiracies); §2E5.1 (Offering, Accepting, or Soliciting a Bribe or Gratuity Affecting the Operation of an Employee Welfare or Pension Benefit Plan); §2N1.1 (Tampering or Attempting to Tamper Involving Risk of Death or Serious Injury); §2Q1.4 (Tampering or Attempted Tampering with Public Water System).

Offense guidelines that expressly cover conspiracies include: §2A2.1 (Assault With Intent to Commit Murder; Conspiracy or Solicitation to Commit Murder; Attempted Murder); §2D1.4 (Attempts and Conspiracies); §2H1.2 (Conspiracy to Interfere with Civil Rights); §2T1.9 (Conspiracy to Impair, Impede or Defeat Tax).

Offense guidelines that expressly cover solicitations include: §2A2.1 (Assault with Intent to Commit Murder; Conspiracy or Solicitation to Commit Murder; Attempted Murder); §2C1.1 (Offering, Giving, Soliciting, or Receiving a Bribe; Extortion Under Color of Official Right); §2C1.2 (Offering, Giving, Soliciting, or Receiving a Gratuity); §2E5.1 (Offering, Accepting, or Soliciting a Bribe or Gratuity Affecting the Operation of an Employee Welfare or Pension Benefit Plan).".

The purpose of this amendment is to clarify the guideline. **The effective date of this amendment is November 1, 1989.**

240. The Commentary to §2X1.1 captioned "Application Notes" is amended by deleting:

"4. If the defendant was convicted of conspiracy or solicitation and also for the completed offense, the conviction for the conspiracy or solicitation shall be imposed to run concurrently with the sentence for the object offense, except in cases where it is otherwise specifically provided for by the guidelines or by law. 28 U.S.C. § 994(l)(2).".

The purpose of this amendment is to delete an application note that does not apply to any determination under this section. The circumstances which this application note addresses are covered under Chapter Three, Part D and Chapter Five, Part G. **The effective date of this amendment is November 1, 1989.**

241. The Commentary to §2X1.1 captioned "Application Notes" is amended by inserting the following additional note:

"4. In certain cases, the participants may have completed (or have been about to complete but for apprehension or interruption) all of the acts necessary for the successful completion of part, but not all, of the intended offense. In such cases, the offense level for the count (or group of closely-related multiple counts) is whichever of the following is greater: the offense level for the intended offense minus 3 levels (under §2X1.1(b)(1), (b)(2), or (b)(3)(A)), or the offense level for the part of the offense for which the necessary acts were completed (or about to be completed but for apprehension or interruption). For example, where the intended offense was the theft of $800,000 but the participants completed (or were about to complete) only the acts necessary to steal $30,000, the offense level is the offense level for the theft of $800,000 minus 3 levels, or the offense level for the theft of $30,000, whichever is greater.

In the case of multiple counts that are not closely-related counts, whether the 3-level reduction under §2X1.1(b)(1) or (2) applies is determined separately for each count.".

The purpose of this amendment is to clarify how the guidelines are to be applied to partially completed offenses. The effective date of this amendment is November 1, 1989.

242. The Commentary to §2X1.1 captioned "Application Notes" is amended in the last sentence of Note 2 by deleting "intended" and inserting in lieu thereof "attempted".

The purpose of this amendment is to clarify the commentary. **The effective date of this amendment is November 1, 1989.**

243. The Commentary to §2X3.1 captioned "Application Notes" is amended in Note 1 by deleting:

"'Underlying offense' means the offense as to which the defendant was an accessory.",

and inserting in lieu thereof:

"'Underlying offense' means the offense as to which the defendant is convicted of being an accessory. Apply the base offense level plus any applicable specific offense characteristics that were known, or reasonably should have been known, by the defendant; see Application Note 1 of the Commentary to §1B1.3 (Relevant Conduct).".

The purpose of this amendment is to clarify the commentary. **The effective date of this amendment is November 1, 1989.**

244. The Commentary to §2X4.1 captioned "Application Notes" is amended in Note 1 by deleting:

"'Underlying offense' means the offense as to which the misprision was committed.",

and inserting in lieu thereof:

"'Underlying offense' means the offense as to which the defendant is convicted of committing the misprision. Apply the base offense level plus any applicable specific offense characteristics that were known, or reasonably should have been known, by the defendant; see Application Note 1 of the Commentary to §1B1.3 (Relevant Conduct).".

The purpose of this amendment is to clarify the commentary. **The effective date of this amendment is November 1, 1989.**

245. Section 3A1.1 is amended by deleting "the victim" wherever it appears and inserting in lieu thereof in each instance "a victim", and by inserting "otherwise" immediately before "particularly".

The Commentary to §3A1.1 captioned Application Notes is amended in Note 1 by deleting:

"any offense where the victim's vulnerability played any part in the defendant's decision to commit the offense",

and inserting in lieu thereof:

"offenses where an unusually vulnerable victim is made a target of criminal activity by the defendant", and by deleting:

"sold fraudulent securities to the general public and one of the purchasers",

and inserting in lieu thereof:

"sold fraudulent securities by mail to the general public and one of the victims".

The purpose of the amendment is to clarify the guideline and commentary. **The effective date of this amendment is November 1, 1989.**

246. Section 3A1.2 is amended by deleting:

"any law-enforcement or corrections officer, any other official as defined in 18 U.S.C. § 1114, or a member of the immediate family thereof, and",

and inserting in lieu thereof:

"a law enforcement or corrections officer; a former law enforcement or corrections officer; an officer or employee included in 18 U.S.C. § 1114; a former officer or employee included in 18 U.S.C. § 1114; or a member of the immediate family of any of the above, and".

The purpose of this amendment is to expand the coverage of this provision to reflect a statutory revision effected by Section 6487 of the Anti-Drug Abuse Act of 1988. **The effective date of this amendment is November 1, 1989.**

247. Section 3A1.2 is amended by deleting "If the victim" and inserting in lieu thereof:

"If--

(a) the victim",

and by deleting "crime was motivated by such status, increase by 3 levels." and inserting in lieu thereof:

"offense of conviction was motivated by such status; or

(b) during the course of the offense or immediate flight therefrom, the defendant or a person for whose conduct the defendant is otherwise accountable, knowing or having reasonable cause to believe that a person was a law enforcement or corrections officer, assaulted such officer in a manner creating a substantial risk of serious bodily injury,

increase by 3 levels.".

The Commentary to §3A1.2 captioned "Application Notes" is amended by inserting the following additional notes:

"4. 'Motivated by such status' in subdivision (a) means that the offense of conviction was motivated by the fact that the victim was a law enforcement or corrections officer or other person covered under 18 U.S.C. § 1114, or a member of the immediate family thereof. This adjustment would not apply, for example, where both the defendant and victim were employed by the same government agency and the offense was motivated by a personal dispute.

5. Subdivision (b) applies in circumstances tantamount to aggravated assault against a law enforcement or corrections officer, committed in the course of, or in immediate flight following, another offense, such as bank robbery. While this subdivision may apply in connection with a variety of offenses that are not by nature targeted against official victims, its applicability is limited to assaultive conduct against law enforcement or corrections officers that is sufficiently serious to create at least a 'substantial risk of serious bodily injury' and that is proximate in time to the commission of the offense.

6. The phrase 'substantial risk of serious bodily injury' in subdivision (b) is a threshold level of harm that includes any more serious injury that was risked, as well as actual serious bodily injury (or more serious harm) if it occurs.".

The purpose of the amendment is to set forth more clearly the categories of cases to which this adjustment is intended to apply. **The effective date of this amendment is November 1, 1989.**

248. The Commentary to §3A1.2 captioned "Application Notes" is amended in Note 3 by inserting the following additional sentences at the end:

"In most cases, the offenses to which subdivision (a) will apply will be from Chapter Two, Part A (Offenses Against the Person). The only offense guideline in Chapter Two, Part A that specifically incorporates this factor is §2A2.4 (Obstructing or Impeding Officers).".

The purpose of this amendment is to clarify the application of the guideline. **The effective date of this amendment is November 1, 1989.**

249. Section 3A1.3 is amended by deleting "the victim of a crime" and inserting in lieu thereof "a victim".

The Commentary to §3A1.3 captioned "Application Notes" is amended in Note 2 by deleting "the victim" and inserting in lieu thereof "a victim".

The purpose of this amendment is to clarify the guideline. **The effective date of this amendment is November 1, 1989.**

250. The Commentary to §3A1.3 captioned "Application Notes" is amended by inserting the following additional note:

"3. If the restraint was sufficiently egregious, an upward departure may be warranted. <u>See</u> §5K2.4 (Abduction or Unlawful Restraint).".

The purpose of this amendment is to clarify the relationship between §3A1.3 and §5K2.4. **The effective date of this amendment is November 1, 1989.**

251. Section 3C1.1 is amended by deleting "from Chapter Two" immediately following "the offense level".

The purpose of this amendment is to delete an incorrect reference. **The effective date of this amendment is November 1, 1989.**

252. The Commentary to §3C1.1 captioned "Application Notes" is amended in Note 4 by deleting:

> ", except in determining the combined offense level as specified in Chapter Three, Part D (Multiple Counts). Under §3D1.2(e), a count for obstruction will be grouped with the count for the underlying offense. Ordinarily, the offense level for that Group of Closely Related Counts will be the offense level for the underlying offense, as increased by the 2-level adjustment specified by this section. In some instances, however, the offense level for the obstruction offense may be higher, in which case that will be the offense level for the Group. See §3D1.3(a). In cases in which a significant further obstruction occurred during the investigation or prosecution of an obstruction offense itself (one of the above listed offenses), an upward departure may be warranted (e.g., where a witness to an obstruction offense is threatened during the course of the prosecution for the obstruction offense).",

and inserting in lieu thereof:

> "to the offense level for that offense except where a significant further obstruction occurred during the investigation or prosecution of the obstruction offense itself (e.g., where the defendant threatened a witness during the course of the prosecution for the obstruction offense). Where the defendant is convicted both of the obstruction offense and the underlying offense, the count for the obstruction offense will be grouped with the count for the underlying offense under subsection (c) of §3D1.2 (Groups of Closely-Related Counts). The offense level for that Group of Closely-Related Counts will be the offense level for the underlying offense increased by the 2-level adjustment specified by this section, or the offense level for the obstruction offense, whichever is greater.".

The purpose of this amendment is to resolve an inconsistency between the commentary in this section and the Commentaries in Chapter Two, Part J. **The effective date of this amendment is November 1, 1989.**

253. Section 3D1.2(b)(3) is amended by deleting "§ 994(u)" and inserting in lieu thereof "§ 994(v)".

Section 3D1.2(d) is amended in the second paragraph by deleting ", 2D1.3", and in the third paragraph by deleting ", 2G3.2" and ", 2P1.4".

The purposes of this amendment are to correct an erroneous reference, and to delete references to two guidelines covering petty offenses that have been deleted and to a guideline that has been deleted by consolidation with another guideline. **The effective date of this amendment is November 1, 1989.**

254. The Commentary to §3D1.2 captioned "Application Notes" is amended in Note 3 by deleting "(6)", "(7)", and "(8)" and inserting in lieu thereof "(5)", "(6)", and "(7)" respectively.

The purpose of this amendment is to correct a clerical error. **The effective date of this amendment is November 1, 1989.**

255. The Commentary to §3D1.2 captioned "Application Notes" is amended in Note 9 by inserting immediately following the second sentence: "See §1B1.2(d) and accompanying commentary.".

The purpose of this amendment is to cross reference the newly created guideline subsection dealing with a multiple object conspiracy. **The effective date of this amendment is November 1, 1989.**

256. The Commentary to §3D1.2 captioned "Background" is amended in the second paragraph by deleting:

> "In general, counts are grouped together only when they involve both the same victim (or societal harm in 'victimless' offenses) and the same or contemporaneous transactions, except as provided in §3D1.2(c) or (d).",

and inserting in lieu thereof:

> "Counts involving different victims (or societal harms in the case of 'victimless' crimes) are grouped together only as provided in subsection (c) or (d).".

The purpose of this amendment is to clarify the commentary. **The effective date of this amendment is November 1, 1989.**

257. Section 3D1.3(b) is amended in the second sentence by deleting "varying" immediately following "involve", and by inserting "of the same general type to which different guidelines apply (e.g., theft and fraud)" immediately following "offenses".

The purpose of this amendment is to enhance the clarity of the guideline. **The effective date of this amendment is November 1, 1989.**

258. The Commentary to §3E1.1 captioned "Application Notes" is amended by deleting:

> "4. An adjustment under this section is not warranted where a defendant perjures himself, suborns perjury, or otherwise obstructs the trial or the administration of justice (see §3C1.1), regardless of other factors.",

and inserting in lieu thereof:

> "4. Conduct resulting in an enhancement under §3C1.1 (Willfully Obstructing or Impeding Proceedings) ordinarily indicates that the defendant has not accepted responsibility for his criminal conduct. There may, however, be extraordinary cases in which adjustments under both §§3C1.1 and 3E1.1 may apply.".

The purposes of this amendment are to provide for extraordinary cases in which adjustments under both §3C1.1 and §3E1.1 are appropriate, and to clarify the reference to obstructive conduct. **The effective date of this amendment is November 1, 1989.**

259. Section 4A1.1(e) is amended by inserting "or while in imprisonment or escape status on such a sentence" immediately before the period at the end of the first sentence.

The Commentary to §4A1.1 captioned "Application Notes" is amended in the second sentence of Note 5 by deleting "still in confinement" and inserting in lieu thereof "in imprisonment or escape status".

The purpose of this amendment is to clarify that subsection (e) applies to defendants who are still in confinement status at the time of the instant offense (e.g., a defendant who commits the instant offense while in prison or on escape status). **The effective date of this amendment is November 1, 1989.**

260. The Commentary to §4A1.1 captioned "Application Notes" is amended in Note 4 by inserting the following additional sentence at the end: "For the purposes of this item, a 'criminal justice sentence' means a sentence countable under §4A1.2 (Definitions and Instructions for Computing Criminal History).".

The purpose of this amendment is to clarify the application of the guideline. **The effective date of this amendment is November 1, 1989.**

261. The Commentary to §4A1.1 captioned "Background" is amended in the third paragraph by inserting "a" immediately before "criminal", and by deleting "control" and inserting in lieu thereof "sentence".

The purpose of this amendment is to conform the commentary to the guideline. **The effective date of this amendment is November 1, 1989.**

262. Section 4A1.2(e)(1) is amended by inserting ", whenever imposed," immediately before "that resulted", and by deleting "defendant's incarceration" and inserting in lieu thereof "defendant being incarcerated".

The purpose of this amendment is to clarify that "resulted in the defendant's incarceration" applies to any part of the defendant's imprisonment and not only to the commencement of the defendant's imprisonment. **The effective date of this amendment is November 1, 1989.**

263. Section 4A1.2(e) is amended by inserting the following additional subdivision:

"(4) The applicable time period for certain sentences resulting from offenses committed prior to age eighteen is governed by §4A1.2(d)(2).".

The purpose of this amendment is to clarify the relationship between §4A1.2(d)(2) and (e). **The effective date of this amendment is November 1, 1989.**

264. Section 4A1.2(f) is amended by inserting ", or a plea of nolo contendere," immediately following "admission of guilt".

The purpose of this amendment is to clarify that a plea of nolo contendere is equivalent to a finding of guilt for the purpose of §4A1.2(f). **The effective date of this amendment is November 1, 1989.**

265. The Commentary to §4A1.2 captioned "Application Notes" is amended in Note 8 by deleting "4A1.2(e)" and inserting in lieu thereof "4A1.2(d)(2) and (e)", and by inserting immediately following the first sentence:

"As used in §4A1.2(d)(2) and (e), the term 'commencement of the instant offense' includes any relevant conduct. See §1B1.3 (Relevant Conduct).".

The purposes of this amendment are to correct a clerical error by inserting a reference to §4A1.2(d)(2), and to clarify that "commencement of the instant offense" includes any relevant conduct. **The effective date of this amendment is November 1, 1989.**

266. Section 4B1.1 is amended by deleting "Offense Level" and inserting in lieu thereof "Offense Level*", and by inserting at the end:

"*If an adjustment from §3E1.1 (Acceptance of Responsibility) applies, decrease the offense level by 2 levels.".

The purpose of this amendment is to authorize the application of §3E1.1 (Acceptance of Responsibility) to the determination of the offense level under this section to provide an incentive for the acceptance of responsibility by defendants subject to the career offender provision. **The effective date of this amendment is November 1, 1989.**

267. The Commentary to §4B1.1 captioned "Application Note" is amended in Note 1 by deleting "felony conviction" and inserting in lieu thereof "two prior felony convictions".

The Commentary to §4B1.1 captioned "Application Note" is amended by inserting the following additional note:

> "2. 'Offense Statutory Maximum' refers to the maximum term of imprisonment authorized for the offense of conviction that is a crime of violence or controlled substance offense. If more than one count of conviction is of a crime of violence or controlled substance offense, use the maximum authorized term of imprisonment for the count that authorizes the greatest maximum term of imprisonment.",

and in the caption by deleting "Note" and inserting in lieu thereof "Notes".

The Commentary to §4B1.1 captioned "Background" is amended by deleting:

> "128 Cong. Rec. 12792, 97th Cong., 2d Sess. (1982) ('Career Criminals' amendment No. 13 by Senator Kennedy), 12796 (explanation of amendment), and 12798 (remarks by Senator Kennedy)",

and inserting in lieu thereof:

> "128 Cong. Rec. 26, 511-12 (1982) (text of 'Career Criminals' amendment by Senator Kennedy), 26, 515 (brief summary of amendment), 26, 517-18 (statement of Senator Kennedy)".

The purposes of this amendment are to clarify the operation of the guideline and to provide a citation to the more readily available edition of the Congressional Record. **The effective date of this amendment is November 1, 1989.**

268. Section 4B1.2(1) is amended by deleting "as used in this provision is defined under 18 U.S.C. § 16" and inserting in lieu thereof:

> "means any offense under federal or state law punishable by imprisonment for a term exceeding one year that --
>
> (i) has as an element the use, attempted use, or threatened use of physical force against the person of another, or
>
> (ii) is burglary of a dwelling, arson, or extortion, involves use of explosives, or otherwise involves conduct that presents a serious potential risk of physical injury to another".

Section 4B1.2(2) is amended by deleting "as used in this provision" immediately before "means", and by deleting "identified in 21 U.S.C. §§841, 845(b), 856, 952(a), 955, 955(a), 959; and similar offenses" and inserting in lieu thereof:

> "under a federal or state law prohibiting the manufacture, import, export, or distribution of a controlled substance (or a counterfeit substance) or the possession of a controlled substance (or a counterfeit substance) with intent to manufacture, import, export, or distribute".

The Commentary to §4B1.2 captioned "Application Notes" is amended by deleting:

"1. 'Crime of violence' is defined in 18 U.S.C. § 16 to mean an offense that has as an element the use, attempted use, or threatened use of physical force against the person or property of another, or any other offense that is a felony and that by its nature involves a substantial risk that physical force against the person or property of another may be used in committing the offense. The Commission interprets this as follows: murder, manslaughter, kidnapping, aggravated assault, extortionate extension of credit, forcible sex offenses, arson, or robbery are covered by this provision. Other offenses are covered only if the conduct for which the defendant was specifically convicted meets the above definition. For example, conviction for an escape accomplished by force or threat of injury would be covered; conviction for an escape by stealth would not be covered. Conviction for burglary of a dwelling would be covered; conviction for burglary of other structures would not be covered.

2. 'Controlled substance offense' includes any federal or state offense that is substantially similar to any of those listed in subsection (2) of the guideline. These offenses include manufacturing, importing, distributing, dispensing, or possessing with intent to manufacture, import, distribute, or dispense, a controlled substance (or a counterfeit substance). This definition also includes aiding and abetting, conspiring, or attempting to commit such offenses, and other offenses that are substantially equivalent to the offenses listed.",

and inserting in lieu thereof:

"1. The terms 'crime of violence' and 'controlled substance offense' include the offenses of aiding and abetting, conspiring, and attempting to commit such offenses.

2. 'Crime of violence' includes murder, manslaughter, kidnapping, aggravated assault, forcible sex offenses, robbery, arson, extortion, extortionate extension of credit, and burglary of a dwelling. Other offenses are included where (A) that offense has as an element the use attempted use, or threatened use, of physical force against the person of another, or (B) the conduct set forth in the count of which the defendant was convicted involved use of explosives or, by its nature, presented a serious potential risk of physical injury to another.".

The caption of §4B1.2 is amended by deleting "Definitions" and inserting in lieu thereof "Definitions of Terms Used in Section 4B1.1".

The Commentary to §4B1.2 captioned "Application Notes" is amended in Note 4 by deleting "§4A1.2(e) (Applicable Time Period), §4A1.2(h) (Foreign Sentences), and §4A1.2(j) (Expunged Convictions)" and inserting in lieu thereof "§4A1.2 (Definitions and Instructions for Computing Criminal History)", and by deleting the last sentence as follows: "Also applicable is the Commentary to §4A1.2 pertaining to invalid convictions.".

The purpose of this amendment is to clarify the definitions of crime of violence and controlled substance offense used in this guideline. The definition of crime of violence used in this amendment is derived from 18 U.S.C. § 924(e). In addition, the amendment clarifies that all pertinent definitions and instructions in §4A1.2 apply to this section. **The effective date of this amendment is November 1, 1989.**

269. Section 4B1.3 is amended by deleting "from which he derived a substantial portion of his income" and inserting in lieu thereof "engaged in as a livelihood".

The Commentary to §4B1.3 captioned "Application Note" is amended by deleting "Note" and inserting in lieu thereof "Notes", and by inserting the following additional note:

"2. 'Engaged in as a livelihood' means that (1) the defendant derived income from the pattern of criminal conduct that in any twelve-month period exceeded 2,000 times the then existing hourly minimum wage under federal law (currently 2,000 times the hourly minimum wage under federal law is $6,700); and (2) the totality of circumstances shows that such criminal conduct was the defendant's primary occupation in that twelve-month period (e.g., the defendant engaged in criminal conduct rather than regular, legitimate employment; or the defendant's legitimate employment was merely a front for his criminal conduct).".

The Commentary to §4B1.3 captioned "Application Notes" is amended in Note 1 by deleting the last sentence as follows: "This guideline is not intended to apply to minor offenses.".

The Commentary to §4B1.3 captioned "Background" is amended by deleting "proportion" and inserting in lieu thereof "portion".

The purpose of this amendment is to provide a better definition of the intended scope of this enhancement. Compare, for example, United States v. Kerr, 686 F. Supp. 1174 (W.D. Penn. 1988) with United States v. Rivera, 694 F. Supp. 1105 (S.D.N.Y. 1988). The first prong of the definition in application Note 2 above is derived from former 18 U.S.C. § 3575, the provision from which the statutory instruction underlying this guideline (28 U.S.C. § 994 (i)(2)) was itself derived. **The effective date of this amendment is November 1, 1989.**

270. Chapter Five, Part A, is amended in the Sentencing Table by deleting "0-1, 0-2, 0-3, 0-4, and 0-5" wherever it appears, and inserting in each instance "0-6".

Chapter Five, Part A, is amended in the Sentencing Table by inserting "(in months of imprisonment)" immediately under the title "Sentencing Table", by inserting "(Criminal History Points)" immediately following the caption "Criminal History Category", and by enclosing in parentheses each of the six sets of criminal history points displayed under that caption.

This amendment provides that the maximum of the guideline range is six months wherever the minimum of the guideline range is zero months. The court has discretion to impose a sentence of up to 6 months imprisonment for a Class B misdemeanor (Class B or C misdemeanors and infractions are not covered by the guidelines; see §1B1.9). It appears anomalous that the Commission guidelines allow less discretion for certain felonies and Class A misdemeanors. In fact, in certain cases, a plea to a reduced charge of a Class B misdemeanor could result in a higher potential sentence because the sentence for the felony or Class A misdemeanor might be restricted to less than 6 months by the guidelines. This can happen when the Sentencing Table provides a guideline range of 0-1 month, 0-2 months, 0-3, 0-4, or 0-5 months. These very narrow ranges are not required by statute, which allows a 6 month guideline range in such cases. This anomaly is removed by amending the guideline table to provide that whenever the lower limit of the guideline range is 0 months, the upper limit of the guideline range is six months.

In addtion, this amendment makes minor editorial improvements to the title and caption of the Sentencing Table. **The effective date of this amendment is November 1, 1989.**

271. Section 5B1.4(b)(20) is amended by inserting ", but only as a substitute for imprisonment" immediately following "release".

Section 5C2.1(c)(2) is amended by deleting "or community confinement" and inserting in lieu thereof ", community confinement, or home detention".

Section 5C2.1(c)(3) is amended by inserting "or home detention" immediately following "community confinement".

Section 5C2.1(d)(2) is amended by inserting "or home detention" immediately following "community confinement".

Section 5C2.1(e) is amended by inserting the following additional subdivision:

> "(3) One day of home detention for one day of imprisonment.",

and by deleting the period at the end of subsection (e)(2) and inserting a semicolon in lieu thereof.

The Commentary to §5C2.1 captioned "Application Notes" is amended in the first sentence of the second subparagraph of Note 3 by deleting "intermittent confinement or community confinement, or combination of intermittent and community confinement," and inserting in lieu thereof "intermittent confinement, community confinement, or home detention, or combination of intermittent confinement, community confinement, and home detention,".

The Commentary to §5C2.1 captioned "Application Notes" is amended in the second sentence of the second subparagraph of Note 3 by deleting "intermittent or community confinement" and inserting in lieu thereof "intermittent confinement, community confinement, or home detention".

The Commentary to §5C2.1 captioned "Application Notes" is amended in the third subparagraph of Note 3 by inserting "or home detention" immediately following "community confinement", wherever the latter appears.

The Commentary to §5C2.1 captioned "Application Notes" is amended in the last paragraph of Note 3 by inserting "or home detention" immediately following "community confinement", wherever the latter appears.

The Commentary to §5C2.1 captioned "Application Notes" is amended in Note 4 by inserting "or home detention" immediately following "community confinement", wherever the latter appears.

The Commentary to §5C2.1 captioned "Application Notes" is amended in Note 5 by deleting the last sentence as follows: "Home detention may not be substituted for imprisonment.".

Section 5F5.2 is amended by inserting ", but only as a substitute for imprisonment" immediately following "release".

The Commentary to §5F5.2 captioned "Application Notes" is amended in Note 1 by deleting:

> "'Home detention' means a program of confinement and supervision that restricts the defendant to his place of residence continuously, or during specified hours, enforced by appropriate means of surveillance by the probation office. The judge may also impose other conditions of probation or supervised release appropriate to effectuate home detention. If the confinement is only during specified hours, the defendant shall engage exclusively in gainful employment, community service or treatment during the non-residential hours.",

and inserting in lieu thereof:

> "'Home detention' means a program of confinement and supervision that restricts the defendant to his place of residence continuously, except for authorized absences, enforced by appropriate means of surveillance by the probation office. When an order of home detention is imposed, the defendant is required to be in his place of residence at all times except for approved absences for gainful employment, community service, religious services, medical care, educational or training programs, and such other times as may be specifically authorized. Electronic monitoring is an appropriate means of surveillance and ordinarily should be used in connection with

home detention. However, alternative means of surveillance may be used so long as they are as effective as electronic monitoring.".

The Commentary to §5F5.2 captioned "Application Notes" is amended in Note 2 by deleting:

"Home detention generally should not be imposed for a period in excess of six months. However, a longer term may be appropriate for disabled, elderly or extremely ill defendants who would otherwise be imprisoned.",

and inserting in lieu thereof:

"The court may impose other conditions of probation or supervised release appropriate to effectuate home detention. If the court concludes that the amenities available in the residence of a defendant would cause home detention not to be sufficiently punitive, the court may limit the amenities available.".

The Commentary to §5F5.2 captioned "Application Notes" is amended by inserting the following additional note:

"3. The defendant's place of residence, for purposes of home detention, need not be the place where the defendant previously resided. It may be any place of residence, so long as the owner of the residence (and any other person(s) from whom consent is necessary) agrees to any conditions that may be imposed by the court, e.g., conditions that a monitoring system be installed, that there will be no 'call forwarding' or 'call waiting' services, or that there will be no cordless telephones or answering machines.".

The Commentary to §5F5.2 is amended by inserting at the end:

"Background: The Commission has concluded that the surveillance necessary for effective use of home detention ordinarily requires electronic monitoring. However, in some cases home detention may effectively be enforced without electronic monitoring, e.g., when the defendant is physically incapacitated, or where some other effective means of surveillance is available. Accordingly, the Commission has not required that electronic monitoring be a necessary condition for home detention. Nevertheless, before ordering home detention without electronic monitoring, the court should be confident that an alternative form of surveillance will be equally effective.

In the usual case, the Commission assumes that a condition requiring that the defendant seek and maintain gainful employment will be imposed when home detention is ordered.".

Section 5B1.1(a)(2) is amended by deleting "or community confinement" and inserting in lieu thereof ", community confinement, or home detention".

The Commentary to §5B1.1 captioned "Application Notes" is amended in Note 1 by inserting ", home detention," immediately after "community confinement" wherever the latter appears.

Chapter One, Part A, section 4(d) is amended in the third sentence of the third paragraph by deleting "or intermittent confinement" and inserting in lieu thereof ", intermittent confinement, or home detention", and in the fourth sentence of the third paragraph by inserting "or home detention" immediately following "of community confinement".

The purpose of this amendment is to conform the guidelines with Section 7305 of the Anti-Drug Abuse Act of 1988. **The effective date of this amendment is November 1, 1989.**

272. Section 5B1.4(b) is amended by inserting the following additional paragraph at the end:

"(25) Curfew

If the court concludes that restricting the defendant to his place of residence during evening and nighttime hours is necessary to provide just punishment for the offense, to protect the public from crimes that the defendant might commit during those hours, or to assist in the rehabilitation of the defendant, a condition of curfew is recommended. Electronic monitoring may be used as a means of surveillance to ensure compliance with a curfew order.".

Section 5B1.4 is amended by inserting the following commentary:

"Commentary

Application Note:

1. Home detention, as defined by §5F5.2, may only be used as a substitute for imprisonment. See §5C2.1 (Imposition of a Term of Imprisonment). Under home detention, the defendant, with specified exceptions, is restricted to his place of residence during all non-working hours. Curfew, which limits the defendant to his place of residence during evening and nighttime hours, is less restrictive than home detention and may be imposed as a condition of probation whether or not imprisonment could have been ordered.".

The purposes of this amendment are to set forth the conditions under which curfew is a recommended condition of probation and clarify that electronic monitoring may be used as a means of surveillance in connection with an order of curfew. **The effective date of this amendment is November 1, 1989.**

273. Section 5B1.3(c) is amended by inserting immediately before the period at the end of the first sentence:

", unless the court finds on the record that extraordinary circumstances exist that would make such a condition plainly unreasonable, in which event the court shall impose one or more of the other conditions set forth under 18 U.S.C. § 3563(b)".

The purpose of this amendment is to conform the guideline to a statutory revision. **The effective date of this amendment is November 1, 1989.**

274. Section 5B1.3(a) is amended by inserting at the end: "The court shall also impose a condition that the defendant not possess illegal controlled substances. 18 U.S.C. § 3563(a)(3).".

Section 5B1.3 is amended by inserting the following commentary:

"Commentary

A broader form of the condition required under 18 U.S.C. § 3563(a)(3) (pertaining to possession of controlled substances) is set forth as recommended condition (7) at §5B1.4 (Recommended Conditions of Probation and Supervised Release).".

The purpose of this amendment is to reference a mandatory condition of probation added by Section 7303 of the Anti-Drug Abuse Act of 1988. **The effective date of this amendment is November 1, 1989.**

275. Section 5C2.1(e) is amended by deleting "Thirty days" and inserting in lieu thereof "One day", by deleting "one month" wherever it appears and inserting in lieu thereof in each instance "one day", and by deleting "One month" and inserting in lieu thereof "One day".

The purpose of this amendment is to enhance the internal consistency of the guidelines. **The effective date of this amendment is November 1, 1989.**

276. Section 5D3.3 is amended by deleting:

"(b) In order to fulfill any authorized purposes of sentencing, the court may impose other conditions reasonably related to (1) the nature and circumstances of the offense, and (2) the history and characteristics of the defendant. 18 U.S.C. § 3583(d).",

and inserting in lieu thereof:

"(b) The court may impose other conditions of supervised release, to the extent that such conditions are reasonably related to (1) the nature and circumstances of the offense and the history and characteristics of the defendant, and (2) the need for the sentence imposed to afford adequate deterrence to criminal conduct, to protect the public from further crimes of the defendant, and to provide the defendant with needed educational or vocational training, medical care, or other correctional treatment in the most effective manner. 18 U.S.C. §§ 3553(a)(2) and 3583(d).".

The purposes of this amendment are to clarify the guideline and conform it to the statute as amended by Section 7108 of the Anti-Drug Abuse Act of 1988. **The effective date of this amendment is November 1, 1989.**

277. Section 5D3.3(a) is amended by inserting at the end: "The court shall also impose a condition that the defendant not possess illegal controlled substances. 18 U.S.C. § 3563(a)(3).".

The Commentary to §5D3.3 captioned "Background" is amended by inserting the following additional sentence at the end:

"A broader form of the condition required under 18 U.S.C. § 3563(a)(3) (pertaining to possession of controlled substances) is set forth as recommended condition (7) at §5B1.4 (Recommended Conditions of Probation and Supervised Release).".

The purpose of this amendment is to reference a mandatory condition of supervised release added by Section 7303 of the Anti-Drug Abuse Act of 1988. **The effective date of this amendment is November 1, 1989.**

278. Section 5E4.1 is amended by inserting the following additional subsection:

"(c) With the consent of the victim of the offense, the court may order a defendant to perform services for the benefit of the victim in lieu of monetary restitution or in conjunction therewith. 18 U.S.C. § 3663(b)(4).".

The purpose of this amendment is to insert language previously contained in §5F5.3(b) where it had been erroneously placed. **The effective date of this amendment is November 1, 1989.**

279. The Commentary to §5E4.1 captioned "Background" is amended in the first paragraph by deleting:

"See S. Rep. No. 225, 98th Cong., 1st Sess. 95-96.",

and inserting in lieu thereof:

"See 18 U.S.C. § 3563(b)(3) as amended by Section 7110 of Pub. L. No. 100-690 (1988).".

This amendment replaces a reference to legislative history with a citation to a revised statute. Section 7110 of the Anti-Drug Abuse Act of 1988 confirms the authority of a sentencing court to impose restitution as a condition of probation. Previously, such authority was inferred from 18 U.S.C. §3563(b)(20) (defendant may be ordered to "satisfy such other conditions as the court may impose") and from legislative history. **The effective date of this amendment is November 1, 1989.**

280. Section 5E4.2(a) is amended by deleting the second sentence as follows:

"If the guideline for the offense in Chapter Two prescribes a different rule for imposing fines, that rule takes precedence over this subsection.".

Section 5E4.2(b) is amended by inserting at the end:

"If, however, the guideline for the offense in Chapter Two provides a specific rule for imposing a fine, that rule takes precedence over subsection (c) of this section.".

The purpose of this amendment is to clarify the guideline. The last sentence of current §5E4.2(a) is in the wrong place. This amendment moves the content of this sentence to subsection (b) where it belongs. **The effective date of this amendment is November 1, 1989.**

281. Section 5E4.2(c)(3) is amended by deleting:

"1	$ 25	$ 250
2-3	$100	$1,000
4-5	$250	$2,500",

and inserting in lieu thereof:

"3 and below	$100	$5,000
4-5	$250	$5,000".

The purpose of this amendment is to increase the maximum in the fine table for offense levels 5 and below to $5,000, an amount equal to the maximum fine authorized for a petty offense. Moreover, because the guidelines now cover only felonies and class A misdemeanors, the minimum fine guideline is increased to $100. **The effective date of this amendment is November 1, 1989.**

282. The Commentary to Section 5E4.3 captioned "Background" is amended in the first paragraph by inserting at the end:

"Under the Victims of Crime Act, as amended by Section 7085 of the Anti-Drug Abuse Act of 1988, the court is required to impose assessments in the following amounts with respect to offenses committed on or after November 18, 1988:

Individuals:

$5, if the defendant is an individual convicted of an infraction or a Class C misdemeanor;
$10, if the defendant is an individual convicted of a Class B misdemeanor;
$25, if the defendant is an individual convicted of a Class A misdemeanor; and
$50, if the defendant is an individual convicted of a felony.

Organizations:

$50, if the defendant is an organization convicted of a Class B misdemeanor;
$125, if the defendant is an organization convicted of a Class A misdemeanor; and
$200, if the defendant is an organization convicted of a felony. 18 U.S.C. § 3013.",

and in the second paragraph by deleting "The Act requires the court" and inserting in lieu thereof "With respect to offenses committed prior to November 18, 1988, the court is required".

The purpose of this amendment is to conform the commentary to the statute as amended by Section 7085 of the Anti-Drug Abuse Act of 1988. **The effective date of this amendment is November 1, 1989.**

283. Section 5F5.3(a) is amended by deleting "(a)", and by inserting "and sentenced to probation" immediately following "felony".

Section 5F5.3(b) is amended by deleting:

"(b) With the consent of the victim of the offense, the court may order a defendant to perform services for the benefit of the victim in lieu of monetary restitution. 18 U.S.C. § 3663(b)(4).".

The purposes of this amendment are to correct an erroneous statement in §5F5.3(a) and to delete §5F5.3(b), which deals with restitution, and therefore should appear at §5E4.1. **The effective date of this amendment is November 1, 1989.**

284. The Commentary to §5F5.4 captioned "Background" is amended by deleting the third paragraph as follows:

"The legislative history indicates that, although the sanction was designed to provide actual notice to victims, a court might properly limit notice to only those victims who could be most readily identified, if to do otherwise would unduly prolong or complicate the sentencing process.".

The purpose of this amendment is to delete an unnecessary statement that could be subject to misinterpretation. **The effective date of this amendment is November 1, 1989.**

285. Section 5F5.5(a) is amended by deleting:

"(2) there is a risk that, absent such restriction, the defendant will continue to engage in unlawful conduct similar to that for which the defendant was convicted; and

(3) imposition of such a restriction is reasonably necessary to protect the public.",

and inserting in lieu thereof:

"(2) imposition of such a restriction is reasonably necessary to protect the public because there is reason to believe that, absent such restriction, the defendant will continue to engage in unlawful conduct similar to that for which the defendant was convicted.",

and by inserting "and" at the end of subsection (a)(1).

The purpose of this amendment is to clarify the guideline. **The effective date of this amendment is November 1, 1989.**

286. Chapter Five, Part G is amended by deleting §5G1.1 in its entirety as follows:

"§5G1.1. <u>Sentencing on a Single Count of Conviction</u>

(a) If application of the guidelines results in a sentence above the maximum authorized by statute for the offense of conviction, the statutory maximum shall be the guideline sentence.

(b) If application of the guidelines results in a sentence below the minimum sentence required by statute, the statutory minimum shall be the guideline sentence.

(c) In any other case, the sentence imposed shall be the sentence as determined from application of the guidelines.

<u>Commentary</u>

If the statute requires imposition of a sentence other than that required by the guidelines, the statute shall control. The sentence imposed should be consistent with the statute but as close as possible to the guidelines.".

A replacement guideline with accompanying commentary is inserted as §5G1.1 (Sentencing on a Single Count of Conviction).

The purpose of this amendment is to clarify the guideline. **The effective date of this amendment is November 1, 1989.**

287. The Commentary to §5G1.2 is amended in the second paragraph by deleting "any combination of concurrent and consecutive sentences that produces the total punishment may be imposed" and inserting in lieu thereof "consecutive sentences are to be imposed to the extent necessary to achieve the total punishment".

The purpose of this amendment is to clarify the commentary. **The effective date of this amendment is November 1, 1989.**

288. The Commentary to §5G1.2 is amended by inserting the following additional paragraph immediately after the first paragraph:

" This section applies to multiple counts of conviction (1) contained in the same indictment or information, or (2) contained in different indictments or informations for which sentences are to be imposed at the same time or in a consolidated proceeding.".

The purpose of this amendment is to clarify that this guideline applies in the case of separate indictments that are consolidated for purposes of sentencing. **The effective date of this amendment is November 1, 1989.**

289. Chapter Five, Part G is amended by deleting §5G1.3 in its entirety as follows:

"§5G1.3. Convictions on Counts Related to Unexpired Sentences

If at the time of sentencing, the defendant is already serving one or more unexpired sentences, then the sentences for the instant offense(s) shall run consecutively to such unexpired sentences, unless one or more of the instant offenses(s) arose out of the same transactions or occurrences as the unexpired sentences. In the latter case, such instant sentences and the unexpired sentences shall run concurrently, except to the extent otherwise required by law.

Commentary

This section reflects the statutory presumption that sentences imposed at different times ordinarily run consecutively. See 18 U.S.C. § 3584(a). This presumption does not apply when the new counts arise out of the same transaction or occurrence as a prior conviction.

Departure would be warranted when independent prosecutions produce anomalous results that circumvent or defeat the intent of the guidelines.".

A replacement guideline with accompanying commentary is inserted as §5G1.3 (Imposition of a Sentence on a Defendant Serving an Unexpired Term of Imprisonment).

The purpose of this amendment is to specify the circumstances in which a consecutive sentence is required by the guidelines. **The effective date of this amendment is November 1, 1989.**

290. Section 5K1.1 is amended by deleting "made a good faith effort to provide" and inserting in lieu thereof "provided".

Section 5K1.1(a) is amended in the first sentence by deleting "conduct" immediately following "of the following".

The purpose of this amendment is to clarify the Commission's intent that departures under this policy statement be based upon the provision of substantial assistance. The existing policy statement could be interpreted as requiring only a willingness to provide such assistance. The amendment also makes an editorial correction. **The effective date of this amendment is November 1, 1989.**

291. The Commentary to §5K1.2 is deleted in its entirety as follows:

"Commentary

Background: The Commission considered and rejected the use of a defendant's refusal to assist authorities as an aggravating sentencing factor. Refusal to assist authorities based upon continued involvement in criminal activities and association with accomplices may be considered, however, in evaluating a defendant's sincerity in claiming acceptance of responsibility.".

The purpose of this amendment is to delete unnecessary commentary containing an unclear example. **The effective date of this amendment is November 1, 1989.**

292. Chapter Five, Part K, Subpart 2, is amended by inserting an additional policy statement as §5K2.15 (Terrorism (Policy Statement)).

The purpose of this amendment is to add a specific policy statement concerning consideration of an upward departure when the offense is committed for a terroristic purpose. This amendment does not make a substantive change. Such conduct is currently included in the broader policy statement at §5K2.9 (Criminal Purpose) and other policy statements. See United States v. Kikumura, 706 F. Supp. 331 (D. N.J. 1989). **The effective date of this amendment is November 1, 1989.**

293. Section 6A1.1 is amended in the title by inserting at the end "(Policy Statement)".

The purpose of this amendment is to designate §6A1.1 as a policy statement. Designation of this section as a policy statement is more consistent with the nature of the subject matter. **The effective date of this amendment is November 1, 1989.**

294. Section 6A1.3 is amended in the title by inserting at the end "(Policy Statement)".

The purpose of this amendment is to designate §6A1.3 as a policy statement. Designation of this section as a policy statement is more consistent with the nature of the subject matter. **The effective date of this amendment is November 1, 1989.**

295. The Commentary to §6B1.2 is amended in the second paragraph by deleting "and does not undermine the basic purposes of sentencing.", and inserting in lieu thereof "(i.e., that such departure is authorized by 18 U.S.C. § 3553(b)). See generally Chapter 1, Part A (4)(b)(Departures).".

The purpose of this amendment is to clarify the commentary. **The effective date of this amendment is November 1, 1989.**

296. Appendix A (Statutory Index) is amended in the second sentence of the "Introduction" by deleting "conduct" and inserting in lieu thereof "nature of the offense conduct charged in the count", and by deleting "select" and inserting in lieu thereof "use"; and in the third sentence of the "Introduction" by deleting "the court is to apply" and inserting in lieu thereof "use", by deleting "which is" immediately before "most applicable", and by deleting "conduct for" and inserting in lieu thereof "nature of the offense conduct charged in the count of".

The purpose of this amendment is to clarify the operation of the Statutory Index in relation to §§1B1.1 and 1B1.2(a). **The effective date of this amendment is November 1, 1989.**

297. Appendix A is amended by inserting the following additional paragraph at the end of the Introduction:

" The guidelines do not apply to any count of conviction that is a Class B or C misdemeanor or an infraction. (See §1B1.9.)".

Appendix A is amended by deleting:

"7 U.S.C. § 52	2N2.1",
"7 U.S.C. § 60	2N2.1",
"10 U.S.C. § 847	2J1.1, 2J1.5",
"16 U.S.C. § 198c	2B1.1, 2B1.3, 2B2.3",
"16 U.S.C. § 204c	2B1.1, 2B1.3",
"16 U.S.C. § 604	2B1.3",

"16 U.S.C. § 606	2B1.1, 2B1.3",
"16 U.S.C. § 668dd	2Q2.1",
"16 U.S.C. § 670j(a)(1)	2B2.3",
"16 U.S.C. § 676	2B2.3",
"16 U.S.C. § 682	2B2.3",
"16 U.S.C. § 683	2B2.3",
"16 U.S.C. § 685	2B2.3",
"16 U.S.C. § 689b	2B2.3",
"16 U.S.C. § 692a	2B2.3",
"16 U.S.C. § 694a	2B2.3",
"18 U.S.C. § 113(d)	2A2.3",
"18 U.S.C. § 113(e)	2A2.3",
"18 U.S.C. § 290	2F1.1",
"18 U.S.C. § 402	2J1.1",
"18 U.S.C. § 437	2C1.3",
"18 U.S.C. § 1164	2B1.3",
"18 U.S.C. § 1165	2B2.3",
"18 U.S.C. § 1382	2B2.3",
"18 U.S.C. § 1504	2J1.2",
"18 U.S.C. § 1726	2F1.1",
"18 U.S.C. § 1752	2B2.3",
"18 U.S.C. § 1793	2P1.4",
"18 U.S.C. § 1856	2B1.3",
"18 U.S.C. § 1863	2B2.3",
"40 U.S.C. § 193e	2B1.1, 2B1.3",
"42 U.S.C. § 1995	2J1.1",
"42 U.S.C. § 2000h	2J1.1",
"42 U.S.C. § 4912	2Q1.3".

The purposes of this amendment are to clarify that the guidelines do not apply to any count of conviction that is a Class B or C misdemeanor or an infraction, and to delete references to statutes that apply solely to such offenses. **The effective date of this amendment is November 1, 1989.**

298. Appendix A is amended by deleting:

"18 U.S.C. § 1512	2J1.2",

and inserting in lieu thereof:

"18 U.S.C. § 1512(a)	2A1.1, 2A1.2, 2A2.1
18 U.S.C. § 1512(b)	2A2.2, 2J1.2
18 U.S.C. § 1512(c)	2J1.2",

and by deleting:

"21 U.S.C. § 848	2D1.5",

and inserting in lieu thereof:

"21 U.S.C. § 848(a)	2D1.5
21 U.S.C. § 848(b)	2D1.5
21 U.S.C. § 848(e)	2A1.1".

Appendix A is amended by inserting the following statutes in the appropriate place according to statutory title and section number:

"18 U.S.C. § 247	2H1.3",
"18 U.S.C. § 709	2F1.1",
"18 U.S.C. § 930	2K2.5",
"18 U.S.C. § 1460	2G3.1",
"18 U.S.C. § 1466	2G3.1",
"18 U.S.C. § 1516	2J1.2",
"18 U.S.C. § 1716C	2B5.2",
"18 U.S.C. § 1958	2A2.1, 2E1.4",
"18 U.S.C. § 1959	2E1.3",
"42 U.S.C. § 7270b	2B2.3",
"43 U.S.C. § 1733(a) (43 C.F.R. 4140.1(b)(1)(i))	2B2.3",
"49 U.S.C. § 1472(c)	2A5.2".

Appendix A is amended on the line beginning "18 U.S.C. § 371" by inserting "2A2.1, 2D1.4," immediately before "2T1.9".

Appendix A is amended in the line beginning "18 U.S.C. § 1005" by inserting ", 2S1.3" immediately following "2F1.1".

Appendix A is amended in the line beginning "18 U.S.C. § 1028" by inserting ",2L1.2, 2L2.1, 2L2.3" immediately following "2F1.1".

Appendix A is amended in the line beginning "26 U.S.C. § 7203" by inserting "2S1.3," immediately before "2T1.2".

The purpose of this amendment is to make the statutory index more comprehensive. **The effective date of this amendment is November 1, 1989.**

299. **Appendix A is amended in the line beginning "18 U.S.C. § 113(a)" by deleting ", 2A3.1" .**

Appendix A is amended in the line beginning "18 U.S.C. § 1854" by deleting ", 2B2.3".

Appendix A is amended in the line beginning "42 U.S.C. § 2278(a)(c)" by deleting "42 U.S.C. § 2278(a)(c)" and inserting in lieu thereof "42 U.S.C. § 2278a(c)".

The purposes of this amendment are to delete incorrect references and to insert a correct reference. **The effective date of this amendment is November 1, 1989.**

300. **Appendix A is amended by inserting the following statutes in the appropriate place according to statutory title and section number:**

"18 U.S.C. § 2251A	2G2.3",
"21 U.S.C. § 858	2D1.10".

Appendix A is amended on the line beginning "18 U.S.C. §1464" by deleting "2G3.1" and inserting in lieu thereof "2G3.2", and by inserting the following statute in the appropriate place according to statutory title and section number:

"18 U.S.C. § 1468	2G3.2".

Appendix A is amended on the line beginning "21 U.S.C. § 845" by deleting "2D1.3" and inserting in lieu thereof "2D1.2", and on the line beginning "21 U.S.C. § 845a" by deleting "2D1.3" and inserting in lieu thereof "2D1.2".

Appendix A is amended in the line beginning "47 U.S.C. § 223" by deleting "47 U.S.C. § 223" and inserting in lieu thereof "47 U.S.C. § 223(b)(1)(A)".

The purpose of this amendment is to reflect the creation of new offense guidelines. **The effective date of this amendment is November 1, 1989.**

301. Appendix A is amended on the line beginning "18 U.S.C. § 844(h)" by deleting ", 2K1.6" and inserting in lieu thereof "(offenses committed prior to November 18, 1988), 2K1.6, 2K1.7".

The purpose of this amendment is to reflect a revision in the offense covered by 18 U.S.C. § 844(h). **The effective date of this amendment is November 1, 1989.**

302. Sections 5C2.1, 5D3.1, 5D3.2, 5D3.3, 5E4.1, 5E4.2, 5E4.3, 5E4.4, 5F5.1, 5F5.2, 5F5.3, 5F5.4, and 5F5.5, and references thereto, are amended by deleting the number designating the subpart (i.e., the digit immediately following the letter in the section designation) wherever it appears and inserting in lieu thereof "1" in each instance.

The purpose of this amendment is to correct a clerical error. **The effective date of this amendment is November 1, 1989.**

303. The Commentary to §1B1.1 captioned "Application Notes" is amended in the third sentence of Note 4 by deleting "subsection" and inserting in lieu thereof "subdivision" and by deleting "subsections (A), (B) and (C)" and inserting in lieu thereof "subdivisions (A) - (E)".

The Commentary to §1B1.2 captioned "Application Notes" is amended in Note 3 by deleting "at Sentencing)" and inserting in lieu thereof "in Imposing Sentence)".

The Commentary to §1B1.3 captioned "Application Notes" is amended in the first sentence of Note 1 by deleting "is" and inserting in lieu thereof "would be".

The Commentary to §1B1.3 captioned "Application Notes" is amended in Note 4 by deleting "(Assault)" and inserting in lieu thereof "(Aggravated Assault)", and by deleting "(Fraud)" and inserting in lieu thereof "(Fraud and Deceit)".

The Commentary to §1B1.3 captioned "Application Notes" is amended in Note 5 by deleting "§2K2.3" and inserting in lieu thereof "§2K2.2", by deleting "12" and inserting in lieu thereof "16", by deleting "convicted under" and inserting in lieu thereof "the defendant is convicted under 18 U.S.C. § 922(o) or ", by deleting "§2A3.4(b)(2)" and inserting in lieu thereof "§2A3.4(a)(2)", and by deleting "abusive contact was accomplished as defined in 18 U.S.C. § 2242, increase by 4 levels" and inserting in lieu thereof "offense was committed by the means set forth in 18 U.S.C. § 2242".

The Commentary to §1B1.3 captioned "Background" is amended in the fourth sentence of the third paragraph by deleting "are part" and inserting in lieu thereof "were part".

The Commentary to §1B1.4 captioned "Background" is amended by deleting "3557" and inserting in lieu thereof "3577".

The Commentary to §2B3.2 captioned "Application Notes" is amended in the third sentence of Note 3 by inserting "and Racketeering" immediately before the period at the end of the sentence.

The Commentary to §2B3.2 captioned "Application Notes" is amended in Note 5 by deleting "items taken" and inserting in lieu thereof "loss".

The Commentary to §2A5.2 captioned "Background" is amended by inserting "or Aboard" immediately following "Materials While Boarding".

The Introductory Commentary to Chapter 2, Part B is amended by deleting "Order and" immediately before "Safety".

The Commentary to §2B1.1 captioned "Application Notes" is amended in Note 2 by deleting "(Attempt, Solicitation, or Conspiracy Not Covered by a Specific Guideline)" and inserting in lieu thereof "(Attempt, Solicitation, or Conspiracy)".

The Commentary to §2D1.1 captioned "Application Notes" is amended in Note 3 by deleting "§§2D1.2-2D1.4" and inserting in lieu thereof "§§2D1.2, 2D1.4, 2D1.5".

The Commentary to §2D1.1 captioned "Background" is amended in the fifth paragraph by deleting "§§5D1.1-5D1.3" and inserting in lieu thereof "Part D (Supervised Release)".

The Commentary to §2F1.1 captioned "Application Notes" is amended in the third sentence of Note 11 by deleting "Part B" and inserting in lieu thereof "Part B of this Chapter".

The Commentary to §2H1.1 captioned "Application Notes" is amended in the last sentence of Note 1 by deleting "for any" and inserting in lieu thereof "applicable to".

The Commentary to §2H1.2 captioned "Application Notes" is amended in Note 1 by deleting "explained" and inserting in lieu thereof "defined".

The Commentary to §2H1.2 captioned "Background" is amended in the second sentence by deleting ", except where death results, in which case" and inserting in lieu thereof "; except where death results,".

Section 2K1.5(c)(1) is amended by deleting "(Attempt or Conspiracy)" and inserting in lieu thereof "(Attempt, Solicitation, or Conspiracy)".

Section 2K1.6(b)(1) is amended by deleting "(Attempt or Conspiracy)" and inserting in lieu thereof "(Attempt, Solicitation, or Conspiracy)".

The Commentary to §2R1.1 captioned "Application Notes" is amended in Note 7 by inserting "Category" immediately following "Criminal History".

The Commentary to §2T1.4 captioned "Application Notes" is amended in Note 3 by inserting "Use of" immediately before "Special Skill".

The Commentary to §3B1.4 is amended by deleting "(Role in the Offense)" the first time it appears and inserting in lieu thereof "(Aggravating Role)", and by deleting "(Role in the Offense)" the second time it appears and inserting in lieu thereof "(Mitigating Role)".

The Commentary to §3D1.2 captioned "Application Notes" is amended in Note 1 by deleting "25 (18 + 1 + 6) rather than 28" and inserting in lieu thereof "28 (18 + 4 + 6) rather than 31".

The Commentary to §3D1.3 captioned "Application Notes" is amended in the last sentence of Note 4 by deleting "Loss or Damage" and inserting in lieu thereof "Damage or Loss".

The Commentary following §3D1.5 captioned "Illustrations of the Operation of the Multiple-Count Rules" is amended in example 1 by deleting "19" and inserting in lieu thereof "22", by deleting "1-Level" and inserting in lieu thereof "4-Level", by deleting "25." and inserting in lieu thereof "28.", by deleting "(25)" and inserting in lieu thereof "(28)", and by deleting "28" and inserting in lieu thereof "31".

The Commentary following §3D1.5 captioned "Illustrations of the Operation of the Multiple-Count Rules" is amended in the last 2 sentences of example 3 by deleting "10" wherever it appears and inserting in lieu thereof in each instance "8".

The Commentary following §3D1.5 captioned "Illustrations of the Operation of the Multiple-Count Rules" is amended in example 5 by deleting "13" wherever it appears and inserting in lieu thereof "14".

The Commentary following §3D1.5 captioned "Illustrations of the Operation of the Multiple-Count Rules" is amended by deleting:

"2. Defendant B, a federal housing inspector, was convicted on four counts of bribery. Counts one and two charged receiving payments of $3,000 and $2,000 from Landlord X in return for a single action with respect to a single property. Count three charged receipt of $1,500 from Landlord X for taking action with respect to another property, and count four charged receipt of $1,000 from Landlord Y for taking action with respect to a third property. Counts one and two, which arise out of the same transaction, are combined into a single Group involving a $5,000 bribe and hence an offense level of 11 (§2C1.1(a)(1), §2F1.1). Each of the two remaining counts represents a distinct Group, at offense level 10. As there are three Count Units, the offense level for the most serious (11) is increased by 3 levels. The combined offense level is 14.",

by renumbering Illustrations 3, 4, and 5 as 2, 3, and 4, respectively, and by redesignating defendants "C", "D", and "E" as "B", "C", and "D", respectively.

The purposes of this amendment are to conform cross-references and illustrations of the operation of the guidelines to the guidelines, as amended, and to make editorial improvements. **The effective date of this amendment is November 1, 1989.**

304. Section 2D2.1 is amended by inserting the following additional subsection:

"(b) Cross Reference

(1) If the defendant is convicted of possession of more than 5 grams of a mixture or substance containing cocaine base, apply §2D1.1 (Unlawful Manufacturing, Importing, Exporting, or Trafficking) as if the defendant had been convicted of possession of that mixture or substance with intent to distribute.".

The Commentary to §2D2.1 captioned "Background" is amended by deleting the entire text as follows:

"Background: Absent a prior drug related conviction, the maximum term of imprisonment authorized by statute is one year. With a single prior drug related conviction, a mandatory minimum term of imprisonment of fifteen days is required by statute and the maximum term of imprisonment authorized is increased to two years. With two or more prior drug related convictions, a mandatory minimum term of imprisonment of ninety days is required by statute and the maximum term of imprisonment authorized is increased to three years.",

and inserting in lieu thereof:

"Background: Mandatory minimum penalties for several categories of cases, ranging from fifteen days' to five years' imprisonment, are set forth in 21 U.S.C. § 844(a). When a mandatory minimum penalty exceeds the guideline range, the mandatory minimum becomes the guideline sentence. §5G1.1(b).

Section 2D2.1(b)(1) provides a cross reference to §2D1.1 for possession of more than five grams of a mixture or substance containing cocaine base, an offense subject to an enhanced penalty under Section 6371 of the Anti-Drug Abuse Act of 1988. Other cases for which enhanced penalties are provided under Section 6371 of the

Anti-Drug Abuse Act of 1988 (e.g., for a person with one prior conviction, possession of more than three grams of a mixture or substance containing cocaine base; for a person with two or more prior convictions, possession of more than one gram of a mixture or substance containing cocaine base) are to be sentenced in accordance with §5G1.1(b).".

The purpose of this amendment is to reflect revisions in 21 U.S.C. § 844(a) made by Section 6371 of the Anti-Drug Abuse Act of 1988. **The effective date of this amendment is November 1, 1989.**

305. Chapter Five, Part F, is amended by inserting an additional guideline with accompanying commentary as §5F1.6 (Denial of Federal Benefits to Drug Traffickers and Possessors).

The purpose of this amendment is to reflect the enactment of 21 U.S.C. § 853a by Section 5301 of the Anti-Drug Abuse Act of 1988. **The effective date of this amendment is November 1, 1989.**

306. Chapter One, Part B, is amended by inserting an additional policy statement with accompanying commentary as §1B1.10 (Retroactivity of Amended Guideline Range (Policy Statement)).

The purpose of this amendment is to implement the directive in 28 U.S.C. § 994(u). **The effective date of this amendment is November 1, 1989.**

307. Chapter One, Part A, is amended by deleting subparts 2-5 in their entirety as follows:

"2. The Statutory Mission

The Comprehensive Crime Control Act of 1984 foresees guidelines that will further the basic purposes of criminal punishment, i.e., deterring crime, incapacitating the offender, providing just punishment, and rehabilitating the offender. It delegates to the Commission broad authority to review and rationalize the federal sentencing process.

The statute contains many detailed instructions as to how this determination should be made, but the most important of them instructs the Commission to create categories of offense behavior and offender characteristics. An offense behavior category might consist, for example, of 'bank robbery/committed with a gun/$2500 taken.' An offender characteristic category might be 'offender with one prior conviction who was not sentenced to imprisonment.' The Commission is required to prescribe guideline ranges that specify an appropriate sentence for each class of convicted persons, to be determined by coordinating the offense behavior categories with the offender characteristic categories. The statute contemplates the guidelines will establish a range of sentences for every coordination of categories. Where the guidelines call for imprisonment, the range must be narrow: the maximum imprisonment cannot exceed the minimum by more than the greater of 25 percent or six months. 28 U.S.C. § 994(b)(2).

The sentencing judge must select a sentence from within the guideline range. If, however, a particular case presents atypical features, the Act allows the judge to depart from the guidelines and sentence outside the range. In that case, the judge must specify reasons for departure. 18 U.S.C. § 3553(b). If the court sentences within the guideline range, an appellate court may review the sentence to see if the guideline was correctly applied. If the judge departs from the guideline range, an appellate court may review the reasonableness of the departure. 18 U.S.C. § 3742.

The Act requires the offender to serve virtually all of any prison sentence imposed, for it abolishes parole and substantially restructures good behavior adjustments.

The law requires the Commission to send its initial guidelines to Congress by April 13, 1987, and under the present statute they take effect automatically on November 1, 1987. Pub. L. No. 98-473, § 235, reprinted at 18 U.S.C. § 3551. The Commission may submit guideline amendments each year to Congress between the beginning of a regular session and May 1. The amendments will take effect automatically 180 days after submission unless a law is enacted to the contrary. 28 U.S.C. § 994(p).

The Commission, with the aid of its legal and research staff, considerable public testimony, and written commentary, has developed an initial set of guidelines which it now transmits to Congress. The Commission emphasizes, however, that it views the guideline-writing process as evolutionary. It expects, and the governing statute anticipates, that continuing research, experience, and analysis will result in modifications and revisions to the guidelines by submission of amendments to Congress. To this end, the Commission is established as a permanent agency to monitor sentencing practices in the federal courts throughout the nation.

3. The Basic Approach (Policy Statement)

To understand these guidelines and the rationale that underlies them, one must begin with the three objectives that Congress, in enacting the new sentencing law, sought to achieve. Its basic objective was to enhance the ability of the criminal justice system to reduce crime through an effective, fair sentencing system. To achieve this objective, Congress first sought honesty in sentencing. It sought to avoid the confusion and implicit deception that arises out of the present sentencing system which requires a judge to impose an indeterminate sentence that is automatically reduced in most cases by 'good time' credits. In addition, the parole commission is permitted to determine how much of the remainder of any prison sentence an offender actually will serve. This usually results in a substantial reduction in the effective length of the sentence imposed, with defendants often serving only about one-third of the sentence handed down by the court.

Second, Congress sought uniformity in sentencing by narrowing the wide disparity in sentences imposed by different federal courts for similar criminal conduct by similar offenders. Third, Congress sought proportionality in sentencing through a system that imposes appropriately different sentences for criminal conduct of different severity.

Honesty is easy to achieve: The abolition of parole makes the sentence imposed by the court the sentence the offender will serve. There is a tension, however, between the mandate of uniformity (treat similar cases alike) and the mandate of proportionality (treat different cases differently) which, like the historical tension between law and equity, makes it difficult to achieve both goals simultaneously. Perfect uniformity -- sentencing every offender to five years -- destroys proportionality. Having only a few simple categories of crimes would make the guidelines uniform and easy to administer, but might lump together offenses that are different in important respects. For example, a single category for robbery that lumps together armed and unarmed robberies, robberies with and without injuries, robberies of a few dollars and robberies of millions, is far too broad.

At the same time, a sentencing system tailored to fit every conceivable wrinkle of each case can become unworkable and seriously compromise the certainty of punishment and its deterrent effect. A bank robber with (or without) a gun, which the robber kept hidden (or brandished), might have frightened (or merely warned), injured seriously (or less seriously), tied up (or simply pushed) a guard, a teller or a customer, at night (or at noon), for a bad (or arguably less bad) motive, in an effort to obtain money for other crimes (or for other purposes), in the company of a few (or many) other robbers, for the first (or fourth) time that day, while sober (or under the influence of drugs or alcohol), and so forth.

The list of potentially relevant features of criminal behavior is long; the fact that they can occur in multiple combinations means that the list of possible permutations of factors is virtually endless. The appropriate relationships among these different factors are exceedingly difficult to establish, for they are often context specific. Sentencing courts do not treat the occurrence of a simple bruise identically in all cases, irrespective of whether that bruise occurred in the context of a bank robbery or in the context of a breach of peace. This is so, in part, because the risk that such a harm will occur differs depending on the underlying offense with which it is connected (and therefore may already be counted, to a different degree, in the punishment for the underlying offense); and also because, in part, the relationship between punishment and multiple harms is not simply additive. The relation varies, depending on how much other harm has occurred. (Thus, one cannot easily assign points for each kind of harm and simply add them up, irrespective of context and total amounts.)

The larger the number of subcategories, the greater the complexity that is created and the less workable the system. Moreover, the subcategories themselves, sometimes too broad and sometimes too narrow, will apply and interact in unforeseen ways to unforeseen situations, thus failing to cure the unfairness of a simple, broad category system. Finally, and perhaps most importantly, probation officers and courts, in applying a complex system of subcategories, would have to make a host of decisions about whether the underlying facts are sufficient to bring the case within a particular subcategory. The greater the number of decisions required and the greater their complexity, the greater the risk that different judges will apply the guidelines differently to situations that, in fact, are similar, thereby reintroducing the very disparity that the guidelines were designed to eliminate.

In view of the arguments, it is tempting to retreat to the simple, broad-category approach and to grant judges the discretion to select the proper point along a broad sentencing range. Obviously, however, granting such broad discretion risks correspondingly broad disparity in sentencing, for different courts may exercise their discretionary powers in different ways. That is to say, such an approach risks a return to the wide disparity that Congress established the Commission to limit.

In the end, there is no completely satisfying solution to this practical stalemate. The Commission has had to simply balance the comparative virtues and vices of broad, simple categorization and detailed, complex subcategorization, and within the constraints established by that balance, minimize the discretionary powers of the sentencing court. Any ultimate system will, to a degree, enjoy the benefits and suffer from the drawbacks of each approach.

A philosophical problem arose when the Commission attempted to reconcile the differing perceptions of the purposes of criminal punishment. Most observers of the criminal law agree that the ultimate aim of the law itself, and of punishment in particular, is the control of crime. Beyond this point, however, the consensus seems to break down. Some argue that appropriate punishment should be defined primarily on the basis of the moral principle of 'just deserts.' Under this principle, punishment should be scaled to the offender's culpability and the resulting harms. Thus, if a defendant is less culpable, the defendant deserves less punishment. Others argue that punishment should be imposed primarily on the basis of practical 'crime control' considerations. Defendants sentenced under this scheme should receive the punishment that most effectively lessens the likelihood of future crime, either by deterring others or incapacitating the defendant.

Adherents of these points of view have urged the Commission to choose between them, to accord one primacy over the other. Such a choice would be profoundly difficult. The relevant literature is vast, the arguments deep, and each point of view has much to be said in its favor. A clear-cut Commission decision in favor of one of these approaches would diminish the chance that the guidelines would find the widespread acceptance they need for effective implementation. As a practical matter, in most sentencing decisions both philosophies may prove consistent with the same result.

For now, the Commission has sought to solve both the practical and philosophical problems of developing a coherent sentencing system by taking an empirical approach that uses data estimating the existing sentencing system as a starting point. It has analyzed data drawn from 10,000 presentence investigations, crimes as distinguished in substantive criminal statutes, the United States Parole Commission's guidelines and resulting statistics, and data from other relevant sources, in order to determine which distinctions are important in present practice. After examination, the Commission has accepted, modified, or rationalized the more important of these distinctions.

This empirical approach has helped the Commission resolve its practical problem by defining a list of relevant distinctions that, although of considerable length, is short enough to create a manageable set of guidelines. Existing categories are relatively broad and omit many distinctions that some may believe important, yet they include most of the major distinctions that statutes and presentence data suggest make a significant difference in sentencing decisions. Important distinctions that are ignored in existing practice probably occur rarely. A sentencing judge may take this unusual case into account by departing from the guidelines.

The Commission's empirical approach has also helped resolve its philosophical dilemma. Those who adhere to a just deserts philosophy may concede that the lack of moral consensus might make it difficult to say exactly what punishment is deserved for a particular crime, specified in minute detail. Likewise, those who subscribe to a philosophy of crime control may acknowledge that the lack of sufficient, readily available data might make it difficult to say exactly what punishment will best prevent that crime. Both groups might therefore recognize the wisdom of looking to those distinctions that judges and legislators have, in fact, made over the course of time. These established distinctions are ones that the community believes, or has found over time, to be important from either a moral or crime-control perspective.

The Commission has not simply copied estimates of existing practice as revealed by the data (even though establishing offense values on this basis would help eliminate disparity, for the data represent averages). Rather, it has departed from the data at different points for various important reasons. Congressional statutes, for example, may suggest or require departure, as in the case of the new drug law that imposes increased and mandatory minimum sentences. In addition, the data may reveal inconsistencies in treatment, such as punishing economic crime less severely than other apparently equivalent behavior.

Despite these policy-oriented departures from present practice, the guidelines represent an approach that begins with, and builds upon, empirical data. The guidelines will not please those who wish the Commission to adopt a single philosophical theory and then work deductively to establish a simple and perfect set of categorizations and distinctions. The guidelines may prove acceptable, however, to those who seek more modest, incremental improvements in the status quo, who believe the best is often the enemy of the good, and who recognize that these initial guidelines are but the first step in an evolutionary process. After spending considerable time and resources exploring alternative approaches, the Commission has developed these guidelines as a practical effort toward the achievement of a more honest, uniform, equitable, and therefore effective, sentencing system.

4. The Guidelines' Resolution of Major Issues (Policy Statement)

The guideline-writing process has required the Commission to resolve a host of important policy questions, typically involving rather evenly balanced sets of competing considerations. As an aid to understanding the guidelines, this introduction will briefly discuss several of those issues. Commentary in the guidelines explains others.

(a) Real Offense vs. Charge Offense Sentencing.

One of the most important questions for the Commission to decide was whether to base sentences upon the actual conduct in which the defendant engaged regardless of the charges for which he was indicted or convicted ('real offense' sentencing), or upon the conduct that constitutes the elements of the offense with which the defendant was charged and of which he was convicted ('charge offense' sentencing). A bank robber, for example, might have used a gun, frightened bystanders, taken $50,000, injured a teller, refused to stop when ordered, and raced away damaging property during escape. A pure real offense system would sentence on the basis of all identifiable conduct. A pure charge offense system would overlook some of the harms that did not constitute statutory elements of the offenses of which the defendant was convicted.

The Commission initially sought to develop a real offense system. After all, the present sentencing system is, in a sense, a real offense system. The sentencing court (and the parole commission) take account of the conduct in which the defendant actually engaged, as determined in a presentence report, at the sentencing hearing, or before a parole commission hearing officer. The Commission's initial efforts in this direction, carried out in the spring and early summer of 1986, proved unproductive mostly for practical reasons. To make such a system work, even to formalize and rationalize the status quo, would have required the Commission to decide precisely which harms to take into account, how to add them up, and what kinds of procedures the courts should use to determine the presence or absence of disputed factual elements. The Commission found no practical way to combine and account for the large number of diverse harms arising in different circumstances; nor did it find a practical way to reconcile the need for a fair adjudicatory procedure with the need for a speedy sentencing process, given the potential existence of hosts of adjudicated 'real harm' facts in many typical cases. The effort proposed as a solution to these problems required the use of, for example, quadratic roots and other mathematical operations that the Commission considered too complex to be workable, and, in the Commission's view, risked return to wide disparity in practice.

The Commission therefore abandoned the effort to devise a 'pure' real offense system and instead experimented with a 'modified real offense system,' which it published for public comment in a September 1986 preliminary draft.

This version also foundered in several major respects on the rock of practicality. It was highly complex and its mechanical rules for adding harms (e.g., bodily injury added the same punishment irrespective of context) threatened to work considerable unfairness. Ultimately, the Commission decided that it could not find a practical or fair and efficient way to implement either a pure or modified real offense system of the sort it originally wanted, and it abandoned that approach.

The Commission, in its January 1987 Revised Draft and the present guidelines, has moved closer to a 'charge offense' system. The system is not, however, pure; it has a number of real elements. For one thing, the hundreds of overlapping and duplicative statutory provisions that make up the federal criminal law have forced the Commission to write guidelines that are descriptive of generic conduct rather than tracking purely statutory language. For another, the guidelines, both through specific offense characteristics and adjustments, take account of a number of important, commonly occurring real offense elements such as role in the offense, the presence of a gun, or the amount of money actually taken.

Finally, it is important not to overstate the difference in practice between a real and a charge offense system. The federal criminal system, in practice, deals mostly with drug offenses, bank robberies and white collar crimes (such as fraud, embezzlement, and bribery). For the most part, the conduct that an indictment charges approximates the real and relevant conduct in which the offender actually engaged.

The Commission recognizes its system will not completely cure the problems of a real offense system. It may still be necessary, for example, for a court to determine some particular real facts that will make a difference to the sentence. Yet, the Commission believes that the instances of controversial facts will be far fewer; indeed, there will be few enough so that the court system will be able to devise fair procedures for their determination. See United States v. Fatico, 579 F.2d 707 (2d Cir. 1978) (permitting introduction of hearsay evidence at sentencing hearing under certain conditions), on remand, 458 F. Supp. 388 (E.D.N.Y. 1978), aff'd, 603 F.2d 1053 (2d Cir. 1979) (holding that the government need not prove facts at sentencing hearing beyond a reasonable doubt), cert. denied, 444 U.S. 1073 (1980).

The Commission also recognizes that a charge offense system has drawbacks of its own. One of the most important is its potential to turn over to the prosecutor the power to determine the sentence by increasing or decreasing the number (or content) of the counts in an indictment. Of course, the defendant's actual conduct (that which the prosecutor can prove in court) imposes a natural limit upon the prosecutor's ability to increase a defendant's sentence. Moreover, the Commission has written its rules for the treatment of multicount convictions with an eye toward eliminating unfair treatment that might flow from count manipulation. For example, the guidelines treat a three-count indictment, each count of which charges sale of 100 grams of heroin, or theft of $10,000, the same as a single-count indictment charging sale of 300 grams of heroin or theft of $30,000. Further, a sentencing court may control any inappropriate manipulation of the indictment through use of its power to depart from the specific guideline sentence. Finally, the Commission will closely monitor problems arising out of count manipulation and will make appropriate adjustments should they become necessary.

(b) Departures.

The new sentencing statute permits a court to depart from a guideline-specified sentence only when it finds 'an aggravating or mitigating circumstance of a kind, or to a degree, not adequately taken into consideration by the Sentencing Commission . . .'. 18 U.S.C. § 3553(b). Thus, in principle, the Commission, by specifying that it had adequately considered a particular factor, could prevent a court from using it as grounds for departure. In this initial set of guidelines, however, the Commission does not so limit the courts' departure powers. The Commission intends the sentencing courts to treat each guideline as carving out a 'heartland,' a set of typical cases embodying the conduct that each guideline describes. When a court finds an atypical case, one to which a particular guideline linguistically applies but where conduct significantly differs from the norm, the court may consider whether a departure is warranted. Section 5H1.10 (Race, Sex, National Origin, Creed, Religion, Socio-Economic Status), the third sentence of §5H1.4, and the last sentence of §5K2.12, list a few factors that the court cannot take into account as grounds for departure. With those specific exceptions, however, the Commission does not intend to limit the kinds of factors (whether or not mentioned anywhere else in the guidelines) that could constitute grounds for departure in an unusual case.

The Commission has adopted this departure policy for two basic reasons. First is the difficulty of foreseeing and capturing a single set of guidelines that encompasses the vast range of human conduct potentially relevant to a sentencing decision. The Commission also recognizes that in the initial set of guidelines it need not do so. The Commission is a permanent body, empowered by law to write and rewrite guidelines, with progressive changes, over many years. By monitoring when courts depart from the guidelines and by analyzing their stated reasons for doing so, the Commission, over time, will be able to create more accurate guidelines that specify precisely where departures should and should not be permitted.

Second, the Commission believes that despite the courts' legal freedom to depart from the guidelines, they will not do so very often. This is because the guidelines, offense by offense, seek to take account of those factors that the Commission's sentencing data indicate make a significant difference in sentencing at the present time. Thus, for example, where the presence of actual physical injury currently makes an important difference in final sentences, as in the case of robbery, assault, or arson, the guidelines specifically instruct the judge to use this factor to augment the sentence. Where the guidelines do not specify an augmentation or diminution, this is generally because the sentencing data do not permit the Commission, at this time, to conclude that the factor is empirically important in relation to the particular offense. Of course, a factor (say physical injury) may nonetheless sometimes occur in connection with a crime (such as fraud) where it does not often occur. If, however, as the data indicate, such occurrences are rare, they are precisely the type of events that the court's departure powers were designed to cover -- unusual cases outside the range of the more typical offenses for which the guidelines were designed. Of course, the Commission recognizes that even its collection and analysis of 10,000 presentence reports are an imperfect source of data sentencing estimates. Rather than rely heavily at this time upon impressionistic accounts, however, the Commission believes it wiser to wait and collect additional data from our continuing monitoring process that may demonstrate how the guidelines work in practice before further modification.

It is important to note that the guidelines refer to two different kinds of departure.

The first kind involves instances in which the guidelines provide specific guidance for departure, by analogy or by other numerical or non-numerical suggestions. For example, the commentary to §2G1.1 (Transportation for Prostitution), recommends a downward adjustment of eight levels where commercial purpose was not involved. The Commission intends such suggestions as policy guidance for the courts. The Commission expects that most departures will reflect the suggestions, and that the courts of appeals may prove more likely to find departures 'unreasonable' where they fall outside suggested levels.

A second kind of departure will remain unguided. It may rest upon grounds referred to in Chapter 5, Part K (Departures), or on grounds not mentioned in the guidelines. While Chapter 5, Part K lists factors that the Commission believes may constitute grounds for departure, those suggested grounds are not exhaustive. The Commission recognizes that there may be other grounds for departure that are not mentioned; it also believes there may be cases in which a departure outside suggested levels is warranted. In its view, however, such cases will be highly unusual.

(c) <u>Plea Agreements</u>.

Nearly ninety percent of all federal criminal cases involve guilty pleas, and many of these cases involve some form of plea agreement. Some commentators on early Commission guideline drafts have urged the Commission not to attempt any major reforms of the agreement process, on the grounds that any set of guidelines that threatens to radically change present practice also threatens to make the federal system unmanageable. Others, starting with the same facts, have argued that guidelines which fail to control and limit plea agreements would leave untouched a 'loophole' large enough to undo the good that sentencing guidelines may bring. Still other commentators make both sets of arguments.

The Commission has decided that these initial guidelines will not, in general, make significant changes in current plea agreement practices. The court will accept or reject any such agreements primarily in accordance with the rules set forth in Fed.R.Crim.P. 11(e). The Commission will collect data on the courts' plea practices and will analyze this information to determine when and why the courts accept or reject plea agreements. In light of this information and analysis, the Commission will seek to further regulate the plea agreement process as appropriate.

The Commission nonetheless expects the initial set of guidelines to have a positive, rationalizing impact upon plea agreements for two reasons. First, the guidelines create a clear, definite expectation in respect to the sentence that a court will impose if a trial takes place. Insofar as a prosecutor and defense attorney seek to agree about a likely sentence or range of sentences, they will no longer work in the dark. This fact alone should help to reduce irrationality in respect to actual sentencing outcomes. Second, the guidelines create a norm to which judges will likely refer when they decide whether, under Rule 11(e), to accept or to reject a plea agreement or recommendation. Since they will have before them the norm, the relevant factors (as disclosed in the plea agreement), and the reason for the agreement, they will find it easier than at present to determine whether there is sufficient reason to accept a plea agreement that departs from the norm.

(d) Probation and Split Sentences.

The statute provides that the guidelines are to 'reflect the general appropriateness of imposing a sentence other than imprisonment in cases in which the defendant is a first offender who has not been convicted of a crime of violence or an otherwise serious offense . . .' 28 U.S.C. § 994(j). Under present sentencing practice, courts sentence to probation an inappropriately high percentage of offenders guilty of certain economic crimes, such as theft, tax evasion, antitrust offenses, insider trading, fraud, and embezzlement, that in the Commission's view are 'serious.' If the guidelines were to permit courts to impose probation instead of prison in many or all such cases, the present sentences would continue to be ineffective.

The Commission's solution to this problem has been to write guidelines that classify as 'serious' (and therefore subject to mandatory prison sentences) many offenses for which probation is now frequently given. At the same time, the guidelines will permit the sentencing court to impose short prison terms in many such cases. The Commission's view is that the definite prospect of prison, though the term is short, will act as a significant deterrent to many of these crimes, particularly when compared with the status quo where probation, not prison, is the norm.

More specifically, the guidelines work as follows in respect to a first offender. For offense levels one through six, the sentencing court may elect to sentence the offender to probation (with or without confinement conditions) or to a prison term. For offense levels seven through ten, the court may substitute probation for a prison term, but the probation must include confinement conditions (community confinement, intermittent confinement, or home detention). For offense levels eleven and twelve, the court must impose at least one half the minimum confinement sentence in the form of prison confinement, the remainder to be served on supervised release with a condition of community confinement or home detention. The Commission, of course, has not dealt with the single acts of aberrant behavior that still may justify probation at higher offense levels through departures.

(e) Multi-Count Convictions.

The Commission, like other sentencing commissions, has found it particularly difficult to develop rules for sentencing defendants convicted of multiple violations of law, each of which makes up a separate count in an indictment. The reason it is difficult is that when a defendant engages in conduct that causes several harms, each additional harm, even if it increases the extent to which punishment is warranted, does not necessarily warrant a proportionate increase in punishment. A defendant who assaults others during a fight, for example, may warrant more punishment if he injures ten people than if he injures one, but his conduct does not necessarily warrant ten times the punishment. If it did, many of the simplest offenses, for reasons that are often fortuitous, would lead to life sentences of imprisonment--sentences that neither 'just deserts' nor 'crime control' theories of punishment would find justified.

Several individual guidelines provide special instructions for increasing punishment when the conduct that is the subject of that count involves multiple occurrences or has caused several harms. The guidelines also provide general rules for aggravating punishment in light of multiple harms charged separately in separate counts. These rules may produce occasional anomalies, but normally they will permit an appropriate degree of aggravation of punishment when multiple offenses that are the subjects of separate counts take place.

These rules are set out in Chapter Three, Part D. They essentially provide: (1) When the conduct involves fungible items, e.g., separate drug transactions or thefts of money, the amounts are added and the guidelines apply to the total amount. (2) When nonfungible harms are involved, the offense level for the most serious count is increased (according to a somewhat diminishing scale) to reflect the existence of other counts of conviction.

The rules have been written in order to minimize the possibility that an arbitrary casting of a single transaction into several counts will produce a longer sentence. In addition, the sentencing court will have adequate power to prevent such a result through departures where necessary to produce a mitigated sentence.

(f) Regulatory Offenses.

Regulatory statutes, though primarily civil in nature, sometimes contain criminal provisions in respect to particularly harmful activity. Such criminal provisions often describe not only substantive offenses, but also more technical, administratively-related offenses such as failure to keep accurate records or to provide requested information. These criminal statutes pose two problems. First, which criminal regulatory provisions should the Commission initially consider, and second, how should it treat technical or administratively-related criminal violations?

In respect to the first problem, the Commission found that it cannot comprehensively treat all regulatory violations in the initial set of guidelines. There are hundreds of such provisions scattered throughout the United States Code. To find all potential violations would involve examination of each individual federal regulation. Because of this practical difficulty, the Commission has sought to determine, with the assistance of the Department of Justice and several regulatory agencies, which criminal regulatory offenses are particularly important in light of the need for enforcement of the general regulatory scheme. The Commission has sought to treat these offenses in these initial guidelines. It will address the less common regulatory offenses in the future.

In respect to the second problem, the Commission has developed a system for treating technical recordkeeping and reporting offenses, dividing them into four categories.

First, in the simplest of cases, the offender may have failed to fill out a form intentionally, but without knowledge or intent that substantive harm would likely follow. He might fail, for example, to keep an accurate record of toxic substance transport, but that failure may not lead, nor be likely to lead, to the release or improper treatment of any toxic substance. Second, the same failure may be accompanied by a significant likelihood that substantive harm will occur; it may make a release of a toxic substance more likely. Third, the same failure may have led to substantive harm. Fourth, the failure may represent an effort to conceal a substantive harm that has occurred.

The structure of a typical guideline for a regulatory offense is as follows:

(1) The guideline provides a low base offense level (6) aimed at the first type of recordkeeping or reporting offense. It gives the court the legal authority to impose a punishment ranging from probation up to six months of imprisonment.

(2) Specific offense characteristics designed to reflect substantive offenses that do occur (in respect to some regulatory offenses), or that are likely to occur, increase the offense level.

(3) A specific offense characteristic also provides that a recordkeeping or reporting offense that conceals a substantive offense will be treated like the substantive offense.

The Commission views this structure as an initial effort. It may revise its approach in light of further experience and analysis of regulatory crimes.

(g) Sentencing Ranges.

In determining the appropriate sentencing ranges for each offense, the Commission began by estimating the average sentences now being served within each category. It also examined the sentence specified in congressional statutes, in the parole guidelines, and in other relevant, analogous sources. The Commission's forthcoming detailed report will contain a comparison between estimates of existing sentencing practices and sentences under the guidelines.

While the Commission has not considered itself bound by existing sentencing practice, it has not tried to develop an entirely new system of sentencing on the basis of theory alone. Guideline sentences in many instances will approximate existing practice, but adherence to the guidelines will help to eliminate wide disparity. For example, where a high percentage of persons now receive probation, a guideline may include one or more specific offense characteristics in an effort to distinguish those types of defendants who now receive probation from those who receive more severe sentences. In some instances, short sentences of incarceration for all offenders in a category have been substituted for a current sentencing practice of very wide variability in which some defendants receive probation while others receive several years in prison for the same offense. Moreover, inasmuch as those who currently plead guilty often receive lesser sentences, the guidelines also permit the court to impose lesser sentences on those defendants who accept responsibility and those who cooperate with the government.

The Commission has also examined its sentencing ranges in light of their likely impact upon prison population. Specific legislation, such as the new drug law and the career offender provisions of the sentencing law, require the Commission to promulgate rules that will lead to substantial prison population increases. These increases will occur irrespective of any guidelines. The guidelines themselves, insofar as they reflect policy decisions made by the Commission (rather than legislated mandatory minimum, or career offender, sentences), will lead to an increase in prison population that computer models, produced by the Commission and the Bureau of Prisons, estimate at approximately 10 percent, over a period of ten years.

(h) The Sentencing Table.

The Commission has established a sentencing table. For technical and practical reasons it has 43 levels. Each row in the table contains levels that overlap with the levels in the preceding and succeeding rows. By overlapping the levels, the table should discourage unnecessary litigation. Both prosecutor and defendant will realize that the difference between one level and another will not necessarily make a difference in the sentence that the judge imposes. Thus, little purpose will be served in protracted litigation trying to determine, for example, whether $10,000 or $11,000 was obtained as a result of a fraud. At the same time, the rows work to increase a sentence proportionately. A change of 6 levels roughly doubles the sentence irrespective of the level at which one starts. The Commission, aware of the legal requirement that the maximum of any range cannot exceed the minimum by more than the greater of 25 percent or six months, also wishes to permit courts the greatest possible range for exercising discretion. The table overlaps offense levels meaningfully, works proportionately, and at the same time preserves the maximum degree of allowable discretion for the judge within each level.

Similarly, many of the individual guidelines refer to tables that correlate amounts of money with offense levels. These tables often have many, rather than a few levels. Again, the reason is to minimize the likelihood of unnecessary litigation. If a money table were to make only a few distinctions, each distinction would become more important and litigation as to which category an offender fell within would become more likely. Where a table has many smaller monetary distinctions, it minimizes the likelihood of litigation, for the importance of the precise amount of money involved is considerably less.

5. A Concluding Note

The Commission emphasizes that its approach in this initial set of guidelines is one of caution. It has examined the many hundreds of criminal statutes in the United States Code. It has begun with those that are the basis for a significant number of prosecutions. It has sought to place them in a rational order. It has developed additional distinctions relevant to the application of these provisions, and it has applied sentencing ranges to each resulting category. In doing so, it has relied upon estimates of existing sentencing practices as revealed by its own statistical analyses, based on summary reports of some 40,000 convictions, a sample of 10,000 augmented presentence reports, the parole guidelines and policy judgments.

The Commission recognizes that some will criticize this approach as overly cautious, as representing too little a departure from existing practice. Yet, it will cure wide disparity. The Commission is a permanent body that can amend the guidelines each year. Although the data available to it, like all data, are imperfect, experience with these guidelines will lead to additional information and provide a firm empirical basis for revision.

Finally, the guidelines will apply to approximately 90 percent of all cases in the federal courts. Because of time constraints and the nonexistence of statistical information, some offenses that occur infrequently are not considered in this initial set of guidelines. They will, however, be addressed in the near future. Their exclusion from this initial submission does not reflect any judgment about their seriousness. The Commission has also deferred promulgation of guidelines pertaining to fines, probation and other sanctions for organizational defendants, with the exception of antitrust violations. The Commission also expects to address this area in the near future.".

Replacement subparts are inserted as Subparts 2 (The Statutory Mission), 3 (The Basic Approach (Policy Statement)), 4 (The Guidelines' Resolution of Major Issues (Policy Statement)), and 5 (A Concluding Note).

This amendment updates this part to reflect the implementation of guideline sentencing on November 1, 1987, and makes various clarifying and editorial changes to enhance the usefulness of this part both as a historical overview and as an introduction to the structure and operation of the guidelines. For example, in the discussion of departures in subpart 4(b), language concerning what the Commission, in principle, might have done is deleted as unnecessary, but no substantive change is made. **The effective date of this amendment is November 1, 1990.**

308. Section 1B1.8(a) is amended by inserting "as part of that cooperation agreement" immediately following "unlawful activities of others, and"; and by deleting "so provided" and inserting in lieu thereof "provided pursuant to the agreement".

Section 1B1.8(b)(3) is amended by inserting "by the defendant" immediately before the period at the end of the sentence.

Section 1B1.8(b) is amended by renumbering subdivisions (2) and (3) as (3) and (4) respectively; and by inserting the following as subdivision (2):

"(2) concerning the existence of prior convictions and sentences in determining §4A1.1 (Criminal History Category) and §4B1.1 (Career Offender);".

The Commentary to §1B1.8 captioned "Application Notes" is amended in Note 2 by deleting:

"The Commission does not intend this guideline to interfere with determining adjustments under Chapter Four, Part A (Criminal History) or §4B1.1 (Career Offender) (e.g., information concerning the defendant's prior convictions).",

and inserting in lieu thereof:

"Subsection (b)(2) prohibits any cooperation agreement from restricting the use of information as to the existence of prior convictions and sentences in determining adjustments under §4A1.1 (Criminal History Category) and §4B1.1 (Career Offender).".

The Commentary to §1B1.8 captioned "Application Notes" is amended in Note 3 by deleting "408" and inserting in lieu thereof "410".

This amendment clarifies the Commission's intention that the use of information concerning the defendant's prior criminal convictions and sentences not be restricted by a cooperation agreement, makes several additional clarifying changes, and corrects a clerical error. **The effective date of this amendment is November 1, 1990.**

309. The Commentary to §1B1.3 captioned "Application Notes" is amended in Note 2 by deleting:

"This subsection applies to offenses of types for which convictions on multiple counts would be grouped together pursuant to §3D1.2(d); multiple convictions are not required.",

and inserting in lieu thereof:

"'Offenses of a character for which §3D1.2(d) would require grouping of multiple counts,' as used in subsection (a)(2), applies to offenses for which grouping of counts would be required under §3D1.2(d) had the defendant been convicted of multiple counts. Application of this provision does not require the defendant, in fact, to have been convicted of multiple counts. For example, where the defendant engaged in three drug sales of 10, 15, and 20 grams of cocaine, as part of the same course of conduct or common scheme or plan, subsection (a)(2) provides that the total quantity of cocaine involved (45 grams) is to be used to determine the offense level even if the defendant is convicted of a single count charging only one of the sales. If the defendant is convicted of multiple counts for the above noted sales, the grouping rules of Chapter Three, Part D (Multiple Counts) provide that the counts are grouped together. Although Chapter Three, Part D (Multiple Counts) applies to multiple counts of conviction, it does not limit the scope of subsection (a)(2). Subsection (a)(2) merely incorporates by reference the types of offenses set forth in §3D1.2(d); thus, as discussed above, multiple counts of conviction are not required for subsection (a)(2) to apply.".

The Commentary to §3D1.2 captioned "Application Notes" is amended in Note 4 by renumbering example (4) as (5); and by inserting, immediately before "But:", the following:

"(4) The defendant is convicted of two counts of distributing a controlled substance, each count involving a separate sale of 10 grams of cocaine that is part of a common scheme or plan. In addition, a finding is made that there are two other sales, also part of the common scheme or plan, each involving 10 grams of cocaine. The total amount of all four sales (40 grams of cocaine) will be used to determine the offense level for each count under §1B1.3(a)(2). The two counts will then be grouped together under either this subsection or subsection (d) to avoid double counting.".

This amendment clarifies the intended scope of §1B1.3(a)(2) in conjunction with Chapter Three, Part D (Multiple Counts) to ensure that the latter is not read to limit the former only to conduct of which the defendant was convicted. **The effective date of this amendment is November 1, 1990.**

310. The Commentary to §2A1.1 captioned "Statutory Provisions" is amended by deleting "18 U.S.C. § 1111" and inserting in lieu thereof "18 U.S.C. §§ 1111, 2113(e), 2118(c)(2)".

The Commentary to §2A1.1 is amended in the first paragraph of Application Note 1 by deleting "the 'willful, deliberate, malicious, and premeditated killing' to which 18 U.S.C. § 1111 applies" and inserting in lieu thereof: "premeditated killing"; and by deleting:

"However, the same statute applies when death results from certain enumerated felonies -- arson, escape, murder, kidnapping, treason, espionage, sabotage, rape, burglary, or robbery.",

and inserting in lieu thereof:

"However, this guideline also applies when death results from the commission of certain felonies.".

The Commentary to §2A1.1 captioned "Background" is amended in the first paragraph by deleting:

"Prior to the applicability of the Sentencing Reform Act of 1984, a defendant convicted under this statute and sentenced to life imprisonment could be paroled (see 18 U.S.C. § 4205(a)). Because of the abolition of parole by that Act, the language of 18 U.S.C. § 1111(b) (which was not amended by the Act) appears on its face to provide a mandatory minimum sentence of life imprisonment for this offense. Other provisions of the Act, however, classify this offense as a Class A felony (see 18 U.S.C. § 3559(a)(1)), for which a term of imprisonment of any period of time is authorized as an alternative to imprisonment for the duration of the defendant's life (see 18 U.S.C. §§ 3559(b), 3581(b)(1), as amended); hence, the relevance of the discussion in Application Note 1, supra, regarding circumstances in which a sentence less than life may be appropriate for a conviction under this statute.",

and inserting in lieu thereof:

"Whether a mandatory minimum term of life imprisonment is applicable to every defendant convicted of first degree murder under 18 U.S.C. § 1111 is a matter of statutory interpretation for the courts. The discussion in Application Note 1, supra, regarding circumstances in which a downward departure may be warranted is relevant in the event the penalty provisions of 18 U.S.C. § 1111 are construed to permit a sentence less than life imprisonment, or in the event the defendant is convicted under a statute that expressly authorizes a sentence of less than life imprisonment (e.g., 18 U.S.C. §§ 2113(e), 2118(c)(2), 21 U.S.C. § 848(e)).".

This amendment clarifies the commentary with respect to circumstances that may warrant a departure below the guideline range for offenses to which this guideline applies. This amendment also reserves for the courts the issue of whether life imprisonment is the mandatory minimum sentence for first degree murder under 18 U.S.C. § 1111. **The effective date of this amendment is November 1, 1990.**

311. Section 2A2.1 is amended in the title by deleting "Conspiracy or Solicitation to Commit Murder;" immediately before "Attempted Murder".

Section 2A2.1 is amended by deleting:

"(a) Base Offense Level: 20

(b) Specific Offense Characteristics

(1) If an assault involved more than minimal planning, increase by 2 levels.

(2) (A) If a firearm was discharged, increase by 5 levels; (B) if a dangerous weapon (including a firearm) was otherwise used, increase by 4 levels; (C) if a dangerous weapon (including a firearm) was brandished or its use was threatened, increase by 3 levels.

(3) If the victim sustained bodily injury, increase the offense level according to the seriousness of the injury:

	Degree of Bodily Injury	Increase in Level
(A)	Bodily Injury	add 2
(B)	Serious Bodily Injury	add 4
(C)	Permanent or Life-Threatening Bodily Injury	add 6

(D) If the degree of injury is between that specified in subdivisions (A) and (B), add 3 levels; or

(E) If the degree of injury is between that specified in subdivisions (B) and (C), add 5 levels.

Provided, however, that the cumulative adjustments from (2) and (3) shall not exceed 9 levels.

(4) If a conspiracy or assault was motivated by a payment or offer of money or other thing of value, increase by 2 levels.",

and inserting in lieu thereof:

"(a) Base Offense Level:

(1) 28, if the object of the offense would have constituted first degree murder; or

(2) 22, otherwise.

(b) Specific Offense Characteristics

(1) (A) If the victim sustained permanent or life-threatening bodily injury, increase by 4 levels; (B) if the victim sustained serious bodily injury, increase by 2 levels; or (C) if the degree of injury is between that specified in subdivisions (A) and (B), increase by 3 levels.

(2) If the offense involved the offer or the receipt of anything of pecuniary value for undertaking the murder, increase by 4 levels.".

The Commentary to §2A2.1 captioned "Statutory Provisions" is amended by deleting "(d), 373, 1113, 1116(a), 1117, 1751(c), (d), 1952A(a)" and inserting in lieu thereof "1113, 1116(a), 1751(c)".

The Commentary to §2A2.1 captioned "Application Note" is amended in Note 1 by deleting "'more than minimal planning,' 'firearm,' 'dangerous weapon,' 'brandished,' 'otherwise used,' 'bodily injury,' 'serious bodily injury,'" and inserting in lieu thereof "'serious bodily injury'".

The Commentary to §2A2.1 captioned "Application Note" is amended by inserting the following additional note:

"2. 'First degree murder,' as used in subsection (a)(1), means conduct that, if committed within the special maritime and territorial jurisdiction of the United States, would constitute first degree murder under 18 U.S.C. § 1111.";

and in the caption by deleting "Note" and inserting in lieu thereof "Notes".

The Commentary to §2A2.1 captioned "Background" is amended in the first paragraph by deleting ", conspiracy to commit murder, solicitation to commit murder," immediately before "and attempted murder"; and by inserting the following additional sentence at the end:

"An attempted manslaughter, or assault with intent to commit manslaughter, is covered under §2A2.2 (Aggravated Assault).".

The Commentary to §2A2.1 captioned "Background" is amended by deleting the second and third paragraphs as follows:

" The maximum term of imprisonment authorized by statute for conspiracy to murder is life imprisonment (18 U.S.C. § 1117). The maximum term of imprisonment authorized by statute for solicitation to murder is twenty years (18 U.S.C. § 373). The statutes that prohibit attempted murder, or assaults with intent to commit murder, vary widely in the maximum term of imprisonment authorized. Assault with intent to commit murder (18 U.S.C. § 113(a)) carries a maximum authorized term of twenty years imprisonment. An attempted assassination of certain essential government officials (18 U.S.C. § 351(c)) carries a maximum authorized term of life imprisonment. An attempted murder of foreign officials (18 U.S.C. § 1116(a)) carries a maximum authorized term of twenty years imprisonment. An attempt to commit murder, other than an assault with intent to commit murder covered by 18 U.S.C. § 113(a), carries a maximum term of three years imprisonment (18 U.S.C. § 1113).

Enhancements are provided for planning, weapon use, injury, and commission of the crime for hire. All of the factors can apply in the case of an assault; only the last can apply in the case of a conspiracy that does not include an assault; and none can apply in the case of a mere solicitation.".

The Commentary to §2A2.2 captioned "Application Notes" is amended in Note 3 by inserting the following additional sentence as the first sentence: "This guideline also covers attempted manslaughter and assault with intent to commit manslaughter.".

The Commentary to §2A2.2 captioned "Background" is amended in the first sentence of the first paragraph by deleting "where there is no intent to kill" immediately following " assaults".

Chapter Two, Part A, Subpart 1, is amended by inserting an additional guideline with accompanying commentary as §2A1.5 (Conspiracy or Solicitation to Commit Murder).

Section 2E1.4(a)(1) is amended by deleting "23" and inserting in lieu thereof "32".

The Commentary to §2E1.4 captioned "Application Notes" is amended by deleting Note 2 as follows:

"2. If the offense level for the underlying conduct is less than the alternative minimum base offense level specified (i.e., 23), the alternative minimum base offense level is to be used.";

and in the caption by deleting "Notes" and inserting in lieu thereof "Note".

The Commentary to §2X1.1 captioned "Application Notes" is amended in Note 1 in the paragraph beginning "Offense guidelines that expressly cover attempts" by deleting "Conspiracy or Solicitation to Commit Murder;" immediately before "Attempted Murder"; in the paragraph beginning "Offense guidelines that expressly cover conspiracies" by deleting "§2A2.1 (Assault With Intent to Commit Murder; Conspiracy or Solicitation to Commit Murder; Attempted Murder)" and inserting in lieu thereof "§2A1.5 (Conspiracy or Solicitation to Commit Murder)"; and in the paragraph beginning "Offense guidelines that expressly cover solicitations" by deleting "§2A2.1 (Assault With Intent to Commit Murder; Conspiracy or Solicitation to Commit Murder; Attempted Murder)" and inserting in lieu thereof "§2A1.5 (Conspiracy or Solicitation to Commit Murder)".

This amendment restructures §2A2.1, and increases the offense level for attempted murder and assault with intent to commit murder where the intended offense, if successful, would have constituted first degree murder to better reflect the seriousness of this conduct. For the same reason, the enhancement for an offense involving the offer or receipt of anything of pecuniary value for undertaking the murder is increased. For greater clarity, an additional guideline (§2A1.5) is inserted to cover conspiracy or solicitation to commit murder. Section 2E1.4 is amended to conform the offense level to that of §2A1.5. **The effective date of this amendment is November 1, 1990.**

312. Section 2B1.1(b) is amended by transposing subdivisions (4) and (5); and by renumbering the transposed subdivisions accordingly.

Section 2B1.2(b) is amended by transposing subdivisions (3) and (4); and by renumbering the transposed subdivisions accordingly.

Section 2B1.3(b) is amended by transposing subdivisions (2) and (3); and by renumbering the transposed subdivisions accordingly.

This amendment reorders the specific offense characteristics in §§2B1.1, 2B1.2, and 2B1.3 that address offenses involving U.S. mail. In cases involving the theft or destruction of U.S. mail, the theft guideline (§2B1.1), stolen property guideline (§2B1.2), property destruction guideline (§2B1.3), and forgery guideline (§2B5.2) produce identical results if the amount involved more than $1,000, or if the offense did not involve more than minimal planning.

However, because of the ordering of the specific offense characteristics, there is a 1 or 2-level difference between §§2B1.1, 2B1.2 and 2B1.3 on the one hand, and §2B5.2 on the other, in cases of stolen or destroyed mail involving more than minimal planning and a loss of $1,000 or less. In these cases, §§2B1.1, 2B1.2 and 2B1.3 produce a result that is 1 or 2-levels lower than §2B5.2. This amendment corrects this anomaly by conforming the offense levels in §§2B1.1, 2B1.2, and 2B1.3 to that of §2B5.2 in such cases. **The effective date of this amendment is November 1, 1990.**

313. Section 2B1.3 is amended by inserting the following additional subsection:

"(c) Cross Reference

(1) If the offense involved arson, or property damage by use of explosives, apply §2K1.4 (Arson; Property Damage by Use of Explosives).";

and in the title by deleting "(Other than by Arson or Explosives)" immediately following "or Destruction".

The Commentary to §2B1.3 captioned "Statutory Provisions" is amended by deleting the last sentence as follows:

"Arson is treated separately in Part K, Offenses Involving Public Order and Safety.".

The Commentary to §2H1.1 captioned "Application Notes" is amended in Note 1 by deleting "(Other than by Arson or Explosives)" immediately following "or Destruction".

Section 2H3.3(a)(3) is amended by deleting "(Other than by Arson or Explosives)" immediately following "or Destruction".

The Commentary to §2H3.3 captioned "Background" is amended by deleting "(Other than by Arson or Explosives)" immediately following "or Destruction".

Section 2Q1.6(a)(2) is amended by deleting "(Other Than by Arson or Explosives)" immediately following "or Destruction".

This amendment inserts a cross reference providing that offense conduct constituting arson or property destruction by explosives is to be treated under §2K1.4 (Arson, Property Destruction by Explosives). Because arson or property damage by use of explosives is an aggravated form of property destruction, just as armed robbery is an aggravated form of robbery, the use of the same "relevant conduct" standard to determine the offense level is appropriate. **The effective date of this amendment is November 1, 1990.**

314. Section 2B3.1(b)(1) is amended by deleting "offense involved robbery or attempted robbery of the" immediately following "If the"; and by inserting "was taken, or if the taking of such property was an object of the offense" immediately before ", increase".

The Commentary to §2B3.1 captioned "Application Notes" is amended in Note 6 by deleting "actually" immediately following "defendant", and by inserting "; Attempted Murder" immediately following "Assault With Intent to Commit Murder".

This amendment clarifies the guideline and Commentary. **The effective date of this amendment is November 1, 1990.**

315. Section 2B2.1(b)(3) is amended by deleting "obtaining" immediately before "a firearm", and by deleting "an object" and inserting in lieu thereof "taken, or if the taking of such item was an object".

The Commentary to §2B2.1 is amended by inserting between "Commentary" and "Application Notes" the following:

"Statutory Provision: 18 U.S.C. § 1153.".

The Commentary to §2B2.1 captioned "Application Notes" is amended by deleting Note 2 as follows:

"2. Obtaining a weapon or controlled substance is to be presumed to be an object of the offense if such an item was in fact taken.";

and by renumbering Notes 3 and 4 as 2 and 3, respectively.

Section 2B2.2(b)(3) is amended by deleting "obtaining" immediately before "a firearm"; and by deleting "an object" and inserting in lieu thereof "taken, or if the taking of such item was an object".

The Commentary to §2B2.2 captioned "Application Notes" is amended by deleting Note 2 as follows:

"2. Obtaining a weapon or controlled substance is to be presumed to be an object of the offense if such an item was in fact taken.";

and by renumbering Notes 3 and 4 as 2 and 3, respectively.

Section 2B3.1(b)(5) is amended by deleting "obtaining" immediately before "a firearm"; and by deleting "the object" and inserting in lieu thereof "taken, or if the taking of such item was an object".

The Commentary to §2B3.1 captioned "Application Notes" is amended by deleting Note 5 as follows:

"5. Obtaining a weapon or controlled substance is to be presumed to be an object of the offense if such an item was in fact taken.";

and by renumbering Notes 6, 7, and 8 as 5, 6, and 7 respectively.

The Commentary to §2B3.1 captioned "Background" is amended by deleting the second paragraph as follows:

" Obtaining drugs or other controlled substances is often the motive for robberies of a Veterans Administration Hospital, a pharmacy on a military base, or a similar facility. A specific offense characteristic is included for robberies where drugs or weapons were the object of the offense to take account of the dangers involved when such items are taken.".

This amendment provides that the specific offense characteristic related to the taking of a firearm or controlled substance applies whenever such item is taken or is an object of the offense. Also, it inserts additional Commentary to §2B2.1 referencing a statutory provision contained in Appendix A (Statutory Index) to conform the format of this guideline to that of other offense guidelines. **The effective date of this amendment is November 1, 1990.**

316. Section 2B3.2(b)(1) is amended by deleting "§2B3.1" and inserting in lieu thereof "§2B2.1(b)(2)".

This amendment references the loss table to §2B2.1(b)(2) rather than §2B3.1. The amendment to the loss table in §2B3.1, effective November 1, 1989, inadvertently reduced the offense level for certain cases under this guideline by one level. **The effective date of this amendment is November 1, 1990.**

317. Section 2B1.1(b) is amended by inserting the following additional subdivision:

"(7) If the offense substantially jeopardized the safety and soundness of a financial institution, increase by 4 levels. If the resulting offense level is less than level 24, increase to level 24.".

The Commentary to §2B1.1 captioned "Application Notes" is amended by inserting the following additional notes:

"9. 'Financial institution,' as used in this guideline, is defined to include any institution described in 18 U.S.C. §§ 215, 656-657, 1005-1008, 1014, and 1344; any state or foreign bank, trust company, credit union, insurance company, investment company, mutual fund, savings (building and loan) association, union or employee pension fund; any health, medical or hospital insurance association; brokers and dealers registered, or required to be registered, with the Securities and Exchange Commission; futures commodity merchants and commodity pool operators registered, or required to be registered, with the Commodity Futures Trading Commission; and any similar entity, whether or not insured by the federal government. 'Union or employee pension fund' and 'any health, medical, or hospital insurance association,' as used above, primarily include large pension funds that serve many individuals (e.g., pension funds of large national and international organizations, unions, and corporations doing substantial interstate business), and associations that undertake to provide pension, disability, or other benefits (e.g., medical or hospitalization insurance) to large numbers of persons.

10. An offense shall be deemed to have 'substantially jeopardized the safety and soundness of a financial institution' if as a consequence of the offense the institution became insolvent, substantially reduced benefits to pensioners or insureds, was unable on demand to refund fully any deposit, payment or investment, or was so depleted of its assets as to be forced to merge with another institution in order to continue active operations.".

The Commentary to §2B1.1 captioned "Background" is amended by inserting the following additional paragraph at the end:

" Subsection (b)(7) implements, in a broader form, the statutory directive to the Commission in Section 961(m) of Public Law 101-73.".

Section 2B4.1(b) is amended by deleting "Characteristic" and inserting in lieu thereof "Characteristics"; and by inserting the following additional subdivision:

"(2) If the offense substantially jeopardized the safety and soundness of a financial institution, increase by 4 levels. If the resulting offense level is less than level 24, increase to level 24.".

The Commentary to §2B4.1 captioned "Statutory Provisions" is amended by deleting "§§ 1," and inserting in lieu thereof "§§".

The Commentary to §2B4.1 captioned "Application Notes" is amended by inserting the following additional notes:

"3. 'Financial institution,' as used in this guideline, is defined to include any institution described in 18 U.S.C. §§ 215, 656-657, 1005-1008, 1014, and 1344; any state or foreign bank, trust company, credit union, insurance company, investment company, mutual fund, savings (building and loan) association, union or employee pension fund; any health, medical or hospital insurance association; brokers and dealers registered, or required to be registered, with the Securities and Exchange Commission; futures commodity merchants and commodity pool operators registered, or required to be registered, with the Commodity Futures Trading Commission; and any similar entity, whether or not insured by the federal government. 'Union or employee pension fund' and 'any health, medical, or hospital insurance association,' as used above, primarily include large pension funds that serve many individuals (e.g., pension funds of large national and international organizations, unions, and corporations doing substantial interstate business), and associations that undertake to provide pension, disability, or other benefits (e.g., medical or hospitalization insurance) to large numbers of persons.

4. An offense shall be deemed to have 'substantially jeopardized the safety and soundness of a financial institution' if as a consequence of the offense the institution became insolvent, substantially reduced benefits to pensioners or insureds, was unable on demand to refund fully any deposit, payment or investment, or was so depleted of its assets as to be forced to merge with another institution in order to continue active operations.".

The Commentary to §2B4.1 captioned "Background" is amended by inserting the following additional paragraph at the end:

" Subsection (b)(2) implements, in a broader form, the statutory directive to the Commission in Section 961(m) of Public Law 101-73.".

Section 2F1.1(b) is amended by inserting the following additional subdivision:

"(6) If the offense substantially jeopardized the safety and soundness of a financial institution, increase by 4 levels. If the resulting offense level is less than level 24, increase to level 24.".

The Commentary to §2F1.1 captioned "Statutory Provisions" is amended by deleting "290" and inserting in lieu thereof "289".

The Commentary to §2F1.1 captioned "Application Notes" is amended by inserting the following additional notes:

"14. 'Financial institution,' as used in this guideline, is defined to include any institution described in 18 U.S.C. §§ 215, 656-657, 1005-1008, 1014, and 1344; any state or foreign bank, trust company, credit union, insurance company, investment company, mutual fund, savings (building and loan) association, union or employee pension fund; any health, medical or hospital insurance association; brokers and dealers registered, or required to be registered, with the Securities and Exchange Commission; futures commodity merchants and commodity pool operators registered, or required to be registered, with the Commodity Futures Trading Commission; and any similar entity, whether or not insured by the federal government. 'Union or employee pension fund' and 'any health, medical, or hospital insurance association,' as used above, primarily include large pension funds that serve many individuals (e.g., pension funds of large national and international organizations, unions, and corporations doing substantial interstate business), and associations that undertake to provide pension, disability, or other benefits (e.g., medical or hospitalization insurance) to large numbers of persons.

15. An offense shall be deemed to have 'substantially jeopardized the safety and soundness of a financial institution' if as a consequence of the offense the institution became insolvent, substantially reduced benefits to pensioners or

insureds, was unable on demand to refund fully any deposit, payment or investment, or was so depleted of its assets as to be forced to merge with another institution in order to continue active operations.".

The Commentary to §2F1.1 captioned "Background" is amended by inserting the following additional paragraph at the end:

" Subsection (b)(6) implements, in a broader form, the statutory directive to the Commission in Section 961(m) of Public Law 101-73.".

This amendment implements, in a broader form, the following statutory directive in Section 961(m) of Public Law 101-73: "Pursuant to section 994 of title 28, United States Code, and section 21 of the Sentencing Act of 1987, the United States Sentencing Commission shall promulgate guidelines, or amend existing guidelines, to provide for a substantial period of incarceration for a violation of, or a conspiracy to violate, section 215, 656, 657, 1005, 1006, 1007, 1014, 1341, 1343, or 1344 of title 18, United States Code, that substantially jeopardizes the safety and soundness of a federally insured financial institution." In addition, this amendment deletes an incorrect statutory provision in the Commentary to §2B4.1, and deletes a reference to a petty offense in the Commentary to §2F1.1 that was inadvertently retained when other references to petty offenses were deleted. **The effective date of this amendment is November 1, 1990.**

318. The Commentary to §2D1.1 captioned "Application Notes" is amended in Note 10 in the subdivision of the "Drug Equivalency Tables" captioned "Cocaine and Other Schedule I and II Stimulants (and their immediate precursors)" by inserting the following additional entry as the seventh entry: "1 gm of Methamphetamine (Pure) = 50 gm of cocaine/10 gm of heroin".

The Commentary to §2D1.1 captioned "Application Notes" is amended in Note 10 in the subdivision of the "Drug Equivalency Tables" captioned "Cocaine and Other Schedule I and II Stimulants (and their immediate precursors)" in the twelfth (fomerly eleventh) entry by deleting "0.418 gm" and inserting in lieu thereof "0.416 gm".

The Commentary to §2D1.1 captioned "Application Notes" is amended in Note 10 in the subdivision of the "Drug Equivalency Tables" captioned "Schedule IV Substances" by deleting the sixth entry as follows:

"1 gm of Mephobarbital = 0.125 mg of heroin/0.125 gm of marihuana".

The Commentary to §2D1.1 captioned "Application Notes" is amended in Note 11 by inserting "in the table below" immediately before "to estimate"; by deleting "Bufotenine at 1 mg per dose = 100 mg of Bufotenine" and inserting in lieu thereof "Mescaline at 500 mg per dose = 50 gms of mescaline"; and by deleting "common controlled substances" and inserting in lieu thereof "certain controlled substances. Do not use this table if any more reliable estimate of the total weight is available from case-specific information".

The Commentary to §2D1.1 captioned "Application Notes" is amended in Note 11 by deleting the following from the table captioned "Typical Weight Per Unit (Dose, Pill, or Capsule) Table":

"Bufotenine	1 mg
Diethyltryptamine	60 mg
Dimethyltryptamine	50 mg",
"Barbiturates	100 mg
Glutethimide (Doriden)	500 mg",
"Thiobarbital	50 mg";

by inserting an asterisk immediately after each of the following:

"LSD (Lysergic acid diethylamide)", "MDA", "PCP", "Psilocin", "Psilocybin", "2,5-Dimethoxy-4-methylamphetamine (STP, DOM)", "Methaqualone", "Amphetamine", "Methamphetamine", "Phenmetrazine (Preludin)";

and by inserting the following at the end:

"*For controlled substances marked with an asterisk, the weight per unit shown is the weight of the actual controlled substance, and not generally the weight of the mixture or substance containing the controlled substance. Therefore, use of this table provides a very conservative estimate of the total weight.".

This amendment provides an additional equivalency to reflect the distinction between methamphetamine and pure methamphetamine in the Drug Quantity Table at §2D1.1(c), corrects an error in the equivalency for Phenylacetone/P_2P, and deletes a duplicate listing for Mephobarbital.

In addition, this amendment clarifies that the "Typical Weight Per Unit Table" in Note 11 of the Commentary to §2D1.1 is not to be used where a more reliable estimate of the weight of the mixture or substance containing the controlled substance is available from case-specific information. This amendment also clarifies that for certain controlled substances this table provides an estimate of the weight of the actual controlled substance, not necessarily the weight of the mixture or substance containing the controlled substance, and therefore use of this table in such cases will provide a very conservative estimate. Finally, this amendment deletes listings for several controlled substances that are generally legitimately manufactured and then unlawfully diverted; in such cases, more accurate weight estimates can be obtained from other sources (e.g., from the Drug Enforcement Administration or the manufacturer). **The effective date of this amendment is November 1, 1990.**

319. Section 2D1.2(a)(1) is amended by inserting "applicable to the quantity of controlled substances directly involving a protected location or an underage or pregnant individual" immediately following "§2D1.1".

Section §2D1.2(a) is amended by renumbering subdivisions (2) and (3) as (3) and (4), respectively; and by inserting the following as subdivision (2):

"(2) 1 plus the offense level from §2D1.1 applicable to the total quantity of controlled substances involved in the offense; or".

The Commentary to §2D1.2 is amended by inserting, immediately before "Background", the following:

"Application Note:

1. Where only part of the relevant offense conduct directly involved a protected location or an underage or pregnant individual, subsections (a)(1) and (a)(2) may result in different offense levels. For example, if the defendant, as part of the same course of conduct or common scheme or plan, sold 5 grams of heroin near a protected location and 10 grams of heroin elsewhere, the offense level from subsection (a)(1) would be level 16 (2 plus the offense level for the sale of 5 grams of heroin, the amount sold near the protected location); the offense level from subsection (a)(2) would be level 17 (1 plus the offense level for the sale of 15 grams of heroin, the total amount of heroin involved in the offense).".

This amendment provides for the determination of the offense level in cases in which only part of the relevant offense conduct involves a protected location or an underage or pregnant individual. **The effective date of this amendment is November 1, 1990.**

320. Section 2D1.6 is amended by deleting "12" and inserting in lieu thereof: "the offense level applicable to the underlying offense.".

The Commentary to §2D1.6 is amended by inserting, immediately before "Background", the following:

"Application Note:

1. Where the offense level for the underlying offense is to be determined by reference to §2D1.1, see Application Note 12 of the Commentary to §2D1.1, and Application Notes 1 and 2 of the Commentary to §2D1.4, for guidance in determining the scale of the offense. Note that the Drug Quantity Table in §2D1.1 provides a minimum offense level of 12 where the offense involves heroin (or other Schedule I or II Opiates), cocaine (or other Schedule I or II Stimulants), cocaine base, PCP, Methamphetamine, LSD (or other Schedule I or II Hallucinogens), Fentanyl, or Fentanyl Analogue (§2D1.1(c)(16)); and a minimum offense level of 6 otherwise (§2D1.1(c)(19)).".

This amendment is designed to reduce unwarranted disparity by requiring consideration in the guideline of the amount of the controlled substance involved in the offense, thus conforming this guideline section to the structure of §§2D1.1, 2D1.2, 2D1.4, and 2D1.5. The statute to which this guideline applies (21 U.S.C. § 843(b)) prohibits the use of a communications facility to commit, cause, or facilitate a felony controlled substance offense. Frequently, a conviction under this statute is the result of a plea bargain because the statute has a low maximum (four years with no prior felony drug conviction; eight years with a prior felony drug conviction) and no mandatory minimum. The current guideline has a base offense level of 12 and no specific offense characteristics. Therefore, the scale of the underlying drug offense is not reflected in the guideline. This results in a departure from the guideline range frequently being warranted. Without guidance as to whether or how far to depart, the potential for unwarranted disparity is substantial. Under this amendment, the guideline itself will take into account the scale of the underlying offense. **The effective date of this amendment is November 1, 1990.**

321. Section 2D2.1(a)(1) is amended by deleting "or an analogue of these" and inserting in lieu thereof "an analogue of these, or cocaine base".

This amendment specifies the appropriate offense level for possession of cocaine base ("crack") in cases not covered by the enhanced penalties created by section 6371 of the Anti-Drug Abuse Act of 1988. **The effective date of this amendment is November 1, 1990.**

322. Section 2G1.1(c)(1) is amended by deleting "involves" and inserting in lieu thereof "involved".

The Commentary to §2G1.1 captioned "Application Notes" is amended in Note 3 by inserting at the end:

"This factor would apply, for example, where the ability of the person being transported to appraise or control conduct was substantially impaired by drugs or alcohol. In the case of transportation involving an adult, rather than a minor, this characteristic generally will not apply where the alcohol or drug was voluntarily taken.".

The Commentary to §2G1.1 captioned "Application Notes" is amended in Note 5 by deleting ", distinct offense, even if several persons are transported in a single act" and inserting in lieu thereof:

> "victim. Consequently, multiple counts involving the transportation of different persons are not to be grouped together under §3D1.2 (Groups of Closely-Related Counts). Special instruction (c)(1) directs that if the relevant conduct of an offense of conviction includes more than one person being transported, whether specifically cited in the count of conviction or not, each such person shall be treated as if contained in a separate count of conviction".

This amendment clarifies the application of this guideline and corrects a clerical error. **The effective date of this amendment is November 1, 1990.**

323. Section 2G1.2(c)(1) is amended by deleting "involves" and inserting in lieu thereof "involved".

Section 2G1.2 is amended by inserting the following additional subsection:

> "(d) Cross Reference
>
> (1) If the offense involved the defendant causing, transporting, permitting, or offering or seeking by notice or advertisement, a minor to engage in sexually explicit conduct for the purpose of producing a visual depiction of such conduct, apply §2G2.1 (Sexually Exploiting a Minor by Production of Sexually Explicit Visual or Printed Material; Custodian Permitting Minor to Engage in Sexually Explicit Conduct; Advertisement for Minors to Engage in Production).".

The Commentary to §2G1.2 captioned "Statutory Provisions" is amended by deleting "§ 2423" and inserting in lieu thereof "§§ 2421, 2422, 2423".

The Commentary to §2G1.2 captioned "Application Notes" is amended in Note 1 by deleting ", distinct offense, even if several persons are transported in a single act" and inserting in lieu thereof:

> "victim. Consequently, multiple counts involving the transportation of different persons are not to be grouped together under §3D1.2 (Groups of Closely-Related Counts). Special instruction (c)(1) directs that if the relevant conduct of an offense of conviction includes more than one person being transported, whether specifically cited in the count of conviction or not, each such person shall be treated as if contained in a separate count of conviction".

The Commentary to §2G1.2 captioned "Application Notes" is amended in Note 3 by inserting the following at the end:

> "This factor would apply, for example, where the ability of the person being transported to appraise or control conduct was substantially impaired by drugs or alcohol.".

The Commentary to §2G1.2 captioned "Application Notes" is amended by inserting the following additional notes:

> "4. 'Sexually explicit conduct,' as used in this guideline, has the meaning set forth in 18 U.S.C. § 2256.
>
> 5. The cross reference in (d)(1) is to be construed broadly to include all instances where the offense involved employing, using, persuading, inducing, enticing,

coercing, transporting, permitting, or offering or seeking by notice or advertisement, a minor to engage in sexually explicit conduct for the purpose of producing any visual depiction of such conduct.".

This amendment clarifies the application of this guideline and corrects a clerical error. In addition, a cross reference to §2G2.1 is inserted where the offense involves conduct that is more appropriately covered by that guideline to provide an offense level that more appropriately reflects the seriousness of such conduct. **The effective date of this amendment is November 1, 1990.**

324. Section 2G2.1 is amended in the title by inserting "; Custodian Permitting Minor to Engage in Sexually Explicit Conduct; Advertisement for Minors to Engage in Production" immediately following "Printed Material".

Section 2G2.1 is amended by deleting:

"(1) If the minor was under the age of twelve years, increase by 2 levels.";

and inserting in lieu thereof:

"(1) If the offense involved a minor under the age of twelve years, increase by 4 levels; otherwise, if the offense involved a minor under the age of sixteen years, increase by 2 levels.

(2) If the defendant was a parent, relative, or legal guardian of the minor involved in the offense, or if the minor was otherwise in the custody, care, or supervisory control of the defendant, increase by 2 levels.

(c) Special Instruction

(1) If the offense involved the exploitation of more than one minor, Chapter Three, Part D (Multiple Counts) shall be applied as if the exploitation of each minor had been contained in a separate count of conviction.";

and by deleting "Characteristic" and inserting in lieu thereof "Characteristics".

The Commentary to §2G2.1 captioned "Statutory Provisions" is amended by deleting "8 U.S.C. § 1328;"; and by inserting "(a), (b), (c)(1)(B)" immediately following "18 U.S.C. § 2251".

The Commentary to §2G2.1 captioned "Application Notes" is amended in Note 1 by inserting at the end:

"Special instruction (c)(1) directs that if the relevant conduct of an offense of conviction includes more than one minor being exploited, whether specifically cited in the count of conviction or not, each such minor shall be treated as if contained in a separate count of conviction.".

The Commentary to §2G2.1 captioned "Application Note" is amended by inserting the following additional notes:

"2. Specific offense characteristic (b)(2) is intended to have broad application and includes offenses involving a minor entrusted to the defendant, whether temporarily or permanently. For example, teachers, day care providers, baby-sitters, or other temporary caretakers are among those who would be subject to this enhancement. In determining whether to apply this adjustment, the court should look to the actual relationship that existed between the defendant and the child and not simply to the legal status of the defendant-child relationship.

3. If specific offense characteristic (b)(2) applies, no adjustment is to be made under §3B1.3 (Abuse of Position of Trust or Use of Special Skill).";

and in the caption by deleting "Note" and inserting in lieu thereof "Notes".

The Commentary to §2G2.1 captioned "Background" is deleted in its entirety as follows:

"Background: This offense commonly involves the production source of a child pornography enterprise. Because the offense directly involves the exploitation of minors, the base offense level is higher than for the distribution of the sexually explicit material after production. An enhancement is provided when the conduct involves the exploitation of a minor under age twelve to reflect the more serious nature of exploiting young children.".

This amendment revises subsection (b)(1) to provide distinctions for the age of the victim consistent with §2G1.2, and adds subsection (b)(2) to provide an increase for defendants who abuse a position of trust in exploiting minor children. A special instruction is added to conform the operation of the multiple count rule in this guideline with §§2G1.1 and 2G1.2. A revision to the statutory provisions removes 8 U.S.C. § 1328; such offenses are now brought under this guideline by the cross reference appearing in §2G1.2. In addition, the reference in the statutory provisions to 18 U.S.C. § 2251 is made specific to the appropriate subsections. **The effective date of this amendment is November 1, 1990.**

325. Section 2G2.2 is amended by inserting the following at the end:

" (3) If the offense involved material that portrays sadistic or masochistic conduct or other depictions of violence, increase by 4 levels.

(c) Cross Reference

(1) If the offense involved causing, transporting, permitting, or offering or seeking by notice or advertisement, a minor to engage in sexually explicit conduct for the purpose of producing a visual depiction of such conduct, apply §2G2.1 (Sexually Exploiting a Minor by Production of Sexually Explicit Visual or Printed Material; Custodian Permitting Minor to Engage in Sexually Explicit Conduct; Advertisement for Minors to Engage in Production) if the resulting offense level is greater than that determined above.".

The Commentary to §2G2.2 captioned "Statutory Provision" is amended by deleting "Provision" and inserting in lieu thereof "Provisions"; and by inserting "§ 1460, 2251(c)(1)(A)," immediately before "2252".

The Commentary to §2G2.2 captioned "Application Note" is amended by inserting the following additonal notes:

"2. 'Sexually explicit conduct,' as used in this guideline, has the meaning set forth in 18 U.S.C. § 2256.

3. The cross reference in (c)(1) is to be construed broadly to include all instances where the offense involved employing, using, persuading, inducing, enticing, coercing, transporting, permitting, or offering or seeking by notice or advertisement, a minor to engage in sexually explicit conduct for the purpose of producing any visual depiction of such conduct.

4. If the defendant sexually abused a minor at any time, whether or not such sexual abuse occurred during the course of the offense, an upward departure is warranted. In determining the extent of such a departure, the court should take into consideration the offense levels provided in §§2A3.1, 2A3.2, and 2A3.4 most commensurate with the defendant's conduct.";

and in the caption by deleting "Note" and inserting in lieu thereof "Notes".

This amendment provides a specific offense characteristic for materials involving depictions of sadistic or masochistic conduct or other violence, and a cross reference for offenses more appropriately treated under §2G2.1. It also provides Commentary recommending consideration of an upward departure in cases in which the defendant has sexually abused a minor at any time, whether or not such sexual abuse occurred during the course of the instant offense. In addition, it inserts a statutory provision indicating the applicability of this guideline to violations of 18 U.S.C. § 2251(c)(1)(A). **The effective date of this amendment is November 1, 1990.**

326. Section 2G3.1(b)(2) is amended by deleting "sadomasochistic" and inserting in lieu thereof "sadistic or masochistic".

Section 2G3.1(c) is amended by deleting:

"(1) If the offense involved a criminal enterprise, apply the appropriate guideline from Chapter Two, Part E (Offenses Involving Criminal Enterprises and Racketeering) if the resulting offense level is greater than that determined above.",

and inserting in lieu thereof:

"(1) If the offense involved transporting, distributing, receiving, possessing, or advertising to receive material involving the sexual exploitation of a minor, apply §2G2.2 (Transporting, Receiving, or Trafficking in Material Involving the Sexual Exploitation of a Minor).".

This amendment inserts a cross reference to §2G2.2 for offenses involving materials which, in fact, depict children to ensure that the penalties for such offenses adequately reflect their seriousness. The current cross reference at subsection (c)(1) is deleted. In addition, the amendment conforms the terminology of specific offense characteristic (b)(2) to that used in other offense guidelines. **The effective date of this amendment is November 1, 1990.**

327. Section 2H1.1 is amended in the title by inserting "Conspiracy to Interfere with Civil Rights;" immediately before "Going".

Chapter Two, Part H, Subpart 1 is amended by deleting §2H1.2 in its entirety as follows:

"§2H1.2. Conspiracy to Interfere with Civil Rights

(a) Base Offense Level (Apply the greater):

(1) 13; or

(2) 2 plus the offense level applicable to any underlying offense.

(b) Specific Offense Characteristic

(1) If the defendant was a public official at the time of the offense, increase by 4 levels.

Commentary

Statutory Provision: 18 U.S.C. § 241.

Application Notes:

1. '2 plus the offense level applicable to any underlying offense' is defined in the Commentary to §2H1.1.

2. Where the adjustment in §2H1.2(b)(1) is applied, do not apply §3B1.3 (Abuse of Position of Trust or Use of Special Skill).

Background: This section applies to conspiracies to interfere with civil rights. The maximum term of imprisonment authorized by statute is ten years; except where death results, the maximum term of imprisonment authorized by statute is life imprisonment. The base offense level for this guideline assumes threatening or otherwise serious conduct.".

The Commentary to §2X1.1 captioned "Application Notes" is amended in Note 1 in the paragraph beginning "Offense guidelines that expressly cover conspiracies" by deleting "§2H1.2 (Conspiracy to Interfere with Civil Rights)" and inserting in lieu thereof "§2H1.1 (Conspiracy to Interfere With Civil Rights; Going in Disguise to Deprive of Rights)".

This amendment consolidates two guidelines and raises the minimum base offense level from level 13 to level 15 for cases currently covered under §2H1.2 to better reflect the seriousness of this offense. **The effective date of this amendment is November 1, 1990.**

328. The Commentary to §2H1.5 captioned "Statutory Provisions" is amended by deleting "Provisions" and inserting in lieu thereof "Provision"; and by deleting "; 42 U.S.C. § 3631".

The Commentary to §2H1.5 captioned "Application Notes" is amended by deleting Note 3 as follows:

"3. In the case of a violation of 42 U.S.C. § 3631, apply this guideline where the offense did not involve the threat or use of force. If the offense involved the threat or use of force, apply §2H1.3.".

This amendment deletes references to a statute to which this guideline does not apply. **The effective date of this amendment is November 1, 1990.**

329. Section 2J1.6 is amended by deleting:

"(a) Base Offense Level: 6

(b) Specific Offense Characteristics

(1) If the underlying offense is punishable by death or imprisonment for a term of fifteen years or more, increase by 9 levels.

(2) If the underlying offense is punishable by a term of imprisonment of five or more years, but less than fifteen years, increase by 6 levels.

(3) If the underlying offense is a felony punishable by a maximum term of less than five years, increase by 3 levels.",

and inserting in lieu thereof:

"(a) Base Offense Level:

(1) 11, if the offense constituted a failure to report for service of sentence; or

(2) 6, otherwise.

(b) Specific Offense Characteristics

(1) If the base offense level is determined under subsection (a)(1), and the defendant --

(A) voluntarily surrendered within 96 hours of the time he was originally scheduled to report, decrease by 5 levels; or

(B) was ordered to report to a community corrections center, community treatment center, 'halfway house,' or similar facility, and subdivision (A) above does not apply, decrease by 2 levels.

Provided, however, that this reduction shall not apply if the defendant, while away from the facility, committed any federal, state, or local offense punishable by a term of imprisonment of one year or more.

(2) If the base offense level is determined under subsection (a)(2), and the underlying offense is --

(A) punishable by death or imprisonment for a term of fifteen years or more, increase by 9 levels; or

(B) punishable by a term of imprisonment of five years or more, but less than fifteen years, increase by 6 levels; or

(C) a felony punishable by a term of imprisonment of less than five years, increase by 3 levels.".

The Commentary to §2J1.6 captioned "Background" is amended by deleting "The offense level for this offense" and inserting in lieu thereof "Where the base offense level is determined under subsection (a)(2), the offense level".

This amendment provides greater differentiation in the guideline offense levels for the various types of conduct covered by this guideline. **The effective date of this amendment is November 1, 1990.**

330. Chapter Two, Part K, Subpart 1 is amended by deleting §2K1.4 in its entirety as follows:

"§2K1.4. Arson; Property Damage By Use of Explosives

(a) Base Offense Level: 6

(b) Specific Offense Characteristics

If more than one applies, use the greatest:

(1) If the defendant knowingly created a substantial risk of death or serious bodily injury, increase by 18 levels.

(2) If the defendant recklessly endangered the safety of another, increase by 14 levels.

(3) If the offense involved destruction or attempted destruction of a residence, increase by 12 levels.

(4) If the defendant used fire or an explosive to commit another offense that is a felony under federal law, or carried explosives during the commission of any offense that is a felony under federal law (i.e., the defendant is convicted under 18 U.S.C. § 844(h)), increase by 7 levels.

(5) If the defendant endangered the safety of another person, increase by 4 levels.

(6) If a destructive device was used, increase by 2 levels.

(c) Cross References

(1) If the defendant caused death, or intended to cause bodily injury, apply the most analogous guideline from Chapter Two, Part A (Offenses Against the Person) if the resulting offense level is greater than that determined above.

(2) Apply §2B1.3 (Property Damage or Destruction) if the resulting offense level is greater than that determined above.

(d) Note

(1) The specific offense characteristic in subsection (b)(4) applies only in the case of an offense committed prior to November 18, 1988.

Commentary

Statutory Provisions: 18 U.S.C. §§ 32, 33, 81, 844(f), (h) (only in the case of an offense committed prior to November 18, 1988), (i), 1153, 1855, 2275.

Application Notes:

1. 'Destructive device' means any article described in 18 U.S.C. § 921(a)(4) (for example, explosive, incendiary, or poison gas bombs, grenades, mines, and similar devices and certain rockets, missiles, and large bore weapons).

2. If bodily injury resulted, an upward departure may be warranted. See Chapter Five, Part K (Departures).

Background: Review of presentence reports indicates that many arson cases involve 'malicious mischief,' i.e., minor property damage under circumstances that do not present an appreciable danger. A low base offense level is provided for these cases. However, aggravating factors are provided for instances where a defendant knowingly or recklessly endangered others, destroyed or attempted to destroy a residence, used a destructive device, or otherwise endangered others. As amended by Section 6474(b) of the Anti-Drug Abuse Act of 1988 (effective November 18, 1988), 18 U.S.C. § 844(h) sets forth a mandatory sentencing enhancement of five years for the first offense and ten years for subsequent offenses if the defendant was convicted of using fire or an explosive to commit a felony or of carrying an explosive during the commission of a felony. See §2K1.7.".

A replacement guideline with accompanying commentary is inserted as §2K1.4 (Arson; Property Damage by Use of Explosives).

This amendment restructures this guideline to provide more appropriate offense levels for the conduct covered. The Commission has determined that the offense levels provided in the current guideline do not adequately reflect the seriousness of the offenses that are covered under this section. **The effective date of this amendment is November 1, 1990.**

331. Section 2K1.6(a) is amended by deleting "greater" and inserting in lieu thereof "greatest"; and by inserting the following additional subdivision:

"(3) If death resulted, apply the most analogous guideline from Chapter Two, Part A, Subpart 1 (Homicide).".

Section 2K1.6(a)(2) is amended by deleting the period at the end and inserting in lieu thereof "; or".

This amendment adds an additional alternative base offense level to cover the situation in which the commission of this offense results in death. **The effective date of this amendment is November 1, 1990.**

332. Section 2K1.7 is amended by inserting "(a)" immediately before "If"; and by inserting the following additional subsection:

"(b) Special Instruction for Fines

(1) Where there is a federal conviction for the underlying offense, the fine guideline shall be the fine guideline that would have been applicable had there only been a conviction for the underlying offense. This guideline shall be used as a consolidated fine guideline for both the underlying offense and the conviction underlying this section.".

The Commentary to §2K1.7 captioned "Application Notes" is amended by inserting the following additional notes:

"3. Where a sentence under this section is imposed in conjunction with a sentence for an underlying offense, any specific offense characteristic for the use of fire or explosives is not to be applied in respect to the guideline for the underlying offense.

4. Subsection (b) sets forth special provisions concerning the imposition of fines. Where there is also a conviction for the underlying offense, a consolidated fine guideline is determined by the offense level that would have applied to the underlying offense absent a conviction under 18 U.S.C. § 844(h). This is required because the offense level for the underlying offense may be reduced in that any specific offense characteristic for use of fire or explosives would not be applied (see Application Note 3). The Commission has not established a fine guideline range for the unusual case in which there is no conviction for the underlying offense, although a fine is authorized under 18 U.S.C. § 3571.".

The Commentary to §2K2.4 captioned "Application Notes" is amended in Note 4 in the third sentence by inserting "required" immediately before "because"; and by inserting ", although a fine is authorized under 18 U.S.C. § 3571" immediately before the period at the end of the last sentence.

This amendment conforms §2K1.7 to §2K2.4, which includes specific instructions concerning treatment of fines and double counting. Both sections are based upon similarly written statutes that provide for a fixed mandatory, consecutive sentence of imprisonment. In addition, Application Note 4 of the Commentary to §2K2.4 is revised and expanded for greater clarity. **The effective date of this amendment is November 1, 1990.**

333. Section 2K2.1(a)(1) is amended by deleting "16" and inserting in lieu thereof "18".

Section 2K2.1(b)(1) is amended by inserting ", other than a firearm covered in 26 U.S.C. § 5845(a)," immediately following "ammunition".

Section 2K2.2(a)(1) is amended by deleting "16" and inserting in lieu thereof "18".

This amendment provides that the reduction in offense level under subsection (b)(1) for possession of a weapon for sporting purposes or collection may not be applied in the case of any weapon described in 26 U.S.C. § 5845(a). In addition, the amendment increases the base offense level in subsection (a)(1) of §§2K2.1 and 2K2.2 from 16 to 18 to better reflect the seriousness of the conduct covered. **The effective date of this amendment is November 1, 1990.**

334. Chapter Two, Part K, Subpart 3 is amended by inserting an additional guideline with accompanying commentary as §2K3.2 (Feloniously Mailing Injurious Articles).

This amendment adds an additional guideline covering the felony provisions of 18 U.S.C. § 1716. **The effective date of this amendment is November 1, 1990.**

335. Section 2L1.1(b)(1) is amended by deleting "and without knowledge that the alien was excludable under 8 U.S.C. §§ 1182(a)(27), (28), (29)," immediately before "decrease".

The Commentary to §2L1.1 captioned "Application Notes" is amended by deleting:

"7. 8 U.S.C. §§ 1182(a)(27), (a)(28), and (a)(29) concern certain aliens who are excludable because they are subversives.",

and inserting in lieu thereof:

"7. Where the defendant smuggled, transported, or harbored an alien knowing that the alien intended to enter the United States to engage in subversive activity, an upward departure may be warranted.".

The Commentary to §2L1.1 captioned "Background" is amended in the second sentence by deleting "and did not know the alien was excludable as a subversive" immediately following "profit".

This amendment deletes a portion of specific offense characteristic (b)(1) that is unclear in application, and in any event rarely occurs, and replaces it with an application note indicating that an upward departure may be warranted in the circumstances specified. **The effective date of this amendment is November 1, 1990.**

336. Section 2M4.1(b)(1) is amended by deleting "while" and inserting in lieu thereof "at a time when"; and by deleting "into the armed services, other than in time of war or armed conflict" and inserting in lieu thereof "for compulsory military service".

The Commentary to §2M4.1 captioned "Application Notes" is amended by deleting:

"1. 'While persons were being inducted into the armed services' means at a time of compulsory military service under the Selective Service laws.

2. The Commission has not considered the appropriate sanction for this offense when persons are being inducted during time of war or armed conflict.",

and inserting in lieu thereof:

"1. Subsection (b)(1) does not distinguish between whether the offense was committed in peacetime or during time of war or armed conflict. If the offense was committed when persons were being inducted for compulsory military service during time of war or armed conflict, an upward departure may be warranted.";

and in the caption by deleting "Notes" and inserting in lieu thereof "Note".

This amendment clarifies this guideline and deletes language that produced the anomalous result of a lower offense level for failure to register and evasion of military service in time of war or armed conflict than during a peacetime draft. In addition, the amendment makes a technical correction to the language of the guideline that enables the elimination of current Application Note 1. **The effective date of this amendment is November 1, 1990.**

337. Section 2M5.2 is amended by deleting:

"(a) Base Offense Level (Apply the greater):

(1) 22, if sophisticated weaponry was involved; or

(2) 14.",

and inserting in lieu thereof:

"(a) Base Offense Level:

(1) 22, except as provided in subdivision (2) below;

(2) 14, if the offense involved only non-fully-automatic small arms (rifles, handguns, or shotguns), and the number of weapons did not exceed ten.".

The Commentary to §2M5.2 captioned "Statutory Provision" is amended by deleting "Provision" and inserting in lieu thereof "Provisions", and by deleting "§ 2778" and inserting in lieu thereof "§§ 2778, 2780".

The Commentary to §2M5.2 captioned "Application Notes" is amended in Note 1 by inserting, immediately before "In the case of a violation", the following:

"Under 22 U.S.C. § 2778, the President is authorized, through a licensing system administered by the Department of State, to control exports of defense articles and defense services that he deems critical to a security or foreign policy interest of the United States. The items subject to control constitute the United States Munitions List, which is set out in 22 C.F.R. Part 121.1. Included in this list are such things as military aircraft, helicopters, artillery, shells, missiles, rockets, bombs, vessels of war, explosives, military and space electronics, and certain firearms.

The base offense level assumes that the offense conduct was harmful or had the potential to be harmful to a security or foreign policy interest of the United States. In the unusual case where the offense conduct posed no such risk, a downward departure may be warranted.".

The Commentary to §2M5.2 captioned "Application Notes" is amended in the first sentence of Note 2 by inserting "or foreign policy" immediately before "interest".

This amendment revises this guideline to better distinguish the more and less serious forms of offense conduct covered. **The effective date of this amendment is November 1, 1990.**

338. Section 2N1.1 is amended by inserting the following additional subsection:

"(b) Cross Reference

(1) If the offense involved extortion, apply §2B3.2 (Extortion by Force or Threat of Injury or Serious Damage) if the resulting offense level is greater than that determined above.".

This amendment adds a cross reference to ensure that in the case of an offense involving extortion, the offense level will not be lower than that under §2B3.2. **The effective date of this amendment is November 1, 1990.**

339. Section 2N1.2 is amended by deleting:

"(a) Base Offense Level (Apply the greater):

(1) 16;

(2) If the offense involved extortion, apply §2B3.2.",

and inserting in lieu thereof:

"(a) Base Offense Level: 16

(b) Cross Reference

(1) If the offense involved extortion, apply §2B3.2 (Extortion by Force or Threat of Injury or Serious Damage).".

The Commentary to §2N1.2 captioned "Application Notes" is amended by deleting Note 1 as follows:

"1. If the offense involved extortion, apply the guideline from §2B3.2 (Extortion by Force or Threat of Injury or Serious Damage) rather than the guideline from this section.";

by renumbering Note 2 as Note 1; and in the caption by deleting "Notes" and inserting in lieu thereof "Note".

This amendment conforms the structure of this guideline to that used in other guidelines. No substantive change results. **The effective date of this amendment is November 1, 1990.**

340. The Commentary to §2N2.1 captioned "Statutory Provisions" is amended by inserting "(a)(1), (a)(2), (b)" immediately after "333".

The Commentary to §2N2.1 captioned "Application Notes" is amended by inserting the following additional note:

"4. The Commission has not promulgated a guideline for violations of 21 U.S.C. § 333(e) (offenses involving anabolic steroids).".

This amendment provides that §2N2.1 does not apply to convictions under 21 U.S.C. § 333(e). **The effective date of this amendment is November 1, 1990.**

341. Section 2P1.1(b)(2) is amended by inserting the following at the end:

"*Provided*, however, that this reduction shall not apply if the defendant, while away from the facility, committed any federal, state, or local offense punishable by a term of imprisonment of one year or more.".

Section 2P1.1(b) is amended by renumbering subdivision (3) as (4); and by inserting the following as subdivision (3):

"(3) If the defendant escaped from the non-secure custody of a community corrections center, community treatment center, 'halfway house,' or similar facility, and subsection (b)(2) is not applicable, decrease the offense level under subsection (a)(1) by 4 levels or the offense level under subsection (a)(2) by 2 levels. *Provided*, however, that this reduction shall not apply if the defendant, while away from the facility, committed any federal, state, or local offense punishable by a term of imprisonment of one year or more.".

The Commentary to §2P1.1 captioned "Application Notes" is amended in Note 3 by deleting "§2P1.1(b)(3)" and inserting in lieu thereof "subsection (b)(4)".

The Commentary to §2P1.1 captioned "Application Notes" is amended by inserting the following additional note:

"5. Criminal history points under Chapter Four, Part A (Criminal History) are to be determined independently of the application of this guideline. For example, in the case of a defendant serving a one-year sentence of imprisonment at the time of the escape, criminal history points from §4A1.1(b) (for the sentence being served at the time of the escape), §4A1.1(d) (custody status), and §4A1.1(e) (recency) would be applicable.".

This amendment provides greater differentiation in the guideline offense levels for the various types of conduct covered by this guideline. In addition, it clarifies that, where the instant offense is escape, criminal history points from §4A1.1(d) or (e), or both, may be applicable and that the addition of such points does not constitute unintended double counting. **The effective date of this amendment is November 1, 1990.**

342. The Introductory Commentary to Chapter Two, Part S, is deleted in its entirety as follows:

"<u>Introductory Commentary</u>

Money laundering activities are essential to the operation of organized crime. Congress recently enacted new statutes prohibiting these activities and increased the maximum penalties.

The guidelines provide substantially increased punishments for these offenses. In fiscal year 1985, the time served by defendants convicted of felonies involving monetary transaction reporting under 31 U.S.C. §§ 5313, 5316, and 5322 averaged about ten months, and only a few defendants served as much as four to five years.

However, courts have been imposing higher sentences as they come to appreciate the seriousness of this activity, and sentences as long as thirty-five years have been reported. Specifically, Congress made all reporting violations felonies in 1984, and enacted the Money Laundering Control Act of 1986 (18 U.S.C. §§ 1956, 1957), which creates new offenses and provides higher maximum sentences when knowledge, facilitation or concealment of serious criminal activity is proved.".

This amendment deletes the introductory commentary to this part as outdated, inconsistent with the commentaries to other sections, and better covered in the individual commentaries to the offenses contained in the part. **The effective date of this amendment is November 1, 1990.**

343. The Commentary to §2T1.1 captioned "Application Notes" is amended in Note 5 by deleting:

"'racketeering activity' as defined in 18 U.S.C. § 1961. If §2T1.1(b)(1) applies, do not apply §4B1.3 (Criminal Livelihood), which is substantially duplicative",

and inserting in lieu thereof:

"conduct constituting a criminal offense under federal, state, or local law".

The Commentary to §2T1.2 captioned "Application Notes" is amended in Note 1 by deleting:

"'racketeering activity' as defined in 18 U.S.C. § 1961. If §2T1.2(b)(1) applies, do not apply §4B1.3 (Criminal Livelihood), which is substantially duplicative",

and inserting in lieu thereof:

"conduct constituting a criminal offense under federal, state, or local law".

The Commentary to §2T1.3 captioned "Application Notes" is amended in Note 1 by deleting:

"'racketeering activity' as defined in 18 U.S.C. § 1961. If §2T1.3(b)(1) applies, do not apply §4B1.3 (Criminal Livelihood), which is substantially duplicative",

and inserting in lieu thereof:

"conduct constituting a criminal offense under federal, state, or local law".

The Commentary to §2T1.4 captioned "Application Notes" is amended in Note 1 by deleting the last sentence as follows:

"If this subsection applies, do not apply §4B1.3 (Criminal Livelihood) which is substantially duplicative.".

This amendment deletes the portion of these application notes concerning application of §4B1.3 (Criminal Livelihood) because this commentary conflicts with the principle expressed in Application Note 5 of the Commentary to §1B1.1 (when two guideline provisions are equally applicable, the one producing the greater offense level controls). In addition, this amendment broadens the definition of "criminal activity" to cover any criminal violation of federal, state, or local law. **The effective date of this amendment is November 1, 1990.**

344. The Introductory Commentary to Chapter Three, Part A is amended by deleting the second sentence as follows: "They are to be treated as specific offense characteristics.".

The Commentary to §3A1.1 (Vulnerable Victim) captioned "Application Notes" is amended in Note 2 by inserting the following at the end:

"For example, where the offense guideline provides an enhancement for the age of the victim, this guideline should not be applied unless the victim was unusually vulnerable for reasons unrelated to age.".

This amendment clarifies the application of §3A1.1, and eliminates an unnecessary and confusing sentence in the introductory commentary to this part. **The effective date of this amendment is November 1, 1990.**

345. The Introductory Commentary to Chapter Three, Part B, is amended by beginning a new paragraph with the second sentence; and by inserting, immediately after the first sentence, the following:

"The determination of a defendant's role in the offense is to be made on the basis of all conduct within the scope of §1B1.3 (Relevant Conduct), i.e., all conduct included under §1B1.3(a)(1)-(4), and not solely on the basis of elements and acts cited in the count of conviction. However, where the defendant has received mitigation by virtue of being convicted of an offense significantly less serious than his actual criminal conduct, e.g., the defendant is convicted of unlawful possession of a controlled substance but his actual conduct involved drug trafficking, a further reduction in the offense level under §3B1.2 (Mitigating Role) ordinarily is not warranted because the defendant is not substantially less culpable than a defendant whose only conduct involved the less serious offense.".

This amendment clarifies the conduct that is relevant to the determination of Chapter Three, Part B, and clarifies the operation of §3B1.2 in certain cases. **The effective date of this amendment is November 1, 1990.**

346. Section 3B1.3 is amended in the second sentence by deleting "in addition to that provided for in §3B1.1, nor may it be employed" immediately following "may not be employed"; and by inserting the following additional sentence at the end:

"If this adjustment is based upon an abuse of a position of trust, it may be employed in addition to an adjustment under §3B1.1 (Aggravating Role); if this adjustment is based solely on the use of a special skill, it may not be employed in addition to an adjustment under §3B1.1 (Aggravating Role).".

This amendment provides that the enhancement for abuse of a position of trust may apply in addition to an enhancement for an aggravating role under §3B1.1. **The effective date of this amendment is November 1, 1990.**

347. Section 3C1.1 is amended in the title by deleting "Willfully Obstructing or Impeding Proceedings" and inserting in lieu thereof "Obstructing or Impeding the Administration of Justice".

Section 3C1.1 is amended by deleting "impeded or obstructed, or attempted to impede or obstruct" and inserting in lieu thereof "obstructed or impeded, or attempted to obstruct or impede,"; and by deleting "or prosecution" and inserting in lieu thereof ", prosecution, or sentencing".

The Commentary to §3C1.1 is amended by deleting the introductory paragraph immediately before "Application Notes" as follows:

"This section provides a sentence enhancement for a defendant who engages in conduct calculated to mislead or deceive authorities or those involved in a judicial proceeding, or otherwise to willfully interfere with the disposition of criminal charges, in respect to the instant offense.".

The Commentary to §3C1.1 captioned "Application Notes" is amended by deleting Notes 1-4 as follows:

"1. The following conduct, while not exclusive, may provide a basis for applying this adjustment:

(a) destroying or concealing material evidence, or attempting to do so;

(b) directing or procuring another person to destroy or conceal material evidence, or attempting to do so;

(c) testifying untruthfully or suborning untruthful testimony concerning a material fact, or producing or attempting to produce an altered, forged, or counterfeit document or record during a preliminary or grand jury proceeding, trial, sentencing proceeding, or any other judicial proceeding;

(d) threatening, intimidating, or otherwise unlawfully attempting to influence a co-defendant, witness, or juror, directly or indirectly;

(e) furnishing material falsehoods to a probation officer in the course of a presentence or other investigation for the court.

2. In applying this provision, suspect testimony and statements should be evaluated in a light most favorable to the defendant.

3. This provision is not intended to punish a defendant for the exercise of a constitutional right. A defendant's denial of guilt is not a basis for application of this provision.

4. Where the defendant is convicted for an offense covered by §2J1.1 (Contempt), §2J1.2 (Obstruction of Justice), §2J1.3 (Perjury), §2J1.8 (Bribery of Witness), or §2J1.9 (Payment to Witness), this adjustment is not to be applied to the offense level for that offense except where a significant further obstruction occurred during the investigation or prosecution of the obstruction offense itself (e.g., where the defendant threatened a witness during the course of the prosecution for the obstruction offense). Where the defendant is convicted both of the obstruction offense and the underlying offense, the count for the obstruction offense will be grouped with the count for the underlying offense under subsection (c) of §3D1.2 (Groups of Closely-Related Counts). The offense level for that Group of Closely-Related Counts will be the offense level for the underlying offense increased by the 2-level adjustment specified by this section, or the offense level for the obstruction offense, whichever is greater.",

and inserting in lieu thereof:

"1. This provision is not intended to punish a defendant for the exercise of a constitutional right. A defendant's denial of guilt (other than a denial of guilt under oath that constitutes perjury), refusal to admit guilt or provide information to a probation officer, or refusal to enter a plea of guilty is not a basis for application of this provision. In applying this provision, the defendant's testimony and statements should be evaluated in a light most favorable to the defendant.

2. Obstructive conduct can vary widely in nature, degree of planning, and seriousness. Application Note 3 sets forth examples of the types of conduct to which this enhancement is intended to apply. Application Note 4 sets forth examples of less serious forms of conduct to which this enhancement is not intended to apply, but that ordinarily can appropriately be sanctioned by the

determination of the particular sentence within the otherwise applicable guideline range. Although the conduct to which this enhancement applies is not subject to precise definition, comparison of the examples set forth in Application Notes 3 and 4 should assist the court in determining whether application of this enhancement is warranted in a particular case.

3. The following is a non-exhaustive list of examples of the types of conduct to which this enhancement applies:

(a) threatening, intimidating, or otherwise unlawfully influencing a co-defendant, witness, or juror, directly or indirectly, or attempting to do so;

(b) committing, suborning, or attempting to suborn perjury;

(c) producing or attempting to produce a false, altered, or counterfeit document or record during an official investigation or judicial proceeding;

(d) destroying or concealing or directing or procuring another person to destroy or conceal evidence that is material to an official investigation or judicial proceeding (e.g., shredding a document or destroying ledgers upon learning that an official investigation has commenced or is about to commence), or attempting to do so; however, if such conduct occurred contemporaneously with arrest (e.g., attempting to swallow or throw away a controlled substance), it shall not, standing alone, be sufficient to warrant an adjustment for obstruction unless it resulted in a material hindrance to the official investigation or prosecution of the instant offense or the sentencing of the offender;

(e) escaping or attempting to escape from custody before trial or sentencing; or willfully failing to appear, as ordered, for a judicial proceeding;

(f) providing materially false information to a judge or magistrate;

(g) providing a materially false statement to a law enforcement officer that significantly obstructed or impeded the official investigation or prosecution of the instant offense;

(h) providing materially false information to a probation officer in respect to a presentence or other investigation for the court;

(i) conduct prohibited by 18 U.S.C. §§ 1501-1516.

This adjustment also applies to any other obstructive conduct in respect to the official investigation, prosecution, or sentencing of the instant offense where there is a separate count of conviction for such conduct.

4. The following is a non-exhaustive list of examples of the types of conduct that, absent a separate count of conviction for such conduct, do not warrant application of this enhancement, but ordinarily can appropriately be sanctioned by the determination of the particular sentence within the otherwise applicable guideline range:

(a) providing a false name or identification document at arrest, except where such conduct actually resulted in a significant hindrance to the investigation or prosecution of the instant offense;

(b) making false statements, not under oath, to law enforcement officers, unless Application Note 3(g) above applies;

(c) providing incomplete or misleading information, not amounting to a material falsehood, in respect to a presentence investigation;

(d) avoiding or fleeing from arrest (see, however, §3C1.2 (Reckless Endangerment During Flight)).

5. 'Material' evidence, fact, statement, or information, as used in this section, means evidence, fact, statement, or information that, if believed, would tend to influence or affect the issue under determination.

6. Where the defendant is convicted for an offense covered by §2J1.1 (Contempt), §2J1.2 (Obstruction of Justice), §2J1.3 (Perjury or Subornation of Perjury), §2J1.5 (Failure to Appear by Material Witness), §2J1.6 (Failure to Appear by Defendant), §2J1.8 (Bribery of Witness), or §2J1.9 (Payment to Witness), this adjustment is not to be applied to the offense level for that offense except where a significant further obstruction occurred during the investigation or prosecution of the obstruction offense itself (e.g., where the defendant threatened a witness during the course of the prosecution for the obstruction offense). Where the defendant is convicted both of the obstruction offense and the underlying offense, the count for the obstruction offense will be grouped with the count for the underlying offense under subsection (c) of §3D1.2 (Groups of Closely-Related Counts). The offense level for that group of closely-related counts will be the offense level for the underlying offense increased by the 2-level adjustment specified by this section, or the offense level for the obstruction offense, whichever is greater.".

Chapter Three, Part C, is amended by inserting an additional guideline with accompanying commentary as §3C1.2 (Reckless Endangerment During Flight).

This amendment clarifies the operation of §3C1.1 and inserts an additional guideline to address reckless endangerment during flight. The Commission believes that reckless endangerment during flight is sufficiently different from other forms of obstructive conduct to warrant a separate enhancement. **The effective date of this amendment is November 1, 1990.**

348. Section 3D1.1 is amended by inserting "(a)" immediately before "When"; by deleting "(a)", "(b)", and "(c)", and inserting in lieu thereof "(1)", "(2)", and "(3)" respectively; and by inserting the following additional subsection:

"(b) Any count for which the statute mandates imposition of a consecutive sentence is excluded from the operation of §§3D1.2-3D1.5. Sentences for such counts are governed by the provisions of §5G1.2(a).".

The Commentary to §3D1.1 captioned "Application Notes" is amended in Note 1 by deleting:

"Certain offenses, e.g., 18 U.S.C. § 924(c) (use of a deadly or dangerous weapon in relation to a crime of violence or drug trafficking) by law carry mandatory consecutive sentences. Such offenses are exempted from the operation of these rules. See §3D1.2.",

and inserting in lieu thereof:

"Counts for which a statute mandates imposition of a consecutive sentence are excepted from application of the multiple count rules. Convictions on such counts are not used in the determination of a combined offense level under this Part, but may affect the offense level for other counts. A conviction for 18 U.S.C. § 924(c) (use of firearm in commission of a crime of violence) provides a common example. In the case of a conviction under 18 U.S.C. § 924(c), the specific offense characteristic for weapon use in the primary offense is to be disregarded to avoid double counting. See Commentary to §2K2.4. Example: The defendant is convicted of one count of bank robbery (18 U.S.C. § 2113), and one count of use of a firearm in the commission of a crime of violence (18 U.S.C. § 924(c)). The two counts are not grouped together, and the offense level for the bank robbery count is computed without application of an enhancement for weapon possession or use. The mandatory five-year sentence on the weapon-use count runs consecutively, as required by law. See §5G1.2(a).".

Section 3D1.2 is amended by deleting the second sentence as follows:

"A count for which the statute mandates imposition of a consecutive sentence is excluded from such Groups for purposes of §§3D1.2-3D1.5.".

The Commentary to §3D1.2 captioned "Application Notes" is amended by deleting Note 1 as follows:

"1. Counts for which the statute mandates imposition of a consecutive sentence are excepted from application of the multiple count rules. Convictions under such counts are excluded from the determination of the combined offense level. Convictions for 18 U.S.C. § 924(c) (use of firearm in commission of a crime of violence) provide a common example. Note that such a conviction usually does affect the offense level for other counts, however, in that in the event of such a conviction the specific offense characteristic for weapon use in the primary offense is to be disregarded. See Commentary to §2K2.4. Example: The defendant is convicted of one count of bank robbery in which he took $5,000 and discharged a weapon causing permanent bodily injury (18 U.S.C. § 2113), and one count of use of a firearm in the commission of a crime of violence (18 U.S.C. § 924(c)). The two counts are not grouped together, but the offense level for the bank robbery count is 28 (18 + 4 + 6) rather than 31. The mandatory five year sentence on the weapon-use count runs consecutively, as required by law.".

This amendment consolidates the provisions dealing with statutorily required consecutive sentences in §3D1.1 for greater clarity. **The effective date of this amendment is November 1, 1990.**

349. Section 3D1.2(b) is amended by deleting, immediately following "common scheme or plan", the following:

" , including, but not limited to:

(1) A count charging conspiracy or solicitation and a count charging any substantive offense that was the sole object of the conspiracy or solicitation. 28 U.S.C. § 994(l)(2).

(2) A count charging an attempt to commit an offense and a count charging the commission of the offense. 18 U.S.C. § 3584(a).

(3) A count charging an offense based on a general prohibition and a count charging violation of a specific prohibition encompassed in the general prohibition. 28 U.S.C. § 994(v)".

Section 3D1.2(d) is amended by deleting "Counts are grouped together if" and inserting in lieu thereof "When".

Section 3D1.2(d) is amended by deleting "specifically included" and inserting in lieu thereof "to be grouped".

Section 3D1.2(d) is amended in the second paragraph by inserting in the appropriate place: "§2K2.2;".

Section 3D1.2(d) is amended in the third paragraph by inserting "Chapter Two," immediately before "Part A".

The Commentary to §3D1.2 captioned "Application Notes" is amended by inserting the following as Note 1:

> "1. Subsections (a)-(d) set forth circumstances in which counts are to be grouped together into a single Group. Counts are to be grouped together into a single Group if any one or more of the subsections provide for such grouping. Counts for which the statute mandates imposition of a consecutive sentence are excepted from application of the multiple count rules. <u>See</u> §3D1.1(b).".

The Commentary to §3D1.2 captioned "Application Notes" is amended in Note 3 by inserting the following as the second paragraph:

> "When one count charges an attempt to commit an offense and the other charges the commission of that offense, or when one count charges an offense based on a general prohibition and the other charges violation of a specific prohibition encompassed in the general prohibition, the counts will be grouped together under subsection (a).".

The Commentary to §3D1.2 captioned "Application Notes" is amended in Note 4 in the first sentence of the first paragraph by deleting "states the principle" and inserting in lieu thereof "provides".

The Commentary to §3D1.2 captioned "Application Notes" is amended in Note 4 by inserting the following sentence as the second sentence of the first paragraph:

> "This provision does not authorize the grouping of offenses that cannot be considered to represent essentially one composite harm (<u>e.g.</u>, robbery of the same victim on different occasions involves multiple, separate instances of fear and risk of harm, not one composite harm).";

and by inserting the following as the second paragraph:

> "When one count charges a conspiracy or solicitation and the other charges a substantive offense that was the sole object of the conspiracy or solicitation, the counts will be grouped together under subsection (b).".

The Commentary to §3D1.2 captioned "Application Notes" is amended in Note 6 by deleting the third sentence of the first paragraph as follows:

> "The same general type of offense" is to be construed broadly, and would include, for example, larceny, embezzlement, forgery, and fraud.";

and by inserting the following as the second paragraph:

> "Counts involving offenses to which different offense guidelines apply are grouped together under subsection (d) if the offenses are of the same general type and otherwise meet the criteria for grouping under this subsection. In such cases, the offense guideline that results in the highest offense level is used; <u>see</u> §3D1.3(b). The 'same general type' of offense is to be construed broadly, and would include, for example, larceny, embezzlement, forgery, and fraud.".

This amendment clarifies the operation of §3D1.2(b), makes editorial improvements in §3D1.2(d), makes the listing of offenses in §3D1.2(d) more comprehensive, clarifies the interaction of §§ 3D1.2(d) and 3D1.3(b), and clarifies the Commentary of §3D1.2 by making explicit that offenses such as multiple robberies do not fit within the parameters of §3D1.2(b). **The effective date of this amendment is November 1, 1990.**

350. Section 3D1.4 is amended in the fourth line of the Unit table by inserting "2 1/2-" immediately before "3" the first time "3" appears; and in the fifth line of the Unit table by deleting "4 or" and inserting in lieu thereof "3 1/2-".

Section 3D1.4 is amended by deleting:

"(d) Except when the total number of Units is 1 1/2, round up to the next large whole number.".

The Commentary to §3D1.4 captioned "Background" is amended in the first paragraph by deleting the fifth sentence as follows:

"When this approach produces a fraction in the total Units, other than 1 1/2, it is rounded up to the nearest whole number.".

The "Illustrations of the Operation of the Multiple-Count Rules" following §3D1.5 are amended in example 1 in the third sentence by deleting "18" and "4-" and inserting in lieu thereof "20" and "2-" respectively; and in the sixth sentence by deleting "(rounded up to 3)" immediately following "2 1/2 Units".

The "Illustrations of the Operation of the Multiple-Count Rules" following §3D1.5 are amended in example 3 in the sixth sentence by deleting "Obstruction" and inserting in lieu thereof "Obstructing or Impeding the Administration of Justice".

This amendment simplifies the operation of §3D1.4. In addition, the amendment conforms the illustrations of the operation of the multiple-count rules. **The effective date of this amendment is November 1, 1990.**

351. The Commentary to §3E1.1 captioned "Application Notes" is amended by deleting:

"2. Conviction by trial does not preclude a defendant from consideration under this section. A defendant may manifest sincere contrition even if he exercises his constitutional right to a trial. This may occur, for example, where a defendant goes to trial to assert and preserve issues that do not relate to factual guilt (e.g., to make a constitutional challenge to a statute or a challenge to the applicability of a statute to his conduct).

3. A guilty plea may provide some evidence of the defendant's acceptance of responsibility. However, it does not, by itself, entitle a defendant to a reduced sentence under this section.",

and inserting in lieu thereof:

"2. This adjustment is not intended to apply to a defendant who puts the government to its burden of proof at trial by denying the essential factual elements of guilt, is convicted, and only then admits guilt and expresses remorse. Conviction by trial, however, does not automatically preclude a defendant from consideration for such a reduction. In rare situations a defendant may clearly demonstrate an acceptance of responsibility for his criminal conduct even though he exercises his constitutional right to a trial. This may occur, for example, where a defendant goes to trial to assert and preserve issues that do not relate to factual guilt (e.g., to make a constitutional challenge to a statute or a challenge to the applicability of a statute to his conduct). In each such instance, however, a determination that a defendant has accepted responsibility will be based primarily upon pre-trial statements and conduct.

3. Entry of a plea of guilty prior to the commencement of trial combined with truthful admission of involvement in the offense and related conduct will constitute significant evidence of acceptance of responsibility for the purposes of this section. However, this evidence may be outweighed by conduct of the defendant that is inconsistent with such acceptance of responsibility.".

The Commentary to §3E1.1 captioned "Application Notes" is amended in Note 4 in the first sentence by deleting "Willfully Obstructing or Impeding Proceedings" and inserting in lieu thereof "Obstructing or Impeding the Administration of Justice".

The Commentary to §3E1.1 captioned "Application Notes" is amended in Note 5 in the second sentence by deleting "and should not be disturbed unless it is without foundation" immediately following "review".

The Commentary to §3E1.1 captioned "Background" is amended in the first paragraph in the second sentence by inserting "and related conduct" immediately before "by taking"; and in the third sentence by deleting "lesser sentence" and inserting in lieu thereof "lower offense level", and by deleting "sincere remorse" and inserting in lieu thereof "acceptance of responsibility".

The Commentary to §3E1.1 captioned "Background" is amended by deleting the second paragraph as follows:

" The availability of a reduction under §3E1.1 is not controlled by whether the conviction was by trial or plea of guilty. Although a guilty plea may show some evidence of acceptance of responsibility, it does not automatically entitle the defendant to a sentencing adjustment.".

This amendment clarifies the operation of this guideline and conforms the title of a reference to another guideline. **The effective date of this amendment is November 1, 1990.**

352. Section 4A1.2(a)(3) is amended by inserting "or execution" immediately following "imposition".

Section 4A1.2(c)(1) is amended by inserting in the appropriate place by alphabetical order:

"Careless or reckless driving",
"Insufficient funds check".

Section 4A1.2(c)(1) is amended by inserting "(excluding local ordinance violations that are also criminal offenses under state law)" immediately following "Local ordinance violations".

Section 4A1.2(c)(2) is amended by inserting "(e.g., speeding)" immediately following "minor traffic infractions".

The Commentary to §4A1.2 captioned "Application Notes" is amended by inserting the following additional notes:

"12. Local ordinance violations. A number of local jurisdictions have enacted ordinances covering certain offenses (e.g., larceny and assault misdemeanors) that are also violations of state criminal law. This enables a local court (e.g., a municipal court) to exercise jurisdiction over such offenses. Such offenses are excluded from the definition of local ordinance violations in §4A1.2(c)(1) and, therefore, sentences for such offenses are to be treated as if the defendant had been convicted under state law.

13. Insufficient funds check. 'Insufficient funds check,' as used in §4A1.2(c)(1), does not include any conviction establishing that the defendant used a false name or non-existent account.".

This amendment clarifies that, for the purpose of computing criminal history points, there is no difference between the suspension of the "imposition" and "execution" of a prior sentence. This amendment also makes the provisions of §4A1.2(c)(1) more comprehensive in respect to certain vehicular offenses and clarifies the application of §4A1.2(c)(1) in respect to certain offenses prosecuted in municipal courts. In addition, this amendment expands the coverage of §4A1.2(c)(1) to include a misdemeanor or petty offense conviction for an insufficient funds check. **The effective date of this amendment is November 1, 1990.**

353. The Commentary to §4A1.2 captioned "Application Notes" is amended in Note 6 by deleting:

"Any other sentence resulting in a valid conviction is to be counted in the criminal history score. Convictions which the defendant shows to have been constitutionally invalid may not be counted in the criminal history score. Also, if to count an uncounseled misdemeanor conviction would result in the imposition of a sentence of imprisonment under circumstances that would violate the United States Constitution, then such conviction shall not be counted in the criminal history score. Nonetheless, any conviction that is not counted in the criminal history score may be considered pursuant to §4A1.3 if it provides reliable evidence of past criminal activity.",

and inserting in lieu thereof:

"Also, sentences resulting from convictions that a defendant shows to have been previously ruled constitutionally invalid are not to be counted. Nonetheless, the criminal conduct underlying any conviction that is not counted in the criminal history score may be considered pursuant to §4A1.3 (Adequacy of Criminal History Category).".

The Commentary to §4A1.2 captioned "Application Notes" is amended in the caption of Note 6 by deleting "Invalid" and inserting in lieu thereof "Reversed, Vacated, or Invalidated". The Commentary to §4A1.2 is amended by inserting at the end:

"Background: Prior sentences, not otherwise excluded, are to be counted in the criminal history score, including uncounseled misdemeanor sentences where imprisonment was not imposed.

The Commission leaves for court determination the issue of whether a defendant may collaterally attack at sentencing a prior conviction.".

This amendment clarifies the circumstances under which prior sentences are excluded from the criminal history score. In particular, the amendment clarifies the Commission's intent regarding the counting of uncounseled misdemeanor convictions for which counsel constitutionally is not required because the defendant was not imprisoned. Lack of clarity regarding whether these prior sentences are to be counted may result not only in considerable disparity in guideline application, but also in the criminal history score not adequately reflecting the defendant's failure to learn from the application of previous sanctions and his potential for recidivism. This amendment expressly states the Commission's position that such convictions are to be counted for the purposes of criminal history under Chapter Four, Part A. **The effective date of this amendment is November 1, 1990.**

354. The Commentary to §4B1.3 captioned "Application Notes" is amended in Note 2 by deleting "(currently 2,000x the hourly minimum wage under federal law is $6,700)" immediately following "then existing hourly minimum wage under federal law".

This amendment deletes a reference to the federal minimum wage that is now outdated. **The effective date of this amendment is November 1, 1990.**

355. Chapter Four, Part B, is amended by inserting an additional guideline with accompanying commentary as §4B1.4 (Armed Career Criminal).

This amendment adds a new section to address cases subject to a sentence enhancement under 18 U.S.C. § 924(e). **The effective date of this amendment is November 1, 1990.**

356. Section 5E1.2 is amended by deleting:

"(a) Except as provided in subsection (f) below, the court shall impose a fine in all cases.",

and inserting in lieu thereof:

"(a) The court shall impose a fine in all cases, except where the defendant establishes that he is unable to pay and is not likely to become able to pay any fine.".

Section 5E1.2(d)(2) is amended by deleting "the ability of the defendant" and inserting in lieu thereof "any evidence presented as to the defendant's ability".

The Commentary to §5E1.2 captioned "Application Notes" is amended in Note 3 by deleting the fourth sentence as follows:

"In many cases, circumstances will make it unnecessary to consider these standards other than in the most general terms.";

and by inserting the following additional paragraphs at the end:

"Where it is readily ascertainable that the defendant cannot, and is not likely to become able to, pay a fine greater than the maximum fine set forth in Column B of the Fine Table in subsection (c)(3), calculation of the alternative maximum fines under subsections (c)(2)(B) (twice the gross pecuniary loss caused by the offense) and (c)(2)(C) (three times the gross pecuniary gain to all participants in the offense) is unnecessary. In such cases, a statement that 'the alternative maximums of the fine table were not calculated because it is readily ascertainable that the defendant cannot, and is not likely to become able to, pay a fine greater than the maximum set forth in the fine table' is recommended in lieu of such calculations.

The determination of the fine guideline range may be dispensed with entirely upon a court determination of present and future inability to pay any fine. The inability of a defendant to post bail bond (having otherwise been determined eligible for release) and the fact that a defendant is represented by (or was determined eligible for) assigned counsel are significant indicators of present inability to pay any fine. In conjunction with other factors, they may also indicate that the defendant is not likely to become able to pay any fine.".

This amendment clarifies the operation of this guideline. **The effective date of this amendment is November 1, 1990.**

357. The Introductory Commentary to Chapter Five, Part H is amended by inserting the following additional paragraph at the end:

> " In addition, 28 U.S.C. § 994(e) requires the Commission to assure that its guidelines and policy statements reflect the general inappropriateness of considering the defendant's education, vocational skills, employment record, family ties and responsibilities, and community ties in determining whether a term of imprisonment should be imposed or the length of a term of imprisonment.".

This amendment clarifies the relationship of 28 U.S.C. § 994(e) to certain of the policy statements contained in this part. **The effective date of this amendment is November 1, 1990.**

358. Chapter Five, Part K, Subpart 2, is amended in the title by deleting "GENERAL PROVISIONS:" and inserting in lieu thereof "OTHER GROUNDS FOR DEPARTURE".

Section 5K2.0 is amended in the first sentence of the first paragraph by inserting a comma immediately following "degree", and by inserting "that should result in a sentence different from that described" immediately following "the guidelines"; in the third sentence of the first paragraph by deleting "court at the time of sentencing" and inserting in lieu thereof "courts"; in the fourth sentence of the first paragraph by deleting "the present section" and inserting in lieu thereof "this subpart", by deleting "fully" immediately before "take", by inserting "fully" immediately following "account", and by deleting "precise" and inserting in lieu thereof "the"; in the sixth sentence of the first paragraph by deleting "judge" and inserting in lieu thereof "court"; and in the seventh sentence of the first paragraph by deleting "listed elsewhere in the guidelines (e.g., as an adjustment or specific offense characteristic)" and inserting in lieu thereof "taken into consideration in the guidelines (e.g., as a specific offense characteristic or other adjustment)".

Section 5K2.0 is amended in the first sentence of the second paragraph by inserting ", for example," immediately following "Where", by deleting "guidelines, specific offense characteristics," and inserting in lieu thereof "offense guideline", by deleting "part" and inserting in lieu thereof "subpart", by deleting "guideline" and inserting in lieu thereof "applicable guideline range", and by deleting "of conviction" immediately following "the offense"; in the second sentence of the second paragraph by deleting "offense of conviction" and inserting in lieu thereof "applicable offense guideline"; in the third sentence of the second paragraph by deleting "offense of conviction is theft" and inserting in lieu thereof "theft offense guideline is applicable", by deleting "when" immediately before "the theft", and by inserting "range" immediately before "more readily"; and in the fourth sentence of the second paragraph by deleting "offense of conviction is robbery" and inserting in lieu thereof "robbery offense guideline is applicable", and by deleting "sentence" immediately before "adjustment".

Section 5K2.0 is amended by deleting the fourth paragraph as follows:

> "Harms identified as a possible basis for departure from the guidelines should be taken into account only when they are relevant to the offense of conviction, within the limitations set forth in §1B1.3.".

This amendment makes various editorial and clarifying changes. In addition, the last paragraph is deleted as unclear and overly restrictive. **The effective date of this amendment is November 1, 1990.**

359. Appendix A (Statutory Index) is amended by inserting the following in the appropriate place by title and section:

"7 U.S.C. § 136l	2Q1.2",
"18 U.S.C. § 34	2A1.1, 2A1.2, 2A1.3, 2A1.4",
"18 U.S.C. § 35(b)	2A6.1",
"18 U.S.C. § 219	2C1.3",
"18 U.S.C. § 281	2C1.3",
"18 U.S.C. § 332	2B1.1, 2F1.1",
"18 U.S.C. § 335	2F1.1",
"18 U.S.C. § 608	2H2.1",
"18 U.S.C. § 647	2B1.1",
"18 U.S.C. § 650	2B1.1",
"18 U.S.C. § 665(b)	2B3.3, 2C1.1",
"18 U.S.C. § 667	2B1.1, 2B1.2",
"18 U.S.C. § 712	2F1.1",
"18 U.S.C. § 753	2P1.1",
"18 U.S.C. § 915	2F1.1",
"18 U.S.C. § 917	2F1.1",
"18 U.S.C. § 970(a)	2B1.3, 2K1.4",
"18 U.S.C. § 1015	2F1.1, 2J1.3, 2L2.1, 2L2.2",
"18 U.S.C. § 1023	2B1.1, 2F1.1",
"18 U.S.C. § 1024	2B1.2",
"18 U.S.C. § 1031	2F1.1",
"18 U.S.C. § 1091	2H1.3",
"18 U.S.C. § 1115	2A1.4",
"18 U.S.C. § 1167	2B1.1",
"18 U.S.C. § 1168	2B1.1",
"18 U.S.C. § 1201(c), (d)	2X1.1",
"18 U.S.C. § 1364	2K1.4",
"18 U.S.C. § 1422	2C1.2, 2F1.1",
"18 U.S.C. § 1541	2L2.3",
"18 U.S.C. § 1716 (felony provisions only)	2K3.2",
"18 U.S.C. § 1860	2R1.1",
"18 U.S.C. § 1861	2F1.1",
"18 U.S.C. § 1864	2Q1.6",
"18 U.S.C. § 1991	2A2.1, 2X1.1",
"18 U.S.C. § 1992	2A1.1, 2B1.3, 2K1.4, 2X1.1",
"18 U.S.C. § 2072	2F1.1",
"18 U.S.C. § 2118(d)	2X1.1",
"18 U.S.C. § 2197	2B5.2, 2F1.1",
"18 U.S.C. § 2232	2J1.2",
"18 U.S.C. § 2233	2B1.1, 2B3.1",
"18 U.S.C. § 2272	2F1.1",
"18 U.S.C. § 2276	2B1.3, 2B2.2",
"18 U.S.C. § 2331(a)	2A1.1, 2A1.2, 2A1.3, 2A1.4",
"18 U.S.C. § 2331(b)	2A2.1",
"18 U.S.C. § 2331(c)	2A2.2",
"22 U.S.C. § 2780	2M5.2",
"42 U.S.C. § 300i-1	2Q1.4, 2Q1.5",
"42 U.S.C. § 1973j(c)	2X1.1".

Appendix A is amended:

in the line beginning "8 U.S.C. § 1328" by deleting ", 2G2.1, 2G2.2";

in the line beginning "16 U.S.C. § 1029" by deleting ", 2Q2.2";

in the line beginning "16 U.S.C. § 1030" by deleting ", 2Q2.2";

in the line beginning "16 U.S.C. § 1857(2)" by deleting ", 2Q2.2" and inserting in lieu thereof "2Q2.1";

in the line beginning "16 U.S.C. § 1859" by deleting "2Q2.2" and inserting in lieu thereof "2Q2.1";

and in the line beginning "16 U.S.C. § 3373(d)" by deleting "2Q2.2" and inserting in lieu thereof "2Q2.1";

by deleting:

"18 U.S.C. § 32(a)(1)-(4)	2K1.4, 2B1.3
18 U.S.C. § 32(b)	2A1.1-2A2.3, 2A4.1, 2A5.1-2A5.2, 2K1.4, 2B1.3",

and inserting in lieu thereof:

"18 U.S.C. § 32(a),(b)	2A1.1-2A2.3, 2A4.1, 2A5.1, 2A5.2, 2B1.3, 2K1.4";

in the line beginning "18 U.S.C. § 33" by inserting "2A2.1, 2A2.2," immediately before ""2B1.3";

in the line beginning "18 U.S.C. § 112(a)" by inserting "2A2.1," immediately before "2A2.2," and by inserting ", 2A4.1, 2B1.3, 2K1.4" immediately following "2A2.3";

in the line beginning "18 U.S.C. § 152" by deleting "2F1.1," and by inserting ", 2F1.1, 2J1.3" immediately following "2B4.1";

in the line beginning "18 U.S.C. § 201(b)(1)" by deleting ", 2J1.3, 2J1.8, 2J1.9";

in the line beginning "18 U.S.C. § 241" by deleting "2H1.2,";

in the line beginning "18 U.S.C. § 351(d)" by deleting ", 2A2.1" and inserting in lieu thereof "2A1.5";

in the line beginning "18 U.S.C. § 371" by deleting "2A2.1" and inserting in lieu thereof "2A1.5";

in the line beginning "18 U.S.C. § 373" by deleting "2A2.1" and inserting in lieu thereof "2A1.5";

in the line beginning "18 U.S.C. § 474" by inserting ", 2B5.2" immediately following "2B5.1";

in the line beginning "18 U.S.C. § 476" by inserting ", 2B5.2" immediately following "2B5.1";

in the line beginning "18 U.S.C. § 477" by inserting ", 2B5.2" immediately following "2B5.1";

in the line beginning "18 U.S.C. § 496" by deleting "2T3.1" and inserting in lieu thereof "2F1.1, 2T3.1";

in the line beginning "18 U.S.C. § 545" by deleting "2Q2.2" and inserting in lieu thereof "2Q2.1";

in the line beginning "18 U.S.C. § 549" by inserting "2B1.1," immediately before "2T3.1", and by inserting ", 2T3.2" immediately following "2T3.1";

in the line beginning "18 U.S.C. § 551" by inserting "2J1.2," immediately before "2T3.1";

in the line beginning "18 U.S.C. § 642" by inserting ", 2B5.2" immediately following "2B5.1";

by deleting:

"18 U.S.C. § 666(a)	2B1.1, 2C1.1, 2C1.2, 2F1.1",

and inserting in lieu thereof:

"18 U.S.C. § 666(a)(1)(A)	2B1.1, 2F1.1
18 U.S.C. § 666(a)(1)(B)	2C1.1, 2C1.2
18 U.S.C. § 666(a)(1)(C)	2C1.1, 2C1.2";

in the line beginning "18 U.S.C. § 755" by deleting ", 2X2.1";

in the line beginning "18 U.S.C. § 756" by deleting ", 2X2.1";

in the line beginning "18 U.S.C. § 757" by deleting "2X2.1" and inserting in lieu thereof "2X3.1";

in the line beginning "18 U.S.C. § 793(d), (e)" by inserting "2M3.2," immediately before "2M3.3";

in the line beginning "18 U.S.C. § 842(a)" by deleting ",(h),(i)" by inserting in lieu thereof "-(i)";

in the line beginning "18 U.S.C. § 844(f)" by inserting ", 2X1.1" immediately following "2K1.4";

by deleting:

"18 U.S.C. § 922(a)(1)-(5)	2K2.3
18 U.S.C. § 922(a)(6)	2K2.1
18 U.S.C. § 922(b)(1)-(3)	2K2.3
18 U.S.C. § 922(d)	2K2.3
18 U.S.C. § 922(g)	2K2.1
18 U.S.C. § 922(h)	2K2.1
18 U.S.C. § 922(i)	2B1.2, 2K2.3
18 U.S.C. § 922(j)	2B1.2, 2K2.3
18 U.S.C. § 922(k)	2K2.3
18 U.S.C. § 922(l)	2K2.3
18 U.S.C. § 922(n)	2K2.1
18 U.S.C. § 923	2K2.3
18 U.S.C. § 924(c)	2K2.4",

and inserting in lieu thereof:

"18 U.S.C. § 922(a)(1)	2K2.1,2K2.2
18 U.S.C. § 922(a)(2)	2K2.2
18 U.S.C. § 922(a)(3)	2K2.1
18 U.S.C. § 922(a)(4)	2K2.1
18 U.S.C. § 922(a)(5)	2K2.2
18 U.S.C. § 922(a)(6)	2K2.1
18 U.S.C. § 922(b)-(d)	2K2.2
18 U.S.C. § 922(e)	2K2. 1, 2K2.2
18 U.S.C. § 922(f)	2K2.1, 2K2.2
18 U.S.C. § 922(g)	2K2.1
18 U.S.C. § 922(h)	2K2.1
18 U.S.C. § 922(i)-(l)	2K2.1, 2K2.2
18 U.S.C. § 922(m)	2K2.2
18 U.S.C. § 922(n)	2K2.1
18 U.S.C. § 922(o)	2K2.1, 2K2.2

18 U.S.C. § 923(a)	2K2.2
18 U.S.C. § 924(a)(1)(A)	2K2.2
18 U.S.C. § 924(a)(1)(C)	2K2.1, 2K2.2
18 U.S.C. § 924(a)(3)(A)	2K2.2
18 U.S.C. § 924(b)	2K2.3
18 U.S.C. § 924(c)	2K2.4
18 U.S.C. § 924(f)	2K2.3
18 U.S.C. § 924(g)	2K2.3";

in the line beginning "18 U.S.C. § 1012" by inserting "2C1.3," immediately before "2F1.1";

in the line beginning "18 U.S.C. § 1028" by inserting ", 2L2.4 " immediately following "2L2.3";

in the line beginning "18 U.S.C. § 1113" by inserting ", 2A2.2" immediately following "2A2.1";

in the line beginning "18 U.S.C. § 1117" by deleting "2A2.1" and inserting in lieu thereof "2A1.5";

in the line beginning "18 U.S.C. § 1362" by inserting ", 2K1.4" immediately following "2B1.3";

in the line beginning "18 U.S.C. § "1363" by inserting ", 2K1.4" immediately following "2B1.3";

in the line beginning "18 U.S.C. § 1426" by inserting ", 2L2.2" immediately following "2L2.1";

in the line beginning "18 U.S.C. § 1460" by inserting "2G2.2," immediately before "2G3.1";

in the line beginning "18 U.S.C. § 1512(a)" by inserting "2A1.3," immediately following "2A1.2,";

in the line beginning "18 U.S.C. § 1512(b) by inserting "2A1.2," immediately before "2A2.2";

in the line beginning "18 U.S.C. § 1704" by inserting ", 2F1.1" immediately following "2B5.2";

in the line beginning "18 U.S.C. § 1751(c)" by inserting ", 2X1.1" immediately following "2A4.1";

in the line beginning "18 U.S.C. § 1751(d)" by deleting "2A2.1" and inserting in lieu thereof "2A1.5", and by inserting ", 2X1.1" immediately following "2A4.1";

in the line beginning "18 U.S.C. § 1909" by inserting "2C1.3," immediately before "2C1.4";

in the line beginning "18 U.S.C. § 1951" by deleting "2B3.1, 2B3.2, 2C1.1,";

in the line beginning "18 U.S.C. § 1952A" by deleting "2A2.1,";

in the line beginning "18 U.S.C. § 1958" by deleting "2A2.1,";

by deleting:

"18 U.S.C. § 2251	2G2.1",

and inserting in lieu thereof:

"18 U.S.C. § 2251(a), (b)	2G2.1
18 U.S.C. § 2251(c)(1)(A)	2G2.2
18 U.S.C. § 2251(c)(1)(B)	2G2.1";

in the line beginning "18 U.S.C. § 2271" by deleting "2F1.1,";

in the line beginning "18 U.S.C. § 2421" by inserting ", 2G1.2" immediately following "2G1.1";

in the line beginning "18 U.S.C. § 2422" by inserting ", 2G1.2" immediately following "2G1.1";

by deleting "18 U.S.C. § 4082(d) 2P1.1";

by deleting:

"21 U.S.C. § 333	2N2.1",

and inserting in lieu thereof:

"21 U.S.C. § 333(a)(1)	2N2.1
21 U.S.C. § 333(a)(2)	2F1.1, 2N2.1
21 U.S.C. § 333(b)	2N2.1";

by deleting:

"26 U.S.C. § 5861(a)	2K2.3
26 U.S.C. § 5861(b)-(l)	2K2.2",

and inserting in lieu thereof:

"26 U.S.C. § 5861(a)	2K2.2
26 U.S.C. § 5861(b)	2K2.1
26 U.S.C. § 5861(c)	2K2.1
26 U.S.C. § 5861(d)	2K2.1
26 U.S.C. § 5861(e)	2K2.2
26 U.S.C. § 5861(f)	2K2.2
26 U.S.C. § 5861(g)	2K2.2
26 U.S.C. § 5861(h)	2K2.1
26 U.S.C. § 5861(i)	2K2.1
26 U.S.C. § 5861(j)	2K2.1, 2K2.2
26 U.S.C. § 5861(k)	2K2.1
26 U.S.C. § 5861(l)	2K2.2";

in the line beginning "26 U.S.C. § 5871" by deleting "2K2.2, 2K2.3" and inserting in lieu thereof "2K2.1, 2K2.2";

by deleting:

"33 U.S.C. § 1319	2Q1.1, 2Q1.2, 2Q1.3",

and inserting in lieu thereof:

"33 U.S.C. § 1319(c)(1), (c)(2), (c)(4)	2Q1.2, 2Q1.3
33 U.S.C. § 1319(c)(3)	2Q1.1";

and in the line beginning "42 U.S.C. § 3631" by deleting ", 2H1.5".

The Commentary to §2D3.4 captioned "Statutory Provisions" is amended by deleting "Provision" and inserting in lieu thereof "Provisions"; and by deleting "§ 842" and inserting in lieu thereof "§§ 954, 961".

The Commentary to §2M6.2 is amended by inserting between "Commentary" and "Background" the following:

"Statutory Provision: 42 U.S.C. § 2273".

The Commentary to §2T2.2 captioned "Statutory Provisions" is amended by deleting "5601-5605, 5607, 5608" and inserting in lieu thereof "5601, 5603-5605"; and by deleting "5691," immediately before "5762".

The Commentary to §2X2.1 captioned "Statutory Provisions" is amended by deleting "Provisions" and inserting in lieu thereof "Provision"; and by deleting "§§ 2, 755-757" and inserting in lieu thereof "§ 2".

This amendment makes the statutory index more comprehensive, conforms it to amended guidelines, and corrects erroneous references. In addition, this amendment conforms the statutory provisions of §§ 2D3.4, 2T2.2, 2X2.1 to the statutory index, and inserts additional Commentary in §2M6.2 referencing a statutory provision contained in Appendix A (Statutory Index) to conform the format of this guideline to the format of other offense guidelines. **The effective date of this amendment is November 1, 1990.**

360. Section 1B1.10(d) is amended by deleting "and 269" and inserting in lieu thereof "269, 329, and 341".

This amendment implements the directive in 28 U.S.C. § 994(u) in respect to the guideline amendments effective November 1, 1990. **The effective date of this amendment is November 1, 1990.**

361. The Commentary to §1B1.1 captioned "Application Notes" is amended in Note 1 by inserting the following additional subdivision at the end:

"(k) 'Destructive device' means any article described in 18 U.S.C. § 921(a)(4) (including an explosive, incendiary, or poison gas - (i) bomb, (ii) grenade, (iii) rocket having a propellant charge of more than four ounces, (iv) missile having an explosive or incendiary charge of more than one-quarter ounce, (v) mine, or (vi) device similar to any of the devices described in the proceeding clauses).".

The Commentary to §2B1.1 captioned "Application Notes" is amended in Note 1 by deleting "and 'firearm'" and inserting in lieu thereof ",'firearm,' and 'destructive device'", and by deleting the last sentence as follows: "'Destructive device' is defined in the Commentary to §2K1.4 (Arson: Property Damage by Use of Explosives).".

The Commentary to §2B1.2 captioned "Application Notes" is amended in Note 1 by deleting "and 'firearm'" and inserting in lieu thereof ",'firearm,' and 'destructive device'", and by deleting the last sentence as follows: "'Destructive device' is defined in the Commentary to §2K1.4 (Arson: Property Damage by Use of Explosives).".

The Commentary to §2B2.1 captioned "Application Notes" is amended in Note 1 by inserting "'destructive device,'" immediately before "and 'dangerous weapon'", and by deleting the last sentence as follows: "'Destructive device' is defined in the Commentary to §2K1.4 (Arson: Property Damage by Use of Explosives).".

The Commentary to §2B2.2 captioned "Application Notes" is amended in Note 1 by deleting "and 'firearm'" and inserting in lieu thereof ", 'firearm,' 'destructive device,' and 'dangerous weapon'", and by deleting the last sentence as follows: "'Destructive device' is defined in the Commentary to §2K1.4 (Arson: Property Damage by Use of Explosives).".

The Commentary to §2B3.1 captioned "Application Notes" is amended in Note 1 by inserting "'destructive device,'" immediately before "'dangerous weapon,'".

This amendment inserts the definition of a destructive device, formerly in the Commentary to §2K1.4, in the Commentary to §1B1.1, with minor revisions to the examples of the articles prohibited by 18 U.S.C. § 921(a)(4) to better reflect the statutory provision. This amendment also conforms the commentary of various offense guidelines to reference the definitions set forth in Application Note 1 of the Commentary to §1B1.1. **The effective date of this amendment is November 1, 1990.**

362. Chapter Seven is deleted in its entirety as follows:

"CHAPTER SEVEN - VIOLATIONS OF PROBATION AND SUPERVISED RELEASE

§7A1.1. Reporting of Violations of Probation and Supervised Release (Policy Statement)

(a) The Probation Officer shall promptly report to the court any alleged violation of a condition of probation or supervised release that constitutes new criminal conduct, other than conduct that would constitute a petty offense.

(b) The Probation Officer shall promptly report to the court any other alleged violation of a condition of probation or supervised release, unless the officer determines: (1) that such violation is minor, not part of a continuing pattern of violation, and not indicative of a serious adjustment problem; and (2) that non-reporting will not present an undue risk to the public or be inconsistent with any directive of the court relative to the reporting of violations.

Commentary

This policy statement addresses the reporting of violations of probation and supervised release. It is the Commission's intent that significant violations be promptly reported to the court. At the same time, the Commission realizes that it would neither be practical nor desirable to require such reporting for every minor violation.

§7A1.2. Revocation of Probation (Policy Statement)

(a) Upon a finding of a violation of probation involving new criminal conduct, other than criminal conduct constituting a petty offense, the court shall revoke probation.

(b) Upon a finding of a violation of probation involving conduct other than conduct under subsection (a), the court may: (1) revoke probation; or (2) extend the term of probation and/or modify the conditions of probation.

Commentary

This policy statement expresses a presumption that probation is to be revoked in the case of new criminal conduct other than a petty offense. For lesser violations, the policy statements provide that the court may revoke probation, extend the term of supervision, or modify the conditions of supervision.

§7A1.3. Revocation of Supervised Release (Policy Statement)

(a) Upon a finding of a violation of supervised release involving new criminal conduct, other than criminal conduct constituting a petty offense, the court shall revoke supervised release.

(b) Upon a finding of a violation of supervised release involving conduct other than conduct under subsection (a), the court may: (1) revoke supervised release; or (2) extend the term of supervised release and/or modify the conditions of supervised release.

Commentary

This policy statement expresses a presumption that supervised release is to be revoked in the case of new criminal conduct other than a petty offense. For lesser violations, the policy statements provide that the court may revoke supervised release, extend the term of supervision, or modify the conditions of supervision.

§7A1.4. No Credit for Time Under Supervision (Policy Statement)

(a) Upon revocation of probation, no credit shall be given (toward any sentence of imprisonment imposed) for any portion of the term of probation served prior to revocation.

(b) Upon revocation of supervised release, no credit shall be given (toward any term of imprisonment ordered) for time previously served on post-release supervision.

Commentary

This policy statement provides that time served on probation or supervised release is not to be credited in the determination of any term of imprisonment imposed upon revocation.".

A replacement chapter containing policy statements with accompanying commentary is inserted as Chapter Seven (Violations of Probation and Supervised Release).

This amendment replaces Chapter Seven with a set of more detailed policy statemnts applicable to violations of probation and supervised release. Under 28 U.S.C. § 994(a)(3), the Sentencing Commission is required to issue guidelines or policy statements applicable to the revocation of probation and supervised release. At this time, the Commission has chosen to promulgate policy statements only. These policy statements will provide guidance while allowing for the identification of any substantive or procedural issues that require further review. The Commission views these policy statements as evolutionary and will review relevant data and materials concerning revocation determinations under these policy statements. Revocation guidelines will be issued after federal judges, probation officers, practitioners, and others have the opportunity to evaluate and comment on these policy statements. **The effective date of this amendment is November 1, 1990.**

363. Section 2A4.1(b) is amended by deleting:

"(5) If the victim was kidnapped, abducted, or unlawfully restrained to facilitate the commission of another offense: (A) increase by 4 levels; or (B) if the result of applying this guideline is less than that resulting from application of the guideline for such other offense, apply the guideline for such other offense.",

and inserting in lieu thereof:

"(5) If the victim was sexually exploited, increase by 3 levels.

(6) If the victim is a minor and, in exchange for money or other consideration, was placed in the care or custody of another person who had no legal right to such care or custody of the victim, increase by 3 levels.

(7) If the victim was kidnapped, abducted, or unlawfully restrained during the commission of, or in connection with, another offense or escape therefrom; or if another offense was committed during the kidnapping, abduction, or unlawful restraint, increase to --

(A) the offense level from the Chapter Two offense guideline applicable to that other offense if such offense guideline includes an adjustment for kidnapping, abduction, or unlawful restraint, or otherwise takes such conduct into account; or

(B) 4 plus the offense level from the offense guideline applicable to that other offense, but in no event greater than level 43, in any other case,

if the resulting offense level is greater than that determined above.

(c) Cross Reference

(1) If the victim was killed under circumstances that would constitute murder under 18 U.S.C. § 1111 had such killing taken place within the territorial or maritime jurisdiction of the United States, apply §2A1.1 (First Degree Murder).".

The Commentary to §2A4.1 captioned "Application Notes" is amended by inserting the following additional note:

"4. 'Sexually exploited' includes offenses set forth in 18 U.S.C. §§ 2241-2244, 2251, and 2421-2423.".

The Commentary to §2A4.1 captioned "Background" is amended by inserting the following additional paragraph at the end:

" Section 401 of Public Law 101-647 amended 18 U.S.C. § 1201 to require that courts take into account certain specific offense characteristics in cases involving a victim under eighteen years of age and directed the Commission to include those specific offense characteristics within the guidelines. Where the guidelines did not already take into account the conduct identified by the Act, additional specific offense characteristics have been provided.".

This amendment implements the instructions in Section 401 of the Crime Control Act of 1990 (Public Law 101-647), in some cases with a broader scope, by adding specific offense characteristics at subsections (b)(5) and (b)(6). With respect to the portion of the Congressional instruction pertaining to aiders or abettors, no amendment was required because §1B1.3 (Relevant Conduct) provides an offense level greater than that required by the Congressional instruction. A separate amendment (amendment 388) clarifies that maltreatment to a life threatening degree constitutes life-threatening bodily injury. In addition, this amendment replaces the current subsection (b)(5) with a revised subsection (b)(7) that addresses other offenses connected with kidnapping, abduction, or unlawful restraint in a manner that more appropriately reflects the combined seriousness of such offenses, and inserts a cross reference to address the case in which the victim was murdered. **The effective date of this amendment is November 1, 1991.**

364. Section 2B1.1(b)(7) is amended by inserting "-- (A)" immediately before "substantially"; and by deleting the comma immediately following "institution" and inserting in lieu thereof "; or (B) affected a financial institution and the defendant derived more than $1,000,000 in gross receipts from the offense,".

The Commentary to §2B1.1 captioned "Statutory Provisions" is amended by inserting "225," immediately before "641".

The Commentary to §2B1.1 captioned "Application Notes" is amended in Note 9 by deleting "215" and inserting in lieu thereof "20"; and by deleting "1008, 1014, and 1344" and inserting in lieu thereof "1007, and 1014".

The Commentary to §2B1.1 captioned "Application Notes" is amended in Note 10 by deleting:

"as a consequence of the offense the institution became insolvent, substantially reduced benefits to pensioners or insureds, was unable on demand to refund fully any deposit, payment or investment, or was so depleted of its assets as to be forced to merge with another institution in order to continue active operations",

and inserting in lieu thereof:

", as a consequence of the offense, the institution became insolvent; substantially reduced benefits to pensioners or insureds; was unable on demand to refund fully any deposit, payment, or investment; was so depleted of its assets as to be forced to merge with another institution in order to continue active operations; or was placed in substantial jeopardy of any of the above".

The Commentary to §2B1.1 captioned "Application Notes" is amended by inserting the following additional notes:

"11. 'The defendant derived more than $1,000,000 in gross receipts from the offense,' as used in subsection (b)(7)(B), generally means that the gross receipts to the defendant individually, rather than to all participants, exceeded $1,000,000. 'Gross receipts from the offense' includes all property, real or personal, tangible or intangible, which is obtained directly or indirectly as a result of such offense. See 18 U.S.C. § 982(a)(4).

12. If the defendant is convicted under 18 U.S.C. § 225 (relating to a continuing financial crimes enterprise), the offense level is that applicable to the underlying series of offenses comprising the 'continuing financial crimes enterprise.'

13. If subsection (b)(7)(A) or (B) applies, there shall be a rebuttable presumption that the offense involved 'more than minimal planning.'".

The Commentary to §2B1.1 captioned "Background" is amended in the seventh paragraph by deleting "(b)(7)" and inserting in lieu thereof "(b)(7)(A)", and by deleting "statutory directive" and inserting in lieu thereof "instruction"; and by inserting the following additional paragraph at the end:

" Subsection (b)(7)(B) implements the instruction to the Commission in Section 2507 of Public Law 101-647.".

Section 2B4.1(b)(2) is amended by inserting "-- (A)" immediately before "substantially"; and by deleting the comma immediately following "institution" and inserting in lieu thereof "; or (B) affected a financial institution and the defendant derived more than $1,000,000 in gross receipts from the offense,".

The Commentary to §2B4.1 captioned "Statutory Provisions" is amended by inserting ", 225" immediately following "224".

The Commentary to §2B4.1 captioned "Application Notes" is amended in Note 2 by deleting "Bribery" and inserting in lieu thereof "Offering, Giving, Soliciting, or Receiving a Bribe; Extortion Under Color of Official Right".

The Commentary to §2B4.1 captioned "Application Notes" is amended in Note 3 by deleting "215" and inserting in lieu thereof "20"; and by deleting "1008, 1014, and 1344" and inserting in lieu thereof "1007, and 1014".

The Commentary to §2B4.1 captioned "Application Notes" is amended in Note 4 by deleting:

> "as a consequence of the offense the institution became insolvent, substantially reduced benefits to pensioners or insureds, was unable on demand to refund fully any deposit, payment or investment, or was so depleted of its assets as to be forced to merge with another institution in order to continue active operations",

and inserting in lieu thereof:

> ", as a consequence of the offense, the institution became insolvent; substantially reduced benefits to pensioners or insureds; was unable on demand to refund fully any deposit, payment, or investment; was so depleted of its assets as to be forced to merge with another institution in order to continue active operations; or was placed in substantial jeopardy of any of the above".

The Commentary to §2B4.1 captioned "Application Notes" is amended by inserting the following additional notes:

> "5. 'The defendant derived more than $1,000,000 in gross receipts from the offense,' as used in subsection (b)(2)(B), generally means that the gross receipts to the defendant individually, rather than to all participants, exceeded $1,000,000. 'Gross receipts from the offense' includes all property, real or personal, tangible or intangible, which is obtained directly or indirectly as a result of such offense. See 18 U.S.C. § 982(a)(4).
>
> 6. If the defendant is convicted under 18 U.S.C. § 225 (relating to a continuing financial crimes enterprise), the offense level is that applicable to the underlying series of offenses comprising the 'continuing financial crimes enterprise.'".

The Commentary to §2B4.1 captioned "Background" is amended in the second paragraph by deleting the second sentence as follows:

> "As is the case for most other offenses covered by this guideline, the maximum term of imprisonment authorized is five years.";

in the seventh paragraph by deleting "(b)(2)" and inserting in lieu thereof "(b)(2)(A)", and by deleting "statutory directive" and inserting in lieu thereof "instruction"; and by inserting the following additional paragraph at the end:

> " Subsection (b)(2)(B) implements the instruction to the Commission in Section 2507 of Public Law 101-647.".

Section 2F1.1(b)(6) is amended by inserting "-- (A)" immediately before "substantially"; and by deleting the comma immediately following "institution" and inserting in lieu thereof "; or (B) affected a financial institution and the defendant derived more than $1,000,000 in gross receipts from the offense,".

The Commentary to §2F1.1 captioned "Statutory Provisions" is amended by inserting "225," immediately before "285".

The Commentary to §2F1.1 captioned "Application Notes" is amended in Note 14 by deleting "215" and inserting in lieu thereof "20"; and by deleting "1008, 1014, and 1344" and inserting in lieu thereof "1007, and 1014".

The Commentary to §2F1.1 captioned "Application Notes" is amended in Note 15 by deleting:

> "as a consequence of the offense the institution became insolvent, substantially reduced benefits to pensioners or insureds, was unable on demand to refund fully any deposit, payment or investment, or was so depleted of its assets as to be forced to merge with another institution in order to continue active operations",

and inserting in lieu thereof:

> ", as a consequence of the offense, the institution became insolvent; substantially reduced benefits to pensioners or insureds; was unable on demand to refund fully any deposit, payment, or investment; was so depleted of its assets as to be forced to merge with another institution in order to continue active operations; or was placed in substantial jeopardy of any of the above".

The Commentary to §2F1.1 captioned "Application Notes" is amended by inserting the following additional notes:

> "16. 'The defendant derived more than $1,000,000 in gross receipts from the offense,' as used in subsection (b)(6)(B), generally means that the gross receipts to the defendant individually, rather than to all participants, exceeded $1,000,000. 'Gross receipts from the offense' includes all property, real or personal, tangible or intangible, which is obtained directly or indirectly as a result of such offense. <u>See</u> 18 U.S.C. § 982(a)(4).
>
> 17. If the defendant is convicted under 18 U.S.C. § 225 (relating to a continuing financial crimes enterprise), the offense level is that applicable to the underlying series of offenses comprising the 'continuing financial crimes enterprise.'
>
> 18. If subsection (b)(6)(A) or (B) applies, there shall be a rebuttable presumption that the offense involved 'more than minimal planning.'".

The Commentary to §2F1.1 captioned "Background" is amended in the sixth paragraph by deleting "(b)(6)" and inserting in lieu thereof "(b)(6)(A)", and by deleting "statutory directive" and inserting in lieu thereof "instruction"; and by inserting the following additional paragraph at the end:

> " Subsection (b)(6)(B) implements the instruction to the Commission in Section 2507 of Public Law 101-647.".

This amendment implements the instruction to the Commission in Section 2507 of the Crime Control Act of 1990 (Public Law 101-647). It also reflects the new offense relating to a continuing financial crimes enterprise created by Section 2510 of the Crime Control Act of 1990. In addition, it revises the Commentary to §§2B1.1, 2B4.1, and 2F1.1 with respect to the definition of "substantially jeopardized the safety and soundness of a financial institution" so that the commentary is read to include cases in which the offense created a substantial risk of any of the harms described in addition to cases in which such harm actually occurred. **The effective date of this amendment is November 1, 1991.**

365. Section 2B3.1(b) is amended by deleting:

"(2) (A) If a firearm was discharged, increase by 5 levels; (B) if a dangerous weapon (including a firearm) was otherwise used, increase by 4 levels; (C) if a dangerous weapon (including a firearm) was brandished, displayed, or possessed, increase by 3 levels; or (D) if an express threat of death was made, increase by 2 levels.",

and inserting in lieu thereof:

"(2) (A) If a firearm was discharged, increase by 7 levels; (B) if a firearm was otherwise used, increase by 6 levels; (C) if a firearm was brandished, displayed, or possessed, increase by 5 levels; (D) if a dangerous weapon was otherwise used, increase by 4 levels; (E) if a dangerous weapon was brandished, displayed, or possessed, increase by 3 levels; or (F) if an express threat of death was made, increase by 2 levels.".

Section 2B3.1 (b)(3) is amended by deleting "9" and inserting in lieu thereof "11".

The Commentary to §2B3.1 captioned "Application Notes" is amended in Note 1 by inserting "'bodily injury,' 'serious bodily injury,' 'permanent or life-threatening bodily injury,'" immediately before "'abducted'".

The Commentary to §2B3.1 captioned "Application Notes" is amended in Note 2 by deleting "(b)(2)(C)" and inserting in lieu thereof "(b)(2)(E)".

The Commentary to §2B3.1 captioned "Application Notes" is amended in Note 4 by deleting "9" and inserting in lieu thereof "11".

The Commentary to §2B3.1 captioned "Application Notes" is amended in Note 7 by deleting "(b)(2)(D)" and inserting in lieu thereof "(b)(2)(F)".

This amendment increases the offense levels for use or possession of a firearm by 2 levels to better reflect the seriousness of such offenses and to reduce the disparity resulting from the exercise of prosecutorial discretion in the charging of an offense under 18 U.S.C. § 924(c) or § 929(a). In addition, this amendment revises the commentary to make the reference to the terms defined in §1B1.1 more comprehensive. **The effective date of this amendment is November 1, 1991.**

366. Section 2B3.2(b) is amended by deleting subdivisions (1) and (2) as follows:

"(1) If the greater of the amount obtained or demanded exceeded $2,500, increase by the corresponding number of levels from the table in §2B2.1(b)(2).

(2) (A) If a firearm was discharged, increase by 5 levels; (B) if a dangerous weapon (including a firearm) was otherwise used, increase by 4 levels; (C) if a dangerous weapon (including a firearm) was brandished, displayed, or possessed, increase by 3 levels.";

by renumbering subdivisions (3) and (4) as (4) and (5) respectively; by inserting the following as subdivisions (1)-(3):

"(1) If the offense involved an express or implied threat of death, bodily injury, or kidnapping, increase by 2 levels.

(2) If the greater of the amount demanded or the loss to the victim exceeded $10,000, increase by the corresponding number of levels from the table in §2B3.1(b)(6).

(3) (A)(i) If a firearm was discharged, increase by 7 levels; (ii) if a firearm was otherwise used, increase by 6 levels; (iii) if a firearm was brandished, displayed, or possessed, increase by 5 levels; (iv) if a dangerous weapon was otherwise used, increase by 4 levels; or (v) if a dangerous weapon was brandished, displayed, or possessed, increase by 3 levels; or

(B) If the offense involved preparation to carry out a threat of (i) death, (ii) serious bodily injury, (iii) kidnapping, or (iv) product tampering; or if the participant(s) otherwise demonstrated the ability to carry out such threat, increase by 3 levels.";

and in the last sentence of the renumbered subdivision (4) (formerly (3)) by deleting "(2)", "(3)" and "9", and inserting in lieu thereof "(3)", "(4)", and "11", respectively.

Section 2B3.2 is amended by inserting the following additional subsection:

"(c) Cross Reference

(1) If the offense was tantamount to attempted murder, apply §2A2.1 (Assault With Intent to Commit Murder; Attempted Murder) if the resulting offense level is greater than that determined above.".

The Commentary to §2B3.2 captioned "Application Notes" is amended in Note 1 by inserting "'bodily injury,' 'serious bodily injury,' 'permanent or life-threatening bodily injury,'" immediately before "abducted"; and in Note 4 by deleting "9" and inserting in lieu thereof "11".

The Commentary to §2B3.2 captioned "Application Notes" is amended by deleting:

"5. Valuation of loss is discussed in the Commentary to §2B1.1 (Larceny, Embezzlement, and Other Forms of Theft).",

and inserting in lieu thereof:

"5. 'Loss to the victim,' as used in subsection (b)(2), means any demand paid plus any additional consequential loss from the offense (e.g., the cost of defensive measures taken in direct response to the offense).

6. In certain cases, an extortionate demand may be accompanied by conduct that does not qualify as a display of a dangerous weapon under subsection (b)(3)(A)(v) but is nonetheless similar in seriousness, demonstrating the defendant's preparation or ability to carry out the threatened harm (e.g., an extortionate demand containing a threat to tamper with a consumer product accompanied by a workable plan showing how the product's tamper-resistant seals could be defeated, or a threat to kidnap a person accompanied by information showing study of that person's daily routine). Subsection (b)(3)(B) addresses such cases.

7. If the offense involved the threat of death or serious bodily injury to numerous victims (e.g., in the case of a plan to derail a passenger train or poison consumer products), an upward departure may be warranted.

8. If the offense involved organized criminal activity, or a threat to a family member of the victim, an upward departure may be warranted.".

The Commentary to §2B3.2 captioned "Background" is amended in the last sentence by deleting "§ 877" and inserting in lieu thereof "18 U.S.C. § 877".

This amendment provides a specific offense characteristic to distinguish the greater seriousness of offenses that involve an express or implied threat of death, bodily injury, or kidnapping; conforms the loss table to that used in the robbery guideline to reflect that the typical case under the amended guideline will have an offense level that is more closely comparable to robbery; increases the offense levels for offenses involving use or possession of a firearm to conform to an amendment being made to the robbery guideline; adds a subdivision to the specific offense characteristic dealing with use or possession of a dangerous weapon to address cases in which the conduct is tantamount in seriousness to the brandishing, display, or possession of a dangerous weapon, but does not qualify under the current specific offense characteristic for weapon enhancement; modifies subsection (b)(1) to provide that the greater of the amount demanded or the loss to the victim is used; adds a cross reference to §2A2.1 to address cases in which the conduct was tantamount to attempted murder; and sets forth commentary describing certain aggravating factors that may warrant an upward departure. **The effective date of this amendment is November 1, 1991.**

367. Section 2C1.1(b)(1) is amended by inserting "or extortion" immediately following "bribe".

Section 2C1.1(b)(2)(A) is amended by deleting "bribe or the benefit received, or to be received, in return for the bribe" and inserting in lieu thereof "payment, the benefit received or to be received in return for the payment, or the loss to the government from the offense, whichever is greatest,".

Section 2C1.1(b)(2)(B) is amended by deleting "bribe" and inserting in lieu thereof "payment".

Section 2C1.1(c) is amended by deleting:

"(1) If the bribe was for the purpose of concealing or facilitating another criminal offense, or for obstructing justice in respect to another criminal offense, apply §2X3.1 (Accessory After the Fact) in respect to such other criminal offense if the resulting offense level is greater than that determined above.";

by renumbering subsection (c)(2) as (c)(3); and by inserting the following as subsections (c)(1) and (2):

"(1) If the offense was committed for the purpose of facilitating the commission of another criminal offense, apply the offense guideline applicable to a conspiracy to commit that other offense if the resulting offense level is greater than that determined above.

(2) If the offense was committed for the purpose of concealing, or obstructing justice in respect to, another criminal offense, apply §2X3.1 (Accessory After the Fact) or §2J1.2 (Obstruction of Justice), as appropriate, in respect to that other offense if the resulting offense level is greater than that determined above.".

The Commentary to §2C1.1 captioned "Application Notes" is amended by deleting Note 2 as follows:

"2. 'Value of the bribe or the benefit received, or to be received, in return for the bribe' means the greater of the value of the bribe or the value of the benefit received, or to be received, in return for the bribe. The 'value of the benefit received or to be received' means the net value of such benefit. For example, if a $150,000 contract on which $20,000 profit was made was awarded in return for a bribe, the value of the benefit received in return is $20,000.",

and inserting in lieu thereof:

"2. 'Loss' is discussed in the Commentary to §2B1.1 (Larceny, Embezzlement, and Other Forms of Theft) and includes both actual and intended loss. The value of 'the benefit received or to be received' means the net value of such benefit. Examples: (1) A government employee, in return for a $500 bribe, reduces the price of a piece of surplus property offered for sale by the government from $10,000 to $2,000; the value of the benefit received is $8,000. (2) A $150,000 contract on which $20,000 profit was made was awarded in return for a bribe; the value of the benefit received is $20,000. Do not deduct the value of the bribe itself in computing the value of the benefit received or to be received. In the above examples, therefore, the value of the benefit received would be the same regardless of the value of the bribe.";

The Commentary to §2C1.1 captioned "Application Notes" is amended in Note 3 by deleting "§2C1.1(c)(1) or (2)." and inserting in lieu thereof "§2C1.1(c)(1), (2), or (3). In such cases, an adjustment from §3B1.3 (Abuse of Position of Trust or Use of Special Skill) may apply.".

The Commentary to §2C1.1 captioned "Application Notes" is amended in Note 4 by deleting "bribe" and inserting in lieu thereof "unlawful payment"; and by deleting "and (2)" and inserting in lieu thereof ", (2), and (3)".

The Commentary to §2C1.1 captioned "Application Notes" is amended in Note 6 by inserting the following as the first sentence:

"Subsection (b)(1) provides an adjustment for offenses involving more than one incident of either bribery or extortion.";

by deleting "bribe" the first time it occurs and inserting in lieu thereof "incident of bribery or extortion"; and by inserting "or extortion" immediately before ", even if charged".

The Commentary to §2C1.1 captioned "Background" is amended by deleting the third paragraph as follows:

" The amount of the bribe is used as a factor in the guideline not because it directly measures harm to society, but because it is improbable that a large bribe would be given for a favor of little consequence. Moreover, for deterrence purposes, the punishment should be commensurate with the gain.",

and inserting in lieu thereof:

" In determining the net value of the benefit received or to be received, the value of the bribe is not deducted from the gross value of such benefit; the harm is the same regardless of value of the bribe paid to receive the benefit. Where the value of the bribe exceeds the value of the benefit or the value of the benefit cannot be determined, the value of the bribe is used because it is likely that the payer of such a bribe expected something in return that would be worth more than the value of the bribe. Moreover, for deterrence purposes, the punishment should be commensurate with the gain to the payer or the recipient of the bribe, whichever is higher.".

The Commentary to §2C1.1 captioned "Background" is amended in the fourth paragraph by deleting "bribe is" and inserting in lieu thereof "payment was".

The Commentary to §2C1.1 captioned "Background" is amended by deleting the fifth, sixth, and seventh paragraphs as follows:

"Under §2C1.1(c)(1), if the purpose of the bribe involved the facilitation of another criminal offense or the obstruction of justice in respect to another criminal offense, the guideline for §2X3.1 (Accessory After the Fact) in respect to that criminal offense will be applied, if the result is greater than that determined above. For example, if a bribe was given for the purpose of facilitating or covering up the offense of espionage, the guideline for accessory after the fact to espionage would be applied.

Under §2C1.1(c)(2), if the offense involved forcible extortion, the guideline from §2B3.2 (Extortion by Force or Threat of Injury or Serious Damage) will apply if the result is greater than that determined above.

Note that, when applying 2C1.1(c)(1) or (2), an adjustment from Chapter Three, Part B (Role in the Offense) will also apply. This normally will result in an increase of at least 2 levels.",

and inserting in lieu thereof:

" Under §2C1.1(c)(1), if the payment was to facilitate the commission of another criminal offense, the guideline applicable to a conspiracy to commit that other offense will apply if the result is greater than that determined above. For example, if a bribe was given to a law enforcement officer to allow the smuggling of a quantity of cocaine, the guideline for conspiracy to import cocaine would be applied if it resulted in a greater offense level.

Under §2C1.1(c)(2), if the payment was to conceal another criminal offense or obstruct justice in respect to another criminal offense, the guideline from §2X3.1 (Accessory After the Fact) or §2J1.2 (Obstruction of Justice), as appropriate, will apply if the result is greater than that determined above. For example, if a bribe was given for the purpose of concealing the offense of espionage, the guideline for accessory after the fact to espionage would be applied.

Under §2C1.1(c)(3), if the offense involved forcible extortion, the guideline from §2B3.2 (Extortion by Force or Threat of Injury or Serious Damage) will apply if the result is greater than that determined above.

When the offense level is determined under §2C1.1(c)(1), (2), or (3), an adjustment from §3B1.3 (Abuse of Position of Trust or Use of Special Skill) may apply.".

This amendment adds an additional factor in subsection (b)(2)(A) to take into account loss to the government from the offense; expands subsection (c) to distinguish an offense committed for the purpose of facilitating the commission of another offense from an offense committed to cover up or obstruct justice in respect to another offense; clarifies the term "value of the benefit received"; and substitutes "payment" for "bribe" and adds "or extortion" where necessary to reflect that this guideline covers both bribery and extortion under color of official right. **The effective date of this amendment is November 1, 1991.**

368. Chapter Two, Part C, is amended by inserting an additional guideline with accompanying commentary as §2C1.7 (Fraud Involving Deprivation of the Intangible Right to the Honest Services of Public Officials; Conspiracy to Defraud by Interference with Governmental Functions).

This amendment provides an additional guideline to cover certain offenses that involve public corruption but do not fall within the guidelines of Chapter Two, Part C (Official Corruption) as currently written. In some cases, the statutes covered are used to prosecute offenses more appropriately covered under §2C1.1 (Offering, Giving, Soliciting, or Receiving a Bribe; Extortion Under Color of Official Right), §2C1.2 (Offering, Giving, Soliciting, or Receiving a Gratuity), or §2C1.3 (Conflict of Interest). A cross reference is provided to address such cases. **The effective date of this amendment is November 1, 1991.**

369. Section 2D1.1(c)(12) is amended by deleting the period immediately after "Schedule III substances" and inserting in lieu thereof "(except anabolic steroids);", and by inserting the following additional subdivision at the end:

"40,000 or more units of anabolic steroids.".

Section 2D1.1(c)(13) is amended by deleting the period immediately after "Schedule III substances" and inserting in lieu thereof "(except anabolic steroids);", and by inserting the following additional subdivision at the end:

"At least 20,000 but less than 40,000 units of anabolic steroids.".

Section 2D1.1(c)(14) is amended by deleting the period immediately after "Schedule III substances" and inserting in lieu thereof "(except anabolic steroids);", and by inserting the following additional subdivision at the end:

"At least 10,000 but less than 20,000 units of anabolic steroids.".

Section 2D1.1(c)(15) is amended by deleting the period immediately after "Schedule III substances" and inserting in lieu thereof "(except anabolic steroids);", and by inserting the following additional subdivision at the end:

"At least 5,000 but less than 10,000 units of anabolic steroids.".

Section 2D1.1(c)(16) is amended by inserting "(except anabolic steroids)" immediately after "Schedule III substances", and by inserting the following additional subdivision after the next to last subdivision:

"At least 2,500 but less than 5,000 units of anabolic steroids;".

Section 2D1.1(c)(17) is amended by inserting "(except anabolic steroids)" immediately after "Schedule III substances", and by inserting the following additional subdivision after the next to last subdivision:

"At least 1,000 but less than 2,500 units of anabolic steroids;".

Section 2D1.1(c)(18) is amended by inserting "(except anabolic steroids)" immediately after "Schedule III substances", and by inserting the following additional subdivision after the fourth subdivision:

"At least 250 but less than 1,000 units of anabolic steroids;".

Section 2D1.1(c)(19) is amended by inserting "(except anabolic steroids)" immediately after "Schedule III substances", and by inserting the following additional subdivision after the fourth subdivision:

"Less than 250 units of anabolic steroids;".

Section 2D1.1(c) is amended in the note following subdivision (19) by inserting the following additional paragraph at the end:

"In the case of anabolic steroids, one 'unit' means a 10 cc vial of an injectable steroid or fifty tablets. All vials of injectable steroids are to be converted on the basis of their volume to the equivalent number of 10 cc vials (e.g., one 50 cc vial is to be counted as five 10 cc vials).".

This amendment adds offenses involving anabolic steroids to §2D1.1 to reflect that Title XIX of the Crime Control Act of 1990 (Public Law 101-647) reclassified anabolic steroids as Schedule III controlled substances under 21 U.S.C. § 812(c). Because of the variety of substances involved, the Commission has determined that a measure based on quantity unit, rather than weight, provides the most appropriate measure of the scale of the offense. **The effective date of this amendment is November 1, 1991.**

370. Section 2D1.1(c) is amended in subdivision (1) by inserting ", or 30 KG or more of 'Ice'" immediately following "Pure Methamphetamine"; in subdivision (2) by inserting ", or at least 10 KG but less than 30 KG of 'Ice'" immediately following "Pure Methamphetamine"; in subdivision (3) by inserting ", or at least 3 KG but less than 10 KG of 'Ice'" immediately following "Pure Methamphetamine"; in subdivision (4) by inserting ", or at least 1 KG but less than 3 KG of 'Ice'" immediately following "Pure Methamphetamine"; in subdivision (5) by inserting ", or at least 300 G but less than 1 KG of 'Ice'" immediately following "Pure Methamphetamine"; in subdivision (6) by inserting ", or at least 100 G but less than 300 G of 'Ice'" immediately following "Pure Methamphetamine"; in subdivision (7) by inserting ", or at least 70 G but less than 100 G of 'Ice'" immediately following "Pure Methamphetamine"; in subdivision (8) by inserting ", or at least 40 G but less than 70 G of 'Ice'" immediately following "Pure Methamphetamine"; subdivision (9) by inserting ", or at least 10 G but less than 40 G of 'Ice'" immediately following "Pure Methamphetamine"; in subdivision (10) by inserting ", or at least 8 G but less than 10 G of 'Ice'" immediately following "Pure Methamphetamine"; in subdivision (11) by inserting ", or at least 6 G but less than 8 G of 'Ice'" immediately following "Pure Methamphetamine"; in subdivision (12) by inserting ", or at least 4 G but less than 6 G of 'Ice'" immediately following "Pure Methamphetamine"; in subdivision (13) by inserting ", or at least 2 G but less than 4 G of 'Ice'" immediately following "Pure Methamphetamine"; subdivision (14) by inserting ", or at least 1 G but less than 2 G of 'Ice'" immediately following "Pure Methamphetamine"; in subdivision (15) by inserting ", or at least 500 MG but less than 1 G of 'Ice'" immediately following "Pure Methamphetamine"; in subdivision (16) by inserting ", or less than 500 MG of 'Ice'" immediately following "Pure Methamphetamine"; and in the note following subdivision (19) by inserting the following as the second paragraph:

"'Ice,' for the purposes of this guideline, means a mixture or substance containing d-methamphetamine hydrochloride of at least 80% purity.".

This amendment implements the instruction to the Commission in Section 2701 of the Crime Control Act of 1990 (Public Law 101-647) in a form compatible with the structure of the guidelines. **The effective date of this amendment is November 1, 1991.**

371. Chapter Two, Part D, Subpart 1, is amended by inserting additional guidelines with accompanying commentary as §2D1.11 (Unlawfully Distributing, Importing, Exporting or Possessing a Listed Chemical), §2D1.12 (Unlawful Possession, Manufacture, Distribution, or Importation of Prohibited Flask or Equipment), and §2D1.13 (Structuring Chemical Transactions or Creating a Chemical Mixture to Evade Reporting or Recordkeeping Requirements; Presenting False or Fraudulent Identification to Obtain a Listed Chemical).

Chapter Two, Part D, Subpart 3 is amended by inserting an additional guideline with accompanying commentary as §2D3.5 (Violation of Recordkeeping or Reporting Requirements for Listed Chemicals and Certain Machines).

The Commentary to §2D1.1 captioned "Statutory Provisions" is amended by deleting "841, 960" and inserting in lieu thereof "841(a), (b)(1)-(3), 960(a), (b)".

The Commentary to §2D1.1 captioned "Application Notes" is amended by inserting the following additional note:

"14. D-lysergic acid, which is generally used to make LSD, is classified as a Schedule III controlled substance (to which §2D1.1 applies) and as a listed precursor (to which §2D1.11 applies). Where the defendant is convicted under 21 U.S.C. §§ 841(b)(1)(D) or 860(b)(4) of an offense involving d-lysergic acid, apply §2D1.1 or §2D1.11, whichever results in the greater offense level. See Application Note 5 in the Commentary to §1B1.1 (Application Instructions). Where the defendant is accountable for an offense involving the manufacture of LSD, see Application Note 12 above pertaining to the determination of the scale of the offense.".

This amendment makes Chapter Two, Part D more comprehensive by providing additional guidelines to address violations involving listed chemicals, flasks, and certain machines that are used in the manufacture of controlled substances. Conforming changes are made to the Commentary to §2D1.1. **The effective date of this amendment is November 1, 1991.**

372. Chapter Two, Part G, Subpart 2 is amended by inserting additional guidelines with accompanying commentary as §2G2.4 (Receipt or Possession of Materials Depicting a Minor Engaged in Sexually Explicit Conduct) and §2G2.5 (Recordkeeping Offenses Involving the Production of Sexually Explicit Materials).

Section 2G2.2 is amended in the title by deleting "Transporting, Receiving, or"; and by inserting at the end "; Receiving, Transporting, Advertising, or Possessing Material Involving the Sexual Exploitation of a Minor with Intent to Traffic".

The Commentary to §2G2.2 captioned "Statutory Provisions" is amended by deleting "1460,".

Section 2G3.1(c)(1) is amended by deleting "(Transporting, Receiving, or Trafficking in Material Involving the Sexual Exploitation of a Minor)" and inserting in lieu thereof "(Trafficking in Material Involving the Sexual Exploitation of a Minor; Receiving, Transporting, Advertising, or Possessing Material Involving the Sexual Exploitation of a Minor with Intent to Traffic) or §2G2.4 (Receipt or Possession of Materials Depicting a Minor Engaged in Sexually Explicit Conduct), as appropriate".

This amendment inserts an additional guideline at §2G2.4 to address offenses involving receipt or possession of materials depicting a minor engaged in sexually explicit conduct, as distinguished from offenses involving trafficking in such material, which continue to be covered under §2G2.2. Offenses involving receipt or transportation of such material for the purpose of trafficking are referenced to §2G2.2 on the basis of the underlying conduct (subsection (c)(2)). Similarly, offenses in which the underlying conduct is more appropriately addressed as sexual exploitation of a minor are referenced to that guideline (subsection (c)(1)). Among the offenses covered by this guideline is a new offense created by Section 323 of the Crime Control Act of 1990 (Public Law 101-647). In addition, this amendment inserts an additional guideline at §2G2.5 to address a recordkeeping offense created by Section 311 of the Crime Control Act of 1990 (Public Law 101-647). **The effective date of this amendment is November 1, 1991.**

373. Chapter Two, Part K, Subpart 1 is amended by deleting §§2K1.3 and 2K1.6 in their entirety as follows:

"§2K1.3. Unlawfully Trafficking In, Receiving, or Transporting Explosives

(a) Base Offense Level: 6

(b) Specific Offense Characteristics

If more than one applies, use the greatest:

(1) If the defendant"s conduct involved any written or oral false or fictitious statement, false record, or misrepresented identification, increase by 4 levels.

(2) If the offense involved explosives that the defendant knew or had reason to believe were stolen, increase by 6 levels.

(3) If the defendant knowingly distributed explosives to a person under twenty-one years of age, to a person prohibited by state law or ordinance from receiving such explosives at the place of distribution, or to a person the defendant had reason to believe intended to transport such materials into a state in violation of the law of that state, increase by 4 levels.

(4) If the defendant was a person prohibited from receiving explosives under 18 U.S.C. § 842(i), or if the defendant knowingly distributed explosives to a person prohibited from receiving explosives under 18 U.S.C. § 842(i), increase by 10 levels.

(5) If a recordkeeping offense reflected an effort to conceal a substantive offense involving explosives, apply the guideline for the substantive offense.

Commentary

Statutory Provisions: 18 U.S.C. §§ 842(a), (h), (i), 844(b). For additional statutory provision(s), see Appendix A (Statutory Index).

Application Note:

1. 'A person prohibited from receiving explosives under 18 U.S.C. § 842(i)' is anyone who is under indictment for or has been convicted of a crime punishable by imprisonment for more than one year; who is a fugitive from justice; who is an unlawful user of or addicted to marihuana, any depressant or stimulant or narcotic drug; or who has been adjudicated as a mental defective or has been committed to a mental institution.

Background: This section applies to conduct ranging from violations of a regulatory nature pertaining to licensees or persons otherwise lawfully involved in explosives commerce to more serious violations that involve substantial danger to public safety.",

"§2K1.6. Shipping, Transporting, or Receiving Explosives with Felonious Intent or Knowledge; Using or Carrying Explosives in Certain Crimes

(a) Base Offense Level (Apply the greatest):

(1) 18; or

(2) If the defendant committed the offense with intent to commit another offense against a person or property, apply §2X1.1 (Attempt, Solicitation, or Conspiracy) in respect to such other offense; or

(3) If death resulted, apply the most analogous guideline from Chapter Two, Part A, Subpart 1 (Homicide).

Commentary

Statutory Provisions: 18 U.S.C. § 844(d); 26 U.S.C. § 5685. For additional statutory provision(s), see Appendix A (Statutory Index).".

A replacement guideline with accompanying commentary is inserted as §2K1.3 (Unlawful Receipt, Possession, or Transportation of Explosive Materials; Prohibited Transactions Involving Explosive Materials).

Chapter Two, Part K, Subpart 1 is amended by inserting an additional guideline with accompanying commentary as §2K1.6 (Licensee Recordkeeping Violations Involving Explosive Materials).

This amendment consolidates two guidelines, and revises the offense levels and characteristics to more adequately reflect the seriousness of such offenses, including enhancements for defendants previously convicted of felony crimes of violence or controlled substance offenses. In addition, the amendment inserts an additional guideline to cover certain recordkeeping offenses. **The effective date of this amendment is November 1, 1991.**

374. Chapter Two, Part K, Subpart 2 is amended by deleting §§2K2.1, 2K2.2, and 2K2.3 in their entirety as follows:

"§2K2.1. Unlawful Receipt, Possession, or Transportation of Firearms or Ammunition

(a) Base Offense Level (Apply the greatest):

(1) 18, if the defendant is convicted under 18 U.S.C. § 922(o) or 26 U.S.C. § 5861; or

(2) 12, if the defendant is convicted under 18 U.S.C. § 922(g), (h), or (n); or if the defendant, at the time of the offense, had been convicted in any court of an offense punishable by imprisonment for a term exceeding one year; or

(3) 6, otherwise.

(b) Specific Offense Characteristics

(1) If the defendant obtained or possessed the firearm or ammunition, other than a firearm covered in 26 U.S.C. § 5845(a), solely for lawful sporting purposes or collection, decrease the offense level determined above to level 6.

(2) If the firearm was stolen or had an altered or obliterated serial number, increase by 2 levels.

(c) Cross References

(1) If the offense involved the distribution of a firearm or possession with intent to distribute, apply §2K2.2 (Unlawful Trafficking and Other Prohibited Transactions Involving Firearms) if the resulting offense level is greater than that determined above.

(2) If the defendant used or possessed the firearm in connection with commission or attempted commission of another offense, apply §2X1.1 (Attempt, Solicitation, or Conspiracy) in respect to that other offense, if the resulting offense level is greater than that determined above.

Commentary

Statutory Provisions: 18 U.S.C. § 922(a)(1), (a)(3), (a)(4), (a)(6), (e), (f), (g), (h), (i), (j), (k), (l), (n), and (o); 26 U.S.C. § 5861(b), (c), (d), (h), (i), (j), and (k). For additional statutory provision(s), see Appendix A (Statutory Index).

Application Notes:

1. The definition of 'firearm' used in this section is that set forth in 18 U.S.C. § 921(a)(3) (if the defendant is convicted under 18 U.S.C. § 922) and 26 U.S.C. § 5845(a) (if the defendant is convicted under 26 U.S.C. § 5861). These definitions are somewhat broader than that used in Application Note 1(e) of the Commentary to §1B1.1 (Application Instructions). Under 18 U.S.C. § 921(a)(3), the term 'firearm' means (A) any weapon (including a starter gun) which will or is designed to or may readily be converted to expel a projectile by the action of an explosive; (B) the frame or receiver of any such weapon; (C) any firearm muffler or firearm silencer; or (D) any destructive device. Under 26 U.S.C. § 5845(a), the term 'firearm' includes a shotgun, or a weapon made from a shotgun, with a barrel or barrels of less than 18 inches in length; a weapon made from a shotgun or rifle with an overall length of less than 26 inches; a rifle, or weapon made from a rifle, with a barrel or barrels less than 16 inches in length; a machine gun; a muffler or silencer for a firearm; a destructive device; and certain other large bore weapons.

2. Under §2K2.1(b)(1), intended lawful use, as determined by the surrounding circumstances, provides a decrease in the offense level. Relevant circumstances include, among others, the number and type of firearms (sawed-off shotguns, for example, have few legitimate uses) and ammunition, the location and circumstances of possession, the nature of the defendant's criminal history (e.g., whether involving firearms), and the extent to which possession was restricted by local law.

Background: Under pre-guidelines practice, there was substantial sentencing variation for these crimes. From the Commission's investigations, it appeared that the variation was attributable primarily to the wide variety of circumstances under which these offenses occur. Apart from the nature of the defendant's criminal history, his actual or intended use of the firearm was probably the most important factor in determining the sentence.

Statistics showed that pre-guidelines sentences averaged two to three months lower if the firearm involved was a rifle or an unaltered shotgun. This may reflect the fact that these weapons tend to be more suitable than others for recreational activities. However, some rifles or shotguns may be possessed for criminal purposes, while some handguns may be suitable primarily for recreation. Therefore, the guideline is not based upon the type of firearm. Intended lawful use, as determined by the surrounding circumstances, is a mitigating factor.

Available pre-guidelines data were not sufficient to determine the effect a stolen firearm had on the average sentence. However, reviews of pre-guidelines cases suggested that this factor tended to result in more severe sentences. Independent studies show that stolen firearms are used disproportionately in the commission of crimes.

The firearm statutes often are used as a device to enable the federal court to exercise jurisdiction over offenses that otherwise could be prosecuted only under state law. For example, a convicted felon may be prosecuted for possessing a firearm if he used the firearm to rob a gasoline station. In pre-guidelines practice, such prosecutions resulted in high sentences because of the true nature of the underlying conduct. The cross reference at §2K2.1(c)(2) deals with such cases.

§2K2.2. Unlawful Trafficking and Other Prohibited Transactions Involving Firearms

(a) Base Offense Level:

(1) 18, if the defendant is convicted under 18 U.S.C. § 922(o) or 26 U.S.C. § 5861;

(2) 6, otherwise.

(b) Specific Offense Characteristics

(1) If the offense involved distribution of a firearm, or possession with intent to distribute, and the number of firearms unlawfully distributed, or to be distributed, exceeded two, increase as follows:

Number of Firearms	Increase in Level
(A) 3 - 4	add 1
(B) 5 - 7	add 2
(C) 8 - 12	add 3
(D) 13 - 24	add 4
(E) 25 - 49	add 5
(F) 50 or more	add 6.

(2) If any of the firearms was stolen or had an altered or obliterated serial number, increase by 2 levels.

(3) If more than one of the following applies, use the greater:

(A) If the defendant is convicted under 18 U.S.C. § 922(d), increase by 6 levels; or

(B) If the defendant is convicted under 18 U.S.C. § 922(b)(1) or (b)(2), increase by 1 level.

(c) Cross Reference

(1) If the defendant, at the time of the offense, had been convicted in any court of a crime punishable by imprisonment for a term exceeding one year, apply §2K2.1 (Unlawful Receipt, Possession, or Transportation of Firearms or Ammunition) if the resulting offense level is greater than that determined above.

Commentary

Statutory Provisions: 18 U.S.C. § 922(a)(1), (a)(2), (a)(5), (b), (c), (d), (e), (f), (i), (j), (k), (l), (m), (o); 26 U.S.C. § 5861(a), (e), (f), (g), (j), and (l). For additional statutory provision(s), see Appendix A (Statutory Index).

Application Notes:

1. The definition of 'firearm' used in this section is that set forth in 18 U.S.C. § 921(a)(3) (if the defendant is convicted under 18 U.S.C. § 922) and 26 U.S.C. § 5845(a) (if the defendant is convicted under 26 U.S.C § 5861). These

definitions are somewhat broader than that used in Application Note 1(e) of the Commentary to §1B1.1 (Application Instructions). Under 18 U.S.C. § 921(a)(3), the term 'firearm' means (A) any weapon (including a starter gun) which will or is designed to or may readily be converted to expel a projectile by the action of an explosive; (B) the frame or receiver of any such weapon; (C) any firearm muffler or firearm silencer; or (D) any destructive device. Under 26 U.S.C. § 5845(a), the term 'firearm' includes a shotgun, or a weapon made from a shotgun, with a barrel or barrels of less than 18 inches in length; a weapon made from a shotgun or rifle with an overall length of less than 26 inches; a rifle, or weapon made from a rifle, with a barrel or barrels less than 16 inches in length; a machine gun; a muffler or silencer for a firearm; a destructive device; and certain other large bore weapons.

2. If the number of weapons involved exceeded fifty, an upward departure may be warranted. An upward departure especially may be warranted in the case of large numbers of military type weapons (e.g., machine guns, automatic weapons, assault rifles).

Background: This guideline applies to a variety of offenses involving firearms, ranging from unlawful distribution of silencers, machine guns, sawed-off shotguns and destructive devices, to essentially technical violations.

§2K2.3. Receiving, Transporting, Shipping or Transferring a Firearm or Ammunition With Intent to Commit Another Offense, or With Knowledge that It Will Be Used in Committing Another Offense

(a) Base Offense Level (Apply the greatest):

(1) The offense level from §2X1.1 (Attempt, Solicitation, or Conspiracy) in respect to the offense that the defendant intended or knew was to be committed with the firearm; or

(2) The offense level from §2K2.1 (Unlawful Receipt, Possession, or Transportation of Firearms or Ammunition), or §2K2.2 (Unlawful Trafficking and Other Prohibited Transactions Involving Firearms), as applicable; or

(3) 12.

Commentary

Statutory Provisions: 18 U.S.C. § 924(b), (f), (g).".

A replacement guideline with accompanying commentary is inserted as §2K2.1 (Unlawful Receipt, Possession, or Transportation of Firearms or Ammunition; Prohibited Transactions Involving Firearms or Ammunition).

Chapter Two, Part K, Subpart 2 is amended by deleting §2K2.5 in its entirety as follows:

"§2K2.5. Possession of Firearms and Dangerous Weapons in Federal Facilities

(a) Base Offense Level: 6

(b) Cross Reference

(1) If the defendant possessed the firearm or other dangerous weapon with intent to use it in the

commission of another offense, apply §2X1.1 (Attempt, Solicitation, or Conspiracy) in respect to that other offense if the resulting offense level is greater than that determined above.

Commentary

Statutory Provision: 18 U.S.C. § 930.".

A replacement guideline with accompanying commentary is inserted as §2K2.5 (Possession of Firearm or Dangerous Weapon in Federal Facility; Possession or Discharge of Firearm in School Zone).

This amendment consolidates three firearms guidelines and revises the adjustments and offense levels to more adequately reflect the seriousness of such conduct, including enhancements for defendants previously convicted of felony crimes of violence or controlled substance offenses. In addition, §2K1.5 is amended to address offenses committed within a school zone or federal court facility. **The effective date of this amendment is November 1, 1991.**

375. Section 2L1.1(a) is amended by deleting "9" and inserting in lieu thereof:

"(1) 20, if the defendant was convicted under 8 U.S.C. § 1327 of a violation involving an alien who previously was deported after a conviction for an aggravated felony; or

(2) 9, otherwise.".

Section 2L1.1(b)(1) is amended by inserting "and the base offense level is determined under subsection (a)(2)," immediately before "decrease".

The Commentary to §2L1.1 captioned "Application Notes" is amended by inserting the following additional note:

"9. 'Aggravated felony' is defined in the Commentary to §2L1.2 (Unlawfully Entering or Remaining in the United States).".

Section 2L1.2(b) is amended by deleting "Specific Offense Characteristic" and inserting in lieu thereof:

"Specific Offense Characteristics

If more than one applies, use the greater:".

Section 2L1.2(b)(1) is amended by deleting "sustaining" immediately before "a conviction"; and by inserting the following additional subdivision:

"(2) If the defendant previously was deported after a conviction for an aggravated felony, increase by 16 levels.".

The Commentary to §2L1.2 captioned "Statutory Provisions" is amended by deleting "1325" and inserting in lieu thereof "1325(a)".

The Commentary to §2L1.2 captioned "Application Notes" is amended in Note 1 by deleting:

"First offenses under 8 U.S.C. § 1325 are petty offenses for which no guideline has been promulgated.",

and inserting in lieu thereof:

"A first offense under 8 U.S.C. § 1325(a) is a Class B misdemeanor for which no guideline has been promulgated. A prior sentence for such offense, however, is to be considered under the provisions of Chapter Four, Part A (Criminal History).".

The Commentary to §2L1.2 captioned "Application Notes" is amended in Note 3 by deleting "sustaining" immediately before "a conviction"; and by deleting the last sentence as follows:

"In the case of a defendant previously deported after sustaining a conviction for an aggravated felony as defined in 8 U.S.C. § 1101(a), or for any other violent felony, an upward departure may be warranted.".

The Commentary to §2L1.2 captioned "Application Notes" is amended by deleting:

"4. The adjustment under §2L1.2(b)(1) is in addition to any criminal history points added for such conviction in Chapter 4, Part A (Criminal History).",

and inserting in lieu thereof:

"4. A 16-level increase is provided under subsection (b)(2) in the case of a defendant who was previously deported after a conviction for an aggravated felony.

5. An adjustment under subsection (b)(1) or (b)(2) for a prior felony conviction applies in addition to any criminal history points added for such conviction in Chapter Four, Part A (Criminal History).

6. 'Deported after a conviction,' as used in subsections (b)(1) and (b)(2), means that the deportation was subsequent to the conviction, whether or not the deportation was in response to such conviction.

7. 'Aggravated felony,' as used in subsection (b)(2), means murder; any illicit trafficking in any controlled substance (as defined in 21 U.S.C. § 802), including any drug trafficking crime as defined in 18 U.S.C. § 924(c)(2); any illicit trafficking in any firearms or destructive devices as defined in 18 U.S.C. § 921; any offense described in 18 U.S.C. § 1956 (relating to laundering of monetary instruments); any crime of violence (as defined in 18 U.S.C. § 16, not including a purely political offense) for which the term of imprisonment imposed (regardless of any suspension of such imprisonment) is at least five years; or any attempt or conspiracy to commit any such act. The term 'aggravated felony' applies to offenses described in the previous sentence whether in violation of federal or state law and also applies to offenses described in the previous sentence in violation of foreign law for which the term of imprisonment was completed within the previous 15 years. See 8 U.S.C. § 1101(a)(43).".

This amendment adds a specific offense characteristic providing an increase of 16 levels above the base offense level under §2L1.2 for defendants who reenter the United States after having been deported subsequent to a conviction for an aggravated felony. Previously, such cases were addressed by a recommendation for consideration of an upward departure. This amendment also modifies §2L1.1 to provide a base offense level of 20 for a defendant who is convicted under 8 U.S.C. § 1327 for an offense involving the smuggling, transporting, or harboring of an alien who was deported after a conviction for an aggravated felony. The Commission has determined that these increased offense levels are appropriate to reflect the serious nature of these offenses. In addition, this amendment revises the Commentary to §2L1.2 to make the statutory reference more precise, and to clarify the operation of the guidelines in respect to prior criminal history. **The effective date of this amendment is November 1, 1991.**

376. Section 2N1.1 is amended in the title by deleting "Serious" and inserting in lieu thereof "Bodily".

Section 2N1.1 is amended by deleting:

"(b) Cross Reference

(1) If the offense involved extortion, apply §2B3.2 (Extortion by Force or Threat of Injury or Serious Damage) if the resulting offense level is greater than that determined above.",

and inserting in lieu thereof:

"(b) Specific Offense Characteristic

(1) (A) If any victim sustained permanent or life-threatening bodily injury, increase by 4 levels; (B) if any victim sustained serious bodily injury, increase by 2 levels; or (C) if the degree of injury is between that specified in subdivisions (A) and (B), increase by 3 levels.

(c) Cross References

(1) If the offense resulted in death, apply §2A1.1 (First Degree Murder) if the death was caused intentionally or knowingly, or §2A1.2 (Second Degree Murder) in any other case.

(2) If the offense was tantamount to attempted murder, apply §2A2.1 (Assault With Intent to Commit Murder; Attempted Murder) if the resulting offense level is greater than that determined above.

(3) If the offense involved extortion, apply §2B3.2 (Extortion by Force or Threat of Injury or Serious Damage) if the resulting offense level is greater than that determined above.

(d) Special Instruction

(1) If the defendant is convicted of a single count involving (A) the death or permanent, life-threatening, or serious bodily injury of more than one victim, or (B) conduct tantamount to the attempted murder of more than one victim, Chapter Three, Part D (Multiple Counts) shall be applied as if the defendant had been convicted of a separate count for each such victim.".

The Commentary to §2N1.1 captioned "Application Note" is amended by deleting:

"1. If death, bodily injury, extreme psychological injury, or substantial property damage or monetary loss resulted, an upward departure may be warranted. See Chapter Five, Part K (Departures).",

and inserting in lieu thereof:

"1. The base offense level reflects that this offense typically poses a risk of death or serious bodily injury to one or more victims; or causes, or is intended to cause, bodily injury. Where the offense posed a substantial risk of death or serious bodily injury to numerous victims, or caused extreme psychological injury or substantial property damage or monetary loss, an upward departure may be warranted. In the unusual case in which the offense did not cause a risk of death or serious bodily injury, and neither caused nor was intended to cause bodily injury, a downward departure may be warranted.

2. The special instruction in subsection (d)(1) applies whether the offense level is determined under subsection (b)(1) or by use of a cross reference in subsection (c).";

and in the caption by deleting "Note" and inserting in lieu thereof "Notes".

The Commentary to §2N1.1 captioned "Background" is deleted in its entirety as follows:

"Background: The base offense level reflects the risk of death or serious injury posed to significant numbers of people by this type of product tampering.".

This amendment adds a specific offense characteristic for permanent, life-threatening, or serious bodily injury, and adds cross references for cases in which the offense resulted in death or was tantamount to attempted murder. In addition, a special instruction is added to address certain conduct involving multiple victims. Finally, the title of this guideline is revised to reflect more accurately the coverage of the guideline, and the background commentary is revised to clarify the "heartland" conduct to which the guideline applies. **The effective date of this amendment is November 1, 1991.**

377. Section 2R1.1(a) is amended by deleting "9" and inserting in lieu thereof "10".

Section 2R1.1(b)(2) is amended by deleting "less than $1,000,000 or more than $4,000,000" and inserting in lieu thereof "more than $400,000"; and by deleting:

"(A) Less than $1,000,000 subtract 1
(B) $1,000,000 - $4,000,000 no adjustment
(C) More than $4,000,000 add 1
(D) More than $15,000,000 add 2
(E) More than $50,000,000 add 3",

and inserting in lieu thereof:

"(A) More than $400,000 add 1
(B) More than $1,000,000 add 2
(C) More than $2,500,000 add 3
(D) More than $6,250,000 add 4
(E) More than $15,000,000 add 5
(F) More than $37,500,000 add 6
(G) More than $100,000,000 add 7.".

Section 2R1.1 is amended by deleting:

"(c) Fines

A fine shall be imposed in addition to any term of imprisonment. The guideline fine range for an individual conspirator is from 4 to 10 percent of the volume of commerce, but not less than $20,000. The fine range for an organization is from 20 to 50 percent of the volume of commerce, but not less than $100,000.",

and inserting in lieu thereof:

"(c) Special Instruction for Fines

(1) For an individual, the guideline fine range shall be from one to five percent of the volume of commerce, but not less than $20,000.".

The Commentary to §2R1.1 captioned "Application Notes" is amended by deleting:

"1. Because the guideline sentences depend on the volume of commerce done by each firm, role in the offense is implicitly taken into account. Accordingly, the provisions of §3B1.1 (Aggravating Role) are to be applied only in unusual circumstances. An increase for role under §3B1.1 might be appropriate only where a defendant actually coerced others into participating in a conspiracy -- an unusual circumstance. Conversely, a decrease for role under §3B1.2 (Mitigating Role) would not be appropriate merely because an individual defendant or his firm did not profit substantially from the violation. An individual defendant should be considered for a downward adjustment for a mitigating role in the offense only if he was responsible in some minor way for his firm's participation in the conspiracy. A complementary bidder who did not win a bid would not for that reason qualify for a downward adjustment, but a low-level employee who participated in only one of several agreements constituting a conspiracy would.",

and inserting in lieu thereof:

"1. The provisions of §3B1.1 (Aggravating Role) and §3B1.2 (Mitigating Role) should be applied to an individual defendant as appropriate to reflect the individual's role in committing the offense. For example, if a sales manager organizes or leads the price-fixing activity of five or more participants, a 4-level increase is called for under §3B1.1. An individual defendant should be considered for a downward adjustment under §3B1.2 for a mitigating role in the offense only if he was responsible in some minor way for his firm's participation in the conspiracy.".

The Commentary to §2R1.1 captioned "Background" is amended in the third paragraph by deleting "four" and inserting in lieu thereof "six".

The Commentary to §2R1.1 captioned "Background" is amended by deleting the fourth paragraph as follows:

" The guideline imprisonment terms represent a substantial change from pre-guidelines practice. Under pre-guidelines practice, approximately 39 percent of all individuals convicted of antitrust violations were imprisoned. Considering all defendants sentenced, the average time served under pre-guidelines practice was only forty-five days. The guideline prison terms are, however, consistent with the parole guidelines. The fines specified in the guideline represent substantial increases over pre-guidelines practice. Under pre-guidelines practice, the average fine for individuals was only approximately $27,000; for corporations, it was approximately $160,000.".

This amendment increases the offense levels for antitrust violations to make them more comparable to the offense levels for fraud with similar amounts of loss. The base offense level for antitrust violations starts higher than the base offense level for fraud violations to reflect the serious nature of and the difficulty of detecting such violations, but the offense levels for antitrust offenses based on volume of commerce increase less rapidly than the offense levels for fraud, in part, because, on the average, the level of mark-up from an antitrust violation may tend to decline with the volume of commerce involved. This amendment also reduces the minimum guideline fine level based on the volume of commerce to reflect a marginal shift from fines to imprisonment as the more effective means to deter antitrust offenses. The provision addressing fines for organizational defendants in the current guideline is deleted. Such fines are addressed by the provisions pertaining to the sentencing of organizational defendants that are added by a separate amendment (amendment 422). **The effective date of this amendment is November 1, 1991.**

378. Section 2S1.1(a)(1) is amended by deleting "or (a)(2)(A)" and inserting in lieu thereof ", (a)(2)(A), or (a)(3)(A)".

Section 2S1.1(b)(1) is amended by inserting "or believed" immediately following "knew".

The Commentary to §2S1.1 captioned "Background" is amended in the third paragraph by deleting "or (a)(2)(A)" and inserting in lieu thereof ", (a)(2)(A), or (a)(3)(A)"; and by deleting "did not merely conceal a serious crime that had already taken place, but" immediately before "encouraged".

This amendment revises this guideline to reflect the enactment of subsection (a)(3) of 18 U.S.C. § 1956 that authorizes undercover "sting" operations in money laundering cases. Such cases differ from those prosecuted under subsection (a)(1) in that the money being laundered is not actually criminal proceeds, but is government "sting" money that an undercover officer represents to be criminal proceeds. In all other respects, subsections (a)(1) and (a)(3) are the same. **The effective date of this amendment is November 1, 1991.**

379. Section 2S1.3(a)(1) is amended by deleting:

"(B) made false statements to conceal or disguise the evasion of reporting requirements; or

(C) reasonably should have believed that the funds were criminally derived property;",

and inserting in lieu thereof:

"(B) knowingly filed, or caused another to file, a report containing materially false statements; or".

Section 2S1.3(b)(1) is amended by deleting "5 levels." and inserting in lieu thereof "4 levels. If the resulting offense level is less than level 13, increase to level 13.".

The Commentary to §2S1.3 captioned "Statutory Provisions" is amended by deleting "18 U.S.C. § 1005;"; and by deleting "5316," immediately before "5322".

The Commentary to §2S1.3 captioned "Application Notes" is amended by deleting:

"2. Subsection (a)(1)(C) applies where a reasonable person would have believed from the circumstances that the funds were criminally derived property. Subsection (b)(1) applies if the defendant knew or believed the funds were criminally derived property. Subsection (b)(1) applies in addition to, and not in lieu of, subsection (a)(1)(C). Where subsection (b)(1) applies, subsection (a)(1)(C) also will apply. It is possible that a defendant "believed" or "reasonably should have believed" that the funds were criminally derived property even if, in fact, the funds were not so derived (e.g., in a "sting" operation where the defendant is told the funds were derived from the unlawful sale of controlled substances).";

and in the caption by deleting "Notes" and inserting in lieu thereof "Note".

The Commentary to §2S1.3 captioned "Background" is amended by deleting the second and third paragraphs as follows:

" A base offense level of 13 is provided for those offenses where the defendant either structured the transaction to evade reporting requirements, made false statements to conceal or disguise the activity, or reasonably should have believed that the funds were criminally derived property. A lower alternative base offense level of 5 is provided in all other cases. The Commission anticipates that such cases will involve simple recordkeeping or other more minor technical violations of the regulatory scheme governing certain monetary transactions committed by defendants who reasonably believe that the funds at issue emanated from legitimate sources.

Where the defendant actually knew or believed that the funds were criminally derived property, subsection (b)(1) provides for a 5 level increase in the offense level.",

and inserting in lieu thereof:

" A base offense level of 13 is provided for those offenses where the defendant either structured the transaction to evade reporting requirements or knowingly filed, or caused another to file, a report containing materially false statements. A lower alternative base offense level of 5 is provided in all other cases.

Where the defendant actually knew or believed that the funds were criminally derived property, subsection (b)(1) provides for the greater of a 4-level increase or an increase to level 13.".

Chapter Two, Part S is amended by inserting an additional guideline with accompanying commentary as §2S1.4 (Failure to File Currency and Monetary Instrument Report).

This amendment clarifies the scope of the specific offense characteristics in §2S1.3 and modifies subsection (b)(1) so that it does not produce a result that exceeds the comparable offense level under §2S1.2. In addition, this amendment creates an additional offense guideline (§2S1.4) for offenses involving Currency and Monetary Instrument Reports (CMIR). Currently, such offenses are covered by §2S1.3, which deals with all currency transaction reporting requirements. CMIR violations are committed by individuals who, when entering or leaving the country, knowingly conceal $10,000 or more in cash or bearer instruments on their persons or in their personal effects and knowingly fail to file the report required by the U.S. Customs Service. Such criminal conduct is sufficiently different from the other offenses covered by §2S1.3 to merit treatment in a separate guideline. **The effective date of this amendment is November 1, 1991.**

380. Section 2X3.1(a) is amended by inserting the following additional sentence at the end:

"*Provided*, that where the conduct is limited to harboring a fugitive, the offense level shall not be more than level 20.".

This amendment distinguishes harboring a fugitive from other forms of accessory after the fact by providing a lower maximum offense level for such cases reflective, in part, of the lower statutory maximum provided for such offenses. **The effective date of this amendment is November 1, 1991.**

381. The Commentary to §4A1.1 captioned "Application Notes" is amended by inserting the following additional sentence as the second sentence of Note 4 and the third sentence of Note 5:

"Failure to report for service of a sentence of imprisonment is to be treated as an escape from such sentence. <u>See</u> §4A1.2(n).".

The Commentary to §4A1.1 captioned "Application Notes" is amended in the third (formerly second) sentence of Note 4 by inserting the following immediately before the period at the end of the sentence:

> "having a custodial or supervisory component, although active supervision is not required for this item to apply. For example, a term of unsupervised probation would be included; but a sentence to pay a fine, by itself, would not be included. A defendant who commits the instant offense while a violation warrant from a prior sentence is outstanding (e.g., a probation, parole, or supervised release violation warrant) shall be deemed to be under a criminal justice sentence for the purposes of this provision if that sentence is otherwise countable, even if that sentence would have expired absent such warrant. See §4A1.2(m)".

Section 4A1.2(a) is amended by inserting the following additional subdivision:

> "(4) Where a defendant has been convicted of an offense, but not yet sentenced, such conviction shall be counted as if it constituted a prior sentence under §4A1.1(c) if a sentence resulting from that conviction otherwise would be countable. In the case of a conviction for an offense set forth in §4A1.2(c)(1), apply this provision only where the sentence for such offense would be countable regardless of type or length.
>
> 'Convicted of an offense,' for the purposes of this provision, means that the guilt of the defendant has been established, whether by guilty plea, trial, or plea of nolo contendere.".

Section 4A1.2(k)(2) is amended by deleting the last sentence as follows:

> "It may also affect the time period under which certain sentences are counted as provided in §4A1.2(e)(1).";

by inserting "(A)" immediately after "(2)"; and by inserting the following additional subdivision:

> "(B) Revocation of probation, parole, supervised release, special parole, or mandatory release may affect the time period under which certain sentences are counted as provided in §4A1.2(d)(2) and (e). For the purposes of determining the applicable time period, use the following: (i) in the case of an adult term of imprisonment totaling more than one year and one month, the date of last release from incarceration on such sentence (see §4A1.2(e)(1)); (ii) in the case of any other confinement sentence for an offense committed prior to the defendant's eighteenth birthday, the date of the defendant's last release from confinement on such sentence (see §4A1.2(d)(2)(A)); and (iii) in any other case, the date of the original sentence (see §4A1.2(d)(2)(B) and (e)(2)).".

Section 4A1.2 is amended by inserting the following additional subsections:

> "(l) Sentences on Appeal
>
> Prior sentences under appeal are counted except as expressly provided below. In the case of a prior sentence, the execution of which has been stayed pending appeal, §4A1.1(a), (b), (c), (d), and (f) shall apply as if the execution of such sentence had not been stayed; §4A1.1(e) shall not apply.
>
> (m) Effect of a Violation Warrant
>
> For the purposes of §4A1.1(d), a defendant who commits the instant offense while a violation warrant from a prior sentence is outstanding (e.g., a

probation, parole, or supervised release violation warrant) shall be deemed to be under a criminal justice sentence if that sentence is otherwise countable, even if that sentence would have expired absent such warrant.

(n) Failure to Report for Service of Sentence of Imprisonment

For the purposes of §4A1.1(d) and (e), failure to report for service of a sentence of imprisonment shall be treated as an escape from such sentence.

(o) Felony Offense

For the purposes of §4A1.2(c), a 'felony offense' means any federal, state, or local offense punishable by death or a term of imprisonment exceeding one year, regardless of the actual sentence imposed.".

The Commentary to §4A1.2 captioned "Application Notes" is amended in Note 1 by inserting the following additional paragraph:

"Under §4A1.2(a)(4), a conviction for which the defendant has not yet been sentenced is treated as if it were a prior sentence under §4A1.1(c) if a sentence resulting from such conviction otherwise would have been counted. In the case of an offense set forth in §4A1.2(c)(1) (which lists certain misdemeanor and petty offenses), a conviction for which the defendant has not yet been sentenced is treated as if it were a prior sentence under §4A1.2(a)(4) only where the offense is similar to the instant offense (because sentences for other offenses set forth in §4A1.2(c)(1) are counted only if they are of a specified type and length).".

The Commentary to §4A1.2 captioned "Application Notes" is amended in Note 2 by inserting, immediately after "stated maximum", the following:

"(e.g., in the case of a determinate sentence of five years, the stated maximum is five years; in the case of an indeterminate sentence of one to five years, the stated maximum is five years; in the case of an indeterminate sentence for a term not to exceed five years, the stated maximum is five years; in the case of an indeterminate sentence for a term not to exceed the defendant's twenty-first birthday, the stated maximum is the amount of time in pre-trial detention plus the amount of time between the date of sentence and the defendant's twenty-first birthday)".

The Commentary to §4A1.2 is amended in Note 11 by inserting the following additional paragraph at the end:

"Where a revocation applies to multiple sentences, and such sentences are counted separately under §4A1.2(a)(2), add the term of imprisonment imposed upon revocation to the sentence that will result in the greatest increase in criminal history points. Example: A defendant was serving two probationary sentences, each counted separately under §4A1.2(a)(2); probation was revoked on both sentences as a result of the same violation conduct; and the defendant was sentenced to a total of 45 days of imprisonment. If one sentence had been a 'straight' probationary sentence and the other had been a probationary sentence that had required service of 15 days of imprisonment, the revocation term of imprisonment (45 days) would be added to the probationary sentence that had the 15-day term of imprisonment. This would result in a total of 2 criminal history points under §4A1.1(b) (for the combined 60-day term of imprisonment) and 1 criminal history point under §4A1.1(c) (for the other probationary sentence).".

Section 4A1.3(d) is amended by deleting ", sentencing, or appeal" and inserting in lieu thereof "or sentencing".

This amendment clarifies the meaning of the term "under a criminal justice sentence" as used in §4A1.1; inserts a new subdivision in §4A1.2(a) to address the case in which the defendant has been convicted of a prior offense, but has not yet been sentenced for that offense; inserts an additional subdivision in §4A1.2(k) to clarify the determination of the applicable time periods in revocation cases; inserts additional subsections in §4A1.2 to address the counting of sentences stayed pending appeal, the effect of a violation warrant on the counting of points under §4A1.1(d), the counting of a failure to report for service of sentence under §4A1.1(d) and (e), and the definition of a felony offense as used in §4A1.2(c); adds an example to Application Note 2 in the Commentary to §4A1.2 to illustrate the meaning of "stated maximum" sentence; adds an additional application note in the Commentary to §4A1.2 addressing the counting of points in complex revocation cases; and conforms the Commentary of §4A1.3 to the addition of §4A1.2(l). **The effective date of this amendment is November 1, 1991.**

382. Section 4A1.1 is amended by inserting the following additional subsection:

"(f) Add 1 point for each prior sentence resulting from a conviction of a crime of violence that did not receive any points under (a), (b), or (c) above because such sentence was considered related to another sentence resulting from a conviction of a crime of violence, up to a total of 3 points for this item. *Provided*, that this item does not apply where the sentences are considered related because the offenses occurred on the same occasion.".

Section 4A1.1 is amended in the first sentence by deleting "(e)" and inserting in lieu thereof "(f)".

Section 4A1.1(c) is amended by deleting "included" and inserting in lieu thereof "counted".

The Commentary to §4A1.1 captioned "Application Notes" is amended by inserting the following additional note:

"6. <u>§4A1.1(f)</u>. Where the defendant received two or more prior sentences as a result of convictions for crimes of violence that are treated as related cases but did not arise from the same occasion (<u>i.e.</u>, offenses committed on different occasions that were part of a single common scheme or plan or were consolidated for trial or sentencing; <u>see</u> Application Note 3 of the Commentary to §4A1.2), one point is added under §4A1.1(f) for each such sentence that did not result in any additional points under §4A1.1(a), (b), or (c). A total of up to 3 points may be added under §4A1.1(f). 'Crime of violence' is defined in §4B1.2(1); <u>see</u> §4A1.2(p).

For example, a defendant's criminal history includes two robbery convictions for offenses committed on different occasions that were consolidated for sentencing and therefore are treated as related. If the defendant received a five-year sentence of imprisonment for one robbery and a four-year sentence of imprisonment for the other robbery (consecutively or concurrently), a total of 3 points is added under §4A1.1(a). An additional point is added under §4A1.1(f) because the second sentence did not result in any additional point(s) (under §4A1.1(a), (b), or (c)). In contrast, if the defendant received a one-year sentence of imprisonment for one robbery and a nine-month consecutive sentence of imprisonment for the other robbery, a total of 3 points also is added under §4A1.1(a) (a one-year sentence of imprisonment and a consecutive nine-month sentence of imprisonment are treated as a combined one-year-nine-month sentence of imprisonment). But no additional point is added under §4A1.1(f) because the sentence for the second robbery already resulted in an additional point under §4A1.1(a). Without the second sentence, the defendant would only have received two points under §4A1.1(b) for the one-year sentence of imprisonment).".

Section 4A1.2(a)(2) is amended by deleting "the criminal history" and inserting in lieu thereof "§4A1.1(a), (b), and (c)".

Section 4A1.2 is amended by inserting the following additional subsection:

"(p) Crime of Violence Defined

For the purposes of §4A1.1(f), the definition of 'crime of violence' is that set forth in §4B1.2(1).".

The Commentary to §4A1.2 captioned "Application Notes" is amended in Note 3 by deleting:

"Cases are considered related if they (1) occurred on a single occasion,",

and inserting in lieu thereof:

"Prior sentences are not considered related if they were for offenses that were separated by an intervening arrest (i.e., the defendant is arrested for the first offense prior to committing the second offense). Otherwise, prior sentences are considered related if they resulted from offenses that (1) occurred on the same occasion,";

and by deleting:

"For example, if the defendant commits a number of offenses on independent occasions separated by arrests, and the resulting criminal cases are consolidated and result in a combined sentence of eight years, counting merely three points for this factor will not adequately reflect either the seriousness of the defendant's criminal history or the frequency with which he commits crimes. In such circumstances, the court should consider whether departure is warranted. See §4A1.3.",

and inserting in lieu thereof:

"For example, if a defendant was convicted of a number of serious non-violent offenses committed on different occasions, and the resulting sentences were treated as related because the cases were consolidated for sentencing, the assignment of a single set of points may not adequately reflect the seriousness of the defendant's criminal history or the frequency with which he has committed crimes. In such circumstances, an upward departure may be warranted. Note that the above example refers to serious non-violent offenses. Where prior related sentences result from convictions of crimes of violence, §4A1.1(f) will apply.".

This amendment provides for a specific enhancement under §4A1.2(f) in certain cases having prior convictions of crimes of violence not arising from the same incident that otherwise would be treated as related under §4A1.2. In addition, the definition of related cases in Application Note 3 in the Commentary to §4A1.2 is amended to provide that cases separated by an intervening arrest for one of the offenses are not treated as related cases. **The effective date of this amendment is November 1, 1991.**

383. Section 5E1.1 is amended by redesignating subsections (b) and (c) as (c) and (d), respectively; and by deleting:

"(a) Restitution shall be ordered for convictions under Title 18 of the United States Code or under 49 U.S.C. § 1472(h), (i), (j) or (n) in accordance with 18 U.S.C. § 3663(d), and may be ordered as a condition of probation or supervised release in any other case.",

and inserting in lieu thereof:

"(a) The court shall --

(1) enter a restitution order if such order is authorized under 18 U.S.C. §§ 3663-3664; or

(2) if a restitution order would be authorized under 18 U.S.C. §§ 3663-3664, except for the fact that the offense of conviction is not an offense set forth in Title 18, United States Code, or 49 U.S.C. § 1472(h), (i), (j), or (n), impose a term of probation or supervised release with a condition requiring restitution.

(b) *Provided*, that the provisions of subsection (a) do not apply when full restitution has been made, or to the extent the court determines that the complication and prolongation of the sentencing process resulting from the fashioning of a restitution requirement outweighs the need to provide restitution to any victims through the criminal process.".

The Commentary to §5E1.1 captioned "Background" is amended in the first paragraph by deleting the last sentence as follows:

"An order of restitution may be appropriate in offenses not specifically referenced in 18 U.S.C. § 3663 where victims require relief more promptly than the civil justice system provides.".

The Commentary to §5E1.1 captioned "Background" is amended in the second paragraph by deleting "5E1.1 requires the court to order restitution for offenses under Title 18, or 49 U.S.C. § 1472(h), (i), (j) or (n), unless" and inserting in lieu thereof "(a)(1) of this guideline requires the court to order restitution for offenses under Title 18, United States Code, or 49 U.S.C. § 1472(h), (i), (j) or (n), unless full restitution has already been made or".

The Commentary to §5E1.1 captioned "Background" is amended in the sixth paragraph by deleting "how and to whom" and by inserting in lieu thereof "the manner in which, and the persons to whom,".

The Commentary to §5E1.1. captioned "Background" is amended by inserting the following additional paragraph at the end:

" Subsection (a)(2) provides for restitution as a condition of probation or supervised release for offenses not set forth in Title 18, United States Code, or 49 U.S.C. § 1472(h), (i), (j), or (n).".

This amendment expands §5E1.1 to require restitution as a condition of probation or supervised release for offenses not set forth in Title 18 and 49 U.S.C. § 1472(h), (i), (j), and (n). Currently, §5E1.1 permits, but does not require, restitution to be ordered as a condition of probation or supervised release for offenses not set forth in Title 18, United States Code, or 49 U.S.C. § 1472(h) (i), (j), and (n). **The effective date of this amendment is November 1, 1991.**

384. Section 5E1.2(c) is amended by deleting:

"(1) The minimum of the fine range is the greater of:

(A) the amount shown in column A of the table below; or

(B) the pecuniary gain to the defendant, less restitution made or ordered.

(2) Except as specified in (4) below, the maximum of the fine range is the greater of:

(A) the amount shown in column B of the table below;

(B) twice the gross pecuniary loss caused by the offense; or

(C) three times the gross pecuniary gain to all participants in the offense.",

and inserting in lieu thereof:

"(1) The minimum of the fine range is the amount shown in column A of the table below.

(2) Except as specified in (4) below, the maximum of the fine range is the amount shown in column B of the table below.".

The Commentary to §5E1.2 captioned "Application Notes" is amended in Note 3 by deleting the first two paragraphs as follows:

"Alternative fine limits are provided in subsection (c). The terms 'pecuniary gain' and 'pecuniary loss' are taken from 18 U.S.C. § 3571(d). The Commission does not intend precise or detailed calculation of the gain or loss in using the alternative fine limits.

Where it is readily ascertainable that the defendant cannot, and is not likely to become able to, pay a fine greater than the maximum fine set forth in Column B of the Fine Table in subsection (c)(3), calculation of the alternative maximum fines under subsections (c)(2)(B) (twice the gross pecuniary loss caused by the offense) and (c)(2)(C) (three times the gross pecuniary gain to all participants in the offense) is unnecessary. In such cases, a statement that "the alternative maximums of the fine table were not calculated because it is readily ascertainable that the defendant cannot, and is not likely to become able to, pay a fine greater than the maximum set forth in the fine table" is recommended in lieu of such calculations.".

The Commentary to §5E1.2 captioned "Application Notes" is amended by deleting:

"4. 'Restitution made or ordered' refers to restitution for the instant offense made before or at the time of sentencing, as well as any restitution ordered at the time of sentencing for the instant offense.",

and inserting in lieu thereof:

"4. The Commission envisions that for most defendants, the maximum of the guideline fine range from subsection (c) will be at least twice the amount of gain or loss resulting from the offense. Where, however, two times either the amount of gain to the defendant or the amount of loss caused by the offense exceeds the maximum of the fine guideline, an upward departure from the fine guideline may be warranted.

Moreover, where a sentence within the applicable fine guideline range would not be sufficient to ensure both the disgorgement of any gain from the offense that otherwise would not be disgorged (e.g., by restitution or forfeiture) and an adequate punitive fine, an upward departure from the fine guideline range may be warranted.".

The Commentary to §5E1.2 captioned "Background" is deleted in its entirety as follows:

"Background: These guidelines permit a relatively wide range of fines. The Commission may promulgate more detailed guidelines for the imposition of fines after analyzing practice under these initial guidelines.

Recent legislation provides for substantial increases in fines. 18 U.S.C. § 3571(b). With few restrictions, 42 U.S.C. § 10601(b), and (c) authorize fine payments up to $100 million to be deposited in the Crime Victims Fund in the United States Treasury. With vigorous enforcement, higher fines should be effective punitive and deterrent sanctions.

A larger multiple of the gain than of the loss is used in subsection (c)(2) because most offenses result in losses to society that exceed the gain to the participants. In addition, in many such cases restitution will not be feasible. These larger fines authorized under subsection (c)(2) are, of course, subject to the absolute limits on fines that are imposed by statute.

The Commission has not attempted to define gain or loss precisely. It is expected that the terms will be used flexibly and consistently with their use in the criminal code, including former 18 U.S.C. § 3623(c)(1).".

This amendment is designed to simplify the operation of this guideline and conserve probation and court resources by eliminating the need for the determination of loss and gain under this section in most cases. Experience has shown that for the vast majority of defendants, the amount from the fine table in subsection (c)(3) or the amount from subsection (c)(4), as applicable, is more than twice the gain or loss from the offense. This amendment provides that the guideline fine range is to be determined from subsection (c)(3) or (c)(4), as applicable. In the unusual case in which twice the defendant's gain from the offense or twice the loss caused by the offense exceeds the maximum of the guideline range, an upward departure may be considered. **The effective date of this amendment is November 1, 1991.**

385. Chapter Five, Part G is amended by deleting §5G1.3 in its entirety as follows:

"§5G1.3. Imposition of a Sentence on a Defendant Serving an Unexpired Term of Imprisonment

If the instant offense was committed while the defendant was serving a term of imprisonment (including work release, furlough, or escape status), the sentence for the instant offense shall be imposed to run consecutively to the unexpired term of imprisonment.

Commentary

Under this guideline, the court shall impose a consecutive sentence where the instant offense (or any part thereof) was committed while the defendant was serving an unexpired term of imprisonment.

Where the defendant is serving an unexpired term of imprisonment, but did not commit the instant offense while serving that term of imprisonment, the sentence for the instant offense may be imposed to run consecutively or concurrently with the unexpired term of imprisonment. The court may consider imposing a sentence for the instant offense that results in a combined sentence that approximates the total punishment that would have been imposed under §5G1.2 (Sentencing on Multiple Counts of Conviction) had all of the offenses been federal offenses for which sentences were being imposed at the same time. Where the defendant is serving a term of imprisonment for a state offense, the information available may permit only a rough estimate of the total punishment that would have been imposed under the guidelines. It is not intended that the above methodology be applied in a manner that unduly complicates or prolongs the sentencing process.".

A replacement guideline with accompanying commentary is inserted as §5G1.3 (Imposition of a Sentence on a Defendant Subject to an Undischarged Term of Imprisonment).

This amendment provides additional structure and guidance for the decision to impose a consecutive or concurrent sentence upon a defendant subject to an undischarged term of imprisonment to reduce the potential for unwarranted disparity in such determinations. **The effective date of this amendment is November 1, 1991.**

386. The Introductory Commentary to Chapter Five, Part H is amended by deleting:

" Congress has directed the Commission to consider whether certain specific offender characteristics 'have any relevance to the nature, extent, place of service, or other incidents of an appropriate sentence' and to take them into account only to the extent they are determined relevant by the Commission. 28 U.S.C. § 994(d).",

and inserting in lieu thereof:

" The following policy statements address the relevance of certain offender characteristics to the determination of whether a sentence should be outside the applicable guideline range and, in certain cases, to the determination of a sentence within the applicable guideline range. Under 28 U.S.C. § 994(d), the Commission is directed to consider whether certain specific offender characteristics 'have any relevance to the nature, extent, place of service, or other incidents of an appropriate sentence' and to take them into account only to the extent they are determined to be relevant by the Commission.

The Commission has determined that certain factors are not ordinarily relevant to the determination of whether a sentence should be outside the applicable guideline range. Unless expressly stated, this does not mean that the Commission views such factors as necessarily inappropriate to the determination of the sentence within the applicable guideline range or to the determination of various other incidents of an appropriate sentence (e.g., the appropriate conditions of probation or supervised release).".

Section 5H1.1 is amended by deleting:

"Age is not ordinarily relevant in determining whether a sentence should be outside the guidelines. Neither is it ordinarily relevant in determining the type of sentence to be imposed when the guidelines provide sentencing options. Age may be a reason to go below the guidelines when the offender is elderly and infirm and where a form of punishment (e.g., home confinement) might be equally efficient as and less costly than incarceration. If, independent of the consideration of age, a defendant is sentenced to probation or supervised release, age may be relevant in the determination of the length and conditions of supervision.",

and inserting in lieu thereof:

"Age (including youth) is not ordinarily relevant in determining whether a sentence should be outside the applicable guideline range. Age may be a reason to impose a sentence below the applicable guideline range when the defendant is elderly and infirm and where a form of punishment such as home confinement might be equally efficient as and less costly than incarceration. Physical condition, which may be related to age, is addressed at §5H1.4 (Physical Condition, Including Drug or Alcohol Dependence or Abuse).

The guidelines are not applicable to a person sentenced as a juvenile delinquent under the provisions of 18 U.S.C. § 5037.".

Section 5H1.2 is amended by deleting:

"Education and vocational skills are not ordinarily relevant in determining whether a sentence should be outside the guidelines, but the extent to which a defendant may have misused special training or education to facilitate criminal activity is an express guideline factor. See §3B1.3 (Abuse of Position of Trust or Use of Special Skill). Neither are education and vocational skills relevant in determining the type of sentence to be imposed when the guidelines provide sentencing options. If, independent of consideration of education and vocational skills, a defendant is sentenced to probation or supervised release, these considerations may be relevant in the determination of the length and conditions of supervision for rehabilitative purposes, for public protection by restricting activities that allow for the utilization of a certain skill, or in determining the type or length of community service.",

and by inserting in lieu thereof:

"Education and vocational skills are not ordinarily relevant in determining whether a sentence should be outside the applicable guideline range, but the extent to which a defendant may have misused special training or education to facilitate criminal activity is an express guideline factor. See §3B1.3 (Abuse of Position of Trust or Use of Special Skill).

Education and vocational skills may be relevant in determining the conditions of probation or supervised release for rehabilitative purposes, for public protection by restricting activities that allow for the utilization of a certain skill, or in determining the appropriate type of community service.".

Section 5H1.3 is amended by deleting:

"Mental and emotional conditions are not ordinarily relevant in determining whether a sentence should be outside the guidelines, except as provided in the general provisions in Chapter Five. Mental and emotional conditions, whether mitigating or aggravating, may be relevant in determining the length and conditions of probation or supervised release.",

and inserting in lieu thereof:

"Mental and emotional conditions are not ordinarily relevant in determining whether a sentence should be outside the applicable guideline range, except as provided in Chapter Five, Part K, Subpart 2 (Other Grounds for Departure).

Mental and emotional conditions may be relevant in determining the conditions of probation or supervised release; e.g., participation in a mental health program (see recommended condition (24) at §5B1.4 (Recommended Conditions of Probation and Supervised Release)).".

Section 5H1.4 is amended by deleting:

"Physical Condition, Including Drug Dependence and Alcohol Abuse (Policy Statement)

Physical condition is not ordinarily relevant in determining whether a sentence should be outside the guidelines or where within the guidelines a sentence should fall. However, an extraordinary physical impairment may be a reason to impose a sentence other than imprisonment.

Drug dependence or alcohol abuse is not a reason for imposing a sentence below the guidelines. Substance abuse is highly correlated to an increased propensity to commit crime. Due to this increased risk, it is highly recommended that a defendant who is incarcerated also be sentenced to supervised release with a requirement that the defendant participate in an appropriate substance abuse program. If participation in a substance abuse program is required, the length of supervised release should take into account the length of time necessary for the supervisory body to judge the success of the program.

This provision would also apply in cases where the defendant received a sentence of probation. The substance abuse condition is strongly recommended and the length of probation should be adjusted accordingly. Failure to comply would normally result in revocation of probation.",

and inserting in lieu thereof:

"Physical Condition, Including Drug or Alcohol Dependence or Abuse (Policy Statement)

Physical condition or appearance, including physique, is not ordinarily relevant in determining whether a sentence should be outside the applicable guideline range. However, an extraordinary physical impairment may be a reason to impose a sentence below the applicable guideline range; e.g., in the case of a seriously infirm defendant, home detention may be as efficient as, and less costly than, imprisonment.

Drug or alcohol dependence or abuse is not a reason for imposing a sentence below the guidelines. Substance abuse is highly correlated to an increased propensity to commit crime. Due to this increased risk, it is highly recommended that a defendant who is incarcerated also be sentenced to supervised release with a requirement that the defendant participate in an appropriate substance abuse program (see recommended condition (23) at §5B1.4 (Recommended Conditions of Probation and Supervised Release)). If participation in a substance abuse program is required, the length of supervised release should take into account the length of time necessary for the supervisory body to judge the success of the program.

Similarly, where a defendant who is a substance abuser is sentenced to probation, it is strongly recommended that the conditions of probation contain a requirement that the defendant participate in an appropriate substance abuse program (see recommended condition (23) at §5B1.4 (Recommended Conditions of Probation and Supervised Release)).".

Section 5H1.5 is amended by deleting:

"Employment record is not ordinarily relevant in determining whether a sentence should be outside the guidelines or where within the guidelines a sentence should fall. Employment record may be relevant in determining the type of sentence to be imposed when the guidelines provide for sentencing options. If, independent of the consideration of employment record, a defendant is sentenced to probation or supervised release, considerations of employment record may be relevant in the determination of the length and conditions of supervision.",

and inserting in lieu thereof:

"Employment record is not ordinarily relevant in determining whether a sentence should be outside the applicable guideline range.

Employment record may be relevant in determining the conditions of probation or supervised release (e.g., the appropriate hours of home detention).".

Section 5H1.6 is amended by deleting:

"Family ties and responsibilities and community ties are not ordinarily relevant in determining whether a sentence should be outside the guidelines. Family responsibilities that are complied with are relevant in determining whether to impose restitution and fines. Where the guidelines provide probation as an option, these factors may be relevant in this determination. If a defendant is sentenced to probation or supervised release, family ties and responsibilities that are met may be relevant in the determination of the length and conditions of supervision.",

and inserting in lieu thereof:

"Family ties and responsibilities and community ties are not ordinarily relevant in determining whether a sentence should be outside the applicable guideline range.

Family responsibilities that are complied with may be relevant to the determination of the amount of restitution or fine.".

Chapter Five, Part H is amended by inserting an additional policy statement as §5H1.11 (Military, Civic, Charitable, or Public Service; Employment-Related Contributions; Record of Prior Good Works (Policy Statement)).

This amendment expresses the Commission's intent that the factors set forth in this part are not ordinarily relevant in determining whether a sentence should be outside the applicable guideline range; but that, unless expressly stated, these policy statements do not mean that the Commission views such factors as necessarily inappropriate to the determination of the sentence within the applicable guideline range. The language within these sections is revised for clarity and consistency. In addition, this amendment adds language that expressly states that the guidelines do not apply to defendants sentenced as juvenile delinquents; and sets forth the Commission's position that physical appearance, including physique, military, civic, charitable, or public service, employment-related contributions, and record of prior good works are not ordinarily relevant in determining whether a sentence should be outside the applicable guideline range. **The effective date of this amendment is November 1, 1991.**

387. The Commentary to §6A1.3 is amended by inserting the following additional paragraph as the third paragraph:

"The Commission believes that use of a preponderance of the evidence standard is appropriate to meet due process requirements and policy concerns in resolving disputes regarding application of the guidelines to the facts of a case.".

This amendment expresses the Commission's approval of the use of a preponderance of the evidence standard in resolving disputes regarding application of the guidelines to the facts of a case. **The effective date of this amendment is November 1, 1991.**

388. The Commentary to §1B1.1 captioned "Application Notes" is amended in Note 1 in the first sentence by inserting immediately before the colon:

"and are of general applicability (except to the extent expressly modified in respect to a particular guideline or policy statement)".

The Commentary to §1B1.1 captioned "Application Notes" is amended in Note 2 by deleting the first two sentences as follows:

"Definitions or explanations of terms may also appear within the commentary to specific guidelines. Such commentary is not of general applicability.",

and inserting in lieu thereof:

> "Definitions of terms also may appear in other sections. Such definitions are not designed for general applicability; therefore, their applicability to sections other than those expressly referenced must be determined on a case by case basis.";

and by beginning a new paragraph with the third sentence.

The Commentary to §1B1.1 captioned "Application Notes" is amended in Note 1(e) by deleting:

> "'Firearm' means any weapon which is designed to or may readily be converted to expel any projectile by the action of an explosive.",

and inserting in lieu thereof:

> "'Firearm' means (i) any weapon (including a starter gun) which will or is designed to or may readily be converted to expel a projectile by the action of an explosive; (ii) the frame or receiver of any such weapon; (iii) any firearm muffler or silencer; or (iv) any destructive device.";

and by inserting "a" immediately before "'BB' or pellet gun".

The Commentary to §1B1.1 captioned "Application Notes" is amended in Note (1)(f) by inserting ", other than conduct to which §3C1.1 (Obstructing or Impeding the Administration of Justice) applies." immediately following "conceal the offense".

The Commentary to §1B1.1 captioned "Application Notes" is amended in Note 1(h) by inserting the following additional sentence at the end:

> "In the case of a kidnapping, for example, maltreatment to a life-threatening degree (e.g., by denial of food or medical care) would constitute life-threatening bodily injury.".

The Commentary to §1B1.1 captioned "Application Notes" is amended in Note 1(k) by deleting "18 U.S.C. § 921(a)(4)" and inserting in lieu thereof "26 U.S.C. § 5845(f)"; and by deleting "proceeding" and inserting in lieu thereof "preceding".

The Commentary to §1B1.1 captioned "Application Notes" is amended in Note 1 by inserting the following additional subdivision:

> "(l) 'Offense' means the offense of conviction and all relevant conduct under §1B1.3 (Relevant Conduct) unless a different meaning is specified or is otherwise clear from the context.".

This amendment revises the definition of firearm in Note 1(e) to track more closely the definition of firearm in 18 U.S.C. § 921; clarifies Note 1(f) to prevent inappropriate "double counting;" clarifies in Note 1(h) that maltreatment to a life-threatening degree constitutes life-threatening bodily injury; conforms the statutory reference in Note 1(k) to conform to that used in §2K2.1; and inserts an additional subdivision in Note 1 (subdivision (l)) that describes how the term "offense" is used in the guidelines. In addition, this amendment correct clerical errors and makes editorial improvements. **The effective date of this amendment is November 1, 1991.**

389. The Commentary to §1B1.3 captioned "Application Notes" is amended in Note 2 in the first sentence by inserting "that were part of the same course of conduct or common scheme or plan as the offense of conviction" immediately following "'Such acts and omissions"; and by

inserting ", that were part of the same course of conduct or common scheme or plan as the offense of conviction" immediately following "otherwise accountable".

The Commentary to §1B1.3 captioned "Application Notes" is amended in Note 2 by inserting the following additional paragraph at the end:

> "As noted above, subsection (a)(2) applies to offenses of a character for which §3D1.2(d) would require grouping of multiple counts, had the defendant been convicted of multiple counts. For example, the defendant sells 30 grams of cocaine (a violation of 21 U.S.C. § 841) on one occasion and, as part of the same course of conduct or common scheme or plan, attempts to sell an additional 15 grams of cocaine (a violation of 21 U.S.C. 846) on another occasion. The defendant is convicted of one count charging the completed sale of 30 grams of cocaine. The two offenses (sale of cocaine and attempted sale of cocaine), although covered by different statutory provisions, are of a character for which §3D1.2(d) would require the grouping of counts, had the defendant been convicted of both counts. Therefore, subsection (a)(2) applies and the total amount of cocaine (45 grams) involved is used to determine the offense level.".

The Commentary to §1B1.3 captioned "Application Notes" is amended in Note 4 by inserting "; Property Damage by Use of Explosives" immediately following "Arson".

The Commentary to §1B1.3 captioned "Application Notes is amended in Note 5 by deleting:

> "E.g., in §2K2.2, a base offense level of 16 is used 'if the defendant is convicted under 18 U.S.C. § 922(o) or 26 U.S.C. § 5861.'",

and inserting in lieu thereof:

> "For example, in §2K1.5, subsection (b)(1) applies 'If the defendant is convicted under 49 U.S.C. § 1472(l)(2).'";

by deleting:

> "Examples of this usage are found in §2K1.3(b)(4) ('If the defendant was a person prohibited from receiving explosives under 18 U.S.C. § 842(i), or if the defendant knowingly distributed explosives to a person prohibited from receiving explosives under 18 U.S.C. § 842(i), increase by 10 levels'); and",

and inserting in lieu thereof "An example of this usage is found in"; and by inserting the following additional paragraph at the end:

> "An express direction to apply a particular factor only if the defendant was convicted of a particular statute includes the determination of the offense level where the defendant was convicted of conspiracy, attempt, solicitation, aiding or abetting, accessory after the fact, or misprision of felony in respect to that particular statute. For example, §2K1.5(b)(1) (which is applicable only if the defendant is convicted under 49 U.S.C. § 1472(l)(2)) would be applied in determining the offense level under §2X3.1 (Accessory After the Fact) where the defendant was convicted of accessory after the fact to a violation of 49 U.S.C. § 1472(l)(2).".

The Commentary to §1B1.3 captioned "Application Notes" is amended by inserting the following additional notes:

> "6. In the case of a partially completed offense (e.g., an offense involving an attempted theft of \$800,000 and a completed theft of \$30,000), the offense level is to be determined in accordance with §2X1.1 (Attempt, Solicitation, or Conspiracy) whether the conviction is for the substantive offense, the inchoate offense (attempt, solicitation, or conspiracy), or both. See Application Note

4 in the Commentary to §2X1.1. Note, however, that Application Note 4 is not applicable where the offense level is determined under §2X1.1(c)(1).

7. For the purposes of subsection (a)(2), offense conduct associated with a sentence that was imposed prior to the acts or omissions constituting the instant federal offense (the offense of conviction) is not considered as part of the same course of conduct or common scheme or plan as the offense of conviction.

Examples: (1) The defendant was convicted for the sale of cocaine and sentenced to state prison. Immediately upon release from prison, he again sold cocaine to the same person, using the same accomplices and modus operandi. The instant federal offense (the offense of conviction) charges this latter sale. In this example, the offense conduct relevant to the state prison sentence is considered as prior criminal history, not as part of the same course of conduct or common scheme or plan as the offense of conviction. The prior state prison sentence is counted under Chapter Four (Criminal History and Criminal Livelihood). (2) The defendant engaged in two cocaine sales constituting part of the same course of conduct or common scheme or plan. Subsequently, he is arrested by state authorities for the first sale and by federal authorities for the second sale. He is convicted in state court for the first sale and sentenced to imprisonment; he is then convicted in federal court for the second sale. In this case, the cocaine sales are not separated by an intervening sentence. Therefore, under subsection (a)(2), the cocaine sale associated with the state conviction is considered as relevant conduct to the instant federal offense. The state prison sentence for that sale is not counted as a prior sentence; see §4A1.2(a)(1).

Note, however, in certain cases, offense conduct associated with a previously imposed sentence may be expressly charged in the offense of conviction. Unless otherwise provided, such conduct will be considered relevant conduct under subsection (a)(1), not (a)(2).".

The Commentary to §1B1.3 captioned "Background" is amended by deleting the last paragraph as follows:

"This guideline and §1B1.4 clarify the intent underlying §1B1.3 as originally promulgated.".

This amendment makes editorial improvements in Application Notes 1 and 2; inserts an additional paragraph in Application Note 2 to clarify that "offenses of a character for which §3D1.2(d) would require grouping of multiple counts" is not limited to offenses proscribed by the same statutory provision; conforms a reference in Application Note 4 to the correct title of the guideline; conforms examples in Application Note 5 to amended guidelines and clarifies how a direction to apply a particular factor only if the defendant is convicted of a particular statute applies to the offenses of conspiracy, attempt, solicitation, aiding or abetting, accessory after the fact, and misprision of felony; inserts an additional application note (Note 6) that highlights the provision in §2X1.1 dealing with cases of partially completed conduct; inserts an additional application note (Note 7) that clarifies the treatment of conduct for which the defendant has previously been sentenced; and deletes a surplus sentence of Background Commentary more appropriately contained in Appendix C in the paragraph describing the reason for amendment 3. **The effective date of this amendment is November 1, 1991.**

390. The Commentary to §1B1.8 captioned "Application Notes" is amended by inserting the following additional notes:

"5. This guideline limits the use of certain incriminating information furnished by a defendant in the context of a defendant-government agreement for the defendant to provide information concerning the unlawful activities of other persons. The guideline operates as a limitation on the use of such incriminating information in determining the applicable guideline range, and not merely as a restriction of the government's presentation of such information (e.g., where the defendant, subsequent to having entered into a cooperation agreement, repeats such information to the probation officer preparing the presentence report, the use of such information remains protected by this section).

6. Unless the cooperation agreement relates to the provision of information concerning the unlawful activities of others, this guideline does not apply (i.e., an agreement by the defendant simply to detail the extent of his own unlawful activities, not involving an agreement to provide information concerning the unlawful activity of another person, is not covered by this guideline).".

This amendment clarifies the operation of this guideline. **The effective date of this amendment is November 1, 1991.**

391. The Commentary to §2A2.1 captioned "Application Notes" is amended by inserting the following additional note:

"3. If the offense created a substantial risk of death or serious bodily injury to more than one person, an upward departure may be warranted.".

This amendment adds commentary to address the case in which an attempted murder results in a substantial risk of death or serious bodily injury to more than one person. **The effective date of this amendment is November 1, 1991.**

392. The Commentary to §2A3.1 captioned "Application Notes" is amended by inserting the following additional note:

"3. If the adjustment in subsection (b)(3) applies, do not apply §3B1.3 (Abuse of Position of Trust or Use of Special Skill).".

Section 2A3.2(b)(1) is amended by deleting "1 level" and inserting in lieu thereof "2 levels".

The Commentary to §2A3.2 captioned "Application Note" is amended by inserting the following additional note:

"2. If the adjustment in subsection (b)(1) applies, do not apply §3B1.3 (Abuse of Position of Trust or Use of Special Skill).";

and in the caption by deleting "Note" and inserting in lieu thereof "Notes".

Section 2A3.4(b) is amended by inserting the following additional subdivision:

"(3) If the victim was in the custody, care, or supervisory control of the defendant, increase by 2 levels.".

The Commentary to §2A3.4 captioned "Application Notes" is amended by inserting the following additional note:

"3. If the adjustment in subsection (b)(3) applies, do not apply §3B1.3 (Abuse of Position of Trust or Use of Special Skill).".

This amendment provides for consistency among §§2A3.1, 2A3.2, and 2A3.4 with respect to an adjustment for a victim in the custody, care, or supervisory control of the defendant. In addition, the amendment adds an application note clarifying that when this adjustment applies, an adjustment from §3B1.3 will not apply. **The effective date of this amendment is November 1, 1991.**

393. The Commentary to §2B1.1 captioned "Application Notes" is amended in Note 2 by deleting:

> "In cases of partially completed conduct, the loss is to be determined in accordance with the provisions of §2X1.1 (Attempt, Solicitation, or Conspiracy). E.g., in the case of the theft of a government check or money order, loss refers to the loss level that would have occurred if the check or money order had been cashed. Similarly, if a defendant is apprehended in the process of taking a vehicle, the loss refers to the value of the vehicle even if the vehicle is recovered immediately.",

and inserting in lieu thereof:

> "Examples: (1) In the case of a theft of a check or money order, the loss is the loss that would have occurred if the check or money order had been cashed. (2) In the case of a defendant apprehended taking a vehicle, the loss is the value of the vehicle even if the vehicle is recovered immediately.
>
> In the case of a partially completed offense (e.g., an offense involving a completed theft that is part of a larger, attempted theft), the offense level is to be determined in accordance with the provisions of §2X1.1 (Attempt, Solicitation, or Conspiracy) whether the conviction is for the substantive offense, the inchoate offense (attempt, solicitation, or conspiracy), or both; see Application Note 4 in the Commentary to §2X1.1.".

The Commentary to §2B1.1 captioned "Application Notes" is amended in Note 4 by deleting "Attempts" and inserting in lieu thereof "Attempt, Solicitation, or Conspiracy"; and by inserting "and Deceit" immediately following "Fraud".

The Commentary to §2F1.1 is amended by deleting Notes 7 and 8 as follows:

> "7. Valuation of loss is discussed in the Commentary to §2B1.1 (Larceny, Embezzlement, and Other Forms of Theft). In keeping with the Commission's policy on attempts, if a probable or intended loss that the defendant was attempting to inflict can be determined, that figure would be used if it was larger than the actual loss. For example, if the fraud consisted of attempting to sell $40,000 in worthless securities, or representing that a forged check for $40,000 was genuine, the "loss" would be treated as $40,000 for purposes of this guideline.
>
> 8. The amount of loss need not be precise. The court is not expected to identify each victim and the loss he suffered to arrive at an exact figure. The court need only make a reasonable estimate of the range of loss, given the available information. The estimate may be based on the approximate number of victims and an estimate of the average loss to each victim, or on more general factors, such as the nature and duration of the fraud and the revenues generated by similar operations. Estimates based upon aggregate 'market loss' (e.g., the aggregate decline in market value of a stock resulting from disclosure of information that was wrongfully withheld or misrepresented) are especially appropriate for securities cases. The offender's gross gain from committing the fraud is an alternative estimate that ordinarily will understate the loss.";

by deleting Note 10 as follows:

"10. In a few instances, the total dollar loss that results from the offense may overstate its seriousness. Such situations typically occur when a misrepresentation is of limited materiality or is not the sole cause of the loss. Examples would include understating debts to a limited degree in order to obtain a substantial loan which the defendant genuinely expected to repay; attempting to negotiate an instrument that was so obviously fraudulent that no one would seriously consider honoring it; and making a misrepresentation in a securities offering that enabled the securities to be sold at inflated prices, but where the value of the securities subsequently declined in substantial part for other reasons. In such instances, a downward departure may be warranted.";

by renumbering Note 9 as Note 10; by inserting the following as Notes 7, 8 and 9:

"7. Valuation of loss is discussed in the Commentary to §2B1.1 (Larceny, Embezzlement, and Other Forms of Theft). Consistent with the provisions of §2X1.1 (Attempt, Solicitation or Conspiracy), if an intended loss that the defendant was attempting to inflict can be determined, this figure will be used if it is greater than the actual loss. Frequently, loss in a fraud case will be the same as in a theft case. For example, if the fraud consisted of selling or attempting to sell $40,000 in worthless securities, or representing that a forged check for $40,000 was genuine, the loss would be $40,000.

There are, however, instances where additional factors are to be considered in determining the loss or intended loss:

(a) Fraud Involving Misrepresentation of the Value of an Item or Product Substitution

A fraud may involve the misrepresentation of the value of an item that does have some value (in contrast to an item that is worthless). Where, for example, a defendant fraudulently represents that stock is worth $40,000 and the stock is worth only $10,000, the loss is the amount by which the stock was overvalued (i.e., $30,000). In a case involving a misrepresentation concerning the quality of a consumer product, the loss is the difference between the amount paid by the victim for the product and the amount for which the victim could resell the product received.

(b) Fraudulent Loan Application and Contract Procurement Cases

In fraudulent loan application cases and contract procurement cases where the defendant's capabilities are fraudulently represented, the loss is the actual loss to the victim (or if the loss has not yet come about, the expected loss). For example, if a defendant fraudulently obtains a loan by misrepresenting the value of his assets, the loss is the amount of the loan not repaid at the time the offense is discovered, reduced by the amount the lending institution has recovered, or can expect to recover, from any assets pledged to secure the loan.

In some cases, the loss determined above may significantly understate or overstate the seriousness of the defendant's conduct. For example, where the defendant substantially understated his debts to obtain a loan, which he nevertheless repaid, the loss determined above (zero loss) will tend not to reflect adequately the risk of loss created by the defendant's conduct. Conversely, a defendant may understate his debts to a limited degree to obtain a loan (e.g., to expand a grain export business), which he genuinely expected to repay and for which he would have qualified at a higher interest rate had he made truthful disclosure, but he is unable to repay the loan because of some unforeseen event (e.g., an embargo imposed on grain exports) which would have caused a default in any event. In such a case, the loss determined above may overstate the seriousness of the defendant's conduct.

(c) Consequential Damages in Procurement Fraud and Product Substitution Cases

In contrast to other types of cases, loss in a procurement fraud or product substitution case includes not only direct damages, but also consequential damages that were reasonably foreseeable. For example, in a case involving a defense product substitution offense, the loss includes the government's reasonably foreseeable costs of making substitute transactions and handling or disposing of the product delivered or retrofitting the product so that it can be used for its intended purpose, plus the government's reasonably foreseeable cost of rectifying the actual or potential disruption to government operations caused by the product substitution. Similarly, in the case of fraud affecting a defense contract award, loss includes the reasonably foreseeable administrative cost to the government and other participants of repeating or correcting the procurement action affected, plus any increased cost to procure the product or service involved that was reasonably foreseeable. Inclusion of reasonably foreseeable consequential damages directly in the calculation of loss in procurement fraud and product substitution cases reflects that such damages frequently are substantial in such cases.

(d) Diversion of Government Program Benefits

In a case involving diversion of government program benefits, loss is the value of the benefits diverted from intended recipients or uses.

(e) Davis-Bacon Act Cases

In a case involving a Davis-Bacon Act violation (a violation of 40 U.S.C. § 276a, criminally prosecuted under 18 U.S.C. § 1001), the loss is the difference between the legally required and actual wages paid.

8. For the purposes of subsection (b)(1), the loss need not be determined with precision. The court need only make a reasonable estimate of the loss, given the available information. This estimate, for example, may be based on the approximate number of victims and an estimate of the average loss to each victim, or on more general factors, such as the nature and duration of the fraud and the revenues generated by similar operations. The offender's gain from committing the fraud is an alternative estimate that ordinarily will underestimate the loss.

9. In the case of a partially completed offense (e.g., an offense involving a completed fraud that is part of a larger, attempted fraud), the offense level is to be determined in accordance with the provisions of §2X1.1 (Attempt, Solicitation, or Conspiracy) whether the conviction is for the substantive offense, the inchoate offense (attempt, solicitation, or conspiracy), or both; see Application Note 4 in the Commentary to §2X1.1.";

and in the renumbered Note 10 (formerly Note 9) by deleting:

"Dollar loss often does not fully capture the harmfulness and seriousness of the conduct. In such instances, an upward departure may be warranted.",

and inserting in lieu thereof:

> "In cases in which the loss determined under subsection (b)(1) does not fully capture the harmfulness and seriousness of the conduct, an upward departure may be warranted.";

by deleting subdivision (f) as follows:

> "(f) completion of the offense was prevented, or the offense was interrupted before it caused serious harm.";

by deleting the semicolon at the end of subdivision (e) and inserting in lieu thereof a period; and by inserting the following additional paragraph at the end:

> "In a few instances, the loss determined under subsection (b)(1) may overstate the seriousness of the offense. This may occur, for example, where a defendant attempted to negotiate an instrument that was so obviously fraudulent that no one would seriously consider honoring it.".

This amendment provides a more precise reference in the commentary of these guidelines to the discussion in §2X1.1 that applies in the case of a partially completed offense. In addition, the amendment reorders the material in these notes, and divides them into separate paragraphs for greater clarity. The amendment also conforms the wording of Application Note 7 of the Commentary to §2F1.1 to Application Note 2 of the Commentary to §2B1.1 to make clear that the treatment of attempts in cases of fraud and theft is identical. Finally, this amendment provides additional guidance with respect to the determination of loss, and makes editorial improvements. **The effective date of this amendment is November 1, 1991.**

394. Section 2D1.1(b)(1) is amended by deleting "during commission of the offense" immediately after "possessed".

The Commentary to §2D1.1 captioned "Application Notes" is amended in Note 3 by deleting ". The adjustment is to be applied even if several counts are involved and the weapon was present in any of them." and inserting in lieu thereof ", 2D1.6, 2D1.7(b)(1).".

Section 2D1.8(b)(1) is amended by deleting "during commission of the offense" immediately after "possessed".

This amendment clarifies that the provisions of §1B1.3(a)(2) apply to the adjustments in §§2D1.1(b)(1) and 2D1.8(b)(1), and updates the list of referenced offense guidelines in Application Note 3 of the Commentary to §2D1.1. **The effective date of this amendment is November 1, 1991.**

395. Section 2D1.1(c) is amended in the Drug Quantity Table by deleting "Pure PCP" wherever it appears and inserting in lieu thereof "PCP (actual)"; and by deleting "Pure Methamphetamine" wherever it appears and inserting in lieu thereof "Methamphetamine (actual)".

Section 2D1.1(c) is amended in the note designated by a single asterisk by inserting the following additional sentences as the third and fourth sentences of the first paragraph:

> "The terms 'PCP (actual)' and 'Methamphetamine (actual)' refer to the weight of the controlled substance, itself, contained in the mixture or substance. For example, a mixture weighing 10 grams containing PCP at 50% purity contains 5 grams of PCP (actual).";

and in the last sentence of the first paragraph by deleting "pure PCP or methamphetamine" and inserting in lieu thereof "PCP (actual) or methamphetamine (actual)".

Section 2D1.1(c) is amended by deleting "Schedule I or II Depressants" wherever it appears and inserting in lieu thereof "Secobarbital (or the equivalent amount of other Schedule I or II Depressants)".

This amendment clarifies the operation of the guideline in cases involving methamphetamine or PCP by replacing the terms "Pure PCP" and "pure methamphetamine" with "PCP (actual)" and "methamphetamine (actual)," and by providing an example of their application. This amendment also clarifies the interaction of the guideline and drug equivalency tables with respect to Schedule I and II Depressants by using Secobarbital as the referenced substance. **The effective date of this amendment is November 1, 1991.**

396. The Commentary to §2D1.1 captioned "Application Notes" is amended in Note 10 in the first paragraph by deleting "grams of a substance containing heroin" and inserting in lieu thereof "kilograms of marihuana"; in the second paragraph by deleting:

> "If all the drugs are 'equivalents' of the same drug, e.g., stimulants that are grouped with cocaine, convert them to that drug. In other cases, convert each of the drugs to either the heroin or marihuana equivalents, add the quantities, and look up the total in the Drug Quantity Table to obtain the combined offense level. Use the marihuana equivalents when the only substances involved are 'Schedule I Marihuana,' 'Schedule III Substances,' 'Schedule IV Substances,' 'Schedule V Substances' or 'Schedule I or II Depressants.' Otherwise, use the heroin equivalents.",

and inserting in lieu thereof:

> "In each case, convert each of the drugs to its marihuana equivalent, add the quantities, and look up the total in the Drug Quantity Table to obtain the combined offense level.";

in the first example by deleting:

> "a. The defendant is convicted of selling seventy grams of a substance containing PCP (Level 22) and 250 milligrams of a substance containing LSD (Level 18). Both PCP and LSD are grouped together in the Drug Equivalency Tables under the heading "LSD, PCP, and Other Schedule I and II Hallucinogens," which provide PCP equivalencies. The 250 milligrams of LSD is equivalent to twenty-five grams of PCP. The total is therefore ninety-five grams of PCP, for which the Drug Quantity Table provides an offense level of 24.",

and inserting in lieu thereof:

> "a. The defendant is convicted of selling 70 grams of a substance containing PCP (Level 22) and 250 milligrams of a substance containing LSD (Level 18). The PCP converts to 70 kilograms of marihuana; the LSD converts to 25 kilograms of marihuana. The total is therefore equivalent to 95 kilograms of marihuana, for which the Drug Quantity Table provides an offense level of 24.";

and in the third example by deleting:

> "c. The defendant is convicted of selling eighty grams of cocaine (Level 16) and five kilograms of marihuana (Level 14). The cocaine is equivalent to sixteen grams of heroin; the marihuana, to five grams of heroin. The total equivalent is twenty-one grams of heroin, which has an offense level of 18 in the Drug Quantity Table.",

and inserting in lieu thereof:

"c. The defendant is convicted of selling 80 grams of cocaine (Level 16) and five kilograms of marihuana (Level 14). The cocaine is equivalent to 16 kilograms of marihuana. The total is therefore equivalent to 21 kilograms of marihuana, which has an offense level of 18 in the Drug Quantity Table.".

The Commentary to §2D1.1 captioned "Application Notes" is amended in Note 10 by inserting the following additional paragraph as the third paragraph:

"For certain types of controlled substances, the marihuana equivalencies in the Drug Equivalency Tables are 'capped' at specified amounts (e.g., the combined equivalent weight of all Schedule V controlled substances shall not exceed 999 grams of marihuana). Where there are controlled substances from more than one schedule (e.g., a quantity of a Schedule IV substance and a quantity of a Schedule V substance), determine the marihuana equivalency for each schedule separately (subject to the cap, if any, applicable to that schedule). Then add the marihuana equivalencies to determine the combined marihuana equivalency (subject to the cap, if any, applicable to the combined amounts).".

The Commentary to §2D1.1 captioned "Application Notes" is amended in Note 10 by inserting the following additional example immediately after example (c):

"d. The defendant is convicted of selling 28 kilograms of a Schedule III substance, 50 kilograms of a Schedule IV substance, and 100 kilograms of a Schedule V substance. The marihuana equivalency for the Schedule III substance is 56 kilograms of marihuana (below the cap of 59.99 kilograms of marihuana set forth as the maximum equivalent weight for Schedule III substances). The marihuana equivalency for the Schedule IV substance is subject to a cap of 4.99 kilograms of marihuana set forth as the maximum equivalent weight for Schedule IV substances (without the cap it would have been 6.25 kilograms). The marihuana equivalency for the Schedule V substance is subject to the cap of 999 grams of marihuana set forth as the maximum equivalent weight for Schedule V substances (without the cap it would have been 1.25 kilograms). The combined equivalent weight, determined by adding together the above amounts, is subject to the cap of 59.99 kilograms of marihuana set forth as the maximum combined equivalent weight for Schedule III, IV, and V substances. Without the cap, the combined equivalent weight would have been 61.99 (56 + 4.99 + .999) kilograms.".

The Commentary to §2D1.1 captioned "Application Notes" is amended in Note 10 by deleting:

"DRUG EQUIVALENCY TABLES

Schedule I or II Opiates

1 gm of Alpha-Methylfentanyl =	10 gm of heroin
1 gm of Dextromoramide =	0.67 gm of heroin
1 gm of Dipipanone =	0.25 gm of heroin
1 gm of 3-Methylfentanyl =	10 gm of heroin
1 gm of 1-Methyl-4-phenyl-4-propionoxypiperidine/MPPP =	0.7 gm of heroin
1 gm of 1-(2-Phenylethyl)-4-phenyl-4-acetyloxypiperidine/ PEPAP =	0.7 gm of heroin
1 gm of Alphaprodine =	0.1 gm of heroin
1 gm of Fentanyl (N-phenyl-N-[1-(2-phenylethyl)-4-piperidinyl] Propanamide) =	2.5 gm of heroin
1 gm of Hydromorphone/Dihydromorphinone =	2.5 gm of heroin
1 gm of Levorphanol =	2.5 gm of heroin
1 gm of Meperidine/Pethidine =	0.05 gm of heroin
1 gm of Methadone =	0.5 gm of heroin
1 gm of 6-Monoacetylmorphine =	1 gm of heroin

1 gm of Morphine =	0.5 gm of heroin
1 gm of Oxycodone =	0.5 gm of heroin
1 gm of Oxymorphone =	5 gm of heroin
1 gm of Racemorphan =	0.8 gm of heroin
1 gm of Codeine =	0.08 gm of heroin
1 gm of Dextropropoxyphene/Propoxyphene-Bulk =	0.05 gm of heroin
1 gm of Ethylmorphine =	0.165 gm of heroin
1 gm of Hydrocodone/Dihydrocodeinone =	0.5 gm of heroin
1 gm of Mixed Alkaloids of Opium/Papaveretum =	0.25 gm of heroin
1 gm of Opium =	0.05 gm of heroin

Cocaine and Other Schedule I and II Stimulants (and their immediate precursors)

1 gm of Cocaine =	0.2 gm of heroin
1 gm of N-Ethylamphetamine =	0.4 gm of cocaine/0.08 gm of heroin
1 gm of Fenethylline =	0.2 gm of cocaine/0.04 gm of heroin
1 gm of Amphetamine =	1.0 gm of cocaine/0.2 gm of heroin
1 gm of Dextroamphetamine =	1.0 gm of cocaine/0.2 gm of heroin
1 gm of Methamphetamine =	5.0 gm of cocaine/1.0 gm of heroin
1 gm of Methamphetamine (Pure) =	50 gm of cocaine/10 gm of heroin
1 gm of L-Methamphetamine/Levo-methamphetamine/ L-Desoxyephedrine =	0.2 gm of cocaine/0.04 gm of heroin
1 gm of 4-Methylaminorex ("Euphoria") =	0.5 gm of cocaine/0.1 gm of heroin
1 gm of Methylphenidate (Ritalin) =	0.5 gm of cocaine/0.1 gm of heroin
1 gm of Phenmetrazine =	0.4 gm of cocaine/0.08 gm of heroin
1 gm Phenylacetone/P_2P (when possessed for the purpose of manufacturing methamphetamine) =	2.08 gm of cocaine/0.416 gm of heroin
1 gm Phenylacetone/P_2P (in any other case) =	0.375 gm of cocaine/0.075 gm of heroin
1 gm of Cocaine Base ("Crack") =	100 gm of cocaine/20 gm of heroin

LSD, PCP, and Other Schedule I and II Hallucinogens (and their immediate precursors)

1 gm of Bufotenine =	0.07 gm of heroin or PCP
1 gm of D-Lysergic Acid Diethylamide/Lysergide/LSD =	100 gm of heroin or PCP
1 gm of Diethyltryptamine/DET =	0.08 gm of heroin or PCP
1 gm of Dimethyltryptamine/DMT =	0.1 gm of heroin or PCP
1 gm of Mescaline =	0.01 gm of heroin or PCP
1 gm of Mushrooms containing Psilocin and/or Psilocybin (Dry) =	0.001 gm of heroin or PCP
1 gm of Mushrooms containing Psilocin and/or Psilocybin (Wet) =	0.0001 gm of heroin or PCP
1 gm of Peyote (Dry) =	0.0005 gm of heroin or PCP
1 gm of Peyote (Wet) =	0.00005 gm of heroin or PCP
1 gm of Phencyclidine/PCP =	1 gm of heroin
1 gm of Phencyclidine (Pure PCP) =	10 gm of heroin or PCP
1 gm of Psilocin =	0.5 gm of heroin or PCP
1 gm of Psilocybin =	0.5 gm of heroin or PCP
1 gm of Pyrrolidine Analog of Phencyclidine/PHP =	1 gm of heroin or PCP
1 gm of Thiophene Analog of Phencyclidine/TCP =	1 gm of heroin or PCP
1 gm of 4-Bromo-2,5-Dimethoxyamphetamine/DOB =	2.5 gm of heroin or PCP
1 gm of 2,5-Dimethoxy-4-methylamphetamine/DOM =	1.67 gm of heroin or PCP
1 gm of 3,4-Methylenedioxyamphetamine/MDA =	0.05 gm of heroin or PCP
1 gm of 3,4-Methylenedioxymethamphetamine/MDMA =	0.035 gm of heroin or PCP
1 gm of 3,4-Methylenedioxy-N-ethylamphetamine/MDEA =	0.03 gm of heroin or PCP
1 gm of 1-Piperidinocyclohexanecarbonitrile/PCC =	0.68 gm of heroin or PCP

Schedule I Marihuana

1 gm of Marihuana/Cannabis =	1 mg of heroin
1 gm of Marihuana/Cannabis, granulated, powdered, etc. =	1 mg of heroin/1 gm of marihuana
1 gm of Hashish Oil =	0.05 gm of heroin/50 gm of marihuana
1 gm of Cannabis Resin or Hashish =	5 mg of heroin/5 gm of marihuana
1 gm of Tetrahydrocannabinol, Organic =	0.167 gm of heroin/167 gm of marihuana
1 gm of Tetrahydrocannabinol, Synthetic =	0.167 gm of heroin/167 gm of marihuana

Schedule I or II Depressants

1 gm of Methaqualone =	0.7 mg of heroin/700 mg of marihuana
1 gm of Amobarbital =	2 mg of heroin/2 gm of marihuana

1 gm of Pentobarbital =	2 mg of heroin/2 gm of marihuana
1 gm of Secobarbital =	2 mg of heroin/2 gm of marihuana

Schedule III Substances

1 gm of Allobarbital =	2 mg of heroin/2 gm of marihuana
1 gm of Aprobarbital =	2 mg of heroin/2 gm of marihuana
1 gm of Barbiturate =	2 mg of heroin/2 gm of marihuana
1 gm of Benzphetamine =	4 mg of heroin/4 gm of marihuana
1 gm of Butabarbital =	2 mg of heroin/2 gm of marihuana
1 gm of Butalbital =	2 mg of heroin/2 gm of marihuana
1 gm of Butobarbital/butethal =	2 mg of heroin/2 gm of marihuana
1 gm of Cyclobarbital =	2 mg of heroin/2 gm of marihuana
1 gm of Cyclopentobarbital =	2 mg of heroin/2 gm of marihuana
1 gm of Glutethimide =	0.4 mg of heroin/0.4 gm of marihuana
1 gm of Heptabarbital =	2 mg of heroin/2 gm of marihuana
1 gm of Hexethal =	2 mg of heroin/2 gm of marihuana
1 gm of Hexobarbital =	2 mg of heroin/2 gm of marihuana
1 gm of Metharbital =	2 mg of heroin/2 gm of marihuana
1 gm of Talbutal =	2 mg of heroin/2 gm of marihuana
1 gm of Thialbarbital =	2 mg of heroin/2 gm of marihuana
1 gm of Thiamylal =	2 mg of heroin/2 gm of marihuana
1 gm of Thiobarbital =	2 mg of heroin/2 gm of marihuana
1 gm of Thiopental =	2 mg of heroin/2 gm of marihuana
1 gm of Vinbarbital =	2 mg of heroin/2 gm of marihuana
1 gm of Vinylbital =	2 mg of heroin/2 gm of marihuana
1 gm of Phendimetrazine =	2 mg of heroin/2 gm of marihuana
1 ml of Paregoric =	0.25 mg of heroin/0.25 gm of marihuana
1 ml of Hydrocodone Cough Syrup =	1 mg of heroin/1 gm of marihuana

Schedule IV Substances

1 gm of Phentermine =	0.125 mg of heroin/0.125 gm of marihuana
1 gm of Pentazocine =	0.125 mg of heroin/0.125 gm of marihuana
1 gm of Barbital =	0.125 mg of heroin/0.125 gm of marihuana
1 gm of Diazepam =	0.125 mg of heroin/0.125 gm of marihuana
1 gm of Phenobarbital =	0.125 mg of heroin/0.125 gm of marihuana
1 gm of Methohexital =	0.125 mg of heroin/0.125 gm of marihuana
1 gm of Methylphenobarbital/Mephobarbital =	0.125 mg of heroin/0.125 gm of marihuana
1 gm of Nitrazepam =	0.125 mg of heroin/0.125 gm of marihuana

Schedule V Substances

1 gm of codeine cough syrup =	0.0125 mg of heroin/12.5 mg of marihuana.",

and inserting in lieu thereof:

"DRUG EQUIVALENCY TABLES

Schedule I or II Opiates

1 gm of Heroin =	1 kg of marihuana
1 gm of Alpha-Methylfentanyl =	10 kg of marihuana
1 gm of Dextromoramide =	670 gm of marihuana
1 gm of Dipipanone =	250 gm of marihuana
1 gm of 3-Methylfentanyl =	10 kg of marihuana
1 gm of 1-Methyl-4-phenyl-4-propionoxypiperidine/MPPP =	700 gm of marihuana

1 gm of 1-(2-Phenylethyl)-4-phenyl-4-acetyloxypiperidine/ PEPAP =	700 gm of marihuana
1 gm of Alphaprodine =	100 gm of marihuana
1 gm of Fentanyl (N-phenyl-N-[1-(2-phenylethyl)-4-piperidinyl] Propanamide) =	2.5 kg of marihuana
1 gm of Hydromorphone/Dihydromorphinone =	2.5 kg of marihuana
1 gm of Levorphanol =	2.5 kg of marihuana
1 gm of Meperidine/Pethidine =	50 gm of marihuana
1 gm of Methadone =	500 gm of marihuana
1 gm of 6-Monoacetylmorphine =	1 kg of marihuana
1 gm of Morphine =	500 gm of marihuana
1 gm of Oxycodone =	500 gm of marihuana
1 gm of Oxymorphone =	5 kg of marihuana
1 gm of Racemorphan =	800 gm of marihuana
1 gm of Codeine =	80 gm of marihuana
1 gm of Dextropropoxyphene/Propoxyphene-Bulk =	50 gm of marihuana
1 gm of Ethylmorphine =	165 gm of marihuana
1 gm of Hydrocodone/Dihydrocodeinone =	500 gm of marihuana
1 gm of Mixed Alkaloids of Opium/Papaveretum =	250 gm of marihuana
1 gm of Opium =	50 gm of marihuana

<u>Cocaine and Other Schedule I and II Stimulants (and their immediate precursors)</u>

1 gm of Cocaine =	200 gm of marihuana
1 gm of N-Ethylamphetamine =	80 gm of marihuana
1 gm of Fenethylline =	40 gm of marihuana
1 gm of Amphetamine =	200 gm of marihuana
1 gm of Dextroamphetamine =	200 gm of marihuana
1 gm of Methamphetamine =	1 kg of marihuana
1 gm of Methamphetamine (Actual) =	10 kg of marihuana
1 gm of "Ice" =	10 kg of marihuana
1 gm of L-Methamphetamine/Levo-methamphetamine/ L-Desoxyephedrine=	40 gm of marihuana
1 gm of 4-Methylaminorex ("Euphoria")=	100 gm of marihuana
1 gm of Methylphenidate (Ritalin)=	100 gm of marihuana
1 gm of Phenmetrazine =	80 gm of marihuana
1 gm Phenylacetone/P_2P (when possessed for the purpose of manufacturing methamphetamine) =	416 gm of marihuana
1 gm Phenylacetone/P_2P (in any other case) =	75 gm of marihuana
1 gm of Cocaine Base ("Crack") =	20 kg of marihuana

<u>LSD, PCP, and Other Schedule I and II Hallucinogens (and their immediate precursors)</u>

1 gm of Bufotenine =	70 gm of marihuana
1 gm of D-Lysergic Acid Diethylamide/Lysergide/LSD =	100 kg of marihuana
1 gm of Diethyltryptamine/DET =	80 gm of marihuana
1 gm of Dimethyltryptamine/DMT =	100 gm of marihuana
1 gm of Mescaline =	10 gm of marihuana
1 gm of Mushrooms containing Psilocin and/or Psilocybin (Dry) =	1 gm of marihuana
1 gm of Mushrooms containing Psilocin and/or Psilocybin (Wet) =	0.1 gm of marihuana
1 gm of Peyote (Dry) =	0.5 gm of marihuana
1 gm of Peyote (Wet) =	0.05 gm of marihuana
1 gm of Phencyclidine/PCP =	1 kg of marihuana
1 gm of Phencyclidine (actual) /PCP (actual) =	10 kg of marihuana
1 gm of Psilocin =	500 gm of marihuana
1 gm of Psilocybin =	500 gm of marihuana
1 gm of Pyrrolidine Analog of Phencyclidine/PHP =	1 kg of marihuana
1 gm of Thiophene Analog of Phencyclidine/TCP =	1 kg of marihuana
1 gm of 4-Bromo-2,5-Dimethoxyamphetamine/DOB =	2.5 kg of marihuana
1 gm of 2,5-Dimethoxy-4-methylamphetamine/DOM =	1.67 kg of marihuana
1 gm of 3,4-Methylenedioxyamphetamine/MDA =	50 gm of marihuana
1 gm of 3,4-Methylenedioxymethamphetamine/MDMA =	35 gm of marihuana
1 gm of 3,4-Methylenedioxy-N-ethylamphetamine/MDEA=	30 gm of marihuana
1 gm of 1-Piperidinocyclohexanecarbonitrile/PCC =	680 gm of marihuana

<u>Schedule I Marihuana</u>

1 gm of Marihuana/Cannabis, granulated, powdered, etc. =	1 gm of marihuana
1 gm of Hashish Oil =	50 gm of marihuana
1 gm of Cannabis Resin or Hashish =	5 gm of marihuana
1 gm of Tetrahydrocannabinol, Organic =	167 gm of marihuana
1 gm of Tetrahydrocannabinol, Synthetic =	167 gm of marihuana

Secobarbital and Other Schedule I or II Depressants*

1 gm of Amobarbital =	2 gm of marihuana
1 gm of Glutethimide =	0.4 gm of marihuana
1 gm of Methaqualone =	0.7 gm of marihuana
1 gm of Pentobarbital =	2 gm of marihuana
1 gm of Secobarbital =	2 gm of marihuana

**Provided*, that the combined equivalent weight of all Schedule I or II depressants, Schedule III substances, Schedule IV substances, and Schedule V substances shall not exceed 59.99 kilograms of marihuana.

Schedule III Substances**

1 gm of a Schedule III Substance (except anabolic steroids) =	2 gm of marihuana
1 unit of anabolic steroids =	1 gm of marihuana

***Provided*, that the combined equivalent weight of all Schedule III substances, Schedule I or II depressants, Schedule IV substances, and Schedule V substances shall not exceed 59.99 kilograms of marihuana.

Schedule IV Substances***

1 gm of a Schedule IV Substance =	0.125 gm of marihuana

****Provided*, that the combined equivalent weight of all Schedule IV and V substances shall not exceed 4.99 kilograms of marihuana.

Schedule V Substances****

1 gm of a Schedule V Substance =	0.0125 gm of marihuana

*****Provided*, that the combined equivalent weight of Schedule V substances shall not exceed 999 grams of marihuana.".

The Commentary to §2D1.1 captioned "Background" is amended by inserting the following additional paragraph as the fourth paragraph:

> " In cases involving fifty or more marihuana plants, an equivalency of one plant to one kilogram of marihuana is derived from the statutory penalty provisions of 21 U.S.C. § 841(b)(1)(A), (B), and (D). In cases involving fewer than fifty plants, the statute is silent as to the equivalency. For cases involving fewer than fifty plants, the Commission has adopted an equivalency of 100 grams per plant, or the actual weight of the usable marihuana, whichever is greater. The decision to treat each plant as equal to 100 grams is premised on the fact that the average yield from a mature marihuana plant equals 100 grams of marihuana. In controlled substance offenses, an attempt is assigned the same offense level as the object of the attempt (see §2D1.4). Consequently, the Commission adopted the policy that, in the case of fewer than fifty marihuana plants, each plant is to be treated as the equivalent of an attempt to produce 100 grams of marihuana, except where the actual weight of the usable marihuana is greater.".

This amendment substitutes a single conversion for Schedule III substances (1 gm of a Schedule III substance = 2 gms of marihuana) that will simplify application of the guidelines as well as address currently unlisted Schedule III substances. Because the equivalencies for Schedule III substances are not statutorily based, nor are the pharmacological equivalencies as clear as with Schedule I or II Substances, a generic listing was deemed appropriate. For the same reasons, the amendment provides a single conversion for Schedule IV substances (1 gm of a Schedule IV substance = 0.125 gm of marihuana) and Schedule V substances (1 gm of a Schedule V substance = 0.0125 gm of marihuana). The amendment also adds a conversion for anabolic steroids consistent with their treatment in the Drug Quantity Table. In addition, the amendment adds footnotes to the Drug Equivalency Tables for Schedule I or II depressants and Schedule III, IV, and V substances to remove an ambiguity in guideline application by expressly limiting the combined equivalent weight of such substances to the marihuana amount consistent with the highest offense level for such substances provided in the Drug Quantity Table. See United States v. Gurgliolo, 894 F.2d 56 (3d Cir. 1990). The amendment inserts an additional listing under "Secobarbital and Other Schedule

I and II Depressants" to reflect that glutethimide has been changed from a Schedule III to a Schedule II controlled substance under 21 C.F.R. §1308.12. In addition, the amendment simplifies the application of the Drug Equivalency Table by referencing the conversions to one substance (marihuana) rather than to four substances; the use of one referent rather than four makes no substantive change but will make the required computations easier and reduce the likelihood of computational error. Finally, the amendment sets forth the rationale for the Commission's treatment of fewer than fifty marihuana plants. **The effective date of this amendment is November 1, 1991.**

397. Section 2D1.7 is amended in the title by deleting "Interstate Sale and Transporting" and inserting in lieu thereof "Sale or Transportation".

Section 2D1.7 is amended by inserting the following additional subsection:

"(b) Cross Reference

(1) If the offense involved a controlled substance, apply §2D1.1 (Unlawful Manufacturing, Importing, Exporting, or Trafficking) or §2D2.1 (Unlawful Possession), as appropriate, if the resulting offense level is greater than that determined above.".

The Commentary to §2D1.7 captioned "Statutory Provision" is amended by deleting "21 U.S.C. § 857" and inserting in lieu thereof "21 U.S.C. § 863 (formerly 21 U.S.C. § 857)".

The Commentary to §2D1.7 is amended by inserting the following at the end:

"Application Note:

1. The typical case addressed by this guideline involves small-scale trafficking in drug paraphernalia (generally from a retail establishment that also sells items that are not unlawful). In a case involving a large-scale dealer, distributor, or manufacturer, an upward departure may be warranted. Conversely, where the offense was not committed for pecuniary gain (e.g., transportation for the defendant's personal use), a downward departure may be warranted.".

This amendment revises the title of the guideline to address the expanded coverage of the underlying statute, as amended by Section 2401 of the Crime Control Act of 1990 (Public Law 101-647), adds a cross reference to address cases in which the underlying conduct involves a controlled substance offense, and adds an application note to specify the "heartland" types of cases addressed by the offense level set forth in the guideline. **The effective date of this amendment is November 1, 1991.**

398. Amendment: Section 2E2.1 is amended in the title by deleting ", Financing, or Collecting an Extortionate Extension of Credit" and inserting in lieu thereof "or Financing an Extortionate Extension of Credit; Collecting an Extension of Credit by Extortionate Means".

Section 2E2.1(b)(3)(A) is amended by deleting "the commission of the offense or an escape from the scene of the crime" and inserting in lieu thereof "commission of the offense or to facilitate escape".

This amendment corrects an error in the title of this section, and conforms the wording in subsection (b)(3)(A) with the wording used in subsection (b)(3)(B) and other guidelines. **The effective date of this amendment is November 1, 1991.**

399. The Commentary to §2E5.2 captioned "Application Notes" is amended in Note 1 by deleting "had a fiduciary obligation under the Employee Retirement Income Security Act" and

inserting in lieu thereof "was a fiduciary of the benefit plan"; and by deleting "would" and inserting in lieu thereof "will".

The Commentary to §2E5.2 captioned "Application Notes" is amended by deleting Note 2 as follows:

"2. 'Fiduciary of the benefit plan' is defined in 29 U.S.C. § 1002(21)(A) to mean a person who exercises any discretionary authority or control in respect to the management of such plan or exercises authority or control in respect to management or disposition of its assets, or who renders investment advice for a fee or other direct or indirect compensation with respect to any moneys or other property of such plan, or has any authority or responsibility to do so, or who has any discretionary authority or responsibility in the administration of such plan.";

by inserting the text of former Note 2 as the last sentence of Note 1; and, in the caption, by deleting "Notes" and inserting in lieu thereof "Note".

This amendment makes an editorial improvement in the language of this commentary. **The effective date of this amendment is November 1, 1991.**

400. Section 2G1.2(b) is amended by inserting the following additional subdivision:

"(4) If the defendant was a parent, relative, or legal guardian of the minor involved in the offense, or if the minor was otherwise in the custody, care, or supervisory control of the defendant, increase by 2 levels.".

Sections 2G1.2(c) and (d) are transposed and redesignated accordingly.

Section 2G1.2(c) (formerly §2G1.2(d)) is amended in the caption by deleting "Reference" and inserting in lieu thereof "References"; and by inserting the following additional subsections:

"(2) If the offense involved criminal sexual abuse, attempted criminal sexual abuse, or assault with intent to commit criminal sexual abuse, apply §2A3.1 (Criminal Sexual Abuse; Attempt or Assault with the Intent to Commit Criminal Sexual Abuse).

(3) If neither subsection (c)(1) nor (c)(2) is applicable, and the offense did not involve transportation for the purpose of prostitution, apply §2A3.2 (Criminal Sexual Abuse of a Minor or Attempt to Commit Such Acts) or §2A3.4 (Abusive Sexual Contact or Attempt to Commit Abusive Sexual Contact), as appropriate.".

Section 2G1.2(c)(1) (formerly §2G1.2(d)(1)) is amended by deleting "the defendant" immediately before "causing".

The Commentary to §2G1.2 captioned "Application Notes" is amended by renumbering Note 5 as Note 7, and by inserting the following additional notes:

"5. Subsection (b)(4) is intended to have broad application and includes offenses involving a minor entrusted to the defendant, whether temporarily or permanently. For example, teachers, day care providers, baby-sitters, or other temporary caretakers are among those who would be subject to this enhancement. In determining whether to apply this adjustment, the court should look to the actual relationship that existed between the defendant and the child and not simply to the legal status of the defendant-child relationship.

6. If the adjustment in subsection (b)(4) applies, do not apply §3B1.3 (Abuse of Position of Trust or Use of Special Skill).".

The commentary to §2G1.2 captioned "Application Notes" is amended in Note 1 by deleting "(c)(1)" and inserting in lieu thereof "(d)(1)"; and in Note 7 (formerly Note 5) by deleting "(d)(1)" and inserting in lieu thereof "subsection (c)(1)".

The Commentary to §2G2.1 captioned "Application Notes" is amended in Note 2 by deleting "Specific offense characteristic" and inserting in lieu thereof "Subsection".

The Commentary to §2G2.1 captioned "Application Notes" is amended by deleting:

"3. If specific offense characteristic (b)(2) applies, no adjustment is to be made under §3B1.3 (Abuse of Position of Trust or Use of Special Skill).",

and inserting in lieu thereof:

"3. If the adjustment in subsection (b)(2) applies, do not apply §3B1.3 (Abuse of Position of Trust or Use of Special Skill).".

This amendment adds a specific offense characteristic and commentary to provide consistent treatment for similar conduct among the guidelines in this part, conforms the language used in §2G1.2(c)(1) (formerly §2G1.2(d)(1)) with the language used elsewhere in the guidelines, and makes editorial changes to improve clarity. In addition, as statutes referenced to §2G1.2 may be used as "jurisdictional" statutes in some cases to prosecute conduct that is more appropriately covered under other guidelines (§§2A3.1, 2A3.2, and 2A3.4), this amendment inserts cross references as §2G1.2(c)(2) and (3) to provide consistent offense levels in such cases. **The effective date of this amendment is November 1, 1991.**

401. The Commentary to §2J1.2 captioned "Application Notes" is amended in Note 1 by deleting:

", an indictment or verdict based upon perjury, false testimony, or other false evidence,"

and inserting in lieu thereof:

"; an indictment, verdict, or any judicial determination based upon perjury, false testimony, or other false evidence;".

The Commentary to §2J1.2 captioned "Application Notes" is amended by inserting the following additional note:

"5. The inclusion of 'property damage' under subsection (b)(1) is designed to address cases in which property damage is caused or threatened as a means of intimidation or retaliation (e.g., to intimidate a witness from, or retaliate against a witness for, testifying). Subsection (b)(1) is not intended to apply, for example, where the offense consisted of destroying a ledger containing an incriminating entry.".

The Commentary to §2J1.2 captioned "Background" is amended in the second paragraph by deleting:

"assist another person to escape punishment for a crime he has committed, an alternative reference to the guideline for accessory after the fact is made",

and inserting in lieu thereof:

"avoid punishment for an offense that the defendant has committed or to assist another person to escape punishment for an offense, a cross reference to §2X3.1 (Accessory After the Fact) is provided. Use of this cross reference will provide an enhanced offense level when the obstruction is in respect to, a particularly serious offense, whether such offense was committed by the defendant or another person".

The Commentary to §2J1.3 captioned "Application Notes" is amended in Note 1 by deleting:

", an indictment or verdict based upon perjury, false testimony, or other false evidence,"

and inserting in lieu thereof:

"; an indictment, verdict, or any judicial determination based upon perjury, false testimony, or other false evidence;".

The Commentary to §2J1.5 captioned "Application Notes" is amended in Note 1 by deleting:

", an indictment or verdict based upon perjury, false testimony, or other false evidence,"

and inserting in lieu thereof:

"; an indictment, verdict, or any judicial determination based upon perjury, false testimony, or other false evidence;".

The Commentary to §2J1.8 captioned "Application Notes" is amended in Note 1 by deleting:

", an indictment or verdict based upon perjury, false testimony, or other false evidence,"

and inserting in lieu thereof:

"; an indictment, verdict, or any judicial determination based upon perjury, false testimony, or other false evidence;".

This amendment clarifies the types of circumstances to which §§2J1.2(b)(1) and 2J1.2(c)(1) apply. This amendment also clarifies the scope of the enhancement for "substantial interference with the administration of justice" in §§2J1.2, 2J1.3, 2J1.5, and 2J1.8. **The effective date of this amendment is November 1, 1991.**

402. Section 2J1.3 is amended by inserting the following additional subsection:

"(d) Special Instruction

(1) In the case of counts of perjury or subornation of perjury arising from testimony given, or to be given, in separate proceedings, do not group the counts together under §3D1.2 (Groups of Closely-Related Counts).".

The Commentary to §2J1.3 captioned "Application Notes" is amended by inserting the following additional note:

"5. 'Separate proceedings,' as used in subsection (d)(1), includes different proceedings in the same case or matter (e.g., a grand jury proceeding and a trial, or a trial and retrial), and proceedings in separate cases or matters (e.g., separate trials of codefendants), but does not include multiple grand jury proceedings in the same case.".

This amendment provides a special instruction addressing the appropriate treatment of multiple instances of perjury under Chapter Three, Part D (Multiple Counts). **The effective date of this amendment is November 1, 1991.**

403. The Commentary to §2J1.6 captioned "Application Notes" is amended by deleting:

"2. By statute, a term of imprisonment imposed for this offense runs consecutively to any other term of imprisonment imposed. 18 U.S.C. § 3146(b)(1).";

by renumbering Note 3 as Note 2; and by inserting the following additional notes:

"3. In the case of a failure to appear for service of sentence, any term of imprisonment imposed on the failure to appear count is to be imposed consecutively to any term of imprisonment imposed for the underlying offense. See §5G1.3(a). The guideline range for the failure to appear count is to be determined independently and the grouping rules of §§ 3D1.2-3D1.5 do not apply.

Otherwise, in the case of a conviction on both the underlying offense and the failure to appear, the failure to appear is treated under §3C1.1 (Obstructing or Impeding the Administration of Justice) as an obstruction of the underlying offense; and the failure to appear count and the count(s) for the underlying offense are grouped together under §3D1.2(c). Note that although 18 U.S.C. § 3146(b)(2) does not require a sentence of imprisonment on a failure to appear count, it does require that any sentence of imprisonment on a failure to appear count be imposed consecutively to any other sentence of imprisonment. Therefore, in such cases, the combined sentence must be constructed to provide a 'total punishment' that satisfies the requirements both of §5G1.2 (Sentencing on Multiple Counts of Conviction) and 18 U.S.C. § 3146(b)(2). For example, where the combined applicable guideline range for both counts is 30-37 months and the court determines a 'total punishment' of 36 months is appropriate, a sentence of thirty months for the underlying offense plus a consecutive six months sentence for the failure to appear count would satisfy these requirements.

4. In some cases, the defendant may be sentenced on the underlying offense (the offense in respect to which the defendant failed to appear) before being sentenced on the failure to appear offense. In such cases, criminal history points for the sentence imposed on the underlying offense are to be counted in determining the guideline range on the failure to appear offense only where the offense level is determined under subsection (a)(1) (i.e., where the offense constituted a failure to report for service of sentence).".

This amendment inserts an application note (Note 3) to clarify the interaction of §§2J1.6, 3C1.1, 5G1.2, and 5G1.3; and inserts an application note (Note 4) to clarify the interaction of §§2J1.6 and 4A1.1. **The effective date of this amendment is November 1, 1991.**

404. Section 2K1.1 is amended in the title by deleting "Explosives" and inserting in lieu thereof "Explosive Materials".

Section 2K1.2 is amended in the title by deleting "Explosives" and inserting in lieu thereof "Explosive Materials".

The Commentary to §2K1.4 captioned "Application Notes" is amended by inserting the following additional note:

"3. 'Explosives,' as used in the title of this guideline, includes any explosive, explosive material, or destructive device.".

Section 2K1.5(c)(1) is amended by inserting "or possessed" immediately following "used"; and by inserting ", as appropriate," immediately before "if the".

This amendment revises the titles of §2K1.1 and §2K1.2, and the Commentary to §2K1.4 to clarify that the term explosives, as used in those guidelines, includes explosives materials. In addition, this amendment clarifies the application of the cross reference in §2K1.5(c)(1). **The effective date of this amendment is November 1, 1991.**

405. The Commentary to §2K2.4 captioned "Application Notes" is amended in Note 2 by deleting "§2B3.1(b)(2)" and inserting in lieu thereof "§2B3.1(b)(2)(A)-(F)"; and by inserting the following additional paragraphs at the end:

"*Provided*, that where the maximum of the guideline range from Chapter Five, Part A (Sentencing Table) determined by an offense level adjusted under the procedure described in the preceding paragraph, plus the term of imprisonment required under 18 U.S.C. § 924(c) or § 929(a), is less than the maximum of the guideline range that would apply to the underlying offense absent such adjustment, the procedure described in the preceding paragraph does not apply. Instead, the guideline range applicable to the underlying offense absent such adjustment is to be used after subtracting the term of imprisonment imposed under 18 U.S.C. § 924(c) or § 929(a) from both the minimum and maximum of such range.

Example: A defendant, is to be sentenced under the robbery guideline; his unadjusted offense level from §2B3.1 is 30, including a 7-level enhancement for discharging a firearm; no Chapter Three adjustments are applicable; and his criminal history category is Category IV. His unadjusted guideline range from Chapter Five, Part A (Sentencing Table) is 135-168 months. This defendant has also been convicted under 18 U.S.C. § 924(c) arising from the possession of a weapon during the robbery, and therefore must be sentenced to an additional consecutive five-year term of imprisonment. The defendant's adjusted guideline range, which takes into account the conviction under 18 U.S.C. § 924(c) by eliminating the 7-level weapon enhancement, is 70-87 months. Because the maximum of the defendant's adjusted guideline range plus the five year consecutive sentence (87 months + 60 months = 147 months) is less than the maximum of the defendant's unadjusted guideline range (168 months), the defendant is to be sentenced using the unadjusted guideline range after subtracting the 60 month sentence to be imposed under 18 U.S.C. § 924(c) from both the minimum and maximum of the unadjusted range (e.g., 135 months - 60 months = 75 months; 168 months - 60 months = 108 months). A sentence imposed for the underlying offense using the guideline range determined in this manner (75-108 months) when combined with the consecutive sentence imposed under 18 U.S.C. § 924(c) or § 929(a), will produce the appropriate total term of imprisonment.".

This amendment provides an additional instruction for the determination of the offense level in cases in which the defendant is convicted under 18 U.S.C. § 924(c) or §929(a) in addition to a count for the offense in respect to which the firearm was used or possessed. The amendment is designed to prevent the anomalous result of the total punishment being less when there are convictions on both such counts than if the defendant was convicted only of the offense in respect to which the weapon was used or possessed. **The effective date of this amendment is November 1, 1991.**

406. The Commentary to §2P1.1 captioned "Application Notes" is amended by inserting the following additional note:

"6. If the adjustment in subsection (b)(1) applies as a result of conduct that involves an official victim, do not apply §3A1.2 (Official Victim).".

This amendment addresses the issue raised in United States v. Dugan, 912 F.2d 942 (8th Cir. 1990) concerning the interaction between §2P1.1(b)(1) and §3A1.2 by expressly providing that where an enhancement from subsection (b)(1) applies, §3A1.2 does not apply. **The effective date of this amendment is November 1, 1991.**

407. Section 2Q2.1(b)(3)(A) is amended by deleting "specially protected" immediately before "fish".

This amendment removes language inadvertently retained when this guideline was consolidated with the former §2Q2.2. **The effective date of this amendment is November 1, 1991.**

408. The Commentary to §2T1.2 captioned "Background" is amended in the third paragraph by deleting:

"difficulty of computing the tax loss, which may become the subject of protracted civil litigation. It is expected that the measure used will generally understate the tax due, and will not call for a sentence approaching the maximum unless very large incomes are involved. Thus, the burden will remain on the prosecution to provide a more accurate estimate of the tax loss if it seeks enhanced punishment",

and inserting in lieu thereof:

"potential difficulty of determining the amount of tax the taxpayer owed. It is expected that this alternative measure generally will understate the amount of tax owed".

This amendment clarifies the meaning of the commentary and deletes surplus material. **The effective date of this amendment is November 1, 1991.**

409. Section 2T1.6 is amended by inserting the following additional subsection:

"(b) Cross Reference

(1) Where the offense involved embezzlement by withholding tax from an employee's earnings and willfully failing to account to the employee for it, apply §2B1.1 (Larceny, Embezzlement, and Other Forms of Theft) if the resulting offense level is greater than that determined above.".

The Commentary to §2T1.6 captioned "Application Note" is amended in Note 1 by deleting "In such instances, an upward departure may be warranted" and inserting in lieu thereof "Subsection (b)(1) addresses such cases".

This amendment replaces the recommendation in the commentary of this guideline concerning consideration of an upward departure where the court finds that the offense involved embezzlement of an employee's funds with a cross reference that provides for the application of §2B1.1 (Larceny, Embezzlement, and Other Forms of Theft) in such cases where that guideline results in the greater offense level. **The effective date of this amendment is November 1, 1991.**

410. Section 2T3.1(a) is amended by deleting "Level from §2T4.1 (Tax Table) corresponding to the tax loss." and inserting in lieu thereof:

"(1) The level from §2T4.1 (Tax Table) corresponding to the tax loss, if the tax loss exceeded $1,000; or

(2) 5, if the tax loss exceeded $100 but did not exceed $1,000; or

(3) 4, if the tax loss did not exceed $100.".

Section 2T3.1 is amended by inserting the following additional subsection:

"(b) Specific Offense Characteristic

(1) If sophisticated means were used to impede discovery of the nature or existence of the offense, increase by 2 levels.".

Section 2T3.2(a) is amended by deleting "Level from §2T4.1 (Tax Table) corresponding to the tax loss." and inserting in lieu thereof:

"(1) The level from §2T4.1 (Tax Table) corresponding to the tax loss, if the tax loss exceeded $1,000; or

(2) 5, if the tax loss exceeded $100 but did not exceed $1,000; or

(3) 4, if the tax loss did not exceed $100.".

Section 2T3.2 is amended by inserting the following additional subsection:

"(b) Specific Offense Characteristic

(1) If sophisticated means were used to impede discovery of the nature or existence of the offense, increase by 2 levels.".

This amendment lowers the offense level for the least serious offenses (evasion of import duty of $1,000 or less without use of sophisticated means) to provide an offense level equal to the offense level for theft of the same amount without more than minimal planning. In addition, it adds an adjustment for "sophisticated means" to conform with other tax evasion guidelines (e.g., §2T1.1). **The effective date of this amendment is November 1, 1991.**

411. Section 2X1.1(a) and (b)(3) are amended by deleting "object" wherever it appears and inserting in lieu thereof in each instance "substantive".

Section 2X1.1(b)(1) is amended by inserting "substantive" immediately before "offense".

Section 2X1.1(b)(2) is amended by inserting "substantive" immediately before "offense".

Section 2X1.1(b)(3) is amended by deleting "the offense" the first two times it appears and inserting in lieu thereof in each instance "the substantive offense".

The Commentary to §2X1.1 captioned "Application Notes" is amended in Note 2 by deleting:

"Under §2X1.1(a) the base offense level will be the same as that for the object offense which the defendant solicited, or conspired or attempted to commit.",

and inserting in lieu thereof:

"'Substantive offense,' as used in this guideline, means the offense that the defendant was convicted of soliciting, attempting, or conspiring to commit. Under §2X1.1(a), the base offense level will be the same as that for the substantive offense.".

The Commentary to §2X1.1 is amended by deleting "object" wherever it appears and inserting in lieu thereof "substantive".

The Commentary to §2X1.1 captioned "Application Notes" is amended in Note 4 in the second paragraph by deleting "or (2)" and inserting in lieu thereof ", (b)(2), or (b)(3)(A)".

The Commentary to §2X1.1 captioned "Background" is amended by deleting "necessary acts of" and inserting in lieu thereof "acts necessary for".

This amendment replaces the term "object offense" with the more commonly used term "substantive offense," and makes clarifying and editorial changes. **The effective date of this amendment is November 1, 1991.**

412. Section 2X5.1 is amended by inserting, immediately before the period at the end of the second sentence, the following:

", except that any guidelines and policy statements that can be applied meaningfully in the absence of a Chapter Two offense guideline shall remain applicable".

The Commentary to §2X5.1 is amended by inserting, immediately after "Commentary", the following:

"Application Note:

1. Guidelines and policy statements that can be applied meaningfully in the absence of a Chapter Two offense guideline include: §5B1.3 (Conditions of Probation); §5B1.4 (Recommended Conditions of Probation and Supervised Release); §5D1.1 (Imposition of a Term of Supervised Release); §5D1.2 (Term of Supervised Release); §5D1.3 (Conditions of Supervised Release); §5E1.1 (Restitution); §5E1.3 (Special Assessments); §5E1.4 (Forfeiture); Chapter Five, Part F (Sentencing Options); §5G1.3 (Imposition of a Sentence on a Defendant Subject to an Undischarged Term of Imprisonment); Chapter Five, Part H (Specific Offender Characteristics); Chapter Five, Part J (Relief from Disability); Chapter Five, Part K (Departures); Chapter Six, Part A (Sentencing Procedures); Chapter Six, Part B (Plea Agreements).".

The Commentary to §2X5.1 captioned "Background" is amended by inserting the following additional paragraph:

" The sentencing guidelines apply to convictions under 18 U.S.C. § 13 (Assimilative Crimes Act) and 18 U.S.C. § 1153 (Indian Major Crimes Act); see 18 U.S.C. § 3551(a), as amended by section 1602 of Public Law 101-647.".

This amendment inserts an application note to clarify that, in the case of an offense for which there is no sufficiently analogous offense guideline, any guidelines and policy statements that can be meaningfully applied in the absence of a Chapter Two offense guideline remain applicable. This amendment also clarifies the applicability of the sentencing guidelines to convictions under 18 U.S.C. §§ 13 (Assimilative Crimes Act) and 1153 (Indian Major Crimes Act). Section 1602 of the Crime Control Act of 1990 (Public Law 101-647) resolved this issue by amending 18 U.S.C. § 3551(a) to provide expressly that Chapter 227 of Title 18, United States Code (including the sentencing guidelines) applies to convictions under these statutes. **The effective date of this amendment is November 1, 1991.**

413. The Commentary to §3A1.3 captioned "Application Notes" is amended by deleting:

"2. This adjustment applies to any offense in which a victim was physically restrained in the course of the offense, except where such restraint is an element of the offense, specifically incorporated into the base offense level, or listed as a specific offense characteristic.",

and inserting in lieu thereof:

"2. Do not apply this adjustment where the offense guideline specifically incorporates this factor, or where the unlawful restraint of a victim is an element of the offense itself (e.g., this adjustment does not apply to offenses covered by §2A4.1 (Kidnapping, Abduction, Unlawful Restraint)).".

This amendment clarifies the application of this guideline. **The effective date of this amendment is November 1, 1991.**

414. The Commentary to §3B1.1 captioned "Application Notes" is amended in Note 1 by inserting the following additional sentence at the end:

"A person who is not criminally responsible for the commission of the offense (e.g., an undercover law enforcement officer) is not a participant.".

This amendment clarifies the operation of this guideline in accord with the holding in United States v. Carroll, 893 F.2d 1502 (6th Cir. 1990). **The effective date of this amendment is November 1, 1991.**

415. The Commentary to §3C1.1 captioned "Application Notes" is amended in Note 1 in the last sentence by deleting ", the defendant's testimony and" and inserting in lieu thereof "in respect to alleged false testimony or statements by the defendant, such testimony or".

This amendment more precisely states the meaning of this commentary. **The effective date of this amendment is November 1, 1991.**

416. The Commentary to §3C1.2 captioned "Application Notes" is amended by redesignating note 3 as note 4; and by inserting the following additional note:

"3. 'During flight' is to be construed broadly and includes preparation for flight. Therefore, this adjustment also is applicable where the conduct occurs in the course of resisting arrest.".

This amendment clarifies that reckless endangerment in the course of resisting arrest that does not receive a 3-level enhancement under §3A1.2 (Official Victim) may be considered under this section. **The effective date of this amendment is November 1, 1991.**

417. Section 3D1.2(d) is amended in the second paragraph by inserting ", 2C1.7" immediately following "2C1.2"; by inserting ", 2D1.11, 2D1.13" immediately following "2D1.5"; and by deleting "2K2.2" and inserting in lieu thereof "2K2.1".

The Commentary to §3D1.2 captioned "Application Notes" is amended in Note 2 by inserting the following immediately after the second sentence:

"For offenses in which there are no identifiable victims (e.g., drug or immigration offenses, where society at large is the victim), the 'victim' for purposes of subsections (a) and (b) is the societal interest that is harmed. In such cases, the counts are grouped together when the societal interests that are harmed are closely related. Where one count, for example, involves unlawfully entering the United States and the other involves possession of fraudulent evidence of citizenship, the counts are grouped together because the societal interests harmed (the interests protected by laws governing immigration) are closely related. In contrast, where one count involves the sale of controlled substances and the other involves an immigration law violation, the counts are not grouped together because different societal interests are harmed.";

and by deleting the last sentence as follows:

"Thus, for so-called 'victimless' crimes (crimes in which society at large is the victim), the grouping decision must be based primarily upon the nature of the interest invaded by each offense.".

The Commentary to §3D1.2 captioned "Application Notes" is amended by deleting Note 8, inserting the text of deleted Note 8 as the second paragraph of Note 5, and by renumbering Note 9 as Note 8.

The Commentary to §3D1.2 captioned "Application Notes" is amended in the third (formerly second) paragraph of Note 5 by deleting "accessory after the fact for" and inserting in lieu thereof "a conspiracy to commit".

The Commentary to §3D1.2 captioned "Application Notes" is amended in Note 6 by inserting the following additional paragraph as the second paragraph:

"A conspiracy, attempt, or solicitation to commit an offense is covered under subsection (d) if the offense that is the object of the conspiracy, attempt, or solicitation is covered under subsection (d).".

The Commentary following §3D1.5 captioned "Illustrations of the Operation of the Multiple-Count Rules" is amended in example 1 by deleting "gun was discharged" and inserting in lieu thereof "firearm was displayed".

The Commentary following §3D1.5 captioned "Illustrations of the Operation of the Multiple-Count Rules" is amended in example 2 by deleting:

"The base offense level is 6, and there is an aggravator of 1 level for property value. However, because the conduct involved repeated acts with some planning, the offense level is raised to 8 (§2F1.1(b)(2)(B)). The combined offense level therefore is 8.",

and inserting in lieu thereof:

"The base offense level is 6; 1 level is added because of the value of the property (§2F1.1(b)(1)); and 2 levels are added because the conduct involved repeated acts with some planning (§2F1.1(b)(2)(A)). The resulting offense level is 9.".

The Commentary following §3D1.5 captioned "Illustrations of the Operation of the Multiple-Count Rules" is amended in example 4 by deleting "§2B4.1 (Commercial Bribery)" and inserting in lieu thereof "§2B4.1 (Bribery in Procurement of Bank Loan and Other Commercial Bribery)".

This amendment revises §3D1.2(d) to reflect amendments to the offense guidelines of Chapter Two; clarifies the commentary in Note 1 to expressly state that a conspiracy, attempt, or solicitation to commit an offense covered under subsection (d) is also covered under subsection (d); clarifies the commentary in Note 2 with respect to the meaning of the term "victim" where society at large is the victim; merges former Note 8 with Note 5 for greater clarity; conforms two illustrations of the operation of the guidelines to the guidelines, as amended; corrects an inaccurate illustration; and corrects a reference to the title of an offense guideline. **The effective date of this amendment is November 1, 1991.**

418. The Commentary to Chapter Five, Part A (Sentencing Table) captioned "Application Notes" is amended in Note 3 by inserting ", except as provided in §§4B1.1 (Career Offender) and

4B1.4 (Armed Career Criminal)" immediately before the period at the end of the first sentence.

This amendment conforms the commentary of this section to the provisions concerning the determination of the criminal history category set forth in §§4B1.1 and 4B1.4. No substantive change results. **The effective date of this amendment is November 1, 1991.**

419. Section 5F1.3 is amended by deleting:

"If the defendant was convicted of a felony and sentenced to probation, the court must order one or more of the following sanctions: a fine, restitution, or community service. 18 U.S.C. § 3563(a)(2).".

This amendment deletes a sentence in this guideline that is unnecessary and no longer accurate because of a change in the statute. The correct reference is found at §5B1.3(a). **The effective date of this amendment is November 1, 1991.**

420. Chapter Five, Part K, Subpart 2 is amended by inserting an additional policy statement as §5K2.16 (Voluntary Disclosure of Offense (Policy Statement)).

This amendment sets forth an additional policy statement regarding a mitigating factor that may warrant a downward departure. **The effective date of this amendment is November 1, 1991.**

421. Appendix A (Statutory Index) is amended by inserting, in the appropriate place by title and section, the following:

"8 U.S.C. § 1160(b)(7)(A)	2L2.1, 2L2.2";
"18 U.S.C. § 225	2B1.1, 2B4.1, 2F1.1";
"18 U.S.C. § 403	2J1.1";
"18 U.S.C. § 1032	2B4.1, 2F1.1";
"18 U.S.C. § 1346	2C1.7";
"18 U.S.C. § 1517	2J1.2";
"18 U.S.C. § 2257	2G2.5";
"21 U.S.C. § 841(g)(1)	2D1.11, 2D1.13";
"21 U.S.C. § 843(a)(4)(B)	2D1.13";
"21 U.S.C. § 843(a)(6), (7)	2D1.12";
"21 U.S.C. § 843(a)(8)	2D1.13";
"21 U.S.C. § 859	2D1.2";
"21 U.S.C. § 860	2D1.2";
"21 U.S.C. § 861	2D1.2";
"21 U.S.C. § 863	2D1.7";
"42 U.S.C. § 1320a-7b	2B1.1, 2B4.1, 2F1.1".

Appendix A (Statutory Index) is amended in the line beginning "18 U.S.C. § 371" by inserting "2C1.7," immediately before "2D1.4";

by deleting:

"18 U.S.C. § 842(a)-(i)	2K1.3",

and inserting in lieu thereof:

"18 U.S.C. § 842(a)-(e)	2K1.3
18 U.S.C. § 842(f)	2K1.6

18 U.S.C. § 842(g)	2K1.6
18 U.S.C. § 842(h), (i)	2K1.3";

by deleting:

"18 U.S.C. § 844(a)	2K1.3
18 U.S.C. § 844(b)	2K1.1, 2K1.2, 2K1.3";

in the line beginning "18 U.S.C. § 844(d)" by deleting "§2K1.6" and inserting in lieu thereof "§2K1.3";

by deleting:

"18 U.S.C. § 922(a)(1)	2K2.1, 2K2.2
18 U.S.C. § 922(a)(2)	2K2.2
18 U.S.C. § 922(a)(3)	2K2.1
18 U.S.C. § 922(a)(4)	2K2.1
18 U.S.C. § 922(a)(5)	2K2.2
18 U.S.C. § 922(a)(6)	2K2.1
18 U.S.C. § 922(b)-(d)	2K2.2
18 U.S.C. § 922(e)	2K2.1, 2K2.2
18 U.S.C. § 922(f)	2K2.1, 2K2.2
18 U.S.C. § 922(g)	2K2.1
18 U.S.C. § 922(h)	2K2.1
18 U.S.C. § 922(i)-(l)	2K2.1, 2K2.2
18 U.S.C. § 922(m)	2K2.2
18 U.S.C. § 922(n)	2K2.1
18 U.S.C. § 922(o)	2K2.1, 2K2.2
18 U.S.C. § 923(a)	2K2.2
18 U.S.C. § 924(a)(1)(A)	2K2.2
18 U.S.C. § 924(a)(1)(C)	2K2.1, 2K2.2
18 U.S.C. § 924(a)(3)(A)	2K2.2
18 U.S.C. § 924(b)	2K2.3",

and inserting in lieu thereof:

"18 U.S.C. § 922(a)-(p)	2K2.1
18 U.S.C. § 922(q)	2K2.5
18 U.S.C. § 922(r)	2K2.1
18 U.S.C. § 923	2K2.1
18 U.S.C. § 924(a)	2K2.1
18 U.S.C. § 924(b)	2K2.1";

by deleting:

"18 U.S.C. § 924(f)	2K2.3
18 U.S.C. § 924(g)	2K2.3",

and inserting in lieu thereof:

"18 U.S.C. § 924(e)	2K2.1 (see also 4B1.4)
18 U.S.C. § 924(f)	2K2.1
18 U.S.C. § 924(g)	2K2.1";

in the line beginning "18 U.S.C. § 1005" by deleting ", 2S1.3";

in the line beginning "18 U.S.C. § 1341" by inserting "2C1.7," immediately before "2F1.1";

in the line beginning "18 U.S.C. § 1342" by inserting "2C1.7," immediately before "2F1.1";

in the line beginning "18 U.S.C. § 1343" by inserting "2C1.7," immediately before "2F1.1";

in the line beginning "18 U.S.C. § 1460" by deleting "2G2.2,";

in the line beginning "18 U.S.C. § 1543" by inserting "2L2.3," immediately before "2L2.4";

in the line beginning "18 U.S.C. § 1716" by inserting "2K1.3," immediately before "2K3.2";

in the line beginning "18 U.S.C. § 2252" by inserting ", 2G2.4" immediately following "2G2.2";

by deleting:

"21 U.S.C. § 841(d) 2D1.1",

and inserting in lieu thereof:

"21 U.S.C. § 841(d)(1), (2) 2D1.11
21 U.S.C. § 841(d)(3) 2D1.13";

by deleting:

"21 U.S.C. § 842(a) 2D3.1, 2D3.2, 2D3.3",

and inserting in lieu thereof:

"21 U.S.C. § 842(a)(1) 2D3.1
21 U.S.C. § 842(a)(2) 2D3.3
21 U.S.C. § 842(a)(9), (10) 2D3.5";

in the line beginning "21 U.S.C. § 843(a)(1), (2), (4)" by deleting ", (1), (2), (4)" and inserting in lieu thereof "(1), (2)";

by deleting:

"21 U.S.C. § 960 2D1.1",

and inserting in lieu thereof:

"21 U.S.C. § 960(a), (b) 2D1.1
21 U.S.C. § 960(d)(1), (2) 2D1.11";

in the line beginning 26 U.S.C. § 5685 by deleting "2K1.6,", and by deleting "2K2.2" and inserting in lieu thereof "2K2.1";

by deleting:

"26 U.S.C. § 5861(a) 2K2.2
26 U.S.C. § 5861(b) 2K2.1
26 U.S.C. § 5861(c) 2K2.1
26 U.S.C. § 5861(d) 2K2.1
26 U.S.C. § 5861(e) 2K2.2
26 U.S.C. § 5861(f) 2K2.2
26 U.S.C. § 5861(g) 2K2.2
26 U.S.C. § 5861(h) 2K2.1
26 U.S.C. § 5861(i) 2K2.1
26 U.S.C. § 5861(j) 2K2.1, 2K2.2
26 U.S.C. § 5861(k) 2K2.1
26 U.S.C. § 5861(l) 2K2.2
26 U.S.C. § 5871 2K2.1, 2K2.2",

and inserting in lieu thereof:

"26 U.S.C. § 5861(a)-(l) 2K2.1
26 U.S.C. § 5871 2K2.1";

by deleting:

"31 U.S.C. § 5316(a) 2S1.3",

and inserting in lieu thereof:

"31 U.S.C. § 5316 2S1.4";

by deleting:

"46 U.S.C. § App. 1903 2D1.1",

and inserting in lieu thereof:

"46 U.S.C. App. § 1903(a) 2D1.1
46 U.S.C. App. § 1903(g) 2D1.1
46 U.S.C. App. § 1903(j) 2D1.4"; and

in the line beginning "47 U.S.C. § 605" by inserting "2B5.3," immediately before "2H3.1".

The Commentary to §2D1.2 captioned "Statutory Provisions" is amended by deleting "21 U.S.C. §§ 845, 845a, 845b" and inserting in lieu thereof "21 U.S.C. §§ 859 (formerly 21 U.S.C. § 845), 860 (formerly 21 U.S.C. § 845a), 861 (formerly 21 U.S.C. § 845b)".

The Commentary to §2D3.1 captioned "Statutory Provision" is amended by deleting "843(a). For additional statutory provision(s), see Appendix A (Statutory Index)." and inserting in lieu thereof "842(a)(1), 843(a)(1), (2)."; and by deleting "Provision" and inserting in lieu thereof "Provisions".

The Commentary to §2D3.2 captioned "Statutory Provision" is amended by deleting "842" and inserting in lieu thereof "842(b), 843(a)(3)"; and by deleting "Provision" and inserting in lieu thereof "Provisions".

The Commentary to §2D3.3 captioned "Statutory Provision" is amended by deleting "842" and inserting in lieu thereof "842(a)(2)".

This amendment makes the statutory index more comprehensive, and conforms it to the offense guidelines, as amended. **The effective date of this amendment is November 1, 1991.**

422. The Guidelines Manual is amended by inserting an additional chapter containing guidelines, policy statements, and accompanying commentary as Chapter Eight (Sentencing of Organizations).

Section 2B4.1 is amended by inserting the following additional subsection:

"(c) Special Instruction for Fines - Organizations

(1) In lieu of the pecuniary loss under subsection (a)(3) of §8C2.4 (Base Fine), use the greatest of: (A) the value of the unlawful payment; (B) the value of the benefit received or to be received in return for the unlawful payment; or (C) the consequential damages resulting from the unlawful payment.".

Section 2C1.1 is amended by inserting the following additional subsection:

"(d) Special Instruction for Fines - Organizations

(1) In lieu of the pecuniary loss under subsection (a)(3) of §8C2.4 (Base Fine), use the greatest of: (A) the value of the unlawful payment; (B) the value of the benefit received or to be received in return for the unlawful payment; or (C) the consequential damages resulting from the unlawful payment.".

Section 2C1.2 is amended by inserting the following additional subsection:

"(c) Special Instruction for Fines - Organizations

(1) In lieu of the pecuniary loss under subsection (a)(3) of §8C2.4 (Base Fine), use the value of the unlawful payment.".

Section 2E5.1 is amended by inserting the following additional subsection:

"(c) Special Instruction for Fines - Organizations

(1) In lieu of the pecuniary loss under subsection (a)(3) of §8C2.4 (Base Fine), use the greatest of: (A) the value of the unlawful payment; (B) if a bribe, the value of the benefit received or to be received in return for the unlawful payment; or (C) if a bribe, the consequential damages resulting from the unlawful payment.".

Section 2E5.6 is amended by inserting the following additional subsection:

"(c) Special Instruction for Fines - Organizations

(1) In lieu of the pecuniary loss under subsection (a)(3) of §8C2.4 (Base Fine), use the greatest of: (A) the value of the unlawful payment; (B) if a bribe, the value of the benefit received or to be received in return for the unlawful payment; or (C) if a bribe, the consequential damages resulting from the unlawful payment.".

Section 2R1.1 is amended by inserting the following additional subsection:

"(d) Special Instructions for Fines - Organizations

(1) In lieu of the pecuniary loss under subsection (a)(3) of §8C2.4 (Base Fine), use 20 percent of the volume of affected commerce.

(2) When applying §8C2.6 (Minimum and Maximum Multipliers), neither the minimum nor maximum multiplier shall be less than 0.75.

(3) In a bid-rigging case in which the organization submitted one or more complementary bids, use as the organization's volume of commerce the greater of (A) the volume of commerce done by the organization in the goods or services that were affected by the violation, or (B) the largest contract on which the organization submitted a complementary bid in connection with the bid-rigging conspiracy.".

The Commentary to §2R1.1 captioned "Application Notes" is amended by deleting:

"3. In setting the fine for an organization, the court should consider whether the organization encouraged or took steps to prevent the violation, whether high-level management was aware of the violation, and whether the organization previously engaged in antitrust violations.",

and inserting in lieu thereof:

"3. The fine for an organization is determined by applying Chapter Eight (Sentencing of Organizations). In selecting a fine for an organization within the guideline fine range, the court should consider both the gain to the organization from the offense and the loss caused by the organization. It is estimated that the average gain from price-fixing is 10 percent of the selling price. The loss from price-fixing exceeds the gain because, among other things, injury is inflicted upon consumers who are unable or for other reasons do not buy the product at the higher prices. Because the loss from price-fixing exceeds the gain, subsection (d)(1) provides that 20 percent of the volume of affected commerce is to be used in lieu of the pecuniary loss under §8C2.4(a)(3). The purpose for specifying a percent of the volume of commerce is to avoid the time and expense that would be required for the court to determine the actual gain or loss. In cases in which the actual monopoly overcharge appears to be either substantially more or substantially less than 10 percent, this factor should be considered in setting the fine within the guideline fine range.".

The Commentary to §2R1.1 captioned "Background" is amended by deleting the last paragraph as follows:

" Substantial fines are an essential part of the sanction. It is estimated that the average additional profit attributable to price fixing is 10 percent of the selling price. The Commission has specified that a fine from two to five times that amount be imposed on organizational defendants as a deterrent because of the difficulty in identifying violators. Additional monetary penalties can be provided through private treble damage actions. A lower fine is specified for individuals. The Commission believes that most antitrust defendants have the resources and earning capacity to pay these fines, at least over time. The statutory maximum fine is $250,000 for individuals and $1,000,000 for organizations, but is increased when there are convictions on multiple counts.",

and inserting in lieu thereof:

" Substantial fines are an essential part of the sentence. For an individual, the guideline fine range is from one to five percent of the volume of commerce, but not less than $20,000. For an organization, the guideline fine range is determined under Chapter Eight (Sentencing of Organizations), but pursuant to subsection (d)(2), the minimum multiplier is at least 0.75. This multiplier, which requires a minimum fine of 15 percent of the volume of commerce for the least serious case, was selected to provide an effective deterrent to antitrust offenses. At the same time, this minimum multiplier maintains incentives for desired organizational behavior. Because the Department of Justice has a well-established amnesty program for organizations that self-report antitrust offenses, no lower minimum multiplier is needed as an incentive for self-reporting. A minimum multiplier of at least 0.75 ensures that fines imposed in antitrust cases will exceed the average monopoly overcharge.

The Commission believes that most antitrust defendants have the resources and earning capacity to pay the fines called for by this guideline, at least over time on an installment basis. The statutory maximum fine is $350,000 for individuals and $10,000,000 for organizations, but is increased when there are convictions on multiple counts.".

Section 2S1.1 is amended by inserting the following additional subsection:

"(c) Special Instruction for Fines - Organizations

(1) In lieu of the applicable amount from the table in subsection (d) of §8C2.4 (Base Fine), use:

(A) the greater of $250,000 or 100 percent of the value of the funds if subsections (a)(1) and (b)(1) are used to determine the offense level; or

(B) the greater of $200,000 or 70 percent of the value of the funds if subsections (a)(2) and (b)(1) are used to determine the offense level; or

(C) the greater of $200,000 or 70 percent of the value of the funds if subsection (a)(1) but not (b)(1) is used to determine the offense level; or

(D) the greater of $150,000 or 50 percent of the value of the funds if subsection (a)(2) but not (b)(1) is used to determine the offense level.".

Section 2S1.2 is amended by inserting the following additional subsection:

"(c) Special Instruction for Fines - Organizations

(1) In lieu of the applicable amount from the table in subsection (d) of §8C2.4 (Base Fine), use:

(A) the greater of $175,000 or 60 percent of the value of the funds if subsection (b)(1)(A) is used to determine the offense level; or

(B) the greater of $150,000 or 50 percent of the value of the funds if subsection (b)(1)(B) is used to determine the offense level.".

Section 2S1.3 is amended by inserting the following additional subsection:

"(c) Special Instruction for Fines - Organizations

(1) In lieu of the applicable amount from the table in subsection (d) of §8C2.4 (Base Fine), use:

(A) the greater of $125,000 or 30 percent of the value of the funds if subsections (a)(1) and (b)(1) are used to determine the offense level; or

(B) the greater of $50,000 or 20 percent of the value of the funds if subsection (a)(1) but not (b)(1) are used to determine the offense level.".

Section 2S1.4 is amended by inserting the following additional subsection:

"(c) Special Instruction for Fines - Organizations

(1) In lieu of the applicable amount from the table in subsection (d) of §8C2.4 (Base Fine), use:

(A) the greater of $50,000 or 20 percent of the value of the funds if subsection (b)(1) or (b)(2) is used to determine the offense level; or

(B) the greater of $15,000 or 10 percent of the value of the funds, otherwise.".

This amendment adds guidelines and policy statements to address the sentencing of organizational defendants. **The effective date of this amendment is November 1, 1991.**

423. Section 1B1.10(c) is amended by deleting:

"(c) *Provided*, however, that a reduction in a defendant's term of imprisonment --

(1) is not authorized unless the maximum of the guideline range applicable to the defendant (from Chapter Five, Part A) has been lowered by at least six months; and

(2) may, in no event, exceed the number of months by which the maximum of the guideline range applicable to the defendant (from Chapter Five, Part A) has been lowered.",

and inserting in lieu thereof:

"(c) *Provided*, that a reduction in a defendant's term of imprisonment may, in no event, exceed the number of months by which the maximum of the guideline range applicable to the defendant (from Chapter Five, Part A) has been lowered.".

Section 1B1.10(d) is amended by deleting "and 341" and inserting in lieu thereof "341, 379, and 380".

The Commentary to §1B1.10 captioned "Background" is amended in the fourth paragraph by deleting:

"The requirement in subsection (c)(1) that the maximum of the guideline range be lowered by at least six months for a reduction to be considered",

and inserting in lieu thereof:

"The Commission has not included in this policy statement amendments that generally reduce the maximum of the guideline range by less than six months. This criterion".

This amendment expands the listing in subsection (d) to implement the directive in 28 U.S.C. § 994(u) in respect to the guideline amendments effective November 1, 1991. In addition, the amendment modifies subsection (c) to simplify the operation of this policy statement, expand eligibility under the policy statement to a few additional cases, and remove the potential for an anomalous result. **The effective date of this amendment is November 1, 1991.**

424. Chapter Five, Part F, is amended by inserting an additional policy statement as §5F1.7 (Shock Incarceration Program (Policy Statement)).

This amendment adds a policy statement at §5F1.7 to reflect the provisions and implementation of 18 U.S.C. § 4046. **The effective date of this amendment is November 1, 1991.**

425. The Commentary to §6A1.2 is amended by inserting, immediately after "Commentary", the following:

"Application Note:

1. Under Rule 32, Fed.R.Crim. P., if the court intends to consider a sentence outside the applicable guideline range on a ground not identified as a ground for departure either in the presentence report or a pre-hearing submission, it shall provide reasonable notice that it is contemplating such ruling, specifically identifying the ground for the departure. Burns v. United States, __ U.S.__, 111 S.Ct. 2182 (1991).";

and by inserting "Background:" immediately before "In order".

This amendment adds an application note to reflect the recent Supreme Court decision in Burns v. United States, __ U.S. __, 111 S.Ct. 2182 (1991). **The effective date of this amendment is November 1, 1991.**

426. The Commentary to §2T1.3 captioned "Application Notes" is amended by inserting the following additional note:

"4. The amount by which the greater of gross income and taxable income was understated, plus 100 percent of the total amount of any false credits claimed against tax is calculated as follows: (1) determine the amount, if any, by which the gross income was understated; (2) determine the amount, if any, by which the taxable income was understated; and (3) determine the amount of any false credit(s) claimed (a tax 'credit' is an item that reduces the amount of tax directly; in contrast, a 'deduction' is an item that reduces the amount of taxable income). Use the amount determined under step (1) or (2), whichever is greater, plus any amount determined under step (3).".

This amendment clarifies the operation of the guideline. **The effective date of this amendment is November 1, 1991.**

427. Section 7B1.3 is amended by redesignating subsection (c)(1)(1) as (c)(1)(A), (c)(1)(2) as (c)(1)(B), (c)(2)(1) as (c)(2)(A), and (c)(2)(2) as (c)(2)(B).

The Commentary to §7B1.3 captioned "Application Notes" is amended in Note 2 by deleting "§7B1.3(f)(2)" and inserting in lieu thereof "§7B1.3(g)(2)".

The Commentary to §7B1.3 captioned "Application Notes" is amended in Note 3 by deleting "No. 89-10529 (9th Cir. July 3, 1990)" and inserting in lieu thereof "907 F.2d 896 (9th Cir. 1990)".

The Commentary to §7B1.3 captioned "Application Notes" is amended by inserting the following additional note:

"7. 'Maximum term of imprisonment imposable upon revocation,' as used in subsection (g)(2), refers to the maximum term of imprisonment authorized by statute for the violation of supervised release, not to the maximum of the guideline range.".

This amendment clarifies the operation of this policy statement, makes editorial improvements, and corrects a clerical error. **The effective date of this amendment is November 1, 1991.**

428. The Commentary to §5F1.5 captioned "Background" is amended by deleting the last paragraph as follows:

" The Comprehensive Crime Control Act expressly authorizes promulgation of policy statements regarding the appropriate use of conditions of probation and supervised release. 28 U.S.C. § 994(a)(2)(B). The Act does not expressly grant the authority to issue guidelines on the subject. The appellate review provisions of the Act, however, authorize appeals of occupational restrictions that deviate from the minimum and maximum limitations 'established in the guideline' (emphasis added).".

This amendment deletes an outdated paragraph. Section 7103(b)(3) of Public Law 100-690 amended 28 U.S.C. § 994 by adding subsection (a)(1)(E), which expressly authorizes the Commission to promulgate guidelines addressing occupational restrictions as a condition of probation or supervised release. **The effective date of this amendment is November 1, 1991.**

429. The Commentary to §1B1.5 captioned "Application Note" is amended in Note 1 by deleting "2D1.2(a)(1), 2H1.2(a)(2)" and inserting in lieu thereof "2D1.2(a)(1), (2), and 2H1.1(a)(2)"; by deleting "§§2A4.1(b)(5)(B), 2Q1.2(b)(5)" and inserting in lieu thereof "§2A4.1(b)(7)"; and by inserting the following additional paragraph:

"A reference may also be to a specific subsection of another guideline; e.g., the reference in §2D1.10(a)(1) to '3 plus the offense level from the Drug Quantity Table in §2D1.1'. In such case, only the specific subsection of that other guideline is used.".

The Commentary to §1B1.5 captioned "Application Note" is amended by inserting the following additional notes:

"2. A reference may require that the offense level be determined under another offense guideline. In such case, the adjustments in Chapter Three, Parts A (Victim-Related Adjustments), B (Role in the Offense), and E (Acceptance of Responsibility) are also to be determined in respect to that other offense guideline. For example, a defendant convicted of possession of a firearm by a felon, to which §2K2.1 (Unlawful Receipt, Possession, or Transportation of Firearms or Ammunition; Prohibited Transactions Involving Firearms or Ammunition) applies, is found to have used that firearm in the commission of a robbery. The cross reference at §2K2.1(c) directs that the robbery offense guideline be used. The adjustments in Chapter Three, Parts A, B and E are to be applied as if the offense of conviction had directly referenced the robbery guideline.

3. A reference to another guideline may direct that such reference is to be used only if it results in a greater offense level. In such cases, the greater offense level means the greater final offense level (i.e., the greater offense level taking into account both the Chapter Two offense level and any applicable Chapter Three adjustments). Although the offense guideline that results in the greater offense level under Chapter Two will most frequently result in the greater final offense level, this will not always be the case. If, for example, a role or abuse of trust adjustment applies to the cross-referenced offense guideline, but not to the guideline initially applied, the greater Chapter Two offense level may not necessarily result in a greater final offense level.

4. A reference may direct that, if the conduct involved another offense, the offense guideline for such other offense is to be applied. Where there is more than one such other offense, the most serious such offense (or group of closely-related offenses in the case of offenses that would be grouped together under §3D1.2(d)) is to be used. For example, if a defendant convicted of possession of a firearm by a felon, to which §2K2.1 (Unlawful Receipt, Possession, or Transportation of Firearms or Ammunition; Prohibited

Transactions Involving Firearms or Ammunition) applies, is found to have possessed that firearm during commission of a series of offenses, the cross reference at §2K2.1(c) is applied to the offense resulting in the greatest offense level.";

and in the caption by deleting "Note" and inserting in lieu thereof "Notes".

This amendment clarifies the operation of this guideline. **The effective date of this amendment is November 1, 1991.**

430. The Commentary to §2H1.1 captioned "Application Notes" is amended by inserting the following additional paragraph as the first paragraph of Note 1:

> "'Underlying offense,' as used in this guideline, includes any offense under federal, state, or local law other than an offense that is itself covered under Chapter Two, Part H, Subpart 1, 2, or 4. For example, in the case of a conspiracy to interfere with a person's civil rights (a violation of 18 U.S.C. § 241) that involved an aggravated assault (the use of force) to deny certain rights or benefits in furtherance of discrimination (a violation of 18 U.S.C. § 245), the underlying offense in respect to both the violation of 18 U.S.C. § 241 (to which §2H1.1 applies) and the violation of 18 U.S.C. § 245 (to which §2H1.3 applies) would be the aggravated assault.".

The Commentary to §2H1.1 captioned "Application Notes" is amended in Note 1 by inserting the following additional paragraph at the end:

> "In certain cases, the count of which the defendant is convicted may set forth conduct that constitutes more than one underlying offense (e.g., two instances of assault, or one instance of assault and one instance of arson). In such cases, determine the offense level for the underlying offense by treating each underlying offense as if contained in a separate count of conviction. To determine which of the alternative base offense levels (e.g., §2H1.1(a)(1) or (a)(2)) results in the greater offense level, apply Chapter Three, Parts A, B, C, and D to each alternative base offense level. Use whichever results in the greater offense level. Example: The defendant is convicted of one count of conspiracy to violate civil rights that included two level 12 underlying offenses (of a type not grouped together under Chapter Three, Part D). No adjustment from Chapter Three, Parts A, B, or C applies. The base offense level from §2H1.1(a)(1) is 15. The offense level for each underlying offense from §2H1.1(a)(2) is 14 (2 + 12). Under Chapter Three, Part D (Multiple Counts), the two level 14 underlying offenses result in a combined offense level of 16. This offense level is greater than the alternative base offense level of 15 under §2H1.1(a)(1). Therefore, the case is treated as if there were two counts, one for each underlying offense, with a base offense level under §2H1.1(a)(2) of 14 for each underlying offense.".

The Commentary to §2H1.1 captioned "Application Notes" is amended in the first sentence of the second paragraph of Note 1 (formerly the first paragraph) by deleting "contained in the particular guideline in Chapter Two) for any underlying criminal conduct" and inserting in lieu thereof "and cross references) from the offense guideline in Chapter Two that most closely corresponds to the underlying offense"; in the last sentence of the second paragraph of Note 1 (formerly the first paragraph) by deleting "an offense" and "that offense" and inserting in lieu thereof "arson" in each instance.

This amendment clarifies the operation of this guideline. **The effective date of this amendment is November 1, 1991.**

431. The Commentary to §2J1.7 captioned "Background" is amended by deleting the first paragraph as follows:

"An enhancement under 18 U.S.C. § 3147 may be imposed only upon application of the government; it cannot be imposed on the court's own motion. In this respect, it is similar to a separate count of conviction and, for this reason, is placed in Chapter Two of the guidelines.",

and inserting in lieu thereof:

"An enhancement under 18 U.S.C. § 3147 may be imposed only after sufficient notice to the defendant by the government or the court, and applies only in the case of a conviction for a federal offense that is committed while on release on another federal charge.".

This amendment corrects the description in the Background Commentary of the operation of the statute to which this guideline applies. **The effective date of this amendment is November 1, 1991.**

432. The Commentary to §2N2.1 captioned "Application Notes" is amended in Note 1 by inserting "or reckless" immediately before "conduct".

The Commentary to §2N2.1 captioned "Application Notes" is amended in Note 4 by deleting "anabolic steroids" and inserting in lieu thereof "human growth hormones", and by inserting at the end:

"Offenses involving anabolic steroids are covered by Chapter Two, Part D (Offenses Involving Drugs). In the case of an offense involving a substance purported to be an anabolic steroid, but not containing any active ingredient, apply §2F1.1 (Fraud and Deceit) with 'loss' measured by the amount paid, or to be paid, by the victim for such substance.".

This amendment clarifies Application Note 1 with respect to reckless conduct, conforms Application Note 4 to reflect that offenses involving anabolic steroids will be covered under §2D1.1 (Amendment 369), and clarifies the treatment of an offense involving a substance purported to be an anabolic steroid, but containing no active ingredient. **The effective date of this amendment is November 1, 1991.**

433. Section 4B1.2(2) is amended by deleting "or distribution" and inserting in lieu thereof "distribution, or dispensing"; and by deleting "or distribute" and inserting in lieu thereof "distribute, or dispense".

Section 4B1.2(3) is amended by deleting "Part A of this Chapter" and inserting in lieu thereof "§4A1.1(a), (b), or (c)".

The Commentary to §4B1.2 captioned "Application Notes" is amended in Note 2 by inserting "(i.e., expressly charged)" immediately following "set forth"; by inserting the following at the end:

"Under this section, the conduct of which the defendant was convicted is the focus of inquiry.

The term 'crime of violence' does not include the offense of unlawful possession of a firearm by a felon. Where the instant offense is the unlawful possession of a firearm by a felon, the specific offense characteristics of §2K2.1 (Unlawful Receipt, Possession, or Transportation of Firearms or Ammunition; Prohibited Transactions Involving Firearms or Ammunition) provide an increase in offense level if the defendant has one or more prior felony convictions for a crime of violence or controlled substance offense; and, if the defendant is sentenced under the provisions of 18 U.S.C. § 924(e), §4B1.4 (Armed Career Criminal) will apply.".

The Commentary to §4B1.2 captioned "Application Notes" is amended in Note 2 by inserting "(including any explosive material or destructive device)" immediately following "explosives".

The Commentary to §4B1.2 captioned "Application Notes" is amended in Note 3 by inserting the following additional sentences at the end:

> "A conviction for an offense committed at age eighteen or older is an adult conviction. A conviction for an offense committed prior to age eighteen is an adult conviction if it is classified as an adult conviction under the laws of the jurisdiction in which the defendant was convicted (e.g., a federal conviction for an offense committed prior to the defendant's eighteenth birthday is an adult conviction if the defendant was expressly proceeded against as an adult).".

This amendment clarifies that the application of §4B1.2 is determined by the offense of conviction (i.e., the conduct charged in the count of which the defendant was convicted); clarifies that the offense of unlawful possession of a weapon is not a crime of violence for the purposes of this section; clarifies the definition of a prior adult conviction; makes the definitions in §4B1.2(2) more comprehensive; and clarifies the application of §4B1.2(3) by specifying the particular provisions of Chapter Four, Part A to which this subsection refers. **The effective date of this amendment is November 1, 1991.**

434. The Commentary to §1B1.2 captioned "Application Notes" is amended in Note 1 in the second sentence of the second paragraph by deleting "as part of a plea of guilty or nolo contendere" and inserting in lieu thereof "that is set forth in a written plea agreement or made between the parties on the record during a plea proceeding"; in the second sentence of the third paragraph by deleting "the plea" and inserting in lieu thereof "a plea agreement"; and in the third sentence of the third paragraph by inserting "agreement" immediately following "plea".

This amendment clarifies the meaning of the term "stipulation" used in §1B1.2(a) and (c). **The effective date of this amendment is November 1, 1991.**

435. Section 2G2.2 is amended in the title by deleting "Advertising, or" and inserting in lieu thereof "Shipping, or Advertising Material Involving the Sexual Exploitation of a Minor;".

Section 2G2.2(a) is amended by deleting "13" and inserting in lieu thereof "15".

Section 2G2.2(b) is amended by inserting the following additional subdivision:

> "(4) If the defendant engaged in a pattern of activity involving the sexual abuse or exploitation of a minor, increase by 5 levels.".

Section 2G2.2(b)(2) is amended by inserting "by" immediately following "event".

The Commentary to §2G2.2 captioned "Statutory Provisions" is amended by deleting "2252" and inserting in lieu thereof "2252(a)(1)-(3)".

The Commentary to §2G2.2 captioned "Application Notes" is amended by redesignating Note 4 as Note 5; by inserting the following as Note 4:

> "'Pattern of activity involving the sexual abuse or exploitation of a minor,' for the purposes of subsection (b)(4), means any combination of two or more separate instances of the sexual abuse or the sexual exploitation of a minor, whether involving the same or different victims.";

and in Note 5 (formerly Note 4) by inserting "exploited or" immediately before "abused"; by deleting "is warranted" and inserting in lieu thereof "may be warranted"; and by inserting ", as well as whether the defendant has received an enhancement under subsection (b)(4) on account of such conduct" immediately after "conduct".

This amendment implements the instructions to the Commission in Section 632 of Public Law 102-141, the Treasury, Postal Service and General Government Appropriations Act of 1992. **The effective date of this amendment is November 27, 1991.**

436. Section 2G2.4 is amended in the title by deleting "Receipt or" immediately before "Possession".

Section 2G2.4(a) is amended by deleting "10" and inserting in lieu thereof "13".

Section 2G2.4(b) is amended by inserting the following additional subdivision:

"(2) If the offense involved possessing ten or more books, magazines, periodicals, films, video tapes, or other items, containing a visual depiction involving the sexual exploitation of a minor, increase by 2 levels.";

and in the caption by deleting "Characteristic" and inserting in lieu thereof "Characteristics".

Section 2G2.4(c)(2) is amended by inserting "shipping," immediately before "advertising, or"; and by deleting "Advertising, or" and inserting in lieu thereof "Shipping, or Advertising Material Involving the Sexual Exploitation of a Minor;".

The Commentary to §2G2.4 captioned "Statutory Provision" is amended by deleting "2252" and inserting in lieu thereof "2252(a)(4)".

The Commentary to §2G2.4 captioned "Application Note" is deleted in its entirety as follows:

"Application Note:

1. This guideline assumes that the offense involved a small number of prohibited items. If the defendant possessed 50 or more books, magazines, periodicals, films, video tapes, or other items containing a visual depiction involving the sexual exploitation of a minor, and subsection (c)(1) or (c)(2) does not apply, an upward departure may be warranted.".

This amendment implements the instructions to the Commission in Section 632 of Public Law 102-141, the Treasury, Postal Service and General Government Appropriations Act of 1992. **The effective date of this amendment is November 27, 1991.**

437. Section 2G3.1(a) is amended by deleting "6" and inserting in lieu thereof "10".

Section 2G3.1(c) is amended by deleting "Advertising, or" and inserting in lieu thereof "Shipping, or Advertising Material Involving the Sexual Exploitation of a Minor;"; and by deleting "Receipt or" immediately before "Possession".

The Commentary to §2G3.1 captioned "Background" is amended by deleting "11" and inserting in lieu thereof "15".

This amendment implements the instructions to the Commission in Section 632 of Public Law 102-141, the Treasury, Postal Service and General Government Appropriations Act of 1992. **The effective date of this amendment is November 27, 1991.**

438. Section 1B1.2(a) is amended by deleting "conviction by a plea of guilty or nolo contendere" and inserting in lieu thereof "a plea agreement (written or made orally on the record)".

Section 1B1.2(c) is amended by deleting "conviction by a plea of guilty or nolo contendere" and inserting in lieu thereof "plea agreement (written or made orally on the record)".

The Commentary to §1B1.2 captioned "Application Notes" is amended in Note 5 by deleting "jury's verdict" and inserting in lieu thereof "verdict or plea".

This amendment revises the language of this guideline to clarify the meaning of the term "stipulation," complementing an amendment to the commentary of this guideline effective November 1, 1991 (amendment 434). Both this amendment and amendment 434 were made in response to Braxton v. United States, 111 S.Ct. 1854 (1991). In addition, the term "jury's verdict" in the commentary of this section is deleted and replaced with the more appropriate term "verdict or plea". **The effective date of this amendment is November 1, 1992.**

439. Section 1B1.3(a) is amended by deleting:

"(1) all acts and omissions committed or aided and abetted by the defendant, or for which the defendant would be otherwise accountable, that occurred during the commission of the offense of conviction, in preparation for that offense, or in the course of attempting to avoid detection or responsibility for that offense, or that otherwise were in furtherance of that offense;

(2) solely with respect to offenses of a character for which §3D1.2(d) would require grouping of multiple counts, all such acts and omissions that were part of the same course of conduct or common scheme or plan as the offense of conviction;

(3) all harm that resulted from the acts or omissions specified in subsections (a)(1) and (a)(2) above, and all harm that was the object of such acts or omissions; and",

and inserting in lieu thereof:

"(1) (A) all acts and omissions committed, aided, abetted, counseled, commanded, induced, procured, or willfully caused by the defendant; and

(B) in the case of a jointly undertaken criminal activity (a criminal plan, scheme, endeavor, or enterprise undertaken by the defendant in concert with others, whether or not charged as a conspiracy), all reasonably foreseeable acts and omissions of others in furtherance of the jointly undertaken criminal activity,

that occurred during the commission of the offense of conviction, in preparation for that offense, or in the course of attempting to avoid detection or responsibility for that offense;

(2) solely with respect to offenses of a character for which §3D1.2(d) would require grouping of multiple counts, all acts and omissions described in subdivisions (1)(A) and (1)(B) above that were part of the same course of conduct or common scheme or plan as the offense of conviction;

(3) all harm that resulted from the acts and omissions specified in subsections (a)(1) and (a)(2) above, and all harm that was the object of such acts and omissions; and".

The Commentary to §1B1.3 captioned "Application Notes" is amended by renumbering Notes 2-7 as Notes 3-8, respectively; and by deleting Note 1 as follows:

"1. Conduct 'for which the defendant would be otherwise accountable,' as used in subsection (a)(1), includes conduct that the defendant counseled, commanded, induced, procured, or willfully caused. (Cf. 18 U.S.C. § 2.) In the case of criminal activity undertaken in concert with others, whether or not charged as a conspiracy, the conduct for which the defendant 'would be otherwise accountable' also includes conduct of others in furtherance of the execution of the jointly-undertaken criminal activity that was reasonably foreseeable by the defendant. Because a count may be broadly worded and include the conduct of many participants over a substantial period of time, the scope of the jointly-undertaken criminal activity, and hence relevant conduct, is not necessarily the same for every participant. Where it is established that the conduct was neither within the scope of the defendant's agreement, nor was reasonably foreseeable in connection with the criminal activity the defendant agreed to jointly undertake, such conduct is not included in establishing the defendant's offense level under this guideline.

In the case of solicitation, misprision, or accessory after the fact, the conduct for which the defendant 'would be otherwise accountable' includes all conduct relevant to determining the offense level for the underlying offense that was known, or reasonably should have been known, by the defendant.

Illustrations of Conduct for Which the Defendant is Accountable

a. Defendant A, one of ten off-loaders hired by Defendant B, was convicted of importation of marihuana, as a result of his assistance in off-loading a boat containing a one-ton shipment of marihuana. Regardless of the number of bales of marihuana that he actually unloaded, and notwithstanding any claim on his part that he was neither aware of, nor could reasonably foresee, that the boat contained this quantity of marihuana, Defendant A is held accountable for the entire one-ton quantity of marihuana on the boat because he aided and abetted the unloading, and hence the importation, of the entire shipment.

b. Defendant C, the getaway driver in an armed bank robbery in which $15,000 is taken and a teller is injured, is convicted of the substantive count of bank robbery. Defendant C is accountable for the money taken because he aided and abetted the taking of the money. He is accountable for the injury inflicted because he participated in concerted criminal conduct that he could reasonably foresee might result in the infliction of injury.

c. Defendant D pays Defendant E a small amount to forge an endorsement on an $800 stolen government check. Unknown to Defendant E, Defendant D then uses that check as a down payment in a scheme to fraudulently obtain $15,000 worth of merchandise. Defendant E is convicted of forging the $800 check. Defendant E is not accountable for the $15,000 because the fraudulent scheme to obtain $15,000 was beyond the scope of, and not reasonably foreseeable in connection with, the criminal activity he jointly undertook with Defendant D.

d. Defendants F and G, working together, design and execute a scheme to sell fraudulent stocks by telephone. Defendant F fraudulently obtains $20,000. Defendant G fraudulently obtains $35,000. Each is convicted of mail fraud. Each defendant is accountable for the entire amount ($55,000) because each aided and abetted the other in the fraudulent conduct. Alternatively, because Defendants F and G engaged in concerted criminal activity, each is accountable for the entire $55,000 loss because the conduct of each was in furtherance of the jointly undertaken criminal activity and was reasonably foreseeable.

e. Defendants H and I engaged in an ongoing marihuana importation conspiracy in which Defendant J was hired only to help off-load a single shipment. Defendants H, I, and J are included in a single count charging conspiracy to import marihuana. For the purposes of determining the offense level under this guideline, Defendant J is accountable for the entire single shipment of marihuana he conspired to help import and any acts or omissions in furtherance of the importation that were reasonably foreseeable. He is not accountable for prior or subsequent shipments of marihuana imported by Defendants H or I if those acts were beyond the scope of, and not reasonably foreseeable in connection with, the criminal activity he agreed to jointly undertake with Defendants H and I (i.e., the importation of the single shipment of marihuana).",

and inserting in lieu thereof:

"1. The principles and limits of sentencing accountability under this guideline are not always the same as the principles and limits of criminal liability. Under subsections (a)(1) and (a)(2), the focus is on the specific acts and omissions for which the defendant is to be held accountable in determining the applicable guideline range, rather than on whether the defendant is criminally liable for an offense as a principal, accomplice, or conspirator.

2. A 'jointly undertaken criminal activity' is a criminal plan, scheme, endeavor, or enterprise undertaken by the defendant in concert with others, whether or not charged as a conspiracy.

In the case of a jointly undertaken criminal activity, subsection (a)(1)(B) provides that a defendant is accountable for the conduct (acts and omissions) of others that was both:

(i) in furtherance of the jointly undertaken criminal activity; and

(ii) reasonably foreseeable in connection with that criminal activity.

Because a count may be worded broadly and include the conduct of many participants over a period of time, the scope of the criminal activity jointly undertaken by the defendant (the 'jointly undertaken criminal activity') is not necessarily the same as the scope of the entire conspiracy, and hence relevant conduct is not necessarily the same for every participant. In order to determine the defendant's accountability for the conduct of others under subsection (a)(1)(B), the court must first determine the scope of the criminal activity the particular defendant agreed to jointly undertake (i.e., the scope of the specific conduct and objectives embraced by the defendant's agreement). The conduct of others that was both in furtherance of, and reasonably foreseeable in connection with, the criminal activity jointly undertaken by the defendant is relevant conduct under this provision. The conduct of others that was not in furtherance of the criminal activity jointly undertaken by the defendant, or was not reasonably foreseeable in connection with that criminal activity, is not relevant conduct under this provision.

In determining the scope of the criminal activity that the particular defendant agreed to jointly undertake (i.e., the scope of the specific conduct and objectives embraced by the defendant's agreement), the court may consider any explicit agreement or implicit agreement fairly inferred from the conduct of the defendant and others.

Note that the criminal activity that the defendant agreed to jointly undertake, and the reasonably foreseeable conduct of others in furtherance of that criminal activity, are not necessarily identical. For example, two defendants agree to commit a robbery and, during the course of that robbery, the first defendant assaults and injures a victim. The second defendant is accountable for the assault and injury to the victim (even if the second defendant had not agreed to the assault and had cautioned the first defendant to be careful not to hurt anyone) because the assaultive conduct was in furtherance of the jointly undertaken criminal activity (the robbery) and was reasonably foreseeable in connection with that criminal activity (given the nature of the offense).

With respect to offenses involving contraband (including controlled substances), the defendant is accountable for all quantities of contraband with which he was directly involved and, in the case of a jointly undertaken criminal activity, all reasonably foreseeable quantities of contraband that were within the scope of the criminal activity that he jointly undertook.

The requirement of reasonable foreseeability applies only in respect to the conduct (i.e., acts and omissions) of others under subsection (a)(1)(B). It does not apply to conduct that the defendant personally undertakes, aids, abets, counsels, commands, induces, procures, or willfully causes; such conduct is addressed under subsection (a)(1)(A).

Illustrations of Conduct for Which the Defendant is Accountable

(a) Acts and omissions aided or abetted by the defendant

(1) Defendant A is one of ten persons hired by Defendant B to off-load a ship containing marihuana. The off-loading of the ship is interrupted by law enforcement officers and one ton of marihuana is seized (the amount on the ship as well as the amount off-loaded). Defendant A and the other off-loaders are arrested and convicted of importation of marihuana. Regardless of the number of bales he personally unloaded, Defendant A is accountable for the entire one-ton quantity of marihuana. Defendant A aided and abetted the off-loading of the entire shipment of marihuana by directly participating in the off-loading of that shipment (i.e., the specific objective of the criminal activity he joined was the off-loading of the entire shipment). Therefore, he is accountable for the entire shipment under subsection (a)(1)(A) without regard to the issue of reasonable foreseeability. This is conceptually similar to the case of a defendant who transports a suitcase knowing that it contains a controlled substance and, therefore, is accountable for the controlled substance in the suitcase regardless of his knowledge or lack of knowledge of the actual type or amount of that controlled substance.

In certain cases, a defendant may be accountable for particular conduct under more than one subsection of this guideline. As noted in the preceding paragraph, Defendant A is accountable for the entire one-ton shipment of marihuana under subsection (a)(1)(A). Defendant A also is accountable for the entire one-ton shipment of marihuana on the basis of subsection (a)(1)(B)(applying to a jointly undertaken criminal activity). Defendant A engaged in a jointly undertaken criminal activity (the scope of which was the importation of the shipment of marihuana). A finding that the one-ton quantity of marihuana was reasonably foreseeable is warranted from the nature of the undertaking itself (the importation of marihuana by ship typically involves very large quantities of marihuana). The specific circumstances of the case (the defendant was one of ten persons off-loading the marihuana in bales) also support this finding. In an actual case, of course, if a defendant's accountability for particular conduct is established under one provision of this guideline, it is not necessary to review alternative provisions under which such accountability might be established.

(b) Acts and omissions aided or abetted by the defendant; requirement that the conduct of others be in furtherance of the jointly undertaken criminal activity and reasonably foreseeable

(1) Defendant C is the getaway driver in an armed bank robbery in which $15,000 is taken and a teller is assaulted and injured. Defendant C is accountable for the money taken under subsection (a)(1)(A) because he aided and abetted the act of taking the money (the taking of money was the specific objective of the offense he joined). Defendant C is accountable for the injury to the teller under subsection (a)(1)(B) because the assault on the teller was in furtherance of the jointly undertaken criminal activity (the robbery) and was reasonably foreseeable in connection with that criminal activity (given the nature of the offense).

As noted earlier, a defendant may be accountable for particular conduct under more than one subsection. In this example, Defendant C also is accountable for the money taken on the basis of subsection (a)(1)(B) because the taking of money was in furtherance of the jointly undertaken criminal activity (the robbery) and was reasonably foreseeable (as noted, the taking of money was the specific objective of the jointly undertaken criminal activity).

(c) Requirement that the conduct of others be in furtherance of the jointly undertaken criminal activity and reasonably foreseeable; scope of the criminal activity

(1) Defendant D pays Defendant E a small amount to forge an endorsement on an $800 stolen government check. Unknown to Defendant E, Defendant D then uses that check as a down payment in a scheme to fraudulently obtain $15,000 worth of merchandise. Defendant E is convicted of forging the $800 check and is accountable for the forgery of this check under subsection (a)(1)(A). Defendant E is not accountable for the $15,000 because the fraudulent scheme to obtain $15,000 was not in furtherance of the criminal activity he jointly undertook with Defendant D (i.e., the forgery of the $800 check).

(2) Defendants F and G, working together, design and execute a scheme to sell fraudulent stocks by telephone. Defendant F fraudulently obtains $20,000. Defendant G fraudulently obtains $35,000. Each is convicted of mail fraud. Defendants F and G each are accountable for the entire amount ($55,000). Each defendant is accountable for the amount he personally obtained under subsection (a)(1)(A). Each defendant is accountable for the amount obtained by his accomplice under subsection (a)(1)(B) because the conduct of each was in furtherance of

the jointly undertaken criminal activity and was reasonably foreseeable in connection with that criminal activity.

(3) Defendants H and I engaged in an ongoing marihuana importation conspiracy in which Defendant J was hired only to help off-load a single shipment. Defendants H, I, and J are included in a single count charging conspiracy to import marihuana. Defendant J is accountable for the entire single shipment of marihuana he helped import under subsection (a)(1)(A) and any acts and omissions in furtherance of the importation of that shipment that were reasonably foreseeable (see the discussion in example (a)(1) above). He is not accountable for prior or subsequent shipments of marihuana imported by Defendants H or I because those acts were not in furtherance of his jointly undertaken criminal activity (the importation of the single shipment of marihuana).

(4) Defendant K is a wholesale distributor of child pornography. Defendant L is a retail-level dealer who purchases child pornography from Defendant K and resells it, but otherwise operates independently of Defendant K. Similarly, Defendant M is a retail-level dealer who purchases child pornography from Defendant K and resells it, but otherwise operates independently of Defendant K. Defendants L and M are aware of each other's criminal activity but operate independently. Defendant N is Defendant K's assistant who recruits customers for Defendant K and frequently supervises the deliveries to Defendant K's customers. Each defendant is convicted of a count charging conspiracy to distribute child pornography. Defendant K is accountable under subsection (a)(1)(A) for the entire quantity of child pornography sold to Defendants L and M. Defendant N also is accountable for the entire quantity sold to those defendants under subsection (a)(1)(B) because the entire quantity was within the scope of his jointly undertaken criminal activity and reasonably foreseeable. Defendant L is accountable under subsection (a)(1)(A) only for the quantity of child pornography that he purchased from Defendant K because the scope of his jointly undertaken criminal activity is limited to that amount. For the same reason, Defendant M is accountable under subsection (a)(1)(A) only for the quantity of child pornography that he purchased from Defendant K.

(5) Defendant O knows about her boyfriend's ongoing drug-trafficking activity, but agrees to participate on only one occasion by making a delivery for him at his request when he was ill. Defendant O is accountable under subsection (a)(1)(A) for the drug quantity involved on that one occasion. Defendant O is not accountable for the other drug sales made by her boyfriend because those sales were not in furtherance of her jointly undertaken criminal activity (i.e., the one delivery).

(6) Defendant P is a street-level drug dealer who knows of other street-level drug dealers in the same geographic area who sell the same type of drug as he sells. Defendant P and the other dealers share a common source of supply, but otherwise operate independently. Defendant P is not accountable for the quantities of drugs sold by the other street-level drug dealers

because he is not engaged in a jointly undertaken criminal activity with them. In contrast, Defendant Q, another street-level drug dealer, pools his resources and profits with four other street-level drug dealers. Defendant Q is engaged in a jointly undertaken criminal activity and, therefore, he is accountable under subsection (a)(1)(B) for the quantities of drugs sold by the four other dealers during the course of his joint undertaking with them because those sales were in furtherance of the jointly undertaken criminal activity and reasonably foreseeable in connection with that criminal activity.

(7) Defendant R recruits Defendant S to distribute 500 grams of cocaine. Defendant S knows that Defendant R is the prime figure in a conspiracy involved in importing much larger quantities of cocaine. As long as Defendant S's agreement and conduct is limited to the distribution of the 500 grams, Defendant S is accountable only for that 500 gram amount (under subsection (a)(1)(A)), rather than the much larger quantity imported by Defendant R.

(8) Defendants T, U, V, and W are hired by a supplier to backpack a quantity of marihuana across the border from Mexico into the United States. Defendants T, U, V, and W receive their individual shipments from the supplier at the same time and coordinate their importation efforts by walking across the border together for mutual assistance and protection. Each defendant is accountable for the aggregate quantity of marihuana transported by the four defendants. The four defendants engaged in a jointly undertaken criminal activity, the object of which was the importation of the four backpacks containing marihuana (subsection (a)(1)(B)), and aided and abetted each other's actions (subsection (a)(1)(A)) in carrying out the jointly undertaken criminal activity. In contrast, if Defendants T, U, V, and W were hired individually, transported their individual shipments at different times, and otherwise operated independently, each defendant would be accountable only for the quantity of marihuana he personally transported (subsection (a)(1)(A)). As this example illustrates, in cases involving contraband (including controlled substances), the scope of the jointly undertaken criminal activity (and thus the accountability of the defendant for the contraband that was the object of that jointly undertaken activity) may depend upon whether, in the particular circumstances, the nature of the offense is more appropriately viewed as one jointly undertaken criminal activity or as a number of separate criminal activities.".

The Commentary to §1B1.3 captioned "Application Notes" is amended in Note 3 (formerly Note 2) by deleting the first sentence as follows:

"'Such acts and omissions that were part of the same course of conduct or common scheme or plan as the offense of conviction,' as used in subsection (a)(2), refers to acts and omissions committed or aided and abetted by the defendant, or for which the defendant would be otherwise accountable, that were part of the same course of conduct or common scheme or plan as the offense of conviction.".

The Commentary to §1B1.3 captioned "Application Notes" is amended in Note 6 (formerly Note 5) in the first paragraph by deleting:

"For example, in §2K1.5, subsection (b)(1) applies 'If the defendant is convicted under 49 U.S.C. § 1472(l)(2).'",

and inserting in lieu thereof:

"For example, in §2S1.1, subsection (a)(1) applies if the defendant 'is convicted under 18 U.S.C. § 1956(a)(1)(A), (a)(2)(A), or (a)(3)(A).'";

and in the second paragraph by deleting:

"For example, §2K1.5(b)(1) (which is applicable only if the defendant is convicted under 49 U.S.C. § 1472(l)(2)) would be applied in determining the offense level under §2X3.1 (Accessory After the Fact) where the defendant was convicted of accessory after the fact to a violation of 49 U.S.C. § 1472(l)(2).",

and inserting in lieu thereof:

"For example, §2S1.1(a)(1) (which is applicable only if the defendant is convicted under 18 U.S.C. § 1956(a)(1)(A), (a)(2)(A), or (a)(3)(A)) would be applied in determining the offense level under §2X3.1 (Accessory After the Fact) where the defendant was convicted of accessory after the fact to a violation of 18 U.S.C. § 1956(a)(1)(A), (a)(2)(A), or (a)(3)(A).".

The Commentary to §1B1.3 captioned "Application Notes" is amended by inserting the following additional notes:

"9. 'Common scheme or plan' and 'same course of conduct' are two closely-related concepts.

(A) Common scheme or plan. For two or more offenses to constitute part of a common scheme or plan, they must be substantially connected to each other by at least one common factor, such as common victims, common accomplices, common purpose, or similar modus operandi. For example, the conduct of five defendants who together defrauded a group of investors by computer manipulations that unlawfully transferred funds over an eighteen-month period would qualify as a common scheme or plan on the basis of any of the above listed factors; i.e., the commonality of victims (the same investors were defrauded on an ongoing basis), commonality of offenders (the conduct constituted an ongoing conspiracy), commonality of purpose (to defraud the group of investors), or similarity of modus operandi (the same or similar computer manipulations were used to execute the scheme).

(B) Same course of conduct. Offenses that do not qualify as part of a common scheme or plan may nonetheless qualify as part of the same course of conduct if they are sufficiently connected or related to each other as to warrant the conclusion that they are part of a single episode, spree, or ongoing series of offenses. Factors that are appropriate to the determination of whether offenses are sufficiently connected or related to each other to be considered as part of the same course of conduct include the degree of similarity of the offenses and the time interval between the offenses. The nature of the offenses may also be a relevant consideration (e.g., a defendant's failure to file tax returns in three consecutive years appropriately would be considered as part of the same course of conduct because such returns are only required at yearly intervals).

10. In the case of solicitation, misprision, or accessory after the fact, the conduct for which the defendant is accountable includes all conduct relevant to determining the offense level for the underlying offense that was known, or reasonably should have been known, by the defendant.".

This amendment clarifies and more fully illustrates the operation of this guideline. Material is moved from the commentary to the guideline itself and rephrased for greater clarity, the discussion of the application of this provision in the commentary is expanded, and additional examples are inserted. In addition, this amendment provides definitions of the terms "same course of conduct" and "common scheme or plan." Finally, this amendment conforms an example in Application Note 6 of the Commentary to a revision of a Chapter Two offense guideline. **The effective date of this amendment is November 1, 1992.**

440. Section 1B1.5 is amended by deleting:

"Unless otherwise expressly indicated, a reference to another guideline, or an instruction to apply another guideline, refers to the entire guideline, i.e., the base offense level plus all applicable specific offense characteristics and cross references.",

and inserting in lieu thereof:

"(a) A cross reference (an instruction to apply another offense guideline) refers to the entire offense guideline (i.e., the base offense level, specific offense characteristics, cross references, and special instructions).

(b) (1) An instruction to use the offense level from another offense guideline refers to the offense level from the entire offense guideline (i.e., the base offense level, specific offense characteristics, cross references, and special instructions), except as provided in subdivision (2) below.

(2) An instruction to use a particular subsection or table from another offense guideline refers only to the particular subsection or table referenced, and not to the entire offense guideline.

(c) If the offense level is determined by a reference to another guideline under subsection (a) or (b)(1) above, the adjustments in Chapter Three (Adjustments) also are determined in respect to the referenced offense guideline, except as otherwise expressly provided.

(d) A reference to another guideline under subsection (a) or (b)(1) above may direct that it be applied only if it results in the greater offense level. In such case, the greater offense level means the greater final offense level (i.e., the greater offense level taking into account both the Chapter Two offense level and any applicable Chapter Three adjustments).".

The Commentary to §1B1.5 captioned "Application Notes" is amended in Note 1 by deleting:

"are to be construed to incorporate the specific offense characteristics and cross references",

and inserting in lieu thereof:

"incorporate the specific offense characteristics, cross references, and special instructions".

The Commentary to §1B1.5 captioned "Application Notes" is amended by deleting Note 2 as follows:

"2. A reference may require that the offense level be determined under another offense guideline. In such case, the adjustments in Chapter Three, Parts A (Victim-Related Adjustments), B (Role in the Offense), and E (Acceptance of Responsibility) are also to be determined in respect to that other offense guideline. For example, a defendant convicted of possession of a firearm by a felon, to which §2K2.1 (Unlawful Receipt, Possession, or Transportation of Firearms or Ammunition; Prohibited Transactions Involving Firearms or Ammunition) applies, is found to have used that firearm in the commission of a robbery. The cross reference at §2K2.1(c) directs that the robbery offense guideline be used. The adjustments in Chapter Three, Parts A, B and E are to be applied as if the offense of conviction had directly referenced the robbery guideline.";

and by renumbering Notes 3 and 4 as Notes 2 and 3, respectively.

This amendment clarifies the operation of this guideline and moves an instruction currently contained in the commentary into the guideline itself. **The effective date of this amendment is November 1, 1992.**

441. Section 1B1.8(b) is amended in subdivision (3) by deleting "or" immediately following the semicolon; in subdivision (4) by deleting the period at the end and inserting in lieu thereof "; or"; and by inserting the following additional subdivision:

"(5) in determining whether, or to what extent, a downward departure from the guidelines is warranted pursuant to a government motion under §5K1.1 (Substantial Assistance to Authorities).".

The Commentary to §1B1.8 captioned "Application Notes" is amended in Note 1 by deleting the third sentence as follows:

"Although this guideline, consistent with the general structure of these guidelines, affects only the determination of the guideline range, the policy of the Commission is that where a defendant as a result of a cooperation agreement with the government to assist in the investigation or prosecution of other offenders reveals information that implicates him in unlawful conduct not already known to the government, such defendant should not be subject to an increased sentence by virtue of that cooperation where the government agreed that the information revealed would not be used for such purpose.",

and inserting in lieu thereof:

"Although the guideline itself affects only the determination of the guideline range, the policy of the Commission, as a corollary, is that information prohibited from being used to determine the applicable guideline range shall not be used to increase the defendant's sentence above the applicable guideline range by upward departure. In contrast, subsection (b)(5) provides that consideration of such information is appropriate in determining whether, and to what extent, a downward departure is warranted pursuant to a government motion under §5K1.1 (Substantial Assistance to Authorities); e.g., a court may refuse to depart below the applicable guideline range on the basis of such information.".

The Commentary to §1B1.8 captioned "Application Notes" is amended in Note 3 in the second sentence by deleting:

"is governed by the provisions of Rule 11 of the Federal Rules of Criminal Procedure and Rule 410",

and inserting in lieu thereof:

"in a sentencing proceeding is restricted by Rule 11(e)(6) (Inadmissibility of Pleas, Plea Discussions, and Related Statements) of the Federal Rules of Criminal Procedure and Rule 410 (Inadmissibility of Pleas, Plea Discussions, and Related Statements)".

The Commentary to §1B1.8 captioned "Application Notes" is amended in Note 5 in the second sentence by deleting "repeats" and inserting in lieu thereof "provides".

This amendment clarifies the operation of this guideline. Information protected by this guideline may not be used to determine the applicable guideline range. An upward departure on the basis of such information would be contrary to the Commission's policy (and, consequently, would be appealable under 18 U.S.C. § 3742(a)(2) and (3). See Williams v. United States, 112 S.Ct. 1112 (1992)). In contrast, the use of information covered by this guideline is appropriate in considering whether, and to what extent, a downward departure under §5K1.1 (Substantial Assistance to Authorities) is appropriate. In addition, this amendment makes minor editorial improvements. **The effective date of this amendment is November 1, 1992.**

442. Chapter One, Part B, is amended by inserting an additional policy statement with accompanying commentary as §1B1.11 (Use of Guidelines Manual in Effect on Date of Sentencing (Policy Statement)).

This amendment inserts a policy statement addressing the use of the Guidelines Manual when the Guidelines Manual has been amended between the date the offense was committed and the date of sentencing. **The effective date of this amendment is November 1, 1992.**

443. Section 2A2.4(c)(1) is amended by deleting "defendant is convicted under 18 U.S.C. § 111 and the" immediately before "conduct".

Section 2K1.5(b)(1) is amended by deleting:

> "defendant is convicted under 49 U.S.C. § 1472(l)(2) (i.e., the defendant acted willfully and without regard for the safety of human life, or with reckless disregard for the safety of human life)",

and inserting in lieu thereof:

> "offense was committed willfully and without regard for the safety of human life, or with reckless disregard for the safety of human life".

This amendment deletes the requirement of a conviction under a specific statute for these specific offense characteristics to apply and, consistent with the overall structure of the guidelines, provides for their application on the basis of the underlying conduct. **The effective date of this amendment is November 1, 1992.**

444. Section 2A3.1 is amended in the title by deleting "or Assault with the Intent" immediately following "Attempt".

Section 2A3.1(b)(3) is amended by deleting:

> "in the custody, care, or supervisory control of the defendant, was a corrections employee, or",

and by inserting in lieu thereof:

> "(A) in the custody, care, or supervisory control of the defendant; or (B)".

Section 2A3.1 is amended by inserting the following additional subsection:

"(c) Special Instruction

(1) If the offense occurred in a correctional facility and the victim was a corrections employee, the offense shall be deemed to have an official victim for purposes of subsection (a) of §3A1.2 (Official Victim).".

The Commentary to §2A3.1 captioned "Application Notes" is amended by renumbering Note 3 as Note 4; and by inserting the following additional note:

"3. Subsection (b)(3), as it pertains to a victim in the custody, care, or supervisory control of the defendant, is intended to have broad application and is to be applied whenever the victim is entrusted to the defendant, whether temporarily or permanently. For example, teachers, day care providers, baby-sitters, or other temporary caretakers are among those who would be subject to this enhancement. In determining whether to apply this enhancement, the court should look to the actual relationship that existed between the defendant and the victim and not simply to the legal status of the defendant-victim relationship.".

Section 2A3.2 is amended by inserting the following additional subsection:

"(c) Cross Reference

(1) If the offense involved criminal sexual abuse or attempt to commit criminal sexual abuse (as defined in 18 U.S.C. § 2241 or § 2242), apply §2A3.1 (Criminal Sexual Abuse; Attempt to Commit Criminal Sexual Abuse).".

The Commentary to §2A3.2 captioned "Application Notes" is amended by renumbering Note 2 as Note 3; and by inserting the following as Note 2:

"2. Subsection (b)(1) is intended to have broad application and is to be applied whenever the victim is entrusted to the defendant, whether temporarily or permanently. For example, teachers, day care providers, baby-sitters, or other temporary caretakers are among those who would be subject to this enhancement. In determining whether to apply this enhancement, the court should look to the actual relationship that existed between the defendant and the victim and not simply to the legal status of the defendant-victim relationship.".

Section 2A3.4 is amended by inserting the following additional subsection:

"(c) Cross References

(1) If the offense involved criminal sexual abuse or attempt to commit criminal sexual abuse (as defined in 18 U.S.C. § 2241 or § 2242), apply §2A3.1 (Criminal Sexual Abuse; Attempt to Commit Criminal Sexual Abuse).

(2) If the offense involved criminal sexual abuse of a minor or attempt to commit criminal sexual abuse of a minor (as defined in 18 U.S.C. § 2243(a)), apply §2A3.2 (Criminal Sexual Abuse of a Minor or Attempt to Commit Such Acts), if the resulting offense level is greater than that determined above.".

The Commentary to §2A3.4 captioned "Application Notes" is amended by renumbering Note 3 as Note 4; and by inserting the following as Note 3:

"3. Subsection (b)(3) is intended to have broad application and is to be applied whenever the victim is entrusted to the defendant, whether temporarily or permanently. For example, teachers, day care providers, baby-sitters, or other temporary caretakers are among those who would be subject to this enhancement. In determining whether to apply this enhancement, the court should look to the actual relationship that existed between the defendant and the victim and not simply to the legal status of the defendant-victim relationship.".

Section 2G1.2(c)(2) is amended by deleting "or Assault with the Intent" immediately before "to Commit Criminal Sexual Abuse".

The Commentary to §2X1.1 captioned "Application Notes" is amended in Note 1 in the second paragraph by deleting "or Assault with the Intent" immediately before "to Commit Criminal Sexual Abuse".

This amendment cross references §2A3.2 to §2A3.1, and §2A3.4 to §§2A3.1 and 2A3.2. A review of cases sentenced under these guidelines indicated that a significant proportion of cases sentenced under §2A3.2 and §2A3.4 clearly involved conduct that would more appropriately be covered under an offense guideline applicable to more serious sexual abuse cases. The addition of these cross references is designed to address this issue. In addition, this amendment removes an anomaly between §2A3.1(b)(3) and §3A1.2(a), and adds application notes to clarify the scope of §§2A3.1(b)(3), 2A3.2(b)(1), and 2A3.4(b)(3), using language derived from application notes pertaining to similar specific offense characteristics in Chapter Two, Part G. **The effective date of this amendment is November 1, 1992.**

445. The Commentary to §2A4.1 captioned "Application Notes" is amended by inserting the following additional note:

"5. In the case of a conspiracy, attempt, or solicitation to kidnap, §2X1.1 (Attempt, Solicitation, or Conspiracy) requires that the court apply any adjustment that can be determined with reasonable certainty. Therefore, for example, if an offense involved conspiracy to kidnap for the purpose of committing murder, subsection (b)(7) would reference first degree murder (resulting in an offense level of 43, subject to a possible 3-level reduction under §2X1.1(b)). Similarly, for example, if an offense involved a kidnapping during which a participant attempted to murder the victim under circumstances that would have constituted first degree murder had death occurred, the offense referenced under subsection (b)(7) would be the offense of first degree murder.".

This amendment clarifies the operation of this guideline. **The effective date of this amendment is November 1, 1992.**

446. Section 2D1.1(b)(2) is amended by deleting "is convicted of violating 21 U.S.C. § 960(a)" and inserting in lieu thereof "unlawfully imported or exported a controlled substance"; and by inserting "or export" immediately following "to import".

The Commentary to §2D1.1 captioned "Application Notes" is amended in Note 10 in the "Drug Equivalency Tables" in the subdivision captioned "Cocaine and Other Schedule I and II Stimulants" by inserting the following additional entries at the end:

"1 gm of Aminorex =	100 gm of marihuana
1 gm of Methcathinone =	380 gm of marihuana
1 gm of N-N-Dimethylamphetamine =	40 gm of marihuana";

and in the subdivision captioned "LSD, PCP, and Other Schedule I and II Hallucinogens" by inserting the following additional entry as the last entry:

"1 gm of Phenylcyclohexamine (PCE) = 5.79 kg of marihuana".

The Commentary to §2D1.1 captioned "Application Notes" is amended in Note 10 in the "Drug Equivalency Tables" by inserting an asterisk immediately following each of the following subdivision captions: "Schedule I or II Opiates", "Cocaine and Other Schedule I or II Stimulants (and their immediate precursors)", and "LSD, PCP, and Other Schedule I and II Hallucinogens (and their immediate precursors)"; and by inserting the following additional sentence at the end of each of the above noted subdivisions:

"**Provided*, that the minimum offense level from the Drug Quantity Table for any of these controlled substances individually, or in combination with another controlled substance, is level 12.".

The Commentary to §2D1.1 captioned "Application Notes" is amended by inserting the following additional note:

"15. Certain pharmaceutical preparations are classified as Schedule III, IV, or V controlled substances by the Drug Enforcement Administration under 21 C.F.R. § 1308.13-15 even though they contain a small amount of a Schedule I or II controlled substance. For example, Tylenol 3 is classified as a Schedule III controlled substance even though it contains a small amount of codeine, a Schedule II opiate. For the purposes of the guidelines, the classification of the controlled substance under 21 C.F.R. § 1308.13-15 is the appropriate classification.".

The Commentary to §2D1.1 captioned "Background" is amended in the fifth paragraph by deleting "mandated by" and inserting in lieu thereof "derived from".

This amendment deletes the requirement of a conviction under a specific statute for the specific offense characteristic in subsection (b)(2) to apply and, consistent with the overall structure of the guidelines, provides for the application of this specific offense characteristic on the basis of the underlying conduct. In addition, this amendment adds equivalencies for four controlled substances to make the Drug Equivalency Tables more comprehensive, adds notes to the Drug Equivalency Tables to make clear the interaction between the minimum offense level for certain types of controlled substances in the Drug Quantity Table and the instructions for determining a combined offense level in a case with multiple controlled substances, and clarifies the treatment of certain pharmaceutical preparations that are classified as Schedule III, IV, or V substances under 21 C.F.R. § 1308.13-15. **The effective date of this amendment is November 1, 1992.**

447. Sections 2D1.1, 2D1.2, 2D1.5, 2D1.6, 2D1.7, 2D1.8, 2D1.9, 2D1.10, 2D1.11, 2D1.12, 2D1.13, 2D2.1, 2D2.2, 2D3.1, 2D3.2, 2D3.3, 2D3.4, and 2D3.5 are amended in their titles by inserting at the end thereof in each instance "; Attempt or Conspiracy".

Section 2D1.4, including accompanying commentary, is deleted as follows:

"§2D1.4. Attempts and Conspiracies

(a) Base Offense Level: If a defendant is convicted of a conspiracy or an attempt to commit any offense involving a controlled substance, the offense level shall be the same as if the object of the conspiracy or attempt had been completed.

Commentary

Statutory Provisions: 21 U.S.C. §§ 846, 963. For additional statutory provision(s), see Appendix A (Statutory Index).

Application Notes:

1. If the defendant is convicted of a conspiracy that includes transactions in controlled substances in addition to those that are the subject of substantive counts of conviction, each conspiracy transaction shall be included with those of the substantive counts of conviction to determine scale. If the defendant is convicted of an offense involving negotiation to traffic in a controlled substance, the weight under negotiation in an uncompleted distribution shall be used to calculate the applicable amount. However, where the court finds that the defendant did not intend to produce and was not reasonably capable of producing the negotiated amount, the court shall exclude from the guideline calculation the amount that it finds the defendant did not intend to produce and was not reasonably capable of producing. If the defendant is convicted of conspiracy, see Application Note 1 to §1B1.3 (Relevant Conduct).

2. Where there is no drug seizure or the amount seized does not reflect the scale of the offense, the sentencing judge shall approximate the quantity of the controlled substance. In making this determination, the judge may consider, for example, the price generally obtained for the controlled substance, financial or other records, similar transactions in controlled substances by the defendant, and the size or capability of any laboratory involved.

3. See Commentary to §2D1.1 regarding weapon possession.".

The Commentary to §2D1.1 captioned "Application Notes" is amended in Note 3 by deleting "reference §2D1.1, i.e., §§2D1.2, 2D1.4, 2D1.5, 2D1.6, 2D1.7(b)(1)" and inserting in lieu thereof "are referenced to §2D1.1; see §§2D1.2(a)(1) and (2), 2D1.5(a)(1), 2D1.6, 2D1.7(b)(1), 2D1.8, 2D1.11(c)(1), 2D1.12(b)(1), and 2D2.1(b)(1)".

The Commentary to §2D1.1 captioned "Application Notes" is amended in Note 12 by deleting:

"If the amount seized does not reflect the scale of the offense, see Application Note 2 of the Commentary to §2D1.4. If the offense involved negotiation to traffic in a controlled substance, see Application Note 1 of the Commentary to §2D1.4.",

and inserting in lieu thereof:

"Where there is no drug seizure or the amount seized does not reflect the scale of the offense, the court shall approximate the quantity of the controlled substance. In making this determination, the court may consider, for example, the price generally obtained for the controlled substance, financial or other records, similar transactions in controlled substances by the defendant, and the size or capability of any laboratory involved.

If the offense involved both a substantive drug offense and an attempt or conspiracy (e.g., sale of five grams of heroin and an attempt to sell an additional ten grams of heroin), the total quantity involved shall be aggregated to determine the scale of the offense.

In an offense involving negotiation to traffic in a controlled substance, the weight under negotiation in an uncompleted distribution shall be used to calculate the applicable amount. However, where the court finds that the defendant did not intend to produce and was not reasonably capable of producing the negotiated amount, the court shall exclude from the guideline calculation the amount that it finds the defendant did not intend to produce and was not reasonably capable of producing.".

The Commentary to §2D1.1 captioned "Background" is amended in the fifth sentence of the fourth paragraph by deleting "(see §2D1.4)" immediately following "object of the attempt".

The Commentary to §2D1.6 captioned "Application Note" is amended in the first sentence of Note 1 by deleting "Commentary to §2D1.1, and Application Notes 1 and 2 of the Commentary to §2D1.4," and inserting in lieu thereof "Commentary to §2D1.1".

Section 2D1.11(c) is amended by deleting ", or §2D1.4 (Attempts and Conspiracies), as appropriate," immediately before "if the resulting".

Section 2D1.12(b) is amended by deleting ", or §2D1.4 (Attempts and Conspiracies), as appropriate," immediately before "if the resulting".

The Commentary to §2X1.1 captioned "Application Notes" is amended in Note 1 by deleting "§2D1.4 (Attempts and Conspiracies)" wherever it appears and inserting in lieu thereof in each instance:

"§2D1.1 (Unlawful Manufacturing, Importing, Exporting, or Trafficking, Including Possession with Intent to Commit These Offenses; Attempt or Conspiracy); §2D1.2 (Drug Offenses Occurring Near Protected Locations or Involving Underage or Pregnant Individuals; Attempt or Conspiracy); §2D1.5 (Continuing Criminal Enterprise; Attempt or Conspiracy); §2D1.6 (Use of Communication Facility in Committing Drug Offense; Attempt or Conspiracy); §2D1.7 (Unlawful Sale or Transportation of Drug Paraphernalia; Attempt or Conspiracy); §2D1.8 (Renting or Managing a Drug Establishment; Attempt or Conspiracy); §2D1.9 (Placing or Maintaining Dangerous Devices on Federal Property to Protect the Unlawful Production of Controlled Substances; Attempt or Conspiracy); §2D1.10 (Endangering Human Life While Illegally Manufacturing a Controlled Substance; Attempt or Conspiracy); §2D1.11 (Unlawfully Distributing, Importing, Exporting or Possessing a Listed Chemical; Attempt or Conspiracy); §2D1.12 (Unlawful Possession, Manufacture, Distribution, or Importation of Prohibited Flask or Equipment; Attempt or Conspiracy); §2D1.13 (Structuring Chemical Transactions or Creating a Chemical Mixture to Evade Reporting or Recordkeeping Requirements; Presenting False or Fraudulent Identification to Obtain a Listed Chemical; Attempt or Conspiracy); §2D2.1 (Unlawful Possession; Attempt or Conspiracy); §2D2.2 (Acquiring a Controlled Substance by Forgery, Fraud, Deception, or Subterfuge; Attempt or Conspiracy); §2D3.1 (Illegal Use of Registration Number to Manufacture, Distribute, Acquire, or Dispense a Controlled Substance; Attempt or Conspiracy); §2D3.2 (Manufacture of Controlled Substance in Excess of or Unauthorized by Registration Quota; Attempt or Conspiracy); §2D3.3 (Illegal Use of Registration Number to Distribute or Dispense a Controlled Substance to Another Registrant or Authorized Person; Attempt or Conspiracy); §2D3.4 (Illegal Transfer or Transshipment of a Controlled Substance; Attempt or Conspiracy); and §2D3.5 (Violation of Recordkeeping or Reporting Requirements for Listed Chemicals and Certain Machines; Attempt or Conspiracy)".

This amendment clarifies and simplifies the guideline provisions dealing with attempts and conspiracies in drug cases and conforms the structure of these provisions to that of other offense guidelines that specifically address attempts and conspiracies (i.e., offense guidelines referenced by §2X1.1(c)). **The effective date of this amendment is November 1, 1992.**

448. Section 2D1.8 is amended by deleting subsections (a) and (b) as follows:

"(a) Base Offense Level: 16

(b) Specific Offense Characteristic

(1) If a firearm or other dangerous weapon was possessed, increase by 2 levels.",

and inserting in lieu thereof:

"(a) Base Offense Level:

(1) The offense level from §2D1.1 applicable to the underlying controlled substance offense, except as provided below.

(2) If the defendant had no participation in the underlying controlled substance offense other than allowing use of the premises, the offense level shall be 4 levels less than the offense level from §2D1.1 applicable to the underlying controlled substance offense, but not greater than level 16.

(b) Special Instruction

(1) If the offense level is determined under subsection (a)(2), do not apply an adjustment under §3B1.2 (Mitigating Role).".

The Commentary to §2D1.8 captioned "Application Note" is amended by deleting Note 1 as follows:

"1. Definitions of "firearm" and "dangerous weapon" are found in the Commentary to §1B1.1 (Application Instructions).",

and inserting in lieu thereof:

"1. Subsection (a)(2) does not apply unless the defendant had no participation in the underlying controlled substance offense other than allowing use of the premises. For example, subsection (a)(2) would not apply to a defendant who possessed a dangerous weapon in connection with the offense, a defendant who guarded the cache of controlled substances, a defendant who arranged for the use of the premises for the purpose of facilitating a drug transaction, a defendant who allowed the use of more than one premises, a defendant who made telephone calls to facilitate the underlying controlled substance offense, or a defendant who otherwise assisted in the commission of the underlying controlled substance offense. Furthermore, subsection (a)(2) does not apply unless the defendant initially leased, rented, purchased, or otherwise acquired a possessory interest in the premises for a legitimate purpose. Finally, subsection (a)(2) does not apply if the defendant had previously allowed any premises to be used as a drug establishment without regard to whether such prior misconduct resulted in a conviction.".

This amendment is designed to reduce unwarranted disparity by requiring consideration in the guideline of the scale of the underlying controlled substance offense. The amendment parallels an amendment to §2D1.6 made in 1990 (amendment 320). The effective date of this amendment is November 1, 1992.

449. The Commentary to §2E1.4 captioned "Background" is amended by deleting:

"The statute does not require that a murder covered by this section has been committed. The maximum term of imprisonment authorized by statute ranges from five years to life imprisonment.",

and inserting in lieu thereof:

> "This guideline and the statute to which it applies do not require that a murder actually have been committed.".

This amendment makes editorial improvements, and deletes a reference to the length of the maximum term of imprisonment authorized by statute for the offense covered by this section that is no longer accurate. The effective date of this amendment is November 1, 1992.

450. Section 2L1.1(b)(2) is amended by deleting:

> "If the defendant previously has been convicted of smuggling, transporting, or harboring an unlawful alien, or a related offense, increase by 2 levels.",

and inserting in lieu thereof:

> "If the offense involved the smuggling, transporting, or harboring of six or more unlawful aliens, increase as follows:

	Number of Unlawful Aliens Smuggled, Transported, or Harbored	Increase in Level
(A)	6-24	add 2
(B)	25-99	add 4
(C)	100 or more	add 6.".

The Commentary to §2L1.1 captioned "Application Notes" is amended in Note 1 by inserting the following additional sentence at the end:

> "The 'number of unlawful aliens smuggled, transported, or harbored' does not include the defendant.".

The Commentary to §2L1.1 captioned "Application Notes" is amended by deleting Notes 2, 3, and 4 as follows:

> "2. 'Convicted of smuggling, transporting, or harboring an unlawful alien, or a related offense' includes any conviction for smuggling, transporting, or harboring an unlawful alien, and any conviction for aiding and abetting, conspiring or attempting to commit such offense.
>
> 3. If the defendant was convicted under 8 U.S.C. § 1328, apply the applicable guideline from Part G (see Statutory Index) rather than this guideline.
>
> 4. The adjustment under §2L1.1(b)(2) for a previous conviction is in addition to any points added to the criminal history score for such conviction in Chapter Four, Part A (Criminal History). This adjustment is to be applied only if the previous conviction occurred prior to the last overt act of the instant offense.";

and by renumbering Notes 5, 6, 7, 8 and 9, as Notes 2, 3, 4, 5, and 6, respectively.

The Commentary to §2L1.1 captioned "Application Notes" is amended in Note 4 (formerly Note 7) by inserting "drug trafficking, or other serious criminal behavior," immediately following "subversive activity,".

The Commentary to §2L1.1 captioned "Application Notes" is amended by deleting the text of Note 5 (formerly Note 8) as follows:

"The Commission has not considered offenses involving large numbers of aliens or dangerous or inhumane treatment. An upward departure should be considered in those circumstances.",

and inserting in lieu thereof:

"If the offense involved dangerous or inhumane treatment, death or bodily injury, possession of a dangerous weapon, or substantially more than 100 aliens, an upward departure may be warranted.".

The Commentary to §2L1.1 captioned "Background" is amended by deleting:

"A second specific offense characteristic provides an enhancement if the defendant was previously convicted of a similar offense.",

and inserting in lieu thereof:

"The offense level increases with the number of unlawful aliens smuggled, transported, or harbored. In large scale cases, an additional adjustment from §3B1.1 (Aggravating Role) typically will apply to the most culpable defendants.".

The title of §2L2.1 is amended by deleting "Evidence of Citizenship or Documents Authorizing Entry" and inserting in lieu thereof "Documents Relating to Naturalization, Citizenship, or Legal Resident Status; False Statement in Respect to the Citizenship or Immigration Status of Another; Fraudulent Marriage to Assist Alien to Evade Immigration Law".

Section 2L2.1(b) is amended by deleting "Characteristic" and inserting in lieu thereof "Characteristics"; and by inserting the following additional specific offense characteristic:

"(2) If the offense involved six or more sets of documents, increase as follows:

	Number of Sets of Documents	Increase in Level
(A)	6-24	add 2
(B)	25-99	add 4
(C)	100 or more	add 6.".

The Commentary to §2L2.1 captioned "Statutory Provisions" is amended by deleting "18 U.S.C. §§ 1425-1427, 1546. For additional statutory provision(s), see Appendix A (Statutory Index)" and inserting in lieu thereof "8 U.S.C. §§ 1160(b)(7)(A), 1185(a)(3), (4), 1325(b), (c); 18 U.S.C. §§ 1015, 1028, 1425-1427, 1546".

The Commentary to §2L2.1 captioned "Application Note" is amended by deleting "Note" and inserting in lieu thereof "Notes"; and by inserting the following additional note:

"2. Where it is established that multiple documents are part of a set intended for use by a single person, treat the set as one document.".

The title of §2L2.2 is amended by deleting "Evidence of Citizenship or Documents Authorizing Entry for Own Use" and inserting in lieu thereof "Documents Relating to Naturalization, Citizenship, or Legal Resident Status for Own Use; False Personation or Fraudulent Marriage by Alien to Evade Immigration Law".

The Commentary to §2L2.2 captioned "Statutory Provisions" is amended by deleting "18 U.S.C. §§ 1423, 1425, 1546. For additional statutory provision(s), see Appendix A (Statutory Index)" and inserting in lieu thereof "8 U.S.C. §§ 1160(b)(7)(A), 1185(a)(3), (5), 1325(b), (c); 18 U.S.C. §§ 911, 1015, 1028, 1423-1426, 1546".

Section 2L2.3(b) is amended by deleting "Characteristic" and inserting in lieu thereof "Characteristics"; and by inserting the following additional specific offense characteristic:

"(2) If the offense involved six or more passports, increase as follows:

	Number of Passports	Increase in Level
(A)	6-24	add 2
(B)	25-99	add 4
(C)	100 or more	add 6.".

Prior to this amendment, §2L1.1 provided the same offense level for a defendant who smuggles, transports, or harbors 1, 5, 25, 50, or any number of unlawful aliens. The inclusion of specific offense characteristic (b)(2) in §2L1.1 in the guidelines as initially promulgated in April 1987 was intended to conform the guidelines to the offense level indicated by past practices data for "ongoing criminal conduct." However, further study has convinced the Commission that the specific offense characteristic "prior conviction for the same or similar offense" is not a good proxy for such conduct. Moreover, the inclusion of a prior criminal record variable in the offense guideline is inconsistent with the general treatment of prior record as a separate dimension in the guidelines.

This amendment addresses these issues by providing an enhancement in the guideline for the number of aliens smuggled, transported, or harbored as a more direct measure of the scope of the offense. Consistent with the Commission's general approach throughout the guidelines, the offense level increases gradually with the number of aliens. It should be noted that §3B1.1 (Aggravating Role) generally provides an additional increase of 2, 3, or 4 levels for organizers, managers, and supervisors in large-scale cases. The enhancement in this amendment pertaining to the number of aliens is designed to work in conjunction with the operation of the role enhancements from §3B1.1. Sections 2L2.1 and 2L2.3 are amended to follow the same structure.

In addition, this amendment expands the titles of §§2L2.1 and 2L2.2, and the statutory provisions to these sections, to include additional statutes appropriately covered by these guidelines. **The effective date of this amendment is November 1, 1992.**

451. Section 2N2.1 is amended by inserting the following additional subsection:

"(b) Cross References

(1) If the offense involved fraud, apply §2F1.1 (Fraud and Deceit).

(2) If the offense was committed in furtherance of, or to conceal, an offense covered by another offense guideline, apply that other offense guideline if the resulting offense level is greater than that determined above.".

The Commentary to §2N2.1 captioned "Application Notes" is amended by deleting Note 2 as follows:

"2. If the offense involved theft, fraud, bribery, revealing trade secrets, or destruction of property, apply the guideline applicable to the underlying conduct, rather than this guideline.",

and inserting in lieu thereof:

"2. The cross reference at subsection (b)(1) addresses cases in which the offense involved fraud. The cross reference at subsection (b)(2) addresses cases in which the offense was committed in furtherance of, or to conceal, an offense covered by another offense guideline (e.g., theft, bribery, revealing trade secrets, or destruction of property).".

This amendment inserts cross references to cover cases more appropriately addressed by other offense guidelines. Previously, a similar instruction addressing such cases was contained in the commentary to this section. **The effective date of this amendment is November 1, 1992.**

452. Section 2Q2.1(b)(1) is amended by deleting "involved a commercial purpose" and inserting in lieu thereof "(A) was committed for pecuniary gain or otherwise involved a commercial purpose; or (B) involved a pattern of similar violations".

Section 2Q2.1(b)(2) is amended by deleting:

"involved fish, wildlife, or plants that were not quarantined as required by law",

and inserting in lieu thereof:

"(A) involved fish, wildlife, or plants that were not quarantined as required by law; or (B) otherwise created a significant risk of infestation or disease transmission potentially harmful to humans, fish, wildlife, or plants".

Section 2Q2.1(b)(3)(B) is amended by deleting:

"a quantity of fish, wildlife, or plants that was substantial in relation either to the overall population of the species or to a discrete subpopulation",

and inserting in lieu thereof:

"(i) marine mammals that are listed as depleted under the Marine Mammal Protection Act (as set forth in 50 C.F.R. § 216.15); (ii) fish, wildlife, or plants that are listed as endangered or threatened by the Endangered Species Act (as set forth in 50 C.F.R. Part 17); or (iii) fish, wildlife, or plants that are listed in Appendix I to the Convention on International Trade in Endangered Species of Wild Fauna or Flora (as set forth in 50 C.F.R. Part 23)".

The Commentary to §2Q2.1 is amended by inserting, immediately before "Background", the following:

"Application Notes:

1. 'For pecuniary gain' means for receipt of, or in anticipation of receipt of, anything of value, whether monetary or in goods or services. Thus, offenses committed for pecuniary gain include both monetary and barter transactions. Similarly, activities designed to increase gross revenue are considered to be committed for pecuniary gain.

2. The acquisition of fish, wildlife, or plants for display to the public, whether for a fee or donation and whether by an individual or an organization, including a governmental entity, a private non-profit organization, or a private for-profit organization, shall be considered to involve a 'commercial purpose.'

3. For purposes of subsection (b)(2), the quarantine requirements include those set forth in 9 C.F.R. Part 92, and 7 C.F.R. Chapter III. State quarantine laws are included as well.

4. When information is reasonably available, 'market value' under subsection (b)(3)(A) shall be based on the fair-market retail price. Where the fair-market retail price is difficult to ascertain, the court may make a reasonable estimate using any reliable information, such as the reasonable replacement or restitution cost or the acquisition and preservation (e.g., taxidermy) cost. Market value, however, shall not be based on measurement of aesthetic loss (so called 'contingent valuation' methods).

5. If the offense involved the destruction of a substantial quantity of fish, wildlife, or plants, and the seriousness of the offense is not adequately measured by the market value, an upward departure may be warranted.".

The Commentary to §2Q2.1 captioned "Background" is amended by deleting the last two sentences as follows:

"Enhancements are provided where the offense involved a commercial purpose, and where the fish, wildlife, or plants were not quarantined as required by law. An additional enhancement is provided where the market value of the species exceeded $2,000 or the offense involved a quantity of fish, wildlife, or plants that was substantial in relation either to the population of the species or to a discrete subpopulation of the species.".

This amendment is designed to strengthen the deterrent effect of the sanctions for violations covered by this guideline. The amendment expands the specific offense characteristic in subsection (b)(1) to cover categories of offenses that appear to be equally serious to those committed for a commercial purpose. In addition, the amendment expands the specific offense characteristic in subsection (b)(2) to cover other comparable types of risk of harm. Furthermore, the amendment modifies the specific offense characteristic in subsection (b)(3) to better encompass the types of cases that the Commission intended to cover. **The effective date of this amendment is November 1, 1992.**

453. The Introductory Commentary to Chapter Two, Part T, Subpart 3, is amended by deleting "This part" and inserting in lieu thereof "This Subpart"; by deleting:

". These guidelines are primarily aimed at revenue collection or trade regulation. They are",

and inserting in lieu thereof:

", and is designed to address violations involving revenue collection or trade regulation. It is";

by deleting "legislation generally applies" and inserting in lieu thereof "criminal statutes apply"; and by deleting:

"or for imposing a sentence above that specified in these guidelines",

and inserting in lieu thereof:

"if applicable, or for imposing a sentence above that specified in the guideline in this Subpart".

Section 2T3.1 is amended in the title by inserting at the end "; Receiving or Trafficking in Smuggled Property".

Section 2T3.1 is amended by inserting the following additional subsection:

"(c) Cross Reference

(1) If the offense involves a contraband item covered by another offense guideline, apply that offense guideline if the resulting offense level is greater than that determined above.".

The Commentary to §2T3.1 captioned "Application Notes" is amended in the third sentence of Note 2 by deleting "the court should impose a sentence above the guideline" and inserting in lieu thereof "an upward departure may be warranted".

Section 2T3.2, including accompanying commentary, is deleted as follows:

"§2T3.2. <u>Receiving or Trafficking in Smuggled Property</u>

(a) Base Offense Level:

(1) The level from §2T4.1 (Tax Table) corresponding to the tax loss, if the tax loss exceeded $1,000; or

(2) 5, if the tax loss exceeded $100 but did not exceed $1,000; or

(3) 4, if the tax loss did not exceed $100.

For purposes of this guideline, the 'tax loss' is the amount of the duty.

(b) Specific Offense Characteristic

(1) If sophisticated means were used to impede discovery of the nature or existence of the offense, increase by 2 levels.

<u>Commentary</u>

<u>Statutory Provision</u>: 18 U.S.C. § 545. For additional statutory provision(s), <u>see</u> Appendix A (Statutory Index).

<u>Application Note</u>:

1. Particular attention should be given to those items for which entry is prohibited, limited, or restricted. Especially when such items are harmful or protective quotas are in effect, the duties evaded on such items may not adequately reflect the harm to society or protected industries resulting from their importation. In such instances, the court should impose a sentence above the guideline. A sentence based upon an alternative measure of the 'duty' evaded, such as the increase in market value due to importation, or 25 percent of the items' fair market value in the United States if the increase in market value due to importation is not readily ascertainable, might be considered.".

Section 8C2.1(a) is amended by deleting ", 2T3.2" immediately following "2T3.1".

This amendment inserts a cross reference in §2T3.1 to cover cases more appropriately addressed by other offense guidelines. Previously, a similar instruction was set forth in the Introductory Commentary to this part. In addition, this amendment consolidates §§2T3.1 and 2T3.2 into one guideline as each contains the same offense levels and adjustments. **The effective date of this amendment is November 1, 1992.**

454. The Commentary to §3A1.1 captioned "Application Notes" is amended in Note 1 by inserting the following additional sentence at the end:

> "Similarly, for example, a bank teller is not an unusually vulnerable victim solely by virtue of the teller's position in a bank.".

This amendment clarifies the circumstances in which the vulnerable victim adjustment is intended to be applied. **The effective date of this amendment is November 1, 1992.**

455. Section 3A1.2(a) is amended by deleting:

> "a law enforcement or corrections officer; a former law enforcement or corrections officer; an officer or employee included in 18 U.S.C. § 1114; a former officer or employee included in 18 U.S.C. § 1114",

and inserting in lieu thereof:

> "a government officer or employee; a former government officer or employee".

The Commentary to §3A1.2 captioned "Application Notes" is amended in Note 2 by deleting:

> "are not expressly covered by this section. The court should make an upward departure of at least three levels in those unusual cases in which such persons are victims",

and inserting in lieu thereof:

> "although covered by this section, do not represent the heartland of the conduct covered. An upward departure to reflect the potential disruption of the governmental function in such cases typically would be warranted".

The Commentary to §3A1.2 captioned "Application Notes" is amended in Note 4 by deleting "law enforcement or corrections officer or other person covered under 18 U.S.C. § 1114" and inserting in lieu thereof "government officer or employee"; and by inserting the following additional sentence at the end:

> "This adjustment also would not apply in the case of a robbery of a postal employee because the offense guideline for robbery contains an enhancement (§2B3.1(a)) that takes such conduct into account.".

This amendment expands the coverage of this guideline to apply in the case of any government officer or employee, former government officer or employee, or a member of the immediate family of any of the above, who is targeted because of the official conduct or position of that officer or employee. **The effective date of this amendment is November 1, 1992.**

456. The Introductory Commentary to Chapter Three, Part B is amended by deleting the third sentence of the first paragraph as follows:

> "However, where the defendant has received mitigation by virtue of being convicted of an offense significantly less serious than his actual criminal conduct, e.g., the defendant is convicted of unlawful possession of a controlled substance but his actual conduct involved drug trafficking, a further reduction in the offense level under §3B1.2 (Mitigating Role) ordinarily is not warranted because the defendant is not substantially less culpable than a defendant whose only conduct involved the less serious offense.".

The Commentary to §3B1.2 captioned "Application Notes" is amended by inserting the following additional note:

"4. If a defendant has received a lower offense level by virtue of being convicted of an offense significantly less serious than warranted by his actual criminal conduct, a reduction for a mitigating role under this section ordinarily is not warranted because such defendant is not substantially less culpable than a defendant whose only conduct involved the less serious offense. For example, if a defendant whose actual conduct involved a minimal role in the distribution of 25 grams of cocaine (an offense having a Chapter Two offense level of 14 under §2D1.1) is convicted of simple possession of cocaine (an offense having a Chapter Two offense level of 6 under §2D2.1), no reduction for a mitigating role is warranted because the defendant is not substantially less culpable than a defendant whose only conduct involved the simple possession of cocaine.".

This amendment clarifies a situation in which a defendant is not ordinarily eligible for a reduction under §3B1.2 (Mitigating Role) and moves the discussion of this issue from the Introductory Commentary of Chapter Three, Part B, to the Commentary of §3B1.2, where it more appropriately belongs. **The effective date of this amendment is November 1, 1992.**

457. The Commentary to §3C1.1 captioned "Application Notes" is amended by inserting the following additional note:

"7. Under this section, the defendant is accountable for his own conduct and for conduct that he aided or abetted, counseled, commanded, induced, procured, or willfully caused.".

The Commentary to §3C1.2 captioned "Application Notes" is amended by inserting the following additional notes:

"5. Under this section, the defendant is accountable for his own conduct and for conduct that he aided or abetted, counseled, commanded, induced, procured, or willfully caused.

6. If death or bodily injury results or the conduct posed a substantial risk of death or bodily injury to more than one person, an upward departure may be warranted. <u>See</u> Chapter Five, Part K (Departures).".

This amendment clarifies the scope of the conduct for which the defendant is accountable under §§3C1.1 and 3C1.2. In addition, this amendment adds an application note to the Commentary of §3C1.2 that describes circumstances in which an upward departure may be warranted. **The effective date of this amendment is November 1, 1992.**

458. Section 3D1.2(d) is amended in the second paragraph by inserting "§§2L1.1, 2L2.1, 2L2.3;" in the appropriate place by section; by inserting "§2Q2.1" in the appropriate place by section; and by deleting ", 2T3.2" immediately following "2T3.1".

Section 3D1.2(d) is amended in the third paragraph by deleting "§§2L1.1, 2L2.1, 2L2.2, 2L2.3" and inserting in lieu thereof "2L2.2".

The Commentary to §3D1.2 captioned "Application Notes" is amended in Note 3 by deleting example 7 as follows:

"(7) The defendant is convicted of two counts, each for unlawfully bringing one alien into the United States, but on different occasions. The counts <u>are</u> <u>not</u> to be grouped together.".

This amendment revises §3D1.2(d) to reflect amendments to §§2L1.1, 2L2.1, and 2L2.3 (amendment 450); to clarify that offenses under §2Q2.1 are to be grouped under this subsection; and to delete the reference to §2T3.2 made obsolete by the deletion of that guideline (amendment 453). **The effective date of this amendment is November 1, 1992.**

459. Section 3E1.1 is amended by deleting:

"(a) If the defendant clearly demonstrates a recognition and affirmative acceptance of personal responsibility for his criminal conduct, reduce the offense level by 2 levels.

(b) A defendant may be given consideration under this section without regard to whether his conviction is based upon a guilty plea or a finding of guilt by the court or jury or the practical certainty of conviction at trial.

(c) A defendant who enters a guilty plea is not entitled to a sentencing reduction under this section as a matter of right.",

and inserting in lieu thereof:

"(a) If the defendant clearly demonstrates acceptance of responsibility for his offense, decrease the offense level by 2 levels.

(b) If the defendant qualifies for a decrease under subsection (a), the offense level determined prior to the operation of subsection (a) is level 16 or greater, and the defendant has assisted authorities in the investigation or prosecution of his own misconduct by taking one or more of the following steps:

(1) timely providing complete information to the government concerning his own involvement in the offense; or

(2) timely notifying authorities of his intention to enter a plea of guilty, thereby permitting the government to avoid preparing for trial and permitting the court to allocate its resources efficiently,

decrease the offense level by 1 additional level.".

The Commentary to §3E1.1 captioned "Application Notes" is amended in Note 1 by deleting "for this provision" and inserting in lieu thereof "under subsection (a)"; by deleting subdivision (c) as follows:

"(c) voluntary and truthful admission to authorities of involvement in the offense and related conduct;";

by redesignating subdivisions (a) and (b) as subdivisions (b) and (c), respectively; by inserting the following as subdivision (a):

"(a) truthfully admitting the conduct comprising the offense(s) of conviction, and truthfully admitting or not falsely denying any additional relevant conduct for which the defendant is accountable under §1B1.3 (Relevant Conduct). Note that a defendant is not required to volunteer, or affirmatively admit, relevant conduct beyond the offense of conviction in order to obtain a reduction under subsection (a). A defendant may remain silent in respect to relevant conduct beyond the offense of conviction without affecting his ability to obtain a reduction under this subsection. However, a defendant who falsely denies, or frivolously contests, relevant conduct that the court determines to be true has acted in a manner inconsistent with acceptance of responsibility;";

in subdivision (f) by deleting "and" immediately following "offense;";

by redesignating subdivision (g) as subdivision (h); and by inserting the following as subdivision (g):

> "(g) post-offense rehabilitative efforts (e.g., counseling or drug treatment); and".

The Commentary to §3E1.1 captioned "Application Notes" is amended by deleting Note 3 as follows:

> "3. Entry of a plea of guilty prior to the commencement of trial combined with truthful admission of involvement in the offense and related conduct will constitute significant evidence of acceptance of responsibility for the purposes of this section. However, this evidence may be outweighed by conduct of the defendant that is inconsistent with such acceptance of responsibility.",

and by inserting in lieu thereof:

> "3. Entry of a plea of guilty prior to the commencement of trial combined with truthfully admitting the conduct comprising the offense of conviction, and truthfully admitting or not falsely denying any additional relevant conduct for which he is accountable under §1B1.3 (Relevant Conduct) (see Application Note 1(a)), will constitute significant evidence of acceptance of responsibility for the purposes of subsection (a). However, this evidence may be outweighed by conduct of the defendant that is inconsistent with such acceptance of responsibility. A defendant who enters a guilty plea is not entitled to an adjustment under this section as a matter of right.".

The Commentary to §3E1.1 captioned "Application Notes" is amended by inserting the following additional note:

> "6. Subsection (a) provides a 2-level decrease in offense level. Subsection (b) provides an additional 1-level decrease in offense level for a defendant at offense level 16 or greater prior to the operation of subsection (a) who both qualifies for a decrease under subsection (a) and who has assisted authorities in the investigation or prosecution of his own misconduct by taking one or both of the steps set forth in subsection (b). The timeliness of the defendant's acceptance of responsibility is a consideration under both subsections, and is context specific. In general, the conduct qualifying for a decrease in offense level under subsection (b)(1) or (2) will occur particularly early in the case. For example, to qualify under subsection (b)(2), the defendant must have notified authorities of his intention to enter a plea of guilty at a sufficiently early point in the process so that the government may avoid preparing for trial and the court may schedule its calendar efficiently.".

The Commentary to §3E1.1 captioned "Background" is amended by deleting "a recognition and affirmative acceptance of personal responsibility for the offense and related conduct" and inserting in lieu thereof "acceptance of responsibility for his offense"; and by inserting the following additional paragraph at the end:

> " Subsection (a) provides a 2-level decrease in offense level. Subsection (b) provides an additional 1-level decrease for a defendant at offense level 16 or greater prior to operation of subsection (a) who both qualifies for a decrease under subsection (a) and has assisted authorities in the investigation or prosecution of his own misconduct by taking one or more of the steps specified in subsection (b). Such a defendant has accepted responsibility in a way that ensures the certainty of his just punishment in a timely manner, thereby appropriately meriting an additional reduction. Subsection (b) does not apply, however, to a defendant whose offense level is level 15 or lower prior to application of subsection (a). At offense level 15 or

lower, the reduction in the guideline range provided by a 2-level decrease in offense level under subsection (a) (which is a greater proportional reduction in the guideline range than at higher offense levels due to the structure of the Sentencing Table) is adequate for the court to take into account the factors set forth in subsection (b) within the applicable guideline range.".

Section 4B1.1 is amended in the last sentence by deleting "2-levels" and inserting in lieu thereof "the number of levels corresponding to that adjustment".

Section 4B1.4(b) is amended by deleting the last sentence as follows:

"*If §3E1.1 (Acceptance of Responsibility) applies, reduce by 2 levels.",

and inserting in lieu thereof:

"*If an adjustment from §3E1.1 (Acceptance of Responsibility) applies, decrease the offense level by the number of levels corresponding to that adjustment.".

This amendment provides an additional reduction of one level for certain defendants whose acceptance of responsibility includes assistance to the government in the investigation or prosecution of their own misconduct. In addition, it replaces the term "offense and related conduct" with the term "offense" and provides guidance as to the meaning of this term in the context of this guideline. **The effective date of this amendment is November 1, 1992.**

460. Section 4A1.3 is amended in the fourth paragraph by deleting "a Category IV criminal history" wherever it appears and inserting in lieu thereof in each instance "Criminal History Category IV"; and by deleting:

"The Commission contemplates that there may, on occasion, be a case of an egregious, serious criminal record in which even the guideline range for a Category VI criminal history is not adequate to reflect the seriousness of the defendant's criminal history. In such a case, a decision above the guideline range for a defendant with a Category VI criminal history may be warranted. However, this provision is not symmetrical. The lower limit of the range for a Category I criminal history is set for a first offender with the lowest risk of recidivism. Therefore, a departure below the lower limit of the guideline range for a Category I criminal history on the basis of the adequacy of criminal history cannot be appropriate.",

and inserting in lieu thereof:

"The Commission contemplates that there may, on occasion, be a case of an egregious, serious criminal record in which even the guideline range for Criminal History Category VI is not adequate to reflect the seriousness of the defendant's criminal history. In such a case, a departure above the guideline range for a defendant with Criminal History Category VI may be warranted. In determining whether an upward departure from Criminal History Category VI is warranted, the court should consider that the nature of the prior offenses rather than simply their number is often more indicative of the seriousness of the defendant's criminal record. For example, a defendant with five prior sentences for very large-scale fraud offenses may have 15 criminal history points, within the range of points typical for Criminal History Category VI, yet have a substantially more serious criminal history overall because of the nature of the prior offenses. On the other hand, a defendant with nine prior 60-day jail sentences for offenses such as petty larceny, prostitution, or possession of gambling slips has a higher number of criminal history points (18 points) than the typical Criminal History Category VI defendant, but not necessarily a more serious criminal history overall. Where the court determines that the extent and nature of the defendant's criminal history, taken together, are sufficient to warrant an upward departure from Criminal History Category VI, the court should structure the departure by moving incrementally down the sentencing table to the next higher offense level in Criminal History Category VI until it finds a guideline range appropriate to the case.

However, this provision is not symmetrical. The lower limit of the range for Criminal History Category I is set for a first offender with the lowest risk of recidivism. Therefore, a departure below the lower limit of the guideline range for Criminal History Category I on the basis of the adequacy of criminal history cannot be appropriate.".

This amendment provides additional guidance concerning upward departure from Criminal History Category VI on the basis of adequacy of criminal history category, and makes minor editorial changes. **The effective date of this amendment is November 1, 1992.**

461. Section 4B1.2(3) is amended by deleting the last sentence as follows:

"The date that a defendant sustained a conviction shall be the date the judgment of conviction was entered.",

and inserting in lieu thereof:

"The date that a defendant sustained a conviction shall be the date that the guilt of the defendant has been established, whether by guilty plea, trial, or plea of nolo contendere.".

The Commentary to §4B1.2 captioned "Application Notes" is amended by deleting the text of Note 2 as follows:

"'Crime of violence' includes murder, manslaughter, kidnapping, aggravated assault, forcible sex offenses, robbery, arson, extortion, extortionate extension of credit, and burglary of a dwelling. Other offenses are included where (A) that offense has as an element the use, attempted use, or threatened use of physical force against the person of another, or (B) the conduct set forth (i.e., expressly charged) in the count of which the defendant was convicted involved use of explosives (including any explosive material or destructive device) or, by its nature, presented a serious potential risk of physical injury to another. Under this section, the conduct of which the defendant was convicted is the focus of inquiry.

The term 'crime of violence' does not include the offense of unlawful possession of a firearm by a felon. Where the instant offense is the unlawful possession of a firearm by a felon, the specific offense characteristics of §2K2.1 (Unlawful Receipt, Possession, or Transportation of Firearms or Ammunition; Prohibited Transactions Involving Firearms or Ammunition) provide an increase in offense level if the defendant has one or more prior felony convictions for a crime of violence or controlled substance offense; and, if the defendant is sentenced under the provisions of 18 U.S.C. § 924(e), §4B1.4 (Armed Career Criminal) will apply.",

and inserting in lieu thereof:

"'Crime of violence' includes murder, manslaughter, kidnapping, aggravated assault, forcible sex offenses, robbery, arson, extortion, extortionate extension of credit, and burglary of a dwelling. Other offenses are included where (A) that offense has as an element the use, attempted use, or threatened use of physical force against the person of another, or (B) the conduct set forth (i.e., expressly charged) in the count of which the defendant was convicted involved use of explosives (including any explosive material or destructive device) or, by its nature, presented a serious potential risk of physical injury to another. Under this section, the conduct of which the defendant was convicted is the focus of inquiry.

The term 'crime of violence' does not include the offense of unlawful possession of a firearm by a felon. Where the instant offense is the unlawful possession of a firearm by a felon, §2K2.1 (Unlawful Receipt, Possession, or Transportation of Firearms or Ammunition; Prohibited Transactions Involving Firearms or Ammunition) provides an increase in offense level if the defendant has one or more prior felony convictions for a crime of violence or controlled substance offense; and, if the defendant is sentenced under the provisions of 18 U.S.C. § 924(e), §4B1.4 (Armed Career Criminal) will apply.".

This amendment conforms the definition of "sustaining a conviction" in §4B1.2 to the definition of "convicted of an offense" in §4A1.2. In addition, this amendment ratifies a previous amendment to the commentary to §4B1.2 (amendment 433, effective November 1, 1991) and corrects a clerical error in a reference in that commentary to §2K2.1. The previous amendment to the text of Application Note 2 clarified that application of §4B1.2 is governed by the offense of conviction, and that the offense of being a felon in possession of a firearm is not a crime of violence within the meaning of this guideline. As a clarifying and conforming change, the previous commentary amendment reflected Commission intent that the term "crime of violence," as that term is used in §§4B1.1 and 4B1.2, be interpreted consistently with that term as used in other provisions of the Guidelines Manual. For example, §4B1.4, as promulgated by amendment 355, effective November 1, 1990, provides an increased offense level for a "felon-in-possession" defendant who is subject to an enhanced sentence under 18 U.S.C. § 924(e) and who used or possessed the firearm in connection with a crime of violence (§4B1.4(b)(3)(A)). This action to ratify a previous commentary amendment was taken because of concerns raised by United States v. Stinson, 957 F.2d 813 (11th Cir. 1992), in which the court stated it would not follow amendment 433 because the commentary amendment was not submitted to Congress. **The effective date of this amendment is November 1, 1992.**

462. Chapter Five, Part A, is amended in the Sentencing Table at Offense Level 7, Criminal History Category I, by deleting "1-7" and inserting in lieu thereof "0-6"; and at Offense Level 8, Criminal History Category I, by deleting "2-8" and inserting in lieu thereof "0-6".

Chapter Five, Part A is amended in the Sentencing Table by designating four zones as follows: Zone A (containing all guideline ranges having a minimum of zero months); Zone B (containing all guideline ranges having a minimum of at least one but not more than six months); Zone C (containing all guideline ranges having a minimum of eight, nine, or ten months); and Zone D (containing all guideline ranges having a minimum of twelve months or more).

Section 5B1.1 is amended by deleting:

"(a) Subject to the statutory restrictions in subsection (b) below, sentence of probation is authorized:

(1) if the minimum term of imprisonment in the range specified by the Sentencing Table in Part A, is zero months;

(2) if the minimum term of imprisonment specified by the Sentencing Table is at least one but not more than six months, provided that the court imposes a condition or combination of conditions requiring intermittent confinement, community confinement, or home detention as provided in §5C1.1(c)(2) (Imposition of a Term of Imprisonment).",

and inserting in lieu thereof:

"(a) Subject to the statutory restrictions in subsection (b) below, a sentence of probation is authorized if:

(1) the applicable guideline range is in Zone A of the Sentencing Table; or

(2) the applicable guideline range is in Zone B of the Sentencing Table and the court imposes a condition or combination of conditions requiring intermittent confinement, community confinement, or home detention as provided in subsection (c)(3) of §5C1.1 (Imposition of a Term of Imprisonment).".

The Commentary to §5B1.1 captioned "Application Notes" is amended in Note 1 by deleting:

"(a) Where the minimum term of imprisonment specified in the guideline range from the Sentencing Table is zero months. In such case, a condition requiring a period of community confinement, home detention, or intermittent confinement may be imposed but is not required.

(b) Where the minimum term of imprisonment specified in the guideline range from the Sentencing Table is at least one but not more than six months.",

and inserting in lieu thereof:

"(a) Where the applicable guideline range is in Zone A of the Sentencing Table (i.e., the minimum term of imprisonment specified in the applicable guideline range is zero months). In such cases, a condition requiring a period of community confinement, home detention, or intermittent confinement may be imposed but is not required.

(b) Where the applicable guideline range is in Zone B of the Sentencing Table (i.e., the minimum term of imprisonment specified in the applicable guideline range is at least one but not more than six months).";

and by deleting "Offense Level is 8 and the Criminal History Category is I" and inserting in lieu thereof "offense level is 7 and the criminal history category is II".

The Commentary to §5B1.1 captioned "Application Notes" is amended in Note 2 by deleting:

"Where the minimum term of imprisonment specified in the guideline range from the Sentencing Table is more than six months",

and inserting in lieu thereof:

"Where the applicable guideline range is in Zone C or D of the Sentencing Table (i.e., the minimum term of imprisonment specified in the applicable guideline range is eight months or more)".

The Commentary to §5B1.1 captioned "Background" is amended by deleting "1st Sess. 89). Subsection" and inserting in lieu thereof "1st Sess. 89 (1983)). Section".

Section 5C1.1(a) is amended by inserting "applicable" immediately before "guideline range".

Section 5C1.1(b) is amended by deleting "minimum term of imprisonment in the applicable guideline range in the Sentencing Table is zero months" and inserting in lieu thereof "applicable guideline range is in Zone A of the Sentencing Table".

Sections 5C1.1 is amended by deleting:

"(c) If the minimum term of imprisonment in the applicable guideline range in the Sentencing Table is at least one but not more than six months, the minimum term may be satisfied by (1) a sentence of imprisonment; (2) a sentence of probation that includes a condition or combination of conditions that substitute intermittent confinement, community confinement, or home detention for imprisonment according to the schedule in §5C1.1(e); or (3) a sentence of imprisonment that includes a term of supervised release with a condition that substitutes community confinement or home detention according to the schedule in §5C1.1(e), provided that at least one-half of the minimum term, but in no event less than one month, is satisfied by imprisonment.

(d) If the minimum term of imprisonment in the applicable guideline range in the Sentencing Table is more than six months but not more than ten months, the minimum term may be satisfied by (1) a sentence of imprisonment; or (2) a sentence of imprisonment that includes a term of supervised release with a condition that substitutes community confinement or home detention according to the schedule in §5C1.1(e), provided that at least one-half of the minimum term is satisfied by imprisonment.",

and inserting in lieu thereof:

"(c) If the applicable guideline range is in Zone B of the Sentencing Table, the minimum term may be satisfied by --

(1) a sentence of imprisonment; or

(2) a sentence of imprisonment that includes a term of supervised release with a condition that substitutes community confinement or home detention according to the schedule in subsection (e), provided that at least one month is satisfied by imprisonment; or

(3) a sentence of probation that includes a condition or combination of conditions that substitute intermittent confinement, community confinement, or home detention for imprisonment according to the schedule in subsection (e).

(d) If the applicable guideline range is in Zone C of the Sentencing Table, the minimum term may be satisfied by --

(1) a sentence of imprisonment; or

(2) a sentence of imprisonment that includes a term of supervised release with a condition that substitutes community confinement or home detention according to the schedule in subsection (e), provided that at least one-half of the minimum term is satisfied by imprisonment.".

Section 5C1.1 is amended by deleting:

"(f) If the minimum term of imprisonment in the applicable guideline range in the Sentencing Table is more than ten months, the guidelines require that the minimum term be satisfied by a sentence of imprisonment.",

and inserting in lieu thereof:

"(f) If the applicable guideline range is in Zone D of the Sentencing Table, the minimum term shall be satisfied by a sentence of imprisonment.".

The Commentary to §5C1.1 captioned "Application Notes" is amended in Note 1 by deleting the first sentence as follows:

"Subsection 5C1.1(a) provides that a sentence conforms with the guidelines for imprisonment if it is within the minimum and maximum terms of the guideline range specified in the Sentencing Table.",

and inserting in lieu thereof:

"Subsection (a) provides that a sentence conforms with the guidelines for imprisonment if it is within the minimum and maximum terms of the applicable guideline range specified in the Sentencing Table in Part A of this Chapter.".

The Commentary to §5C1.1 captioned "Application Notes" is amended in Note 2 by deleting:

"Subsection 5C1.1(b) provides that where the minimum term of imprisonment specified in the guideline range from the Sentencing Table is zero months",

and inserting in lieu thereof:

"Subsection (b) provides that where the applicable guideline range is in Zone A of the Sentencing Table (i.e., the minimum term of imprisonment specified in the applicable guideline range is zero months)";

and by deleting "may, for example," and inserting in lieu thereof ", for example, may".

The Commentary to §5C1.1 captioned "Application Notes" is amended in Note 3 by deleting:

"Subsection 5C1.1(c) provides that where the minimum term of imprisonment specified in the guideline range from the Sentencing Table is at least one but not more than six months",

and inserting in lieu thereof:

"Subsection (c) provides that where the applicable guideline range is in Zone B of the Sentencing Table (i.e., the minimum term of imprisonment specified in the applicable guideline range is at least one but not more than six months)";

by deleting:

"For example, where the guideline range is 3-9 months, a sentence of probation with a condition requiring at least three",

and inserting in lieu thereof:

"For example, where the guideline range is 4-10 months, a sentence of probation with a condition requiring at least four";

by deleting "one-half of the minimum term specified in the guideline range from the Sentencing Table, but in no event less than one month," and inserting in lieu thereof "one month"; by deleting "two months followed by a term of supervised release with a condition requiring two" and inserting in lieu thereof "one month followed by a term of supervised release with a condition requiring three"; and by deleting:

"For example, where the guideline range is 3-9 months, both a sentence of probation with a condition requiring six months of community confinement or home detention (under §5C1.1(c)(2)) and a sentence of two months imprisonment followed by a term of supervised release with a condition requiring four months of community confinement or home detention (under §5C1.1(c)(3)",

and inserting in lieu thereof:

"For example, where the guideline range is 4-10 months, both a sentence of probation with a condition requiring six months of community confinement or home detention (under subsection (c)(3)) and a sentence of two months imprisonment followed by a term of supervised release with a condition requiring four months of community confinement or home detention (under subsection (c)(2)".

The Commentary to §5C1.1 captioned "Application Notes" is amended in Note 4 by deleting:

"Subsection 5C1.1(d) provides that where the minimum term specified in the guideline range from the Sentencing Table is more than six but not more than ten months",

and inserting in lieu thereof:

"Subsection (d) provides that where the applicable guideline range is in Zone C of the Sentencing Table (i.e., the minimum term specified in the applicable guideline range is eight, nine, or ten months)";

and by deleting "under §5C1.1(d)" wherever it appears and inserting in lieu thereof in each instance "under subsection (d)".

The Commentary to §5C1.1 captioned "Application Notes" is amended in Note 5 by deleting "Subsection 5C1.1(e)" and inserting in lieu thereof "Subsection (e)".

The Commentary to §5C1.1 captioned "Application Notes" is amended in Note 7 by deleting "§5C1.1(c)" and inserting in lieu thereof "subsections (c)".

The Commentary to §5C1.1 captioned "Application Notes" is amended by deleting Note 8 as follows:

"8. Subsection 5C1.1(f) provides that, if the minimum term of imprisonment set forth in the Sentencing Table is more than ten months, the minimum term must be satisfied by a sentence of imprisonment without the use of any of the incarceration alternatives in §5C1.1(e).",

and inserting in lieu thereof:

"8. Subsection (f) provides that, where the applicable guideline range is in Zone D of the Sentencing Table (i.e., the minimum term of imprisonment specified in the applicable guideline range is twelve months or more), the minimum term must be satisfied by a sentence of imprisonment without the use of any of the imprisonment substitutes in subsection (e).".

This amendment expands the number of categories in the Sentencing Table in Criminal History Category I in which the court has discretion to impose a sentence without imprisonment or confinement conditions. In addition, it removes the requirement that a "split sentence" include a term of imprisonment of at least one-half of the minimum of the guideline range for less serious categories of offenses and offenders and substitutes a requirement that such term of imprisonment be at least one month. Finally, this amendment reformats these sections to make their operation clearer. **The effective date of this amendment is November 1, 1992.**

463. Chapter Five, Part E, is amended by inserting an additional policy statement as §5E1.5 (Costs of Prosecution (Policy Statement)).

This amendment makes the Guidelines Manual more comprehensive by adding a section to provide notice of certain statutory requirements pertaining to the imposition of the costs of prosecution. **The effective date of this amendment is November 1, 1992.**

464. Section 5F1.6 is amended by deleting "21 U.S.C. § 853a" and inserting in lieu thereof "21 U.S.C. § 862".

The Commentary to §5F1.6 captioned "Application Notes" is amended in Note 1 by deleting "21 U.S.C. § 853a(d)" and inserting in lieu thereof "21 U.S.C. § 862(d)".

The Commentary to §5F1.6 captioned "Background" is amended by deleting "21 U.S.C. § 853a" wherever it appears and inserting in lieu thereof in each instance "21 U.S.C. § 862"; by deleting "21 U.S.C. § 853a(a)(1)" and inserting in lieu thereof "21 U.S.C. § 862(a)(1)"; by deleting "(a)(2)" and inserting in lieu thereof "(b)(1)"; by deleting "21 U.S.C. § 853a(a)(1)(C)" and inserting in lieu thereof "21 U.S.C. § 862(a)(1)(C)"; and by deleting "21 U.S.C. § 853a(c)" and inserting in lieu thereof "21 U.S.C. § 862(c)".

This amendment conforms the references to the statutory provisions underlying this guideline as such provisions were renumbered by the Comprehensive Crime Control Act of 1990. **The effective date of this amendment is November 1, 1992.**

465. Section 5G1.3 is amended by deleting subsection (b) as follows:

"(b) If subsection (a) does not apply, and the undischarged term of imprisonment resulted from offense(s) that constituted part of the same course of conduct as the instant offense and have been fully taken into account in the determination of the offense level for the instant offense, or if the prior undischarged term of imprisonment resulted from a federal offense and was imposed pursuant to the Sentencing Reform Act, the sentence for the instant offense shall be imposed to result in a combined sentence equal to the total punishment that would have been imposed under §5G1.2 (Sentencing on Multiple Counts of Conviction) had all the sentences been imposed at the same time.",

and inserting in lieu thereof:

"(b) If subsection (a) does not apply, and the undischarged term of imprisonment resulted from offense(s) that have been fully taken into account in the determination of the offense level for the instant offense, the sentence for the instant offense shall be imposed to run concurrently to the undischarged term of imprisonment.".

Section 5G1.3(c) is amended by inserting "(Policy Statement)" immediately before "In"; and by deleting "unexpired" and inserting in lieu thereof "undischarged".

The Commentary to §5G1.3 captioned "Application Notes" is amended by deleting Notes 2-4 as follows:

"2. Subsection (b) (which applies only if subsection (a) does not apply), applies in two situations. First, it applies if the sentence resulting in the undischarged term of imprisonment was a federal sentence imposed pursuant to the Sentencing Reform Act. In such cases, the court shall fashion a sentence equal to the total punishment that would have been imposed had both sentences been imposed at the same time. Second, it applies if the conduct resulting in the undischarged term of imprisonment was part of the same course of conduct as the instant offense and has been fully taken into account in determining the offense level for the instant offense (e.g., where a defendant is prosecuted in both federal and state court for the same criminal conduct; or where a defendant is prosecuted in federal and state court for different criminal transactions that are part of the same course of conduct, such as two drug sales, but the conduct underlying both transactions is fully taken into account under §1B1.3 (Relevant Conduct) in determining the offense level for the instant offense).

3. When a sentence is imposed pursuant to subsection (b), the court should adjust for any term of imprisonment already served as a result of the conduct taken into account in determining the instant sentence (e.g., if the appropriate total punishment determined under this subsection for all offenses is 30 months and the defendant has already served 10 months of the prior undischarged term of imprisonment, the court should impose a sentence of 20 months concurrent with the prior undischarged term).

4. Where the defendant is serving an unexpired term of imprisonment in circumstances other than those set forth in subsections (a) or (b), the court shall impose a consecutive sentence to the extent necessary to fashion a sentence resulting in incremental punishment for the multiple offenses. To the extent practicable, the court shall impose a sentence for the instant offense that results in a combined sentence that approximates the total punishment that would have been imposed under §5G1.2 (Sentencing on Multiple Counts of Conviction) had all of the offenses been federal offenses for which sentences were being imposed at the same time. Where the defendant is serving a term of imprisonment for a state offense, the information available may permit only a rough estimate of the total punishment that would have been imposed under the guidelines. It is not intended that the above methodology be applied in a manner that unduly complicates or prolongs the sentencing process. In fashioning an appropriate incremental punishment, the court should consider whether the offense was committed while the defendant was on bail or other release status from another offense. In such cases, a reasonable incremental penalty appropriately would include an additional enhancement equivalent to that provided in §2J1.7 (Commission of Offense While on Release).",

and inserting in lieu thereof:

"2. Subsection (b) (which may apply only if subsection (a) does not apply), addresses cases in which the conduct resulting in the undischarged term of imprisonment has been fully taken into account under §1B1.3 (Relevant Conduct) in determining the offense level for the instant offense. This can occur, for example, where a defendant is prosecuted in both federal and state court, or in two or more federal jurisdictions, for the same criminal conduct or for different criminal transactions that were part of the same course of conduct.

When a sentence is imposed pursuant to subsection (b), the court should adjust for any term of imprisonment already served as a result of the conduct taken into account in determining the sentence for the instant offense. Example: The defendant has been convicted of a federal offense charging the sale of 40 grams of cocaine. Under §1B1.3 (Relevant Conduct), the defendant is held accountable for the sale of an additional 15 grams of cocaine that is part of the same course of conduct for which the defendant has been convicted and sentenced in state court (the defendant received a nine-month sentence of imprisonment, of which he has served six months at the time of sentencing on the instant federal offense). The guideline range applicable to the defendant is 10-16 months (Chapter Two offense level of 14 for sale of 55 grams of cocaine; 2-level reduction for acceptance of responsibility; final offense level of 12; Criminal History Category I). The court determines that a sentence of 13 months provides the appropriate total punishment. Because the defendant has already served six months on the related state charge, a sentence of seven months, imposed to run concurrently with the remainder of the defendant's state sentence, achieves this result. For clarity, the court should note on the Judgment in a Criminal Case Order that the sentence imposed is not a departure from the guidelines because the defendant has been credited for guideline purposes under §5G1.3(b) with six months served in state custody.

3. Where the defendant is subject to an undischarged term of imprisonment in circumstances other than those set forth in subsections (a) or (b), subsection (c) applies and the court shall impose a consecutive sentence to the extent necessary to fashion a sentence resulting in a reasonable incremental punishment for the multiple offenses. In some circumstances, such incremental punishment can be achieved by the imposition of a sentence that is concurrent with the remainder of the unexpired term of imprisonment. In such cases, a consecutive sentence is not required. To the extent practicable, the court should consider a reasonable incremental penalty to be a sentence for the instant offense that results in a combined sentence of imprisonment that approximates the total punishment that would have been imposed under §5G1.2 (Sentencing on Multiple Counts of Conviction) had all of the offenses been federal offenses for which sentences were being imposed at the same time. It is recognized that this determination frequently will require an approximation. Where the defendant is serving a term of imprisonment for a state offense, the information available may permit only a rough estimate of the total punishment that would have been imposed under the guidelines. Where the offense resulting in the undischarged term of imprisonment is a federal offense for which a guideline determination has previously been made, the task will be somewhat more straightforward, although even in such cases a precise determination may not be possible.

It is not intended that the above methodology be applied in a manner that unduly complicates or prolongs the sentencing process. Additionally, this methodology does not, itself, require the court to depart from the guideline range established for the instant federal offense. Rather, this methodology is meant to assist the court in determining the appropriate sentence (e.g., the appropriate point within the applicable guideline range, whether to order the sentence to run concurrently or consecutively to the undischarged term of imprisonment, or whether a departure is warranted). Generally, the court may achieve an appropriate sentence through its determination of an appropriate point within the applicable guideline range for the instant federal offense, combined with its determination of whether that sentence will run concurrently or consecutively to the undischarged term of imprisonment.

Illustrations of the Application of Subsection (c):

(A) The guideline range applicable to the instant federal offense is 24-30 months. The court determines that a total punishment of 36 months' imprisonment would appropriately reflect the instant federal offense and the offense resulting in the undischarged term of imprisonment. The undischarged term of imprisonment is an indeterminate sentence of imprisonment with a 60-month maximum. At the time of sentencing on the instant federal offense, the defendant has served ten months on the undischarged term of imprisonment. In this case, a sentence of 26 months' imprisonment to be served concurrently with the remainder of the undischarged term of imprisonment would (1) be within the guideline range for the instant federal offense, and (2) achieve an appropriate total punishment (36 months).

(B) The applicable guideline range for the instant federal offense is 24-30 months. The court determines that a total punishment of 36 months' imprisonment would appropriately reflect the instant federal offense and the offense resulting in the undischarged term of imprisonment. The undischarged term of imprisonment is a six-month determinate sentence. At the time of sentencing on the instant federal offense, the defendant has served three months on the undischarged term of imprisonment. In this case, a sentence of 30 months' imprisonment to be served consecutively to the undischarged term of imprisonment would (1) be within the guideline range for the instant federal offense, and (2) achieve an appropriate total punishment (36 months).

(C) The applicable guideline range for the instant federal offense is 24-30 months. The court determines that a total punishment of 60 months' imprisonment would appropriately reflect the instant federal offense and the offense resulting in the undischarged term of imprisonment. The undischarged term of imprisonment is a 12-month determinate sentence. In this case, a sentence of 30 months' imprisonment to be served consecutively to the undischarged term of imprisonment would be the greatest sentence imposable without departure for the instant federal offense.

(D) The applicable guideline range for the instant federal offense is 24-30 months. The court determines that a total punishment of 36 months' imprisonment would appropriately reflect the instant federal offense and the offense resulting in the undischarged term of imprisonment. The undischarged term of imprisonment is an indeterminate sentence with a 60-month maximum. At the time of sentencing on the instant federal offense, the defendant has served 22 months on the undischarged term of imprisonment. In this case, a sentence of 24 months to be served concurrently with the remainder of the undischarged term of imprisonment would be the lowest sentence imposable without departure for the instant federal offense.".

This amendment deletes the prong of §5G1.3(b) pertaining to the sentencing of a defendant subject to an undischarged term of imprisonment previously imposed pursuant to the Sentencing Reform Act because the Commission found a number of problems in implementation. Cases previously addressed by this prong henceforth will be addressed by subsection (c), which is designed to produce a similar result but requires less precise calculations. Consistent with the structure of the Guidelines Manual, subsection (c) is expressly designated a policy statement. In addition, this amendment provides additional commentary explaining, and providing examples of, the operation of this section. **The effective date of this amendment is November 1, 1992.**

466. Chapter 5, Part H is amended by inserting an additional policy statement as §5H1.12 (Lack of Guidance as a Youth and Similar Circumstances (Policy Statement)).

Chapter 1, Part A, Subpart 4(b) is amended in the first paragraph by inserting "§5H1.12 (Lack of Guidance as a Youth and Similar Circumstances)," immediately following "§5H1.10 (Race, Sex, National Origin, Creed, Religion, and Socio-Economic Status),".

This amendment provides that the factors specified are not appropriate grounds for departure. **The effective date of this amendment is November 1, 1992.**

467. Section 6B1.2(a) is amended by inserting "or the sentencing guidelines" immediately following "statutory purposes of sentencing".

Section 6B1.2(a) is amended by inserting the following additional paragraph at the end:

"*Provided*, that a plea agreement that includes the dismissal of a charge or a plea agreement not to pursue a potential charge shall not preclude the conduct underlying such charge from being considered under the provisions of §1B1.3 (Relevant Conuuct) in connection with the count(s) of which the defendant is convicted.".

The Commentary to §6B1.2 is amended in the first paragraph by deleting:

"This section makes clear that a court may accept a plea agreement provided that the judge complies with the obligations imposed by Rule 11(e), Fed. R. Crim. P. A judge",

and inserting in lieu thereof "The court".

The Commentary to §6B1.2 is amended in the second paragraph by deleting:

"will accept a recommended sentence or a plea agreement requiring imposition of a specific sentence only if the court is satisfied either that the contemplated sentence is within the guidelines or, if not, that the recommended sentence or agreement",

and inserting in lieu thereof:

"should accept a recommended sentence or a plea agreement requiring imposition of a specific sentence only if the court is satisfied either that such sentence is an appropriate sentence within the applicable guideline range or, if not, that the sentence".

The Commentary to §6B1.2 is amended by inserting the following additional paragraphs at the end:

" A defendant who enters a plea of guilty in a timely manner will enhance the likelihood of his receiving a reduction in offense level under §3E1.1 (Acceptance of Responsibility). Further reduction in offense level (or sentence) due to a plea agreement will tend to undermine the sentencing guidelines.

The second paragraph of subsection (a) provides that a plea agreement that includes the dismissal of a charge, or a plea agreement not to pursue a potential charge, shall not prevent the conduct underlying that charge from being considered under the provisions of §1B1.3 (Relevant Conduct) in connection with the count(s) of which the defendant is convicted. This paragraph prevents a plea agreement from restricting consideration of conduct that is within the scope of §1B1.3 (Relevant Conduct) in respect to the count(s) of which the defendant is convicted; it does not in any way expand or modify the scope of §1B1.3 (Relevant Conduct).".

This amendment clarifies that a plea agreement to dismiss a charge or not to pursue a potential charge does not insulate the conduct underlying such charge from the operation of §1B1.3 (Relevant Conduct) in respect to the count(s) of which the defendant is convicted. In addition, this amendment makes clearer the Commission's policy that plea agreements should not undermine the sentencing guidelines. **The effective date of this amendment is November 1, 1992.**

468. Appendix A (Statutory Index) is amended by deleting:

"8 U.S.C. § 1325 2L1.2",

and inserting in lieu thereof:

"8 U.S.C. § 1325(a) 2L1.2
8 U.S.C. § 1325(b) 2L2.1, 2L2.2
8 U.S.C. § 1325(c) 2L2.1, 2L2.2";

in the line beginning "18 U.S.C. § 245(b)" by inserting ", 2J1.2" immediately following "2H2.1";

in the line beginning "18 U.S.C. § 371" by deleting "2D1.4," immediately following "2C1.7,";

in the line beginning "18 U.S.C. § 545" by deleting ", 2T3.2";

in the line beginning "18 U.S.C. § 547" by deleting ", 2T3.2";

in the line beginning "18 U.S.C. § 549" by deleting ", 2T3.2";

in the line beginning "18 U.S.C. § 656" by inserting ", 2F1.1" immediately following "2B1.1";

in the line beginning "18 U.S.C. § 657" by inserting ", 2F1.1" immediately following "2B1.1";

in the line beginning "18 U.S.C. § 1028" by deleting "2L1.2, 2L2.1" and inserting in lieu thereof "2L2.1, 2L2.2";

by deleting:

"18 U.S.C. § 1346 2C1.7";

in the line beginning "18 U.S.C. § 2331(a)" by deleting "18 U.S.C. § 2331(a)" and inserting in lieu thereof "18 U.S.C. § 2332(a)";

by deleting:

"18 U.S.C. § 2331(b) 2A2.1",

and inserting in lieu thereof:

"18 U.S.C. § 2332(b)(1) 2A2.1
18 U.S.C. § 2332(b)(2) 2A1.5";

in the line beginning "18 U.S.C. § 2331(c)" by deleting "18 U.S.C. § 2331(c)" and inserting in lieu thereof "18 U.S.C. § 2332(c)";

in the line beginning "19 U.S.C. § 1464" by deleting ", 2T3.2";

in the line beginning "21 U.S.C. § 846" by deleting "2D1.4" and inserting in lieu thereof "2D1.1, 2D1.2, 2D1.5, 2D1.6, 2D1.7, 2D1.8, 2D1.9, 2D1.10, 2D1.11, 2D1.12, 2D1.13, 2D2.1, 2D2.2, 2D3.1, 2D3.2, 2D3.3, 2D3.4, 2D3.5";

in the line beginning "21 U.S.C. § 963" by deleting "2D1.4" and inserting in lieu thereof "2D1.1, 2D1.2, 2D1.5, 2D1.6, 2D1.7, 2D1.8, 2D1.9, 2D1.10, 2D1.11, 2D1.12, 2D1.13, 2D2.1, 2D2.2, 2D3.1, 2D3.2, 2D3.3, 2D3.4, 2D3.5";

in the line beginning "31 U.S.C. § 5322" by inserting ", 2S1.4" immediately following "2S1.3";

and in the line beginning "46 U.S.C. App. § 1903(j)" by deleting "2D1.4" and inserting in lieu thereof "2D1.1".

The Commentary to §2B4.1 captioned "Background" is amended in the sixth paragraph by deleting "§§77d-1 and 77d-2" and inserting in lieu thereof "78dd-1 and 78dd-2".

The Commentary to §2C1.7 captioned "Statutory Provisions" is amended by deleting ", 1346".

The Commentary to §2C1.7 captioned "Application Notes" is amended in Note 1 by inserting "(A)" immediately following "involve"; and by deleting ", 1346), or" and inserting in lieu thereof "), or (B)".

The Commentary to §2C1.7 captioned "Background" is amended by deleting ", 1341-1343, and 1346" and inserting in lieu thereof "and 1341-1343".

The Commentary to §2T1.1 captioned "Background" is amended in the fifth paragraph by deleting "28 U.S.C. § 994(n)" and inserting in lieu thereof "28 U.S.C. § 994(i)(2)".

This amendment makes the statutory index more comprehensive, and conforms it to the amendments of the Chapter Two offense guidelines. In addition, it corrects clerical errors and makes an editorial improvement. **The effective date of this amendment is November 1, 1992.**

469. Section 1B1.10(d) is amended by deleting "and 380" and inserting in lieu thereof "380, 433, and 461".

This amendment expands the listing in subsection (d) to implement the directive in 28 U.S.C. § 994(u) in respect to guideline amendments that may be considered for retroactive application. **The effective date of this amendment is November 1, 1992.**

470. The Commentary to §2F1.1 captioned "Application Notes" is amended in Note 7 in the first paragraph by inserting the following additional sentence as the second sentence:

> "As in theft cases, loss is the value of the money, property, or services unlawfully taken; it does not, for example, include interest the victim could have earned on such funds had the offense not occurred.".

The Commentary to §2F1.1 captioned "Application Notes" is amended in Note 7(b) by deleting:

> "In fraudulent loan application cases and contract procurement cases where the defendant's capabilities are fraudulently represented, the loss is the actual loss to the victim (or if the loss has not yet come about, the expected loss). For example, if a defendant fraudulently obtains a loan by misrepresenting the value of his assets, the loss is the amount of the loan not repaid at the time the offense is discovered, reduced by the amount the lending institution has recovered, or can expect to recover, from any assets pledged to secure the loan.",

and inserting in lieu thereof:

> "In fraudulent loan application cases and contract procurement cases, the loss is the actual loss to the victim (or if the loss has not yet come about, the expected loss). For example, if a defendant fraudulently obtains a loan by misrepresenting the value of his assets, the loss is the amount of the loan not repaid at the time the offense is discovered, reduced by the amount the lending institution has recovered (or can expect to recover) from any assets pledged to secure the loan. However, where the intended loss is greater than the actual loss, the intended loss is to be used.".

This amendment clarifies that interest is not included in the determination of loss. In, addition, it clarifies that in fraudulent loan application cases, as in other types of fraud, if the intended loss is greater than the actual loss, the intended loss is used. Finally, it makes an editorial improvement in this commentary by deleting an unnecessary phrase. **The effective date of this amendment is November 1, 1992.**

471. The Commentary to §2K1.3 captioned "Application Notes" is amended by inserting the following additional note:

> "11. As used in subsections (b)(3) and (c)(1), 'another felony offense' and 'another offense' refer to offenses other than explosives or firearms possession or trafficking offenses. However, where the defendant used or possessed a firearm or explosive to facilitate another firearms or explosives offense (e.g.,

the defendant used or possessed a firearm to protect the delivery of an unlawful shipment of explosives), an upward departure under §5K2.6 (Weapons and Dangerous Instrumentalities) may be warranted.".

The Commentary to §2K2.1 captioned "Application Notes" is amended in Note 15 by deleting "or (a)(5)" and inserting in lieu thereof "(a)(4)(B), or (a)(6)".

The Commentary to 2K2.1 captioned "Application Notes" is amended by inserting the following additional note:

"18. As used in subsections (b)(5) and (c)(1), 'another felony offense' and 'another offense' refer to offenses other than explosives or firearms possession or trafficking offenses. However, where the defendant used or possessed a firearm or explosive to facilitate another firearms or explosives offense (e.g., the defendant used or possessed a firearm to protect the delivery of an unlawful shipment of explosives), an upward departure under §5K2.6 (Weapons and Dangerous Instrumentalities) may be warranted.".

This amendment clarifies the meaning of the terms "another felony offense' and "another offense," and corrects a clerical error. **The effective date of this amendment is November 1, 1992.**

472. The Commentary to §4A1.2 captioned "Application Notes" is amended in Note 8 by deleting the last sentence as follows:

"If the government is able to show that a sentence imposed outside this time period is evidence of similar misconduct or the defendant's receipt of a substantial portion of income from criminal livelihood, the court may consider this information in determining whether to depart and sentence above the applicable guideline range.",

and by inserting in lieu thereof:

"If the court finds that a sentence imposed outside this time period is evidence of similar, or serious dissimilar, criminal conduct, the court may consider this information in determining whether an upward departure is warranted under §4A1.3 (Adequacy of Criminal History Category).".

This amendment clarifies that dissimilar, serious prior offenses outside the applicable time period may be considered in determining whether an upward departure is warranted under §4A1.3. The amendment provides additional Commission guidance on an issue that has produced conflicting decisions among the courts of appeals. Compare, e.g., United States v. Leake, 908 F.2d 550, 554 (9th Cir. 1990) (upward departure impermissible for remote prior convictions dissimilar to instant offense) and United States v. Samuels, 938 F.2d 210, 215 (D.C. Cir. 1991) (suggesting the same) with United States v. Williams, 910 F.2d 1574, 1579 (7th Cir. 1990) (although older prior crimes dissimilar to instant offense, upward departure permissible if convictions are reliable information of increased recidivism risk), rev'd on other grounds, 112 S. Ct. 1112 (1992) and United States v. Russell, 905 F.2d 1439, 1444 (10th Cir. 1990) (same). **The effective date of this amendment is November 1, 1992.**

473. The Commentary to §7B1.1 captioned "Application Notes" is amended by deleting Notes 2 and 3 as follows:

"2. 'Crime of violence' has the same meaning as set forth in §4B1.2(1), and includes any offense under federal or state law punishable by imprisonment for a term exceeding one year that --

(i) has as an element the use, attempted use, or threatened use of physical force against the person of another; or

(ii) is burglary of a dwelling, arson, or extortion, involves use of explosives, or otherwise involves conduct that presents a serious potential risk of physical injury to another.

A crime of violence includes murder, manslaughter, kidnapping, aggravated assault, forcible sex offenses, robbery, arson, extortion, extortionate extension of credit, and burglary of a dwelling. Other offenses are included where (A) that offense has as an element the use, attempted use, or threatened use of physical force against the person of another, or (B) the conduct set forth in the violation charged involved use of explosives or, by its nature, presented a serious potential risk of physical injury to another. A crime of violence also includes the offenses of aiding and abetting, conspiring, and attempting to commit such offenses.

3. 'Controlled substance offense' includes any offense under a federal or state law prohibiting the manufacture, import, export, distribution, or dispensing of a controlled substance (or a counterfeit substance) or the possession of a controlled substance (or a counterfeit substance) with the intent to manufacture, import, export, distribute, or dispense. A controlled substance offense also includes the offenses of aiding and abetting, conspiring, and attempting to commit such offenses.",

and by inserting in lieu thereof:

"2. 'Crime of violence' is defined in §4B1.2 (Definitions of Terms Used in Section 4B1.1). See §4B1.2(1) and Application Notes 1 and 2 of the Commentary to §4B1.2.

3. 'Controlled substance offense' is defined in §4B1.2 (Definitions of Terms Used in Section 4B1.1). See §4B1.2(2) and Application Note 1 of the Commentary to §4B1.2.".

This amendment clarifies the Commission's intent that the terms "crime of violence" and "controlled substance offense" in §7B1.1 have the same meaning as these terms have in §4B1.2. **The effective date of this amendment is November 1, 1992.**

474. Section 1B1.11(b) is amended by inserting the following additional subdivision:

"(3) If the defendant is convicted of two offenses, the first committed before, and the second after, a revised edition of the Guidelines Manual became effective, the revised edition of the Guidelines Manual is to be applied to both offenses.".

The Commentary to §1B1.11 captioned "Application Note" is amended by inserting the following additional note:

"2. Under subsection (b)(1), the last date of the offense of conviction is the controlling date for ex post facto purposes. For example, if the offense of conviction (i.e., the conduct charged in the count of the indictment or information of which the defendant was convicted) was determined by the court to have been committed between October 15, 1991 and October 28, 1991, the date of October 28, 1991 is the controlling date for ex post facto purposes. This is true even if the defendant's conduct relevant to the determination of the guideline range under §1B1.3 (Relevant Conduct) included an act that occurred on November 2, 1991 (after a revised Guideline Manual took effect).";

and in the caption by deleting "Note" and inserting in lieu thereof "Notes".

The Commentary to §1B1.11 captioned "Background" is amended by inserting the following additional sentence as the first sentence of the first paragraph:

"Subsections (a) and (b)(1) provide that the court should apply the Guidelines Manual in effect on the date the defendant is sentenced unless the court determines that doing so would violate the ex post facto clause in Article I, § 9 of the United States Constitution.";

and by inserting the following additional paragraphs at the end:

" Subsection (b)(2) provides that the Guidelines Manual in effect on a particular date shall be applied in its entirety.

Subsection (b)(3) provides that where the defendant is convicted of two offenses, the first committed before, and the second after, a revised edition of the Guidelines Manual became effective, the revised edition of the Guidelines Manual is to be applied to both offenses, even if the revised edition results in an increased penalty for the first offense. Because the defendant completed the second offense after the amendment to the guidelines took effect, the ex post facto clause does not prevent determining the sentence for that count based on the amended guidelines. For example, if a defendant pleads guilty to a single count of embezzlement that occurred after the most recent edition of the Guidelines Manual became effective, the guideline range applicable in sentencing will encompass any relevant conduct (e.g., related embezzlement offenses that may have occurred prior to the effective date of the guideline amendments) for the offense of conviction. The same would be true for a defendant convicted of two counts of embezzlement, one committed before the amendments were enacted, and the second after. In this example, the ex post facto clause would not bar application of the amended guideline to the first conviction; a contrary conclusion would mean that such defendant was subject to a lower guideline range than if convicted only of the second offense. Decisions from several appellate courts addressing the analogous situation of the constitutionality of counting pre-guidelines criminal activity as relevant conduct for a guidelines sentence support this approach. See United States v. Ykema, 887 F.2d 697 (6th Cir. 1989) (upholding inclusion of pre-November 1, 1987, drug quantities as relevant conduct for the count of conviction, noting that habitual offender statutes routinely augment punishment for an offense of conviction based on acts committed before a law is passed), cert. denied, 493 U.S. 1062 (1990); United States v. Allen, 886 F.2d 143 (8th Cir. 1989) (similar); see also United States v. Cusack, 901 F.2d 29 (4th Cir. 1990) (similar).

Moreover, the approach set forth in subsection (b)(3) should be followed regardless of whether the offenses of conviction are the type in which the conduct is grouped under §3D1.2(d). The ex post facto clause does not distinguish between groupable and nongroupable offenses, and unless that clause would be violated, Congress' directive to apply the sentencing guidelines in effect at the time of sentencing must be followed. Under the guideline sentencing system, a single sentencing range is determined based on the defendant's overall conduct, even if there are multiple counts of conviction (see §§3D1.1-3D1.5, 5G1.2). Thus, if a defendant is sentenced in January 1992 for a bank robbery committed in October 1988 and one committed in November 1991, the November 1991 Guidelines Manual should be used to determine a combined guideline range for both counts. See generally United States v. Stephenson, 921 F.2d 438 (2d Cir. 1990) (holding that the Sentencing Commission and Congress intended that the applicable version of the guidelines be applied as a 'cohesive and integrated whole' rather than in a piecemeal fashion).

Consequently, even in a complex case involving multiple counts that occurred under several different versions of the Guidelines Manual, it will not be necessary to compare more than two manuals to determine the applicable guideline range -- the manual in effect at the time the last offense of conviction was completed and the manual in effect at the time of sentencing.".

This amendment expands §1B1.11 to address what has become a frequently asked hotline question and troublesome application issue -- the application of amended guidelines to multiple count cases in which the effective date of guideline revision(s) occurs between the offenses of conviction. The issue has also produced litigation before several appellate courts. See United States v. Castro, 972 F.2d 1107 (9th Cir. 1992), cert. denied, 113 S. Ct. 1350 (1993); United States v. Seligsohn, 981 F.2d 1418 (3d Cir. 1992); United States v. Hartzog, 983 F.2d 604 (4th Cir. 1993). This amendment extends the Commission's "one book" rule to multiple count cases and sets forth the rationale for this policy. **The effective date of this amendment is November 1, 1993.**

475. Chapter One, Part B, is amended by inserting an additional policy statement as §1B1.12 (Persons Sentenced Under the Federal Juvenile Delinquency Act (Policy Statement)).

Section 5H1.1 is amended by deleting the last paragraph as follows:

"The guidelines are not applicable to a person sentenced as a juvenile delinquent under the provisions of 18 U.S.C. § 5037.".

This amendment adds a policy statement as §1B1.12 to address the determination of the maximum imposable sentence in the case of a juvenile delinquent. The Supreme Court's decision in United States v. R.L.C., 112 S. Ct. 1329 (1992), requires calculation of the guideline range in order to determine the maximum sentence imposable on a juvenile delinquent. **The effective date of this amendment is November 1, 1993.**

476. The Commentary to §2A1.1 captioned "Background" is deleted as follows:

"Background: The maximum penalty authorized by 18 U.S.C. § 1111 for first degree murder is death or life imprisonment. Whether a mandatory minimum term of life imprisonment is applicable to every defendant convicted of first degree murder under 18 U.S.C. § 1111 is a matter of statutory interpretation for the courts. The discussion in Application Note 1, supra, regarding circumstances in which a downward departure may be warranted is relevant in the event the penalty provisions of 18 U.S.C. § 1111 are construed to permit a sentence less than life imprisonment, or in the event the defendant is convicted under a statute that expressly authorizes a sentence of less than life imprisonment (e.g., 18 U.S.C. §§ 2113(e), 2118(c)(2), 21 U.S.C. § 848(e)).

The maximum penalty authorized under 21 U.S.C. § 848(e) is death or life imprisonment. If a term of imprisonment is imposed, the statutorily required minimum term is twenty years.".

This amendment deletes commentary that highlighted the question of whether 18 U.S.C. § 1111 provides a mandatory minimum term of life imprisonment. Since this commentary was written, appellate courts uniformly have held that 18 U.S.C. § 1111 does provide a mandatory minimum term of life imprisonment. See United States v. Sands, 968 F.2d 1058 (10th Cir. 1992), cert. denied, 113 S. Ct. 987 (1993); United States v. LaFleur, 952 F.2d 1537 (9th Cir), modfied and reh'g denied, 971 F.2d 200 (9th Cir. 1991); United States v. Gonzalez, 922 F.2d 1044 (2d Cir.), cert. denied, 112 S. Ct. 660 (1991); United States v. Donley, 878 F.2d 735 (3d Cir. 1989), cert. denied, 494 U.S. 1058 (1990). In addition, this amendment deletes, as unnecessary, several sentences of commentary that merely recite statutory penalties. **The effective date of this amendment is November 1, 1993.**

477. Section 2A3.1 is amended by redesignating subsection (c) as subsection (d); and by inserting the following additional subsection:

"(c) Cross Reference

(1) If a victim was killed under circumstances that would constitute murder under 18 U.S.C. § 1111 had such killing taken place within the territorial or maritime jurisdiction of the United States, apply §2A1.1 (First Degree Murder).".

Section 2A3.1(b)(2) is amended by deleting "otherwise, (B) if the victim was under the age of sixteen" and inserting in lieu thereof "or (B) if the victim had attained the age of twelve years but had not attained the age of sixteen years".

The Commentary to §2A3.1 captioned "Application Notes" is amended by inserting the following additional note:

"5. If the defendant was convicted (A) of more than one act of criminal sexual abuse and the counts are grouped under §3D1.2 (Groups of Closely Related Counts), or (B) of only one such act but the court determines that the offense involved multiple acts of criminal sexual abuse of the same victim or different victims, an upward departure would be warranted.".

This amendment adds a cross reference to §2A3.1 to address the circumstance in which a victim is murdered during the offense. In addition, an editorial change in §2A3.1(b)(2) is made to conform the phraseology used in this subsection to that used elsewhere in the guidelines. This amendment also authorizes an upward departure where the offense involved multiple acts of criminal sexual abuse that do not result in an increase in offense level under the multiple count rules in Chapter Three, Part D. **The effective date of this amendment is November 1, 1993.**

478. The Commentary to §2A4.1 captioned "Background" is amended in the third paragraph by deleting:

"or to facilitate the commission of another offense. Should the application of this guideline result in a penalty less than the result achieved by applying the guideline for the underlying offense, apply the guideline for the underlying offense (e.g., §2A3.1, Criminal Sexual Abuse).",

and inserting in lieu thereof:

"(subsection (b)(1)) or involves another federal, state, or local offense that results in a greater offense level (subsections (b)(7) and (c)(1)).".

The Commentary to §2K1.3 captioned "Application Notes" is amended in Note 4 by inserting "(federal, state, or local)" immediately following "any offense".

The Commentary to §2K1.3 captioned "Application Notes" is amended in Note 8 by inserting "(which may be a federal, state, or local offense)" immediately before "is".

The Commentary to §2K2.1 captioned "Application Notes" is amended in Note 7 by inserting "(federal, state, or local)" immediately following "any offense".

The Commentary to §2K2.1 captioned "Application Notes" is amended in Note 14 by inserting "(which may be a federal, state, or local offense)" immediately before "is".

The Commentary to §2K2.1 captioned "Application Notes" is amended by inserting the following additional note:

"19. The enhancement under subsection (b)(4) for a stolen firearm or a firearm with an altered or obliterated serial number applies whether or not the defendant knew or had reason to believe that the firearm was stolen or had an altered or obliterated serial number.".

This amendment clarifies that the terms "another offense" and "other offense" in §2A4.1(b)(7), and "felony offense," "another felony offense," "another offense," and "other offense" in §§2K1.3 and 2K2.1, refer to federal, state, or local offenses. In addition, this amendment clarifies that the enhancement in §2K2.1(b)(4) applies whether or not the defendant knew or had reason to believe the firearm was stolen or had an altered or obliterated serial number. **The effective date of this amendment is November 1, 1993.**

479. Section 2A4.2 is amended by inserting the following additional subsection:

"(b) Cross Reference

(1) If the defendant was a participant in the kidnapping offense, apply §2A4.1 (Kidnapping; Abduction; Unlawful Restraint).".

The Commentary to §2A4.2 is amended by inserting the following immediately before "Background".

"Application Note:

1. A 'participant' is a person who is criminally responsible for the commission of the offense, but need not have been convicted.".

Section 2B3.2(c) is amended by deleting "Reference" and inserting in lieu thereof "References"; by renumbering subdivision (1) as subdivision (2); and by inserting the following additional subdivision:

"(1) If a victim was killed under circumstances that would constitute murder under 18 U.S.C. § 1111 had such killing taken place within the territorial or maritime jurisdiction of the United States, apply §2A1.1 (First Degree Murder).".

Section 2B3.3 is amended by inserting the following additional subsection:

"(c) Cross References

(1) If the offense involved extortion under color of official right, apply §2C1.1 (Offering, Giving, Soliciting, or Receiving a Bribe; Extortion Under Color of Official Right).

(2) If the offense involved extortion by force or threat of injury or serious damage, apply §2B3.2 (Extortion by Force or Threat of Injury or Serious Damage).".

Section 2D1.1 is amended by inserting the following additional subsection:

"(d) Cross Reference

(1) If a victim was killed under circumstances that would constitute murder under 18 U.S.C. § 1111 had such killing taken place within the territorial or maritime jurisdiction of the United States, apply §2A1.1 (First Degree Murder).".

Section 2E2.1 is amended by inserting the following additional subsection:

"(c) Cross Reference

(1) If a victim was killed under circumstances that would constitute murder under 18 U.S.C. § 1111 had such killing taken place within the territorial or maritime jurisdiction of the United States, apply §2A1.1 (First Degree Murder).".

This amendment adds a cross reference to §2A4.2 to address the circumstance in which the defendant was a participant in the underlying kidnapping offense. This amendment also adds cross references to §§2B3.2, 2D1.1, and 2E2.1 to address the circumstance in which a victim is murdered during the offense. Finally, this amendment adds cross references to §2B3.3 to ensure the selection of the appropriate guideline. **The effective date of this amendment is November 1, 1993.**

480. Section 2A5.2(a)(1) is amended by deleting "defendant intentionally endangered" and inserting in lieu thereof "offense involved intentionally endangering".

Section 2A5.2(a)(2) is amended by deleting "defendant recklessly endangered" and inserting in lieu thereof "offense involved recklessly endangering".

Section 2A6.1(b)(1) is amended by deleting "defendant engaged in" and inserting in lieu thereof "offense involved".

Section 2A6.1(b)(2) is amended by deleting "the defendant's conduct" and inserting in lieu thereof "the offense".

This amendment deletes language that could be construed as a limitation on the scope of conduct for which a defendant is accountable under §1B1.3 (Relevant Conduct) and replaces it with language consistent with that used in other offense guidelines. **The effective date of this amendment is November 1, 1993.**

481. Section 2B1.1 is amended in the title by inserting "; Receiving, Transporting, Transferring, Transmitting, or Possessing Stolen Property" at the end thereof.

Section 2B1.1(b)(2) is amended by inserting "(A)" immediately following "If"; and by inserting "or the taking of such item was an object of the offense; or (B) the stolen property received, transported, transferred, transmitted, or possessed was a firearm, destructive device, or controlled substance," immediately following "taken,".

Section 2B1.1(b)(4) is amended by inserting "(A)" immediately following "If"; and by inserting "or the taking of such item was an object of the offense; or (B) the stolen property received, transported, transferred, transmitted, or possessed was undelivered United States mail," immediately following "taken,".

Section 2B1.1(b)(5) is amended by inserting "(A)" immediately before "If"; and by inserting "; or (B) If the offense involved receiving stolen property, and the defendant was a person in the business of receiving and selling stolen property, increase by 4 levels." immediately following "levels".

The Commentary to §2B1.1 captioned "Statutory Provisions" is amended by inserting "553(a)(1)," immediately following "225,"; by inserting "662, 664," immediately before "1702"; and by deleting ", 2317" and inserting in lieu thereof "-2317; 29 U.S.C. § 501(c)".

The Commentary to §2B1.1 captioned "Application Notes" is amended in Note 2 by inserting the following additional paragraph as the next to the last paragraph:

"In stolen property offenses (receiving, transporting, transferring, transmitting, or possessing stolen property), the loss is the value of the stolen property determined as in a theft offense.".

The Commentary to §2B1.1 captioned "Application Notes" is amended by inserting the following additional note:

"14. If the offense involved theft or embezzlement from an employee pension or welfare benefit plan (a violation of 18 U.S.C. § 664) and the defendant was a fiduciary of the benefit plan, an adjustment under §3B1.3 (Abuse of Position of Trust or Use of Special Skill) will apply. 'Fiduciary of the benefit plan' is defined in 29 U.S.C. § 1002(21)(A) to mean a person who exercises any discretionary authority or control in respect to the management of such plan or exercises authority or control in respect to management or disposition of its assets, or who renders investment advice for a fee or other direct or indirect compensation with respect to any moneys or other property of such plan, or has any authority or responsibility to do so, or who has any discretionary authority or responsibility in the administration of such plan.

If the offense involved theft or embezzlement from a labor union (a violation of 29 U.S.C. § 501(c)) and the defendant was a union officer or occupied a position of trust in the union as set forth in 29 U.S.C. § 501(a), an adjustment under §3B1.3 (Abuse of Position of Trust or Use of Special Skill) will apply.".

The Commentary to §2B1.1 captioned "Background" is amended in the first paragraph by deleting "property taken" and inserting in lieu thereof "the property stolen"; by deleting "theft offenses," and inserting in lieu thereof "theft and other offenses involving stolen property"; and by deleting "loss from the theft" and inserting in lieu thereof "loss".

Section 2B1.2 is deleted in its entirety as follows:

"§2B1.2. <u>Receiving, Transporting, Transferring, Transmitting, or Possessing Stolen Property</u>

(a) Base Offense Level: 4

(b) Specific Offense Characteristics

(1) If the value of the stolen property exceeded $100, increase by the corresponding number of levels from the table in §2B1.1.

(2) If the property included a firearm, destructive device, or controlled substance, increase by 1 level; but if the resulting offense level is less than 7, increase to 7.

(3) If the property included undelivered United States mail and the offense level as determined above is less than level 6, increase to level 6.

(4) (A) If the offense was committed by a person in the business of receiving and selling stolen property, increase by 4 levels; or

(B) If the offense involved more than minimal planning, increase by 2 levels.

(5) If the offense involved an organized scheme to receive stolen vehicles or vehicle parts, and the offense level as

determined above is less than level 14, increase to level 14.

Commentary

Statutory Provisions: 18 U.S.C. §§ 553(a)(1), 659, 662, 1708, 2312-2317. For additional statutory provision(s), see Appendix A (Statutory Index).

Application Notes:

1. 'More than minimal planning,' 'firearm,' and 'destructive device' are defined in the Commentary to §1B1.1 (Application Instructions).

2. Valuation of property is discussed in the Commentary to §2B1.1.

3. 'Undelivered United States mail' means mail that has not actually been received by the addressee or his agent (e.g., it includes mail that is in the addressee's mail box).

4. Subsection (b)(5), referring to an 'organized scheme to receive stolen vehicles or vehicle parts,' provides an alternative minimum measure of loss in the case of an ongoing, sophisticated operation such as an auto theft ring or 'chop shop.' 'Vehicles' refers to all forms of vehicles, including aircraft and watercraft. See Commentary to §2B1.1 (Larceny, Embezzlement, and Other Forms of Theft).

Background: The treatment accorded receiving stolen property parallels that given theft. Persons who receive stolen property for resale receive a sentence enhancement because the amount of property is likely to underrepresent the scope of their criminality and the extent to which they encourage or facilitate other crimes.".

Section 2B2.1 is amended in the title by inserting "or a Structure Other than a Residence" at the end thereof.

Section 2B2.1(a) is amended by deleting "Base Offense Level: 17" and inserting in lieu thereof:

"Base Offense Level:

(1) 17, if a residence; or

(2) 12, if a structure other than a residence.".

The Commentary to §2B2.1 captioned "Statutory Provision" is amended by deleting "Provision: 18 U.S.C. § 1153" and inserting in lieu thereof "Provisions: 18 U.S.C. §§ 1153, 2113(a), 2115, 2117, 2118(b). For additional statutory provision(s), see Appendix A (Statutory Index)".

Section 2B2.2 is deleted in its entirety as follows:

"§2B2.2. Burglary of Other Structures

(a) Base Offense Level: 12

(b) Specific Offense Characteristics

(1) If the offense involved more than minimal planning, increase by 2 levels.

(2) If the loss exceeded $2,500, increase by the corresponding number of levels from the table in §2B2.1.

(3) If a firearm, destructive device, or controlled substance was taken, or if the taking of such item was an object of the offense, increase by 1 level.

(4) If a dangerous weapon (including a firearm) was possessed, increase by 2 levels.

Commentary

Statutory Provisions: 18 U.S.C. §§ 2113(a), 2115, 2117, 2118(b). For additional statutory provision(s), see Appendix A (Statutory Index).

Application Notes:

1. 'More than minimal planning,' 'firearm,' 'destructive device,' and 'dangerous weapon' are defined in the Commentary to §1B1.1 (Application Instructions).

2. Valuation of loss is discussed in the Commentary to §2B1.1 (Larceny, Embezzlement, and Other Forms of Theft).

3. Subsection (b)(4) does not apply to possession of a dangerous weapon (including a firearm) that was stolen during the course of the offense.

Background: The offense level for burglary is significantly higher than that for theft for low losses, but is approximately the same for very high losses. Weapon possession, but not use, is a specific offense characteristic because use of a weapon (including to threaten) ordinarily would make the offense robbery. Weapon use would be a ground for upward departure.".

Chapter Two, Part B, Subpart 5 is amended in the title by deleting ", FORGERY," immediately before "AND".

Section 2B5.2 is deleted in its entirety as follows:

"§2B5.2. Forgery; Offenses Involving Altered or Counterfeit Instruments Other than Counterfeit Bearer Obligations of the United States

Apply §2F1.1 (Fraud and Deceit).

Commentary

Statutory Provisions: 18 U.S.C. §§ 471-473, 500, 510, 1003, 2314, 2315. For additional statutory provision(s), see Appendix A (Statutory Index).".

Section 2B5.3 is amended in the title by inserting "or Trademark" at the end thereof.

The Commentary to §2B5.3 captioned "Statutory Provisions" is amended by deleting "2319" and inserting in lieu thereof "2318-2320".

The Commentary to §2B5.3 captioned "Background" is amended in the first paragraph by inserting "and trademark" immediately following "copyright".

Section 2B5.4 is deleted in its entirety as follows:

"§2B5.4. Criminal Infringement of Trademark

(a) Base Offense Level: 6

(b) Specific Offense Characteristic

(1) If the retail value of the infringing items exceeded $2,000, increase by the corresponding number of levels from the table in §2F1.1 (Fraud and Deceit).

Commentary

Statutory Provisions: 18 U.S.C. §§ 2318, 2320.

Background: The Commission concluded that trademark infringement is roughly comparable to copyright infringement.".

Section 2D3.2 is amended in the title by deleting "Manufacture of Controlled Substance in Excess of or Unauthorized by Registration Quota; Attempt or Conspiracy" and inserting in lieu thereof "Regulatory Offenses Involving Controlled Substances; Attempt or Conspiracy".

The Commentary to §2D3.2 captioned "Statutory Provisions" is amended by deleting "842(b), 843(a)(3)" and inserting in lieu thereof "842(a)(2), (9), (10), (b), 954, 961".

The Commentary to §2D3.2 captioned "Background" is amended by deleting "This offense is a misdemeanor" and inserting in lieu thereof "These offenses are misdemeanors".

Sections 2D3.3, 2D3.4, and 2D3.5 are deleted in their entirety as follows:

"§2D3.3. Illegal Use of Registration Number to Distribute or Dispense a Controlled Substance to Another Registrant or Authorized Person; Attempt or Conspiracy

(a) Base Offense Level: 4

Commentary

Statutory Provision: 21 U.S.C. § 842(a)(2).

Background: This offense is a misdemeanor. The maximum term of imprisonment authorized by statute is one year.

§2D3.4. Illegal Transfer or Transshipment of a Controlled Substance; Attempt or Conspiracy

(a) Base Offense Level: 4

Commentary

Statutory Provisions: 21 U.S.C. §§ 954, 961.

Background: This offense is a misdemeanor. The maximum term of imprisonment authorized by statute is one year.

§2D3.5. Violation of Recordkeeping or Reporting Requirements for Listed Chemicals and Certain Machines; Attempt or Conspiracy

(a) Base Offense Level: 4

Commentary

Statutory Provisions: 21 U.S.C. § 842(a)(9), (10).".

Section 2E1.5 is deleted in its entirety as follows:

"§2E1.5. Hobbs Act Extortion or Robbery

Apply §2B3.1 (Robbery), §2B3.2 (Extortion by Force or Threat of Injury or Serious Damage), §2B3.3 (Blackmail and Similar Forms of Extortion), or §2C1.1 (Offering, Giving, Soliciting, or Receiving a Bribe; Extortion Under Color of Official Right), as applicable.

Commentary

Statutory Provision: 18 U.S.C. § 1951.".

Section 2E3.1 is amended in the title by deleting "Engaging in a Gambling Business" and inserting in lieu thereof "Gambling Offenses".

Section 2E3.1(a) is amended by deleting "12" and inserting in lieu thereof:

"(1) 12, if the offense was (A) engaging in a gambling business; (B) transmission of wagering information; or (C) committed as part of, or to facilitate, a commercial gambling operation; or

(2) 6, otherwise.".

The Commentary to §2E3.1 captioned "Statutory Provision" is amended by deleting "Provision: 18 U.S.C. § 1955" and inserting in lieu thereof "Provisions: 15 U.S.C. §§ 1172-1175; 18 U.S.C. §§ 1082, 1301-1304, 1306, 1511, 1953, 1955. For additional statutory provision(s), see Appendix A (Statutory Index)".

Sections 2E3.2 and 2E3.3 are deleted in their entirety as follows:

"§2E3.2. Transmission of Wagering Information

(a) Base Offense Level: 12

Commentary

Statutory Provision: 18 U.S.C. § 1084.

§2E3.3. Other Gambling Offenses

(a) Base Offense Level: 6

(b) Specific Offense Characteristic

(1) If the offense is committed as part of, or to facilitate, a commercial gambling operation, increase by 6 levels.

Commentary

Statutory Provisions: 15 U.S.C. §§ 1172-1175; 18 U.S.C. §§ 1082, 1301-1304, 1306, 1511, 1953. For additional statutory provision(s), see Appendix A (Statutory Index).

Background: This section includes a wide variety of conduct. A specific offense characteristic has been included to distinguish commercial from other gambling offenses.".

Section 2E5.1 is amended in the title by inserting "; Prohibited Payments or Lending of Money by Employer or Agent to Employees, Representatives, or Labor Organizations" at the end thereof.

Section 2E5.1(b)(1) is amended by inserting "or labor organization" immediately following "plan".

The Commentary to §2E5.1 captioned "Statutory Provision" is amended by deleting "Provision: 18 U.S.C. § 1954" and inserting in lieu thereof "Provisions: 18 U.S.C. § 1954; 29 U.S.C. § 186".

The Commentary to §2E5.1 captioned "Background" is amended by inserting ", or labor organizations" immediately following "plans"; and by deleting the last sentence as follows:

"A more severe penalty is warranted in a bribery where the payment is the primary motivation for an action to be taken, as opposed to graft, where the prohibited payment is given because of a person's actions, duties, or decisions without a prior understanding that the recipient's performance will be directly influenced by the gift.".

Section 2E5.2 is deleted in its entirety as follows:

"§2E5.2. Theft or Embezzlement from Employee Pension and Welfare Benefit Plans

Apply §2B1.1 (Larceny, Embezzlement, and Other Forms of Theft).

Commentary

Statutory Provision: 18 U.S.C. § 664.

Application Note:

1. In the case of a defendant who was a fiduciary of the benefit plan, an adjustment under §3B1.3 (Abuse of Position of Trust or Use of Special Skill) will apply. 'Fiduciary of the benefit plan' is defined in 29 U.S.C. § 1002(21)(A) to mean a person who exercises any discretionary authority or control in respect to the management of such plan or exercises authority or control in respect to management or disposition of its assets, or who renders investment advice for a fee or other direct or indirect compensation with respect to any moneys or other property of such plan, or has any authority or responsibility to do so, or who has any discretionary authority or responsibility in the administration of such plan.

Background: This section covers theft or conversion from employee benefit plans by fiduciaries, or by any person, including borrowers to whom loans are disbursed based upon materially defective loan applications, service providers who are paid on inflated billings, and beneficiaries paid as the result of fraudulent claims.".

Section 2E5.3 is amended in the title by inserting "; Failure to Maintain and Falsification of Records Required by the Labor Management Reporting and Disclosure Act" at the end thereof.

Section 2E5.3(a)(2) is amended by deleting "relating to the operation of an employee benefit plan, apply §2E5.2" and inserting in lieu thereof ", apply §2B1.1".

The Commentary to §2E5.3 captioned "Statutory Provision" is amended by deleting "Provision: 18 U.S.C. § 1027" and inserting in lieu thereof "Provisions: 18 U.S.C. § 1027; 29 U.S.C. §§ 439, 461, 1131. For additional statutory provision(s), see Appendix A (Statutory Index)".

The Commentary to §2E5.3 captioned "Background" is amended by inserting the following additional sentence as the second sentence:

"It also covers failure to maintain proper documents required by the LMRDA or falsification of such documents.".

Sections 2E5.4, 2E5.5, and 2E5.6 are deleted in their entirety as follows:

"§2E5.4. Embezzlement or Theft from Labor Unions in the Private Sector

Apply §2B1.1 (Larceny, Embezzlement, and Other Forms of Theft).

Commentary

Statutory Provision: 29 U.S.C. § 501(c).

Application Note:

1. In the case of a defendant who was a union officer or occupied a position of trust in the union, as set forth in 29 U.S.C. § 501(a), an adjustment under §3B1.3 (Abuse of Position of Trust or Use of Special Skill) would apply.

Background: This section includes embezzlement or theft from a labor organization. It is directed at union officers and persons employed by a union.

§2E5.5. Failure to Maintain and Falsification of Records Required by the Labor Management Reporting and Disclosure Act

(a) Base Offense Level (Apply the greater):

(1) 6; or

(2) If the offense was committed to facilitate or conceal a theft or embezzlement, or an offense involving a bribe or gratuity, apply §2E5.4 or §2E5.6, as applicable.

Commentary

Statutory Provisions: 29 U.S.C. §§ 439, 461. For additional statutory provision(s), see Appendix A (Statutory Index).

Background: This section covers failure to maintain proper documents required by the LMRDA or falsification of such documents. This offense is a misdemeanor.

§2E5.6. Prohibited Payments or Lending of Money by Employer or Agent to Employees, Representatives, or Labor Organizations

(a) Base Offense Level:

(1) 10, if a bribe; or

(2) 6, if a gratuity.

(b) Specific Offense Characteristic

(1) Increase by the number of levels from the table in §2F1.1 (Fraud and Deceit) corresponding to the value of the prohibited payment or the value of the improper benefit to the payer, whichever is greater.

(c) Special Instruction for Fines - Organizations

(1) In lieu of the pecuniary loss under subsection (a)(3) of §8C2.4 (Base Fine), use the greatest of: (A) the value of the unlawful payment; (B) if a bribe, the value of the benefit received or to be received in return for the unlawful payment; or (C) if a bribe, the consequential damages resulting from the unlawful payment.

Commentary

Statutory Provision: 29 U.S.C. § 186.

Application Notes:

1. 'Bribe' refers to the offer or acceptance of an unlawful payment with the specific understanding that it will corruptly affect an official action of the recipient.

2. 'Gratuity' refers to the offer or acceptance of an unlawful payment other than a bribe.

3. 'Value of the improper benefit to the payer' is explained in the Commentary to §2C1.1 (Offering, Giving, Soliciting, or Receiving a Bribe; Extortion Under Color of Official Right).".

Section 2F1.1 is amended in the title by inserting "; Forgery; Offenses Involving Altered or Counterfeit Instruments Other than Counterfeit Bearer Obligations of the United States" at the end thereof.

The Commentary to §2F1.1 captioned "Statutory Provisions" is amended by inserting "471-473, 500, 510," immediately following "289,"; and by inserting ", 2314, 2315" immediately following "1344".

Section 2J1.3 is amended in the title by inserting "; Bribery of Witness" at the end thereof.

Section 2J1.3(b)(2) is amended by deleting "perjury or subornation of perjury" and inserting in lieu thereof "perjury, subornation of perjury, or witness bribery".

Section 2J1.3(c)(1) is amended by deleting "perjury or subornation of perjury" and inserting in lieu thereof "perjury, subornation of perjury, or witness bribery".

The Commentary to §2J1.3 captioned "Statutory Provisions" is amended by inserting "201 (b)(3), (4)," immediately before "1621".

The Commentary to §2J1.3 captioned "Application Notes" is amended in Note 3 by inserting ", subornation of perjury, or witness bribery" immediately following "perjury".

The Commentary to §2J1.3 captioned "Background" is amended by deleting "perjury and subornation of perjury" and inserting in lieu thereof "perjury, subornation of perjury, and witness bribery".

Section 2J1.8 is deleted in its entirety as follows:

"§2J1.8. Bribery of Witness

(a) Base Offense Level: 12

(b) Specific Offense Characteristic

(1) If the offense resulted in substantial interference with the administration of justice, increase by 3 levels.

(c) Cross Reference

(1) If the offense involved bribery of a witness in respect to a criminal offense, apply §2X3.1 (Accessory After the Fact) in respect to that criminal offense, if the resulting offense level is greater than that determined above.

Commentary

Statutory Provisions: 18 U.S.C. § 201(b)(3), (4).

Application Notes:

1. 'Substantial interference with the administration of justice' includes a premature or improper termination of a felony investigation; an indictment, verdict, or any judicial determination based upon perjury, false testimony, or other false evidence; or the unnecessary expenditure of substantial governmental or court resources.

2. For offenses covered under this section, Chapter Three, Part C (Obstruction) does not apply, unless the defendant obstructed the investigation or trial of the witness bribery count.

3. In the event that the defendant is convicted under this section as well as for the underlying offense (i.e., the offense with respect to which the bribery occurred), see the Commentary to Chapter Three, Part C (Obstruction), and to §3D1.2(c) (Groups of Closely Related Counts).

Background: This section applies to witness bribery. The offense levels correspond to those for perjury (§2J1.3).".

Section 2K1.1 is amended in the title by inserting "; Improper Storage of Explosive Materials" at the end thereof.

The Commentary to §2K1.1 captioned "Statutory Provisions" is amended by deleting "842(k), 844(b)" and inserting in lieu thereof "842(j), (k), 844(b). For additional statutory provision(s), see Appendix A (Statutory Index)".

Section 2K1.2 is deleted in its entirety as follows:

"§2K1.2. Improper Storage of Explosive Materials

(a) Base Offense Level: 6

Commentary

Statutory Provision: 18 U.S.C. § 842(j). For additional statutory provision(s), see Appendix A (Statutory Index).

Background: The above-referenced provision is a misdemeanor. The maximum term of imprisonment authorized by statute is one year.".

Section 2K1.7 is deleted in its entirety as follows:

"§2K1.7. Use of Fire or Explosives to Commit a Federal Felony

(a) If the defendant, whether or not convicted of another crime, was convicted under 18 U.S.C. § 844(h), the term of imprisonment is that required by statute.

(b) Special Instruction for Fines

(1) Where there is a federal conviction for the underlying offense, the fine guideline shall be the fine guideline that would have been applicable had there only been a conviction for the underlying offense. This guideline shall be used as a consolidated fine guideline for both the underlying offense and the conviction underlying this section.

Commentary

Statutory Provision: 18 U.S.C. § 844(h).

Application Notes:

1. The statute requires a term of imprisonment imposed under this section to run consecutively to any other term of imprisonment.

2. Imposition of a term of supervised release is governed by the provisions of §5D1.1 (Imposition of a Term of Supervised Release).

3. Where a sentence under this section is imposed in conjunction with a sentence for an underlying offense, any specific offense characteristic for the use of fire or explosives is not to be applied in respect to the guideline for the underlying offense.

4. Subsection (b) sets forth special provisions concerning the imposition of fines. Where there is also a conviction for the underlying offense, a consolidated fine guideline is determined by the offense level that would have applied to the underlying offense absent a conviction under 18 U.S.C. § 844(h). This is required because the offense level for the underlying offense may be reduced in that any specific offense characteristic for use of fire or explosives would not be applied (see Application Note 3). The Commission has not established a fine guideline range for the unusual case in which there is no conviction for the underlying offense, although a fine is authorized under 18 U.S.C. § 3571.".

Section 2K2.4 is amended in the title by deleting "Firearms or Armor-Piercing Ammunition" and inserting in lieu thereof "Firearm, Armor-Piercing Ammunition, or Explosive".

Section 2K2.4(a) is amended by deleting "§ 924(c)" and inserting in lieu thereof "§ 844(h), § 924(c),".

The Commentary to §2K2.4 captioned "Statutory Provisions" is amended by inserting "844(h)," immediately before "924(c)".

The Commentary to §2K2.4 captioned "Application Notes" is amended in Note 2 in the first paragraph by deleting "a firearm" and inserting in lieu thereof "an explosive or firearm"; and by deleting the comma immediately following "(Robbery))".

The Commentary to §2K2.4 captioned "Application Notes" is amended in Note 4 by deleting "§ 924(c)" wherever it occurs and inserting in lieu thereof in each instance "§ 844(h), § 924(c),".

The Commentary to §2K2.4 captioned "Background" is amended by deleting "924(c)" and inserting in lieu thereof "844(h), 924(c),"; and by inserting "explosive or" immediately before "firearm".

Chapter Two, Part K, Subpart 3 is amended in the title by deleting "TRANSPORTATION OF HAZARDOUS MATERIALS" and inserting in lieu thereof "MAILING INJURIOUS ARTICLES".

Section 2K3.1 is deleted in its entirety as follows:

"§2K3.1. Unlawfully Transporting Hazardous Materials in Commerce

Apply the guideline provision for §2Q1.2 (Mishandling of Hazardous or Toxic Substances or Pesticides; Recordkeeping, Tampering, and Falsification).

Commentary

Statutory Provision: 49 U.S.C. § 1809(b). For additional statutory provision(s), see Appendix A (Statutory Index).

Background: This conduct involves the same risks as the conduct covered under §2Q1.2 (Mishandling of Hazardous or Toxic Substances or Pesticides; Recordkeeping, Tampering, and Falsification). Accordingly, that guideline applies.".

Section 2L2.1 is amended in the title by deleting "Documents" and inserting in lieu thereof "a Document"; and by inserting ", or a United States Passport" immediately following "Status".

Section 2L2.1(b)(2) is amended by inserting "or passports" immediately following "documents"; and by inserting "/Passports" immediately following "Documents".

The Commentary to §2L2.1 captioned "Statutory Provisions" is amended by inserting "1542, 1544," immediately following "1427,".

The Commentary to §2L2.1 captioned "Application Notes" is amended in Note 2 by deleting "set as one document" and inserting in lieu thereof "documents as one set".

Section 2L2.2 is amended in the title by inserting "; Fraudulently Acquiring or Improperly Using a United States Passport" at the end thereof.

The Commentary to §2L2.2 captioned "Statutory Provisions" is amended by inserting "1542-1544," immediately before "1546.".

Sections 2L2.3 and 2L2.4 are deleted in their entirety as follows:

"§2L2.3. Trafficking in a United States Passport

(a) Base Offense Level: 9

(b) Specific Offense Characteristics

(1) If the defendant committed the offense other than for profit, decrease by 3 levels.

(2) If the offense involved six or more passports, increase as follows:

	Number of Passports	Increase in Level
(A)	6-24	add 2
(B)	25-99	add 4
(C)	100 or more	add 6.

Commentary

Statutory Provisions: 18 U.S.C. §§ 1542, 1544. For additional statutory provision(s), see Appendix A (Statutory Index).

Application Note:

1. 'For profit' means for financial gain or commercial advantage.

§2L2.4. Fraudulently Acquiring or Improperly Using a United States Passport

(a) Base Offense Level: 6

(b) Specific Offense Characteristic

(1) If the defendant is an unlawful alien who has been deported (voluntarily or involuntarily) on one or more occasions prior to the instant offense, increase by 2 levels.

Commentary

Statutory Provisions: 18 U.S.C. §§ 1543, 1544. For additional statutory provision(s), see Appendix A (Statutory Index).

Application Note:

1. For the purposes of Chapter Three, Part D (Multiple Counts), a conviction for unlawfully entering or remaining in the United States (§2L1.2) arising from the same course of conduct is treated as a closely related count, and is therefore grouped with an offense covered by this guideline.".

Section 2M2.1 is amended in the title by inserting ", or Production of Defective," immediately following "Destruction of".

The Commentary to §2M2.1 captioned "Statutory Provisions" is amended by inserting ", 2154" immediately following "2153".

Section 2M2.2 is deleted in its entirety as follows:

"§2M2.2. Production of Defective War Material, Premises, or Utilities

(a) Base Offense Level: 32

Commentary

Statutory Provision: 18 U.S.C. § 2154.".

Section 2M2.3 is amended in the title by inserting ", or Production of Defective," immediately following "Destruction of".

The Commentary to §2M2.3 captioned "Statutory Provisions" is amended by inserting ", 2156" immediately following "2155".

Section 2M2.4 is deleted in its entirety as follows:

"§2M2.4. Production of Defective National Defense Material, Premises, or Utilities

(a) Base Offense Level: 26

Commentary

Statutory Provision: 18 U.S.C. § 2156.".

Section 2M3.3 is amended in the title by inserting "; Disclosure of Classified Cryptographic Information; Unauthorized Disclosure to a Foreign Government or a Communist Organization of Classified Information by Government Employee; Unauthorized Receipt of Classified Information" at the end thereof.

Section 2M3.3(a)(1) is amended by deleting "was transmitted" immediately following "information".

The Commentary to §2M3.3 captioned "Statutory Provisions" is amended by deleting ". For additional statutory provision(s), see Appendix A (Statutory Index)" and inserting in lieu thereof ", 798; 50 U.S.C. § 783(b), (c)".

The Commentary to §2M3.3 captioned "Background" is amended by inserting the following additional paragraph at the end:

" This section also covers statutes that proscribe the disclosure of classified information concerning cryptographic or communication intelligence to the detriment of the United States or for the benefit of a foreign government, the unauthorized disclosure to a foreign government or a communist organization of classified information by a government employee, and the unauthorized receipt of classified information.".

Sections 2M3.6, 2M3.7, and 2M3.8 are deleted in their entirety as follows:

"§2M3.6. Disclosure of Classified Cryptographic Information

(a) Base Offense Level:

(1) 29, if top secret information was disclosed; or

(2) 24, otherwise.

Commentary

Statutory Provision: 18 U.S.C. § 798.

Application Note:

1. See Commentary to §2M3.1.

Background: The statute covered in this section proscribes the disclosure of classified information concerning cryptographic or communication intelligence to the detriment of the United States or for the benefit of a foreign government.

§2M3.7. Unauthorized Disclosure to Foreign Government or a Communist Organization of Classified Information by Government Employee

(a) Base Offense Level:

(1) 29, if top secret information was disclosed; or

(2) 24, otherwise.

Commentary

Statutory Provision: 50 U.S.C. § 783(b).

Application Note:

1. See Commentary to §2M3.1.

§2M3.8. Receipt of Classified Information

(a) Base Offense Level:

(1) 29, if top secret information was received; or

(2) 24, otherwise.

Commentary

Statutory Provision: 50 U.S.C. § 783(c).

Application Note:

1. See Commentary to §2M3.1.".

Section 2Q1.2 is amended in the title by inserting "; Unlawfully Transporting Hazardous Materials in Commerce" at the end thereof.

The Commentary to §2Q1.2 captioned "Statutory Provisions" is amended by inserting "; 49 U.S.C. § 1809(b)" immediately following "1822(b)".

This amendment deletes 25 offense guidelines by consolidating them with other offense guidelines that cover similar offense conduct and have identical or very similar base offense levels and adjustments. Consolidation of offense guidelines in this manner has a number of practical advantages: it shortens and simplifies the Guidelines Manual and reduces the likelihood of inconsistency in phraseology and definitions from section to section; it will reduce possible confusion and litigation as to which guideline applies to particular conduct; it will reduce the number of conforming amendments required whenever similar sections are amended; and it will aid the development of case law because cases involving similar or identical concepts and definitions can be referenced under one guideline rather than different guidelines. **The effective date of this amendment is November 1, 1993.**

482. The Commentary to §2B1.1 captioned "Application Notes" is amended in Note 2 by inserting the following additional sentence as the fourth sentence of the first paragraph:

"Loss does not include the interest that could have been earned had the funds not been stolen.";

and by inserting the following additional paragraphs as the second and third paragraphs:

"Where the offense involved making a fraudulent loan or credit card application, or other unlawful conduct involving a loan or credit card, the loss is to be determined under the principles set forth in the Commentary to §2F1.1 (Fraud and Deceit).

In certain cases, an offense may involve a series of transactions without a corresponding increase in loss. For example, a defendant may embezzle $5,000 from a bank and conceal this embezzlement by shifting this amount from one account to another in a series of nine transactions over a six-month period. In this example, the loss is $5,000 (the amount taken), not $45,000 (the sum of the nine transactions), because the additional transactions did not increase the actual or potential loss.".

The Commentary to §2B1.1 captioned "Application Notes" is amended by deleting Note 3 as follows:

"3. The loss need not be determined with precision, and may be inferred from any reasonably reliable information available, including the scope of the operation.",

and inserting in lieu thereof:

"3. For the purposes of subsection (b)(1), the loss need not be determined with precision. The court need only make a reasonable estimate of the loss, given the available information. This estimate, for example, may be based upon the approximate number of victims and the average loss to each victim, or on more general factors such as the scope and duration of the offense.".

The Commentary to §2B5.3 is amended by inserting the following immediately before "Background":

"Application Note:

1. 'Infringing items' means the items that violate the copyright or trademark laws (not the legitimate items that are infringed upon).".

The Commentary to §2B6.1 captioned "Application Note" is amended in the caption by deleting "Note" and inserting in lieu thereof "Notes"; and by inserting the following additional Note:

"2. The 'corresponding number of levels from the table in §2F1.1 (Fraud and Deceit),' as used in subsection (b)(1), refers to the number of levels corresponding to the retail value of the motor vehicles or parts involved.".

Section 2F1.1(b)(3) is amended by deleting "or process" and by inserting in lieu thereof ", or process not addressed elsewhere in the guidelines".

The Commentary to §2F1.1 captioned "Application Notes" is amended in Note 5 in the first sentence by inserting a comma immediately following "decree"; and by inserting the following additional sentence at the end:

"This subsection does not apply to conduct addressed elsewhere in the guidelines; e.g., a violation of a condition of release (addressed in §2J1.7 (Offense Committed While on Release)) or a violation of probation (addressed in §4A1.1 (Criminal History Category)).".

The Commentary to §2F1.1 captioned "Application Notes" is amended in Note 7(b) in the second paragraph by inserting the following additional sentence at the end:

> "Where the loss determined above significantly understates or overstates the seriousness of the defendant's conduct, an upward or downward departure may be warranted.".

The Commentary to §2F1.1 captioned "Application Notes" is amended in Note 10 by deleting "the primary" and inserting in lieu thereof "a primary"; by inserting "; or the fraud caused or risked reasonably foreseeable, substantial non-monetary harm" immediately following "was non-monetary"; by deleting "physical or psychological harm" and inserting in lieu thereof "reasonably foreseeable, physical or psychological harm or severe emotional trauma"; by deleting the period immediately following "institution" and inserting in lieu thereof a semicolon; by inserting a new subdivision, immediately following subdivision (e), as follows:

> "(f) the offense involved the knowing endangerment of the solvency of one or more victims.";

and by inserting the following additional sentence at the end of the last paragraph:

> "In such cases, a downward departure may be warranted.".

The Commentary to §2F1.1 captioned "Application Notes" is amended in Note 11 by deleting the last two sentences as follows:

> "The statutes provide for increased maximum terms of imprisonment for the use or possession of device-making equipment and the production or transfer of more than five identification documents or fifteen access devices. The court may find it appropriate to enhance the sentence for violations of these statutes in a manner similar to the treatment of analogous counterfeiting offenses under Part B of this Chapter.",

and inserting in lieu thereof:

> "Where the primary purpose of the offense involved the unlawful production, transfer, possession, or use of identification documents for the purpose of violating, or assisting another to violate, the laws relating to naturalization, citizenship, or legal resident status, apply §2L2.1 or §2L2.2, as appropriate, rather than §2F1.1. In the case of an offense involving false identification documents or access devices, an upward departure may be warranted where the actual loss does not adequately reflect the seriousness of the conduct.".

This amendment makes the definitions of loss in §§2B1.1 (Larceny, Embezzlement, and Other Forms of Theft) and 2F1.1 (Fraud and Deceit) more consistent. Although the term "reasonably reliable information" is deleted from §2B1.1 (there is no corresponding term in §2F1.1), no substantive change results because the reliability of the information considered in respect to all cases is already addressed in §6A1.3 (Resolution of Disputed Factors). In addition, this amendment provides additional guidance for the determination of loss in cases that are referenced to §2B1.1, but have loss characteristics closely resembling offenses referenced to §2F1.1, and in cases in which simply adding the amounts from a series of transactions does not reflect the amount taken or put at risk. This amendment also clarifies the meaning of the term "infringing items" in §2B5.3, and expressly provides that the reference in §2B6.1 to the table in §2F1.1 is to be applied using the retail value of the stolen parts. In addition, this amendment clarifies the operation of §2F1.1(b)(3) to avoid inappropriate double counting. Finally, this amendment revises the Commentary to §2F1.1 by expanding Application Note 10 to provide guidance in cases in which the monetary loss does not adequately reflect the seriousness of the offense, and by clarifying Application Note 11 and conforming the phraseology in this application note to that used elsewhere in the guidelines. **The effective date of this amendment is November 1, 1993.**

483. Section 2B3.1(b)(1) is amended by inserting "(A)" immediately following "If"; and by inserting "or (B) the offense involved carjacking," immediately before "increase".

Section 2B3.1 is amended by inserting the following additional subsection:

"(c) Cross Reference

(1) If a victim was killed under circumstances that would constitute murder under 18 U.S.C. § 1111 had such killing taken place within the territorial or maritime jurisdiction of the United States, apply §2A1.1 (First Degree Murder).".

The Commentary to §2B3.1 captioned "Statutory Provisions" is amended by inserting ", 2119" immediately following "2118(a)".

The Commentary to §2B3.1 captioned "Application Notes" is amended in Note 1 by inserting the following additional paragraph at the end:

"'Carjacking' means the taking or attempted taking of a motor vehicle from the person or presence of another by force and violence or by intimidation.".

The Commentary to §2B3.1 captioned "Application Notes" is amended by deleting Note 6 as follows:

"6. If the defendant was convicted under 18 U.S.C. § 2113(e) and in committing the offense or attempting to flee or escape, a participant killed any person, apply §2A1.1 (First Degree Murder). Otherwise, if death results, see Chapter Five, Part K (Departures).";

and by renumbering Note 7 as Note 6.

This amendment adds a specific offense characteristic for carjacking to §2B3.1, references 18 U.S.C. § 2119 (carjacking offenses) to this guideline, and adds a cross reference to this guideline to address the circumstance in which a victim is murdered during the offense. **The effective date of this amendment is November 1, 1993.**

484. The Commentary to §2D1.1 captioned "Application Notes" is amended in Note 1 by deleting "21 U.S.C. § 841." and inserting in lieu thereof:

"21 U.S.C. § 841, except as expressly provided. Mixture or substance does not include materials that must be separated from the controlled substance before the controlled substance can be used. Examples of such materials include the fiberglass in a cocaine/fiberglass bonded suitcase, beeswax in a cocaine/beeswax statue, and waste water from an illicit laboratory used to manufacture a controlled substance. If such material cannot readily be separated from the mixture or substance that appropriately is counted in the Drug Quantity Table, the court may use any reasonable method to approximate the weight of the mixture or substance to be counted.

An upward departure nonetheless may be warranted when the mixture or substance counted in the Drug Quantity Table is combined with other, non-countable material in an unusually sophisticated manner in order to avoid detection.".

This amendment addresses an inter-circuit conflict regarding the meaning of the term "mixture or substance," as used in §2D1.1 by expressly providing that this term does not include portions of a drug mixture that have to be separated from the controlled substance before the controlled substance can be used. This issue has arisen, subsequent to the United States Supreme Court decision in Chapman v. United States, 111 S. Ct. 1919 (1991), in two types of cases. The first type of case involves a controlled substance bonded to, or suspended in, another substance (e.g., cocaine mixed with beeswax); however, the controlled substance is not usable until it is separated from the other substance. See, e.g., United States v. Mahecha-Onofre, 936 F.2d 623 (1st Cir.), cert. denied, 112 S. Ct. 648 (1991); United States v. Restrepo-Contreras, 942 F.2d 96 (1st Cir. 1991), cert. denied, 112 S. Ct. 955 (1992). The second type of case involves the waste produced from an illicit laboratory used to manufacture a controlled substance or chemicals confiscated before the chemical processing of the controlled substance is completed. The waste product is typically water or chemicals used to either remove impurities or form a precipitate (the precipitate, in some cases, being the controlled substance). Typically, a small amount of controlled substance remains in the waste water; often this amount is too small to quantify and is listed as a trace amount (no weight given) in DEA reports. In these types of cases, the waste product is not consumable. The chemicals seized before the end of processing are also not usable in that form because further processing must take place before they can be used. See, e.g., United States v. Sherrod, 964 F.2d 1501 (5th Cir.), cert. denied sub nom. Cooper v. United States, 113 S. Ct. 832 (1992) (White and Blackmun, JJ., dissenting from denial of cert.), and cert. denied sub nom. United States v. Sewell, 113 S. Ct. 1367 (1993) (White and Blackmun, JJ., opinion dissenting from denial of cert.). **The effective date of this amendment is November 1, 1993.**

485. The Commentary to §2D1.1 captioned "Application Notes" is amended by inserting the following additional note:

"16. Where (A) the amount of the controlled substance for which the defendant is accountable under §1B1.3 (Relevant Conduct) results in a base offense level greater than 36, (B) the court finds that this offense level overrepresents the defendant's culpability in the criminal activity, and (C) the defendant qualifies for a mitigating role adjustment under §3B1.2 (Mitigating Role), a downward departure may be warranted. The court may depart to a sentence no lower than the guideline range that would have resulted if the defendant's Chapter Two offense level had been offense level 36. Provided, that a defendant is not eligible for a downward departure under this provision if the defendant:

(a) has one or more prior felony convictions for a crime of violence or a controlled substance offense as defined in §4B1.2 (Definitions of Terms Used in Section 4B1.1);

(b) qualifies for an adjustment under §3B1.3 (Abuse of Position of Trust or Use of Special Skill);

(c) possessed or induced another participant to use or possess a firearm in the offense;

(d) had decision-making authority;

(e) owned the controlled substance or financed any part of the offense; or

(f) sold the controlled substance or played a substantial part in negotiating the terms of the sale.

Example: A defendant, who the court finds meets the criteria for a downward departure under this provision, has a Chapter Two offense level of 40, a 2-level reduction for a minor role from §3B1.2, and a 3-level reduction for acceptance of responsibility from §3E1.1. His final offense level is 35. If the defendant's Chapter Two offense level had been 36, the 2-level reduction for a minor role and 3-level reduction for acceptance of responsibility would have resulted in a final offense level of 31. Therefore, under this provision, a downward departure not to exceed 4 levels (from level 35 to level 31) would be authorized.".

Where a defendant's base offense level is greater than level 36 and the defendant had a minimal or minor role in the offense (and meets certain other qualifications), the quantity of the controlled substance for which the defendant is held accountable under §1B1.3 (Relevant Conduct) may overrepresent the defendant's culpability in the criminal activity. To address this issue, this amendment adds an application note to §2D1.1 that authorizes a downward departure in the specific circumstances described and sets forth the extent of a departure authorized on this basis. **The effective date of this amendment is November 1, 1993.**

486. The Commentary to §2D1.1 captioned "Application Notes" is amended by inserting the following additional note:

"17. If, in a reverse sting (an operation in which a government agent sells or negotiates to sell a controlled substance to a defendant), the court finds that the government agent set a price for the controlled substance that was substantially below the market value of the controlled substance, thereby leading to the defendant's purchase of a significantly greater quantity of the controlled substance than his available resources would have allowed him to purchase except for the artificially low price set by the government agent, a downward departure may be warranted.".

This amendment adds an application note to §2D1.1 authorizing a downward departure if, in a reverse sting operation, the court finds that the government agent set a price for the controlled substance that was substantially below market value and thereby significantly inflated the quantity of controlled substance purchased by the defendant beyond the amount the defendant otherwise could have afforded. **The effective date of this amendment is November 1, 1993.**

487. Section 2D1.1(c) is amended in the notes following the Drug Quantity Table by inserting the following additional paragraph as the third paragraph.

"'Cocaine base,' for the purposes of this guideline, means 'crack.' 'Crack' is the street name for a form of cocaine base, usually prepared by processing cocaine hydrochloride and sodium bicarbonate, and usually appearing in a lumpy, rocklike form.".

This amendment provides that, for purposes of the guidelines, "cocaine base" means "crack." The amendment addresses an inter-circuit conflict. Compare, e.g., United States v. Shaw, 936 F.2d 412 (9th Cir. 1991) (cocaine base means crack) with United States v. Jackson, 968 F.2d 158 (2d Cir) (cocaine base has a scientific, chemical definition that is more inclusive than crack), cert. denied, 113 S. Ct. 664 (1992). Under this amendment, forms of cocaine base other than crack (e.g., coca paste, an intermediate step in the processing of coca leaves into cocaine hydrochloride, scientifically is a base form of cocaine, but it is not crack) will be treated as cocaine. **The effective date of this amendment is November 1, 1993.**

488. Section 2D1.1(c) is amended in the notes following the Drug Quantity Table by inserting the following additional paragraph at the end:

"In the case of LSD on a carrier medium (e.g., a sheet of blotter paper), do not use the weight of the LSD/carrier medium. Instead, treat each dose of LSD on the carrier medium as equal to 0.4 mg of LSD for the purposes of the Drug Quantity Table.".

The Commentary to §2D1.1 captioned "Application Notes" is amended in note 11 by deleting the first entry in the "Typical Weight Per Unit Table" as follows:

"LSD (Lysergic acid diethylamide) 0.05 mg".

The Commentary to §2D1.1 captioned "Application Notes" is amended by inserting the following additional note:

"18. LSD on a blotter paper carrier medium typically is marked so that the number of doses ('hits') per sheet readily can be determined. When this is not the case, it is to be presumed that each 1/4 inch by 1/4 inch section of the blotter paper is equal to one dose.

In the case of liquid LSD (LSD that has not been placed onto a carrier medium), using the weight of the LSD alone to calculate the offense level may not adequately reflect the seriousness of the offense. In such a case, an upward departure may be warranted.".

The Commentary to §2D1.1 captioned "Background" is amended by inserting the following paragraphs at the end:

"Because the weights of LSD carrier media vary widely and typically far exceed the weight of the controlled substance itself, the Commission has determined that basing offense levels on the entire weight of the LSD and carrier medium would produce unwarranted disparity among offenses involving the same quantity of actual LSD (but different carrier weights), as well as sentences disproportionate to those for other, more dangerous controlled substances, such as PCP. Consequently, in cases involving LSD contained in a carrier medium, the Commission has established a weight per dose of 0.4 milligram for purposes of determining the base offense level.

The dosage weight of LSD selected exceeds the Drug Enforcement Administration's standard dosage unit for LSD of 0.05 milligram (i.e., the quantity of actual LSD per dose) in order to assign some weight to the carrier medium. Because LSD typically is marketed and consumed orally on a carrier medium, the inclusion of some weight attributable to the carrier medium recognizes (A) that offense levels for most other controlled substances are based upon the weight of the mixture containing the controlled substance without regard to purity, and (B) the decision in Chapman v. United States, 111 S. Ct. 1919 (1991) (holding that the term 'mixture or substance' in 21 U.S.C. § 841(b)(1) includes the carrier medium in which LSD is absorbed). At the same time, the weight per dose selected is less than the weight per dose that would equate the offense level for LSD on a carrier medium with that for the same number of doses of PCP, a controlled substance that comparative assessments indicate is more likely to induce violent acts and ancillary crime than is LSD. (Treating LSD on a carrier medium as weighing 0.5 milligram per dose would produce offense levels equivalent to those for PCP.) Thus, the approach decided upon by the Commission will harmonize offense levels for LSD offenses with those for other controlled substances and avoid an undue influence of varied carrier weight on the applicable offense level. Nonetheless, this approach does not override the applicability of 'mixture or substance' for the purpose of applying any mandatory minimum sentence (see Chapman; §5G1.1(b)).".

The Commission has found that the weights of LSD carrier media vary widely and typically far exceed the weight of the controlled substance itself (e.g., LSD is typically placed on blotter paper which generally weighs from 5 to 10 milligrams per dose; the weight of the LSD itself per dose is generally from 0.02 to 0.08 milligram; the Drug Enforcement Administration describes a standard dose of LSD as containing 0.05 milligram of LSD). As a result, basing the offense level on the entire weight of the LSD and carrier medium produces unwarranted disparity among offenses involving the same quantity of actual LSD but different carrier weights, as well as sentences that are disproportionate to those for other, more dangerous controlled substances, such as PCP, heroin, and cocaine. Under the guidelines prior to the amendment, for example, 100 grams of heroin or 500 grams of cocaine (weights that correspond to several thousand doses, the number depending upon the purity) result in the same offense level as 125 doses of LSD on blotter paper (which has an average weight of 8 milligrams per dose) or 1 dose of LSD on a sugar cube (2000 milligrams per dose).

Consequently, in cases involving LSD contained in a carrier medium, this amendment establishes a weight per dose of 0.4 milligram to be used for purposes of determining the base offense level. The dosage weight of LSD selected by the Commission exceeds the Drug Enforcement Administration's standard dosage unit for LSD of 0.05 milligram (i.e., the quantity of actual LSD per dose) in order to assign some weight to the carrier medium. Because LSD typically is marketed and consumed orally on a carrier medium, the inclusion of some weight attributable to the carrier medium recognizes (A) that offense levels for most other controlled substances are based upon the weight of the mixture containing the controlled substance without regard to purity, and (B) the decision in Chapman v. United States, 111 S. Ct. 1919 (1991) (holding that the term "mixture or substance" in 21 U.S.C. § 841(b)(1) includes the carrier medium in which LSD is absorbed). At the same time, the weight per dose selected is less than the weight per dose that would equate the offense level for LSD on a carrier medium with that for the same number of doses of PCP, a controlled substance that comparative assessments indicate is more likely to induce violent acts and ancillary crime than is LSD. Treating LSD on a carrier medium as weighing 0.5 milligram per dose would produce offense levels equivalent to those for PCP (for example, 2000 doses of LSD at 0.5 milligram per dose equals 1 gram of LSD -- corresponding to the lower limit of offense level 26; similarly, 2000 doses of PCP at 5 milligrams per dose, the standard amount of actual PCP in a dose, equals 10 grams of actual PCP -- corresponding to the lower limit of offense level 26). Thus, the approach decided upon by the Commission will harmonize offense levels for LSD offenses with those for other controlled substances and avoid an undue influence of varied carrier weight on the applicable offense level. Nonetheless, this approach does not override the definition of mixture or substance for purposes of applying any mandatory minimum sentence (see Chapman; §5G1.1(b)). **The effective date of this amendment is November 1, 1993.**

489. The Commentary to §2K2.4 captioned "Application Notes" is amended in Note 2 by deleting:

"Provided, that where the maximum of the guideline range from Chapter Five, Part A (Sentencing Table) determined by an offense level adjusted under the procedure described in the preceding paragraph, plus the term of imprisonment required under 18 U.S.C. § 924(c) or § 929(a), is less than the maximum of the guideline range that would apply to the underlying offense absent such adjustment, the procedure described in the preceding paragraph does not apply. Instead, the guideline range applicable to the underlying offense absent such adjustment is to be used after subtracting the term of imprisonment imposed under 18 U.S.C. § 924(c) or § 929(a) from both the minimum and maximum of such range.

Example: A defendant, is to be sentenced under the robbery guideline; his unadjusted offense level from §2B3.1 is 30, including a 7-level enhancement for discharging a firearm; no Chapter Three adjustments are applicable; and his criminal history category is Category IV. His unadjusted guideline range from Chapter Five, Part A (Sentencing Table) is 135-168 months. This defendant has also been convicted under 18 U.S.C. § 924(c) arising from the possession of a weapon during the robbery, and therefore must be sentenced to an additional consecutive five-year term of imprisonment. The defendant's adjusted guideline range, which takes into account the conviction under 18 U.S.C. § 924(c) by eliminating the 7-level weapon enhancement, is 70-87 months. Because the maximum of the defendant's adjusted guideline range plus the five year consecutive sentence (87 months + 60 months = 147 months) is less than the maximum of the defendant's unadjusted guideline range (168 months), the defendant is to be sentenced using the unadjusted guideline range after subtracting the 60 month sentence to be imposed under 18 U.S.C. § 924(c) from both the minimum and maximum of the unadjusted range (e.g., 135 months - 60 months = 75 months; 168 months - 60 months = 108 months). A sentence imposed for the underlying offense using the guideline range determined in this manner (75-108 months) when combined with the consecutive sentence imposed under 18 U.S.C. § 924(c) or § 929(a), will produce the appropriate total term of imprisonment.",

and inserting in lieu thereof:

"In a few cases, the offense level for the underlying offense determined under the preceding paragraph may result in a guideline range that, when combined with the mandatory consecutive sentence under 18 U.S.C. § 844(h), § 924(c), or § 929(a), produces a total maximum penalty that is less than the maximum of the guideline range that would have resulted had there not been a count of conviction under 18 U.S.C. § 844(h), § 924(c), or § 929(a) (i.e., the guideline range that would have resulted if the enhancements for possession, use, or discharge of a firearm had been applied). In such a case, an upward departure may be warranted so that the conviction under 18 U.S.C. § 844(h), § 924(c), or § 929(a) does not result in a decrease in the total punishment. An upward departure under this paragraph shall not exceed the maximum of the guideline range that would have resulted had there not been a count of conviction under 18 U.S.C. § 844(h), § 924(c), or § 929(a).".

This amendment simplifies the operation of §2K2.4 in order to reduce erroneous application by deleting the proviso in Application Note 2 and, in lieu thereof, authorizing an upward departure in the unusual case in which the combined sentence for an underlying offense and a firearms or explosives offense (under 18 U.S.C. § 844(h), §924(c), or § 929(a)) is less than the maximum of the guideline range that would have resulted if there had been no additional conviction for the firearms or explosives offense. **The effective date of this amendment is November 1, 1993.**

490. Sections 2S1.3 and 2S1.4 are deleted in their entirety as follows:

"§2S1.3. Failure to Report Monetary Transactions; Structuring Transactions to Evade Reporting Requirements

(a) Base Offense Level:

(1) 13, if the defendant:

(A) structured transactions to evade reporting requirements; or

(B) knowingly filed, or caused another to file, a report containing materially false statements; or

(2) 5, otherwise.

(b) Specific Offense Characteristics

(1) If the defendant knew or believed that the funds were criminally derived property, increase by 4 levels. If the resulting offense level is less than level 13, increase to level 13.

(2) If the base offense level is from (a)(1) above and the value of the funds exceeded $100,000, increase the offense level as specified in §2S1.1(b)(2).

(c) Special Instruction for Fines - Organizations

(1) In lieu of the applicable amount from the table in subsection (d) of §8C2.4 (Base Fine), use:

(A) the greater of $125,000 or 30 percent of the value of the funds if subsections (a)(1) and (b)(1) are used to determine the offense level; or

(B) the greater of $50,000 or 20 percent of the value of the funds if subsection (a)(1) but not (b)(1) are used to determine the offense level.

Commentary

Statutory Provisions: 26 U.S.C. § 7203 (if a willful violation of 26 U.S.C. § 6050I); 31 U.S.C. §§ 5313, 5314, 5322, 5324. For additional statutory provision(s), see Appendix A (Statutory Index).

Application Note:

1. 'Criminally derived property' means any property constituting, or derived from, proceeds obtained from a criminal offense. See 18 U.S.C. § 1957(f)(2).

Background: The offenses covered by this guideline relate to records and reports of certain transactions involving currency and monetary instruments. The maximum prison sentence for these offenses is ten years if there is any pattern of unlawful activity, and five years otherwise.

A base offense level of 13 is provided for those offenses where the defendant either structured the transaction to evade reporting requirements or knowingly filed, or caused another to file, a report containing materially false statements. A lower alternative base offense level of 5 is provided in all other cases.

Where the defendant actually knew or believed that the funds were criminally derived property, subsection (b)(1) provides for the greater of a 4-level increase or an increase to level 13.

Except in rare cases, the dollar value of the transactions not reported is an important indicator of several factors that are pertinent to the sentence, including the size of the criminal enterprise, and the extent to which the defendant aided the enterprise.

§2S1.4. Failure to File Currency and Monetary Instrument Report

(a) Base Offense Level: 9

(b) Specific Offense Characteristics

(1) If the defendant knew or believed that the funds were criminally derived property, increase by 4 levels.

(2) If the defendant knew or believed that the funds were intended to be used to promote criminal activity, increase by 4 levels.

(3) If the value of the funds exceeded $100,000, increase the offense level as specified in §2S1.1(b)(2).

(c) Special Instruction for Fines - Organizations

(1) In lieu of the applicable amount from the table in subsection (d) of §8C2.4 (Base Fine), use:

(A) the greater of $50,000 or 20 percent of the value of the funds if subsection (b)(1) or (b)(2) is used to determine the offense level; or

(B) the greater of $15,000 or 10 percent of the value of the funds, otherwise.

Commentary

Statutory Provision: 31 U.S.C. § 5316. For additional statutory provision(s), see Appendix A (Statutory Index).

Application Note:

1. 'Criminally derived property' means any property constituting, or derived from, proceeds obtained from a criminal offense. See 18 U.S.C. § 1957(f)(2).".

A replacement guideline with accompanying commentary is inserted as "§2S1.3 (Structuring Transactions to Evade Reporting Requirements; Failure to Report Cash or Monetary Transactions; Failure to File Currency and Monetary Instrument Report; Knowingly Filing False Reports)".

This amendment consolidates existing §§2S1.3 and 2S1.4 and modifies these guidelines to assure greater consistency of punishment for similar offenses and greater sensitivity to indicia of offense seriousness. **The effective date of this amendment is November 1, 1993.**

491. Chapter Two, Part T, Subpart 1 is amended in the title by inserting ", EMPLOYMENT TAXES, ESTATE TAXES, GIFT TAXES, AND EXCISE TAXES (OTHER THAN ALCOHOL, TOBACCO, AND CUSTOMS TAXES)" at the end thereof.

Section 2T1.1 is amended in the title by inserting "; Willful Failure to File Return, Supply Information, or Pay Tax; Fraudulent or False Returns, Statements, or Other Documents" at the end thereof.

Section 2T1.1(a) is amended by deleting:

"Base Offense Level: Level from §2T4.1 (Tax Table) corresponding to the tax loss.

For purposes of this guideline, the 'tax loss' is the greater of: (A) the total amount of tax that the taxpayer evaded or attempted to evade; and (B) the 'tax loss' defined in §2T1.3.",

and inserting in lieu thereof:

"(a) Base Offense Level:

(1) Level from §2T4.1 (Tax Table) corresponding to the tax loss; or

(2) 6, if there is no tax loss.".

Section 2T1.1(b)(2) is amended by deleting "nature" and inserting in lieu thereof "existence".

Section 2T1.1 is amended by inserting the following additional subsection:

"(c) Special Instructions

For the purposes of this guideline --

(1) If the offense involved tax evasion or a fraudulent or false return, statement, or other document, the tax loss is the total amount of loss that was the object of the offense (i.e., the loss that would have resulted had the offense been successfully completed).

Notes:

(A) If the offense involved filing a tax return in which gross income was underreported, the tax loss shall be treated as equal to 28% of the unreported gross income (34% if the taxpayer is a corporation) plus 100% of any false credits claimed against tax, unless a more accurate determination of the tax loss can be made.

(B) If the offense involved improperly claiming a deduction or an exemption, the tax loss shall be treated as equal to 28% of the amount of the improperly claimed deduction or exemption (34% if the taxpayer is a corporation) plus 100% of any false credits claimed against tax, unless a more accurate determination of the tax loss can be made.

(C) If the offense involved improperly claiming a deduction to provide a basis for tax evasion in the future, the tax loss shall be treated as equal to 28% of the amount of the improperly claimed deduction (34% if the taxpayer is a corporation) plus 100% of any false credits claimed against tax, unless a more accurate determination of the tax loss can be made.

(2) If the offense involved failure to file a tax return, the tax loss is the amount of tax that the taxpayer owed and did not pay.

Note: If the offense involved failure to file a tax return, the tax loss shall be treated as equal to 20% of the gross income (25% if the taxpayer is a corporation) less any tax withheld or otherwise paid, unless a more accurate determination of the tax loss can be made.

(3) If the offense involved willful failure to pay tax, the tax loss is the amount of tax that the taxpayer owed and did not pay.

(4) If the offense involved improperly claiming a refund to which the claimant was not entitled, the tax loss is the amount of the claimed refund to which the claimant was not entitled.

(5) The tax loss is not reduced by any payment of the tax subsequent to the commission of the offense.".

The Commentary to §2T1.1 captioned "Statutory Provision" is amended by deleting "Provision: 26 U.S.C. § 7201" and inserting in lieu thereof "Provisions: 26 U.S.C. §§ 7201, 7203 (other than a violation based upon 26 U.S.C. § 6050I), 7206 (other than a violation based upon 26 U.S.C. § 6050I or § 7206(2)), and 7207".

The Commentary to §2T1.1 captioned "Application Notes" is amended by deleting Notes 1 and 4 as follows:

> "1. False statements in furtherance of the evasion (<u>see</u> §§2T1.3, 2T1.5, and 2T1.8) are considered part of the offense for purposes of this guideline.",
>
> "4. The guideline refers to §2T1.3 to provide an alternative minimum standard for the tax loss, which is based on a percentage of the dollar amounts of certain misstatements made in returns filed by the taxpayer. This alternative standard may be easier to determine, and should make irrelevant the issue of whether the taxpayer was entitled to offsetting adjustments that he failed to claim.";

and by renumbering the remaining notes accordingly.

The Commentary to §2T1.1 captioned "Application Notes" is amended in Note 1 (formerly Note 2) by deleting "For purposes of the guideline, the tax loss is the amount of tax that the taxpayer evaded or attempted to evade" and inserting in lieu thereof "'Tax loss' is defined in subsection (c)"; by deleting "deficiency" and inserting in lieu thereof "figures"; and by inserting the following additional paragraphs at the end:

> "Notes under subsections (c)(1) and (c)(2) address certain situations in income tax cases in which the tax loss may not be reasonably ascertainable. In these situations, the 'presumptions' set forth are to be used unless the government or defense provides sufficient information for a more accurate assessment of the tax loss. In cases involving other types of taxes, the presumptions in the notes under subsections (c)(1) and (c)(2) do not apply.
>
> <u>Example 1</u>: A defendant files a tax return reporting income of $40,000 when his income was actually $90,000. Under Note (A) to subsection (c)(1), the tax loss is treated as $14,000 ($90,000 of actual gross income minus $40,000 of reported gross income = $50,000 x 28%) unless sufficient information is available to make a more accurate assessment of the tax loss.
>
> <u>Example 2</u>: A defendant files a tax return reporting income of $60,000 when his income was actually $130,000. In addition, the defendant claims $10,000 in false tax credits. Under Note (A) to subsection (c)(1), the tax loss is treated as $29,600 ($130,000 of actual gross income minus $60,000 of reported gross income = $70,000 x 28% = $19,600, plus $10,000 of false tax credits) unless sufficient information is available to make a more accurate assessment of the tax loss.
>
> <u>Example 3</u>: A defendant fails to file a tax return for a year in which his salary was $24,000, and $2,600 in income tax was withheld by his employer. Under the note to subsection (c)(2), the tax loss is treated as $2,200 ($24,000 of gross income x 20% = $4,800, minus $2,600 of tax withheld) unless sufficient information is available to make a more accurate assessment of the tax loss.
>
> In determining the tax loss attributable to the offense, the court should use as many methods set forth in subsection (c) and this commentary as are necessary given the circumstances of the particular case. If none of the methods of determining the tax loss set forth fit the circumstances of the particular case, the court should use any method of determining the tax loss that appears appropriate to reasonably calculate the loss that would have resulted had the offense been successfully completed.".

The Commentary to §2T1.1 captioned "Application Notes" is amended in Note 3 (formerly Note 5) by deleting "or local" and inserting in lieu thereof "local, or foreign".

The Commentary to §2T1.1 captioned "Application Notes" is amended in Note 4 (formerly Note 6) by deleting "§2T1.1(b)(2)" and inserting in lieu thereof "subsection (b)(2)"; by inserting a comma immediately following "applied"; and by inserting "or fictitious entities" immediately following "shells".

The Commentary to §2T1.1 captioned "Application Notes" is amended by inserting the following additional notes:

"5. A 'credit claimed against tax' is an item that reduces the amount of tax directly. In contrast, a 'deduction' is an item that reduces the amount of taxable income.

6. 'Gross income,' for the purposes of this section, has the same meaning as it has in 26 U.S.C. § 61 and 26 C.F.R. § 1.61.

7. If the offense involves both individual and corporate tax returns, the tax loss is the aggregate tax loss from the offenses taken together.".

The Commentary to §2T1.1 captioned "Background" is amended by deleting:

" This guideline relies most heavily on the amount of tax evaded because the chief interest protected by the statute is the collection of taxes. A greater evasion is obviously more harmful to the treasury, and more serious than a smaller one with otherwise similar characteristics. Furthermore, as the potential benefit from tax evasion increases, the sanction necessary to deter also increases.

The overlapping imprisonment ranges in the Sentencing Table are intended to minimize the significance of disputes. The consequence of an inexact estimate of the tax loss is never severe, even when the tax loss is near the boundary of a range. For example, although the difference between $39,999 and $40,001 results in a change from level 10 to level 11, any sentence of eight to twelve months would be within the guidelines regardless of the offense level determination made by the court. Indeed, any sentence between ten and twelve months would be within the guidelines for a tax loss ranging from $20,000 to $150,000. As a consequence, for all dollar amounts, the Sentencing Table affords the court considerable latitude in evaluating other factors, even when the amount of the tax loss is uncertain.

Under pre-guidelines practice, roughly half of all tax evaders were sentenced to probation without imprisonment, while the other half received sentences that required them to serve an average prison term of twelve months. This guideline is intended to reduce disparity in sentencing for tax evasion and to somewhat increase average sentence length. As a result, the number of purely probationary sentences will be reduced. The Commission believes that any additional costs of imprisonment that may be incurred as a result of the increase in the average term of imprisonment for tax evasion are inconsequential in relation to the potential increase in revenue. According to estimates current at the time this guideline was originally developed (1987), income taxes are underpaid by approximately $90 billion annually.

Although under pre-guidelines practice some large-scale evaders served as much as five years in prison, the average sentence length for defendants sentenced to a term of imprisonment did not increase rapidly with the amount of tax evaded. Thus, the average time served by those sentenced to a term of imprisonment for evading less than $10,000 in taxes was about nine months, while the corresponding figure for those evading over $100,000 in taxes was about sixteen months. Guideline sentences should result in small increases in the average length of imprisonment for most tax cases that involve less than $100,000 in tax evaded. The increase is expected to be somewhat larger for cases involving more taxes.

Failure to report criminally derived income is included as a factor for deterrence purposes. Criminally derived income is generally difficult to establish, so that the tax loss in such cases will tend to be substantially understated. An enhancement for offenders who violate the tax laws as part of a pattern of criminal activity from which they derive a substantial portion of their income also serves to implement the mandate of 28 U.S.C. § 994(i)(2). Estimates from pre-guidelines practice were that, on average, the presence of this factor increased time served by the equivalent of 2 levels.

Although tax evasion always involves some planning, unusually sophisticated efforts to conceal the evasion decrease the likelihood of detection and therefore warrant an additional sanction for deterrence purposes. Analyses of pre-guidelines data for other frauds and property crimes showed that careful planning or sophistication generally resulted in an average increase of at least 2 levels.",

and inserting in lieu thereof:

" This guideline relies most heavily on the amount of loss that was the object of the offense. Tax offenses, in and of themselves, are serious offenses; however, a greater tax loss is obviously more harmful to the treasury and more serious than a smaller one with otherwise similar characteristics. Furthermore, as the potential benefit from the offense increases, the sanction necessary to deter also increases.

Under pre-guidelines practice, roughly half of all tax evaders were sentenced to probation without imprisonment, while the other half received sentences that required them to serve an average prison term of twelve months. This guideline is intended to reduce disparity in sentencing for tax offenses and to somewhat increase average sentence length. As a result, the number of purely probationary sentences will be reduced. The Commission believes that any additional costs of imprisonment that may be incurred as a result of the increase in the average term of imprisonment for tax offenses are inconsequential in relation to the potential increase in revenue. According to estimates current at the time this guideline was originally developed (1987), income taxes are underpaid by approximately $90 billion annually. Guideline sentences should result in small increases in the average length of imprisonment for most tax cases that involve less than $100,000 in tax loss. The increase is expected to be somewhat larger for cases involving more taxes.

Failure to report criminally derived income is included as a factor for deterrence purposes. Criminally derived income is generally difficult to establish, so that the tax loss in such cases will tend to be substantially understated. An enhancement for offenders who violate the tax laws as part of a pattern of criminal activity from which they derive a substantial portion of their income also serves to implement the mandate of 28 U.S.C. § 994(i)(2).

Although tax offenses always involve some planning, unusually sophisticated efforts to conceal the offense decrease the likelihood of detection and therefore warrant an additional sanction for deterrence purposes.".

Sections 2T1.2 and 2T1.3 are deleted in their entirety as follows:

"§2T1.2. Willful Failure To File Return, Supply Information, or Pay Tax

(a) Base Offense Level:

(1) 1 level less than the level from §2T4.1 (Tax Table) corresponding to the tax loss; or

(2) 5, if there is no tax loss.

For purposes of this guideline, 'tax loss' means the total amount of tax that the taxpayer owed and did not pay, but, in the event of a failure to file in any year, not less than 10 percent of the amount by which the taxpayer's gross income for that year exceeded $20,000.

(b) Specific Offense Characteristics

(1) If the defendant failed to report or to correctly identify the source of income exceeding $10,000 in any year from criminal activity, increase by 2 levels. If the resulting offense level is less than level 12, increase to level 12.

(2) If sophisticated means were used to impede discovery of the nature or extent of the offense, increase by 2 levels.

(c) Cross Reference

(1) If the defendant is convicted of a willful violation of 26 U.S.C. § 6050I, apply §2S1.3 (Failure to Report Monetary Transactions) in lieu of this guideline.

Commentary

Statutory Provision: 26 U.S.C. § 7203 (other than a willful violation of 26 U.S.C. § 6050I).

Application Notes:

1. 'Criminal activity' means any conduct constituting a criminal offense under federal, state, or local law.

2. 'Sophisticated means,' as used in §2T1.2(b)(2), includes conduct that is more complex or demonstrates greater intricacy or planning than a routine tax-evasion case. An enhancement would be applied, for example, where the defendant used offshore bank accounts or transactions through corporate shells.

3. In determining the total tax loss attributable to the offense (see §1B1.3(a)(2)), all conduct violating the tax laws should be considered as part of the same course of conduct or common scheme or plan unless the evidence demonstrates that the conduct is clearly unrelated. See Application Note 3 of the Commentary to §2T1.1.

Background: Violations of 26 U.S.C. § 7203 are usually serious misdemeanors that are similar to tax evasion, except that there need be no affirmative act in support of the offense. They are rarely prosecuted unless the defendant also owed taxes that he failed to pay.

Because the conduct generally is tantamount to tax evasion, the guideline is similar to §2T1.1. Because the offense is a misdemeanor, the offense level has been set at one below the level corresponding to evasion of the same amount of taxes.

An alternative measure of the tax loss, 10 percent of gross income in excess of $20,000, has been provided because of the potential difficulty of determining the amount of tax the taxpayer owed. It is expected that this alternative measure generally will understate the amount of tax owed.

The intended impact of this guideline is to increase the average time served for this offense, and to increase significantly the number of violators who receive a term of imprisonment. Under pre-guidelines practice, the average time served for this offense was approximately 2.5 months, including those who were not sentenced to prison. Considering only those who did serve a term of imprisonment, the average term was about six to seven months.

§2T1.3. Fraud and False Statements Under Penalty of Perjury

(a) Base Offense Level:

(1) Level from §2T4.1 (Tax Table) corresponding to the tax loss, if the offense was committed in order to facilitate evasion of a tax; or

(2) 6, otherwise.

For purposes of this guideline, the 'tax loss' is 28 percent of the amount by which the greater of gross income and taxable income was understated, plus 100 percent of the total amount of any false credits claimed against tax. If the taxpayer is a corporation, use 34 percent in lieu of 28 percent.

(b) Specific Offense Characteristics

(1) If the defendant failed to report or to correctly identify the source of income exceeding $10,000 in any year from criminal activity, increase by 2 levels. If the resulting offense level is less than level 12, increase to level 12.

(2) If sophisticated means were used to impede discovery of the nature or extent of the offense, increase by 2 levels.

Commentary

Statutory Provision: 26 U.S.C. § 7206, except § 7206(2). For additional statutory provision(s), see Appendix A (Statutory Index).

Application Notes:

1. 'Criminal activity' means any conduct constituting a criminal offense under federal, state, or local law.

2. 'Sophisticated means,' as used in §2T1.3(b)(2), includes conduct that is more complex or demonstrates greater intricacy or planning than a routine tax-evasion case. An enhancement would be applied, for example, where the defendant used offshore bank accounts or transactions through corporate shells.

3. In determining the total tax loss attributable to the offense (see §1B1.3(a)(2)), all conduct violating the tax laws should be considered as part of the same course of conduct or common scheme or plan unless the evidence demonstrates that the conduct is clearly unrelated. See Application Note 3 of the Commentary to §2T1.1.

4. The amount by which the greater of gross income and taxable income was understated, plus 100 percent of the total amount of any false credits claimed against tax is calculated as follows: (1) determine the amount, if any, by which the gross income was understated; (2) determine the amount, if any, by which the taxable income was understated; and (3) determine the amount of any false credit(s) claimed (a tax 'credit' is an item that reduces the amount of tax directly; in contrast, a 'deduction' is an item that reduces the amount of taxable income). Use the amount determined under step (1) or (2), whichever is greater, plus any amount determined under step (3).

<u>Background</u>: This guideline covers conduct that usually is analogous to tax evasion, although the elements differ. Accordingly, the offense is treated much like tax evasion.

Existence of a tax loss is not an element of these offenses. Furthermore, in instances where the defendant is setting the groundwork for evasion of a tax that is expected to become due in the future, he may make false statements that underreport income that as of the time of conviction may not yet have resulted in a tax loss. In order to gauge the seriousness of these offenses, the guidelines establish a rule for determining a 'tax loss' based on the nature and magnitude of the false statements made. Use of this approach also avoids complex problems of proof and invasion of privacy when returns of persons other than the defendant and co-defendants are involved.".

Section 2T1.4(a)(1) is amended by deleting "resulting tax loss, if any" and inserting in lieu thereof "tax loss".

Section 2T1.4(a)(2) is amended by deleting "otherwise" and inserting in lieu thereof "if there is no tax loss".

Section 2T1.4(a) is amended by deleting "§2T1.3" and inserting in lieu thereof "§2T1.1".

Section 2T1.4(b)(1) is amended by inserting "(A)" immediately following "If"; and by inserting "; or (B) the defendant was in the business of preparing or assisting in the preparation of tax returns" immediately before ", increase".

Section 2T1.4(b)(2) is amended by deleting "nature" and inserting in lieu thereof "existence".

Section 2T1.4(b) is amended by deleting:

"(3) If the defendant was in the business of preparing or assisting in the preparation of tax returns, increase by 2 levels.".

The Commentary to §2T1.4 captioned "Statutory Provision" is amended by inserting "(other than a violation based upon 26 U.S.C. § 6050I)" immediately following "§ 7206(2)".

The Commentary to §2T1.4 captioned "Application Notes" is amended by deleting Notes 1, 3, and 4 as follows:

"1. Subsection (b)(1) applies to persons who derive a substantial portion of their income through the promotion of tax fraud or tax evasion, <u>e.g.</u>, through promoting fraudulent tax shelters.",

"3. Subsection (b)(3) applies to persons who regularly act as tax preparers or advisers for profit. Do not employ §3B1.3 (Abuse of Position of Trust or Use of Special Skill) if this adjustment applies. Subsection (b)(1) may also apply to such persons.

4. In certain instances, such as promotion of a tax shelter scheme, the defendant may advise other persons to violate their tax obligations through filing returns that find no support in the tax laws. If this type of conduct can be shown to have resulted in the filing of false returns (regardless of whether the principals were aware of their falsity), the misstatements in all such returns will contribute to one aggregate 'tax loss.'";

by renumbering Note 2 as Note 3; and by inserting the following as Notes 1 and 2:

"1. For the general principles underlying the determination of tax loss, see §2T1.1(c) and Application Note 1 of the Commentary to §2T1.1 (Tax Evasion; Willful Failure to File Return, Supply Information, or Pay Tax; Fraudulent or False Returns, Statements, or Other Documents). In certain instances, such as promotion of a tax shelter scheme, the defendant may advise other persons to violate their tax obligations through filing returns that find no support in the tax laws. If this type of conduct can be shown to have resulted in the filing of false returns (regardless of whether the principals were aware of their falsity), the misstatements in all such returns will contribute to one aggregate 'tax loss.'

2. Subsection (b)(1) has two prongs. The first prong applies to persons who derive a substantial portion of their income through the promotion of tax schemes, e.g., through promoting fraudulent tax shelters. The second prong applies to persons who regularly prepare or assist in the preparation of tax returns for profit. If an enhancement from this subsection applies, do not apply §3B1.3 (Abuse of Position of Trust or Use of Special Skill).".

The Commentary to §2T1.4 captioned "Application Notes" is amended in Note 3 (formerly Note 2) by inserting "or fictitious entities" immediately following "corporate shells".

The Commentary to §2T1.4 captioned "Background" is amended by deleting "tax preparers and advisers" and inserting in lieu thereof "those in the business of preparing or assisting in the preparation of tax returns and those who make a business of promoting tax fraud"; and by deleting "§2T1.3" and inserting in lieu thereof "2T1.1".

Section 2T1.5 is deleted in its entirety as follows:

"§2T1.5. Fraudulent Returns, Statements, or Other Documents

(a) Base Offense Level: 6

Commentary

Statutory Provision: 26 U.S.C. § 7207.

Background: The offense is a misdemeanor. It is to be distinguished from 26 U.S.C. § 7206(1) (§2T1.3), which is a felony involving a false statement under penalty of perjury. The offense level has been set at 6 in order to give the sentencing judge considerable latitude because the conduct could be similar to tax evasion.".

Section 2T1.9 is amended in the title by deleting "Impair, Impede" and inserting in lieu thereof "Impede, Impair, Obstruct,".

Section 2T1.9(a)(1) is amended by deleting "§2T1.3, as applicable" and inserting in lieu thereof "§2T1.4, as appropriate".

Section 2T1.9(b)(1) is amended by inserting "to impede, impair, obstruct, or defeat the ascertainment, computation, assessment, or collection of revenue" immediately following "violence".

Section 2T1.9(b)(2) is amended by deleting "impede or impair the Internal Revenue Service in the assessment and" and inserting in lieu thereof "impede, impair, obstruct, or defeat the ascertainment, computation, assessment, or"; and by inserting the following additional sentence at the end:

> "Do not, however, apply this adjustment if an adjustment from §2T1.4(b)(1) is applied.".

The Commentary to §2T1.9 captioned "Application Notes" is amended in Note 2 by deleting "§2T1.3 (whichever is applicable to the underlying conduct)" and inserting in lieu thereof "§2T1.4 (whichever guideline most closely addresses the harm that would have resulted had the conspirators succeeded in impeding, impairing, obstructing, or defeating the Internal Revenue Service)".

The Commentary to §2T1.9 captioned "Application Notes" is amended by inserting the following additional note:

> "4. Subsection (b)(2) provides an enhancement where the conduct was intended to encourage persons, other than the participants directly involved in the offense, to violate the tax laws (e.g., an offense involving a 'tax protest' group that encourages persons to violate the tax laws, or an offense involving the marketing of fraudulent tax shelters or schemes).".

Section 2T4.1 is amended by deleting:

	"Tax Loss (Apply the Greatest)	Offense Level
(A)	$2,000 or less	6
(B)	More than $2,000	7
(C)	More than $5,000	8
(D)	More than $10,000	9
(E)	More than $20,000	10
(F)	More than $40,000	11
(G)	More than $70,000	12
(H)	More than $120,000	13
(I)	More than $200,000	14
(J)	More than $350,000	15
(K)	More than $500,000	16
(L)	More than $800,000	17
(M)	More than $1,500,000	18
(N)	More than $2,500,000	19
(O)	More than $5,000,000	20
(P)	More than $10,000,000	21
(Q)	More than $20,000,000	22
(R)	More than $40,000,000	23
(S)	More than $80,000,000	24.",

and inserting in lieu thereof:

	"Tax Loss (Apply the Greatest)	Offense Level
(A)	$1,700 or less	6
(B)	More than $1,700	7
(C)	More than $3,000	8
(D)	More than $5,000	9
(E)	More than $8,000	10
(F)	More than $13,500	11
(G)	More than $23,500	12
(H)	More than $40,000	13

(I)	More than $70,000	14
(J)	More than $120,000	15
(K)	More than $200,000	16
(L)	More than $325,000	17
(M)	More than $550,000	18
(N)	More than $950,000	19
(O)	More than $1,500,000	20
(P)	More than $2,500,000	21
(Q)	More than $5,000,000	22
(R)	More than $10,000,000	23
(S)	More than $20,000,000	24
(T)	More than $40,000,000	25
(U)	More than $80,000,000	26.".

This amendment consolidates §§2T1.1, 2T1.2, 2T1.3, and 2T1.5, thereby eliminating the confusion that has arisen in some cases regarding which guideline applies. In addition, by adopting a uniform definition of tax loss, this amendment eliminates the anomaly of using actual tax loss in some cases and an amount that differs from actual tax loss in others. Furthermore, this amendment consolidates §2T1.4(b)(1) and (b)(3) to reflect the substantial overlap between these subsections. Finally, this amendment adopts a revised "tax loss" table to provide increased deterrence for tax offenses. **The effective date of this amendment is November 1, 1993.**

492. The Commentary to §3B1.3 captioned "Application Notes" is amended by deleting Note 1 as follows:

"1. The position of trust must have contributed in some substantial way to facilitating the crime and not merely have provided an opportunity that could as easily have been afforded to other persons. This adjustment, for example, would not apply to an embezzlement by an ordinary bank teller.",

and inserting in lieu thereof:

"1. 'Public or private trust' refers to a position of public or private trust characterized by professional or managerial discretion (i.e., substantial discretionary judgment that is ordinarily given considerable deference). Persons holding such positions ordinarily are subject to significantly less supervision than employees whose responsibilities are primarily non-discretionary in nature. For this enhancement to apply, the position of trust must have contributed in some significant way to facilitating the commission or concealment of the offense (e.g., by making the detection of the offense or the defendant's responsibility for the offense more difficult). This adjustment, for example, would apply in the case of an embezzlement of a client's funds by an attorney serving as a guardian, a bank executive's fraudulent loan scheme, or the criminal sexual abuse of a patient by a physician under the guise of an examination. This adjustment would not apply in the case of an embezzlement or theft by an ordinary bank teller or hotel clerk because such positions are not characterized by the above-described factors.

Notwithstanding the preceding paragraph, because of the special nature of the United States mail an adjustment for an abuse of a position of trust will apply to any employee of the U.S. Postal Service who engages in the theft or destruction of undelivered United States mail.".

This amendment reformulates the definition of an abuse of position of trust to better distinguish cases warranting this enhancement. **The effective date of this amendment is November 1, 1993.**

493. The Commentary to §4A1.2 captioned "Application Notes" is amended in Note 1 by inserting the following additional sentence at the end of the first paragraph:

> "Conduct that is part of the instant offense means conduct that is relevant conduct to the instant offense under the provisions of §1B1.3 (Relevant Conduct).".

The Commentary to §4A1.2 captioned "Application Notes" is amended in Note 6 in the first sentence of the first paragraph by inserting "(A)" immediately before "have been reversed"; by deleting the comma following "law"; and by inserting "or (B) have been ruled constitutionally invalid in a prior case" immediately before "are not to be counted";

The Commentary to §4A1.2 captioned "Application Notes" is amended in Note 6 by deleting the second sentence as follows:

> "Also, sentences resulting from convictions that a defendant shows to have been previously ruled constitutionally invalid are not to be counted.",

and inserting in lieu thereof:

> "With respect to the current sentencing proceeding, this guideline and commentary do not confer upon the defendant any right to attack collaterally a prior conviction or sentence beyond any such rights otherwise recognized in law (e.g., 21 U.S.C. § 851 expressly provides that a defendant may collaterally attack certain prior convictions).";

and by beginning a new paragraph with the third sentence.

The Commentary to §4A1.2 captioned "Background" is amended by deleting the second paragraph as follows:

> "The Commission leaves for court determination the issue of whether a defendant may collaterally attack at sentencing a prior conviction.".

This amendment expressly provides that the term "part of the instant offense" in §4A1.2(a)(1) means relevant conduct as defined in §1B1.3 (Relevant Conduct) to avoid double counting and ensure consistency with other guideline provisions.

This amendment also clarifies the Commission's intent with respect to whether §4A1.2 confers on defendants a right to attack prior convictions collaterally at sentencing, an issue on which the appellate courts have differed. Compare, e.g., United States v. Canales, 960 F.2d 1311, 1316 (5th Cir. 1992) (Section 4A1.2 commentary indicates Commission intended to grant sentencing courts discretion to entertain initial defendant challenges to prior convictions); United States v. Jacobetz, 955 F.2d 786, 805 (2d Cir.) (similar), cert. denied, 113 S. Ct. 104 (1992); United States v. Cornog, 945 F.2d 1504, 1511 (11th Cir. 1991) (similar) with United States v. Hewitt, 942 F.2d 1270, 1276 (8th Cir. 1991) (commentary indicates defendants may only challenge use of prior convictions at sentencing by showing such conviction previously ruled invalid). This amendment addresses this inter-circuit conflict in interpreting the commentary by stating more clearly that the Commission does not intend to enlarge a defendant's right to attack collaterally a prior conviction at the current sentencing proceeding beyond any right otherwise recognized in law. **The effective date of this amendment is November 1, 1993.**

494. The Commentary to §5G1.3 captioned "Application Notes" is amended in the second paragraph of Note 2 by deleting "40" and inserting in lieu thereof "30", and by deleting "55" and inserting in lieu thereof "45".

The Commentary to §5G1.3 captioned "Application Notes" is amended by inserting the following additional note:

"4. If the defendant was on federal or state probation, parole, or supervised release at the time of the instant offense, and has had such probation, parole, or supervised release revoked, the sentence for the instant offense should be imposed to be served consecutively to the term imposed for the violation of probation, parole, or supervised release in order to provide an incremental penalty for the violation of probation, parole, or supervised release (in accord with the policy expressed in §§7B1.3 and 7B1.4).".

This amendment adds an application note to §5G1.3 to provide guidance in the case of a defendant who was on federal or state probation, parole, or supervised release at the time of the instant federal offense and has had such term of supervision revoked prior to sentencing on the instant federal offense. In addition, this amendment corrects a mathematical error in an example. **The effective date of this amendment is November 1, 1993.**

495. The Commentary to §6B1.2 is amended by inserting the following additional paragraph at the end:

" The Commission encourages the prosecuting attorney prior to the entry of a plea of guilty or nolo contendere under Rule 11 of the Federal Rules of Criminal Procedure to disclose to the defendant the facts and circumstances of the offense and offender characteristics, then known to the prosecuting attorney, that are relevant to the application of the sentencing guidelines. This recommendation, however, shall not be construed to confer upon the defendant any right not otherwise recognized in law.".

This amendment adds commentary to §6B1.2 recommending that the prosecuting attorney disclose to the defendant the facts and circumstances of the offense and offender characteristics then known to the prosecuting attorney that are relevant to the application of the guidelines in order to encourage plea negotiations that realistically reflect probable outcomes. **The effective date of this amendment is November 1, 1993.**

496. Appendix A (Statutory Index) is amended in the second paragraph of the introduction by deleting "or an attempt" and inserting in lieu thereof ", attempt, or solicitation".

Appendix A (Statutory Index) is amended by inserting the following at the appropriate place by title and section:

"16 U.S.C. § 742j-1(a)	2Q2.1",
"16 U.S.C. § 773e(a)(2), (3),(4),(6)	2A2.4",
"16 U.S.C. § 773g	2A2.4",
"16 U.S.C. § 916c	2Q2.1",
"16 U.S.C. § 916f	2Q2.1",
"16 U.S.C. § 973c(a)(8), (10),(11),(12)	2A2.4",
"16 U.S.C. § 973e	2A2.4",
"16 U.S.C. § 1417(a)(5),(6), (b)(2)	2A2.4",
"16 U.S.C. § 3606	2A2.4",
"16 U.S.C. § 3637(a)(2), (3),(4),(6),(c)	2A2.4",
"16 U.S.C. § 4223	2Q2.1",
"16 U.S.C. § 4224	2Q2.1",
"16 U.S.C. § 4910(a)	2Q2.1",
"16 U.S.C. § 4912(a)(2)(A)	2Q2.1",

"16 U.S.C. § 5009(5),(6), (7),(8)	2A2.4",
"16 U.S.C. § 5010(b)	2A2.4",
"18 U.S.C. § 43	2B1.3",
"18 U.S.C. § 228	2J1.1",
"18 U.S.C. § 924(h)	2K2.1",
"18 U.S.C. § 2119	2B3.1",
"18 U.S.C. § 2322	2B6.1",
"22 U.S.C. § 2197(n)	2F1.1",
"26 U.S.C. § 7208	2F1.1",
"26 U.S.C. § 7212(a) (omnibus clause)	2J1.2, 2T1.1",
"26 U.S.C. § 7232	2F1.1",
"29 U.S.C. § 530	2B3.2",
"29 U.S.C. § 1131	2E5.3",
"30 U.S.C. § 1461(a)(3), (4),(5),(7)	2A2.4",
"30 U.S.C. § 1463	2A2.4",
"42 U.S.C. § 1973gg-10	2H2.1",
"42 U.S.C. § 9151(2),(3), (4),(5),	2A2.4",
"42 U.S.C. § 9152(d)	2A2.4",
"46 U.S.C. App. § 1707a (f)(2)	2B1.1",
"49 U.S.C. App. § 1687(g)	2B1.3"

Appendix A (Statutory Index) is amended by deleting:

"7 U.S.C. § 13(a)	2B1.1
7 U.S.C. § 13(b)	2F1.1
7 U.S.C. § 13(c)	2F1.1
7 U.S.C. § 13(e)	2F1.2",

and inserting in lieu thereof:

"7 U.S.C. § 13(a)(1)	2B1.1
7 U.S.C. § 13(a)(2)	2F1.1
7 U.S.C. § 13(a)(3)	2F1.1
7 U.S.C. § 13(a)(4)	2F1.1
7 U.S.C. § 13(c)	2C1.3
7 U.S.C. § 13(d)	2F1.2
7 U.S.C. § 13(f)	2F1.2";

in the lines referenced to 15 U.S.C. §§ 1172, 1173, 1174, 1175, and 1176 by deleting "2E3.3" and inserting in lieu thereof "2E3.1";

in the lines referenced to 16 U.S.C. §§ 1029 and 1030 by deleting "2A2.2, 2A2.3, 2Q2.1" and inserting in lieu thereof "2A2.4";

in the line referenced to 16 U.S.C. § 1857(1)(D) by deleting "2A2.3" and inserting in lieu thereof "2A2.4";

in the line referenced to 16 U.S.C. § 1857(1)(E) by deleting "2A2.2, 2A2.3" and inserting in lieu thereof "2A2.4";

in the line referenced to 16 U.S.C. § 1857(1)(F) by deleting "2A2.3" and inserting in lieu thereof "2A2.4";

in the line referenced to 16 U.S.C. § 1857(1)(H) by deleting "2A2.2, 2A2.3" and inserting in lieu thereof "2A2.4";

by deleting:

"16 U.S.C. § 1857(2) 2Q2.1";

in the line referenced to 16 U.S.C. § 1859 by deleting "2A2.2, 2A2.3, 2Q2.1" and inserting in lieu thereof "2A2.4";

in the line referenced to 16 U.S.C. § 2435(4) by deleting "2A2.3" and inserting in lieu thereof "2A2.4";

in the lines referenced to 16 U.S.C. §§ 2435(5), 2435(6), 2435(7), and 2438 by deleting "2A2.2, 2A2.3" and inserting in lieu thereof "2A2.4";

in the line referenced to 18 U.S.C. § 32(a),(b) by deleting "2A1.1-2A2.3" and inserting in lieu thereof "2A1.1, 2A1.2, 2A1.3, 2A1.4, 2A2.1, 2A2.2, 2A2.3".

in the lines referenced to 18 U.S.C. §§ 201(b)(3) and 201(b)(4) by deleting "2J1.8" and inserting in lieu thereof "2J1.3";

in the lines referenced to 18 U.S.C. §§ 471, 472, 473, 474, 476, 477, 478, 479, 480, 481, 482, 483, 484, 485, 486, 488, 493, 494, 497, 498, 499, 500, 502, 503, 505, 506, 507, 508, 509, 510, and 513 by deleting "2B5.2" and inserting in lieu thereof "2F1.1";

in the lines referenced to 18 U.S.C. §§ 553(a)(1) and 553(a)(2) by deleting "2B1.2" and inserting in lieu thereof "2B1.1";

in the line referenced to 18 U.S.C. § 641 by deleting ", 2B1.2";

in the line referenced to 18 U.S.C. § 642 by deleting "2B5.2" and inserting in lieu thereof "2F1.1";

in the line referenced to 18 U.S.C. § 659 by deleting ", 2B1.2";

in the line referenced to 18 U.S.C. § 662 by deleting "2B1.2" and inserting in lieu thereof "2B1.1";

in the line referenced to 18 U.S.C. § 664 by deleting "2E5.2" and inserting in lieu thereof "2B1.1";

in the line referenced to 18 U.S.C. § 666(a)(1)(C) by deleting "18 U.S.C. § 666(a)(1)(C)"and inserting in lieu thereof "18 U.S.C. § 666(a)(2)";

in the line referenced to 18 U.S.C. § 667 by deleting ", 2B1.2";

in the line referenced to 18 U.S.C. § 798 by deleting ", 2M3.6";

in the line referenced to 18 U.S.C. § 842(j) by deleting "2K1.2" and inserting in lieu thereof "2K1.1";

in the line referenced to 18 U.S.C. § 844(h) by deleting "2K1.4 (offenses committed prior to November 18, 1988), 2K1.6, 2K1.7" and inserting in lieu thereof "2K2.4 (2K1.4 for offenses committed prior to November 18, 1988)";

in the lines referenced to 18 U.S.C. §§ 1003 and 1010 by deleting "2B5.2,";

in the line referenced to 18 U.S.C. § 1024 by deleting "2B1.2" and inserting in lieu thereof "2B1.1";

in the line referenced to 18 U.S.C. § 1028 by deleting ", 2L2.3, 2L2.4";

in the line referenced to 18 U.S.C. § 1082 by deleting "2E3.3" and inserting in lieu thereof "2E3.1";

in the line referenced to 18 U.S.C. § 1084 by deleting "2E3.2" and inserting in lieu thereof "2E3.1";

in the line referenced to 18 U.S.C. § 1153 by deleting "2B2.2,";

in the line referenced to 18 U.S.C. § 1163 by deleting ", 2B1.2";

in the lines referenced to 18 U.S.C. §§ 1301, 1302, 1303, 1304, 1306, and 1511 by deleting "2E3.3" and inserting in lieu thereof "2E3.1";

in the line referenced to 18 U.S.C. § 1541 by deleting "2L2.3" and inserting in lieu thereof "2L2.1";

in the lines referenced to 18 U.S.C. §§ 1542, 1543, and 1544 by deleting "2L2.3, 2L2.4" and inserting in lieu thereof "2L2.1, 2L2.2";

in the line referenced to 18 U.S.C. § 1704 by deleting "2B5.2,";

in the line referenced to 18 U.S.C. § 1708 by deleting "2B1.2,";

in the line referenced to 18 U.S.C. § 1716C by deleting "2B5.2" and inserting in lieu thereof "2F1.1";

in the lines referenced to 18 U.S.C. §§ 1852 and 1854 by deleting "2B1.2,";

in the line referenced to 18 U.S.C. § 1951 by deleting "2E1.5" and inserting in lieu thereof "2B3.1, 2B3.2, 2B3.3, 2C1.1";

in the line referenced to 18 U.S.C. § 1953 by deleting "2E3.3" and inserting in lieu thereof "2E3.1";

in the line referenced to 18 U.S.C. § 2113(a) by deleting "2B2.2" and inserting in lieu thereof "2B2.1";

in the line referenced to 18 U.S.C. § 2113(c) by deleting ", 2B1.2";

in the lines referenced to 18 U.S.C. §§ 2115, 2116, 2117, and 2118(b) by deleting "2B2.2" and inserting in lieu thereof "2B2.1";

in the line referenced to 18 U.S.C. § 2154 by deleting "2M2.2" and inserting in lieu thereof "2M2.1";

in the line referenced to 18 U.S.C. § 2156 by deleting "2M2.4" and inserting in lieu thereof "2M2.3";

in the line referenced to 18 U.S.C. § 2197 by deleting "2B5.2,";

in the line referenced to 18 U.S.C. § 2276 by deleting "2B2.2" and inserting in lieu thereof "2B2.1";

in the lines referenced to 18 U.S.C. §§ 2312 and 2313 by deleting ", 2B1.2";

in the lines referenced to 18 U.S.C. §§ 2314 and 2315 by deleting "2B1.2, 2B5.2,";

in the lines referenced to 18 U.S.C. §§ 2316 and 2317 by deleting ", 2B1.2";

in the lines referenced to 18 U.S.C. §§ 2318 and 2320 by deleting "2B5.4" and inserting in lieu thereof "2B5.3";

in the line referenced to 20 U.S.C. § 1097(a) by deleting "2B5.2,";

by deleting:

"21 U.S.C. § 842(a)(2)	2D3.3
21 U.S.C. § 842(a)(9),(10)	2D3.5",

and inserting in lieu thereof:

"21 U.S.C. § 842(a)(2),(9),(10)	2D3.2";

in the line referenced to 21 U.S.C. § 846 by deleting ", 2D3.3, 2D3.4, 2D3.5";

in the lines referenced to 21 U.S.C. §§ 954 and 961 by deleting "2D3.4" and inserting in lieu thereof "2D3.2";

in the line referenced to 21 U.S.C. § 963 by deleting ", 2D3.3, 2D3.4, 2D3.5";

in the line referenced to 22 U.S.C. § 4221 by deleting "2B5.2" and inserting in lieu thereof "2F1.1";

in the line referenced to 26 U.S.C. § 7203 by deleting "2T1.2" and inserting in lieu thereof "2T1.1";

in the line referenced to 26 U.S.C. § 7206(1),(3),(4),(5) by deleting "2T1.3" and inserting in lieu thereof "2S1.3, 2T1.1";

in the line referenced to 26 U.S.C. § 7206(2) by inserting "2S1.3," immediately before "2T1.4";

in the line referenced to 26 U.S.C. § 7207 by deleting "2T1.5" and inserting in lieu thereof "2T1.1";

in the line referenced to 26 U.S.C. § 7211 by deleting "2T1.3" and inserting in lieu thereof "2T1.1";

in the line referenced to 26 U.S.C. § 7212(a) by deleting "2A2.2, 2A2.3" and inserting in lieu thereof "2A2.4";

in the line referenced to 29 U.S.C. § 186 by deleting "2E5.6" and inserting in lieu thereof "2E5.1";

in the lines referenced to 29 U.S.C. §§ 431, 432, 433, 439, and 461 by deleting "2E5.5" and inserting in lieu thereof "2E5.3";

in the line referenced to 29 U.S.C. § 501(c) by deleting "2E5.4" and inserting in lieu thereof "2B1.1";

in the line referenced to 31 U.S.C. § 5316 by deleting "2S1.4" and inserting in lieu thereof "2S1.3";

in the line referenced to 31 U.S.C. § 5322 by deleting ", 2S1.4";

in the line referenced to 33 U.S.C. § 1232(b)(2) by deleting "2A2.2, 2A2.3" and inserting in lieu thereof "2A2.4";

in the line referenced to 33 U.S.C. § 1415(b) by inserting "§2Q1.2," immediately before "2Q1.3";

in the line referenced to 46 U.S.C. § 3718(b) by deleting "2K3.1" and inserting in lieu thereof "2Q1.2";

in the lines referenced to 49 U.S.C. §§ 1472(h)(2) and 1809(b) by deleting "2K3.1" and inserting in lieu thereof "2Q1.2";

in the line referenced to 50 U.S.C. § 783(b) by deleting "2M3.7" and inserting in lieu thereof "2M3.3"; and

in the line referenced to 50 U.S.C. § 783(c) by deleting "2M3.8" and inserting in lieu thereof "2M3.3".

The Commentary to §2J1.1 captioned "Statutory Provision" is amended by deleting "Provision: 18 U.S.C. § 401" and inserting lieu thereof "Provisions: 18 U.S.C. §§ 401, 228".

The Commentary to §2J1.1 captioned "Application Note" is amended in the caption by deleting "Note" and inserting lieu thereof "Notes"; and by inserting the following additional note:

"2. For offenses involving the willful failure to pay court-ordered child support (violations of 18 U.S.C. § 228), the most analogous guideline is §2B1.1 (Larceny, Embezzlement, and Other Forms of Theft). The amount of the loss is the amount of child support that the defendant willfully failed to pay. Note: This guideline applies to second and subsequent offenses under 18 U.S.C. § 228. A first offense under 18 U.S.C. § 228 is not covered by this guideline because it is a Class B misdemeanor.".

The Commentary to §2X1.1 captioned "Application Notes" is amended in Note 1 by deleting:

"Offense guidelines that expressly cover attempts include: §2A2.1 (Assault With Intent to Commit Murder; Attempted Murder); §2A3.1 (Criminal Sexual Abuse; Attempt to Commit Criminal Sexual Abuse); §2A3.2 (Criminal Sexual Abuse of a Minor (Statutory Rape) or Attempt to Commit Such Acts); §2A3.3 (Criminal Sexual Abuse of a Ward or Attempt to Commit Such Acts); §2A3.4 (Abusive Sexual Contact or Attempt to Commit Abusive Sexual Contact); §2A4.2 (Demanding or Receiving Ransom Money); §2A5.1 (Aircraft Piracy or Attempted Aircraft Piracy); §2C1.1 (Offering, Giving, Soliciting, or Receiving a Bribe; Extortion Under Color of Official Right); §2C1.2 (Offering, Giving, Soliciting, or Receiving a Gratuity); §2D1.1 (Unlawful Manufacturing, Importing, Exporting, or Trafficking, Including Possession with Intent to Commit These Offenses; Attempt or Conspiracy); §2D1.2 (Drug Offenses Occurring Near Protected Locations or Involving Underage or Pregnant Individuals; Attempt or Conspiracy); §2D1.5 (Continuing Criminal Enterprise; Attempt or Conspiracy); §2D1.6 (Use of Communication Facility in Committing Drug Offense; Attempt or Conspiracy); §2D1.7 (Unlawful Sale or Transportation of Drug Paraphernalia; Attempt or Conspiracy); §2D1.8 (Renting or Managing a Drug Establishment; Attempt or Conspiracy); §2D1.9 (Placing or Maintaining Dangerous Devices on Federal Property to Protect the Unlawful Production of Controlled Substances; Attempt or Conspiracy); §2D1.10 (Endangering Human Life While Illegally Manufacturing a Controlled Substance; Attempt or Conspiracy); §2D1.11 (Unlawfully Distributing, Importing, Exporting or Possessing a Listed Chemical; Attempt or Conspiracy); §2D1.12 (Unlawful Possession, Manufacture, Distribution, or Importation of Prohibited Flask or Equipment; Attempt or Conspiracy); §2D1.13 (Structuring Chemical Transactions or Creating a Chemical Mixture to Evade

Reporting or Recordkeeping Requirements; Presenting False or Fraudulent Identification to Obtain a Listed Chemical; Attempt or Conspiracy); §2D2.1 (Unlawful Possession; Attempt or Conspiracy); §2D2.2 (Acquiring a Controlled Substance by Forgery, Fraud, Deception, or Subterfuge; Attempt or Conspiracy); §2D3.1 (Illegal Use of Registration Number to Manufacture, Distribute, Acquire, or Dispense a Controlled Substance; Attempt or Conspiracy); §2D3.2 (Manufacture of Controlled Substance in Excess of or Unauthorized by Registration Quota; Attempt or Conspiracy); §2D3.3 (Illegal Use of Registration Number to Distribute or Dispense a Controlled Substance to Another Registrant or Authorized Person; Attempt or Conspiracy); §2D3.4 (Illegal Transfer or Transshipment of a Controlled Substance; Attempt or Conspiracy); and §2D3.5 (Violation of Recordkeeping or Reporting Requirements for Listed Chemicals and Certain Machines; Attempt or Conspiracy); §2E5.1 (Offering, Accepting, or Soliciting a Bribe or Gratuity Affecting the Operation of an Employee Welfare or Pension Benefit Plan); §2N1.1 (Tampering or Attempting to Tamper Involving Risk of Death or Serious Injury); §2Q1.4 (Tampering or Attempted Tampering with Public Water System).

Offense guidelines that expressly cover conspiracies include: §2A1.5 (Conspiracy or Solicitation to Commit Murder); §2D1.1 (Unlawful Manufacturing, Importing, Exporting, or Trafficking, Including Possession with Intent to Commit These Offenses; Attempt or Conspiracy); §2D1.2 (Drug Offenses Occurring Near Protected Locations or Involving Underage or Pregnant Individuals; Attempt or Conspiracy); §2D1.5 (Continuing Criminal Enterprise; Attempt or Conspiracy); §2D1.6 (Use of Communication Facility in Committing Drug Offense; Attempt or Conspiracy); §2D1.7 (Unlawful Sale or Transportation of Drug Paraphernalia; Attempt or Conspiracy); §2D1.8 (Renting or Managing a Drug Establishment; Attempt or Conspiracy); §2D1.9 (Placing or Maintaining Dangerous Devices on Federal Property to Protect the Unlawful Production of Controlled Substances; Attempt or Conspiracy); §2D1.10 (Endangering Human Life While Illegally Manufacturing a Controlled Substance; Attempt or Conspiracy); §2D1.11 (Unlawfully Distributing, Importing, Exporting or Possessing a Listed Chemical; Attempt or Conspiracy); §2D1.12 (Unlawful Possession, Manufacture, Distribution, or Importation of Prohibited Flask or Equipment; Attempt or Conspiracy); §2D1.13 (Structuring Chemical Transactions or Creating a Chemical Mixture to Evade Reporting or Recordkeeping Requirements; Presenting False or Fraudulent Identification to Obtain a Listed Chemical; Attempt or Conspiracy); §2D2.1 (Unlawful Possession; Attempt or Conspiracy); §2D2.2 (Acquiring a Controlled Substance by Forgery, Fraud, Deception, or Subterfuge; Attempt or Conspiracy); §2D3.1 (Illegal Use of Registration Number to Manufacture, Distribute, Acquire, or Dispense a Controlled Substance; Attempt or Conspiracy); §2D3.2 (Manufacture of Controlled Substance in Excess of or Unauthorized by Registration Quota; Attempt or Conspiracy); §2D3.3 (Illegal Use of Registration Number to Distribute or Dispense a Controlled Substance to Another Registrant or Authorized Person; Attempt or Conspiracy); §2D3.4 (Illegal Transfer or Transshipment of a Controlled Substance; Attempt or Conspiracy); and §2D3.5 (Violation of Recordkeeping or Reporting Requirements for Listed Chemicals and Certain Machines; Attempt or Conspiracy); §2H1.1 (Conspiracy to Interfere with Civil Rights; Going in Disguise to Deprive of Rights); §2T1.9 (Conspiracy to Impair, Impede or Defeat Tax).

Offense guidelines that expressly cover solicitations include: §2A1.5 (Conspiracy or Solicitation to Commit Murder); §2C1.1 (Offering, Giving, Soliciting, or Receiving a Bribe; Extortion Under Color of Official Right); §2C1.2 (Offering, Giving, Soliciting, or Receiving a Gratuity); §2E5.1 (Offering, Accepting, or Soliciting a Bribe or Gratuity Affecting the Operation of an Employee Welfare or Pension Benefit Plan).",

and inserting in lieu thereof:

"Offense guidelines that expressly cover attempts include:

§§2A2.1, 2A3.1, 2A3.2, 2A3.3, 2A3.4, 2A4.2, 2A5.1;
§§2C1.1, 2C1.2;
§§2D1.1, 2D1.2, 2D1.5, 2D1.6, 2D1.7, 2D1.8, 2D1.9, 2D1.10, 2D1.11, 2D1.12, 2D1.13, 2D2.1, 2D2.2, 2D3.1, 2D3.2;
§2E5.1;
§2N1.1;
§2Q1.4.

Offense guidelines that expressly cover conspiracies include:

§2A1.5;
§§2D1.1, 2D1.2, 2D1.5, 2D1.6, 2D1.7, 2D1.8, 2D1.9, 2D1.10, 2D1.11, 2D1.12, 2D1.13, 2D2.1, 2D2.2, 2D3.1, 2D3.2;
§2H1.1;
§2T1.9.

Offense guidelines that expressly cover solicitations include:

§2A1.5;
§§2C1.1, 2C1.2;
§2E5.1.".

The Commentary to §2X3.1 captioned "Application Notes" is amended in Note 1 in the second sentence by deleting "Note 1" and inserting in lieu thereof "Note 10".

The Commentary to §2X4.1 captioned "Application Notes" is amended in Note 1 in the second sentence by deleting "Note 1" and inserting in lieu thereof "Note 10".

The Commentary to §3C1.1 captioned "Application Notes" is amended in Note 6 by inserting "; Bribery of Witness" immediately following "of Perjury"; by deleting "§2J1.8 (Bribery of Witness, or §2J1.9 (Payment to Witness)" and inserting in lieu thereof "§2J1.9 (Payment to Witness), §2X3.1 (Accessory After the Fact), or §2X4.1 (Misprision of Felony)"; and by deleting "or prosecution" and inserting in lieu thereof ", prosecution, or sentencing".

Section 3D1.2(d) is amended in the second paragraph by deleting "2B1.2,", "2B5.2,", "2B5.4,", "2E5.2, 2E5.4, 2E5.6", ", 2L2.3", and "2T1.2, 2T1.3,"; and in the third paragraph by deleting "2B2.2,", "2E1.5,", "2L2.4,", and "2M3.6, 2M3.7, 2M3.8,".

Section 8C2.1(a) is amended by deleting "2B1.2,", "2B5.4,", ", 2D3.4", "2E3.2, 2E3.3,", "2E5.2,", ", 2E5.4, 2E5.5, 2E5.6", "2K1.2,", ", 2S1.4", "2T1.2, 2T1.3," and "2T1.5,".

The Commentary to §8C2.4 captioned "Application Notes" is amended in Note 5 by inserting "; Prohibited Payments or Lending of Money by Employer or Agent to Employees, Representatives, or Labor Organizations" immediately following "Plan"; and by deleting "§2S1.3 (Failure to Report Monetary Transactions; Structuring Transactions to Evade Reporting Requirements); and §2S1.4 (Failure to File Currency and Monetary Instrument Report)" and inserting in lieu thereof "and §2S1.3 (Structuring Transactions to Evade Reporting Requirements; Failure to Report Cash or Monetary Transactions; Failure to File Currency and Monetary Instrument Report; Knowingly Filing False Reports)".

This amendment makes Appendix A more comprehensive, conforms it to the consolidation of offense guidelines under amendments 481, 490, and 491, and deletes references to several Class B and C misdemeanor offenses to which the guidelines do not apply. In addition, this amendment conforms §3D1.2(d), §8C2.1, and the Commentary to §§2X1.1, 3C1.1, and 8C2.4 to the consolidation of offense guidelines under amendments 481, 490, and 491. In addition, this amendment reformats the Commentary to 2X1.1 for ease in application; corrects an omission in the second paragraph of the Introduction to Appendix A; revises Application

Note 6 of the Commentary to §3C1.1 to make the listing of offense guidelines more comprehensive and correct the omission of a reference to the sentencing of the instant offense; and revises a reference in the Commentary to §§2X3.1 and 2X4.1 to conform to a previous revision in the referenced provision. **The effective date of this amendment is November 1, 1993.**

497. The Commentary to §1B1.1 captioned "Application Notes" is amended in Note 4 by inserting the following additional paragraph as the second paragraph:

> "Absent an instruction to the contrary, the adjustments from different guideline sections are applied cumulatively (added together). For example, the adjustments from §2F1.1(b)(2) (more than minimal planning) and §3B1.1 (aggravating role) are applied cumulatively.".

This amendment clarifies the Commission's intent that, absent an instruction to the contrary, adjustments from different guideline sections are to be applied cumulatively. **The effective date of this amendment is November 1, 1993.**

498. The Commentary to §1B1.7 is amended by deleting the second paragraph as follows:

> " In stating that failure to follow certain commentary 'could constitute an incorrect application of the guidelines,' the Commission simply means that in seeking to understand the meaning of the guidelines courts likely will look to the commentary for guidance as an indication of the intent of those who wrote them. In such instances, the courts will treat the commentary much like legislative history or other legal material that helps determine the intent of a drafter.",

and inserting in lieu thereof:

> " '[C]ommentary in the Guidelines Manual that interprets or explains a guideline is authoritative unless it violates the Constitution or a federal statute, or is inconsistent with, or a plainly erroneous reading of, that guideline.' Stinson v. United States, 113 S. Ct. 1913, 1915 (1993).".

This amendment revises the commentary to this section to reflect the decision of the Supreme Court in Stinson v. United States, 113 S. Ct. 1913, 1915 (1993). **The effective date of this amendment is November 1, 1993.**

499. The Commentary to §2D1.1 captioned "Application Notes" is amended in Note 10 in the "Drug Equivalency Tables" in the subdivision captioned "LSD, PCP, and other Schedule I and II Hallucinogens" by deleting:

> "Phenylcyclohexamine (PCE) = 5.79 kg of marihuana"

and inserting in lieu thereof:

> "N-ethyl-1-phenylcyclohexylamine (PCE) = 1 kg of marihuana".

This amendment revises the equivalency for PCE to reflect a reassessment of the potency of this controlled substance by the Drug Enforcement Administration. In addition, this amendment corrects an error in the scientific name for this controlled substance. **The effective date of this amendment is November 1, 1993.**

500. The Commentary to §3B1.1 captioned "Application Notes" is amended by renumbering Notes 2 and 3 as 3 and 4, respectively; and by inserting the following additional note:

"2. To qualify for an adjustment under this section, the defendant must have been the organizer, leader, manager, or supervisor of one or more other participants. An upward departure may be warranted, however, in the case of a defendant who did not organize, lead, manage, or supervise another participant, but who nevertheless exercised management responsibility over the property, assets, or activities of a criminal organization.".

This amendment clarifies the operation of this section to resolve a split among the courts of appeal. Compare United States v. Carroll, 893 F.2d 1502 (6th Cir. 1990) (requiring degree of control over other persons for §3B1.1 to apply); United States v. Fuller, 897 F.2d 1217 (1st Cir. 1990) (same); United States v. Mares-Molina, 913 F.2d 770 (9th Cir. 1990) (same) and United States v. Fuentes, 954 F.2d 151 (3d Cir.) (same), cert. denied, 112 S.Ct. 2950 (1992) with United States v. Chambers, 985 F.2d 1263 (4th Cir.) (defendant may be a "manager" even though he did not directly supervise other persons), petition for cert. filed, No. 92-8737 (U.S. May 17, 1993). **The effective date of this amendment is November 1, 1993.**

501. The Commentary to §5E1.1 captioned "Background" is amended in the second paragraph by inserting the following additional sentence as the first sentence:

"A court's authority to decline to order restitution is limited.";

by inserting, immediately after "18 U.S.C. § 3663(d).", the following:

"The legislative history of 18 U.S.C. § 3579, the precursor of 18 U.S.C. § 3663, states that even '[i]n those unusual cases where the precise amount owed is difficult to determine, the section authorizes the court to reach an expeditious, reasonable determination of appropriate restitution by resolving uncertainties with a view toward achieving fairness to the victim.' S. Rep. No. 532, 97th Cong., 2d Sess. 31, reprinted in 1982 U.S. Code Cong. & Ad. News 2515, 2537.";

and by inserting the following additional sentence as the last sentence:

"Subsection (a)(2) provides for restitution as a condition of probation or supervised release for offenses not set forth in Title 18, United States Code, or 49 U.S.C. § 1472(h), (i), (j), or (n).".

The Commentary to §5E1.1 captioned "Background" is amended by deleting the fifth paragraph as follows:

" A court's authority to deny restitution is limited. Even 'in those unusual cases where the precise amount owed is difficult to determine, section 3579(d) authorizes the court to reach an expeditious, reasonable determination of appropriate restitution by resolving uncertainties with a view toward achieving fairness to the victim.' S. Rep. No. 532, 97th Cong., 2d Sess. 31, reprinted in 1982 U.S. Code Cong. & Ad. News 2515, 2537.";

and by deleting the seventh paragraph as follows:

" Subsection (a)(2) provides for restitution as a condition of probation or supervised release for offenses not set forth in Title 18, United States Code, or 49 U.S.C. § 1472(h), (i), (j), or (n).".

This amendment updates the background commentary of §5E1.1 to reflect the redesignation of 18 U.S.C. § 3579 as 18 U.S.C. § 3663. In addition, it moves material from the fifth and seventh paragraphs to the second paragraph to enhance clarity. **The effective date of this amendment is November 1, 1993.**

502. Section 1B1.10(d) is amended by deleting "and 461" and inserting in lieu thereof "454, 461, 484, 488, 490, and 499".

This amendment expands the listing in §1B1.10(d) to implement the directive in 28 U.S.C. § 994(u) in respect to guideline amendments that may be considered for retroactive application. **The effective date of this amendment is November 1, 1993.**

503. The Commentary to §1B1.3 captioned "Application Notes" is amended in Note 2 by inserting the following additional paragraph as the eighth paragraph:

"A defendant's relevant conduct does not include the conduct of members of a conspiracy prior to the defendant joining the conspiracy, even if the defendant knows of that conduct (e.g., in the case of a defendant who joins an ongoing drug distribution conspiracy knowing that it had been selling two kilograms of cocaine per week, the cocaine sold prior to the defendant joining the conspiracy is not included as relevant conduct in determining the defendant's offense level). The Commission does not foreclose the possibility that there may be some unusual set of circumstances in which the exclusion of such conduct may not adequately reflect the defendant's culpability; in such a case, an upward departure may be warranted.".

The Commentary to §1B1.3 captioned "Application Notes" is amended in Note 9(B) by deleting "and the time interval between the offenses" and inserting in lieu thereof:

", the regularity (repetitions) of the offenses, and the time interval between the offenses. When one of the above factors is absent, a stronger presence of at least one of the other factors is required. For example, where the conduct alleged to be relevant is relatively remote to the offense of conviction, a stronger showing of similarity or regularity is necessary to compensate for the absence of temporal proximity".

This amendment clarifies the operation of §1B1.3 with respect to the defendant's accountability for the actions of other conspirators prior to the defendant joining the conspiracy. The amendment is in accord with the rule stated in recent caselaw. See, e.g., United States v. Carreon, 11 F.3d 1225 (5th Cir. 1994); United States v. Petty, 982 F.2d 1374, 1377 (9th Cir. 1993); United States v. O'Campo, 973 F.2d 1015, 1026 (1st Cir. 1992). Cf. United States v. Miranda-Ortiz, 926 F.2d 172, 178 (2d Cir. 1991); United States v. Edwards, 945 F.2d 1387, 1393 (7th Cir. 1991)) (applying earlier versions of §1B1.3). In addition, this amendment adds a well-phrased formulation, developed by the Ninth Circuit in United States v. Hahn, 960 F.2d 903 (9th Cir. 1992), addressing the circumstances in which multiple acts constitute the "same course of conduct." **The effective date of this amendment is November 1, 1994.**

504. Section 1B1.10(a) is amended by deleting "guidelines" and inserting in lieu thereof "Guidelines Manual"; by deleting "may be considered" and inserting in lieu thereof "is authorized"; by inserting "and thus is not authorized" immediately following "policy statement"; and by deleting "subsection (d)" wherever it appears and inserting in lieu thereof in each instance "subsection (c)".

Section 1B1.10(b) is amended by inserting ", and to what extent," immediately before "a reduction"; and by deleting:

"originally imposed had the guidelines, as amended, been in effect at that time",

and inserting in lieu thereof:

"imposed had the amendment(s) to the guidelines listed in subsection (c) been in effect at the time the defendant was sentenced".

Section 1B1.10 is amended by deleting:

"(c) *Provided*, that a reduction in a defendant's term of imprisonment may, in no event, exceed the number of months by which the maximum of the guideline range applicable to the defendant (from Chapter Five, Part A) has been lowered.";

and by redesignating subsection (d) as subsection (c).

Section 1B1.10(c)(formerly subsection (d)) is amended by inserting "371," immediately before "379"; and by deleting "and 499" and inserting in lieu thereof "499, and 506".

The Commentary to §1B1.10 captioned "Application Note" is amended by deleting "Note" and inserting in lieu thereof "Notes"; and by deleting:

"1. Although eligibility for consideration under 18 U.S.C. § 3582(c)(2) is triggered only by an amendment listed in subsection (d) of this section, the amended guideline range referred to in subsections (b) and (c) of this section is to be determined by applying all amendments to the guidelines (i.e., as if the defendant was being sentenced under the guidelines currently in effect).",

and inserting in lieu thereof:

"1. Eligibility for consideration under 18 U.S.C. § 3582(c)(2) is triggered only by an amendment listed in subsection (c) that lowers the applicable guideline range.

2. In determining the amended guideline range under subsection (b), the court shall substitute only the amendments listed in subsection (c) for the corresponding guideline provisions that were applied when the defendant was sentenced. All other guideline application decisions remain unaffected.".

The Commentary to §1B1.10 captioned "Background" is amended in the third paragraph by deleting "subsection (d)" and inserting in lieu thereof "subsection (c)".

This amendment simplifies the operation of §1B1.10 by providing that, in determining an amended guideline range, the court will use only those amendments expressly designated as retroactive. In addition, this amendment deletes §1B1.10(c), a rather complex subsection, as an unnecessary restriction on the court's consideration of a revised sentence, redesignates §1B1.10(d) as §1B1.10(c), and makes a number of minor clarifying revisions. This amendment also expands the listing in §1B1.10(c) (formerly §1B1.10(d)) to implement the directive in 28 U.S.C. § 994(u) with respect to guideline amendments that may be considered for retroactive application. **The effective date of this amendment is November 1, 1994.**

505. Section 2D1.1(c) is amended by deleting:

"(1) 300 KG or more of Heroin (or the equivalent amount of other Schedule I or II Opiates); Level 42
1500 KG or more of Cocaine (or the equivalent amount of other Schedule I or II Stimulants);
15 KG or more of Cocaine Base;
300 KG or more of PCP, or 30 KG or more of PCP (actual);
300 KG or more of Methamphetamine, or 30 KG or more of Methamphetamine (actual), or 30 KG or more of "Ice";
3 KG or more of LSD (or the equivalent amount of other Schedule I or II Hallucinogens);
120 KG or more of Fentanyl;
30 KG or more of a Fentanyl Analogue;

300,000 KG or more of Marihuana;
60,000 KG or more of Hashish;
6,000 KG or more of Hashish Oil.

(2) At least 100 KG but less than 300 KG of Heroin (or the equivalent amount of other Schedule I or II Opiates);
At least 500 KG but less than 1500 KG of Cocaine (or the equivalent amount of other Schedule I or II Stimulants);
At least 5 KG but less than 15 KG of Cocaine Base;
At least 100 KG but less than 300 KG of PCP, or at least 10 KG but less than 30 KG of PCP (actual);
At least 100 KG but less than 300 KG of Methamphetamine, or at least 10 KG but less than 30 KG of Methamphetamine (actual), or at least 10 KG but less than 30 KG of "Ice";
At least 1 KG but less than 3 KG of LSD (or the equivalent amount of other Schedule I or II Hallucinogens);
At least 40 KG but less than 120 KG of Fentanyl;
At least 10 KG but less than 30 KG of a Fentanyl Analogue;
At least 100,000 KG but less than 300,000 KG of Marihuana;
At least 20,000 KG but less than 60,000 KG of Hashish;
At least 2,000 KG but less than 6,000 KG of Hashish Oil. — Level 40

(3) At least 30 KG but less than 100 KG of Heroin (or the equivalent amount of other Schedule I or II Opiates);
At least 150 KG but less than 500 KG of Cocaine (or the equivalent amount of other Schedule I or II Stimulants);
At least 1.5 KG but less than 5 KG of Cocaine Base;
At least 30 KG but less than 100 KG of PCP, or at least 3 KG but less than 10 KG of PCP (actual);
At least 30 KG but less than 100 KG of Methamphetamine, or at least 3 KG but less than 10 KG of Methamphetamine (actual), or at least 3 KG but less than 10 KG of "Ice";
At least 300 G but less than 1 KG of LSD (or the equivalent amount of other Schedule I or II Hallucinogens);
At least 12 KG but less than 40 KG of Fentanyl;
At least 3 KG but less than 10 KG of a Fentanyl Analogue;
At least 30,000 KG but less than 100,000 KG of Marihuana;
At least 6,000 KG but less than 20,000 KG of Hashish;
At least 600 KG but less than 2,000 KG of Hashish Oil.", — Level 38

and inserting in lieu thereof:

"(1) 30 KG or more of Heroin (or the equivalent amount of other Schedule I or II Opiates);
150 KG or more of Cocaine (or the equivalent amount of other Schedule I or II Stimulants);
1.5 KG or more of Cocaine Base;
30 KG or more of PCP, or 3 KG or more of PCP (actual);
30 KG or more of Methamphetamine, or 3 KG or more of Methamphetamine (actual), or 3 KG or more of 'Ice';
300 G or more of LSD (or the equivalent amount of other Schedule I or II Hallucinogens);
12 KG or more of Fentanyl;
3 KG or more of a Fentanyl Analogue;
30,000 KG or more of Marihuana; — Level 38

6,000 KG or more of Hashish;
600 KG or more of Hashish Oil.";

and by renumbering subdivisions 4-19 as 2-17, respectively.

The Commentary to §2D1.1 captioned "Application Notes" is amended in Note 14 by deleting "860(b)(4)" and inserting in lieu thereof "960(b)(4)".

The Commentary to §2D1.1 captioned "Application Notes" is amended in Note 16 by deleting "40" and inserting in lieu thereof "38"; by deleting "35" wherever it appears and inserting in lieu thereof in each instance "33"; and by deleting "4 levels" and inserting in lieu thereof "2 levels".

The Commentary to §2D1.1 captioned "Application Notes" is amended by inserting the following additional note:

> "19. In an extraordinary case, an upward departure above offense level 38 on the basis of drug quantity may be warranted. For example, an upward departure may be warranted where the quantity is at least ten times the minimum quantity required for level 38.".

The Commentary to §2D1.6 captioned "Application Note" is amended in Note 1 by deleting "(§2D1.1(c)(16))" and inserting in lieu thereof "(§2D1.1(c)(14))"; and by deleting "(§2D1.1(c)(19))" and inserting in lieu thereof "(§2D1.1(c)(17))".

This amendment sets the upper limit of the Drug Quantity Table in §2D1.1 at level 38. The Commission has determined that the extension of the Drug Quantity Table above level 38 for quantity itself is not required to ensure adequate punishment given that organizers, leaders, managers, and supervisors of such offenses will receive a 4-, 3-, or 2-level enhancement for their role in the offense, and any participant will receive an additional 2-level enhancement if a dangerous weapon is possessed in the offense. The Commission, however, has not foreclosed the possibility of an upward departure above offense level 38 on the basis of drug quantity in an extraordinary case. In addition, this amendment corrects a typographical error in a statutory reference. **The effective date of this amendment is November 1, 1994.**

506. The Commentary to §4B1.1 captioned "Application Notes" is amended in Note 2 by deleting:

> "'Offense Statutory Maximum' refers to the maximum term of imprisonment authorized for the offense of conviction that is a crime of violence or controlled substance offense.",

and inserting in lieu thereof:

> "'Offense Statutory Maximum,' for the purposes of this guideline, refers to the maximum term of imprisonment authorized for the offense of conviction that is a crime of violence or controlled substance offense, not including any increase in that maximum term under a sentencing enhancement provision that applies because of the defendant's prior criminal record (such sentencing enhancement provisions are contained, for example, in 21 U.S.C. § 841(b)(1)(A), (b)(1)(B), (b)(1)(C), and (b)(1)(D)). For example, where the statutory maximum term of imprisonment under 21 U.S.C. § 841(b)(1)(C) is increased from twenty years to thirty years because the defendant has one or more qualifying prior drug convictions, the 'Offense Statutory Maximum' for the purposes of this guideline is twenty years and not thirty years.".

This amendment defines the term "offense statutory maximum" in §4B1.1 to mean the statutory maximum prior to any enhancement based on prior criminal record (<u>i.e.</u>, an enhancement of the statutory maximum sentence that itself was based upon the defendant's prior criminal record will not be used in determining the alternative offense level under this guideline). This rule avoids unwarranted double counting as well as unwarranted disparity associated with variations in the exercise of prosecutorial discretion in seeking enhanced penalties based on prior convictions. It is noted that when the instruction to the Commission that underlies §4B1.1 (28 U.S.C. § 994(h)) was enacted by the Congress in 1984, the enhanced maximum sentences provided for recidivist drug offenders (e.g., under 21 U.S.C. § 841) did not exist. **The effective date of this amendment is November 1, 1994.**

507. The Commentary to §5G1.2 is amended in the fourth paragraph by deleting "3D1.2" and inserting in lieu thereof "3D1.1"; and by inserting the following additional sentences at the end:

> "Note, however, that even in the case of a consecutive term of imprisonment imposed under subsection (a), any term of supervised release imposed is to run concurrently with any other term of supervised release imposed. See 18 U.S.C. § 3624(e).".

This amendment revises the Commentary to §5G1.2 to clarify that the Commission's interpretation is that 18 U.S.C. § 3624(e) requires multiple terms of supervised release to run concurrently in all cases. This interpretation is in accord with the view stated in United States v. Gullickson, 982 F.2d 1231, 1236 (8th Cir. 1993). In contrast, two courts of appeals have cited the current commentary as supporting the view that, notwithstanding the language in 18 U.S.C. § 3624(e) stating that terms of supervised release run concurrently, a court may order that supervised release terms run consecutively under certain circumstances. See United States v. Shorthouse, 7 F.3d 149 (9th Cir. 1993); United States v. Maxwell, 966 F.2d 545, 551 (10th Cir. 1992). **The effective date of this amendment is November 1, 1994.**

508. The Introductory Commentary to Chapter Five, Part H, is amended in the second paragraph by inserting the following additional sentences at the end:

> "Furthermore, although these factors are not ordinarily relevant to the determination of whether a sentence should be outside the applicable guideline range, they may be relevant to this determination in exceptional cases. See §5K2.0 (Grounds for Departure).".

Section 5K2.0 is amended by inserting the following additional paragraph as the fourth paragraph:

> "An offender characteristic or other circumstance that is not ordinarily relevant in determining whether a sentence should be outside the applicable guideline range may be relevant to this determination if such characteristic or circumstance is present to an unusual degree and distinguishes the case from the 'heartland' cases covered by the guidelines in a way that is important to the statutory purposes of sentencing.".

Section 5K2.0 is amended by inserting the following commentary at the end:

> "Commentary
>
> The last paragraph of this policy statement sets forth the conditions under which an offender characteristic or other circumstance that is not ordinarily relevant to a departure from the applicable guideline range may be relevant to this determination. The Commission does not foreclose the possibility of an extraordinary case that, because of a combination of such characteristics or circumstances, differs significantly from the 'heartland' cases covered by the guidelines in a way that is important to the statutory purposes of sentencing, even though none of the characteristics or circumstances individually distinguishes the case. However, the Commission believes that such cases will be extremely rare.

In the absence of a characteristic or circumstance that distinguishes a case as sufficiently atypical to warrant a sentence different from that called for under the guidelines, a sentence outside the guideline range is not authorized. See 18 U.S.C. § 3553(b). For example, dissatisfaction with the available sentencing range or a preference for a different sentence than that authorized by the guidelines is not an appropriate basis for a sentence outside the applicable guideline range.".

This amendment revises §5K2.0 and the Introductory Commentary to Chapter Five, Part H to provide guidance as to when an offender characteristic or other circumstance (or combination of such characteristics or circumstances) that is not ordinarily relevant to a determination of whether a sentence should be outside the applicable guideline range may be relevant to this determination. **The effective date of this amendment is November 1, 1994.**

509. The Commentary to §2D1.1 captioned "Application Notes" is amended in Note 7 by inserting the following additional sentences at the end:

"In addition, 18 U.S.C. § 3553(f) provides an exception to the applicability of mandatory minimum sentences in certain cases. See §5C1.2 (Limitation on Applicability of Statutory Minimum Sentences in Certain Cases).".

The Commentary to §2D2.1 captioned "Background" is amended in the first paragraph by inserting "(statutory)" immediately following "Mandatory"; and by deleting "§5G1.1(b)" and inserting in lieu thereof:

"See §5G1.1(b). Note, however, that 18 U.S.C. § 3553(f) provides an exception to the applicability of mandatory minimum sentences in certain cases. See §5C1.2 (Limitation on Applicability of Statutory Minimum Sentences in Certain Cases).".

Chapter Five, Part C, is amended by inserting an additional guideline with accompanying commentary as §5C1.2 (Limitation on Applicability of Statutory Minimum Sentences in Certain Cases).

This amendment adds a new guideline as §5C1.2, and revises the commentary in §§2D1.1 and 2D1.2, to reflect the addition of 18 U.S.C. § 3553(f) by section 80001 of the Violent Crime Control and Law Enforcement Act of 1994. **The effective date of this amendment is September 23, 1994.**

APPENDIX D*

SENTENCING WORKSHEETS

*Publisher's Note: These Sentencing Worksheets (as revised October, 1994) were prepared by the United States Sentencing Commission.

Worksheet A (Offense Level)

Defendant ______________________ District/Office ______________________

Docket Number (Year-Sequence-Defendant No.) ___ ___-___ ___ ___ ___ ___-___ ___

Count Number(s) ________ U.S. Code Title & Section ________: ______________________

________: ______________________

Guidelines Manual Edition Used: 19____

Instructions:

For each count of conviction (or stipulated offense), complete a separate Worksheet A. Exception: Use only a single Worksheet A where the offense level for a group of closely related counts is based primarily on aggregate value or quantity (see §3D1.2(d)) or where a count of conspiracy, solicitation, or attempt is grouped with a substantive count that was the sole object of the conspiracy, solicitation, or attempt (see §3D1.2(a) and (b)).

1. **Offense Level** (See Chapter Two)
Enter the applicable base offense level and any specific offense characteristics from Chapter Two and explain the bases for these determinations. Enter the sum in the box provided.

Guideline	Description	Level	
			(base)

Notes: ______________________

Sum ☐

2. **Victim-Related Adjustments** (See Chapter Three, Part A) § ________ ☐
Enter the applicable section and adjustment. If more than one section is applicable, list each section and enter the combined adjustment. If no adjustment is applicable, enter "0."

3. **Role in the Offense Adjustment** (See Chapter Three, Part B) § ________ ☐
Enter the applicable section and adjustment. If more than one section is applicable, list each section and enter the combined adjustment. If the adjustment reduces the offense level, enter a minus (-) sign in front of the adjustment. If no adjustment is applicable, enter "0."

4. **Obstruction Adjustment** (See Chapter Three, Part C) § ________ ☐
Enter the applicable section and adjustment. If more than one section is applicable, list each section and enter the combined adjustment. If no adjustment is applicable, enter "0."

5. **Adjusted Offense Level** ☐
Enter the sum of Items 1-4. If this worksheet does not cover all counts of conviction or stipulated offenses, complete Worksheet B. Otherwise, enter this result on Worksheet D, Item 1.

☐ *Check if the defendant is convicted of a single count. In such case, Worksheet B need not be completed.*

☐ *If the defendant has no criminal history, enter criminal history "I" here and on Item 4, Worksheet D. In such case, Worksheet C need not be completed.*

Worksheet B
(Multiple Counts or Stipulation to Additional Offenses)

Defendant ______________________ Docket Number ______________

Instructions

Step 1: Enter the adjusted offense level from Worksheet A in the box(es) provided for: (1) counts grouped under §3D1.2(d) or (2) a count charging conspiracy, solicitation, or attempt that is grouped with the substantive count of conviction (see §3D1.2(a)).

Step 2: Combine the remaining counts resulting in conviction into distinct groups of closely related counts by applying the rules specified in §3D1.2 and explain the reasons for grouping below.

NOTES: ____

____

Step 3: For every group of closely related counts determined at Step 2, enter from Worksheet A the count with the highest adjusted offense level (see §3D1.3).

Step 4: Enter the number of units to be assigned to each group (see §3D1.4) as follows:

- One unit (1) for the group of closely related counts with the highest offense level
- An additional unit (1) for each group that is equally serious or 1 to 4 levels less serious
- An additional half unit (1/2) for each group that is 5 to 8 levels less serious
- No increase in units for groups that are 9 or more levels less serious

1. **Adjusted Offense Level for the First Group of Closely Related Counts**
   Count number(s):______________ ☐ ______(unit)

2. **Adjusted Offense Level for the Second Group of Closely Related Counts**
   Count number(s):______________ ☐ ______(unit)

3. **Adjusted Offense Level for the Third Group of Closely Related Counts**
   Count number(s):______________ ☐ ______(unit)

4. **Adjusted Offense Level for the Fourth Group of Closely Related Counts**
   Count number(s):______________ ☐ ______(unit)

5. **Adjusted Offense Level for the Fifth Group of Closely Related Counts**
   Count number(s):______________ ☐ ______(unit)

6. **Total Units** ______ **(total units)**

7. **Increase in Offense Level Based on Total Units (See §3D1.4)** ☐

1 unit:	no increase	2 1/2 - 3 units:	add 3 levels
1 1/2 units:	add 1 level	3 1/2 - 5 units:	add 4 levels
2 units:	add 2 levels	More than 5 units:	add 5 levels

8. **Highest of the Adjusted Offense Levels from Items 1-5 Above** ☐

9. **Combined Adjusted Offense Level (See §3D1.4)** ☐
   Enter the sum of Items 7 and 8 here and on Worksheet D, Item 1.

Worksheet C (Criminal History)

Defendant ______________________ Docket Number ______________

Date Defendant Commenced Participation in Instant Offense (Earliest Date of Relevant Conduct) __________

1. 3 Points for each prior ADULT sentence of imprisonment exceeding ONE YEAR and ONE MONTH imposed within 15 YEARS of the defendant's commencement of the instant offense OR resulting in incarceration during any part of that 15-YEAR period. (See §§4A1.1(a) and 4A1.2.)

2. 2 Points for each prior sentence of imprisonment of at least 60 DAYS resulting from an offense committed ON OR AFTER the defendant's 18th birthday not counted under §4A1.1(a) imposed within 10 YEARS of the instant offense; and

   2 Points for each prior sentence of imprisonment of at least 60 DAYS resulting from an offense committed BEFORE the defendant's 18th birthday not counted under §4A1.1(a) from which the defendant was released from confinement within 5 YEARS of the instant offense. (See §§4A1.1(b) and 4A1.2.)

3. 1 Point for each prior sentence resulting from an offense committed ON OR AFTER the defendant's 18th birthday not counted under §4A1.1(a) or §4A1.1(b) imposed within 10 YEARS of the instant offense; and

   1 Point for each prior sentence resulting from an offense committed BEFORE the defendant's 18th birthday not counted under §4A1.1(a) or §4A1.1(b) imposed within 5 YEARS of the instant offense. (See §§4A1.1 (c) and 4A1.2.)

   NOTE: A maximum of 4 Points may be imposed for the prior sentences in Item 3.

Date of Imposition	Offense	Sentence	Release Date**	Guideline Section	Criminal History Pts.

* Indicate with an asterisk those offenses where defendant was sentenced as a juvenile.

** A release date is required in only three instances:

a. When a sentence covered under §4A1.1(a) was imposed more than 15 years prior to the commencement of the instant offense but release from incarceration occurred within such 15-year period;

b. When a sentence counted under §4A1.1(b) was imposed for an offense committed prior to age 18 and more than 5 years prior to the commencement of the instant offense, but release from incarceration occurred within such 5-year period; and

c. When §4A1.1(e) applies because the defendant was released from custody on a sentence counted under 4A1.1(a) or 4A1.1 (b) within 2 years of the instant offense or was still in custody at the time of the instant offense (see Item 5).

Total Criminal History Points for §§4A1.1(a), 4A1.1(b), and 4A1.1(c) (Items 1,2,3) ☐

Rev. 10/94

Worksheet C

Defendant ______________________ Docket Number ______________

4. 2 Points if the defendant committed the instant offense while under any criminal justice sentence (e.g., probation, parole, supervised release, imprisonment, work release, escape status). (See §§4A1.1(d) and 4A1.2.) List the type of control and identify the sentence from which control resulted. Otherwise, enter 0 Points.

5. 2 Points if the defendant committed the instant offense less than 2 YEARS after release from imprisonment on a sentence counted under §4A1.1(a) or (b) or while in imprisonment or escape status on such a sentence. However, enter only 1 Point for this item if 2 points were added at Item 4 under §4A1.1(d). (See §§4A1.1(e) and 4A1.2.) List the date of release and identify the sentence from which release resulted. Otherwise, enter 0 Points.

6. 1 Point for each prior sentence resulting from a conviction of a crime of violence that did not receive any points under §4A1.1(a), (b), or (c) because such sentence was considered related to another sentence resulting from a conviction of a crime of violence. *Provided,* that this item does not apply where the sentences are considered related because the offenses occurred on the same occasion. (See §§4A1.1(f) and 4A1.2.) Identify the crimes of violence and briefly explain why the cases are considered related. Otherwise, enter 0 Points.

   Note: A maximum of 3 Points may be imposed for Item 6.

7. **Total Criminal History Points** (Sum of Items 1-6)

8. **Criminal History Category** (Enter here and on Worksheet D, Item 4)

Total Points	Criminal History Category
0-1	I
2-3	II
4-6	III
7-9	IV
10-12	V
13 or more	VI

Worksheet D (Guideline Worksheet)

Defendant ______________________ District ______________________

Docket Number ______________________

1. **Adjusted Offense Level** (From Worksheet A or B)
   If Worksheet B is required, enter the result from Worksheet B, Item 9. Otherwise, enter the result from Worksheet A, Item 5.

2. **Acceptance of Responsibility** (See Chapter Three, Part E)
   Enter the applicable reduction. —

3. **Offense Level Total** (Item 1 less Item 2)

4. **Criminal History Category** (From Worksheet C)
   Enter the result from Worksheet C, Item 8.

5. **Career Offender/Criminal Livelihood/Armed Career Criminal** (see Chapter Four, Part B)

   a. Offense Level Total

   If the provision for Career Offender (§4B1.1), Criminal Livelihood (§4B1.3), or Armed Career Criminal (§4B1.4) results in an offense level total higher than Item 3, enter the offense level total. Otherwise, enter "N/A."

   b. Criminal History Category

   If the provision for Career Offender (§4B1.1) or Armed Career Criminal (§4B1.4) results in a criminal history category higher than Item 4, enter the applicable criminal history category. Otherwise, enter "N/A."

6. **Guideline Range from Sentencing Table**
   Enter the applicable guideline range from Chapter Five, Part A. Months

7. **Restricted Guideline Range** (See Chapter Five, Part G)
   If the statutorily authorized maximum sentence or the statutorily required minimum sentence restricts the guideline range (Item 6) (see §§5G1.1 and 5G1.2), enter either the restricted guideline range or any statutory maximum or minimum penalty that would modify the guideline range. Otherwise, enter "N/A." Months

   ☐ Check here if §5C1.2 (Limitation on Applicabiity of Statutory Minimum Penalties in Certain Cases) applies.

8. **Undischarged Term of Imprisonment** (See §5G1.3)

   ☐ If the defendant is subject to an undischarged term of imprisonment, check this box and list the undischarged term(s) below.

   ____

   ____

   ____

Rev. 10/94

Worksheet D

Defendant ______________________ Docket Number ______________

9. **Sentencing Options** (Check the applicable box that corresponds to the Guideline Range entered in Item 6.) (See Chapter Five, Sentencing Table)

☐ Zone A — If checked, the following options are available (see §5B1.1):

- Fine (See §5E1.2(a))
- "Straight" Probation
- Imprisonment

☐ Zone B — If checked, the minimum term may be satisfied by:

- Imprisonment
- Imprisonment of at least one month plus supervised release with a condition that substitutes community confinement or home detention for imprisonment (see §5C1.1(c)(2))
- Probation with a condition that substitutes intermittent confinement, community confinement, or home detention for imprisonment (see §5B1.1(a)(2) and §5C1.1(c)(3))

☐ Zone C — If checked, the minimum term may be satisfied by:

- Imprisonment
- Imprisonment of at least one-half of the minimum term plus supervised release with a condition that substitutes community confinement or home detention for imprisonment (see §5C1.1(d)(2))

☐ Zone D — If checked, the minimum term shall be satisfied by a sentence of imprisonment (see §5C1.1(f))

10. **Length of a Term of Probation** (See §5B1.2)

If probation is authorized, the guideline for the length of such term of probation is: (Check applicable box)

☐ At least one year, but not more than five years (if the offense level total is 6 or more)

☐ No more than three years (if the offense level total is 5 or less)

11. **Conditions of Probation** (See §§5B1.3 and 5B1.4)

A defendant serving any term of probation shall not commit a federal, state, or local crime. In addition to standard conditions (1-13), list any applicable special conditions:

____

____

____

____

____

Worksheet D

Defendant ______________________ Docket Number ______________________

12. **Supervised Release** (See §§5D1.1 and 5D1.2)

a. A term of supervised release is: (Check applicable box)

☐ Required because a term of imprisonment of more than one year is to be imposed

☐ Authorized but not required because a term of imprisonment of one year or less is to be imposed

b. Length of Term (Check applicable box)

☐ If the defendant is convicted under a statute that requires a term of supervised release, the term shall be at least three years but not more than five years or the minimum period required by statute, whichever is greater (see §5D1.2(a)) List the applicable term: ______________.

☐ Class A or B Felony: Three to Five Year Term

☐ Class C or D Felony: Two to Three Year Term

☐ Class E Felony or Class A Misdemeanor: One Year Term

13. **Conditions of Supervised Release** (See §5D1.3)
A defendant serving any term of supervised release shall not commit a federal, state, or local crime. In addition to standard conditions (1-13), list any applicable special conditions:

____

____

14. **Restitution** (See §5E1.1)
If an order of restitution is applicable, enter the amount. Otherwise, enter "N/A."

____

15. **Fines**

a. Fines for Individual Defendants (See §5E1.2)	Minimum	Maximum
(1) If any of the counts of conviction has a statutory maximum penalty that exceeds $250,000 list the aggregate statutory maximum penalties for those counts.		$__________
(2) Fine Table:	$__________	$__________
(3) Guideline Range for Fines: (determined by the minimum and greater maximum above)	$__________	$__________

b. Cost of imprisonment $__________ (See §5E1.2(i))

Cost of probation, supervised release $__________

Cost of community confinement $__________

Worksheet D

Page 4

Defendant ______________________ Docket Number ______________________

16. **Special Assessments** (See §5E1.3)

Enter the total amount of special assessments required for all counts of conviction:

- $25 for each misdemeanor count of conviction
- $50 for each felony count of conviction

$__________

17. **Additional Factors**

List any additional applicable guidelines, policy statements, and statutory provisions. Also list any applicable aggravating and mitigating factors that may warrant a sentence at a particular point either within or outside the applicable guideline range. Attach additional sheets as required.

Completed by ______________________ Date ______________________

Rev. 10/94

ORGANIZATIONAL WORKSHEET A*
(Offense Level)

Defendant ______________________ Docket Number ______________________

District/Office ______________________

For each count of conviction (or stipulated offense) listed at §8C2.1, complete a separate Worksheet A. Exception: Use only a single Worksheet A where the offense level for a group of closely related counts is based primarily on aggregate value or quantity (see §3D1.2(d)) or where there is a count of conspiracy, solicitation, or attempt and a substantive count that was the sole object of the conspiracy, solicitation, or attempt (see §3D1.2(a) and (b)).

For counts of conviction (or stipulated offenses) not listed at §8C2.1, skip to Worksheet D, Item 1.

Count Number(s) __________ U.S. Code Title & Section ____ - ______ - ____

____ - ______ - ____

1. **Offense Level** (See §8C2.3)

Enter the applicable base offense level and any specific offense characteristics from Chapter Two and explain the bases for these determinations. Enter the sum in the box provided below. Exception: Do not enter a sum if the applicable Chapter Two guideline is §§2S1.1, 2S1.2, 2S1.3 or 2S1.4. Instead, enter "N/A" and complete Item 2.

Guideline	Description	Level
__________	__________	__________
__________	__________	__________
__________	__________	__________

If this worksheet does not cover all counts of conviction or stipulated offenses listed at §8C2.1, complete Worksheet B. Otherwise, enter this result on Worksheet C, Item 1.

Sum [ ]

Notes: ______________________

____

Note: Chapter Three Parts A,B,C, and E, do not apply to organizational defendants.

2. **Special Instructions for Offenses Covered by §§2S1.1, 2S1.2, 2S1.3, or 2S1.4.**

Determine the applicable special instruction for fines using the base offense level and applicable specific offense characteristic(s) from Item 1 above, and enter at (a) below. Apply the special instruction to determine the amount to be used at §8C2.4(a)(1). Enter this amount at (b) below and on Worksheet C, Item 2(a).

(a) ______________________

(b) ______________________

* *Publisher's Note:* These Organizational Worksheets were prepared by the United States Sentencing Commission.

ORGANIZATIONAL WORKSHEET B
(Multiple Counts or Stipulation to Additional Offenses)

Defendant ______________________ Docket Number ______________________

District/Office ____

Notes explaining grouping decision(s): ____

____

____

Instructions for Items 1-5:

If the offense level for the Group is based primarily on aggregate value or quantity, or is the offense level for a count charging conspiracy, solicitation, or attempt, and a substantive offense that was the sole object of the conspiracy, solicitation, or attempt, enter the adjusted offense level from Worksheet A. Otherwise, enter the adjusted offense level from Worksheet A for the count in the Group having the highest adjusted offense level (*see* §3D1.3). List the count number(s) for each of the counts in the Group.

Then enter the number of units to be assigned to each group as follows (*See* §3D1.4):

- One unit (1) for the Count Group with the highest offense level
- One unit (1) for each additional Group equally serious or 1 to 4 levels less serious
- One-half unit (1/2) for each Group 5 to 8 levels less serious
- No increase in units for each Group 9 or more levels less serious

1. **Adjusted Offense Level for the First Group of Closely Related Counts**
   Count number(s): ______ [ ] ______(unit)
2. **Adjusted Offense Level for the Second Group of Closely Related Counts**
   Count number(s): ______ [ ] ______(unit)
3. **Adjusted Offense Level for the Third Group of Closely Related Counts**
   Count number(s): ______ [ ] ______(unit)
4. **Adjusted Offense Level for the Fourth Group of Closely Related Counts**
   Count number(s): ______ [ ] ______(unit)
5. **Adjusted Offense Level for the Fifth Group of Closely Related Counts**
   Count number(s): ______ [ ] ______(unit)
6. **Total Units** ______ (Total Units)
7. **Increase in Offense Level Based on Total Units (*see* §3D1.4)** [ ]

1 unit - no increase	2 1/2 to 3 units - add 3 levels
1 1/2 units - add 1 level	3 1/2 to 5 units - add 4 levels
2 units - add 2 levels	More than 5 units - add 5 levels

8. **Highest of the Adjusted Offense Levels from Items 1-5 Above** [ ]
9. **Combined Adjusted Offense Level (*see* §3D1.4)**
   Enter the sum of Items 7 and 8 here and on Worksheet C, Item 1. [ ]

ORGANIZATIONAL WORKSHEET C
(Base Fine, Culpability Score and Fine Range)

Defendant________________ Docket Number __________

District/Office________________

1. **Offense Level Total** (From Worksheet A or B)

   If Worksheet B is required, enter the result from Item 9. Otherwise, enter the result from Worksheet A, Item 1. If only applicable Chapter Two guidelines are §§2S1.1, 2S1.2, 2S1.3, or 2S1.4, enter "N/A". [ ]

2. **Base Fine** (See §8C2.4)

   (a) Enter the amount from the Offense Level Fine Table (See §8C2.4(d)). Note: If the only applicable Chapter Two guidelines are §§2S1.1, 2S1.2, 2S1.3, or 2S1.4, enter the result from Worksheet A, Item 2(b) instead. If §§2S1.1, 2S1.2, 2S1.3, or 2S1.4 apply as well as another offense guideline and the counts are grouped together, enter the greater of the amounts from the Offense Level Fine Table or Worksheet A, Item 2(b). $________

   (b) Enter the pecuniary gain to the organization (See §8C2.4(a)(2)). $________

   (c) Enter the pecuniary loss caused by the organization to the extent the loss was caused intentionally, knowingly, or recklessly (See §8C2.4(a)(3)). Note: the following Chapter Two guidelines have special instructions regarding the determination of pecuniary loss: §§2B4.1, 2C1.1, 2C1.2, 2E5.1, 2E5.6, and 2R1.1. $________

   (d) Enter the amount from Item (a), (b), or (c) above, whichever is greatest. $________

3. **Culpability Score** (See §8C2.5)

   (a) Start with five points and apply (b) through (g) below. [5]

   (b) Involvement/Tolerance (See §8C2.5(b))

   Enter the specific subdivision and points applicable. If more than one subdivision is applicable, use the greatest. If no adjustment is applicable, enter "0". §______ [ ]

   (c) Prior History (See §8C2.5(c))

   Enter the specific subdivision and points applicable. If more than one subdivision is applicable, use the greater. If no adjustment is applicable, enter "0". §______ [ ]

   Earliest date of relevant conduct for the instant offense: ________

Organizational Worksheet C, Page Two

Defendant ______________________ Docket Number ______________________

District/Office ______________________

d) Violation of an Order (See §8C2.5(d))

Enter the specific subdivision and points applicable. If more than one subdivision is applicable, use the greater. If no adjustment is applicable, enter "0".

§__________ [ ]

(e) Obstruction of Justice (See §8C2.5(e))

If no adjustment is applicable, enter "0". [ ]

(f) Effective Program to Prevent and Detect Violations of Law (See §8C2.5(f))

If no adjustment is applicable, enter "0". [ ]

(g) Self-Reporting, Cooperation and Acceptance of Responsibility (See §8C2.5(g))

Enter the specific subdivision and points applicable. If more than one subdivision is applicable, use the greatest. If no adjustment is applicable, enter "0".

§__________ [ ]

4. **Total Culpability Score**

Enter the sum of Items 3(a) thru 3(g). [ ]

5. **Minimum and Maximum Multipliers** (See §8C2.6)

Enter the minimum and the maximum multipliers from the table at §8C2.6 corresponding to the total culpability score (Item 4 above). Note: If the applicable Chapter Two guideline is §2R1.1, neither the minimum nor the maximum multiplier shall be less than 0.75 (See §2R1.1(d)(2)).

(a) Minimum Multiplier __________

(b) Maximum Multiplier __________

Organizational Worksheet C, Page Three

Defendant____________________________ Docket Number __________________

District/Office ____

6. **Fine Range** (See §8C2.7)

   (a) Multiply the base fine (Item 2(d) above) by the minimum multiplier (Item 5(a) above) to establish the minimum of the fine range. Enter the result here and at Worksheet D, Item 4(a).

   Minimum of fine range ____________________

   (b) Multiply the base fine (Item 2(d) above) by the maximum multiplier (Item 5(b) above) to establish the maximum of the fine range. Enter the result here and at Worksheet D, Item 4(a).

   Maximum of fine range ____________________

7. **Disgorgement** (See §8C2.9)

   Skip this item if any pending or anticipated civil or administrative proceeding is expected to deprive the defendant of its gain from the offense.

   (a) Enter the amount of pecuniary gain from Item 2(b).

   $________________

   (b) Enter the amount of restitution already made and remedial costs already incurred.

   $________________

   (c) Enter the amount of restitution and other remedial costs to be ordered by the court. (See §§8B1.1, 8B1.2)

   $________________

   (d) Add Items (b) and (c) and enter the result.

   $________________

   (e) Subtract the amount of total restitution and remedial costs (Item (d)) from the amount of pecuniary gain to the defendant (Item (a)) to determine undisgorged gain. Enter the result here and at Worksheet D, Item 4(b). Note: If the amount of undisgorged gain is less than zero, enter zero.

   $________________

ORGANIZATIONAL WORKSHEET D
(Guideline Worksheet)

Defendant ______________________________ Docket Number ____________________

District/Office ____

Note: Unless otherwise specfied, all items on Worksheet D are applicable to all counts of conviction.

1. **Restitution** (See §8B1.1)

   If an order of restitution is applicable, enter the amount corresponding to the count(s) of conviction. Otherwise, enter "N/A".

   $ ____________________

2. **Remedial Orders** (See §8B1.2), **Community Service** (See §8B1.3), **Order of Notice to Victims** (See §8B1.4)

   List if applicable. Otherwise, enter "N/A".

   ____

   ____

3. **Criminal Purpose Organization Calculation** (See §8C1.1)

   If a preliminary determination indicates that the organization operated primarily for a criminal purpose or primarily by criminal means, enter the amount of the organization's net assets below. This amount shall be the fine (subject to the statutory maximum) for all counts of conviction.

   $ ____

4. **Fine Calculation** (Only for counts listed under §8C2.1)

   (a) Guideline Fine Range (From Worksheet C, Item 6)

   $ ____________________ to $ ____________________

   (b) Disgorgement (See §8C2.9)

   Enter the result from the Worksheet C, Item 7(e). The court shall add to the fine determined under §8C2.1 (Determining the Fine Within the Range) any undisgorged gain to the organization from the offense.

   $ ____________________

5. **Counts Not Listed Under §8C2.1** (See §8C2.10)

   Enter the counts not listed under §8C2.1and the statutory maximum for each count. The court may impose an additional fine for these counts.

   ____

Organizational Worksheet D, Page Two

Defendant ______________________________ Docket Number ______________________

District/Office ____

6. **Fine Offset** (See §8C3.4)

Multiply the total fines imposed upon individuals who each own at least five percent interest in the organization by those individuals' total percentage interest in the organization and enter the result below.

$______________________

The court may reduce the fine imposed on a closely held organization by an amount not to exceed the fine offset.

7. **Imposition of a Sentence of Probation**. (See §8D1.1)

(a) Probation is required if any of the following apply: (Check the applicable line(s)).

_____(1) Probation is necessary as a mechanism to secure payment of restitution (§8B1.1), enforce a remedial order (§8B1.2), or ensure completion of community service (§8B1.3).

_____(2) Any monetary penalty imposed (i.e., restitution, fine or special assessment) is not paid in full at the time of sentencing and restrictions appear necessary to safeguard the defendant's ability to make payments.

_____(3) At the time of sentencing the organization has 50 or more employees and does not have an effective program to prevent and detect violations of law.

_____(4) Within the last five years prior to sentencing, the organization has engaged in similar misconduct, as determined by a prior criminal adjudication, and any part of the misconduct underlying the instant offense occurred after that adjudication.

_____(5) An individual within high-level personnel of the organization or the unit of the organization within which the instant offense was committed participated in the misconduct underlying the instant offense; and that individual within five years prior to sentencing engaged in similar misconduct, as determined by a prior criminal adjudication; and any part of the misconduct underlying the instant offense occurred after that adjudication.

_____(6) Probation is necessary to ensure that changes are made within the organization to reduce the likelihood of future criminal conduct.

_____(7) The sentence imposed upon the organization does not include a fine.

_____(8) Probation is necessary to accomplish one or more of the purposes of sentencing set forth in 18 U.S.C. §3553(a)(2).

State purpose(s): ____

____

____

Organizational Worksheet D, Page Three

Defendant ______________________________ Docket Number ____________________

District/Office ____

(b) Length of Term of Probation (See §8D1.2)

If probation is authorized, the guideline for the length of such term of probation is: (Check the applicable line).

_____(1) At least one year, but not more than five years (if the offense is a felony)

_____(2) No more than five years (if the offense is a Class A misdemeanor)

(c) Conditions of Probation (See §8D1.4)

In addition to standard conditions (See §8D1.3), list any applicable special conditions:

____

____

____

8. **Special Assessments** (See §8E1.1)

Enter the total amount of special assessments required for all counts of conviction:

$_______________

9. **Additional Applicable Guidelines, Policy Statements, Statutory Provisions, and Aggravating and Mitigating Factors.**

List any additional applicable guidelines, policy statements, and statutory provisions. Also, list any applicable aggravating and mitigating factors that may warrant a sentence at a particular point within the applicable guideline range or outside the applicable guideline range. Attach additional sheets as required.

____

____

____

____

____

____

Completed by ______________________________ Date ____________________

[If a plea agreement is accepted by the court, attach a copy to the worksheet.]

APPENDIX E*

QUESTIONS MOST FREQUENTLY ASKED ABOUT THE SENTENCING GUIDELINES

Questions Most Frequently Asked About

The Sentencing Guidelines

United States Sentencing Commission
Washington, D.C.

Volume VII — June 1, 1994
(replaces volumes I-VI)

Disclaimer: Information provided by the Commission's Training Staff is offered to assist in understanding and applying the sentencing guidelines. The information does not necessarily represent the official position of the Commission, should not be considered definitive, and is not binding upon the Commission, the court, or the parties in any case.

---

* **Publisher's Note:** **These materials were prepared by the United States Sentencing Commission.**

INDEX: MOST FREQUENTLY ASKED QUESTIONS, SEVENTH EDITION

(✓ *indicates new question for this edition*)

I. CHAPTER ONE: *Introduction and General Application Principles*

Guideline	MFAQ #	Summary of Topic
1B1.1	1	Statutory Provisions listed not inclusive
1B1.2	2	Conspiracy to commit more than one offense
1B1.2/6B1.4	3	Effect of stipulations on guideline application
1B1.3	4	Reasonable foreseeability and relevant conduct
1B1.3	5	Drug conspiracy, amount of drugs for each defendant
1B1.3	6	Drug amounts from prior convictions and relevant conduct
✓1B1.3	7	Conduct of co-conspirators prior to defendant joining conspiracy
1B1.3(a)(1)	8	Loss caused during flight from scene of crime is relevant conduct
1B1.3(a)(1)	9	Adding drug amounts when no conspiracy conviction; evidentiary legal standard
1B1.5	10	Underlying offense includes base offense level plus specific offense characteristics
1B1.5	11	Cross references and applicability of Chapter Three adjustments
1B1.9	12	Class B and C misdemeanors and infractions not subject to guidelines
1B1.10	13	Retroactivity of amended guidelines
1B1.10	14	Calculation of amended guideline range

II. CHAPTER TWO: *Offense Conduct*

Guideline	MFAQ #	Summary of Topic
2A3.1/1B1.3	15	Conviction under particular statute not required for application of specific offense characteristic
2B3.1	16	Toy gun in bank robbery; gun enhancement possible
2B3.1/5K2.0	17	Injury to multiple robbery victims; departure possible
2B5.3/2B5.4	18	Definition of "infringing items"
2C1.1	19	Offerer and recipient not distinguished in bribery
2D1.1	20	Weight of drug packaging not included
✓2D1.1	21	LSD/carrier medium
✓2D1.1	22	Materials that must be separated from controlled substance before controlled substance can be used
✓2D1.1	23	Cocaine base means crack
✓2D1.1	24	Mandatory minimums and drug analogs
✓2D1.1	25	Fraudulent drug transactions
2D1.1/2D1.11	26	Controlled substances not listed in guidelines
2D1.1	27	When to use the Typical Weight Per Unit Table
2D1.1	28	Base offense level for mixture of different drugs
2D1.1	29	Tylenol 3 is Schedule III controlled substance
2D1.1	30	Treatment of anomalies when combining drugs
2D1.2	31	Weapon enhancement possible under §2D1.2
2D2.1	32	Amount of drugs not relevant for simple possession
2E1.1	33	Alternative base offense levels for "RICO"

2F1.1	34	Actual and intended loss
2F1.1	35	Reduction of loss amount due to loan payments
2F1.1/2T1.1/3D1.2	36	Grouping rule for differing definitions of loss
2H1.1	37	Underlying offense in civil rights guidelines
2K2.1	38	Conviction for underlying offense not a factor in applicability of cross-references in firearm guidelines
✓2K2.1	39	Defendant unaware firearm was stolen
✓2K2.1	40	"Felony offense" means federal, state, or local offense
2K2.1/3D1.2	41	When to group counts of felon in possession of a firearm
2L1.2	42	Deportation after conviction for aggravated felony
✓2L1.2	43	Felony or aggravated felony convictions need not be "countable" under Chapter Four
2S1.1	44	"Value of funds" in money laundering
2T1.1/3D1.2	45	Tax evasion count grouped with count for underlying offense
2T1.3	46	Calculation of "tax loss"
2X1.1	47	Cross-reference to 2X1.1 and completed conduct
2X3.1	48	Cross-reference for Accessory After the Fact
2X5.1	49	Procedure when statute not listed in Appendix A
2X5.1	50	Guidelines applicable to Assimilative Crimes, Indian Major Crimes Acts
2X5.1	51	No analogous guideline for DWI

III. CHAPTER THREE: ***Adjustments***

Guideline	MFAQ #	Summary of Topic
3A1.1	52	Vulnerable Victim enhancement for sexual exploitation of a minor
3A1.2	53	Official Victim enhancement with Aggravated Assault
3A1.2/2B3.1	54	Official Victim enhancement possible in addition to bodily injury adjustment
3A1.3	55	Illegal aliens as "victims"
3B1.2	56	Role adjustments based on relevant conduct
✓3B1.3	57	Abuse of Position of Trust and postal carriers
3C1.1	58	No obstruction for bribery in separate case
3C1.1	59	Drug + perjury = obstruction, counts grouped
3C1.1	60	Obstruction enhancement for destruction of evidence contemporaneous with arrest
3C1.1	61	Chapter Three adjustments to counts grouped under §3D1.2(d) to which different guidelines apply
3C1.1/1B1.3	62	Enhancement for obstructive conduct of co-defendant
3D1.1/2K2.1/2K2.4	63	Grouping of 18 USC § 922(g) and 18 USC § 924(c)
3D1.2	64	Use of alternative grouping rule
3D1.2	65	Grouping for money laundering and drug distribution
3D1.2(c)	66	Grouping under rule (c)
3D1.2(c)/2J1.6	67	Grouping for drug distribution and failure to appear
3E1.1	68	Acceptance of Responsibility not automatic upon guilty plea
3E1.1	69	Applying Acceptance of Responsibility to multiple counts of conviction
✓3E1.1	70	Acceptance of Responsibility amendment not retroactive
✓3E1.1	71	Applying the three-level acceptance reduction
3E1.1/legal	72	Acceptance of Responsibility in the plea agreement

IV. CHAPTER FOUR: *Criminal History, Career Offender, and Criminal Livelihood*

Guideline	MFAQ #	Summary of Topic
4A1.1	73	Sentence of "time served" and criminal history
4A1.1	74	Prior civil adjudications and criminal history
4A1.1(a)	75	Criminal history points while on appeal bond
4A1.1(c)	76	Work release and criminal history
4A1.1(d)	77	Criminal history points while on active warrant
4A1.1(d)	78	Criminal history points for unsupervised probation
4A1.1(d) & (e)	79	Criminal history points for escape
4A1.2	80	Later offense as a "prior sentence"
4A1.2	81	Offense while on bond pending trial
4A1.2	82	Points based on new sentence pronounced
4A1.2	83	Counting uncounseled misdemeanors
4A1.2	84	Cases separated by intervening arrest not treated as related
4A1.2(a)(2)	85	Concurrent sentences that are not related
4A1.2(a)(2)	86	Cases consolidated for sentencing
4A1.2(c)	87	Assigning points to local ordinance violations
4A1.2(c)	88	DWI not considered "minor traffic infraction"
4A1.2(f)	89	Diversionary sentences
4A1.2(k)	90	Revocation may affect counting of certain sentences
4A1.3(e)	91	Prior criminal conduct with no conviction
4B1.1	92	Multiple count Career Offender
4B1.1/4B1.2	93	Definitional differences in career offender and armed career criminal guidelines
4B1.2	94	Time periods for Career Offenders
4B1.2	95	Offense of conviction for Career Offender
4B1.2	96	Simple possession not "controlled substance" for Career Offender
4B1.2	97	Prior felony convictions need not be sentences of imprisonment for Career Offender
4B1.2	98	Career Offender and "telephone count"
4B1.2	99	Felon in possession not crime of violence for Career Offender purposes
4B1.2(3)	100	Timetable for "prior sentences" for Career Offender
4B1.2(3)	101	Date defendant "sustained a conviction"
4B1.4	102	Guideline sentences for Armed Career Criminal

V. CHAPTER FIVE: *Determining the Sentence*

Guideline	MFAQ #	Summary of Topic
5B1.3	103	Guidelines permit unsupervised probation
5C1.1	104	Home detention
5C1.1(c) & (d)	105	Sentencing options available at any point within range
5C1.1(d)	106	"Split sentence" option
5D1.1	107	Supervised release on multiple counts
5D1.1/2K2.4	108	Supervised release for conviction under 18 USC § 924(c)
5D1.2	109	18 USC § 3581 versus 18 USC § 3559: follow § 3559
5D1.2(a)	110	Supervised release; statute and guideline range
5D1.3	111	Community confinement with guideline maximum sentence
5D1.3/7B1.3	112	Intermittent confinement not available as condition of supervised release
5E1.1	113	Restitution with non-title 18 or 49 crimes

5E1.2	114	Determining maximum of guideline fine range
5E1.2	115	Fine as sole sanction
5E1.2(f)	116	Effect of not imposing a fine
5E1.2(i)	117	Imprisonment/supervision costs constitute additional fine amount
5G1.1	118	Guidelines and statutory minimums or maximums
5G1.2	119	Mandatory consecutive sentences
5G1.2	120	Counts from separate indictments consolidated
✓5G1.3	121	Explanation of provision
✓5G1.3	122	Sentence for instant offense in light of revocation
✓5G1.3	123	Provision inapplicable to defendant not serving term of imprisonment
✓5G1.3	124	Adjusting guideline sentence to reflect time served
✓5G1.3	125	Incremental punishment procedure in Application Note 3

VI. CHAPTER SIX: *Sentencing Procedures and Plea Agreements*

Guideline	MFAQ #	Summary of Topic
6A1.3/ legal	126	Standard of evidence when facts are disputed
6A1.3/ legal	127	Burden of persuasion when facts are disputed

VII. CHAPTER SEVEN: *Violations of Probation and Supervised Release*

Guideline	MFAQ #	Summary of Topic
Chapter 7	128	Sentencing range in revocation cases
Chapter 7	129	Revocation of probation and supervised release
7B1.1	130	Determination of grade of violation
7B1.3	131	Grade A violation of probation or supervised release
7B1.3(e)	132	Credit for time in official detention
7B1.4	133	Definition of "original sentence"
7B1.4	134	Maximum imprisonment on revocation of supervised release

VIII. CHAPTER EIGHT: *Sentencing of Organizations*

Guideline	MFAQ #	Summary of Topic
8A1.1	135	Applicability of Chapter Eight to felonies and Class A misdemeanors
8B1.1	136	Exceptions to guideline restitution requirement
8C2.2-.7/8C3.3	137	When fine range calculations not required
8C2.4	138	Determining fines for organizational defendants
8C2.4	139	Base fine
8C2.9	140	Disgorgement of profits
8D1.1	141	Mandatory bases for organizational probation

IX. STATUTORY ISSUES

Statute	MFAQ #	Summary of Topic
18 USC § 19	142	Definition of petty offense
18 USC § 3553(c)(1)	143	When judges must state reasons for sentence
18 USC § 3561	144	Probation for a Class A or B felony
18 USC §§ 3565(a), 3583(g)	145	Revocation of supervision based on positive drug test

18 USC § 3583	146	Supervised release with statutory maximum sentence
18 USC § 3624	147	Amount of "good time"

X. LEGAL ISSUES

Issue	MFAQ #	Summary of Topic
Old law/New law	148	Separate pre- and post-guideline counts
Old law/New law	149	Conspiracies extending beyond November 1, 1987
Legal	150	Amendments and Ex Post Facto issues
✓Legal	151	Historical notes and Ex Post Facto analysis
Legal	152	Amended guidelines and multiple counts
Legal	153	Applicability of guidelines when all overt acts of conspiracy are pre-November 1, 1987
Legal	154	Effective date and applicability of organizational guidelines
✓Legal	155	Drug quantity for mandatory minimum determined by court at sentencing
✓Legal	156	Court not bound by drug amount cited in indictment

XI. MISCELLANEOUS

Issue	MFAQ #	Summary of Topic
✓Guidelines	157	Submission of worksheets not required in all cases
Guidelines	158	Documentation to be submitted to Commission upon violation of probation or supervised release
Guidelines	159	Cross-references in Chapter Two not optional
Guidelines	160	Applicability to defendants with mental disease or defect
✓Guidelines	161	Binding nature of guideline commentary
Juveniles	162	Guidelines do not apply for juvenile sentencing

(✓ *indicates new question for this edition*)

1. **QUESTION:** Are the Statutory Provisions listed under each guideline inclusive?

   ANSWER: *No. Application Note 3 to §1B1.1 states "[t]he list of 'Statutory Provisions' in the Commentary to each offense guideline does not necessarily include every statute covered by that guideline. In addition, some statutes may be covered by more than one guideline."*

2. **QUESTION:** How do the guidelines apply to a count charging a conspiracy to commit more than one offense?

   ANSWER: *Subsection (d) of §1B1.2 (Applicable Guidelines) instructs that a conviction on a count charging a conspiracy to commit more than one offense shall be treated as if the defendant had been convicted on a separate count of conspiracy for each offense that the defendant conspired to commit. For example, if the defendant is convicted of one count of conspiracy to commit offenses A, B, and C, treat this as if the defendant were convicted of (1) conspiracy to commit offense A; (2) conspiracy to commit offense B; and (3) conspiracy to commit offense C. These "pseudo counts" are then subject to the multiple count rules in Chapter Three, Part D (<u>see</u> Application Note 9 to §3D1.2 (Groups of Closely-Related Counts)).*

   Application Note 5 to §1B1.2 instructs that for cases in which the verdict does not establish which offense(s) was the object of the conspiracy, subsection (d) should only be applied with respect to an object offense alleged in the conspiracy count if the court, were it sitting as a trier of fact, would convict the defendant of conspiring to commit that object offense (<u>i.e.</u>, applying a "beyond a reasonable doubt" standard of proof, rather than a preponderance of the evidence standard). Application Note 5 further instructs that if the object offenses specified in the conspiracy count would be grouped together under §3D1.2(d), it is not necessary to engage in the foregoing analysis because subsection (a)(2) of §1B1.3 (Relevant Conduct) governs consideration of the defendant's conduct.

3. **QUESTION:** A plea agreement contains several stipulations as to the amount of drugs, role in the offense, and so forth. Must the court automatically accept the stipulations as binding?

   ANSWER: *No. Policy Statement 6B1.4(d) states that "The court is not bound by the stipulation, but may with the aid of the presentence report, determine the facts relevant to sentencing." The commentary under §6B1.4 further instructs that in determining the factual basis for the sentence, the court will consider the stipulation, together with the results of the presentence investigation, and any other relevant information. Therefore, the probation officer should calculate the guideline sentence on the basis of all the relevant facts.*

   In the event of conviction by a plea of guilty or <u>nolo contendere</u> containing a stipulation that specifically establishes a more serious offense than the offense of conviction, §1B1.2 states that the court shall apply the guideline most applicable to the stipulated offense.

   <u>See</u> <u>United States v. Bennett</u>, 990 F.2d 998 (7th Cir. 1993)(district court not bound by parties' stipulation that defendant was not a career offender); <u>United States v. Isirov</u>, 986 F.2d 183 (7th Cir. 1993)(defendant's stipulation to drug quantity did not bar defendant's challenge to the pre-sentence report's quantity determination because "a court is not bound by a stipulation of facts, but may, with the aid of the presentence report, determine the facts relevant to sentencing."); and <u>United States v. Wagner</u>, 994 F.2d 1467 (10th Cir. May 18, 1993) (defendant who stipulated that she was a career offender properly sentenced under regular sentencing guidelines when it was shown that stipulation was in error).

4. **QUESTION:** Is the concept of reasonable foreseeability as used in §1B1.3 (Relevant Conduct) based upon what is reasonably foreseeable to a particular defendant?

ANSWER: *No. The determination of whether the conduct of others was reasonably foreseeable to a defendant should be made using an objective standard of what would have been foreseeable to a reasonable person in the position of the defendant, rather than the subjective standard of what the particular defendant foresaw. This is illustrated by the use of the phrase "reasonably foreseeable in connection with the offense" in Application Note 2 of the commentary to §1B1.3 (see especially Illustration (b)(1) that explains reasonable foreseeability in relation to the nature of the offense.*

5. **QUESTION:** If multiple defendants are convicted of drug conspiracy, are all the drugs in the conspiracy used in calculating the guideline ranges for all defendants?

ANSWER: *It depends. Guideline 1B1.3 was amended effective November 1, 1992, to clarify a defendant's accountability under the provisions of relevant conduct. Under §1B1.3(a)(1)(A), all defendants are accountable for acts and omissions that they themselves committed, aided, abetted, counseled, commanded, induced, procured, or willfully caused. Application Note 2 clarifies that "[i]n order to determine the defendant's accountability for the conduct of others under subsection (a)(1)(B), the court must first determine the scope of the criminal activity the particular defendant agreed to jointly undertake (i.e., the scope of the specific conduct and objectives embraced by the defendant's agreement). The conduct of others that was both in furtherance of, and reasonably foreseeable in connection with, the criminal activity jointly undertaken by the defendant is relevant conduct under this provision." Thus, the amount of drugs used in calculating the guideline range for each defendant may vary accordingly. The note further states that "[t]he conduct of others that was not in furtherance of the criminal activity jointly undertaken by the defendant, or was not reasonably foreseeable in connection with that criminal activity, is not relevant conduct under this provision" (see illustrations (c)(3) and (c)(5)-(c)(8) under Application Note 2 to §1B1.3.) See also, United States v. Collado, (3rd Cir. 1992) ("accomplice attribution is permitted only when the facts indicated that drug transactions conducted by co-conspirators were within the scope and in furtherance of the activity the defendant agreed to undertake").*

6. **QUESTION:** Can §1B1.3 (Relevant Conduct) be used to include drug amounts from prior drug distribution convictions in calculating the base offense level for the instant offense of drug distribution?

ANSWER: *It depends. Effective November 1, 1991, Application Note 8 to §1B1.3 (Relevant Conduct) instructs that for the purposes of subsection (a)(2) to §1B1.3, offense conduct associated with a sentence that was imposed prior to the acts or omissions constituting the instant federal offense (the offense of conviction) generally is not considered as part of the same course of conduct or common scheme or plan as the offense of conviction. The application note provides two illustrative examples and also outlines a limited exception to this rule in the case of previously sentenced offense conduct that is expressly charged in the offense of conviction.*

✓7. **QUESTION:** Does a defendant's relevant conduct include the conduct of other members of a conspiracy that occurred prior to the defendant's joining the conspiracy?

ANSWER: *No. Under §1B1.3, a defendant's relevant conduct does not include the conduct of other co-conspirators that occurred prior to the defendant's joining the conspiracy, even if the defendant* *knows of that conduct (e.g., in the case of a defendant who joins an ongoing drug distribution conspiracy knowing that it had been selling two kilograms of cocaine per week, the cocaine sold prior to the defendant's joining the conspiracy is not included in determining relevant conduct for his distribution of controlled substances.) However, an unusual set of circumstances in which application of the provision does not adequately reflect the defendant's culpability may appropriately be addressed through a departure. Note that on April 28, 1994, the Commission sent to Congress an amendment to the commentary in §1B1.3 that clarifies that prior conduct of others is generally not to be counted as relevant conduct. This amendment will take effect November 1, 1994, unless rejected by Congress.*

8. **QUESTION:** Fleeing from the scene of a bank robbery, the defendant crashed into another vehicle, causing extensive damage. In applying the specific offense characteristics under robbery, does the value of the automobile figure into the determination of loss?

ANSWER: *Yes. Section 1B1.3(a)(1) directs that conduct relevant to determining the applicable guideline range includes all acts committed by the defendant in the course of attempting to avoid detection or responsibility for the offense. If the destruction of the car fits this criterion, the monetary damage to the car would be added to the amount of money stolen from the bank in determining the total loss under §2B3.1(b)(6) because "loss" is defined as the value of the property taken, damaged, or destroyed (see Application Note 2 to §2B1.1).*

9. **QUESTION:** If the defendant is indicted on a drug conspiracy charge and multiple substantive counts of drug distribution and pleads to only one substantive count, are the amounts of drugs from the conspiracy and other substantive counts added to the drugs in the count of conviction for purposes of guideline calculation?

ANSWER: *Yes, if they meet the criteria for relevant conduct under §1B1.3 and are supported by a preponderance of the evidence. (Of course, if a quantity of drugs is the subject of both a substantive count and a conspiracy count, the quantity of drugs is to be counted only once.) Guideline 1B1.3(a)(2) states that when considering offenses of a character that would require grouping of multiple counts under the aggregation principles of §3D1.2(d), the court should look to "all such acts and omissions that were part of the same course of conduct or common scheme or plan as the offense of conviction." Application Note 3 to §1B1.3 clarifies that application of subsection (a)(2), which references the types of offenses described in §3D1.2(d), does not require the defendant to have been convicted of multiple counts. In addition, the Background notes to §1B1.3 state that "conduct that is not formally charged or is not an element of the offense of conviction may enter into the determination of the applicable guideline sentencing range," provided it is within the parameters of relevant conduct. The Commentary to the policy statement at §6A1.3 (Resolution of Disputed Factors), amended November 1, 1991, states the Commission's view that use of a preponderance of the evidence standard is appropriate to meet due process requirements and policy concerns in resolving disputes regarding application of the guidelines to the facts of a case.*

10. **QUESTION:** When the guidelines instruct the court to use the "underlying offense" to determine the base offense level, does this include the base offense level plus all specific offense characteristics for the underlying offense?

ANSWER: *Yes. As clarified effective November 1, 1992, §1B1.5(b)(1) states that "[a]n instruction to use the offense level from another offense guideline refers to the offense level from the entire* *offense guideline (i.e., the base offense level, specific offense characteristics, cross references, and special instructions)...".*

11. **QUESTION:** How are Chapter Three adjustments applied when a Chapter Two guideline for the offense of conviction cross references another Chapter Two guideline?

    ANSWER: *In such a case, adjustments in Chapter Three are to be determined with respect to the guideline applied through the cross reference (see clarification to §1B1.5, effective November 1, 1992).*

12. **QUESTION:** Are Class B and C misdemeanors and infractions subject to the guidelines?

    ANSWER: *No. Effective June 15, 1988, all Class B and C misdemeanors and infractions (offenses that include but are not limited to petty offenses) are not subject to the guidelines (see §1B1.9 (Class B and C Misdemeanors and Infractions).*

13. **QUESTION:** Can the court reduce a defendant's sentence of imprisonment when a guideline has been subsequently amended by the Commission?

    ANSWER: *Possibly. Section 3582(c)(2) of title 18 provides that the court may reduce the term of imprisonment of a defendant sentenced to a term of imprisonment based on a sentencing range that has subsequently been lowered by the Commission after considering the factors set forth in 18 U.S.C. § 3553(a) to the extent they are applicable if such a reduction is consistent with applicable policy statements issued by the Commission. The Commission's policy statement in response to this provision is set forth at §1B1.10 (Retroactivity of Amended Guideline Range).*

14. **QUESTION:** The defendant is currently serving a term of imprisonment imposed in 1990. In 1993, the Commission amended the offense guideline under which the defendant was sentenced, a change that results in a lower guideline range. The amendment effecting this change is listed in §1B1.10 (Retroactivity of Amended Guideline Range). Can the defendant petition the court for a reduction in sentence? How is the amended guideline range calculated?

    ANSWER: *Yes, the defendant is eligible to apply for a reduction in sentence under 18 U.S.C. § 3582(c)(2) and the Commission's policy statement at §1B1.10. The statute provides: "[I]n the case of a defendant who has been sentenced to a term of imprisonment based on a sentencing range that has subsequently been lowered by the Sentencing Commission pursuant to 28 U.S.C. § 994(o), upon motion of the defendant or the Director of the Bureau of Prisons, or on its own motion, the court may reduce the term of imprisonment, after considering the factors set forth in section 3553(a) to the extent that they are applicable, if such a reduction is consistent with applicable policy statements issued by the Sentencing Commission."*

    Effective November 1, 1994, the Commission amended §1B1.10 to substantially simplify its operation. Under this amendment, the amended guideline range is calculated by substituting only the applicable retroactive amendments listed under §1B1.10(c) for the corresponding guideline provisions that were applied when the defendant was sentenced. All other guideline application decisions remain unaffected.

Although the applicable statute and policy statement prescribe the circumstances under which an imprisoned defendant may be considered for a sentence reduction, the decision of whether to grant any reduction is discretionary with the court.

Example: The defendant was convicted of manufacturing 3 kilos of methamphetamine in 1990. At the time of sentencing, the court found that the 3 kilos of methamphetamine included 1 kilo of waste water which contained a detectable amount of methamphetamine. The offense level calculated under §2D1.1 was 34. The defendant also received a two-level reduction for acceptance of responsibility under §3E1.1. No other Chapter three adjustments were applicable. The defendant had a criminal history category of I. The guideline range was 121-151. The court sentenced the defendant to 124 months imprisonment.

Effective November 1, 1993, the Commission amended the Commentary to §2D1.1 (Unlawful Manufacturing, Importing, Exporting, or Trafficking (Including Possession with Intent to Commit These Offenses); Attempt or Conspiracy) to state that the term "mixture or substance" as used in §2D1.1 does not include materials that must be separated from the controlled substance before the substance can be used (amendment 484). This amendment is listed under §1B1.10 as available for potential retroactive application.

Because of the above noted amendment, the additional 1 kilo of waste water would not be used to calculate the defendant's offense level under §2D1.1. Therefore, the defendant is now subject to a lower guideline range of 97-121 months (offense level 32 for one kilogram of methamphetamine, reduced by two levels for acceptance of responsibility; Criminal History Category I). Under §1B1.10, the court may reduce the term of imprisonment consistent with the amended guideline range of 97-121 months. Although several other amendments were made to the guidelines between 1990 and 1993, the defendant only receives the benefit of amendments that are listed in §1B1.10 for retroactive application. The defendant would not, for example, receive the additional one-level reduction for acceptance of responsibility (even if he qualifies under §3E1.1) because this amendment is not listed for retroactive application under §1B1.10.

15. **QUESTION:** The defendant is convicted of one count of criminal sexual abuse of a child under the age of 12 (see 18 U.S.C. § 2241(c)). Force was used against the victim in the commission of this offense. Subsection (b)(1) of §2A3.1 (Criminal Sexual Abuse) provides a 4-level increase if the offense was committed "by the means set forth in 18 U.S.C. § 2241(a) or (b)," which includes the use of force against the victim. Is this specific offense characteristic applied even though the defendant was not convicted of either 18 U.S.C. § 2241(a) or (b)?

    ANSWER: *Yes. Subsection (b)(1) to §2A3.1 does not expressly require a conviction under 18 U.S.C. § 2241(a) or (b); rather, it uses a statutory reference to describe a particular set of circumstances that, if met, will require application of the specific offense characteristic. Application Note 6 to §1B1.3 (Relevant Conduct) states that while a guideline may expressly direct that a particular factor be applied only if the defendant was convicted of a specific statute, conviction under the statute is not required unless such an express direction is included in a base offense level or specific offense characteristic.*

16. **QUESTION:** Does the weapon enhancement apply in a bank robbery case if the defendant used a toy gun?

ANSWER: *It may. Application Note 2 to §2B3.1 (Robbery) states that "[w]hen an object that appeared to be a dangerous weapon was brandished, displayed, or possessed, treat the object as a dangerous weapon for the purposes of subsection (b)(2)(E)." Therefore, if the court determines that the toy gun appeared to be a dangerous weapon, the enhancement under §2B3.1(b)(2)(E) would apply.*

See United States v. Faulkner, 934 F.2d 190 (9th Cir. 1991)(applying enhancement when defendant used a toy gun); and United States v. Laughy, 886 F.2d 28 (2nd Cir. 1989) (upholding enhancement when defendant used an inoperable pellet gun).

17. **QUESTION:** The defendant was convicted of one count of armed bank robbery. During the course of the robbery, the defendant pistol-whipped a teller causing severe facial lacerations requiring 35 stitches. The defendant punched another teller in the face causing a black eye. Does the robbery guideline at §2B3.1 account for injuries to multiple victims?

ANSWER: *No. The specific offense characteristic at subsection (b)(3) of §2B3.1 sanctions for the most serious bodily injury sustained by any single victim. In this case, the teller with facial lacerations sustained the more serious injury; consequently, the seriousness of this injury would determine the increase in offense level under subsection (b)(3).*

Application Notes 4 and 5 to §1B1.1 (Application Instructions) explain that offense level adjustments within each specific offense characteristic are alternative, not cumulative. The adjustments for degrees of bodily injury are never added together; only the one that best describes the most serious conduct is to be used.

Where multiple victims sustain bodily injury and no separate counts of conviction capture the assaultive behavior, an upward departure may be warranted. The policy statement at §5K2.0 (Grounds for Departure) specifically states that "because the robbery guideline does not deal with injury to more than one victim, departure would be warranted if several persons were injured."

18. **QUESTION:** What does the term "infringing items" mean at §§2B5.3?

ANSWER: *"Infringing items" are, for example, imitation products that are represented as being legitimate products. To illustrate, if a defendant produced 1,000 unauthorized copies of copyrighted videotapes for retail sale at $5 per tape, the value of the infringing items for purposes of §2B5.3(b)(1) would be $5,000. If a defendant sold $4,000 worth of tennis shoes that were falsely labelled with another company's trademark, the value of the infringing items would be $4,000.*

19. **QUESTION:** The defendant is a sheriff convicted of accepting a bribe, an offense covered by §2C1.1 (Offering, Giving, Soliciting, or Receiving a Bribe; Extortion Under Color of Official Right). Subsection (b)(2)(B) provides an 8-level increase if the offense involved a payment for the purpose of influencing an elected official or any official holding a high level decision-making or sensitive position. Does this subsection apply to both the official who receives a payment as well as the person who pays the official?

ANSWER: *Yes.*

20. **QUESTION:** When using the drug table, is the weight of the drug's packaging added to determine the drug amount?

ANSWER: *No. The footnote to the Drug Quantity Table in §2D1.1 designated by a single asterisk states that "the entire weight of any mixture or substance containing a detectable amount of the controlled substance" is to be used in determining the guideline offense level (emphasis added). Packaging materials are not part of the "mixture or substance" and are therefore not used to determine weight for purposes of applying the guidelines or drug statutes.*

✓21. **QUESTION:** In a drug trafficking case involving LSD on a carrier medium, how is the offense level determined using the Drug Quantity Table?

ANSWER: *Effective November 1, 1993, §2D1.1(c) instructs that each dose of LSD on a carrier medium is to be treated as 0.4 mg of LSD for purposes of the Drug Quantity Table (see the Background Commentary to §2D1.1 for a discussion of the Commission's determination of 0.4 mg as the appropriate dosage weight). The weights of LSD carrier media vary widely and typically far exceed the weight of the controlled substance itself. As a result, basing the offense level on the entire weight of the LSD and carrier medium produces unwarranted disparity in offenses involving the same quantity of actual LSD but different carrier weights. It also results in sentences that are disproportionate to those for other, more dangerous controlled substances (e.g., PCP).*

The Commission has listed this amendment for retroactive application in §1B1.10 (Retroactivity of Amended Guideline Range), allowing the court to consider a reduction in a defendant's previously imposed sentence under 18 U.S.C. § 3582(c)(2). Nonetheless, this approach does not override the applicability of "mixture or substance" in 21 U.S.C. § 841(b)(1) for the purposes of applying any mandatory minimum sentence (see Chapman v. United States, 111 S.Ct. 1919 (1991)).

✓22. **QUESTION:** Federal agents seized 15 grams of methamphetamine and one liter of waste water with trace amounts of methamphetamine during the defendant's arrest at his drug manufacturing lab. Is this waste water considered a "mixture or substance" within the meaning of §2D1.1 (Unlawful Manufacturing, Importing, Exporting, or Trafficking; Attempt or Conspiracy), and therefore counted when computing the base offense level from the Drug Quantity Table?

ANSWER: *No. Effective November 1, 1993, Application Note 1 of §2D1.1 expressly specifies that the term "mixture or substance" does not include materials that must be separated from the controlled substance before the controlled substance can be used (e.g., waste water from an illicit laboratory).*

The Commission has listed this amendment for retroactive application in §1B1.10 (Retroactivity of Amended Guideline Range), allowing the court to consider a reduction in a defendant's previously imposed sentence under 18 U.S.C. § 3582(c)(2).

✓23. **QUESTION:** Does the term "cocaine base," as used in §2D1.1 (Unlawful Manufacturing, Importing, Exporting, or Trafficking (Including Possession with Intent to Commit These Offenses; Attempt or Conspiracy), include forms of cocaine base other than crack?

ANSWER: *No. To address an inter-circuit conflict on this issue, §2D1.1(c) was amended effective November 1, 1993, to instruct that, for purposes of the guidelines, the term "cocaine base" includes only that form of cocaine base known as "crack." Crack is a form of cocaine base usually prepared by processing cocaine hydrochloride and sodium bicarbonate and typically appears in a lumpy, rock-like form. Under this amendment, other forms of cocaine base (e.g., coca paste) will be treated as cocaine for the purpose of determining the offense level from the Drug Quantity Table found in §2D1.1.*

✓24. **QUESTION:** The defendant was convicted of distribution of an analog of methamphetamine (in this case, methcathinone). Are the mandatory minimum penalties for methamphetamine listed in 21 U.S.C. § 841 applicable to these analog substances?

ANSWER: *No. The mandatory minimum penalties §§ 841(b)(1)(A) and (B) apply only to the controlled substances specifically listed in those subsections. In this case, the Drug Equivalency Table would be consulted to determine the marijuana equivalency for methcathinone. The defendant's base offense level would then be determined under the Drug Quantity Table without regard to any mandatory minimum penalty.*

✓25. **QUESTION:** The defendant distributed cocaine on two occasions to federal agents and on a third occasion distributed two kilos of 100 percent cornstarch which the defendant fraudulently claimed to be cocaine. When calculating the offense level at §2D1.1, is the weight of the cornstarch added to the weight of the cocaine that was distributed?

ANSWER: *No. In determining the sentence for drug trafficking, both the statute and guideline (see 21 U.S.C. § 841 and §2D1.1) direct that the "weight of any mixture or substance containing a detectable amount" of a drug or controlled substance is considered. In this example, the cornstarch distribution may be fraudulent conduct but it is not drug trafficking. Accordingly, the weight of the cornstarch should not be added to the weight of the illegally distributed substances. However, the court may wish to consider whether the fraudulent behavior involved in the cornstarch distribution warrants a sentence at a higher point in the guideline range or whether, in an extreme case, this factor warrants departure.*

26. **QUESTION:** A case involves a controlled substance or listed chemical not expressly enumerated in the guidelines. How should the probation officer proceed?

ANSWER: *If a controlled substance or listed chemical is not enumerated in §§2D1.1 or 2D1.11, the probation officer handling the case should contact the Commission. Staff will consult with the Drug Enforcement Administration and will forward the resulting information to the probation officer for the court's consideration.*

27. **QUESTION:** When is the Typical Weight Per Unit Table in §2D1.1 to be used?

ANSWER: *As instructed in Application Note 11 to §2D1.1, the Typical Weight Per Unit Table is to be used only if the number of doses, pills, or capsules is known but not the weight of the controlled substance. For example, if the defendant is convicted of conspiracy to distribute 100 "hits" of methamphetamine but there is no actual methamphetamine to weigh, the table is used to calculate the weight (i.e, 100 doses at 5 mg. per dose = .5 gm. of methamphetamine). Do not use this table if a more reliable estimate of the total weight is available from case-specific information (e.g., the case involved the distribution of methamphetamines obtained by prescription and an average weight per pill is available from the pharmaceutical company).*

For controlled substances marked with an asterisk (e.g., methamphetamine), the table provides a very conservative estimate of the total weight (i.e., the weight shown only reflects the weight of the actual controlled substance and not the weight of the mixture or substance containing the controlled substance). In the example above, the .5 gm. of methamphetamine would not include the weight of the capsule containing the methamphetamine or the cutting agent mixed with the methamphetamine.

28. **QUESTION:** The defendant was convicted of possession with intent to distribute marijuana and hashish. The hashish was mixed in with the marijuana for a combined weight of 1 kilogram. How should the base offense level be calculated?

ANSWER: *The footnote to the Drug Quantity Table at §2D1.1(c) designated by a single asterisk instructs that if a mixture or substance contains more than one controlled substance, the weight of the entire mixture or substance is assigned to the controlled substance that results in the greater offense level. In this case, because 1 kilogram of hashish results in a base offense level of 14 and 1 kilogram of marijuana results in a base offense level of 10, the base offense level for the entire mixture is level 14.*

29. **QUESTION:** The defendant was convicted of possession with intent to distribute Tylenol 3 (Tylenol with codeine). Although the indictment states that Tylenol 3 is a Schedule III controlled substance, codeine is listed in the drug equivalency table of §2D1.1 under Schedule I and II Opiates. Should the court use the equivalency for codeine listed under Schedule I and II Opiates?

ANSWER: *No. Tylenol 3 is a Schedule III controlled substance and should be treated as such under the guidelines. Certain pharmaceutical preparations such as Tylenol 3 that contain a Schedule I or II controlled substance are nevertheless classified as Schedule III, IV, or V controlled substances by the Drug Enforcement Administration due to the extremely small amounts of Schedule I or II controlled substance in the compounds. For purposes of the guidelines, such pharmaceutical preparations are to be treated as Schedule III, IV, or V substances as set forth in 21 C.F.R. 1308.13 - .15. Effective November 1, 1992, the Commission clarified this issue by adding Application Note 15 to §2D1.1.*

30. **QUESTION:** The defendant is convicted of possession with intent to distribute 10 grams of cocaine and 4 grams of methamphetamine. The drug quantity table at §2D1.1(c) assigns a level 12 to both 10 grams of cocaine and to 4 grams of methamphetamine. However, when these two substances are converted into their marijuana equivalent amounts using the drug equivalency tables to reach a single offense level (as instructed in Application Note 10 to §2D1.1), the total amount of marijuana (2,160 grams) corresponds to Level 10. Which offense level should be used?

ANSWER: *Offense level 12. The drug quantity table in the Guidelines Manual sets forth a minimum offense level of 12 for cocaine and methamphetamine, and this minimum offense level controls. Obviously, it would be anomalous for guideline application to result in a lower offense level for a combination of 10 grams of cocaine and 4 grams of methamphetamine than for either the 10 grams of cocaine or 4 grams of methamphetamine alone. The Commission has clarified this point in an amendment to the Drug Equivalency Tables effective November 1, 1992 (see amendment 446.)*

31. **QUESTION:** The defendant was convicted of one count of drug distribution near a school, an offense covered under §2D1.2 (Drug Offenses Occurring Near Protected Locations or Involving Underage or Pregnant Individuals). The defendant possessed a firearm during the offense. Does §2D1.2 sanction for possession of a weapon?

ANSWER: *Yes, if the base offense level is determined under subsections (a)(1) or (a)(2) of §2D1.2, both of which reference the offense level from §2D1.1 (Unlawful Manufacturing, Importing, Exporting, or Trafficking (Including Possession with Intent to Commit These Offenses; Attempt or Conspiracy)). Application Note 3 to §2D1.1 instructs that the enhancement for weapon possession at subsection (b)(1) also applies to offenses that reference §2D1.1(a)(1) and (2).*

32. **QUESTION:** If the offender is indicted for possession with intent to distribute, but is only convicted of simple possession, does the amount of drugs affect the sentence?

ANSWER: *The guideline section utilized to compute the guideline range must be determined by the offense of conviction (§1B1.2(a)). Except for possession of cocaine base (crack), the simple possession guideline (§2D2.1) does not utilize the amount of drugs to determine the appropriate offense level. Of course, the amount of drugs may be considered by the court for the purposes of determining the appropriate sentence within the guideline range or for possible departure.*

33. **QUESTION:** The defendant was convicted of RICO (18 U.S.C. § 1962). How is the alternative base offense level at §2E1.1(a)(2) determined?

ANSWER: *Application Note 1 to §2E1.1 instructs that where there is more than one underlying offense (i.e., predicate act), each underlying offense should be treated as if contained in a separate count of conviction for the purposes of subsection (a)(2). The RICO count is to be treated as if it were a conspiracy count (see §1B1.2(d) and Application Note 5). Each of the underlying offenses, whether or not charged in substantive counts of conviction, are treated as if they were substantive counts of conviction, or "pseudo counts."*

Application Note 1 to §2E1.1 also states that to determine whether subsection (a)(1) or (a)(2) results in the greater offense level, apply Chapter Three, Parts A, B, C, and D to both (a)(1) and (a)(2). For example, if there were three "pseudo counts" of residential burglary, each having an offense level of 17 and no adjustments from Chapter Three, Parts A, B, or C, subsection (a)(2) would produce an offense level of 20 after applying Chapter Three, Part D, while subsection (a)(1) would produce an offense level of 19. In many instances, the determination as to whether subsection (a)(1) or (a)(2) will result in the higher offense level is obvious, making this comparative calculation unnecessary. If the higher offense level is determined through application of (a)(2), do not apply these Chapter Three adjustments a second time.

34. **QUESTION:** Defendant A falsifies various loan documents to secure a loan of $500,000 to purchase a commercial property whose value she has overstated by approximately $100,000. Defendant A leases the property and makes mortgage payments as required. Two years later Defendant A loses her tenant and, unable to secure a new tenant, defaults on the $450,000 balance of the loan. The lender sells the property, as provided by law, and recovers only $375,000. What amount of loss should be used in the calculation of Defendant A's offense level in applying the fraud guideline when the actual loss exceeds the intended loss?

ANSWER: *$75,000. Under Application Note 7(b) to §2F1.1, in fraudulent loan cases the loss is the amount of the loan less any amount repaid at the time the offense is discovered, and less the value of the property serving as security for the loan.*

Thus, Defendant A's fraud resulted in an actual loss to the lender of $75,000 (i.e., loan amount ($500,000) less amount repaid ($50,000) less value of security ($375,000)). It is not relevant for this loss determination that the defendant put the lender at risk for the $100,000 overstatement of property value at the time of the fraudulent loan application. Note that the lender is not obligated to maximize the return on the sale (e.g., by delaying the foreclosure sale until market conditions improve).

35. **QUESTION:** The defendant made loan payments before and after authorities discovered that he fraudulently obtained the loan by misrepresenting the value of his assets. Should the loss amount calculated under §2F1.1 be reduced by the total of these payments?

ANSWER: *No. The loss amount is reduced by the payments made before, but not after, the offense is discovered. Application Note 7(b) to §2F1.1 states that in a fraudulent loan application case, the loss is the amount of the loan not repaid "at the time the offense is discovered," reduced by the value of any assets pledged to the lending institution to secure the loan. Amounts paid toward the loan subsequent to the discovery of the offense would be considered restitution.*

36. **QUESTION:** Can tax evasion (§2T1.1) be grouped with fraud (§2F1.1) pursuant to §3D1.2(d)?

ANSWER: *No. Although fraud (§2F1.1) and tax evasion (§2T1.1) are both listed as "aggregatable" offenses under §3D1.2(d), these two counts may not be grouped together under this rule. This does not, however, preclude grouping under another rule.*

Guideline 3D1.3 (Offense Level Applicable to Each Group of Closely-Related Counts) states that when counts are groupable under §3D1.2(d) and the counts involve offenses of the same general type to which different guidelines apply (e.g., theft and fraud), apply the offense guideline that produces the highest offense level. The fraud table and the tax table are driven by different guideline definitions of "loss." Thus, tax evasion and fraud are not "of the same general type," and therefore may not be grouped according to rule (d).

37. **QUESTION:** When calculating the alternative base offense level for §2H1.1(a)(2) (Conspiracy to Interfere with Civil Rights; Going in Disguise to Deprive of Rights), does "any underlying offense" include another civil rights offense?

ANSWER: *No. Subsection (a)(2) refers to offenses other than a civil rights offense (see the first paragraph of Application Note 1 as amended November 1, 1991). As the second paragraph of the introductory commentary to Chapter H, Subpart One, points out, "[t]he addition of two levels to the offense level applicable to the underlying offense in this subpart reflects the fact that the harm involved both the underlying conduct and activity intended to deprive a person of his civil rights."*

Application Note 1 to §2H1.1 instructs that if the defendant is convicted of conspiracy to interfere with civil rights, and the underlying offense was damage to property by means of arson, two levels would be added to the offense level determined under §2K1.4 (Arson; Property Damage by Use of Explosives). The offense level for the underlying offense would not be determined through application of §2H1.3 (Use of Force or Threat of Force to Deny Benefits or Rights in Furtherance of Discrimination; Damage to Religious Real Property), §2H1.4 (Interference with Civil Rights Under Color of Law), or §2H1.5 (Other Deprivations of Rights or Benefits in Furtherance of Discrimination).

38. **QUESTION:** Guideline 2K2.1 (Unlawful Receipt, Possession, or Transportation of Firearms or Ammunition; Prohibited Transactions Involving Firearms or Ammunition) provides cross references to the underlying offense. Are the cross references to be applied even if the defendant has been convicted and sentenced on the underlying offense in state court?

ANSWER: *Yes. The firearm statutes are often used as a mechanism to allow the federal court to exercise jurisdiction over offenses that otherwise could be prosecuted only under state law. The cross reference is designed to handle such situations.*

There are two mechanisms built into the guidelines to avoid double counting in such cases. First, the state conviction would not be counted in the calculation of the criminal history score. The term "prior sentence" is defined in §4A1.2(a)(1) as "any sentence previously imposed upon adjudication of guilt, whether by guilty plea, trial, or plea of <u>nolo</u> <u>contendere</u> for conduct not part of the instant offense." In this case, the prior state conviction would be part of the instant offense and thus would not meet the definition of "prior offense" for the purposes of applying criminal history points.

Second, if the instant offense was not committed while the defendant was serving a term of imprisonment, §5G1.3(b) instructs that if the undischarged term of imprisonment resulted from offense(s) that constituted part of the same course of conduct as the instant offense and have been fully taken into account in the determination of the offense level for the instant offense, then the sentence for the instant offense shall be imposed to result in a combined sentence equal to the total punishment that would have been imposed under §5G1.2 (Sentencing on Multiple Counts of Conviction) had all the sentences been imposed at the same time. In imposing sentence, the court should adjust for any term of imprisonment already served as a result of the conduct taken into account in determining the instant sentence (<u>see</u> Application Note 2 to §5G1.3).

✓39. **QUESTION:** The defendant, a convicted felon, is charged in the instant offense with illegal possession of a firearm. The defendant states that he did not know the firearm he bought from a co-defendant was stolen – a claim substantiated by the co-defendant. Does the enhancement for a stolen firearm at subsection (b)(4) of §2K2.1 (Unlawful Receipt, Possession, or Transportation of Firearms or Ammunition; Prohibited Transactions Involving Firearms or Ammunition) still apply?

ANSWER: *Yes. The Commentary to §2K2.1 was amended effective November 1, 1993, to clarify this situation. Application Note 19 clarifies that the enhancement at §2K2.1(b)(4) for a stolen firearm or a firearm with an altered or obliterated serial number applies "whether or not the defendant knew or had reason to believe that the firearm was stolen or had an altered or obliterated serial number."*

✓40. **QUESTION:** Subsection (b)(5) of §2K2.1 (Unlawful Receipt, Possession, or Transportation of Firearms or Ammunition; Prohibited Transactions Involving Firearms of Ammunition) provides an enhancement if the defendant used or possessed any firearm or explosive in connection with another felony offense. Does this enhancement apply even if the underlying offense is a state offense?

ANSWER: *Yes. Application Note 7 was amended effective November 1, 1993, to clarify that "felony offense" as used in subsection (b)(5) may refer to a federal, state, or local offense.*

41. **QUESTION:** How do the grouping rules apply to multiple counts of felon in possession of a firearm (18 U.S.C. § 922(g))?

ANSWER: *Effective November 1, 1991, the counts are grouped together under §3D1.2(d) unless each count involves a different underlying offense covered under the cross reference at §2K2.1(c). In such case, whether or not the counts are grouped together depends upon whether the underlying offenses (i.e., the cross-referenced offenses) would be grouped together.*

42. **QUESTION:** Guideline 2L1.2 (Unlawfully Entering or Remaining in the United States) provides an enhancement at specific offense characteristic (b)(2) for a defendant who was previously deported after a conviction for an "aggravated felony." Application Note 7 to §2L1.2 provides a list of offenses (e.g., murder, drug trafficking) that qualify as aggravated felonies for purposes of the enhancement. One offense on the list is "any crime of violence" for which the term of imprisonment imposed was at least five years (regardless of any suspension of such term of imprisonment). Do all of the offenses listed in the Application Note require imposition of at least five years imprisonment to qualify as aggravated felonies?

ANSWER: *No. The five-year imprisonment requirement (regardless of any suspension of such term of imprisonment) applies only to crimes of violence as defined in 18 U.S.C. § 16 not otherwise listed in Application Note 7.*

✓43. **QUESTION:** Do the specific offense characteristics for deportation after a conviction for a felony or aggravated felony under §2L1.2 (Unlawfully Entering or Remaining in the United States) require that these convictions be "countable" under the provisions of Chapter Four, Part A (Criminal History)?

ANSWER: *No. The applicability of specific offense characteristics (b)(1) and/or (b)(2) is not dependent on whether the felony or aggravated felony conviction resulted in a sentence countable under the criminal history provisions of Chapter Four.*

44. **QUESTION:** The defendant pleaded guilty to one count of money laundering and is facing sentencing under §2S1.1. The offense was discovered after the defendant had successfully laundered $70,000 of funds derived from a $125,000 fraud. In applying §2S1.1(b)(2), what is the "value of the funds?"

ANSWER: *The "value of funds" would be $70,000 unless the government established that the defendant attempted to launder a larger amount. In such an event, consistent with the provisions of §1B1.3 (Relevant Conduct) and §2X1.1 (Attempt, Solicitation, or Conspiracy), the "value of funds" would be the total of the amount successfully laundered and any additional amount the defendant attempted to launder.*

45. **QUESTION:** In a case involving one count of tax evasion and another count embodying criminal conduct that generated the income on which tax was evaded, can the tax evasion count be grouped with the underlying offense?

ANSWER: *Yes. The counts can be grouped under §3D1.2(c). Grouping rule (c) instructs that counts are to be grouped when one of the counts embodies conduct that is treated as a specific offense characteristic in, or other adjustment to, the guideline applicable to another of the counts. Specific offense characteristic (b)(1) at §2T1.1 (Tax Evasion) provides an enhancement if the defendant failed to report or correctly to identify the source of income exceeding $10,000 in any year from criminal activity. Tax evasion is always grouped with the underlying offense according to rule (c), regardless of whether (b)(1) was actually applied (But see United States v. Borone, 913 F.2d 46 (2nd Cir. 1990)* *and United States v. Astorri, 923 F.2d 1052 (3d Cir. 1991) (holding that tax evasion is to be grouped separately from the offense that generated the income)).*

46. **QUESTION:** The defendant has been convicted of filing a false tax return. The Internal Revenue Agent has indicated that the tax loss is $20,000. Both the government and defense counsel agree with this figure. However, if the special instruction for calculating "tax loss" at §2T1.1(c)(1) is used, the loss is more than $20,000. Which figure should be used?

ANSWER: *$20,000, which is the actual tax loss in this example. The special instructions at §2T1.1 address situations in which the tax loss may not be reasonably ascertainable. In this case, the application of the special instruction is not necessary since sufficient information is available to determine the tax loss. In cases where tax loss cannot be readily determined, Application Note 1 provides that the "presumptions" at §2T1.1(c)(1) are to be used unless the government or the defendant provides sufficient information for a more accurate assessment of the tax loss.*

47. **QUESTION:** When a Chapter Two guideline contains a cross reference to §2X1.1 (Attempt, Solicitation, or Conspiracy Not Covered by a Specific Guideline), should §2X1.1 be applied even when the underlying offense conduct constitutes a completed substantive offense as opposed to an attempt, conspiracy, or solicitation?

ANSWER: *Yes. The fact that the offense did not involve an attempt, solicitation, or conspiracy does not preclude application of this guideline. Completed conduct is covered under subsection (a) of §2X1.1. Subsections (b)(1), (b)(2), and (b)(3) provide adjustments for certain attempts, solicitations, and conspiracies. Use of §2X1.1 ensures that if the underlying offense in fact involves completed conduct, the guideline applicable to such conduct will be applied.*

48. **QUESTION:** A girlfriend-witness of a drug dealer perjured herself at his trial by providing him with a false alibi. The boyfriend was subsequently convicted of drug trafficking and the girlfriend of perjury. The guideline for perjury (§2J1.3) lists a cross reference instructing, "[i]f the offense involved perjury or subornation of perjury in respect to a criminal offense, apply §2X3.1 (Accessory After the Fact) in respect to that criminal offense, if the resulting offense level is greater than that determined above." The boyfriend was convicted of cocaine trafficking in an amount that resulted in a Chapter Two offense level of 34. Would the girlfriend's offense level for the perjury conviction be 6 levels less than the boyfriend's offense level of 34?

ANSWER: *Yes. According to §2X3.1 (Accessory After the Fact), the underlying offense means "the offense as to which the defendant is convicted of being an accessory." The underlying offense in this case is drug distribution carrying an offense level of 34. Therefore, the girlfriend's offense level would be 28, 6 levels less than the boyfriend's Chapter Two offense level of 34.*

49. **QUESTION:** What should be done if the statute of conviction is not listed in the Statutory Index?

ANSWER: *Appendix A (the Statutory Index) refers to §2X5.1 for offenses not listed in the index. Guideline 2X5.1 states that if the offense is a felony or a Class A misdemeanor, the most analogous guideline should be applied. In determining the most analogous guideline, the court should consider the conduct for which the defendant was convicted (§1B1.2(a) and the statute(s) that the potentially analogous guidelines reflect) (see Statutory Provisions listed under each offense guideline).*

If no sufficiently analogous guideline exists for the felony or Class A misdemeanor, the provisions of 18 U.S.C. § 3553(b) shall control. However, Application Note 1 to §2X5.1, effective November 1, 1991, clarifies that any guidelines and policy statements (such as the guidelines on supervised release) that can be applied meaningfully in the absence of a Chapter Two offense guideline shall remain applicable. Class B and C misdemeanors and infractions are excluded from sentencing under the guidelines effective June 15, 1988.

50. QUESTION: Do the guidelines apply to cases prosecuted under the Assimilative Crimes Act and the Indian Major Crimes Act?

ANSWER: *Yes. Refer to §2X5.1, which states that if the offense is a felony or a Class A misdemeanor, the most analogous guideline should be applied. If no sufficiently analogous guideline exists for the felony or Class A misdemeanor, the provisions of 18 U.S.C. § 3553(b) shall control, except that any guidelines and policy statements that can be applied meaningfully in the absence of a Chapter Two offense guideline shall remain applicable (see Application Note 1 to §2X5.1.). Class B and C misdemeanors and infractions are excluded from sentencing under the guidelines effective June 15, 1988 (see §1B1.9).*

51. QUESTION: Is there an analogous guideline for Driving While Intoxicated (DWI)?

ANSWER: *No.*

52. QUESTION: The defendant was convicted of sexually exploiting a minor (18 U.S.C. § 2251) and §2G2.1 has been applied. Is the Chapter Three adjustment for vulnerable victim applied due to the victim's young age?

ANSWER: *No. Certain guidelines for sex offenses in Chapter Two, Parts A and G, consider the victim's young age through the base offense level and specific offense characteristics. Application Note 2 to §3A1.1 (Vulnerable Victim) instructs that this adjustment should not be applied where the Chapter Two offense guideline already provides an enhancement for the age of the victim.*

53. QUESTION: The defendant assaulted a law enforcement officer and is convicted of 18 U.S.C. § 111. Guideline 2A2.2 (Aggravated Assault) has been applied. Is the Chapter Three adjustment for official victim (§3A1.2) applicable or has the enhancement for official victim been taken into account under §2A2.2?

ANSWER: *The offense level determined through application of §2A2.2 does not include consideration of an official victim. The aggravated assault guideline (§2A2.2) was developed to cover numerous statutory provisions, including 18 U.S.C. §§ 111, 112, 113, and 114 and other statutes that do not ordinarily involve official victims (see Statutory Provisions under §2A2.2). Therefore, if an official victim is involved, the enhancement at §3A1.2 would be applied.*

54. QUESTION: The defendant was convicted of one count of armed bank robbery. In an attempt to avoid arrest the defendant shot a police officer in the leg. Does the adjustment at subsection (b) of §3A1.2 (Official Victim) apply in addition to the specific offense characteristic for bodily injury at subsection (b)(3) of §2B3.1 (Robbery)?

ANSWER: *Yes. Application Note 5 to §3A1.2 explains that subsection (b) applies in circumstances tantamount to aggravated assault against a law enforcement or corrections officer committed in the course of, or in immediate flight following, another offense. Application Note 3 states that this adjustment would not apply where the Chapter Two offense guideline specifically incorporates this factor. The robbery guideline at §2B3.1 does not specifically incorporate assaultive behavior against a law enforcement officer. Therefore, it would be appropriate to enhance for both victim injury and official victim (see United States v. Muhammad, 948 F.2d 1449 (6th Cir. 1991), cert. denied, 112 S. Ct. 1239 (1992)).*

55. QUESTION: The defendant was convicted of smuggling illegal aliens into the United States. Upon their entry, the smuggled aliens were locked in a room for two weeks before being released. Can the aliens be considered "victims" for the purposes of applying §3A1.3 (Restraint of Victim)?

ANSWER: *Yes. The adjustment is not barred because the "victims" initially were willing participants in the illegal entry offense. In this case, the aliens became victims during the course of the instant smuggling offense. This adjustment applies to any offense in which a victim was physically restrained in the course of the offense, except where such restraint is an element of the offense, specifically incorporated into the base offense level, or listed as a specific offense characteristic (see Application Note 2 to §3A1.3).*

Be aware that the term "victim" is defined differently throughout the Guidelines Manual and that these definitions are not necessarily interchangeable. For example, while the aliens in this example may be considered victims for the purpose of applying §3A1.3, they would not be considered victims for the purpose of applying the multiple count rules in Chapter Three, Part D. In the latter case, the "victim" would be a societal interest invaded by the illegal smuggling of aliens.

56. QUESTION: Is the determination of a role in the offense adjustment under Chapter Three, Part B, based on the defendant's relevant conduct in conspiracy cases?

ANSWER: *Yes. The first sentence in §1B1.3(a) states that, unless otherwise specified, adjustments in Chapter Three shall be determined on the basis of information within the scope of relevant conduct. Therefore, the real offense parameters of relevant conduct are used to determine the defendant's role in the offense of conviction.*

The Introductory Commentary to Chapter Three, Part B, clarifies that a defendant's role in the offense is to be assessed on the basis of all conduct within the scope of §1B1.3 (Relevant Conduct) and not solely on the basis of elements and acts encompassed within the count(s) of conviction. Application Note 4 to §3B1.2 clarifies that where the defendant has received a lower offense level by virtue of being convicted of an offense significantly less serious than warranted by his actual criminal conduct, a reduction in the offense level under §3B1.2 (Mitigating Role) ordinarily is not warranted.

✓57. QUESTION: The defendant was a postal carrier convicted of stealing undelivered United States mail containing Social Security checks. Should she receive an enhancement under §3B1.3 (Abuse of Position of Trust or Use of Special Skill)?

ANSWER: *Yes. Effective November 1, 1993, the Commentary to §3B1.3 was amended to reformulate the definition of an abuse of position of trust to better distinguish cases warranting this enhancement. Under Application Note 1 of the revised guidelines, a position of public or private trust is defined as* *being characterized by "professional or managerial discretion (i.e., substantial discretionary judgment that is ordinarily given considerable deference). Persons holding such positions ordinarily are subject to significantly less supervision than employees whose responsibilities are primarily non-discretionary in nature."*

Although postal carriers do not ordinarily meet the above definition, paragraph two of Application Note 1 expressly covers postal employees, providing "because of the special nature of the United States mail an adjustment for an abuse of position of trust will apply to any employee of the U.S. Postal Service who engages in the theft or destruction of undelivered Unites States mail."

58. **QUESTION:** The instant offense is bribery of a witness. The defendant bribed the witness not to testify against him in another case. Does the enhancement for obstruction of justice apply?

ANSWER: *No. Section 3C1.1 states that the obstruction must have taken place "during the investigation or prosecution of the instant offense" (emphasis added). For offenses covered under Part J (Offenses Involving the Administration of Justice), the Chapter Three adjustment for obstruction does not apply unless the defendant obstructed the investigation or trial of the obstruction of justice count.*

59. **QUESTION**: The defendant faces sentencing on one count of drug distribution and one count of perjury. The perjury count involves lying on the witness stand during the trial for the drug distribution. Would these two counts be grouped together in applying the guidelines?

ANSWER: *Testifying untruthfully during the drug distribution trial provides grounds for applying the obstruction enhancement (§3C1.1) when calculating the adjusted offense level for the drug count (see §3C1.1, Application Note 3(b)). Assuming that the obstruction enhancement is applied to the drug count, the perjury count would subsequently be grouped with the drug count pursuant to §3D1.2(c). This rule calls for grouping when one of the counts embodies conduct that is treated as a specific offense characteristic in, or other adjustment to, the guideline applicable to another of the counts.*

60. **QUESTION:** The defendant flushed cocaine down the toilet immediately before being arrested by DEA agents. Does §3C1.1 (Obstructing or Impeding the Administration of Justice) apply?

ANSWER: *Generally, no. This guideline was amended effective November 1, 1990. Application Note 3 to §3C1.1 instructs that destroying evidence contemporaneously with arrest may only be counted if such conduct results in a material hindrance to the official investigation or prosecution of the instant offense or to the sentencing of the offender. "Material" is defined in Application Note 5 to §3C1.1.*

Less serious forms of obstructive conduct to which the enhancement is not intended to apply may be ordinarily sanctioned by the choice of a particular sentence from the otherwise applicable guideline range (see Application Note 2).

61. **QUESTION:** The defendant was convicted of one count of theft and one count of fraud. These counts are groupable under the provisions of §3D1.2(d). The defendant obstructed justice on the theft count but not on the fraud count. Does the defendant receive a 2-level enhancement under §3C1.1 (Obstructing or Impeding the Administration of Justice)?

ANSWER: *Yes. Subsection (b) of §3D1.3 (Offense Level Applicable to Each Group of Closely-Related Counts) instructs that when counts grouped according to §3D1.2(d) involve offenses of the same general type to which different guidelines apply (e.g., theft and fraud), the offense guideline that produces the highest offense level should be applied. Application Note 3 to §3D1.3 states that specific offense characteristics from Chapter Two and adjustments from Chapter Three, Parts A (Victim), B (Role), and C (Obstruction) are to be applied based upon the combined offense behavior taken as a whole. Thus, the dollar amounts from the theft and fraud should be added and the 2-level enhancement for obstruction (§3C1.1) should be applied to both §2B1.1 (Theft) and §2F1.1 (Fraud) when determining which guideline produces the higher offense level.*

62. **QUESTION:** Because §1B1.3 (Relevant Conduct) applies to Chapter Three adjustments, can the obstructive conduct of a codefendant be used to enhance the defendant's offense level under §3C1.1 (Obstructing or Impeding the Administration of Justice)?

ANSWER: *Perhaps. Section 1B1.3(a) instructs that Chapter Three adjustments are to be determined under the provisions of relevant conduct "unless otherwise specified." Section 3C1.1 is an example of an adjustment that otherwise specifies how relevant conduct is to be applied (i.e., the offense level is to be increased by 2 levels "[i]f the defendant" obstructed or impeded the administration of justice). The language "[i]f the defendant" thus limits the scope of relevant conduct.*

Therefore, the defendant cannot be held accountable for a codefendant's obstructive conduct unless the defendant aided or abetted, counseled, commanded, induced, procured, or willfully caused the obstructive conduct (see §1B1.3(a)(1)(A) and Application Note 7 to §3C1.1). This principle also applies to §3C1.2 (Reckless Endangerment During Flight).

63. **QUESTION:** The defendant was convicted of drug distribution (21 U.S.C. § 841), felon in possession of a firearm (18 U.S.C. § 922(g)), and use of a weapon during a drug trafficking offense (18 U.S.C. § 924(c)). The two firearms forming the basis of the weapons counts were both used in the drug distribution scheme. How would these counts be grouped?

ANSWER: *Guideline 3D1.1 instructs that counts carrying mandatory consecutive sentences, such as 18 U.S.C. § 924(c), are exempted from operation of the grouping rules. Therefore, the 924(c) count is not taken into account in the process of grouping these counts.*

The guidelines applied to the drug distribution count and the felon-in-possession count are §2D1.1 (Unlawful Manufacturing, Importing, Exporting, or Trafficking) and §2K2.1 (Unlawful Receipt, Possession, or Transportation of Firearms or Ammunition; Prohibited Transactions Involving Firearms or Ammunition), respectively. In applying §2K2.1 in this example, the cross reference at §2K2.1(c) to the underlying drug offense would apply if the resulting offense level from §2D1.1 was greater than that determined from the application of §2K2.1. In such a case, the drug distribution count and the felon-in-possession count would be grouped together under §3D1.2(a), because the use of the cross reference has resulted in the application of §2D1.1 to both counts for the same criminal conduct, and thus represents an instance where "counts involve the same victim and the same act or transaction."

If, however, the cross reference at §2K2.1(c) is not applied because the offense level from application of §2K2.1 is higher than that determined for the underlying drug offense, the drug distribution count and the felon-in-possession count would be grouped under §3D1.2(c) because the felon-in-possession count embodies conduct that §2D1.1 treats as a specific offense characteristic (possession of a dangerous weapon, including a firearm). Application Note 2 to §2K2.4 prevents the application of this specific offense characteristic; however this does not prevent the counts from being grouped under §3D1.2(c).

64. QUESTION: Is it possible to group multiple counts using another rule if an offense is excluded from the §3D1.2(d) grouping rule?

ANSWER: *Yes. As stated in the final sentence of §3D1.2(d), exclusion of an offense from grouping under this subsection (i.e., §3D1.2(d) only) does not necessarily preclude grouping under another subsection. Grouping under any of the remaining rules (§3D1.2(a), (b) or (c)) may be appropriate. For example, convictions for Chapter Two, Part A offenses are excluded from grouping under §3D1.2(d). However, suppose a defendant is convicted of assault with intent to commit murder and assault with a dangerous weapon, both counts related to a single incident involving the same victim. These counts would appropriately be grouped under §3D1.2(a) (same act or transaction and same victim) even though they are excluded from §3D1.2(d) grouping.*

65. QUESTION: Can a count of money laundering be grouped with a count of drug distribution when the offense behavior involved laundering the proceeds of a drug distribution scheme?

ANSWER: *In most cases it will be appropriate to group a money laundering count with a drug distribution count under grouping rule (a) or (b) of §3D1.2. The introductory commentary to Chapter Three, Part D (Multiple Counts) states that "[s]ome offenses that may be charged in multiple-count indictments are so closely intertwined with other offenses that conviction for them ordinarily would not warrant increasing the guideline range." This underlying principle should be given consideration when resolving ambiguities in a grouping decision.*

Because the societal interests underlying the drug distribution and laundering of drug proceeds are the same or closely related (see Application Note 2 to §3D1.2), the offenses are considered to have the "same victim" within the meaning of §3D1.2(a) and (b). In other words, because money laundering is a type of statutory offense that facilitates the completion of some other underlying offense, it is conceptually appropriate to treat a money laundering offense as "closely intertwined" and groupable with the underlying offense. Accordingly, grouping under rule (a) would appear appropriate in the case of a defendant convicted of a drug conspiracy and money laundering whose sole function in the drug operation was to "clean" the money in a single transaction. Grouping under rule (b) would appear appropriate in other cases in which the defendant is involved in both the trafficking offense (in some fashion beyond laundering the proceeds) and the money laundering offense.

Rule (b) at §3D1.2 (Groups of Closely-Related Counts) states that counts are to be grouped when they involve the same victim and two or more acts or transactions connected by a common criminal objective or constituting part of a common scheme or plan. Application Note 4 instructs that counts that are part of a single course of conduct with a single criminal objective and that represent essentially one composite harm to the same victim are to be grouped together, even if they constitute legally distinct offenses occurring at different times.

For example, grouping rule (b) may apply where the offense conduct involved the defendant's purchase of a luxury automobile with the proceeds of his ongoing drug distribution scheme. These two offenses are so closely intertwined that it can be argued that they constitute one composite harm that invades the same societal interest, thereby meeting the definition of being connected by a common criminal objective.

Grouping rule (c) provides an alternative approach to grouping money laundering and drug trafficking counts in some scenarios. Rule (c) instructs that counts are to be grouped when one of the counts embodies conduct that is treated as a specific offense characteristic in, or other adjustment to, the guideline applicable to another of the counts. Subsection (b)(1) of §2S1.1 (Laundering of Monetary Instruments) provides a 3-level increase if the defendant knew the funds were the proceeds of an unlawful activity involving the manufacture, importation, or distribution of narcotics or other controlled substances (see also §2S1.2(b)(1), providing a similar 5-level adjustment).

Grouping rule (c) may apply, for example, as an alternative to grouping under rule (a) or (b) in the case of a defendant convicted of drug conspiracy and money laundering whose sole function in the drug operation was to "clean" the money. His conduct in the drug conspiracy clearly embodies the conduct described in subsection (b)(1) of §2S1.1. If, however, the defendant was both distributing drugs and laundering money, it becomes conceptually problematic to say that the specific offense characteristic in the money laundering guidelines treats the conduct embodied in a related drug distribution; distributing drugs is not conduct equivalent to knowledge that funds were the proceeds of drug distribution. Thus, in such cases, grouping under rule (b) may be more appropriate.

In summary, §3D1.2 would call for grouping of related drug trafficking and money laundering counts under one or more of rules (a), (b), or (c). In a case in which the underlying conduct is not intertwined by a common criminal objective, plan, or scheme, grouping of the counts would not be appropriate.

66. **QUESTION:** Is it possible to group two counts under §3D1.2(c) if the conduct cited in one count is embodied in a specific offense characteristic or other adjustment to the guideline applicable to the other count, without that specific offense characteristic or other adjustment being applied?

ANSWER: *Yes. If the conduct cited in one count is clearly considered by a specific offense characteristic or other adjustment in the guideline covering the other count, but has not risen to the level of warranting application of a specific offense characteristic or an adjustment, the two counts should be grouped under rule (c). For example, a defendant is convicted of one count of bank robbery and one count of assault, with the assault occurring during the commission of the robbery when the defendant pushed a teller to the floor but did not injure her. Because there was no victim injury, the specific offense characteristic for bodily injury at subsection (b)(3) of §2B3.1 (Robbery) is not applied. While the assault does not rise to the level of warranting an adjustment under subsection (b)(3) of the robbery guideline, that specific offense characteristic clearly considers the type of conduct embodied in the assault count. Therefore, the two counts should be grouped under rule §3D1.2(c).*

67. **QUESTION:** The defendant is sentenced for one count of drug distribution and one count of failure to appear for trial on the drug charge. Are the two counts grouped together under the grouping rules in Chapter Three, Part D?

ANSWER: *Yes. Effective November 1, 1991, Application Note 3 to §2J1.6 (Failure to Appear by Defendant) instructs that in such a case, the failure to appear is treated under §3C1.1 (Obstructing or Impeding the Administration of Justice) as an obstruction of the underlying offense. Therefore, the failure to appear count and the count(s) for the underlying offense are grouped together under §3D1.2(c) (see also Application Note 6 to §3C1.1).*

Application Note 3 further explains that although 18 U.S.C. § 3146(b)(2) does not require a sentence of imprisonment on a failure to appear count, any sentence of imprisonment imposed on such a count must be imposed consecutively to any other sentence of imprisonment. Therefore, in such cases the combined sentence must be constructed to provide a "total punishment" that satisfies the requirements of §5G1.2 (Sentencing on Multiple Counts of Conviction) and 18 U.S.C. § 3146(b)(2). For example, where the combined applicable guideline range for both counts (after grouping) is 30-37 months and the court determines that a "total punishment" of 36 months is appropriate, a sentence of 30 months for the underlying offense plus a consecutive six-month sentence for the failure to appear count would satisfy these requirements.

Note, however, that in the case of a failure to appear for service of sentence, the grouping rules of §§3D1.2 and 3D1.5 do not apply; the guideline range for the failure to appear count is determined independently and the sentence imposed consecutively to any imprisonment sentence for the underlying offense (see Application Note 2 to §2J1.6 and §5G1.3(a)).

68. **QUESTION:** Does a guilty plea, in and of itself, entitle a defendant to a reduction for acceptance of responsibility?

ANSWER: *No. Effective November 1, 1992, Application Note 3 to §3E1.1 states that a defendant who pleads guilty prior to the commencement of trial and truthfully admits the conduct comprising the offense of conviction (while truthfully admitting or not falsely denying any additional relevant conduct for which he is accountable under §1B1.3 (Relevant Conduct)) has provided significant evidence of acceptance of responsibility for the purposes of the two-level reduction under subsection (a) (emphasis added).*

69. **QUESTION:** The defendant is convicted of two counts of assault involving different victims, but affirmatively accepts personal responsibility for only one of the assaults. For guideline application purposes, does the court apply §3E1.1 (Acceptance of Responsibility) separately to each count of conviction?

ANSWER: *No. Guideline 1B1.1 (Application Instructions) lists the order in which the Guidelines Manual is to be applied. Part E of Chapter Three (Acceptance of Responsibility) is applied after Part D of Chapter Three (Multiple Counts) has produced a single combined offense level for all counts of conviction (see §1B1.1(d) and (e)). At this point in the guideline application process, the court must decide whether the defendant, based on the considerations identified in §3E1.1 in respect to both offenses, merits a downward adjustment for Acceptance of Responsibility.*

✓70. **QUESTION:** Did the Commission make retroactive the amendment to §3E1.1 (Acceptance of Responsibility) which became effective November 1, 1992, providing an additional 1-level reduction for certain defendants?

ANSWER: *No. The amendment to §3E1.1 is not one the Commission determined would be retroactive and is therefore not listed under subsection (d) of §1B1.10 (Retroactivity of Amended Guideline Range). Only those defendants affected by an amendment listed under subsection (d) are eligible for consideration of a reduction in their term of imprisonment.*

✓71. **QUESTION:** Defendants who qualify for the 2-level reduction for Acceptance of Responsibility under §3E1.1(a) may be eligible to receive an additional 1-level reduction under §3E1.1(b) if their offense level was 16 or greater "prior to the operation of subsection (a)" of §3E1.1. Does this mean the offense level determined after application of only Chapter Two adjustments?

ANSWER: *No. Because the guidelines are applied in sequential order, an offense level determined prior to the operation of §3E1.1(a) would include all appropriate Chapter Two adjustments and all appropriate Chapter Three adjustments up to §3E1.1, i.e., Parts A (Victim-Related Adjustments), B (Role in the Offense), C (Obstruction of Justice), and D (Multiple Counts) (see §1B1.1 (Application Instructions)).*

72. **QUESTION:** If the probation officer does not find that the defendant has demonstrated a recognition and affirmative acceptance of personal responsibility, must he or she nevertheless recommend a reduction in offense level when there is a plea agreement that stipulates that the defendant has accepted responsibility for the offense of conviction?

ANSWER: *No. Rule 32(c)(2) states that the presentence investigation shall contain "the classification of the offense and of the defendant under the categories established by the Sentencing Commission pursuant to § 994(a) of title 28, that the probation officer believes to be applicable to the defendant's case..." (emphasis added). Neither the probation officer nor the court is bound by a stipulation of guideline factors by the parties (see §6B1.4(d)).*

73. **QUESTION:** The defendant has a prior conviction for which he was sentenced to "time served." Does this time in custody count for purposes of applying criminal history points?

ANSWER: *Yes. The amount of time served should be considered when determining the length of the prior sentence of imprisonment under §4A1.1(a), (b), or (c).*

74. **QUESTION:** Are criminal history points assessed for a defendant's prior civil adjudications?

ANSWER: *No. Chapter Four, Part A (Criminal History) applies only to prior criminal convictions and adjudications.*

75. **QUESTION:** The defendant was convicted in 1984 and sentenced in state court to 20 years imprisonment. He served 90 days and was released on appeal bond, which is still pending when he commits the instant offense. Would he receive any criminal history points under §4A1.1(a)?

ANSWER: *Yes. The possibility that the prior conviction may be overturned on appeal is irrelevant in application of the guidelines to the instant offense. Therefore, the defendant should receive 3 points under §4A1.1(a). Application Note 2 of §4A1.2 states that "criminal history points are based on the sentence pronounced, not the length of time actually served." Effective November 1, 1991, §4A1.2(l) clarifies that "[i]n the case of a prior sentence, the execution of which has been stayed pending appeal, §4A1.1(a), (b), (c), (d), and (f) shall apply as if the execution of such sentence had not been stayed; §4A1.1(e) shall not apply."*

76. **QUESTION:** When calculating criminal history points, does work release count as imprisonment?

ANSWER: *If the offender was sentenced to imprisonment and as part of the term of imprisonment was placed on work release status, this would be treated as a sentence of imprisonment. If the sentence did not involve a term of imprisonment (e.g., a sentence of probation with a condition requiring residency in a halfway house), the sentence would not be considered imprisonment and would fall under §4A1.1(c).*

A sentence of residency in a halfway house is not considered imprisonment (see Background Commentary to §4A1.1 (second paragraph)).

77. **QUESTION:** In computing criminal history, should a defendant whose probation term has expired but who committed the instant offense when subject to an active warrant issued for absconding from probation supervision receive 2 points under §4A1.1(d)?

ANSWER: *Yes. For the purposes of §4A1.1(d), the defendant in the above example remains under a criminal justice sentence until discharged from the probationary sentence. Even though the term of probation may have expired, a defendant subject to an active warrant has not been discharged from criminal justice control (see clarifying language added to Application Note 4 to §4A1.1, effective November 1, 1991).*

78. **QUESTION:** Does a defendant serving unsupervised probation at the time of the instant offense receive 2 criminal history points under §4A1.1(d) for being under a criminal justice sentence?

ANSWER: *Yes. Under §4A1.1(d), 2 points would be added if at the time the defendant committed the instant offense he was under a criminal justice sentence. A criminal justice sentence includes probation, as stated in Application Note 4 to §4A1.1. Keep in mind that the prior offense must meet the definition of prior sentence at §4A1.2. Whether or not the defendant was being actually supervised at the time of the instant offense is not a determining factor (see clarifying language added to Application Note 4 to §4A1.1, effective November 1, 1991).*

79. **QUESTION:** If the instant offense involved escape from prison (or work release), does the defendant receive 2 criminal history points for §4A1.1(d) and one more for §4A1.1(e)?

ANSWER: *Yes, providing the prior sentence of imprisonment or work release from confinement is at least 60 days and is otherwise a countable sentence. The defendant receives 2 points pursuant to §4A1.1(d) for committing the instant offense while under any criminal justice sentence. Another point is received for committing the offense less than two years after release from imprisonment on a sentence of at least 60 days (§4A1.1(e)). As stated in Application Note 5, §4A1.1(e) "also applies if the defendant committed the instant offense while still in imprisonment or escape status on such a sentence" (see also Application Note 5 to §2P1.1).*

If the escape was from a halfway house (or work release from the halfway house) and the residence is not a portion of a sentence of imprisonment of at least 60 days, the defendant would only receive 2 points under §4A1.1(d) for being under a criminal justice sentence. No points would be given for §4A1.1(e) for this prior sentence.

80. **QUESTION:** If a defendant commits an offense after the instant offense but is sentenced for the subsequent offense prior to sentencing on the instant offense, can it be counted under criminal history as a prior sentence?

ANSWER: *Yes. According to §4A1.2, Application Note 1, a sentence imposed after the defendant's commencement of the instant offense, but prior to sentencing on the instant offense, is a prior sentence if it was a sentence for conduct other than conduct that was part of the instant offense.*

81. **QUESTION**: The defendant committed the instant offense while on bond pending trial for an unrelated offense. Does the offense for which he was on bond qualify as a prior sentence in calculating criminal history points in the instant case?

ANSWER: *It depends on whether, at the time of sentencing for the instant offense, the defendant has been convicted or sentenced for the offense for which he was released on bond. According to Application Note 1 to §4A1.2, a sentence imposed after the defendant's commencement of the instant offense, but prior to sentencing on the instant offense, is a prior sentence if it was for conduct other than conduct that was part of the instant offense. If sentencing for the earlier behavior occurs after or in conjunction with sentencing on the instant offense, it would not be considered a prior sentence under §4A1.1(a) or (b). Effective November 1, 1991, §4A1.2(a)(4) instructs that where a defendant has been convicted of an offense, but not yet sentenced, such conviction shall be counted as if it constituted a prior sentence under §4A1.1(c) (i.e., receiving 1 point) if a sentence resulting from that conviction otherwise would be countable (see also Application Note 1 to §4A1.2).*

82. **QUESTION:** A defendant's prior two-year custody sentence was modified after service of three months imprisonment and the balance suspended with the defendant placed on three years probation. How many criminal history points should be assigned?

ANSWER: *Two. Criminal history points are based upon the sentence imposed. However, if part of a sentence of imprisonment was suspended, "sentence of imprisonment" refers only to the portion that was not suspended (§4A1.2(b)(2)). In this example, the defendant served three months imprisonment before the court suspended the balance through a sentence modification. Applying §4A1.1(b), 2 criminal history points would be assigned based on the three-month portion of the imprisonment sentence that was not suspended.*

83. **QUESTION:** Are prior uncounseled convictions considered invalid convictions and therefore not countable under criminal history?

ANSWER: *Not necessarily. If a prior conviction is shown by the defendant to have been previously ruled constitutionally invalid, it is not counted in the criminal history score (see §4A1.2, Application Note 6). Otherwise, the fact that a conviction was uncounseled does not automatically mean that the conviction was constitutionally invalid. In the case of a felony or misdemeanor, for example, the defendant may have waived counsel. Or, in the case of a misdemeanor, a term of imprisonment may not have been imposed and thus provision of counsel would not have been constitutionally required. The Background Commentary to §4A1.2 expressly states the Commission's intent that prior sentences not otherwise excluded are to be counted in the calculation of the defendant's criminal history score, including uncounseled misdemeanors where imprisonment was not imposed.*

See United States v. Eckford, 910 F.2d 216 (5th Cir.), reh'g en banc denied 915 F.2d 695 (5th Cir. 1990) (prior uncounseled but valid misdemeanor convictions may be counted in criminal history score); United States v. Castro-Vega, 945 F.2d 496 (2d Cir. 1991), cert. denied Cintron-Rodriguez v. United States, 113 S. Ct. 1250 (1993); United States v. Follin, 979 F.2d 369 (5th Cir. 1990). But see United States v. Lee, 995 F.2d 887 (9th Cir. 1993) (barring use of uncounseled conviction unless defendant knowingly waived assistance of counsel).

84. **QUESTION:** The defendant's prior record includes two robberies, the second committed while he was out on bail release for the first. The two robbery offenses subsequently were consolidated for

sentencing. Are these two prior sentences considered "related cases" for purposes of computing criminal history points?

ANSWER: *No. The definition of related cases in Application Note 3 to §4A1.2 (Definitions and Instructions for Computing Criminal History) was amended effective November 1, 1991, to provide that cases separated by an intervening arrest are not treated as related cases, even if they otherwise meet the definition.*

85. QUESTION: The defendant was sentenced in state court to five years imprisonment for burglary. Two days later, before he began serving his imprisonment term, he was sentenced in the same court to three years imprisonment for possession of cocaine to run concurrently with the burglary sentence. Are these two sentences considered related and therefore considered one sentence for purposes of assigning criminal history points?

ANSWER: *No. Guideline 4A1.2(a)(2) directs that "prior sentences imposed in unrelated cases are to be counted separately. Prior sentences imposed in related cases are to be treated as one sentence for purposes of the criminal history." Related cases are defined in Application Note 3 to §4A1.2 as prior sentences resulting from offenses not separated by an intervening arrest that "(1) occurred on the same occasion, (2) were part of a single common scheme or plan, or (3) were consolidated for trial or sentencing." The example fits none of these circumstances. Therefore, the convictions would be considered "unrelated" and each would receive 3 criminal history points.*

86. QUESTION: A defendant was sentenced for two separate larcenies on the same day in the same court and received consecutive sentences. Can each larceny be counted individually when calculating criminal history points?

ANSWER: *Yes, but only if the larcenies were separated by an intervening arrest (i.e., the defendant was arrested for the first larceny prior to committing the second). Guideline 4A1.2(a)(2) states that prior sentences imposed in related cases are to be treated as one sentence for purposes of computing the criminal history score. The guideline further states that the "aggregate sentence of imprisonment imposed" should be used when consecutive sentences are imposed. Furthermore, Application Note 3 to §4A1.2 states that "prior sentences are considered related if they (1) occurred on the same occasion; (2) were part of a single common scheme or plan; or (3) were consolidated for trial or sentencing." Thus, if the two larceny cases were consolidated for sentencing they would be considered one sentence for the purpose of calculating criminal history, with one important exception. Application Note 3 to §4A1.2, amended November 1, 1991, instructs that prior sentences are not considered related if they were for offenses that were separated by an intervening arrest (i.e., the defendant is arrested for the first offense prior to committing the second offense).*

87. QUESTION: Should criminal history points be assigned if the defendant was convicted of a local ordinance violation for simple assault?

ANSWER: *Yes. Local courts in several jurisdictions adjudicate violations of ordinances that mirror state law. Where the conduct could have been prosecuted under state or local law, the fact that the conviction was obtained under a local ordinance should not result in the exclusion of the conviction from the criminal history score unless conviction under similar state law would also be excluded. Such exceptions include zoning, nuisance, and leash law violations (see §4A1.2(c)(1) and (c)(2)).*

88. **QUESTION:** The defendant has a prior conviction for driving under the influence of alcohol. Does this sentence count for the purpose of calculating the criminal history score?

ANSWER: *Yes, provided it falls within the applicable time frames (§4A1.2(d) and (e)). Application Note 5 to §4A1.2 states that such convictions are not minor traffic infractions within the meaning of §4A1.2(c).*

89. **QUESTION:** Is a diversionary sentence based upon a plea of <u>nolo</u> <u>contendere</u> – adjudication withheld – considered a prior sentence for the purpose of criminal history computation?

ANSWER: *Yes. Guideline 4A1.2(f) and its accompanying commentary state that a diversionary disposition, other than diversion from juvenile court, that involves a finding of guilt or admission of guilt is counted as a prior sentence under §4A1.1(c). Guideline 4A1.2(a)(1) states that a plea of <u>nolo contendere</u> is treated the same as a guilty plea or finding of guilt after trial for the purpose of defining the term "prior sentence." This is in accord with the Federal Rules of Criminal Procedure (<u>see</u> Rule 11 in particular) that generally treat a <u>nolo</u> <u>contendere</u> plea the same as a guilty plea or determination of guilt for sentencing purposes.*

90. **QUESTION:** The defendant committed the instant offense on January 1, 1990. In 1974, he received a three-year sentence of imprisonment for drug distribution and was released on parole later that year. Subsequently, in 1975, the parole term was revoked and the defendant was imprisoned until January 1, 1976, when he was released on parole. Is the drug distribution sentence counted for purposes of computing criminal history points?

ANSWER: *Yes. Guideline 4A1.2(k) (Revocations of Probation, Parole, Mandatory Release, or Supervised Release) states that revocation may affect the time period under which certain sentences are counted. Effective November 1, 1991, §4A1.2(k)(2)(B) clarifies that the date of last release from incarceration is used to determine the applicable time period in the case of an adult term of imprisonment totaling more than one year and one month. In this example, January 1, 1976, was the date the defendant was last released from the total term of imprisonment that resulted from the drug distribution sentence. Because the defendant was incarcerated on a sentence exceeding one year and one month within the applicable 15-year time period, the sentence is counted under §4A1.1(a) (<u>see</u> §4A1.2(e)(1)).*

91. **QUESTION**: During the presentence interview, the defendant provides information about his past criminal conduct for which he was never arrested. While unrelated to the instant offense, it is similar in nature. Can this information be considered in determining the defendant's criminal history category?

ANSWER: *No, this activity would not be used to calculate the criminal history category. However, the court may consider such behavior as criteria for a specific point within the guideline range or as grounds for departure. Adequacy of Criminal History (Policy Statement 4A1.3(e)) states that the court may consider imposing a sentence that departs from the otherwise applicable guideline range if there is reliable information of "... prior similar adult criminal conduct not resulting in a criminal conviction."*

92. **QUESTION**: The defendant, having met the requirements for classification as a career offender, is set for sentencing on two counts. Are the statutory maxima for the two counts added together to determine the adjusted offense level under §4B1.1?

ANSWER: *No. As provided in Application Note 2 to §4B1.1, only the count for the crime of violence or controlled substance offense carrying the greater statutory maximum is used in determining the offense level via the Offense Statutory Maximum table of §4B1.1. Note, however, that if the combined adjusted offense level for the counts determined in Chapters Two and Three is greater than that determined through the table, the combined adjusted offense level controls.*

93. **QUESTION:** Are the terms "crime of violence" and "controlled substance offense" as used in the career offender guideline (§§4B1.1-4B1.2) identical to the terms "violent felony" and "serious drug offense" as used to determine if a defendant is an armed career criminal under 18 U.S.C. § 924(e) and guideline 4B1.4?

ANSWER: *No. Section 4B1.4 (the armed career criminal guideline) implements 18 U.S.C. § 924(e), a mandatory minimum sentencing enhancement that applies to a defendant whose instant offense of conviction is 18 U.S.C. § 922(g) (felon in possession) and who has three previous convictions for violent felonies or serious drug offenses. The terms "violent felony" and "serious drug offense" are defined at 18 U.S.C. § 924(e)(2). The definitions of these terms are similar but not identical to the definitions of "crime of violence" and "controlled substance offense" used in §§4B1.1-4B1.2 (the career offender guidelines) (see Application Note 1 to §4B1.4).*

In addition, the three previous convictions that qualify a defendant for armed career criminal status under section 924(e) are counted irrespective of when they were sustained and whether or not they would be considered "related" within the meaning of §4A1.2 (Definitions and Instructions for Computing Criminal History). In contrast, prior sentences under the career offender guideline (§§4B1.1-4B1.2) are controlled by the time limits and other rules applicable to the counting of prior sentences set forth in §4A1.2 (see Application Note 4 to §4B1.2).

94. **QUESTION:** Do the time periods that apply to criminal history calculations also apply to career offender determinations?

ANSWER: *Yes. Application Note 4 under §4B1.2 indicates that the applicable time periods provision of §4A1.2(e) also applies to the counting of convictions under §4B1.1 (Career Offender).*

95. **QUESTION:** Is bank larceny considered a crime of violence when applying the career offender enhancement? What if the defendant actually committed bank robbery but is charged with bank larceny?

ANSWER: *The career offender provision of the guidelines requires use of the offense of conviction (i.e., the statutory violation for which the defendant was convicted). Guideline 4B1.2(1) states that "[t]he term 'crime of violence' means any offense under federal or state law punishable by imprisonment for a term exceeding one year that (1) has as an element the use, attempted use, or threatened use of physical force against the person of another, or (2) is burglary of a dwelling, arson, or extortion, involves use of explosives, or otherwise involves conduct that presents a serious potential risk of physical injury to another."*

This definition is virtually identical to the definition of "violent felony" in 18 U.S.C. § 924(e)(2)(B) (except that the guideline definition excludes non-residential burglaries). In determining whether a crime is a "violent felony" within the meaning of that statute, courts have focused on the elements and inherent nature of the offense of conviction as denominated by the statute, rather than on underlying real offense conduct. Application Note 2 to §4B1.2 lists several offenses that the Commission considers to be crimes of violence; bank larceny is not among them. However, the commentary advises that other offenses are to be considered crimes of violence "... where (A) that offense has as an element the use, attempted use, or threatened use of physical force against the person of another, or (B) the conduct set forth in the count of which the defendant was convicted involved the use of explosives or, by its nature, presented a serious potential risk of physical injury to another." Thus, the court must determine whether the conduct expressly charged in the count of which the defendant is convicted meets these criteria.

96. **QUESTION:** Does a conviction for simple possession of a controlled substance qualify as a "controlled substance offense" within the meaning of the career offender guideline?

ANSWER: *No. A conviction for possession of a controlled substance does not meet the definitional criteria of §4B1.2. Even if the real offense conduct involved trafficking in controlled substances, the career offender enhancement is applied only if the offense of conviction is for a controlled substance offense as defined by the guidelines. According to §4B1.2(2), the term "controlled substance offense" means an offense "under a federal or state law prohibiting the manufacture, import, export, distribution, or dispensing of a controlled substance (or a counterfeit substance) or the possession of a controlled substance (or a counterfeit substance) with intent to manufacture, import, export, distribute, or dispense." This definition does not include simple possession.*

97. **QUESTION:** If the defendant has two prior felony convictions for crimes of violence but received probationary sentences on each, can these prior sentences be considered in determining career offender status?

ANSWER: *Yes. For purposes of applying the career offender guideline, the prior felony convictions need not have resulted in sentences of imprisonment. Probation sentences counted under §4A1.1(c) may be considered prior convictions for determination of career offender status provided that they are felony convictions and meet the definitions of "crime of violence" or "controlled substance offense," and "two prior felony convictions" in §4B1.2.*

98. **QUESTION:** Can a conviction for 21 U.S.C. § 843(b) (communication facility) be used to determine whether the defendant qualifies for career offender status?

ANSWER: *Possibly. Application Note 1 to §4B1.2 explains that the terms "crime of violence" and "controlled substance offense," for purposes of the career offender guideline determinations, "include the offenses of aiding and abetting, conspiring, and attempting to commit such offenses." The offense of using a communication facility "in committing or in causing or facilitating the commission of any act or acts constituting a felony under [subchapters I or II of Chapter 13 of title 21, U.S. Code]" may be likened to aiding and abetting a drug offense. Thus, a "telephone count" may be appropriately considered a "controlled substance offense" for career offender purposes if the felony caused or facilitated by use of the communication's facility would be so considered.*

99. **QUESTION:** Is a felon-in-possession conviction (18 U.S.C. § 922(g)(1)) a qualifying "crime of violence" for purposes of the career offender provision?

ANSWER: *No. The commentary to §4B1.2 was clarified effective November 1, 1991, to state specifically that the term "crime of violence" does not include the offense of unlawful possession of a firearm by a felon (see amendment 461, effective November 1, 1992. See also United States v. Stinson, 113 S. Ct. 1913 (1993) (citing Commission Commentary in reversing Eleventh Circuit decision holding that being a felon-in-possession is a crime of violence)).*

100. **QUESTION:** The defendant's instant offense is for distributing drugs. He has two prior sentences for the same type of offense, but one of the prior convictions came after he committed the instant offense. Should he be treated as a career offender?

ANSWER: *No. Although the defendant may be awarded criminal history points under §4A1.1, he would not qualify as a career offender under §4B1.1. The definition of "two prior felony convictions" at §4B1.2(3) states that the defendant must have already been convicted of the prior offenses before he committed the instant offense.*

101. **QUESTION:** What does the phrase "the date the defendant sustained a conviction" mean in §4B1.2, definitions of terms used in the career offender guideline?

ANSWER: *The date a defendant "sustained a conviction" is the date that the guilt of the defendant has been established, whether by guilty plea, trial, or plea of nolo contendere. Guideline 4B1.2 was amended effective November 1, 1992, to conform the definition of "sustained a conviction" to the definition of "convicted of an offense" in §4A1.2 (Definitions and Instructions for Computing Criminal History).*

102. **QUESTION:** Can a defendant convicted under 18 U.S.C. § 924(e) (armed career criminal) receive a guideline sentence greater than the mandatory minimum of 15 years imprisonment?

ANSWER: *Perhaps. Guideline 4B1.4 (Armed Career Criminal), effective November 1, 1990, applies to those defendants subject to an enhanced sentence under the provisions of 18 U.S.C. § 924(e). This statute provides a mandatory minimum sentence of imprisonment of at least 15 years for a defendant who violates 18 U.S.C. § 922(g) and has three prior convictions for either a violent felony or a serious drug offense. Guideline 4B1.4 provides for a range of sentences to reflect the varying severity of the offense conduct and criminal history of such defendants.*

103. **QUESTION:** Do the guidelines permit "unsupervised" probation?

ANSWER: *Yes. Supervision is not a mandatory condition of probation listed under §5B1.3. Recommended conditions of probation are included in a policy statement at §5B1.4. The recommended conditions are generally those that address reporting and necessitate supervision. While the conditions listed in §5B1.4 are recommended, they are not required.*

104. **QUESTION:** Can home detention (house arrest) be substituted for imprisonment?

ANSWER: *Yes. As of November 1, 1989, home detention (house arrest) may be substituted for imprisonment when imposing a term of probation or supervised release as described under §5C1.1. As indicated in §5C1.1(e), one day of home detention is a substitute for one day of imprisonment. Home* *detention may be imposed as a condition of probation or supervised release, but only as a substitute for imprisonment, not simply as a more limiting condition of probation or supervised release (see §5F1.2).*

Application Note 1 to §5B1.4 indicates that "[u]nder home detention, the defendant, with specified exceptions, is restricted to his place of residence during all non-working hours. Curfew, which limits the defendant to his place of residence during evening and nighttime hours, is less restrictive than home detention and may be imposed as a condition of probation whether or not imprisonment could have been ordered."

105. QUESTION: Sections (c) and (d) of §5C1.1 (Imposition of a Term of Imprisonment) outline various sentencing options to satisfy minimum terms of imprisonment. Are these options available only when the court chooses the minimum of the guideline range as the appropriate total punishment, or are they available when the court chooses any point within the applicable guideline range?

ANSWER: *The sentencing options described in those sections are available for any point chosen by the court within the guideline range, provided that the minimum term of the applicable guideline range falls within the limits set by sections (c) and (d). For example, if the defendant's guideline range is 8-14 months and the court wishes to impose a sentence equivalent to 14 months, the following options are available under §5C1.1(d): (1) a sentence of 14 months imprisonment; or (2) a sentence of at least four months' imprisonment (one-half of the minimum term of the applicable guideline range must be satisfied by imprisonment under this option) followed by a term of supervised release that substitutes community confinement or home detention for the remainder of the 14 months (e.g., four months imprisonment plus ten months home detention).*

106. QUESTION: The defendant has a guideline range of 8-14 months. Can the minimum of the guideline range be satisfied by ordering the defendant to serve the entire eight months in community confinement?

ANSWER: *No. Under the "split sentence" option described at §5C1.1(d), at least one-half of the minimum term must be satisfied by imprisonment without benefit of the incarceration alternatives outlined in §5C1.1(e). The schedule of substitute punishments at §5C1.1(e) is only available to satisfy incarceration requirements imposed as a condition of probation or supervised release.*

107. QUESTION: Do the guidelines require imposition of a term of supervised release on each count when sentencing on multiple counts?

ANSWER: *No. The guidelines do not require a term of supervised release on each count. According to §5D1.1, the court is required to impose a term of supervised release in conjunction with sentences of more than one year. Section 5D1.2 identifies the appropriate terms of supervised release. While the court's final sentence must be within the guideline range as determined in §5D1.2, no instructions are provided as to how the term of supervised release is to be allocated among multiple counts. The guidelines do not require nor do they prohibit imposition of a term of supervised release on each count. Note: 18 U.S.C. § 3624(e) requires that terms of supervised release imposed on more than one count run concurrently, commencing on the day the defendant is released from imprisonment.*

108. QUESTION: Should a term of supervised release be ordered for a defendant convicted solely of 18 U.S.C. § 924(c)?

ANSWER: *Yes. Application Note 3 to §2K2.4 states that the imposition of a term of supervised release is governed by the provisions of §5D1.1 (Imposition of a Term of Supervised Release) (but see U.S. v. Allison, 953 F.2d 870 (5th Cir.), cert. denied, 112 S. Ct. 2319 (1992), corrected, 986 F.2d 896 (5th Cir. 1993) (supervised release not allowed under the penalty provisions of 18 U.S.C. § 924(c)).*

109. **QUESTION:** There appears to be a disagreement between 18 U.S.C. § 3559 and 18 U.S.C. § 3581 regarding the classification of crimes and the authorized terms of imprisonment. Which statute should we follow?

ANSWER: *Section 3559 is the more relevant provision for present sentencing purposes. Subsection (a) of this section establishes the classification for sentencing purposes of each criminal offense, based upon the maximum term of imprisonment authorized in the statute(s) describing the offense. The sentencing classification (whether the offense is a Class B or C felony, for example) then determines (1) whether a sentence of probation is authorized by law (see 18 U.S.C. § 3561(a)(1)); (2) the statutory maximum fine (see 18 U.S.C. § 3571); (3) the statutory maximum term of supervised release (see 18 U.S.C. § 3583(b)); (4) the sentencing guideline term of supervised release (see §5D1.2); and (5) the maximum term of imprisonment imposable upon revocation of supervised release (see 18 U.S.C. § 3583(e)(3)). Section 3559(b) specifically states that the maximum imprisonment term for any offense is the maximum stated in the law describing the offense (rather than the maximum listed in § 3581).*

Section 3581 of title 18 is a provision of the Sentencing Reform Act that was intended to be used in conjunction with the once-planned, later-abandoned comprehensive revision of the Federal Criminal Code. Under that contemplated scheme, Congress would have graded existing crimes by sentencing classification without specifying a maximum penalty in the provisions describing the offense. Section 3581 would then have been used to determine the maximum authorized imprisonment term for each offense (e.g., an offense classified as a Class C felony would, under § 3581, have carried a maximum imprisonment of 12 years). Section 3581 remains a dormant provision because Congress, subsequent to the 1984 Sentencing Reform Act, has continued to specify maximum penalties rather than simply classifying offenses by letter grade.

110. **QUESTION:** The defendant was convicted under a statute that requires a four-year mandatory minimum term of supervised release. What is the maximum term of supervised release permitted by the guidelines?

ANSWER: *According to §5D1.2(a), when a defendant is convicted under a statute that requires a minimum term of supervised release, the term shall be "at least three years but not more than five years, or the minimum period required by statute, whichever is greater." In the example cited, the minimum period required by statute (four years) is not greater than the upper end of the guideline range. Therefore, since the court cannot impose less than the four-year mandatory minimum sentence required by statute, the effective guideline range is four to five years.*

111. **QUESTION:** The defendant has a guideline range of 8-14 months. Is it a departure for the court to order 14 months imprisonment followed by a term of supervised release with a special condition that the defendant reside for six months in a community treatment center, halfway house, or similar facility?

ANSWER: *Technically, no. Although the total period of imprisonment and residency in such a community facility would be 20 months (which is above the guideline range), such a sentence is authorized under the applicable statutory provisions and does not contravene any express provision of* *the guidelines. According to 18 U.S.C. § 3583(d), the court may order, as a further condition of supervised release, any condition set forth as a discretionary condition of probation in 18 U.S.C. § 3563(b). Section 3563(b)(10) of title 18 authorizes the court to order the defendant to "undergo available medical, psychiatric, or psychological treatment, including treatment for drug or alcohol dependency, as specified by the court, and remain in a specified institution if required for that purpose." Nevertheless, since the total period during which a defendant is deprived of his liberty exceeds the maximum in the applicable guideline range, the court should impose such a sentence only when consistent with the purposes of sentencing (see 18 U.S.C. § 3565(b) referencing § 3553(a)(1) and (a)(2)).*

112. QUESTION: Is intermittent confinement available as a condition of supervised release?

ANSWER: *No. Intermittent confinement is authorized only as a condition of probation during the first year of the term of probation (see 18 U.S.C. § 3563(b)(11) and Application Note 6 to §7B1.3 (Revocation of Probation or Supervised Release)). Intermittent confinement is not authorized as a condition of supervised release (see 18 U.S.C. § 3583(d)).*

113. QUESTION: Must restitution be ordered for offenses not under titles 18 or 49 U.S.C. §§ 1472(h), (j), or (n)?

ANSWER: *Yes. Effective November 1, 1991, §5E1.1 (Restitution) requires the court to impose a term of probation or supervised release with a condition requiring restitution. Senate Report Number 225, 98th Congress, 1st Session 95-96, indicates that restitution for other offenses is authorized by section 3563(b)(20) of title 18 as a condition of probation or supervised release.*

114. QUESTION: Can a statutory maximum fine of $250,000 be used to determine the maximum of the guideline fine range?

ANSWER: *No. Subsection (c)(4) of §5E1.2 (Fines for Individual Defendants) instructs that only statutory maximum fines greater than $250,000 are to be used in the determination of the maximum of the guideline fine range. Statutory maximum fines in excess of $250,000 are cumulative for the purposes of making this determination.*

For example, if the defendant was convicted of one count with a statutory maximum fine of $250,000, this amount would not be used to calculate the maximum of the guideline fine range. Statutory maximum fines of $250,000 are not to be added together to determine the maximum of the guideline fine range. If the defendant was convicted of two counts that carry statutory maximum fines of $250,000 and $1,000,000, respectively, the maximum guideline fine would be $1,000,000. Note that the $250,000 maximum fine is not added to the $1,000,000 maximum fine. If the defendant was convicted of two counts that each carry a statutory maximum fine of $1,000,000, the guideline maximum would be $2,000,000.

115. QUESTION: Can a fine be the sole sanction for a defendant sentenced under the Sentencing Reform Act?

ANSWER: *Yes. Application Note 1 to §5E1.2 instructs that a fine may be the sole sanction if the guidelines do not require a term of imprisonment (i.e., where the guideline range is 0-6 months).*

However, Application Note 1 also states that if the fine is not paid in full at the time of sentencing, the court is encouraged to sentence the defendant to a term of probation, with payment of the fine as a condition of probation.

116. QUESTION: If the court does not impose a fine, is the sentence a departure?

ANSWER: *It depends upon whether the defendant had the ability to pay a fine. If a defendant has the ability to pay a fine but one was not imposed, the sentence would be a departure. However, if the fine was waived due to an inability to pay, the sentence would not be a departure. The guidelines require a fine in every case unless the defendant demonstrates an inability to pay or that imposition of a fine would unduly burden the defendant's dependents. In such a case the court may impose a lesser fine or waive the fine (see §5E1.2(f)).*

Application Note 3 to §5E1.2 instructs that the calculation of the guideline fine range may be dispensed with entirely upon a court determination that the defendant is unable, and is unlikely to become able, to pay any fine.

117. QUESTION: Is the cost of imprisonment and supervision considered a fine?

ANSWER: *Yes. The guidelines provide that the court shall order a fine within the guideline fine range and the court "shall impose an additional fine amount that is at least sufficient to pay the cost to the government of any imprisonment, probation, or supervised release ordered" (emphasis added). Of course, the guideline fine and the costs of imprisonment/supervision fine cannot total more than the maximum fine provided by statute (see §5E1.2(i)).*

118. QUESTION: What should be done if the guideline range is below a statutory minimum mandatory sentence or above a statutory maximum?

ANSWER: *If the guideline range is below a statutory minimum mandatory sentence, the statutory minimum is controlling and becomes the guideline sentence. If the guideline range is above a statutory maximum, the statutory maximum is controlling and becomes the guideline sentence (see §5G1.1).*

119. QUESTION: What should be done when a statute mandates that a term of imprisonment be imposed and that the term of imprisonment run consecutively to any other sentence (e.g., 18 U.S.C. § 924(c))?

ANSWER: *Under §5G1.2, the mandatory term of imprisonment runs consecutively to any other sentences imposed under the guidelines (see §3D1.1(b) and Application Note 1 to §3D1.1). To avoid double counting, special adjustments to the offense levels and guideline range may be required (see Application Note 2 to §2K2.4).*

Note that this provision only applies where the statute mandates both that a term of imprisonment be imposed and that it run consecutively to any other term of imprisonment. Certain statutes (e.g., 18 U.S.C. §§ 3146, 3147) that require a consecutive sentence only if imprisonment is imposed are not included under this provision (see Application Note 3 to §2J1.6 and Application Note 2 to §2J1.7).

120. QUESTION: The defendant is awaiting sentencing in federal court on two unrelated guideline convictions. Does the court treat each conviction individually and compute a separate guideline range for each case?

ANSWER: *No. The multiple count rules are applied to separate indictments consolidated for sentencing (see Commentary to §5G1.2). The same procedure is used when an indictment has been transferred via Rule 20 and is to be sentenced with another unrelated guideline conviction. The guidelines do not dictate the decision to consolidate separate indictments for sentencing. However, if the court decides to do so, the multiple count rules would apply and the separate indictments should be treated as if they were counts contained in a single indictment.*

✓**121. QUESTION:** Why is §5G1.3 (Imposition of a Sentence on a Defendant Subject to an Undischarged Term of Imprisonment) necessary?

ANSWER: *For several reasons. First, Congress specifically directed the Commission (at 28 U.S.C. § 994(a)(1)(D)) to determine "whether multiple sentences to terms of imprisonment should be ordered to run concurrently or consecutively." Congress further directed that the Commission shall ensure that the guidelines reflect the "appropriateness of imposing an incremental penalty for each offense in a case in which a defendant is convicted of – (A) multiple offenses committed in the same course of conduct that result in the exercise of ancillary jurisdiction over one or more of the offenses; and (B) multiple offenses committed at different times..." (see 28 U.S.C. § 994(l)(1)).*

Second, a primary goal of the Sentencing Reform Act was the elimination of unwarranted sentencing disparity. Without §5G1.3, substantial disparity could result if one court orders a guideline sentence to be served concurrently and another court orders the sentence to be served consecutively to an undischarged term of imprisonment. Consider two similar defendants who have committed identical offenses and who have the same guideline range of 30-37 months. Both are awaiting federal sentencing and both are serving undischarged terms of imprisonment of three years. Both are sentenced to 36 months on the instant federal offense; however, one defendant receives a concurrent sentence and the other a consecutive sentence. Ultimately, one defendant serves three years and the other six years. Without §5G1.3, the uniformity and proportionality that the guidelines are designed to produce can be severely undermined.

Finally, §5G1.3 accomplishes the congressional goal of imposing an incremental penalty while safeguarding the defendant from the over-punishment that could result from multiple federal prosecutions for criminal conduct that occurred in multiple federal jurisdictions. For example, if a defendant is convicted of drug trafficking that occurred in New Mexico, Arizona, and Colorado, federal prosecution could occur in each federal district. The drug guideline, however, is written to consider all the criminal acts that were part of the same course of conduct or common scheme or plan as the offense of conviction, regardless of jurisdictional boundaries. The offense level for the drug trafficking offense charged in Arizona, for example, would be determined on the basis of all of the criminal behavior involved in all three jurisdictions if they were found to be part of the same course of conduct or common scheme or plan. An incremental penalty is provided through determining the offense level by aggregating all the drugs distributed. If federal prosecutors charge this defendant with drug trafficking in New Mexico and Colorado, the offense level again is determined on the basis of all of the drugs distributed. However, §5G1.3(b) would ensure that concurrent sentences are imposed in New Mexico and Colorado. Without this guideline, the defendant could be subject to the imposition of consecutive sentences, doubling or tripling the punishment imposed.

Application Note 3 recognizes that the application of §5G1.3 is sometimes difficult and notes that the suggested methodology (reliance on the same rules used for sentencing on multiple counts) is not intended to complicate unduly or prolong the sentencing process. For this reason the Commission has designated subsection (c) as a policy statement, not a guideline, thereby providing the sentencing court with more latitude in determining whether a concurrent or consecutive sentence would best achieve a reasonable incremental punishment. As a policy statement, §5G1.3(c) achieves the congressional and Commission goal of a reasonable incremental punishment without binding the court to a practice that may be of limited value in some cases.

✓122. **QUESTION:** The defendant was serving a term of supervised release when she committed the instant federal offense. The term of supervision was subsequently revoked and the defendant imprisoned prior to sentencing on the instant offense. Do the provisions of §5G1.3 (Imposition of a Sentence on a Defendant Subject to an Undischarged Term of Imprisonment) apply when the defendant is sentenced on the instant offense?

ANSWER: *Yes. As of November 1, 1993, Application Note 4 to §5G1.3 specifies that if the defendant was on federal or state probation, parole, or supervised release at the time of the instant offense and has had such term of supervision revoked prior to sentencing on the instant offense, the sentence for the instant offense should be imposed to run consecutive to the term imposed for the revocation. Such a consecutive sentence would provide incremental punishment within the meaning of §5G1.3 for the violation of probation, parole, or supervised release in accord with the policy expressed in §§7B1.3 (Revocation of Probation or Supervised Release) and 7B1.4 (Term of Imprisonment).*

✓123. **QUESTION:** The defendant has been recently paroled on a state offense. He is scheduled for sentencing on the instant federal offense, which occurred prior to the period of imprisonment on the state offense. Will the provisions of §5G1.3 (Imposition of a Sentence on a Defendant Subject to an Undischarged Term of Imprisonment) apply when the defendant is sentenced on the instant offense?

ANSWER: *No. A defendant who is not serving a term of imprisonment is not subject to the provisions of §5G1.3, which only apply to a defendant serving an undischarged term of imprisonment at the time of sentencing on the instant federal offense.*

✓124. **QUESTION:** Subsection (b) of §5G1.3 (Imposition of a Sentence on a Defendant Subject to an Undischarged Term of Imprisonment) provides instruction for imposing a sentence in cases in which an undischarged term of imprisonment resulted from offense(s) that have been fully taken into account in determining the offense level for the instant offense. Is it a departure if the court adjusts the guideline sentence for the instant offense to reflect any period of imprisonment already served on the undischarged term?

ANSWER: *No. The purpose of subsection (b) is to allow the court to achieve the appropriate total punishment for the instant offense and the offense(s) for which the defendant is serving an undischarged term without punishing the defendant twice for the same conduct. Therefore, the court must adjust the total punishment chosen from the applicable guideline range to reflect any term of imprisonment already served as a result of conduct taken into account in determining the sentence for the instant offense (see Application Note 2 to §5G1.3). Further, the guideline sentence must be imposed to run concurrently to the undischarged term of imprisonment. If such an adjustment results in a sentence outside of the applicable guideline range, this is not considered a departure.*

For example, at the time of sentencing for the instant offense the defendant has served six months of a nine-month state sentence for conduct that has been taken into account in determining the guideline range for the instant federal offense. The court determines that, from a guideline range of 10-16 months, 13 months is the appropriate total punishment for all of the conduct represented in the applicable guideline range. The court should adjust the total punishment to account for the six months served on the undischarged term and impose a sentence of seven months to run concurrently to the remainder of the state term. Application Note 2 instructs that, for clarity, the court should note on the Judgment in a Criminal Case Order that the sentence imposed is not a departure from the guidelines because the defendant has been credited for guideline purposes under §5G1.3(b) with six months served in state custody.

✓125. **QUESTION**: The court is imposing a sentence pursuant to the policy statement at subsection (c) of §5G1.3 (Imposition of a Sentence on a Defendant Subject to an Undischarged Term of Imprisonment). The presentence report contains two guideline ranges: 1) the guideline range for the instant offense that was calculated prior to consideration of §5G1.3; and 2) the total punishment guideline range calculated according to the instruction in Application Note 3 of §5G1.3. Should the court impose sentence within the instant offense range or the total punishment range?

ANSWER: *The guideline range for the instant offense is to be used for imposing sentence. The sole purpose of calculating the total punishment range (as outlined in Application Note 3) is to provide the court guidance in determining how to fashion a sentence for the instant offense that will provide a reasonable incremental punishment for both the instant offense and the offense for which the defendant is serving an unexpired term of imprisonment.*

Application Note 3 states that, to the extent practicable, the court should consider a reasonable incremental punishment to be a sentence for the instant offense that results in a combined sentence of imprisonment that approximates the total punishment that would have been imposed under §5G1.2 (Sentencing on Multiple Counts of Conviction) had all of the offenses been federal offenses for which sentence was being imposed at the same time. Therefore, the court would calculate a "hypothetical" guideline range and determine the point within that range that would have been appropriate as the total punishment. As outlined in Application Note 3, this methodology is meant to assist the court in determining: 1) the appropriate point within the guideline range for the instant offense; 2) whether to order the sentence to run concurrently or consecutively to the undischarged term of imprisonment; or 3) whether a departure is warranted. The application note stresses that this methodology is not meant to be applied in a manner that unduly complicates or prolongs the sentencing process. Calculation of a "hypothetical" range will often be imprecise and require an approximation, particularly when the undischarged term is for a state offense.

126. **QUESTION:** What is the standard of evidence used by the court to settle disputed factors as outlined in §6A1.3, Resolution of Disputed Factors?

ANSWER: *Prior to implementation of the guidelines, the U.S. Supreme Court held in McMillan v. Pennsylvania that a preponderance of the evidence standard satisfied constitutional due process requirements at sentencing. The decided trend among courts of appeals decisions is that this standard is also adequate for guideline application purposes (see, e.g., United States v. Wright, 873 F.2d 437 (1st Cir. 1989); United States v. Guerra, 888 F.2d 247 (2nd Cir. 1989), cert. denied, 494 U.S. 1090 (1991); United States v. McDowell, 888 F.2d 285 (3d Cir. 1989); United States v. Urrego-Linares, 879 F.2d 1234 (4th Cir. 1989), cert. denied, 493 U.S. 943 (1989); United States v. Casto, 889 F.2d 562 (5th Cir. 1989), cert. denied, 493 U.S. 1092 (1990); United States v. Barrett, 890 F.2d 855 (6th Cir.*

1989); United States v. White, 888 F.2d 490 (7th Cir. 1989); United States v. Gooden, 892 F.2d 725 (8th Cir. 1989), cert. denied, 496 U.S. 908 (1990); United States v. Kirk, 894 F.2d 1162 (10th Cir. 1990); United States v. Alston, 895 F.2d 1362 (11th Cir. 1990); United States v. Chandler, 894 F.2d 463 (D.C. Cir. 1990); United States v. Restrepo, 946 F.2d 654 (9th Cir. 1991), cert. denied, 112 S. Ct. 1564 (1992). But see United States v. Kikumura, 918 F.2d 1084 (3d Cir. 1990) (clear and convincing standard necessary to support upward departure of great magnitude)).

Effective November 1, 1991, the Commentary to the policy statement at §6A1.3 (Resolution of Disputed Factors) clarifies that the Commission believes that use of a preponderance of the evidence standard is appropriate to meet due process requirements and policy concerns in resolving disputes regarding application of the guidelines to the facts of a case.

127. **QUESTION:** Does the government have the burden of persuasion in resolving guideline application disputes when the guideline adjustment would enhance (aggravate) the sentence? Likewise, does the burden of persuasion rest with the defendant if the adjustment would reduce (mitigate) the sentence?

ANSWER: *Generally, yes. The Commission notes court decisions holding that the burden of persuasion in resolving guideline application disputes rests with the government if the guideline adjustment would enhance the sentence and with the defendant if the adjustment would reduce the sentence (see, e.g., United States v. Rodriguez, 975 F.2d 999 (3d Cir.), reh'g denied, 1992 US App LEXIS 29972 (3d Cir., Nov. 3, 1992); United States v. Pierson, 946 F.2d 1044 (4th Cir. 1991); United States v. Bailey, 961 F.2d 180 (11th Cir. 1992); United States v. Morrison, 983 F.2d 730 (6th Cir. 1993)). However, this does not prevent the sentencing judge from taking an independent position that would result in a sentence adjustment (enhancement or reduction) that was not argued by either party.*

128. **QUESTION:** In supervised release revocation cases, is the court bound by the original guideline range for the offense being revoked?

ANSWER: *No. Upon revocation of supervised release under 18 U.S.C. § 3583(e), a court is required by virtue of the cross reference to 18 U.S.C. § 3553(a)(4) and (5) to consider any applicable sentencing guidelines and policy statements. The Commission has not yet issued revocation guidelines, but has promulgated policy statements effective November 1, 1990, that are specifically intended to guide courts in supervised release revocation decisions. The issuance of policy statements, which have their own sentencing ranges, should make clear that the Commission does not intend that courts impose a revocation sanction in accord with the guidelines applicable to initial sentencing decisions. Moreover, when revoking supervised release, the appellate courts have held that the statute does not require that courts observe the guideline range for the initial sentence (see United States v. Bermudez, 974 F.2d 12 (2nd Cir. 1992); United States v. Dillard, 910 F.2d 461 (7th Cir. 1990); United States v. Smeathers, 930 F.2d 18 (8th Cir. 1991); United States v. Scroggins, 910 F.2d 768 (11th Cir. 1990)).*

129. **QUESTION:** Upon revocation of probation or supervised release, how does the court impose sentence?

ANSWER: *Effective November 1, 1990, the Commission promulgated a new Chapter Seven of the Guidelines Manual containing detailed Policy Statements for violations and revocation of probation and supervised release. According to 18 U.S.C. § 3553(a)(5), the court is required to consider any applicable policy statements issued by the Commission when imposing sentence.*

130. QUESTION: Is the grade of probation or supervised release violation in Chapter Seven determined by the criminal charges, the count(s) of conviction, or the actual conduct of the defendant?

ANSWER: *Application Note 1 to policy statement §7B1.1 (Classification of Violations) explains that the grade of violation does not depend upon the criminal charges or counts of conviction, but rather is to be based upon the defendant's actual conduct. It should be noted that the evidentiary standard applicable to revocation determinations is a preponderance of the evidence.*

131. QUESTION: What options are available to the court upon a finding of a Grade A violation of probation or supervised release?

ANSWER: *According to subsection (a)(1) of the policy statement at §7B1.3 (Revocation of Probation or Supervised Release), the court shall revoke probation or supervised release upon finding a Grade A or B violation. Absent a "departure," the court must sentence the defendant to a term of imprisonment according to the Revocation Table at §7B1.4. Alternatives to imprisonment upon revocation are only available for defendants found to have committed Grade B or C violations (see §7B1.3(c)).*

132. QUESTION: The defendant's probation was revoked and a term of imprisonment is to be imposed. Does time in official detention affect the length of imprisonment term called for under the Chapter Seven policy statements (Probation and Supervised Release Violations)?

ANSWER: *It may. The policy statement at §7B1.3(e) instructs that where the court revokes probation or supervised release and imposes a term of imprisonment, it shall increase the term of imprisonment determined under subsections (b), (c), and (d) by the amount of time in official detention that will be credited toward service of the term of imprisonment under 18 U.S.C. § 3585(b), other than time in official detention resulting from the federal probation or supervised release violation warrant or proceeding.*

In a case in which the defendant has spent time in detention that might call for an adjustment under §7B1.3(e), the Bureau of Prisons should be consulted to verify the amount of time, if any, that will be credited to the defendant. According to the Bureau, there are two instances currently in which credit will be granted for time in official detention other than time in official detention resulting from the federal probation or supervised release violation warrant or proceeding: 1) where the defendant served time in pretrial detention before receiving the original term of probation; and 2) where the defendant, while serving a term of probation or supervised release, was arrested and held for new criminal behavior, but was released without the charges being pursued.

To apply the policy statement at §7B1.3(e), the court should choose a sentence within the applicable range from the revocation table at §7B1.4 (Term of Imprisonment), and add to it the amount of time that will be credited to the defendant by the Bureau of Prisons.

133. QUESTION: Application Note 5 to policy statement §7B1.4 (Term of Imprisonment) instructs that under 18 U.S.C. § 3565(a) the court is required "to revoke the sentence of probation and sentence the defendant to not less than one-third of the original sentence" upon a finding that a defendant violated a condition of probation by being in possession of a controlled substance. Does "original sentence" refer to the original term of probation?

ANSWER: *No. According to U.S. v. Granderson, 114 S.Ct. 1259 (1994), the term "original sentence" refers to the applicable guideline sentence of imprisonment, not the revoked term of probation.*

Therefore, upon a finding by the court that a defendant violated a condition of probation by being in possession of a controlled substance, the court is required to impose a minimum sentence of one-third of the maximum of the original guideline range. For example, where the original guideline range was 6-12 months, one-third of the maximum of the original range would be 4 months imprisonment.

134. **QUESTION:** The defendant's one-year term of supervised release is being revoked, and the applicable range of imprisonment from the policy statement at §7B1.4 (Term of Imprisonment) is 8-14 months. What is the maximum amount of imprisonment that the defendant can receive upon revocation?

ANSWER: *According to 18 U.S.C. § 3583(e)(3), upon revocation of supervised release the court can require the person to serve in prison all or part of the term of supervised release with specified maximums or "caps" for Class B, C, and D felonies. Thus, under the statute, either the term of supervised release (as initially imposed or as later modified and extended) or the "cap" for the felony classification of the initial offense sets the maximum statutory period of imprisonment that a defendant can be ordered to serve upon revocation. The court should then consider the Commission's policy statements. According to Policy Statement 7B1.4(b)(3)(A), the court may impose any penalty within the applicable range upon revocation, provided that the penalty is not greater than the maximum term of imprisonment authorized by statute. Because the defendant's original term of supervised release was one year, the maximum statutory penalty upon revocation is one year of imprisonment and, therefore, the court may not impose more than 12 months imprisonment upon revocation.*

135. **QUESTION:** Do the provisions of Chapter Eight (Sentencing of Organizations) apply to all felony and Class A misdemeanor offenses committed by organizations?

ANSWER: *Yes (see §8A1.1 (Applicability of Chapter Eight)). Although certain offenses are presently exempt from application of Chapter Eight's fine range calculations (§§8C2.2 through 8C2.9), the remainder of Chapter Eight is applicable to all offenses. Offenses for which calculation of a guideline fine range is required are listed in subsection (a) of §8C2.1 (Applicability of Fine Guidelines).*

136. **QUESTION**: The Introductory Commentary to Chapter Eight, Part B (Remedying the Harm from Criminal Conduct) states that "[a]s a general principle, the court should require that the organization take all appropriate steps to provide compensation to victims...." Assuming that victims have been harmed economically by the offense, when could a court appropriately determine not to order restitution?

ANSWER: *Restitution is generally mandatory under §8B1.1. Subsection (a) of this guideline expressly states that the court "shall" order restitution. Subsection (b) states two narrow exceptions to this general rule. Under subsection (b), the court need not order restitution if the organization has already made full restitution. Additionally, restitution is not required if "the complication and prolongation of the sentencing process resulting from the fashioning of a restitution requirement outweighs the need to provide restitution to any victims through the criminal process." This language closely tracks a provision found at 18 U.S.C. § 3663(d). Under this exception, a court might conclude, for example, that in sentencing an antitrust defendant the complication and prolongation of the sentencing process would outweigh the need to compensate victims "through the criminal process" because a civil antitrust action has been filed that can be expected to compensate victims.*

137. **QUESTION:** An organizational defendant is convicted of an offense for which calculation of a guideline fine range under §8C2.1 is applicable. If it is clear that the defendant organization will not be able to pay a fine, must a guideline fine range be calculated?

ANSWER: *No, although the remainder of Chapter Eight remains applicable. Commission research indicates that historically many organizational defendants have been unable to pay a fine. To avoid requiring courts to make unnecessary calculations, §8C2.2 authorizes courts to bypass full guideline fine range calculations under either of two circumstances. First, subsection (a) states that no guideline fine determination is required "[w]here it is readily ascertainable the organization cannot and is not likely to become able (even on an installment schedule) to pay restitution." The policy of allowing courts to avoid making fine calculations when it is readily ascertainable that restitution will not be paid reflects the guidelines' policy of putting the payment of restitution to victims first. In other words, under the guidelines, if an organization cannot pay restitution, no fine calculation is necessary because restitution must be paid before any of the organization's funds are directed toward payment of the fine (see §8C3.3(a)). Thus, in cases in which restitution cannot be paid, no fine calculation is required.*

Subsection (b) provides that "[w]here it is readily ascertainable through a preliminary determination of the minimum of the guideline fine range" that the organization cannot and likely will not be able to pay the minimum guideline fine, a further determination of the guideline fine range is unnecessary. In this circumstance, the court is directed to use a preliminary determination of the minimum fine as a starting point and then consider a reduction in the fine, as appropriate, under §8C3.3.

In making a preliminary minimum fine determination, the court is directed to consider the provisions of §§8C2.3 through 8C2.7. In addition, for this preliminary determination, the court should resolve all reasonable factual inferences in favor of the defendant organization. The reason for giving the defendant organization the benefit of all reasonable factual inferences is to ensure that the preliminary minimum fine determination will identify the lowest reasonably possible applicable guideline fine. If, after giving all reasonable factual inferences to the defendant organization, it is apparent the organization will not be able to pay the minimum fine, the requirements of §8C2.2(b) are clearly met and no further fine range calculation is necessary. Application Notes 1 and 2 to §8C2.2 recommend language a court may wish to consider to note on the record its conclusion that a full guideline fine range determination was not necessary.

138. **QUESTION:** How are fines determined under the organizational guidelines?

ANSWER: *In most cases, fines are based on two distinct analyses. The first analysis yields a "base fine" that is a measure of the seriousness of the offense involved (see §8C2.4 (Base Fine)). The second analysis yields a "culpability score" that is a measure of how culpable the organization was in committing and responding to the occurrence of the offense (see §8C2.5 (Culpability Score)). Together, these two determinations yield a "guideline fine range" from which the court has discretion to select the precise fine amount to be imposed (see §§8C2.6 - 8C2.8).*

If an organization has no lawful purpose (e.g., a front for a scheme to commit fraud or sell drugs), the guidelines require that the fine be set sufficiently high to divest the organization of its assets (see §8C1.1 (Determining the Fine — Criminal Purpose Organizations)).

139. **QUESTION:** How does the base fine reflect the seriousness of the offense?

ANSWER: *Under the guidelines, the base fine for an offense will generally be the highest of three measures of offense seriousness: the loss caused by the offense, the gain to the organization from the* *offense, or an amount from a table corresponding to the applicable "offense level" (a generic offense seriousness measure already used in the individual guidelines) (see §8C2.4).*

For a few offenses, the guidelines employ a "special instruction" to measure offense seriousness and therefore determine the base fine (see §8C2.4(b)). For example, in money laundering cases, the base fine is tied to the amount of money laundered (see §2S1.1(c)). In antitrust cases, the base fine is 20 percent of the volume of affected commerce (see §2R1.1(d)).

140. **QUESTION:** Do the organizational guidelines ever permit monetary sanctions that would be less than the organization's profit from the offense?

ANSWER: *No. Even when the culpability score determined under §8C2.5 dictates that a fine be relatively low due to an organization's efforts to prevent an offense and bring it to the attention of authorities, §8C2.9 (Disgorgement) mandates that the total sanction will always be greater than the gain from the offense. This is to ensure that under no circumstances will an organization profit from crime.*

141. **QUESTION:** Under what circumstances would the guidelines call for an organization to be placed on probation?

ANSWER: *There are two general mandatory bases for organizational probation under the guidelines: 1) when it is needed to ensure that another sanction will be fully implemented (see §8D1.1(a)(1),(2)); and 2) to ensure that steps will be taken within the organization to reduce the likelihood of future criminal conduct (see §8D1.1(a)(3)-(6)).*

For example, probation would be ordered to ensure that a fine an organization was unable to pay at sentencing will be paid on an installment basis. Additionally, probation would be ordered if the defendant (other than a small organization) lacked an effective program to prevent and detect violations of law.

142. **QUESTION:** What is the definition of a petty offense?

ANSWER: *Section 7089 of the Anti-Drug Abuse Act of 1988 (codified at 18 U.S.C. § 19) revised the definition of petty offense so that it no longer exactly corresponds with Class B or C misdemeanors or infractions. Under the revised definition, a Class B or C misdemeanor or infraction that does not provide for a fine in excess of $5,000 for an individual and $10,000 for a corporation is considered a petty offense (see Appendix C, Amendment 81).*

143. **QUESTION:** When must a judge state a reason for a sentence within the guideline range?

ANSWER: *In every case. Title 18 U.S.C. § 3553(c)(1), as amended by section 17 of the Sentencing Act of 1987, states: "The court, at the time of sentencing, shall state in open court the reasons for its imposition of the particular sentence, and, if the sentence is of the kind, and within the range, described in subsection (a)(4), and that range exceeds 24 months, the reason for imposing a sentence at a particular point within the range..." (emphasis added).*

Thus, it appears that (1) the court must always state its reasons for imposing the particular sentence, and (2) if the range exceeds 24 months, the court must also state a reason for imposing the sentence at a particular point in the range.

144. **QUESTION:** Can the court depart downward and impose probation on a defendant convicted of a Class A or B felony?

ANSWER: *Possibly. Under 18 U.S.C. § 3561, a defendant may not be sentenced to a term of probation if convicted of a Class A or B felony. Subsequent to the enactment of that provision in the Sentencing Reform Act of 1984, the Anti-Drug Abuse Act of 1986 added a provision codified as 18 U.S.C. § 3553(e), an amendment to Rule 35(b) of the Rules of Criminal Procedure, and a provision codified as 28 U.S.C. § 994(n). These provisions were intended to permit a defendant to have his sentence reduced upon motion of the government – even below the level of an applicable statutory minimum – to reflect a defendant's substantial assistance in the investigation or prosecution of another offender. The legislative history is not clear as to whether Congress intended the prohibition on probation for Class A or B felonies to be treated in the same manner as a mandatory minimum term of imprisonment.*

Even if 18 U.S.C. § 3553(e) is interpreted by a court to permit "override" of 18 U.S.C. § 3561, there is a further question as to the authority to grant probation for some drug offenses for which the statutory language specifically prohibits a court from sentencing a defendant to probation. However, at least one court of appeals has determined that the probation prohibition in 18 U.S.C. § 3561 is akin to a mandatory minimum and no longer constrains the court once the government makes a substantial assistance motion (see United States v. Daiagi, 892 F.2d 31 (4th Cir. 1989)). Specifically, 21 U.S.C. § 841(b) prohibits the imposition of probation "notwithstanding any other provision of law," a phrase that has been interpreted by another court of appeals to require an imprisonment sentence for offenses under that statute even if the government makes a substantial assistance motion (see United States v. Thomas, 930 F.2d 526 (7th Cir. 1991), cert. denied, 112 S. Ct. 171 (1991)).

145. **QUESTION:** The court is required to revoke supervision and impose a mandatory period of imprisonment upon finding that a defendant violated a condition of supervision by being in possession of a controlled substance (see 18 U.S.C. §§ 3565(a) and 3583(g)). Does evidence of drug usage established solely by laboratory analysis constitute "possession of a controlled substance" as set forth in 18 U.S.C. §§ 3565(a) and 3583(g)?

ANSWER: *It may. As stated in Application Note 5 to §7B1.4 (Term of Imprisonment), the court must make this determination. The Third Circuit has held that a positive drug test constitutes circumstantial evidence of possession of a controlled substance and may therefore be used to support a finding of a supervision violation under 18 U.S.C. § 3583(g). (see United States v. Dow, 990 F.2d 22 (1st Cir. 1993); United States v. Blackston, 940 F.2d 877 (3d Cir. 1991), cert. denied, 112 S. Ct. 611 (1991); United States v. Battle, 993 F.2d 49 (4th Cir. 1993); United States v. Smith, 978 F.2d 181 (5th Cir. 1992)). The same analysis would appear to apply to probation violations under 18 U.S.C. § 3565(a) (see United States v. Gordon, 961 F.2d 426 (3d Cir. 1992)).*

146. **QUESTION:** Can the court impose the maximum statutory sentence for an offense and also impose a term of supervised release?

ANSWER: *Yes. When Congress abolished parole and created supervised release (18 U.S.C. § 3583), a term of supervised release was intended as separate from, and in addition to, the statutory maximum penalty for the offense. It is possible, therefore, for a defendant to be sentenced to the statutory maximum term of imprisonment for the offense and after release be subject to further imprisonment if supervised release is revoked. Supervised release is analogous to former provisions for a "special parole term" following imprisonment for a drug trafficking offense.*

147. QUESTION: Under the Sentencing Reform Act, how much "good time" can an inmate receive toward service of sentence?

ANSWER: *No good time credit is available for a prisoner serving a sentence of one year or less, or a life sentence. An inmate serving a sentence of at least one year and one day to any determinate number of years is eligible for 54 days of good time credit each year, beginning after service of the first year of the term (18 U.S.C. § 3624(b)).*

148. QUESTION: If an indictment includes separate counts under pre-guideline law and post-guideline law, how should the defendant be sentenced?

ANSWER: *The Sentencing Reform Act of 1987, passed on December 7, 1987, (Public Law 100-182), included a provision that the guidelines apply to offenses occurring on or after November 1, 1987. The pre-guideline counts would therefore be sentenced under pre-guideline provisions and counts that pertain to offenses occurring on or after November 1, 1987, would be sentenced under the guidelines.*

Relevant conduct for offenses subject to the guidelines is to be determined without regard to the November 1 implementation date. If the relevant conduct for an offense committed on or after November 1, 1987, overlaps with conduct sanctioned as part of a pre-November 1 count, there would be a potential for double counting unless the pre-guideline counts were sentenced concurrently. The court will have to fashion the sentence carefully with these concerns in mind.

149. QUESTION: Do the guidelines apply to conspiracies that began prior to November 1, 1987, and continued past that date?

ANSWER: *The Sentencing Commission's legal staff agrees with the opinion of the Department of Justice and an opinion by legal counsel for the Administrative Office of the U.S. Courts that a defendant convicted of a continuing offense, such as a conspiracy, that began prior to November 1, 1987, but concluded after that date should be sentenced under the guidelines. It is the consensus of these opinions that such an application does not violate the ex post facto clause of the Constitution (see Prosecutors Handbook on Sentencing Guidelines, pg. 72; see also, "Looking at the Law," Federal Probation, (December 1987) addressing this issue).*

150. QUESTION: The Commission has amended the Guidelines Manual yearly since November 1, 1987, in some cases increasing offense levels for guidelines applicable to certain defendants after they have committed an offense but prior to sentencing. Should courts use the guidelines in effect at the time of sentencing or those in effect when the offense was completed?

ANSWER: *In general, the Guidelines Manual in effect at the time of sentencing is to be used, as directed by the Sentencing Reform Act of 1984 (see 18 U.S.C. § 3553(a)(4) and (5) and S. Rep. No.*

225, 98th Cong., 1st Sess. 77-78 (1983)). This directive may be constrained by the limits of the ex post facto clause, however. The Supreme Court ruled in Miller v. Florida, 482 U.S. 423 (1987) that the ex post facto clause precluded the application of a Florida sentencing guideline amendment that was enacted after the date of the defendant's offense and increased the range of imprisonment for the type of offense he committed. A number of courts have held that Miller similarly prevents a federal judge from using a Guidelines Manual that was amended after the defendant completed his offense if the amended guidelines would result in a higher sentencing range (see United States v. Lam Kwong-Wah, 924 F.2d 298 (D.C. Cir. 1991), cert. denied, 113 S. Ct. 287 (1992); United States v. McAllister, 927 F.2d 136 (3d Cir. 1991), cert. denied, 112 S. Ct. 111 (1991); United States v. Morrow, 925 F.2d 779 (4th Cir. 1991); United States v. Gullickson, 981 F.2d 344 (8th Cir. 1992);United States v. Smith, 930 F.2d 1450 (10th Cir. 1991), cert. denied, 112 S. Ct. 225 (1991)); (but see United States v. Bader, 956 F.2d 708 (7th Cir. 1992) (holding that ex post facto concerns not implicated by a guideline amendment resulting in a higher guideline sentencing range because affect the maximum punishment that could have been imposed under the statute of conviction).

If the Guidelines Manual has been amended since a defendant's offense, courts have held that the ex post facto clause appears to preclude use of the version of the Manual in effect at the time of sentencing if the sentencing range dictated by that version is higher than the pre-amendment sentencing range. A sentencing range may not be calculated by mixing provisions from different editions of the Guidelines Manual because each edition of the Manual is meant to operate as a cohesive document containing interrelated provisions that produce a single sentencing range for a particular defendant (see United States v. Stephenson, 921 F.2d 438 (2d Cir. 1990)) and because the proper test for an ex post facto clause violation is whether the overall punishment for an offense was increased after the fact (see Dobbert v. Florida, 432 U.S. 282, 294 (1977) (comparing the two statutes in toto to determine whether the new one is more onerous)). If amendments are neutral or clarifying in nature, or if the interaction of all applicable guideline amendments does not raise the bottom of the guideline range, a Miller problem does not arise, even if a single amendment might be more harsh than its predecessor.

For example, suppose a defendant commits an offense before the most recent amendments go into effect. Furthermore, suppose that the amendments lower the base offense level in Chapter Two, eliminate a specific offense characteristic that would have mitigated the offense level, broaden the reach of the victim adjustment in Chapter Three, and lower the criminal history points in Chapter Four. The court should make two guidelines calculations – one using all of the guidelines in effect at the time of the offense and another using all of the guidelines in effect at the time of sentencing. The lower of the two ranges would apply, and the guidelines should be interpreted with the aid of any clarifying amendments in effect at the time of sentencing. (Several appellate courts have approved the application at sentencing of clarifying amendments that were not in effect at the time of the offense (see, e.g., United States v. Thompson, 944 F.2d 1331 (7th Cir. 1991), cert. denied, 112 S. Ct. 1177 (1992); United States v. Deigert, 916 F.2d 916 (4th Cir. 1990); United States v. Aguilera-Zapata, 901 F.2d 1209 (5th Cir. 1990); United States v. Nissen, 928 F.2d 690 (5th Cir. 1991)).

✓151. **QUESTION:** What role can the historical note at the end of each guideline section play in the court's ex post facto analysis?

ANSWER: *The historical note provides the following information: (1) the effective date the guideline section; (2) the dates of any amendments; and (3) the amendment history of the guideline. If the guideline has been amended, the corresponding amendment number allows the reader to use Appendix C to determine the date of and specific nature of the amendment. This is useful in making comparisons for the purposes of ex post facto analysis.*

152. **QUESTION:** Suppose a defendant is convicted of two offenses, one completed after the most recent version of the Guidelines Manual went into effect, and the other completed before that effective date. If the guidelines for the pre-amendment offense are now more harsh than they were when that offense was committed, which version(s) of the guidelines should the court apply?

ANSWER: *The court should apply only one version of the guidelines in any particular case. In the scenario outlined above, the court should apply the version in effect at the time of sentencing because that version was in effect before the defendant completed his last offense of conviction. As noted in the answer to question 142, the Guidelines Manual in effect at the time of sentencing is to be used unless doing so would violate the ex post facto clause of the U.S. Constitution. If the defendant completes the second offense after the guidelines have been amended, clearly there is no constitutional impediment to determining his sentence for that count based on the new guidelines. Moreover, under the guideline sentencing system, a single sentencing range is determined based on the defendant's overall conduct, even if there are multiple counts of conviction (see §§3D1.1 – 3D1.5, 5G1.2). Thus, the guideline range applicable in sentencing the defendant for the second offense necessarily will encompass relevant conduct for both counts.*

If, for example, a defendant pleads guilty to a single count of embezzlement that occurred after the effective date of amendments to the Guidelines Manual, the relevant conduct and, ultimately, the guideline range applicable at sentencing will encompass any relevant conduct (e.g., related embezzlement offenses) that may have occurred prior to the effective date of the guideline amendments for the offense of conviction. The same would be true for a defendant convicted of two counts of embezzlement, one committed before the amendments were enacted, and the second after. In this scenario, it would not follow that the ex post facto clause somehow bars application of the amended guideline to the first conviction and that the defendant was thereby subject to a lower guideline range than if he had been convicted only of the second offense.

Decisions from several appellate courts addressing the analogous situation of the constitutionality of counting pre-guidelines criminal activity as relevant conduct for a guidelines sentence support this approach (see United States v. Ykema, 887 F.2d 697 (6th Cir. 1989), cert. denied, 493 U.S. 1062 (1990) (upholding inclusion of pre-November 1, 1987, drug quantities as relevant conduct for the count of conviction, noting that habitual offender statutes routinely augment punishment for an offense of conviction based on acts committed before a law is passed); United States v. Allen, 886 F.2d 143 (8th Cir.1989); United States v. Cusack, 901 F.2d 29 (4th Cir. 1990); United States v. Moscony, 927 F.2d 742 (3d Cir. 1991)).

Furthermore, this approach should be followed regardless of whether the offenses of conviction are the type in which the conduct is aggregated under §3D1.2(d). The ex post facto clause does not distinguish between aggregable and non-aggregable offenses, and unless that clause would be violated, Congress' directive to apply the sentencing guidelines in effect at the time of sentencing must be followed. Thus, if a defendant was sentenced in January 1992 for two bank robberies committed in October 1988 and one committed on November 1, 1991, the November 1991 Guidelines Manual should be used to determine a combined guideline range for all three counts (see generally United States v. Stephenson, 921 F.2d 438 (2d Cir. 1990) (holding that the Sentencing Commission and Congress intended that the applicable version of the guidelines be applied as a "cohesive and integrated whole" rather than in a piecemeal fashion). Accord, United States v. Gordon, 997 F.2d 263 (7th Cir. 1993); United States v. Warren, 980 F.2d 1300 (9th Cir. 1992). In summary, even in a complex case involving multiple counts that occurred under several different versions of the Guidelines Manual, it should not be necessary to use more than two Manuals to determine the applicable guideline range – the Manual in effect at the time the last offense was completed and the one in effect at sentencing (if different from the former). See Question 142.

153. QUESTION: A broadly written conspiracy count that began before November 1, 1987, and continued after that date cites the defendant for committing only pre-guideline overt acts. Must the defendant be sentenced under the guidelines?

ANSWER: *Not necessarily. It is settled law that a crime that continues past the effective date of a new statute comes under the new statute. Applying that principle, the appellate courts appear to be uniformly holding that a conspiracy that continues beyond November 1, 1987, is subject to the Sentencing Reform Act and the guidelines. A more difficult question is presented in the case of a defendant who, while convicted of participation in such a conspiracy, cannot be shown to have committed any post-November 1, 1987, overt acts or otherwise to have actively participated in the conspiracy on or after that date. The general legal principle appears to be that a defendant must show that he effectively withdrew from or renounced involvement in the conspiracy to avoid legal accountability. Under that principle, a defendant convicted of a conspiracy that spans the November 1, 1987, guideline effective date would be sentenced under the guidelines unless the defendant withdrew or renounced the conspiracy before November 1, 1987.*

154. QUESTION: The Commission promulgated Chapter Eight of the Guidelines Manual in 1991 to govern the sentencing of organizational defendants. When should courts begin applying Chapter Eight to organizational defendants?

ANSWER: *In its transmittal letter to Congress, the Commission specified that the new organizational guidelines would have an effective date of November 1, 1991. In addition, 18 U.S.C. § 3553(a)(4) states that courts are to apply guidelines "that are in effect on the date the defendant is sentenced." These two facts provide an initial indication that organizations sentenced on or after November 1, 1991, should be sentenced pursuant to Chapter Eight of the guidelines, as applicable.*

However, legal considerations may dictate that Chapter Eight will be applied only to offenses that occurred on or after November 1, 1991. As explained in more detail in the answer to question 142, courts have held that the ex post facto clause precludes application of a guideline amendment that became effective after the defendant's offense if the amended version of the guidelines would result in a higher sentence than the pre-amendment version of the guidelines. This issue potentially could be raised with respect to some antitrust offenses committed by organizations because the Guidelines Manual already contained guidelines applicable to antitrust offenses committed by organizations when Chapter Eight was adopted, and the new guidelines may call for higher fines (see §2R1.1(c), 1990 Guidelines Manual).

Moreover, the Department of Justice has stated that application of Chapter Eight to all organizational offenses, regardless of whether these offenses were previously addressed in the Guidelines Manual, would raise ex post facto concerns. While the courts have not addressed the broader issue of whether ex post facto problems arise when guidelines are made applicable to offenses not previously covered by the guidelines, the Department of Justice has stated that it will seek to have Chapter Eight of the guidelines applied only to offenses occurring on or after November 1, 1991. The Department has further indicated that it will follow this policy irrespective of whether application of Chapter Eight would be advantageous or disadvantageous to the defendant organization. Moreover, whether the guidelines would be disadvantageous to a defendant in some respect may be difficult or impossible to determine in almost every case. Thus, legal considerations may lead to Chapter Eight's application only on a prospective basis (i.e., only to offenses occurring on or after November 1, 1991). To the extent a court concludes that ex post facto considerations bar application of Chapter Eight in a particular case, the court may, in its discretion, consider the provisions of Chapter Eight on an advisory basis for appropriate policy guidance.

✓155. **QUESTION:** Do the mandatory minimum penalties found in the drug trafficking statutes require that the amount of drugs be cited in the charging indictment?

ANSWER: *No. The circuit courts that have addressed this issue have held uniformly that drug quantity for determining a mandatory minimum sentence is not an element of the offense. Rather, the amount is a sentencing factor to be determined by the court. In other words, at sentencing the court is not bound by an indictment that lists a specific amount of drugs (see United States v. McNeese, 901 F.2d 585 (7th Cir. 1990) (quantity of the controlled substance is not an essential element of crimes proscribed under 841(a)(1) and 846); United States v. Uwaeme, 975 F.2d 1016 (4th Cir. 1992); United States v. Underwood, 982 F.2d 426 (10th Cir. 1992); United States v. McCann, 940 F.2d 1352 (10th Cir. 1991); United States v. Gibbs, 813 F.2d 596 (3d Cir. 1989); United States v. Cross, 916 F.2d 622 (11th Cir. 1990); United States v. Campuzano, 905 F.2d 677 (2d Cir. 1990); United States v. Sotelo-Rivera, 931 F.2d 1317 (9th Cir. 1991); United States v. Wood, 834 F.2d 1382 (8th Cir. 1987)).*

Similarly, a growing body of case law also holds that mandatory minimum and maximum penalties are not necessarily the same for all defendants in a drug conspiracy. This case law has endorsed the use of relevant conduct principles to compute not only the guideline range for defendants convicted of a drug conspiracy offense, but also the appropriate mandatory minimum penalty for each defendant under 21 U.S.C. § 841(b) (see United States v. Martinez, 987 F.2d 920 (2nd Cir. 1993); United States v. Irvin, No. 91-5454 (4th Cir. August 23, 1993); United States v. Young, No. 92-1431 (7th Cir. June 24, 1993); United States v. Jones, 965 F.2d 1507 (8th Cir. 1992); see also United States v. Conkins, 987 F.2d 564 (9th Cir. 1993); United States v. Becerra, 992 F. 2d 960 (9th Cir. 1993)).

Note, however, that if the defendant is convicted only of a substantive count charging distribution on a certain date, drug amounts from other distribution activity may not be aggregated to achieve the quantity necessary to trigger a mandatory minimum penalty under section 841(b), although the drugs may be aggregated to determine the applicable offense level under §1B1.3. In other words, the mandatory minimum penalty provisions of section 841(b) are based solely upon the amount of drugs that the court finds was actually involved in the substantive distribution count. Similarly, a conviction for a specific conspiracy under 21 U.S.C. § 846 does not permit inclusion of drugs from outside that conspiracy in determining whether a mandatory minimum penalty is applicable (see United States v. Darmand 3 F.3d 157 (2nd Cir. 1993)).

✓156. **QUESTION:** If a drug amount is cited in the charging instrument, is the court bound by that amount when applying the guidelines to a defendant convicted of drug trafficking or importation, or conspiring to commit these acts?

ANSWER: *No. The Sentencing Commission and the circuit courts agree that the district court should determine at sentencing the amount of drugs involved in the offense. Guideline 1B1.3 (Relevant Conduct) provides that if the defendant is found guilty of a broadly worded conspiracy count, the defendant may not necessarily be accountable at sentencing for the entire quantity of drugs distributed during the conspiracy. Instead, the provisions of §1B1.3 should be used to determine the quantity for which the defendant should appropriately be held accountable.*

Appellate courts have concurred with this standard in ruling that at sentencing, to determine the drug amount, the court must make a separate determination of the scope of each defendant's agreement and the acts in furtherance of and reasonably foreseeable in connection with that agreement. Consequently, every co-conspirator is not necessarily given the same sentence (see United States v. O'Campo, 973 F.2d 101 (1st Cir. 1992); United States v. Lanni, 970 F.2d 1092 (2d Cir. 1992); United States v. Collado, 975 F.2d 985 (3d Cir. 1992); United States v. Edwards, 945 F.2d 1387 (7th Cir. 1991); United States v. Thompson, 944 F.2d 1331 (7th Cir. 1991); United States v. Jones, 965 F.2d 1507 (8th Cir. 1992); United States v. Navarro, 979 F.2d 786 (9th Cir. 1992); United States v. Medina, F.2d 573 (6th Cir. 1993)).

✓157. **QUESTION:** Does the Commission still require submission of guideline worksheets for all cases sentenced under the Sentencing Reform Act?

ANSWER: *No. The Commission no longer requires submission of guideline worksheets for cases in which the guideline calculations are included in the presentence reports. However, the Commission continues to request worksheets for cases in which the presentence report was waived.*

This new policy is part of a larger change in the Commission's policy regarding requests for documentation. Following consultation with the Criminal Law Committee of the Judicial Conference and the Administrative Office of the U.S. Courts (AO), the Commission and the AO issued a joint memo to district judges and chief probation officers dated July 7, 1993, officially requesting (in addition to the continued submission of Presentence Reports, Statements of Reasons for Imposing Sentence, Judgment of Conviction Orders, and any written Plea Agreements) the following documents:

1) Indictments or informations (including any superseding indictments or informations);

2) Modification of Sentence (a copy of the amended judgment or court order in all cases in which any portion of the sentence has been modified); and

3) Documents related to revocation of probation and supervised release, including (a) violation worksheets submitted to the court; (b) violation report or petition for action; (c) summary of the violation hearing form; and (d) judgment order. This documentation is required for all violation hearings, even if a revocation does not result.

158. **QUESTION:** Upon a court finding of a violation of probation or supervised release, must all applicable documentation be sent to the Sentencing Commission even if the court determines that revocation is not warranted?

ANSWER: *Yes. It is essential to the Commission's evaluation of the revocation policy statements that probation officers submit the following forms on all violation hearings, regardless of whether the hearing results in a revocation: revocation worksheets submitted to the court, violation report submitted to the court, summary of violation form, and judgment order.*

159. **QUESTION:** Are the cross references in Chapter Two guidelines optional?

ANSWER: *No. For example, in the firearms guideline (§2K2.1), if the defendant used a firearm in connection with a robbery, the court is to apply the robbery guideline (§2B3.1) if it results in an offense level greater than that otherwise obtained under §2K2.1.*

160. QUESTION: Do the guidelines apply to a defendant who has been hospitalized for mental disease or defect under the provisions of 18 U.S.C. § 4244(d)?

ANSWER: *No. However, if the defendant recovers and is resentenced under the provisions of 18 U.S.C. § 4244(e), the guidelines apply.*

✓161. QUESTION: Is the commentary to the Guidelines Manual binding?

ANSWER: *Yes, in certain circumstances. In Stinson v. United States, 113 S. Ct. 1913 (1993), the Supreme Court held that commentary in the Guidelines Manual that interprets or explains a guideline is authoritative unless it violates the Constitution or a federal statute or is inconsistent with, or a plainly erroneous reading of, that guideline. Note that this ruling is limited to commentary that interprets or explains a guideline. It does not apply to other types of commentary, (e.g. commentary that suggests a possible ground for a departure or informational background commentary).*

162. QUESTION: Do the Guidelines apply when sentencing individuals as juveniles?

ANSWER: *No, not in the same way that they apply to adults. In United States v. R.L.C., 112 S.Ct. 1329 (1992), the Supreme Court held that the maximum term of imprisonment applicable to a juvenile sentenced under the Juvenile Delinquency Act was the maximum sentence a similarly situated adult could receive under the guidelines absent a basis for departure. Therefore, although the guidelines are not to be applied in juvenile proceedings, a court will need to calculate the guideline range to determine the maximum permissible sentence. Effective November 1, 1993, the Commission added the policy statement at §1B1.12 (Persons Sentenced Under the Federal Juvenile Delinquency Act) to address this issue.*

APPENDIX F*

FEDERAL RULES OF CRIMINAL PROCEDURE RELATING TO SENTENCING

VII. JUDGMENT

Rule 32. Sentence and Judgment

(a) IN GENERAL; TIME FOR SENTENCING. When a presentence investigation and report are made under subdivision (b)(1), sentence should be imposed without unnecessary delay following completion of the process prescribed by subdivision (b)(6). The time limits prescribed in subdivision (b)(6) may be either shortened or lengthened for good cause.

(b) PRESENTENCE INVESTIGATION AND REPORT.

(1) When Made. The probation officer must make a presentence investigation and submit a report to the court before the sentence is imposed, unless:

(A) the court finds that the information in the record enables it to exercise its sentencing authority meaningfully under 18 U.S.C. § 3553; and

(B) the court explains this finding on the record.

(2) Presence of Counsel. On request, the defendant's counsel is entitled to notice and a reasonable opportunity to attend any interview of the defendant by a probation officer in the course of a presentence investigation.

(3) Nondisclosure. The report must not be submitted to the court or its contents disclosed to anyone unless the defendant has consented in writing, has pleaded guilty or nolo contendere, or has been found guilty.

(4) Contents of the Presentence Report. The presentence report must contain—

(A) information about the defendant's history and characteristics, including any prior criminal record, financial condition, and any circumstances that, because they affect the defendant's behavior, may be helpful in imposing sentence or in correctional treatment;

(B) the classification of the offense and of the defendant under the categories established by the Sentencing Commission under 28 U.S.C. § 994(a), as the probation officer believes to be applicable to the defendant's case; the kinds of sentence and the sentencing range suggested for such a category of offense committed by such a category of defendant as set forth in the guidelines issued by the Sentencing Commission under 28 U.S.C. § 994(a)(1); and the probation officer's explanation of any factors that may suggest a different sentence—within or without the applicable guideline—that would be more appropriate, given all the circumstances;

(C) a reference to any pertinent policy statement issued by the Sentencing Commission under 28 U.S.C. § 994(a)(2);

**Publisher's Note:* This Appendix has been added by the Publisher. It is not included in the Commission's *Guidelines Manual.*

(D) verified information, stated in a nonargumentative style, containing an assessment of the financial, social, psychological, and medical impact on any individual against whom the offense has been committed;

(E) in appropriate cases, information about the nature and extent of nonprison programs and resources available for the defendant;

(F) any report and recommendation resulting from a study ordered by the court under 18 U.S.C. § 3552(b); and

(G) any other information required by the court.

(5) Exclusions. The presentence report must exclude:

(A) any diagnostic opinions that, if disclosed, might seriously disrupt a program of rehabilitation;

(B) sources of information obtained upon a promise of confidentiality; or

(C) any other information that, if disclosed, might result in harm, physical or otherwise, to the defendant or other persons.

(6) Disclosure and Objections.

(A) Not less than 35 days before the sentencing hearing—unless the defendant waives this minimum period—the probation officer must furnish the presentence report to the defendant, the defendant's counsel, and the attorney for the Government. The court may, by local rule or in individual cases, direct that the probation officer not disclose the probation officer's recommendation, if any, on the sentence.

(B) Within 14 days after receiving the presentence report, the parties shall communicate in writing to the probation officer, and to each other, any objections to any material information, sentencing classifications, sentencing guideline ranges, and policy statements contained in or omitted from the presentence report. After receiving objections, the probation officer may meet with the defendant, the defendant's counsel, and the attorney for the Government to discuss those objections. The probation officer may also conduct a further investigation and revise the presentence report as appropriate.

(C) Not later than 7 days before the sentencing hearing, the probation officer must submit the presentence report to the court, together with an addendum setting forth any unresolved objections, the grounds for those objections, and the probation officer's comments on the objections. At the same time, the probation officer must furnish the revisions of the presentence report and the addendum to the defendant, the defendant's counsel, and the attorney for the Government.

(D) Except for any unresolved objection under subdivision (b)(6)(B), the court may, at the hearing, accept the presentence report as its findings of fact. For good cause shown, the court may allow a new objection to be raised at any time before imposing sentence.

(c) SENTENCE.

(1) Sentencing Hearing. At the sentence hearing, the court must afford counsel for the defendant and for the Government an opportunity to comment on the probation officer's determinations and on other matters relating to the appropriate sentence, and must rule on any unresolved objections to the presentence report. The court may, in its discretion, permit the parties to introduce testimony or other evidence on the objections. For each matter controverted, the court must make either a finding on the allegation or a determination that no finding is necessary because the controverted matter will not be taken into account in, or will not affect, sentencing. A written record of these findings and determinations must be appended to any copy of the presentence report made available to the Bureau of Prisons.

(2) Production of Statements at Sentencing Hearing. Rule 26.2(a)–(d) and (f) applies at a sentencing hearing under this rule. If a party elects not to comply with an order under Rule 26.2(a) to deliver a statement to the movant, the court may not consider the affidavit or testimony of the witness whose statement is withheld.

(3) Imposition of Sentence. Before imposing sentence, the court must:

(A) verify that the defendant and defendant's counsel have read and discussed the presentence report made available under subdivision (b)(6)(A). If the court has received information excluded from the presentence report under subdivision (b)(5) the court—in lieu of making that information available—must summarize it in writing, if the information will be relied on in determining sentence. The court must also give the defendant and the defendant's counsel a reasonable opportunity to comment on that information;

(B) afford defendant's counsel an opportunity to speak on behalf of the defendant;

(C) address the defendant personally and determine whether the defendant wishes to make a statement and to present any information in mitigation of the sentence;

(D) afford the attorney for the Government an opportunity equivalent to that of the defendant's counsel to speak to the court; and

(E) if sentence is to be imposed for a crime of violence or sexual abuse, address the victim personally if the victim is present at the sentencing hearing and determine if the victim wishes to make a statement or present any information in relation to the sentence.

(4) In Camera Proceedings. The court's summary of information under subdivision (c)(3)(A) may be in camera. Upon joint motion by the defendant and by the attorney for the Government, the court may hear in camera the statements—made under subdivision (c)(3)(B), (C), (D), and (E)—by the defendant, the defendant's counsel, the victim, or the attorney for the Government.

(5) Notification of Right to Appeal. After imposing sentence in a case which has gone to trial on a plea of not guilty, the court must advise the defendant of the right to appeal. After imposing sentence in any case, the court must advise the defendant of any right to appeal the sentence, and of the right of a person who is unable to pay the cost of an appeal to apply for leave to appeal in forma pauperis. If the defendant so requests, the clerk of the court must immediately prepare and file a notice of appeal on behalf of the defendant.

(d) JUDGMENT.

(1) In General. A judgment of conviction must set forth the plea, the verdict or findings, the adjudication, and the sentence. If the defendant is found not guilty or for any other reason is entitled to be discharged, judgment must be entered accordingly. The judgment must be signed by the judge and entered by the clerk.

(2) Criminal Forfeiture. When a verdict contains a finding of criminal forfeiture, the judgment must authorize the Attorney General to seize the interest or property subject to forfeiture on terms that the court considers proper.

(e) PLEA WITHDRAWAL. If a motion to withdraw a plea of guilty or nolo contendere is made before sentence is imposed, the court may permit the plea to be withdrawn if the defendant shows any fair and just reason. At any later time, a plea may be set aside only on direct appeal or by motion under 28 U.S.C. § 2255.

"**(f) DEFINITIONS.**—For purposes of this rule—

"(1) 'victim' means any individual against whom an offense has been committed for which a sentence is to be imposed, but the right of allocution under subdivision (c)(3)(E) may be exercised instead by—

"(A) a parent or legal guardian if the victim is below the age of eighteen years or incompetent; or

"(B) one or more family members or relatives designated by the court if the victim is deceased or incapacitated;

if such person or persons are present at the sentencing hearing, regardless of whether the victim is present; and

"(2) 'crime of violence or sexual abuse' means a crime that involved the use or attempted or threatened use of physical force against the person or property of another, or a crime under chapter 109A of title 18, United States Code.".

Amended effective December 1, 1994.

Rule 32.1 Revocation or Modification of Probation or Supervised Release

(a) Revocation of Probation or Supervised Release.

(1) Preliminary Hearing. Whenever a person is held in custody on the ground that the person has violated a condition of probation or supervised release, the person shall be afforded a prompt hearing before any judge, or a United States magistrate who has been given authority pursuant to 28 U.S.C. § 636 to conduct such hearings, in order to determine whether there is probable cause to hold the person for a revocation hearing. The person shall be given

(A) notice of the preliminary hearing and its purpose and of the alleged violation;

(B) an opportunity to appear at the hearing and present evidence in the person's own behalf;

(C) upon request, the opportunity to question witnesses against the person unless, for good cause, the federal magistrate decides that justice does not require the appearance of the witness; and

(D) notice of the person's right to be represented by counsel.

The proceedings shall be recorded stenographically or by an electronic recording device. If probable cause is found to exist, the person shall be held for a revocation hearing. The person may be released pursuant to Rule 46(c) pending the revocation hearing. If probable cause is not found to exist, the proceeding shall be dismissed.

(2) Revocation Hearing. The revocation hearing, unless waived by the person, shall be held within a reasonable time in the district of jurisdiction. The person shall be given

(A) written notice of the alleged violation;

(B) disclosure of the evidence against the person;

(C) an opportunity to appear and to present evidence in the person's own behalf;

(D) the opportunity to question adverse witnesses; and

(E) notice of the person's right to be represented by counsel.

(b) Modification of Probation or Supervised Release. A hearing and assistance of counsel are required before the terms or conditions of probation or supervised release can be modified, unless the relief to be granted to the person on probation or supervised release upon the person's request or the court's own motion is favorable to the person, and the attorney for the government, after having been given notice of the proposed relief and a reasonable opportunity to object, has not objected. An extension of the term of probation or supervised release is not favorable to the person for the purposes of this rule.

Amended effective December 1, 1991.

Rule 35. Correction or Reduction of Sentence

(a) Correction of a Sentence on Remand. The court shall correct a sentence that is determined on appeal under 18 U.S.C. [§] 3742 to have been imposed in violation of law, to have been imposed as a result of an incorrect application of the sentencing guidelines, or to be unreasonable, upon remand to the case to the court—

(1) for imposition of a sentence in accord with the findings of the court of appeals; or

(2) for further sentencing proceedings if, after such proceedings, the court determines that the original sentence was incorrect.

(b) Reduction of Sentence for Changed Circumstances. The court, on motion of the Government made within one year after the imposition of the sentence, may reduce a sentence to reflect a defendant's subsequent, substantial assistance in the investigation or prosecution of another person who has committed an offense, in accordance with the guidelines and policy statements issued by the Sentencing Commission pursuant to section 994 of title 28, United States Code. The court may consider a government motion to reduce a sentence made one year or more after imposition of the sentence where the defendant's substantial assistance involves information or evidence not known by the defendant until one year or more after imposition of sentence. The court's authority to reduce a sentence under this subsection includes the authority to reduce such sentence to a level below that established by statute as a minimum sentence.

(c) Correction of Sentence by Sentencing Court. The court, acting within 7 days after the imposition of sentence, may correct a sentence that was imposed as a result of arithmetical, technical, or other clear error.

Amended effective December 1, 1991.

VIII. APPEAL

Rule 38. Stay of Execution

(a) Death. A sentence of death shall be stayed if an appeal is taken from the conviction or sentence.

(b) Imprisonment. A sentence of imprisonment shall be stayed if an appeal is taken from the conviction or sentence and the defendant is released pending disposition of appeal pursuant to Rule 9(b) of the Federal Rules of Appellate Procedure. If not stayed, the court may recommend to the Attorney General that the defendant be retained at, or transferred to, a place of confinement near the place of trial or the place where an appeal is to be heard, for a period reasonably necessary to permit the defendant to assist in the preparation of an appeal to the court of appeals.

(c) Fine. A sentence to pay a fine or a fine and costs, if an appeal is taken, may be stayed by the district court or by the court of appeals upon such terms as the court deems proper. The court may require the defendant pending appeal to deposit the whole or any part of the fine and costs in the registry of the district court, or to give bond for the payment thereof, or to submit to an examination of assets, and it may make any appropriate order to restrain the defendant from dissipating such defendant's assets.

(d) Probation. A sentence of probation may be stayed if an appeal from the conviction or sentence is taken. If the sentence is stayed, the court shall fix the terms of the stay.

(e) Criminal Forfeiture, Notice to Victims, and Restitution. A sanction imposed as part of the sentence pursuant to 18 U.S.C. [§§] 3554, 3555, or 3556 may, if an appeal of the conviction or sentence is taken, be stayed by the district court or by the court of appeals upon such terms as the court finds appropriate. The court may issue such orders as may be reasonably necessary to ensure compliance with the sanction upon disposition of the appeal, including the entering of a restraining order or an injunction or requiring a deposit in whole or in part of the monetary amount involved into the registry of the district court or execution of a performance bond.

(f) Disabilities. A civil or employment disability arising under a Federal statute by reason of the defendant's conviction or sentence, may, if an appeal is taken, be stayed by the district court or by the court of appeals upon such terms as the court finds appropriate. The court may enter a restraining order or an injunction, or take any other action that may be reasonably necessary to protect the interest represented by the disability pending disposition of the appeal.

X. GENERAL PROVISIONS

Rule 58. Procedure for Misdemeanors and Other Petty Offenses

(a) Scope.

(1) In General. This rule governs the procedure and practice for the conduct of proceedings involving misdemeanors and other petty offenses, and for appeals to judges of the district courts in such cases tried by magistrates.

(2) Applicability of Other Federal Rules of Criminal Procedure. In proceedings concerning petty offenses for which no sentence of imprisonment will be imposed the court may follow such provisions of these rules as it deems appropriate, to the extent not inconsistent with this rule. In all other proceedings the other rules govern except as specifically provided in this rule.

(3) Definition. The term "petty offenses for which no sentence of imprisonment will be imposed" as used in this rule, means any petty offenses as defined in 18 U.S.C. § 19 as to which the court determines, that, in the event of conviction, no sentence of imprisonment will actually be imposed.

(b) Pretrial Procedures.

(1) Trial Document. The trial of a misdemeanor may proceed on an indictment, information, or complaint or, in the case of a petty offense, on a citation or violation notice.

(2) Initial Appearance. At the defendant's initial appearance on a misdemeanor or other petty offense charge, the court shall inform the defendant of:

(A) the charge, and the maximum possible penalties provided by law, including payment of a special assessment under 18 U.S.C § 3013, and restitution under 18 U.S.C. § 3663;

(B) the right to retain counsel;

(C) unless the charge is a petty offense for which appointment of counsel is not required, the right to request the assignment of counsel if the defendant is unable to obtain counsel;

(D) the right to remain silent and that any statement made by the defendant may be used against the defendant;

(E) the right to trial, judgment, and sentencing before a judge of the district court, unless the defendant consents to trial, judgment, and sentencing before a magistrate;

(F) unless the charge is a petty offense, the right to trial by jury before either a magistrate or a judge of the district court; and

(G) if the defendant is held in custody and charged with a misdemeanor other than a petty offense, the right to a preliminary examination in accordance with 18 U.S.C. § 3060, and the general circumstances under which the defendant may secure pretrial release.

(3) Consent and Arraignment.

(A) Trial Before a Magistrate. If the defendant signs a written consent to be tried before the magistrate which specifically waives trial before a judge of the district court, the magistrate shall take the defendant's plea. The defendant may plead not guilty, guilty, or with the consent of the magistrate, nolo contendere.

(B) Failure to Consent. If the defendant does not consent to trial before the magistrate, the defendant shall be ordered to appear before a judge of the district court for further proceedings on notice.

(c) Additional Procedures Applicable Only to Petty Offenses for Which no Sentence of Imprisonment Will Be Imposed. With respect to petty offenses for which no sentence of imprisonment will be imposed, the following additional procedures are applicable:

(1) Plea of Guilty or Nolo Contendere. No plea of guilty or nolo contendere shall be accepted unless the court is satisfied that the defendant understands the nature of the charge and the maximum possible penalties provided by law.

(2) Waiver of Venue for Plea and Sentence. A defendant who is arrested, held, or present in a district other than that in which the indictment, information, complaint, citation or violation notice is pending against that defendant may state in writing a wish to plead guilty or nolo contendere, to waive venue and trial in the district in which the proceeding is pending, and to consent to disposition of the case in the district in which that defendant was arrested, is held, or is present. Unless the defendant thereafter pleads not guilty, the prosecution shall be had as if venue were in such district, and notice of the same shall be given to the magistrate in the district where the proceeding was originally commenced. The defendant's statement of a desire to plead guilty or nolo contendere is not admissible against the defendant.

(3) Sentence. The court shall afford the defendant an opportunity to be heard in mitigation. The court shall then immediately proceed to sentence the defendant, except that in the discretion of the court, sentencing may be continued to allow an investigation by the probation service or submission of additional information by either party.

(4) Notification of Right to Appeal. After imposing sentence in a case which has gone to trial on a plea of not guilty, the court shall advise the defendant of the defendant's right to appeal including any right to appeal the sentence. There shall be no duty on the court to advise the defendant of any right of appeal after sentence is imposed following a plea of guilty or nolo contendere, except that the court shall advise the defendant of any right to appeal the sentence.

(d) Securing the Defendant's Appearance; Payment in Lieu of Appearance.

(1) Forfeiture of Collateral. When authorized by local rules of the district court, payment of a fixed sum may be accepted in suitable cases in lieu of appearance and as authorizing the termination of the proceedings. Local rules may make provision for increases in fixed sums not to exceed the maximum fine which could be imposed.

(2) Notice to Appear. If a defendant fails to pay a fixed sum, request a hearing, or appear in response to a citation or violation notice, the clerk or a magistrate may issue a notice for the defendant to appear before the court on a date certain. The notice may also afford the defendant an additional opportunity to pay a fixed sum in lieu of appearance, and shall be served upon the defendant by mailing a copy to the defendant's last known address.

(3) Summons or Warrant. Upon an indictment or a showing by one of the other documents specified in subdivision (b)(1) of probable cause to believe that an offense has been committed and that the defendant has committed it, the court may issue an arrest warrant or, if no warrant is requested by the attorney for the prosecution, a summons. The showing of probable cause shall be made in writing upon oath or under penalty for perjury, but the affiant need not appear before the court. If the defendant fails to appear before the court in response to a summons, the court may summarily issue a warrant for the defendant's immediate arrest and appearance before the court.

(e) Record. Proceedings under this rule shall be taken down by a reporter or recorded by suitable sound equipment.

(f) New Trial. The provisions of Rule 33 shall apply.

(g) Appeal.

(1) Decision, Order, Judgment or Sentence by a District Judge. An appeal from a decision, order, judgment or conviction or sentence by a judge of the district court shall be taken in accordance with the Federal Rules of Appellate Procedure.

(2) Decision, Order, Judgment or Sentence by a Magistrate.

(A) Interlocutory Appeal. A decision or order by a magistrate which, if made by a judge of the district court, could be appealed by the government or defendant under any provision of law, shall be subject to an appeal to a judge of the district court provided such appeal is taken within 10 days of the entry of the decision or order. An appeal shall be taken by filing with the clerk of court a statement copy with the magistrate.

(B) Appeal From Conviction or Sentence. An appeal from a judgment of conviction or sentence by a magistrate to a judge of the district court shall be taken within 10 days after entry of the judgment. An appeal shall be taken by filing with the clerk of court a statement specifying the judgment from which an appeal is taken, and by serving a copy of the statement upon the United States Attorney, personally or by mail, and by filing a copy with the magistrate.

(C) Record. The record shall consist of the original papers and exhibits in the case together with any transcript, tape, or other recording of the proceedings and a certified copy of the docket entries which shall be transmitted promptly to the clerk of court. For

purposes of the appeal, a copy of the record of such proceedings shall be made available at the expense of the United States to a person who establishes by affidavit the inability to pay or give security therefor, and the expense of such copy shall be paid by the Director of the Administrative Office of the United States Courts.

(D) Scope of Appeal. The defendant shall not be entitled to a trial de novo by a judge of the district court. The scope of the appeal shall be the same as an appeal from a judgment of a district court to a court of appeals.

(3) Stay of Execution; Release Pending Appeal. The provisions of Rule 38 relating to stay of execution shall be applicable to a judgment of conviction or sentence. The defendant may be released pending appeal in accordance with the provisions of law relating to release pending appeal from a judgment of a district court to a court of appeals.

Amended effective December 1, 1991.

APPENDIX G*

Selected Provisions of the Violent Crime Control and Law Enforcement Act of 1994 Relating to the Federal Sentencing Guidelines and the United States Sentencing Commission

**Publisher's Note:* This Appendix has been added by the Publisher. It is not included in the Commission's *Guidelines Manual.*

Violent Crime Control and Law Enforcement Act of 1994

* * *

TITLE II—PRISONS

Subtitle D—Miscellaneous Provisions

* * *

SEC. 20402. PRISON IMPACT ASSESSMENTS.

(a) **IN GENERAL.**—Chapter 303 of title 18, United States Code is amended by adding at the end the following new section:

"§ 4047. Prison impact assessments

"(a) Any submission of legislation by the Judicial or Executive branch which could increase or decrease the number of persons incarcerated in Federal penal institutions shall be accompanied by a prison impact statement (as defined in subsection(b)).

"(b) The Attorney General shall, in consultation with the Sentencing Commission and the Administrative Office of the United States Courts, prepare and furnish prison impact assessments under subsection (c) of this section, and in response to requests from Congress for information relating to a pending measure or matter that might affect the number of defendants processed through the Federal criminal justice system. A prison impact assessment on pending legislation must be supplied within 21 days of any request. A prison impact assessment shall include—

"(1) projections of the impact on prison, probation, and post prison supervision populations;

"(2) an estimate of the fiscal impact of such population changes on Federal expenditures, including those for construction and operation of correctional facilities for the current fiscal year and 5 succeeding fiscal years;

"(3) an analysis of any other significant factor affecting the cost of the measure and its impact on the operations of components of the criminal justice system; and

"(4) a statement of the methodologies and assumptions utilized in preparing the assessment.

"(c) The Attorney General shall prepare and transmit to the Congress, by March 1 of each year, a prison impact assessment reflecting the cumulative effect of all relevant changes in the law taking effect during the preceding calendar year."

(b) **TECHNICAL AMENDMENT.**—The chapter analysis for chapter 303 is amended by adding at the end the following new item:

"4047. Prison impact assessments.".

SEC. 20403. SENTENCES TO ACCOUNT FOR COSTS TO THE GOVERNMENT OF IMPRISONMENT, RELEASE, AND PROBATION.

(a) **IMPOSITION OF SENTENCE.**—Section 3572(a) of title 18, United States Code, is amended—

(1) by redesignating paragraphs (6) and (7) as paragraphs (7) and (8), respectively; and

(2) by inserting after paragraph (5) the following new paragraph:

"(6) the expected costs to the government of any imprisonment, supervised release, or probation component of the sentence;".

(b) **DUTIES OF THE SENTENCING COMMISSION.**—Section 994 of title 28, United States Code, is amended by adding at the end the following new subsection:

"(y) The Commission, in promulgating guidelines pursuant to subsection (a)(1), may include, as a component of a fine, the expected costs to the Government of any imprisonment, supervised release, or probation sentence that is ordered.".

SEC. 20405. CREDITING OF "GOOD TIME".

Section 3624 of title 18, United States Code, is amended—

(1) by striking "he" each place it appears and inserting "the prisoner";

(2) by striking "his" each place it appears and inserting "the prisoner's";

(3) in subsection (d) by striking "him" and inserting "the prisoner"; and

(4) in subsection (b)—

(A) in the first sentence by inserting "(other than a prisoner serving a sentence for a crime of violence)" after "A prisoner"; and

(B) by inserting after the first sentence the following: "A prisoner who is serving a term of imprisonment of more than 1 year for a crime of violence, other than a term of imprisonment for the duration of the prisoner's life, may receive credit toward the service of the prisoner's sentence, beyond the time served, of up to 54 days at the end of each year of the prisoner's term of imprisonment, beginning at the end of the first year of the term, subject to determination by the Bureau of Prisons that, during that year, the prisoner has displayed exemplary compliance with such institutional disciplinary regulations.".

* * *

SEC. 20412. EDUCATION REQUIREMENT FOR EARLY RELEASE.

Section 3624(b) of title 18, United States Code, is amended—

(1) by inserting "(1)" after "behavior.—";

(2) by striking "Such credit toward service of sentence vests at the time that it is received. Credit that has vested may not later be withdrawn, and credit that has not been earned may not later be granted." and inserting "Credit that has not been earned may not later be granted."; and

(3) by adding at the end the following:

"(2) Credit toward a prisoner's service of sentence shall not be vested unless the prisoner has earned or is making satisfactory progress toward a high school diploma or an equivalent degree.

"(3) The Attorney General shall ensure that the Bureau of Prisons has in effect an optional General Educational Development program for inmates who have not earned a high school diploma or its equivalent.

"(4) Exemptions to the General Educational Development requirement may be made as deemed appropriate by the Director of the Federal Bureau of Prisons.".

* * *

SEC. 20414. POST-CONVICTION RELEASE DRUG TESTING—FEDERAL OFFENDERS.

(a) **DRUG TESTING PROGRAM.**—

(1) **IN GENERAL.**—Subchapter A of chapter 229 of title 18, United States Code, is amended by adding at the end of the following new section:

"§ 3608. Drug testing of Federal offenders on post-conviction release

"The Director of the Administrative Office of the United States Courts, in consultation with the Attorney General and the Secretary of Health and Human Services, shall, subject to the availability of appropriations, establish a program of drug testing of Federal offenders on post-conviction release. The program shall include such standards and guidelines as the Director may determine necessary to ensure the reliability and accuracy of the drug testing programs. In each judicial district the chief probation officer shall arrange for the drug testing of defendants on post-conviction release pursuant to a conviction for a felony or other offense described in section 3563(a)(4).".

(2) **TECHNICAL AMENDMENT.**—The subchapter analysis for subchapter A of chapter 229 of title 18, United States Code, is amended by adding at the end the following new item:

"3608. Drug testing of Federal offenders on post-conviction release.".

(b) **CONDITIONS OF PROBATION.**—Section 3563(a) of title 18, United States Code, is amended—

(1) in paragraph (2) by striking "and" after the semicolon;

(2) in paragraph (3) by striking the period and inserting "; and";

(3) by adding at the end the following new paragraph:

"(4) for a felony, a misdemeanor, or an infraction, that the defendant refrain from any unlawful use of a controlled substance and submit to one drug test within 15 days of release on probation and at least 2 periodic drug tests thereafter (as determined by the court) for use of a controlled substance, but the condition stated in this paragraph may be ameliorated or suspended by the court for any individual defendant if the defendant's presentence report or other reliable sentencing information indicates a low risk of future substance abuse by the defendant."; and

(4) by adding at the end the following: "The results of a drug test administered in accordance with paragraph (4) shall be subject to confirmation only if the results are positive, the defendant is subject to possible imprisonment for such failure, and either the defendant denies the accuracy of such test or there is some other reason to question the results of the test. A defendant who tests positive may be detained pending verification of a positive drug test result. A drug test confirmation shall be a urine drug test confirmed using gas chromatography/mass spectrometry techniques or such test as the Director of the Administrative Office of the United States Courts after consultation with the Secretary of Health and Human Services may determine to be of equivalent accuracy. The court shall consider whether the availability of appropriate substance abuse treatment programs, or an individual's current or past participation in such programs, warrants an exception in accordance with United States Sentencing Commission guidelines from the rule of section 3565(b), when considering any action against a defendant who fails a drug test administered in accordance with paragraph (4).".

(c) **CONDITIONS OF SUPERVISED RELEASE.**—Section 3583(d) of title 18, United States Code, is amended by inserting after the first sentence the following: "The court shall also order, as an explicit condition of supervised release, that the defendant refrain from any unlawful use of a controlled substance and submit to a drug test within 15 days of release on supervised release and at least 2 periodic drug tests thereafter (as determined by the court) for use of a controlled substance. The condition stated in the preceding sentence may be ameliorated or suspended by the court as provided in section 3563(a)(4). The results of a drug test administered in accordance with the preceding subsection shall be subject to confirmation only if the results are positive, the defendant is subject to possible imprisonment for such failure, and either the defendant denies the accuracy of such test or there is some other reason to question the results of the test. A drug test confirmation shall be a urine drug test confirmed using gas chromatography/mass spectrometry techniques or such test as the Director of the Administrative Office of the United States Courts after consultation with the Secretary of Health and Human Services may determine to be of equivalent accuracy. The court shall consider whether the availability of appropriate substance abuse treatment programs, or an individual's current or past participation in such programs, warrants an exception in accordance with United States Sentencing Commission guidelines from the rule of section 3583(g) when considering any action against a defendant who fails a drug test.".

(d) **CONDITIONS OF PAROLE.**—Section 4209(a) of title 18, United States Code, is amended by inserting after the first sentence the following: "In every case, the Commission shall also impose as a condition of parole that the parolee pass a drug test prior to release and refrain from any unlawful use of a controlled substance and submit to at least 2 periodic drug tests (as determined by the Commission) for use of a controlled substance. The condition stated in the preceding sentence may be ameliorated or suspended by the Commission for any individual parolee if it determines that there is good cause for doing so. The results of a drug test administered in accordance with the provisions of the preceding sentence shall be subject to confirmation only if the results are positive, the defendant is subject to possible imprisonment for such failure, and either the defendant denies the accuracy of such test or there is some other reason to question the results of the test. A drug test confirmation shall be a urine drug test confirmed using gas chromatography/mass spectrometry techniques or such test as the Director of the Administrative Office of the United States Courts after consultation with the Secretary of Health and Human Services may determine to be of equivalent accuracy. The Commission shall consider whether the availability of appropriate substance abuse treatment programs, or an individual's current or past participation in such programs, warrants an exception in accordance with United States Sentencing Commission guidelines from the rule of section 4214(f) when considering any action against a defendant who fails a drug test.".

TITLE IV—VIOLENCE AGAINST WOMEN

Subtitle A—Safe Streets for Women

* * *

CHAPTER 1—FEDERAL PENALTIES FOR SEX CRIMES

SEC. 40111. REPEAT OFFENDERS.

(a) **IN GENERAL.**—Chapter 109A of title 18, United States Code, is amended by adding at the end the following new section:

"§ 2247. Repeat offenders

"Any person who violates a provision of this chapter, after one or more prior convictions for an offense punishable under this chapter, or after one or more prior convictions under the laws of any State relating to aggravated sexual abuse, sexual abuse, or abusive sexual contact have become final, is punishable by a term of imprisonment up to twice that otherwise authorized.".

(b) **AMENDMENT OF SENTENCING GUIDELINES.**—The Sentencing Commission shall implement the amendment made by subsection (a) by promulgating amendments, if appropriate, in the sentencing guidelines applicable to chapter 109A offenses.

(c) **CHAPTER ANALYSIS.**—The chapter analysis for chapter 109A of title 18, United States Code, is amended by adding at the end the following new item:

"2247. Repeat offenders.".

SEC. 40112. FEDERAL PENALTIES.

(A) **AMENDMENT OF SENTENCING GUIDELINES.**—Pursuant to its authority under section 994(p) of title 28, United States Code, the United States Sentencing Commission shall review and amend, where necessary, its sentencing guidelines on aggravated sexual abuse under section 2241 of title 18, United States Code, or sexual abuse under section 2242 of title 18, United States Code, as follows:

(1) The Commission shall review and promulgate amendments to the guidelines, if appropriate, to enhance penalties if more than 1 offender is involved in the offense.

(2) The Commission shall review and promulgate amendments to the guidelines, if appropriate, to reduce unwarranted disparities between the sentences for sex offenders who are known to the victim and sentences for sex offenders who are not known to the victim.

(3) The Commission shall review and promulgate amendments to the guidelines to enhance penalties, if appropriate, to render Federal penalties on Federal territory commensurate with penalties for similar offenses in the States.

(4) The Commission shall review and promulgate amendments to the guidelines, if appropriate, to account for the general problem of recidivism in cases of sex offenses, the severity of the offense, and its devastating effects on survivors.

(b) **REPORT**.—Not later than 180 days after the date of enactment of this Act, the United States Sentencing Commission shall review and submit to Congress a report containing an analysis of Federal rape sentencing, accompanied by comment from independent experts in the field, describing—

(1) comparative Federal sentences for cases in which the rape victim is known to the defendant and cases in which the rape victim is not known to the defendant;

(2) comparative Federal sentences for cases on Federal territory and sentences in surrounding States; and

(3) an analysis of the effect of rape sentences on populations residing primarily on Federal territory relative to the impact of other Federal offenses in which the existence of Federal jurisdiction depends upon the offense's being committed on Federal territory.

SEC. 40113. MANDATORY RESTITUTION FOR SEX CRIMES.

(a) **SEXUAL ABUSE.**—

(1) **IN GENERAL.**—Chapter 109A of title 18, United States Code, is amended by adding at the end the following new section:

"§ 2248. Mandatory restitution

"(a) **IN GENERAL.**—Notwithstanding section 3663, and in addition to any other civil or criminal penalty authorized by law, the court shall order restitution for any offense under this chapter.

"(b) **SCOPE AND NATURE OF ORDER.**—

"(1) **DIRECTIONS.**—The order of restitution under this section shall direct that—

"(A) the defendant pay to the victim (through the appropriate court mechanism) the full amount of the victim's losses as determined by the court, pursuant to paragraph (3); and

"(B) The United States Attorney enforce the restitution order by all available and reasonable means.

"(2) **ENFORCEMENT BY VICTIM.**—An order of restitution also may be enforced by a victim named in the order to receive the restitution in the same manner as a judgment in a civil action.

"(3) **DEFINITION.**—For purposes of this subsection, the term 'full amount of the victim's losses' includes any costs incurred by the victim for—

"(A) medical services relating to physical, psychiatric, or psychological care;

"(B) physical and occupational therapy or rehabilitation;

"(C) necessary transportation, temporary housing, and child care expenses;

"(D) lost income;

"(E) attorneys' fees, plus any costs incurred in obtaining a civil protection order; and

"(F) any other losses suffered by the victim as a proximate result of the offense.

"(4) **ORDER MANDATORY.**—(A) The issuance of a restitution order under this section is mandatory.

"(B) A court may not decline to issue an order under this section because of—

"(i) the economic circumstances of the defendant; or

"(ii) the fact that a victim has, or is entitled to, receive compensation for his or her injuries from the proceeds of insurance or any other source.

"(C)(i) Notwithstanding subparagraph (A), the court may take into account the economic circumstances of the defendant in determining the manner in which and the schedule according to which the restitution is to be paid.

"(ii) For purposes of this subparagraph, the term 'economic circumstances' includes—

"(I) the financial resources and other assets of the defendant;

"(II) projected earnings, earning capacity, and other income of the defendant; and

"(III) any financial obligations of the defendant, including obligations to dependents.

"(D) Subparagraph (A) does not apply if—

"(i) the court finds on the record that the economic circumstances of the defendant do not allow for the payment of any amount of a restitution order, and do not allow for the payment of any or some portion of the amount of a restitution order in the foreseeable future (under any reasonable schedule of payments); and

"(ii) the court enters in its order the amount of the victim's losses, and provides a nominal restitution award.

"(5) **MORE THAN 1 OFFENDER.**—When the court finds that more than 1 offender has contributed to the loss of a victim, the court may make each offender liable for payment of the full amount of restitution or may apportion liability among the offenders to reflect the level of contribution and economic circumstances of each offender.

"(6) **MORE THAN 1 VICTIM**.—When the court finds that more than 1 victim has sustained a loss requiring restitution by an offender, the court shall order full restitution of each victim but may provide for different payment schedules to reflect the economic circumstances of each victim.

"(7) **PAYMENT SCHEDULE**.—An order under this section may direct the defendant to make a single lump-sum payment or partial payments at specified intervals.

"(8) **SETOFF**.—Any amount paid to a victim under this section shall be set off against any amount later recovered as compensatory damages by the victim from the defendant in—

"(A) any Federal civil proceeding; and

"(B) any State civil proceeding, to the extent provided by the law of the State.

"(9) **EFFECT ON OTHER SOURCES OF COMPENSATION**.—The issuance of a restitution order shall not affect the entitlement of a victim to receive compensation with respect to a loss from insurance or any other source until the payments actually received by the victim under the restitution order fully compensate the victim for the loss.

"(10) **CONDITION OF PROBATION OR SUPERVISED RELEASE**.—Compliance with a restitution order issued under this section shall be a condition of any probation or supervised release of a defendant. If an offender fails to comply with a restitution order, the court may, after a hearing, revoke probation or a term of supervised release, modify the terms or conditions of probation or a term of supervised release, or hold the defendant in contempt pursuant to section 3583(e). In determining whether to revoke probation or a term of supervised release, modify the terms or conditions of probation or supervised release or hold a defendant serving a term of supervised release in contempt, the court shall consider the defendant's employment status, earning ability and financial resources, the willfulness of the defendant's failure to comply, and any other circumstances that may have a bearing on the defendant's ability to comply.

"(c) **PROOF OF CLAIM**.—

"(1) **AFFIDAVIT**.—Within 60 days after conviction and, in any event, not later than 10 days prior to sentencing, the United States Attorney (or the United States Attorney's delegee), after consulting with the victim, shall prepare and file an affidavit with the court listing the amounts subject to restitution under this section. The affidavit shall be signed by the United States Attorney (or the United States Attorney's delegee) and the victim. Should the victim object to any of the information included in the affidavit, the United States Attorney (or the United States Attorney's delegee) shall advise the victim that the victim may file a separate affidavit and shall provide the victim with an affidavit form which may be used to do so.

"(2) **OBJECTION**.—If, after the defendant has been notified of the affidavit, no objection is raised by the defendant, the amounts attested to in the affidavit filed pursuant to paragraph (1) shall be entered in the court's restitution order. If objection is raised, the court may require the victim or the United States Attorney (or the United States Attorney's delegee) to submit further affidavits or other supporting documents, demonstrating the victim's losses.

"(3) **ADDITIONAL DOCUMENTATION AND TESTIMONY**.—If the court concludes, after reviewing the supporting documentation and considering the defendant's objections, that there is a substantial reason for doubting the authenticity or veracity of the records submitted, the court may require additional documentation or hear testimony on those questions. The privacy of any records filed, or testimony heard, pursuant to this section shall be maintained to the greatest extent possible, and such records may be filed or testimony heard in camera.

"(4) **FINAL DETERMINATION OF LOSSES.**—If the victim's losses are not ascertainable by the date that is 10 days prior to sentencing as provided in paragraph (1), the United States Attorney (or the United States Attorney's delegee) shall so inform the court, and the court shall set a date for the final determination of the victim's losses, not to exceed 90 days after sentencing. If the victim subsequently discovers further losses, the victim shall have 60 days after discovery of those losses in which to petition the court for an amended restitution order. Such order may be granted only upon a showing of good cause for the failure to include such losses in the initial claim for restitutionary relief.

"(d) **MODIFICATION OF ORDER.**—A victim or the offender may petition the court at any time to modify a restitution order as appropriate in view of a change in the economic circumstances of the offender.

"(e) **REFERENCE TO MAGISTRATE OR SPECIAL MASTER.**—The court may refer any issue arising in connection with a proposed order of restitution to a magistrate or special master for proposed findings of fact and recommendations as to disposition, subject to a de novo determination of the issue by the court.

"(f) **DEFINITION.**—For purposes of this section, the term 'victim' means the individual harmed as a result of a commission of a crime under this chapter, including, in the case of a victim who is under 18 years of age, incompetent, incapacitated, or deceased, the legal guardian of the victim or representative of the victim's estate, another family member, or any other person appointed as suitable by the court, but in no event shall the defendant be named as such representative or guardian.".

(2) **TECHNICAL AMENDMENT.**—The chapter analysis for chapter 109A of title 18, United States Code, is amended by adding at the end the following new item:

"2248. Mandatory restitution.".

(b) **SEXUAL EXPLOITATION AND OTHER ABUSE OF CHILDREN.**—

(1) **IN GENERAL.**—Chapter 110 of title 18, United States Code, is amended by adding at the end the following new section:

"§ 2259. Mandatory restitution

"(a) **IN GENERAL.**—Notwithstanding section 3663, and in addition to any other civil or criminal penalty authorized by law, the court shall order restitution for any offense under this chapter.

"(b) **SCOPE AND NATURE OF ORDER.**—

"(1) **DIRECTIONS.**—The order of restitution under this section shall direct that—

"(A) the defendant pay to the victim (through the appropriate court mechanism) the full amount of the victim's losses as determined by the court, pursuant to paragraph (3); and

"(B) the United States Attorney enforce the restitution order by all available and reasonable means.

"(2) **ENFORCEMENT BY VICTIM.**—An order of restitution may also be enforced by a victim named in the order to receive the restitution in the same manner as a judgment in a civil action.

"(3) **DEFINITION.**—For purposes of this subsection, the term 'full amount of the victim's losses' includes any costs incurred by the victim for—

"(A) medical services relating to physical, psychiatric, or psychological care;

"(B) physical and occupational therapy or rehabilitation;

"(C) necessary transportation, temporary housing, and child care expenses;

"(D) lost income;

"(E) attorneys' fees, as well as other costs incurred; and

"(F) any other losses suffered by the victim as a proximate result of the offense.

"(4) **ORDER MANDATORY.**—(A) The issuance of a restitution order under this section is mandatory.

"(B) A court may not decline to issue an order under this section because of—

"(i) the economic circumstances of the defendant; or

"(ii) the fact that a victim has, or is entitled to, receive compensation for his or her injuries from the proceeds of insurance or any other source.

"(C)(i) Notwithstanding subparagraph (A), the court may take into account the economic circumstances of the defendant in determining the manner in which and the schedule according to which the restitution is to be paid.

"(ii) For purposes of this subparagraph, the term 'economic circumstances' includes—

"(I) the financial resources and other assets of the defendant;

"(II) projected earnings, earning capacity, and other income of the defendant; and

"(III) any financial obligations of the defendant, including obligations to dependents.

"(D) Subparagraph (A) does not apply if—

"(i) the court finds on the record that the economic circumstances of the defendant do not allow for the payment of any amount of a restitution order, and do not allow for the payment of any or some portion of the amount of a restitution order in the foreseeable future (under any reasonable schedule of payments); and

"(ii) the court enters in its order the amount of the victim's losses, and provides a nominal restitution award.

"(5) **MORE THAN 1 OFFENDER.**—When the court finds that more than 1 offender has contributed to the loss of a victim, the court may make each offender liable for payment of the full amount of restitution or may apportion liability among the offenders to reflect the level of contribution and economic circumstances of each offender.

"(6) **MORE THAN 1 VICTIM.**—When the court finds that more than 1 victim has sustained a loss requiring restitution by an offender, the court shall order full restitution of each victim but may provide for different payment schedules to reflect the economic circumstances of each victim.

"(7) **PAYMENT SCHEDULE.**—An order under this section may direct the defendant to make a single lump-sum payment or partial payments at specified intervals.

"(8) **SETOFF.**—Any amount paid to a victim under this section shall be set off against any amount later recovered as compensatory damages by the victim from the defendant in—

"(A) any Federal civil proceeding; and

"(B) any State civil proceeding, to the extent provided by the law of the State.

"(9) **EFFECT ON OTHER SOURCES OF COMPENSATION.**—The issuance of a restitution order shall not affect the entitlement of a victim to receive compensation with respect to a loss from insurance or any other source until the payments actually received by the victim under the restitution order fully compensate the victim for the loss.

"(10) **CONDITION OF PROBATION OR SUPERVISED RELEASE.**—Compliance with a restitution order issued under this section shall be a condition of any probation or supervised release of a defendant. If an offender fails to comply with a restitution order, the court may, after a hearing, revoke probation or a term of supervised release, modify the terms or conditions of probation or a term of supervised release, or hold the defendant in contempt pursuant to section 3583(e). In determining whether to revoke probation or a term of supervised release, modify the terms or conditions of probation or supervised release or hold a defendant serving a term of supervised release in contempt, the court shall consider the defendant's employment status, earning ability and financial resources, the willfulness of the defendant's failure to comply, and any other circumstances that may have a bearing on the defendant's ability to comply.

"(c) **PROOF OF CLAIM.**—

"(1) **AFFIDAVIT.**—Within 60 days after conviction and, in any event, not later than 10 days prior to sentencing, the United States Attorney (or the United States Attorney's delegee), after consulting with the victim, shall prepare and file an affidavit with the court listing the amounts subject to restitution under this section. The affidavit shall be signed by the United States Attorney (or the United States Attorney's delegee) and the victim. Should the victim object to any of the information included in the affidavit, the United States Attorney (or the United States Attorney's delegee) shall advise the victim that the victim may file a separate affidavit and shall provide the victim with an affidavit form which may be used to do so.

"(2) **OBJECTION.**—If, after the defendant has been notified of the affidavit, no objection is raised by the defendant, the amounts attested to in the affidavit filed pursuant to paragraph (1) shall be entered in the court's restitution order. If objection is raised, the court may require the victim or the United States Attorney (or the United States Attorney's delegee) to submit further affidavits or other supporting documents, demonstrating the victim's losses.

"(3) **ADDITIONAL DOCUMENTATION AND TESTIMONY.**—If the court concludes, after reviewing the supporting documentation and considering the defendant's objections, that there is a substantial reason for doubting the authenticity or veracity of the records submitted, the court may require additional documentation or hear testimony on those questions. The privacy of any records filed, or testimony heard, pursuant to this section shall be maintained to the greatest extent possible, and such records may be filed or testimony heard in camera.

"(4) **FINAL DETERMINATION OF LOSSES.**—If the victim's losses are not ascertainable by the date that is 10 days prior to sentencing as provided in paragraph (1), the United States Attorney (or the United States Attorney's delegee) shall so inform the court, and the court shall set a date for the final determination of the victim's losses, not to exceed 90 days after sentencing. If the victim subsequently discovers further losses, the victim shall have 60 days after discovery of those losses in which to petition the court for an amended restitution order. Such order may be granted only upon a showing of good cause for the failure to include such losses in the initial claim for restitutionary relief.

"(d) **MODIFICATION OF ORDER.**—A victim or the offender may petition the court at any time to modify a restitution order as appropriate in view of a change in the economic circumstances of the offender.

"(e) **REFERENCE TO MAGISTRATE OR SPECIAL MASTER.**—The court may refer any issue arising in connection with a proposed order of restitution to a magistrate or special master for proposed findings of fact and recommendations as to disposition, subject to a de novo determination of the issue by the court.

"(f) **DEFINITION.**—For the purposes of this section, the term 'victim' means the individual harmed as a result of a commission of a crime under this chapter, including, in the case of a victim who is under 18 years of age, incompetent, incapacitated, or deceased, the legal guardian of the victim or representative of the victim's estate, another family member, or any other person appointed as suitable by the court, but in no event shall the defendant be named as such representative or guardian.".

(2) **TECHNICAL AMENDMENT.**—The chapter analysis for chapter 110 of title 18, United States Code, is amended by adding at the end the following new item:

"2259. Mandatory restitution.".

Subtitle E—Violence Against Women Act Improvements

* * *

SEC. 40503. PAYMENT OF COST OF TESTING FOR SEXUALLY TRANSMITTED DISEASES.

(a) **FOR VICTIMS IN SEX OFFENSE CASES.**—Section 503(c)(7) of the Victims' Rights and Restitution Act of 1990 (42 U.S.C. 10607(c)(7)) is amended by adding at the end the following: "The Attorney General shall provide for the payment of the cost of up to 2 anonymous and confidential tests of the victim for sexually transmitted diseases, including HIV, gonorrhea, herpes, chlamydia, and syphilis, during the 12 months following sexual assaults that pose a risk of transmission, and the cost of a counseling session by a medically trained professional on the accuracy of such tests and the risk of transmission of sexually transmitted diseases to the victim as the result of the assault. A victim may waive anonymity and confidentiality of any tests paid for under this section.".

(b) **LIMITED TESTING OF DEFENDANTS.**—

(1) **COURT ORDER.**—The victim of an offense of the type referred to in subsection (a) may obtain an order in the district court of the United States for the district in which charges are brought against the defendant charged with the offense, after notice to the defendant and an opportunity to be heard, requiring that the defendant be tested for the presence of the etiologic agent for acquired immune deficiency

syndrome, and that the results of the test be communicated to the victim and the defendant. Any test result of the defendant given to the victim or the defendant must be accompanied by appropriate counseling.

(2) **SHOWING REQUIRED**.—To obtain an order under paragraph (1), the victim must demonstrate that—

(A) the defendant has been charged with the offense in a State or Federal court, and if the defendant has been arrested without a warrant, a probable cause determination has been made;

(B) the test for the etiologic agent for acquired immune deficiency syndrome is requested by the victim after appropriate counseling; and

(C) the test would provide information necessary for the health of the victim of the alleged offense and the court determines that the alleged conduct of the defendant created a risk of transmission, as determined by the Centers for Disease Control, of the etiologic agent for acquired immune deficiency syndrome to the victim.

(3) **FOLLOW–UP TESTING**.—The court may order follow-up tests and counseling under paragraph (b)(1) if the initial test was negative. Such follow-up tests and counseling shall be performed at the request of the victim on dates that occur six months and twelve months following the initial test.

(4) **TERMINATION OF TESTING REQUIREMENTS**.—An order for follow-up testing under paragraph (3) shall be terminated if the person obtains an acquittal on, or dismissal of, all charges of the type referred to in subsection (a).

(5) **CONFIDENTIALITY OF TEST**.—The results of any test ordered under this subsection shall be disclosed only to the victim or, where the court deems appropriate, to the parent or legal guardian of the victim, and to the person tested. The victim may disclose the test results only to any medical professional, counselor, family member or sexual partner(s) the victim may have had since the attack. Any such individual to whom the test results are disclosed by the victim shall maintain the confidentiality of such information.

(6) **DISCLOSURE OF TEST RESULTS**.—The court shall issue an order to prohibit the disclosure by the victim of the results of any test performed under this subsection to anyone other than those mentioned in paragraph (5). The contents of the court proceedings and test results pursuant to this section shall be sealed. The results of such test performed on the defendant under this section shall not be used as evidence in any criminal trial.

(7) **CONTEMPT FOR DISCLOSURE**.—Any person who discloses the results of a test in violation of this subsection may be held in contempt of court.

(c) **PENALTIES FOR INTENTIONAL TRANSMISSION OF HIV**.—Not later than 6 months after the date of enactment of this Act, the United States Sentencing Commission shall conduct a study and prepare and submit to the committees on the Judiciary of the Senate and the House of Representatives a report concerning recommendations for the revision of sentencing guidelines that relate to offenses in which an HIV infected individual engages in sexual activity if the individual known that he or she is infected with HIV and intends, through such sexual activity, to expose another to HIV.

SEC. 40504. EXTENSION AND STRENGTHENING OF RESTITUTION.

Section 3663(b) of title 18, United States Code, is amended—

(1) in paragraph (2) by inserting "including an offense under chapter 109A or chapter 110" after "an offense resulting in bodily injury to a victim";

(2) by striking "and" at the end of paragraph (3);

(3) by redesignating paragraph (4) as paragraph (5); and

(4) by inserting after paragraph (3) the following new paragraph:

"(4) in any case, reimburse the victim for lost income and necessary child care, transportation, and other expenses related to participation in the investigation or prosecution of the offense or attendance at proceedings related to the offense; and".

SEC. 40505. ENFORCEMENT OF RESTITUTION ORDERS THROUGH SUSPENSION OF FEDERAL BENEFITS.

Section 3663 of title 18, United States Code, is amended by adding at the end the following new subsection:

"(i)(1) A Federal agency shall immediately suspend all Federal benefits provided by the agency to the defendant, and shall terminate the defendant's eligibility for Federal benefits administered by that agency, upon receipt of a certified copy of a written judicial finding that the defendant is delinquent in making restitution in accordance with any schedule of payments or any requirement of immediate payment imposed under this section.

"(2) Any written finding of delinquency described in paragraph (1) shall be made by a court, after a hearing, upon motion of the victim named in the order to receive the restitution or upon motion of the United States.

"(3) A defendant found to be delinquent may subsequently seek a written finding from the court that the defendant has rectified the delinquency or that the defendant has made and will make good faith efforts to rectify the delinquency. The defendant's eligibility for Federal benefits shall be reinstated upon receipt by the agency of a certified copy of such a finding.

"(4) In this subsection, 'Federal benefit' means a grant, contract, loan, professional license, or commercial license provided by an agency of the United States.".

* * *

TITLE VII—MANDATORY LIFE IMPRISONMENT FOR PERSONS CONVICTED OF CERTAIN FELONIES

SEC. 70001. MANDATORY LIFE IMPRISONMENT FOR PERSONS CONVICTED OF CERTAIN FELONIES.

Section 3559 of title 18, United States Code, is amended—

(1) in subsection (b), by striking "An" and inserting "Except as provided in subsection (c), an" in lieu thereof; and

(2) by adding the following new subsection at the end:

"(c) **IMPRISONMENT OF CERTAIN VIOLENT FELONS.**—

"(1) **MANDATORY LIFE IMPRISONMENT.**—Notwithstanding any other provision of law, a person who is convicted in a court of the United States of a serious violent felony shall be sentenced to life imprisonment if—

"(A) the person has been convicted (and those convictions have become final) on separate prior occasions in a court of the United States or of a State of—

"(i) 2 or more serious violent felonies; or

"(ii) one or more serious violent felonies and one or more serious drug offenses; and

"(B) each serious violent felony or serious drug offense used as a basis for sentencing under this subsection, other than the first, was committed after the defendant's conviction of the preceding serious violent felony or serious drug offense.

"(2) **DEFINITIONS.**—For purposes of this subsection—

"(A) the term 'assault with intent to commit rape' means an offense that has as its elements engaging in physical contact with another person or using or brandishing a weapon against another person with intent to commit aggravated sexual abuse or sexual abuse (as described in sections 2241 and 2242);

"(B) the term 'arson' means an offense that has as its elements maliciously damaging or destroying any building, inhabited structure, vehicle, vessel, or real property by means of fire or an explosive;

"(C) the term 'extortion' means an offense that has as its elements the extraction of anything of value from another person by threatening or placing that person in fear of injury to any person or kidnapping of any person;

"(D) the term 'firearms use' means an offense that has as its elements those described in section 924(c) or 929(a), if the firearm was brandished, discharged, or otherwise used as a weapon and the crime of violence or drug trafficking crime during and relation to which the firearm was used was subject to prosecution in a court of the United States or a court of a State, or both;

"(E) the term 'kidnapping' means an offense that has as its elements the abduction, restraining, confining, or carrying away of another person by force or threat of force;

"(F) the term 'serious violent felony' means—

"(i) a Federal or State offense, by whatever designation and wherever committed, consisting of murder (as described in section 1111); manslaughter other than involuntary manslaughter (as described in section 1112); assault with intent to commit murder (as described in section 113(a)); assault with intent to commit rape; aggravated sexual abuse and sexual abuse (as described in sections 2241 and 2242); abusive sexual contact (as described in sections 2244(a)(1) and (a)(2)); kidnapping; aircraft piracy (as described in section 46502 of Title 49); robbery (as described in section 2111, 2113, or 2118); carjacking (as described in section 2119); extortion; arson; firearms use; or attempt, conspiracy, or solicitation to commit any of the above offenses; and

"(ii) any other offense punishable by a maximum term of imprisonment of 10 years or more that has as an element the use, attempted use, or threatened use of physical force against the person of another or that, by its nature, involves a substantial risk that physical force against the person of another may be used in the course of committing the offense;

"(G) the term 'State' means a State of the United States, the District of Columbia, and a commonwealth, territory, or possession of the United States; and

"(H) the term 'serious drug offense' means—

"(i) an offense that is punishable under section 401(b)(1)(A) or 408 of the Controlled Substances Act (21 U.S.C. 841(b)(1)(A), 848) or section 1010(b)(1)(A) of the Controlled Substances Import and Export Act (21 U.S.C. 960(b)(1)(A)); or

"(ii) an offense under State law that, had the offense been prosecuted in a court of the United States, would have been punishable under 401(b)(1)(A) or 408 of the Controlled Substances Act (21 U.S.C. 841(b)(1)(A), 848) or section 1010(b)(1)(A) of the Controlled Substances Import and Export Act (21 U.S.C. 960(b)(1)(A)); or

"(3) **NONQUALIFYING FELONIES.**—

"(A) **ROBBERY IN CERTAIN CASES.**—Robbery, an attempt, conspiracy, or solicitation to commit robbery; or an offense described in paragraph (2)(F)(ii) shall not serve as a basis for sentencing under this subsection if the defendant establishes by clear and convincing evidence that—

"(i) no firearm or other dangerous weapon was used in the offense and no threat of use of a firearm or other dangerous weapon was involved in the offense; and

"(ii) the offense did not result in death or serious bodily injury (as defined in section 1365) to any person.

"(B) **ARSON IN CERTAIN CASES.**—Arson shall not serve as a basis for sentencing under this subsection if the defendant establishes by clear and convincing evidence that—

"(i) the offense posed no threat to human life; and

"(ii) the defendant reasonably believed the offense posed no threat to human life.

"(4) **INFORMATION FILED BY UNITED STATES ATTORNEY.**—The provisions of section 411(a) of the Controlled Substances Act (21 U.S.C. 851(a)) shall apply to the imposition of sentence under this subsection.

"(5) **RULE OF CONSTRUCTION.**—This subsection shall not be construed to preclude imposition of the death penalty.

"(6) **SPECIAL PROVISION FOR INDIAN COUNTRY.**—No person subject to the criminal jurisdiction of an Indian tribal government shall be subject to this subsection for any offense for which Federal jurisdiction is solely predicated on Indian country (as defined in section 1151) and which occurs within the boundaries of such Indian country unless the governing body of the tribe has elected that this subsection have effect over land and persons subject to the criminal jurisdiction of the tribe.

"(7) **RESENTENCING UPON OVERTURNING OF PRIOR CONVICTION.**—If the conviction for a serious violent felony or serious drug offense that was a basis for sentencing under this subsection is found, pursuant to any appropriate State or Federal procedure, to be unconstitutional or is vitiated on the explicit basis of innocence, or if the convicted person is pardoned on the explicit basis of innocence, the person serving a sentence imposed under this subsection shall be resentenced to any sentence that was available at the time of the original sentencing.".

TITLE VIII—APPLICABILITY OF MANDATORY MINIMUM PENALTIES IN CERTAIN CASES

SEC. 80001. LIMITATION ON APPLICABILITY OF MANDATORY MINIMUM PENALTIES IN CERTAIN CASES.

(a) IN GENERAL.—Section 3553 of title 18, United States Code, is amended by adding at the end the following new subsection:

"(f) **LIMITATION ON APPLICABILITY OF STATUTORY MINIMUMS IN CERTAIN CASES.**—Notwithstanding any other provision of law, in the case of an offense under section 401, 404, or 406 of the Controlled Substances Act (21 U.S.C. 841, 844, 846) or section 1010 or 1013 of the Controlled Substances Import and Export Act (21 U.S.C. 961, 963), the court shall impose a sentence pursuant to guidelines promulgated by the United States Sentencing Commission under section 994 of title 28 without regard to any statutory minimum sentence, if the court finds at sentencing, after the Government has been afforded the opportunity to make a recommendation, that—

"(1) the defendant does not have more than 1 criminal history point, as determined under the sentencing guidelines;

"(2) the defendant did not use violence or credible threats of violence or possess a firearm or other dangerous weapon (or induce another participant to do so) in connection with the offense;

"(3) the offense did not result in death or serious bodily injury to any person;

"(4) the defendant was not an organizer, leader, manager, or supervisor of others in the offense, as determined under the sentencing guidelines and was not engaged in a continuing criminal enterprise, as defined in 21 U.S.C. 848; and

"(5) not later than the time of the sentencing hearing, the defendant has truthfully provided to the Government all information and evidence the defendant has concerning the offense or offenses that were part of the same course of conduct or of a common scheme or plan, but the fact that the defendant has no relevant or useful other information to provide or that the Government is already aware of the information shall not preclude a determination by the court that the defendant has complied with this requirement."

(b) **SENTENCING COMMISSION AUTHORITY.**—

(1) **IN GENERAL.**—(A) The United States Sentencing Commission (referred to in this subsection as the "Commission"), under section 994(a)(1) and (p) of title 28—

(i) shall promulgate guidelines, or amendments to guidelines, to carry out the purposes of this section and the amendment made by this section; and

(ii) may promulgate policy statements, or amendments to policy statements, to assist in the application of this section and that amendment.

(B) In the case of a defendant for whom the statutorily required minimum sentence is 5 years, such guidelines and amendments to guidelines issued under subparagraph (A) shall call for a guideline range in which the lowest term of imprisonment is at lease 24 months.

(2) **PROCEDURES.**—If the Commission determines that it is necessary to do so in order that the amendments made under paragraph (1) may take effect on the effective date of the amendment made by subsection (a), the Commission may promulgate the amendments made under paragraph (1) in accordance with the procedures set forth in section 21(a) of the Sentencing Act of 1987, as though the authority under that section had not expired.

(c) **EFFECTIVE DATE AND APPLICATION.**—The amendment made by subsection (a) shall apply to all sentences imposed on or after the 10th day beginning after the date of enactment of this Act.

TITLE IX—DRUG CONTROL

Subtitle A—Enhanced Penalties and General Provisions

SEC. 90101. ENHANCEMENT OF PENALTIES FOR DRUG TRAFFICKING IN PRISONS.

Section 1791 of title 18, United States Code, is amended—

(1) in subsection (c), by inserting before "Any" the following new sentence: "Any punishment imposed under subsection (b) for a violation of this section involving a controlled substance shall be consecutive to any other sentence imposed by any court for an offense involving such a controlled substance.";

(2) in subsection (d)(1)(A), by inserting after "a firearm or destructive device" the following: "or a controlled substance in schedule I or II, other than marijuana or a controlled substance referred to in subparagraph (C) of this subsection";

(3) in subsection (d)(1)(B), by inserting before "ammunition," the following: "marijuana or a controlled substance in schedule III, other than a controlled substance referred to in subparagraph (C) of this subsection,";

(4) in subsection (d)(1)(C), by inserting "methamphetamine, its salts, isomers, and salts of its isomers," after "a narcotic drug,";

(5) in subsection (d)(1)(D), by inserting "(A), (B), or" before "(C)"; and

(6) in subsection (b), by striking "(c)" each place it appears and inserting "(d)".

SEC. 90102. INCREASED PENALTIES FOR DRUG-DEALING IN "DRUG-FREE" ZONES.

Pursuant to its authority under section 994 of title 28, United States Code, the United States Sentencing Commission shall amend its sentencing guidelines to provide an appropriate enhancement for a defendant convicted of violating section 419 of the Controlled Substances Act (21 U.S.C. 860).

SEC. 90103. ENHANCED PENALTIES FOR ILLEGAL DRUG USE IN FEDERAL PRISONS AND FOR SMUGGLING DRUGS INTO FEDERAL PRISONS.

(a) **DECLARATION OF POLICY.**—It is the policy of the Federal Government that the use or distribution of illegal drugs in the Nation's Federal prisons will not be tolerated and that such crimes shall be prosecuted to the fullest extent of the law.

(b) **SENTENCING GUIDELINES.**—Pursuant to its authority under section 994 of title 28, United States Code, the United States Sentencing Commission shall amend its sentencing guidelines to appropriately enhance the penalty for a person convicted of an offense—

(1) under section 404 of the Controlled Substances Act involving simple possession of a controlled substance within a Federal prison or other Federal detention facility; or

(2) under section 401(b) of the Controlled Substances Act involving the smuggling of a controlled substance into a Federal prison or other Federal detention facility or the distribution or intended distribution of a controlled substance within a Federal prison or other Federal detention facility.

(c) **NO PROBATION.**—Notwithstanding any other law, the court shall not sentence a person convicted of an offense described in subsection (b) to probation.

* * *

TITLE XI—FIREARMS

Subtitle E—Gun Crime Penalties

SEC. 110501. ENHANCED PENALTY FOR USE OF A SEMIAUTOMATIC FIREARM DURING A CRIME OF VIOLENCE OR A DRUG TRAFFICKING CRIME.

(a) **AMENDMENT TO SENTENCING GUIDELINES.**—Pursuant to its authority under section 994 of title 28, United States Code, the United States Sentencing Commission shall amend its sentencing guidelines to provide an appropriate enhancement of the punishment for a crime of violence (as defined in section 924(c)(3) of title 18, United States Code) or a drug trafficking crime (as defined in section 924(c)(2) of title 18, United States Code) if a semiautomatic firearm is involved.

(b) **SEMIAUTOMATIC FIREARM.**—In subsection (a), "semiautomatic firearm" means any repeating firearm that utilizes a portion of the energy of a firing cartridge to extract the fired cartridge case and chamber the next round and that requires a separate pull of the trigger to fire each cartridge.

SEC. 110502. ENHANCED PENALTY FOR SECOND OFFENSE OF USING AN EXPLOSIVE TO COMMIT A FELONY.

Pursuant to its authority under section 994 of title 28, United States Code, the United States Sentencing Commission shall promulgate amendments to the sentencing guidelines to appropriately enhance penalties in a case in which a defendant convicted under section 844(h) of title 18, United States Code, has previously been convicted under that section.

* * *

SEC. 110505. REVOCATION OF SUPERVISED RELEASE AFTER IMPRISONMENT.

Section 3583 of title 18, United States Code, is amended—

(1) in subsection (d) by striking "possess illegal controlled substances" and inserting "unlawfully possess a controlled substance";

(2) in subsection (e)—

(A) by striking "person" each place such term appears in such subsection and inserting "defendant"; and

(B) by amending paragraph (3) to read as follows:

"(3) revoke a term of supervised release, and require the defendant to serve in prison all or part of the term of supervised release authorized by statute for the offense that resulted in such term of supervised release without credit for time previously served on postrelease supervision, if the court, pursuant to the Federal Rules of Criminal Procedure applicable to revocation of probation or supervised release, finds by a preponderance of the evidence that the defendant violated a condition of supervised release, except that a defendant whose term is revoked under this paragraph may not be required to serve more than 5 years in prison if the offense that resulted in the term of supervised release is a class A felony, more than 3 years in prison if such offense is a class B felony, more than 2 years in prison if such offense is a class C or D felony, or more than one year in any other case; or"; and

(3) by striking subsection (g) and inserting the following:

"(g) **MANDATORY REVOCATION FOR POSSESSION OF CONTROLLED SUBSTANCE OR FIREARM OR FOR REFUSAL TO COMPLY WITH DRUG TESTING.**—If the defendant—

"(1) possesses a controlled substance in violation of the condition set forth in subsection (d);

"(2) possesses a firearm, as such term is defined in section 921 of this title, in violation of Federal law, or otherwise violates a condition of supervised release prohibiting the defendant from possessing a firearm; or

"(3) refuses to comply with drug testing imposed as a condition of supervised release;

the court shall revoke the term of supervised release and require the defendant to serve a term of imprisonment not to exceed the maximum term of imprisonment authorized under subsection (e)(3).

"(h) **SUPERVISED RELEASE FOLLOWING REVOCATION.**—When a term of supervised release is revoked and the defendant is required to serve a term of imprisonment that is less than the maximum term of imprisonment authorized under subsection (e)(3), the court may include a requirement that the defendant be placed on a term of supervised release after imprisonment. The length of such a term of supervised release shall not exceed the term of supervised release authorized by statute for the offense that resulted in the original term of supervised release, less any term of imprisonment that was imposed upon revocation of supervised release.

"(i) **DELAYED REVOCATION.**—The power of the court to revoke a term of supervised release for violation of a condition of supervised release, and to order the defendant to serve a term of imprisonment and, subject to the limitations in subsection (h), a further term of supervised release, extends beyond the expiration of the term of supervised release for any period reasonably necessary for the adjudication of matters arising before its expiration if, before its expiration, a warrant or summons has been issued on the basis of an allegation of such a violation.".

SEC. 110506. REVOCATION OF PROBATION.

(a) **IN GENERAL.**—Section 3565(a) of title 18, United States Code, is amended—

(1) in paragraph (2) by striking "impose any other sentence that was available under subchapter A at the time of the initial sentencing" and inserting "resentence the defendant under subchapter A"; and

(2) by striking the last sentence.

(b) **MANDATORY REVOCATION.**—Section 3565(b) of title 18, United States Code, is amended to read as follows:

"(b) **MANDATORY REVOCATION FOR POSSESSION OF CONTROLLED SUBSTANCE OR FIREARM OR REFUSAL TO COMPLY WITH DRUG TESTING.**—If the defendant—

"(1) possesses a controlled substance in violation of the condition set forth in section 3563(a)(3);

"(2) possesses a firearm, as such term is defined in section 921 of this title, in violation of Federal law, or otherwise violates a condition of probation prohibiting the defendant from possessing a firearm; or

"(3) refuses to comply with drug testing, thereby violating the condition imposed by section 3563(a)(4),

the court shall revoke the sentence of probation and resentence the defendant under subchapter A to a sentence that includes a term of imprisonment.".

* * *

SEC. 110512. USING A FIREARM IN THE COMMISSION OF COUNTERFEITING OR FORGERY.

Pursuant to its authority under section 994 of title 28, United States Code, the United States Sentencing Commission shall amend its sentencing guidelines to provide an appropriate enhancement of the punishment for a defendant convicted of a felony under chapter 25 of title 18, United States Code, if the defendant used or carried a firearm (as defined in section 921(a)(3) of title 18, United States Code) during and in relation to the felony.

SEC. 110513. ENHANCED PENALTIES FOR FIREARMS POSSESSION BY VIOLENT FELONS AND SERIOUS DRUG OFFENDERS.

Pursuant to its authority under section 994 of title 28, United States Code, the United States Sentencing Commission shall amend its sentencing guidelines to—

(1) appropriately enhance penalties in cases in which a defendant convicted under section 922(g) of title 18, United States Code, has 1 prior conviction by any court referred to in section 922(g)(1) of title 18 for a violent felony (as defined in section 924(e)(2)(B) of that title) or a serious drug offense (as defined in section 924(e)(2)(A) of that title); and

(2) appropriately enhance penalties in cases in which such a defendant has 2 prior convictions for violent felony (as so defined) or a serious drug offense (as so defined).

* * *

TITLE XII—TERRORISM

* * *

SEC. 120004. SENTENCING GUIDELINES INCREASE FOR TERRORIST CRIMES.

The United States Sentencing Commission is directed to amend its sentencing guidelines to provide an appropriate enhancement for any felony, whether committed within or outside the United States, that involves or is intended to promote international terrorism, unless such involvement or intent is itself an element of the crime.

* * *

TITLE XIV—YOUTH VIOLENCE

* * *

SEC. 140008. SOLICITATION OF MINOR TO COMMIT CRIME.

(a) **DIRECTIVE TO SENTENCING COMMISSION.**—(1) The United States Sentencing Commission shall promulgate guidelines or amend existing guidelines to provide that a defendant 21 years of age or older who has been convicted of an offense shall receive an appropriate sentence enhancement if the defendant involved a minor in the commission of the offense.

(2) The Commission shall provide that the guideline enhancement promulgated pursuant to paragraph (1) shall apply for any offense in relation to which the defendant has solicited, procured, recruited, counseled, encouraged, trained, directed, commanded, intimidated, or otherwise used or attempted to use any person less than 18 years of age with the intent that the minor would commit a Federal offense.

(b) **RELEVANT CONSIDERATIONS.**—In implementing the directive in subsection (a), the Sentencing Commission shall consider—

(1) the severity of the crime that the defendant intended the minor to commit;

(2) the number of minors that the defendant used or attempted to use in relation to the offense;

(3) the fact that involving a minor in a crime of violence is frequently of even greater seriousness than involving a minor in a drug trafficking offense, for which the guidelines already provide a two-level enhancement; and

(4) the possible relevance of the proximity in age between the offender and the minor(s) involved in the offense.

* * *

TITLE XVIII—RURAL CRIME

* * *

Subtitle B—Drug Free Truck Stops and Safety Rest Areas

SEC. 180201. DRUG FREE TRUCK STOPS AND SAFETY REST AREAS.

(a) **SHORT TITLE.**—This section may be cited as the "Drug Free Truck Stop Act".

(b) **AMENDMENT TO CONTROLLED SUBSTANCES ACT.**—

(1) **IN GENERAL.**—Part D of the Controlled Substances Act (21 U.S.C. 801 et seq.) is amended by inserting after section 408 the following new section:

"TRANSPORTATION SAFETY OFFENSES

"SEC. 409. (a) DEFINITIONS.—In this section—

"'safety rest area' means a roadside facility with parking facilities for the rest or other needs of motorists.

"'truck stop' means a facility (including any parking lot appurtenant thereto) that—

"(A) has the capacity to provide fuel or service, or both, to any commercial motor vehicle (as defined in section 31301 of title 49, United States Code), operating in commerce (as defined in that section); and

"(B) is located within 2,500 feet of the Nation System of Interstate and Defense Highways or the Federal-Aid Primary System.

"(B) **FIRST OFFENSE.**—A person who violates section 401(a)(1) or section 416 by distributing or possessing with intent to distribute a controlled substance in or on, or within 1,00 feet or, a truck stop or safety rest area is (except as provided in subsection (b)) subject to—

"(1) twice the maximum punishment authorized by section 401(b); and

"(2) twice any term of supervised release authorized by section 401(b) for a first offense.

"(c) **SUBSEQUENT OFFENSE.**—A person who violates section 401(a)(1) or section 416 by distributing or possessing with intent to distribute a controlled substance in or on, or within 1,000 feet of, a truck stop or a safety rest area after a prior conviction or convictions under subsection (a) have become final is subject to—

"(1) 3 time the maximum punishment authorized by section 401(b); and

"(2) 3 time any term of supervised release authorized by section 401(b) for a first offense.".

(2) **TECHNICAL AMENDMENTS.**—

(A) **CROSS REFERENCE.**—Section 401(b) of the Controlled Substances Act (21 U.S.C. 841 (b)) is amended by inserting "409," before "418," each place it appears.

(B) **TABLE OF CONTENTS.**—The table of contents of the Comprehensive Drug Abuse Prevention and Control Act of 1970 is amended by striking the item relating to section 409 and inserting the following new item:

"Sec. 409. Transportation safety offenses.".

(c) **SENTENCING GUIDELINES.**—Pursuant to its authority under section 994 of title 28, United States Code, and section 21 of the Sentencing Act of 1987 (28 U.S.C. 994 note), the United States Sentencing Commission shall promulgate guidelines, or shall amend existing guidelines, to provide an appropriate enhancement of punishment for a defendant convicted of violation section 409 of the Controlled Substances Act, as added by subsection (b).

* * *

TITLE XXIII—VICTIMS OF CRIME

Subtitle A—Victims of Crime

SEC. 230101. VICTIM'S RIGHT OF ALLOCUTION IN SENTENCING.

(a) **MODIFICATION OF PROPOSED AMENDMENTS.**—The proposed amendments to the Federal Rules of Criminal Procedure which are embraced by an order entered by the Supreme Court of the United States on April 29, 1994, shall take effect on December 1, 1994, as otherwise provided by law, but with the following amendments:

(b) **IN GENERAL.**—Rule 32 of the Federal Rules of Criminal Procedure is amended by—

(1) striking "and" following the semicolon in subdivision (c)(3)(C);

(2) striking the period at the end of subdivision (c)(3)(D) and inserting "; and";

(3) inserting after subdivision (c)(3)(D) the following:

"(E) if sentence is to be imposed for a crime of violence or sexual abuse, address the victim personally if the victim is present at the sentencing hearing and determine if the victim wishes to make a statement or present any information in relation to the sentence.";

(4) in subdivision (c)(3)(D), striking "equivalent opportunity" and inserting in lieu thereof "opportunity equivalent to that of the defendant's counsel";

(5) in the last sentence of subdivision (c)(4), striking "and (D)" and inserting "(D), and (E)";

(6) in the last sentence of subdivision (c)(4), inserting "the victim," before "or the attorney for the Government."; and

(7) adding at the end the following:

"(f) **DEFINITIONS.**—For purposes of this rule—

"(1) 'victim' means any individual against whom an offense has been committed for which a sentence is to be imposed, but the right of allocution under subdivision (c)(3)(E) may be exercised instead by—

"(A) a parent or legal guardian if the victim is below the age of eighteen years or incompetent; or

"(B) one or more family members or relatives designated by the court if the victim is deceased or incapacitated;

if such person or persons are present at the sentencing hearing, regardless of whether the victim is present; and

"(2) 'crime of violence or sexual abuse' means a crime that involved the use or attempted or threatened use of physical force against the person or property of another, or a crime under chapter 109A of title 18, United States Code.".

(c) **EFFECTIVE DATE.**—The amendments made by subsection (b) shall become effective on December 1, 1994.

* * *

TITLE XXIV—PROTECTIONS FOR THE ELDERLY

* * *

SEC. 24002. CRIMES AGAINST THE ELDERLY.

(a) **IN GENERAL.**—Pursuant to its authority under the Sentencing Reform Act of 1984 and section 21 of the Sentencing Act of 1987 (including its authority to amend the sentencing guidelines and policy statements) and its authority to make such amendments on an emergency basis, the United States Sentencing Commission shall ensure that the applicable guideline range for a defendant convicted of a crime of violence against an elderly victim is sufficiently stringent to deter such a crime, to protect the public from additional crimes of such a defendant, and to adequately reflect the heinous nature of such an offense.

(b) **CRITERIA.**—In carrying out subsection (a), the United States Sentencing Commission shall ensure that—

(1) the guidelines provide for increasingly severe punishment for a defendant commensurate with the degree of physical harm caused to the elderly victim;

(2) the guidelines take appropriate account of the vulnerability of the victim; and

(3) the guidelines provide enhanced punishment for a defendant convicted of a crime of violence against an elderly victim who has previously been convicted of a crime of violence against an elderly victim, regardless of whether the conviction occurred in Federal or State court.

(c) **DEFINITIONS**.—In this section—

"crime of violence" means an offense under section 113, 114, 1111, 1112, 1113, 1117, 2241, 2242, or 2244 of title 18, United States Code.

"elderly victim" means a victim who is 65 years of age or older at the time of an offense.

TITLE XXV—SENIOR CITIZENS AGAINST MARKETING SCAMS

* * *

"CHAPTER 113B—TERRORISM".

SEC. 250003. INCREASED PENALTIES FOR FRAUD AGAINST OLDER VICTIMS.

(a) **REVIEW**.—The United States Sentencing Commission shall review and, if necessary, amend the sentencing guidelines to ensure that victim related adjustments for fraud offenses against older victims over the age of 55 are adequate.

(b) **REPORT**.—Not later than 180 days after the date of enactment of this Act, the Sentencing Commission shall report to Congress the result of its review under subsection (a).

* * *

TITLE XXVIII—SENTENCING PROVISIONS

SEC. 280001. IMPOSITION OF SENTENCE.

Section 3553(a)(4) of title 18, United States Code, is amended to read as follows:

"(4) the kinds of sentence and the sentencing range established for—

"(A) the applicable category of offense committed by the applicable category of defendant as set forth in the guidelines issued by the Sentencing Commission pursuant to section 994(a)(1) of title 28, United States Code, and that are in effect on the date the defendant is sentenced; or

"(B) in the case of a violation of a probation or supervised release, the applicable guidelines or policy statements issued by the Sentencing Commission pursuant to section 994(a)(3) of title 28, United States Code;".

SEC. 280002. TECHNICAL AMENDMENT TO MANDATORY CONDITIONS OF PROBATION.

Section 3563(a)(3) of title 18, United States Code, is amended by striking "possess illegal controlled substances" and inserting "unlawfully possess a controlled substance".

SEC. 280003. DIRECTION TO UNITED STATES SENTENCING COMMISSION REGARDING SENTENCING ENHANCEMENTS FOR HATE CRIMES.

(a) **DEFINITION.**—In this section, "hate crime" means a crime in which the defendant intentionally selects a victim, or in the case of a property crime, the property that is the object of the crime, because of the actual or perceived race, color, religion, national origin, ethnicity, gender, disability, or sexual orientation of any person.

(b) **SENTENCING ENHANCEMENT.**—Pursuant to section 994 of title 28, United States Code, the United States Sentencing Commission shall promulgate guidelines or amend existing guidelines to provide sentencing enhancements of not less than 3 offense levels for offenses that the finder of fact at trial determines beyond a reasonable doubt are hate crimes. In carrying out this section, the United States Sentencing Commission shall ensure that there is reasonable consistency with other guidelines, avoid duplicative punishments for substantially the same offense, and take into account any mitigating circumstances that might justify exceptions.

SEC. 280004. AUTHORIZATION OF PROBATION FOR PETTY OFFENSES IN CERTAIN CASES.

Section 3561(a)(3) of title 18, United States Code, is amended by inserting "that is not a petty offense" before the period.

SEC. 280005. FULL–TIME VICE CHAIRS OF THE UNITED STATES SENTENCING COMMISSION.

(a) **ESTABLISHMENT OF POSITIONS.**—Section 991(a) of title 28, United States Code, is amended—

(1) in the second sentence by striking the period and inserting "and three of whom shall be designated by the President as Vice Chairs.";

(2) in the fourth sentence by striking the period and inserting ", and of the three Vice Chairs, no more than two shall be members of the same political party."; and

(3) in the sixth sentence by striking "Chairman" and inserting "Chair, Vice Chairs,".

(b) **TERMS AND COMPENSATION.**—Section 992(c) of title 28, United States Code, is amended—

(1) by amending the first sentence to read as follows: "The Chair and Vice Chairs of the Commission shall hold full-time positions and shall be compensated during their terms of office at the annual rate at which judges of the United States courts of appeals are compensated.";

(2) in the second sentence by striking "Chairman" and inserting "Chair and Vice Chairs"; and

(3) in the third sentence by striking "Chairman" and inserting "Chair and Vice Chairs,".

(c) **TECHNICAL AMENDMENTS.**—Chapter 58 of title 28, United States Code, is amended—

(1) by striking "Chairman" each place it appears and inserting "Chair";

(2) in the fifth sentence of section 991(a) by striking "his" and inserting "the Attorney General's";

(3) in the fourth sentence of section 992(c) by striking "his" and inserting "the judge's";

(4) in section 994(i)(2) by striking "he" and inserting "the defendant" and striking "his" and inserting "the defendant's"; and

(5) in section 996(a) by striking "him" and inserting "the Staff Director".

SEC. 280006. COCAINE PENALTY STUDY.

Not later than December 31, 1994, the United States Sentencing Commission shall submit a report to Congress on issues relating to sentences applicable to offenses involving the possession or distribution of all forms of cocaine. The report shall address the differences in penalty levels that apply to different forms of cocaine and include any recommendations that the Commission may have for retention or modification of such differences in penalty levels.

APPENDIX H*

MODEL SENTENCING FORMS UNDER THE SENTENCING REFORM ACT OF 1984

Introduction

The sentencing forms that follow are intended to provide assistance in imposing sentences under the Sentencing Reform Act of 1984. As under prior law, it is important that the judge's intentions be unambiguously expressed, but no particular litany is required in imposing sentence. Note, however, that at the time of sentencing the court must "state in open court the reasons for its imposition of the particular sentence." If the guideline sentencing range exceeds 24 months, the court must state "the reason for imposing a sentence at a particular point within the range," and if the court departs from the guideline range, it must state "the specific reason for the imposition" of that sentence. 18 U.S.C. § 3553(c).

Forms 1-10 are modules that are to be combined to formulate a sentence. Most sentences will begin with Form 1 (imprisonment) or Form 2 (probation) and will include one or more of the subsequent forms. These ten forms should be adequate for the vast majority of sentences.

The remaining forms cover various special authorities. Forms 11-13 are for dispositions under 18 U.S.C. § 3607, which carries forward the authority to defer judgment on certain convictions of simple possession of controlled substances. Form 14 is for dispositions of juvenile delinquents. Form 15 covers commitments under 18 U.S.C. § 4244 for care or treatment of a mental disease or defect.

Of necessity, some of the language in the forms is only illustrative; modifications may be needed to fit individual cases, particularly where there are multiple counts.

As the forms indicate, it is suggested that the sentence be introduced with a statement that it is imposed pursuant to the Sentencing Reform Act. The purpose of such a statement is to create an unambiguous record of the fact that the sentence is imposed under the new law. This will of course be critical information in the subsequent administration of the sentence, especially in imprisonment cases. When sentences under the old law are rendered after Nov. 1, 1987, a parallel statement would be useful (i.e., that the sentence is not imposed under the Sentencing Reform Act but under prior law).

Where the conviction is on multiple counts, the Sentencing Commission's guideline ranges for prison terms, probation terms, and fine amounts are to be determined on the basis of a "combined offense level" calculated under part D of chapter 3 of the guidelines. The guideline sentence is thus based on consideration of all counts together. Nevertheless, § 5G1.2 of the guidelines calls for a sentence of imprisonment to be imposed count by count rather than as a general sentence. For the sake of consistency, the suggested forms follow the count-by-count approach for probation, supervised release, and fines as well.

10/94

***Publisher's Note**: These Model Sentencing Forms have been developed by a Federal Judicial Center committee to assist judges in rendering sentences under the Sentencing Reform Act of 1984.

SENTENCING REFORM ACT FORMS

Contents

FORM 1: IMPRISONMENT AND SUPERVISED RELEASE

One-Count Convictions

Pursuant to the Sentencing Reform Act of 1984, it is the judgment of the court that the defendant, _ ___________________, is hereby committed to the custody of the Bureau of Prisons to be imprisoned for a term of ___ months.

Upon release from imprisonment, the defendant shall be placed on supervised release for a term of _ years. Within 72 hours of release from the custody of the Bureau of Prisons, the defendant shall report in person to the probation office in the district to which the defendant is released. [Omit if supervised release is not ordered.]

Multiple-Count Convictions

Pursuant to the Sentencing Reform Act of 1984, it is the judgment of the court that the defendant, _ ___________________, is hereby committed to the custody of the Bureau of Prisons to be imprisoned for a term of _____ months. This term consists of . . .

Alternatives

terms of ___ months on each count, to be served concurrently. [Use if every count carries a maximum that encompasses the total term.]

terms of ___ months on each of Counts ____________ and terms of ____ months on each of Counts ______________, all to be served concurrently. [Use, modified as necessary, if at least one count carries a maximum that encompasses the total term but others carry lower maximums.]

terms of ___ months on each of Counts _________ to be served concurrently, and terms of __ months on each of Counts ______, to be served concurrently with each other but consecutively to the terms imposed on Counts __________ to the extent necessary to produce a total term of ___ months. [Use, modified as necessary, if no count carries a maximum that encompasses the total term or if a statute requires consecutive sentences.]

Upon release from imprisonment, the defendant shall be placed on supervised release for a term of __ years. This term consists of terms of __ years on each of Counts ______ and terms of __ years on each of Counts ______________ all such terms to run concurrently. Within 72 hours of release from the custody of the Bureau of Prisons, the defendant shall report in person to the probation office in the district to which the defendant is released. [Omit if supervised release is not ordered.]

Sentence Consecutive to Prior Sentences

The term(s) of imprisonment imposed by this judgment shall run consecutively to the defendant's imprisonment under any previous state or federal sentence.

Sentence Concurrent With Prior Federal Sentence

The term(s) of imprisonment imposed by this judgment shall run concurrently with the defendant's term of imprisonment pursuant to the judgment in Docket Number _________ , __________ District of __________.

Sentence Concurrent With Prior State Sentence

The court recommends that the Bureau of Prisons designate [institution where defendant is serving state sentence] to be the place of service of this sentence, thereby making this sentence concurrent with the defendant's imprisonment pursuant to the judgment in Docket Number _____________ , [court] .

NOTES:

1. Under 18 U.S.C. § 3621(a), a person sentenced to a term of imprisonment is to be committed to the custody of the Bureau of Prisons rather than, as formerly, the custody of the Attorney General.

2. The suggested form for a multiple-count sentence reflects the fact that the guideline term of imprisonment is first determined for all counts taken together and is then translated into a count-by-count sentence. The three alternative statements implement the instructions in § 5G1.2 of the guidelines for determining the sentence on each count. Except where a statute mandates a consecutive sentence, and subject to statutory maximum and minimum terms, § 5G1.2(b) states that the sentence imposed on each count should equal the total term of imprisonment. The sentences should run concurrently, § 5G1.2(c), unless the sentence on the count with the highest statutory maximum term cannot accommodate the total term. In that case, § 5G1.2(d) instructs that "the sentence imposed on one or more of the other counts shall run consecutively, but only to the extent necessary to produce" the total sentence. Thus, it is apparently contemplated that sentences on some counts will be partly concurrent and partly consecutive.

3. In some situations, adherence to the guideline rules about multiple-count sentences may limit the sentencing court's authority to resentence if the convictions or sentences on one or more counts are overturned on appeal or collateral attack. If a defendant is convicted on one count under a 20-year statute and two counts under a 5-year statute and the guideline sentence is 12 years, the guideline method calls for a 12-year sentence on one count and concurrent 5-year sentences on the other counts. If the conviction on the 20-year count were reversed, the court might then be limited to a total sentence of 5 years. See U.S. v. Frady, 607 F.2d 383 (D.C. Cir. 1979) (concurrent sentences on two counts cannot be made consecutive when one sentence is reduced after appeal); cf. U.S. v. Pisani, 787 F.2d 71 (2d Cir. 1986) (sentence on one count cannot be increased when convictions on other counts are reversed); U.S. v. Rosen, 764 F.2d 763 (11th Cir. 1985) (where trial court imposes illegal sentence on one count, appellate court can remand for resentencing on all counts, but similar power does not exist when illegal sentence on one count is collaterally attacked), cert. denied, 106 S. Ct. 806 (1986).

4. Terms of supervised release run "concurrently with any federal, state, or local term of probation or supervised release or parole for another offense to which the person is subject or becomes subject during the term of supervised release." 18 U.S.C. § 3624(e).

5. Multiple terms of imprisonment imposed at different times run consecutively unless the court orders that they are to run concurrently. 18 U.S.C. § 3584(a). When an offense was "committed while the defendant was serving a term of imprisonment (including work release, furlough, or escape status)," the sentence "shall be imposed to run consecutively to the undischarged term of imprisonment." U.S.S.G. § 5G1.3(a). If the defendant was not serving a term of imprisonment at the time of the offense and the undischarged term of imprisonment resulted from conduct accounted for in the offense level for the instant offense, the sentence "shall be imposed to run concurrently to the undischarged term of imprisonment." U.S.S.G. § 5G1.3(b).

6. Concurrency with a state sentence is achieved only by designating the state institution as the place of service of the federal sentence. Designation is within the discretion of the Bureau of Prisons. 18 U.S.C. § 3621(b). The Bureau will attempt to designate a state institution when requested to do so by the sentencing federal judge; in the absence of such a request, federal and state sentences will be served consecutively.

FORM 2: PROBATION

One-Count Convictions

Pursuant to the Sentencing Reform Act of 1984, it is the judgment of the court that the defendant, __________ , is hereby placed on probation for a term of ___ months.

Multiple-Count Convictions

Pursuant to the Sentencing Reform Act of 1984, it is the judgment of the court that the defendant, ___________ , is hereby placed on probation for a term of ___ months. This term consists of terms of ___ months on each of Counts _______ and terms of ___ months on each of Counts _________ , all such terms to run concurrently.

NOTES:

1. Under 18 U.S.C. § 3561, probation is a sentence in its own right. The traditional language about suspension of imposition or execution of sentence is not used.

2. Terms of probation, "whether imposed at the same time or at different times, run concurrently with each other" and also with "any Federal, State, or local term of probation, supervised release, or parole for another offense to which the defendant is subject or becomes subject during the term of probation." 18 U.S.C. § 3564(b).

3. Probation is not authorized for defendant if the offense carries a maximum sentence of 20 years or more for offenses committed before Nov. 18, 1988, or carries a maximum penalty of life, 25 years or more imprisonment, or death for offenses committed on or after Nov. 18, 1988 (see 1 U.S.C. § 109; 18 U.S.C. § 3561(a)(1)).

4. Probation may not be imposed if the defendant is sentenced at the same time to a term of imprisonment for the same or a different offense. 18 U.S.C. § 3561(a)(3). Where a period of supervision in the community is to follow a term of imprisonment, supervised release should be used.

FORM 3: CONDITIONS OF PROBATION OR SUPERVISED RELEASE

While on (probation) (supervised release), the defendant shall not commit another federal, state, or local crime, shall comply with the standard conditions that have been adopted by this court, and shall comply with the following additional conditions:

Community Confinement

The defendant shall reside for a period of ___ months, to commence (immediately) (immediately following release from imprisonment) (on __[date]__), in [name of community treatment center, halfway house, or similar residential facility] and shall observe the rules of that facility.

Intermittent Confinement (probation only)

The defendant shall be confined in the custody of the Bureau of Prisons . . .

Alternatives

from ___ p.m. each Friday until ___ a.m. each Monday for _____ consecutive weekends, commencing ___________ .

from _____ p.m. each evening to _____ a.m. each morning for a period of ____ weeks, commencing ___________ .

from ____ p.m. each evening Monday through Thursday to ____ a.m. the following morning, and from ____ p.m. each Friday until ____ a.m. each Monday, for a period of ____ weeks, commencing ___________ .

The defendant shall report to custody pursuant to this schedule at a facility designated by the Bureau of Prisons and shall comply with the rules of the facility in which confined.

Payment of Fine or Restitution

The defendant shall pay any (restitution and special assessment) (fine and special assessment) (restitution, fine, and special assessment) that is imposed by this judgment (and that remains unpaid at the commencement of the term of supervised release).

Requirement of Community Service

The defendant shall perform ____ hours of community service as directed by the probation officer.

Requirement of Drug or Alcohol Treatment

The defendant shall participate in a program of testing and treatment for (drug) (alcohol) abuse, as directed by the probation officer, until such time as the defendant is released from the program by the probation officer.

Compliance with Order of Notice to Victims

The defendant shall comply with the portion of this judgment that requires that notice be given to victims of the offense.

NOTES:

1. This form assumes that the court has adopted standard conditions, reflecting provisions of the Anti-Drug Abuse Act of 1988, that prohibit illegal possession of controlled substances and prohibit possession of firearms (including destructive devices). The prohibition of illegal possession of controlled substances is mandatory under 18 U.S.C. §§ 3563(a)(3) and 3583(d). The firearms condition is implicitly required for probationers, since 18 U.S.C. § 3565(b) mandates revocation of probation for possession of a firearm; there is no similar provision governing supervised releasees.

2. Conditions simply prohibiting certain conduct are not listed. Authorized probation conditions are found at 18 U.S.C. § 3563; all except intermittent confinement are authorized for supervised release under 18 U.S.C. § 3583(d). The Sentencing Commission recommends conditions, including 13 as "standard" conditions, at § 5B1.4 of the guidelines.

3. U.S.S.G. § 5C1.1(b), (c), and (d) provide for alternatives to straight imprisonment, including probation, intermittent confinement, community confinement, and home detention.

4. If the defendant is placed on probation for a felony, the conditions of probation must include one or more of a restitution condition, a fine condition, and a community service condition, unless the court finds on the record that extraordinary circumstances make such a condition plainly unreasonable. 18 U.S.C. § 3563(a)(2). If the court finds such extraordinary circumstances, it must impose one or more of the other conditions listed in § 3563(b).

FORM 4: DEATH

It is the judgment of the court that the defendant is sentenced to death.

The time, place, and manner of execution are to be determined by the Attorney General, provided that the time shall not be sooner than 61 days nor later than 90 days after the date of this judgment. If an appeal is taken from the conviction or sentence, execution of the judgment shall be stayed pending further order of this court upon receipt of the mandate of the court of appeals.

The defendant is hereby committed to the custody of the Bureau of Prisons to be confined until the sentence is carried out.

NOTES:

1. The death penalty is authorized by 21 U.S.C. § 848(e). No statute prescribes the time, place, or manner of execution; the language suggested in this form reflects the view that the executive branch should be permitted a reasonable degree of discretion in implementing the sentence. Former 18 U.S.C. § 3566, which was in effect before Furman v. Georgia, 408 U.S. 238 (1972), and was repealed before enactment of § 848(e), provided that "the manner of inflicting the punishment of death shall be that prescribed by the laws of the place within which the sentence is imposed." If the sentence was imposed in a place that did not have the death penalty, the court was authorized to designate another place.

2. The 61-day delay is intended to allow time for an appeal to be filed. There is some ambiguity about the time for appeal because 21 U.S.C. § 848(q)(1) states that the notice of appeal must be filed within the time prescribed by 28 U.S.C. § 2107, a provision that governs only appeals in civil cases. A 90-day period is prescribed for admiralty appeals, and a 60-day period is prescribed for appeals in other civil cases in which the United States is a party.

3. The 90-day maximum period is suggested to provide a reasonable period within which the sentence can be carried out. If the judge wishes, it is probably proper to set the date of execution.

FORM 5: RESTITUTION

Obligation to Make Restitution

Alternatives—Single Defendant Cases

It is further ordered that the defendant shall make restitution to ____________ in the amount of $ _________ .

It is further ordered that the defendant shall make restitution to the following persons in the following amounts: [List victims and amounts.] Any payment made that is not payment in full shall be divided proportionately among the persons named.

Alternatives—Multiple Defendant Cases

It is further ordered that the defendant shall make restitution to ______________ in the amount of $ _____ . The defendant's restitution obligations shall not be affected by any restitution payments that may be made by other defendants in this case. [Use in one-victim cases if restitution obligation is apportioned among defendants rather than imposed as joint and several liability.]

It is further ordered that the defendant shall make restitution to the following persons in the amounts indicated: [List victims and amounts.] Any payment made that is not payment in full shall be divided proportionately among the persons named. The defendant's restitution obligations shall not be affected by any restitution payments that may be made by other defendants in this case. [Use in multiple-victim cases if restitution obligation is apportioned among defendants rather than imposed as joint and several liability.]

The court finds that ___________ has suffered injury compensable under the Victim and Witness Protection Act in the amount of $____. It is ordered that the defendant make restitution to ________ of $ _____ , except that no further payment shall be required after the sum of the amounts actually paid by all defendants has fully covered the compensable injury. [Use in one-victim cases if restitution obligation is to be joint and several.]

The court finds that the following persons have suffered injuries compensable under the Victim and Witness Protection Act in the amounts indicated: [List victims and amounts.] It is ordered that the defendant make restitution to such persons totalling $ ____ , except that no further payment shall be required after the sum of the amounts actually paid by all defendants has fully covered all of the compensable injuries. Any payment made by the defendant shall be divided among the persons named in proportion to their compensable injuries. [Use in multiple-victim cases if restitution obligation is to be joint and several.]

Timing and Mode of Payment

The restitution shall be paid . . .

Alternatives

immediately.
within ____ days.
in installments of $ ____ per (week) (month) until paid.

Payment shall be made . . .

Alternatives

directly to ____________________ .
to the Department of Justice for transfer to ____________ .

The defendant shall notify the United States Attorney for this district within 30 days of any change of mailing or residence address that occurs while any portion of the restitution remains unpaid.

NOTES:

1. If neither imprisonment nor probation is imposed, the introductory language in this form must be modified.

2. 18 U.S.C. § 3551(b) states that imprisonment, probation, or a fine must be imposed in every case and that restitution may be imposed in addition. 18 U.S.C. § 3663(a) permits restitution to be imposed "in lieu of any other penalty authorized by law" in misdemeanor cases. The limitation of "in lieu" restitution to misdemeanor cases was added to § 3663 in 1986, Pub. L. No. 99-646, § 20(a), 100 Stat. 3592, 3596, and presumably prevails as the later enactment. Thus, restitution may not be used as the entire sentence in felony cases but probably may be in misdemeanor cases.

3. If restitution is ordered and the defendant is placed on probation or ordered to serve a term of supervised release, payment of the restitution must be made a condition of supervision. 18 U.S.C. § 3663(g); see Form 3.

4. The limited body of case law suggests that if an offense was committed jointly, it is within the discretion of the court to determine whether to apportion the restitution obligation among defendants or to impose joint and several liability. U.S. v. Trettenaro, 601 F. Supp. 183 (D. Colo. 1985); see U.S. v. Tzakis, 736 F.2d 867 (2d Cir. 1984) (under the former probation statute), followed in U.S. v. Van Cauwenberghe, 827 F.2d 424, 435 (9th Cir. 1987), cert. denied 108 S. Ct. 773 (1988). The alternative statements of the restitution obligation for multi-defendant cases are intended to accommodate that discretion. The last two alternatives also accommodate a modified form of joint and several liability, in which an individual defendant's exposure is limited to an amount smaller than the entire compensable injury. The court may wish to impose such a limitation after considering the defendant's financial resources and the financial needs of the defendant and dependents. See 18 U.S.C. § 3664(a).

5. If more than one victim is to be paid, the court may wish to establish priorities among victims as an alternative to proportionate sharing of payments. The differing needs of victims may suggest that some

victims be given priority over others. In addition, if there are victims whose proportionate shares of individual payments would be very small, an alternative should be fashioned as to them to avoid administrative problems, particularly if the Justice Department is to serve as an intermediary.

6. 18 U.S.C. § 3663(h) provides that an order of restitution "may be enforced by the United States in the manner provided" for the collection of fines. When the Fine Enforcement Act was in effect, the Department of Justice took the position that the quoted language made interest payable on installment payments of restitution to the same extent as on installment payments of fines. W. Weld, W. Hendricks, D. Foster & M. Schnell, Restitution Pursuant to the Victim and Witness Protection Act 44-45 (U.S. Dept. of Justice 1987). The Department may seek to collect interest under present law on restitution amounts of more than $2,500. See Form 6, notes 4 & 5.

FORM 6: FINE

One-Count Convictions

It is further ordered that the defendant shall pay to the United States a fine of $ ______ .

Multiple-Count Conviction

It is further ordered that the defendant shall pay to the United States a total fine of $ ______, consisting of the following:

On count 1, a fine of $ _______ .
On count 2, a fine of $ _______ .
Etc.

Terms of Payment

Alternatives

This sum shall be paid immediately.

This fine (including any interest required by law) shall be paid in full within ____ days. The defendant shall notify the United States Attorney for this district within 30 days of any change of mailing or residence address that occurs while any portion of the sum remains unpaid.

This fine shall be paid in installments of $ _____ the first installment to be paid on _________ and later installments to be paid each (week) (month) until the full amount (including any interest required by law) has been paid. The defendant shall notify the United States Attorney for this district within 30 days of any change of mailing or residence address that occurs while any portion of the sum remains unpaid.

NOTES:

1. If the sentence is for a fine only, the introductory language in this form must be modified.

2. If immediate payment of the fine is not ordered, the period for payment may not exceed five years, excluding any period of imprisonment for the offense. 18 U.S.C. § 3572(d). This limitation apparently applies only to the payment of principal; see note 3.

3. Under 18 U.S.C. § 3612(f), interest will accrue on a fine of more than $2,500 beginning 15 days after sentencing unless the fine is paid in full before that date. Payments made will be allocated to principal until the principal has been fully paid; interest is not compounded. The rate of interest is tied to the auction price for 52-week Treasury bills and will not always be known precisely at the time of sentencing. As a rule of thumb, if the fine is to be paid in equal installments starting shortly after sentencing, the amount of interest payable will be half the amount of the fine (i.e., the average unpaid balance), times the anticipated annual interest rate, times the number of years allowed for payment. For example, if a $6,000 fine is to be paid in equal monthly installments of $100 over five years and the interest rate is 7%, the interest will be approximately $3,000 x .07 x 5 years, or $1,050; the interest would in this case add nearly a year to the

payment period.

4. If the court determines that the defendant does not have the ability to pay interest, the court may waive the interest requirement or modify it in prescribed ways. 18 U.S.C. § 3612(f)(3).

5. If probation is imposed, payment of the fine must be made a condition. 18 U.S.C. § 3563(a); see Form 3.

6. 18 U.S.C. § 3572(e) was apparently intended to prohibit the practice of ordering a defendant to stand committed until a fine is paid. See S. Rep. No. 98-225, 98th Cong., 1st Sess. 109 n.251 (1983) (subsection is "in opposition to" old § 3565, which referred to cases in which "the judgment directs imprisonment until the fine or penalty imposed is paid").

7. If the fine exceeds $100, the written judgment must include the defendant's Social Security number, mailing address, and residence address. 18 U.S.C. § 3612(b).

FORM 7: INJUNCTION PROHIBITING REGULATED TRANSACTIONS INVOLVING LISTED CHEMICALS

It is further ordered that the defendant is hereby enjoined, for a period of _____ (months) (years) [not to exceed 10 years], from distributing, receiving, selling, importing, or exporting a threshold amount of any chemical as specified by regulation of the Attorney General, that is used in manufacturing a controlled substance, and from distributing, importing, or exporting a tableting or encapsulating machine. This injunction shall not apply to transactions that are excluded from the definition of regulated transactions under 21 U.S.C. § 802(39).

FORM 8: ORDER OF NOTICE TO VICTIMS

It is further ordered that the defendant shall notify the victims of the offense of this conviction. The text of the notice shall be as follows:

[Insert text]

Alternatives

The notice shall be sent by first-class mail to [definition of class] at their last-known addresses.

The notice shall be published through paid advertisements in [describe media, number of advertisements, size, and placement].

NOTES:

1. Orders of notice, authorized for offenses involving fraud or other intentionally deceptive practices, are in addition to any other penalties imposed. 18 U.S.C. § 3555.

2. An order of notice can be imposed only if the court has given notice to the parties that it is considering such an order and has provided them an opportunity to respond. 18 U.S.C. § 3553(d).

FORM 9: SPECIAL ASSESSMENT

It is further ordered that the defendant shall pay to the United States a special assessment of $ ______ , which shall be due immediately.

NOTE:

1. If the defendant is unable to pay immediately, adapt language from Form 6 about deferred payment of fines.

10/94

FORM 10: VOLUNTARY SURRENDER; SURRENDER TO MARSHALL

Voluntary Surrender at Institution

It is further ordered that the defendant, ____________________ , surrender himself or herself at the institution designated by the Bureau of Prisons . . .

Alternatives

before 2 p.m. on ___[date]___.
as notified by the United States Marshal.
as notified by the Probation Office.

Surrender to United States Marshal

It is further ordered that the defendant, __________ , surrender himself to the United States Marshal for this district . . .

Alternatives

at ___[time]___ on ___[date]___.
as notified by the Marshal.

NOTES:

1. Before ordering that the defendant report for sentence at a future date, the judge must find by clear and convincing evidence that the defendant is not likely to flee or pose a danger to the safety of any other person or the community if released. 18 U.S.C. § 3143(a). If such a finding is made, the defendant is released under the provisions of 18 U.S.C. § 3142(b) or (c), governing conditions of release before trial. Failure to surrender for service of sentence pursuant to the court's order is a violation of the bail-jumping statute. 18 U.S.C. § 3146(a)(2).

2. The Judicial Conference urged at its September 1980 meeting that courts make increased use of voluntary surrender after considering the guidelines found by the Bureau of Prisons to be appropriate criteria for security classification, namely, seriousness of the offense, length of sentence, extent of prior record, detainers, history of escape, and history of violence. An offender without sufficient funds to pay his or her own subsistence and transportation expenses may petition the court for an order directing the Marshal to pay such expenses. Memorandum of Rowland F. Kirks, Director, Administrative Office of the U.S. Courts, Sept. 26, 1974. It is important that the judgment arrive at the designated institution before the defendant does.

3. Leaving the reporting date open avoids the possibility that the defendant will be required to start service of sentence before the Bureau of Prisons has determined where he or she will be confined. However, the practice is disapproved in the Third Circuit. U.S. v. Golden, 795 F.2d 19 (3d Cir. 1986).

FORM 11: PROBATION WITHOUT JUDGMENT UPON CONVICTION OF SIMPLE POSSESSION OF CONTROLLED SUBSTANCE

It is ordered that the defendant, ______________ , is hereby placed on probation for a term of (one year) (___ months). The entry of judgment is deferred. If the defendant completes the term of probation without violation of the conditions imposed, the proceedings will be dismissed.

NOTES:

1. The maximum probation term that may be imposed under this procedure is one year. 18 U.S.C. § 3607(a).

2. The defendant's consent is required. Id.

10/94

FORM 12: DISMISSAL OF CASE UPON SUCCESSFUL COMPLETION OF PROBATION WITHOUT JUDGMENT

The court, pursuant to 18 U.S.C. § 3607, hereby discharges the defendant from probation and dismisses those proceedings under which probation had been ordered, and orders that the case files and other court records pertinent to this case be sealed and turned over to the clerk of this court.

NOTE:

1. This form has been adapted from a standard order that was approved by the Judicial Conference for use under former 21 U.S.C. § 844(b)(1), the predecessor of 18 U.S.C. § 3607(a) and (b). (Conf. Rpt., April 1973, at 14-15.)

FORM 13: EXPUNGEMENT OF OFFICIAL RECORDS OF CERTAIN YOUTHFUL DRUG OFFENDERS

Upon application of the defendant, it is ordered that there be expunged from all official records, except the nonpublic records referred to in 18 U.S.C. § 3607(b), all references to the defendant's arrest for the offense of which the defendant was found guilty in this case and all references to the institution of criminal proceedings and to the conduct and outcome of those proceedings.

NOTE:

1. The following instruction to clerks of court was approved by the Judicial Conference under former 21 U.S.C. § 844(b)(2), the predecessor of 18 U.S.C. § 3607(c):

> Pursuant to an order under this section, the Clerk shall first obliterate the name of the individual from all indexes, and shall withdraw the docket sheets and the file containing the papers of the case from the court records. He then shall notify the Administrative Office, the court reporter, the probation officer and the magistrate of the order[,] instructing them to make a similar obliteration and withdrawal of the papers in the case and delivery of the papers to the Clerk.
>
> All the papers shall thereupon be expunged by being placed in the sealed records of the court to be opened only upon court order, and shall be physically destroyed after 10 years.

(Conf. Rpt., March 1971, at 5.)

FORM 14: DISPOSITION OF JUVENILE DELINQUENT

It is adjudged that the defendant, ___________ , is a juvenile delinquent. Disposition is made under 18 U.S.C. § 5037, as amended effective Nov. 1, 1987.

Alternatives

It is the judgment of the court that the defendant, __________ , is hereby committed to official detention in the custody of the Attorney General of the United States (until defendant's twenty-first birthday) (for a term of ___ years).

It is the judgment of the court that the defendant, ___________ , is hereby placed on probation (until defendant's twenty-first birthday) (for a term of ___ years).

It is the judgment of the court that the defendant, _________ , shall make restitution . . . . [Use alternatives from Form 5.]

NOTES:

1. Although the sentencing guidelines do not apply to adjudications of delinquency, the Sentencing Reform Act repealed the section authorizing parole release. Juveniles committed to custody will accordingly serve the full sentence, reduced only by good time. See 18 U.S.C. § 5037(c). There is no provision for supervised release. It is particularly important in custody cases to make clear whether the sentence is under the old law or the new.

2. If the juvenile is placed on probation, use Form 3 for the conditions.

3. Authorized periods of probation and detention are set forth in 18 U.S.C. § 5037(b) and (c). If the juvenile is 18 or older, terms may in some cases extend beyond the twenty-first birthday.

4. Restitution orders were not specifically authorized under the old law, but restitution under the Victim and Witness Protection Act is authorized by the new law. The disjunctive language in 18 U.S.C. § 5037(a) may imply that restitution cannot be combined with detention or probation.

5. In addition to the dispositions covered by the above forms, 18 U.S.C. § 5037(a) authorizes the court to "suspend the findings of juvenile delinquency." The former § 5037(b) authorized the court to "suspend the adjudication of delinquency or the disposition of the delinquent on such conditions as it deems proper." Elimination of the "such conditions" language suggests that suspension may have the effect of an unconditional discharge.

FORM 15: COMMITMENT FOR CARE OR TREATMENT UPON FINDING OF MENTAL DISEASE OR DEFECT

It is the judgment of the court that the defendant, __________ , is hereby committed to the custody of the Attorney General of the United States to be hospitalized in a suitable facility pursuant to 18 U.S.C. § 4244 in lieu of a sentence of imprisonment. If not sooner released under 18 U.S.C. § 4244(e), the defendant shall be released upon expiration of the maximum term that could have been imposed for the offense of conviction.

It is further ordered that the defendant shall pay to the United States a special assessment of $ ______ , which shall be due immediately.

NOTES:

1. 18 U.S.C. § 4244, which took effect Oct. 12, 1984, sets forth the procedures that must be followed before ordering a commitment of this type. See Mental Competency in Criminal Matters, Sec. 1.26, supra.

2. 18 U.S.C. 4244(d) states that commitment under this section "constitutes a provisional sentence of imprisonment to the maximum term authorized by law for the offense for which the defendant was found guilty." 18 U.S.C. § 4244(e), relating to discharge, does not state that the defendant must be discharged upon expiration of the provisional sentence. The second sentence of the above form is intended to fill that gap. It should be observed that it has been drafted for one-count convictions; the application to multiple-count convictions of the language quoted above is not free from doubt.

3. The defendant having been convicted, the mandatory special assessment is applicable. If the defendant is unable to pay immediately, adapt language from Form 6 about deferred payment of fines.

4. Defendants who are committed under § 4244 are generally assigned to mental hospitals within prisons and are not treated differently from those in need of care who have been sentenced to imprisonment. Hence, the principal effect of using this procedure is that it invokes different provisions about release from custody. Also, there does not appear to be authority to impose a term of supervised release following custody.

5. Since a defendant is committed under this section "in lieu of being sentenced to imprisonment," 18 U.S.C. § 4244(d), it may be argued that restitution and/or a fine may also be imposed.

APPENDIX I

TABLE OF GUIDELINES CASES APPLYING SPECIFIC SENTENCING GUIDELINES

CHAPTER ONE—INTRODUCTION AND GENERAL PRINCIPLES

Part A: Introduction

1A Sentencing Table—798 F.Supp. 291
1A comment—885 F.2d 483
1A comment—885 F.2d 1417
1A comment—921 F.2d 985
1A comment—946 F.2d 654
1A comment—970 F.2d 1312
1A comment—999 F.2d 1192
1A comment—735 F.Supp. 928
1A comment—798 F.Supp. 861
1A1.1 et seq.—956 F.2d 1555
1A.1 et seq.—857 F.2d 122
1A.1 et seq.—870 F.2d 52
1A.1 et seq.—878 F.2d 68
1A.1 et seq.—884 F.2d 121
1A.1 et seq.—885 F.2d 246
1A.1 et seq.—888 F.2d 490
1A.1 et seq.—890 F.2d 212
1A.1 et seq.—890 F.2d 1413
1A.1 et seq.[1988]—892 F.2d 691
1A.1 et seq.[1988]—895 F.2d 702
1A.1 et seq.—897 F.2d 414
1A.1 et seq.—902 F.2d 133
1A.1 et seq.—914 F.2d 1131
1A.1 et seq.—934 F.2d 1237
1A.1 et seq.—724 F.Supp. 1118
1A.1 et seq.—730 F.Supp. 45
1A.1 et seq.—730 F.Supp. 329
1A.1 et seq.—730 F.Supp. 398
1A.1 et seq.—754 F.Supp. 827
1A.2—905 F.2d 599
1A.2—695 F.Supp. 856
1A.3—857 F.2d 1245
1A.3—874 F.2d 43
1A.3—891 F.2d 962
1A.3 [1988]—897 F.2d 981
1A.3—899 F.2d 503
1A.3 [1988]—900 F.2d 1357
1A.3—901 F.2d 741
1A.3 [1988]—906 F.2d 1356
1A.3—907 F.2d 121
1A.3—908 F.2d 1491
1A.3—945 F.2d 989
1A.3—972 F.2d 281
1A.3—7 F.3d 1458
1A.3—18 F.3d 1190
1A.3—691 F.Supp. 1036
1A.3—692 F.Supp. 331
1A.3—728 F.Supp. 632
1A.4—857 F.2d 1245
1A.4—927 F.2d 197
1A.4—941 F.2d 1047
1A.4—971 F.2d 562
1A.4—985 F.2d 65
1A.4—692 F.Supp. 331
1A.4—730 F.Supp. 35
1A.4—817 F.Supp. 321
1A.4(a)—860 F.2d 35
1A.4(a)—863 F.2d 245
1A.4(a)—866 F.2d 604
1A.4(a)—867 F.2d 783
1A.4(a)—876 F.2d 377
1A.4(a)—890 F.2d 176
1A.4(a)—918 F.2d 1084
1A.4(a)—945 F.2d 1145
1A.4(a)—965 F.2d 1112
1A.4(a)—994 F.2d 1088
1A.4(a)—18 F.3d 1190
1A.4(b)—857 F.2d 1245
1A.4(b)—860 F.2d 35
1A.4(b)—866 F.2d 604
1A.4(b)—867 F.2d 783
1A.4(b)—870 F.2d 52
1A.4(b)—877 F.2d 1409
1A.4(b)—884 F.2d 1314

Publisher's Note: This Appendix has been added by the Publisher. It is not included in the Commission's Guidelines Manual.

1A.4(b)—889 F.2d 916
1A.4(b)—890 F.2d 176
1A.4(b)—895 F.2d 184
1A.4(b)—895 F.2d 1198
1A.4(b)—895 F.2d 1375
1A.4(b)—897 F.2d 981
1A.4(b)—898 F.2d 91
1A.4(b)—899 F.2d 582
1A.4(b)—900 F.2d 1057
1A.4(b) [1988]—900 F.2d 1357
1A.4(b)—901 F.2d 728
1A.4(b) [1988]—906 F.2d 1356
1A.4(b)—907 F.2d 87
1A.4(b)—909 F.2d 235
1A.4(b)—911 F.2d 542
1A.4(b)—916 F.2d 916
1A.4(b)—918 F.2d 1084
1A.4(b)—918 F.2d 1268
1A.4(b)—919 F.2d 1325
1A.4(b)—920 F.2d 562
1A.4(b)—928 F.2d 844
1A.4(b)—930 F.2d 1368
1A.4(b)—930 F.2d 1427
1A.4(b)—932 F.2d 651
1A.4(b)—932 F.2d 1155
1A.4(b)—936 F.2d 1124
1A.4(b)—938 F.2d 149
1A.4(b)—941 F.2d 738
1A.4(b)—946 F.2d 176
1A.4(b)—947 F.2d 956
1A.4(b)—954 F.2d 155
1A.4(b)—961 F.2d 1110
1A.4(b)—964 F.2d 124
1A.4(b)—965 F.2d 1112
1A.4(b)—968 F.2d 1193
1A.4(b)—970 F.2d 444
1A.4(b)—975 F.2d 664
1A.4(b)—980 F.2d 980
1A.4(b)—985 F.2d 732
1A.4(b)—994 F.2d 942
1A.4(b) [1988]—994 F.2d 942
1A.4(b)—994 F.2d 1088
1A.4(b)—998 F.2d 917
1A.4(b)—4 F.3d 70
1A.4(b)—7 F.3d 1471
1A.4(b)—13 F.3d 1308
1A.4(b)—16 F.3d 45
1A.4(b)—16 F.3d 498
1A.4(b)—18 F.3d 41
1A.4(b)—18 F.3d 301
1A.4(b)—20 F.3d 918
1A.4(b)—22 F.3d 1040
1A.4(b)—687 F.Supp. 1403
1A.4(b)—708 F.Supp. 964
1A.4(b)—710 F.Supp. 106
1A.4(b)—728 F.Supp. 632
1A.4(b) [1988]—733 F.Supp. 1307
1A.4(b)—821 F.Supp. 1400
1A.4(b)—833 F.Supp. 769
1A.4(b)—835 F.supp. 1335
1A.4(b)—840 F.Supp. 1404
1A.4(b)—841 F.Supp. 734
1A.4(c)—969 F.2d 1419
1A.4(c)—684 F.Supp. 1048
1A.4(d)—895 F.2d 318
1A.4(d)—900 F.2d 481
1A.4(d)—924 F.2d 836
1A.4(d)—930 F.2d 1486
1A.4(d)—940 F.2d 985
1A.4(d)—941 F.2d 738
1A.4(d)—946 F.2d 335
1A.4(d)—964 F.2d 640
1A.4(d)—972 F.2d 1007
1A.4(d)—992 F.2d 108
1A.4(d)—13 F.3d 752
1A.4(d)—18 F.3d 301
1A.4(d)—687 F.Supp. 1403
1A.4(d)—840 F.Supp. 1404
1A.4(e)—883 F.2d 781
1A.4(e)—888 F.2d 907
1A.4(e)—984 F.2d 298
1A.4(e)—7 F.3d 813
1A.4(g)—926 F.2d 125
1A.4(h)—855 F.2d 925
1A.4 comment—953 F.2d 443
1A.4 comment—971 F.2d 989
1A.4(b)—952 F.2d 1090
1A.6—994 F.2d 1380

Part B: General Application Principles

1B1.1—855 F.2d 925
1B1.1—867 F.2d 783
1B1.1—868 F.2d 698
1B1.1—874 F.2d 43
1B1.1—874 F.2d 248
1B1.1—881 F.2d 114
1B1.1—888 F.2d 285
1B1.1—890 F.2d 1284
1B1.1—891 F.2d 300

1B1.1—895 F.2d 615
1B1.1—897 F.2d 13
1B1.1—913 F.2d 201
1B1.1—915 F.2d 269
1B1.1—916 F.2d 553
1B1.1—920 F.2d 1218
1B1.1—921 F.2d 1095
1B1.1—929 F.2d 1235
1B1.1—932 F.2d 651
1B1.1—935 F.2d 47
1B1.1—936 F.2d 154
1B1.1—936 F.2d 1292
1B1.1—937 F.2d 1041
1B1.1—959 F.2d 54
1B1.1—995 F.2d 1414
1B1.1—4 F.3d 70
1B1.1—16 F.3d 247
1B1.1—20 F.3d 538
1B1.1—709 F.Supp. 653
1B1.1—819 F.Supp. 250
1B1.1(a)—891 F.2d 82
1B1.1(a)—913 F.2d 193
1B1.1(a) [1988]—913 F.2d 193
1B1.1(a)—915 F.2d 811
1B1.1(a) [1988]—917 F.2d 841
1B1.1(a)—920 F.2d 363
1B1.1(a)—933 F.2d 752
1B1.1(a)—994 F.2d 1088
1B1.1(a)—14 F.3d 502
1B1.1(a-d)—819 F.Supp. 250
1B1.1(a-e)—873 F.2d 495
1B1.1(a-g)—880 F.2d 1204
1B1.1(a-i)—891 F.2d 300
1B1.1(a-i)—819 F.Supp. 250
1B1.1(b)—900 F.2d 1350
1B1.1(b)—954 F.2d 204
1B1.1(b)—985 F.2d 371
1B1.1(b-e)—918 F.2d 1084
1B1.1(c)—900 F.2d 1350
1B1.1(c)—985 F.2d 371
1B1.1(d)—888 F.2d 285
1B1.1(d)—953 F.2d 870
1B1.1(e)—888 F.2d 285
1B1.1(e)—900 F.2d 1350
1B1.1(e)—18 F.3d 826
1B1.1(f)—889 F.2d 357
1B1.1(f)—900 F.2d 1350
1B1.1(g)—855 F.2d 925
1B1.1(g)—873 F.2d 495
1B1.1(g)—874 F.2d 248
1B1.1(h)—855 F.2d 925
1B1.1(h)—874 F.2d 248
1B1.1(i)—855 F.2d 925
1B1.1(i)—926 F.2d 588
1B1.1(i)—960 F.2d 212
1B1.1(i)—18 F.3d 826
1B1.1 et seq.—109 S.Ct. 647
1B1.1 et seq.—112 S.Ct. 1112
1B1.1 et seq.—112 S.Ct. 1329
1B1.1 et seq.—113 S.Ct. 1913
1B1.1 et seq.—114 S.Ct. 1921
1B1.1 et seq.—831 F.2d 156
1B1.1 et seq.—831 F.2d 1355
1B1.1 et seq.—835 F.2d 215
1B1.1 et seq.—845 F.2d 1132
1B1.1 et seq.—846 F.2d 329
1B1.1 et seq.—846 F.2d 995
1B1.1 et seq.—847 F.2d 991
1B1.1 et seq.—851 F.2d 890
1B1.1 et seq.—855 F.2d 199
1B1.1 et seq.—855 F.2d 201
1B1.1 et seq.—855 F.2d 707
1B1.1 et seq.—855 F.2d 925
1B1.1 et seq.—857 F.2d 367
1B1.1 et seq.—858 F.2d 1512
1B1.1 et seq.—860 F.2d 779
1B1.1 et seq.—861 F.2d 206
1B1.1 et seq.—862 F.2d 423
1B1.1 et seq.—863 F.2d 36
1B1.1 et seq.—863 F.2d 1149
1B1.1 et seq.—865 F.2d 115
1B1.1 et seq.—865 F.2d 450
1B1.1 et seq.—866 F.2d 610
1B1.1 et seq.—866 F.2d 747
1B1.1 et seq.—867 F.2d 209
1B1.1 et seq.—867 F.2d 213
1B1.1 et seq.—867 F.2d 216
1B1.1 et seq.—867 F.2d 830
1B1.1 et seq.—868 F.2d 157
1B1.1 et seq.—868 F.2d 807
1B1.1 et seq.—868 F.2d 1121
1B1.1 et seq.—868 F.2d 1390
1B1.1 et seq.—869 F.2d 805
1B1.1 et seq.—869 F.2d 822
1B1.1 et seq.—870 F.2d 18
1B1.1 et seq.—870 F.2d 52
1B1.1 et seq.—870 F.2d 615
1B1.1 et seq.—871 F.2d 45
1B1.1 et seq.—872 F.2d 597
1B1.1 et seq.—872 F.2d 632

1B1.1 et seq.—872 F.2d 827
1B1.1 et seq.—873 F.2d 15
1B1.1 et seq.—873 F.2d 182
1B1.1 et seq.—873 F.2d 205
1B1.1 et seq.—873 F.2d 743
1B1.1 et seq.—873 F.2d 765
1B1.1 et seq.—873 F.2d 963
1B1.1 et seq.—873 F.2d 1157
1B1.1 et seq.—874 F.2d 371
1B1.1 et seq.—874 F.2d 591
1B1.1 et seq.—875 F.2d 1124
1B1.1 et seq.—876 F.2d 21
1B1.1 et seq.—876 F.2d 372
1B1.1 et seq.—876 F.2d 734
1B1.1 et seq.—876 F.2d 1411
1B1.1 et seq.—876 F.2d 1502
1B1.1 et seq.—877 F.2d 338
1B1.1 et seq.—877 F.2d 460
1B1.1 et seq.—877 F.2d 664
1B1.1 et seq.—877 F.2d 1138
1B1.1 et seq.—877 F.2d 1409
1B1.1 et seq.—878 F.2d 50
1B1.1 et seq.—878 F.2d 256
1B1.1 et seq.—878 F.2d 921
1B1.1 et seq.—878 F.2d 997
1B1.1 et seq.—878 F.2d 1232
1B1.1 et seq.—879 F.2d 391
1B1.1 et seq.—879 F.2d 415
1B1.1 et seq.—879 F.2d 541
1B1.1 et seq.—879 F.2d 1234
1B1.1 et seq.—879 F.2d 1268
1B1.1 et seq.—879 F.2d 1562
1B1.1 et seq.—880 F.2d 1204
1B1.1 et seq.—881 F.2d 114
1B1.1 et seq.—881 F.2d 386
1B1.1 et seq.—881 F.2d 586
1B1.1 et seq.—881 F.2d 684
1B1.1 et seq.—882 F.2d 441
1B1.1 et seq.—882 F.2d 471
1B1.1 et seq.—883 F.2d 43
1B1.1 et seq.—884 F.2d 75
1B1.1 et seq.—884 F.2d 181
1B1.1 et seq.—884 F.2d 540
1B1.1 et seq.—885 F.2d 483
1B1.1 et seq.—885 F.2d 720
1B1.1 et seq.—885 F.2d 1353
1B1.1 et seq.—886 F.2d 973
1B1.1 et seq.—886 F.2d 1036
1B1.1 et seq.—887 F.2d 697
1B1.1 et seq.—887 F.2d 1262
1B1.1 et seq.—888 F.2d 720
1B1.1 et seq.—888 F.2d 862
1B1.1 et seq.—888 F.2d 1049
1B1.1 et seq.—888 F.2d 1100
1B1.1 et seq.—889 F.2d 88
1B1.1 et seq.—889 F.2d 562
1B1.1 et seq.—889 F.2d 803
1B1.1 et seq.—889 F.2d 1032
1B1.1 et seq.—889 F.2d 1336
1B1.1 et seq.—889 F.2d 1417
1B1.1 et seq.—889 F.2d 1570
1B1.1 et seq.—890 F.2d 672
1B1.1 et seq.—890 F.2d 968
1B1.1 et seq.—890 F.2d 1245
1B1.1 et seq.—891 F.2d 667
1B1.1 et seq.—891 F.2d 921
1B1.1 et seq.—891 F.2d 988
1B1.1 et seq.—891 F.2d 1063
1B1.1 et seq.—892 F.2d 8
1B1.1 et seq.—892 F.2d 31
1B1.1 et seq.—892 F.2d 233
1B1.1 et seq.—892 F.2d 269
1B1.1 et seq.—892 F.2d 696
1B1.1 et seq. [1988]—892 F.2d 725
1B1.1 et seq.—892 F.2d 969
1B1.1 et seq.—893 F.2d 46
1B1.1 et seq.—893 F.2d 250
1B1.1 et seq.—893 F.2d 314
1B1.1 et seq.—893 F.2d 479
1B1.1 et seq.—893 F.2d 669
1B1.1 et seq.—893 F.2d 825
1B1.1 et seq.—893 F.2d 1502
1B1.1 et seq.—894 F.2d 373
1B1.1 et seq.—894 F.2d 665
1B1.1 et seq.—894 F.2d 957
1B1.1 et seq.—894 F.2d 1043
1B1.1 et seq.—894 F.2d 1085
1B1.1 et seq.—895 F.2d 205
1B1.1 et seq.—895 F.2d 399
1B1.1 et seq.—895 F.2d 538
1B1.1 et seq.—895 F.2d 1030
1B1.1 et seq.—895 F.2d 1297
1B1.1 et seq.—895 F.2d 1362
1B1.1 et seq.—896 F.2d 842
1B1.1 et seq.—896 F.2d 1031
1B1.1 et seq.—897 F.2d 490
1B1.1 et seq. [1988]—897 F.2d 981
1B1.1 et seq.—897 F.2d 1018
1B1.1 et seq.—897 F.2d 1092
1B1.1 et seq.—897 F.2d 1413

1B1.1 et seq.—897 F.2d 1444
1B1.1 et seq.—897 F.2d 1558
1B1.1 et seq.—898 F.2d 3
1B1.1 et seq.—898 F.2d 91
1B1.1 et seq.—898 F.2d 99
1B1.1 et seq.—898 F.2d 110
1B1.1 et seq.—898 F.2d 119
1B1.1 et seq.—898 F.2d 130
1B1.1 et seq.—898 F.2d 368
1B1.1 et seq.—898 F.2d 450
1B1.1 et seq.—898 F.2d 968
1B1.1 et seq.—898 F.2d 987
1B1.1 et seq.—899 F.2d 582
1B1.1 et seq.—899 F.2d 677
1B1.1 et seq.—899 F.2d 714
1B1.1 et seq.—899 F.2d 1526
1B1.1 et seq.—900 F.2d 22
1B1.1 et seq.—900 F.2d 45
1B1.1 et seq.—900 F.2d 139
1B1.1 et seq.—900 F.2d 213
1B1.1 et seq.—900 F.2d 1350
1B1.1 et seq.—900 F.2d 1524
1B1.1 et seq.—900 F.2d 1531
1B1.1 et seq.—901 F.2d 85
1B1.1 et seq.—901 F.2d 647
1B1.1 et seq.—901 F.2d 1000
1B1.1 et seq.—901 F.2d 1201
1B1.1 et seq.—901 F.2d 1433
1B1.1 et seq.—901 F.2d 1498
1B1.1 et seq.—902 F.2d 90
1B1.1 et seq.—902 F.2d 336
1B1.1 et seq.—902 F.2d 489
1B1.1 et seq.—902 F.2d 501
1B1.1 et seq.—902 F.2d 873
1B1.1 et seq.—902 F.2d 894
1B1.1 et seq.—902 F.2d 912
1B1.1 et seq.—902 F.2d 1129
1B1.1 et seq.—902 F.2d 1169
1B1.1 et seq.—902 F.2d 1176
1B1.1 et seq.—902 F.2d 1344
1B1.1 et seq.—902 F.2d 1383
1B1.1 et seq.—902 F.2d 1427
1B1.1 et seq.—903 F.2d 91
1B1.1 et seq.—903 F.2d 334
1B1.1 et seq.—903 F.2d 341
1B1.1 et seq.—903 F.2d 1022
1B1.1 et seq.—903 F.2d 1084
1B1.1 et seq.—903 F.2d 1188
1B1.1 et seq.—903 F.2d 1313
1B1.1 et seq.—903 F.2d 1478
1B1.1 et seq.—904 F.2d 306
1B1.1 et seq.—904 F.2d 403
1B1.1 et seq.—904 F.2d 1490
1B1.1 et seq.—904 F.2d 1534
1B1.1 et seq.—905 F.2d 54
1B1.1 et seq.—905 F.2d 350
1B1.1 et seq.—905 F.2d 580
1B1.1 et seq.—905 F.2d 599
1B1.1 et seq.—905 F.2d 638
1B1.1 et seq.—905 F.2d 867
1B1.1 et seq.—905 F.2d 1050
1B1.1 et seq.—905 F.2d 1092
1B1.1 et seq.—905 F.2d 1157
1B1.1 et seq.—905 F.2d 1304
1B1.1 et seq.—905 F.2d 1335
1B1.1 et seq.—905 F.2d 1432
1B1.1 et seq.—905 F.2d 1439
1B1.1 et seq.—905 F.2d 1448
1B1.1 et seq.—905 F.2d 1450
1B1.1 et seq.—905 F.2d 1513
1B1.1 et seq.—906 F.2d 139
1B1.1 et seq.—906 F.2d 147
1B1.1 et seq.—906 F.2d 323
1B1.1 et seq.—906 F.2d 359
1B1.1 et seq.—906 F.2d 776
1B1.1 et seq.—906 F.2d 867
1B1.1 et seq.—906 F.2d 1261
1B1.1 et seq.—906 F.2d 1285
1B1.1 et seq.—906 F.2d 1424
1B1.1 et seq.—906 F.2d 1531
1B1.1 et seq.—907 F.2d 31
1B1.1 et seq.—907 F.2d 91
1B1.1 et seq.—907 F.2d 99
1B1.1 et seq.—907 F.2d 121
1B1.1 et seq.—907 F.2d 254
1B1.1 et seq.—907 F.2d 282
1B1.1 et seq. [1988]—907 F.2d 294
1B1.1 et seq.—907 F.2d 671
1B1.1 et seq.—907 F.2d 781
1B1.1 et seq.—907 F.2d 1494
1B1.1 et seq.—907 F.2d 1540
1B1.1 et seq.—908 F.2d 56
1B1.1 et seq.—908 F.2d 179
1B1.1 et seq.—908 F.2d 230
1B1.1 et seq.—908 F.2d 304
1B1.1 et seq.—908 F.2d 396
1B1.1 et seq.—908 F.2d 795
1B1.1 et seq.—908 F.2d 816
1B1.1 et seq.—908 F.2d 1229
1B1.1 et seq.—908 F.2d 1289

1B1.1 et seq.—908 F.2d 1312
1B1.1 et seq.—908 F.2d 1491
1B1.1 et seq.—909 F.2d 61
1B1.1 et seq.—909 F.2d 196
1B1.1 et seq.—909 F.2d 235
1B1.1 et seq.—909 F.2d 359
1B1.1 et seq.—909 F.2d 392
1B1.1 et seq.—909 F.2d 395
1B1.1 et seq.—909 F.2d 412
1B1.1 et seq.—909 F.2d 780
1B1.1 et seq.—909 F.2d 1143
1B1.1 et seq.—909 F.2d 1164
1B1.1 et seq.—910 F.2d 164
1B1.1 et seq.—910 F.2d 221
1B1.1 et seq.—910 F.2d 309
1B1.1 et seq.—910 F.2d 530
1B1.1 et seq.—910 F.2d 542
1B1.1 et seq.—910 F.2d 547
1B1.1 et seq.—910 F.2d 587
1B1.1 et seq.—910 F.2d 703
1B1.1 et seq.—910 F.2d 749
1B1.1 et seq.—910 F.2d 1016
1B1.1 et seq.—910 F.2d 1069
1B1.1 et seq.—910 F.2d 1241
1B1.1 et seq.—910 F.2d 1309
1B1.1 et seq.—910 F.2d 1342
1B1.1 et seq.—910 F.2d 1484
1B1.1 et seq.—910 F.2d 1574
1B1.1 et seq.—911 F.2d 50
1B1.1 et seq.—911 F.2d 129
1B1.1 et seq.—911 F.2d 186
1B1.1 et seq.—911 F.2d 227
1B1.1 et seq.—911 F.2d 350
1B1.1 et seq.—911 F.2d 403
1B1.1 et seq.—911 F.2d 542
1B1.1 et seq.—911 F.2d 847
1B1.1 et seq.—911 F.2d 985
1B1.1 et seq.—911 F.2d 1016
1B1.1 et seq.—911 F.2d 1023
1B1.1 et seq.—911 F.2d 1025
1B1.1 et seq.—911 F.2d 1567
1B1.1 et seq.—912 F.2d 156
1B1.1 et seq.—912 F.2d 204
1B1.1 et seq.—912 F.2d 424
1B1.1 et seq.—912 F.2d 448
1B1.1 et seq.—912 F.2d 1119
1B1.1 et seq.—912 F.2d 1210
1B1.1 et seq.—912 F.2d 1365
1B1.1 et seq.—913 F.2d 59
1B1.1 et seq.—913 F.2d 193
1B1.1 et seq.—913 F.2d 466
1B1.1 et seq.—913 F.2d 839
1B1.1 et seq.—913 F.2d 1172
1B1.1 et seq.—914 F.2d 20
1B1.1 et seq.—914 F.2d 98
1B1.1 et seq. [1988]—914 F.2d 208
1B1.1 et seq.—914 F.2d 696
1B1.1 et seq.—914 F.2d 699
1B1.1 et seq.—914 F.2d 915
1B1.1 et seq.—914 F.2d 950
1B1.1 et seq.—914 F.2d 966
1B1.1 et seq.—914 F.2d 1131
1B1.1 et seq.—914 F.2d 1288
1B1.1 et seq.—914 F.2d 1352
1B1.1 et seq.—914 F.2d 1355
1B1.1 et seq.—914 F.2d 1527
1B1.1 et seq.—915 F.2d 1
1B1.1 et seq.—915 F.2d 132
1B1.1 et seq.—915 F.2d 402
1B1.1 et seq.—915 F.2d 599
1B1.1 et seq.—915 F.2d 774
1B1.1 et seq.—915 F.2d 811
1B1.1 et seq.—915 F.2d 1164
1B1.1 et seq.—915 F.2d 1220
1B1.1 et seq.—915 F.2d 1254
1B1.1 et seq.—915 F.2d 1259
1B1.1 et seq.—915 F.2d 1501
1B1.1 et seq.—915 F.2d 1514
1B1.1 et seq.—916 F.2d 27
1B1.1 et seq.—916 F.2d 129
1B1.1 et seq.—916 F.2d 147
1B1.1 et seq.—916 F.2d 157
1B1.1 et seq.—916 F.2d 186
1B1.1 et seq.—916 F.2d 219
1B1.1 et seq.—916 F.2d 464
1B1.1 et seq.—916 F.2d 497
1B1.1 et seq.—916 F.2d 628
1B1.1 et seq.—916 F.2d 725
1B1.1 et seq.—916 F.2d 916
1B1.1 et seq.—916 F.2d 1020
1B1.1 et seq.—917 F.2d 112
1B1.1 et seq.—917 F.2d 165
1B1.1 et seq.—917 F.2d 181
1B1.1 et seq.—917 F.2d 369
1B1.1 et seq.—917 F.2d 477
1B1.1 et seq.—917 F.2d 502
1B1.1 et seq.—917 F.2d 507
1B1.1 et seq.—917 F.2d 607
1B1.1 et seq.—917 F.2d 683
1B1.1 et seq.—917 F.2d 846

1B1.1 et seq.—917 F.2d 997
1B1.1 et seq.—917 F.2d 1133
1B1.1 et seq.—917 F.2d 1220
1B1.1 et seq.—917 F.2d 1280
1B1.1 et seq.—917 F.2d 1521
1B1.1 et seq.—918 F.2d 30
1B1.1 et seq.—918 F.2d 244
1B1.1 et seq.—918 F.2d 631
1B1.1 et seq.—918 F.2d 647
1B1.1 et seq.—918 F.2d 664
1B1.1 et seq.—918 F.2d 745
1B1.1 et seq.—918 F.2d 789
1B1.1 et seq.—918 F.2d 848
1B1.1 et seq.—918 F.2d 882
1B1.1 et seq.—918 F.2d 895
1B1.1 et seq.—918 F.2d 1156
1B1.1 et seq. [1990]—918 F.2d 1268
1B1.1 et seq.—918 F.2d 1329
1B1.1 et seq.—918 F.2d 1551
1B1.1 et seq.—919 F.2d 19
1B1.1 et seq.—919 F.2d 94
1B1.1 et seq.—919 F.2d 123
1B1.1 et seq.—919 F.2d 258
1B1.1 et seq.—919 F.2d 461
1B1.1 et seq.—919 F.2d 568
1B1.1 et seq.—919 F.2d 842
1B1.1 et seq.—919 F.2d 881
1B1.1 et seq.—919 F.2d 896
1B1.1 et seq.—919 F.2d 940
1B1.1 et seq.—919 F.2d 946
1B1.1 et seq.—919 F.2d 962
1B1.1 et seq.—919 F.2d 969
1B1.1 et seq.—919 F.2d 1365
1B1.1 et seq.—919 F.2d 1451
1B1.1 et seq.—920 F.2d 139
1B1.1 et seq.—920 F.2d 167
1B1.1 et seq.—920 F.2d 714
1B1.1 et seq.—920 F.2d 810
1B1.1 et seq.—920 F.2d 1040
1B1.1 et seq.—920 F.2d 1100
1B1.1 et seq.—920 F.2d 1218
1B1.1 et seq.—920 F.2d 1231
1B1.1 et seq.—920 F.2d 1330
1B1.1 et seq.—920 F.2d 1570
1B1.1 et seq.—921 F.2d 143
1B1.1 et seq.—921 F.2d 168
1B1.1 et seq.—921 F.2d 196
1B1.1 et seq.—921 F.2d 204
1B1.1 et seq.—921 F.2d 330
1B1.1 et seq.—921 F.2d 438
1B1.1 et seq.—921 F.2d 580
1B1.1 et seq.—921 F.2d 1064
1B1.1 et seq.—921 F.2d 1073
1B1.1 et seq.—921 F.2d 1095
1B1.1 et seq.—922 F.2d 311
1B1.1 et seq.—922 F.2d 404
1B1.1 et seq.—922 F.2d 549
1B1.1 et seq.—922 F.2d 563
1B1.1 et seq.—922 F.2d 624
1B1.1 et seq.—922 F.2d 748
1B1.1 et seq.—922 F.2d 765
1B1.1 et seq.—922 F.2d 910
1B1.1 et seq.—922 F.2d 1044
1B1.1 et seq.—922 F.2d 1385
1B1.1 et seq.—922 F.2d 1443
1B1.1 et seq.—922 F.2d 1501
1B1.1 et seq.—923 F.2d 13
1B1.1 et seq.—923 F.2d 47
1B1.1 et seq.—923 F.2d 76
1B1.1 et seq.—923 F.2d 369
1B1.1 et seq.—923 F.2d 1079
1B1.1 et seq.—923 F.2d 1293
1B1.1 et seq.—923 F.2d 1346
1B1.1 et seq.—923 F.2d 1371
1B1.1 et seq.—923 F.2d 1500
1B1.1 et seq.—924 F.2d 68
1B1.1 et seq.—924 F.2d 112
1B1.1 et seq.—924 F.2d 187
1B1.1 et seq.—924 F.2d 298
1B1.1 et seq.—924 F.2d 395
1B1.1 et seq.—924 F.2d 721
1B1.1 et seq.—924 F.2d 800
1B1.1 et seq.—924 F.2d 921
1B1.1 et seq.—924 F.2d 1289
1B1.1 et seq.—924 F.2d 1362
1B1.1 et seq.—925 F.2d 107
1B1.1 et seq.—925 F.2d 112
1B1.1 et seq.—925 F.2d 270
1B1.1 et seq.—925 F.2d 359
1B1.1 et seq.—925 F.2d 610
1B1.1 et seq.—925 F.2d 728
1B1.1 et seq.—925 F.2d 1131
1B1.1 et seq.—925 F.2d 1191
1B1.1 et seq.—926 F.2d 64
1B1.1 et seq.—926 F.2d 112
1B1.1 et seq.—926 F.2d 172
1B1.1 et seq.—926 F.2d 204
1B1.1 et seq.—926 F.2d 410
1B1.1 et seq.—926 F.2d 588
1B1.1 et seq.—926 F.2d 649

1B1.1 et seq.—926 F.2d 838
1B1.1 et seq.—926 F.2d 899
1B1.1 et seq.—926 F.2d 1323
1B1.1 et seq.—927 F.2d 111
1B1.1 et seq.—927 F.2d 136
1B1.1 et seq.—927 F.2d 303
1B1.1 et seq.—927 F.2d 453
1B1.1 et seq.—927 F.2d 489
1B1.1 et seq.—927 F.2d 742
1B1.1 et seq.—927 F.2d 1058
1B1.1 et seq.—927 F.2d 1361
1B1.1 et seq.—927 F.2d 1376
1B1.1 et seq.—927 F.2d 1463
1B1.1 et seq.—928 F.2d 150
1B1.1 et seq.—928 F.2d 310
1B1.1 et seq.—928 F.2d 324
1B1.1 et seq.—928 F.2d 339
1B1.1 et seq.—928 F.2d 349
1B1.1 et seq.—928 F.2d 690
1B1.1 et seq.—928 F.2d 728
1B1.1 et seq.—928 F.2d 780
1B1.1 et seq.—928 F.2d 1450
1B1.1 et seq.—929 F.2d 56
1B1.1 et seq.—929 F.2d 254
1B1.1 et seq.—929 F.2d 307
1B1.1 et seq.—929 F.2d 334
1B1.1 et seq.—929 F.2d 364
1B1.1 et seq.—929 F.2d 436
1B1.1 et seq.—929 F.2d 518
1B1.1 et seq.—929 F.2d 741
1B1.1 et seq.—929 F.2d 798
1B1.1 et seq.—929 F.2d 858
1B1.1 et seq.—929 F.2d 1030
1B1.1 et seq.—929 F.2d 1275
1B1.1 et seq.—929 F.2d 1425
1B1.1 et seq.—929 F.2d 1466
1B1.1 et seq.—929 F.2d 1476
1B1.1 et seq.—930 F.2d 18
1B1.1 et seq.—930 F.2d 216
1B1.1 et seq.—930 F.2d 413
1B1.1 et seq.—930 F.2d 495
1B1.1 et seq.—930 F.2d 567
1B1.1 et seq.—930 F.2d 639
1B1.1 et seq.—930 F.2d 744
1B1.1 et seq.—930 F.2d 795
1B1.1 et seq.—930 F.2d 811
1B1.1 et seq.—930 F.2d 1257
1B1.1 et seq.—930 F.2d 1447
1B1.1 et seq.—930 F.2d 1486
1B1.1 et seq.—931 F.2d 3
1B1.1 et seq.—931 F.2d 31
1B1.1 et seq.—931 F.2d 33
1B1.1 et seq.—931 F.2d 308
1B1.1 et seq.—931 F.2d 359
1B1.1 et seq. [1990]—931 F.2d 463
1B1.1 et seq.—931 F.2d 851
1B1.1 et seq.—931 F.2d 964
1B1.1 et seq.—931 F.2d 1139
1B1.1 et seq.—931 F.2d 1250
1B1.1 et seq.—932 F.2d 31
1B1.1 et seq.—932 F.2d 67
1B1.1 et seq.—932 F.2d 244
1B1.1 et seq.—932 F.2d 358
1B1.1 et seq.—932 F.2d 364
1B1.1 et seq.—932 F.2d 752
1B1.1 et seq.—932 F.2d 823
1B1.1 et seq.—932 F.2d 1029
1B1.1 et seq.—932 F.2d 1049
1B1.1 et seq.—932 F.2d 1073
1B1.1 et seq.—932 F.2d 1085
1B1.1 et seq.—932 F.2d 1167
1B1.1 et seq.—932 F.2d 1343
1B1.1 et seq.—932 F.2d 1515
1B1.1 et seq.—932 F.2d 1529
1B1.1 et seq.—933 F.2d 362
1B1.1 et seq.—933 F.2d 742
1B1.1 et seq.—933 F.2d 916
1B1.1 et seq.—933 F.2d 962
1B1.1 et seq.—933 F.2d 1117
1B1.1 et seq.—933 F.2d 1219
1B1.1 et seq.—934 F.2d 148
1B1.1 et seq.—934 F.2d 196
1B1.1 et seq.—934 F.2d 553
1B1.1 et seq.—934 F.2d 847
1B1.1 et seq.—934 F.2d 875
1B1.1 et seq.—934 F.2d 1077
1B1.1 et seq.—934 F.2d 1226
1B1.1 et seq.—934 F.2d 1325
1B1.1 et seq.—935 F.2d 32
1B1.1 et seq.—935 F.2d 39
1B1.1 et seq.—935 F.2d 47
1B1.1 et seq.—935 F.2d 143
1B1.1 et seq.—935 F.2d 644
1B1.1 et seq.—935 F.2d 719
1B1.1 et seq.—935 F.2d 739
1B1.1 et seq.—935 F.2d 822
1B1.1 et seq.—935 F.2d 1139
1B1.1 et seq.—935 F.2d 1199
1B1.1 et seq.—936 F.2d 85
1B1.1 et seq.—936 F.2d 165

1B1.1 et seq.—936 F.2d 227
1B1.1 et seq.—936 F.2d 412
1B1.1 et seq.—936 F.2d 648
1B1.1 et seq.—936 F.2d 661
1B1.1 et seq.—936 F.2d 950
1B1.1 et seq.—936 F.2d 1124
1B1.1 et seq.—936 F.2d 1138
1B1.1 et seq.—936 F.2d 1238
1B1.1 et seq.—936 F.2d 1281
1B1.1 et seq.—936 F.2d 1292
1B1.1 et seq.—936 F.2d 1403
1B1.1 et seq.—937 F.2d 151
1B1.1 et seq.—937 F.2d 515
1B1.1 et seq.—937 F.2d 716
1B1.1 et seq.—937 F.2d 979
1B1.1 et seq.—937 F.2d 1196
1B1.1 et seq.—937 F.2d 1369
1B1.1 et seq.—937 F.2d 1514
1B1.1 et seq.—937 F.2d 1528
1B1.1 et seq.—938 F.2d 139
1B1.1 et seq.—938 F.2d 149
1B1.1 et seq.—938 F.2d 168
1B1.1 et seq.—938 F.2d 172
1B1.1 et seq.—938 F.2d 175
1B1.1 et seq.—938 F.2d 210
1B1.1 et seq.—938 F.2d 326
1B1.1 et seq.—938 F.2d 456
1B1.1 et seq.—938 F.2d 579
1B1.1 et seq.—938 F.2d 744
1B1.1 et seq.—938 F.2d 972
1B1.1 et seq.—938 F.2d 1020
1B1.1 et seq.—938 F.2d 1086
1B1.1 et seq.—938 F.2d 1164
1B1.1 et seq.—938 F.2d 1431
1B1.1 et seq.—938 F.2d 1446
1B1.1 et seq.—939 F.2d 244
1B1.1 et seq.—939 F.2d 721
1B1.1 et seq.—939 F.2d 929
1B1.1 et seq.—940 F.2d 107
1B1.1 et seq.—940 F.2d 286
1B1.1 et seq.—940 F.2d 478
1B1.1 et seq.—940 F.2d 985
1B1.1 et seq.—940 F.2d 1061
1B1.1 et seq.—940 F.2d 1141
1B1.1 et seq.—940 F.2d 1159
1B1.1 et seq.—940 F.2d 1352
1B1.1 et seq.—941 F.2d 8
1B1.1 et seq.—941 F.2d 60
1B1.1 et seq.—941 F.2d 133
1B1.1 et seq.—941 F.2d 267
1B1.1 et seq.—941 F.2d 480
1B1.1 et seq.—941 F.2d 738
1B1.1 et seq.—941 F.2d 761
1B1.1 et seq.—941 F.2d 858
1B1.1 et seq.—941 F.2d 905
1B1.1 et seq.—941 F.2d 1047
1B1.1 et seq.—941 F.2d 1090
1B1.1 et seq.—942 F.2d 454
1B1.1 et seq.—942 F.2d 528
1B1.1 et seq.—942 F.2d 556
1B1.1 et seq.—942 F.2d 606
1B1.1 et seq.—942 F.2d 751
1B1.1 et seq.—942 F.2d 775
1B1.1 et seq.—942 F.2d 800
1B1.1 et seq.—942 F.2d 878
1B1.1 et seq.—942 F.2d 894
1B1.1 et seq.—942 F.2d 1217
1B1.1 et seq.—942 F.2d 1270
1B1.1 et seq.—943 F.2d 43
1B1.1 et seq.—943 F.2d 215
1B1.1 et seq.—943 F.2d 383
1B1.1 et seq.—943 F.2d 428
1B1.1 et seq.—943 F.2d 692
1B1.1 et seq.—943 F.2d 798
1B1.1 et seq.—943 F.2d 836
1B1.1 et seq.—943 F.2d 873
1B1.1 et seq.—943 F.2d 1007
1B1.1 et seq.—943 F.2d 1032
1B1.1 et seq.—943 F.2d 1218
1B1.1 et seq.—943 F.2d 1422
1B1.1 et seq.—944 F.2d 14
1B1.1 et seq.—944 F.2d 33
1B1.1 et seq.—944 F.2d 42
1B1.1 et seq.—944 F.2d 414
1B1.1 et seq.—944 F.2d 959
1B1.1 et seq.—944 F.2d 1106
1B1.1 et seq.—944 F.2d 1253
1B1.1 et seq.—945 F.2d 14
1B1.1 et seq.—945 F.2d 100
1B1.1 et seq.—945 F.2d 300
1B1.1 et seq.—945 F.2d 365
1B1.1 et seq.—945 F.2d 378
1B1.1 et seq.—945 F.2d 496
1B1.1 et seq.—945 F.2d 650
1B1.1 et seq.—945 F.2d 967
1B1.1 et seq.—945 F.2d 989
1B1.1 et seq.—945 F.2d 1052
1B1.1 et seq.—945 F.2d 1214
1B1.1 et seq.—945 F.2d 1337
1B1.1 et seq.—945 F.2d 1387

1B1.1 et seq.—945 F.2d 1504
1B1.1 et seq.—946 F.2d 13
1B1.1 et seq.—946 F.2d 23
1B1.1 et seq.—946 F.2d 97
1B1.1 et seq.—946 F.2d 100
1B1.1 et seq.—946 F.2d 142
1B1.1 et seq.—946 F.2d 335
1B1.1 et seq.—946 F.2d 362
1B1.1 et seq.—946 F.2d 505
1B1.1 et seq.—946 F.2d 729
1B1.1 et seq.—946 F.2d 1105
1B1.1 et seq.—946 F.2d 1191
1B1.1 et seq.—946 F.2d 1428
1B1.1 et seq.—947 F.2d 130
1B1.1 et seq.—947 F.2d 139
1B1.1 et seq.—947 F.2d 306
1B1.1 et seq.—947 F.2d 644
1B1.1 et seq.—947 F.2d 739
1B1.1 et seq.—947 F.2d 742
1B1.1 et seq.—947 F.2d 1263
1B1.1 et seq.—947 F.2d 1424
1B1.1 et seq.—947 F.2d 1479
1B1.1 et seq.—948 F.2d 241
1B1.1 et seq.—948 F.2d 370
1B1.1 et seq.—948 F.2d 448
1B1.1 et seq.—948 F.2d 732
1B1.1 et seq.—948 F.2d 1046
1B1.1 et seq.—948 F.2d 1074
1B1.1 et seq.—948 F.2d 1093
1B1.1 et seq.—948 F.2d 1107
1B1.1 et seq.—948 F.2d 1196
1B1.1 et seq.—948 F.2d 1449
1B1.1 et seq.—949 F.2d 61
1B1.1 et seq.—949 F.2d 289
1B1.1 et seq.—949 F.2d 722
1B1.1 et seq.—949 F.2d 777
1B1.1 et seq.—949 F.2d 860
1B1.1 et seq.—949 F.2d 973
1B1.1 et seq.—949 F.2d 1121
1B1.1 et seq.—949 F.2d 1183
1B1.1 et seq.—949 F.2d 1465
1B1.1 et seq.—950 F.2d 72
1B1.1 et seq.—950 F.2d 226
1B1.1 et seq.—950 F.2d 444
1B1.1 et seq.—950 F.2d 508
1B1.1 et seq.—950 F.2d 633
1B1.1 et seq.—950 F.2d 969
1B1.1 et seq.—950 F.2d 1095
1B1.1 et seq.—950 F.2d 1255
1B1.1 et seq.—950 F.2d 1267
1B1.1 et seq.—950 F.2d 1508
1B1.1 et seq.—951 F.2d 26
1B1.1 et seq.—951 F.2d 161
1B1.1 et seq.—951 F.2d 751
1B1.1 et seq.—951 F.2d 867
1B1.1 et seq.—951 F.2d 887
1B1.1 et seq.—951 F.2d 902
1B1.1 et seq.—951 F.2d 988
1B1.1 et seq.—951 F.2d 1057
1B1.1 et seq.—951 F.2d 1164
1B1.1 et seq.—951 F.2d 1182
1B1.1 et seq.—951 F.2d 1451
1B1.1 et seq.—952 F.2d 50
1B1.1 et seq.—952 F.2d 155
1B1.1 et seq.—952 F.2d 190
1B1.1 et seq.—952 F.2d 260
1B1.1 et seq.—952 F.2d 289
1B1.1 et seq.—952 F.2d 514
1B1.1 et seq.—952 F.2d 591
1B1.1 et seq.—952 F.2d 672
1B1.1 et seq.—952 F.2d 827
1B1.1 et seq.—952 F.2d 934
1B1.1 et seq.—952 F.2d 1049
1B1.1 et seq.—952 F.2d 1066
1B1.1 et seq.—952 F.2d 1090
1B1.1 et seq.—952 F.2d 1101
1B1.1 et seq.—953 F.2d 321
1B1.1 et seq.—953 F.2d 443
1B1.1 et seq.—953 F.2d 452
1B1.1 et seq.—953 F.2d 461
1B1.1 et seq.—953 F.2d 526
1B1.1 et seq.—953 F.2d 559
1B1.1 et seq.—953 F.2d 753
1B1.1 et seq.—953 F.2d 895
1B1.1 et seq.—953 F.2d 898
1B1.1 et seq.—953 F.2d 939
1B1.1 et seq.—953 F.2d 1060
1B1.1 et seq.—953 F.2d 1089
1B1.1 et seq.—953 F.2d 1184
1B1.1 et seq.—954 F.2d 204
1B1.1 et seq.—954 F.2d 482
1B1.1 et seq.—954 F.2d 951
1B1.1 et seq.—954 F.2d 1005
1B1.1 et seq.—954 F.2d 1012
1B1.1 et seq.—954 F.2d 1015
1B1.1 et seq.—954 F.2d 1386
1B1.1 et seq.—955 F.2d 14
1B1.1 et seq.—955 F.2d 99
1B1.1 et seq.—955 F.2d 182
1B1.1 et seq.—955 F.2d 270

1B1.1 et seq.—955 F.2d 288
1B1.1 et seq.—955 F.2d 291
1B1.1 et seq.—955 F.2d 397
1B1.1 et seq.—955 F.2d 586
1B1.1 et seq.—955 F.2d 1098
1B1.1 et seq.—955 F.2d 1492
1B1.1 et seq.—955 F.2d 1500
1B1.1 et seq.—956 F.2d 450
1B1.1 et seq.—956 F.2d 643
1B1.1 et seq.—956 F.2d 891
1B1.1 et seq.—956 F.2d 907
1B1.1 et seq.—956 F.2d 939
1B1.1 et seq.—956 F.2d 954
1B1.1 et seq.—956 F.2d 1007
1B1.1 et seq.—956 F.2d 1079
1B1.1 et seq.—956 F.2d 1098
1B1.1 et seq.—956 F.2d 1408
1B1.1 et seq.—956 F.2d 1534
1B1.1 et seq.—956 F.2d 1555
1B1.1 et seq.—957 F.2d 36
1B1.1 et seq.—957 F.2d 497
1B1.1 et seq.—957 F.2d 525
1B1.1 et seq.—957 F.2d 671
1B1.1 et seq.—957 F.2d 677
1B1.1 et seq.—957 F.2d 681
1B1.1 et seq.—957 F.2d 813
1B1.1 et seq.—957 F.2d 831
1B1.1 et seq.—957 F.2d 1488
1B1.1 et seq.—958 F.2d 26
1B1.1 et seq.—958 F.2d 66
1B1.1 et seq.—958 F.2d 804
1B1.1 et seq.—958 F.2d 806
1B1.1 et seq.—959 F.2d 26
1B1.1 et seq.—959 F.2d 81
1B1.1 et seq.—959 F.2d 189
1B1.1 et seq.—959 F.2d 246
1B1.1 et seq.—959 F.2d 516
1B1.1 et seq.—959 F.2d 1324
1B1.1 et seq.—960 F.2d 55
1B1.1 et seq.—960 F.2d 256
1B1.1 et seq.—960 F.2d 409
1B1.1 et seq.—960 F.2d 449
1B1.1 et seq.—960 F.2d 716
1B1.1 et seq.—960 F.2d 955
1B1.1 et seq.—960 F.2d 965
1B1.1 et seq.—960 F.2d 1055
1B1.1 et seq.—960 F.2d 1075
1B1.1 et seq.—960 F.2d 1099
1B1.1 et seq.—960 F.2d 1301
1B1.1 et seq.—960 F.2d 1348
1B1.1 et seq.—960 F.2d 1501
1B1.1 et seq.—961 F.2d 41
1B1.1 et seq.—961 F.2d 82
1B1.1 et seq.—961 F.2d 103
1B1.1 et seq.—961 F.2d 164
1B1.1 et seq.—961 F.2d 180
1B1.1 et seq.—961 F.2d 288
1B1.1 et seq.—961 F.2d 462
1B1.1 et seq.—961 F.2d 493
1B1.1 et seq.—961 F.2d 685
1B1.1 et seq.—961 F.2d 710
1B1.1 et seq.—961 F.2d 756
1B1.1 et seq.—961 F.2d 882
1B1.1 et seq.—961 F.2d 1058
1B1.1 et seq.—961 F.2d 1327
1B1.1 et seq.—961 F.2d 1351
1B1.1 et seq.—961 F.2d 1390
1B1.1 et seq.—961 F.2d 1399
1B1.1 et seq.—961 F.2d 1460
1B1.1 et seq.—961 F.2d 1476
1B1.1 et seq.—962 F.2d 409
1B1.1 et seq.—962 F.2d 560
1B1.1 et seq.—962 F.2d 767
1B1.1 et seq.—962 F.2d 894
1B1.1 et seq.—962 F.2d 1410
1B1.1 et seq.—962 F.2d 1418
1B1.1 et seq.—962 F.2d 1548
1B1.1 et seq.—963 F.2d 132
1B1.1 et seq.—963 F.2d 268
1B1.1 et seq.—963 F.2d 476
1B1.1 et seq.—963 F.2d 546
1B1.1 et seq.—963 F.2d 641
1B1.1 et seq.—963 F.2d 693
1B1.1 et seq.—963 F.2d 711
1B1.1 et seq.—963 F.2d 777
1B1.1 et seq.—963 F.2d 1184
1B1.1 et seq.—963 F.2d 1320
1B1.1 et seq.—963 F.2d 1323
1B1.1 et seq.—963 F.2d 1337
1B1.1 et seq.—964 F.2d 167
1B1.1 et seq.—964 F.2d 381
1B1.1 et seq.—964 F.2d 640
1B1.1 et seq.—964 F.2d 763
1B1.1 et seq.—964 F.2d 1065
1B1.1 et seq.—964 F.2d 1186
1B1.1 et seq.—964 F.2d 1492
1B1.1 et seq.—964 F.2d 1501
1B1.1 et seq.—965 F.2d 206
1B1.1 et seq.—965 F.2d 222
1B1.1 et seq.—965 F.2d 262

1B1.1 et seq.—965 F.2d 283
1B1.1 et seq.—965 F.2d 480
1B1.1 et seq.—965 F.2d 604
1B1.1 et seq.—965 F.2d 1124
1B1.1 et seq.—966 F.2d 201
1B1.1 et seq.—966 F.2d 380
1B1.1 et seq.—966 F.2d 398
1B1.1 et seq.—966 F.2d 403
1B1.1 et seq.—966 F.2d 508
1B1.1 et seq.—966 F.2d 559
1B1.1 et seq.—966 F.2d 591
1B1.1 et seq.—966 F.2d 682
1B1.1 et seq.—966 F.2d 703
1B1.1 et seq.—966 F.2d 707
1B1.1 et seq.—966 F.2d 959
1B1.1 et seq.—966 F.2d 1270
1B1.1 et seq.—966 F.2d 1354
1B1.1 et seq.—966 F.2d 1366
1B1.1 et seq.—966 F.2d 1383
1B1.1 et seq.—966 F.2d 1390
1B1.1 et seq.—966 F.2d 1500
1B1.1 et seq.—966 F.2d 1575
1B1.1 et seq.—967 F.2d 287
1B1.1 et seq.—967 F.2d 561
1B1.1 et seq.—967 F.2d 572
1B1.1 et seq.—967 F.2d 724
1B1.1 et seq.—967 F.2d 1028
1B1.1 et seq.—967 F.2d 1098
1B1.1 et seq.—967 F.2d 1220
1B1.1 et seq.—967 F.2d 1321
1B1.1 et seq.—967 F.2d 1351
1B1.1 et seq.—967 F.2d 1468
1B1.1 et seq.—968 F.2d 216
1B1.1 et seq.—968 F.2d 242
1B1.1 et seq.—968 F.2d 729
1B1.1 et seq.—968 F.2d 947
1B1.1 et seq.—968 F.2d 1047
1B1.1 et seq.—968 F.2d 1154
1B1.1 et seq.—969 F.2d 187
1B1.1 et seq.—969 F.2d 223
1B1.1 et seq.—969 F.2d 733
1B1.1 et seq.—969 F.2d 757
1B1.1 et seq.—969 F.2d 980
1B1.1 et seq.—970 F.2d 164
1B1.1 et seq.—970 F.2d 444
1B1.1 et seq.—971 F.2d 89
1B1.1 et seq.—971 F.2d 357
1B1.1 et seq.—971 F.2d 667
1B1.1 et seq.—971 F.2d 961
1B1.1 et seq.—971 F.2d 989
1B1.1 et seq.—971 F.2d 1257
1B1.1 et seq.—971 F.2d 1302
1B1.1 et seq.—972 F.2d 218
1B1.1 et seq.—972 F.2d 271
1B1.1 et seq.—972 F.2d 273
1B1.1 et seq.—972 F.2d 284
1B1.1 et seq.—972 F.2d 294
1B1.1 et seq.—972 F.2d 548
1B1.1 et seq.—972 F.2d 958
1B1.1 et seq.—972 F.2d 1000
1B1.1 et seq.—972 F.2d 1007
1B1.1 et seq.—972 F.2d 1107
1B1.1 et seq.—973 F.2d 1
1B1.1 et seq.—973 F.2d 600
1B1.1 et seq.—973 F.2d 1152
1B1.1 et seq.—973 F.2d 1354
1B1.1 et seq.—974 F.2d 19
1B1.1 et seq.—974 F.2d 22
1B1.1 et seq.—974 F.2d 25
1B1.1 et seq.—974 F.2d 55
1B1.1 et seq.—974 F.2d 246
1B1.1 et seq.—974 F.2d 948
1B1.1 et seq.—974 F.2d 961
1B1.1 et seq.—974 F.2d 1270
1B1.1 et seq.—975 F.2d 17
1B1.1 et seq.—975 F.2d 305
1B1.1 et seq.—975 F.2d 596
1B1.1 et seq.—975 F.2d 944
1B1.1 et seq.—975 F.2d 958
1B1.1 et seq.—975 F.2d 1061
1B1.1 et seq.—975 F.2d 1120
1B1.1 et seq.—975 F.2d 1554
1B1.1 et seq.—976 F.2d 393
1B1.1 et seq.—976 F.2d 414
1B1.1 et seq.—976 F.2d 844
1B1.1 et seq.—976 F.2d 1096
1B1.1 et seq.—976 F.2d 1226
1B1.1 et seq.—976 F.2d 1446
1B1.1 et seq.—977 F.2d 69
1B1.1 et seq.—977 F.2d 331
1B1.1 et seq.—977 F.2d 457
1B1.1 et seq.—977 F.2d 861
1B1.1 et seq.—977 F.2d 905
1B1.1 et seq.—977 F.2d 1061
1B1.1 et seq.—977 F.2d 1360
1B1.1 et seq.—978 F.2d 78
1B1.1 et seq.—978 F.2d 166
1B1.1 et seq.—978 F.2d 185
1B1.1 et seq.—978 F.2d 281
1B1.1 et seq.—978 F.2d 341

1B1.1 et seq.—978 F.2d 433
1B1.1 et seq.—978 F.2d 557
1B1.1 et seq.—978 F.2d 881
1B1.1 et seq.—978 F.2d 903
1B1.1 et seq.—978 F.2d 1112
1B1.1 et seq.—978 F.2d 1133
1B1.1 et seq.—978 F.2d 1554
1B1.1 et seq.—979 F.2d 116
1B1.1 et seq.—979 F.2d 396
1B1.1 et seq.—979 F.2d 402
1B1.1 et seq.—979 F.2d 469
1B1.1 et seq.—979 F.2d 786
1B1.1 et seq.—979 F.2d 790
1B1.1 et seq.—979 F.2d 816
1B1.1 et seq.—979 F.2d 921
1B1.1 et seq.—979 F.2d 1048
1B1.1 et seq.—979 F.2d 1219
1B1.1 et seq.—979 F.2d 1227
1B1.1 et seq.—980 F.2d 8
1B1.1 et seq.—980 F.2d 312
1B1.1 et seq.—980 F.2d 506
1B1.1 et seq.—980 F.2d 847
1B1.1 et seq.—980 F.2d 1400
1B1.1 et seq.—981 F.2d 92
1B1.1 et seq.—981 F.2d 569
1B1.1 et seq.—981 F.2d 1123
1B1.1 et seq.—981 F.2d 1382
1B1.1 et seq.—981 F.2d 1398
1B1.1 et seq.—982 F.2d 116
1B1.1 et seq.—982 F.2d 216
1B1.1 et seq.—982 F.2d 317
1B1.1 et seq.—982 F.2d 325
1B1.1 et seq.—982 F.2d 483
1B1.1 et seq.—982 F.2d 665
1B1.1 et seq.—982 F.2d 959
1B1.1 et seq.—982 F.2d 1365
1B1.1 et seq.—983 F.2d 206
1B1.1 et seq.—983 F.2d 369
1B1.1 et seq.—983 F.2d 730
1B1.1 et seq.—983 F.2d 757
1B1.1 et seq.—983 F.2d 1380
1B1.1 et seq.—983 F.2d 1425
1B1.1 et seq.—983 F.2d 1563
1B1.1 et seq.—984 F.2d 143
1B1.1 et seq.—984 F.2d 298
1B1.1 et seq.—984 F.2d 597
1B1.1 et seq.—984 F.2d 635
1B1.1 et seq.—984 F.2d 651
1B1.1 et seq.—984 F.2d 899
1B1.1 et seq.—984 F.2d 989
1B1.1 et seq.—984 F.2d 1067
1B1.1 et seq.—984 F.2d 1162
1B1.1 et seq.—984 F.2d 1339
1B1.1 et seq.—985 F.2d 535
1B1.1 et seq.—985 F.2d 612
1B1.1 et seq.—985 F.2d 732
1B1.1 et seq.—985 F.2d 763
1B1.1 et seq.—985 F.2d 945
1B1.1 et seq.—985 F.2d 1175
1B1.1 et seq. [1988]—986 F.2d 21
1B1.1 et seq.—986 F.2d 35
1B1.1 et seq.—986 F.2d 44
1B1.1 et seq.—986 F.2d 65
1B1.1 et seq.—986 F.2d 151
1B1.1 et seq.—986 F.2d 349
1B1.1 et seq.—986 F.2d 439
1B1.1 et seq.—986 F.2d 875
1B1.1 et seq.—986 F.2d 916
1B1.1 et seq.—986 F.2d 1225
1B1.1 et seq.—987 F.2d 251
1B1.1 et seq.—987 F.2d 564
1B1.1 et seq.—987 F.2d 631
1B1.1 et seq.—987 F.2d 1129
1B1.1 et seq.—987 F.2d 1225
1B1.1 et seq.—987 F.2d 1462
1B1.1 et seq.—987 F.2d 1497
1B1.1 et seq.—988 F.2d 16
1B1.1 et seq.—988 F.2d 107
1B1.1 et seq.—988 F.2d 280
1B1.1 et seq.—988 F.2d 544
1B1.1 et seq.—988 F.2d 712
1B1.1 et seq.—988 F.2d 746
1B1.1 et seq.—988 F.2d 998
1B1.1 et seq.—988 F.2d 1002
1B1.1 et seq.—988 F.2d 1374
1B1.1 et seq.—989 F.2d 52
1B1.1 et seq.—989 F.2d 180
1B1.1 et seq.—989 F.2d 261
1B1.1 et seq.—989 F.2d 384
1B1.1 et seq.—989 F.2d 438
1B1.1 et seq.—989 F.2d 454
1B1.1 et seq.—989 F.2d 1117
1B1.1 et seq.—989 F.2d 1137
1B1.1 et seq.—990 F.2d 178
1B1.1 et seq.—990 F.2d 251
1B1.1 et seq.—990 F.2d 1179
1B1.1 et seq.—991 F.2d 55
1B1.1 et seq.—991 F.2d 181
1B1.1 et seq.—991 F.2d 443
1B1.1 et seq.—991 F.2d 533

1B1.1 et seq. [1992]—991 F.2d 590
1B1.1 et seq.—991 F.2d 627
1B1.1 et seq.—991 F.2d 702
1B1.1 et seq.—991 F.2d 819
1B1.1 et seq.—991 F.2d 1468
1B1.1 et seq.—992 F.2d 87
1B1.1 et seq.—992 F.2d 91
1B1.1 et seq.—992 F.2d 108
1B1.1 et seq.—992 F.2d 164
1B1.1 et seq.—992 F.2d 301
1B1.1 et seq.—992 F.2d 573
1B1.1 et seq.—992 F.2d 678
1B1.1 et seq.—992 F.2d 793
1B1.1 et seq.—992 F.2d 896
1B1.1 et seq.—992 F.2d 967
1B1.1 et seq.—992 F.2d 982
1B1.1 et seq.—992 F.2d 1143
1B1.1 et seq.—992 F.2d 1459
1B1.1 et seq.—992 F.2d 1472
1B1.1 et seq.—993 F.2d 187
1B1.1 et seq.—993 F.2d 338
1B1.1 et seq.—993 F.2d 680
1B1.1 et seq.—993 F.2d 1522
1B1.1 et seq.—994 F.2d 386
1B1.1 et seq.—994 F.2d 609
1B1.1 et seq.—994 F.2d 714
1B1.1 et seq.—994 F.2d 918
1B1.1 et seq.—994 F.2d 1088
1B1.1 et seq.—994 F.2d 1129
1B1.1 et seq.—994 F.2d 1192
1B1.1 et seq.—994 F.2d 1380
1B1.1 et seq.—995 F.2d 173
1B1.1 et seq.—995 F.2d 182
1B1.1 et seq.—995 F.2d 307
1B1.1 et seq.—995 F.2d 746
1B1.1 et seq.—995 F.2d 931
1B1.1 et seq.—995 F.2d 936
1B1.1 et seq.—995 F.2d 1006
1B1.1 et seq.—995 F.2d 1414
1B1.1 et seq.—995 F.2d 1448
1B1.1 et seq.—996 F.2d 75
1B1.1 et seq.—996 F.2d 284
1B1.1 et seq.—996 F.2d 827
1B1.1 et seq.—996 F.2d 906
1B1.1 et seq.—996 F.2d 937
1B1.1 et seq.—996 F.2d 993
1B1.1 et seq.—996 F.2d 1009
1B1.1 et seq.—996 F.2d 1541
1B1.1 et seq.—997 F.2d 30
1B1.1 et seq.—997 F.2d 139
1B1.1 et seq.—997 F.2d 263
1B1.1 et seq.—997 F.2d 407
1B1.1 et seq.—997 F.2d 475
1B1.1 et seq.—997 F.2d 594
1B1.1 et seq.—997 F.2d 632
1B1.1 et seq.—997 F.2d 687
1B1.1 et seq.—997 F.2d 967
1B1.1 et seq.—997 F.2d 970
1B1.1 et seq.—997 F.2d 1130
1B1.1 et seq.—997 F.2d 1213
1B1.1 et seq.—997 F.2d 1426
1B1.1 et seq.—998 F.2d 42
1B1.1 et seq.—998 F.2d 453
1B1.1 et seq.—998 F.2d 497
1B1.1 et seq.—998 F.2d 572
1B1.1 et seq.—998 F.2d 604
1B1.1 et seq.—998 F.2d 634
1B1.1 et seq.—998 F.2d 917
1B1.1 et seq.—998 F.2d 1377
1B1.1 et seq.—998 F.2d 1491
1B1.1 et seq.—999 F.2d 38
1B1.1 et seq.—999 F.2d 312
1B1.1 et seq.—999 F.2d 639
1B1.1 et seq.—999 F.2d 640
1B1.1 et seq.—999 F.2d 1048
1B1.1 et seq.—999 F.2d 1053
1B1.1 et seq.—999 F.2d 1150
1B1.1 et seq.—999 F.2d 1175
1B1.1 et seq.—999 F.2d 1192
1B1.1 et seq.—999 F.2d 1225
1B1.1 et seq.—999 F.2d 1246
1B1.1 et seq.—999 F.2d 1326
1B1.1 et seq.—999 F.2d 1334
1B1.1 et seq.—1 F.3d 46
1B1.1 et seq.—1 F.3d 51
1B1.1 et seq.—1 F.3d 192
1B1.1 et seq.—1 F.3d 330
1B1.1 et seq.—1 F.3d 414
1B1.1 et seq.—1 F.3d 654
1B1.1 et seq.—1 F.3d 729
1B1.1 et seq.—1 F.3d 972
1B1.1 et seq.—1 F.3d 1044
1B1.1 et seq.—1 F.3d 1098
1B1.1 et seq.—1 F.3d 1112
1B1.1 et seq.—1 F.3d 1161
1B1.1 et seq.—2 F.3d 200
1B1.1 et seq.—2 F.3d 557
1B1.1 et seq.—2 F.3d 574
1B1.1 et seq.—2 F.3d 827
1B1.1 et seq.—2 F.3d 942

1B1.1 et seq.—2 F.3d 1094
1B1.1 et seq.—2 F.3d 1318
1B1.1 et seq.—3 F.3d 311
1B1.1 et seq.—3 F.3d 314
1B1.1 et seq.—3 F.3d 667
1B1.1 et seq.—3 F.3d 1149
1B1.1 et seq.—3 F.3d 1468
1B1.1 et seq.—4 F.3d 549
1B1.1 et seq.—4 F.3d 628
1B1.1 et seq.—4 F.3d 647
1B1.1 et seq.—4 F.3d 891
1B1.1 et seq.—4 F.3d 941
1B1.1 et seq.—4 F.3d 1358
1B1.1 et seq.—5 F.3d 44
1B1.1 et seq.—5 F.3d 48
1B1.1 et seq.—5 F.3d 192
1B1.1 et seq.—5 F.3d 292
1B1.1 et seq.—5 F.3d 365
1B1.1 et seq.—5 F.3d 467
1B1.1 et seq.—5 F.3d 563
1B1.1 et seq.—5 F.3d 715
1B1.1 et seq.—5 F.3d 795
1B1.1 et seq.—5 F.3d 986
1B1.1 et seq.—5 F.3d 1070
1B1.1 et seq.—5 F.3d 1267
1B1.1 et seq.—5 F.3d 1338
1B1.1 et seq.—5 F.3d 1365
1B1.1 et seq.—5 F.3d 1369
1B1.1 et seq.—5 F.3d 1420
1B1.1 et seq.—6 F.3d 431
1B1.1 et seq.—6 F.3d 554
1B1.1 et seq.—6 F.3d 601
1B1.1 et seq.—6 F.3d 611
1B1.1 et seq.—6 F.3d 715
1B1.1 et seq.—6 F.3d 735
1B1.1 et seq.—6 F.3d 911
1B1.1 et seq.—6 F.3d 1201
1B1.1 et seq.—6 F.3d 1218
1B1.1 et seq.—6 F.3d 1400
1B1.1 et seq.—7 F.3d 49
1B1.1 et seq.—7 F.3d 101
1B1.1 et seq.—7 F.3d 144
1B1.1 et seq.—7 F.3d 149
1B1.1 et seq.—7 F.3d 254
1B1.1 et seq.—7 F.3d 527
1B1.1 et seq.—7 F.3d 629
1B1.1 et seq.—7 F.3d 744
1B1.1 et seq.—7 F.3d 813
1B1.1 et seq.—7 F.3d 840
1B1.1 et seq.—7 F.3d 927
1B1.1 et seq.—7 F.3d 957
1B1.1 et seq.—7 F.3d 1155
1B1.1 et seq.—7 F.3d 1193
1B1.1 et seq.—7 F.3d 1279
1B1.1 et seq.—7 F.3d 1331
1B1.1 et seq.—7 F.3d 1471
1B1.1 et seq.—7 F.3d 1483
1B1.1 et seq.—8 F.3d 11
1B1.1 et seq.—8 F.3d 39
1B1.1 et seq.—8 F.3d 186
1B1.1 et seq.—8 F.3d 785
1B1.1 et seq.—8 F.3d 839
1B1.1 et seq.—8 F.3d 1379
1B1.1 et seq.—8 F.3d 1488
1B1.1 et seq.—9 F.3d 368
1B1.1 et seq.—9 F.3d 531
1B1.1 et seq.—9 F.3d 543
1B1.1 et seq.—9 F.3d 741
1B1.1 et seq.—9 F.3d 761
1B1.1 et seq.—9 F.3d 875
1B1.1 et seq.—9 F.3d 1377
1B1.1 et seq.—9 F.3d 1422
1B1.1 et seq.—9 F.3d 1438
1B1.1 et seq.—9 F.3d 1442
1B1.1 et seq.—10 F.3d 263
1B1.1 et seq.—10 F.3d 485
1B1.1 et seq.—10 F.3d 630
1B1.1 et seq.—10 F.3d 1003
1B1.1 et seq.—10 F.3d 1044
1B1.1 et seq.—10 F.3d 1086
1B1.1 et seq.—10 F.3d 1197
1B1.1 et seq.—11 F.3d 18
1B1.1 et seq.—11 F.3d 52
1B1.1 et seq.—11 F.3d 140
1B1.1 et seq.—11 F.3d 315
1B1.1 et seq.—11 F.3d 505
1B1.1 et seq.—11 F.3d 602
1B1.1 et seq.—11 F.3d 777
1B1.1 et seq.—11 F.3d 973
1B1.1 et seq.—11 F.3d 1225
1B1.1 et seq.—11 F.3d 1510
1B1.1 et seq.—12 F.3d 70
1B1.1 et seq.—12 F.3d 139
1B1.1 et seq.—12 F.3d 273
1B1.1 et seq.—12 F.3d 298
1B1.1 et seq.—12 F.3d 746
1B1.1 et seq.—12 F.3d 836
1B1.1 et seq.—12 F.3d 1116
1B1.1 et seq.—12 F.3d 1350
1B1.1 et seq.—13 F.3d 147

1B1.1 et seq.—13 F.3d 154
1B1.1 et seq.—13 F.3d 207
1B1.1 et seq.—13 F.3d 369
1B1.1 et seq.—13 F.3d 860
1B1.1 et seq.—13 F.3d 1043
1B1.1 et seq.—13 F.3d 1117
1B1.1 et seq.—13 F.3d 1126
1B1.1 et seq.—13 F.3d 1305
1B1.1 et seq.—13 F.3d 1354
1B1.1 et seq.—13 F.3d 1381
1B1.1 et seq.—14 F.3d 30
1B1.1 et seq.—14 F.3d 79
1B1.1 et seq.—14 F.3d 337
1B1.1 et seq.—14 F.3d 502
1B1.1 et seq.—14 F.3d 662
1B1.1 et seq.—14 F.3d 1030
1B1.1 et seq.—14 F.3d 1093
1B1.1 et seq.—14 F.3d 1189
1B1.1 et seq.—14 F.3d 1200
1B1.1 et seq.—14 F.3d 1283
1B1.1 et seq.—14 F.3d 1364
1B1.1 et seq.—14 F.3d 1502
1B1.1 et seq.—15 F.3d 68
1B1.1 et seq.—15 F.3d 825
1B1.1 et seq.—15 F.3d 830
1B1.1 et seq.—15 F.3d 1002
1B1.1 et seq.—15 F.3d 1161
1B1.1 et seq.—15 F.3d 1356
1B1.1 et seq.—15 F.3d 1380
1B1.1 et seq.—16 F.3d 45
1B1.1 et seq.—16 F.3d 193
1B1.1 et seq.—16 F.3d 317
1B1.1 et seq.—16 F.3d 494
1B1.1 et seq.—16 F.3d 599
1B1.1 et seq.—16 F.3d 795
1B1.1 et seq.—16 F.3d 1110
1B1.1 et seq.—16 F.3d 1168
1B1.1 et seq.—17 F.3d 53
1B1.1 et seq.—17 F.3d 70
1B1.1 et seq.—17 F.3d 146
1B1.1 et seq.—17 F.3d 230
1B1.1 et seq.—17 F.3d 306
1B1.1 et seq.—17 F.3d 351
1B1.1 et seq.—17 F.3d 462
1B1.1 et seq.—17 F.3d 496
1B1.1 et seq.—17 F.3d 660
1B1.1 et seq.—17 F.3d 737
1B1.1 et seq.—17 F.3d 865
1B1.1 et seq.—17 F.3d 1294
1B1.1 et seq.—18 F.3d 301
1B1.1 et seq.—18 F.3d 363
1B1.1 et seq.—18 F.3d 465
1B1.1 et seq.—18 F.3d 588
1B1.1 et seq.—18 F.3d 595
1B1.1 et seq.—18 F.3d 612
1B1.1 et seq.—18 F.3d 807
1B1.1 et seq.—18 F.3d 1123
1B1.1 et seq.—18 F.3d 1145
1B1.1 et seq.—18 F.3d 1156
1B1.1 et seq.—18 F.3d 1254
1B1.1 et seq.—18 F.3d 1488
1B1.1 et seq.—19 F.3d 350
1B1.1 et seq.—19 F.3d 482
1B1.1 et seq.—19 F.3d 605
1B1.1 et seq.—19 F.3d 917
1B1.1 et seq.—19 F.3d 982
1B1.1 et seq.—19 F.3d 1210
1B1.1 et seq.—19 F.3d 1385
1B1.1 et seq.—20 F.3d 204
1B1.1 et seq.—20 F.3d 229
1B1.1 et seq.—20 F.3d 521
1B1.1 et seq.—20 F.3d 610
1B1.1 et seq.—20 F.3d 615
1B1.1 et seq.—20 F.3d 709
1B1.1 et seq.—20 F.3d 831
1B1.1 et seq.—20 F.3d 999
1B1.1 et seq.—20 F.3d 1325
1B1.1 et seq.—20 F.3d 1336
1B1.1 et seq.—21 F.3d 7
1B1.1 et seq.—21 F.3d 632
1B1.1 et seq.—21 F.3d 714
1B1.1 et seq.—21 F.3d 747
1B1.1 et seq.—21 F.3d 759
1B1.1 et seq.—21 F.3d 850
1B1.1 et seq.—21 F.3d 885
1B1.1 et seq.—22 F.3d 93
1B1.1 et seq.—22 F.3d 170
1B1.1 et seq.—22 F.3d 218
1B1.1 et seq.—22 F.3d 330
1B1.1 et seq.—22 F.3d 409
1B1.1 et seq.—22 F.3d 583
1B1.1 et seq.—22 F.3d 662
1B1.1 et seq.—22 F.3d 674
1B1.1 et seq.—22 F.3d 744
1B1.1 et seq.—22 F.3d 790
1B1.1 et seq.—22 F.3d 846
1B1.1 et seq.—22 F.3d 981
1B1.1 et seq.—22 F.3d 1040
1B1.1 et seq.—22 F.3d 1048
1B1.1 et seq.—22 F.3d 1504

1B1.1 et seq.—23 F.3d 47
1B1.1 et seq.—23 F.3d 87
1B1.1 et seq.—23 F.3d 135
1B1.1 et seq.—23 F.3d 216
1B1.1 et seq.—23 F.3d 269
1B1.1 et seq.—23 F.3d 300
1B1.1 et seq.—23 F.3d 343
1B1.1 et seq.—23 F.3d 370
1B1.1 et seq.—670 F.Supp. 1056
1B1.1 et seq.—672 F.Supp. 812
1B1.1 et seq.—677 F.Supp. 1386
1B1.1 et seq.—678 F.Supp. 1463
1B1.1 et seq.—680 F.Supp. 26
1B1.1 et seq.—680 F.Supp. 119
1B1.1 et seq.—680 F.Supp. 1411
1B1.1 et seq.—681 F.Supp. 126
1B1.1 et seq.—681 F.Supp. 1510
1B1.1 et seq.—682 F.Supp. 29
1B1.1 et seq.—682 F.Supp. 815
1B1.1 et seq.—682 F.Supp. 1033
1B1.1 et seq.—682 F.Supp. 1517
1B1.1 et seq.—683 F.Supp. 701
1B1.1 et seq.—683 F.Supp. 1003
1B1.1 et seq.—684 F.Supp. 634
1B1.1 et seq.—685 F.Supp. 111
1B1.1 et seq.—685 F.Supp. 179
1B1.1 et seq.—685 F.Supp. 725
1B1.1 et seq.—685 F.Supp. 827
1B1.1 et seq.—685 F.Supp. 1213
1B1.1 et seq.—685 F.Supp. 1245
1B1.1 et seq.—685 F.Supp. 1479
1B1.1 et seq.—686 F.Supp. 284
1B1.1 et seq.—686 F.Supp. 296
1B1.1 et seq.—686 F.Supp. 847
1B1.1 et seq.—686 F.Supp. 1246
1B1.1 et seq.—687 F.Supp. 38
1B1.1 et seq.—687 F.Supp. 426
1B1.1 et seq.—687 F.Supp. 1145
1B1.1 et seq.—688 F.Supp. 70
1B1.1 et seq.—688 F.Supp. 542
1B1.1 et seq.—688 F.Supp. 819
1B1.1 et seq.—688 F.Supp. 1398
1B1.1 et seq.—688 F.Supp. 1483
1B1.1 et seq.—689 F.Supp. 954
1B1.1 et seq.—689 F.Supp. 1319
1B1.1 et seq.—690 F.Supp. 272
1B1.1 et seq.—690 F.Supp. 1030
1B1.1 et seq.—690 F.Supp. 1274
1B1.1 et seq.—690 F.Supp. 1303
1B1.1 et seq.—690 F.Supp. 1423
1B1.1 et seq.—691 F.Supp. 36
1B1.1 et seq.—691 F.Supp. 277
1B1.1 et seq.—691 F.Supp. 341
1B1.1 et seq.—691 F.Supp. 525
1B1.1 et seq.—691 F.Supp. 584
1B1.1 et seq.—692 F.Supp. 968
1B1.1 et seq.—693 F.Supp. 687
1B1.1 et seq.—693 F.Supp. 1102
1B1.1 et seq.—694 F.supp. 512
1B1.1 et seq.—694 F.Supp. 635
1B1.1 et seq.—694 F.Supp. 777
1B1.1 et seq.—694 F.Supp. 786
1B1.1 et seq.—694 F.Supp. 1194
1B1.1 et seq.—694 F.Supp. 1218
1B1.1 et seq.—694 F.Supp. 1406
1B1.1 et seq.—695 F.Supp. 1140
1B1.1 et seq.—696 F.Supp. 55
1B1.1 et seq.—696 F.Supp. 781
1B1.1 et seq.—697 F.Supp. 1305
1B1.1 et seq.—698 F.Supp. 153
1B1.1 et seq.—699 F.Supp. 147
1B1.1 et seq.—701 F.Supp. 148
1B1.1 et seq.—702 F.Supp. 549
1B1.1 et seq.—702 F.Supp. 605
1B1.1 et seq.—704 F.Supp. 175
1B1.1 et seq.—704 F.Supp. 787
1B1.1 et seq.—704 F.Supp. 910
1B1.1 et seq.—706 F.Supp. 91
1B1.1 et seq.—706 F.Supp. 331
1B1.1 et seq.—707 F.Supp. 1101
1B1.1 et seq.—707 F.Supp. 1582
1B1.1 et seq.—708 F.Supp. 425
1B1.1 et seq.—708 F.Supp. 964
1B1.1 et seq.—708 F.Supp. 1064
1B1.1 et seq.—709 F.Supp. 10
1B1.1 et seq.—709 F.Supp. 653
1B1.1 et seq.—709 F.Supp. 908
1B1.1 et seq.—710 F.Supp. 106
1B1.1 et seq.—710 F.Supp. 551
1B1.1 et seq.—713 F.Supp. 565
1B1.1 et seq.—713 F.Supp. 1315
1B1.1 et seq.—715 F.Supp. 193
1B1.1 et seq.—715 F.Supp. 203
1B1.1 et seq.—715 F.Supp. 261
1B1.1 et seq.—715 F.Supp. 854
1B1.1 et seq.—716 F.Supp. 1137
1B1.1 et seq.—716 F.Supp. 1452
1B1.1 et seq.—718 F.Supp. 8
1B1.1 et seq.—718 F.Supp. 493
1B1.1 et seq.—725 F.Supp. 878

1B1.1 et seq.—725 F.Supp. 1459
1B1.1 et seq.—726 F.Supp. 1359
1B1.1 et seq.—731 F.Supp. 262
1B1.1 et seq.—731 F.Supp. 944
1B1.1 et seq.—733 F.Supp. 496
1B1.1 et seq.—733 F.Supp. 1195
1B1.1 et seq.—733 F.Supp. 1256
1B1.1 et seq.—734 F.Supp. 312
1B1.1 et seq.—734 F.Supp. 599
1B1.1 et seq.—734 F.Supp. 842
1B1.1 et seq.—735 F.Supp. 874
1B1.1 et seq.—735 F.Supp. 1057
1B1.1 et seq.—740 F.Supp. 1332
1B1.1 et seq.—740 F.Supp. 1502
1B1.1 et seq.—741 F.Supp. 622
1B1.1 et seq.—741 F.Supp. 1200
1B1.1 et seq.—742 F.Supp. 1003
1B1.1 et seq.—746 F.Supp. 1076
1B1.1 et seq.—747 F.Supp. 493
1B1.1 et seq.—749 F.Supp. 53
1B1.1 et seq.—749 F.Supp. 1450
1B1.1 et seq.—751 F.Supp. 1195
1B1.1 et seq.—751 F.Supp. 1350
1B1.1 et seq.—753 F.Supp. 23
1B1.1 et seq.—755 F.Supp. 304
1B1.1 et seq.—756 F.Supp. 23
1B1.1 et seq.—756 F.Supp. 134
1B1.1 et seq.—756 F.Supp. 217
1B1.1 et seq.—756 F.Supp. 470
1B1.1 et seq.—760 F.Supp. 777
1B1.1 et seq.—760 F.Supp. 1322
1B1.1 et seq.—763 F.Supp. 645
1B1.1 et seq.—764 F.Supp. 1451
1B1.1 et seq.—765 F.Supp. 1499
1B1.1 et seq.—770 F.Supp. 598
1B1.1 et seq.—771 F.Supp. 324
1B1.1 et seq.—773 F.Supp. 479
1B1.1 et seq.—774 F.Supp. 1582
1B1.1 et seq.—776 F.Supp. 1030
1B1.1 et seq.—777 F.Supp. 293
1B1.1 et seq.—777 F.Supp. 1229
1B1.1 et seq.—778 F.Supp. 393
1B1.1 et seq.—778 F.Supp. 931
1B1.1 et seq.—779 F.Supp. 561
1B1.1 et seq.—782 F.Supp. 747
1B1.1 et seq.—783 F.Supp. 203
1B1.1 et seq.—784 F.Supp. 1373
1B1.1 et seq.—786 F.Supp. 1105
1B1.1 et seq.—788 F.Supp. 132
1B1.1 et seq.—788 F.Supp. 158
1B1.1 et seq.—788 F.Supp. 413
1B1.1 et seq.—788 F.Supp. 756
1B1.1 et seq.—791 F.Supp. 380
1B1.1 et seq.—791 F.Supp. 843
1B1.1 et seq.—792 F.Supp. 637
1B1.1 et seq.—792 F.Supp. 922
1B1.1 et seq.—793 F.Supp. 64
1B1.1 et seq.—794 F.Supp. 539
1B1.1 et seq.—795 F.Supp. 1262
1B1.1 et seq.—796 F.Supp. 268
1B1.1 et seq.—796 F.Supp. 853
1B1.1 et seq.—796 F.Supp. 1036
1B1.1 et seq.—799 F.Supp. 646
1B1.1 et seq.—801 F.Supp. 1407
1B1.1 et seq.—802 F.Supp. 781
1B1.1 et seq.—803 F.Supp. 53
1B1.1 et seq.—803 F.Supp. 70
1B1.1 et seq.—803 F.Supp. 592
1B1.1 et seq.—806 F.Supp. 1567
1B1.1 et seq.—807 F.Supp. 156
1B1.1 et seq.—807 F.Supp. 1063
1B1.1 et seq.—808 F.Supp. 166
1B1.1 et seq.—810 F.Supp. 230
1B1.1 et seq.—811 F.Supp. 578
1B1.1 et seq.—811 F.Supp. 762
1B1.1 et seq.—812 F.Supp. 183
1B1.1 et seq.—813 F.Supp. 1175
1B1.1 et seq.—814 F.Supp. 760
1B1.1 et seq.—814 F.Supp. 1249
1B1.1-7A1.4—897 F.2d 1034
1B1.1 comment—888 F.2d 862
1B1.1 comment—893 F.2d 950
1B1.1 comment—893 F.2d 1343
1B1.1 comment—894 F.2d 74
1B1.1 comment—895 F.2d 1225
1B1.1 comment—897 F.2d 13
1B1.1 comment—898 F.2d 25
1B1.1 comment—898 F.2d 1465
1B1.1 comment—903 F.2d 457
1B1.1 comment—905 F.2d 935
1B1.1 comment—905 F.2d 1296
1B1.1 comment—907 F.2d 91
1B1.1 comment—911 F.2d 985
1B1.1 comment—913 F.2d 193
1B1.1 comment—913 F.2d 201
1B1.1 comment—913 F.2d 1053
1B1.1 comment—914 F.2d 206
1B1.1 comment [1988]—914 F.2d 208
1B1.1 comment—918 F.2d 1084
1B1.1 comment—921 F.2d 25

1B1.1 comment—922 F.2d 748
1B1.1 comment—929 F.2d 389
1B1.1 comment—929 F.2d 1126
1B1.1 comment—932 F.2d 651
1B1.1 comment—933 F.2d 824
1B1.1 comment—934 F.2d 190
1B1.1 comment—934 F.2d 553
1B1.1 comment—936 F.2d 227
1B1.1 comment—942 F.2d 528
1B1.1 comment—943 F.2d 29
1B1.1 comment—943 F.2d 1543
1B1.1 comment—947 F.2d 112
1B1.1 comment—948 F.2d 1125
1B1.1 comment—948 F.2d 1449
1B1.1 comment—951 F.2d 1451
1B1.1 comment—952 F.2d 1066
1B1.1 comment—954 F.2d 928
1B1.1 comment—955 F.2d 547
1B1.1 comment—956 F.2d 341
1B1.1 comment—960 F.2d 115
1B1.1 comment—960 F.2d 599
1B1.1 comment—964 F.2d 911
1B1.1 comment—965 F.2d 404
1B1.1 comment—966 F.2d 262
1B1.1 comment—966 F.2d 555
1B1.1 comment—966 F.2d 1383
1B1.1 comment—969 F.2d 425
1B1.1 comment—973 F.2d 832
1B1.1 comment—973 F.2d 835
1B1.1 comment [1988]—975 F.2d 985
1B1.1 comment—976 F.2d 55
1B1.1 comment—976 F.2d 608
1B1.1 comment [1988]—977 F.2d 672
1B1.1 comment—978 F.2d 861
1B1.1 comment—981 F.2d 1153
1B1.1 comment—985 F.2d 463
1B1.1 comment—986 F.2d 1
1B1.1 comment—987 F.2d 104
1B1.1 comment—988 F.2d 13
1B1.1 comment—989 F.2d 454
1B1.1 comment—989 F.2d 948
1B1.1 comment—990 F.2d 1090
1B1.1 comment—990 F.2d 1545
1B1.1 comment—991 F.2d 409
1B1.1 comment [1991]—991 F.2d 700
1B1.1 comment—993 F.2d 1444
1B1.1 comment—997 F.2d 30
1B1.1 comment—998 F.2d 74
1B1.1 comment—1 F.3d 729
1B1.1 comment—2 F.3d 870
1B1.1 comment—4 F.3d 697
1B1.1 comment—5 F.3d 295
1B1.1 comment—6 F.3d 208
1B1.1 comment—7 F.3d 319
1B1.1 comment—7 F.3d 691
1B1.1 comment—7 F.3d 1155
1B1.1 comment—11 F.3d 140
1B1.1 comment—13 F.3d 1126
1B1.1 comment—16 F.3d 358
1B1.1 comment—16 F.3d 599
1B1.1 comment [1988]—17 F.3d 409
1B1.1 comment—18 F.3d 1367
1B1.1 comment—19 F.3d 166
1B1.1 comment—19 F.3d 1387
1B1.1 comment—20 F.3d 270
1B1.1 comment—684 F.Supp. 1048
1B1.1 comment—733 F.Supp. 1307
1B1.1 comment—803 F.Supp. 53
1B1.1 comment—814 F.Supp. 964
1B1.1 comment—819 F.Supp. 250
1B1.1 comment—833 F.Supp. 769
1B1.2—860 F.2d 35
1B1.2—863 F.2d 245
1B1.2—867 F.2d 783
1B1.2—872 F.2d 101
1B1.2—887 F.2d 104
1B1.2—891 F.2d 82
1B1.2—903 F.2d 292
1B1.2—912 F.2d 754
1B1.2 [1988]—916 F.2d 916
1B1.2—917 F.2d 841
1B1.2 [1990]—920 F.2d 1290
1B1.2—943 F.2d 1306
1B1.2—971 F.2d 115
1B1.2—995 F.2d 1020
1B1.2—684 F.Supp. 1048
1B1.2—776 F.Supp. 1030
1B1.2—815 F.Supp. 84
1B1.2(a)—111 S.Ct. 1854
1B1.2(a)—863 F.2d 245
1B1.2(a)—866 F.2d 604
1B1.2(a)—875 F.2d 1124
1B1.2(a)—877 F.2d 688
1B1.2(a)—882 F.2d 151
1B1.2(a)—884 F.2d 181
1B1.2(a)—885 F.2d 1266
1B1.2(a)—887 F.2d 697
1B1.2(a)—891 F.2d 405
1B1.2(a)—893 F.2d 73
1B1.2(a)—897 F.2d 1558

1B1.2(a)—898 F.2d 705
1B1.2(a)—898 F.2d 1465
1B1.2(a)—904 F.2d 441
1B1.2(a)—913 F.2d 193
1B1.2(a)—914 F.2d 67
1B1.2(a)—917 F.2d 683
1B1.2(a)—917 F.2d 1178
1B1.2(a)—919 F.2d 461
1B1.2(a)—920 F.2d 363
1B1.2(a)—943 F.2d 587
1B1.2(a)—947 F.2d 1031
1B1.2(a)—954 F.2d 586
1B1.2(a)—959 F.2d 1324
1B1.2(a)—962 F.2d 1236
1B1.2(a)—965 F.2d 460
1B1.2(a)—983 F.2d 1507
1B1.2(a)—988 F.2d 94
1B1.2(a)—991 F.2d 725
1B1.2(a)—993 F.2d 752
1B1.2(a)—994 F.2d 1088
1B1.2(a)—999 F.2d 674
1B1.2(a) [1990]—3 F.3d 98
1B1.2(a)—7 F.3d 1496
1B1.2(a)—684 F.Supp. 1048
1B1.2(a)—698 F.Supp. 563
1B1.2(a)—815 F.Supp. 84
1B1.2(b)—863 F.2d 245
1B1.2(b)—872 F.2d 101
1B1.2(b)—875 F.2d 1124
1B1.2(b)—877 F.2d 688
1B1.2(b)—897 F.2d 1558
1B1.2(b)—898 F.2d 705
1B1.2(b)—917 F.2d 683
1B1.2(b)—917 F.2d 841
1B1.2(b)—923 F.2d 1079
1B1.2(b)—959 F.2d 1324
1B1.2(b) [1990]—3 F.3d 98
1B1.2(c)—905 F.2d 337
1B1.2(c)—925 F.2d 205
1B1.2(c)—948 F.2d 732
1B1.2(c)—6 F.3d 715
1B1.2(c)—12 F.3d 160
1B1.2(d)—927 F.2d 1272
1B1.2(d)—948 F.2d 1107
1B1.2(d)—954 F.2d 1413
1B1.2(d)—960 F.2d 1391
1B1.2(d)—962 F.2d 1308
1B1.2(d)—965 F.2d 1001
1B1.2(d)—966 F.2d 936
1B1.2(d)—995 F.2d 1020
1B1.2(d)—22 F.3d 574
1B1.2(d)—815 F.Supp. 158
1B1.2(d)—817 F.Supp. 321
1B1.2 comment—875 F.2d 1124
1B1.2 comment—884 F.2d 181
1B1.2 comment—904 F.2d 441
1B1.2 comment [1990]—920 F.2d 1290
1B1.2 comment—925 F.2d 205
1B1.2 comment—948 F.2d 1107
1B1.2 comment—960 F.2d 1391
1B1.2 comment—966 F.2d 936
1B1.2 comment—991 F.2d 819
1B1.2 comment—994 F.2d 1088
1B1.2 comment—995 F.2d 1020
1B1.2 comment [1990]—3 F.3d 98
1B1.2 comment—3 F.3d 325
1B1.2 comment—4 F.3d 70
1B1.2 comment—6 F.3d 715
1B1.2 comment—817 F.Supp. 321
1B1.3—863 F.2d 245
1B1.3—866 F.2d 604
1B1.3—872 F.2d 101
1B1.3—872 F.2d 597
1B1.3—872 F.2d 735
1B1.3—873 F.2d 23
1B1.3—873 F.2d 437
1B1.3—874 F.2d 213
1B1.3—875 F.2d 1124
1B1.3—877 F.2d 688
1B1.3—877 F.2d 1138
1B1.3—879 F.2d 454
1B1.3—880 F.2d 1204
1B1.3—884 F.2d 1355
1B1.3—887 F.2d 104
1B1.3—887 F.2d 697
1B1.3—888 F.2d 223
1B1.3—888 F.2d 247
1B1.3 [1988]—888 F.2d 862
1B1.3—888 F.2d 907
1B1.3—889 F.2d 357
1B1.3—889 F.2d 1531
1B1.3—891 F.2d 364
1B1.3—893 F.2d 314
1B1.3—894 F.2d 261
1B1.3—895 F.2d 867
1B1.3—895 F.2d 1362
1B1.3—896 F.2d 99
1B1.3—896 F.2d 912
1B1.3—896 F.2d 1071
1B1.3—897 F.2d 490

1B1.3 [1987]—897 F.2d 490
1B1.3—897 F.2d 1099
1B1.3—898 F.2d 373
1B1.3—898 F.2d 705
1B1.3—901 F.2d 29
1B1.3—902 F.2d 451
1B1.3—902 F.2d 1046
1B1.3—903 F.2d 648
1B1.3—904 F.2d 1490
1B1.3—905 F.2d 295
1B1.3—906 F.2d 867
1B1.3—906 F.2d 879
1B1.3—906 F.2d 1285
1B1.3—909 F.2d 436
1B1.3 [1988]—911 F.2d 1016
1B1.3—913 F.2d 1288
1B1.3—914 F.2d 1527
1B1.3—915 F.2d 402
1B1.3 [1988]—916 F.2d 916
1B1.3—917 F.2d 112
1B1.3—917 F.2d 507
1B1.3—917 F.2d 601
1B1.3—917 F.2d 683
1B1.3—917 F.2d 879
1B1.3 [1988]—917 F.2d 879
1B1.3—917 F.2d 1495
1B1.3—918 F.2d 1084
1B1.3—919 F.2d 286
1B1.3—919 F.2d 940
1B1.3—920 F.2d 1231
1B1.3—922 F.2d 630
1B1.3—922 F.2d 1411
1B1.3—924 F.2d 298
1B1.3—924 F.2d 454
1B1.3—925 F.2d 828
1B1.3—926 F.2d 172
1B1.3—927 F.2d 825
1B1.3—928 F.2d 1548
1B1.3—929 F.2d 55
1B1.3—929 F.2d 285
1B1.3—929 F.2d 365
1B1.3—929 F.2d 1453
1B1.3—930 F.2d 1450
1B1.3—931 F.2d 1440
1B1.3—932 F.2d 342
1B1.3—932 F.2d 1174
1B1.3—933 F.2d 898
1B1.3—934 F.2d 875
1B1.3—935 F.2d 201
1B1.3—935 F.2d 766
1B1.3—936 F.2d 333
1B1.3—937 F.2d 54
1B1.3—937 F.2d 95
1B1.3—938 F.2d 678
1B1.3—938 F.2d 764
1B1.3 [1988]—938 F.2d 1086
1B1.3—938 F.2d 1327
1B1.3—939 F.2d 416
1B1.3—939 F.2d 780
1B1.3—941 F.2d 133
1B1.3—943 F.2d 444
1B1.3—944 F.2d 1377
1B1.3—945 F.2d 650
1B1.3—945 F.2d 826
1B1.3—946 F.2d 484
1B1.3—946 F.2d 505
1B1.3 [1990]—948 F.2d 776
1B1.3—948 F.2d 1042
1B1.3—949 F.2d 968
1B1.3—950 F.2d 72
1B1.3—952 F.2d 281
1B1.3—953 F.2d 1312
1B1.3—954 F.2d 12
1B1.3—954 F.2d 374
1B1.3—954 F.2d 586
1B1.3—956 F.2d 894
1B1.3—956 F.2d 954
1B1.3—957 F.2d 577
1B1.3—960 F.2d 955
1B1.3—961 F.2d 1476
1B1.3—962 F.2d 165
1B1.3—963 F.2d 976
1B1.3—964 F.2d 325
1B1.3—964 F.2d 687
1B1.3—966 F.2d 945
1B1.3—967 F.2d 68
1B1.3—967 F.2d 1383
1B1.3—968 F.2d 278
1B1.3—968 F.2d 575
1B1.3—969 F.2d 352
1B1.3—970 F.2d 960
1B1.3—970 F.2d 1490
1B1.3—971 F.2d 115
1B1.3—971 F.2d 562
1B1.3—971 F.2d 626
1B1.3—971 F.2d 1138
1B1.3—973 F.2d 1015
1B1.3—973 F.2d 1152
1B1.3—975 F.2d 580
1B1.3—975 F.2d 596

1B1.3—975 F.2d 985
1B1.3—975 F.2d 1225
1B1.3—976 F.2d 235
1B1.3—976 F.2d 414
1B1.3—977 F.2d 1350
1B1.3—978 F.2d 166
1B1.3—979 F.2d 402
1B1.3—979 F.2d 1289
1B1.3—979 F.2d 1406
1B1.3—979 F.2d 1557
1B1.3—982 F.2d 4
1B1.3—982 F.2d 354
1B1.3—982 F.2d 426
1B1.3 [1992]—982 F.2d 1374
1B1.3—983 F.2d 625
1B1.3—983 F.2d 893
1B1.3—984 F.2d 338
1B1.3—985 F.2d 860
1B1.3—987 F.2d 564
1B1.3—987 F.2d 1009
1B1.3—988 F.2d 228
1B1.3—989 F.2d 583
1B1.3—989 F.2d 659
1B1.3—990 F.2d 419
1B1.3 [1992]—990 F.2d 1456
1B1.3—990 F.2d 1545
1B1.3—991 F.2d 725
1B1.3—991 F.2d 1445
1B1.3—991 F.2d 1468
1B1.3—992 F.2d 70
1B1.3 [1992]—992 F.2d 70
1B1.3—992 F.2d 887
1B1.3—992 F.2d 1029
1B1.3—996 F.2d 88
1B1.3—997 F.2d 78
1B1.3—997 F.2d 139
1B1.3—997 F.2d 396
1B1.3—998 F.2d 74
1B1.3—998 F.2d 253
1B1.3—998 F.2d 584
1B1.3—998 F.2d 776
1B1.3—999 F.2d 154
1B1.3—999 F.2d 392
1B1.3—999 F.2d 483
1B1.3—1 F.3d 386
1B1.3—2 F.3d 72
1B1.3—2 F.3d 927
1B1.3 [1990]—3 F.3d 98
1B1.3—3 F.3d 506
1B1.3—3 F.3d 827
1B1.3—3 F.3d 1578
1B1.3—4 F.3d 70
1B1.3—4 F.3d 1338
1B1.3—5 F.3d 1070
1B1.3—6 F.3d 431
1B1.3—6 F.3d 1201
1B1.3—7 F.3d 254
1B1.3—7 F.3d 1496
1B1.3—8 F.3d 186
1B1.3 [1992]—9 F.3d 368
1B1.3—9 F.3d 1377
1B1.3—10 F.3d 910
1B1.3—10 F.3d 1044
1B1.3 [1990]—10 F.3d 1044
1B1.3 [1992]—10 F.3d 1252
1B1.3—13 F.3d 949
1B1.3—13 F.3d 1305
1B1.3—14 F.3d 277
1B1.3—14 F.3d 502
1B1.3—15 F.3d 856
1B1.3—16 F.3d 604
1B1.3—17 F.3d 27
1B1.3—17 F.3d 146
1B1.3—17 F.3d 502
1B1.3—18 F.3d 541
1B1.3—20 F.3d 242
1B1.3—22 F.3d 1066
1B1.3—684 F.Supp. 1048
1B1.3—692 F.Supp. 788
1B1.3—709 F.Supp. 908
1B1.3—727 F.Supp. 1023
1B1.3—732 F.Supp. 878
1B1.3—733 F.Supp. 29
1B1.3—734 F.Supp. 842
1B1.3—740 F.Supp. 1502
1B1.3—760 F.Supp. 1322
1B1.3—761 F.Supp. 697
1B1.3—763 F.Supp. 645
1B1.3—776 F.Supp. 1030
1B1.3—781 F.Supp. 428
1B1.3—791 F.Supp. 348
1B1.3—802 F.Supp. 859
1B1.3—811 F.Supp. 1106
1B1.3—813 F.Supp. 1175
1B1.3—832 F.Supp. 1426
1B1.3—834 F.Supp. 659
1B1.3—835 F.Supp. 1501
1B1.3—838 F.Supp. 709
1B1.3—845 F.Supp. 270
1B1.3(a)—885 F.2d 441

1B1.3(a)—887 F.2d 697
1B1.3(a)—888 F.2d 907
1B1.3(a)—889 F.2d 357
1B1.3(a)—897 F.2d 490
1B1.3(a) [1987]—897 F.2d 490
1B1.3(a)—899 F.2d 465
1B1.3(a)—901 F.2d 842
1B1.3(a)—910 F.2d 1241
1B1.3(a)—913 F.2d 705
1B1.3(a)—913 F.2d 1288
1B1.3(a)—915 F.2d 1174
1B1.3(a)—916 F.2d 219
1B1.3(a)—917 F.2d 841
1B1.3(a)—922 F.2d 675
1B1.3(a)—922 F.2d 910
1B1.3(a)—927 F.2d 197
1B1.3(a)—928 F.2d 339
1B1.3(a)—934 F.2d 1325
1B1.3(a)—936 F.2d 1292
1B1.3(a)—938 F.2d 1446
1B1.3(a)—939 F.2d 135
1B1.3(a)—940 F.2d 1141
1B1.3(a)—945 F.2d 650
1B1.3(a)—952 F.2d 934
1B1.3(a)—964 F.2d 124
1B1.3(a)—964 F.2d 454
1B1.3(a)—967 F.2d 728
1B1.3(a)—970 F.2d 960
1B1.3(a)—971 F.2d 115
1B1.3(a)—977 F.2d 698
1B1.3(a)—979 F.2d 402
1B1.3(a) [1991]—982 F.2d 116
1B1.3(a)—982 F.2d 354
1B1.3(a)—984 F.2d 1426
1B1.3(a) [1991]—987 F.2d 874
1B1.3(a) [1991]—991 F.2d 700
1B1.3(a)—994 F.2d 1204
1B1.3(a)—996 F.2d 88
1B1.3(a)—996 F.2d 284
1B1.3(a)—999 F.2d 706
1B1.3(a)—4 F.3d 70
1B1.3(a)—4 F.3d 697
1B1.3(a)—5 F.3d 795
1B1.3(a) [1992]—7 F.3d 285
1B1.3(a)—10 F.3d 1
1B1.3(a)—12 F.3d 70
1B1.3(a)—14 F.3d 502
1B1.3(a)—16 F.3d 228
1B1.3(a)—18 F.3d 1156
1B1.3(a)—21 F.3d 194
1B1.3(a) [1992]—21 F.3d 714
1B1.3(a)—778 F.Supp. 931
1B1.3(a)—800 F.Supp. 648
1B1.3(a)—836 F.Supp. 812
1B1.3(a)(i) [1992]—9 F.3d 368
1B1.3(a)(ii)—937 F.2d 95
1B1.3(a)(ii)—970 F.2d 960
1B1.3(a)(iii)—970 F.2d 960
1B1.3(a)(iii)(1)—994 F.2d 456
1B1.3(a)(1)—863 F.2d 245
1B1.3(a)(1)—872 F.2d 101
1B1.3(a)(1)—894 F.2d 965
1B1.3(a)(1)—897 F.2d 909
1B1.3(a)(1)—899 F.2d 503
1B1.3(a)(1)—899 F.2d 873
1B1.3(a)(1)—901 F.2d 1209
1B1.3(a)(1)—902 F.2d 451
1B1.3(a)(1)—903 F.2d 457
1B1.3(a)(1)—904 F.2d 365
1B1.3(a)(1)—906 F.2d 1531
1B1.3(a)(1)—907 F.2d 1540
1B1.3(a)(1)—909 F.2d 1346
1B1.3(a)(1)—911 F.2d 149
1B1.3(a)(1)—913 F.2d 705
1B1.3(a)(1)—914 F.2d 699
1B1.3(a)(1)—915 F.2d 1174
1B1.3(a)(1)—920 F.2d 1395
1B1.3(a)(1)—922 F.2d 311
1B1.3(a)(1)—922 F.2d 910
1B1.3(a)(1)—924 F.2d 454
1B1.3(a)(1)—925 F.2d 112
1B1.3(a)(1)—925 F.2d 205
1B1.3(a)(1)—928 F.2d 339
1B1.3(a)(1)—928 F.2d 1450
1B1.3(a)(1)—928 F.2d 1548
1B1.3(a)(1)—929 F.2d 213
1B1.3(a)(1)—929 F.2d 839
1B1.3(a)(1)—930 F.2d 63
1B1.3(a)(1)—930 F.2d 1450
1B1.3(a)(1)—933 F.2d 641
1B1.3(a)(1)—933 F.2d 701
1B1.3(a)(1)—936 F.2d 1292
1B1.3(a)(1)—937 F.2d 1514
1B1.3(a)(1)—940 F.2d 286
1B1.3(a)(1)—941 F.2d 133
1B1.3(a)(1)—941 F.2d 761
1B1.3(a)(1)—943 F.2d 1543
1B1.3(a)(1)—944 F.2d 1106
1B1.3(a)(1)—945 F.2d 1387
1B1.3(a)(1)—948 F.2d 776

1B1.3(a)(1)—950 F.2d 72
1B1.3(a)(1)—953 F.2d 1184
1B1.3(a)(1)—953 F.2d 1312
1B1.3(a)(1)—955 F.2d 547
1B1.3(a)(1)—958 F.2d 315
1B1.3(a)(1)—959 F.2d 375
1B1.3(a)(1)—959 F.2d 1324
1B1.3(a)(1)—961 F.2d 11
1B1.3(a)(1)—961 F.2d 756
1B1.3(a)(1)—961 F.2d 1476
1B1.3(a)(1)—962 F.2d 409
1B1.3(a)(1)—962 F.2d 767
1B1.3(a)(1)—967 F.2d 68
1B1.3(a)(1)—967 F.2d 1550
1B1.3(a)(1)—968 F.2d 278
1B1.3(a)(1)—968 F.2d 1143
1B1.3(a)(1)—969 F.2d 858
1B1.3(a)(1)—970 F.2d 960
1B1.3(a)(1)—970 F.2d 1328
1B1.3(a)(1)—971 F.2d 562
1B1.3(a)(1)—973 F.2d 1015
1B1.3(a)(1)—974 F.2d 61
1B1.3(a)(1)—975 F.2d 985
1B1.3(a)(1)—980 F.2d 259
1B1.3(a)(1)—980 F.2d 847
1B1.3(a)(1) [1991]—982 F.2d 116
1B1.3(a)(1)—982 F.2d 1241
1B1.3(a)(1) [1992]—986 F.2d 44
1B1.3(a)(1) [1992]—986 F.2d 880
1B1.3(a)(1)—987 F.2d 1009
1B1.3(a)(1)—989 F.2d 583
1B1.3(a)(1) [1992]—989 F.2d 948
1B1.3(a)(1) [1992]—990 F.2d 1456
1B1.3(a)(1)—993 F.2d 1498
1B1.3(a)(1) [1992]—994 F.2d 63
1B1.3(a)(1) [1991]—996 F.2d 116
1B1.3(a)(1)—996 F.2d 209
1B1.3(a)(1) [1990]—996 F.2d 456
1B1.3(a)(1) [1992]—998 F.2d 1377
1B1.3(a)(1)—998 F.2d 1491
1B1.3(a)(1)—1 F.3d 662
1B1.3(a)(1) [1990]—1 F.3d 1566
1B1.3(a)(1)—7 F.3d 66
1B1.3(a)(1) [1992]—7 F.3d 285
1B1.3(a)(1)—8 F.3d 186
1B1.3(a)(1) [1992]—9 F.3d 368
1B1.3(a)(1) [1992]—10 F.3d 1252
1B1.3(a)(1) [1992]—12 F.3d 1350
1B1.3(a)(1)—14 F.3d 1264
1B1.3(a)(1)—15 F.3d 1161
1B1.3(a)(1) [1992]—17 F.3d 333
1B1.3(a)(1)—18 F.3d 795
1B1.3(a)(1)—18 F.3d 807
1B1.3(a)(1) [1991]—19 F.3d 929
1B1.3(a)(1)—19 F.3d 1283
1B1.3(a)(1)—684 F.Supp. 1048
1B1.3(a)(1)—716 F.Supp. 1137
1B1.3(a)(1)—730 F.Supp. 35
1B1.3(a)(1)—730 F.Supp. 45
1B1.3(a)(1)—753 F.Supp. 917
1B1.3(a)(1)—753 F.Supp. 1191
1B1.3(a)(1)—763 F.Supp. 645
1B1.3(a)(1)—776 F.Supp. 1030
1B1.3(a)(1)—779 F.Supp. 422
1B1.3(a)(1)—781 F.Supp. 428
1B1.3(a)(1)—807 F.Supp. 165
1B1.3(a)(1)—814 F.Supp. 964
1B1.3(a)(1)—826 F.Supp. 1536
1B1.3(a)(1)—834 F.Supp. 659
1B1.3(a)(1)(A)—993 F.2d 1522
1B1.3(a)(1)(A)—995 F.2d 1006
1B1.3(a)(1)(A)—5 F.3d 868
1B1.3(a)(1)(A)—16 F.3d 202
1B1.3(a)(1)(A)—16 F.3d 897
1B1.3(a)(1)(A)—21 F.3d 632
1B1.3(a)(1)(A)—827 F.Supp. 205
1B1.3(a)(1)(A)—833 F.Supp. 1454
1B1.3(a)(1)(B)—982 F.2d 426
1B1.3(a)(1)(B)—985 F.2d 21
1B1.3(a)(1)(B)—987 F.2d 920
1B1.3(a)(1)(B)—992 F.2d 573
1B1.3(a)(1)(B)—995 F.2d 1006
1B1.3(a)(1)(B)—995 F.2d 1448
1B1.3(a)(1)(B)—1 F.3d 330
1B1.3(a)(1)(B)—2 F.3d 1551
1B1.3(a)(1)(B)—4 F.3d 70
1B1.3(a)(1)(B)—4 F.3d 1338
1B1.3(a)(1)(B)—5 F.3d 633
1B1.3(a)(1)(B)—5 F.3d 868
1B1.3(a)(1)(B)—6 F.3d 431
1B1.3(a)(1)(B)—8 F.3d 1313
1B1.3(a)(1)(B)—10 F.3d 1044
1B1.3(a)(1)(B)—10 F.3d 1236
1B1.3(a)(1)(B)—11 F.3d 1225
1B1.3(a)(1)(B)—13 F.3d 860
1B1.3(a)(1)(B)—14 F.3d 300
1B1.3(a)(1)(B)—14 F.3d 1128
1B1.3(a)(1)(B)—15 F.3d 149
1B1.3(a)(1)(B)—16 F.3d 193
1B1.3(a)(1)(B)—16 F.3d 897

1B1.3(a)(1)(B)—19 F.3d 166
1B1.3(a)(1)(B)—19 F.3d 409
1B1.3(a)(1)(B) [1991]—19 F.3d 929
1B1.3(a)(1)(B)—21 F.3d 632
1B1.3(a)(1)(B)—22 F.3d 47
1B1.3(a)(1)(B)—22 F.3d 580
1B1.3(a)(1)(B)—813 F.Supp. 168
1B1.3(a)(1)(B)—817 F.Supp. 321
1B1.3(a)(1)(B)—832 F.Supp. 1426
1B1.3(a)(1)(B)—833 F.Supp. 1454
1B1.3(a)(1-4)—15 F.3d 131
1B1.3(a)(2)—863 F.2d 245
1B1.3(a)(2)—869 F.2d 805
1B1.3(a)(2)—877 F.2d 688
1B1.3(a)(2)—878 F.2d 73
1B1.3(a)(2)—879 F.2d 391
1B1.3(a)(2)—880 F.2d 804
1B1.3(a)(2)—884 F.2d 349
1B1.3(a)(2)—884 F.2d 1355
1B1.3(a)(2)—886 F.2d 143
1B1.3(a)(2)—888 F.2d 490
1B1.3(a)(2)—888 F.2d 907
1B1.3(a)(2)—891 F.2d 13
1B1.3(a)(2)—891 F.2d 155
1B1.3(a)(2)—891 F.2d 364
1B1.3(a)(2)—891 F.2d 405
1B1.3(a)(2) [1988]—892 F.2d 725
1B1.3(a)(2)—893 F.2d 947
1B1.3(a)(2)—894 F.2d 74
1B1.3(a)(2)—894 F.2d 225
1B1.3(a)(2)—895 F.2d 1362
1B1.3(a)(2)—897 F.2d 490
1B1.3(a)(2)—897 F.2d 1558
1B1.3(a)(2)—898 F.2d 705
1B1.3(a)(2)—900 F.2d 1127
1B1.3(a)(2)—900 F.2d 1225
1B1.3(a)(2)—901 F.2d 29
1B1.3(a)(2)—902 F.2d 483
1B1.3(a)(2)—902 F.2d 501
1B1.3(a)(2)—903 F.2d 648
1B1.3(a)(2)—903 F.2d 891
1B1.3(a)(2)—906 F.2d 879
1B1.3(a)(2)—906 F.2d 1456
1B1.3(a)(2)—907 F.2d 781
1B1.3(a)(2)—908 F.2d 230
1B1.3(a)(2)—910 F.2d 1321
1B1.3(a)(2)—913 F.2d 1288
1B1.3(a)(2)—915 F.2d 402
1B1.3(a)(2)—917 F.2d 601
1B1.3(a)(2)—917 F.2d 841
1B1.3(a)(2)—917 F.2d 879
1B1.3(a)(2)—919 F.2d 286
1B1.3(a)(2)—919 F.2d 461
1B1.3(a)(2)—919 F.2d 606
1B1.3(a)(2)—920 F.2d 1530
1B1.3(a)(2)—922 F.2d 1490
1B1.3(a)(2)—924 F.2d 68
1B1.3(a)(2)—924 F.2d 399
1B1.3(a)(2)—924 F.2d 454
1B1.3(a)(2)—926 F.2d 112
1B1.3(a)(2)—926 F.2d 321
1B1.3(a)(2)—926 F.2d 734
1B1.3(a)(2)—926 F.2d 838
1B1.3(a)(2)—927 F.2d 111
1B1.3(a)(2)—928 F.2d 339
1B1.3(a)(2)—928 F.2d 372
1B1.3(a)(2)—928 F.2d 383
1B1.3(a)(2)—928 F.2d 1548
1B1.3(a)(2)—929 F.2d 55
1B1.3(a)(2)—929 F.2d 64
1B1.3(a)(2)—929 F.2d 365
1B1.3(a)(2)—929 F.2d 500
1B1.3(a)(2)—930 F.2d 63
1B1.3(a)(2)—931 F.2d 251
1B1.3(a)(2)—931 F.2d 308
1B1.3(a)(2)—931 F.2d 964
1B1.3(a)(2)—933 F.2d 362
1B1.3(a)(2)—936 F.2d 227
1B1.3(a)(2)—936 F.2d 1021
1B1.3(a)(2)—936 F.2d 1124
1B1.3(a)(2)—937 F.2d 95
1B1.3(a)(2)—937 F.2d 1041
1B1.3(a)(2)—937 F.2d 1208
1B1.3(a)(2)—937 F.2d 1227
1B1.3(a)(2) [1988]—938 F.2d 1086
1B1.3(a)(2)—942 F.2d 454
1B1.3(a)(2)—942 F.2d 779
1B1.3(a)(2)—943 F.2d 444
1B1.3(a)(2)—943 F.2d 897
1B1.3(a)(2)—944 F.2d 265
1B1.3(a)(2)—945 F.2d 826
1B1.3(a)(2)—946 F.2d 13
1B1.3(a)(2)—946 F.2d 110
1B1.3(a)(2)—946 F.2d 650
1B1.3(a)(2)—946 F.2d 654
1B1.3(a)(2)—947 F.2d 1320
1B1.3(a)(2)—948 F.2d 1
1B1.3(a)(2)—948 F.2d 352
1B1.3(a)(2)—948 F.2d 732
1B1.3(a)(2)—948 F.2d 776

1B1.3(a)(2)—948 F.2d 877
1B1.3(a)(2)—949 F.2d 968
1B1.3(a)(2)—950 F.2d 508
1B1.3(a)(2)—950 F.2d 1255
1B1.3(a)(2)—951 F.2d 405
1B1.3(a)(2)—951 F.2d 1220
1B1.3(a)(2)—952 F.2d 226
1B1.3(a)(2)—952 F.2d 281
1B1.3(a)(2)—952 F.2d 289
1B1.3(a)(2)—954 F.2d 12
1B1.3(a)(2)—954 F.2d 1224
1B1.3(a)(2)—956 F.2d 643
1B1.3(a)(2)—956 F.2d 1534
1B1.3(a)(2)—957 F.2d 577
1B1.3(a)(2)—958 F.2d 196
1B1.3(a)(2)—958 F.2d 315
1B1.3(a)(2)—959 F.2d 637
1B1.3(a)(2)—959 F.2d 1489
1B1.3(a)(2)—960 F.2d 903
1B1.3(a)(2)—961 F.2d 11
1B1.3(a)(2)—961 F.2d 41
1B1.3(a)(2)—961 F.2d 1476
1B1.3(a)(2)—963 F.2d 63
1B1.3(a)(2)—964 F.2d 778
1B1.3(a)(2)—965 F.2d 283
1B1.3(a)(2)—967 F.2d 1383
1B1.3(a)(2)—968 F.2d 278
1B1.3(a)(2)—968 F.2d 1250
1B1.3(a)(2)—970 F.2d 1490
1B1.3(a)(2)—971 F.2d 562
1B1.3(a)(2)—971 F.2d 876
1B1.3(a)(2)—971 F.2d 1138
1B1.3(a)(2)—973 F.2d 396
1B1.3(a)(2)—973 F.2d 852
1B1.3(a)(2)—973 F.2d 1015
1B1.3(a)(2)—975 F.2d 580
1B1.3(a)(2)—975 F.2d 596
1B1.3(a)(2)—975 F.2d 1061
1B1.3(a)(2)—976 F.2d 414
1B1.3(a)(2)—976 F.2d 1446
1B1.3(a)(2)—977 F.2d 222
1B1.3(a)(2)—977 F.2d 624
1B1.3(a)(2)—977 F.2d 866
1B1.3(a)(2)—977 F.2d 1077
1B1.3(a)(2)—977 F.2d 1350
1B1.3(a)(2)—979 F.2d 116
1B1.3(a)(2)—979 F.2d 119
1B1.3(a)(2)—979 F.2d 402
1B1.3(a)(2)—981 F.2d 192
1B1.3(a)(2)—981 F.2d 790
1B1.3(a)(2)—982 F.2d 4
1B1.3(a)(2) [1982]—982 F.2d 4
1B1.3(a)(2)—982 F.2d 292
1B1.3(a)(2)—982 F.2d 354
1B1.3(a)(2)—983 F.2d 893
1B1.3(a)(2)—984 F.2d 298
1B1.3(a)(2) [1992]—985 F.2d 463
1B1.3(a)(2)—986 F.2d 297
1B1.3(a)(2)—986 F.2d 1199
1B1.3(a)(2)—987 F.2d 564
1B1.3(a)(2)—987 F.2d 1349
1B1.3(a)(2)—988 F.2d 681
1B1.3(a)(2) [1992]—988 F.2d 1374
1B1.3(a)(2)—989 F.2d 44
1B1.3(a)(2)—990 F.2d 707
1B1.3(a)(2)—991 F.2d 171
1B1.3(a)(2)—991 F.2d 1328
1B1.3(a)(2)—991 F.2d 1468
1B1.3(a)(2)—992 F.2d 207
1B1.3(a)(2)—992 F.2d 437
1B1.3(a)(2)—992 F.2d 967
1B1.3(a)(2)—993 F.2d 1012
1B1.3(a)(2)—996 F.2d 1541
1B1.3(a)(2)—997 F.2d 139
1B1.3(a)(2)—997 F.2d 378
1B1.3(a)(2)—998 F.2d 84
1B1.3(a)(2)—998 F.2d 776
1B1.3(a)(2)—999 F.2d 182
1B1.3(a)(2)—999 F.2d 1175
1B1.3(a)(2)—1 F.3d 473
1B1.3(a)(2)—1 F.3d 644
1B1.3(a)(2)—1 F.3d 1501
1B1.3(a)(2)—2 F.3d 927
1B1.3(a)(2)—3 F.3d 29
1B1.3(a)(2)—3 F.3d 1312
1B1.3(a)(2)—3 F.3d 1578
1B1.3(a)(2)—4 F.3d 1026
1B1.3(a)(2)—7 F.3d 1331
1B1.3(a)(2)—8 F.3d 629
1B1.3(a)(2)—9 F.3d 198
1B1.3(a)(2) [1992]—9 F.3d 368
1B1.3(a)(2)—9 F.3d 1377
1B1.3(a)(2)—10 F.3d 1463
1B1.3(a)(2)—11 F.3d 346
1B1.3(a)(2)—11 F.3d 973
1B1.3(a)(2)—11 F.3d 1510
1B1.3(a)(2)—12 F.3d 30
1B1.3(a)(2)—13 F.3d 1354
1B1.3(a)(2)—13 F.3d 1418
1B1.3(a)(2)—14 F.3d 286

1B1.3(a)(2) [1991]—14 F.3d 1189
1B1.3(a)(2)—15 F.3d 1161
1B1.3(a)(2)—16 F.3d 179
1B1.3(a)(2)—19 F.3d 1283
1B1.3(a)(2)—20 F.3d 367
1B1.3(a)(2)—20 F.3d 1428
1B1.3(a)(2)—21 F.3d 811
1B1.3(a)(2)—23 F.2d 306
1B1.3(a)(2)—684 F.Supp. 1048
1B1.3(a)(2)—692 F.Supp. 788
1B1.3(a)(2)—704 F.Supp. 910
1B1.3(a)(2)—710 F.Supp. 1136
1B1.3(a)(2)—716 F.Supp. 1137
1B1.3(a)(2)—730 F.Supp. 35
1B1.3(a)(2)—730 F.Supp. 45
1B1.3(a)(2)—730 F.Supp. 1418
1B1.3(a)(2)—751 F.Supp. 1350
1B1.3(a)(2)—753 F.Supp. 917
1B1.3(a)(2)—760 F.Supp. 1322
1B1.3(a)(2)—763 F.Supp. 645
1B1.3(a)(2)—781 F.Supp. 428
1B1.3(a)(2)—798 F.Supp. 203
1B1.3(a)(2)—798 F.Supp. 291
1B1.3(a)(2)—813 F.Supp. 168
1B1.3(a)(2)—813 F.Supp. 1423
1B1.3(a)(2)—826 F.Supp. 1536
1B1.3(a)(2)—827 F.Supp. 205
1B1.3(a)(2)—829 F.Supp. 435
1B1.3(a)(3) [1988]—888 F.2d 862
1B1.3(a)(3)—898 F.2d 373
1B1.3(a)(3)—899 F.2d 503
1B1.3(a)(3)—911 F.2d 1016
1B1.3(a)(3)—943 F.2d 1543
1B1.3(a)(3)—953 F.2d 363
1B1.3(a)(3)—957 F.2d 577
1B1.3(a)(3)—971 F.2d 562
1B1.3(a)(3)—977 F.2d 1350
1B1.3(a)(3)—989 F.2d 583
1B1.3(a)(4)—886 F.2d 736
1B1.3(a)(4)—914 F.2d 699
1B1.3(a)(4)—946 F.2d 23
1B1.3(b)—899 F.2d 465
1B1.3(b)—941 F.2d 133
1B1.3(b)—982 F.2d 354
1B1.3(b)—11 F.3d 74
1B1.3 et seq.—883 F.2d 781
1B1.3 comment—877 F.2d 688
1B1.3 comment—880 F.2d 804
1B1.3 comment—888 F.2d 907
1B1.3 comment—889 F.2d 1531
1B1.3 comment—891 F.2d 364
1B1.3 comment—892 F.2d 182
1B1.3 comment [1988]—892 F.2d 725
1B1.3 comment—894 F.2d 208
1B1.3 comment—894 F.2d 261
1B1.3 comment—895 F.2d 1362
1B1.3 comment—896 F.2d 884
1B1.3 comment—898 F.2d 373
1B1.3 comment [1988]—898 F.2d 450
1B1.3 comment—898 F.2d 705
1B1.3 comment—899 F.2d 465
1B1.3 comment—900 F.2d 1225
1B1.3 comment—901 F.2d 1209
1B1.3 comment—903 F.2d 891
1B1.3 comment—904 F.2d 365
1B1.3 comment—905 F.2d 580
1B1.3 comment—906 F.2d 814
1B1.3 comment—907 F.2d 781
1B1.3 comment—909 F.2d 780
1B1.3 comment—909 F.2d 1346
1B1.3 comment—911 F.2d 1456
1B1.3 comment—912 F.2d 424
1B1.3 comment—913 F.2d 1288
1B1.3 comment—914 F.2d 1131
1B1.3 comment—915 F.2d 269
1B1.3 comment—917 F.2d 601
1B1.3 comment—917 F.2d 846
1B1.3 comment [1988]—917 F.2d 846
1B1.3 comment—917 F.2d 1220
1B1.3 comment—918 F.2d 62
1B1.3 comment—918 F.2d 68
1B1.3 comment—919 F.2d 19
1B1.3 comment—922 F.2d 630
1B1.3 comment—923 F.2d 369
1B1.3 comment—923 F.2d 427
1B1.3 comment [1988]—923 F.2d 910
1B1.3 comment—924 F.2d 298
1B1.3 comment—924 F.2d 454
1B1.3 comment—924 F.2d 800
1B1.3 comment—925 F.2d 112
1B1.3 comment—926 F.2d 112
1B1.3 comment—926 F.2d 1323
1B1.3 comment—928 F.2d 339
1B1.3 comment—928 F.2d 372
1B1.3 comment—928 F.2d 1450
1B1.3 comment—929 F.2d 365
1B1.3 comment—929 F.2d 839
1B1.3 comment—932 F.2d 1529
1B1.3 comment—933 F.2d 701
1B1.3 comment—934 F.2d 875

1B1.5—963 F.2d 1388
1B1.5 [1992]—5 F.3d 795
1B1.7—113 S.Ct. 1913
1B1.7—872 F.2d 101
1B1.7—895 F.2d 641
1B1.7—900 F.2d 1442
1B1.7—902 F.2d 1082
1B1.7—904 F.2d 441
1B1.7—909 F.2d 1047
1B1.7—946 F.2d 19
1B1.7—952 F.2d 982
1B1.7—961 F.2d 384
1B1.7—962 F.2d 484
1B1.7—964 F.2d 1079
1B1.7—981 F.2d 281
1B1.7 [1992]—994 F.2d 1380
1B1.7—996 F.2d 17
1B1.7 [1990]—3 F.3d 98
1B1.7 [1991]—15 F.3d 849
1B1.7—710 F.Supp. 1293
1B1.7—753 F.Supp. 1191
1B1.7—762 F.Supp. 441
1B1.7 comment—113 S.Ct. 1913
1B1.7 comment—900 F.2d 1442
1B1.7 comment—710 F.Supp. 1293
1B1.7 comment—753 F.Supp. 1191
1B1.8—887 F.2d 253
1B1.8—887 F.2d 697
1B1.8—898 F.2d 1111
1B1.8—918 F.2d 1383
1B1.8—942 F.2d 1270
1B1.8—963 F.2d 72
1B1.8—984 F.2d 387
1B1.8—985 F.2d 427
1B1.8—998 F.2d 572
1B1.8—723 F.Supp. 66
1B1.8(a)—910 F.2d 1321
1B1.8(a)—917 F.2d 181
1B1.8(a)—921 F.2d 580
1B1.8(a)—924 F.2d 800
1B1.8(a)—946 F.2d 1066
1B1.8(a)—985 F.2d 497
1B1.8(a)—730 F.2d 45
1B1.8(a)—796 F.2d 853
1B1.8(a)—998 F.2d 572
1B1.8(b)—15 F.3d 1292
1B1.8(b)(1)—917 F.2d 181
1B1.8(b)(1)—921 F.2d 580
1B1.8(b)(1)—921 F.2d 1073
1B1.8(b)(1)—946 F.2d 1066
1B1.8(b)(1)—963 F.2d 72
1B1.8(b)(1)—998 F.2d 572
1B1.8 comment— 787 F.2d 253
1B1.8 comment— 942 F.2d 1270
1B1.8 comment— 946 F.2d 1066
1B1.8 comment— 963 F.2d 72
1B1.8 comment—999 F.2d 1246
1B1.9 comment—998 F.2d 692
1B1.9—896 F.2d 206
1B1.9 comment—796 F.2d 206
1B1.9 comment—912 F.2d 1170
1B1.9 comment—968 F.2d 216
1B1.10—903 F.2d 341
1B1.10—960 F.2d 191
1B1.10—989 F.2d 583
1B1.10—997 F.2d 767
1B1.10—18 F.3d 601
1B1.10—762 F.Supp. 658
1B1.10—808 F.Supp. 206
1B1.10—810 F.Supp. 242
1B1.10—812 F.Supp. 612
1B1.10—812 F.Supp. 1092
1B1.10—814 F.Supp. 77
1B1.10—814 F.Supp. 244
1B1.10—814 F.Supp. 488
1B1.10—826 F.Supp. 368
1B1.10—829 F.Supp. 98
1B1.10—834 F.Supp. 550
1B1.10—838 F.Supp. 709
1B1.10(a)—905 F.2d 3
1B1.10(a)—960 F.2d 191
1B1.10(a)—977 F.2d 1323
1B1.10(a)—997 F.2d 429
1B1.10(a)—997 F.2d 767
1B1.10(a)—6 F.3d 601
1B1.10(a)—8 F.3d 1268
1B1.10(a)—9 F.3d 1438
1B1.10(a)—11 F.3d 97
1B1.10(a)—15 F.3d 68
1B1.10(a)—19 F.3d 1340
1B1.10(a)—807 F.Supp. 21
1B1.10(a)—808 F.Supp. 206
1B1.10(a)—809 F.Supp. 480
1B1.10(a)—810 F.Supp. 1231
1B1.10(a)—814 F.Supp. 14
1B1.10(a)—817 F.Supp. 894
1B1.10(a)—826 F.Supp. 368
1B1.10(a)—831 F.Supp. 880
1B1.10(b)—838 F.Supp. 377
1B1.10(d)—905 F.2d 3

1B1.10(d)—938 F.2d 139
1B1.10(d)—951 F.2d 634
1B1.10(d)—960 F.2d 191
1B1.10(d)—977 F.2d 1323
1B1.10(d)—981 F.2d 645
1B1.10(d)—989 F.2d 583
1B1.10(d)—990 F.2d 707
1B1.10(d)—995 F.2d 323
1B1.10(d)—997 F.2d 429
1B1.10(d)—997 F.2d 767
1B1.10(d)—6 F.3d 601
1B1.10(d)—8 F.3d 1268
1B1.10(d)—9 F.3d 1438
1B1.10(d)—13 F.3d 752
1B1.10(d)—15 F.3d 68
1B1.10(d)—808 F.Supp. 206
1B1.10(d)—810 F.Supp. 1231
1B1.10(d)—814 F.Supp. 14
1B1.10(d)—817 F.Supp. 894
1B1.10(d)—826 F.Supp. 368
1B1.10(d)—831 F.Supp. 880
1B1.10(d)—834 F.Supp. 550
1B1.10 comment—951 F.2d 634
1B1.10 comment—8 F.3d 1268
1B1.11—997 F.2d 263
1B1.11—842 F.Supp. 134
1B1.11(a)—8 F.3d 839
1B1.11(a)—23 F.3d 343
1B1.11(a)—834 F.Supp. 550
1B1.11(b)(1)—8 F.3d 839
1B1.11(b)(1)—834 F.Supp. 550
1B1.11(b)(2)—5 F.3d 795
1B1.11 comment—22 F.3d 330
1B1.11 comment—842 F.Supp. 134

CHAPTER TWO—OFFENSE CONDUCT

Part A: Offenses Against the Person

2A1.1—922 F.2d 1044
2A1.1—932 F.2d 1529
2A1.1—970 F.2d 1328
2A1.1—971 F.2d 200
2A1.1—974 F.2d 1389
2A1.1—1 F.3d 1137
2A1.1—9 F.3d 660
2A1.1—16 F.3d 202
2A1.1—16 F.3d 767
2A1.1—741 F.Supp. 215
2A1.1—835 F.Supp. 1466
2A1.1—835 F.Supp. 1543
2A1.1-2A1.4—817 F.Supp. 64
2A1.1 et seq.—881 F.2d 114
2A1.1 et seq.—893 F.2d 314
2A1.1 et seq.—908 F.2d 1229
2A1.1 et seq.—914 F.2d 67
2A1.1 et seq.—920 F.2d 363
2A1.1 et seq.—941 F.2d 133
2A1.1 et seq.—970 F.2d 1312
2A1.1 et seq.—993 F.2d 442
2A1.1 et seq.—684 F.Supp. 1506
2A1.1 et seq.—684 F.Supp. 1535
2A1.1 et seq.—686 F.Supp. 1174
2A1.1 et seq.—845 F.Supp. 270
2A1.1 comment—952 F.2d 1537
2A1.1 comment—956 F.2d 46
2A1.1 comment—968 F.2d 1058
2A1.1 comment—971 F.2d 200
2A1.2—908 F.2d 1229
2A1.2 [1990]—920 F.2d 1290
2A1.2—1 F.3d 1137
2A1.2—5 F.3d 259
2A1.2—16 F.3d 202
2A1.4—975 F.2d 622
2A1.4—993 F.2d 442
2A1.4 comment—975 F.2d 622
2A1.4 comment—12 F.3d 1427
2A1.5—974 F.2d 1389
2A1.5—978 F.2d 281
2A1.5—821 F.Supp. 1400
2A1.5—835 F.Supp. 1466
2A1.5—835 F.Supp. 1501
2A1.5—835 F.Supp. 1543
2A1.5(c)(1)—817 F.Supp. 321
2A2.1—887 F.2d 448
2A2.1—906 F.2d 1531
2A2.1—914 F.2d 1131

2A2.1 [1988]—918 F.2d 1084
2A2.1 [1990]—920 F.2d 1290
2A2.1—932 F.2d 324
2A2.1 [1990]—952 F.2d 1014
2A2.1—956 F.2d 46
2A2.1 [1990]—974 F.2d 1389
2A2.1—978 F.2d 281
2A2.1—751 F.Supp. 1195
2A2.1—755 F.Supp. 914
2A2.1 [1990]—755 F.Supp. 914
2A2.1—835 F.Supp. 1466
2A2.1 [1990]—835 F.Supp. 1466
2A2.1—835 F.Supp. 1543
2A2.1(a)—918 F.2d 1084
2A2.1(a) [1988]—918 F.2d 1084
2A2.1(a) [1988]—817 F.Supp. 1401
2A2.1(b) [1990]—920 F.2d 1290
2A2.1(b)—997 F.2d 30
2A2.1(b)(1) [1988]—918 F.2d 1084
2A2.1(b)(1)—930 F.2d 1450
2A2.1(b)(1)—989 F.2d 948
2A2.1(b)(1)—755 F.Supp. 914
2A2.1(b)(2)—755 F.Supp. 914
2A2.1(b)(2)(A)—906 F.2d 1531
2A2.1(b)(2)(B) [1990]—835 F.Supp. 1466
2A2.1(b)(2)(C) [1990]—943 F.2d 812
2A2.1(b)(3)—855 F.2d 925
2A2.1(b)(3) [1990]—989 F.2d 948
2A2.1(b)(3)(C)—868 F.2d 1121
2A2.1(b)(4) [1990]—943 F.2d 812
2A2.1(b)(4) [1990]—952 F.2d 1014
2A2.1(b)(4) [1990]—989 F.2d 948
2A2.1(b)(4) [1990]—755 F.Supp. 914
2A2.1(b)(4) [1990]—835 F.Supp. 1466
2A2.1 comment—992 F.2d 156
2A2.1 comment—999 F.2d 361
2A2.1 comment [1990]—755 F.Supp. 914
2A2.2—868 F.2d 114
2A2.2—892 F.2d 742
2A2.2—898 F.2d 25
2A2.2—910 F.2d 326
2A2.2—914 F.2d 1355
2A2.2—925 F.2d 359
2A2.2—932 F.2d 342
2A2.2—943 F.2d 1543
2A2.2—948 F.2d 1033
2A2.2—953 F.2d 1060
2A2.2—954 F.2d 204
2A2.2—961 F.2d 322
2A2.2—966 F.2d 945
2A2.2—967 F.2d 572
2A2.2—972 F.2d 504
2A2.2—976 F.2d 1226
2A2.2—981 F.2d 790
2A2.2—983 F.2d 1507
2A2.2—988 F.2d 94
2A2.2—988 F.2d 107
2A2.2—991 F.2d 725
2A2.2—997 F.2d 67
2A2.2—997 F.2d 396
2A2.2—999 F.2d 1144
2A2.2—1 F.3d 414
2A2.2—2 F.3d 870
2A2.2—2 F.3d 942
2A2.2—4 F.3d 1358
2A2.2—733 F.Supp. 1307
2A2.2—833 F.Supp. 769
2A2.2(a)—943 F.2d 836
2A2.2(a)—981 F.2d 1153
2A2.2(a)—4 F.3d 1358
2A2.2(a)—827 F.Supp. 100
2A2.2(b)—972 F.2d 504
2A2.2(b)—4 F.3d 1358
2A2.2(b)(1)—898 F.2d 25
2A2.2(b)(1)—908 F.2d 528
2A2.2(b)(1)—931 F.2d 238
2A2.2(b)(1)—1 F.3d 414
2A2.2(b)(1—4)—972 F.2d 504
2A2.2(b)(2)—914 F.2d 1355
2A2.2(b)(2)—929 F.2d 1126
2A2.2(b)(2)—931 F.2d 238
2A2.2(b)(2)—976 F.2d 1226
2A2.2(b)(2)—2 F.3d 870
2A2.2(b)(2)(A)—4 F.3d 1358
2A2.2(b)(2)(A)—8 F.3d 1264
2A2.2(b)(2)(B)—954 F.2d 204
2A2.2(b)(2)(B)—1 F.3d 414
2A2.2(b)(2)(B)—833 F.Supp. 769
2A2.2(b)(2)(C)—898 F.2d 25
2A2.2(b)(3)—855 F.2d 925
2A2.2(b)(3)—931 F.2d 238
2A2.2(b)(3)—958 F.2d 646
2A2.2(b)(3)—997 F.2d 30
2A2.2(b)(3)—2 F.3d 870
2A2.2(b)(3)(A)—932 F.2d 342
2A2.2(b)(3)(A)—976 F.2d 1249
2A2.2(b)(3)(A)—833 F.Supp. 769
2A2.2(b)(3)(B)—880 F.2d 612
2A2.2(b)(3)(B)—943 F.2d 836
2A2.2(b)(3)(B)—976 F.2d 1226

2A2.2(b)(3)(B)—976 F.2d 1249
2A2.2(b)(3)(B)—982 F.2d 665
2A2.2(b)(3)(B)—1 F.3d 414
2A2.2(b)(3)(C)—981 F.2d 1153
2A2.2-2A2.4—988 F.2d 107
2A2.2 comment—976 F.2d 1226
2A2.2 comment—983 F.2d 1507
2A2.2 comment—988 F.2d 94
2A2.2 comment—993 F.2d 427
2A2.2 comment—997 F.2d 30
2A2.2 comment—997 F.2d 67
2A2.2 comment—827 F.Supp. 100
2A2.2 comment—833 F.Supp. 769
2A2.3—950 F.2d 1348
2A2.3—967 F.2d 572
2A2.3—993 F.2d 427
2A2.3—2 F.3d 870
2A2.3—2 F.3d 942
2A2.3(a)(1)—983 F.2d 1507
2A2.4—914 F.2d 1355
2A2.4—961 F.2d 322
2A2.4—962 F.2d 894
2A2.4—966 F.2d 945
2A2.4—981 F.2d 790
2A2.4—988 F.2d 94
2A2.4—991 F.2d 450
2A2.4—991 F.2d 725
2A2.4—997 F.2d 67
2A2.4—14 F.3d 30
2A2.4(b)(1)—972 F.2d 890
2A2.4(b)(1)—983 F.2d 1380
2A2.4(b)(1)—997 F.2d 67
2A2.4(c)—961 F.2d 322
2A3.1—925 F.2d 270
2A3.1—938 F.2d 748
2A3.1—942 F.2d 775
2A3.1—957 F.2d 679
2A3.1—965 F.2d 575
2A3.1—974 F.2d 897
2A3.1—997 F.2d 1234
2A3.1—5 F.3d 795
2A3.1—13 F.3d 369
2A3.1—15 F.3d 740
2A3.1—20 F.3d 610
2A3.1(a)(1)—974 F.2d 897
2A3.1(b)—929 F.2d 1235
2A3.1(b)—965 F.2d 575
2A3.1(b)(1) [1988]—893 F.2d 950
2A3.1(b)(1)—952 F.2d 992
2A3.1(b)(1)—965 F.2d 575
2A3.1(b)(1)—982 F.2d 305
2A3.1(b)(1)—987 F.2d 475
2A3.1(b)(1)—997 F.2d 419
2A3.1(b)(1)—997 F.2d 1234
2A3.1(b)(1)—4 F.3d 450
2A3.1(b)(1) [1988]—733 F.Supp. 1307
2A3.1(b)(2)—965 F.2d 575
2A3.1(b)(2)(A)—942 F.2d 775
2A3.1(b)(2)(B)—929 F.2d 1235
2A3.1(b)(3)—902 F.2d 873
2A3.1(b)(3)—964 F.2d 942
2A3.1(b)(3)—965 F.2d 575
2A3.1(b)(3)—965 F.2d 586
2A3.1(b)(3)—982 F.2d 305
2A3.1(b)(4)—986 F.2d 1225
2A3.1(b)(5)—963 F.2d 1388
2A3.1(b)(5)—997 F.2d 1234
2A3.1 comment—893 F.2d 950
2A3.1 comment—964 F.2d 942
2A3.1 comment—965 F.2d 575
2A3.1 comment—965 F.2d 586
2A3.1 note [1988]—893 F.2d 950
2A3.2—925 F.2d 270
2A3.2—942 F.2d 775
2A3.4—935 F.2d 143
2A3.4—733 F.Supp. 1307
2A3.4 [1988]—733 F.Supp. 1307
2A3.4(a)(1)—987 F.2d 631
2A3.4(a)(1)—9 F.3d 705
2A3.4(a)(1)—22 F.3d 981
2A3.4(b)(1) [1988]—908 F.2d 272
2A3.4(b)(1)—957 F.2d 737
2A3.4(b)(1)—22 F.3d 981
2A3.4(b)(1) [1988]—733 F.Supp. 1307
2A3.4(b)(2) [1988]—733 F.Supp. 1307
2A3.4(b)(3)—23 F.3d 337
2A3.4 comment—23 F.3d 337
2A4.1—932 F.2d 324
2A4.1—944 F.2d 88
2A4.1—962 F.2d 263
2A4.1—963 F.2d 1388
2A4.1—974 F.2d 1389
2A4.1—975 F.2d 275
2A4.1—978 F.2d 903
2A4.1—5 F.3d 795
2A4.1—751 F.Supp. 1195
2A4.1(b)(1)—916 F.2d 219
2A4.1(b)(2)—962 F.2d 263
2A4.1(b)(2)—975 F.2d 275
2A4.1(b)(2)(B)—19 F.3d 166

2A4.1(b)(3)—911 F.2d 985
2A4.1(b)(3)—937 F.2d 542
2A4.1(b)(3)—975 F.2d 275
2A4.1(b)(3)—996 F.2d 88
2A4.1(b)(3)—19 F.3d 166
2A4.1(b)(3)—19 F.3d 1387
2A4.1(b)(3)—799 F.Supp. 646
2A4.1(b)(4)(A)—894 F.2d 1307
2A4.1(b)(4)(C)—903 F.2d 457
2A4.1(b)(5)—903 F.2d 457
2A4.1(b)(5)—916 F.2d 219
2A4.1(b)(5)—932 F.2d 324
2A4.1(b)(5) [1991]—963 F.2d 1388
2A4.1(b)(5) [1991]—975 F.2d 275
2A4.1(b)(5)—996 F.2d 939
2A4.1(b)(5)(A)—903 F.2d 457
2A4.1(b)(5)(A) [1991]—975 F.2d 275
2A4.1(b)(5)(B) [1991]—975 F.2d 275
2A4.1(b)(5)(B)—751 F.Supp. 1195
2A4.1(b)(7)—962 F.2d 263
2A4.1(b)(7)—5 F.3d 795
2A4.1(b)(7)(B)—16 F.3d 681
2A4.1 comment—903 F.2d 457
2A4.1 comment—911 F.2d 985
2A4.1 comment—5 F.3d 795
2A4.1 comment—19 F.3d 166
2A4.1 comment—21 F.3d 874
2A5.2—975 F.2d 622
2A5.2(a)—975 F.2d 622
2A5.2(a)(2)—7 F.3d 953
2A6.1—914 F.2d 966
2A6.1—950 F.2d 1348
2A6.1—951 F.2d 1182
2A6.1—954 F.2d 586
2A6.1—965 F.2d 460
2A6.1—967 F.2d 539
2A6.1—994 F.2d 1380
2A6.1—1 F.3d 452
2A6.1—5 F.3d 275
2A6.1—14 F.3d 30
2A6.1—801 F.Supp. 263
2A6.1—835 F.Supp. 1501
2A6.1(a)—763 F.Supp 546
2A6.1(b)(1)—898 F.2d 813
2A6.1(b)(1)—942 F.2d 105
2A6.1(b)(1)—947 F.2d 1467
2A6.1(b)(1)—763 F.Supp. 546
2A6.1(b)(1)—16 F.3d 45
2A6.1(b)(1)—18 F.3d 1123
2A6.1(b)(2)—801 F.Supp. 263

Part B: Offenses Involving Property

2B1.1—881 F.2d 980
2B1.1—893 F.2d 1343
2B1.1—894 F.2d 74
2B1.1—894 F.2d 334
2B1.1—899 F.2d 1097
2B1.1—900 F.2d 45
2B1.1—901 F.2d 85
2B1.1—901 F.2d 1075
2B1.1—903 F.2d 457
2B1.1—911 F.2d 398
2B1.1—912 F.2d 204
2B1.1—912 F.2d 448
2B1.1—913 F.2d 201
2B1.1—917 F.2d 369
2B1.1—918 F.2d 707
2B1.1—919 F.2d 286
2B1.1—923 F.2d 910
2B1.1—925 F.2d 56
2B1.1—927 F.2d 1376
2B1.1—929 F.2d 629
2B1.1—951 F.2d 1164
2B1.1—952 F.2d 267
2B1.1—955 F.2d 170
2B1.1—956 F.2d 197
2B1.1—956 F.2d 994
2B1.1—956 F.2d 1534
2B1.1—962 F.2d 409
2B1.1—962 F.2d 1548
2B1.1—967 F.2d 5
2B1.1—971 F.2d 562
2B1.1—973 F.2d 1152
2B1.1—975 F.2d 1028
2B1.1—979 F.2d 1289
2B1.1—983 F.2d 893
2B1.1—984 F.2d 1339
2B1.1—989 F.2d 28
2B1.1—993 F.2d 1358
2B1.1—994 F.2d 942
2B1.1—995 F.2d 759
2B1.1—998 F.2d 249
2B1.1—6 F.3d 623
2B1.1—7 F.3d 285
2B1.1—9 F.3d 198
2B1.1—13 F.3d 154
2B1.1—15 F.3d 1380
2B1.1—16 F.3d 166
2B1.1—22 F.3d 76
2B1.1—684 F.Supp. 1048

2B1.1—716 F.Supp. 1452
2B1.1—751 F.Supp. 368
2B1.1—753 F.Supp. 1260
2B1.1—765 F.Supp. 945
2B1.1—803 F.Supp. 53
2B1.1—819 F.Supp. 250
2B1.1—830 F.Supp. 841
2B1.1 [1988]—832 F.Supp. 1426
2B1.1(a)—874 F.2d 174
2B1.1(a)—896 F.2d 678
2B1.1(a)—912 F.2d 204
2B1.1(a)—930 F.2d 555
2B1.1(a)—934 F.2d 553
2B1.1(a)—712 F.Supp. 707
2B1.1(b)—880 F.2d 612
2B1.1(b)—880 F.2d 1204
2B1.1(b)—920 F.2d 1040
2B1.1(b)—934 F.2d 553
2B1.1(b)(1)—855 F.2d 925
2B1.1(b)(1)—880 F.2d 1204
2B1.1(b)(1)—898 F.2d 373
2B1.1(b)(1)—911 F.2d 398
2B1.1(b)(1)—920 F.2d 1040
2B1.1(b)(1)—925 F.2d 828
2B1.1(b)(1)—930 F.2d 555
2B1.1(b)(1)—933 F.2d 1219
2B1.1(b)(1)—934 F.2d 248
2B1.1(b)(1)—989 F.2d 44
2B1.1(b)(1)—998 F.2d 249
2B1.1(b)(1) [1991]—7 F.3d 1458
2B1.1(b)(1)—17 F.3d 1531
2B1.1(b)(1)(A) [1991]—7 F.3d 1458
2B1.1(b)(1)—765 F.Supp. 945
2B1.1(b)(1)(B)—943 F.2d 1543
2B1.1(b)(1)(E)—995 F.2d 759
2B1.1(b)(1)(E)—22 F.3d 76
2B1.1(b)(1)(F)—966 F.2d 161
2B1.1(b)(1)(F)—671 F.Supp. 79
2B1.1(b)(1)(G)—874 F.2d 174
2B1.1(b)(1)(G)—899 F.2d 503
2B1.1(b)(1)(H)—995 F.2d 759
2B1.1(b)(1)(H) [1988]—15 F.3d 1380
2B1.1(b)(1)(I)—15 F.3d 1380
2B1.1(b)(1)(J)—924 F.2d 68
2B1.1(b)(1)(J)—22 F.3d 76
2B1.1(b)(1)(K)—894 F.2d 1015
2B1.1(b)(1)(K)—14 F.3d 666
2B1.1(b)(1)(L)—795 F.Supp. 1262
2B1.1(b)(1)(M)—961 F.2d 11
2B1.1(b)(1)(N)—934 F.2d 248
2B1.1(b)(1)(N)—13 F.3d 154
2B1.1(b)(1)(U) [1991]—7 F.3d 1458
2B1.1(b)(2)—901 F.2d 85
2B1.1(b)(3)—903 F.2d 457
2B1.1(b)(3)—769 F.Supp. 137
2B1.1(b)(4)—880 F.2d 1204
2B1.1(b)(4)—890 F.2d 1042
2B1.1(b)(4)—894 F.2d 1015
2B1.1(b)(4)—899 F.2d 503
2B1.1(b)(4)—903 F.2d 457
2B1.1(b)(4)—911 F.2d 398
2B1.1(b)(4)—911 F.2d 403
2B1.1(b)(4)—913 F.2d 201
2B1.1(b)(4)—934 F.2d 248
2B1.1(b)(4)—934 F.2d 553
2B1.1(b)(4)—955 F.2d 170
2B1.1(b)(4) [1990]—989 F.2d 44
2B1.1(b)(4)—801 F.Supp. 59
2B1.1(b)(5)—933 F.2d 1219
2B1.1(b)(5)—949 F.2d 966
2B1.1(b)(5)—955 F.2d 170
2B1.1(b)(5)—957 F.2d 248
2B1.1(b)(5)—965 F.2d 404
2B1.1(b)(5)—966 F.2d 555
2B1.1(b)(5)—976 F.2d 608
2B1.1(b)(5)—973 F.2d 832
2B1.1(b)(5)—991 F.2d 409
2B1.1(b)(5)—3 F.2d 667
2B1.1(b)(5)—803 F.Supp. 53
2B1.1(b)(5)(B)—14 F.3d 666
2B1.1(b)(7)(B)—3 F.3d 667
2B1.1 et seq.—894 F.2d 1092
2B1.1 et seq.—899 F.2d 714
2B1.1 et seq.—911 F.2d 227
2B1.1 et seq.—971 F.2d 357
2B1.1 comment—855 F.2d 925
2B1.1 comment [1988]—894 F.2d 74
2B1.1 comment—894 F.2d 334
2B1.1 comment—898 F.2d 373
2B1.1 comment—903 F.2d 457
2B1.1 comment—904 F.2d 515
2B1.1 comment—909 F.2d 176
2B1.1 comment—911 F.2d 398
2B1.1 comment—912 F.2d 448
2B1.1 comment—913 F.2d 1288
2B1.1 comment—915 F.2d 269
2B1.1 comment—919 F.2d 286
2B1.1 comment—941 F.2d 1102
2B1.1 comment—942 F.2d 141
2B1.1 comment—952 F.2d 267

2B1.1 comment—952 F.2d 1110
2B1.1 comment—961 F.2d 145
2B1.1 comment—964 F.2d 167
2B1.1 comment—966 F.2d 262
2B1.1 comment—967 F.2d 1460
2B1.1 comment—969 F.2d 1283
2B1.1 comment—974 F.2d 496
2B1.1 comment—977 F.2d 517
2B1.1 comment—980 F.2d 312
2B1.1 comment—981 F.2d 281
2B1.1 comment—983 F.2d 893
2B1.1 comment—984 F.2d 1339
2B1.1 comment—985 F.2d 930
2B1.1 comment—989 F.2d 28
2B1.1 comment—992 F.2d 1472
2B1.1 comment [1988]—993 F.2d 214
2B1.1 comment—993 F.2d 702
2B1.1 comment—993 F.2d 1358
2B1.1 comment—998 F.2d 249
2B1.1 comment—4 F.3d 658
2B1.1 comment—5 F.3d 614
2B1.1 comment—9 F.3d 198
2B1.1 comment—12 F.3d 1
2B1.1 comment—15 F.3d 1380
2B1.1 comment—17 F.3d 177
2B1.1 comment—20 F.3d 204
2B1.1 comment—22 F.3d 76
2B1.1 comment—22 F.3d 195
2B1.1 comment—22 F.3d 1504
2B1.1 comment—684 F.Supp. 1048
2B1.1 comment—753 F.Supp. 1260
2B1.1 comment—769 F.Supp. 137
2B1.1 comment—775 F.Supp. 348
2B1.1 comment—777 F.Supp. 6
2B1.1 comment—791 F.Supp. 348
2B1.1 comment—819 F.Supp. 250
2B1.1 comment—830 F.Supp. 841
2B1.1 comment—848 F.Supp. 639
2B1.2—898 F.2d 373
2B1.2—913 F.2d 1288
2B1.2—962 F.2d 409
2B1.2—977 F.2d 698
2B1.2—980 F.2d 312
2B1.2—7 F.3d 285
2B1.2(a)—904 F.2d 515
2B1.2(b)—904 F.2d 515
2B1.2(b)(1)—898 F.2d 373
2B1.2(b)(1)—929 F.2d 389
2B1.2(b)(1)—987 F.2d 104
2B1.2(b)(1)—7 F.3d 285
2B1.2(b)(3)(A)—913 F.2d 466
2B1.2(b)(3)(A)—913 F.2d 1288
2B1.2(b)(3)(A) [1990]—919 F.2d 957
2B1.2(b)(3)(A)—950 F.2d 1267
2B1.2(b)(3)(A)—835 F.Supp. 253
2B1.2(b)(3)(B)—684 F.2d 1048
2B1.2(b)(3)(B) [1990]—13 F.3d 1464
2B1.2(b)(4)—913 F.2d 1288
2B1.2(b)(4)—709 F.Supp. 1062
2B1.2(b)(4)(A)—977 F.2d 698
2B1.2(b)(4)(A) [1993]—17 F.3d 1531
2B1.2(b)(4)(A) [1993]—20 F.3d 204
2B1.2(b)(4)(A) [1993]—21 F.3d 1302
2B1.2(b)(4)(A) [1992]—848 F.Supp. 639
2B1.2(b)(4)(B)—929 F.2d 389
2B1.2(b)(4)(B)—955 F.2d 547
2B1.2(b)(4)(B)—974 F.2d 906
2B1.2(b)(4)(B)—987 F.2d 104
2B1.2(b)(4)(B)—996 F.2d 1170
2B1.2(b)(4)(B) [1993]—17 F.3d 1531
2B1.2(b)(4)(B) [1992]—23 F.3d 278
2B1.1(b)(5)—913 F.2d 1288
2B1.2 comment—798 F.2d 373
2B1.2 comment—904 F.2d 515
2B1.2 comment—913 F.2d 466
2B1.2 comment—977 F.2d 698
2B1.3—948 F.2d 1033
2B1.3—969 F.2d 980
2B1.3—994 F.2d 1088
2B1.3—6 F.3d 623
2B1.3 [1991]—7 F.3d 1458
2B1.3 comment—6 F.3d 623
2B2.1—917 F.2d 369
2B2.1 comment—7 F.3d 285
2B2.1(b)(2)—855 F.2d 925
2B2.1(b)(2)—915 F.2d 269
2B2.1(b)(2)(B)—917 F.2d 369
2B2.2—915 F.2d 269
2B2.2—1 F.3d 414
2B2.2(b)(1)—960 F.2d 599
2B2.2(b)(2)—915 F.2d 269
2B2.2(b)(4)—960 F.2d 599
2B2.2 comment—960 F.2d 599
2B2.2 comment—7 F.3d 285
2B3.1—835 F.2d 1195
2B3.1—867 F.2d 222
2B3.1—869 F.2d 54
2B3.1—891 F.2d 75
2B3.1—891 F.2d 962
2B3.1—898 F.2d 1003

2B3.1—903 F.2d 457
2B3.1—913 F.2d 1288
2B3.1—914 F.2d 67
2B3.1—914 F.2d 98
2B3.1—916 F.2d 186
2B3.1—943 F.2d 1543
2B3.1—945 F.2d 650
2B3.1—961 F.2d 145
2B3.1 [1991]—982 F.2d 116
2B3.1—4 F.3d 800
2B3.1—7 F.3d 1471
2B3.1—21 F.3d 998
2B3.1—791 F.Supp. 348
2B3.1(a)—867 F.2d 222
2B3.1(a)—873 F.2d 709
2B3.1(a)—891 F.2d 962
2B3.1(a) [1988]—922 F.2d 578
2B3.1(a)—16 F.3d 1168
2B3.1(b) [1988]—914 F.2d 208
2B3.1(b)—965 F.2d 1001
2B3.1(b)(1)—867 F.2d 222
2B3.1(b)(1)—905 F.2d 1296
2B3.1(b)(1) [1988]—930 F.2d 820
2B3.1(b)(1)—12 F.3d 139
2B3.1(b)(1)—20 F.3d 886
2B3.1(b)(1)—791 F.Supp. 348
2B3.1(b)(1)—816 F.Supp. 623
2B3.1(b)(1-4)—16 F.3d 1168
2B3.1(b)(1)(B) [1988]—922 F.2d 578
2B3.1(b)(1)(C)—873 F.2d 709
2B3.1(b)(1)(C)—924 F.2d 945
2B3.1(b)(2)—905 F.2d 935
2B3.1(b)(2) [1988]—914 F.2d 208
2B3.1(b)(2)—948 F.2d 1125
2B3.1(b)(2)—962 F.2d 1308
2B3.1(b)(2)—992 F.2d 853
2B3.1(b)(2)—20 F.3d 538
2B3.1(b)(2)—716 F.Supp. 1207
2B3.1(b)(2)(A-F)—1 F.3d 729
2B3.1(b)(2)(B)—948 F.2d 1125
2B3.1(b)(2)(B)—950 F.2d 1309
2B3.1(b)(2)(B)—998 F.2d 74
2B3.1(b)(2)(B) [1991]—788 F.Supp. 433
2B3.1(b)(2)(B)—807 F.Supp. 1063
2B3.1(b)(2)(C)—886 F.2d 28
2B3.1(b)(2)(C)—891 F.2d 75
2B3.1(b)(2)(C)—895 F.2d 1225
2B3.1(b)(2)(C)—905 F.2d 1296
2B3.1(b)(2)(C)—924 F.2d 945
2B3.1(b)(2)(C)—937 F.2d 1528
2B3.1(b)(2)(C) [1988]—965 F.2d 1001
2B3.1(b)(2)(C) [1990]—966 F.2d 1383
2B3.1(b)(2)(C) [1990]—968 F.2d 242
2B3.1(b)(2)(C) [1991]—982 F.2d 116
2B3.1(b)(2)(C)—991 F.2d 693
2B3.1(b)(2)(C)—998 F.2d 53
2B3.1(b)(2)(C)—998 F.2d 74
2B3.1(b)(2)(C)—998 F.2d 453
2B3.1(b)(2)(C)—7 F.3d 285
2B3.1(b)(2)(C)—15 F.3d 825
2B3.1(b)(2)(C)—16 F.3d 358
2B3.1(b)(2)(C)—19 F.3d 350
2B3.1(b)(2)(C) [1991]—788 F.Supp. 433
2B3.1(b)(2)(D)—964 F.2d 896
2B3.1(b)(2)(D) [1990]—964 F.2d 1079
2B3.1(b)(2)(D) [1990]—969 F.2d 733
2B3.1(b)(2)(D) [1991]—973 F.2d 1374
2B3.1(b)(2)(D) [1991]—981 F.2d 887
2B3.1(b)(2)(D) [1990]—994 F.2d 773
2B3.1(b)(2)(D)—11 F.3d 140
2B3.1(b)(2)(D)—16 F.3d 952
2B3.1(b)(2)(E)—991 F.2d 693
2B3.1(b)(2)(E)—20 F.3d 270
2B3.1(b)(2)(E)—791 F.Supp. 348
2B3.1(b)(2)(F)—952 F.2d 1149
2B3.1(b)(2)(F)—964 F.2d 1079
2B3.1(b)(2)(F)—973 F.2d 1374
2B3.1(b)(2)(F)—998 F.2d 648
2B3.1(b)(2)(F)—4 F.3d 800
2B3.1(b)(2)(F)—6 F.3d 715
2B3.1(b)(2)(F)—12 F.3d 139
2B3.1(b)(2)(F) [1993]—20 F.3d 270
2B3.1(b)(2)(F)—20 F.3d 1336
2B3.1(b)(3)—933 F.2d 924
2B3.1(b)(3)—948 F.2d 1449
2B3.1(b)(3)—984 F.2d 933
2B3.1(b)(3)—997 F.2d 30
2B3.1(b)(3)—6 F.3d 208
2B3.1(b)(3)—7 F.3d 744
2B3.1(b)(3)—807 F.Supp. 1063
2B3.1(b)(3)(A)—896 F.2d 1009
2B3.1(b)(3)(A)—964 F.2d 911
2B3.1(b)(3)(A)—13 F.3d 1126
2B3.1(b)(3)(A)—20 F.3d 270
2B3.1(b)(3)(B)—972 F.2d 271
2B3.1(b)(4)—788 F.Supp. 433
2B3.1(b)(4)(A)—16 F.3d 952
2B3.1(b)(4)(B)—948 F.2d 1125
2B3.1(b)(4)(B)—950 F.2d 1309
2B3.1(b)(4)(B)—969 F.2d 341

2B3.1(b)(4)(B)—986 F.2d 285
2B3.1(b)(4)(B)—993 F.2d 1444
2B3.1(b)(4)(B)—1 F.3d 729
2B3.1(b)(4)(B)—7 F.3d 319
2B3.1(b)(4)(B)—16 F.3d 952
2B3.1(b)(4)(B)—20 F.3d 270
2B3.1(b)(6)—903 F.2d 91
2B3.1(b)(6)—989 F.2d 28
2B3.1(b)(6)—16 F.3d 1168
2B3.1(b)(6)—21 F.3d 354
2B3.1(b)(6)(A)—791 F.Supp. 348
2B3.1(b)(6)(B)—12 F.3d 1
2B3.1(b)(6)(H)—791 F.Supp. 348
2B3.1 comment—867 F.2d 222
2B3.1 comment [1988]—930 F.2d 820
2B3.1 comment [1990]—934 F.2d 1077
2B3.1 comment—952 F.2d 1149
2B3.1 comment—964 F.2d 1079
2B3.1 comment [1991]—982 F.2d 116
2B3.1 comment—989 F.2d 28
2B3.1 comment—998 F.2d 648
2B3.1 comment—6 F.3d 715
2B3.1 comment—7 F.3d 1471
2B3.1 comment [1993]—20 F.3d 270
2B3.1 comment—20 F.3d 538
2B3.2—896 F.2d 789
2B3.2—914 F.2d 966
2B3.2—916 F.2d 186
2B3.2—925 F.2d 641
2B3.2—952 F.2d 1504
2B3.2—965 F.2d 460
2B3.2—966 F.2d 55
2B3.2—967 F.2d 539
2B3.2—975 F.2d 1120
2B3.2—994 F.2d 1088
2B3.2—997 F.2d 967
2B3.2—10 F.3d 1
2B3.2—733 F.Supp. 1174
2B3.2—788 F.Supp. 756
2B3.2—835 F.Supp. 1501
2B3.2(a)—971 F.2d 1302
2B3.2(a)—997 F.2d 967
2B3.2(b)—971 F.2d 1302
2B3.2(b)(1)—916 F.2d 186
2B3.2(b)(1)—997 F.2d 967
2B3.2(b)(2)(A) [1991]—971 F.2d 1302
2B3.2(b)(2)(A)—975 F.2d 1120
2B3.2(b)(2)(C)—960 F.2d 115
2B3.2(b)(3)—855 F.2d 925
2B3.2(b)(3)(A)(iii)—23 F.3d 47
2B3.2(b)(4)—997 F.2d 30
2B3.2 comment—896 F.2d 789
2B3.2 comment—960 F.2d 115
2B3.2 comment—965 F.2d 460
2B3.2 comment—966 F.2d 55
2B3.3—925 F.2d 641
2B3.3—671 F.Supp. 79
2B3.3—966 F.2d 55
2B3.3—684 F.Supp. 1535
2B4.1—882 F.2d 151
2B4.1—913 F.2d 193
2B4.1 comment—882 F.2d 151
2B4.2—882 F.2d 151
2B5.1—896 F.2d 678
2B5.1—980 F.2d 506
2B5.1—989 F.2d 583
2B5.1(a)—874 F.2d 213
2B5.1(a)—901 F.2d 867
2B5.1(a)—952 F.2d 827
2B5.1(b)(1)—874 F.2d 213
2B5.1(b)(1)—896 F.2d 678
2B5.1(b)(1)—901 F.2d 867
2B5.1(b)(1)—952 F.2d 827
2B5.1(b)(1)—980 F.2d 506
2B5.1(b)(1)—989 F.2d 583
2B5.1(b)(1) [1992]—994 F.2d 63
2B5.1(b)(1)—15 F.3d 75
2B5.1(b)(2)—878 F.2d 1377
2B5.1(b)(2)—886 F.2d 736
2B5.1(b)(2)—893 F.2d 996
2B5.1(b)(2)—914 F.2d 212
2B5.1(b)(2)—928 F.2d 1106
2B5.1(b)(2)—991 F.2d 533
2B5.1 comment—914 F.2d 212
2B5.1 comment—980 F.2d 506
2B5.1 comment—991 F.2d 533
2B5.1 comment—1 F.3d 1040
2B5.2—881 F.2d 980
2B5.2—980 F.2d 506
2B5.3—952 F.2d 672
2B5.3 comment—952 F.2d 672
2B5.4(b)(1)—963 F.2d 65
2B6.1—962 F.2d 409
2B6.1—973 F.2d 1152
2B6.1—982 F.2d 1411
2B6.1(b)(3)—931 F.2d 631
2B6.1 comment—931 F.2d 631
2B6.1 comment—973 F.2d 1152

Part C: Offenses Involving Public Officials

2C comment—857 F.2d 1245
2C1.1—931 F.2d 282
2C1.1—946 F.2d 267
2C1.1—952 F.2d 1504
2C1.1 [1991]—973 F.2d 600
2C1.1—983 F.2d 1150
2C1.1—989 F.2d 447
2C1.1—995 F.2d 759
2C1.1—996 F.2d 17
2C1.1—10 F.3d 1
2C1.1—848 F.Supp. 369
2C1.1(a)—972 F.2d 1385
2C1.1(b)(1)—906 F.2d 814
2C1.1(b)(1)—964 F.2d 756
2C1.1(b)(1)—11 F.3d 915
2C1.1(b)(2)—882 F.2d 151
2C1.1(b)(2)—895 F.2d 867
2C1.1(b)(2)—992 F.2d 793
2C1.1(b)(2)(A)—931 F.2d 282
2C1.1(b)(2)(A)—951 F.2d 580
2C1.1(b)(2)(A)—5 F.3d 44
2C1.1(b)(2)(A)—779 F.Supp. 385
2C1.1(b)(2)(B)—992 F.2d 793
2C1.1(b)(2)(B)—14 F.3d 580
2C1.1(b)(2)(B)—14 F.3d 1014
2C1.1(b)(2)(B)—788 F.Supp. 756
2C1.1(c)(1)—946 F.2d 122
2C1.1(c)(1) [1991]—972 F.2d 1385
2C1.1(c)(1)—6 F.3d 1415
2C1.1(c)(1)—16 F.3d 985
2C1.1(c)(2)—17 F.3d 351
2C1.1(c)(3)—788 F.Supp. 756
2C1.1 et seq.—882 F.2d 151
2C1.1 comment—930 F.2d 1427
2C1.1 comment—931 F.2d 282
2C1.1 comment—946 F.2d 267
2C1.1 comment [1991]—973 F.2d 600
2C1.1 comment—983 F.2d 1150
2C1.1 comment [1990]—992 F.2d 793
2C1.1 comment [1991]—992 F.2d 793
2C1.1 comment—996 F.2d 17
2C1.1 comment—5 F.3d 44
2C1.1 comment—6 F.3d 1415
2C1.1 comment—11 F.3d 915
2C1.1 comment—16 F.3d 985
2C1.1 comment—21 F.3d 759
2C1.2—996 F.2d 17
2C1.2 comment—983 F.2d 1150

Part D: Offenses Involving Drugs

2D1.1—838 F.2d 585
2D1.1—863 F.2d 245
2D1.1—866 F.2d 604
2D1.1—868 F.2d 125
2D1.1—868 F.2d 135
2D1.1—868 F.2d 1390
2D1.1—868 F.2d 1409
2D1.1—868 F.2d 1412
2D1.1—869 F.2d 797
2D1.1—869 F.2d 805
2D1.1—872 F.2d 735
2D1.1—872 F.2d 1365
2D1.1—873 F.2d 23
2D1.1—873 F.2d 437
2D1.1—874 F.2d 43
2D1.1—875 F.2d 143
2D1.1—877 F.2d 1138
2D1.1—878 F.2d 73
2D1.1—881 F.2d 970
2D1.1—882 F.2d 474
2D1.1—883 F.2d 313
2D1.1—883 F.2d 781
2D1.1—884 F.2d 354
2D1.1—888 F.2d 907
2D1.1—889 F.2d 1454
2D1.1—891 F.2d 13
2D1.1—891 F.2d 82
2D1.1—891 F.2d 364
2D1.1—894 F.2d 56
2D1.1—894 F.2d 208
2D1.1—894 F.2d 981
2D1.1—896 F.2d 856
2D1.1—898 F.2d 43
2D1.1—898 F.2d 442
2D1.1—900 F.2d 204
2D1.1—900 F.2d 571
2D1.1—900 F.2d 1000
2D1.1 [1988]—901 F.2d 27
2D1.1—901 F.2d 85
2D1.1—901 F.2d 1204
2D1.1—902 F.2d 336
2D1.1—902 F.2d 693
2D1.1—904 F.2d 411
2D1.1—905 F.2d 677
2D1.1—906 F.2d 129
2D1.1—906 F.2d 1261

2D1.1—907 F.2d 94
2D1.1—907 F.2d 781
2D1.1—908 F.2d 1312
2D1.1—909 F.2d 235
2D1.1—914 F.2d 1050
2D1.1—915 F.2d 402
2D1.1 [1988]—915 F.2d 1462
2D1.1—917 F.2d 683
2D1.1—917 F.2d 841
2D1.1—917 F.2d 1220
2D1.1—920 F.2d 107
2D1.1—920 F.2d 1530
2D1.1 [1988]—922 F.2d 1234
2D1.1—923 F.2d 427
2D1.1—923 F.2d 1293
2D1.1 [1988]—923 F.2d 1293
2D1.1—926 F.2d 172
2D1.1—926 F.2d 838
2D1.1—927 F.2d 176
2D1.1—928 F.2d 1450
2D1.1—929 F.2d 334
2D1.1—929 F.2d 546
2D1.1—932 F.2d 1529
2D1.1—933 F.2d 362
2D1.1—933 F.2d 1029
2D1.1—936 F.2d 333
2D1.1—936 F.2d 412
2D1.1—936 F.2d 623
2D1.1—936 F.2d 1124
2D1.1—936 F.2d 1403
2D1.1—937 F.2d 979
2D1.1—938 F.2d 149
2D1.1—938 F.2d 1231
2D1.1—942 F.2d 96
2D1.1—942 F.2d 363
2D1.1—944 F.2d 356
2D1.1—945 F.2d 129
2D1.1—945 F.2d 967
2D1.1—945 F.2d 1145
2D1.1—945 F.2d 1378
2D1.1—946 F.2d 100
2D1.1—948 F.2d 1046
2D1.1—950 F.2d 508
2D1.1—951 F.2d 64
2D1.1—954 F.2d 1160
2D1.1—954 F.2d 1224
2D1.1—955 F.2d 1116
2D1.1—955 F.2d 1500
2D1.1—956 F.2d 1007
2D1.1—957 F.2d 671
2D1.1—958 F.2d 315
2D1.1—959 F.2d 206
2D1.1—959 F.2d 246
2D1.1—959 F.2d 375
2D1.1—959 F.2d 1377
2D1.1—959 F.2d 1489
2D1.1—960 F.2d 409
2D1.1—960 F.2d 950
2D1.1—961 F.2d 41
2D1.1—961 F.2d 599
2D1.1—961 F.2d 972
2D1.1—962 F.2d 100
2D1.1—963 F.2d 63
2D1.1—963 F.2d 551
2D1.1—964 F.2d 787
2D1.1—964 F.2d 944
2D1.1—966 F.2d 398
2D1.1—966 F.2d 682
2D1.1—967 F.2d 27
2D1.1—967 F.2d 45
2D1.1—967 F.2d 68
2D1.1—967 F.2d 728
2D1.1 [1990]—968 F.2d 130
2D1.1—968 F.2d 158
2D1.1—970 F.2d 1490
2D1.1—971 F.2d 626
2D1.1—972 F.2d 281
2D1.1—972 F.2d 927
2D1.1—973 F.2d 611
2D1.1—974 F.2d 97
2D1.1—974 F.2d 971
2D1.1—974 F.2d 1270
2D1.1—975 F.2d 999
2D1.1—975 F.2d 1016
2D1.1—976 F.2d 666
2D1.1—977 F.2d 1436
2D1.1—978 F.2d 1300
2D1.1—979 F.2d 402
2D1.1—979 F.2d 1522
2D1.1—980 F.2d 1375
2D1.1—981 F.2d 92
2D1.1—981 F.2d 202
2D1.1—981 F.2d 1123
2D1.1—981 F.2d 1549
2D1.1—982 F.2d 1374
2D1.1—983 F.2d 206
2D1.1—984 F.2d 635
2D1.1—984 F.2d 989
2D1.1—984 F.2d 1426
2D1.1—985 F.2d 371

2D1.1—985 F.2d 1175
2D1.1—986 F.2d 1199
2D1.1 [1992]—987 F.2d 463
2D1.1 [1992]—987 F.2d 1225
2D1.1—988 F.2d 1374
2D1.1—989 F.2d 84
2D1.1—989 F.2d 760
2D1.1—990 F.2d 266
2D1.1—990 F.2d 1456
2D1.1—991 F.2d 702
2D1.1—991 F.2d 1328
2D1.1—992 F.2d 887
2D1.1—993 F.2d 713
2D1.1—994 F.2d 277
2D1.1—994 F.2d 1467
2D1.1—995 F.2d 380
2D1.1 [1990]—996 F.2d 456
2D1.1—996 F.2d 1307
2D1.1—997 F.2d 429
2D1.1—997 F.2d 687
2D1.1—998 F.2d 584
2D1.1—999 F.2d 182
2D1.1—999 F.2d 596
2D1.1—999 F.2d 1192
2D1.1—1 F.3d 192
2D1.1—1 F.3d 473
2D1.1—3 F.3d 769
2D1.1—4 F.3d 115
2D1.1—4 F.3d 150
2D1.1—5 F.3d 20
2D1.1—5 F.3d 1161
2D1.1—5 F.3d 1369
2D1.1—6 F.3d 294
2D1.1—7 F.3d 164
2D1.1—7 F.3d 285
2D1.1—7 F.3d 927
2D1.1—7 F.3d 947
2D1.1—7 F.3d 957
2D1.1—7 F.3d 1523
2D1.1—9 F.3d 1442
2D1.1—11 F.3d 1218
2D1.1—12 F.3d 605
2D1.1—13 F.3d 1391
2D1.1 [1988]—14 F.3d 1030
2D1.1—15 F.3d 25
2D1.1—16 F.3d 795
2D1.1—17 F.3d 1294
2D1.1—20 F.3d 229
2D1.1—20 F.3d 670
2D1.1—22 F.3d 1410
2D1.1—23 F.3d 306
2D1.1—692 F.Supp. 788
2D1.1—700 F.Supp. 292
2D1.1—708 F.Supp. 461
2D1.1—710 F.Supp. 1290
2D1.1—746 F.Supp. 200
2D1.1—750 F.Supp. 1
2D1.1—756 F.Supp. 571
2D1.1—762 F.Supp. 1314
2D1.1—763 F.Supp. 645
2D1.1—774 F.Supp. 594
2D1.1—776 F.Supp. 1030
2D1.1—778 F.Supp. 219
2D1.1—778 F.Supp. 393
2D1.1—779 F.Supp. 561
2D1.1—781 F.Supp. 81
2D1.1—783 F.Supp. 39
2D1.1—786 F.Supp. 1105
2D1.1—788 F.Supp. 1165
2D1.1—796 F.Supp. 1456
2D1.1—809 F.Supp. 843
2D1.1—810 F.Supp. 230
2D1.1—811 F.Supp. 1106
2D1.1—815 F.Supp. 84
2D1.1—819 F.Supp. 1076
2D1.1—836 F.Supp. 812
2D1.1—840 F.Supp. 1
2D1.1—842 F.Supp. 1031
2D1.1—845 F.Supp. 270
2D1.1—845 F.Supp. 725
2D1.1(a)—942 F.2d 243
2D1.1(a)—959 F.2d 246
2D1.1(a)—753 F.Supp. 23
2D1.1(a)(2)—970 F.2d 1328
2D1.1(a)(3)—860 F.2d 35
2D1.1(a)(3)—863 F.2d 245
2D1.1(a)(3)—867 F.2d 213
2D1.1(a)(3)—872 F.2d 101
2D1.1(a)(3)—875 F.2d 674
2D1.1(a)(3)—876 F.2d 1121
2D1.1(a)(3)—877 F.2d 688
2D1.1(a)(3)—878 F.2d 256
2D1.1(a)(3)—880 F.2d 612
2D1.1(a)(3)—881 F.2d 95
2D1.1(a)(3)—882 F.2d 474
2D1.1(a)(3)—884 F.2d 95
2D1.1(a)(3)—884 F.2d 181
2D1.1(a)(3)—884 F.2d 349
2D1.1(a)(3)—885 F.2d 1266
2D1.1(a)(3)—891 F.2d 300

2D1.1(a)(3)—891 F.2d 364
2D1.1(a)(3)—891 F.2d 686
2D1.1(a)(3)—894 F.2d 975
2D1.1(a)(3)—895 F.2d 24
2D1.1(a)(3)—898 F.2d 705
2D1.1(a)(3)—902 F.2d 501
2D1.1(a)(3)—903 F.2d 648
2D1.1(a)(3)—905 F.2d 195
2D1.1(a)(3)—905 F.2d 359
2D1.1(a)(3)—905 F.2d 499
2D1.1(a)(3)—905 F.2d 970
2D1.1(a)(3) [1988]—906 F.2d 477
2D1.1(a)(3)—907 F.2d 781
2D1.1(a)(3)—907 F.2d 1441
2D1.1(a)(3)—909 F.2d 759
2D1.1(a)(3)—909 F.2d 1109
2D1.1(a)(3)—917 F.2d 841
2D1.1(a)(3)—918 F.2d 789
2D1.1(a)(3)—918 F.2d 1129
2D1.1(a)(3)—927 F.2d 202
2D1.1(a)(3)—928 F.2d 956
2D1.1(a)(3)—929 F.2d 1466
2D1.1(a)(3)—930 F.2d 1486
2D1.1(a)(3)—931 F.2d 1017
2D1.1(a)(3)—932 F.2d 1029
2D1.1(a)(3)—934 F.2d 411
2D1.1(a)(3)—945 F.2d 1145
2D1.1(a)(3)—946 F.2d 13
2D1.1(a)(3)—946 F.2d 362
2D1.1(a)(3)—947 F.2d 224
2D1.1(a)(3)—947 F.2d 1031
2D1.1(a)(3)—947 F.2d 1424
2D1.1(a)(3)—948 F.2d 877
2D1.1(a)(3)—950 F.2d 1223
2D1.1(a)(3)—953 F.2d 363
2D1.1(a)(3)—964 F.2d 454
2D1.1(a)(3)—967 F.2d 27
2D1.1(a)(3)—967 F.2d 497
2D1.1(a)(3)—969 F.2d 569
2D1.1(a)(3)—969 F.2d 858
2D1.1(a)(3)—970 F.2d 1328
2D1.1(a)(3)—971 F.2d 626
2D1.1(a)(3)—973 F.2d 459
2D1.1(a)(3)—974 F.2d 55
2D1.1(a)(3)—981 F.2d 1123
2D1.1(a)(3)—982 F.2d 1209
2D1.1(a)(3)—984 F.2d 1095
2D1.1(a)(3)—985 F.2d 341
2D1.1(a)(3)—988 F.2d 712
2D1.1(a)(3)—990 F.2d 360
2D1.1(a)(3)—992 F.2d 22
2D1.1(a)(3)—994 F.2d 942
2D1.1(a)(3)—998 F.2d 791
2D1.1(a)(3) [1991]—5 F.3d 445
2D1.1(a)(3)—6 F.3d 1201
2D1.1(a)(3)—7 F.3d 66
2D1.1(a)(3)—8 F.3d 943
2D1.1(a)(3) [1992]—9 F.3d 368
2D1.1(a)(3)—11 F.3d 1225
2D1.1(a)(3) [1988]—14 F.3d 165
2D1.1(a)(3) [1991]—14 F.3d 1189
2D1.1(a)(3)—14 F.3d 1264
2D1.1(a)(3) [1993]—17 F.3d 735
2D1.1(a)(3) [1991]—19 F.3d 929
2D1.1(a)(3)—21 F.3d 194
2D1.1(a)(3)—22 F.3d 195
2D1.1(a)(3)—704 F.Supp. 910
2D1.1(a)(3)—709 F.Supp. 908
2D1.1(a)(3)—710 F.Supp. 1290
2D1.1(a)(3)—728 F.Supp. 632
2D1.1(a)(3)—730 F.Supp. 45
2D1.1(a)(3)—761 F.Supp. 697
2D1.1(a)(3)—773 F.Supp. 479
2D1.1(a)(3)—782 F.Supp. 747
2D1.1(a)(3)—801 F.Supp. 1407
2D1.1(a)(3)—808 F.Supp. 1572
2D1.1(a)(3)—833 F.Supp. 1454
2D1.1(a)(3)—834 F.Supp. 550
2D1.1(a)(3)—845 F.Supp. 270
2D1.1(a)(3)—846 F.Supp. 768
2D1.1(b)—868 F.2d 1412
2D1.1(b)—877 F.2d 3
2D1.1(b)—882 F.2d 1095
2D1.1(b)—883 F.2d 13
2D1.1(b)—888 F.2d 862
2D1.1(b)—890 F.2d 45
2D1.1(b)—890 F.2d 366
2D1.1(b)—896 F.2d 1122
2D1.1(b)—902 F.2d 336
2D1.1(b)—911 F.2d 1016
2D1.1(b)—913 F.2d 378
2D1.1(b)—918 F.2d 647
2D1.1(b)—926 F.2d 649
2D1.1(b)—931 F.2d 308
2D1.1(b)—947 F.2d 1424
2D1.1(b)—952 F.2d 934
2D1.1(b)—958 F.2d 196
2D1.1(b) [1988]—959 F.2d 246
2D1.1(b)—959 F.2d 1181
2D1.1(b)—7 F.3d 629

2D1.1(b)—14 F.3d 286
2D1.1(b)—18 F.3d 1156
2D1.1(b)(1)—869 F.2d 797
2D1.1(b)(1)—874 F.2d 250
2D1.1(b)(1)—875 F.2d 427
2D1.1(b)(1)—875 F.2d 674
2D1.1(b)(1)—875 F.2d 1294
2D1.1(b)(1)—880 F.2d 827
2D1.1(b)(1)—884 F.2d 349
2D1.1(b)(1)—884 F.2d 1090
2D1.1(b)(1)—884 F.2d 1294
2D1.1(b)(1)—886 F.2d 220
2D1.1(b)(1)—887 F.2d 358
2D1.1(b)(1)—891 F.2d 13
2D1.1(b)(1)—894 F.2d 208
2D1.1(b)(1)—896 F.2d 1063
2D1.1(b)(1)—896 F.2d 1122
2D1.1(b)(1)—898 F.2d 442
2D1.1(b)(1)—899 F.2d 177
2D1.1(b)(1)—899 F.2d 465
2D1.1(b)(1)—899 F.2d 515
2D1.1(b)(1)—899 F.2d 714
2D1.1(b)(1)—899 F.2d 873
2D1.1(b)(1)—900 F.2d 131
2D1.1(b)(1)—900 F.2d 1211
2D1.1(b)(1)—901 F.2d 1209
2D1.1(b)(1)—902 F.2d 873
2D1.1(b)(1)—902 F.2d 1221
2D1.1(b)(1)—903 F.2d 891
2D1.i(b)(1)—903 F.2d 1188
2D1.1(b)(1)—904 F.2d 1219
2D1.1(b)(1)—905 F.2d 499
2D1.1(b)(1)—906 F.2d 129
2D1.1(b)(1)—906 F.2d 359
2D1.1(b)(1)—907 F.2d 7
2D1.1(b)(1)—907 F.2d 53
2D1.1(b)(1)—907 F.2d 91
2D1.1(b)(1)—909 F.2d 1346
2D1.1(b)(1)—910 F.2d 1321
2D1.1(b)(1)—911 F.2d 1016
2D1.1(b)(1)—913 F.2d 300
2D1.1(b)(1)—913 F.2d 378
2D1.1(b)(1)—915 F.2d 899
2D1.1(b)(1)—917 F.2d 879
2D1.1(b)(1)—918 F.2d 1004
2D1.1(b)(1)—919 F.2d 461
2D1.1(b)(1)—919 F.2d 606
2D1.1(b)(1)—920 F.2d 480
2D1.1(b)(1)—920 F.2d 1218
2D1.1(b)(1)—920 F.2d 1377
2D1.1(b)(1)—921 F.2d 25
2D1.1(b)(1)—922 F.2d 910
2D1.1(b)(1)—924 F.2d 209
2D1.1(b)(1)—925 F.2d 170
2D1.1(b)(1)—926 F.2d 380
2D1.1(b)(1)—926 F.2d 899
2D1.1(b)(1)—927 F.2d 1361
2D1.1(b)(1)—928 F.2d 250
2D1.1(b)(1)—928 F.2d 1450
2D1.1(b)(1)—928 F.2d 1548
2D1.1(b)(1)—929 F.2d 55
2D1.1(b)(1)—929 F.2d 285
2D1.1(b)(1)—929 F.2d 356
2D1.1(b)(1)—932 F.2d 358
2D1.1(b)(1)—933 F.2d 701
2D1.1(b)(1)—933 F.2d 898
2D1.1(b)(1)—934 F.2d 148
2D1.1(b)(1)—934 F.2d 1226
2D1.1(b)(1)—934 F.2d 1325
2D1.1(b)(1)—935 F.2d 161
2D1.1(b)(1)—935 F.2d 766
2D1.1(b)(1)—936 F.2d 387
2D1.1(b)(1)—937 F.2d 95
2D1.1(b)(1)—938 F.2d 1086
2D1.1(b)(1)—940 F.2d 172
2D1.1(b)(1)—940 F.2d 382
2D1.1(b)(1)—940 F.2d 1061
2D1.1(b)(1)—941 F.2d 220
2D1.1(b)(1)—942 F.2d 243
2D1.1(b)(1)—942 F.2d 363
2D1.1(b)(1)—942 F.2d 556
2D1.1(b)(1)—942 F.2d 878
2D1.1(b)(1)—943 F.2d 383
2D1.1(b)(1)—945 F.2d 1145
2D1.1(b)(1)—945 F.2d 1378
2D1.1(b)(1)—946 F.2d 1191
2D1.1(b)(1)—947 F.2d 635
2D1.1(b)(1)—947 F.2d 1424
2D1.1(b)(1)—949 F.2d 156
2D1.1(b)(1)—949 F.2d 713
2D1.1(b)(1)—950 F.2d 1508
2D1.1(b)(1)--952 F.2d 20
2D1.1(b)(1)—952 F.2d 190
2D1.1(b)(1)—953 F.2d 363
2D1.1(b)(1)—935 F.2d 1449
2D1.1(b)(1)—954 F.2d 788
2D1.1(b)(1)—954 F.2d 1224
2D1.1(b)(1)—956 F.2d 643
2D1.1(b)(1)—957 F.2d 1138
2D1.1(b)(1)—959 F.2d 246

2D1.1(b)(1) [1988]—959 F.2d 246
2D1.1(b)(1)—959 F.2d 1181
2D1.1(b)(1)—959 F.2d 1489
2D1.1(b)(1)—960 F.2d 587
2D1.1(b)(1)—960 F.2d 599
2D1.1(b)(1)—960 F.2d 1301
2D1.1(b)(1)—962 F.2d 335
2D1.1(b)(1)—962 F.2d 420
2D1.1(b)(1)—962 F.2d 1332
2D1.1(b)(1) [1990]—965 F.2d 887
2D1.1(b)(1)—966 F.2d 403
2D1.1(b)(1)—966 F.2d 868
2D1.1(b)(1)—967 F.2d 497
2D1.1(b)(1)—967 F.2d 724
2D1.1(b)(1)—967 F.2d 728
2D1.1(b)(1)—967 F.2d 1508
2D1.1(b)(1)—967 F.2d 1550
2D1.1(b)(1)—968 F.2d 729
2D1.1(b)(1)—971 F.2d 626
2D1.1(b)(1)—971 F.2d 1206
2D1.1(b)(1)—975 F.2d 1357
2D1.1(b)(1)—978 F.2d 1554
2D1.1(b)(1)—979 F.2d 8
2D1.1(b)(1)—979 F.2d 402
2D1.1(b)(1)—979 F.2d 1234
2D1.1(b)(1)—980 F.2d 645
2D1.1(b)(1)—981 F.2d 569
2D1.1(b)(1)—982 F.2d 426
2D1.1(b)(1)—984 F.2d 928
2D1.1(b)(1)—985 F.2d 371
2D1.1(b)(1)—985 F.2d 766
2D1.1(b)(1)—985 F.2d 1175
2D1.1(b)(1) [1992]—987 F.2d 463
2D1.1(b)(1)—988 F.2d 13
2D1.1(b)(1)—989 F.2d 760
2D1.1(b)(1)—990 F.2d 583
2D1.1(b)(1)—990 F.2d 1083
2D1.1(b)(1)—991 F.2d 702
2D1.1(b)(1)—991 F.2d 1350
2D1.1(b)(1)—992 F.2d 573
2D1.1(b)(1)—994 F.2d 1184
2D1.1(b)(1)—994 F.2d 1510
2D1.1(b)(1)—995 F.2d 808
2D1.1(b)(1)—995 F.2d 1285
2D1.1(b)(1)—995 F.2d 1407
2D1.1(b)(1)—997 F.2d 78
2D1.1(b)(1)—997 F.2d 248
2D1.1(b)(1)—997 F.2d 378
2D1.1(b)(1)—998 F.2d 42
2D1.1(b)(1)—998 F.2d 791
2D1.1(b)(1)—998 F.2d 1491
2D1.1(b)(1)—998 F.2d 1571
2D1.1(b)(1)—1 F.3d 972
2D1.1(b)(1)—2 F.3d 574
2D1.1(b)(1)—3 F.3d 266
2D1.1(b)(1)—3 F.3d 506
2D1.1(b)(1)—3 F.3d 1496
2D1.1(b)(1)—4 F.3d 337
2D1.1(b)(1)—4 F.3d 1026
2D1.1(b)(1)—5 F.3d 295
2D1.1(b)(1)—5 F.3d 715
2D1.1(b)(1)—5 F.3d 1161
2D1.1(b)(1)—6 F.3d 1366
2D1.1(b)(1)—7 F.3d 1171
2D1.1(b)(1)—10 F.3d 590
2D1.1(b)(1)—11 F.3d 824
2D1.1(b)(1)—11 F.3d 953
2D1.1(b)(1)—11 F.3d 973
2D1.1(b)(1)—12 F.2d 39
2D1.1(b)(1)—12 F.2d 1186
2D1.1(b)(1)—12 F.2d 1427
2D1.1(b)(1)—13 F.3d 711
2D1.1(b)(1)—14 F.3d 502
2D1.1(b)(1)—14 F.3d 1128
2D1.1(b)(1) [1991]—14 F.3d 1189
2D1.1(b)(1)—15 F.3d 125
2D1.1(b)(1)—15 F.3d 540
2D1.1(b)(1)—18 F.3d 541
2D1.1(b)(1)—19 F.3d 895
2D1.1(b)(1)—22 F.3d 182
2D1.1(b)(1)—703 F.Supp. 1350
2D1.1(b)(1)—710 F.Supp. 1136
2D1.1(b)(1)—724 F.Supp. 1110
2D1.1(b)(1)—726 F.Supp. 861
2D1.1(b)(1)—738 F.Supp. 572
2D1.1(b)(1)—741 F.Supp. 12
2D1.1(b)(1)—746 F.Supp. 200
2D1.1(b)(1)—753 F.Supp. 1191
2D1.1(b)(1)—759 F.Supp. 1258
2D1.1(b)(1)—767 F.Supp. 11
2D1.1(b)(1)—784 F.Supp. 1373
2D1.1(b)(1)—811 F.Supp. 1106
2D1.1(b)(1)—815 F.Supp. 84
2D1.1(b)(1)—818 F.Supp. 812
2D1.1(b)(1)—829 F.Supp. 435
2D1.1(b)(1)—833 F.Supp. 1454
2D1.1(b)(1)—845 F.Supp. 270
2D1.1(b)(2)—7 F.3d 174
2D1.1(b)(2)—815 F.Supp. 84
2D1.1(b)(2)—917 F.Supp. 879

2D1.1(b)(8)—965 F.2d 1124
2D1.1(c)—891 F.2d 1265
2D1.1(c)—898 F.2d 28
2D1.1(c)—899 F.2d 515
2D1.1(c)—900 F.2d 1225
2D1.1(c)—902 F.2d 860
2D1.1(c)—905 F.2d 499
2D1.1(c)—906 F.2d 477
2D1.1(c)—907 F.2d 94
2D1.1(c)—909 F.2d 235
2D1.1(c)—917 F.2d 841
2D1.1(c)—921 F.2d 785
2D1.1(c)—925 F.2d 170
2D1.1(c)—926 F.2d 172
2D1.1(c)—926 F.2d 838
2D1.1(c)—927 F.2d 498
2D1.1(c)—927 F.2d 1272
2D1.1(c)—929 F.2d 839
2D1.1(c)—932 F.2d 1029
2D1.1(c)—933 F.2d 1029
2D1.1(c)—934 F.2d 411
2D1.1(c) [1990]—935 F.2d 739
2D1.1(c)—936 F.2d 1403
2D1.1(c)—939 F.2d 603
2D1.1(c)—942 F.2d 697
2D1.1(c)—943 F.2d 622
2D1.1(c)—944 F.2d 356
2D1.1(c)—947 F.2d 224
2D1.1(c)—947 F.2d 635
2D1.1(c)—947 F.2d 1361
2D1.1(c)—948 F.2d 877
2D1.1(c)—955 F.2d 1500
2D1.1(c)—956 F.2d 63
2D1.1(c)—961 F.2d 1389
2D1.1(c)—962 F.2d 1218
2D1.1(c)—964 F.2d 763
2D1.1(c)—964 F.2d 944
2D1.1(c)—964 F.2d 1088
2D1.1(c)—965 F.2d 610
2D1.1(c)—966 F.2d 1045
2D1.1(c)—969 F.2d 569
2D1.1(c)—970 F.2d 1336
2D1.1(c)—972 F.2d 64
2D1.1(c)—974 F.2d 19
2D1.1(c)—974 F.2d 55
2D1.1(c)—974 F.2d 61
2D1.1(c)—975 F.2d 999
2D1.1(c)—975 F.2d 1225
2D1.1(c)—978 F.2d 1520
2D1.1(c)—979 F.2d 287
2D1.1(c)—982 F.2d 290
2D1.1(c)—982 F.2d 1241
2D1.1(c)—984 F.2d 1426
2D1.1(c)—985 F.2d 3
2D1.1(c)—985 F.2d 21
2D1.1(c)—985 F.2d 371
2D1.1(c)—989 F.2d 447
2D1.1(c)—989 F.2d 871
2D1.1(c)—991 F.2d 1308
2D1.1(c)—993 F.2d 625
2D1.1(c)—994 F.2d 1467
2D1.1(c) [1990]—996 F.2d 456
2D1.1(c)—996 F.2d 917
2D1.1(c)—998 F.2d 84
2D1.1(c)—998 F.2d 791
2D1.1(c)—1 F.3d 644
2D1.1(c)—1 F.3d 920
2D1.1(c)—4 F.3d 1026
2D1.1(c)—6 F.3d 735
2D1.1(c)—7 F.3d 1506
2D1.1(c) [1992]—9 F.3d 368
2D1.1(c)—10 F.3d 1463
2D1.1(c)—11 F.3d 97
2D1.1(c)—11 F.3d 806
2D1.1(c)—11 F.3d 953
2D1.1(c)—12 F.3d 605
2D1.1(c)—13 F.3d 1217
2D1.1(c)—14 F.3d 1264
2D1.1(c) [1988]—14 F.3d 1264
2D1.1(c)—15 F.3d 4
2D1.1(c)—19 F.3d 93
2D1.1(c)—20 F.3d 242
2D1.1(c)—21 F.3d 375
2D1.1(c)—730 F.Supp. 45
2D1.1(c)—753 F.Supp. 23
2D1.1(c)—753 F.Supp. 1191
2D1.1(c)—773 F.Supp. 479
2D1.1(c)—778 F.Supp. 393
2D1.1(c)—782 F.Supp. 609
2D1.1(c)—782 F.Supp. 761
2D1.1(c)—783 F.Supp. 39
2D1.1(c)—784 F.Supp. 1373
2D1.1(c)—794 F.Supp. 874
2D1.1(c)—795 F.Supp. 665
2D1.1(c)—801 F.Supp. 1407
2D1.1(c)—811 F.Supp. 1106
2D1.1(c)—813 F.Supp. 168
2D1.1(c)—821 F.Supp. 868
2D1.1(c)—827 F.Supp. 205
2D1.1(c)—838 F.Supp. 377

2D1.1(c)—845 F.Supp. 270
2D1.1(c)—847 F.Supp. 613
2D1.1(c)(1)—994 F.2d 1510
2D1.1(c)(2)—991 F.2d 702
2D1.1(c)(2)—1 F.3d 920
2D1.1(c)(2)—11 F.3d 1510
2D1.1(c)(2)—13 F.3d 711
2D1.1(c)(2)—14 F.3d 1030
2D1.1(c)(2)—782 F.Supp. 609
2D1.1(c)(2)—833 F.Supp. 1454
2D1.1(c)(3)—961 F.2d 784
2D1.1(c)(3)—966 F.2d 403
2D1.1(c)(3)—968 F.2d 715
2D1.1(c)(3)—975 F.2d 1384
2D1.1(c)(3)—11 F.3d 346
2D1.1(c)(4)—940 F.2d 1134
2D1.1(c)(4)—947 F.2d 1424
2D1.1(c)(4)—950 F.2d 1223
2D1.1(c)(4)—959 F.2d 246
2D1.1(c)(4)—991 F.2d 702
2D1.1(c)(4)—996 F.2d 320
2D1.1(c)(4)—15 F.3d 563
2D1.1(c)(5)—936 F.2d 1124
2D1.1(c)(5)—947 F.2d 224
2D1.1(c)(5)—950 F.2d 1223
2D1.1(c)(5)—964 F.2d 763
2D1.1(c)(5)—981 F.2d 1123
2D1.1(c)(5)—988 F.2d 1374
2D1.1(c)(5)—996 F.2d 116
2D1.1(c)(5)—11 F.3d 346
2D1.1(c)(5)—13 F.3d 1
2D1.1(c)(5)—19 F.3d 409
2D1.1(c)(5)—784 F.Supp. 1373
2D1.1(c)(6)—919 F.2d 652
2D1.1(c)(6)—921 F.2d 340
2D1.1(c)(6)—930 F.2d 310
2D1.1(c)(6)—947 F.2d 224
2D1.1(c)(6)—953 F.2d 363
2D1.1(c)(6)—972 F.2d 1259
2D1.1(c)(6)—979 F.2d 317
2D1.1(c)(6)—981 F.2d 1123
2D1.1(c)(6)—986 F.2d 86
2D1.1(c)(6)—989 F.2d 659
2D1.1(c)(6)—5 F.3d 1306
2D1.1(c)(6)—11 F.3d 346
2D1.1(c)(6)—11 F.3d 1510
2D1.1(c)(6)—15 F.3d 1161
2D1.1(c)(6)—19 F.3d 1283
2D1.1(c)(6)—813 F.Supp. 168
2D1.1(c)(6)—829 F.Supp. 435
2D1.1(c)(7)—946 F.2d 362
2D1.1(c)(7)—5 F.3d 1306
2D1.1(c)(7)—7 F.3d 101
2D1.1(c)(7)—834 F.Supp. 550
2D1.1(c)(8)—910 F.2d 703
2D1.1(c)(8)—932 F.2d 1029
2D1.1(c)(8)—968 F.2d 216
2D1.1(c)(8)—753 F.Supp. 23
2D1.1(c)(8)—813 F.Supp. 168
2D1.1(c)(8)—998 F.Supp. 42
2D1.1(c)(9)—917 F.2d 601
2D1.1(c)(9)—937 F.2d 1041
2D1.1(c)(9)—946 F.2d 362
2D1.1(c)(9)—951 F.2d 26
2D1.1(c)(9)—954 F.2d 12
2D1.1(c)(9)—961 F.2d 738
2D1.1(c)(9)—965 F.2d 1037
2D1.1(c)(9)—967 F.2d 1383
2D1.1(c)(9)—979 F.2d 1406
2D1.1(c)(9)—982 F.2d 290
2D1.1(c)(9)—987 F.2d 1493
2D1.1(c)(9)—992 F.2d 22
2D1.1(c)(9)—818 F.Supp. 812
2D1.1(c)(10)—969 F.2d 858
2D1.1(c)(10)—994 F.2d 942
2D1.1(c)(11)—969 F.2d 609
2D1.1(c)(11)—969 F.2d 858
2D1.1(c)(11)—972 F.2d 1580
2D1.1(c)(11)—7 F.3d 66
2D1.1(c)(12)—919 F.2d 940
2D1.1(c)(12)—953 F.2d 1184
2D1.1(c)(12)—958 F.2d 315
2D1.1(c)(12)—966 F.2d 1366
2D1.1(c)(12)—969 F.2d 609
2D1.1(c)(12)—982 F.2d 315
2D1.1(c)(13)—937 F.2d 496
2D1.1(c)(13)—951 F.2d 636
2D1.1(c)(13)—953 F.2d 1184
2D1.1(c)(13)—972 F.2d 1259
2D1.1(c)(13)—974 F.2d 97
2D1.1(c)(13)—833 F.Supp. 1454
2D1.1(c)(13)—846 F.Supp. 768
2D1.1(c)(14)—951 F.2d 636
2D1.1(c)(15)—990 F.2d 419
2D1.1(c)(16)—967 F.2d 1383
2D1.1(c)(16)—976 F.2d 666
2D1.1(c)(16)—3 F.3d 325
2D1.1 Table—967 F.2d 27
2D1.1 Table—969 F.2d 569
2D1.1 Table—998 F.2d 1571

2D1.1 comment—974 F.2d 971
2D1.1 comment—975 F.2d 999
2D1.1 comment—976 F.2d 666
2D1.1 comment—977 F.2d 222
2D1.1 comment—978 F.2d 433
2D1.1 comment—978 F.2d 577
2D1.1 comment—980 F.2d 645
2D1.1 comment—982 F.2d 290
2D1.1 comment—982 F.2d 325
2D1.1 comment—983 F.2d 625
2D1.1 comment—983 F.2d 1468
2D1.1 comment—984 F.2d 705
2D1.1 comment—984 F.2d 989
2D1.1 comment—985 F.2d 1175
2D1.1 comment—986 F.2d 1199
2D1.1 comment—989 F.2d 1279
2D1.1 comment—991 F.2d 1328
2D1.1 comment—992 F.2d 1459
2D1.1 comment—993 F.2d 204
2D1.1 comment—994 F.2d 1129
2D1.1 comment—994 F.2d 1467
2D1.1 comment—994 F.2d 1510
2D1.1 comment—996 F.2d 1300
2D1.1 comment—997 F.2d 248
2D1.1 comment—997 F.2d 475
2D1.1 comment—998 F.2d 1571
2D1.1 comment—999 F.2d 1192
2D1.1 comment—1 F.3d 920
2D1.1 comment—1 F.3d 972
2D1.1 comment—1 F.3d 1105
2D1.1 comment—2 F.3d 849
2D1.1 comment—3 F.3d 506
2D1.1 comment—4 F.3d 150
2D1.1 comment—5 F.3d 295
2D1.1 comment—5 F.3d 1161
2D1.1 comment—6 F.3d 554
2D1.1 comment—7 F.3d 101
2D1.1 comment—7 F.3d 164
2D1.1 comment—7 F.3d 516
2D1.1 comment—7 F.3d 957
2D1.1 comment—8 F.3d 17
2D1.1 comment—10 F.3d 590
2D1.1 comment—11 F.3d 97
2D1.1 comment—11 F.3d 824
2D1.1 comment—11 F.3d 953
2D1.1 comment—12 F.3d 1186
2D1.1 comment—12 F.3d 1350
2D1.1 comment—12 F.3d 1427
2D1.1 comment—13 F.3d 711
2D1.1 comment—13 F.3d 1217
2D1.1 comment—13 F.3d 1391
2D1.1 comment—13 F.3d 1418
2D1.1 comment—14 F.3d 300
2D1.1 comment—14 F.3d 331
2D1.1 comment—14 F.3d 502
2D1.1 comment—14 F.3d 1128
2D1.1 comment—16 F.3d 317
2D1.1 comment—17 F.3d 496
2D1.1 comment—19 F.3d 1246
2D1.1 comment—20 F.3d 1428
2D1.1 comment—22 F.3d 779
2D1.1 comment—23 F.3d 1024
2D1.1 comment—703 F.Supp. 1350
2D1.1 comment—704 F.Supp. 910
2D1.1 comment—709 F.Supp. 908
2D1.1 comment—726 F.Supp. 861
2D1.1 comment—729 F.Supp. 140
2D1.1 comment—730 F.Supp. 35
2D1.1 comment—730 F.Supp. 45
2D1.1 comment—732 F.Supp. 878
2D1.1 comment—738 F.Supp. 1256
2D1.1 comment—740 F.Supp. 1502
2D1.1 comment—753 F.Supp. 23
2D1.1 comment—756 F.Supp. 310
2D1.1 comment—784 F.Supp. 1373
2D1.1 comment—796 F.Supp. 366
2D1.1 comment—818 F.Supp. 812
2D1.1 comment—833 F.Supp. 1454
2D1.2—866 F.2d 604
2D1.2—874 F.2d 43
2D1.2—922 F.2d 1490
2D1.2—923 F.2d 1293
2D1.2—937 F.2d 979
2D1.2—995 F.2d 562
2D1.2—998 F.2d 584
2D1.2—5 F.3d 467
2D1.2—756 F.Supp. 310
2D1.2—814 F.Supp. 1249
2D1.2—836 F.Supp. 812
2D1.2(a)(1)—981 F.2d 613
2D1.2(a)(1)—992 F.2d 22
2D1.2(a)(1)—993 F.2d 196
2D1.2(a)(1)—995 F.2d 562
2D1.2(a)(1)—13 F.3d 1217
2D1.2(a)(2) [1988]—959 F.2d 246
2D1.2 comment—932 F.2d 1529
2D1.3—866 F.2d 604
2D1.3 [1988]—902 F.2d 451
2D1.3 [1988]—935 F.2d 766
2D1.3(a)(2)(B) [1988]—923 F.2d 1293

2D1.4—869 F.2d 797
2D1.4—870 F.2d 174
2D1.4—876 F.2d 1121
2D1.4—884 F.2d 1090
2D1.4—885 F.2d 1266
2D1.4—887 F.2d 57
2D1.4—888 F.2d 1255
2D1.4—889 F.2d 1454
2D1.4—893 F.2d 669
2D1.4—893 F.2d 690
2D1.4—894 F.2d 208
2D1.4—894 F.2d 261
2D1.4—894 F.2d 1035
2D1.4—895 F.2d 1362
2D1.4—896 F.2d 99
2D1.4—897 F.2d 1099
2D1.4—898 F.2d 659
2D1.4—898 F.2d 705
2D1.4—901 F.2d 85
2D1.4 [1988]—902 F.2d 451
2D1.4—902 F.2d 734
2D1.4 [1988]—902 F.2d 734
2D1.4—904 F.2d 1070
2D1.4—905 F.2d 1050
2D1.4—906 F.2d 1261
2D1.4—909 F.2d 780
2D1.4—909 F.2d 1042
2D1.4—911 F.2d 1456
2D1.4—915 F.2d 402
2D1.4—917 F.2d 112
2D1.4—920 F.2d 139
2D1.4—922 F.2d 404
2D1.4—926 F.2d 172
2D1.4—926 F.2d 204
2D1.4—927 F.2d 176
2D1.4—927 F.2d 1272
2D1.4—930 F.2d 1375
2D1.4—932 F.2d 1029
2D1.4—932 F.2d 1174
2D1.4—934 F.2d 411
2D1.4—935 F.2d 39
2D1.4—937 F.2d 151
2D1.4—941 F.2d 267
2D1.4—944 F.2d 442
2D1.4—945 F.2d 1387
2D1.4—946 F.2d 122
2D1.4—946 F.2d 484
2D1.4—950 F.2d 508
2D1.4—953 F.2d 1312
2D1.4—955 F.2d 182
2D1.4—955 F.2d 1116
2D1.4—956 F.2d 1256
2D1.4—957 F.2d 1138
2D1.4—959 F.2d 246
2D1.4—959 F.2d 1489
2D1.4—960 F.2d 256
2D1.4—961 F.2d 41
2D1.4—961 F.2d 972
2D1.4—961 F.2d 1380
2D1.4—961 F.2d 1476
2D1.4—963 F.2d 1027
2D1.4—964 F.2d 454
2D1.4—968 F.2d 216
2D1.4—971 F.2d 1257
2D1.4—973 F.2d 1015
2D1.4—974 F.2d 61
2D1.4—975 F.2d 1225
2D1.4—977 F.2d 1436
2D1.4—978 F.2d 881
2D1.4—979 F.2d 786
2D1.4—979 F.2d 1406
2D1.4 [1992]—982 F.2d 1374
2D1.4 [1988]—983 F.2d 1468
2D1.4 [1992]—984 F.2d 1426
2D1.4 [1992]—985 F.2d 371
2D1.4 [1990]—985 F.2d 391
2D1.4—985 F.2d 766
2D1.4 [1992]—986 F.2d 349
2D1.4 [1992]—986 F.2d 1091
2D1.4 [1992]—987 F.2d 1225
2D1.4 [1991]—989 F.2d 546
2D1.4—990 F.2d 1005
2D1.4 [1992]—991 F.2d 1328
2D1.4 [1992]—992 F.2d 573
2D1.4—992 F.2d 887
2D1.4 [1992]—994 F.2d 1129
2D1.4 [1992]—995 F.2d 380
2D1.4 [1990]—996 F.2d 456
2D1.4—996 F.2d 1307
2D1.4 [1991]—997 F.2d 475
2D1.4—998 F.2d 584
2D1.4 [1992]—3 F.3d 1496
2D1.4—5 F.3d 633
2D1.4 [1992]—5 F.3d 1306
2D1.4—6 F.3d 431
2D1.4 [1992]—7 F.3d 164
2D1.4 [1992]—7 F.3d 1506
2D1.4—9 F.3d 1422
2D1.4 [1991]—19 F.3d 929
2D1.4—710 F.Supp. 1136

2D1.4—715 F.Supp. 1473
2D1.4—727 F.Supp. 134
2D1.4—756 F.Supp. 310
2D1.4—760 F.Supp. 1322
2D1.4—761 F.Supp. 697
2D1.4—801 F.Supp. 1407
2D1.4(a)—888 F.2d 490
2D1.4(a)—910 F.2d 703
2D1.4(a)—915 F.2d 402
2D1.4(a)—918 F.2d 1129
2D1.4(a)—926 F.2d 838
2D1.4(a)—930 F.2d 567
2D1.4(a)—940 F.2d 593
2D1.4(a)—941 F.2d 761
2D1.4(a)—943 F.2d 1007
2D1.4(a)—946 F.2d 505
2D1.4(a)—951 F.2d 26
2D1.4(a)—956 F.2d 1256
2D1.4(a)—959 F.2d 637
2D1.4(a) [1988]—959 F.2d 246
2D1.4(a)—967 F.2d 497
2D1.4(a)—970 F.2d 1490
2D1.4(a)—974 F.2d 61
2D1.4(a)—981 F.2d 906
2D1.4(a)—981 F.2d 1123
2D1.4(a)—983 F.2d 778
2D1.4(a) [1992]—985 F.2d 1001
2D1.4(a)—985 F.2d 1175
2D1.4(a) [1992]—988 F.2d 228
2D1.4(a) [1992]—988 F.2d 493
2D1.4(a) [1992]—989 F.2d 1061
2D1.4(a) [1992]—993 F.2d 680
2D1.4(a) [1991]—997 F.2d 475
2D1.4(a) [1992]—5 F.3d 1306
2D1.4(a)—21 F.3d 194
2D1.4(a)—784 F.Supp. 1373
2D1.4(c)(4)—996 F.2d 1541
2D1.4 comment—869 F.2d 805
2D1.4 comment—870 F.2d 174
2D1.4 comment—880 F.2d 376
2D1.4 comment—885 F.2d 441
2D1.4 comment—885 F.2d 1266
2D1.4 comment—886 F.2d 740
2D1.4 comment—886 F.2d 998
2D1.4 comment—886 F.2d 1041
2D1.4 comment—891 F.2d 145
2D1.4 comment—891 F.2d 155
2D1.4 comment—891 F.2d 364
2D1.4 comment—892 F.2d 182
2D1.4 comment—893 F.2d 669
2D1.4 comment—894 F.2d 208
2D1.4 comment—894 F.2d 261
2D1.4 comment—895 F.2d 1216
2D1.4 comment—895 F.2d 1362
2D1.4 comment [1988]—895 F.2d 1362
2D1.4 comment—896 F.2d 1031
2D1.4 comment—897 F.2d 1099
2D1.4 comment—898 F.2d 659
2D1.4 comment—898 F.2d 705
2D1.4 comment—900 F.2d 131
2D1.4 comment—901 F.2d 11
2D1.4 comment—902 F.2d 734
2D1.4 comment—903 F.2d 891
2D1.4 comment—905 F.2d 1050
2D1.4 comment—906 F.2d 129
2D1.4 comment [1988]—907 F.2d 1441
2D1.4 comment [1988]—908 F.2d 1289
2D1.4 comment—909 F.2d 1042
2D1.4 comment—911 F.2d 1456
2D1.4 comment—912 F.2d 424
2D1.4 comment—915 F.2d 402
2D1.4 comment [1988]—916 F.2d 464
2D1.4 comment—917 F.2d 601
2D1.4 comment—917 F.2d 683
2D1.4 comment [1988]—918 F.2d 1501
2D1.4 comment—920 F.2d 1231
2D1.4 comment—922 F.2d 311
2D1.4 comment—922 F.2d 404
2D1.4 comment—924 F.2d 298
2D1.4 comment—924 F.2d 753
2D1.4 comment—926 F.2d 204
2D1.4 comment—926 F.2d 838
2D1.4 comment—926 F.2d 1323
2D1.4 comment—927 F.2d 176
2D1.4 comment—927 F.2d 202
2D1.4 comment—927 F.2d 1272
2D1.4 comment—928 F.2d 372
2D1.4 comment—929 F.2d 64
2D1.4 comment—929 F.2d 213
2D1.4 comment—929 F.2d 356
2D1.4 comment—930 F.2d 310
2D1.4 comment [1988]—930 F.2d 1375
2D1.4 comment—931 F.2d 964
2D1.4 comment—931 F.2d 1201
2D1.4 comment—932 F.2d 1029
2D1.4 comment—934 F.2d 148
2D1.4 comment—934 F.2d 411
2D1.4 comment—934 F.2d 1440
2D1.4 comment—935 F.2d 39
2D1.4 comment—935 F.2d 739

2D1.4 comment—936 F.2d 387
2D1.4 comment—936 F.2d 1138
2D1.4 comment—937 F.2d 151
2D1.4 comment—937 F.2d 716
2D1.4 comment—939 F.2d 135
2D1.4 comment—940 F.2d 593
2D1.4 comment—940 F.2d 722
2D1.4 comment—941 F.2d 761
2D1.4 comment—942 F.2d 1298
2D1.4 comment—943 F.2d 383
2D1.4 comment—943 F.2d 824
2D1.4 comment—946 F.2d 122
2D1.4 comment—947 F.2d 1445
2D1.4 comment—948 F.2d 877
2D1.4 comment—949 F.2d 289
2D1.4 comment—950 F.2d 70
2D1.4 comment—951 F.2d 405
2D1.4 comment—953 F.2d 452
2D1.4 comment—953 F.2d 1184
2D1.4 comment—955 F.2d 182
2D1.4 comment—956 F.2d 894
2D1.4 comment—957 F.2d 671
2D1.4 comment—957 F.2d 1138
2D1.4 comment [1988]—959 F.2d 246
2D1.4 comment—959 F.2d 375
2D1.4 comment—959 F.2d 1489
2D1.4 comment—960 F.2d 256
2D1.4 comment—961 F.2d 41
2D1.4 comment—961 F.2d 93
2D1.4 comment—961 F.2d 972
2D1.4 comment—961 F.2d 1380
2D1.4 comment—961 F.2d 1476
2D1.4 comment—962 F.2d 767
2D1.4 comment—963 F.2d 1027
2D1.4 comment—964 F.2d 778
2D1.4 comment—964 F.2d 944
2D1.4 comment—966 F.2d 403
2D1.4 comment—967 F.2d 497
2D1.4 comment—970 F.2d 227
2D1.4 comment—970 F.2d 1490
2D1.4 comment—971 F.2d 454
2D1.4 comment—971 F.2d 1257
2D1.4 comment—972 F.2d 139
2D1.4 comment—974 F.2d 61
2D1.4 comment—975 F.2d 1225
2D1.4 comment—976 F.2d 1446
2D1.4 comment—977 F.2d 1077
2D1.4 comment—979 F.2d 1406
2D1.4 comment [1992]—982 F.2d 57
2D1.4 comment [1992]—982 F.2d 325
2D1.4 comment [1992]—982 F.2d 1374
2D1.4 comment [1992]—985 F.2d 427
2D1.4 comment [1992]—985 F.2d 766
2D1.4 comment [1992]—985 F.2d 1001
2D1.4 comment—985 F.2d 1175
2D1.4 comment [1992]—987 F.2d 1225
2D1.4 comment [1991]—987 F.2d 1349
2D1.4 comment [1992]—988 F.2d 1494
2D1.4 comment [1991]—989 F.2d 546
2D1.4 comment [1992]—989 F.2d 1061
2D1.4 comment [1992]—990 F.2d 251
2D1.4 comment—990 F.2d 1005
2D1.4 comment—992 F.2d 887
2D1.4 comment [1992]—993 F.2d 680
2D1.4 comment—994 F.2d 1287
2D1.4 comment [1992]—995 F.2d 380
2D1.4 comment [1992]—995 F.2d 808
2D1.4 comment—996 F.2d 1300
2D1.4 comment [1992]—996 F.2d 1541
2D1.4 comment [1992]—997 F.2d 78
2D1.4 comment [1992]—997 F.2d 248
2D1.4 comment [1992]—998 F.2d 42
2D1.4 comment [1992]—999 F.2d 1175
2D1.4 comment [1991]—3 F.3d 506
2D1.4 comment [1992]—3 F.3d 1496
2D1.4 comment [1991]—4 F.3d 1026
2D1.4 comment—5 F.3d 633
2D1.4 comment [1992]—5 F.3d 1306
2D1.4 comment [1992]—6 F.3d 431
2D1.4 comment [1992]—6 F.3d 735
2D1.4 comment [1991]—8 F.3d 1246
2D1.4 comment [1992]—9 F.3d 368
2D1.4 comment [1992]—9 F.3d 531
2D1.4 comment [1992]—15 F.3d 1161
2D1.4 comment [1992]—22 F.3d 195
2D1.4 comment—23 F.3d 135
2D1.4 comment—715 F.Supp. 1473
2D1.4 comment—730 F.Supp. 45
2D1.4 comment—740 F.Supp. 1502
2D1.4 comment—756 F.Supp. 310
2D1.4 comment—760 F.Supp. 1322
2D1.4 comment—761 F.Supp. 697
2D1.4 comment—784 F.Supp. 1373
2D1.5—918 F.2d 895
2D1.5—949 F.2d 1465
2D1.5—11 F.3d 1218
2D1.5—845 F.Supp. 270
2D1.5(a)(1)—845 F.Supp. 270
2D1.5 comment—899 F.2d 515
2D1.5 comment—913 F.2d 313

2D1.5 comment—988 F.2d 750
2D1.5 comment—845 F.Supp. 270
2D1.6—860 F.2d 35
2D1.6—863 F.2d 245
2D1.6—866 F.2d 604
2D1.6—891 F.2d 82
2D1.6—900 F.2d 204
2D1.6—929 F.2d 334
2D1.6—931 F.2d 1017
2D1.6—938 F.2d 1431
2D1.7—982 F.2d 1020
2D1.8—912 F.2d 1210
2D1.8—922 F.2d 563
2D1.8—922 F.2d 616
2D1.8—927 F.2d 453
2D1.8—941 F.2d 770
2D1.8—972 F.2d 64
2D1.8 [1992]—987 F.2d 463
2D1.8(b)(1) [1992]—987 F.2d 463
2D1.8 (b)(1)—19 F.3d 1452
2D1.10—936 F.2d 1403
2D1.11—979 F.2d 1522
2D1.11—981 F.2d 202
2D1.11—985 F.2d 466
2D1.11—988 F.2d 1374
2D1.11—993 F.2d 713
2D1.11—994 F.2d 1467
2D1.11—7 F.3d 164
2D1.11—9 F.3d 1442
2D1.11—11 F.3d 505
2D1.11—22 F.3d 1410
2D1.11(c)—994 F.2d 1467
2D1.11(c)(1)—7 F.3d 164
2D1.11(d)—994 F.2d 1467
2D1.11 comment—988 F.2d 1374
2D1.11 comment—994 F.2d 1467
2D2.1—866 F.2d 604
2D2.1—952 F.2d 414
2D2.1—973 F.2d 852
2D2.1—981 F.2d 92
2D2.1—698 F.Supp. 563
2D2.1(a)(2)—883 F.2d 963
2D2.1(b)—12 F.3d 605
2D2.1(b)—15 F.3d 25
2D2.1 comment—781 F.Supp. 281
2E1.1—899 F.2d 149
2E1.1—946 F.2d 484
2E1.1—954 F.2d 114
2E1.1—959 F.2d 1137
2E1.1—960 F.2d 1099

Part E: Offenses Involving Criminal Enterprises and Racketeering

2E1.1—979 F.2d 469
2E1.1—4 F.3d 70
2E1.1—713 F.Supp. 1278
2E1.1—751 F.Supp. 368
2E1.1—768 F.Supp. 1277
2E1.1—807 F.Supp. 165
2E1.1—834 F.Supp. 659
2E1.1—835 F.Supp. 1501
2E1.1(a)—22 F.3d 783
2E1.1(a)(1)—955 F.2d 77
2E1.1(a)(1)—4 F.3d 70
2E1.1(a)(1)—768 F.Supp. 1277
2E1.1(a)(2)—4 F.3d 70
2E1.1(a)(2)—751 F.Supp. 368
2E1.1(a)(2)—799 F.Supp. 900
2E1.1 comment—960 F.2d 1099
2E1.1 comment—751 F.Supp. 368
2E1.1 comment—835 F.Supp. 1466
2E1.2—919 F.2d 926
2E1.2—807 F.Supp. 165
2E1.2(a)—908 F.2d 1229
2E1.2(a)(2)—755 F.Supp. 914
2E1.2 comment—908 F.2d 1229
2E1.2 comment—919 F.2d 926
2E1.2 comment—817 F.Supp. 321
2E1.2(a)—908 F.2d 1229
2E1.2(a)(2)—755 F.Supp. 914
2E1.2 comment—908 F.2d 1229
2E1.2 comment—919 F.2d 926
2E1.4 [1990]—920 F.2d 1290
2E1.4—741 F.Supp. 215
2E1.4(a) [1990]—920 F.2d 1290
2E1.4 comment [1990]—920 F.2d 1290
2E1.4 comment—741 F.Supp. 215
2E1.5—968 F.2d 242
2E1.5—971 F.2d 1302
2E1.5 [1992]—8 F.3d 1552
2E1.5—791 F.Supp. 348
2E1.5 [1993]—848 F.Supp. 369
2E2.1—914 F.2d 966
2E2.1—943 F.2d 1543
2E2.1—835 F.Supp. 1466
2E2.1(b)(1)(C)—890 F.2d 1284
2E2.1(b)(1)(C)—915 F.2d 1174
2E2.1(b)(2)—855 F.2d 925
2E2.1(b)(2)—947 F.2d 112
2E2.1 et seq.—814 F.Supp. 382

2E3.1—825 F.Supp. 422
2E3.1—828 F.Supp. 3
2E3.1—835 F.Supp. 1466
2E3.2—814 F.Supp. 382
2E3.2—825 F.Supp. 422
2E3.2—828 F.Supp. 3
2E5.2—994 F.2d 942

Part F: Offenses Involving Fraud or Deceit

2F1.1—872 F.2d 597
2F1.1—878 F.2d 164
2F1.1—881 F.2d 823
2F1.1—881 F.2d 980
2F1.1—893 F.2d 1343
2F1.1—894 F.2d 334
2F1.1—894 F.2d 554
2F1.1—895 F.2d 1030
2F1.1—897 F.2d 909
2F1.1—900 F.2d 1350
2F1.1—908 F.2d 396
2F1.1—908 F.2d 561
2F1.1—909 F.2d 235
2F1.1—912 F.2d 204
2F1.1—912 F.2d 448
2F1.1—912 F.2d 979
2F1.1—913 F.2d 193
2F1.1—922 F.2d 1385
2F1.1—923 F.2d 1052
2F1.1—927 F.2d 942
2F1.1—930 F.2d 1527
2F1.1—932 F.2d 324
2F1.1—932 F.2d 651
2F1.1—933 F.2d 752
2F1.1—933 F.2d 807
2F1.1—937 F.2d 58
2F1.1—937 F.2d 1196
2F1.1 [1988]—943 F.2d 692
2F1.1—945 F.2d 1214
2F1.1—946 F.2d 267
2F1.1—947 F.2d 139
2F1.1—948 F.2d 74
2F1.1—949 F.2d 722
2F1.1—949 F.2d 1183
2F1.1—951 F.2d 521
2F1.1—951 F.2d 1164
2F1.1—951 F.2d 1182
2F1.1—951 F.2d 1451
2F1.1—952 F.2d 267
2F1.1—952 F.2d 289
2F1.1—952 F.2d 827
2F1.1—952 F.2d 1090
2F1.1—952 F.2d 1110
2F1.1—954 F.2d 217
2F1.1—956 F.2d 994
2F1.1—956 F.2d 1534
2F1.1—957 F.2d 577
2F1.1—957 F.2d 841
2F1.1—957 F.2d 1488
2F1.1—962 F.2d 409
2F1.1—962 F.2d 739
2F1.1—962 F.2d 1236
2F1.1—962 F.2d 1548
2F1.1—964 F.2d 1065
2F1.1—966 F.2d 1270
2F1.1—967 F.2d 572
2F1.1—969 F.2d 218
2F1.1—970 F.2d 681
2F1.1—971 F.2d 799
2F1.1—973 F.2d 835
2F1.1—973 F.2d 1152
2F1.1—975 F.2d 580
2F1.1—975 F.2d 596
2F1.1—975 F.2d 710
2F1.1—975 F.2d 1028
2F1.1 [1990]—975 F.2d 1028
2F1.1—977 F.2d 517
2F1.1—977 F.2d 1350
2F1.1—979 F.2d 1008
2F1.1—979 F.2d 1289
2F1.1—980 F.2d 8
2F1.1—980 F.2d 312
2F1.1—981 F.2d 281
2F1.1—983 F.2d 893
2F1.1—983 F.2d 1497
2F1.1—984 F.2d 338
2F1.1—984 F.2d 701
2F1.1—986 F.2d 916
2F1.1—986 F.2d 1176
2F1.1—987 F.2d 1311
2F1.1—987 F.2d 1497
2F1.1—989 F.2d 438
2F1.1 [1991]—989 F.2d 438
2F1.1—990 F.2d 822
2F1.1—991 F.2d 55
2F1.1—992 F.2d 1472
2F1.1—993 F.2d 147
2F1.1—994 F.2d 1192
2F1.1—994 F.2d 1332

2F1.1—994 F.2d 1380
2F1.1—995 F.2d 109
2F1.1—995 F.2d 759
2F1.1—995 F.2d 1448
2F1.1—997 F.2d 263
2F1.1—997 F.2d 407
2F1.1—999 F.2d 194
2F1.1—999 F.2d 483
2F1.1—1 F.3d 1112
2F1.1—2 F.3d 927
2F1.1—3 F.3d 311
2F1.1—4 F.3d 925
2F1.1—5 F.3d 467
2F1.1—5 F.3d 986
2F1.1—5 F.3d 1420
2F1.1—6 F.3d 1095
2F1.1—7 F.3d 1155
2F1.1—9 F.3d 686
2F1.1—10 F.3d 910
2F1.1—11 F.3d 74
2F1.1—11 F.3d 915
2F1.1—12 F.3d 17
2F1.1—12 F.3d 950
2F1.1 [1988]—13 F.3d 489
2F1.1—13 F.3d 595
2F1.1—13 F.3d 1043
2F1.1—16 F.3d 193
2F1.1—17 F.3d 247
2F1.1—18 F.3d 562
2F1.1—19 F.3d 1117
2F1.1—20 F.3d 1054
2F1.1—21 F.3d 7
2F1.1—21 F.3d 1228
2F1.1—22 F.3d 783
2F1.1—23 F.3d 343
2F1.1—671 F.Supp. 79
2F1.1—684 F.Supp. 1535
2F1.1—751 F.Supp. 368
2F1.1—755 F.Supp. 942
2F1.1—775 F.Supp. 348
2F1.1—794 F.Supp. 539
2F1.1—803 F.Supp. 53
2F1.1—814 F.Supp. 964
2F1.1—819 F.Supp. 250
2F1.1—832 F.Supp. 1400
2F1.1 [1988]—832 F.Supp. 1426
2F1.1—841 F.Supp. 734
2F1.1 [1988]—841 F.Supp. 734
2F1.1—848 F.Supp. 287
2F1.1(a)—908 F.2d 396
2F1.1(a)—909 F.2d 176
2F1.1(a)—912 F.2d 204
2F1.1(a)—930 F.2d 555
2F1.1(a)—937 F.2d 1196
2F1.1(a)—942 F.2d 141
2F1.1(a)—943 F.2d 692
2F1.1(a)—957 F.2d 577
2F1.1(a)—978 F.2d 759
2F1.1(a)—7 F.3d 1155
2F1.1(a)—9 F.3d 353
2F1.1(a)—692 F.Supp. 1427
2F1.1(a)—768 F.Supp. 1277
2F1.1(a)—775 F.Supp. 348
2F1.1(a)—777 F.Supp. 1229
2F1.1(a)—779 F.Supp. 422
2F1.1(a)—787 F.Supp. 819
2F1.1(a)—819 F.Supp. 250
2F1.1(b)—872 F.2d 597
2F1.1(b)—942 F.2d 528
2F1.1(b)—946 F.2d 650
2F1.1(b)—954 F.2d 928
2F1.1(b)—957 F.2d 577
2F1.1(b)—975 F.2d 580
2F1.1(b)—980 F.2d 259
2F1.1(b)—981 F.2d 1398
2F1.1(b)—984 F.2d 651
2F1.1(b)—1 F.3d 1112
2F1.1(b) [1991]—9 F.3d 452
2F1.1(b)—753 F.Supp. 1260
2F1.1(b)—779 F.Supp. 422
2F1.1(b)—798 F.Supp. 556
2F1.1(b)(1)—855 F.2d 925
2F1.1(b)(1)—889 F.2d 1336
2F1.1(b)(1)—901 F.2d 867
2F1.1(b)(1)—908 F.2d 396
2F1.1(b)(1)—912 F.2d 448
2F1.1(b)(1)—930 F.2d 555
2F1.1(b)(1)—933 F.2d 353
2F1.1(b)(1)—937 F.2d 58
2F1.1(b)(1)—937 F.2d 1196
2F1.1(b)(1)—952 F.2d 827
2F1.1(b)(1)—952 F.2d 1090
2F1.1(b)(1)—954 F.2d 217
2F1.1(b)(1)—961 F.2d 1012
2F1.1(b)(1)—966 F.2d 262
2F1.1(b)(1)—967 F.2d 1460
2F1.1(b)(1)—974 F.2d 496
2F1.1(b)(1)—975 F.2d 1028
2F1.1(b)(1)—981 F.2d 1398
2F1.1(b)(1)—984 F.2d 651

2F1.1(b)(1)—986 F.2d 65
2F1.1(b)(1)—993 F.2d 147
2F1.1(b)(1)—997 F.2d 263
2F1.1(b)(1)—1 F.3d 581
2F1.1(b)(1)—4 F.3d 658
2F1.1(b)(1)—5 F.3d 614
2F1.1(b)(1)—17 F.3d 409
2F1.1(b)(1) [1988]—18 F.3d 374
2F1.1(b)(1) [1988]—766 F.Supp. 227
2F1.1(b)(1)—775 F.Supp. 348
2F1.1(b)(1)—777 F.Supp. 6
2F1.1(b)(1)—818 F.Supp. 1306
2F1.1(b)(1)—819 F.Supp. 250
2F1.1(b)(1)(A)—973 F.2d 1
2F1.1(b)(1)(A-S)—981 F.2d 1398
2F1.1(b)(1)(A-S)—19 F.3d 1102
2F1.1(b)(1)(B)—896 F.2d 678
2F1.1(b)(1)(B)—957 F.2d 577
2F1.1(b)(1)(C)—995 F.2d 759
2F1.1(b)(1)(C)—1 F.3d 1112
2F1.1(b)(1)(C)—7 F.3d 1155
2F1.1(b)(1)(C)—783 F.Supp. 1109
2F1.1(b)(1)(D)—944 F.2d 472
2F1.1(b)(1)(D)—977 F.2d 517
2F1.1(b)(1)(D)—15 F.3d 784
2F1.1(b)(1)(E)—937 F.2d 1196
2F1.1(b)(1)(E)—948 F.2d 74
2F1.1(b)(1)(E)—961 F.2d 1354
2F1.1(b)(1)(F)—930 F.2d 1527
2F1.1(b)(1)(F)—967 F.2d 1028
2F1.1(b)(1)(F)—980 F.2d 8
2F1.1(b)(1)(F)—993 F.2d 1012
2F1.1(b)(1)(F)—995 F.2d 759
2F1.1(b)(1)(F)—11 F.3d 74
2F1.1(b)(1)(G)—894 F.2d 334
2F1.1(b)(1)(G)—906 F.2d 814
2F1.1(b)(1)(G)—909 F.2d 176
2F1.1(b)(1)(G)—955 F.2d 1175
2F1.1(b)(1)(G) [1988]—977 F.2d 1350
2F1.1(b)(1)(G)—753 F.Supp. 1260
2F1.1(b)(1)(H)—933 F.2d 752
2F1.1(b)(1)(H)—952 F.2d 672
2F1.1(b)(1)(H)—971 F.2d 89
2F1.1(b)(1)(H)—975 F.2d 580
2F1.1(b)(1)(H) [1988]—977 F.2d 1350
2F1.1(b)(1)(H)—819 F.Supp. 250
2F1.1(b)(1)(I)—941 F.2d 1102
2F1.1(b)(1)(I)—950 F.2d 50
2F1.1(b)(1)(I)—961 F.2d 1012
2F1.1(b)(1)(I)—962 F.2d 739
2F1.1(b)(1)(I) [1988]—22 F.3d 1504
2F1.1(b)(1)(I) [1988]—797 F.Supp. 672
2F1.1(b)(1)(J)—893 F.2d 314
2F1.1(b)(1)(J)—951 F.2d 1164
2F1.1(b)(1)(J)—957 F.2d 577
2F1.1(b)(1)(J)—964 F.2d 756
2F1.1(b)(1)(J)—995 F.2d 711
2F1.1(b)(1)(J)—819 F.Supp. 250
2F1.1(b)(1)(K)—926 F.2d 562
2F1.1(b)(1)(K)—995 F.2d 109
2F1.1(b)(1)(K)—7 F.3d 113
2F1.1(b)(1)(K)—12 F.3d 17
2F1.1(b)(1)(K)—775 F.Supp. 348
2F1.1(b)(1)(K)—819 F.Supp. 250
2F1.1(b)(1)(L)—964 F.2d 756
2F1.1(b)(1)(L)—969 F.2d 1283
2F1.1(b)(1)(L)—995 F.2d 109
2F1.1(b)(1)(L)—995 F.2d 711
2F1.1(b)(1)(L)—787 F.Supp. 819
2F1.1(b)(1)(L)—819 F.Supp. 250
2F1.1(b)(1)(M)—13 F.3d 15
2F1.1(b)(1)(N)—993 F.2d 1012
2F1.1(b)(1)(N)—798 F.Supp. 203
2F1.1(b)(1)(P) [1992]—994 F.2d 63
2F1.1(b)(1)(P)—989 F.Supp. 583
2F1.1(b)(2)—889 F.2d 1336
2F1.1(b)(2)—892 F.2d 756
2F1.1(b)(2)—909 F.2d 176
2F1.1(b)(2)—922 F.2d 748
2F1.1(b)(2)—923 F.2d 1052
2F1.1(b)(2)—930 F.2d 1527
2F1.1(b)(2) [1988]—932 F.2d 651
2F1.1(b)(2)—933 F.2d 353
2F1.1(b)(2)—936 F.2d 227
2F1.1(b)(2)—942 F.2d 528
2F1.1(b)(2)—952 F.2d 827
2F1.1(b)(2)—954 F.2d 928
2F1.1(b)(2)—955 F.2d 1175
2F1.1(b)(2)—957 F.2d 577
2F1.1(b)(2)—957 F.2d 681
2F1.1(b)(2)—969 F.2d 1283
2F1.1(b)(2)—970 F.2d 164
2F1.1(b)(2)—973 F.2d 835
2F1.1(b)(2)—976 F.2d 55
2F1.1(b)(2)—984 F.2d 651
2F1.1(b)(2)—986 F.2d 281
2F1.1(b)(2)—989 F.2d 20
2F1.1(b)(2)—989 F.2d 454
2F1.1(b)(2)—993 F.2d 702
2F1.1(b)(2)—994 F.2d 1332

2F1.1(b)(2)—997 F.2d 407
2F1.1(b)(2)—999 F.2d 1043
2F1.1(b)(2)—1 F.3d 1501
2F1.1(b)(2)—5 F.3d 986
2F1.1(b)(2)—7 F.3d 691
2F1.1(b)(2)—7 F.3d 1155
2F1.1(b)(2)—11 F.3d 74
2F1.1(b)(2) [1988]—13 F.3d 1421
2F1.1(b)(2)—16 F.3d 599
2F1.1(b)(2)—17 F.3d 177
2F1.1(b)(2)—18 F.3d 374
2F1.1(b)(2)—751 F.Supp. 368
2F1.1(b)(2)—777 F.Supp. 1229
2F1.1(b)(2) [1988]—797 F.Supp. 672
2F1.1(b)(2)—824 F.Supp. 26
2F1.1(b)(2)(A)—894 F.2d 74
2F1.1(b)(2)(A)—908 F.2d 281
2F1.1(b)(2)(A)—913 F.2d 1053
2F1.1(b)(2)(A)—914 F.2d 206
2F1.1(b)(2)(A)—916 F.2d 388
2F1.1(b)(2)(A)—917 F.2d 974
2F1.1(b)(2)(A)—938 F.2d 456
2F1.1(b)(2)(A)—942 F.2d 141
2F1.1(b)(2)(A)—944 F.2d 545
2F1.1(b)(2)(A)—956 F.2d 341
2F1.1(b)(2)(A)—969 F.2d 425
2F1.1(b)(2)(A)—972 F.2d 904
2F1.1(b)(2)(A)—978 F.2d 759
2F1.1(b)(2)(A)—981 F.2d 367
2F1.1(b)(2)(A)—983 F.2d 1497
2F1.1(b)(2)(A)—984 F.2d 701
2F1.1(b)(2)(A)—986 F.2d 1
2F1.1(b)(2)(A)—989 F.2d 347
2F1.1(b)(2)(A)—990 F.2d 1090
2F1.1(b)(2)(A)—990 F.2d 1545
2F1.1(b)(2)(A) [1988]—993 F.2d 214
2F1.1(b)(2)(A)—994 F.2d 1332
2F1.1(b)(2)(A)—997 F.2d 139
2F1.1(b)(2)(A)—999 F.2d 57
2F1.1(b)(2)(A)—5 F.3d 467
2F1.1(b)(2)(A)—9 F.3d 686
2F1.1(b)(2)(A)—13 F.3d 15
2F1.1(b)(2)(A)—15 F.3d 784
2F1.1(b)(2)(A)—17 F.3d 409
2F1.1(b)(2)(A)—18 F.3d 153
2F1.1(b)(2)(A)—18 F.3d 1367
2F1.1(b)(2)(A)—19 F.3d 1178
2F1.1(b)(2)(A)—787 F.Supp. 819
2F1.1(b)(2)(A)—819 F.Supp. 250
2F1.1(b)(2)(B)—908 F.2d 281
2F1.1(b)(2)(B)—926 F.2d 562
2F1.1(b)(2)(B)—944 F.2d 472
2F1.1(b)(2)(B) [1988]—977 F.2d 1350
2F1.1(b)(2)(B) [1988]—993 F.2d 214
2F1.1(b)(2)(B)—787 F.Supp. 819
2F1.1(b)(2)(1) [1988]—774 F.Supp. 506
2F1.1(b)(3)—930 F.2d 1527
2F1.1(b)(3)—996 F.2d 284
2F1.1(b)(3)—15 F.3d 599
2F1.1(b)(3)(A)—913 F.2d 1053
2F1.1(b)(3)(B)—947 F.2d 339
2F1.1(b)(3)(B)—975 F.2d 580
2F1.1(b)(3)(B)—984 F.2d 701
2F1.1(b)(3)(B)—987 F.2d 878
2F1.1(b)(3)(B)—5 F.3d 467
2F1.1(b)(3)(B)—10 F.3d 630
2F1.1(b)(4)—978 F.2d 861
2F1.1(b)(4)—9 F.3d 49
2F1.1(b)(6)(B)—6 F.3d 118
2F1.1 et seq.—818 F.Supp. 1306
2F1.1 comment—881 F.2d 823
2F1.1 comment—894 F.2d 334
2F1.1 comment—895 F.2d 318
2F1.1 comment—908 F.2d 396
2F1.1 comment—911 F.2d 793
2F1.1 comment—912 F.2d 448
2F1.1 comment—914 F.2d 206
2F1.1 comment—915 F.2d 774
2F1.1 comment—917 F.2d 1178
2F1.1 comment—923 F.2d 1052
2F1.1 comment—926 F.2d 562
2F1.1 comment—930 F.2d 555
2F1.1 comment—930 F.2d 1527
2F1.1 comment—932 F.2d 651
2F1.1 comment [1988]—932 F.2d 651
2F1.1 comment—936 F.2d 661
2F1.1 comment—938 F.2d 456
2F1.1 comment—941 F.2d 1047
2F1.1 comment—942 F.2d 141
2F1.1 comment—942 F.2d 528
2F1.1 comment—945 F.2d 1214
2F1.1 comment—948 F.2d 74
2F1.1 comment—950 F.2d 50
2F1.1 comment—951 F.2d 1164
2F1.1 comment—951 F.2d 1451
2F1.1 comment—952 F.2d 267
2F1.1 comment—952 F.2d 289
2F1.1 comment—952 F.2d 1090
2F1.1 comment—954 F.2d 217
2F1.1 comment—956 F.2d 341

Part G: Offenses Involving Prostitution, Sexual Exploitation of Minors, and Obscenity

2G1.1—943 F.2d 94
2G1.1—946 F.2d 230
2G1.1—950 F.2d 72
2G1.1 [1992]—994 F.2d 1380
2G1.1(c)—950 F.2d 72
2G1.1 comment—941 F.2d 738
2G1.1 comment—956 F.2d 864
2G1.1 comment—975 F.2d 1120
2G1.1 comment—994 F.2d 942
2G1.2—946 F.2d 230
2G1.2—956 F.2d 864
2G1.2—979 F.2d 539
2G1.2(b)(1)—901 F.2d 1161
2G1.2(b)(1)—902 F.2d 873
2G1.2(b)(1)—989 F.2d 980
2G1.2(b)(3)—901 F.2d 399
2G1.2 comment—956 F.2d 864
2G2.1—901 F.2d 1161
2G2.1—994 F.2d 456
2G2.1—5 F.3d 64
2G2.1(a)—994 F.2d 456
2G2.2—970 F.2d 960
2G2.2—987 F.2d 345
2G2.2—994 F.2d 456
2G2.2(b)(1)—901 F.2d 399
2G2.2(b)(1)—949 F.2d 283
2G2.2(b)(1)—959 F.2d 198
2G2.2(b)(1)—20 F.3d 610
2G2.2(b)(2)—973 F.2d 608
2G2.2(b)(3)—970 F.2d 960
2G2.2(c)(1)—994 F.2d 456
2G2.4—2 F.3d 1318
2G2.4(c)(1)—2 F.3d 1318
2G3.1—970 F.2d 960
2G3.1—987 F.2d 345
2G3.1(b)(2)—970 F.2d 960
2G3.1(c)(1)—970 F.2d 960

Part H: Offenses Involving Individual Rights

2H comment—994 F.2d 1380
2H1.1-2H4.1 [1992]—994 F.2d 1380
2H1.1 comment—976 F.2d 1226
2H1.2—893 F.2d 113
2H1.2—2 F.3d 870
2H1.3—935 F.2d 96
2H1.3—954 F.2d 586
2H1.3—976 F.2d 1226
2H1.3—827 F.Supp. 100
2H1.3(a)—954 F.2d 586
2H1.3(a)—976 F.2d 1226
2H1.3(a)(2)—976 F.2d 1226
2H1.3(a)(3)—976 F.2d 1226
2H1.3 comment—976 F.2d 1226
2H1.4—968 F.2d 1503
2H1.4—2 F.3d 870
2H1.4—833 F.Supp. 769
2H1.4(a)(2)—982 F.2d 665
2H1.4 comment—968 F.2d 1503
2H3.2—908 F.2d 561

Part J: Offenses Involving the Administration of Justice

2J1.1—880 F.2d 612
2J1.1 [1988]—923 F.2d 1536
2J1.1—945 F.2d 1214
2J1.2—967 F.2d 754
2J1.1—983 F.2d 1306
2J1.1—967 F.2d 754
2J1.1—731 F.Supp. 1051
2J1.1 comment—780 F.2d 612
2J1.1 comment [1988]—923 F.2d 1536
2J1.1 comment—731 F.Supp. 1051
2J1.2—880 F.2d 612
2J1.2—971 F.2d 717
2J1.2—977 F.2d 1420
2J1.2—983 F.2d 1306
2J1.2—991 F.2d 450
2J1.2—15 F.3d 272
2J1.2—731 F.Supp. 1051
2J1.2—821 F.Supp. 1400
2J1.27—89 F.Supp. 957
2J1.2(a)—712 F.Supp. 707
2J1.2(b)(1)—917 F.2d 1057
2J1.2(b)(1)—927 F.2d 1376
2J1.2(b)(1)—960 F.2d 212
2J1.2(b)(1)—977 F.2d 449
2J1.2(b)(1)—977 F.2d 1420
2J1.2(c)(1)—917 F.2d 507
2J1.2(c)(1)—983 F.2d 1306
2J1.2 comment—983 F.2d 1306
2J1.3—913 F.2d 193
2J1.3—919 F.2d 1365
2J1.3—933 F.2d 807

2J1.3—946 F.2d 1044
2J1.3—974 F.2d 127
2J1.3—996 F.2d 698
2J1.3—19 F.3d 1117
2J1.3(b)(2)—886 F.2d 293
2J1.3(b)(2)—889 F.2d 1374
2J1.3(b)(2)—900 F.2d 512
2J1.3(b)(2)—908 F.2d 230
2J1.3(b)(2)—919 F.2d 1365
2J1.3(b)(2)—931 F.2d 1035
2J1.3(b)(2)—941 F.2d 260
2J1.3(b)(2)—949 F.2d 1461
2J1.3(b)(2)—955 F.2d 77
2J1.3(c)—946 F.2d 1044
2J1.3(c)—974 F.2d 1270
2J1.3(c)—996 F.2d 698
2J1.3(c)(1)—929 F.2d 254
2J1.3(c)(1)—956 F.2d 80
2J1.3(c)(1)—974 F.2d 1270
2J1.3(c)(1)—977 F.2d 203
2J1.3(c)(1)—977 F.2d 1042
2J1.3 comment—789 F.2d 1374
2J1.3 comment—900 F.2d 512
2J1.3 comment—919 F.2d 1365
2J1.3 comment—941 F.2d 260
2J1.3 comment—948 F.2d 145
2J1.3 comment—949 F.2d 1461
2J1.4—895 F.2d 1178
2J1.4—948 F.2d 74
2J1.4(c)—934 F.2d 553
2J1.4(c)(1)—948 F.2d 74
2J1.5—880 F.2d 612
2J1.5—967 F.2d 754
2J1.5—731 F.Supp. 1051
2J1.5 comment—780 F.2d 612
2J1.6—887 F.2d 888
2J1.6—888 F.2d 528
2J1.6—900 F.2d 877
2J1.6—919 F.2d 1381
2J1.6—923 F.2d 1536
2J1.6—929 F.2d 505
2J1.6—930 F.2d 1447
2J1.6—932 F.2d 1073
2J1.6 [1988]—932 F.2d 1073
2J1.6—932 F.2d 1515
2J1.6—959 F.2d 54
2J1.6—977 F.2d 1284
2J1.6—995 F.2d 468
2J1.6—10 F.3d 1003
2J1.6(a)—921 F.2d 254
2J1.6(b)—921 F.2d 254
2J1.6(b) [1988]—955 F.2d 1492
2J1.6(b)(1)(B)—977 F.2d 1284
2J1.6(b)(2)(A)—995 F.2d 468
2J1.6(b)(2)(A)—834 F.Supp. 292
2J1.6(b)(2)(A)—843 F.Supp. 223
2J1.6 comment [1988]—932 F.2d 1073
2J1.6 comment [1988]—955 F.2d 1492
2J1.6 comment—975 F.2d 397
2J1.6 comment—10 F.3d 1003
2J1.6 comment—834 F.Supp. 292
2J1.7—928 F.2d 65
2J1.7—956 F.2d 1465
2J1.7—964 F.2d 325
2J1.7—966 F.2d 243
2J1.7—975 F.2d 1120
2J1.7—14 F.3d 1502
2J1.7—751 F.Supp. 803
2J1.7 comment—956 F.2d 1465
2J1.7 comment—966 F.2d 243

Part K: Offenses Involving Public Safety

2K1.1 et seq.—941 F.2d 114
2K1.3.—918 F.2d 1084
2K1.3—929 F.2d 1030
2K1.3—706 F.Supp. 331
2K1.3(b)(1) [1991]—7 F.3d 1458
2K1.3(b)(2)—946 F.2d 23
2K1.3(b)(3)—946 F.2d 23
2K1.3 comment—929 F.2d 1030
2K1.4—881 F.2d 114
2K1.4—908 F.2d 1229
2K1.4—915 F.2d 1514
2K1.4—917 F.2d 1178
2K1.4—935 F.2d 96
2K1.4—943 F.2d 1306
2K1.4—948 F.2d 1033
2K1.4—952 F.2d 565
2K1.4 [1990]—954 F.2d 1413
2K1.4—966 F.2d 1158
2K1.4 [1990]—966 F.2d 1158
2K1.4—970 F.2d 214
2K1.4—985 F.2d 1342
2K1.4 [1990]—985 F.2d 1342
2K1.4—997 F.2d 564
2K1.4—997 F.2d 594
2K1.4 [1990]—4 F.3d 891
2K1.4 [1990]—6 F.3d 623
2K1.4—7 F.3d 1279

2K1.4—8 F.3d 785
2K1.4—817 F.Supp. 64
2K1.4(a)—849 F.2d 1259
2K1.4(a)—995 F.2d 1357
2K1.4(a)—8 F.3d 785
2K1.4(a)(1)—8 F.3d 785
2K1.4(a)(1)—16 F.3d 202
2K1.4(a)(2)—943 F.2d 1306
2K1.4(a)(2)—967 F.2d 1468
2K1.4(a)(2)—993 F.2d 442
2K1.4(a)(2)—8 F.3d 785
2K1.4(b)—881 F.2d 114
2K1.4(b)—897 F.2d 13
2K1.4(b)(1)—917 F.2d 1178
2K1.4(b)(1) [1990]—927 F.2d 1188
2K1.4(b)(1) [1990]—956 F.2d 708
2K1.4(b)(1)—997 F.2d 564
2K1.4(b)(1) [1990]—4 F.3d 891
2K1.4(b)(2)—897 F.2d 13
2K1.4(b)(2) [1990]—927 F.2d 617
2K1.4(b)(2) [1990]—956 F.2d 1188
2K1.4(b)(2)—997 F.2d 564
2K1.4(b)(2) [1990]—4 F.3d 891
2K1.4(b)(4)—849 F.2d 1259
2K1.4(b)(4)—915 F.2d 1514
2K1.4(b)(4) [1990]—922 F.2d 1370
2K1.4(b)(5)—897 F.2d 13
2K1.4(b)(5) [1990]—927 F.2d 1188
2K1.4(c)—993 F.2d 442
2K1.4(c)—16 F.3d 767
2K1.4(c)(1)—908 F.2d 1229
2K1.4(c)(1)—918 F.2d 1084
2K1.4(c)(1)—929 F.2d 307
2K1.4(c)(1)—9 F.3d 660
2K1.4(c)(1)—817 F.Supp. 64
2K1.4(c)(2) [1990]—6 F.3d 623
2K1.4 comment—917 F.2d 1178
2K1.4 comment—985 F.2d 1342
2K1.5—951 F.2d 1182
2K1.5(b)(3)—984 F.2d 1402
2K1.6 [1988]—914 F.2d 208
2K1.6—918 F.2d 1084
2K1.6—956 F.2d 46
2K1.6—706 F.Supp. 331
2K1.6(a)(1)—918 F.2d 1084
2K1.6(a)(2)—918 F.2d 1084
2K1.6(a)(2) [1991]—956 F.2d 46
2K2.1—835 F.2d 1195
2K2.1—867 F.2d 783
2K2.1—871 F.2d 506
2K2.1—892 F.2d 742
2K2.1—894 F.2d 1162
2K2.1—898 F.2d 642
2K2.1—898 F.2d 1111
2K2.1 [1988]—906 F.2d 1356
2K2.1—908 F.2d 1491
2K2.1—914 F.2d 67
2K2.1—914 F.2d 959
2K2.1 [1988]—914 F.2d 959
2K2.1—917 F.2d 301
2K2.1—918 F.2d 226
2K2.1 [1988]—918 F.2d 925
2K2.1—918 F.2d 1084
2K2.1 [1988]—918 F.2d 1084
2K2.1—931 F.2d 705
2K2.1—941 F.2d 114
2K2.1—956 F.2d 46
2K2.1 [1991]—956 F.2d 450
2K2.1 [1991]—957 F.2d 72
2K2.1—958 F.2d 66
2K2.1 [1990]—959 F.2d 1489
2K2.1—967 F.2d 370
2K2.1 [1988]—971 F.2d 717
2K2.1—974 F.2d 897
2K2.1 [1988]—983 F.2d 369
2K2.1—986 F.2d 44
2K2.1—997 F.2d 396
2K2.1—999 F.2d 1144
2K2.1—4 F.3d 504
2K2.1 [1991]—4 F.3d 504
2K2.1—7 F.3d 854
2K2.1—8 F.3d 1264
2K2.1—706 F.Supp. 331
2K2.1—751 F.Supp. 803
2K2.1—788 F.Supp. 413
2K2.1—797 F.Supp. 539
2K2.1(a) [1988]—918 F.2d 925
2K2.1(a) [1988]—918 F.2d 1084
2K2.1(a)—937 F.2d 1514
2K2.1(a) [1990]—937 F.2d 1514
2K2.1(a)—956 F.2d 1216
2K2.1(a) [1988]—983 F.2d 369
2K2.1(a)—17 F.3d 6
2K2.1(a)—20 F.3d 999
2K2.1(a) [1991]—798 F.Supp. 291
2K2.1(a)(1) [1990]—954 F.2d 482
2K2.1(a)(1)—991 F.2d 1308
2K2.1(a)(2)—941 F.2d 114
2K2.1(a)(2) [1989]—980 F.2d 1300
2K2.1(a)(2)—982 F.2d 419

2K2.1(a)(2)—999 F.2d 1144
2K2.1(a)(2) [1990]—7 F.3d 66
2K2.1(a)(2) [1991]—18 F.3d 41
2K2.1(a)(4)—991 F.2d 1445
2K2.1(a)(4)—22 F.3d 583
2K2.1(a)(4)(A)—22 F.3d 736
2K2.1(a)(5)—5 F.3d 1378
2K2.1(a)(7)—959 F.2d 1489
2K2.1(a)(7)—797 F.Supp. 539
2K2.1(b)—939 F.2d 844
2K2.1(b)—18 F.3d 1190
2K2.1(b)—797 F.Supp. 539
2K2.1(b)(1)—886 F.2d 215
2K2.1(b)(1)—894 F.2d 1162
2K2.1(b)(1) [1988]—898 F.2d 681
2K2.1(b)(1)—908 F.2d 1491
2K2.1(b)(1)—917 F.2d 1133
2K2.1(b)(1)—942 F.2d 800
2K2.1(b)(1)—946 F.2d 23
2K2.1(b)(1)—946 F.2d 97
2K2.1(b)(1) [1990]—954 F.2d 482
2K2.1(b)(1)—966 F.2d 530
2K2.1(b)(1)—968 F.2d 1154
2K2.1(b)(1) [1991]—971 F.2d 548
2K2.1(b)(1) [1991]—986 F.2d 1244
2K2.1(b)(1)—5 F.3d 1378
2K2.1(b)(1) [1990]—22 F.3d 1048
2K2.1(b)(1)—818 F.Supp. 785
2K2.1(b)(1)(A)—20 F.3d 521
2K2.1(b)(1)(B)—20 F.3d 521
2K2.1(b)(2)—878 F.2d 921
2K2.1(b)(2)—884 F.2d 363
2K2.1(b)(2)—904 F.2d 23
2K2.1(b)(2) [1988]—918 F.2d 925
2K2.1(b)(2) [1988]—918 F.2d 1084
2K2.1(b)(2)—921 F.2d 204
2K2.1(b)(2) [1988]—928 F.2d 150
2K2.1(b)(2)—937 F.2d 676
2K2.1(b)(2)—939 F.2d 844
2K2.1(b)(2)—942 F.2d 800
2K2.1(b)(2) [1988]—947 F.2d 739
2K2.1(b)(2)—947 F.2d 1232
2K2.1(b)(2) [1990]—956 F.2d 450
2K2.1(b)(2)—972 F.2d 885
2K2.1(b)(2)—981 F.2d 989
2K2.1(b)(2)—983 F.2d 730
2K2.1(b)(2) [1988]—986 F.2d 21
2K2.1(b)(2) [1988]—990 F.2d 497
2K2.1(b)(2)—5 F.3d 1378
2K2.1(b)(2)—12 F.3d 28
2K2.1(b)(2)—12 F.3d 298
2K2.1(b)(2)—15 F.3d 52
2K2.1(b)(2)—20 F.3d 999
2K2.1(b)(2) [1990]—22 F.3d 1048
2K2.1(b)(2)—780 F.Supp. 1366
2K2.1(b)(4)—982 F.2d 216
2K2.1(b)(4)—990 F.2d 582
2K2.1(b)(4)—8 F.3d 769
2K2.1(b)(4)—23 F.3d 300
2K2.1 (b)(5)—990 F.2d 582
2K2.1 (b)(5)—991 F.2d 1445
2K2.1(b)(5)—995 F.2d 166
2K2.1(b)(5)—1 F.3d 51
2K2.1(b)(5)—5 F.3d 464
2K2.1(b)(5)—18 F.3d 1190
2K2.1(c)—971 F.2d 717
2K2.1(c) [1992]—998 F.2d 1377
2K2.1(c)—4 F.3d 1358
2K2.1(c)—5 F.3d 259
2K2.1(c)—797 F.Supp. 539
2K2.1(c) [1991]—798 F.Supp. 291
2K2.1(c)(1)—892 F.2d 742
2K2.1(c)(1) [1988]—895 F.2d 247
2K2.1(c)(1) [1988]—901 F.2d 555
2K2.1(c)(1)—918 F.2d 226
2K2.1(c)(1)—937 F.2d 1514
2K2.1(c)(1) [1991]—957 F.2d 72
2K2.1(c)(1)—967 F.2d 370
2K2.1(c)(1)—974 F.2d 897
2K2.1(c)(1) [1988]—983 F.2d 369
2K2.1(c)(1)—996 F.2d 88
2K2.1(c)(1)—4 F.3d 1358
2K2.1(c)(2)—895 F.2d 247
2K2.1(c)(2)—914 F.2d 67
2K2.1(c)(2)—925 F.2d 359
2K2.1(c)(2)—928 F.2d 323
2K2.1(c)(2)—932 F.2d 1529
2K2.1(c)(2)—947 F.2d 635
2K2.1(c)(2)—953 F.2d 898
2K2.1(c)(2) [1991]—956 F.2d 46
2K2.1(c)(2)—961 F.2d 1421
2K2.1(c)(2)—973 F.2d 459
2K2.1(c)(2) [1992]—997 F.2d 396
2K2.1(c)(2) [1990]—3 F.3d 98
2K2.1(c)(2) [1990]—7 F.3d 66
2K2.1(c)(2)—755 F.Supp. 914
2K2.1–2K2.3 [1988]—906 F.2d 1356
2K2.1 comment—884 F.2d 363
2K2.1 comment—894 F.2d 1162
2K2.1 comment [1988]—906 F.2d 1356

2K2.1 comment—914 F.2d 67
2K2.1 comment—917 F.2d 301
2K2.1 comment [1988]—918 F.2d 925
2K2.1 comment [1988]—918 F.2d 1084
2K2.1 comment—961 F.2d 1421
2K2.1 comment—974 F.2d 897
2K2.1 comment [1990]—3 F.3d 98
2K2.1 comment—5 F.3d 464
2K2.1 comment—17 F.3d 6
2K2.1 comment—20 F.3d 521
2K2.1 comment [1990]—818 F.Supp. 785
2K2.2—897 F.2d 751
2K2.2 [1988]—897 F.2d 751
2K2.2—906 F.2d 1531
2K2.2 [1988]—907 F.2d 294
2K2.2—918 F.2d 1084
2K2.2 [1988]—918 F.2d 1084
2K2.2—922 F.2d 1411
2K2.2—937 F.2d 1514
2K2.2—940 F.2d 107
2K2.2—941 F.2d 114
2K2.2 [1988]—957 F.2d 831
2K2.2 [1991]—957 F.2d 72
2K2.2 [1988]—975 F.2d 275
2K2.2 [1988]—983 F.2d 369
2K2.2 [1991]—992 F.2d 367
2K2.2 [1990]—7 F.3d 1458
2K2.2—706 F.Supp. 331
2K2.2 [1988]—817 F.Supp. 1406
2K2.2(a)—875 F.2d 1124
2K2.2(a) [1988]—918 F.2d 1084
2K2.2(a) [1988]—983 F.2d 369
2K2.2(a)(1)—940 F.2d 107
2K2.2(b)—940 F.2d 107
2K2.2(b)(1)—875 F.2d 1124
2K2.2(b)(1)—879 F.2d 454
2K2.2(b)(1)—941 F.2d 114
2K2.2(b)(1) [1991]—992 F.2d 967
2K2.2(b)(1)(B)—926 F.2d 768
2K2.2(b)(1-3)—875 F.2d 1124
2K2.2(b)(1-3)—922 F.2d 1411
2K2.2(b)(2)—913 F.2d 1053
2K2.2(b)(2)—926 F.2d 768
2K2.2(b)(2)—941 F.2d 114
2K2.2(b)(2)—946 F.2d 23
2K2.2(b)(3)—871 F.2d 506
2K2.2(b)(3) [1988]—918 F.2d 1084
2K2.2(b)(3)—922 F.2d 1411
2K2.2(b)(3) [1988]—957 F.2d 677
2K2.2(b)(3)—703 F.Supp. 62
2K2.2(b)(3)—719 F.Supp. 789
2K2.2(c) [1988]—925 F.2d 359
2K2.2(c)(1)—910 F.2d 326
2K2.2(c)(1) [1988]—925 F.2d 359
2K2.2(c)(1)—941 F.2d 114
2K2.2(c)(1) [1988]—975 F.2d 275
2K2.2(c)(1) [1988]—983 F.2d 369
2K2.2(c)(1)(A)—997 F.2d 396
2K2.2 comment—871 F.2d 506
2K2.2 comment [1988]—893 F.2d 30
2K2.2 comment [1988]—918 F.2d 1084
2K2.2 comment—922 F.2d 1411
2K2.2 comment—753 F.Supp. 1191
2K2.2 comment [1990]—980 F.2d 980
2K2.3—867 F.2d 783
2K2.3 [1988]—918 F.2d 1084
2K2.3—941 F.2d 419
2K2.3 [1988]—975 F.2d 275
2K2.3 [1991]—975 F.2d 275
2K2.3 [1990]—995 F.2d 91
2K2.3(b)(1)—867 F.2d 783
2K2.3(b)(1)(E) [1988]—907 F.2d 294
2K2.3(b)(2)—867 F.2d 783
2K2.3(b)(2)(A) [1988]—946 F.2d 23
2K2.3(b)(2)(A)—952 F.2d 591
2K2.3(b)(2)(B) [1988]—946 F.2d 23
2K2.3(b)(2)(C)—867 F.2d 783
2K2.3(c)(1)—918 F.2d 1084
2K2.3(c)(1) [1988]—918 F.2d 1084
2K2.4—835 F.2d 1195
2K2.4—872 F.2d 1365
2K2.4—875 F.2d 1294
2K2.4—898 F.2d 659
2K2.4—921 F.2d 650
2K2.4—923 F.2d 1371
2K2.4—959 F.2d 246
2K2.4—959 F.2d 1489
2K2.4—965 F.2d 1001
2K2.4—976 F.2d 1226
2K2.4—4 F.3d 800
2K2.4—716 F.Supp. 1207
2K2.4—719 F.Supp. 1015
2K2.4—767 F.Supp. 11
2K2.4(a)—959 F.2d 1489
2K2.4(a)—987 F.2d 1493
2K2.4(a)—7 F.3d 1471
2K2.4(a)—20 F.3d 229
2K2.4 comment—921 F.2d 650
2K2.4 comment—928 F.2d 575
2K2.4 comment—943 F.2d 35

2K2.4 comment—945 F.2d 1013
2K2.4 comment—959 F.2d 246
2K2.4 comment—976 F.2d 1226
2K2.4 comment—981 F.2d 497
2K2.4 comment [1991]—981 F.2d 887
2K2.4 comment—982 F.2d 4
2K2.4 comment—998 F.2d 42
2K2.4 comment—998 F.2d 453
2K2.4 comment—1 F.3d 729
2K2.4 comment—4 F.3d 800
2K2.4 comment—7 F.3d 1471
2K2.4 comment—758 F.Supp. 195
2K2.4 comment—767 F.Supp. 11
2K3.1—883 F.2d 1142

Part L: Offenses Involving Immigration, Naturalization, and Passports

2L1.1—868 F.2d 698
2L1.1—872 F.2d 632
2L1.1—879 F.2d 1247
2L1.1—877 F.2d 1409
2L1.1—922 F.2d 1443
2L1.1—935 F.2d 4
2L1.1—962 F.2d 873
2L1.1—975 F.2d 622
2L1.1—975 F.2d 1120
2L1.1(a)—868 F.2d 1121
2L1.1(a)—916 F.2d 27
2L1.1(a)(2)—968 F.2d 1042
2L1.1(b)(1)—975 F.2d 622
2L1.1(b)(1)—979 F.2d 249
2L1.1(b)(2)—868 F.2d 698
2L1.1(b)(2)—873 F.2d 1177
2L1.1(b)(2)—879 F.2d 1247
2L1.1(b)(2)—922 F.2d 1443
2L1.1(b)(2)—975 F.2d 1120
2L1.1(b)(2)—979 F.2d 146
2L1.1(b)(2) [1991]—3 F.3d 316
2L1.1(b)(3)—802 F.2d 781
2L1.1(b)(3)—999 F.2d 640
2L1.1(b)(3)—3 F.3d 314
2L1.1 et seq.—902 F.2d 734
2L1.1 comment—868 F.2d 1121
2L1.1 comment—872 F.2d 632
2L1.1 comment—873 F.2d 1177
2L1.1 comment—879 F.2d 1247
2L1.1 comment—884 F.2d 170
2L1.1 comment [1988]—897 F.2d 981
2L1.1 comment—901 F.2d 728
2L1.1 comment—916 F.2d 27
2L1.1 comment—927 F.2d 48
2L1.1 comment—929 F.2d 518
2L1.1 comment—941 F.2d 114
2L1.1 comment—943 F.2d 1
2L1.1 comment—962 F.2d 873
2L1.1 comment—967 F.2d 1321
2L1.1 comment—975 F.2d 622
2L1.1 comment—975 F.2d 1120
2L1.1 comment—977 F.2d 540
2L1.1 comment—979 F.2d 146
2L1.1 comment—979 F.2d 249
2L1.1 comment—766 F.Supp. 1227
2L1.1 comment—802 F.Supp. 657
2L1.2—855 F.2d 925
2L1.2—857 F.2d 1245
2L1.2—908 F.2d 425
2L1.2—908 F.2d 996
2L1.2—941 F.2d 1451
2L1.2—960 F.2d 101
2L1.2—967 F.2d 20
2L1.2—968 F.2d 1159
2L1.2—977 F.2d 540
2L1.2—987 F.2d 1129
2L1.2—999 F.2d 38
2L1.2 [1991]—999 F.2d 38
2L1.2—9 F.3d 875
2L1.2—16 F.3d 1294
2L1.2—18 F.3d 730
2L1.2—18 F.3d 1173
2L1.2—803 F.Supp. 675
2L1.2—815 F.Supp. 920
2L1.2—838 F.Supp. 142
2L1.2(a)—855 F.2d 925
2L1.2(a)—1 F.3d 46
2L1.2(b)—10 F.3d 544
2L1.2(b)(1)—855 F.2d 925
2L1.2(b)(1)—926 F.2d 64
2L1.2(b)(1)—941 F.2d 996
2L1.2(b)(1)—952 F.2d 514
2L1.2(b)(1)—963 F.2d 1284
2L1.2(b)(1)—968 F.2d 1159
2L1.2(b)(1)—9 F.3d 875
2L1.2(b)(2)—967 F.2d 20
2L1.2(b)(2)—979 F.2d 138
2L1.2(b)(2)—988 F.2d 16
2L1.2(b)(2)—1 F.3d 46
2L1.2(b)(2)—9 F.3d 875
2L1.2(b)(2)—10 F.3d 544
2L1.2(b)(2)—18 F.3d 1173

2L1.2(b)(2)—788 F.Supp. 132
2L1.2(b)(2)—803 F.Supp. 675
2L1.2(b)(2)—815 F.Supp. 920
2L1.2 comment—908 F.2d 425
2L1.2 comment—968 F.2d 1159
2L1.2 comment—999 F.2d 38
2L1.2 comment [1991]—999 F.2d 38
2L1.2 comment—9 F.3d 875
2L1.2 comment—18 F.3d 730
2L1.2 comment—815 F.Supp. 920
2L1.2 comment—967 F.Supp. 20
2L1.2 comment—803 F.Supp. 675
2L2.1—6 F.3d 1400
2L2.1(b)—890 F.2d 176
2L2.1 comment—6 F.3d 1400
2L2.2—951 F.2d 1451
2L2.2(a)—876 F.2d 24
2L2.2(a)—692 F.Supp. 1427
2L2.2(b)(1)—999 F.2d 640
2L2.3—1 F.3d 13
2L2.4—918 F.2d 1084
2L2.4—941 F.2d 1047
2L2.4(b)(1)—959 F.2d 850
2L2.4(b)(1)—999 F.2d 640

Part M: Offenses Involving National Defense

2M1.1 et seq.—954 F.2d 155
2M3.1—3M6.1 et seq.—954 F.2d 155
2M4.1—838 F.2d 932
2M5.2—928 F.2d 690
2M5.2 [1988]—931 F.2d 43
2M5.2—951 F.2d 988
2M5.2—952 F.2d 565
2M5.2—954 F.2d 155
2M5.2—958 F.2d 66
2M5.2—978 F.2d 166
2M5.2 [1988]—978 F.2d 166
2M5.2—978 F.2d 457
2M5.2 comment—952 F.2d 565
2M5.2 comment—954 F.2d 155
2M5.2 comment—978 F.2d 457

Part N: Offenses Involving Food, Drugs, Agricultural Products, and Odometer Laws

2N1.2—916 F.2d 186
2N1.2—939 F.2d 780
2N1.2(b)(1)—925 F.2d 186
2N1.2 comment—916 F.2d 186
2N2.1—933 F.2d 752
2N2.1—939 F.2d 780
2N2.1—947 F.2d 139
2N2.1—984 F.2d 338
2N2.1 comment—947 F.2d 139
2N3.1(b)—979 F.2d 1008

Part P: Offenses Involving Prisons and Correctional Facilities

2P1.1—879 F.2d 811
2P1.1—894 F.2d 1000
2P1.1—908 F.2d 861
2P1.1—943 F.2d 1543
2P1.1—960 F.2d 846
2P1.1—704 F.Supp. 175
2P1.1—710 F.Supp. 106
2P1.1—768 F.Supp. 339
2P1.1(a)—884 F.2d 75
2P1.1(a)—936 F.2d 85
2P1.1(a)—708 F.Supp. 964
2P1.1(a)(1)—894 F.2d 1000
2P1.1(a)(1)—920 F.2d 1570
2P1.1(a)(1)—936 F.2d 85
2P1.1(a)(1)—5 F.3d 1139
2P1.1(a)(1)—709 F.Supp. 1064
2P1.1(a)(1)—711 F.Supp. 736
2P1.1(a)(1)—716 F.Supp. 1207
2P1.1(a)(1)—976 F.Supp. 242
2P1.1(a)(2)—894 F.2d 1000
2P1.1(a)(2)—5 F.3d 1139
2P1.1(b)—979 F.2d 41
2P1.1(b)(1)—704 F.Supp. 175
2P1.1(b)(1)—710 F.Supp. 106
2P1.1(b)(2)—884 F.2d 75
2P1.1(b)(2)—920 F.2d 1570
2P1.1(b)(2)—5 F.3d 331
2P1.1(b)(2)—5 F.3d 1139
2P1.1(b)(2)—709 F.Supp. 1064
2P1.1(b)(3)—960 F.2d 846
2P1.1(b)(3)—968 F.2d 1161
2P1.1(b)(3)—970 F.2d 764
2P1.1(b)(3)—981 F.2d 1194
2P1.1(b)(3)—988 F.2d 448
2P1.1(b)(3)—5 F.3d 331
2P1.1(b)(3)—5 F.3d 1139
2P1.1(b)(3)—14 F.3d 41
2P1.1(b)(3)—709 F.Supp. 1064

2P1.1(b)(3)—762 F.Supp. 658
2P1.1(b)(3)—768 F.Supp. 339
2P1.1(b)(3)—789 F.Supp. 373
2P1.1(b)(3)—822 F.Supp. 198
2P1.1(b)(3)—837 F.Supp. 1324
2P1.1 et seq.—970 F.2d 764
2P1.1 comment—960 F.2d 846
2P1.1 comment—988 F.2d 448
2P1.1 comment—5 F.3d 1139
2P1.1 comment—709 F.Supp. 1064
2P1.1 comment—768 F.Supp. 339
2P1.1 comment—981 F.Supp. 1194
2P1.2—899 F.2d 983
2P1.2—953 F.2d 939
2P1.2—963 F.2d 1506
2P1.2(a)(3)—963 F.2d 1506
2P1.2(b)(1)—953 F.2d 939
2P1.2(c)(1)—990 F.2d 58

2P1.3—943 F.2d 1543
2P1.3(a)(2)—943 F.2d 1543
2P1.4—870 F.2d 174

Part Q: Offenses Involving the Environment

2Q1.2—883 F.2d 1142
2Q1.2—920 F.2d 363
2Q1.2—922 F.2d 54
2Q1.2—926 F.2d 410
2Q1.2—932 F.2d 1155
2Q1.2—959 F.2d 1324
2Q1.2—751 F.Supp. 368
2Q1.2(b)(1)—959 F.2d 1324
2Q1.2(b)(1)—994 F.2d 658
2Q1.2(b)(1)(A)—922 F.2d 54
2Q1.2(b)(1)(A)—959 F.2d 1324
2Q1.2(b)(1)(A)—751 F.Supp. 368
2Q1.2(b)(1)(B)—920 F.2d 363
2Q1.2(b)(1)(B)—926 F.2d 410
2Q1.2(b)(1)(B)—731 F.Supp. 242
2Q1.2(b)(3)—883 F.2d 1142
2Q1.2(b)(3)—888 F.2d 223
2Q1.2(b)(3)—920 F.2d 363
2Q1.2(b)(3)—922 F.2d 54
2Q1.2(b)(3)—18 F.3d 363
2Q1.2(b)(3)—731 F.Supp. 242
2Q1.2(b)(3)—751 F.Supp. 368
2Q1.2(b)(4)—959 F.2d 1324
2Q1.2(b)(4)—978 F.2d 643
2Q1.2(b)(4)—994 F.2d 658
2Q1.2(b)(4)—731 F.Supp. 242
2Q1.2(b)(4)—751 F.Supp. 368
2Q1.2 comment—920 F.2d 363
2Q1.2 comment—922 F.2d 54
2Q1.2 comment—926 F.2d 410
2Q1.2 comment—932 F.2d 1155
2Q1.2 comment—959 F.2d 1324
2Q1.2 comment—978 F.2d 643
2Q1.2 comment—994 F.2d 658
2Q1.2 comment—751 F.Supp. 368
2Q1.3—959 F.2d 1324
2Q1.3—993 F.2d 395
2Q1.3(a)—993 F.2d 395
2Q1.3(b)(1)—993 F.2d 395
2Q1.3(b)(1)(A)—961 F.2d 462
2Q1.3(b)(4)—961 F.2d 462
2Q1.3(b)(4)—987 F.2d 225
2Q1.3 comment—993 F.2d 395
2Q2.1—966 F.2d 1270
2Q2.1—998 F.2d 692
2Q2.1—11 F.3d 632
2Q2.1—753 F.Supp. 1260
2Q2.1(b)(1) [1992]—11 F.3d 632
2Q2.1(b)(1)—753 F.Supp. 1260
2Q2.1(b)(3)—10 F.3d 1058
2Q2.1(b)(3)—955 F.2d 288
2Q2.1(b)(3)(A)—966 F.2d 1270
2Q2.1(b)(3)(A)—986 F.2d 65
2Q2.1(b)(3)(A)—753 F.Supp. 1260
2Q2.1(b)(3)(B) [1992]—11 F.3d 632
2Q2.1(b)(3)(B)—753 F.Supp. 1260
2Q2.1(b)(3)(B)—765 F.Supp. 356
2Q2.1 comment—753 F.Supp. 1260

Part R: Antitrust Offenses

2R1.1—903 F.2d 1478
2R1.1—999 F.2d 194
2R1.1 [1991]—22 F.2d 790
2R1.1(a)—777 F.Supp. 1229
2R1.1(b)(1)—777 F.Supp. 1229
2R1.1(b)(2) [1991]—22 F.2d 790
2R1.1(b)(2)—777 F.Supp. 1229
2R1.1(c)—777 F.Supp. 1229
2R1.1 comment—903 F.2d 1478

Part S: Money Laundering and Monetary Transaction Reporting

2S1.1—962 F.2d 1228
2S1.1—966 F.2d 201
2S1.1—971 F.2d 562
2S1.1—986 F.2d 880
2S1.1—18 F.3d 562
2S1.1—20 F.3d 367
2S1.1—20 F.3d 918
2S1.1—21 F.3d 7
2S1.1(a)(1)—926 F.2d 649
2S1.1(a)(1)—9 F.3d 543
2S1.1(a)(1)—19 F.3d 616
2S1.1(a)(2)—966 F.2d 201
2S1.1(a)(2)—974 F.2d 1474
2S1.1(a)(2)—9 F.3d 543
2S1.1(a)(2)—19 F.3d 616
2S1.1(b)—925 F.2d 112
2S1.1(b)—971 F.2d 562
2S1.1(b)—986 F.2d 880
2S1.1(b)(1)—926 F.2d 649
2S1.1(b)(1)—964 F.2d 381
2S1.1(b)(1)—966 F.2d 201
2S1.1(b)(1)—977 F.2d 1264
2S1.1(b)(1)—992 F.2d 295
2S1.1(b)(1) [1991]—992 F.2d 295
2S1.1(b)(1)—20 F.3d 1325
2S1.1(b)(2)—925 F.2d 112
2S1.1(b)(2)—926 F.2d 649
2S1.1(b)(2)—984 F.2d 899
2S1.1(b)(2)—993 F.2d 1522
2S1.1(b)(2)—787 F.Supp. 155
2S1.1(b)(2)(B)—926 F.2d 649
2S1.1(b)(2)(C)—909 F.2d 789
2S1.1(b)(2)(E)—993 F.2d 1522
2S1.1(b)(2)(G)—974 F.2d 1474
2S1.1(b)(2)(K)—971 F.2d 562
2S1.1-2S1.3—825 F.Supp. 422
2S1.1-2S1.3—828 F.Supp. 3
2S1.1 comment—925 F.2d 112
2S1.1 comment—936 F.2d 661
2S1.1 comment—946 F.2d 176
2S1.1 comment—993 F.2d 1522
2S1.1 comment—9 F.3d 543
2S1.2—984 F.2d 298
2S1.2—5 F.3d 467
2S1.2(b)(1)(B)—984 F.2d 298
2S1.2(b)(1)(B)—5 F.3d 467
2S1.2(b)(1)(B)—5 F.3d 568
2S1.3—951 F.2d 634
2S1.3—960 F.2d 191
2S1.3 [1991]—962 F.2d 1236
2S1.3—963 F.2d 1316
2S1.3—968 F.2d 232
2S1.3—13 F.3d 752
2S1.3—807 F.Supp. 21
2S1.3—837 F.Supp. 490
2S1.3(a) [1991]—962 F.2d 1236
2S1.3(a)—981 F.2d 1382
2S1.3(a)(1) [1991]—962 F.2d 1236
2S1.3(a)(1)—981 F.2d 1382
2S1.3(a)(1)—762 F.Supp. 441
2S1.3(a)(1)(A)—917 F.2d 507
2S1.3(a)(1)(A)—919 F.2d 258
2S1.3(a)(1)(A)—981 F.2d 1382
2S1.3(a)(1)(A)—762 F.Supp. 441
2S1.3(a)(1)(b)—944 F.2d 475
2S1.3(a)(1)(B) [1991]—962 F.2d 1236
2S1.3(a)(1)(B)—977 F.2d 1323
2S1.3(a)(1)(C)—914 F.2d 699
2S1.3(a)(1)(C)—939 F.2d 244
2S1.3(a)(1)(C) [1991]—807 F.Supp. 21
2S1.3(a)(2)—919 F.2d 258
2S1.3(a)(2)—981 F.2d 1382
2S1.3(a)(2)—762 F.Supp. 441
2S1.3(b)(1)—914 F.2d 699
2S1.3(b)(1)—922 F.2d 664
2S1.3(b)(1)—927 F.2d 303
2S1.3(b)(1)—942 F.2d 894
2S1.3(b)(1)—943 F.2d 1422
2S1.3(b)(1) [1991]—957 F.2d 636
2S1.3(b)(1)—960 F.2d 191
2S1.3(b)(1) [1988]—969 F.2d 136
2S1.3(b)(1)—981 F.2d 1382
2S1.3(b)(1)—982 F.2d 970
2S1.3(b)(1) [1991]—807 F.Supp. 21
2S1.3(b)(2)—981 F.2d 1382
2S1.3(b)(2)—787 F.Supp. 155
2S1.3(b)(2)(E)—981 F.2d 1382
2S1.3 comment—922 F.2d 664
2S1.3 comment—960 F.2d 191
2S1.3 comment—968 F.2d 232
2S1.3 comment [1988]—969 F.2d 136
2S1.3 comment—981 F.2d 1382
2S1.3 comment—982 F.2d 970
2S1.3 comment [1988]—762 F.Supp. 441
2S1.4—951 F.2d 634
2S1.4—977 F.2d 1323
2S1.4—4 F.3d 815

2S1.4—807 F.Supp. 21

Part T: Offenses Involving Taxation

2T1.1—855 F.2d 925
2T1.1—956 F.2d 540
2T1.1—961 F.2d 1286
2T1.1—991 F.2d 819
2T1.1—2 F.3d 1094
2T1.1(a)—980 F.2d 496
2T1.1(a)—998 F.2d 776
2T1.1(b)(2)—3 F.3d 1081
2T1.1(b)(2)—17 F.3d 146
2T1.1 comment—956 F.2d 540
2T1.1 comment—2 F.3d 1094
2T1.1 comment [1993]—19 F.3d 463
2T1.2(b)(2)—965 F.2d 383
2T1.2(b)(2)—835 F.Supp. 1466
2T1.3—934 F.2d 169
2T1.3—961 F.2d 1286
2T1.3—963 F.2d 1316
2T1.3—964 F.2d 318
2T1.3—3 F.3d 827
2T1.3(a)—935 F.2d 1440
2T1.3(a)—996 F.2d 919
2T1.3(a)(1)—968 F.2d 936
2T1.3(a)(1) [1993]—19 F.3d 463
2T1.3(a)(1)—786 F.Supp. 1151
2T1.3(a)(1)—800 F.Supp. 648
2T1.3(a)(2)—835 F.Supp. 1466
2T1.3(a)(2)—786 F.Supp. 1151
2T1.3(b)—935 F.2d 1440
2T1.3(b)—989 F.2d 347
2T1.3(b)(1)—989 F.2d 347
2T1.3(b)(1)—800 F.Supp. 648
2T1.3(b)(2)—989 F.2d 347
2T1.3(b)(2)—998 F.2d 279
2T1.3(b)(2)—3 F.3d 827
2T1.3(b)(2)—800 F.Supp. 648
2T1.3(b)(2)—835 F.Supp. 1466
2T1.3 comment—964 F.2d 318
2T1.3 comment—989 F.2d 347
2T1.4(b)(1)—19 F.3d 192
2T1.4(b)(2)—978 F.2d 1032
2T1.4(b)(3) [1993]—19 F.3d 192
2T1.4 comment—978 F.2d 1032
2T1.5—2 F.3d 942
2T1.9—934 F.2d 169
2T1.9—2 F.3d 942
2T1.9(a)(2)—980 F.2d 496
2T1.9(b)—908 F.2d 816
2T1.9(b)(2)—985 F.2d 962
2T3.1—896 F.2d 678
2T3.1—918 F.2d 52
2T3.1—4 F.3d 815
2T3.1 comment—896 F.2d 678
2T4.1—855 F.2d 925
2T4.1—935 F.2d 1440
2T4.1—964 F.2d 318
2T4.1—980 F.2d 496
2T4.1—991 F.2d 819
2T4.1—17 F.3d 146
2T4.1 [1992]—17 F.3d 146
2T4.1—800 F.Supp. 648
2T4.1(F)—998 F.2d 776
2T4.1(H)—998 F.2d 776
2T4.1(M)—838 F.Supp. 709

Part X: Other Offenses

2X1.1—867 F.2d 222
2X1.1—891 F.2d 300
2X1.1—891 F.2d 962
2X1.1—897 F.2d 13
2X1.1—912 F.2d 448
2X1.1—917 F.2d 301
2X1.1—918 F.2d 1084
2X1.1—922 F.2d 1385
2X1.1—925 F.2d 359
2X1.1—932 F.2d 324
2X1.1—932 F.2d 1529
2X1.1—935 F.2d 822
2X1.1—937 F.2d 58
2X1.1—952 F.2d 267
2X1.1—956 F.2d 46
2X1.1—956 F.2d 1007
2X1.1—959 F.2d 1489
2X1.1—967 F.2d 370
2X1.1—968 F.2d 242
2X1.1—971 F.2d 562
2X1.1—971 F.2d 717
2X1.1—974 F.2d 897
2X1.1—974 F.2d 1389
2X1.1 [1991]—975 F.2d 275
2X1.1 [1988]—983 F.2d 369
2X1.1—983 F.2d 1468
2X1.1—988 F.2d 318
2X1.1—990 F.2d 58
2X1.1—995 F.2d 109
2X1.1—996 F.2d 88

2X1.1—997 F.2d 396
2X1.1—998 F.2d 53
2X1.1—999 F.2d 1144
2X1.1—4 F.3d 1358
2X1.1 [1990]—7 F.3d 66
2X1.1—8 F.3d 1552
2X1.1—11 F.3d 74
2X1.1—22 F.3d 662
2X1.1—751 F.Supp. 1195
2X1.1—755 F.Supp. 914
2X1.1—768 F.Supp. 1277
2X1.1—791 F.Supp. 348
2X1.1—814 F.Supp. 964
2X1.1(a)—908 F.2d 561
2X1.1(a)—917 F.2d 301
2X1.1(a)—925 F.2d 359
2X1.1(a)—932 F.2d 324
2X1.1(a)—935 F.2d 822
2X1.1(a)—952 F.2d 267
2X1.1(a)—956 F.2d 46
2X1.1(a)—959 F.2d 246
2X1.1(a)—959 F.2d 1489
2X1.1(a)—962 F.2d 263
2X1.1(a)—974 F.2d 897
2X1.1(a)—989 F.2d 28
2X1.1(a)—990 F.2d 58
2X1.1(a) [1992]—994 F.2d 63
2X1.1(a) [1992]—998 F.2d 1377
2X1.1(a)—4 F.3d 1358
2X1.1(a)—5 F.3d 445
2X1.1(a)—22 F.3d 662
2X1.1(a-c)—956 F.2d 46
2X1.1(b)—867 F.2d 222
2X1.1(b)—952 F.2d 267
2X1.1(b)—962 F.2d 263
2X1.1(b)—989 F.2d 28
2X1.1(b)(1)—914 F.2d 67
2X1.1(b)(1)—950 F.2d 444
2X1.1(b)(1)—961 F.2d 11
2X1.1(b)(1) [1991]—975 F.2d 275
2X1.1(b)(1)—977 F.2d 517
2X1.1(b)(1)—981 F.2d 281
2X1.1(b)(1)—989 F.2d 28
2X1.1(b)(1)—9 F.3d 353
2X1.1(b)(1)—11 F.3d 74
2X1.1(b)(2)—914 F.2d 708
2X1.1(b)(2)—932 F.2d 324
2X1.1(b)(2)—935 F.2d 822
2X1.1(b)(2)—962 F.2d 1308
2X1.1(b)(2)—973 F.2d 1422
2X1.1(b)(2) [1990]—973 F.2d 1422
2X1.1(b)(2)—974 F.2d 1389
2X1.1(b)(2)—989 F.2d 28
2X1.1(b)(2)—991 F.2d 819
2X1.1(b)(2)—17 F.3d 1531
2X1.1(b)(2)—751 F.Supp. 1195
2X1.1(b)(2)—755 F.Supp. 914
2X1.1(b)(2)—768 F.Supp. 1277
2X1.1(b)(2)—791 F.Supp. 348
2X1.1(b)(2)—814 F.Supp. 964
2X1.1(c)—768 F.Supp. 1277
2X1.1(c)(1)—932 F.2d 1529
2X1.1(c)(1)—8 F.3d 1552
2X1.1 comment—867 F.2d 222
2X1.1 comment—897 F.2d 13
2X1.1 comment—912 F.2d 448
2X1.1 comment—932 F.2d 324
2X1.1 comment—952 F.2d 267
2X1.1 comment—956 F.2d 46
2X1.1 comment—959 F.2d 1489
2X1.1 comment—961 F.2d 145
2X1.1 comment—962 F.2d 1308
2X1.1 comment—968 F.2d 242
2X1.1 comment—973 F.2d 1422
2X1.1 comment [1991]—975 F.2d 275
2X1.1 comment—977 F.2d 517
2X1.1 comment—981 F.2d 1398
2X1.1 comment—989 F.2d 28
2X1.1 comment—997 F.2d 396
2X1.1 comment—998 F.2d 53
2X1.1 comment—998 F.2d 249
2X1.1 comment—11 F.3d 74
2X1.1 comment—791 F.Supp. 348
2X1.1 comment—821 F.Supp. 1400
2X1.5—789 F.Supp. 957
2X2.1—962 F.2d 652
2X2.1—8 F.3d 731
2X2.1 comment—8 F.3d 731
2X3.1—906 F.2d 251
2X3.1—929 F.2d 254
2X3.1—946 F.2d 122
2X3.1—946 F.2d 1044
2X3.1—972 F.2d 1385
2X3.1—974 F.2d 1270
2X3.1 [1991]—977 F.2d 203
2X3.1—977 F.2d 1042
2X3.1—983 F.2d 1306
2X3.1—989 F.2d 447
2X3.1—996 F.2d 698
2X3.1—2 F.3d 369

2X3.1—712 F.Supp. 707
2X3.1—798 F.Supp. 513
2X3.1(a)—956 F.2d 80
2X3.1(a)—17 F.3d 351
2X3.1 comment—929 F.2d 254
2X4.1—885 F.2d 1266
2X4.1 comment—885 F.2d 1266
2X5.1—880 F.2d 612
2X5.1—894 F.2d 1035
2X5.1—923 F.2d 1536
2X5.1—925 F.2d 270
2X5.1—945 F.2d 1214
2X5.1—951 F.2d 1182
2X5.1—954 F.2d 264
2X5.1—956 F.2d 1007
2X5.1—959 F.2d 1489
2X5.1—963 F.2d 1316
2X5.1—967 F.2d 754
2X5.1—974 F.2d 897
2X5.1—975 F.2d 275
2X5.1—994 F.2d 1088
2X5.1—10 F.3d 1003
2X5.1—731 F.Supp. 1051
2X5.1 [1988]—817 F.Supp. 1406
2X5.1 comment—893 F.2d 250
2X5.1 comment—925 F.2d 270
2X5.1 comment—938 F.2d 149
2X5.1 comment—10 F.3d 1003

CHAPTER THREE—ADJUSTMENTS

Part A: Victim-Related Adjustments

3A comment—919 F.2d 1365
3A1.1—868 F.2d 807
3A1.1—872 F.2d 597
3A1.1—872 F.2d 632
3A1.1—893 F.2d 113
3A1.1—897 F.2d 1329
3A1.1—899 F.2d 1097
3A1.1—901 F.2d 1161
3A1.1—903 F.2d 457
3A1.1—905 F.2d 1137
3A1.1—913 F.2d 136
3A1.1—913 F.2d 780
3A1.1—914 F.2d 345
3A1.1—915 F.2d 352
3A1.1—916 F.2d 219
3A1.1—916 F.2d 497
3A1.1—922 F.2d 1370
3A1.1—923 F.2d 112
3A1.1—923 F.2d 1052
3A1.1—926 F.2d 999
3A1.1—930 F.2d 1450
3A1.1—932 F.2d 324
3A1.1—935 F.2d 1207
3A1.1—939 F.2d 1076
3A1.1—943 F.2d 29
3A1.1—943 F.2d 94
3A1.1—948 F.2d 74
3A1.1—949 F.2d 722
3A1.1—955 F.2d 25
3A1.1—957 F.2d 681
3A1.1—960 F.2d 955
3A1.1—962 F.2d 1410
3A1.1—965 F.2d 206
3A1.1—967 F.2d 434
3A1.1—967 F.2d 516
3A1.1—968 F.2d 1503
3A1.1—971 F.2d 667
3A1.1—972 F.2d 904
3A1.1—973 F.2d 832
3A1.1—974 F.2d 1135
3A1.1—979 F.2d 539
3A1.1—981 F.2d 1418
3A1.1—983 F.2d 1507
3A1.1—984 F.2d 1136
3A1.1—989 F.2d 936
3A1.1 [1988]—993 F.2d 214
3A1.1—994 F.2d 1332
3A1.1 [1992]—994 F.2d 1380
3A1.1—996 F.2d 939
3A1.1—999 F.2d 14
3A1.1—5 F.3d 467
3A1.1—6 F.3d 1218
3A1.1—7 F.3d 1155
3A1.1—10 F.3d 1
3A1.1—11 F.3d 1207
3A1.1—12 F.3d 70
3A1.1—14 F.3d 1364
3A1.1—18 F.2d 1123
3A1.1—684 F.Supp. 1535
3A1.1—734 F.Supp. 687
3A1.1—751 F.Supp. 1195
3A1.1—755 F.Supp. 914

3A1.1—787 F.Supp. 819
3A1.1—788 F.Supp. 756
3A1.1—827 F.Supp. 100
3A1.1(a)—948 F.2d 74
3A1.1 et seq.—918 F.2d 1084
3A1.1 et seq.—941 F.2d 133
3A1.1 et seq.—952 F.2d 1090
3A1.1 et seq.—968 F.2d 411
3A1.1 et seq.—970 F.2d 1312
3A1.1 et seq.—982 F.2d 4
3A1.1 et seq.—988 F.2d 1374
3A1.1 et seq.—819 F.Supp. 250
3A1.1 et seq.—684 F.Supp. 1535
3A1.1-3A1.3—833 F.Supp. 769
3A1.1-3C1.1—684 F.Supp. 1506
3A1.1-3C1.2—845 F.Supp. 270
3A1.1-3P1.2—872 F.2d 632
3A1.1 comment—893 F.2d 113
3A1.1 comment—901 F.2d 1161
3A1.1 comment—914 F.2d 345
3A1.1 comment—923 F.2d 1052
3A1.1 comment—934 F.2d 553
3A1.1 comment—935 F.2d 1207
3A1.1 comment—927 F.2d 681
3A1.1 comment—996 F.2d 939
3A1.1 comment—999 F.2d 14
3A1.1 comment—1 F.3d 46
3A1.1 comment—704 F.Supp. 175
3A1.2 [1992]—994 F.2d 1380
3A1.2—997 F.2d 67
3A1.2 [1992]—6 F.3d 611
3A1.2 [1992]—10 F.3d 1003
3A1.2—12 F.3d 39
3A1.2—14 F.3d 30
3A1.2(a)—20 F.3d 911
3A1.2(b)—996 F.2d 88
3A1.2(b)—1 F.3d 414
3A1.2(b)—6 F.3d 611
3A1.2(b)—8 F.3d 1240
3A1.2(b)—8 F.3d 1264
3A1.2(b)—12 F.3d 39
3A1.2(b)—19 F.3d 149
3A1.2 comment [1992]—994 F.2d 1380
3A1.2 comment—6 F.3d 611
3A1.2 comment—10 F.3d 1003
3A1.2 comment [1992]—10 F.3d 1003
3A1.2 comment—12 F.3d 39
3A1.3—881 F.2d 114
3A1.3—895 F.2d 1178
3A1.3—903 F.2d 457
3A1.3—929 F.2d 1235
3A1.3—936 F.2d 153
3A1.3 [1988]—959 F.2d 246
3A1.3—1 F.3d 1137
3A1.3—733 F.Supp. 1307
3A1.3—740 F.Supp. 1502
3A1.3—788 F.Supp. 756
3A1.3—835 F.Supp. 1466
3A1.3 comment—934 F.2d 553
3A1.3 comment—969 F.2d 341
3A1.3 comment—1 F.3d 46
3A1.3 comment—733 F.Supp. 1307
3A2.2—902 F.2d 1469
3A2.2—903 F.2d 292
3A2.2—906 F.2d 1531
3A2.2—908 F.2d 176
3A2.2—914 F.2d 1355
3A2.2—930 F.2d 744
3A2.2—934 F.2d 169
3A2.2—948 F.2d 1449
3A2.2 [1988]—948 F.2d 1449
3A2.2—950 F.2d 1348
3A2.2—951 F.2d 899
3A2.2—961 F.2d 116
3A2.2—961 F.2d 322
3A2.2—704 F.Supp. 175
3A2.2(a)—961 F.2d 180
3A2.2(b)—924 F.2d 1227
3A2.2(b)—925 F.2d 779
3A2.2 comment—908 F.2d 176
3A2.2 comment—934 F.2d 553
3A2.2 comment—961 F.2d 180

Part B: Role in the Offense

3B Sentencing Table—956 F.2d 352
3B comment—895 F.2d 641
3B comment—899 F.2d 1531
3B comment—903 F.2d 1336
3B comment—922 F.2d 1061
3B comment—932 F.2d 1529
3B comment—936 F.2d 1292
3B comment—950 F.2d 1508
3B comment—952 F.2d 171
3B comment—963 F.2d 56
3B comment—969 F.2d 858
3B comment—971 F.2d 1302
3B comment—973 F.2d 1422
3B comment—975 F.2d 580
3B comment—985 F.2d 612

3B comment—986 F.2d 1199
3B comment—996 F.2d 209
3B comment [1992]—999 F.2d 392
3B comment—9 F.3d 728
3B comment—753 F.Supp. 1260
3B1.1—855 F.2d 925
3B1.1—867 F.2d 216
3B1.1—868 F.2d 135
3B1.1—868 F.2d 711
3B1.1—868 F.2d 1390
3B1.1—870 F.2d 174
3B1.1—871 F.2d 511
3B1.1—873 F.2d 437
3B1.1—873 F.2d 765
3B1.1—874 F.2d 43
3B1.1—874 F.2d 213
3B1.1—878 F.2d 997
3B1.1—880 F.2d 376
3B1.1—881 F.2d 95
3B1.1—883 F.2d 963
3B1.1—884 F.2d 354
3B1.1—889 F.2d 1531
3B1.1—890 F.2d 855
3B1.1—893 F.2d 30
3B1.1—893 F.2d 314
3B1.1—893 F.2d 1502
3B1.1—895 F.2d 641
3B1.1—896 F.2d 842
3B1.1—897 F.2d 1324
3B1.1—899 F.2d 1531
3B1.1—900 F.2d 1211
3B1.1—900 F.2d 1531
3B1.1—902 F.2d 336
3B1.1—902 F.2d 675
3B1.1—902 F.2d 1501
3B1.1—903 F.2d 1336
3B1.1—907 F.2d 7
3B1.1—907 F.2d 781
3B1.1—908 F.2d 1229
3B1.1—908 F.2d 1312
3B1.1—908 F.2d 1443
3B1.1—909 F.2d 1042
3B1.1—911 F.2d 222
3B1.1—911 F.2d 1456
3B1.1—913 F.2d 770
3B1.1—913 F.2d 1288
3B1.1—914 F.2d 1527
3B1.1—915 F.2d 1164
3B1.1—916 F.2d 182
3B1.1—917 F.2d 494
3B1.1—918 F.2d 1129
3B1.1 [1990]—918 F.2d 1268
3B1.1—919 F.2d 962
3B1.1—919 F.2d 1181
3B1.1—920 F.2d 538
3B1.1—922 F.2d 675
3B1.1—922 F.2d 1061
3B1.1—923 F.2d 95
3B1.1—923 F.2d 1500
3B1.1—924 F.2d 454
3B1.1—924 F.2d 721
3B1.1—926 F.2d 7
3B1.1—926 F.2d 649
3B1.1—927 F.2d 111
3B1.1—927 F.2d 300
3B1.1—927 F.2d 1079
3B1.1—928 F.2d 383
3B1.1—929 F.2d 334
3B1.1—929 F.2d 500
3B1.1—931 F.2d 282
3B1.1—932 F.2d 611
3B1.1—932 F.2d 651
3B1.1—933 F.2d 195
3B1.1—933 F.2d 641
3B1.1—933 F.2d 1541
3B1.1—934 F.2d 553
3B1.1—935 F.2d 9
3B1.1—935 F.2d 739
3B1.1—936 F.2d 648
3B1.1—938 F.2d 175
3B1.1—939 F.2d 780
3B1.1—940 F.2d 261
3B1.1—941 F.2d 8
3B1.1—942 F.2d 606
3B1.1—942 F.2d 1200
3B1.1—943 F.2d 1007
3B1.1—944 F.2d 1377
3B1.1—947 F.2d 224
3B1.1—947 F.2d 742
3B1.1—950 F.2d 1508
3B1.1—952 F.2d 155
3B1.1—952 F.2d 267
3B1.1—952 F.2d 1026
3B1.1—954 F.2d 151
3B1.1—954 F.2d 674
3B1.1—954 F.2d 928
3B1.1—954 F.2d 1413
3B1.1 [1988]—955 F.2d 1492
3B1.1—959 F.2d 83
3B1.1—959 F.2d 1187

3B1.1—959 F.2d 1514
3B1.1—960 F.2d 51
3B1.1—960 F.2d 256
3B1.1—960 F.2d 263
3B1.1—961 F.2d 121
3B1.1—961 F.2d 972
3B1.1—961 F.2d 1354
3B1.1—962 F.2d 1218
3B1.1—962 F.2d 1410
3B1.1—963 F.2d 56
3B1.1—963 F.2d 72
3B1.1—966 F.2d 1270
3B1.1—967 F.2d 456
3B1.1—968 F.2d 415
3B1.1—968 F.2d 1193
3B1.1—969 F.2d 858
3B1.1—970 F.2d 164
3B1.1—970 F.2d 681
3B1.1—970 F.2d 1328
3B1.1—971 F.2d 562
3B1.1—971 F.2d 656
3B1.1—971 F.2d 961
3B1.1—971 F.2d 1302
3B1.1—973 F.2d 885
3B1.1—975 F.2d 1357
3B1.1—978 F.2d 341
3B1.1—979 F.2d 116
3B1.1—979 F.2d 921
3B1.1—981 F.2d 1398
3B1.1—984 F.2d 705
3B1.1—985 F.2d 15
3B1.1—985 F.2d 860
3B1.1—985 F.2d 1175
3B1.1—986 F.2d 439
3B1.1—986 F.2d 916
3B1.1—986 F.2d 1091
3B1.1—990 F.2d 98
3B1.1—990 F.2d 178
3B1.1—990 F.2d 1099
3B1.1—991 F.2d 374
3B1.1—991 F.2d 819
3B1.1—991 F.2d 1065
3B1.1—991 F.2d 1110
3B1.1—991 F.2d 1445
3B1.1—993 F.2d 442
3B1.1—993 F.2d 1224
3B1.1—994 F.2d 417
3B1.1—994 F.2d 658
3B1.1—994 F.2d 1184
3B1.1—994 F.2d 1204
3B1.1—995 F.2d 182
3B1.1—995 F.2d 1407
3B1.1—996 F.2d 209
3B1.1—997 F.2d 407
3B1.1—997 F.2d 687
3B1.1—999 F.2d 392
3B1.1—1 F.3d 662
3B1.1—1 F.3d 1098
3B1.1—1 F.3d 1105
3B1.1—5 F.3d 365
3B1.1—5 F.3d 1161
3B1.1—6 F.3d 1262
3B1.1—7 F.3d 1155
3B1.1—7 F.3d 1171
3B1.1—8 F.3d 316
3B1.1—8 F.3d 731
3B1.1—9 F.3d 686
3B1.1—9 F.3d 728
3B1.1—11 F.3d 632
3B1.1—11 F.3d 769
3B1.1—11 F.3d 1207
3B1.1 [1993]—12 F.3d 1162
3B1.1—13 F.3d 855
3B1.1—14 F.3d 1093
3B1.1—14 F.3d 1264
3B1.1—16 F.3d 892
3B1.1—17 F.3d 865
3B1.1—17 F.3d 1531
3B1.1—19 F.3d 1123
3B1.1—20 F.2d 367
3B1.1—21 F.3d 70
3B1.1—21 F.3d 759
3B1.1—22 F.3d 1040
3B1.1—733 F.Supp. 1174
3B1.1—733 F.Supp. 1195
3B1.1—751 F.Supp. 368
3B1.1—753 F.Supp. 1260
3B1.1—755 F.Supp. 914
3B1.1—756 F.Supp. 23
3B1.1—796 F.Supp. 853
3B1.1—824 F.Supp. 26
3B1.1—835 F.Supp. 1466
3B1.1—845 F.Supp. 270
3B1.1(a)—872 F.2d 632
3B1.1(a)—878 F.2d 125
3B1.1(a)—881 F.2d 95
3B1.1(a)—881 F.2d 586
3B1.1(a)—884 F.2d 181
3B1.1(a)—890 F.2d 366
3B1.1(a)—893 F.2d 479

3B1.1(a)—893 F.2d 1177
3B1.1(a)—897 F.2d 1034
3B1.1(a)—903 F.2d 1188
3B1.1(a)—905 F.2d 295
3B1.1(a)—907 F.2d 7
3B1.1(a)—907 F.2d 1494
3B1.1(a)—908 F.2d 85
3B1.1(a)—909 F.2d 1143
3B1.1(a)—910 F.2d 530
3B1.1(a)—911 F.2d 1456
3B1.1(a)—913 F.2d 1130
3B1.1(a)—915 F.2d 1150
3B1.1(a)—918 F.2d 1004
3B1.1(a)—918 F.2d 1371
3B1.1(a)—919 F.2d 76
3B1.1(a)—919 F.2d 940
3B1.1(a)—920 F.2d 1179
3B1.1(a)—922 F.2d 748
3B1.1(a)—922 F.2d 1323
3B1.1(a)—923 F.2d 86
3B1.1(a)—924 F.2d 889
3B1.1(a)—924 F.2d 1148
3B1.1(a)—925 F.2d 107
3B1.1(a)—925 F.2d 641
3B1.1(a)—929 F.2d 582
3B1.1(a)—930 F.2d 495
3B1.1(a)—931 F.2d 127
3B1.1(a)—931 F.2d 631
3B1.1(a)—933 F.2d 641
3B1.1(a)—934 F.2d 1114
3B1.1(a)—938 F.2d 456
3B1.1(a)—939 F.2d 135
3B1.1(a)—939 F.2d 244
3B1.1(a)—942 F.2d 454
3B1.1(a)—943 F.2d 94
3B1.1(a)—944 F.2d 1331
3B1.1(a)—947 F.2d 1120
3B1.1(a)—950 F.2d 50
3B1.1(a)—951 F.2d 1164
3B1.1(a)—952 F.2d 1026
3B1.1(a)—954 F.2d 1436
3B1.1(a)—955 F.2d 586
3B1.1(a)—956 F.2d 1388
3B1.1(a)—957 F.2d 577
3B1.1(a)—959 F.2d 1187
3B1.1(a)—959 F.2d 1514
3B1.1(a)—960 F.2d 51
3B1.1(a)—960 F.2d 256
3B1.1(a)—960 F.2d 1112
3B1.1(a)—961 F.2d 784
3B1.1(a)—962 F.2d 739
3B1.1(a)—964 F.2d 763
3B1.1(a)—965 F.2d 262
3B1.1(a)—966 F.2d 1270
3B1.1(a)—969 F.2d 685
3B1.1(a)—969 F.2d 858
3B1.1(a)—970 F.2d 164
3B1.1(a)—971 F.2d 562
3B1.1(a)—971 F.2d 656
3B1.1(a)—971 F.2d 667
3B1.1(a)—971 F.2d 1302
3B1.1(a)—972 F.2d 889
3B1.1(a)—972 F.2d 1107
3B1.1(a)—974 F.2d 520
3B1.1(a)—976 F.2d 393
3B1.1(a)—977 F.2d 455
3B1.1(a)—977 F.2d 664
3B1.1(a)—978 F.2d 78
3B1.1(a)—978 F.2d 573
3B1.1(a)—978 F.2d 1032
3B1.1(a)—978 F.2d 1520
3B1.1(a)—979 F.2d 1008
3B1.1(a)—981 F.2d 664
3B1.1(a)—981 F.2d 1199
3B1.1(a)—983 F.2d 165
3B1.1(a)—983 F.2d 1468
3B1.1(a)—984 F.2d 1339
3B1.1(a)—985 F.2d 371
3B1.1(a)—986 F.2d 183
3B1.1(a)—986 F.2d 1199
3B1.1(a)—987 F.2d 1311
3B1.1(a)—988 F.2d 544
3B1.1(a)—988 F.2d 712
3B1.1(a)—988 F.2d 750
3B1.1(a)—990 F.2d 663
3B1.1(a)—990 F.2d 1179
3B1.1(a)—992 F.2d 1472
3B1.1(a)—993 F.2d 620
3B1.1(a)—993 F.2d 680
3B1.1(a)—993 F.2d 702
3B1.1(a)—994 F.2d 417
3B1.1(a)—994 F.2d 1204
3B1.1(a)—995 F.2d 793
3B1.1(a)—995 F.2d 1285
3B1.1(a)—996 F.2d 284
3B1.1(a)—999 F.2d 57
3B1.1(a)—1 F.3d 473
3B1.1(a)—3 F.3d 1081
3B1.1(a)—4 F.3d 70
3B1.1(a)—4 F.3d 337

3B1.1(a)—5 F.3d 715
3B1.1(a)—5 F.3d 986
3B1.1(a)—7 F.3d 783
3B1.1(a)—8 F.3d 11
3B1.1(a)—8 F.3d 186
3B1.1(a)—9 F.3d 49
3B1.1(a)—9 F.3d 576
3B1.1(a)—11 F.3d 74
3B1.1(a)—11 F.3d 315
3B1.1(a)—11 F.3d 346
3B1.1(a)—11 F.3d 777
3B1.1(a)—13 F.3d 1
3B1.1(a)—13 F.3d 15
3B1.1(a)—13 F.3d 949
3B1.1(a) [1988]—13 F.3d 1421
3B1.1(a) [1988]—14 F.3d 165
3B1.1(a)—14 F.3d 502
3B1.1(a)—15 F.3d 1292
3B1.1(a)—16 F.3d 193
3B1.1(a)—16 F.3d 599
3B1.1(a)—16 F.3d 1324
3B1.1(a)—18 F.3d 153
3B1.1(a)—19 F.3d 166
3B1.1(a)—20 F.3d 367
3B1.1(a)—20 F.3d 615
3B1.1(a)—20 F.3d 670
3B1.1(a)—21 F.3d 813
3B1.1(a)—22 F.3d 1040
3B1.1(a)—703 F.Supp. 1350
3B1.1(a)—731 F.Supp. 242
3B1.1(a)—733 F.Supp. 1195
3B1.1(a)—740 F.Supp. 1502
3B1.1(a)—751 F.Supp. 368
3B1.1(a)—784 F.Supp. 1373
3B1.1(a)—787 F.Supp. 819
3B1.1(a)—824 F.Supp. 26
3B1.1(a)—833 F.Supp. 1454
3B1.1(a)—835 F.Supp. 1466
3B1.1(a)—845 F.Supp. 270
3B1.1(a-c)—895 F.2d 641
3B1.1(a-c)—899 F.2d 1531
3B1.1(a-c)—971 F.2d 1441
3B1.1(a-c)—979 F.2d 921
3B1.1(a-c)—11 F.3d 777
3B1.1(a-c)—14 F.3d 1093
3B1.1(a-c)—704 F.Supp. 175
3B1.1(b)—878 F.2d 125
3B1.1(b)—889 F.2d 1531
3B1.1(b)—890 F.2d 1284
3B1.1(b)—893 F.2d 669
3B1.1(b)—893 F.2d 1269
3B1.1(b)—899 F.2d 714
3B1.1(b)—905 F.2d 970
3B1.1(b)—906 F.2d 1285
3B1.1(b)—907 F.2d 7
3B1.1(b)—907 F.2d 56
3B1.1(b)—911 F.2d 1025
3B1.1(b)—913 F.2d 1288
3B1.1(b)—918 F.2d 68
3B1.1(b)—920 F.2d 1377
3B1.1(b)—927 F.2d 111
3B1.1(b)—927 F.2d 176
3B1.1(b)—928 F.2d 243
3B1.1(b)—929 F.2d 334
3B1.1(b)—933 F.2d 641
3B1.1(b)—934 F.2d 169
3B1.1(b)—935 F.2d 739
3B1.1(b)—935 F.2d 832
3B1.1(b)—937 F.2d 54
3B1.1(b)—942 F.2d 528
3B1.1(b)—942 F.2d 1217
3B1.1(b)—943 F.2d 428
3B1.1(b)—944 F.2d 1253
3B1.1(b)—944 F.2d 1331
3B1.1(b)—945 F.2d 236
3B1.1(b)—947 F.2d 849
3B1.1(b)—950 F.2d 1508
3B1.1(b)—951 F.2d 988
3B1.1(b)—951 F.2d 1220
3B1.1(b)—957 F.2d 310
3B1.1(b)—957 F.2d 1138
3B1.1(b)—958 F.2d 240
3B1.1(b)—959 F.2d 246
3B1.1(b)—960 F.2d 51
3B1.1(b)—960 F.2d 256
3B1.1(b)—960 F.2d 263
3B1.1(b)—960 F.2d 449
3B1.1(b)—961 F.2d 599
3B1.1(b)—962 F.2d 1152
3B1.1(b)—962 F.2d 1332
3B1.1(b)—964 F.2d 1501
3B1.1(b)—966 F.2d 403
3B1.1(b)—966 F.2d 945
3B1.1(b)—969 F.2d 187
3B1.1(b)—975 F.2d 580
3B1.1(b)—979 F.2d 136
3B1.1(b)—979 F.2d 921
3B1.1(b)—983 F.2d 1468
3B1.1(b)—985 F.2d 15
3B1.1(b)—985 F.2d 612

3B1.1(b)—985 F.2d 1263
3B1.1(b)—986 F.2d 880
3B1.1(b)—988 F.2d 750
3B1.1(b)—989 F.2d 760
3B1.1(b)—990 F.2d 663
3B1.1(b)—991 F.2d 120
3B1.1(b)—993 F.2d 680
3B1.1(b)—995 F.2d 865
3B1.1(b)—995 F.2d 1407
3B1.1(b)—996 F.2d 116
3B1.1(b)—997 F.2d 248
3B1.1(b)—997 F.2d 632
3B1.1(b)—997 F.2d 884
3B1.1(b)—997 F.2d 1204
3B1.1(b)—998 F.2d 253
3B1.1(b)—998 F.2d 1491
3B1.1(b)—999 F.2d 1192
3B1.1(b)—1 F.3d 662
3B1.1(b)—2 F.3d 1551
3B1.1(b)—4 F.3d 904
3B1.1(b)—5 F.3d 288
3B1.1(b)—9 F.3d 576
3B1.1(b)—9 F.3d 728
3B1.1(b)—11 F.3d 777
3B1.1(b)—14 F.3d 502
3B1.1(b)—16 F.3d 155
3B1.1(b)—18 F.3d 374
3B1.1(b)—18 F.3d 1332
3B1.1(b)—21 F.3d 243
3B1.1(b)—23 F.3d 135
3B1.1(b)—733 F.Supp. 1195
3B1.1(b)—740 F.Supp. 1502
3B1.1(b)—778 F.Supp. 393
3B1.1(b)—784 F.Supp. 1373
3B1.1(b)—814 F.Supp. 964
3B1.1(b)—833 F.Supp. 1454
3B1.1(b)—835 F.Supp. 1501
3B1.1(c)—871 F.2d 511
3B1.1(c)—873 F.2d 709
3B1.1(c)—874 F.2d 43
3B1.1(c)—874 F.2d 250
3B1.1(c)—878 F.2d 164
3B1.1(c)—878 F.2d 997
3B1.1(c)—884 F.2d 1090
3B1.1(c)—888 F.2d 117
3B1.1(c)—889 F.2d 1056
3B1.1(c)—891 F.2d 921
3B1.1(c)—893 F.2d 690
3B1.1(c)—894 F.2d 208
3B1.1(c)—895 F.2d 24
3B1.1(c)—895 F.2d 641
3B1.1(c)—896 F.2d 1071
3B1.1(c)—897 F.2d 1217
3B1.1(c)—897 F.2d 1558
3B1.1(c)—898 F.2d 987
3B1.1(c)—899 F.2d 177
3B1.1(c)—899 F.2d 1531
3B1.1(c)—900 F.2d 1098
3B1.1(c)—900 F.2d 1207
3B1.1(c)—901 F.2d 867
3B1.1(c)—901 F.2d 1528
3B1.1(c)—902 F.2d 1501
3B1.1(c)—903 F.2d 1336
3B1.1(c)—904 F.2d 441
3B1.1(c)—905 F.2d 1292
3B1.1(c)—908 F.2d 179
3B1.1(c)—908 F.2d 1312
3B1.1(c)—909 F.2d 1443
3B1.1(c)—911 F.2d 403
3B1.1(c)—911 F.2d 613
3B1.1(c)—911 F.2d 1456
3B1.1(c)—912 F.2d 204
3B1.1(c)—913 F.2d 770
3B1.1(c)—914 F.2d 565
3B1.1(c)—914 F.2d 699
3B1.1(c)—914 F.2d 1288
3B1.1(c)—918 F.2d 52
3B1.1(c)—919 F.2d 1471
3B1.1(c)—919 F.2d 461
3B1.1(c)—920 F.2d 1218
3B1.1(c)—922 F.2d 675
3B1.1(c)—923 F.2d 221
3B1.1(c)—925 F.2d 107
3B1.1(c)—926 F.2d 649
3B1.1(c)—927 F.2d 8
3B1.1(c)—927 F.2d 139
3B1.1(c)—928 F.2d 769
3B1.1(c)—928 F.2d 810
3B1.1(c)—929 F.2d 213
3B1.1(c)—930 F.2d 795
3B1.1(c)—931 F.2d 16
3B1.1(c)—932 F.2d 1174
3B1.1(c)—934 F.2d 411
3B1.1(c)—934 F.2d 553
3B1.1(c)—935 F.2d 9
3B1.1(c)—935 F.2d 739
3B1.1(c)—936 F.2d 648
3B1.1(c)—936 F.2d 1021
3B1.1(c)—936 F.2d 1561
3B1.1(c)—941 F.2d 8

3B1.1(c)—941 F.2d 770
3B1.1(c)—942 F.2d 606
3B1.1(c)—943 F.2d 305
3B1.1(c)—945 F.2d 378
3B1.1(c)—945 F.2d 1378
3B1.1(c)—946 F.2d 362
3B1.1(c)—946 F.2d 430
3B1.1(c)—946 F.2d 1191
3B1.1(c)—947 F.2d 224
3B1.1(c)—947 F.2d 893
3B1.1(c)—948 F.2d 66
3B1.1(c)—948 F.2d 352
3B1.1(c)—949 F.2d 522
3B1.1(c)—950 F.2d 70
3B1.1(c)—951 F.2d 887
3B1.1(c)—952 F.2d 171
3B1.1(c)—952 F.2d 289
3B1.1(c)—953 F.2d 351
3B1.1(c)—954 F.2d 155
3B1.1(c)—954 F.2d 340
3B1.1(c)—954 F.2d 928
3B1.1(c)—954 F.2d 1386
3B1.1(c)—954 F.2d 1413
3B1.1(c)—955 F.2d 1116
3B1.1(c)—956 F.2d 351
3B1.1(c)—956 F.2d 1079
3B1.1(c)—956 F.2d 1465
3B1.1(c)—957 F.2d 694
3B1.1(c)—958 F.2d 624
3B1.1(c)—959 F.2d 375
3B1.1(c)—962 F.2d 409
3B1.1(c)—962 F.2d 1410
3B1.1(c)—964 F.2d 325
3B1.1(c)—966 F.2d 707
3B1.1(c)—967 F.2d 456
3B1.1(c)—968 F.2d 729
3B1.1(c)—969 F.2d 689
3B1.1(c)—970 F.2d 960
3B1.1(c)—970 F.2d 1414
3B1.1(c)—971 F.2d 706
3B1.1(c)—971 F.2d 876
3B1.1(c)—973 F.2d 611
3B1.1(c)—974 F.2d 57
3B1.1(c)—974 F.2d 140
3B1.1(c)—976 F.2d 198
3B1.1(c)—978 F.2d 166
3B1.1(c)—978 F.2d 643
3B1.1(c)—979 F.2d 116
3B1.1(c)—979 F.2d 790
3B1.1(c)—981 F.2d 1398
3B1.1(c)—982 F.2d 970
3B1.1(c)—983 F.2d 604
3B1.1(c)—983 F.2d 757
3B1.1(c)—983 F.2d 1468
3B1.1(c)—984 F.2d 928
3B1.1(c)—985 F.2d 21
3B1.1(c)—985 F.2d 962
3B1.1(c)—986 F.2d 379
3B1.1(c)—986 F.2d 1091
3B1.1(c)—988 F.2d 641
3B1.1(c)—989 F.2d 20
3B1.1(c)—989 F.2d 180
3B1.1(c)—990 F.2d 1099
3B1.1(c)—990 F.2d 1456
3B1.1(c)—992 F.2d 573
3B1.1(c)—993 F.2d 620
3B1.1(c) [1992]—994 F.2d 63
3B1.1(c)—994 F.2d 386
3B1.1(c)—994 F.2d 417
3B1.1(c)—994 F.2d 1510
3B1.1(c)—995 F.2d 182
3B1.1(c)—995 F.2d 1493
3B1.1(c)—996 F.2d 1009
3B1.1(c)—996 F.2d 1307
3B1.1(c)—997 F.2d 78
3B1.1(c)—997 F.2d 687
3B1.1(c)—999 F.2d 814
3B1.1(c)—1 F.3d 998
3B1.1(c)—1 F.3d 1501
3B1.1(c)—3 F.3d 667
3B1.1(c)—4 F.3d 579
3B1.1(c)—5 F.3d 345
3B1.1(c)—8 F.3d 864
3B1.1(c)—9 F.3d 54
3B1.1(c)—10 F.3d 1058
3B1.1(c)—11 F.3d 1133
3B1.1(c)—14 F.3d 300
3B1.1(c)—14 F.3d 802
3B1.1(c)—15 F.3d 75
3B1.1(c)—16 F.3d 897
3B1.1(c)—17 F.3d 865
3B1.1(c)—18 F.3d 562
3B1.1(c)—21 F.3d 1302
3B1.1(c)—22 F.3d 182
3B1.1(c)—23 F.3d 278
3B1.1(c)—701 F.Supp. 138
3B1.1(c)—733 F.Supp. 1195
3B1.1(c)—761 F.Supp. 697
3B1.1(c)—819 F.Supp. 250
3B1.1-3B1.4—14 F.3d -1030

3B1.1-3B1.4—877 F.2d 3
3B1.1 et seq.—895 F.2d 932
3B1.1 et seq.—922 F.2d 1061
3B1.1 et seq.—956 F.2d 1555
3B1.1 et seq.—970 F.2d 614
3B1.1 et seq.—1 F.3d 998
3B1.1 et seq.—814 F.Supp. 382
3B1.1 et seq.—819 F.Supp. 250
3B1.1 comment—871 F.2d 511
3B1.1 comment—884 F.2d 1090
3B1.1 comment—890 F.2d 855
3B1.1 comment—894 F.2d 208
3B1.1 comment—895 F.2d 641
3B1.1 comment—896 F.2d 842
3B1.1 comment—899 F.2d 1531
3B1.1 comment—904 F.2d 441
3B1.1 comment—907 F.2d 7
3B1.1 comment—907 F.2d 1494
3B1.1 comment—908 F.2d 1229
3B1.1 comment—911 F.2d 1456
3B1.1 comment—913 F.2d 770
3B1.1 comment—920 F.2d 538
3B1.1 comment—920 F.2d 1179
3B1.1 comment—922 F.2d 748
3B1.1 comment—922 F.2d 1061
3B1.1 comment—926 F.2d 649
3B1.1 comment—928 F.2d 810
3B1.1 comment—929 F.2d 213
3B1.1 comment—931 F.2d 631
3B1.1 comment—932 F.2d 651
3B1.1 comment—934 F.2d 553
3B1.1 comment—934 F.2d 1114
3B1.1 comment—935 F.2d 832
3B1.1 comment—936 F.2d 648
3B1.1 comment—936 F.2d 1292
3B1.1 comment—939 F.2d 135
3B1.1 comment—942 F.2d 528
3B1.1 comment—943 F.2d 1543
3B1.1 comment—944 F.2d 1106
3B1.1 comment—947 F.2d 224
3B1.1 comment—947 F.2d 1120
3B1.1 comment—950 F.2d 70
3B1.1 comment—951 F.2d 580
3B1.1 comment—951 F.2d 1164
3B1.1 comment—952 F.2d 267
3B1.1 comment—952 F.2d 1026
3B1.1 comment—954 F.2d 155
3B1.1 comment—954 F.2d 674
3B1.1 comment—956 F.2d 864
3B1.1 comment—959 F.2d 375
3B1.1 comment—959 F.2d 1187
3B1.1 comment—959 F.2d 1514
3B1.1 comment—960 F.2d 51
3B1.1 comment—960 F.2d 256
3B1.1 comment—960 F.2d 449
3B1.1 comment—960 F.2d 1112
3B1.1 comment—961 F.2d 121
3B1.1 comment—961 F.2d 787
3B1.1 comment—962 F.2d 739
3B1.1 comment—964 F.2d 687
3B1.1 comment—966 F.2d 1270
3B1.1 comment—968 F.2d 575
3B1.1 comment—969 F.2d 685
3B1.1 comment—969 F.2d 858
3B1.1 comment—971 F.2d 562
3B1.1 comment—971 F.2d 656
3B1.1 comment—971 F.2d 1302
3B1.1 comment—971 F.2d 1441
3B1.1 comment—978 F.2d 166
3B1.1 comment—978 F.2d 573
3B1.1 comment—979 F.2d 116
3B1.1 comment—979 F.2d 790
3B1.1 comment—981 F.2d 664
3B1.1 comment—983 F.2d 165
3B1.1 comment—983 F.2d 1468
3B1.1 comment—985 F.2d 15
3B1.1 comment—985 F.2d 612
3B1.1 comment—985 F.2d 860
3B1.1 comment—985 F.2d 1263
3B1.1 comment—986 F.2d 439
3B1.1 comment—988 F.2d 544
3B1.1 comment—988 F.2d 750
3B1.1 comment—988 F.2d 970
3B1.1 comment—989 F.2d 20
3B1.1 comment—992 F.2d 1472
3B1.1 comment—994 F.2d 63
3B1.1 comment—995 F.2d 182
3B1.1 comment—995 F.2d 1407
3B1.1 comment—995 F.2d 1493
3B1.1 comment—996 F.2d 209
3B1.1 comment—1 F.3d 473
3B1.1 comment—1 F.3d 662
3B1.1 comment—1 F.3d 998
3B1.1 comment—5 F.3d 254
3B1.1 comment—8 F.3d 186
3B1.1 comment—9 F.3d 576
3B1.1 comment—11 F.3d 777
3B1.1 comment—11 F.3d 1411
3B1.1 comment [1993]—12 F.3d 1162
3B1.1 comment—13 F.3d 1

3B1.1 comment—13 F.3d 855
3B1.1 comment—14 F.3d 502
3B1.1 comment [1991]—19 F.3d 929
3B1.1 comment—20 F.3d 670
3B1.1 comment—21 F.3d 1302
3B1.1 comment—740 F.Supp. 1502
3B1.1 comment—753 F.Supp. 1260
3B1.1 comment—756 F.Supp. 23
3B1.1 comment—778 F.Supp. 393
3B1.1 comment—784 F.Supp. 1373
3B1.1 comment—796 F.Supp. 853
3B1.1 comment—814 F.Supp. 964
3B1.2—863 F.2d 245
3B1.2—867 F.2d 213
3B1.2—867 F.2d 216
3B1.2—868 F.2d 135
3B1.2—868 F.2d 711
3B1.2—868 F.2d 1409
3B1.2—868 F.2d 1410
3B1.2—869 F.2d 797
3B1.2—870 F.2d 174
3B1.2—873 F.2d 437
3B1.2—874 F.2d 213
3B1.2—875 F.2d 427
3B1.2—876 F.2d 1121
3B1.2—878 F.2d 1299
3B1.2—879 F.2d 454
3B1.2—879 F.2d 541
3B1.2—880 F.2d 376
3B1.2—883 F.2d 781
3B1.2—883 F.2d 963
3B1.2—886 F.2d 220
3B1.2—886 F.2d 736
3B1.2—887 F.2d 485
3B1.2—887 F.2d 568
3B1.2—888 F.2d 752
3B1.2—888 F.2d 1122
3B1.2—890 F.2d 102
3B1.2—890 F.2d 717
3B1.2—890 F.2d 1040
3B1.2—891 F.2d 300
3B1.2—891 F.2d 364
3B1.2—894 F.2d 340
3B1.2—894 F.2d 1085
3B1.2—895 F.2d 932
3B1.2—895 F.2d 1178
3B1.2—895 F.2d 1362
3B1.2—897 F.2d 47
3B1.2—898 F.2d 373
3B1.2—898 F.2d 442
3B1.2—898 F.2d 1400
3B1.2—899 F.2d 465
3B1.2—899 F.2d 582
3B1.2—900 F.2d 1207
3B1.2—901 F.2d 11
3B1.2—901 F.2d 85
3B1.2—902 F.2d 336
3B1.2—902 F.2d 501
3B1.2—903 F.2d 91
3B1.2—903 F.2d 1336
3B1.2—905 F.2d 195
3B1.2—905 F.2d 1034
3B1.2—905 F.2d 1296
3B1.2—906 F.2d 597
3B1.2—906 F.2d 1261
3B1.2—907 F.2d 11
3B1.2—907 F.2d 94
3B1.2—907 F.2d 671
3B1.2—908 F.2d 56
3B1.2—908 F.2d 1443
3B1.2—910 F.2d 601
3B1.2—911 F.2d 421
3B1.2—913 F.2d 705
3B1.2—913 F.2d 1278
3B1.2—914 F.2d 213
3B1.2—915 F.2d 612
3B1.2—916 F.2d 27
3B1.2—917 F.2d 797
3B1.2—918 F.2d 664
3B1.2 [1990]—918 F.2d 1268
3B1.2—918 F.2d 1551
3B1.2—919 F.2d 606
3B1.2—919 F.2d 652
3B1.2—920 F.2d 153
3B1.2—920 F.2d 714
3B1.2—921 F.2d 1569
3B1.2—922 F.2d 1061
3B1.2—923 F.2d 369
3B1.2—923 F.2d 1079
3B1.2—923 F.2d 1397
3B1.2—924 F.2d 201
3B1.2—924 F.2d 298
3B1.2—924 F.2d 454
3B1.2—925 F.2d 335
3B1.2—925 F.2d 1242
3B1.2—927 F.2d 1
3B1.2—927 F.2d 14
3B1.2—927 F.2d 139
3B1.2—927 F.2d 170
3B1.2—928 F.2d 1450

3B1.2—929 F.2d 563
3B1.2—929 F.2d 753
3B1.2—930 F.2d 1096
3B1.2—930 F.2d 1375
3B1.2—931 F.2d 1139
3B1.2—931 F.2d 1201
3B1.2—932 F.2d 1529
3B1.2—933 F.2d 1117
3B1.2—934 F.2d 1325
3B1.2—934 F.2d 1440
3B1.2—935 F.2d 39
3B1.2—935 F.2d 766
3B1.2—936 F.2d 292
3B1.2—936 F.2d 661
3B1.2—936 F.2d 1292
3B1.2—938 F.2d 456
3B1.2—938 F.2d 744
3B1.2—939 F.2d 244
3B1.2—939 F.2d 416
3B1.2—940 F.2d 1128
3B1.2—940 F.2d 1134
3B1.2—940 F.2d 1352
3B1.2—941 F.2d 770
3B1.2—941 F.2d 844
3B1.2—942 F.2d 1200
3B1.2—945 F.2d 264
3B1.2—946 F.2d 129
3B1.2—947 F.2d 211
3B1.2—948 F.2d 1
3B1.2—948 F.2d 444
3B1.2—948 F.2d 776
3B1.2—949 F.2d 817
3B1.2—949 F.2d 247
3B1.2—949 F.2d 532
3B1.2—950 F.2d 70
3B1.2—951 F.2d 308
3B1.2—952 F.2d 934
3B1.2—953 F.2d 452
3B1.2—954 F.2d 12
3B1.2—954 F.2d 788
3B1.2—954 F.2d 928
3B1.2—954 F.2d 1375
3B1.2—955 F.2d 441
3B1.2 [1988]—955 F.2d 1492
3B1.2—957 F.2d 36
3B1.2—957 F.2d 643
3B1.2—960 F.2d 1112
3B1.2—963 F.2d 63
3B1.2—963 F.2d 1027
3B1.2—965 F.2d 20
3B1.2—965 F.2d 460
3B1.2—966 F.2d 707
3B1.2—967 F.2d 728
3B1.2—968 F.2d 1193
3B1.2—971 F.2d 597
3B1.2—971 F.2d 1189
3B1.2—973 F.2d 396
3B1.2—973 F.2d 769
3B1.2—973 F.2d 1422
3B1.2—973 F.2d 1441
3B1.2—974 F.2d 84
3B1.2—974 F.2d 246
3B1.2—975 F.2d 1225
3B1.2—976 F.2d 1446
3B1.2—977 F.2d 331
3B1.2—978 F.2d 1463
3B1.2—979 F.2d 51
3B1.2—979 F.2d 1557
3B1.2—981 F.2d 1398
3B1.2—983 F.2d 968
3B1.2—984 F.2d 769
3B1.2—984 F.2d 1476
3B1.2—987 F.2d 1459
3B1.2—988 F.2d 206
3B1.2—990 F.2d 72
3B1.2—990 F.2d 1099
3B1.2—990 F.2d 1456
3B1.2—991 F.2d 1
3B1.2—991 F.2d 1065
3B1.2—991 F.2d 1493
3B1.2—991 F.2d 1519
3B1.2—993 F.2d 196
3B1.2—996 F.2d 209
3B1.2—996 F.2d 436
3B1.2—997 F.2d 248
3B1.2—997 F.2d 525
3B1.2—998 F.2d 84
3B1.2—999 F.2d 392
3B1.2—999 F.2d 663
3B1.2—1 F.3d 330
3B1.2—1 F.3d 423
3B1.2—1 F.3d 1098
3B1.2—2 F.3d 574
3B1.2—3 F.3d 506
3B1.2—4 F.3d 1026
3B1.2—5 F.3d 192
3B1.2—5 F.3d 480
3B1.2—6 F.3d 1201
3B1.2 [1992]—6 F.3d 1201
3B1.2—8 F.3d 186

3B1.2—10 F.3d 1463
3B1.2—11 F.3d 1411
3B1.2—12 F.3d 1350
3B1.2—13 F.3d 203
3B1.2—13 F.3d 711
3B1.2—13 F.3d 1381
3B1.2—14 F.3d 1128
3B1.2—15 F.3d 856
3B1.2—15 F.3d 902
3B1.2—16 F.3d 1110
3B1.2—18 F.3d 374
3B1.2—18 F.3d 541
3B1.2—18 F.3d 1254
3B1.2—19 F.3d 166
3B1.2—20 F.3d 320
3B1.2—22 F.3d 139
3B1.2—732 F.Supp. 878
3B1.2—740 F.Supp. 1502
3B1.2—756 F.supp. 23
3B1.2—760 F.Supp. 1322
3B1.2—768 F.Supp. 1277
3B1.2—776 F.Supp. 1030
3B1.2—802 F.Supp. 859
3B1.2—804 F.Supp. 19
3B1.2—811 F.Supp. 1106
3B1.2—814 F.Supp. 382
3B1.2—817 F.Supp. 839
3B1.2—818 F.Supp. 812
3B1.2—827 F.Supp. 205
3B1.2(a)—868 F.2d 135
3B1.2(a)—873 F.2d 23
3B1.2(a)—873 F.2d 182
3B1.2(a)—884 F.2d 1550
3B1.2(a)—885 F.2d 243
3B1.2(a)—891 F.2d 300
3B1.2(a)—891 F.2d 396
3B1.2(a)—895 F.2d 51
3B1.2(a)—899 F.2d 371
3B1.2(a)—902 F.2d 867
3B1.2(a)—909 F.2d 176
3B1.2(a)—913 F.2d 1278
3B1.2(a)—917 F.2d 1370
3B1.2(a)—925 F.2d 535
3B1.2(a)—928 F.2d 339
3B1.2(a)—930 F.2d 811
3B1.2(a)—939 F.2d 412
3B1.2(a)—939 F.2d 416
3B1.2(a)—939 F.2d 591
3B1.2(a)—940 F.2d 176
3B1.2(a)—944 F.2d 545
3B1.2(a)—946 F.2d 129
3B1.2(a)—948 F.2d 1033
3B1.2(a)—951 F.2d 405
3B1.2(a)—961 F.2d 685
3B1.2(a)—962 F.2d 1228
3B1.2(a)—965 F.2d 460
3B1.2(a)—967 F.2d 728
3B1.2(a)—971 F.2d 597
3B1.2(a)—973 F.2d 1422
3B1.2(a)—973 F.2d 1441
3B1.2(a)—976 F.2d 1446
3B1.2(a)—986 F.2d 349
3B1.2(a)—989 F.2d 20
3B1.2(a)—990 F.2d 1083
3B1.2(a)—994 F.2d 942
3B1.2(a) [1990]—996 F.2d 456
3B1.2(a)—996 F.2d 1307
3B1.2(a)—997 F.2d 248
3B1.2(a)—998 F.2d 53
3B1.2(a)—998 F.2d 791
3B1.2(a)—3 F.3d 1496
3B1.2(a)—8 F.3d 186
3B1.2(a)—14 F.3d 1030
3B1.2(a)—22 F.3d 76
3B1.2(a)—22 F.3d 783
3B1.2(a)—704 F.Supp. 175
3B1.2(a)—728 F.Supp. 632
3B1.2(a)—756 F.Supp. 23
3B1.2(a)—776 F.Supp. 1030
3B1.2(a)—782 F.Supp. 747
3B1.2(a)—784 F.Supp. 849
3B1.2(a)—814 F.Supp. 382
3B1.2(b)—868 F.2d 714
3B1.2(b)—875 F.2d 427
3B1.2(b)—875 F.2d 674
3B1.2(b)—885 F.2d 1353
3B1.2(b)—890 F.2d 1040
3B1.2(b)—891 F.2d 396
3B1.2(b)—891 F.2d 1265
3B1.2(b)—894 F.2d 1085
3B1.2(b)—895 F.2d 51
3B1.2(b)—896 F.2d 392
3B1.2(b)—898 F.2d 659
3B1.2(b)—898 F.2d 675
3B1.2(b)—902 F.2d 133
3B1.2(b)—902 F.2d 867
3B1.2(b)—903 F.2d 1280
3B1.2(b)—905 F.2d 1092
3B1.2(b)—906 F.2d 139
3B1.2(b)—907 F.2d 1028

3B1.2(b)—909 F.2d 176
3B1.2(b)—909 F.2d 417
3B1.2(b)—911 F.2d 424
3B1.2(b)—914 F.2d 206
3B1.2(b)—914 F.2d 330
3B1.2(b)—914 F.2d 966
3B1.2(b)—917 F.2d 1370
3B1.2(b)—922 F.2d 1234
3B1.2(b)—927 F.2d 14
3B1.2(b)—928 F.2d 339
3B1.2(b)—930 F.2d 811
3B1.2(b)—932 F.2d 1029
3B1.2(b)—934 F.2d 875
3B1.2(b)—936 F.2d 1292
3B1.2(b)—937 F.2d 485
3B1.2(b)—938 F.2d 1
3B1.2(b)—939 F.2d 591
3B1.2(b)—940 F.2d 176
3B1.2(b)—942 F.2d 528
3B1.2(b)—942 F.2d 556
3B1.2(b)—944 F.2d 545
3B1.2(b)—945 F.2d 826
3B1.2(b)—946 F.2d 129
3B1.2(b)—946 F.2d 162
3B1.2(b)—951 F.2d 405
3B1.2(b)—954 F.2d 155
3B1.2(b)—956 F.2d 341
3B1.2(b)—956 F.2d 939
3B1.2(b)—957 F.2d 671
3B1.2(b)—957 F.2d 1138
3B1.2(b)—959 F.2d 1181
3B1.2(b)—960 F.2d 226
3B1.2(b)—961 F.2d 685
3B1.2(b)—962 F.2d 100
3B1.2(b)—963 F.2d 1027
3B1.2(b)—965 F.2d 460
3B1.2(b)—965 F.2d 1124
3B1.2(b)—967 F.2d 101
3B1.2(b)—967 F.2d 497
3B1.2(b)—967 F.2d 728
3B1.2(b)—968 F.2d 1042
3B1.2(b)—971 F.2d 1206
3B1.2(b)—973 F.2d 1422
3B1.2(b)—973 F.2d 1441
3B1.2(b)—978 F.2d 759
3B1.2(b)—981 F.2d 1123
3B1.2(b)—986 F.2d 349
3B1.2(b)—987 F.2d 475
3B1.2(b)—988 F.2d 1494
3B1.2(b)—989 F.2d 20
3B1.2(b)—990 F.2d 419
3B1.2(b)—995 F.2d 711
3B1.2(b)—995 F.2d 1493
3B1.2(b) [1990]—996 F.2d 456
3B1.2(b)—996 F.2d 1307
3B1.2(b)—998 F.2d 53
3B1.2(b)—999 F.2d 663
3B1.2(b)—999 F.2d 1073
3B1.2(b)—1 F.3d 423
3B1.2(b)—1 F.3d 473
3B1.2(b)—1 F.3d 662
3B1.2(b)—1 F.3d 691
3B1.2(b)—2 F.3d 286
3B1.2(b)—2 F.3d 723
3B1.2(b)—3 F.3d 266
3B1.2(b)—3 F.3d 1005
3B1.2(b)—8 F.3d 186
3B1.2(b)—11 F.3d 315
3B1.2(b)—14 F.3d 1030
3B1.2(b)—15 F.3d 825
3B1.2(b)—17 F.3d 409
3B1.2(b)—21 F.3d 309
3B1.2(b)—22 F.3d 76
3B1.2(b)—22 F.3d 783
3B1.2(b)—704 F.Supp. 175
3B1.2(b)—793 F.Supp. 64
3B1.2(b)—814 F.Supp. 382
3B1.2(b)—816 F.Supp. 26
3B1.2 comment—867 F.2d 213
3B1.2 comment—868 F.2d 711
3B1.2 comment—873 F.2d 182
3B1.2 comment—880 F.2d 376
3B1.2 comment—888 F.2d 752
3B1.2 comment—890 F.2d 102
3B1.2 comment—890 F.2d 717
3B1.2 comment—893 F.2d 690
3B1.2 comment—894 F.2d 1085
3B1.2 comment—895 F.2d 932
3B1.2 comment—898 F.2d 373
3B1.2 comment—898 F.2d 1400
3B1.2 comment—899 F.2d 371
3B1.2 comment—899 F.2d 465
3B1.2 comment—901 F.2d 85
3B1.2 comment—902 F.2d 501
3B1.2 comment—902 F.2d 867
3B1.2 comment—905 F.2d 1144
3B1.2 comment—905 F.2d 1429
3B1.2 comment—907 F.2d 1028
3B1.2 comment—908 F.2d 56
3B1.2 comment—910 F.2d 703

3B1.2 comment—911 F.2d 149
3B1.2 comment—911 F.2d 421
3B1.2 comment—911 F.2d 424
3B1.2 comment—913 F.2d 1278
3B1.2 comment—917 F.2d 502
3B1.2 comment—918 F.2d 1551
3B1.2 comment—921 F.2d 1569
3B1.2 comment—925 F.2d 101
3B1.2 comment—925 F.2d 112
3B1.2 comment—925 F.2d 335
3B1.2 comment—927 F.2d 14
3B1.2 comment—928 F.2d 339
3B1.2 comment—928 F.2d 1450
3B1.2 comment—930 F.2d 1486
3B1.2 comment—931 F.2d 1139
3B1.2 comment—932 F.2d 1029
3B1.2 comment—932 F.2d 1529
3B1.2 comment—933 F.2d 1117
3B1.2 comment—934 F.2d 875
3B1.2 comment—935 F.2d 766
3B1.2 comment—936 F.2d 661
3B1.2 comment—937 F.2d 485
3B1.2 comment—937 F.2d 716
3B1.2 comment—939 F.2d 244
3B1.2 comment—942 F.2d 528
3B1.2 comment—945 F.2d 264
3B1.2 comment—946 F.2d 129
3B1.2 comment—948 F.2d 817
3B1.2 comment—948 F.2d 1033
3B1.2 comment—950 F.2d 70
3B1.2 comment—951 F.2d 308
3B1.2 comment—951 F.2d 405
3B1.2 comment—953 F.2d 452
3B1.2 comment—954 F.2d 1375
3B1.2 comment—955 F.2d 547
3B1.2 comment—957 F.2d 671
3B1.2 comment—962 F.2d 100
3B1.2 comment—963 F.2d 63
3B1.2 comment—963 F.2d 1027
3B1.2 comment—965 F.2d 460
3B1.2 comment—965 F.2d 1124
3B1.2 comment—967 F.2d 497
3B1.2 comment—973 F.2d 1422
3B1.2 comment—973 F.2d 1441
3B1.2 comment—975 F.2d 1225
3B1.2 comment—977 F.2d 331
3B1.2 comment—978 F.2d 1463
3B1.2 comment—979 F.2d 369
3B1.2 comment—983 F.2d 968
3B1.2 comment—985 F.2d 271
3B1.2 comment—986 F.2d 349
3B1.2 comment—990 F.2d 1099
3B1.2 comment—991 F.2d 409
3B1.2 comment—995 F.2d 1493
3B1.2 comment—996 F.2d 436
3B1.2 comment [1990]—996 F.2d 456
3B1.2 comment—997 F.2d 78
3B1.2 comment—997 F.2d 248
3B1.2 comment—997 F.2d 651
3B1.2 comment—998 F.2d 84
3B1.2 comment—999 F.2d 663
3B1.2 comment—999 F.2d 1053
3B1.2 comment—3 F.3d 1496
3B1.2 comment—4 F.3d 1006
3B1.2 comment—4 F.3d 1026
3B1.2 comment [1992]—6 F.3d 1201
3B1.2 comment—8 F.3d 186
3B1.2 comment—10 F.3d 1197
3B1.2 comment—12 F.3d 1540
3B1.2 comment—14 F.3d 1030
3B1.2 comment—14 F.3d 1128
3B1.2 comment—15 F.3d 825
3B1.2 comment—17 F.3d 409
3B1.2 comment—18 F.3d 541
3B1.2 comment—22 F.3d 76
3B1.2 comment—740 F.Supp. 1502
3B1.2 comment—784 F.Supp. 849
3B1.2 comment—811 F.Supp. 1106
3B1.3—867 F.2d 216
3B1.3—876 F.2d 377
3B1.3—878 F.2d 1377
3B1.3—902 F.2d 327
3B1.3—902 F.2d 1129
3B1.3—903 F.2d 91
3B1.3—905 F.2d 337
3B1.3—905 F.2d 1304
3B1.3—905 F.2d 1335
3B1.3—906 F.2d 323
3B1.3—909 F.2d 176
3B1.3—910 F.2d 1016
3B1.3—913 F.2d 59
3B1.3—913 F.2d 705
3B1.3—915 F.2d 502
3B1.3—915 F.2d 942
3B1.3—917 F.2d 773
3B1.3—918 F.2d 707
3B1.3—922 F.2d 1162
3B1.3—926 F.2d 387
3B1.3—926 F.2d 792
3B1.3—929 F.2d 307

3B1.3—929 F.2d 389
3B1.3—931 F.2d 1035
3B1.3—932 F.2d 1035
3B1.3—932 F.2d 1510
3B1.3—933 F.2d 1219
3B1.3—934 F.2d 248
3B1.3—936 F.2d 57
3B1.3—938 F.2d 764
3B1.3—940 F.2d 1
3B1.3—941 F.2d 1300
3B1.3—943 F.2d 798
3B1.3—943 F.2d 1032
3B1.3—944 F.2d 14
3B1.3—953 F.2d 867
3B1.3—953 F.2d 939
3B1.3—955 F.2d 77
3B1.3—955 F.2d 170
3B1.3—958 F.2d 285
3B1.3—958 F.2d 345
3B1.3—960 F.2d 191
3B1.3—960 F.2d 587
3B1.3—961 F.2d 462
3B1.3—961 F.2d 892
3B1.3—962 F.2d 938
3B1.3—963 F.2d 641
3B1.3—965 F.2d 887
3B1.3—966 F.2d 555
3B1.3—969 F.2d 1283
3B1.3—971 F.2d 989
3B1.3—972 F.2d 590
3B1.3—973 F.2d 832
3B1.3—976 F.2d 608
3B1.3—978 F.2d 421
3B1.3—979 F.2d 21
3B1.3—979 F.2d 469
3B1.3—979 F.2d 816
3B1.3—982 F.2d 269
3B1.3—983 F.2d 92
3B1.3—985 F.2d 930
3B1.3—989 F.2d 44
3B1.3—989 F.2d 447
3B1.3—990 F.2d 98
3B1.3—991 F.2d 1110
3B1.3—992 F.2d 171
3B1.3—992 F.2d 1081
3B1.3—993 F.2d 338
3B1.3—993 F.2d 902
3B1.3—993 F.2d 1224
3B1.3—994 F.2d 658
3B1.3—994 F.2d 942
3B1.3—996 F.2d 17
3B1.3 [1990]—996 F.2d 456
3B1.3—996 F.2d 1395
3B1.3—997 F.2d 139
3B1.3—999 F.2d 361
3B1.3—999 F.2d 483
3B1.3—999 F.2d 674
3B1.3—999 F.2d 1396
3B1.3—1 F.3d 46
3B1.3—2 F.3d 716
3B1.3—2 F.3d 1107
3B1.3—4 F.3d 115
3B1.3—4 F.3d 904
3B1.3 [1991]—4 F.3d 925
3B1.3 [1991]—5 F.3d 404
3B1.3—5 F.3d 467
3B1.3—6 F.3d 415
3B1.3—6 F.3d 1415
3B1.3—7 F.3d 69
3B1.3—7 F.3d 1155
3B1.3—10 F.3d 1
3B1.3—10 F.3d 485
3B1.3—14 F.3d 1364
3B1.3—15 F.3d 131
3B1.3—15 F.3d 740
3B1.3—15 F.3d 784
3B1.3—16 F.3d 599
3B1.3—16 F.3d 985
3B1.3—18 F.3d 562
3B1.3—21 F.3d 759
3B1.3—22 F.3d 330
3B1.3—22 F.3d 783
3B1.3—712 F.Supp. 707
3B1.3—751 F.Supp. 315
3B1.3—759 F.Supp. 1258
3B1.3—765 F.Supp. 945
3B1.3—768 F.Supp. 1277
3B1.3—800 F.Supp. 648
3B1.3—801 F.Supp. 59
3B1.3—803 F.Supp. 53
3B1.3—837 F.Supp. 916
3B1.3 comment—902 F.2d 327
3B1.3 comment—915 F.2d 502
3B1.3 comment—916 F.2d 186
3B1.3 comment—918 F.2d 707
3B1.3 comment—926 F.2d 792
3B1.3 comment—936 F.2d 57
3B1.3 comment—940 F.2d 261
3B1.3 comment—941 F.2d 1300
3B1.3 comment—943 F.2d 1032

3B1.3 comment—955 F.2d 170
3B1.3 comment—960 F.2d 191
3B1.3 comment—961 F.2d 462
3B1.3 comment—962 F.2d 938
3B1.3 comment—966 F.2d 555
3B1.3 comment—972 F.2d 591
3B1.3 comment—976 F.2d 608
3B1.3 comment—979 F.2d 21
3B1.3 comment—979 F.2d 469
3B1.3 comment—982 F.2d 269
3B1.3 comment—983 F.2d 92
3B1.3 comment—990 F.2d 98
3B1.3 comment—993 F.2d 902
3B1.3 comment—994 F.2d 1262
3B1.3 comment—996 F.2d 1395
3B1.3 comment—997 F.2d 139
3B1.3 comment—999 F.2d 361
3B1.3 comment—999 F.2d 483
3B1.3 comment—1 F.3d 13
3B1.3 comment—2 F.3d 1107
3B1.3 comment—6 F.3d 415
3B1.3 comment—7 F.3d 1155
3B1.3 comment—10 F.3d 485
3B1.3 comment—22 F.3d 330
3B1.3 comment—755 F.Supp. 942
3B1.4—874 F.2d 213
3B1.4—895 F.2d 932
3B1.4—939 F.2d 416
3B1.4—957 F.2d 643
3B1.4—971 F.2d 1441
3B1.4 comment—874 F.2d 213
3B1.4 comment—922 F.2d 1061
3B1.4 comment—971 F.2d 1441

Part C: Obstruction

3C1.1—113 S.Ct. 1111
3C1.1 [1990]—113 S.Ct. 1111
3C1.1—869 F.2d 797
3C1.1—872 F.2d 597
3C1.1—872 F.2d 632
3C1.1—872 F.2d 638
3C1.1—872 F.2d 1365
3C1.1—875 F.2d 427
3C1.1—878 F.2d 945
3C1.1—879 F.2d 454
3C1.1—879 F.2d 1247
3C1.1—880 F.2d 636
3C1.1—881 F.2d 980
3C1.1—884 F.2d 354
3C1.1—884 F.2d 1090
3C1.1—886 F.2d 474
3C1.1—887 F.2d 23
3C1.1—889 F.2d 441
3C1.1—890 F.2d 69
3C1.1—890 F.2d 968
3C1.1—891 F.2d 530
3C1.1—893 F.2d 504
3C1.1—893 F.2d 669
3C1.1—893 F.2d 996
3C1.1—894 F.2d 340
3C1.1—894 F.2d 554
3C1.1—894 F.2d 965
3C1.1—894 F.2d 1083
3C1.1—895 F.2d 882
3C1.1—897 F.2d 309
3C1.1—897 F.2d 1034
3C1.1—899 F.2d 983
3C1.1—900 F.2d 1000
3C1.1—900 F.2d 1098
3C1.1—900 F.2d 1537
3C1.1—901 F.2d 1161
3C1.1—902 F.2d 324
3C1.1—902 F.2d 501
3C1.1—903 F.2d 457
3C1.1—904 F.2d 234
3C1.1—904 F.2d 603
3C1.1—904 F.2d 1250
3C1.1—905 F.2d 295
3C1.1—905 F.2d 1034
3C1.1—905 F.2d 1315
3C1.1—906 F.2d 1366
3C1.1—907 F.2d 53
3C1.1—907 F.2d 274
3C1.1—907 F.2d 282
3C1.1—908 F.2d 56
3C1.1—908 F.2d 230
3C1.1—908 F.2d 281
3C1.1—908 F.2d 816
3C1.1—909 F.2d 119
3C1.1—909 F.2d 196
3C1.1—909 F.2d 389
3C1.1—909 F.2d 1047
3C1.1—909 F.2d 1143
3C1.1—910 F.2d 530
3C1.1—910 F.2d 1231
3C1.1—911 F.2d 227
3C1.1—911 F.2d 1031
3C1.1—911 F.2d 1456
3C1.1—912 F.2d 344

3C1.1—913 F.2d 193
3C1.1—914 F.2d 1204
3C1.1—914 F.2d 1340
3C1.1—915 F.2d 1046
3C1.1—916 F.2d 388
3C1.1—917 F.2d 165
3C1.1—917 F.2d 494
3C1.1—917 F.2d 683
3C1.1 [1990]—918 F.2d 68
3C1.1—918 F.2d 226
3C1.1—918 F.2d 707
3C1.1 [1990]—918 F.2d 1268
3C1.1—918 F.2d 1329
3C1.1—918 F.2d 1371
3C1.1—919 F.2d 842
3C1.1—919 F.2d 1325
3C1.1—919 F.2d 1365
3C1.1—919 F.2d 1390
3C1.1—920 F.2d 1377
3C1.1—922 F.2d 563
3C1.1—922 F.2d 737
3C1.1—922 F.2d 914
3C1.1—922 F.2d 1283
3C1.1—923 F.2d 112
3C1.1—923 F.2d 221
3C1.1—923 F.2d 548
3C1.1—923 F.2d 629
3C1.1—923 F.2d 1500
3C1.1—923 F.2d 1557
3C1.1—924 F.2d 116
3C1.1 [1990]—924 F.2d 223
3C1.1—925 F.2d 205
3C1.1—926 F.2d 64
3C1.1—927 F.2d 14
3C1.1—927 F.2d 111
3C1.1 [1990]—927 F.2d 300
3C1.1 [1990]—927 F.2d 303
3C1.1—927 F.2d 1361
3C1.1—927 F.2d 1463
3C1.1—928 F.2d 383
3C1.1—928 F.2d 1450
3C1.1 [1990]—928 F.2d 1450
3C1.1—929 F.2d 285
3C1.1—929 F.2d 334
3C1.1—929 F.2d 356
3C1.1—929 F.2d 1126
3C1.1—929 F.2d 1224
3C1.1—930 F.2d 526
3C1.1 [1990]—930 F.2d 1375
3C1.1—931 F.2d 33
3C1.1—931 F.2d 43
3C1.1—931 F.2d 1035
3C1.1—931 F.2d 1139
3C1.1—931 F.2d 1216
3C1.1—931 F.2d 1256
3C1.1—932 F.2d 358
3C1.1—932 F.2d 803
3C1.1—932 F.2d 1093
3C1.1—933 F.2d 152
3C1.1—933 F.2d 916
3C1.1—934 F.2d 1075
3C1.1—934 F.2d 1080
3C1.1—935 F.2d 161
3C1.1 [1990]—935 F.2d 644
3C1.1—935 F.2d 832
3C1.1—935 F.2d 1212
3C1.1—936 F.2d 23
3C1.1—936 F.2d 303
3C1.1—936 F.2d 433
3C1.1—936 F.2d 1561
3C1.1—937 F.2d 58
3C1.1—937 F.2d 1191
3C1.1—937 F.2d 1196
3C1.1—937 F.2d 1227
3C1.1—938 F.2d 29
3C1.1—938 F.2d 744
3C1.1—938 F.2d 748
3C1.1—938 F.2d 1327
3C1.1—939 F.2d 405
3C1.1—940 F.2d 1
3C1.1—940 F.2d 176
3C1.1—940 F.2d 332
3C1.1—940 F.2d 1027
3C1.1—940 F.2d 1128
3C1.1—940 F.2d 1136
3C1.1—940 F.2d 1352
3C1.1—941 F.2d 1047
3C1.1—942 F.2d 141
3C1.1—942 F.2d 899
3C1.1—942 F.2d 120
3C1.1—943 F.2d 94
3C1.1—943 F.2d 215
3C1.1—943 F.2d 305
3C1.1—943 F.2d 692
3C1.1—944 F.2d 858
3C1.1—944 F.2d 1032
3C1.1—944 F.2d 14
3C1.1—944 F.2d 88
3C1.1—944 F.2d 178
3C1.1 [1990]—944 F.2d 828

3C1.1—944 F.2d 959
3C1.1—944 F.2d 1331
3C1.1—944 F.2d 1377
3C1.1—945 F.2d 264
3C1.1—945 F.2d 1378
3C1.1—946 F.2d 650
3C1.1—947 F.2d 7
3C1.1—947 F.2d 339
3C1.1—948 F.2d 145
3C1.1—948 F.2d 783
3C1.1—948 F.2d 817
3C1.1 [1988]—948 F.2d 877
3C1.1—949 F.2d 289
3C1.1—949 F.2d 522
3C1.1—949 F.2d 713
3C1.1—949 F.2d 1013
3C1.1—949 F.2d 1023
3C1.1—950 F.2d 1267
3C1.1—951 F.2d 405
3C1.1—951 F.2d 751
3C1.1—952 F.2d 155
3C1.1—952 F.2d 164
3C1.1—952 F.2d 992
3C1.1—952 F.2d 1026
3C1.1—952 F.2d 1086
3C1.1—952 F.2d 1504
3C1.1—953 F.2d 6
3C1.1—955 F.2d 770
3C1.1—955 F.2d 1116
3C1.1—955 F.2d 1492
3C1.1 [1988]—955 F.2d 1492
3C1.1—956 F.2d 65
3C1.1—956 F.2d 135
3C1.1—956 F.2d 954
3C1.1—957 F.2d 577
3C1.1—957 F.2d 1138
3C1.1—958 F.2d 231
3C1.1—958 F.2d 806
3C1.1—959 F.2d 83
3C1.1—959 F.2d 503
3C1.1—959 F.2d 701
3C1.1—959 F.2d 1137
3C1.1—959 F.2d 1324
3C1.1—959 F.2d 1514
3C1.1—960 F.2d 226
3C1.1—960 F.2d 1384
3C1.1—961 F.2d 164
3C1.1—961 F.2d 707
3C1.1—962 F.2d 1069
3C1.1—962 F.2d 1308
3C1.1—962 F.2d 1418
3C1.1—963 F.2d 207
3C1.1—964 F.2d 365
3C1.1—964 F.2d 1017
3C1.1—965 F.2d 383
3C1.1—966 F.2d 1270
3C1.1—966 F.2d 1383
3C1.1—967 F.2d 456
3C1.1—967 F.2d 572
3C1.1—968 F.2d 208
3C1.1—968 F.2d 411
3C1.1—969 F.2d 341
3C1.1—969 F.2d 689
3C1.1—969 F.2d 926
3C1.1—969 F.2d 1419
3C1.1—970 F.2d 371
3C1.1—970 F.2d 494
3C1.1—970 F.2d 1328
3C1.1—970 F.2d 1414
3C1.1 [1990]—971 F.2d 656
3C1.1—971 F.2d 876
3C1.1—971 F.2d 1368
3C1.1 [1990]—971 F.2d 1441
3C1.1—972 F.2d 184
3C1.1—972 F.2d 201
3C1.1—972 F.2d 244
3C1.1—972 F.2d 1385
3C1.1—972 F.2d 1580
3C1.1—973 F.2d 1
3C1.1—973 F.2d 396
3C1.1—973 F.2d 611
3C1.1—973 F.2d 885
3C1.1—974 F.2d 961
3C1.1—974 F.2d 1026
3C1.1—974 F.2d 1135
3C1.1—974 F.2d 57
3C1.1—974 F.2d 104
3C1.1—975 F.2d 305
3C1.1—975 F.2d 622
3C1.1—976 F.2d 242
3C1.1—976 F.2d 1096
3C1.1—976 F.2d 1249
3C1.1—977 F.2d 283
3C1.1—977 F.2d 698
3C1.1—977 F.2d 1330
3C1.1—978 F.2d 421
3C1.1—978 F.2d 1021
3C1.1—978 F.2d 1554
3C1.1—980 F.2d 506
3C1.1—980 F.2d 705

3C1.1—980 F.2d 855
3C1.1—981 F.2d 92
3C1.1—981 F.2d 491
3C1.1—981 F.2d 569
3C1.1—981 F.2d 874
3C1.1—981 F.2d 1382
3C1.1—982 F.2d 187
3C1.1—982 F.2d 196
3C1.1—982 F.2d 965
3C1.1—983 F.2d 757
3C1.1—983 F.2d 1425
3C1.1—984 F.2d 701
3C1.1—984 F.2d 705
3C1.1—984 F.2d 1476
3C1.1—985 F.2d 341
3C1.1—985 F.2d 348
3C1.1—985 F.2d 371
3C1.1—985 F.2d 395
3C1.1—985 F.2d 427
3C1.1—985 F.2d 535
3C1.1—985 F.2d 884
3C1.1—985 F.2d 1175
3C1.1—985 F.2d 1293
3C1.1 [1988]—985 F.2d 1293
3C1.1—985 F.2d 1333
3C1.1—986 F.2d 1
3C1.1—986 F.2d 35
3C1.1—986 F.2d 151
3C1.1—987 F.2d 225
3C1.1—987 F.2d 472
3C1.1—987 F.2d 634
3C1.1 [1991]—987 F.2d 874
3C1.1—987 F.2d 1311
3C1.1—988 F.2d 82
3C1.1—988 F.2d 537
3C1.1—988 F.2d 712
3C1.1—989 F.2d 347
3C1.1—989 F.2d 454
3C1.1—989 F.2d 936
3C1.1—989 F.2d 1279
3C1.1—990 F.2d 355
3C1.1—990 F.2d 1011
3C1.1—990 F.2d 1370
3C1.1—990 F.2d 1456
3C1.1—991 F.2d 120
3C1.1—991 F.2d 304
3C1.1—991 F.2d 493
3C1.1—991 F.2d 907
3C1.1—991 F.2d 1369
3C1.1—992 F.2d 171
3C1.1—992 F.2d 573
3C1.1—992 F.2d 678
3C1.1—992 F.2d 1081
3C1.1—993 F.2d 902
3C1.1—994 F.2d 918
3C1.1—994 F.2d 980
3C1.1—994 F.2d 1262
3C1.1—994 F.2d 1499
3C1.1—994 F.2d 1510
3C1.1—995 F.2d 694
3C1.1—995 F.2d 746
3C1.1—995 F.2d 776
3C1.1—996 F.2d 982
3C1.1—996 F.2d 1288
3C1.1—996 F.2d 1395
3C1.1—997 F.2d 78
3C1.1—997 F.2d 407
3C1.1—997 F.2d 421
3C1.1—997 F.2d 1551
3C1.1—998 F.2d 53
3C1.1—998 F.2d 84
3C1.1—998 F.2d 563
3C1.1—998 F.2d 584
3C1.1—998 F.2d 1491
3C1.1—998 F.2d 1571
3C1.1—999 F.2d 14
3C1.1—999 F.2d 182
3C1.1—999 F.2d 339
3C1.1—999 F.2d 1334
3C1.1—1 F.3d 13
3C1.1—1 F.3d 382
3C1.1—1 F.3d 473
3C1.1—1 F.3d 1523
3C1.1—2 F.3d 723
3C1.1—3 F.3d 244
3C1.1—4 F.3d 100
3C1.1—4 F.3d 697
3C1.1—4 F.3d 891
3C1.1—5 F.3d 345
3C1.1—5 F.3d 467
3C1.1—5 F.3d 1365
3C1.1—5 F.3d 1546
3C1.1—6 F.3d 1262
3C1.1—7 F.3d 1186
3C1.1—8 F.3d 236
3C1.1—8 F.3d 633
3C1.1—9 F.3d 204
3C1.1—9 F.3d 576
3C1.1—9 F.3d 660
3C1.1—9 F.3d 1119

3C1.1—9 F.3d 1442
3C1.1—10 F.3d 578
3C1.1—10 F.3d 1003
3C1.1—10 F.3d 1252
3C1.1—11 F.3d 74
3C1.1—11 F.3d 152
3C1.1—11 F.3d 505
3C1.1—11 F.3d 583
3C1.1—11 F.3d 1392
3C1.1—12 F.3d 298
3C1.1—12 F.3d 618
3C1.1—12 F.3d 1436
3C1.1—13 F.3d 340
3C1.1—13 F.3d 1126
3C1.1 [1990]—13 F.3d 1464
3C1.1—14 F.3d 79
3C1.1—14 F.3d 300
3C1.1—14 F.3d 1200
3C1.1—14 F.3d 1264
3C1.1—14 F.3d 1283
3C1.1—14 F.3d 1364
3C1.1—15 F.3d 272
3C1.1—15 F.3d 784
3C1.1—15 F.3d 1292
3C1.1—16 F.3d 193
3C1.1—16 F.3d 892
3C1.1—16 F.3d 1110
3C1.1—16 F.3d 1324
3C1.1—17 F.3d 660
3C1.1—18 F.3d 581
3C1.1—19 F.3d 417
3C1.1—20 F.3d 670
3C1.1—21 F.3d 120
3C1.1—21 F.3d 250
3C1.1—21 F.3d 281
3C1.1—21 F.3d 309
3C1.1—21 F.3d 998
3C1.1—23 F.3d 300
3C1.1—684 F.Supp. 1048
3C1.1—684 F.Supp. 1535
3C1.1—710 F.Supp. 1293
3C1.1—716 F.Supp. 1009
3C1.1—731 F.Supp. 242
3C1.1—733 F.Supp. 1256
3C1.1—734 F.Supp. 842
3C1.1—737 F.Supp. 819
3C1.1—740 F.Supp. 1502
3C1.1—751 F.Supp. 368
3C1.1—751 F.Supp. 1161
3C1.1—753 F.Supp. 1260
3C1.1—761 F.Supp. 697
3C1.1—766 F.Supp. 617
3C1.1—768 F.Supp. 101
3C1.1—768 F.Supp. 1277
3C1.1—792 F.Supp. 206
3C1.1—792 F.Supp. 637
3C1.1 [1988]—797 F.Supp. 672
3C1.1—801 F.Supp. 263
3C1.1—801 F.Supp. 1407
3C1.1—802 F.Supp. 859
3C1.1—807 F.Supp. 1238
3C1.1—817 F.Supp. 1401
3C1.1—818 F.Supp. 785
3C1.1—819 F.Supp. 250
3C1.1—833 F.Supp. 769
3C1.1—834 F.Supp. 292
3C1.1—835 F.Supp. 227
3C1.1—835 F.Supp. 1466
3C1.1—835 F.Supp. 1501
3C1.1—836 F.Supp. 221
3C1.1—842 F.Supp. 92
3C1.1 et seq.—968 F.2d 411
3C1.1 et seq.—819 F.Supp. 250
3C1.1 comment—113 S.Ct. 1111
3C1.1 comment [1990]—113 S.Ct. 1111
3C1.1 comment—869 F.2d 797
3C1.1 comment—879 F.2d 1247
3C1.1 comment—884 F.2d 1090
3C1.1 comment—888 F.2d 285
3C1.1 comment—894 F.2d 1083
3C1.1 comment—900 F.2d 1000
3C1.1 comment—900 F.2d 1098
3C1.1 comment—900 F.2d 1537
3C1.1 comment—901 F.2d 1161
3C1.1 comment—904 F.2d 603
3C1.1 comment—904 F.2d 1166
3C1.1 comment—905 F.2d 1315
3C1.1 comment—907 F.2d 274
3C1.1 comment—907 F.2d 282
3C1.1 comment—908 F.2d 56
3C1.1 comment—909 F.2d 119
3C1.1 comment—909 F.2d 389
3C1.1 comment—909 F.2d 1047
3C1.1 comment—913 F.2d 1053
3C1.1 comment—914 F.2d 1340
3C1.1 comment—915 F.2d 1046
3C1.1 comment [1990]—918 F.2d 68
3C1.1 comment—918 F.2d 707
3C1.1 comment—918 F.2d 1329
3C1.1 comment [1990]—919 F.2d 1365

3C1.1 comment—922 F.2d 737
3C1.1 comment—923 F.2d 112
3C1.1 comment—923 F.2d 221
3C1.1 comment [1990]—924 F.2d 223
3C1.1 comment—926 F.2d 64
3C1.1 comment [1990]—927 F.2d 14
3C1.1 comment [1990]—927 F.2d 303
3C1.1 comment—927 F.2d 1361
3C1.1 comment—927 F.2d 1463
3C1.1 comment—928 F.2d 1450
3C1.1 comment—929 F.2d 285
3C1.1 comment—929 F.2d 1126
3C1.1 comment—929 F.2d 1224
3C1.1 comment [1990]—930 F.2d 1375
3C1.1 comment—930 F.2d 1512
3C1.1 comment—931 F.2d 33
3C1.1 comment [1988]—931 F.2d 300
3C1.1 comment—931 F.2d 1256
3C1.1 comment—932 F.2d 358
3C1.1 comment [1990]—933 F.2d 152
3C1.1 comment—935 F.2d 161
3C1.1 comment [1990]—935 F.2d 1212
3C1.1 comment—937 F.2d 58
3C1.1 comment [1990]—937 F.2d 1196
3C1.1 comment—937 F.2d 1227
3C1.1 comment—938 F.2d 748
3C1.1 comment—940 F.2d 1128
3C1.1 comment—940 F.2d 1136
3C1.1 comment—942 F.2d 899
3C1.1 comment—943 F.2d 215
3C1.1 comment [1990]—943 F.2d 873
3C1.1 comment [1990]—943 F.2d 1543
3C1.1 comment—944 F.2d 14
3C1.1 comment—944 F.2d 959
3C1.1 comment [1990]—944 F.2d 959
3C1.1 comment—944 F.2d 1331
3C1.1 comment [1990]—945 F.2d 1331
3C1.1 comment—944 F.2d 1377
3C1.1 comment—945 F.2d 264
3C1.1 comment—946 F.2d 650
3C1.1 comment [1988]—948 F.2d 877
3C1.1 comment—949 F.2d 289
3C1.1 comment—949 F.2d 1023
3C1.1 comment—949 F.2d 1465
3C1.1 comment—950 F.2d 444
3C1.1 comment—950 F.2d 1309
3C1.1 comment—951 F.2d 405
3C1.1 comment [1989]—951 F.2d 751
3C1.1 comment—952 F.2d 164
3C1.1 comment—952 F.2d 514
3C1.1 comment—952 F.2d 992
3C1.1 comment—952 F.2d 1026
3C1.1 comment—953 F.2d 6
3C1.1 comment—954 F.2d 122
3C1.1 comment—955 F.2d 1492
3C1.1 comment [1988]—955 F.2d 1492
3C1.1 comment—956 F.2d 1465
3C1.1 comment—957 F.2d 577
3C1.1 comment—957 F.2d 1138
3C1.1 comment—958 F.2d 231
3C1.1 comment—959 F.2d 701
3C1.1 comment—959 F.2d 1324
3C1.1 comment—960 F.2d 226
3C1.1 comment—961 F.2d 972
3C1.1 comment—962 F.2d 1069
3C1.1 comment—962 F.2d 1418
3C1.1 comment—964 F.2d 390
3C1.1 comment—964 F.2d 687
3C1.1 comment—964 F.2d 778
3C1.1 comment—964 F.2d 1017
3C1.1 comment—966 F.2d 1383
3C1.1 comment—967 F.2d 1550
3C1.1 comment [1988]—967 F.2d 1550
3C1.1 comment—968 F.2d 208
3C1.1 comment—969 F.2d 858
3C1.1 comment—969 F.2d 1419
3C1.1 comment—970 F.2d 1328
3C1.1 comment [1990]—971 F.2d 656
3C1.1 comment—971 F.2d 876
3C1.1 comment—971 F.2d 1368
3C1.1 comment—972 F.2d 201
3C1.1 comment—973 F.2d 1
3C1.1 comment—974 F.2d 94
3C1.1 comment—974 F.2d 1026
3C1.1 comment [1990]—974 F.2d 1135
3C1.1 comment—975 F.2d 305
3C1.1 comment—975 F.2d 397
3C1.1 comment—976 F.2d 242
3C1.1 comment—976 F.2d 1096
3C1.1 comment—977 F.2d 283
3C1.1 comment [1990]—977 F.2d 283
3C1.1 comment—977 F.2d 698
3C1.1 comment—977 F.2d 1330
3C1.1 comment—978 F.2d 421
3C1.1 comment—978 F.2d 1021
3C1.1 comment—978 F.2d 1554
3C1.1 comment—980 F.2d 60
3C1.1 comment—980 F.2d 506
3C1.1 comment—980 F.2d 705
3C1.1 comment—980 F.2d 855

3C1.1 comment—981 F.2d 569
3C1.1 comment—981 F.2d 874
3C1.1 comment—981 F.2d 1382
3C1.1 comment—982 F.2d 187
3C1.1 comment—982 F.2d 965
3C1.1 comment—983 F.2d 1468
3C1.1 comment—984 F.2d 1067
3C1.1 comment [1990]—985 F.2d 341
3C1.1 comment—985 F.2d 395
3C1.1 comment—985 F.2d 427
3C1.1 comment—985 F.2d 463
3C1.1 comment—985 F.2d 884
3C1.1 comment [1988]—985 F.2d 1293
3C1.1 comment—986 F.2d 1
3C1.1 comment—986 F.2d 1225
3C1.1 comment—988 F.2d 712
3C1.1 comment—989 F.2d 454
3C1.1 comment—989 F.2d 1279
3C1.1 comment [1991]—990 F.2d 1011
3C1.1 comment—990 F.2d 1370
3C1.1 comment—991 F.2d 304
3C1.1 comment [1990]—992 F.2d 678
3C1.1 comment—992 F.2d 1459
3C1.1 comment—993 F.2d 902
3C1.1 comment—995 F.2d 746
3C1.1 comment—996 F.2d 982
3C1.1 comment—997 F.2d 78
3C1.1 comment—997 F.2d 1288
3C1.1 comment—997 F.2d 1343
3C1.1 comment—997 F.2d 1551
3C1.1 comment—998 F.2d 184
3C1.1 comment—999 F.2d 14
3C1.1 comment—999 F.2d 182
3C1.1 comment—1 F.3d 46
3C1.1 comment—1 F.3d 382
3C1.1 comment—1 F.3d 473
3C1.1 comment—3 F.3d 244
3C1.1 comment—5 F.3d 1365
3C1.1 comment—5 F.3d 1546
3C1.1 comment—7 F.3d 783
3C1.1 comment—7 F.3d 1186
3C1.1 comment—9 F.3d 707
3C1.1 comment—9 F.3d 1119
3C1.1 comment—10 F.3d 578
3C1.1 comment [1991]—10 F.3d 1003
3C1.1 comment—11 F.3d 74
3C1.1 comment—11 F.3d 505
3C1.1 comment—11 F.3d 1392
3C1.1 comment—12 F.3d 298
3C1.1 comment—14 F.3d 79
3C1.1 comment—15 F.3d 52
3C1.1 comment—15 F.3d 272
3C1.1 comment—16 F.3d 892
3C1.1 comment—16 F.3d 1110
3C1.1 comment—740 F.Supp. 1502
3C1.1 comment—751 F.Supp. 368
3C1.1 comment [1990]—751 F.Supp. 1161
3C1.1 comment—761 F.Supp. 697
3C1.1 comment—766 F.Supp. 617
3C1.1 comment—782 F.Supp. 601
3C1.1 comment—788 F.Supp. 576
3C1.1 comment—792 F.Supp. 637
3C1.1 comment—801 F.Supp. 263
3C1.1 comment—802 F.Supp. 859
3C1.1 comment—807 F.Supp. 1238
3C1.1 comment [1990]—814 F.Supp. 964
3C1.1 comment—818 F.Supp. 812
3C1.1 comment—819 F.Supp. 250
3C1.1 comment [1988]—819 F.Supp. 250
3C1.1 comment—835 F.Supp. 227
3C1.1 note [1988]—952 F.2d 1026
3C1.2—923 F.2d 112
3C1.2—933 F.2d 916
3C1.2—952 F.2d 1086
3C1.2—953 F.2d 6
3C1.2—965 F.2d 651
3C1.2—975 F.2d 622
3C1.2—989 F.2d 180
3C1.2—999 F.2d 14
3C1.2—1 F.3d 414
3C1.2—4 F.3d 697
3C1.2—12 F.3d 1427
3C1.2—13 F.3d 1308
3C1.2—19 F.3d 149
3C1.2—804 F.Supp. 19
3C1.2 comment—953 F.2d 6
3C1.2 comment—965 F.2d 651
3C1.2 comment—975 F.2d 622
3C1.2 comment—12 F.3d 1427
3C1.2 comment—21 F.3d 874
3C2.1—12 F.3d 1128

Part D: Multiple Counts

3D comment—791 F.2d 962
3D comment—922 F.2d 549
3D comment—941 F.2d 1019
3D comment—945 F.2d 167
3D comment—957 F.2d 681
3D comment—960 F.2d 965

3D1.2—969 F.2d 926
3D1.2—971 F.2d 989
3D1.2—971 F.2d 1302
3D1.2—974 F.2d 97
3D1.2—981 F.2d 790
3D1.2—981 F.2d 1123
3D1.2—983 F.2d 757
3D1.2—992 F.2d 437
3D1.2—2 F.3d 927
3D1.2 [1988]—13 F.3d 1421
3D1.2—14 F.3d 337
3D1.2—708 F.Supp. 425
3D1.2—708 F.Supp. 461
3D1.2—712 F.Supp. 707
3D1.2—755 F.Supp. 914
3D1.2—756 F.Supp. 310
3D1.2—776 F.Supp. 1030
3D1.2—817 F.Supp. 321
3D1.2—818 F.Supp. 159
3D1.2—825 F.Supp. 550
3D1.2(a)—896 F.2d 678
3D1.2(a)—901 F.2d 399
3D1.2(a)—903 F.2d 457
3D1.2(a)—916 F.2d 147
3D1.2(a) [1990]—920 F.2d 1290
3D1.2(a) [1988]—921 F.2d 438
3D1.2(a)—922 F.2d 549
3D1.2(a)—929 F.2d 56
3D1.2(a)—945 F.2d 167
3D1.2(a)—956 F.2d 1216
3D1.2(a)—981 F.2d 1418
3D1.2(a)—983 F.2d 1480
3D1.2(a)—751 F.Supp. 1195
3D1.2(a)—825 F.Supp. 550
3D1.2(a) [1990]—835 F.Supp. 1466
3D1.2(a-d)—909 F.2d 789
3D1.2(a-d)—949 F.2d 1461
3D1.2(b)—877 F.2d 651
3D1.2(b)—901 F.2d 399
3D1.2(b) [1990]—920 F.2d 1290
3D1.2(b)—924 F.2d 68
3D1.2(b)—929 F.2d 56
3D1.2(b)—936 F.2d 85
3D1.2(b)—943 F.2d 305
3D1.2(b)—944 F.2d 14
3D1.2(b)—951 F.2d 1182
3D1.2(b)—959 F.2d 1514
3D1.2(b)—970 F.2d 960
3D1.2(b)—972 F.2d 321
3D1.2(b)—978 F.2d 1300
3D1.2(b)—981 F.2d 1418
3D1.2(b)—983 F.2d 920
3D1.2(b)—988 F.2d 1374
3D1.2(b)—989 F.2d 44
3D1.2(b)—993 F.2d 16
3D1.2(b)—994 F.2d 1467
3D1.2(b)—5 F.3d 568
3D1.2(b)—18 F.3d 595
3D1.2(b)—851 F.Supp. 1195
3D1.2(b)—853 F.Supp. 1260
3D1.2(b)—866 F.Supp. 617
3D1.2(b)—877 F.Supp. 1229
3D1.2(b)—825 F.Supp. 550
3D1.2(b)—842 F.Supp. 134
3D1.2(b)(1)—876 F.2d 1121
3D1.2(b)(1) [1990]—776 F.Supp. 1030
3D1.2(b)(2)—913 F.2d 1288
3D1.2(c)—883 F.2d 10
3D1.2(c)—913 F.2d 1053
3D1.2(c)—922 F.2d 549
3D1.2(c)—923 F.2d 1052
3D1.2(c)—924 F.2d 1289
3D1.2(c)—931 F.2d 1256
3D1.2(c)—956 F.2d 1465
3D1.2(c)—975 F.2d 397
3D1.2(c)—983 F.2d 1380
3D1.2(c)—996 F.2d 1288
3D1.2(c)—5 F.3d 568
3D1.2(c)—10 F.3d 578
3D1.2(d)—863 F.2d 245
3D1.2(d)—871 F.2d 506
3D1.2(d)—873 F.2d 437
3D1.2(d)—877 F.2d 688
3D1.2(d)—880 F.2d 804
3D1.2(d)—883 F.2d 781
3D1.2(d)—885 F.2d 1266
3D1.2(d)—888 F.2d 490
3D1.2(d)—888 F.2d 907
3D1.2(d)—889 F.2d 1531
3D1.2(d)—894 F.2d 488
3D1.2(d)—897 F.2d 1558
3D1.2(d)—898 F.2d 705
3D1.2(d)—902 F.2d 501
3D1.2(d)—903 F.2d 648
3D1.2(d)—912 F.2d 204
3D1.2(d)—913 F.2d 1288
3D1.2(d)—917 F.2d 879
3D1.2(d)—919 F.2d 461
3D1.2(d) [1990]—920 F.2d 1290
3D1.2(d)—920 F.2d 1530

3D1.2(d) [1988]—921 F.2d 438
3D1.2(d)—924 F.2d 68
3D1.2(d)—924 F.2d 945
3D1.2(d)—926 F.2d 172
3D1.2(d)—926 F.2d 838
3D1.2(d)—927 F.2d 815
3D1.2(d)—929 F.2d 55
3D1.2(d)—936 F.2d 903
3D1.2(d)—936 F.2d 1021
3D1.2(d)—937 F.2d 1227
3D1.2(d)—942 F.2d 800
3D1.2(d)—944 F.2d 14
3D1.2(d)—945 F.2d 1145
3D1.2(d)—946 F.2d 110
3D1.2(d)—947 F.2d 635
3D1.2(d)—947 F.2d 1320
3D1.2(d)—949 F.2d 968
3D1.2(d)—950 F.2d 508
3D1.2(d)—950 F.2d 1255
3D1.2(d)—951 F.2d 1057
3D1.2(d)—952 F.2d 289
3D1.2(d)—953 F.2d 559
3D1.2(d)—956 F.2d 643
3D1.2(d)—956 F.2d 1534
3D1.2(d)—959 F.2d 637
3D1.2(d)—961 F.2d 1476
3D1.2(d)—962 F.2d 409
3D1.2(d)—968 F.2d 278
3D1.2(d)—968 F.2d 1250
3D1.2(d)—970 F.2d 1490
3D1.2(d)—971 F.2d 562
3D1.2(d)—971 F.2d 876
3D1.2(d)—972 F.2d 321
3D1.2(d)—973 F.2d 852
3D1.2(d)—974 F.2d 97
3D1.2(d)—975 F.2d 596
3D1.2(d)—978 F.2d 1300
3D1.2(d)—979 F.2d 402
3D1.2(d)—981 F.2d 790
3D1.2(d)—981 F.2d 1123
3D1.2(d)—981 F.2d 1418
3D1.2(d)—982 F.2d 4
3D1.2(d)—983 F.2d 1380
3D1.2(d)—984 F.2d 298
3D1.2(d)—984 F.2d 635
3D1.2(d)—988 F.2d 1374
3D1.2(d)—989 F.2d 44
3D1.2(d)—994 F.2d 1204
3D1.2(d)—996 F.2d 1541
3D1.2(d)—999 F.2d 1175
3D1.2(d)—1 F.3d 644
3D1.2(d)—2 F.3d 927
3D1.2(d)—3 F.3d 1578
3D1.2(d)—9 F.3d 761
3D1.2(d)—11 F.3d 973
3D1.2(d) [1988]—14 F.3d 165
3D1.2(d)—18 F.3d 541
3D1.2(d)—20 F.3d 367
3D1.2(d)—684 F.Supp. 1048
3D1.2(d)—692 F.Supp. 788
3D1.2(d)—704 F.Supp. 910
3D1.2(d)—733 F.Supp. 29
3D1.2(d)—760 F.Supp. 1322
3D1.2(d)—777 F.Supp. 1229
3D1.2(d)—787 F.Supp. 819
3D1.2(d)—818 F.Supp. 159
3D1.2(d) [1990]—818 F.Supp. 159
3D1.2(d)—819 F.Supp. 250
3D1.2(d)—827 F.Supp. 205
3D1.2(d)—845 F.Supp. 270
3D1.2 comment—735 F.2d 1195
3D1.2 comment—771 F.2d 506
3D1.2 comment—783 F.2d 10
3D1.2 comment—788 F.2d 490
3D1.2 comment—901 F.2d 399
3D1.2 comment—917 F.2d 841
3D1.2 comment—919 F.2d 255
3D1.2 comment—919 F.2d 435
3D1.2 comment [1990]—920 F.2d 1290
3D1.2 comment—931 F.2d 1256
3D1.2 comment—937 F.2d 1227
3D1.2 comment—944 F.2d 88
3D1.2 comment—945 F.2d 167
3D1.2 comment—950 F.2d 508
3D1.2 comment—951 F.2d 1182
3D1.2 comment—954 F.2d 1413
3D1.2 comment—957 F.2d 681
3D1.2 comment—959 F.2d 1514
3D1.2 comment—962 F.2d 409
3D1.2 comment—972 F.2d 321
3D1.2 comment—975 F.2d 1120
3D1.2 comment—983 F.2d 920
3D1.2 comment—989 F.2d 44
3D1.2 comment—993 F.2d 16
3D1.2 comment—2 F.3d 870
3D1.2 comment—22 F.3d 1066
3D1.2 comment—719 F.Supp. 1015
3D1.2 comment—753 F.Supp. 1260
3D1.2 comment—777 F.Supp. 1229
3D1.2 comment—817 F.Supp. 321

3D1.2 comment—818 F.Supp. 159
3D1.2 comment [1990]—835 F.Supp. 1466
3D1.3—871 F.2d 506
3D1.3—948 F.2d 145
3D1.3—959 F.2d 246
3D1.3—963 F.2d 1506
3D1.3—974 F.2d 97
3D1.3—20 F.3d 367
3D1.3—776 F.Supp. 1030
3D1.3(a)—876 F.2d 1121
3D1.3(a)—883 F.2d 10
3D1.3(a)—903 F.2d 457
3D1.3(a)—920 F.2d 363
3D1.3(a)—935 F.2d 1531
3D1.3(a)—944 F.2d 88
3D1.3(a)—983 F.2d 1480
3D1.3(a)—996 F.2d 1288
3D1.3(a)—756 F.Supp. 310
3D1.3(a)—825 F.Supp. 422
3D1.3(b)—883 F.2d 781
3D1.3(b)—903 F.2d 648
3D1.3(b)—912 F.2d 204
3D1.3(b)—926 F.2d 838
3D1.3(b)—945 F.2d 1145
3D1.3(b)—947 F.2d 635
3D1.3(b)—953 F.2d 559
3D1.3(b)—971 F.2d 562
3D1.3(b)—974 F.2d 97
3D1.3(b)—9 F.3d 1438
3D1.3(b) [1988]—14 F.3d 165
3D1.3(b)—18 F.3d 541
3D1.3(b)—819 F.Supp. 250
3D1.3(b)—828 F.Supp. 3
3D1.3 comment—9 F.3d 1438
3D1.3 comment—819 F.Supp. 250
3D1.4—883 F.2d 10
3D1.4—894 F.2d 488
3D1.4—896 F.2d 678
3D1.4 [1988]—900 F.2d 1357
3D1.4—901 F.2d 399
3D1.4—903 F.2d 341
3D1.4—909 F.2d 789
3D1.4—911 F.2d 186
3D1.4—913 F.2d 46
3D1.4—914 F.2d 345
3D1.4—918 F.2d 1084
3D1.4—924 F.2d 945
3D1.4—924 F.2d 1289
3D1.4—936 F.2d 85
3D1.4—942 F.2d 800
3D1.4—950 F.2d 72
3D1.4—950 F.2d 1267
3D1.4—956 F.2d 165
3D1.4—962 F.2d 894
3D1.4—971 F.2d 1302
3D1.4—988 F.2d 318
3D1.4—994 F.2d 1380
3D1.4—1 F.3d 457
3D1.4—4 F.3d 70
3D1.4—6 F.3d 715
3D1.4—7 F.3d 691
3D1.4—751 F.Supp. 368
3D1.4—817 F.Supp. 321
3D1.4—818 F.Supp. 159
3D1.4—835 F.Supp. 1501
3D1.4(a)—877 F.2d 651
3D1.4(a)—913 F.2d 46
3D1.4(a)—918 F.2d 1084
3D1.4(a)—921 F.2d 772
3D1.4(a)—923 F.2d 1052
3D1.4(a)—931 F.2d 238
3D1.4(a)—944 F.2d 88
3D1.4(a)—751 F.Supp. 368
3D1.4(b)—909 F.2d 789
3D1.4(c)—883 F.2d 10
3D1.4(c)—921 F.2d 772
3D1.4(c)—981 F.2d 790
3D1.4(c)—7 F.3d 691
3D1.4 comment [1988]—900 F.2d 1357
3D1.4 comment—911 F.2d 186
3D1.4 comment—956 F.2d 165
3D1.4 comment—817 F.Supp. 321
3D1.5—918 F.2d 1084
3D1.5—953 F.2d 870
3D1.5—981 F.2d 1123

Part E: Acceptance of Responsibility

3E1.1—867 F.2d 783
3E1.1—868 F.2d 1541
3E1.1—869 F.2d 797
3E1.1—869 F.2d 822
3E1.1—870 F.2d 174
3E1.1—871 F.2d 511
3E1.1—872 F.2d 597
3E1.1—872 F.2d 632
3E1.1—872 F.2d 735
3E1.1—873 F.2d 23
3E1.1—873 F.2d 182
3E1.1—873 F.2d 437

3E1.1—873 F.2d 455
3E1.1—873 F.2d 495
3E1.1—873 F.2d 709
3E1.1—874 F.2d 43
3E1.1—874 F.2d 213
3E1.1—875 F.2d 427
3E1.1—875 F.2d 674
3E1.1—875 F.2d 1124
3E1.1—876 F.2d 1121
3E1.1—877 F.2d 251
3E1.1—878 F.2d 921
3E1.1—878 F.2d 1299
3E1.1—879 F.2d 331
3E1.1—879 F.2d 1247
3E1.1—880 F.2d 612
3E1.1—881 F.2d 155
3E1.1—882 F.2d 141
3E1.1—882 F.2d 151
3E1.1—882 F.2d 902
3E1.1—882 F.2d 922
3E1.1—883 F.2d 963
3E1.1—883 F.2d 1010
3E1.1—884 F.2d 181
3E1.1—884 F.2d 354
3E1.1—884 F.2d 1355
3E1.1—886 F.2d 143
3E1.1—886 F.2d 736
3E1.1—886 F.2d 838
3E1.1—888 F.2d 285
3E1.1—888 F.2d 752
3E1.1—888 F.2d 907
3E1.1—888 F.2d 1252
3E1.1—888 F.2d 1267
3E1.1—889 F.2d 189
3E1.1—889 F.2d 697
3E1.1—889 F.2d 1336
3E1.1—889 F.2d 1523
3E1.1—890 F.2d 855
3E1.1—890 F.2d 1284
3E1.1—890 F.2d 1413
3E1.1—891 F.2d 396
3E1.1—891 F.2d 962
3E1.1—893 F.2d 126
3E1.1—893 F.2d 815
3E1.1—893 F.2d 1502
3E1.1—894 F.2d 554
3E1.1—894 F.2d 1015
3E1.1—895 F.2d 28
3E1.1—895 F.2d 318
3E1.1—895 F.2d 932
3E1.1—895 F.2d 984
3E1.1—896 F.2d 317
3E1.1—897 F.2d 1018
3E1.1—898 F.2d 1120
3E1.1—899 F.2d 503
3E1.1—899 F.2d 731
3E1.1—899 F.2d 917
3E1.1—899 F.2d 1097
3E1.1—900 F.2d 66
3E1.1—900 F.2d 119
3E1.1—900 F.2d 914
3E1.1—900 F.2d 1000
3E1.1—900 F.2d 1211
3E1.1—901 F.2d 29
3E1.1—901 F.2d 1161
3E1.1—902 F.2d 331
3E1.1—902 F.2d 501
3E1.1—902 F.2d 1311
3E1.1—903 F.2d 91
3E1.1—903 F.2d 292
3E1.1—904 F.2d 603
3E1.1—904 F.2d 607
3E1.1—905 F.2d 3
3E1.1—905 F.2d 189
3E1.1—905 F.2d 217
3E1.1—905 F.2d 372
3E1.1—905 F.2d 557
3E1.1—905 F.2d 623
3E1.1—905 F.2d 1034
3E1.1—905 F.2d 1166
3E1.1—905 F.2d 1296
3E1.1—905 F.2d 1429
3E1.1—906 F.2d 621
3E1.1—906 F.2d 814
3E1.1—906 F.2d 1285
3E1.1—906 F.2d 1456
3E1.1—906 F.2d 1531
3E1.1—907 F.2d 53
3E1.1—907 F.2d 781
3E1.1—907 F.2d 1441
3E1.1—908 F.2d 33
3E1.1—908 F.2d 85
3E1.1—908 F.2d 340
3E1.1—908 F.2d 655
3E1.1—908 F.2d 816
3E1.1—908 F.2d 1443
3E1.1—909 F.2d 176
3E1.1—909 F.2d 436
3E1.1—909 F.2d 1047
3E1.1—910 F.2d 524

3E1.1—910 F.2d 587
3E1.1—910 F.2d 707
3E1.1—910 F.2d 1069
3E1.1—911 F.2d 129
3E1.1—911 F.2d 227
3E1.1—911 F.2d 398
3E1.1—911 F.2d 983
3E1.1—911 F.2d 1025
3E1.1—911 F.2d 1031
3E1.1—912 F.2d 344
3E1.1—912 F.2d 448
3E1.1—912 F.2d 942
3E1.1—913 F.2d 193
3E1.1—913 F.2d 300
3E1.1—913 F.2d 1288
3E1.1—914 F.2d 699
3E1.1—915 F.2d 352
3E1.1—915 F.2d 899
3E1.1—915 F.2d 947
3E1.1—915 F.2d 1152
3E1.1—915 F.2d 1164
3E1.1—915 F.2d 1225
3E1.1—916 F.2d 129
3E1.1—916 F.2d 219
3E1.1—916 F.2d 388
3E1.1—916 F.2d 417
3E1.1—917 F.2d 457
3E1.1—917 F.2d 494
3E1.1—917 F.2d 601
3E1.1—917 F.2d 1220
3E1.1—917 F.2d 1370
3E1.1—918 F.2d 68
3E1.1—918 F.2d 226
3E1.1—918 F.2d 839
3E1.1 [1990]—918 F.2d 1268
3E1.1—919 F.2d 842
3E1.1—919 F.2d 962
3E1.1—920 F.2d 107
3E1.1—920 F.2d 202
3E1.1—920 F.2d 1218
3E1.1—920 F.2d 1530
3E1.1—921 F.2d 975
3E1.1—922 F.2d 123
3E1.1—922 F.2d 549
3E1.1—922 F.2d 1026
3E1.1—923 F.2d 112
3E1.1—923 F.2d 595
3E1.1—923 F.2d 1039
3E1.1 [1990]—923 F.2d 1346
3E1.1—923 F.2d 1500
3E1.1—924 F.2d 427
3E1.1—924 F.2d 614
3E1.1—925 F.2d 205
3E1.1—925 F.2d 990
3E1.1—926 F.2d 64
3E1.1—926 F.2d 125
3E1.1—926 F.2d 649
3E1.1—926 F.2d 1323
3E1.1—927 F.2d 48
3E1.1—927 F.2d 726
3E1.1—927 F.2d 1463
3E1.1—928 F.2d 65
3E1.1—928 F.2d 645
3E1.1—928 F.2d 769
3E1.1—928 F.2d 818
3E1.1—928 F.2d 844
3E1.1—928 F.2d 1548
3E1.1—929 F.2d 64
3E1.1—929 F.2d 434
3E1.1—929 F.2d 1275
3E1.1—930 F.2d 526
3E1.1—930 F.2d 705
3E1.1—931 F.2d 1139
3E1.1—931 F.2d 1442
3E1.1—932 F.2d 358
3E1.1—932 F.2d 1029
3E1.1—933 F.2d 152
3E1.1—933 F.2d 278
3E1.1—933 F.2d 293
3E1.1—934 F.2d 105
3E1.1—934 F.2d 411
3E1.1—934 F.2d 553
3E1.1—934 F.2d 1440
3E1.1—935 F.2d 161
3E1.1—935 F.2d 1139
3E1.1—935 F.2d 1199
3E1.1—935 F.2d 1212
3E1.1—936 F.2d 23
3E1.1—936 F.2d 303
3E1.1—936 F.2d 387
3E1.1—936 F.2d 628
3E1.1—936 F.2d 1281
3E1.1—937 F.2d 676
3E1.1—938 F.2d 139
3E1.1—939 F.2d 244
3E1.1—939 F.2d 1053
3E1.1—940 F.2d 176
3E1.1—941 F.2d 133
3E1.1—941 F.2d 220
3E1.1—941 F.2d 761

3E1.1—942 F.2d 878
3E1.1—942 F.2d 1200
3E1.1—942 F.2d 1217
3E1.1—943 F.2d 27
3E1.1—945 F.2d 167
3E1.1—945 F.2d 650
3E1.1—946 F.2d 78
3E1.1—946 F.2d 97
3E1.1—946 F.2d 110
3E1.1—946 F.2d 122
3E1.1—946 F.2d 650
3E1.1—947 F.2d 956
3E1.1—948 F.2d 74
3E1.1—948 F.2d 210
3E1.1—948 F.2d 444
3E1.1—948 F.2d 706
3E1.1—948 F.2d 776
3E1.1—948 F.2d 783
3E1.1—948 F.2d 1093
3E1.1—949 F.2d 283
3E1.1—949 F.2d 905
3E1.1—950 F.2d 969
3E1.1—951 F.2d 164
3E1.1—951 F.2d 405
3E1.1—951 F.2d 1300
3E1.1—952 F.2d 171
3E1.1—952 F.2d 182
3E1.1—952 F.2d 289
3E1.1—952 F.2d 934
3E1.1—952 F.2d 992
3E1.1—952 F.2d 1170
3E1.1—952 F.2d 1504
3E1.1—953 F.2d 906
3E1.1—953 F.2d 1167
3E1.1—954 F.2d 482
3E1.1—954 F.2d 788
3E1.1—955 F.2d 397
3E1.1—956 F.2d 135
3E1.1—956 F.2d 450
3E1.1—956 F.2d 536
3E1.1—956 F.2d 894
3E1.1—956 F.2d 1216
3E1.1—957 F.2d 153
3E1.1—957 F.2d 248
3E1.1—957 F.2d 737
3E1.1—958 F.2d 240
3E1.1—958 F.2d 806
3E1.1—959 F.2d 189
3E1.1—959 F.2d 701
3E1.1—960 F.2d 226
3E1.1—960 F.2d 405
3E1.1—960 F.2d 629
3E1.1—960 F.2d 820
3E1.1—961 F.2d 260
3E1.1—961 F.2d 685
3E1.1—961 F.2d 1393
3E1.1—961 F.2d 1428
3E1.1—962 F.2d 560
3E1.1—962 F.2d 1228
3E1.1—963 F.2d 56
3E1.1—963 F.2d 157
3E1.1—964 F.2d 778
3E1.1—964 F.2d 1017
3E1.1 [1988]—964 F.2d 1199
3E1.1—965 F.2d 222
3E1.1—965 F.2d 408
3E1.1—965 F.2d 1507
3E1.1—966 F.2d 390
3E1.1—966 F.2d 703
3E1.1—966 F.2d 945
3E1.1—966 F.2d 1383
3E1.1—966 F.2d 1390
3E1.1—967 F.2d 5
3E1.1—967 F.2d 68
3E1.1—967 F.2d 456
3E1.1—967 F.2d 754
3E1.1—968 F.2d 411
3E1.1—968 F.2d 715
3E1.1—968 F.2d 947
3E1.1—969 F.2d 512
3E1.1—969 F.2d 1073
3E1.1—970 F.2d 371
3E1.1—970 F.2d 1312
3E1.1—970 F.2d 1414
3E1.1—971 F.2d 667
3E1.1—971 F.2d 989
3E1.1—971 F.2d 1076
3E1.1—971 F.2d 1441
3E1.1—972 F.2d 489
3E1.1—972 F.2d 885
3E1.1—972 F.2d 890
3E1.1—972 F.2d 1007
3E1.1—973 F.2d 611
3E1.1—973 F.2d 769
3E1.1—973 F.2d 928
3E1.1—973 F.2d 1354
3E1.1—974 F.2d 140
3E1.1—974 F.2d 1215
3E1.1—975 F.2d 397
3E1.1—975 F.2d 580

3E1.1—975 F.2d 944
3E1.1—975 F.2d 1357
3E1.1—976 F.2d 242
3E1.1—976 F.2d 666
3E1.1—976 F.2d 1044
3E1.1—976 F.2d 1088
3E1.1—977 F.2d 1042
3E1.1—978 F.2d 341
3E1.1—978 F.2d 453
3E1.1—978 F.2d 759
3E1.1—978 F.2d 1032
3E1.1—979 F.2d 402
3E1.1—980 F.2d 476
3E1.1 [1992]—980 F.2d 977
3E1.1—981 F.2d 367
3E1.1—983 F.2d 1468
3E1.1—984 F.2d 1067
3E1.1—985 F.2d 371
3E1.1—985 F.2d 427
3E1.1 [1992]—985 F.2d 478
3E1.1—985 F.2d 860
3E1.1—985 F.2d 960
3E1.1—986 F.2d 337
3E1.1 [1992]—986 F.2d 1091
3E1.1—986 F.2d 1225
3E1.1 [1991]—987 F.2d 874
3E1.1 [1991]—987 F.2d 1362
3E1.1—987 F.2d 1459
3E1.1—988 F.2d 798
3E1.1—988 F.2d 1298
3E1.1—988 F.2d 1374
3E1.1—988 F.2d 1494
3E1.1—989 F.2d 277
3E1.1—989 F.2d 347
3E1.1—989 F.2d 583
3E1.1—989 F.2d 1061
3E1.1—990 F.2d 707
3E1.1—990 F.2d 1011
3E1.1—990 F.2d 1456
3E1.1 [1992]—991 F.2d 1
3E1.1—991 F.2d 120
3E1.1—991 F.2d 552
3E1.1—991 F.2d 1369
3E1.1—991 F.2d 1445
3E1.1—992 F.2d 171
3E1.1—992 F.2d 739
3E1.1—992 F.2d 860
3E1.1—993 F.2d 147
3E1.1—993 F.2d 395
3E1.1—993 F.2d 620
3E1.1—994 F.2d 942
3E1.1—995 F.2d 109
3E1.1—995 F.2d 323
3E1.1 [1991]—995 F.2d 323
3E1.1—996 F.2d 244
3E1.1—996 F.2d 906
3E1.1—996 F.2d 937
3E1.1 [1992]—996 F.2d 937
3E1.1—997 F.2d 139
3E1.1—997 F.2d 767
3E1.1—997 F.2d 1234
3E1.1—997 F.2d 1475
3E1.1—997 F.2d 1576
3E1.1—998 F.2d 594
3E1.1—998 F.2d 599
3E1.1 [1992]—998 F.2d 1377
3E1.1—999 F.2d 154
3E1.1—999 F.2d 456
3E1.1—999 F.2d 615
3E1.1—999 F.2d 1053
3E1.1—1 F.3d 330
3E1.1—1 F.3d 382
3E1.1—1 F.3d 581
3E1.1 [1990]—1 F.3d 581
3E1.1—1 F.3d 729
3E1.1—1 F.3d 1040
3E1.1—1 F.3d 1044
3E1.1—2 F.3d 21
3E1.1—2 F.3d 723
3E1.1—3 F.3d 244
3E1.1—3 F.3d 1081
3E1.1—4 F.3d 1567
3E1.1—5 F.3d 214
3E1.1—5 F.3d 1161
3E1.1—6 F.3d 554
3E1.1—6 F.3d 1415
3E1.1—7 F.3d 609
3E1.1—7 F.3d 691
3E1.1—7 F.3d 800
3E1.1—7 F.3d 811
3E1.1—7 F.3d 854
3E1.1—7 F.3d 1483
3E1.1—7 F.3d 1528
3E1.1 [1991]—7 F.3d 1528
3E1.1 [1989]—8 F.3d 530
3E1.1—8 F.3d 864
3E1.1—9 F.3d 1
3E1.1—9 F.3d 275
3E1.1—9 F.3d 728
3E1.1—9 F.3d 1119

3E1.1 [1992]—9 F.3d 1119
3E1.1—9 F.3d 1132
3E1.1—9 F.3d 1438
3E1.1—9 F.3d 1442
3E1.1—10 F.3d 485
3E1.1—11 F.3d 505
3E1.1—11 F.3d 769
3E1.1—12 F.3d 298
3E1.1—12 F.3d 968
3E1.1 [1992]—12 F.3d 1540
3E1.1—13 F.3d 154
3E1.1—13 F.3d 369
3E1.1—13 F.3d 555
3E1.1—13 F.3d 638
3E1.1—13 F.3d 711
3E1.1—13 F.3d 860
3E1.1—13 F.3d 1391
3E1.1 [1992]—13 F.3d 1450
3E1.1—14 F.3d 1200
3E1.1—15 F.3d 68
3E1.1 [1991]—15 F.3d 68
3E1.1—15 F.3d 272
3E1.1—15 F.3d 646
3E1.1 [1991]—15 F.3d 849
3E1.1—15 F.3d 902
3E1.1—15 F.3d 979
3E1.1—16 F.3d 247
3E1.1—16 F.3d 795
3E1.1—16 F.3d 985
3E1.1—17 F.3d 27
3E1.1—17 F.3d 341
3E1.1—17 F.3d 1100
3E1.1—18 F.3d 541
3E1.1—18 F.3d 595
3E1.1—18 F.3d 601
3E1.1—18 F.3d 1367
3E1.1—19 F.3d 226
3E1.1—19 F.3d 982
3E1.1—19 F.3d 1210
3E1.1—19 F.3d 1283
3E1.1—20 F.3d 229
3E1.1—20 F.3d 266
3E1.1—20 F.3d 320
3E1.1—20 F.3d 393
3E1.1—20 F.3d 670
3E1.1—20 F.3d 1035
3E1.1—21 F.3d 998
3E1.1—22 F.3d 790
3E1.1—22 F.3d 981
3E1.1—22 F.3d 1075
3E1.1—23 F.3d 343
3E1.1—23 F.3d 368
3E1.1—684 F.Supp. 1048
3E1.1—684 F.Supp. 1535
3E1.1—686 F.Supp. 941
3E1.1—694 F.Supp. 1488
3E1.1—701 F.Supp. 138
3E1.1—708 F.Supp. 461
3E1.1—709 F.Supp. 1064
3E1.1—710 F.Supp. 1293
3E1.1—712 F.Supp. 707
3E1.1—716 F.Supp. 1009
3E1.1—719 F.Supp. 1015
3E1.1—726 F.Supp. 861
3E1.1—728 F.Supp. 632
3E1.1—731 F.Supp. 242
3E1.1—732 F.Supp. 878
3E1.1—738 F.Supp. 1256
3E1.1—741 F.Supp. 12
3E1.1—751 F.Supp. 1161
3E1.1—755 F.Supp. 914
3E1.1—760 F.Supp. 1322
3E1.1—760 F.Supp. 1332
3E1.1—763 F.Supp. 546
3E1.1—763 F.Supp. 645
3E1.1—766 F.Supp. 227
3E1.1—766 F.Supp. 617
3E1.1—768 F.Supp. 1277
3E1.1—777 F.Supp. 1229
3E1.1—782 F.Supp. 913
3E1.1—788 F.Supp. 756
3E1.1—791 F.Supp. 843
3E1.1 [1988]—797 F.Supp. 672
3E1.1—798 F.Supp. 513
3E1.1—801 F.Supp. 1407
3E1.1—808 F.Supp. 206
3E1.1—808 F.Supp. 883
3E1.1—809 F.Supp. 480
3E1.1—810 F.Supp. 242
3E1.1—810 F.Supp. 1231
3E1.1—811 F.Supp. 1106
3E1.1—812 F.Supp. 612
3E1.1—812 F.Supp. 1092
3E1.1—814 F.Supp. 14
3E1.1—814 F.Supp. 244
3E1.1—814 F.Supp. 488
3E1.1—816 F.Supp. 26
3E1.1—817 F.Supp. 894
3E1.1—818 F.Supp. 785
3E1.1—818 F.Supp. 812

3E1.1—825 F.Supp. 119
3E1.1—829 F.Supp. 98
3E1.1—831 F.Supp. 880
3E1.1 [1989]—832 F.Supp. 1426
3E1.1—833 F.Supp. 769
3E1.1—833 F.Supp. 1454
3E1.1—834 F.supp. 550
3E1.1—835 F.Supp. 1335
3E1.1—835 F.Supp. 1501
3E1.1—838 F.Supp. 145
3E1.1—838 F.Supp. 377
3E1.1—842 F.Supp. 92
3E1.1(a)—849 F.2d 1259
3E1.1(a)—855 F.2d 925
3E1.1(a)—863 F.2d 245
3E1.1(a)—867 F.2d 222
3E1.1(a)—868 F.2d 698
3E1.1(a)—868 F.2d 1121
3E1.1(a)—868 F.2d 1541
3E1.1(a)—873 F.2d 182
3E1.1(a)—873 F.2d 495
3E1.1(a)—874 F.2d 174
3E1.1(a)—874 F.2d 248
3E1.1(a)—875 F.2d 427
3E1.1(a)—876 F.2d 1381
3E1.1(a)—878 F.2d 125
3E1.1(a)—878 F.2d 164
3E1.1(a)—879 F.2d 1234
3E1.1(a)—880 F.2d 1204
3E1.1(a)—882 F.2d 902
3E1.1(a)—885 F.2d 243
3E1.1(a)—886 F.2d 215
3E1.1(a)—887 F.2d 568
3E1.1(a)—888 F.2d 76
3E1.1(a)—890 F.2d 855
3E1.1(a)—890 F.2d 968
3E1.1(a)—891 F.2d 300
3E1.1(a)—893 F.2d 156
3E1.1(a)—893 F.2d 479
3E1.1(a)—894 F.2d 74
3E1.1(a)—894 F.2d 208
3E1.1(a)—894 F.2d 1000
3E1.1(a)—895 F.2d 615
3E1.1(a)—898 F.2d 1011
3E1.1(a)—898 F.2d 1326
3E1.1(a)—899 F.2d 503
3E1.1(a)—901 F.2d 29
3E1.1(a)—901 F.2d 374
3E1.1(a)—901 F.2d 867
3E1.1(a)—902 F.2d 331
3E1.1(a)—904 F.2d 1036
3E1.1(a)—905 F.2d 217
3E1.1(a)—905 F.2d 623
3E1.1(a)—905 F.2d 970
3E1.1(a)—906 F.2d 139
3E1.1(a)—906 F.2d 814
3E1.1(a)—906 F.2d 867
3E1.1(a)—907 F.2d 11
3E1.1(a)—907 F.2d 94
3E1.1(a)—907 F.2d 1038
3E1.1(a)—908 F.2d 179
3E1.1(a)—908 F.2d 304
3E1.1(a)—909 F.2d 1047
3E1.1(a)—910 F.2d 707
3E1.1(a)—913 F.2d 300
3E1.1(a)—915 F.2d 899
3E1.1(a)—917 F.2d 683
3E1.1(a)—917 F.2d 1370
3E1.1(a)—918 F.2d 1430
3E1.1(a)—919 F.2d 1365
3E1.1(a)—920 F.2d 1570
3E1.1(a)—922 F.2d 311
3E1.1(a)—922 F.2d 549
3E1.1(a)—922 F.2d 675
3E1.1(a)—922 F.2d 1323
3E1.1(a)—922 F.2d 1370
3E1.1(a)—923 F.2d 129
3E1.1(a)—923 F.2d 607
3E1.1(a)—923 F.2d 1039
3E1.1(a)—927 F.2d 48
3E1.1(a)—927 F.2d 735
3E1.1(a)—927 F.2d 1361
3E1.1(a)—928 F.2d 420
3E1.1(a)—928 F.2d 844
3E1.1(a)—928 F.2d 1548
3E1.1(a)—929 F.2d 267
3E1.1(a)—934 F.2d 248
3E1.1(a)—934 F.2d 553
3E1.1(a)—934 F.2d 1077
3E1.1(a)--935 F.2d 766
3E1.1(a)—936 F.2d 599
3E1.1(a)—936 F.2d 648
3E1.1(a)—937 F.2d 1
3E1.1(a)—937 F.2d 559
3E1.1(a)—937 F.2d 716
3E1.1(a)—938 F.2d 139
3E1.1(a)—939 F.2d 1053
3E1.1(a)—942 F.2d 899
3E1.1(a)—944 F.2d 1106
3E1.1(a)—944 F.2d 1253

3E1.1(a)—946 F.2d 122
3E1.1(a)—946 F.2d 162
3E1.1(a)—946 F.2d 362
3E1.1(a)—947 F.2d 1320
3E1.1(a)—948 F.2d 241
3E1.1(a)—950 F.2d 444
3E1.1(a)—950 F.2d 1095
3E1.1(a)—951 F.2d 97
3E1.1(a)—951 F.2d 1300
3E1.1(a)—952 F.2d 1170
3E1.1(a)—953 F.2d 461
3E1.1(a)—955 F.2d 397
3E1.1(a)—956 F.2d 1465
3E1.1(a)—957 F.2d 310
3E1.1(a)—959 F.2d 63
3E1.1(a)—959 F.2d 637
3E1.1(a)—962 F.2d 560
3E1.1(a)—962 F.2d 720
3E1.1(a)—962 F.2d 824
3E1.1(a)—962 F.2d 873
3E1.1(a)—963 F.2d 56
3E1.1(a)—963 F.2d 641
3E1.1(a)—964 F.2d 390
3E1.1(a)—965 F.2d 1037
3E1.1(a)—966 F.2d 945
3E1.1(a)—967 F.2d 254
3E1.1(a)—968 F.2d 216
3E1.1(a)—970 F.2d 214
3E1.1(a)—970 F.2d 1328
3E1.1(a)—970 F.2d 1336
3E1.1(a)—971 F.2d 89
3E1.1(a)—971 F.2d 200
3E1.1(a)—971 F.2d 667
3E1.1(a)—971 F.2d 989
3E1.1(a)—971 F.2d 1206
3E1.1(a)—973 F.2d 459
3E1.1(a)—973 F.2d 928
3E1.1(a)—975 F.2d 999
3E1.1(a)—975 F.2d 1120
3E1.1(a)—976 F.2d 198
3E1.1(a)—976 F.2d 608
3E1.1(a)—976 F.2d 1088
3E1.1(a)—978 F.2d 722
3E1.1(a)—979 F.2d 402
3E1.1(a)—980 F.2d 476
3E1.1(a)—981 F.2d 569
3E1.1(a)—983 F.2d 730
3E1.1(a)—983 F.2d 1425
3E1.1(a)—984 F.2d 933
3E1.1(a)—985 F.2d 371
3E1.1(a) [1992]—985 F.2d 478
3E1.1(a)—988 F.2d 641
3E1.1(a)—988 F.2d 712
3E1.1(a)—988 F.2d 1494
3E1.1(a)—989 F.2d 347
3E1.1(a)—989 F.2d 1279
3E1.1(a) [1991]—990 F.2d 1011
3E1.1(a)—990 F.2d 1090
3E1.1(a) [1991]—990 F.2d 1370
3E1.1(a) [1992]—994 F.2d 63
3E1.1(a)—994 F.2d 1192
3E1.1(a) [1992]—996 F.2d 1169
3E1.1(a)—997 F.2d 1475
3E1.1(a)—998 F.2d 1460
3E1.1(a)—998 F.2d 1491
3E1.1(a)—999 F.2d 339
3E1.1(a) [1990]—1 F.3d 581
3E1.1(a)—5 F.3d 467
3E1.1(a) [1992]—5 F.3d 1161
3E1.1(a)—5 F.3d 1229
3E1.1(a) [1990]—5 F.3d 1229
3E1.1(a) [1992]—6 F.3d 294
3E1.1(a)—6 F.3d 735
3E1.1(a) [1990]—7 F.3d 840
3E1.1(a)—7 F.3d 1155
3E1.1(a)—7 F.3d 1533
3E1.1(a) [1989]—8 F.3d 530
3E1.1(a)—8 F.3d 864
3E1.1(a)—9 F.3d 275
3E1.1(a)—9 F.3d 1119
3E1.1(a)—9 F.3d 1132
3E1.1(a)—11 F.3d 769
3E1.1(a)—11 F.3d 824
3E1.1(a) [1992]—12 F.3d 1350
3E1.1(a)—12 F.3d 1427
3E1.1(a)—13 F.3d 203
3E1.1(a)—13 F.3d 447
3E1.1(a)—13 F.3d 1391
3E1.1(a) [1991]—15 F.3d 849
3E1.1(a)—15 F.3d 902
3E1.1(a)—15 F.3d 1292
3E1.1(a)—17 F.3d 27
3E1.1(a)—17 F.3d 177
3E1.1(a) [1992]—18 F.3d 1380
3E1.1(a)—22 F.3d 139
3E1.1(a)—22 F.3d 1410
3E1.1(a)—703 F.Supp. 1350
3E1.1(a)—733 F.Supp. 1195
3E1.1(a)—751 F.Supp. 368
3E1.1(a)—751 F.Supp. 1350

3E1.1(a)—753 F.Supp. 23
3E1.1(a)—755 F.Supp. 914
3E1.1(a)—760 F.Supp. 1322
3E1.1(a)—766 F.Supp. 617
3E1.1(a)—773 F.Supp. 55
3E1.1(a)—782 F.Supp. 747
3E1.1(a)—793 F.Supp. 64
3E1.1(a)—799 F.Supp. 646
3E1.1(a)—800 F.Supp. 648
3E1.1(a)—816 F.Supp. 26
3E1.1(a)—834 F.Supp. 292
3E1.1(a)—834 F.Supp. 550
3E1.1(a)—835 F.Supp. 253
3E1.1(a-c)—914 F.2d 699
3E1.1(a-c)—925 F.2d 18
3E1.1(a-c)—925 F.2d 990
3E1.1(a-c)—800 F.Supp. 648
3E1.1(b)—870 F.2d 174
3E1.1(b)—875 F.2d 1357
3E1.1(b)—876 F.2d 1057
3E1.1(b)—882 F.2d 147
3E1.1(b)—898 F.2d 1326
3E1.1(b)—900 F.2d 914
3E1.1(b) [1988]—906 F.2d 814
3E1.1(b)—917 F.2d 1370
3E1.1(b)—918 F.2d 1430
3E1.1(b)—919 F.2d 842
3E1.1(b)—922 F.2d 549
3E1.1(b)—947 F.2d 956
3E1.1(b)—956 F.2d 894
3E1.1(b)—963 F.2d 56
3E1.1(b)—975 F.2d 999
3E1.1(b)—987 F.2d 215
3E1.1(b)—996 F.2d 1343
3E1.1(b)—996 F.2d 1395
3E1.1(b)—998 F.2d 599
3E1.1(b)—999 F.2d 339
3E1.1(b)—999 F.2d 1043
3E1.1(b)—1 F.3d 729
3E1.1(b)—5 F.3d 568
3E1.1(b) [1990]—5 F.3d 1229
3E1.1(b) [1992]—5 F.3d 1420
3E1.1(b) [1992]—6 F.3d 294
3E1.1(b)—7 F.3d 744
3E1.1(b)—7 F.3d 800
3E1.1(b)—8 F.3d 864
3E1.1(b)—9 F.3d 1119
3E1.1(b)—9 F.3d 1132
3E1.1(b)—9 F.3d 1438
3E1.1(b)—11 F.3d 824
3E1.1(b) [199]—15 F.3d 849
3E1.1(b)—18 F.3d 826
3E1.1(b)—19 F.3d 1340
3E1.1(b)—20 F.3d 270
3E1.1(b)—20 F.3d 393
3E1.1(b)—22 F.3d 218
3E1.1(b)—773 F.Supp. 55
3E1.1(b)—808 F.Supp. 206
3E1.1(b)—809 F.Supp. 480
3E1.1(b)—813 F.Supp. 168
3E1.1(b)—814 F.Supp. 14
3E1.1(b)—818 F.Supp. 159
3E1.1(b)—826 F.Supp. 368
3E1.1(b)—827 F.Supp. 205
3E1.1(b)—848 F.Supp. 639
3E1.1(b)(1)—966 F.2d 1343
3E1.1(b)(1)—7 F.3d 900
3E1.1(b)(1)—9 F.3d 1119
3E1.1(b)(1)—9 F.3d 1132
3E1.1(b)(1)—818 F.Supp. 159
3E1.1(b)(1)—827 F.Supp. 205
3E1.1(b)(2)—996 F.2d 1343
3E1.1(b)(2)—6 F.3d 554
3E1.1(b)(2)—6 F.3d 601
3E1.1(b)(2)—7 F.3d 800
3E1.1(b)(2)—9 F.3d 1119
3E1.1(b)(2)—9 F.3d 1132
3E1.1(b)(2)—14 F.3d 1200
3E1.1(b)(2)—19 F.3d 982
3E1.1(b)(2)—23 F.3d 351
3E1.1(b)(2)—818 F.Supp. 159
3E1.1(b)(2)—827 F.Supp. 205
3E1.1(c)—868 F.2d 1541
3E1.1(c)—873 F.2d 182
3E1.1(c)—875 F.2d 427
3E1.1(c)—875 F.2d 1357
3E1.1(c)—878 F.2d 125
3E1.1(c)—882 F.2d 902
3E1.1(c)—887 F.2d 23
3E1.1(c)—890 F.2d 855
3E1.1(c)—891 F.2d 530
3E1.1(c)—893 F.2d 156
3E1.1(c)—893 F.2d 479
3E1.1(c)—894 F.2d 1000
3E1.1(c)—900 F.2d 914
3E1.1(c)—901 F.2d 29
3E1.1(c)—904 F.2d 1036
3E1.1(c)—908 F.2d 1229
3E1.1(c)—909 F.2d 1047
3E1.1(c)—914 F.2d 67

3E1.1(c)—915 F.2d 774
3E1.1(c)—915 F.2d 899
3E1.1(c)—915 F.2d 1046
3E1.1(c)—918 F.2d 664
3E1.1(c) [1990]—923 F.2d 1346
3E1.1(c)—925 F.2d 990
3E1.1(c)—927 F.2d 48
3E1.1(c)—927 F.2d 735
3E1.1(c)—934 F.2d 943
3E1.1(c)—936 F.2d 599
3E1.1(c)—942 F.2d 899
3E1.1(c)—946 F.2d 122
3E1.1(c)—947 F.2d 956
3E1.1(c)—950 F.2d 1095
3E1.1(c)—952 F.2d 1170
3E1.1(c)—955 F.2d 397
3E1.1(c)—956 F.2d 1465
3E1.1(c)—959 F.2d 83
3E1.1(c)—962 F.2d 720
3E1.1(c)—973 F.2d 459
3E1.1(c)—976 F.2d 242
3E1.1(c)—978 F.2d 1032
3E1.1(c)—980 F.2d 476
3E1.1(c) [1991]—990 F.2d 1011
3E1.1(c) [1990]—995 F.2d 91
3E1.1(c) [1992]—988 F.2d 544
3E1.1(c) [1989]—8 F.3d 530
3E1.1(c) [1992]—13 F.3d 1391
3E1.1(c)—760 F.Supp. 1322
3E1.1 et seq.—956 F.2d 1555
3E1.1 et seq.—684 F.Supp. 1506
3E1.1 et seq.—720 F.Supp. 619
3E1.1 comment—868 F.2d 1541
3E1.1 comment—869 F.2d 822
3E1.1 comment—870 F.2d 174
3E1.1 comment—871 F.2d 511
3E1.1 comment—872 F.2d 632
3E1.1 comment—873 F.2d 437
3E1.1 comment—875 F.2d 674
3E1.1 comment—875 F.2d 1357
3E1.1 comment—876 F.2d 1057
3E1.1 comment—878 F.2d 1299
3E1.1 comment—879 F.2d 331
3E1.1 comment—879 F.2d 1234
3E1.1 comment—882 F.2d 902
3E1.1 comment—883 F.2d 1142
3E1.1 comment—888 F.2d 76
3E1.1 comment—888 F.2d 1252
3E1.1 comment—890 F.2d 855
3E1.1 comment—891 F.2d 962
3E1.1 comment—893 F.2d 156
3E1.1 comment—893 F.2d 479
3E1.1 comment—893 F.2d 679
3E1.1 comment—894 F.2d 554
3E1.1 comment—894 F.2d 965
3E1.1 comment [1988]—894 F.2d 965
3E1.1 comment—894 F.2d 1000
3E1.1 comment—895 F.2d 932
3E1.1 comment—895 F.2d 1216
3E1.1 comment—897 F.2d 1018
3E1.1 comment—898 F.2d 373
3E1.1 comment—898 F.2d 1326
3E1.1 comment—899 F.2d 503
3E1.1 comment—900 F.2d 914
3E1.1 comment—900 F.2d 1000
3E1.1 comment [1988]—900 F.2d 1000
3E1.1 comment—901 F.2d 29
3E1.1 comment—901 F.2d 374
3E1.1 comment—901 F.2d 778
3E1.1 comment—901 F.2d 1161
3E1.1 comment—904 F.2d 603
3E1.1 comment—905 F.2d 295
3E1.1 comment [1988]—905 F.2d 295
3E1.1 comment—905 F.2d 1034
3E1.1 comment—905 F.2d 1296
3E1.1 comment—905 F.2d 1429
3E1.1 comment [1988]—906 F.2d 814
3E1.1 comment—906 F.2d 1456
3E1.1 comment—907 F.2d 11
3E1.1 comment—907 F.2d 1038
3E1.1 comment—908 F.2d 230
3E1.1 comment—908 F.2d 1229
3E1.1 comment [1988]—908 F.2d 1229
3E1.1 comment—909 F.2d 1047
3E1.1 comment—909 F.2d 436
3E1.1 comment—911 F.2d 983
3E1.1 comment—911 F.2d 1456
3E1.1 comment—912 F.2d 448
3E1.1 comment—913 F.2d 1288
3E1.1 comment—914 F.2d 699
3E1.1 comment—915 F.2d 774
3E1.1 comment [1988]—915 F.2d 774
3E1.1 comment—916 F.2d 1536
3E1.1 comment [1990]—917 F.2d 1220
3E1.1 comment—917 F.2d 1370
3E1.1 comment—919 F.2d 842
3E1.1 comment—921 F.2d 772
3E1.1 comment—921 F.2d 975
3E1.1 comment—922 F.2d 549
3E1.1 comment—923 F.2d 129

3E1.1 comment—923 F.2d 607
3E1.1 comment—923 F.2d 621
3E1.1 comment—923 F.2d 629
3E1.1 comment—923 F.2d 1039
3E1.1 comment—923 F.2d 1346
3E1.1 comment [1990]—923 F.2d 1346
3E1.1 comment—923 F.2d 1500
3E1.1 comment—924 F.2d 427
3E1.1 comment—924 F.2d 545
3E1.1 comment—925 F.2d 205
3E1.1 comment—925 F.2d 990
3E1.1 comment—926 F.2d 125
3E1.1 comment—927 F.2d 735
3E1.1 comment—928 F.2d 383
3E1.1 comment—928 F.2d 1548
3E1.1 comment—930 F.2d 705
3E1.1 comment—930 F.2d 1527
3E1.1 comment—932 F.2d 358
3E1.1 comment—934 F.2d 553
3E1.1 comment—934 F.2d 943
3E1.1 comment—934 F.2d 1080
3E1.1 comment—934 F.2d 1440
3E1.1 comment—935 F.2d 161
3E1.1 comment—935 F.2d 1139
3E1.1 comment—936 F.2d 628
3E1.1 comment—936 F.2d 661
3E1.1 comment—937 F.2d 559
3E1.1 comment—939 F.2d 1053
3E1.1 comment—940 F.2d 1136
3E1.1 comment—941 F.2d 220
3E1.1 comment—942 F.2d 899
3E1.1 comment—942 F.2d 1217
3E1.1 comment—943 F.2d 27
3E1.1 comment—943 F.2d 1543
3E1.1 comment [1990]—944 F.2d 828
3E1.1 comment—945 F.2d 167
3E1.1 comment—946 F.2d 122
3E1.1 comment—946 F.2d 162
3E1.1 comment—946 F.2d 650
3E1.1 comment—946 F.2d 1191
3E1.1 comment—947 F.2d 956
3E1.1 comment—948 F.2d 74
3E1.1 comment—948 F.2d 210
3E1.1 comment—948 F.2d 241
3E1.1 comment—948 F.2d 877
3E1.1 comment—949 F.2d 1465
3E1.1 comment—950 F.2d 444
3E1.1 comment—951 F.2d 161
3E1.1 comment—951 F.2d 164
3E1.1 comment—951 F.2d 405
3E1.1 comment—951 F.2d 1300
3E1.1 comment—952 F.2d 1170
3E1.1 comment—953 F.2d 452
3E1.1 comment—953 F.2d 906
3E1.1 comment [1990]—953 F.2d 906
3E1.1 comment—953 F.2d 1082
3E1.1 comment—954 F.2d 79
3E1.1 comment—954 F.2d 122
3E1.1 comment—956 F.2d 894
3E1.1 comment—957 F.2d 153
3E1.1 comment—957 F.2d 310
3E1.1 comment—957 F.2d 577
3E1.1 comment—958 F.2d 240
3E1.1 comment—958 F.2d 806
3E1.1 comment—959 F.2d 63
3E1.1 comment—959 F.2d 637
3E1.1 comment—959 F.2d 1324
3E1.1 comment—960 F.2d 629
3E1.1 comment—961 F.2d 1428
3E1.1 comment—962 F.2d 720
3E1.1 comment—962 F.2d 873
3E1.1 comment—964 F.2d 167
3E1.1 comment—964 F.2d 390
3E1.1 comment—965 F.2d 222
3E1.1 comment—966 F.2d 1390
3E1.1 comment—966 F.2d 390
3E1.1 comment—967 F.2d 754
3E1.1 comment—967 F.2d 1028
3E1.1 comment—970 F.2d 214
3E1.1 comment—970 F.2d 371
3E1.1 comment—970 F.2d 1328
3E1.1 comment—970 F.2d 1336
3E1.1 comment—971 F.2d 89
3E1.1 comment—971 F.2d 989
3E1.1 comment—971 F.2d 1076
3E1.1 comment—973 F.2d 459
3E1.1 comment—976 F.2d 235
3E1.1 comment—976 F.2d 1096
3E1.1 comment—977 F.2d 1230
3E1.1 comment—980 F.2d 32
3E1.1 comment—980 F.2d 476
3E1.1 comment—984 F.2d 1067
3E1.1 comment [1992]—985 F.2d 478
3E1.1 comment—985 F.2d 860
3E1.1 comment [1992]—986 F.2d 1091
3E1.1 comment—987 F.2d 215
3E1.1 comment—988 F.2d 1374
3E1.1 comment—989 F.2d 347
3E1.1 comment—989 F.2d 936
3E1.1 comment—989 F.2d 1279

3E1.1 comment—990 F.2d 1370
3E1.1 comment—991 F.2d 181
3E1.1 comment [1992]—991 F.2d 552
3E1.1 comment—991 F.2d 702
3E1.1 comment—992 F.2d 739
3E1.1 comment—993 F.2d 620
3E1.1 comment [1990]—993 F.2d 620
3E1.1 comment—994 F.2d 456
3E1.1 comment—995 F.2d 565
3E1.1 comment [1992]—996 F.2d 1169
3E1.1 comment—996 F.2d 1395
3E1.1 comment—997 F.2d 139
3E1.1 comment—997 F.2d 1475
3E1.1 comment—998 F.2d 53
3E1.1 comment—998 F.2d 599
3E1.1 comment—999 F.2d 456
3E1.1 comment—999 F.2d 615
3E1.1 comment—999 F.2d 1053
3E1.1 comment [1992]—999 F.2d 1175
3E1.1 comment—1 F.3d 473
3E1.1 comment—1 F.3d 581
3E1.1 comment [1990]—1 F.3d 581
3E1.1 comment—1 F.3d 1044
3E1.1 comment—3 F.3d 244
3E1.1 comment—5 F.3d 1161
3E1.1 comment—5 F.3d 1420
3E1.1 comment—7 F.3d 691
3E1.1 comment—7 F.3d 800
3E1.1 comment—7 F.3d 813
3E1.1 comment—7 F.3d 1528
3E1.1 comment [1991]—7 F.3d 1528
3E1.1 comment—7 F.3d 1533
3E1.1 comment—9 F.3d 275
3E1.1 comment—9 F.3d 1132
3E1.1 comment—10 F.3d 485
3E1.1 comment—11 F.3d 505
3E1.1 comment—11 F.3d 769
3E1.1 comment—12 F.3d 298
3E1.1 comment [1992]—12 F.3d 1318
3E1.1 comment—12 F.3d 1350
3E1.1 comment—12 F.3d 1427
3E1.1 comment—13 F.3d 711
3E1.1 comment—13 F.3d 1391
3E1.1 comment—14 F.3d 286
3E1.1 comment—15 F.3d 272
3E1.1 comment [1991]—15 F.3d 849
3E1.1 comment—15 F.3d 1292
3E1.1 comment—17 F.3d 27
3E1.1 comment—17 F.3d 1531
3E1.1 comment—18 F.3d 541
3E1.1 comment—18 F.3d 581
3E1.1 comment—18 F.3d 1367
3E1.1 comment—18 F.3d 1380
3E1.1 comment—19 F.3d 1210
3E1.1 comment—20 F.3d 229
3E1.1 comment—20 F.3d 270
3E1.1 comment—20 F.3d 610
3E1.1 comment—20 F.3d 670
3E1.1 comment—21 F.3d 998
3E1.1 comment—22 F.3d 139
3E1.1 comment—22 F.3d 170
3E1.1 comment—22 F.3d 1075
3E1.1 comment—684 F.Supp. 1535
3E1.1 comment—701 F.Supp. 138
3E1.1 comment—704 F.Supp. 175
3E1.1 comment—710 F.Supp. 1293
3E1.1 comment—720 F.Supp. 619
3E1.1 comment—731 F.Supp. 242
3E1.1 comment—737 F.Supp. 819
3E1.1 comment—740 F.Supp. 1502
3E1.1 comment—751 F.Supp. 1161
3E1.1 comment—755 F.Supp. 914
3E1.1 comment—760 F.Supp. 1322
3E1.1 comment—763 F.Supp. 546
3E1.1 comment—766 F.Supp. 617
3E1.1 comment [1990]—766 F.Supp. 617
3E1.1 comment—768 F.Supp. 1277
3E1.1 comment—807 F.Supp. 1063
3E1.1 comment—808 F.Supp. 883
3E1.1 comment—811 F.Supp. 1106
3E1.1 comment—814 F.Supp. 964
3E1.1 comment—818 F.Supp. 785
3E1.1 comment—81—8 F.Supp. 812
3E1.1 comment—827 F.Supp. 205
3E1.1 comment [1988]—832 F.Supp. 1426
3E1.1 comment—835 F.Supp. 1335
3E1.1 comment—842 F.Supp. 92
3E1.1 comment—848 F.Supp. 639
3E1.1 note—880 F.2d 612
3E1.1 note—6 F.3d 294
3E1.2—872 F.2d 735

CHAPTER 4—CRIMINAL HISTORY AND CRIMINAL LIVELIHOOD

Part A: Criminal History

4A comment—873 F.2d 765
4A comment—899 F.2d 515
4A comment—903 F.2d 1313
4A comment—907 F.2d 254
4A comment—967 F.2d 20
4A comment—983 F.2d 1507
4A comment—988 F.2d 80
4A comment—4 F.3d 636
4A comment—22 F.3d 409
4A1.1—872 F.2d 597
4A1.1—874 F.2d 43
4A1.1—874 F.2d 466
4A1.1—875 F.2d 1110
4A1.1—887 F.2d 485
4A1.1—891 F.2d 300
4A1.1—893 F.2d 63
4A1.1—894 F.2d 1057
4A1.1—894 F.2d 1083
4A1.1—897 F.2d 47
4A1.1—900 F.2d 1442
4A1.1—900 F.2d 877
4A1.1—901 F.2d 988
4A1.1—905 F.2d 1450
4A1.1—906 F.2d 555
4A1.1—907 F.2d 456
4A1.1—908 F.2d 861
4A1.1—921 F.2d 985
4A1.1—928 F.2d 383
4A1.1—932 F.2d 1343
4A1.1—932 F.2d 342
4A1.1—932 F.2d 358
4A1.1—936 F.2d 469
4A1.1—942 F.2d 517
4A1.1—945 F.2d 1214
4A1.1—946 F.2d 484
4A1.1—946 F.2d 650
4A1.1—948 F.2d 1093
4A1.1—948 F.2d 1449
4A1.1—950 F.2d 226
4A1.1—954 F.2d 1275
4A1.1—954 F.2d 1386
4A1.1—955 F.2d 786
4A1.1—959 F.2d 375
4A1.1—962 F.2d 1308
4A1.1—962 F.2d 873
4A1.1—964 F.2d 778
4A1.1—974 F.2d 25
4A1.1—975 F.2d 1120
4A1.1—975 F.2d 305
4A1.1—977 F.2d 861
4A1.1—982 F.2d 419
4A1.1—984 F.2d 899
4A1.1—988 F.2d 493
4A1.1—988 F.2d 80
4A1.1—994 F.2d 864
4A1.1—997 F.2d 1213
4A1.1—2 F.3d 1318
4A1.1—2 F.3d 200
4A1.1—3 F.3d 325
4A1.1—4 F.3d 636
4A1.1—6 F.3d 1201
4A1.1—8 F.3d 1037
4A1.1—12 F.3d 1350
4A1.1—13 F.3d 447
4A1.1—13 F.3d 1182
4A1.1—15 F.3d 526
4A1.1—18 F.3d 465
4A1.1—18 F.3d 1173
4A1.1—691 F.Supp. 656
4A1.1—691 F.Supp. 1036
4A1.1—708 F.Supp. 461
4A1.1—712 F.Supp. 707
4A1.1—802 F.Supp. 657
4A1.1—803 F.Supp. 1041
4A1.1—815 F.Supp. 920
4A1.1(a) [1990]—996 F.2d 456
4A1.1(a)—892 F.2d 742
4A1.1(a)—894 F.2d 1057
4A1.1(a)—897 F.2d 414
4A1.1(a)—901 F.2d 1394
4A1.1(a)—903 F.2d 1313
4A1.1(a)—903 F.2d 341
4A1.1(a)—905 F.2d 1432
4A1.1(a)—908 F.2d 425
4A1.1(a)—912 F.2d 1119
4A1.1(a)—912 F.2d 1365
4A1.1(a)—913 F.2d 770
4A1.1(a)—914 F.2d 330
4A1.1(a)—915 F.2d 1471
4A1.1(a)—918 F.2d 925
4A1.1(a)—930 F.2d 542
4A1.1(a)—931 F.2d 564
4A1.1(a)—931 F.2d 851
4A1.1(a)—932 F.2d 1343

4A1.1(a)—932 F.2d 364
4A1.1(a)—938 F.2d 1164
4A1.1(a)—947 F.2d 1424
4A1.1(a)—948 F.2d 732
4A1.1(a)—950 F.2d 1267
4A1.1(a)—952 F.2d 187
4A1.1(a)—958 F.2d 246
4A1.1(a)—962 F.2d 894
4A1.1(a)—979 F.2d 116
4A1.1(a)—982 F.2d 419
4A1.1(a)—986 F.2d 285
4A1.1(a)—988 F.2d 80
4A1.1(a)—991 F.2d 171
4A1.1(a)—992 F.2d 87
4A1.1(a) [1990]—996 F.2d 456
4A1.1(a)—7 F.3d 783
4A1.1(a)—10 F.3d 1003
4A1.1(a)—10 F.3d 544
4A1.1(a)—18 F.3d 1173
4A1.1(a)—19 F.3d 1271
4A1.1(a)—709 F.Supp. 1064
4A1.1(a)—773 F.Supp. 55
4A1.1(a)—815 F.Supp. 920
4A1.1(a-c)—900 F.2d 1442
4A1.1(a-c)—936 F.2d 469
4A1.1(a-c)—973 F.2d 1
4A1.1(a-c)—985 F.2d 1175
4A1.1(a-c)—988 F.2d 493
4A1.1(a-c)—997 F.2d 343
4A1.1(a-c)—4 F.3d 636
4A1.1(a-e)—893 F.2d 63
4A1.1(a-e)—975 F.2d 305
4A1.1(b)—868 F.2d 698
4A1.1(b)—891 F.2d 212
4A1.1(b)—893 F.2d 867
4A1.1(b)—901 F.2d 1394
4A1.1(b)—911 F.2d 1456
4A1.1(b)—912 F.2d 156
4A1.1(b)—913 F.2d 770
4A1.1(b)—914 F.2d 330
4A1.1(b)—924 F.2d 836
4A1.1(b)—929 F.2d 505
4A1.1(b)—938 F.2d 175
4A1.1(b)—941 F.2d 114
4A1.1(b)—942 F.2d 517
4A1.1(b)—945 F.2d 1214
4A1.1(b)—958 F.2d 246
4A1.1(b)—982 F.2d 354
4A1.1(b)—987 F.2d 475
4A1.1(b)—991 F.2d 171
4A1.1(b)—995 F.2d 315
4A1.1(b)—1 F.3d 46
4A1.1(b)—6 F.3d 1201
4A1.1(b)—15 F.3d 715
4A1.1(b)—22 F.3d 109
4A1.1(b)—740 F.Supp. 1502
4A1.1(b)—847 F.Supp. 580
4A1.1(c) [1993]—12 F.3d 618
4A1.1(c)—912 F.2d 1170
4A1.1(c)—913 F.2d 136
4A1.1(c)—913 F.2d 313
4A1.1(c)—919 F.2d 1451
4A1.1(c)—921 F.2d 254
4A1.1(c)—923 F.2d 47
4A1.1(c)—924 F.2d 753
4A1.1(c)—924 F.2d 836
4A1.1(c)—929 F.2d 505
4A1.1(c)—931 F.2d 3
4A1.1(c)—932 F.2d 700
4A1.1(c)—932 F.2d 1343
4A1.1(c)—950 F.2d 50
4A1.1(c)—962 F.2d 824
4A1.1(c)—962 F.2d 1308
4A1.1(c)—965 F.2d 480
4A1.1(c)—979 F.2d 116
4A1.1(c)—989 F.2d 979
4A1.1(c)—993 F.2d 811
4A1.1(c)—999 F.2d 80
4A1.1(c)—999 F.2d 348
4A1.1(c)—12 F.3d 760
4A1.1(c)—13 F.3d 1
4A1.1(c)—19 F.3d 1283
4A1.1(c)—22 F.3d 109
4A1.1(c)—740 F.Supp. 1502
4A1.1(c)—800 F.Supp. 648
4A1.1(d)—877 F.2d 251
4A1.1(d)—879 F.2d 811
4A1.1(d)—884 F.2d 75
4A1.1(d)—891 F.2d 86
4A1.1(d)—891 F.2d 209
4A1.1(d)—891 F.2d 405
4A1.1(d)—893 F.2d 1502
4A1.1(d)—894 F.2d 338
4A1.1(d) [1988]—897 F.2d 160
4A1.1(d)—897 F.2d 286
4A1.1(d)—900 F.2d 877
4A1.1(d)—901 F.2d 285
4A1.1(d)—905 F.2d 251
4A1.1(d)—905 F.2d 482
4A1.1(d)—905 F.2d 1034

4A1.1(d)—908 F.2d 861
4A1.1(d)—911 F.2d 793
4A1.1(d)—912 F.2d 156
4A1.1(d)—913 F.2d 174
4A1.1(d)—913 F.2d 313
4A1.1(d)—914 F.2d 330
4A1.1(d)—914 F.2d 1355
4A1.1(d)—917 F.2d 970
4A1.1(d)—919 F.2d 80
4A1.1(d)—919 F.2d 1451
4A1.1(d)—922 F.2d 578
4A1.1(d)—923 F.2d 369
4A1.1(d)—924 F.2d 753
4A1.1(d)—925 F.2d 234
4A1.1(d)—929 F.2d 500
4A1.1(d)—930 F.2d 12
4A1.1(d)—931 F.2d 8
4A1.1(d)—931 F.2d 851
4A1.1(d)—932 F.2d 1529
4A1.1(d)—933 F.2d 307
4A1.1(d)—934 F.2d 1114
4A1.1(d)—938 F.2d 175
4A1.1(d)—938 F.2d 1164
4A1.1(d)—941 F.2d 114
4A1.1(d)—941 F.2d 571
4A1.1(d)—944 F.2d 414
4A1.1(d)—946 F.2d 1105
4A1.1(d)—947 F.2d 1236
4A1.1(d)—950 F.2d 50
4A1.1(d)—950 F.2d 1267
4A1.1(d)—952 F.2d 187
4A1.1(d)—952 F.2d 289
4A1.1(d)—952 F.2d 514
4A1.1(d)—955 F.2d 28
4A1.1(d)—957 F.2d 525
4A1.1(d)—957 F.2d 677
4A1.1(d)—959 F.2d 83
4A1.1(d)—962 F.2d 1308
4A1.1(d)—963 F.2d 1506
4A1.1(d)—971 F.2d 357
4A1.1(d)—981 F.2d 790
4A1.1(d)—981 F.2d 1123
4A1.1(d)—982 F.2d 354
4A1.1(d)—986 F.2d 285
4A1.1(d)—988 F.2d 1494
4A1.1(d)—989 F.2d 52
4A1.1(d)—991 F.2d 1468
4A1.1(d)—992 F.2d 1116
4A1.1(d)—999 F.2d 80
4A1.1(d)—2 F.3d 286
4A1.1(d)—10 F.3d 1463
4A1.1(d)—11 F.3d 769
4A1.1(d)—14 F.3d 502
4A1.1(d)—18 F.3d 41
4A1.1(d)—18 F.3d 1156
4A1.1(d)—18 F.3d 1173
4A1.1(d)—710 F.Supp. 106
4A1.1(d)—711 F.Supp. 736
4A1.1(d)—716 F.Supp. 1207
4A1.1(d)—729 F.Supp. 1120
4A1.1(d)—773 F.Supp. 55
4A1.1(d) [1988]—797 F.Supp. 672
4A1.1(d)—815 F.Supp. 920
4A1.1(e)—877 F.2d 251
4A1.1(e)—879 F.2d 811
4A1.1(e)—884 F.2d 75
4A1.1(e)—891 F.2d 86
4A1.1(e)—891 F.2d 209
4A1.1(e)—891 F.2d 405
4A1.1(e)—893 F.2d 867
4A1.1(e)—893 F.2d 1502
4A1.1(e) [1988]—897 F.2d 160
4A1.1(e)—897 F.2d 286
4A1.1(e)—903 F.2d 457
4A1.1(e)—906 F.2d 116
4A1.1(e)—911 F.2d 1456
4A1.1(e)—915 F.2d 759
4A1.1(e)—918 F.2d 925
4A1.1(e)—922 F.2d 578
4A1.1(e)—930 F.2d 12
4A1.1(e)—932 F.2d 1529
4A1.1(e)—933 F.2d 307
4A1.1(e)—935 F.2d 4
4A1.1(e)—941 F.2d 114
4A1.1(e)—945 F.2d 1214
4A1.1(e)—948 F.2d 732
4A1.1(e)—950 F.2d 1267
4A1.1(e)—957 F.2d 677
4A1.1(e)—981 F.2d 790
4A1.1(e)—982 F.2d 354
4A1.1(e)—986 F.2d 285
4A1.1(e)—991 F.2d 1468
4A1.1(e)—11 F.3d 769
4A1.1(e)—13 F.3d 447
4A1.1(e)—18 F.3d 41
4A1.1(e)—18 F.3d 1173
4A1.1(e)—710 F.Supp. 106
4A1.1(e)—740 F.Supp. 1502
4A1.1(e)—815 F.Supp. 920
4A1.1 et seq.—868 F.2d 1541

4A1.1 et seq.—879 F.2d 811
4A1.1 et seq.—893 F.2d 825
4A1.1 et seq.—895 F.2d 1198
4A1.1 et seq.—901 F.2d 867
4A1.1 et seq.—908 F.2d 365
4A1.1 et seq.—915 F.2d 759
4A1.1 et seq.—917 F.2d 80
4A1.1 et seq.—921 F.2d 438
4A1.1 et seq.—936 F.2d 1124
4A1.1 et seq.—941 F.2d 133
4A1.1 et seq.—960 F.2d 226
4A1.1 et seq.—967 F.2d 20
4A1.1 et seq.—982 F.2d 354
4A1.1 et seq.—684 F.Supp. 1506
4A1.1 et seq.—684 F.Supp. 1535
4A1.1 et seq.—686 F.Supp. 1174
4A1.1 et seq.—709 F.Supp. 908
4A1.1 et seq.—733 F.Supp. 1003
4A1.1-4B1.3 [1990]—918 F.2d 1268
4A1.1 comment—869 F.2d 822
4A1.1 comment—875 F.2d 1110
4A1.1 comment—879 F.2d 811
4A1.1 comment—889 F.2d 441
4A1.1 comment—893 F.2d 63
4A1.1 comment [1988]—897 F.2d 160
4A1.1 comment—897 F.2d 286
4A1.1 comment—903 F.2d 1313
4A1.1 comment—905 F.2d 1034
4A1.1 comment—905 F.2d 1432
4A1.1 comment—907 F.2d 121
4A1.1 comment—919 F.2d 80
4A1.1 comment—932 F.2d 1529
4A1.1 comment—936 F.2d 628
4A1.1 comment—938 F.2d 175
4A1.1 comment—942 F.2d 1270
4A1.1 comment—943 F.2d 909
4A1.1 comment—962 F.2d 1308
4A1.1 comment—965 F.2d 65
4A1.1 comment—976 F.2d 1096
4A1.1 comment—982 F.2d 354
4A1.1 comment—2 F.3d 574
4A1.1 comment—4 F.3d 636
4A1.1 comment—751 F.Supp. 1161
4A1.1 comment—773 F.Supp. 55
4A1.2 [1988]—797 F.2d 672
4A1.2—868 F.2d 122
4A1.2—879 F.2d 410
4A1.2—900 F.2d 1442
4A1.2—903 F.2d 341
4A1.2—905 F.2d 1034
4A1.2—905 F.2d 1432
4A1.2—907 F.2d 456
4A1.2—909 F.2d 363
4A1.2—910 F.2d 1484
4A1.2—910 F.2d 1574
4A1.2—919 F.2d 80
4A1.2—928 F.2d 250
4A1.2—928 F.2d 310
4A1.2—932 F.2d 358
4A1.2—933 F.2d 362
4A1.2—934 F.2d 1114
4A1.2—938 F.2d 210
4A1.2—943 F.2d 348
4A1.2—943 F.2d 914
4A1.2—946 F.2d 584
4A1.2—946 F.2d 650
4A1.2—947 F.2d 1018
4A1.2—950 F.2d 214
4A1.2—957 F.2d 841
4A1.2—959 F.2d 375
4A1.2—961 F.2d 384
4A1.2—962 F.2d 479
4A1.2—962 F.2d 560
4A1.2—962 F.2d 1308
4A1.2—963 F.2d 224
4A1.2—964 F.2d 778
4A1.2—964 F.2d 896
4A1.2—968 F.2d 216
4A1.2—970 F.2d 1017
4A1.2—975 F.2d 580
4A1.2—976 F.2d 1069
4A1.2—979 F.2d 402
4A1.2—982 F.2d 187
4A1.2—986 F.2d 337
4A1.2—988 F.2d 80
4A1.2—989 F.2d 1117
4A1.2—991 F.2d 195
4A1.2—991 F.2d 1162
4A1.2—995 F.2d 536
4A1.2—2 F.3d 200
4A1.2—3 F.3d 325
4A1.2 [1991]—5 F.3d 781
4A1.2—7 F.3d 66
4A1.2—8 F.3d 1037
4A1.2—9 F.3d 890
4A1.2—11 F.3d 505
4A1.2—13 F.3d 203
4A1.2—13 F.3d 447
4A1.2—13 F.3d 638
4A1.2—14 F.3d 1093

4A1.2—15 F.3d 526
4A1.2—15 F.3d 715
4A1.2 [1992]—18 F.3d 1355
4A1.2—22 F.3d 662
4A1.2—694 F.Supp. 1488
4A1.2—709 F.Supp. 908
4A1.2—734 F.Supp. 312
4A1.2—760 F.Supp. 1332
4A1.2—763 F.Supp. 277
4A1.2—782 F.Supp. 515
4A1.2—843 F.Supp. 38
4A1.2(a)—905 F.2d 482
4A1.2(a)—923 F.2d 47
4A1.2(a)—929 F.2d 505
4A1.2(a)—964 F.2d 564
4A1.2(a)—4 F.3d 636
4A1.2(a)—4 F.3d 1358
4A1.2(a)—5 F.3d 435
4A1.2(a)—796 F.Supp. 366
4A1.2(a)—813 F.Supp. 496
4A1.2(a)(1)—893 F.2d 867
4A1.2(a)(1)—900 F.2d 1442
4A1.2(a)(1)—909 F.2d 389
4A1.2(a)(1)—919 F.2d 19
4A1.2(a)(1)—928 F.2d 349
4A1.2(a)(1)—928 F.2d 383
4A1.2(a)(1)—932 F.2d 364
4A1.2(a)(1)—932 F.2d 1343
4A1.2(a)(1)—934 F.2d 1114
4A1.2(a)(1)—936 F.2d 469
4A1.2(a)(1)—941 F.2d 114
4A1.2(a)(1)—942 F.2d 517
4A1.2(a)(1)—947 F.2d 1424
4A1.2(a)(1)—950 F.2d 214
4A1.2(a)(1)—953 F.2d 443
4A1.2(a)(1)—957 F.2d 1330
4A1.2(a)(1)—966 F.2d 559
4A1.2(a)(1)—970 F.2d 907
4A1.2(a)(1)—973 F.2d 1152
4A1.2(a)(1)—975 F.2d 1120
4A1.2(a)(1)—977 F.2d 861
4A1.2(a)(1)—982 F.2d 100
4A1.2(a)(1)—982 F.2d 419
4A1.2(a)(1)—986 F.2d 321
4A1.2(a)(1)—988 F.2d 80
4A1.2(a)(1)—989 F.2d 979
4A1.2(a)(1)—993 F.2d 811
4A1.2(a)(1)—995 F.2d 315
4A1.2(a)(1)—999 F.2d 1326
4A1.2(a)(1)—1 F.3d 46
4A1.2(a)(1)—7 F.3d 783
4A1.2(a)(1)—10 F.3d 261
4A1.2(a)(1)—13 F.3d 1
4A1.2(a)(1)—16 F.3d 795
4A1.2(a)(1)—18 F.3d 465
4A1.2(a)(1)—800 F.Supp. 648
4A1.2(a)(2)—875 F.2d 1110
4A1.2(a)(2)—883 F.2d 1007
4A1.2(a)(2)—888 F.2d 79
4A1.2(a)(2)—893 F.2d 276
4A1.2(a)(2)—897 F.2d 414
4A1.2(a)(2)—898 F.2d 43
4A1.2(a)(2)—898 F.2d 1461
4A1.2(a)(2)—905 F.2d 217
4A1.2(a)(2)—909 F.2d 389
4A1.2(a)(2)—914 F.2d 330
4A1.2(a)(2)—915 F.2d 1471
4A1.2(a)(2)—920 F.2d 810
4A1.2(a)(2)—921 F.2d 254
4A1.2(a)(2)—922 F.2d 578
4A1.2(a)(2)—922 F.2d 1385
4A1.2(a)(2)—922 F.2d 1501
4A1.2(a)(2)—928 F.2d 349
4A1.2(a)(2)—929 F.2d 116
4A1.2(a)(2)—929 F.2d 136
4A1.2(a)(2)—929 F.2d 930
4A1.2(a)(2)—929 F.2d 1369
4A1.2(a)(2)—930 F.2d 645
4A1.2(a)(2)—932 F.2d 364
4A1.2(a)(2)—933 F.2d 111
4A1.2(a)(2)—936 F.2d 469
4A1.2(a)(2)—941 F.2d 1019
4A1.2(a)(2)—945 F.2d 1504
4A1.2(a)(2)—946 F.2d 97
4A1.2(a)(2)—946 F.2d 650
4A1.2(a)(2)—947 F.2d 1018
4A1.2(a)(2)—947 F.2d 1424
4A1.2(a)(2)—950 F.2d 1267
4A1.2(a)(2)—951 F.2d 827
4A1.2(a)(2)—952 F.2d 982
4A1.2(a)(2) [1991]—957 F.2d 1330
4A1.2(a)(2)—958 F.2d 234
4A1.2(a)(2)—958 F.2d 246
4A1.2(a)(2)—960 F.2d 117
4A1.2(a)(2)—961 F.2d 103
4A1.2(a)(2)—961 F.2d 384
4A1.2(a)(2) [1990]—961 F.2d 1188
4A1.2(a)(2)—963 F.2d 711
4A1.2(a)(2)—964 F.2d 896
4A1.2(a)(2)—967 F.2d 101

4A1.2(a)(2)—969 F.2d 733
4A1.2(a)(2)—970 F.2d 1017
4A1.2(a)(2)—973 F.2d 1
4A1.2(a)(2)—976 F.2d 1096
4A1.2(a)(2)—981 F.2d 367
4A1.2(a)(2)—981 F.2d 1121
4A1.2(a)(2)—981 F.2d 1123
4A1.2(a)(2)—982 F.2d 354
4A1.2(a)(2)—984 F.2d 143
4A1.2(a)(2)—984 F.2d 298
4A1.2(a)(2)—984 F.2d 1289
4A1.2(a)(2)—986 F.2d 14
4A1.2(a)(2)—989 F.2d 303
4A1.2(a)(2)—991 F.2d 171
4A1.2(a)(2)—991 F.2d 1468
4A1.2(a)(2)—996 F.2d 83
4A1.2(a)(2) [1990]—996 F.2d 456
4A1.2(a)(2)—996 F.2d 946
4A1.2(a)(2)—997 F.2d 343
4A1.2(a)(2)—999 F.2d 57
4A1.2(a)(2)—999 F.2d 474
4A1.2(a)(2)—1 F.3d 910
4A1.2(a)(2) [1990]—1 F.3d 910
4A1.2(a)(2)—2 F.3d 200
4A1.2(a)(2)—2 F.3d 218
4A1.2(a)(2)—3 F.3d 325
4A1.2(a)(2)—9 F.3d 1480
4A1.2(a)(2)—10 F.3d 261
4A1.2(a)(2)—13 F.3d 1182
4A1.2(a)(2)—14 F.3d 1030
4A1.2(a)(2)—15 F.3d 526
4A1.2(a)(2)—733 F.Supp. 1003
4A1.2(a)(2)—779 F.Supp. 1285
4A1.2(a)(2)—801 F.Supp. 263
4A1.2(a)(2)—843 F.Supp. 38
4A1.2(a)(3)—962 F.2d 824
4A1.2(a)(3)—999 F.2d 348
4A1.2(a)(3)—999 F.2d 474
4A1.2(a)(3)—4 F.3d 636
4A1.2(a)(3)—12 F.3d 760
4A1.2(a)(4)—985 F.2d 1175
4A1.2(a)(4)—999 F.2d 348
4A1.2(a)(4)—802 F.Supp. 559
4A1.2(b)—929 F.2d 505
4A1.2(b)—941 F.2d 114
4A1.2(b)—942 F.2d 517
4A1.2(b)—4 F.3d 636
4A1.2(b)—15 F.3d 934
4A1.2(b)(1)—892 F.2d 742
4A1.2(b)(1)—893 F.2d 867
4A1.2(b)(1)—941 F.2d 114
4A1.2(b)(1)—959 F.2d 714
4A1.2(b)(1)—19 F.3d 1271
4A1.2(b)(2)—892 F.2d 742
4A1.2(b)(2)—909 F.2d 389
4A1.2(b)(2)—921 F.2d 254
4A1.2(b)(2)—929 F.2d 505
4A1.2(b)(2)—979 F.2d 369
4A1.2(b)(2)—982 F.2d 100
4A1.2(b)(2)—988 F.2d 493
4A1.2(b)(2)—4 F.3d 636
4A1.2(b)(2)—6 F.3d 1201
4A1.2(b)(2)—19 F.3d 1271
4A1.2(c)—895 F.2d 1198
4A1.2(c)—901 F.2d 1000
4A1.2(c)—905 F.2d 251
4A1.2(c)—912 F.2d 1170
4A1.2(c)—915 F.2d 474
4A1.2(c)—915 F.2d 759
4A1.2(c)—916 F.2d 916
4A1.2(c)—920 F.2d 1330
4A1.2(c)—925 F.2d 234
4A1.2(c)—938 F.2d 175
4A1.2(c)—938 F.2d 1020
4A1.2(c)—941 F.2d 690
4A1.2(c)—942 F.2d 454
4A1.2(c)—955 F.2d 786
4A1.2(c)—957 F.2d 525
4A1.2(c)—964 F.2d 756
4A1.2(c)—974 F.2d 140
4A1.2(c)—997 F.2d 30
4A1.2(c)—4 F.3d 636
4A1.2(c)—8 F.3d 186
4A1.2(c) [1993]—12 F.3d 618
4A1.2(c)—19 F.3d 1271
4A1.2(c)—19 F.3d 1283
4A1.2(c)(1)—896 F.2d 246
4A1.2(c)(1)—900 F.2d 582
4A1.2(c)(1)—905 F.2d 1034
4A1.2(c)(1)—913 F.2d 1288
4A1.2(c)(1)—914 F.2d 1527
4A1.2(c)(1)—915 F.2d 474
4A1.2(c)(1)—919 F.2d 1451
4A1.2(c)(1)—920 F.2d 1330
4A1.2(c)(1)—933 F.2d 278
4A1.2(c)(1)—934 F.2d 1114
4A1.2(c)(1)—938 F.2d 1020
4A1.2(c)(1)—950 F.2d 50
4A1.2(c)(1)—954 F.2d 1275
4A1.2(c)(1)—956 F.2d 939

4A1.2(c)(1)—964 F.2d 756
4A1.2(c)(1)—978 F.2d 972
4A1.2(c)(1)—980 F.2d 259
4A1.2(c)(1)—8 F.3d 186
4A1.2(c)(1)—19 F.3d 1238
4A1.2(c)(1) [1990]—818 F.Supp. 785
4A1.2(c)(1)(B)—920 F.2d 1330
4A1.2(c)(2)—871 F.2d 513
4A1.2(c)(2)—881 F.2d 684
4A1.2(c)(2)—905 F.2d 251
4A1.2(c)(2)—914 F.2d 1527
4A1.2(c)(2)—915 F.2d 474
4A1.2(c)(2)—915 F.2d 759
4A1.2(c)(2)—920 F.2d 1330
4A1.2(c)(2)—922 F.2d 1234
4A1.2(c)(2)—934 F.2d 1114
4A1.2(c)(2)—954 F.2d 1275
4A1.2(c)(2)—956 F.2d 891
4A1.2(c)(2)—964 F.2d 756
4A1.2(c)(2)—968 F.2d 216
4A1.2(c)(2)—987 F.2d 1462
4A1.2(c)(2) [1993]—12 F.3d 618
4A1.2(d)—891 F.2d 212
4A1.2(d)—907 F.2d 109
4A1.2(d)—929 F.2d 128
4A1.2(d)—938 F.2d 210
4A1.2(d)—961 F.2d 103
4A1.2(d)—961 F.2d 1110
4A1.2(d)—962 F.2d 1308
4A1.2(d)—988 F.2d 500
4A1.2(d)—3 F.3d 372
4A1.2(d)—3 F.3d 1217
4A1.2(d)(1)—991 F.2d 590
4A1.2(d)(1)—4 F.3d 941
4A1.2(d)(2)—891 F.2d 212
4A1.2(d)(2)—894 F.2d 1057
4A1.2(d)(2)—898 F.2d 368
4A1.2(d)(2)—929 F.2d 930
4A1.2(d)(2)—938 F.2d 210
4A1.2(d)(2)—991 F.2d 700
4A1.2(d)(2)(A)—888 F.2d 1252
4A1.2(d)(2)(A)—893 F.2d 867
4A1.2(d)(2)(A)—906 F.2d 1116
4A1.2(d)(2)(A)—911 F.2d 1456
4A1.2(d)(2)(A)—914 F.2d 1352
4A1.2(d)(2)(A)—938 F.2d 210
4A1.2(d)(2)(A)—961 F.2d 103
4A1.2(d)(2)(A)—987 F.2d 1462
4A1.2(d)(2)(A)—740 F.Supp. 1502
4A1.2(d)(2)(B)—914 F.2d 1352
4A1.2(d)(2)(B)—947 F.2d 1424
4A1.2(d)(2)(B)—12 F.3d 760
4A1.2(e)—868 F.2d 122
4A1.2(e)—900 F.2d 1442
4A1.2(e)—903 F.2d 1313
4A1.2(e)—904 F.2d 365
4A1.2(e)—905 F.2d 1432
4A1.2(e)—905 F.2d 1439
4A1.2(e)—907 F.2d 87
4A1.2(e)—910 F.2d 1241
4A1.2(e)—917 F.2d 607
4A1.2(e)—920 F.2d 1330
4A1.2(e)—921 F.2d 254
4A1.2(e)—922 F.2d 624
4A1.2(e)—923 F.2d 47
4A1.2(e)—923 F.2d 1371
4A1.2(e)—926 F.2d 64
4A1.2(e)—932 F.2d 1343
4A1.2(e)—933 F.2d 742
4A1.2(e)—938 F.2d 210
4A1.2(e)—945 F.2d 989
4A1.2(e)—948 F.2d 215
4A1.2(e)—962 F.2d 560
4A1.2(e)—975 F.2d 1120
4A1.2(e)—988 F.2d 80
4A1.2(e)—997 F.2d 1213
4A1.2(e)—3 F.3d 1217
4A1.2(e)—14 F.3d 1093
4A1.2(e)—773 F.Supp. 55
4A1.2(e)—796 F.Supp. 366
4A1.2(e)(1)—868 F.2d 122
4A1.2(e)(1)—887 F.2d 57
4A1.2(e)(1)—900 F.2d 1442
4A1.2(e)(1)—910 F.2d 530
4A1.2(e)(1)—910 F.2d 1574
4A1.2(e)(1)—912 F.2d 1119
4A1.2(e)(1)—917 F.2d 607
4A1.2(e)(1)—921 F.2d 257
4A1.2(e)(1)—922 F.2d 212
4A1.2(e)(1)—923 F.2d 47
4A1.2(e)(1)—923 F.2d 1371
4A1.2(e)(1)—930 F.2d 542
4A1.2(e)(1)—944 F.2d 1106
4A1.2(e)(1)—945 F.2d 1504
4A1.2(e)(1)—950 F.2d 203
4A1.2(e)(1)—963 F.2d 132
4A1.2(e)(1)—975 F.2d 1120
4A1.2(e)(1)—981 F.2d 664
4A1.2(e)(1)—991 F.2d 1509
4A1.2(e)(1)—7 F.3d 629

4A1.2(e)(1)—7 F.3d 1193
4A1.2(e)(1)—15 F.3d 553
4A1.2(e)(1)--15 F.3d 830
4A1.2(e)(1)—734 F.Supp. 687
4A1.2(e)(1)—773 F.Supp. 1400
4A1.2(e)(1-3)—920 F.2d 1330
4A1.2(e)(2)—868 F.2d 122
4A1.2(e)(2)—871 F.2d 513
4A1.2(e)(2)—898 F.2d 1378
4A1.2(e)(2)—908 F.2d 550
4A1.2(e)(2)—921 F.2d 254
4A1.2(e)(2)—923 F.2d 47
4A1.2(e)(2)—925 F.2d 205
4A1.2(e)(2)—930 F.2d 542
4A1.2(e)(2)—931 F.2d 3
4A1.2(e)(2)—944 F.2d 1106
4A1.2(e)(2)—968 F.2d 216
4A1.2(e)(2)—971 F.2d 357
4A1.2(e)(2)—10 F.3d 261
4A1.2(e)(2)—773 F.Supp. 55
4A1.2(e)(2)—845 F.Supp. 270
4A1.2(e)(3)—908 F.2d 550
4A1.2(e)(3)—930 F.2d 542
4A1.2(e)(3)—965 F.2d 262
4A1.2(e)(3)—975 F.2d 305
4A1.2(e)(3)—984 F.2d 701
4A1.2(f)—919 F.2d 19
4A1.2(f)—923 F.2d 369
4A1.2(f)—932 F.2d 700
4A1.2(f)—934 F.2d 1114
4A1.2(f)—965 F.2d 480
4A1.2(f)—989 F.2d 261
4A1.2(f)—993 F.2d 811
4A1.2(f)—999 F.2d 80
4A1.2(f)—800 F.Supp. 648
4A1.2(f)—802 F.Supp. 559
4A1.2(g)—918 F.2d 841
4A1.2(g)—927 F.2d 1188
4A1.2(g)—930 F.2d 542
4A1.2(h)—889 F.2d 441
4A1.2(h)—946 F.2d 13
4A1.2(h)—986 F.2d 166
4A1.2(h-j)—938 F.2d 210
4A1.2(h-j)—961 F.2d 1110
4A1.2(j)—907 F.2d 87
4A1.2(j)—932 F.2d 805
4A1.2(j)—934 F.2d 1114
4A1.2(j)—945 F.2d 300
4A1.2(j)—959 F.2d 375
4A1.2(j)—989 F.2d 261
4A1.2(j)—991 F.2d 866
4A1.2(j)—993 F.2d 686
4A1.2(j)—999 F.2d 80
4A1.2(j)—20 F.3d 1336
4A1.2(j)—734 F.Supp. 312
4A1.2(k)—909 F.2d 389
4A1.2(k)—933 F.2d 742
4A1.2(k)—945 F.2d 1504
4A1.2(k)—991 F.2d 1509
4A1.2(k)—22 F.3d 109
4A1.2(k)(1)—944 F.2d 1106
4A1.2(k)(2)—991 F.2d 1106
4A1.2(l)—991 F.2d 195
4A1.2 comment—875 F.2d 1110
4A1.2 comment—883 F.2d 1007
4A1.2 comment—888 F.2d 79
4A1.2 comment—889 F.2d 441
4A1.2 comment—893 F.2d 276
4A1.2 comment—897 F.2d 414
4A1.2 comment—898 F.2d 43
4A1.2 comment—898 F.2d 1461
4A1.2 comment—899 F.2d 677
4A1.2 comment—899 F.2d 1097
4A1.2 comment—901 F.2d 1000
4A1.2 comment—905 F.2d 1296
4A1.2 comment—905 F.2d 1432
4A1.2 comment—907 F.2d 87
4A1.2 comment—907 F.2d 109
4A1.2 comment—907 F.2d 121
4A1.2 comment—907 F.2d 456
4A1.2 comment—908 F.2d 550
4A1.2 comment—909 F.2d 196
4A1.2 comment—909 F.2d 389
4A1.2 comment—910 F.2d 1484
4A1.2 comment—912 F.2d 1119
4A1.2 comment—914 F.2d 330
4A1.2 comment—915 F.2d 759
4A1.2 comment—916 F.2d 916
4A1.2 comment—919 F.2d 19
4A1.2 comment—919 F.2d 255
4A1.2 comment—920 F.2d 810
4A1.2 comment—920 F.2d 823
4A1.2 comment—922 F.2d 578
4A1.2 comment—922 F.2d 1385
4A1.2 comment—923 F.2d 369
4A1.2 comment—924 F.2d 462
4A1.2 comment—925 F.2d 205
4A1.2 comment [1990]—928 F.2d 310
4A1.2 comment—928 F.2d 349
4A1.2 comment—929 F.2d 116

4A1.2 comment—929 F.2d 505
4A1.2 comment—929 F.2d 930
4A1.2 comment—929 F.2d 1369
4A1.2 comment—932 F.2d 342
4A1.2 comment—932 F.2d 358
4A1.2 comment—932 F.2d 364
4A1.2 comment—932 F.2d 823
4A1.2 comment—932 F.2d 1343
4A1.2 comment—934 F.2d 1114
4A1.2 comment—936 F.2d 469
4A1.2 comment—936 F.2d 628
4A1.2 comment—938 F.2d 175
4A1.2 comment—938 F.2d 210
4A1.2 comment—942 F.2d 517
4A1.2 comment—944 F.2d 414
4A1.2 comment—945 F.2d 1504
4A1.2 comment [1988]—945 F.2d 1504
4A1.2 comment—945 F.2d 496
4A1.2 comment—946 F.2d 97
4A1.2 comment—946 F.2d 650
4A1.2 comment—947 F.2d 1018
4A1.2 comment—947 F.2d 1424
4A1.2 comment—949 F.2d 973
4A1.2 comment—951 F.2d 827
4A1.2 comment—952 F.2d 982
4A1.2 comment—955 F.2d 786
4A1.2 comment—957 F.2d 1330
4A1.2 comment [1991]—957 F.2d 1330
4A1.2 comment—958 F.2d 234
4A1.2 comment—958 F.2d 246
4A1.2 comment—959 F.2d 714
4A1.2 comment—960 F.2d 117
4A1.2 comment—960 F.2d 130
4A1.2 comment—960 F.2d 1311
4A1.2 comment—961 F.2d 103
4A1.2 comment—961 F.2d 384
4A1.2 comment—961 F.2d 1110
4A1.2 comment [1990]—961 F.2d 1188
4A1.2 comment—962 F.2d 479
4A1.2 comment [1991]—962 F.2d 560
4A1.2 comment—963 F.2d 711
4A1.2 comment—964 F.2d 564
4A1.2 comment—964 F.2d 687
4A1.2 comment—964 F.2d 896
4A1.2 comment—965 F.2d 222
4A1.2 comment—966 F.2d 868
4A1.2 comment—968 F.2d 216
4A1.2 comment—968 F.2d 703
4A1.2 comment—969 F.2d 733
4A1.2 comment [1991]—970 F.2d 1009
4A1.2 comment—970 F.2d 1017
4A1.2 comment—971 F.2d 357
4A1.2 comment—971 F.2d 1302
4A1.2 comment—971 F.2d 1368
4A1.2 comment [1991]—973 F.2d 1
4A1.2 comment—974 F.2d 140
4A1.2 comment—974 F.2d 687
4A1.2 comment [1990]—974 F.2d 687
4A1.2 comment—975 F.2d 1120
4A1.2 comment—976 F.2d 1096
4A1.2 comment—980 F.2d 259
4A1.2 comment—981 F.2d 367
4A1.2 comment—981 F.2d 640
4A1.2 comment—981 F.2d 664
4A1.2 comment—982 F.2d 187
4A1.2 comment [1988]—982 F.2d 187
4A1.2 comment—982 F.2d 354
4A1.2 comment—983 F.2d 558
4A1.2 comment—984 F.2d 701
4A1.2 comment—984 F.2d 1289
4A1.2 comment—986 F.2d 14
4A1.2 comment—986 F.2d 321
4A1.2 comment—986 F.2d 337
4A1.2 comment—988 F.2d 80
4A1.2 comment—988 F.2d 493
4A1.2 comment—988 F.2d 500
4A1.2 comment—988 F.2d 1002
4A1.2 comment—989 F.2d 261
4A1.2 comment—989 F.2d 1117
4A1.2 comment—989 F.2d 1137
4A1.2 comment—991 F.2d 171
4A1.2 comment—991 F.2d 195
4A1.2 comment—991 F.2d 700
4A1.2 comment—991 F.2d 1162
4A1.2 comment [1990]—991 F.2d 1162
4A1.2 comment—991 F.2d 1468
4A1.2 comment—992 F.2d 87
4A1.2 comment—992 F.2d 853
4A1.2 comment—992 F.2d 1008
4A1.2 comment [1992]—994 F.2d 412
4A1.2 comment—995 F.2d 536
4A1.2 comment—996 F.2d 946
4A1.2 comment—997 F.2d 343
4A1.2 comment—999 F.2d 348
4A1.2 comment—999 F.2d 474
4A1.2 comment—999 F.2d 1326
4A1.2 comment—1 F.3d 910
4A1.2 comment—2 F.3d 200
4A1.2 comment—2 F.3d 218
4A1.2 comment—2 F.3d 656

4A1.2 comment—3 F.3d 325
4A1.2 comment—3 F.3d 1217
4A1.2 comment—4 F.3d 636
4A1.2 comment—4 F.3d 941
4A1.2 comment—5 F.3d 435
4A1.2 comment—6 F.3d 1095
4A1.2 comment—6 F.3d 1201
4A1.2 comment—7 F.3d 744
4A1.2 comment—8 F.3d 1037
4A1.2 comment [1993]—12 F.3d 618
4A1.2 comment—13 F.3d 1182
4A1.2 comment [1993]—14 F.3d 18
4A1.2 comment—14 F.3d 106
4A1.2 comment—14 F.3d 1093
4A1.2 comment—15 F.3d 526
4A1.2 comment—15 F.3d 816
4A1.2 comment—17 F.3d 192
4A1.2 comment [1992]—18 F.3d 1355
4A1.2 comment—20 F.3d 817
4A1.2 comment—694 F.Supp. 1488
4A1.2 comment—709 F.Supp. 908
4A1.2 comment—733 F.Supp. 1003
4A1.2 comment—747 F.Supp. 813
4A1.2 comment—763 F.Supp. 277
4A1.2 comment—773 F.Supp. 1400
4A1.2 comment—775 F.Supp. 582
4A1.2 comment—779 F.Supp. 1285
4A1.2 comment—780 F.Supp. 1201
4A1.2 comment—801 F.Supp. 382
4A1.2 comment—802 F.Supp. 559
4A1.2 comment—803 F.Supp. 675
4A1.2 comment—814 F.Supp. 958
4A1.2 comment—843 F.Supp. 38
4A1.3—113 S.Ct. 1913
4A1.3—868 F.2d 122
4A1.3—868 F.2d 128
4A1.3—869 F.2d 54
4A1.3—871 F.2d 513
4A1.3—872 F.2d 597
4A1.3—873 F.2d 765
4A1.3—874 F.2d 43
4A1.3—874 F.2d 466
4A1.3—876 F.2d 784
4A1.3—877 F.2d 664
4A1.3—878 F.2d 50
4A1.3—879 F.2d 1247
4A1.3—882 F.2d 1059
4A1.3—883 F.2d 1007
4A1.3—884 F.2d 170
4A1.3—884 F.2d 1314
4A1.3—886 F.2d 215
4A1.3—886 F.2d 383
4A1.3—888 F.2d 79
4A1.3—889 F.2d 441
4A1.3—889 F.2d 916
4A1.3—891 F.2d 405
4A1.3—891 F.2d 528
4A1.3—891 F.2d 962
4A1.3—892 F.2d 473
4A1.3—893 F.2d 63
4A1.3—893 F.2d 276
4A1.3—893 F.2d 679
4A1.3—895 F.2d 184
4A1.3—895 F.2d 1375
4A1.3—896 F.2d 642
4A1.3—897 F.2d 1300
4A1.3—898 F.2d 91
4A1.3—898 F.2d 203
4A1.3—898 F.2d 642
4A1.3—898 F.2d 878
4A1.3—898 F.2d 968
4A1.3—898 F.2d 1378
4A1.3—899 F.2d 582
4A1.3—899 F.2d 983
4A1.3—901 F.2d 555
4A1.3—901 F.2d 746
4A1.3—901 F.2d 988
4A1.3—901 F.2d 1000
4A1.3—901 F.2d 1394
4A1.3—902 F.2d 501
4A1.3—903 F.2d 540
4A1.3—903 F.2d 1313
4A1.3—904 F.2d 365
4A1.3—904 F.2d 1036
4A1.3—905 F.2d 279
4A1.3—905 F.2d 343
4A1.3—905 F.2d 580
4A1.3—905 F.2d 867
4A1.3—905 F.2d 1432
4A1.3—905 F.2d 1450
4A1.3—907 F.2d 87
4A1.3—907 F.2d 121
4A1.3—907 F.2d 456
4A1.3—908 F.2d 365
4A1.3—908 F.2d 425
4A1.3—908 F.2d 550
4A1.3—909 F.2d 61
4A1.3—909 F.2d 759
4A1.3—910 F.2d 547
4A1.3—910 F.2d 1574

4A1.3—912 F.2d 448
4A1.3—912 F.2d 598
4A1.3—913 F.2d 136
4A1.3—914 F.2d 98
4A1.3—914 F.2d 139
4A1.3—914 F.2d 330
4A1.3—914 F.2d 959
4A1.3—914 F.2d 1340
4A1.3—915 F.2d 474
4A1.3—915 F.2d 618
4A1.3—915 F.2d 1220
4A1.3—916 F.2d 157
4A1.3—916 F.2d 553
4A1.3—916 F.2d 916
4A1.3—916 F.2d 1020
4A1.3—917 F.2d 165
4A1.3—917 F.2d 411
4A1.3—917 F.2d 477
4A1.3—917 F.2d 512
4A1.3—917 F.2d 1057
4A1.3—918 F.2d 1084
4A1.3—920 F.2d 399
4A1.3—920 F.2d 714
4A1.3—920 F.2d 810
4A1.3—920 F.2d 1330
4A1.3—920 F.2d 1570
4A1.3—921 F.2d 985
4A1.3—921 F.2d 1068
4A1.3—922 F.2d 578
4A1.3—922 F.2d 1490
4A1.3—923 F.2d 358
4A1.3—924 F.2d 23
4A1.3—924 F.2d 187
4A1.3—924 F.2d 462
4A1.3—924 F.2d 721
4A1.3—924 F.2d 800
4A1.3—924 F.2d 1148
4A1.3—926 F.2d 64
4A1.3—926 F.2d 128
4A1.3—926 F.2d 734
4A1.3—926 F.2d 999
4A1.3—927 F.2d 1376
4A1.3—928 F.2d 420
4A1.3—928 F.2d 844
4A1.3—929 F.2d 213
4A1.3—929 F.2d 267
4A1.3—929 F.2d 930
4A1.3—929 F.2d 1324
4A1.3—930 F.2d 495
4A1.3—930 F.2d 542
4A1.3—930 F.2d 744
4A1.3—931 F.2d 705
4A1.3—932 F.2d 342
4A1.3—932 F.2d 358
4A1.3—934 F.2d 190
4A1.3—935 F.2d 9
4A1.3—935 F.2d 149
4A1.3—937 F.2d 58
4A1.3—937 F.2d 676
4A1.3—938 F.2d 172
4A1.3—938 F.2d 210
4A1.3—938 F.2d 519
4A1.3—939 F.2d 929
4A1.3—941 F.2d 133
4A1.3—941 F.2d 858
4A1.3—941 F.2d 1019
4A1.3—941 F.2d 1090
4A1.3—944 F.2d 1106
4A1.3—945 F.2d 1096
4A1.3—945 F.2d 1504
4A1.3—946 F.2d 142
4A1.3—946 F.2d 484
4A1.3—948 F.2d 210
4A1.3—948 F.2d 448
4A1.3—948 F.2d 732
4A1.3—948 F.2d 1093
4A1.3—950 F.2d 444
4A1.3—951 F.2d 405
4A1.3—952 F.2d 514
4A1.3—952 F.2d 1066
4A1.3—954 F.2d 1386
4A1.3—955 F.2d 397
4A1.3—957 F.2d 694
4A1.3—958 F.2d 804
4A1.3—961 F.2d 103
4A1.3—961 F.2d 1110
4A1.3—962 F.2d 873
4A1.3—962 F.2d 894
4A1.3—963 F.2d 711
4A1.3—963 F.2d 736
4A1.3—964 F.2d 66
4A1.3—965 F.2d 206
4A1.3—965 F.2d 262
4A1.3—965 F.2d 651
4A1.3—966 F.2d 868
4A1.3—967 F.2d 20
4A1.3—967 F.2d 101
4A1.3—967 F.2d 539
4A1.3—967 F.2d 561
4A1.3—968 F.2d 47

4A1.3—968 F.2d 216
4A1.3—968 F.2d 1159
4A1.3—968 F.2d 1167
4A1.3—968 F.2d 1193
4A1.3—969 F.2d 39
4A1.3—971 F.2d 357
4A1.3—971 F.2d 1302
4A1.3—971 F.2d 1368
4A1.3—972 F.2d 218
4A1.3—972 F.2d 958
4A1.3—975 F.2d 305
4A1.3—977 F.2d 321
4A1.3—977 F.2d 331
4A1.3—977 F.2d 540
4A1.3—977 F.2d 861
4A1.3—978 F.2d 746
4A1.3—979 F.2d 146
4A1.3—979 F.2d 249
4A1.3—979 F.2d 1042
4A1.3—980 F.2d 645
4A1.3—981 F.2d 344
4A1.3—981 F.2d 640
4A1.3—981 F.2d 1123
4A1.3—983 F.2d 106
4A1.3—983 F.2d 558
4A1.3—983 F.2d 851
4A1.3—983 F.2d 1507
4A1.3—984 F.2d 143
4A1.3—984 F.2d 658
4A1.3—984 F.2d 701
4A1.3—984 F.2d 899
4A1.3—985 F.2d 443
4A1.3—985 F.2d 478
4A1.3—985 F.2d 1293
4A1.3—986 F.2d 166
4A1.3—987 F.2d 878
4A1.3—988 F.2d 206
4A1.3—988 F.2d 440
4A1.3—988 F.2d 677
4A1.3—988 F.2d 750
4A1.3—989 F.2d 261
4A1.3—989 F.2d 1137
4A1.3—990 F.2d 178
4A1.3 [1990]—991 F.2d 203
4A1.3—991 F.2d 1110
4A1.3—991 F.2d 1350
4A1.3—991 F.2d 1445
4A1.3—992 F.2d 1008
4A1.3—993 F.2d 187
4A1.3—993 F.2d 821
4A1.3—994 F.2d 942
4A1.3—994 F.2d 1204
4A1.3—995 F.2d 936
4A1.3—996 F.2d 83
4A1.3—996 F.2d 946
4A1.3—997 F.2d 343
4A1.3—998 F.2d 622
4A1.3—999 F.2d 1150
4A1.3—1 F.3d 457
4A1.3—1 F.3d 735
4A1.3—2 F.3d 1218
4A1.3—3 F.3d 316
4A1.3—3 F.3d 1217
4A1.3—5 F.3d 986
4A1.3—6 F.3d 960
4A1.3—6 F.3d 1095
4A1.3—7 F.3d 516
4A1.3—7 F.3d 691
4A1.3—7 F.3d 744
4A1.3—7 F.3d 813
4A1.3—7 F.3d 1394
4A1.3—8 F.3d 839
4A1.3—8 F.3d 1379
4A1.3—9 F.3d 907
4A1.3—9 F.3d 1116
4A1.3—11 F.3d 10
4A1.3—11 F.3d 74
4A1.3—12 F.3d 1540
4A1.3—13 F.3d 447
4A1.3—13 F.3d 555
4A1.3—14 F.3d 128
4A1.3—14 F.3d 1093
4A1.3—15 F.3d 188
4A1.3—15 F.3d 553
4A1.3—15 F.3d 646
4A1.3—16 F.3d 681
4A1.3—18 F.3d 41
4A1.3—19 F.3d 177
4A1.3—20 F.3d 918
4A1.3—20 F.3d 1336
4A1.3—22 F.3d 662
4A1.3—22 F.3d 981
4A1.3—694 F.Supp. 1488
4A1.3—706 F.Supp. 331
4A1.3—712 F.Supp. 707
4A1.3—712 F.Supp. 1327
4A1.3—719 F.Supp. 199
4A1.3—729 F.Supp. 1120
4A1.3—733 F.Supp. 1174
4A1.3—733 F.Supp. 1256

4A1.3—740 F.Supp. 1332
4A1.3—740 F.Supp. 1502
4A1.3—741 F.Supp. 12
4A1.3—751 F.Supp. 168
4A1.3—751 F.Supp. 1161
4A1.3—753 F.Supp. 1289
4A1.3—760 F.Supp. 1332
4A1.3—761 F.Supp. 697
4A1.3—763 F.Supp. 277
4A1.3—794 F.Supp. 425
4A1.3—802 F.Supp. 657
4A1.3—804 F.Supp. 19
4A1.3—825 F.Supp. 866
4A1.3—829 F.Supp. 478
4A1.3—835 F.Supp. 1466
4A1.3—843 F.Supp. 38
4A1.3(a)—928 F.2d 844
4A1.3(a)—938 F.2d 210
4A1.3(a)—946 F.2d 13
4A1.3(a)—966 F.2d 868
4A1.3(a)—979 F.2d 146
4A1.3(a)—983 F.2d 1507
4A1.3(a)—986 F.2d 166
4A1.3(a)—987 F.2d 475
4A1.3(a)—989 F.2d 347
4A1.3(a)—22 F.3d 981
4A1.3(a)—694 F.Supp. 1488
4A1.3(a-c)—941 F.2d 133
4A1.3(b)—868 F.2d 128
4A1.3(b)—879 F.2d 1247
4A1.3(b)—953 F.2d 1449
4A1.3(b)—954 F.2d 1386
4A1.3(c)—901 F.2d 746
4A1.3(c)—918 F.2d 1084
4A1.3(d)—868 F.2d 54
4A1.3(d)—874 F.2d 466
4A1.3(d)—901 F.2d 746
4A1.3(d)—932 F.2d 342
4A1.3(d)—938 F.2d 1164
4A1.3(d)—955 F.2d 14
4A1.3(d)—13 F.3d 447
4A1.3(d)—15 F.3d 646
4A1.3(e)—868 F.2d 128
4A1.3(e)—874 F.2d 466
4A1.3(e)—891 F.2d 405
4A1.3(e)—896 F.2d 678
4A1.3(e)—903 F.2d 341
4A1.3(e)—905 F.2d 337
4A1.3(e)—905 F.2d 1450
4A1.3(e)—908 F.2d 425
4A1.3(e)—909 F.2d 196
4A1.3(e)—910 F.2d 1574
4A1.3(e)—930 F.2d 542
4A1.3(e)—935 F.2d 4
4A1.3(e)—946 F.2d 584
4A1.3(e)—948 F.2d 732
4A1.3(e)—951 F.2d 405
4A1.3(e)—955 F.2d 14
4A1.3(e)—955 F.2d 786
4A1.3(e)—971 F.2d 357
4A1.3(e)—971 F.2d 1302
4A1.3(e)—977 F.2d 331
4A1.3(e)—979 F.2d 146
4A1.3(e)—997 F.2d 343
4A1.3(e)—11 F.3d 10
4A1.3(e)—11 F.3d 1392
4A1.3(e)—13 F.3d 447
4A1.3(e)—22 F.3d 981
4A1.3(e)—733 F.Supp. 1174
4A1.3(e)—802 F.Supp. 559
4A1.3(e)(4)—874 F.2d 466
4A1.3 comment—884 F.2d 1314
4A1.3 comment—903 F.2d 540
4A1.3 comment—907 F.2d 121
4A1.3 comment—912 F.2d 598
4A1.3 comment—917 F.2d 512
4A1.3 comment—938 F.2d 210
4A1.3 comment—941 F.2d 133
4A1.3 comment—955 F.2d 14
4A1.3 comment—956 F.2d 1555
4A1.3 comment—15 F.3d 553
4A1.3 comment—712 F.Supp. 1327
4A1.3 comment—751 F.Supp. 1161
4A1.3 comment—800 F.Supp. 1012

Part B: Career Offenders and Criminal Livelihood

4B1.1—113 S.Ct. 1913
4B1.1—835 F.2d 1195
4B1.1—873 F.2d 495
4B1.1—873 F.2d 709
4B1.1—875 F.2d 143
4B1.1—875 F.2d 1110
4B1.1—879 F.2d 541
4B1.1—881 F.2d 155
4B1.1—881 F.2d 973
4B1.1—882 F.2d 922
4B1.1—884 F.2d 121
4B1.1—886 F.2d 474

4B1.1—888 F.2d 76
4B1.1—888 F.2d 79
4B1.1—889 F.2d 1187
4B1.1—890 F.2d 9
4B1.1—892 F.2d 296
4B1.1—892 F.2d 1170
4B1.1—893 F.2d 815
4B1.1—894 F.2d 996
4B1.1—895 F.2d 487
4B1.1—895 F.2d 615
4B1.1—896 F.2d 906
4B1.1—897 F.2d 1099
4B1.1—898 F.2d 119
4B1.1—898 F.2d 878
4B1.1—898 F.2d 966
4B1.1—898 F.2d 1461
4B1.1—899 F.2d 515
4B1.1—900 F.2d 119
4B1.1—901 F.2d 647
4B1.1—901 F.2d 830
4B1.1—901 F.2d 863
4B1.1—901 F.2d 988
4B1.1—901 F.2d 1394
4B1.1—902 F.2d 570
4B1.1—902 F.2d 1129
4B1.1—902 F.2d 1311
4B1.1—904 F.2d 365
4B1.1—905 F.2d 3
4B1.1—905 F.2d 217
4B1.1—905 F.2d 935
4B1.1—907 F.2d 1
4B1.1—907 F.2d 117
4B1.1—907 F.2d 121
4B1.1—907 F.2d 456
4B1.1—907 F.2d 929
4B1.1—908 F.2d 176
4B1.1—908 F.2d 365
4B1.1—909 F.2d 1164
4B1.1—910 F.2d 221
4B1.1—910 F.2d 530
4B1.1—910 F.2d 663
4B1.1—910 F.2d 760
4B1.1—910 F.2d 1241
4B1.1—910 F.2d 1484
4B1.1—910 F.2d 1524
4B1.1—911 F.2d 542
4B1.1—913 F.2d 982
4B1.1—914 F.2d 213
4B1.1—914 F.2d 696
4B1.1—914 F.2d 915
4B1.1—915 F.2d 132
4B1.1—915 F.2d 392
4B1.1—915 F.2d 1455
4B1.1—916 F.2d 553
4B1.1—917 F.2d 607
4B1.1—917 F.2d 1083
4B1.1—918 F.2d 30
4B1.1—918 F.2d 749
4B1.1—918 F.2d 1343
4B1.1—919 F.2d 568
4B1.1—920 F.2d 495
4B1.1—920 F.2d 569
4B1.1—920 F.2d 810
4B1.1—920 F.2d 823
4B1.1—920 F.2d 1395
4B1.1—921 F.2d 1095
4B1.1—922 F.2d 578
4B1.1—922 F.2d 624
4B1.1—923 F.2d 13
4B1.1—923 F.2d 1371
4B1.1—925 F.2d 535
4B1.1—926 F.2d 328
4B1.1—927 F.2d 136
4B1.1—929 F.2d 116
4B1.1—929 F.2d 213
4B1.1—929 F.2d 1369
4B1.1—930 F.2d 789
4B1.1—931 F.2d 490
4B1.1—931 F.2d 1201
4B1.1—932 F.2d 342
4B1.1—932 F.2d 624
4B1.1—932 F.2d 752
4B1.1—933 F.2d 111
4B1.1—935 F.2d 201
4B1.1—935 F.2d 295
4B1.1—935 F.2d 1053
4B1.1 [1988]—936 F.2d 533
4B1.1—936 F.2d 764
4B1.1—936 F.2d 916
4B1.1—937 F.2d 542
4B1.1—937 F.2d 947
4B1.1—937 F.2d 1369
4B1.1—938 F.2d 96
4B1.1—938 F.2d 139
4B1.1—938 F.2d 519
4B1.1—938 F.2d 1551
4B1.1—939 F.2d 191
4B1.1—940 F.2d 1182
4B1.1—941 F.2d 133
4B1.1—941 F.2d 858

4B1.1—941 F.2d 1019
4B1.1—942 F.2d 439
4B1.1—942 F.2d 644
4B1.1—943 F.2d 348
4B1.1—944 F.2d 73
4B1.1—944 F.2d 1106
4B1.1—945 F.2d 989
4B1.1—945 F.2d 1504
4B1.1—946 F.2d 615
4B1.1—947 F.2d 1018
4B1.1—947 F.2d 1263
4B1.1—948 F.2d 215
4B1.1—948 F.2d 1449
4B1.1—951 F.2d 1300
4B1.1—952 F.2d 914
4B1.1—952 F.2d 1066
4B1.1—953 F.2d 110
4B1.1—953 F.2d 1106
4B1.1—954 F.2d 227
4B1.1—954 F.2d 253
4B1.1—954 F.2d 1005
4B1.1—955 F.2d 291
4B1.1—955 F.2d 814
4B1.1—955 F.2d 858
4B1.1—956 F.2d 85
4B1.1—957 F.2d 520
4B1.1—958 F.2d 234
4B1.1—958 F.2d 268
4B1.1—959 F.2d 1005
4B1.1—960 F.2d 724
4B1.1—960 F.2d 830
4B1.1—961 F.2d 173
4B1.1—961 F.2d 1390
4B1.1—962 F.2d 165
4B1.1—962 F.2d 484
4B1.1—962 F.2d 551
4B1.1—962 F.2d 560
4B1.1—963 F.2d 224
4B1.1—963 F.2d 1467
4B1.1—964 F.2d 390
4B1.1—964 F.2d 564
4B1.1—964 F.2d 677
4B1.1—964 F.2d 751
4B1.1—965 F.2d 262
4B1.1—966 F.2d 703
4B1.1—967 F.2d 287
4B1.1—967 F.2d 314
4B1.1—968 F.2d 47
4B1.1—968 F.2d 216
4B1.1—968 F.2d 703
4B1.1—968 F.2d 1047
4B1.1—968 F.2d 1167
4B1.1—969 F.2d 39
4B1.1—970 F.2d 1009
4B1.1—970 F.2d 1017
4B1.1—970 F.2d 1312
4B1.1—972 F.2d 269
4B1.1—972 F.2d 489
4B1.1—972 F.2d 948
4B1.1—972 F.2d 1000
4B1.1—973 F.2d 1354
4B1.1—974 F.2d 1215
4B1.1—977 F.2d 105
4B1.1—978 F.2d 124
4B1.1—979 F.2d 1042
4B1.1—979 F.2d 1372
4B1.1—981 F.2d 645
4B1.1—981 F.2d 915
4B1.1—982 F.2d 315
4B1.1—982 F.2d 1199
4B1.1—983 F.2d 1
4B1.1—983 F.2d 558
4B1.1—984 F.2d 21
4B1.1—984 F.2d 1084
4B1.1—986 F.2d 312
4B1.1—986 F.2d 321
4B1.1—986 F.2d 1446
4B1.1—988 F.2d 1384
4B1.1—990 F.2d 373
4B1.1—990 F.2d 469
4B1.1—990 F.2d 1367
4B1.1—991 F.2d 590
4B1.1—991 F.2d 1162
4B1.1—992 F.2d 853
4B1.1—993 F.2d 180
4B1.1—993 F.2d 1439
4B1.1—994 F.2d 714
4B1.1—994 F.2d 1467
4B1.1—995 F.2d 142
4B1.1—995 F.2d 323
4B1.1 [1992]—995 F.2d 323
4B1.1—995 F.2d 536
4B1.1—995 F.2d 1285
4B1.1—997 F.2d 146
4B1.1—997 F.2d 343
4B1.1—998 F.2d 42
4B1.1—999 F.2d 966
4B1.1—999 F.2d 1048
4B1.1—999 F.2d 1144
4B1.1—999 F.2d 1326

4B1.1—1 F.3d 735
4B1.1—1 F.3d 889
4B1.1—1 F.3d 1144
4B1.1—2 F.3d 200
4B1.1—2 F.3d 218
4B1.1—3 F.3d 325
4B1.1—4 F.3d 337
4B1.1—4 F.3d 941
4B1.1—5 F.3d 372
4B1.1 [1991]—5 F.3d 781
4B1.1—7 F.3d 144
4B1.1—7 F.3d 516
4B1.1—7 F.3d 783
4B1.1—7 F.3d 840
4B1.1—7 F.3d 957
4B1.1—8 F.3d 688
4B1.1—8 F.3d 839
4B1.1—8 F.3d 1037
4B1.1—8 F.3d 1379
4B1.1—9 F.3d 1
4B1.1—9 F.3d 1480
4B1.1—10 F.3d 724
4B1.1—11 F.3d 505
4B1.1—11 F.3d 788
4B1.1—12 F.3d 280
4B1.1—14 F.3d 1093
4B1.1—15 F.3d 272
4B1.1—15 F.3d 526
4B1.1—15 F.3d 816
4B1.1—15 F.3d 830
4B1.1—16 F.3d 748
4B1.1—16 F.3d 854
4B1.1—17 F.3d 192
4B1.1—17 F.3d 235
4B1.1—17 F.3d 306
4B1.1—18 F.3d 1461
4B1.1—19 F.3d 226
4B1.1—22 F.3d 15
4B1.1—22 F.3d 788
4B1.1—23 F.3d 216
4B1.1—694 F.Supp. 1488
4B1.1—708 F.Supp. 461
4B1.1—715 F.Supp. 261
4B1.1—723 F.Supp. 79
4B1.1—733 F.Supp. 1003
4B1.1—740 F.Supp. 1332
4B1.1—750 F.Supp. 388
4B1.1—753 F.Supp. 1191
4B1.1—756 F.Supp. 470
4B1.1—760 F.Supp. 1332
4B1.1—767 F.Supp. 11
4B1.1—773 F.Supp. 1400
4B1.1—774 F.Supp. 1582
4B1.1—775 F.Supp. 582
4B1.1—794 F.Supp. 425
4B1.1—796 F.Supp. 366
4B1.1—817 F.Supp. 176
4B1.1—835 F.Supp. 1466
4B1.1—843 F.Supp. 38
4B1.1—844 F.Supp. 677
4B1.1(1)—960 F.2d 830
4B1.1(2)—16 F.3d 854
4B1.1(3)—910 F.2d 1484
4B1.1(3)—747 F.Supp. 813
4B1.1(A)—941 F.2d 761
4B1.1(A)—964 F.2d 390
4B1.1(A)—964 F.2d 751
4B1.1(A)—997 F.2d 1426
4B1.1(A)—758 F.Supp. 195
4B1.1(B)—929 F.2d 213
4B1.1(B)—941 F.2d 761
4B1.1(B)—964 F.2d 390
4B1.1(B)—997 F.2d 1426
4B1.1(C)—929 F.2d 213
4B1.1(C)—740 F.Supp. 1332
4B1.1 et seq.—934 F.2d 190
4B1.1 et seq.—947 F.2d 1263
4B1.1 et seq.—956 F.2d 1555
4B1.1 et seq.—962 F.2d 484
4B1.1 et seq.—990 F.2d 1367
4B1.1 et seq.—844 F.Supp. 677
4B1.1 comment—924 F.2d 545
4B1.1 comment—930 F.2d 789
4B1.1 comment—935 F.2d 201
4B1.1 comment—935 F.2d 295
4B1.1 comment—939 F.2d 191
4B1.1 comment—968 F.2d 1167
4B1.1 comment—983 F.2d 851
4B1.2—113 S.Ct. 1913
4B1.2—875 F.2d 143
4Bi.2—898 F.2d 91
4B1.2—900 F.2d 119
4B1.2—900 F.2d 1039
4B1.2 [1988]—901 F.2d 647
4B1.2—902 F.2d 570
4B1.2—902 F.2d 1129
4B1.2—910 F.2d 81
4B1.2—910 F.2d 663
4B1.2—911 F.2d 542
4B1.2—914 F.2d 696

4B1.2—920 F.2d 569
4B1.2—925 F.2d 535
4B1.2—926 F.2d 328
4B1.2—926 F.2d 588
4B1.2—927 F.2d 136
4B1.2—928 F.2d 324
4B1.2—930 F.2d 789
4B1.2—932 F.2d 752
4B1.2—934 F.2d 190
4B1.2—935 F.2d 295
4B1.2—936 F.2d 764
4B1.2—937 F.2d 1369
4B1.2—938 F.2d 519
4B1.2—939 F.2d 191
4B1.2—942 F.2d 439
4B1.2—943 F.2d 348
4B1.2—943 F.2d 1268
4B1.2—944 F.2d 73
4B1.2—944 F.2d 1106
4B1.2—945 F.2d 989
4B1.2—945 F.2d 1504
4B1.2—947 F.2d 1018
4B1.2—947 F.2d 1263
4B1.2—951 F.2d 586
4B1.2—952 F.2d 1066
4B1.2—953 F.2d 110
4B1.2—954 F.2d 253
4B1.2—955 F.2d 291
4B1.2—957 F.2d 520
4B1.2—957 F.2d 813
4B1.2—960 F.2d 117
4B1.2—961 F.2d 1390
4B1.2—962 F.2d 165
4B1.2—963 F.2d 224
4B1.2—964 F.2d 390
4B1.2—965 F.2d 740
4B1.2—966 F.2d 703
4B1.2—967 F.2d 287
4B1.2—967 F.2d 314
4B1.2—982 F.2d 1199
4B1.2—983 F.2d 1
4B1.2—986 F.2d 312
4B1.2—986 F.2d 1026
4B1.2—986 F.2d 1446
4B1.2—990 F.2d 469
4B1.2—990 F.2d 1367
4B1.2—991 F.2d 1162
4B1.2—992 F.2d 356
4B1.2—993 F.2d 180
4B1.2—996 F.2d 993
4B1.2—2 F.3d 200
4B1.2—3 F.3d 325
4B1.2 [1988]—7 F.3d 840
4B1.2—8 F.3d 1268
4B1.2—9 F.3d 1
4B1.2—11 F.3d 788
4B1.2—17 F.3d 6
4B1.2—22 F.3d 15
4B1.2—22 F.3d 736
4B1.2—22 F.3d 788
4B1.2—687 F.Supp. 1329
4B1.2—704 F.Supp. 1398
4B1.2—715 F.Supp. 261
4B1.2—753 F.Supp. 1191
4B1.2—756 F.Supp. 470
4B1.2—801 F.Supp. 382
4B1.2—803 F.Supp. 1041
4B1.2—844 F.Supp. 677
4B1.2(1)—875 F.2d 1110
4B1.2(1)—881 F.2d 973
4B1.2(1)—886 F.2d 383
4B1.2(1)—891 F.2d 507
4B1.2(1)—893 F.2d 815
4B1.2(1) [1988]—901 F.2d 647
4B1.2(1)—908 F.2d 176
4B1.2(1)—910 F.2d 1524
4B1.2(1)—914 F.2d 915
4B1.2(1)—918 F.2d 749
4B1.2(1) [1988]—928 F.2d 324
4B1.2(1)—942 F.2d 439
4B1.2(1)—955 F.2d 858
4B1.2(1)—957 F.2d 520
4B1.2(1)—960 F.2d 830
4B1.2(1)—961 F.2d 173
4B1.2(1)—981 F.2d 915
4B1.2(1)—983 F.2d 1
4B1.2(1)—984 F.2d 21
4B1.2(1)—986 F.2d 1446
4B1.2(1)—990 F.2d 469
4B1.2(1)—994 F.2d 714
4B1.2(1)—997 F.2d 146
4B1.2(1)—999 F.2d 1144
4B1.2(1)—1 F.3d 889
4B1.2(1)—7 F.3d 144
4B1.2(1) [1992]—10 F.3d 724
4B1.2(1)—15 F.3d 272
4B1.2(1)—17 F.3d 6
4B1.2(1)—22 F.3d 583
4B1.2(1)—22 F.3d 736
4B1.2(1)—704 F.Supp. 1398

4B1.2(1)—723 F.Supp. 79
4B1.2(1)—726 F.Supp. 861
4B1.2(1)—832 F.Supp. 1297
4B1.2(1)(i)—925 F.2d 186
4B1.2(1)(i)—931 F.2d 1442
4B1.2(1)(i)—932 F.2d 624
4B1.2(1)(i)—957 F.2d 520
4B1.2(1)(i)—960 F.2d 830
4B1.2(1)(i)—964 F.2d 751
4B1.2(1)(i)—981 F.2d 915
4B1.2(1)(i)—983 F.2d 150
4B1.2(1)(i)—990 F.2d 373
4B1.2(1)(i)—990 F.2d 469
4B1.2(1)(i)—12 F.3d 1506
4B1.2(1)(i)—17 F.3d 6
4B1.2(1)(i)—832 F.Supp. 1297
4B1.2(1)(ii)—925 F.2d 516
4B1.2(1)(ii)—943 F.2d 1268
4B1.2(1)(ii)—954 F.2d 253
4B1.2(1)(ii)—955 F.2d 858
4B1.2(1)(ii)—960 F.2d 830
4B1.2(1)(ii)—964 F.2d 390
4B1.2(1)(ii)—964 F.2d 751
4B1.2(1)(ii)—970 F.2d 1312
4B1.2(1)(ii)—972 F.2d 269
4B1.2(1)(ii)—976 F.2d 844
4B1.2(1)(ii)—983 F.2d 1
4B1.2(1)(ii)—990 F.2d 373
4B1.2(1)(ii)—993 F.2d 180
4B1.2(1)(ii) [1992]—10 F.3d 724
4B1.2(1)(ii)—22 F.3d 15
4B1.2(1)(ii)—767 F.Supp. 11
4B1.2(1)(ii)—791 F.Supp. 244
4B1.2(1)(ii)—803 F.Supp. 1041
4B1.2(1)(ii)—832 F.Supp. 1297
4B1.2(2)—903 F.2d 540
4B1.2(2)—917 F.2d 607
4B1.2(2) [1988]—936 F.2d 533
4B1.2(2)—937 F.2d 542
4B1.2(2)—954 F.2d 1005
4B1.2(2)—956 F.2d 85
4B1.2(2)—960 F.2d 724
4B1.2(2)—983 F.2d 1
4B1.2(2)—986 F.2d 321
4B1.2(2)—990 F.2d 1367
4B1.2(2)—999 F.2d 1326
4B1.2(2)—3 F.3d 325
4B1.2(2)—8 F.3d 1268
4B1.2(2)—11 F.3d 505
4B1.2(2)—12 F.3d 280
4B1.2(3)—875 F.2d 1110
4B1.2(3)—888 F.2d 79
4B1.2(3)—898 F.2d 1461
4B1.2(3)—905 F.2d 217
4B1.2(3)—908 F.2d 365
4B1.2(3)—932 F.2d 342
4B1.2(3)—947 F.2d 1018
4B1.2(3)—970 F.2d 1017
4B1.2(3)—984 F.2d 1289
4B1.2(3)—997 F.2d 343
4B1.2(3)—3 F.3d 325
4B1.2(3)—15 F.3d 526
4B1.2(3)—17 F.3d 192
4B1.2(3)—733 F.Supp. 1003
4B1.2(3)(A)—898 F.2d 1461
4B1.2(3)(A)—902 F.2d 1311
4B1.2(3)(B)—920 F.2d 810
4B1.2(3)(B)—922 F.2d 578
4B1.2(3)(B)—997 F.2d 343
4B1.2 comment—886 F.2d 383
4B1.2 comment—898 F.2d 91
4B1.2 comment [1988]—901 F.2d 647
4B1.2 comment—902 F.2d 570
4B1.2 comment [1988]—903 F.2d 540
4B1.2 comment—904 F.2d 365
4B1.2 comment—905 F.2d 217
4B1.2 comment—907 F.2d 1
4B1.2 comment—909 F.2d 1164
4B1.2 comment—910 F.2d 81
4B1.2 comment—910 F.2d 1484
4B1.2 comment—911 F.2d 542
4B1.2 comment—915 F.2d 132
4B1.2 comment—917 F.2d 607
4B1.2 comment [1988]—917 F.2d 607
4B1.2 comment [1988]—919 F.2d 568
4B1.2 comment—922 F.2d 50
4B1.2 comment—922 F.2d 578
4B1.2 comment—923 F.2d 1371
4B1.2 comment—925 F.2d 516
4B1.2 comment—928 F.2d 310
4B1.2 comment—929 F.2d 116
4B1.2 comment—930 F.2d 789
4B1.2 comment—932 F.2d 624
4B1.2 comment—932 F.2d 752
4B1.2 comment—936 F.2d 916
4B1.2 comment—942 F.2d 439
4B1.2 comment—943 F.2d 1268
4B1.2 comment—947 F.2d 1018
4B1.2 comment—948 F.2d 1450
4B1.2 comment—951 F.2d 586

4B1.2 comment—953 F.2d 110
4B1.2 comment—955 F.2d 291
4B1.2 comment—955 F.2d 814
4B1.2 comment—955 F.2d 858
4B1.2 comment—957 F.2d 520
4B1.2 comment—957 F.2d 813
4B1.2 comment—960 F.2d 724
4B1.2 comment—961 F.2d 173
4B1.2 comment—961 F.2d 1390
4B1.2 comment—962 F.2d 165
4B1.2 comment—962 F.2d 484
4B1.2 comment—964 F.2d 564
4B1.2 comment—970 F.2d 1017
4B1.2 comment—972 F.2d 269
4B1.2 comment—981 F.2d 915
4B1.2 comment—983 F.2d 1
4B1.2 comment—984 F.2d 1289
4B1.2 comment—986 F.2d 321
4B1.2 comment—990 F.2d 1367
4B1.2 comment—991 F.2d 1162
4B1.2 comment—994 F.2d 1467
4B1.2 comment—999 F.2d 1326
4B1.2 comment—3 F.3d 325
4B1.2 comment [1990]—3 F.3d 325
4B1.2 comment—8 F.3d 1268
4B1.2 comment—11 F.3d 505
4B1.2 comment—14 F.3d 1093
4B1.2 comment—15 F.3d 526
4B1.2 comment—15 F.3d 830
4B1.2 comment—18 F.3d 1461
4B1.2 comment—22 F.3d 736
4B1.2 comment—723 F.Supp. 79
4B1.2 comment—753 F.Supp. 1191
4B1.2 comment—760 F.Supp. 1332
4B1.2 comment—767 F.Supp. 11
4B1.2 comment—803 F.Supp. 1041
4B1.2 comment—844 F.Supp. 677
4B1.2 note—835 F.2d 1195
4B1.3—873 F.2d 495
4B1.3—882 F.2d 1059
4B1.3—885 F.2d 441
4B1.3—887 F.2d 140
4B1.3—888 F.2d 1267
4B1.3—889 F.2d 1523
4B1.3—892 F.2d 756
4B1.3 [1988]—894 F.2d 74
4B1.3—899 F.2d 503
4B1.3—902 F.2d 1082
4B1.3 [1988]—902 F.2d 1082
4B1.3—906 F.2d 1424
4B1.3—907 F.2d 121
4B1.3—908 F.2d 260
4B1.3—909 F.2d 1447
4B1.3—912 F.2d 204
4B1.3—939 F.2d 503
4B1.3—946 F.2d 375
4B1.3—949 F.2d 905
4B1.3—951 F.2d 97
4B1.3—956 F.2d 1555
4B1.3—983 F.2d 851
4B1.3—19 F.3d 192
4B1.3—686 F.Supp. 1174
4B1.3—694 F.Supp. 1105
4B1.3—694 F.Supp. 1488
4B1.3—719 F.Supp. 199
4B1.3 comment—888 F.2d 1267
4B1.3 comment—906 F.2d 1424
4B1.3 comment—925 F.2d 828
4B1.3 comment—946 F.2d 375
4B1.3 comment—949 F.2d 905
4B1.3 comment—983 F.2d 851
4B1.4—954 F.2d 253
4B1.4—970 F.2d 1312
4B1.4—975 F.2d 1080
4B1.4—979 F.2d 1042
4B1.4—980 F.2d 980
4B1.4—981 F.2d 645
4B1.4—981 F.2d 1464
4B1.4—982 F.2d 4
4B1.4—984 F.2d 1162
4B1.4—988 F.2d 1002
4B1.4—989 F.2d 303
4B1.4—991 F.2d 524
4B1.4—992 F.2d 785
4B1.4—993 F.2d 1439
4B1.4—998 F.2d 42
4B1.4—7 F.3d 957
4B1.4—9 F.3d 890
4B1.4—13 F.3d 147
4B1.4—19 F.3d 1271
4B1.4—767 F.Supp. 11
4B1.4—829 F.Supp. 478
4B1.4(a)—980 F.2d 980
4B1.4(a) [1991]—1 F.3d 695
4B1.4(a)—20 F.3d 415
4B1.4(a)—758 F.Supp. 195
4B1.4(b)—970 F.2d 1312
4B1.4(b)(1)—970 F.2d 1312
4B1.4(b)(3)—970 F.2d 1312
4B1.4(b)(3)—996 F.2d 83

4B1.4(b)(3)(A)—970 F.2d 1312
4B1.4(b)(3)(A)—982 F.2d 4
4B1.4(b)(3)(A)—5 F.3d 868
4B1.4(b)(3)(A)—758 F.Supp. 195
4B1.4(b)(3)(A)—802 F.Supp. 559
4B1.4(b)(3)(B)—970 F.2d 1312
4B1.4(b)(3)(B) [1991]—1 F.3d 695
4B1.4(b)(3)(B)—7 F.3d 957
4B1.4(c)—982 F.2d 4
4B1.4(c)—19 F.3d 1271
4B1.4(c)(2)—970 F.2d 1312
4B1.4(c)(2)—982 F.2d 4
4B1.4(c)(2)—758 F.Supp. 195
4B1.4(c)(2)—802 F.Supp. 559
4B1.4(c)(2)—829 F.Supp. 478
4B1.4(c)(3) [1991]—1 F.3d 695
4B1.4(c)(3)—7 F.3d 957
4B1.4 comment—7 F.3d 957
4B1.4 comment—9 F.3d 890

CHAPTER 5—DETERMINIG THE SENTENCE

Part A: Sentencing Table

5A Sentencing Table—112 S.Ct. 1112
5A Sentencing Table—838 F.2d 932
5A Sentencing Table—855 F.2d 925
5A Sentencing Table—860 F.2d 35
5A Sentencing Table—867 F.2d 222
5A Sentencing Table—868 F.2d 1121
5A Sentencing Table—868 F.2d 1390
5A Sentencing Table—868 F.2d 1541
5A Sentencing Table—869 F.2d 54
5A Sentencing Table—872 F.2d 735
5A Sentencing Table—878 F.2d 164
5A Sentencing Table—882 F.2d 474
5A Sentencing Table—883 F.2d 963
5A Sentencing Table—889 F.2d 1336
5A Sentencing Table—891 F.2d 212
5A Sentencing Table—891 F.2d 300
5A Sentencing Table—895 F.2d 1198
5A Sentencing Table—897 F.2d 47
5A Sentencing Table—898 F.2d 36
5A Sentencing Table [1988]—900 F.2d 1357
5A Sentencing Table—901 F.2d 867
5A Sentencing Table—901 F.2d 988
5A Sentencing Table—902 F.2d 860
5A Sentencing Table—902 F.2d 873
5A Sentencing Table—903 F.2d 1478
5A Sentencing Table—906 F.2d 555
5A Sentencing Table—906 F.2d 1424
5A Sentencing Table—909 F.2d 392
5A Sentencing Table—913 F.2d 313
5A Sentencing Table—918 F.2d 1084
5A Sentencing Table—921 F.2d 987
5A Sentencing Table [1988]—930 F.2d 1486
5A Sentencing Table—934 F.2d 1114
5A Sentencing Table—948 F.2d 1093
5A Sentencing Table—955 F.2d 270
5A Sentencing Table—961 F.2d 103
5A Sentencing Table—961 F.2d 882
5A Sentencing Table—961 F.2d 1421
5A Sentencing Table—962 F.2d 894
5A Sentencing Table—962 F.2d 938
5A Sentencing Table—965 F.2d 1037
5A Sentencing Table—971 F.2d 200
5A Sentencing Table—978 F.2d 185
5A Sentencing Table—988 F.2d 712
5A Sentencing Table—991 F.2d 171
5A Sentencing Table—991 F.2d 866
5A Sentencing Table—992 F.2d 87
5A Sentencing Table—994 F.2d 412
5A Sentencing Table—994 F.2d 942
5A Sentencing Table—999 F.2d 80
5A Sentencing Table—5 F.3d 192
5A Sentencing Table—5 F.3d 1306
5A Sentencing Table—7 F.3d 1171
5A Sentencing Table—17 F.3d 1294
5A Sentencing Table—21 F.3d 632
5A Sentencing Table—684 F.Supp. 1506
5A Sentencing Table—684 F.Supp. 1535
5A Sentencing Table—686 F.Supp. 1174
5A Sentencing Table—687 F.Supp. 1403
5A Sentencing Table—691 F.Supp. 1036
5A Sentencing Table—692 F.Supp. 1427
5A Sentencing Table—694 F.Supp. 1406
5A Sentencing Table—694 F.Supp. 1488
5A Sentencing Table—703 F.Supp. 1350
5A Sentencing Table—708 F.Supp. 461
5A Sentencing Table—712 F.Supp. 707
5A Sentencing Table—733 F.Supp. 1256
5A Sentencing Table—760 F.Supp. 1332
5A Sentencing Table—776 F.Supp. 1030
5A comment—10 F.3d 263
5A2.0—967 F.2d 20

Part B: Probation

5B1.1—889 F.2d 1336
5B1.1—894 F.2d 1092
5B1.1—11 F.3d 52
5B1.1—694 F.Supp. 1406
5B1.1(a)(1)—22 F.3d 790
5B1.1(a)(2)—903 F.2d 1478
5B1.1(a)(2) [1988]—930 F.2d 1486
5B1.1(a)(2)—984 F.2d 251
5B1.1(a)(2)—688 F.Supp. 191
5B1.1(b)—11 F.3d 52
5B1.1(b)—709 F.Supp. 653
5B1.1(b)(1)—760 F.Supp. 1332
5B1.1 et seq.—902 F.2d 734
5B1.1 et seq.—941 F.2d 133
5B1.1 et seq.—684 F.Supp. 1535
5B1.1 et seq.—686 F.Supp. 1174
5B1.1-5B1.4—927 F.2d 1463
5B1.1-5F1.6—931 F.2d 905
5B1.1-5G1.3—891 F.2d 300
5B1.1 comment—971 F.2d 620
5B1.2—874 F.2d 248
5B1.2(a)(1)—21 F.3d 753
5B1.2(a)(1)—971 F.2d 620
5B1.3(a)—971 F.2d 620
5B1.3(a)—990 F.2d 372
5B1.3(c)—907 F.2d 31
5B1.3(c)—971 F.2d 620
5B1.3(d)—22 F.3d 790
5B1.4(a)—789 F.Supp. 957
5B1.4(a)(1)—960 F.2d 913
5B1.4(b)—994 F.2d 149
5B1.4(b)(14)—994 F.2d 149
5B1.4(b)(16)—922 F.2d 54
5B1.4(b)(20)—22 F.3d 790
5B1.4(b)(22)—959 F.2d 516

Part C: Imprisonment

5C1.1(a)—20 F.3d 193
5C1.1(c)—949 F.2d 905
5C1.1(c)(2)—903 F.2d 1478
5C1.1(c)(2)—984 F.2d 251
5C1.1(c)(3)—20 F.3d 193
5C1.1(d)—925 F.2d 889
5C1.1(d)—940 F.2d 985
5C1.1(d)—949 F.2d 905
5C1.1(d)—17 F.3d 660
5C1.1(d)(2)—940 F.2d 985
5C1.1(d)(2)—18 F.3d 443
5C1.1(e)—903 F.2d 1478
5C1.1(e)(2)—902 F.2d 133
5C1.1(e)(2)—940 F.2d 985
5C1.1(e)(3)—991 F.2d 552
5C1.1(e)(3)—17 F.3d 660
5C1.1(f)—902 F.2d 133
5C1.1(f)—986 F.2d 151
5C1.1 comment—20 F.3d 193
5C1.1 comment—940 F.2d 985
5C1.1 comment—971 F.2d 620
5C2.1(a) [1988]—893 F.2d 504
5C2.1(c) [1988]—930 F.2d 1486
5C2.1(c)—721 F.Supp. 493
5C2.1(c)(2) [1988]—937 F.2d 110
5C2.1(c)(2)—688 F.Supp. 191
5C2.1(c)(3) [1988]—900 F.2d 481
5C2.1(c)(3)—716 F.Supp. 3
5C2.1(d) [1988]—951 F.2d 144
5C2.1(d)—686 F.Supp. 1174
5C2.1(e) [1988]—930 F.2d 1486
5C2.1(f)—686 F.Supp. 1174

Part D: Supervised Release

5D1.1—925 F.2d 205
5D1.1—940 F.2d 985
5D1.1—941 F.2d 745
5D1.1—959 F.2d 516
5D1.1—978 F.2d 557
5D1.1—765 F.Supp. 1499
5D1.1(a)—898 F.2d 1493
5D1.1(a)—907 F.2d 133
5D1.1(a)—927 F.2d 1463
5D1.1(a)—940 F.2d 985
5D1.1(a)—951 F.2d 26
5D1.1(a)—966 F.2d 545
5D1.1(a)—986 F.2d 896
5D1.1(a)—754 F.Supp. 827
5D1.1(a)—833 F.Supp. 769
5D1.1(b)—907 F.2d 133
5D1.1(b)—940 F.2d 985
5D1.1(b)—764 F.Supp. 1067
5D1.1(b)—765 F.Supp. 1499
5D1.1 et seq.—895 F.2d 702
5D1.1 et seq.—941 F.2d 60
5D1.1 comment—959 F.2d 516
5D1.1 comment—966 F.2d 545
5D1.1 comment—754 F.Supp. 827
5D1.1 comment—765 F.Supp. 1499

5D1.2—907 F.2d 133
5D1.2—927 F.2d 1463
5D1.2—957 F.2d 1488
5D1.2—970 F.2d 602
5D1.2—974 F.2d 22
5D1.2—978 F.2d 557
5D1.2—997 F.2d 429
5D1.2(a)—918 F.2d 1156
5D1.2(a)—941 F.2d 60
5D1.2(a)—952 F.2d 995
5D1.2(a)—966 F.2d 91
5D1.2(a)—966 F.2d 545
5D1.2(a)—974 F.2d 22
5D1.2(a)—989 F.2d 384
5D1.2(a)—760 F.Supp. 1332
5D1.2(a)—784 F.Supp. 1366
5D1.2(b)—765 F.Supp. 1499
5D1.2(b)(1)—918 F.2d 1156
5D1.2(b)(2)—898 F.2d 1493
5D1.2(b)(2)—925 F.2d 101
5D1.2(b)(2)—933 F.2d 573
5D1.2(b)(2)—940 F.2d 985
5D1.2(b)(2)—941 F.2d 745
5D1.2(b)(2)—947 F.2d 1263
5D1.2(b)(2)—955 F.2d 291
5D1.2(b)(2)—979 F.2d 1522
5D1.2(b)(2)—994 F.2d 1332
5D1.2(b)(2)—733 F.Supp. 1256
5D1.2(b)(3)—908 F.2d 425
5D1.2(b)(3)—994 F.2d 1332
5D1.2 comment—974 F.2d 22
5D1.3—959 F.2d 516
5D1.3(b)—931 F.2d 1310
5D1.3(b)—978 F.2d 557
5D1.3(b)—998 F.2d 696
5D3.1—867 F.2d 783
5D3.1 [1988]—905 F.2d 82
5D3.1—680 F.Supp. 793
5D3.1—687 F.Supp. 1403
5D3.1(a)—868 F.2d 698
5D3.1(a) [1988]—895 F.2d 702
5D3.1(a) [1988]—898 F.2d 1493
5D3.1(a) [1988]—899 F.2d 371
5D3.1(a) [1988]—927 F.2d 1463
5D3.1(b)—707 F.Supp. 1101
5D3.1 et seq. [1988]—895 F.2d 702
5D3.1 comment [1988]—898 F.2d 91
5D3.1 comment [1988]—899 F.2d 371
5D3.2—867 F.2d 783
5D3.2 [1988]—905 F.2d 82
5D3.2 [1988]—927 F.2d 1463
5D3.2 [1988]—970 F.2d 602
5D3.2(a)—882 F.2d 693
5D3.2(a) [1988]—970 F.2d 602
5D3.2(a) [1988]—14 F.3d 165
5D3.2(b)(1)—884 F.2d 547
5D3.2(b)(1) [1988]—895 F.2d 702
5D3.2(b)(1) [1988]—898 F.2d 91
5D3.2(b)(1) [1988]—918 F.2d 1156
5D3.2(b)(2)—868 F.2d 698
5D3.2(b)(2) [1988]—898 F.2d 1493
5D3.2(b)—882 F.2d 693
5D3.3—867 F.2d 783

Part E: Restitution, Fines, Assessments, Forfeitures

5E1.1—901 F.2d 855
5E1.1—901 F.2d 1457
5E1.1—954 F.2d 79
5E1.1—981 F.2d 1418
5E1.1—9 F.3d 22
5E1.1—788 F.Supp. 433
5E1.1—817 F.Supp. 32
5E1.1(a)—916 F.2d 566
5E1.1(a)—917 F.2d 80
5E1.1(a)—942 F.2d 528
5E1.1(a)—2 F.3d 245
5E1.1(a)(2)—21 F.3d 107
5E1.1(c)—901 F.2d 855
5E1.1(c)—2 F.3d 245
5E1.1-5E1.4—2 F.3d 1318
5E1.1 comment—917 F.2d 80
5E1.1 comment—928 F.2d 243
5E1.1 comment—833 F.Supp. 769
5E1.2—900 F.2d 1201
5E1.2—917 F.2d 901
5E1.2—917 F.2d 1057
5E1.2—919 F.2d 123
5E1.2—924 F.2d 921
5E1.2—941 F.2d 60
5E1.2—942 F.2d 1282
5E1.2—945 F.2d 325
5E1.2—950 F.2d 705
5E1.2—963 F.2d 767
5E1.2—973 F.2d 611
5E1.2—980 F.2d 1110
5E1.2—8 F.3d 1481
5E1.2—9 F.3d 22
5E1.2—11 F.3d 315

5E1.2—15 F.3d 1292
5E1.2—16 F.3d 1110
5E1.2—19 F.3d 409
5E1.2—20 F.3d 1279
5E1.2—21 F.3d 753
5E1.2—22 F.3d 846
5E1.2—833 F.Supp. 769
5E1.2—848 F.Supp. 369
5E1.2(a)—930 F.2d 824
5E1.2(a)—932 F.2d 1155
5E1.2(a)—941 F.2d 60
5E1.2(a)—941 F.2d 220
5E1.2(a)—943 F.2d 1422
5E1.2(a)—946 F.2d 110
5E1.2(a)—962 F.2d 1535
5E1.2(a)—964 F.2d 83
5E1.2(a)—979 F.2d 1037
5E1.2(a)—981 F.2d 569
5E1.2(a)—985 F.2d 612
5E1.2(a)—985 F.2d 1175
5E1.2(a)—991 F.2d 370
5E1.2(a)—994 F.2d 658
5E1.2(a)—998 F.2d 534
5E1.2(a)—998 F.2d 601
5E1.2(a)—2 F.3d 245
5E1.2(a)—3 F.3d 368
5E1.2(a)—9 F.3d 22
5E1.2(a)—11 F.3d 52
5E1.2(a)—11 F.3d 315
5E1.2(a)—16 F.3d 1110
5E1.2(a)—17 F.3d 409
5E1.2(a)—20 F.3d 229
5E1.2(a)—20 F.3d 1030
5E1.2(a)—21 F.3d 7
5E1.2(a)—22 F.3d 430
5E1.2(a)—783 F.Supp. 665
5E1.2(a)—789 F.Supp. 957
5E1.2(b)—946 F.2d 19
5E1.2(c) [1990]—971 F.2d 1441
5E1.2(c)—980 F.2d 1110
5E1.2(c)—998 F.2d 534
5E1.2(c)—20 F.3d 1279
5E1.2(c)—783 F.Supp. 1109
5E1.2(c)—789 F.Supp. 957
5E1.2(c)(1) [1990]—971 F.2d 1441
5E1.2(c)(1)(A)—945 F.2d 851
5E1.2(c)(2)—915 F.2d 474
5E1.2(c)(3)—915 F.2d 474
5E1.2(c)(3)—919 F.2d 123
5E1.2(c)(3)—932 F.2d 1155
5E1.2(c)(3)—935 F.2d 719
5E1.2(c)(3)—943 F.2d 1422
5E1.2(c)(3)—949 F.2d 1461
5E1.2(c)(3)—976 F.2d 155
5E1.2(c)(3)—2 F.3d 245
5E1.2(c)(3)—15 F.3d 119
5E1.2(c)(3)—22 F.3d 846
5E1.2(c)(3)—824 F.Supp. 328
5E1.2(c)(4)—919 F.2d 123
5E1.2(c)(4)—988 F.2d 242
5E1.2(d)—900 F.2d 1201
5E1.2(d)—902 F.2d 331
5E1.2(d)—924 F.2d 1362
5E1.2(d)—935 F.2d 719
5E1.2(d)—941 F.2d 220
5E1.2(d)—945 F.2d 341
5E1.2(d)—946 F.2d 19
5E1.2(d)—983 F.2d 1425
5E1.2(d)—998 F.2d 534
5E1.2(d)—5 F.3d 1100
5E1.2(d)—11 F.3d 52
5E1.2(d)—16 F.3d 155
5E1.2(d)—18 F.3d 1352
5E1.2(d)(1)—900 F.2d 1201
5E1.2(d)(1)—919 F.2d 123
5E1.2(d)(1)—931 F.2d 905
5E1.2(d)(1)—946 F.2d 19
5E1.2(d)(1-3)—19 F.3d 409
5E1.2(d)(1-4)—988 F.2d 798
5E1.2(d)(1-7)—945 F.2d 325
5E1.2(d)(2)—899 F.2d 515
5E1.2(d)(2)—900 F.2d 1201
5E1.2(d)(2)—931 F.2d 905
5E1.2(d)(2)—941 F.2d 60
5E1.2(d)(2)—943 F.2d 1422
5E1.2(d)(2)—950 F.2d 420
5E1.2(d)(2)—5 F.3d 1100
5E1.2(d)(2)—5 F.3d 1338
5E1.2(d)(2)—9 F.2d 22
5E1.2(d)(2)—11 F.3d 52
5E1.2(d)(3)—941 F.2d 419
5E1.2(d)(4)—2 F.3d 245
5E1.2(d)(4)—9 F.3d 1422
5E1.2(d)(5)—9 F.3d 1422
5E1.2(d)(7)—945 F.2d 325
5E1.2(e)—900 F.2d 1201
5E1.2(e)—909 F.2d 412
5E1.2(e)—931 F.2d 905
5E1.2(e)—943 F.2d 1422
5E1.2(e)—946 F.2d 19

5E1.2(e)—995 F.2d 865
5E1.2(f)—903 F.2d 1478
5E1.2(f)—909 F.2d 412
5E1.2(f)—915 F.2d 603
5E1.2(f)—918 F.2d 226
5E1.2(f)—922 F.2d 1290
5E1.2(f)—930 F.2d 824
5E1.2(f)—943 F.2d 1422
5E1.2(f)—945 F.2d 325
5E1.2(f)—946 F.2d 19
5E1.2(f)—979 F.2d 1037
5E1.2(f)—980 F.2d 1110
5E1.2(f)—994 F.2d 149
5E1.2(f)—998 F.2d 534
5E1.2(f)—998 F.2d 601
5E1.2(f)—9 F.3d 22
5E1.2(f)—11 F.3d 52
5E1.2(f)—20 F.3d 1030
5E1.2(f)—758 F.Supp. 195
5E1.2(f)—768 F.Supp. 101
5E1.2(f)—777 F.Supp. 293
5E1.2(f)—783 F.Supp. 665
5E1.2(f)—833 F.Supp. 769
5E1.2(g)—2 F.3d 245
5E1.2(g)—21 F.3d 753
5E1.2(i)—909 F.2d 412
5E1.2(i)—915 F.2d 603
5E1.2(i)—930 F.2d 824
5E1.2(i)—945 F.2d 851
5E1.2(i)—950 F.2d 175
5E1.2(i)—962 F.2d 1535
5E1.2(i)—964 F.2d 83
5E1.2(i)—976 F.2d 155
5E1.2(i)—979 F.2d 1037
5E1.2(i)—998 F.2d 534
5E1.2(i)—2 F.3d 245
5E1.2(i)—3 F.3d 368
5E1.2(i)—4 F.3d 560
5E1.2(i)—6 F.3d 27
5E1.2(i)—777 F.Supp. 1294
5E1.2(i)—833 F.Supp. 769
5E1.2 comment—903 F.2d 1478
5E1.2 comment—945 F.2d 325
5E1.2 comment—985 F.2d 1175
5E1.2 comment—2 F.3d 245
5E1.2 comment—11 F.3d 315
5E1.2 comment—15 F.3d 1292
5E1.2 comment—16 F.3d 1110
5E1.2 comment—777 F.Supp. 1294
5E1.4 comment—10 F.3d 263
5E1.4—981 F.2d 1382
5E1.4—9 F.3d 1422
5E1.4—10 F.3d 263
5E4.1(a) [1988]—893 F.2d 935
5E4.1(a)—901 F.2d 1457
5E4.2—838 F.2d 932
5E4.2—867 F.2d 783
5E4.2—881 F.2d 95
5E4.2 [1988]—895 F.2d 1030
5E4.2 [1988]—910 F.2d 81
5E4.2 [1988]—913 F.2d 193
5E4.2—671 F.Supp. 79
5E4.2—687 F.supp. 1403
5E4.2(a)—857 F.2d 1245
5E4.2(a) [1988]--911 F.2d 227
5E4.2(a)—691 F.Supp. 656
5E4.2(c) [1988]—913 F.2d 193
5E4.2(c)(3)—881 F.2d 95
5E4.2(c)(3) [1988]—896 F.2d 678
5E4.2(c)(3) [1988]—913 F.2d 193
5E4.2(c)(3) [1988]—917 F.2d 901
5E4.2(c)(4)—881 F.2d 95
5E4.2(d) [1988]—947 F.2d 1120
5E4.2(d)(2)—882 F.2d 441
5E4.2(d)(2) [1988]—906 F.2d 621
5E4.2(d)(2) [1988]—911 F.2d 227
5E4.2(d)(2) [1988]—12 F.3d 132
5E4.2(f) [1988]—899 F.2d 371
5E4.2(f) [1988]—906 F.2d 621
5E4.2(f) [1988]—911 F.2d 227
5E4.2(f) [1988]—917 F.2d 901
5E4.2(f) [1988]—10 F.3d 1468
5E4.2(f)—720 F.Supp. 139
5E4.2(i) [1988]—911 F.2d 227
5E4.2(i)—720 F.Supp. 139
5E4.2 comment—886 F.2d 143
5E4.2 comment [1988]—906 F.2d 621
5E4.2 comment [1988]—913 F.2d 193
5E4.3 [1988]—899 F.2d 371

Part F: Sentencing Options

5F1.1—959 F.2d 516
5F1.1—18 F.3d 443
5F1.1 comment—959 F.2d 516
5F1.2—18 F.3d 443
5F1.2—776 F.Supp. 1030
5F1.3 comment—946 F.2d 19
5F1.5—952 F.2d 187
5F1.5—959 F.2d 516

5F5.2 [1988]—22 F.3d 790

Part G: Implementing the Total Sentence of Imprisonment

5G1.1—878 F.2d 735
5G1.1 [1988]—891 F.2d 300
5G1.1—898 F.2d 36
5G1.1—921 F.2d 1095
5G1.1 [1988]—921 F.2d 1095
5G1.1—922 F.2d 1336
5G1.1—930 F.2d 567
5G1.1—938 F.2d 319
5G1.1—939 F.2d 721
5G1.1—942 F.2d 196
5G1.1—952 F.2d 1537
5G1.1—968 F.2d 1058
5G1.1—971 F.2d 200
5G1.1 [1988]—973 F.2d 952
5G1.1—974 F.2d 971
5G1.1—991 F.2d 370
5G1.1—7 F.3d 422
5G1.1—694 F.Supp. 1488
5G1.1(a) [1988]—819 F.2d 250
5G1.1(a)—884 F.2d 181
5G1.1(a)—899 F.2d 177
5G1.1(a)—902 F.2d 291
5G1.1(a)—919 F.2d 1321
5G1.1(a)—938 F.2d 149
5G1.1(a)—946 F.2d 615
5G1.1(a)—949 F.2d 973
5G1.1(a)—975 F.2d 119
5G1.1(a)—981 F.2d 790
5G1.1(a)—992 F.2d 1068
5G1.1(a)—708 F.Supp. 461
5G1.1(a)—819 F.Supp. 250
5G1.1(b)—863 F.2d 595
5G1.1(b)—882 F.2d 1018
5G1.1(b)—898 F.2d 642
5G1.1(b) [1988]—921 F.2d 1095
5G1.1(b)—923 F.2d 358
5G1.1(b)—924 F.2d 187
5G1.1(b)—927 F.2d 697
5G1.1(b)—930 F.2d 234
5G1.1(b)—933 F.2d 362
5G1.1(b)—935 F.2d 149
5G1.1(b)—939 F.2d 509
5G1.1(b)—939 F.2d 721
5G1.1(b)—943 F.2d 39
5G1.1(b)—952 F.2d 414
5G1.1(b)—952 F.2d 1537
5G1.1(b)—956 F.2d 248
5G1.1(b)—960 F.2d 405
5G1.1(b) [1988]—961 F.2d 82
5G1.1(b)—966 F.2d 1045
5G1.1(b)—971 F.2d 200
5G1.1(b)—973 F.2d 769
5G1.1(b)—973 F.2d 857
5G1.1(b)—973 F.2d 1190
5G1.1(b)—979 F.2d 1042
5G1.1(b)—987 F.2d 564
5G1.1(b)—987 F.2d 920
5G1.1(b)—991 F.2d 179
5G1.1(b)—993 F.2d 625
5G1.1(b)—5 F.3d 292
5G1.1(b) [1990]—6 F.3d 363
5G1.1(b)—7 F.3d 203
5G1.1(b)—9 F.3d 1377
5G1.1(b)—16 F.3d 377
5G1.1(b)—753 F.Supp. 1191
5G1.1(b)—771 F.Supp. 324
5G1.1(b)—800 F.Supp. 1012
5G1.1(c)—948 F.2d 1093
5G1.1(c)—16 F.3d 795
5G1.1(c)(2)—938 F.2d 319
5G1.1(c)(2)—965 F.2d 1037
5G1.1 et seq.—884 F.2d 181
5G1.1 et seq.—998 F.2d 1571
5G1.1 et seq.—819 F.Supp. 250
5G1.1 comment [1988]—921 F.2d 1095
5G1.1 comment—939 F.2d 721
5G1.1 comment—961 F.2d 133
5G1.1 comment—973 F.2d 857
5G1.1 comment [1990]—6 F.3d 363
5G1.1 comment—725 F.Supp. 878
5G1.2—894 F.2d 665
5G1.2—903 F.2d 1022
5G1.2—928 F.2d 844
5G1.2—975 F.2d 119
5G1.2—978 F.2d 78
5G1.2—981 F.2d 790
5G1.2—983 F.2d 604
5G1.2—990 F.2d 594
5G1.2—998 F.2d 1571
5G1.2—4 F.3d 1358
5G1.2—12 F.3d 1186
5G1.2—708 F.Supp. 425
5G1.2—729 F.Supp. 11
5G1.2(a)—719 F.Supp. 1015
5G1.2(b)—938 F.2d 1255

5G1.2(b)—975 F.2d 119
5G1.2(c)—936 F.2d 903
5G1.2(c)—952 F.2d 1090
5G1.2(c)—956 F.2d 1216
5G1.2(c)—975 F.2d 119
5G1.2(c)—981 F.2d 790
5G1.2(c)—981 F.2d 1123
5G1.2(c)—985 F.2d 188
5G1.2(d)—884 F.2d 181
5G1.2(d)—917 F.2d 80
5G1.2(d)—924 F.2d 68
5G1.2(d)—924 F.2d 1362
5G1.2(d)—936 F.2d 903
5G1.2(d)—950 F.2d 222
5G1.2(d)—952 F.2d 1090
5G1.2(d)—953 F.2d 870
5G1.2(d)—956 F.2d 1465
5G1.2(d)—962 F.2d 894
5G1.2(d)—966 F.2d 945
5G1.2(d)—971 F.2d 717
5G1.2(d)—977 F.2d 203
5G1.2(d)—708 F.Supp. 461
5G1.2(d)—819 F.Supp. 250
5G1.2 comment—956 F.2d 1465
5G1.2 comment—975 F.2d 119
5G1.2 comment—981 F.2d 790
5G1.2 comment—981 F.2d 1123
5G1.2 comment—998 F.2d 1571
5G1.3—881 F.2d 976
5G1.3—886 F.2d 1034
5G1.3—891 F.2d 86
5G1.3—894 F.2d 334
5G1.3—897 F.2d 134
5G1.3—897 F.2d 963
5G1.3 [1988]—898 F.2d 390
5G1.3—901 F.2d 555
5G1.3 [1988]—903 F.2d 341
5G1.3—909 F.2d 316
5G1.3—912 F.2d 615
5G1.3—917 F.2d 970
5G1.3—936 F.2d 1124
5G1.3—952 F.2d 50
5G1.3—966 F.2d 243
5G1.3 [1988]—973 F.2d 952
5G1.3 [1990]—973 F.2d 952
5G1.3—979 F.2d 1048
5G1.3—979 F.2d 1289
5G1.3—980 F.2d 1300
5G1.3 [1989]—980 F.2d 1300
5G1.3—981 F.2d 344
5G1.3—981 F.2d 1194
5G1.3—987 F.2d 564
5G1.3—992 F.2d 75
5G1.3 [1988]—995 F.2d 315
5G1.3—996 F.2d 1009
5G1.3 [1991]—996 F.2d 1288
5G1.3 [1992]—996 F.2d 1288
5G1.3—4 F.3d 1358
5G1.3—9 F.3d 1377
5G1.3—11 F.3d 309
5G1.3—12 F.3d 139
5G1.3 [1992]—12 F.3d 1186
5G1.3—15 F.3d 610
5G1.3—17 F.3d 230
5G1.3—20 F.3d 874
5G1.3—691 F.Supp. 656
5G1.3—711 F.Supp. 736
5G1.3—716 F.Supp. 1207
5G1.3—726 F.Supp. 861
5G1.3—729 F.Supp. 165
5G1.3 [1988]—733 F.Supp. 1256
5G1.3—789 F.Supp. 957
5G1.3—842 F.Supp. 945
5G1.3(a) [1992]—12 F.3d 1186
5G1.3(b)—975 F.2d 397
5G1.3(b)—979 F.2d 1048
5G1.3(b) [1992]—981 F.2d 973
5G1.3(b)—987 F.2d 564
5G1.3(b) [1992]—990 F.2d 594
5G1.3(b)—992 F.2d 265
5G1.3(b)—1 F.3d 654
5G1.3(b)—4 F.3d 1358
5G1.3(b)—13 F.3d 395
5G1.3(b)—20 F.3d 874
5G1.3(b)—21 F.3d 70
5G1.3(b)—834 F.Supp. 292
5G1.3(c)—981 F.2d 344
5G1.3(c)—993 F.2d 127
5G1.3(c)—12 F.3d 139
5G1.3(c) [1992]—12 F.3d 1186
5G1.3(c)—834 F.Supp. 292
5G1.3 comment—897 F.2d 134
5G1.3 comment—936 F.2d 1124
5G1.3 comment—966 F.2d 243
5G1.3 comment—975 F.2d 397
5G1.3 comment [1992]—981 F.2d 344
5G1.3 comment—993 F.2d 127
5G1.3 comment—999 F.2d 361
5G1.3 comment—1 F.3d 654
5G1.3 comment—4 F.3d 1358

5G1.3 comment—11 F.3d 309
5G1.3 comment—15 F.3d 610

Part H: Specific Offender Characteristics

5H Sentencing Table—788 F.Supp. 413
5H comment—966 F.2d 1488
5H1.1—892 F.2d 31
5H1.1—893 F.2d 63
5H1.1—895 F.2d 318
5H1.1—903 F.2d 540
5H1.1—905 F.2d 599
5H1.1—906 F.2d 814
5H1.1—918 F.2d 664
5H1.1—921 F.2d 340
5H1.1—929 F.2d 116
5H1.1—938 F.2d 1293
5H1.1—940 F.2d 261
5H1.1—941 F.2d 1019
5H1.1—945 F.2d 100
5H1.1—949 F.2d 860
5H1.1—950 F.2d 203
5H1.1—956 F.2d 907
5H1.1—967 F.2d 841
5H1.1—970 F.2d 444
5H1.1—981 F.2d 1418
5H1.1—985 F.2d 478
5H1.1—986 F.2d 278
5H1.1—990 F.2d 178
5H1.1—995 F.2d 960
5H1.1—5 F.3d 568
5H1.1—7 F.3d 1471
5H1.1—13 F.3d 369
5H1.1—18 F.3d 1145
5H1.1—20 F.3d 918
5H1.1—21 F.3d 281
5H1.1—22 F.3d 790
5H1.1—732 F.Supp. 878
5H1.1—760 F.Supp. 1322
5H1.1 [1990]—781 F.Supp. 428
5H1.1—802 F.Supp. 559
5H1.1-5H1.4—902 F.2d 734
5H1.1-5H1.6—916 F.2d 916
5H1.1-5H1.6—927 F.2d 1463
5H1.1-5H1.6—952 F.2d 1101
5H1.1-5H1.6—956 F.2d 1555
5H1.1-5H1.6—682 F.Supp. 815
5H1.1-5H1.6—728 F.Supp. 632
5H1.1-5H1.10—919 F.2d 946
5H1.1-5H1.10—686 F.Supp. 1174
5H1.1-5H1.10—694 F.Supp. 1406
5H1.1 et seq.—882 F.2d 1059
5H1.1 et seq.—902 F.2d 734
5H1.1 et seq.—905 F.2d 599
5H1.1 et seq.—923 F.2d 369
5H1.1 et seq.—994 F.2d 942
5H1.1 et seq.—709 F.Supp. 908
5H1.2—873 F.2d 765
5H1.2—899 F.2d 503
5H1.2—913 F.2d 46
5H1.2—945 F.2d 1096
5H1.2—952 F.2d 182
5H1.2—956 F.2d 1555
5H1.2—996 F.2d 1238
5H1.2—13 F.3d 369
5H1.2—13 F.3d 781
5H1.2—18 F.3d 301
5H1.2—741 F.Supp. 622
5H1.3—895 F.2d 538
5H1.3—905 F.2d 599
5H1.3—907 F.2d 254
5H1.3—909 F.2d 392
5H1.3—917 F.2d 512
5H1.3—927 F.2d 197
5H1.3—929 F.2d 1275
5H1.3—937 F.2d 979
5H1.3—938 F.2d 326
5H1.3—949 F.2d 860
5H1.3—952 F.2d 182
5H1.3—975 F.2d 275
5H1.3—975 F.2d 1554
5H1.3—976 F.2d 1216
5H1.3—979 F.2d 396
5H1.3—986 F.2d 278
5H1.3—992 F.2d 896
5H1.3—18 F.3d 822
5H1.3—19 F.3d 1385
5H1.3—756 F.Supp. 698
5H1.3—793 F.Supp. 64
5H1.4—868 F.2d 125
5H1.4—875 F.2d 1124
5H1.4—891 F.2d 962
5H1.4—895 F.2d 318
5H1.4—897 F.2d 963
5H1.4—898 F.2d 91
5H1.4—898 F.2d 1326
5H1.4—899 F.2d 327
5H1.4—901 F.2d 778
5H1.4—902 F.2d 133
5H1.4—905 F.2d 599

5H1.4—905 F.2d 1448
5H1.4—906 F.2d 814
5H1.4—907 F.2d 1441
5H1.4—909 F.2d 316
5H1.4—916 F.2d 916
5H1.4—922 F.2d 534
5H1.4—928 F.2d 645
5H1.4—933 F.2d 742
5H1.4—937 F.2d 979
5H1.4—938 F.2d 162
5H1.4—938 F.2d 1431
5H1.4—946 F.2d 955
5H1.4—947 F.2d 956
5H1.4—948 F.2d 444
5H1.4—948 F.2d 706
5H1.4—949 F.2d 860
5H1.4—950 F.2d 203
5H1.4—956 F.2d 907
5H1.4—971 F.2d 626
5H1.4—975 F.2d 944
5H1.4 [1991]—977 F.2d 1264
5H1.4—983 F.2d 1507
5H1.4—986 F.2d 278
5H1.4—987 F.2d 618
5H1.4—994 F.2d 942
5H1.4—995 F.2d 960
5H1.4—1 F.3d 1044
5H1.4—5 F.3d 568
5H1.4 [1990]—6 F.3d 363
5H1.4—7 F.3d 813
5H1.4—9 F.3d 60
5H1.4—11 F.3d 777
5H1.4—16 F.3d 927
5H1.4—18 F.3d 1145
5H1.4—20 F.3d 193
5H1.4—733 F.Supp. 1256
5H1.4—736 F.Supp. 71
5H1.4—751 F.Supp. 168
5H1.4—751 F.Supp. 1195
5H1.4—760 F.Supp. 1322
5H1.4—762 F.Supp. 39
5H1.4—763 F.Supp. 645
5H1.4—786 F.Supp. 1267
5H1.4—791 F.Supp. 843
5H1.4—822 F.Supp. 961
5H1.4—836 F.Supp. 965
5H1.4—840 F.Supp. 1404
5H1.4-5H1.6—948 F.2d 1
5H1.5—895 F.2d 538
5H1.5—899 F.2d 503
5H1.5—903 F.2d 564
5H1.5—909 F.2d 61
5H1.5—936 F.2d 41
5H1.5—944 F.2d 1106
5H1.5—952 F.2d 514
5H1.5—956 F.2d 1555
5H1.5—967 F.2d 841
5H1.5—970 F.2d 444
5H1.5—978 F.2d 166
5H1.5—988 F.2d 677
5H1.5—7 F.3d 813
5H1.5—19 F.3d 177
5H1.5—22 F.3d 93
5H1.5—688 F.Supp. 191
5H1.5—703 F.Supp. 1350
5H1.6—872 F.2d 735
5H1.6—890 F.2d 1042
5H1.6—895 F.2d 538
5H1.6—898 F.2d 1326
5H1.6—899 F.2d 503
5H1.6—901 F.2d 1498
5H1.6—902 F.2d 133
5H1.6—902 F.2d 734
5H1.6—903 F.2d 564
5H1.6—907 F.2d 31
5H1.6—907 F.2d 1441
5H1.6—908 F.2d 396
5H1.6—913 F.2d 46
5H1.6—913 F.2d 59
5H1.6—919 F.2d 1325
5H1.6—920 F.2d 244
5H1.6—923 F.2d 1079
5H1.6—929 F.2d 116
5H1.6—929 F.2d 1275
5H1.6—930 F.2d 526
5H1.6—933 F.2d 1117
5H1.6—936 F.2d 41
5H1.6—944 F.2d 1106
5H1.6—945 F.2d 1096
5H1.6—948 F.2d 1093
5H1.6—950 F.2d 969
5H1.6—951 F.2d 308
5H1.6—956 F.2d 907
5H1.6—956 F.2d 1555
5H1.6—960 F.2d 1137
5H1.6—964 F.2d 124
5H1.6—967 F.2d 841
5H1.6—974 F.2d 537
5H1.6—978 F.2d 166
5H1.6—979 F.2d 51

5H1.6—980 F.2d 1296
5H1.6—991 F.2d 82
5H1.6—991 F.2d 552
5H1.6—994 F.2d 942
5H1.6—997 F.2d 970
5H1.6—998 F.2d 601
5H1.6—7 F.3d 813
5H1.6—9 F.3d 60
5H1.6—9 F.3d 1422
5H1.6—11 F.3d 732
5H1.6—19 F.3d 177
5H1.6—20 F.3d 918
5H1.6—21 F.3d 811
5H1.6—22 F.3d 93
5H1.6—22 F.3d 790
5H1.6—691 F.Supp. 1252
5H1.6—703 F.Supp. 1350
5H1.6—732 F.Supp. 878
5H1.6—782 F.Supp. 913
5H1.6—785 F.Supp. 114
5H1.6—790 F.Supp. 1063
5H1.6—795 F.Supp. 1262
5H1.7—918 F.2d 664
5H1.8—898 F.2d 1326
5H1.8—918 F.2d 664
5H1.8—21 F.3d 811
5H1.8—703 F.Supp. 1350
5H1.9—882 F.2d 1059
5H1.9—898 F.2d 1120
5H1.9—956 F.2d 1555
5H1.10—873 F.2d 765
5H1.10—882 F.2d 1059
5H1.10 [1988]—897 F.2d 981
5H1.10—899 F.2d 503
5H1.10—902 F.2d 133
5H1.10—902 F.2d 734
5H1.10—905 F.2d 1448
5H1.10—913 F.2d 46
5H1.10—916 F.2d 916
5H1.10—920 F.2d 244
5H1.10—923 F.2d 369
5H1.10—932 F.2d 1155
5H1.10—933 F.2d 650
5H1.10—936 F.2d 661
5H1.10—938 F.2d 1293
5H1.10—946 F.2d 19
5H1.10—954 F.2d 951
5H1.10—956 F.2d 1555
5H1.10—957 F.2d 643
5H1.10—977 F.2d 69
5H1.10—979 F.2d 51
5H1.10—994 F.2d 942
5H1.10 [1992]—994 F.2d 1380
5H1.10—7 F.3d 420
5H1.10—13 F.3d 369
5H1.10—22 F.3d 790
5H1.10—732 F.Supp. 878
5H1.10—741 F.Supp. 622
5H1.10—802 F.Supp. 781
5H1.10—840 F.Supp. 1404
5H1.11—952 F.2d 514
5H1.11—978 F.2d 166
5H1.11—9 F.3d 60
5H1.11—22 F.3d 790
5H1.12—902 F.2d 133
5H1.12—985 F.2d 65
5H1.12—5 F.3d 1267
5H1.12—8 F.3d 839
5H1.12—840 F.Supp. 1404

Part J: Relief from Disability

5J1.1—753 F.Supp. 239

Part K: Departures

5K Sentencing Table—973 F.2d 857
5K Sentencing Table—788 F.Supp. 413
5K1.1—112 S.Ct. 1840
5K1.1—839 F.2d 175
5K1.1—868 F.2d 125
5K1.1—868 F.2d 1409
5K1.1—869 F.2d 822
5K1.1—873 F.2d 437
5K1.1—874 F.2d 647
5K1.1—877 F.2d 664
5K1.1—878 F.2d 89
5K1.1—885 F.2d 441
5K1.1—886 F.2d 1513
5K1.1—889 F.2d 189
5K1.1—889 F.2d 441
5K1.1—889 F.2d 1341
5K1.1—890 F.2d 1042
5K1.1—892 F.2d 31
5K1.1 [1988]—895 F.2d 501
5K1.1 [1988]—895 F.2d 1335
5K1.1—896 F.2d 246
5K1.1—896 F.2d 710
5K1.1—897 F.2d 351
5K1.1—897 F.2d 691

5K1.1—900 F.2d 1300
5K1.1—901 F.2d 91
5K1.1 [1988]—902 F.2d 61
5K1.1—902 F.2d 221
5K1.1—902 F.2d 259
5K1.1—902 F.2d 894
5K1.1—902 F.2d 1010
5K1.1—903 F.2d 1478
5K1.1—904 F.2d 22
5K1.1—904 F.2d 1026
5K1.1—904 F.2d 1490
5K1.1—905 F.2d 3
5K1.1—905 F.2d 638
5K1.1—905 F.2d 1092
5K1.1—905 F.2d 1192
5K1.1—907 F.2d 1441
5K1.1—908 F.2d 307
5K1.1—908 F.2d 349
5K1.1—908 F.2d 655
5K1.1—908 F.2d 1229
5K1.1—910 F.2d 1239
5K1.1—911 F.2d 126
5K1.1—911 F.2d 129
5K1.1—911 F.2d 1433
5K1.1—912 F.2d 453
5K1.1—913 F.2d 378
5K1.1 [1988]—913 F.2d 897
5K1.1—914 F.2d 330
5K1.1—915 F.2d 599
5K1.1—915 F.2d 1152
5K1.1—918 F.2d 30
5K1.1—918 F.2d 118
5K1.1 [1990]—918 F.2d 1268
5K1.1—918 F.2d 1383
5K1.1—919 F.2d 1181
5K1.1—920 F.2d 107
5K1.1—920 F.2d 1040
5K1.1—920 F.2d 1100
5K1.1—921 F.2d 650
5K1.1—921 F.2d 1569
5K1.1—922 F.2d 588
5K1.1—922 F.2d 1331
5K1.1—922 F.2d 1336
5K1.1—923 F.2d 5
5K1.1—923 F.2d 70
5K1.1—923 F.2d 1039
5K1.1—924 F.2d 21
5K1.1—924 F.2d 721
5K1.1—925 F.2d 354
5K1.1—925 F.2d 1260
5K1.1—926 F.2d 125
5K1.1—926 F.2d 747
5K1.1—927 F.2d 139
5K1.1—927 F.2d 170
5K1.1—927 F.2d 1092
5K1.1—927 F.2d 1361
5K1.1—929 F.2d 116
5K1.1—929 F.2d 128
5K1.1—930 F.2d 526
5K1.1—930 F.2d 705
5K1.1—930 F.2d 1073
5K1.1—930 F.2d 1527
5K1.1—931 F.2d 1310
5K1.1—933 F.2d 711
5K1.1—934 F.2d 353
5K1.1—934 F.2d 1387
5K1.1—936 F.2d 41
5K1.1—936 F.2d 169
5K1.1—936 F.2d 482
5K1.1—937 F.2d 20
5K1.1—938 F.2d 827
5K1.1—939 F.2d 135
5K1.1—939 F.2d 191
5K1.1—939 F.2d 509
5K1.1—940 F.2d 261
5K1.1—941 F.2d 905
5K1.1—942 F.2d 55
5K1.1—942 F.2d 517
5K1.1—946 F.2d 505
5K1.1—946 F.2d 729
5K1.1—946 F.2d 738
5K1.1—948 F.2d 444
5K1.1—948 F.2d 697
5K1.1—949 F.2d 63
5K1.1—951 F.2d 490
5K1.1—953 F.2d 1060
5K1.1—955 F.2d 34
5K1.1—955 F.2d 566
5K1.1—956 F.2d 248
5K1.1—956 F.2d 749
5K1.1—956 F.2d 1555
5K1.1—958 F.2d 1441
5K1.1—961 F.2d 288
5K1.1—962 F.2d 103
5K1.1—963 F.2d 476
5K1.1—963 F.2d 976
5K1.1—963 F.2d 1318
5K1.1—964 F.2d 454
5K1.1—964 F.2d 778
5K1.1—964 F.2d 972

5K1.1—965 F.2d 58
5K1.1—965 F.2d 262
5K1.1—965 F.2d 513
5K1.1—966 F.2d 328
5K1.1—967 F.2d 106
5K1.1—967 F.2d 841
5K1.1—968 F.2d 1193
5K1.1—968 F.2d 1483
5K1.1—969 F.2d 335
5K1.1—969 F.2d 1419
5K1.1—970 F.2d 1095
5K1.1—971 F.2d 89
5K1.1—972 F.2d 294
5K1.1—973 F.2d 611
5K1.1—974 F.2d 123
5K1.1—975 F.2d 149
5K1.1—975 F.2d 556
5K1.1—976 F.2d 155
5K1.1—978 F.2d 166
5K1.1—979 F.2d 1219
5K1.1—980 F.2d 13
5K1.1—980 F.2d 1296
5K1.1—981 F.2d 1549
5K1.1—982 F.2d 283
5K1.1—983 F.2d 1150
5K1.1—983 F.2d 1497
5K1.1—985 F.2d 395
5K1.1—985 F.2d 732
5K1.1—986 F.2d 1042
5K1.1—987 F.2d 538
5K1.1—988 F.2d 206
5K1.1—988 F.2d 544
5K1.1—989 F.2d 261
5K1.1—989 F.2d 377
5K1.1—990 F.2d 397
5K1.1—990 F.2d 1314
5K1.1—991 F.2d 179
5K1.1—991 F.2d 819
5K1.1—991 F.2d 1350
5K1.1—992 F.2d 131
5K1.1—993 F.2d 625
5K1.1—994 F.2d 412
5K1.1—995 F.2d 173
5K1.1—995 F.2d 686
5K1.1—996 F.2d 62
5K1.1—996 F.2d 70
5K1.1—996 F.2d 606
5K1.1—997 F.2d 248
5K1.1—997 F.2d 823
5K1.1—997 F.2d 1343
5K1.1—998 F.2d 228
5K1.1—998 F.2d 253
5K1.1—998 F.2d 1212
5K1.1—2 F.3d 827
5K1.1—3 F.3d 252
5K1.1—4 F.3d 622
5K1.1—5 F.3d 1306
5K1.1—6 F.3d 911
5K1.1—7 F.3d 90
5K1.1—8 F.3d 11
5K1.1—9 F.3d 1422
5K1.1—9 F.3d 1438
5K1.1—9 F.3d 1492
5K1.1—10 F.3d 910
5K1.1—11 F.3d 45
5K1.1—11 F.3d 573
5K1.1—11 F.3d 732
5K1.1—12 F.3d 273
5K1.1—13 F.3d 340
5K1.1—15 F.3d 715
5K1.1—15 F.3d 1033
5K1.1—15 F.3d 1292
5K1.1—16 F.3d 844
5K1.1—17 F.3d 21
5K1.1—17 F.3d 27
5K1.1—17 F.3d 78
5K1.1—17 F.3d 596
5K1.1—18 F.3d 612
5K1.1—19 F.3d 1387
5K1.1—20 F.3d 476
5K1.1—21 F.3d 375
5K1.1—691 F.Supp. 656
5K1.1—703 F.Supp. 1350
5K1.1—704 F.Supp. 661
5K1.1—707 F.Supp. 1101
5K1.1—708 F.Supp. 38
5K1.1—713 F.Supp. 126
5K1.1—717 F.Supp. 682
5K1.1—720 F.Supp. 619
5K1.1—724 F.Supp. 1239
5K1.1—726 F.Supp. 1140
5K1.1—726 F.Supp. 1359
5K1.1—729 F.Supp. 94
5K1.1—732 F.Supp. 878
5K1.1—732 F.Supp. 1151
5K1.1—734 F.Supp. 877
5K1.1—738 F.Supp. 1256
5K1.1—741 F.Supp. 103
5K1.1—741 F.Supp. 1197
5K1.1—742 F.Supp. 1003

5K1.1—749 F.Supp. 1450
5K1.1—750 F.Supp. 388
5K1.1—773 F.Supp. 622
5K1.1—782 F.Supp. 19
5K1.1—796 F.Supp. 853
5K1.1—798 F.Supp. 513
5K1.1—802 F.Supp. 128
5K1.1—802 F.Supp. 843
5K1.1—806 F.Supp. 1567
5K1.1—828 F.Supp. 208
5K1.1—837 F.Supp. 916
5K1.1—838 F.Supp. 709
5K1.1—842 F.Supp. 92
5K1.1—842 F.Supp. 262
5K1.1—843 F.Supp. 158
5K1.1—845 F.Supp. 28
5K1.1—846 F.Supp. 982
5K1.1(a)—922 F.2d 1347
5K1.1(a)—930 F.2d 526
5K1.1(a)—9 F.3d 1492
5K1.1(a)—738 F.Supp. 1256
5K1.1(a)(1)—720 F.Supp. 619
5K1.1(a)(3)—968 F.2d 1193
5K1.1(a)(3)—720 F.Supp. 619
5K1.1(a)(4)—968 F.2d 1193
5K1.1(a)(4)—796 F.Supp. 853
5K1.1 et seq.—867 F.2d 783
5K1.1 et seq.—868 F.2d 125
5K1.1 et seq.—891 F.2d 405
5K1.1 et seq.—893 F.2d 73
5K1.1 et seq.—896 F.2d 856
5K1.1 et seq.—898 F.2d 28
5K1.1 et seq.—917 F.2d 80
5K1.1 et seq.—917 F.2d 1057
5K1.1 et seq.—920 F.2d 562
5K1.1 et seq.—930 F.2d 1368
5K1.1 et seq.—940 F.2d 753
5K1.1 et seq.—961 F.2d 133
5K1.1 et seq.—968 F.2d 130
5K1.1 et seq.—981 F.2d 344
5K1.1 et seq.—993 F.2d 16
5K1.1 et seq.—675 F.Supp. 1127
5K1.1 et seq.—685 F.Supp. 990
5K1.1 et seq.—692 F.Supp. 1427
5K1.1 et seq.—735 F.Supp. 928
5K1.1 et seq.—741 F.Supp. 622
5K1.1 et seq.—803 F.Supp. 53
5K1.1-5K2.14—894 F.2d 225
5K1.1-5K2.14—902 F.2d 483
5K1.1 comment—892 F.2d 31
5K1.1 comment—905 F.2d 1092
5K1.1 comment—911 F.2d 1433
5K1.1 comment—920 F.2d 1100
5K1.1 comment—921 F.2d 1073
5K1.1 comment—921 F.2d 1569
5K1.1 comment—933 F.2d 711
5K1.1 comment—958 F.2d 1441
5K1.1 comment—974 F.2d 123
5K1.1 comment—978 F.2d 166
5K1.1 comment—983 F.2d 1150
5K1.1 comment—989 F.2d 261
5K1.1 comment—8 F.3d 1333
5K1.1 comment—741 F.Supp. 1197
5K1.1 comment—842 F.Supp. 92
5K1.2—889 F.2d 791
5K1.2—907 F.2d 781
5K1.2—915 F.2d 899
5K1.2—927 F.2d 197
5K1.2—943 F.2d 707
5K1.2—971 F.2d 1368
5K2.0—112 S.Ct. 1112
5K2.0—860 F.2d 35
5K2.0—866 F.2d 604
5K2.0—867 F.2d 783
5K2.0—868 F.2d 54
5K2.0—868 F.2d 135
5K2.0—868 F.2d 1121
5K2.0—868 F.2d 1412
5K2.0—869 F.2d 54
5K2.0—870 F.2d 52
5K2.0—873 F.2d 23
5K2.0—873 F.2d 495
5K2.0—874 F.2d 43
5K2.0—876 F.2d 784
5K2.0—878 F.2d 164
5K2.0—882 F.2d 693
5K2.0—883 F.2d 491
5K2.0—884 F.2d 170
5K2.0—887 F.2d 347
5K2.0—889 F.2d 1341
5K2.0—890 F.2d 176
5K2.0—890 F.2d 968
5K2.0—891 F.2d 405
5K2.0—891 F.2d 512
5K2.0—891 F.2d 962
5K2.0—892 F.2d 223
5K2.0—893 F.2d 679
5K2.0—893 F.2d 815
5K2.0—893 F.2d 1343
5K2.0—894 F.2d 317

5K2.0—894 F.2d 965
5K2.0—895 F.2d 318
5K2.0—895 F.2d 435
5K2.0—895 F.2d 597
5K2.0—895 F.2d 1375
5K2.0—896 F.2d 678
5K2.0 [1988]—897 F.2d 981
5K2.0—898 F.2d 1111
5K2.0—899 F.2d 94
5K2.0—899 F.2d 503
5K2.0—900 F.2d 204
5K2.0—901 F.2d 555
5K2.0—901 F.2d 830
5K2.0—902 F.2d 133
5K2.0—902 F.2d 1337
5K2.0—903 F.2d 334
5K2.0—903 F.2d 540
5K2.0—904 F.2d 365
5K2.0—905 F.2d 337
5K2.0—905 F.2d 580
5K2.0—907 F.2d 254
5K2.0—908 F.2d 176
5K2.0—908 F.2d 307
5K2.0—908 F.2d 365
5K2.0—908 F.2d 425
5K2.0—908 F.2d 1491
5K2.0—909 F.2d 235
5K2.0—909 F.2d 1164
5K2.0—911 F.2d 1028
5K2.0—913 F.2d 46
5K2.0—914 F.2d 139
5K2.0 [1988]—914 F.2d 208
5K2.0—914 F.2d 959
5K2.0—914 F.2d 1131
5K2.0—914 F.2d 1288
5K2.0—915 F.2d 899
5K2.0—915 F.2d 947
5K2.0—917 F.2d 477
5K2.0—917 F.2d 502
5K2.0—917 F.2d 512
5K2.0—917 F.2d 1057
5K2.0—918 F.2d 1084
5K2.0 [1990]—918 F.2d 1268
5K2.0—919 F.2d 1365
5K2.0—920 F.2d 1040
5K2.0—920 F.2d 1100
5K2.0—921 F.2d 985
5K2.0 [1990]—921 F.2d 985
5K2.0—922 F.2d 534
5K2.0—922 F.2d 1162
5K2.0—922 F.2d 1283
5K2.0—922 F.2d 1411
5K2.0—922 F.2d 1490
5K2.0—923 F.2d 1545
5K2.0—924 F.2d 395
5K2.0—924 F.2d 1289
5K2.0—925 F.2d 354
5K2.0—925 F.2d 392
5K2.0—925 F.2d 1242
5K2.0—926 F.2d 64
5K2.0—926 F.2d 387
5K2.0—926 F.2d 562
5K2.0—927 F.2d 453
5K2.0—927 F.2d 1092
5K2.0—929 F.2d 213
5K2.0—929 F.2d 267
5K2.0—930 F.2d 1450
5K2.0 [1990]—930 F.2d 1450
5K2.0—930 F.2d 1486
5K2.0—931 F.2d 1396
5K2.0—932 F.2d 651
5K2.0—933 F.2d 1117
5K2.0—934 F.2d 190
5K2.0—934 F.2d 248
5K2.0—935 F.2d 4
5K2.0—935 F.2d 295
5K2.0—935 F.2d 758
5K2.0—935 F.2d 1199
5K2.0—936 F.2d 23
5K2.0—936 F.2d 661
5K2.0—936 F.2d 1124
5K2.0—937 F.2d 20
5K2.0—937 F.2d 979
5K2.0—937 F.2d 1528
5K2.0—938 F.2d 172
5K2.0—938 F.2d 326
5K2.0—938 F.2d 1431
5K2.0—938 F.2d 1446
5K2.0—939 F.2d 780
5K2.0—941 F.2d 133
5K2.0—941 F.2d 905
5K2.0—941 F.2d 1019
5K2.0—941 F.2d 1047
5K2.0—943 F.2d 1032
5K2.0—945 F.2d 264
5K2.0—946 F.2d 176
5K2.0—946 F.2d 955
5K2.0—947 F.2d 956
5K2.0—948 F.2d 706
5K2.0—948 F.2d 776

5K2.0—948 F.2d 1074
5K2.0—949 F.2d 63
5K2.0—949 F.2d 1183
5K2.0—950 F.2d 203
5K2.0—950 F.2d 444
5K2.0—951 F.2d 161
5K2.0—952 F.2d 514
5K2.0—952 F.2d 565
5K2.0—952 F.2d 1066
5K2.0—952 F.2d 1090
5K2.0—952 F.2d 1537
5K2.0—953 F.2d 939
5K2.0—954 F.2d 79
5K2.0—955 F.2d 77
5K2.0—955 F.2d 547
5K2.0—956 F.2d 1555
5K2.0—957 F.2d 681
5K2.0—960 F.2d 191
5K2.0—961 F.2d 882
5K2.0—963 F.2d 1506
5K2.0 [1988]—964 F.2d 66
5K2.0—964 F.2d 124
5K2.0—964 F.2d 167
5K2.0—964 F.2d 778
5K2.0—965 F.2d 513
5K2.0—965 F.2d 906
5K2.0—966 F.2d 243
5K2.0—967 F.2d 841
5K2.0—968 F.2d 411
5K2.0—968 F.2d 1058
5K2.0—968 F.2d 1193
5K2.0—969 F.2d 652
5K2.0—970 F.2d 1095
5K2.0—970 F.2d 1328
5K2.0—970 F.2d 1336
5K2.0—971 F.2d 89
5K2.0—971 F.2d 200
5K2.0—971 F.2d 667
5K2.0—971 F.2d 989
5K2.0—971 F.2d 1302
5K2.0—971 F.2d 1368
5K2.0—972 F.2d 489
5K2.0—972 F.2d 958
5K2.0—973 F.2d 1
5K2.0—973 F.2d 611
5K2.0—974 F.2d 55
5K2.0—975 F.2d 622
5K2.0—975 F.2d 664
5K2.0—975 F.2d 1061
5K2.0—975 F.2d 1120
5K2.0—975 F.2d 1554
5K2.0—977 F.2d 540
5K2.0—978 F.2d 421
5K2.0—978 F.2d 1032
5K2.0—979 F.2d 816
5K2.0—980 F.2d 1296
5K2.0—981 F.2d 1382
5K2.0—983 F.2d 369
5K2.0—983 F.2d 1150
5K2.0—983 F.2d 1507
5K2.0—984 F.2d 649
5K2.0—984 F.2d 933
5K2.0—984 F.2d 1289
5K2.0—985 F.2d 65
5K2.0—985 F.2d 478
5K2.0—985 F.2d 732
5K2.0—985 F.2d 930
5K2.0—986 F.2d 1225
5K2.0—987 F.2d 538
5K2.0—987 F.2d 878
5K2.0—987 F.2d 1497
5K2.0—988 F.2d 440
5K2.0—989 F.2d 180
5K2.0—990 F.2d 397
5K2.0—990 F.2d 1314
5K2.0—991 F.2d 443
5K2.0—991 F.2d 493
5K2.0—991 F.2d 552
5K2.0—991 F.2d 1065
5K2.0—992 F.2d 164
5K2.0—992 F.2d 896
5K2.0 [1988]—993 F.2d 214
5K2.0—994 F.2d 942
5K2.0 [1992]—994 F.2d 1380
5K2.0—996 F.2d 1238
5K2.0—997 F.2d 30
5K2.0 [1990]—997 F.2d 30
5K2.0—997 F.2d 647
5K2.0—998 F.2d 42
5K2.0—1 F.3d 452
5K2.0—1 F.3d 457
5K2.0—1 F.3d 1040
5K2.0—1 F.3d 1137
5K2.0—4 F.3d 622
5K2.0—4 F.3d 901
5K2.0—5 F.3d 795
5K2.0—6 F.3d 1400
5K2.0—7 F.3d 285
5K2.0—7 F.3d 744
5K2.0—7 F.3d 957

5K2.0—8 F.3d 1379
5K2.0—9 F.3d 60
5K2.0—9 F.3d 686
5K2.0—9 F.3d 1422
5K2.0—10 F.3d 575
5K2.0—10 F.3d 1003
5K2.0—11 F.3d 777
5K2.0—11 F.3d 1133
5K2.0—14 F.3d 662
5K2.0—14 F.3d 1438
5K2.0—15 F.3d 1380
5K2.0—16 F.3d 498
5K2.0—16 F.3d 844
5K2.0—16 F.3d 1168
5K2.0—17 F.3d 462
5K2.0—18 F.3d 301
5K2.0—18 F.3d 822
5K2.0—18 F.3d 1367
5K2.0—18 F.3d 1424
5K2.0—19 F.3d 605
5K2.0—19 F.3d 763
5K2.0—19 F.3d 1385
5K2.0—20 F.3d 610
5K2.0—21 F.3d 375
5K2.0—21 F.3d 885
5K2.0—22 F.3d 76
5K2.0—22 F.3d 170
5K2.0—22 F.3d 409
5K2.0—22 F.3d 790
5K2.0—682 F.Supp. 815
5K2.0—692 F.Supp. 1427
5K2.0—696 F.Supp. 781
5K2.0—709 F.Supp. 653
5K2.0—712 F.Supp. 1327
5K2.0—719 F.Supp. 1015
5K2.0—726 F.Supp. 861
5K2.0—729 F.Supp. 487
5K2.0—733 F.Supp. 1195
5K2.0—735 F.Supp. 928
5K2.0—737 F.Supp. 186
5K2.0—740 F.Supp. 1502
5K2.0—741 F.Supp. 968
5K2.0—751 F.Supp. 368
5K2.0—753 F.Supp. 1289
5K2.0—756 F.Supp. 217
5K2.0—756 F.Supp. 698
5K2.0—760 F.Supp. 1322
5K2.0—760 F.Supp. 1332
5K2.0—762 F.Supp. 39
5K2.0—763 F.Supp. 703
5K2.0—766 F.Supp. 1227
5K2.0—768 F.Supp. 1277
5K2.0—773 F.Supp. 55
5K2.0—776 F.Supp. 1030
5K2.0—777 F.Supp. 293
5K2.0—781 F.Supp. 428
5K2.0—782 F.Supp. 19
5K2.0—782 F.Supp. 913
5K2.0—783 F.Supp. 507
5K2.0—784 F.Supp. 849
5K2.0—785 F.Supp. 114
5K2.0—789 F.Supp. 957
5K2.0—794 F.Supp. 425
5K2.0—797 F.Supp. 672
5K2.0—798 F.Supp. 513
5K2.0—798 F.Supp. 861
5K2.0—802 F.Supp. 128
5K2.0—802 F.Supp. 657
5K2.0—803 F.Supp. 53
5K2.0 [1990]—803 F.Supp. 53
5K2.0—803 F.Supp. 657
5K2.0—807 F.Supp. 19
5K2.0—807 F.Supp. 165
5K2.0—807 F.Supp. 515
5K2.0—809 F.Supp. 319
5K2.0—811 F.Supp. 1106
5K2.0—814 F.Supp. 23
5K2.0—817 F.Supp. 321
5K2.0—825 F.Supp. 422
5K2.0—825 F.Supp. 866
5K2.0—833 F.Supp. 1454
5K2.0—834 F.Supp. 292
5K2.0—834 F.Supp. 659
5K2.0—835 F.Supp. 1466
5K2.0—835 F.Supp. 1501
5K2.0—837 F.Supp. 916
5K2.0—840 F.Supp. 1404
5K2.0—842 F.Supp. 92
5K2.0—846 F.Supp. 278
5K2.0 et seq.—886 F.2d 973
5K2.0 et seq.—902 F.2d 734
5K2.0 et seq.—921 F.2d 438
5K2.0 et seq.—999 F.2d 1192
5K2.0 et seq.—835 F.Supp. 1543
5K2.0-5K2.2—872 F.2d 597
5K2.0-5K2.9—891 F.2d 528
5K2.0-5K2.10—872 F.2d 597
5K2.0-5K2.14—883 F.2d 829
5K2.0-5K2.14—686 F.Supp. 1174
5K2.0-5K2.14—696 F.Supp. 781

5K2.0-5K2.14—709 F.Supp. 653
5K2.0-5K2.15—902 F.2d 873
5K2.0-5K2.15—938 F.2d 326
5K2.0-5K2.16—977 F.2d 69
5K2.1—870 F.2d 52
5K2.1—872 F.2d 121
5K2.1—883 F.2d 336
5K2.1—892 F.2d 223
5K2.1—893 F.2d 504
5K2.1—894 F.2d 1307
5K2.1—918 F.2d 1084
5K2.1—925 F.2d 596
5K2.1—928 F.2d 844
5K2.1—933 F.2d 962
5K2.1—959 F.2d 26
5K2.1—970 F.2d 1328
5K2.1—978 F.2d 861
5K2.1—979 F.2d 539
5K2.1—986 F.2d 1287
5K2.1—802 F.Supp. 657
5K2.1—834 F.Supp. 659
5K2.1—835 F.Supp. 1466
5K2.1—835 F.Supp. 1501
5K2.1 et seq.—870 F.2d 52
5K2.1 et seq.—902 F.2d 734
5K2.1-5K2.16—956 F.2d 1555
5K2.2—872 F.2d 121
5K2.2—893 F.2d 504
5K2.2—908 F.2d 425
5K2.2—917 F.2d 411
5K2.2—925 F.2d 392
5K2.2—933 F.2d 962
5K2.2—965 F.2d 206
5K2.2—834 F.Supp. 659
5K2.2(a)—922 F.2d 1411
5K2.3—889 F.2d 697
5K2.3—905 F.2d 337
5K2.3—908 F.2d 272
5K2.3—923 F.2d 1052
5K2.3—929 F.2d 436
5K2.3—930 F.2d 216
5K2.3—930 F.2d 744
5K2.3—935 F.2d 385
5K2.3—946 F.2d 584
5K2.3—965 F.2d 206
5K2.3—975 F.2d 1120
5K2.3—983 F.2d 1507
5K2.3—984 F.2d 933
5K2.3—991 F.2d 55
5K2.3—993 F.2d 16
5K2.3 [1988]—993 F.2d 214
5K2.3—994 F.2d 1380
5K2.3—999 F.2d 361
5K2.3—5 F.3d 795
5K2.3—6 F.3d 1218
5K2.3—7 F.3d 744
5K2.3—18 F.3d 1123
5K2.3—18 F.3d 1438
5K2.3—22 F.3d 662
5K2.3—788 F.Supp. 433
5K2.4—940 F.2d 753
5K2.4—965 F.2d 206
5K2.4—1 F.3d 1137
5K2.5—893 F.2d 504
5K2.5—900 F.2d 45
5K2.5—916 F.2d 186
5K2.5—925 F.2d 392
5K2.5—929 F.2d 436
5K2.5—983 F.2d 1507
5K2.5—987 F.2d 1497
5K2.5 [1988]—993 F.2d 214
5K2.5—18 F.3d 826
5K2.5—751 F.Supp. 368
5K2.6—868 F.2d 1412
5K2.6—875 F.2d 1124
5K2.6—875 F.2d 1294
5K2.6—877 F.2d 1409
5K2.6—898 F.2d 1111
5K2.6—901 F.2d 863
5K2.6—904 F.2d 365
5K2.6—908 F.2d 425
5K2.6—909 F.2d 196
5K2.6 [1988]—914 F.2d 208
5K2.6—914 F.2d 1131
5K2.6—918 F.2d 664
5K2.6—924 F.2d 800
5K2.6—929 F.2d 518
5K2.6—931 F.2d 308
5K2.6—950 F.2d 1267
5K2.6—963 F.2d 711
5K2.6—971 F.2d 667
5K2.6—975 F.2d 1120
5K2.6—980 F.2d 980
5K2.6—989 F.2d 180
5K2.6—994 F.2d 942
5K2.6—1 F.3d 1137
5K2.6 [1988]—5 F.3d 241
5K2.6—7 F.3d 285
5K2.6—13 F.3d 1308
5K2.6—22 F.3d 662

5K2.6—800 F.Supp. 1012
5K2.7—893 F.2d 1343
5K2.7—900 F.2d 45
5K2.7—902 F.2d 1169
5K2.7—913 F.2d 46
5K2.7—917 F.2d 411
5K2.7—918 F.2d 1084
5K2.7—922 F.2d 1283
5K2.7—924 F.2d 1289
5K2.7—926 F.2d 387
5K2.7—934 F.2d 248
5K2.7—943 F.2d 1543
5K2.7—975 F.2d 17
5K2.7—987 F.2d 1497
5K2.7—12 F.3d 1116
5K2.7—18 F.3d 826
5K2.7—706 F.Supp. 331
5K2.7—753 F.Supp. 1289
5K2.7—759 F.Supp. 1258
5K2.7—803 F.Supp. 53
5K2.8—872 F.2d 597
5K2.8—908 F.2d 272
5K2.8—918 F.2d 1084
5K2.8—929 F.2d 436
5K2.8—930 F.2d 216
5K2.8—935 F.2d 385
5K2.8—948 F.2d 241
5K2.8—952 F.2d 565
5K2.8—975 F.2d 1120
5K2.8—983 F.2d 1507
5K2.8—986 F.2d 1287
5K2.8—999 F.2d 361
5K2.8—1 F.3d 1137
5K2.8—5 F.3d 795
5K2.8—18 F.3d 1123
5K2.8—21 F.3d 885
5K2.8—706 F.Supp. 331
5K2.8—753 F.Supp. 1289
5K2.8—834 F.Supp. 659
5K2.9—875 F.2d 1124
5K2.9—893 F.2d 1343
5K2.9—895 F.2d 544
5K2.9—901 F.2d 863
5K2.9—911 F.2d 793
5K2.9—915 F.2d 947
5K2.9—929 F.2d 389
5K2.9—933 F.2d 962
5K2.9—935 F.2d 4
5K2.9—941 F.2d 858
5K2.9—956 F.2d 165
5K2.9—961 F.2d 1421
5K2.9—10 F.3d 1003
5K2.9—22 F.3d 1048
5K2.9—698 F.Supp. 563
5K2.9—753 F.Supp. 1289
5K2.9—803 F.Supp. 53
5K2.10—891 F.2d 650
5K2.10—895 F.2d 1178
5K2.10—901 F.2d 647
5K2.10—914 F.2d 966
5K2.10—917 F.2d 607
5K2.10—919 F.2d 1325
5K2.10—931 F.2d 1250
5K2.10—943 F.2d 836
5K2.10—951 F.2d 887
5K2.10—952 F.2d 182
5K2.10—956 F.2d 857
5K2.10—962 F.2d 824
5K2.10—14 F.3d 1438
5K2.10—833 F.Supp. 769
5K2.10(c)—951 F.2d 887
5K2.10(d)—951 F.2d 887
5K2.11—943 F.2d 1422
5K2.11—998 F.2d 917
5K2.11—10 F.3d 575
5K2.11—13 F.3d 752
5K2.11—732 F.Supp. 878
5K2.11—801 F.Supp. 263
5K2.11—846 F.Supp. 982
5K2.12—887 F.2d 485
5K2.12—889 F.2d 477
5K2.12—902 F.2d 133
5K2.12—917 F.2d 512
5K2.12—927 F.2d 197
5K2.12—931 F.2d 1250
5K2.12—932 F.2d 1155
5K2.12—934 F.2d 371
5K2.12—948 F.2d 776
5K2.12—949 F.2d 190
5K2.12—951 F.2d 887
5K2.12—952 F.2d 914
5K2.12—956 F.2d 894
5K2.12—961 F.2d 288
5K2.12—971 F.2d 1206
5K2.12—976 F.2d 1216
5K2.12—985 F.2d 970
5K2.12—987 F.2d 888
5K2.12—992 F.2d 91
5K2.12—992 F.2d 896
5K2.12—992 F.2d 1091

5K2.12—994 F.2d 942
5K2.12—997 F.2d 594
5K2.12—7 F.3d 1279
5K2.12—20 F.3d 918
5K2.12—21 F.3d 375
5K2.12—22 F.3d 790
5K2.12—709 F.Supp. 653
5K2.12—740 F.Supp. 1502
5K2.12—798 F.Supp. 513
5K2.12—798 F.Supp. 861
5K2.12—804 F.Supp. 476
5K2.12—840 F.Supp. 1404
5K2.12—846 F.Supp. 982
5K2.13—868 F.2d 125
5K2.13—891 F.2d 300
5K2.13—893 F.2d 815
5K2.13—896 F.2d 789
5K2.13—898 F.2d 91
5K2.13—899 F.2d 327
5K2.13—905 F.2d 195
5K2.13—905 F.2d 1448
5K2.13—909 F.2d 392
5K2.13—910 F.2d 707
5K2.13—917 F.2d 512
5K2.13—919 F.2d 95
5K2.13—919 F.2d 1181
5K2.13—920 F.2d 139
5K2.13 [1990]—920 F.2d 1290
5K2.13—924 F.2d 1124
5K2.13—925 F.2d 186
5K2.13—926 F.2d 588
5K2.13—933 F.2d 742
5K2.13—935 F.2d 295
5K2.13—938 F.2d 326
5K2.13—946 F.2d 335
5K2.13—947 F.2d 739
5K2.13—947 F.2d 1467
5K2.13—948 F.2d 1074
5K2.13—949 F.2d 190
5K2.13—951 F.2d 1057
5K2.13—954 F.2d 1012
5K2.13—956 F.2d 907
5K2.13—970 F.2d 1336
5K2.13—975 F.2d 1554
5K2.13—979 F.2d 396
5K2.13—979 F.2d 1227
5K2.13—985 F.2d 1003
5K2.13—986 F.2d 1446
5K2.13—988 F.2d 1005
5K2.13—989 F.2d 44
5K2.13—994 F.2d 942
5K2.13—999 F.2d 1192
5K2.13—12 F.3d 1506
5K2.13—13 F.3d 1117
5K2.13—19 F.3d 1385
5K2.13—723 F.Supp. 79
5K2.13—726 F.Supp. 861
5K2.13—740 F.Supp. 1502
5K2.13—791 F.Supp. 244
5K2.13—793 F.Supp. 64
5K2.13—801 F.Supp. 263
5K2.13—811 F.Supp. 1106
5K2.13—827 F.Supp. 205
5K2.13—833 F.Supp. 1454
5K2.14—867 F.2d 783
5K2.14—891 F.2d 528
5K2.14—901 F.2d 746
5K2.14—902 F.2d 451
5K2.14 [1988]—907 F.2d 294
5K2.14—908 F.2d 425
5K2.14—908 F.2d 438
5K2.14—909 F.2d 395
5K2.14—916 F.2d 186
5K2.14—918 F.2d 1084
5K2.14—922 F.2d 1411
5K2.14—929 F.2d 518
5K2.14—931 F.2d 300
5K2.14—931 F.2d 705
5K2.14—934 F.2d 248
5K2.14—938 F.2d 172
5K2.14—943 F.2d 1543
5K2.14—952 F.2d 565
5K2.14—965 F.2d 262
5K2.14—9 F.3d 907
5K2.14—18 F.3d 41
5K2.14—18 F.3d 826
5K2.14—696 F.Supp. 781
5K2.14—698 F.Supp. 563
5K2.14—706 F.Supp. 331
5K2.14—800 F.Supp. 1012
5K2.15—952 F.2d 565
5K2.15—755 F.Supp. 914
5K2.16—996 F.2d 75

CHAPTER 6—SENTENCING PROCEDURES AND PLEA AGREEMENTS

Part A: Sentencing Procedures

6A comment—905 F.2d 300
6A1.1—886 F.2d 838
6A1.1—905 F.2d 300
6A1.1—907 F.2d 456
6A1.1—908 F.2d 33
6A1.1—918 F.2d 1430
6A1.1—926 F.2d 7
6A1.1 et seq.—976 F.2d 393
6A1.1-6A1.3—923 F.2d 1545
6A1.1-6A1.3—955 F.2d 1098
6A1.2—886 F.2d 838
6A1.2—890 F.2d 855
6A1.2—896 F.2d 856
6A1.2—901 F.2d 21
6A1.2—915 F.2d 474
6A1.2—955 F.2d 77
6A1.2—987 F.2d 104
6A1.2—686 F.Supp. 1174
6A1.2 comment—773 F.2d 765
6A1.2 comment—915 F.2d 474
6A1.2 comment—816 F.Supp. 1102
6A1.3—113 S.Ct. 1111
6A1.3—882 F.2d 693
6A1.3—885 F.2d 1266
6A1.3—887 F.2d 841
6A1.3—889 F.2d 1531
6A1.3—891 F.2d 1265
6A1.3—893 F.2d 1343
6A1.3—894 F.2d 1092
6A1.3—895 F.2d 597
6A1.3—896 F.2d 856
6A1.3—897 F.2d 751
6A1.3—897 F.2d 1558
6A1.3—900 F.2d 571
6A1.3—901 F.2d 21
6A1.3—902 F.2d 336
6A1.3—904 F.2d 1070
6A1.3—907 F.2d 929
6A1.3—909 F.2d 436
6A1.3—910 F.2d 1321
6A1.3—912 F.2d 1210
6A1.3—914 F.2d 67
6A1.3—917 F.2d 477
6A1.3—917 F.2d 601
6A1.3—917 F.2d 1057
6A1.3—920 F.2d 1100
6A1.3 [1990]—920 F.2d 1290
6A1.3—922 F.2d 33
6A1.3—927 F.2d 202
6A1.3—928 F.2d 383
6A1.3—929 F.2d 563
6A1.3—929 F.2d 1453
6A1.3—931 F.2d 1440
6A1.3—935 F.2d 4
6A1.3—935 F.2d 47
6A1.3—943 F.2d 1543
6A1.3—944 F.2d 780
6A1.3—944 F.2d 784
6A1.3—947 F.2d 893
6A1.3—949 F.2d 722
6A1.3—950 F.2d 50
6A1.3—950 F.2d 1508
6A1.3—953 F.2d 127
6A1.3—963 F.2d 693
6A1.3—963 F.2d 1323
6A1.3—963 F.2d 1506
6A1.3—966 F.2d 682
6A1.3—967 F.2d 1
6A1.3—971 F.2d 562
6A1.3—971 F.2d 1206
6A1.3—981 F.2d 180
6A1.3—982 F.2d 1118
6A1.3—985 F.2d 621
6A1.3—994 F.2d 456
6A1.3—995 F.2d 1407
6A1.3—996 F.2d 906
6A1.3—997 F.2d 146
6A1.3—999 F.2d 1225
6A1.3—1 F.3d 341
6A1.3—7 F.3d 1171
6A1.3—12 F.3d 301
6A1.3—12 F.3d 1506
6A1.3—16 F.3d 795
6A1.3—20 F.3d 610
6A1.3—680 F.Supp. 1312
6A1.3—687 F.Supp. 1329
6A1.3—690 F.Supp. 615
6A1.3—701 F.Supp. 138
6A1.3—706 F.Supp. 331
6A1.3—708 F.Supp. 964
6A1.3—734 F.Supp. 552
6A1.3—776 F.Supp. 1030

6A1.3—819 F.Supp. 250
6A1.3(a)—880 F.2d 636
6A1.3(a)—881 F.2d 95
6A1.3(a)—888 F.2d 247
6A1.3(a)—891 F.2d 364
6A1.3(a) [1988]—892 F.2d 725
6A1.3(a)—893 F.2d 950
6A1.3(a)—896 F.2d 392
6A1.3(a)—900 F.2d 1350
6A1.3(a)—903 F.2d 648
6A1.3(a)—903 F.2d 1188
6A1.3(a)—918 F.2d 789
6A1.3(a)—919 F.2d 962
6A1.3(a)—920 F.2d 139
6A1.3(a)—921 F.2d 580
6A1.3(a)—922 F.2d 404
6A1.3(a)—922 F.2d 458
6A1.3(a)—924 F.2d 427
6A1.3(a)—925 F.2d 506
6A1.3(a)—925 F.2d 641
6A1.3(a)—928 F.2d 844
6A1.3(a)—944 F.2d 959
6A1.3(a)—945 F.2d 378
6A1.3(a)—946 F.2d 362
6A1.3(a)—947 F.2d 742
6A1.3(a)—947 F.2d 1424
6A1.3(a)—949 F.2d 283
6A1.3(a)—950 F.2d 50
6A1.3(a)—950 F.2d 1095
6A1.3(a)—951 F.2d 988
6A1.3(a)—952 F.2d 190
6A1.3(a)—954 F.2d 12
6A1.3(a)—956 F.2d 1256
6A1.3(a)—962 F.2d 767
6A1.3(a)—963 F.2d 72
6A1.3(a)—964 F.2d 390
6A1.3(a)—965 F.2d 436
6A1.3(a)—967 F.2d 1
6A1.3(a)—969 F.2d 609
6A1.3(a)—969 F.2d 1283
6A1.3(a)—972 F.2d 904
6A1.3(a)—976 F.2d 393
6A1.3(a)—982 F.2d 317
6A1.3(a)—984 F.2d 899
6A1.3(a)—988 F.2d 228
6A1.3(a)—988 F.2d 641
6A1.3(a)—989 F.2d 44
6A1.3(a)—989 F.2d 659
6A1.3(a)—993 F.2d 204
6A1.3(a)—994 F.2d 386
6A1.3(a)—997 F.2d 78
6A1.3(a)—6 F.3d 554
6A1.3(a)—9 F.3d 705
6A1.3(a)—10 F.3d 910
6A1.3(a)—12 F.3d 1506
6A1.3(a)—13 F.3d 860
6A1.3(a)—14 F.3d 1264
6A1.3(a)—20 F.3d 1428
6A1.3(a)—809 F.Supp. 908
6A1.3(a)—844 F.Supp. 427
6A1.3(b)—873 F.2d 765
6A1.3(b)—894 F.2d 1457
6A1.3(b)—907 F.2d 929
6A1.3(b)—908 F.2d 33
6A1.3(b)—918 F.2d 664
6A1.3(b)—918 F.2d 789
6A1.3(b)—928 F.2d 844
6A1.3(b)—931 F.2d 1139
6A1.3(b)—945 F.2d 1337
6A1.3(b)—963 F.2d 693
6A1.3(b)—987 F.2d 1009
6A1.3(b)—994 F.2d 386
6A1.3(e)—982 F.2d 1118
6A1.3 comment—873 F.2d 765
6A1.3 comment—880 F.2d 636
6A1.3 comment—891 F.2d 92
6A1.3 comment [1988]—892 F.2d 725
6A1.3 comment—893 F.2d 1343
6A1.3 comment—897 F.2d 1324
6A1.3 comment—902 F.2d 336
6A1.3 comment—909 F.2d 363
6A1.3 comment—910 F.2d 1241
6A1.3 comment—911 F.2d 1456
6A1.3 comment—917 F.2d 1057
6A1.3 comment—918 F.2d 789
6A1.3 comment—924 F.2d 427
6A1.3 comment—929 F.2d 389
6A1.3 comment—931 F.2d 1440
6A1.3 comment—935 F.2d 47
6A1.3 comment—936 F.2d 1124
6A1.3 comment—942 F.2d 141
6A1.3 comment—945 F.2d 1337
6A1.3 comment—954 F.2d 12
6A1.3 comment—957 F.2d 942
6A1.3 comment—961 F.2d 1012
6A1.3 comment—964 F.2d 325
6A1.3 comment—964 F.2d 763
6A1.3 comment—966 F.2d 682
6A1.3 comment—969 F.2d 609
6A1.3 comment—976 F.2d 393

6A1.3 comment—981 F.2d 180
6A1.3 comment—989 F.2d 948
6A1.3 comment—993 F.2d 204
6A1.3 comment—996 F.2d 1238
6A1.3 comment—12 F.3d 1506
6A1.3 comment—16 F.3d 1110
6A1.3 comment—682 F.Supp. 815
6A1.3 comment—734 F.Supp. 552
6A1.3 comment—819 F.Supp. 250

Part B: Plea Agreements

6B comment—730 F.Supp. 45
6B comment—893 F.2d 73
6B1.1(b)—894 F.2d 225
6B1.1(b)—898 F.2d 813
6B1.1(b)—902 F.2d 483
6B1.1(b)—925 F.2d 112
6B1.1(b)—950 F.2d 633
6B1.1(c)—908 F.2d 33
6B1.1(c)—979 F.2d 396
6B1.1(c)—988 F.2d 712
6B1.1(c)—731 F.Supp. 262
6B1.1 comment—908 F.2d 33
6B1.1 comment—979 F.2d 396
6B1.1 comment—728 F.Supp. 632
6B1.1 et seq.—952 F.2d 995
6B1.1 et seq.—957 F.2d 115
6B1.1 et seq.—682 F.Supp. 815
6B1.1 et seq.—728 F.Supp. 632
6B1.2—917 F.2d 1178
6B1.2—982 F.2d 216
6B1.2—692 F.Supp. 1427
6B1.2—698 F.Supp. 563
6B1.2—807 F.Supp. 156
6B1.2(a)—875 F.2d 1124
6B1.2(a)—920 F.2d 1231
6B1.2(a)—927 F.2d 1079
6B1.2(a)—934 F.2d 190
6B1.2(a)—937 F.2d 95
6B1.2(a)—952 F.2d 1066
6B1.2(a)—975 F.2d 596
6B1.2(a)—982 F.2d 354
6B1.2(a)—698 F.Supp. 563
6B1.2(a)—730 F.Supp. 45
6B1.2(a)—732 F.Supp. 878
6B1.2(b)—952 F.2d 995
6B1.2(b)(1)—897 F.2d 1558
6B1.2(b)(1)—911 F.2d 1023
6B1.2(c)—908 F.2d 33
6B1.2(c)—4 F.3d 70
6B1.2(c)—698 F.Supp. 563
6B1.2(c)—730 F.Supp. 35
6B1.2 comment—692 F.Supp. 1427
6B1.2 comment—807 F.Supp. 156
6B1.3—908 F.2d 33
6B1.3—963 F.2d 105
6B1.3—684 F.Supp. 1048
6B1.3 comment—4 F.3d 70
6B1.4—874 F.2d 174
6B1.4—888 F.2d 1122
6B1.4—901 F.2d 867
6B1.4—908 F.2d 33
6B1.4—920 F.2d 1231
6B1.4—945 F.2d 1337
6B1.4—962 F.2d 165
6B1.4—684 F.Supp. 1048
6B1.4—716 F.Supp. 1137
6B1.4(a)—921 F.2d 1073
6B1.4(a)—962 F.2d 165
6B1.4(a)—987 F.2d 1009
6B1.4(a)(2)—730 F.Supp. 35
6B1.4(a)(2)—730 F.Supp. 45
6B1.4(b)—730 F.Supp 35
6B1.4(d)—888 F.2d 752
6B1.4(d)—894 F.2d 1085
6B1.4(d)—898 F.2d 813
6B1.4(d)—902 F.2d 324
6B1.4(d)—907 F.2d 1540
6B1.4(d)—908 F.2d 33
6B1.4(d)—913 F.2d 1288
6B1.4(d)—940 F.2d 1352
6B1.4(d)—961 F.2d 1460
6B1.4(d)—962 F.2d 165
6B1.4(d)—973 F.2d 1422
6B1.4(d)—730 F.Supp. 35
6B1.4 comment—888 F.2d 752
6B1.4 comment—894 F.2d 1085
6B1.4 comment—902 F.2d 324
6B1.4 comment—962 F.2d 165
6B1.4 comment—730 F.Supp. 35
6B1.4 comment—730 F.Supp. 45
6B2.2 comment—979 F.2d 517

CHAPTER 7—VIOLATIONS OF PROBATION AND SUPERVISED RELEASE

Part A: Introduction to Chapter Seven

7A comment—957 F.2d 770
7A comment—963 F.2d 777
7A comment—2 F.3d 842
7A comment—11 F.3d 292
7A1.1—946 F.2d 1127
7A1.2—910 F.2d 461
7A1.2(a) [1989]—833 F.Supp. 662
7A1.3—907 F.2d 896
7A1.3—910 F.2d 542
7A1.3—910 F.2d 768
7A1.3 [1988]—925 F.2d 15
7A1.3 [1990]—931 F.2d 463
7A1.3(a)—910 F.2d 542
7A1.3(a) [1988]—930 F.2d 18
7A1.3(a)—946 F.2d 1127
7A1.3(b) [1990]—781 F.Supp. 777
7A1.4—910 F.2d 542
7A1.4(b)—910 F.2d 542
7A—6 F.3d 87
7A—849 F.Supp. 1102
7A.1—23 F.3d 87
7A.1—805 F.Supp. 879
7A.3 [1989]—2 F.3d 842
7A.3—805 F.Supp. 879
7A.3(a)—940 F.2d 877
7A.3(a)—993 F.2d 898
7A.3(a) [1989]—2 F.3d 842
7A.3(d) [1989]—2 F.3d 842
7A.4 [1989]—2 F.3d 842
7A.5—940 F.2d 877

Part B: Probation and Supervised Release Violations

7B1.1(a)—961 F.2d 1421
7B1.1(a)—963 F.2d 777
7B1.1(a)—815 F.Supp. 990
7B1.1(a)(1)—953 F.2d 526
7B1.1(a)(2)—976 F.2d 1380
7B1.1 et seq.—943 F.2d 896
7B1.1 et seq.—963 F.2d 777
7B1.1 et seq.—973 F.2d 605
7B1.1 et seq.—974 F.2d 12
7B1.1 et seq.—976 F.2d 1358
7B1.1 et seq.—2 F.3d 842
7B1.1 et seq.—9 F.3d 741
7B1.1 et seq.—14 F.3d 34
7B1.1 et seq.—19 F.3d 1099
7B1.1-7B1.4—946 F.2d 57
7B1.3—12 F.3d 139
7B1.3(a)—946 F.2d 1127
7B1.3(a)(1)—845 F.Supp. 103
7B1.3(a)(23)—765 F.Supp. 1499
7B1.3(d)—2 F.3d 842
7B1.3(f)—981 F.2d 973
7B1.3(f)—13 F.3d 395
7B1.3(g)—765 F.Supp. 1499
7B1.3(g)(2)—947 F.2d 1461
7B1.3(g)(2)—962 F.2d 339
7B1.3(g)(2)—11 F.3d 292
7B1.3(g)(2)—794 F.Supp. 338
7B1.4—952 F.2d 260
7B1.4—952 F.2d 854
7B1.4—957 F.2d 770
7B1.4—963 F.2d 777
7B1.4—965 F.2d 58
7B1.4—976 F.2d 1380
7B1.4—14 F.3d 34
7B1.4—19 F.3d 482
7B1.4(a)—946 F.2d 1127
7B1.4(a)—948 F.2d 628
7B1.4(a)—961 F.2d 426
7B1.4(a)—961 F.2d 434
7B1.4(a)—973 F.2d 605
7B1.4(a)—17 F.3d 70
7B1.4(a)—830 F.Supp. 1339
7B1.4(a)—833 F.Supp. 662
7B1.4(a)—845 F.Supp. 103
7B1.4(a)(2)—946 F.2d 57
7B1.4(a)(2)—948 F.2d 628
7B1.4(a)(2)—952 F.2d 854

APPENDICES

Appendix C—905 F.2d 3

PROSECUTING ATTORNEY